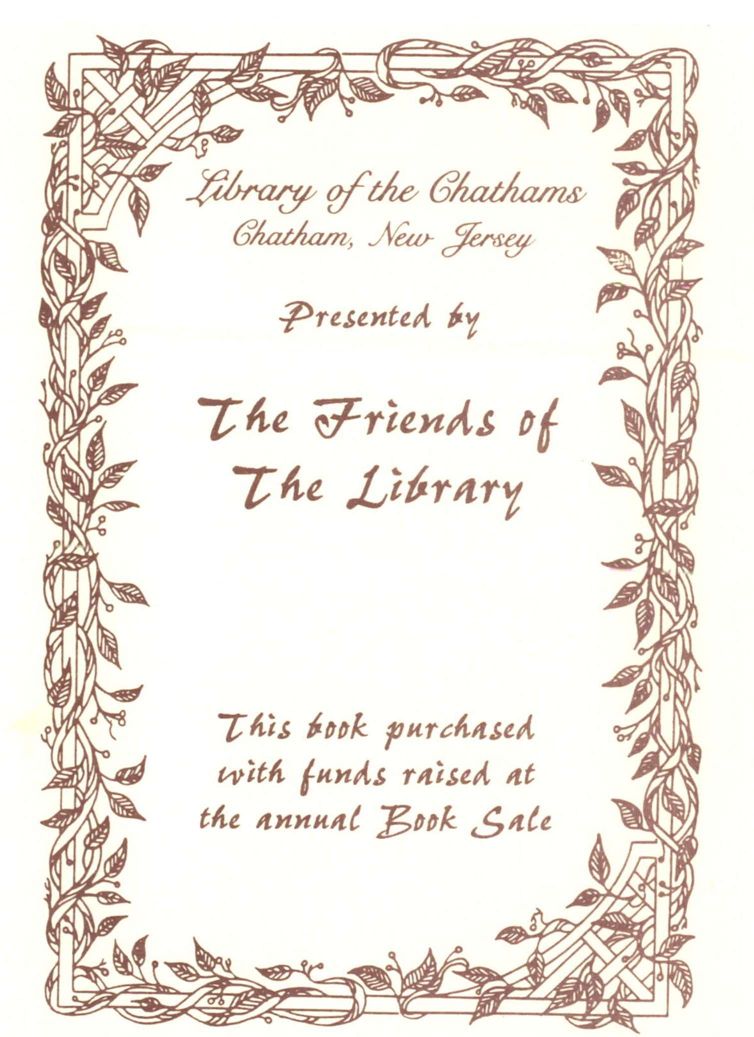

Encyclopedia of

German Literature

Volume 1

A–I

Encyclopedia of

GERMAN LITERATURE

Volume 1
A–I

MATTHIAS KONZETT
Editor

Fitzroy Dearborn Publishers
Chicago and London

For information write to:

FITZROY DEARBORN PUBLISHERS
919 N. Michigan Avenue, Suite 760
Chicago, Illinois 60611
USA

or

FITZROY DEARBORN PUBLISHERS
310 Regent Street
London W1R 5AJ
England

British Library and Library of Congress Cataloging in Publication Data are available.

ISBN 1-57958-138-2

First published in the USA and UK 2000

Index prepared by AEIOU Inc., Pleasantville, New York
Typeset by Sheridan Books Inc., Ann Arbor, Michigan
Printed by Sheridan Books Inc., Ann Arbor, Michigan
Cover design by Chicago Advertising and Design, Chicago, Illinois

Cover illustration: Gabriele Münter, *Zuhören,* 1909 © 1999 Artists Rights Society (ARS),
New York/VG Bild-Kunst, Bonn

CONTENTS

EDITOR'S NOTE

While publication of encyclopedias of German literature is fairly common in German-speaking countries, this cannot be said for English-speaking countries. Although some valuable handbooks providing biographical information or cultural background to areas of German literature and culture are readily available, there has been until now no extensive English encyclopedia that informs readers about German literature, its authors, and its various contexts by means of extended essays and topical discussions.

The *Encyclopedia of German Literature* is unique in that it presents the work of German literature scholars conducted in Anglo-American countries and regions. Not only does it provide an overview of the present state of the field to both layman and expert, it also brings to German culture a transnational perspective, allowing a critical look at German literature and culture from the outside. Although the idea of *Auslandsgermanistik* (German studies abroad) has been in practice for quite some time, its innovative scope and vigor has not been properly documented. Unlike similar and more narrowly defined projects, this encyclopedia amply displays the wide variety of approaches that are brought to German studies in its foreign reception. Transnationalism as a critical perspective is thus understood in its more far-reaching sense and not exclusively as contained in ideological interests. The latter concerns are well represented in this volume, but not to the exclusion of other approaches that have carried forward the legacy of German cultural production.

In its transnational focus, the encyclopedia also pays particular attention to the regional varieties of German literature and does not attempt to reduce its diverse manifestations to national or hegemonic canons alone. A number of topical essays, commenting on intellectual, national, regional, gender, and ethnic traditions help the reader to understand better the multiple overlapping layers and contexts that provide the background for the individual authors. In addition, the discussion of a number of women writers is meant to create for readers new and unexpected affinities in an understanding of literary history heretofore dominated by male voices. However, the encyclopedia does not wish to compete with existing and valuable English encyclopedias of women's literature; instead, it aims to provide a context in which there is a space for all the social and cultural voices to be heard inclusively and in tension with one another.

This inclusive undertaking, however, is by no means innocent and beyond criticism. In drafting the various entries for discussion, problematic decisions were inevitable. Given the size of the volume, our board of editorial advisers had to vote on the inclusion or exclusion of particular authors, works, and topics. The corrective against a one-sided and slanted selection had to be provided by the editor and publisher, and for this reason, scholars of different ideological backgrounds were invited to join the editorial board. These divisive perspectives within the field had to be negotiated in a democratic fashion in an attempt to come to terms with the conflicting claims of various interest groups.

Perhaps even more problematic than the selection of authors of German literature for inclusion in the encyclopedia were the categorizations of our topic entries. Entries aiming to reflect innovative tendencies in the field, such as women's literature and ethnic literatures, were duly considered by the editorial board and the contributors in the interest of doing justice to the complex status of marginalized voices. Categories such as women's literature or ethnic literature often directly or indirectly reaffirm the marginalization they intend to reverse. Entries by Sarah Colvin and Kamakshi Murti are especially helpful in drawing immediate attention to the inherent flaws in trying to construct politically correct categories that camouflage ongoing practices of exclusion. At the same time, it would be equally misleading to deny that such categories are frequently used and would be looked for by readers. In other words, the empirical existence and pragmatic use of these categories make it imperative to include them in the encyclopedia in spite of inviting justifiable criticism.

As German culture moves into an exciting new era of radical transformation, German literature will be a significant tool for cultural orientation, providing both a profound understanding of tradition and a visionary perspective for newly emerging social and cultural contexts. Since literature orchestrates a plurality of voices and discourses in its representation of cultures, if offers a cohesive articulation of social lifeworlds and their complex symbolic exchanges. Our cover illustration, Gabriele Münter's *Zuhören* (Listening, 1909), was chosen to reflect this inclusive and communicative approach of our project. The work, which depicts Münter's fellow painter, the Russian German transnational Alexei von Jawlenski, shows the artist in the act of concentrated listening. In so doing, he takes on the appearance of the objects surrounding him, such as the German sausages, the lamp, and other objects, thereby becoming a part of the world surrounding him.

I hope readers will share the enthusiasm that has gone into this encyclopedia and appreciate its open and informative approach to a large variety of aspects of German culture and its evolving legacy.

Arrangement of Entries and Format within Entries

Entries in the encyclopedia are of three main types (authors, works, and topics) and are arranged alphabetically, as listed in the **Alphabetical List of Entries** (p. xv). Because entries devoted to individual works or groups of related works by the same author are presented immediately after and as part of the author entry, a separate **Alphabetical List of Works** is provided as well. Within the works entries for a given author, these entries are presented in alphabetical order by title.

Each of the three main types of entry consists of a critical essay followed by a list of selected **Further Reading.** In addition, author entries contain a brief **Biography** and a **Selected Works** section, and works entries include an **Editions** section, in which bibliographic information for the first edition, selected critical editions, and selected translations is given.

Throughout the encyclopedia, the first time a work is referred to in an essay, the first date of publication and an English translation of the title are given in parentheses. English translations of the titles of works have been rendered in the following way. If the translation has been published, the translation title appears in italic type: *Die Blechtrommel* (1959; *The Tin Drum*). If the title has not been published in English, it appears in roman type: *Die Fehler des Kopisten* (1997; The Errors of the Copyist). If the title is a poem or short story that normally appears in quotation marks rather than italics, the translation will appear in quotation marks if published or without quotation marks if not published.

In order to facilitate access to the contents of the encyclopedia, a number of indexes and cross references are provided. These are:

1. **Title Index** (p. 1041). This index lists all titles found in the **Selected Works** sections of author entries.

2. **General Index** (p. 1085). This index includes individuals, works, concepts, and topics found throughout the encyclopedia. This index may be particularly useful for locating references to individuals, works, and topics that do not have an entry of their own.

3. **Cross References.** At the end of many entries there are *See also* listings, which refer the reader to entries on related topics. In addition, there are a number of *see* references throughout the book that direct the reader to the location of an entry that might be found under a different word or spelling (e.g., **Richter, Johann Paul Friedrich** *see* **Jean Paul**).

Acknowledgments

For first approaching me about editing the encyclopedia and convincing me of the feasibility of this challenging project, I wish to thank Paul Schellinger and Steven LaRue at Fitzroy Dearborn. I would also like to thank the highly professional staff that has made this publication possible, most notably, Steven LaRue, the in-house editor largely responsible for overseeing the copy-editing, layout, and crucial aspects of publishing, as well as William Weaver, Ann Edahl, Hillary Herzog, and Anne-Marie Bogdan as supporting editorial and research staff. Thanks also should go to editorial coordinators Gretchen Willenberg and Amber Forst, who have assisted in every way and at every stage of the preparation of this publication. Once again thanks to Paul Schellinger, who was of great help in the final stages of the project and guided the book with his professional experience throughout its crucial stages.

This project would not have been possible without the help of our editorial advisory board. Here I would like to thank especially Andrew Barker, Ingeborg Hoestery, Peter Hutchinson, Dagmar Lorenz, Donald Marshall, Moray McGowan, David Midgley, Brian Murdoch, and Jeffrey Sammons for suggesting contributors, writing entries, and providing critical advice and support. For locating and helping to secure the rights for the cover illustration by Gabriele Münter, I would like to thank my former teacher Reinhold Heller. Finally, I would like to acknowledge the many fine contributors who responded enthusiastically to our invitation to contribute to the encyclopedia and who have shaped this book in a truly cooperative effort.

MATTHIAS KONZETT
Assistant Professor of German Literature, Yale University

ADVISERS

CONTRIBUTORS

Scott Abbott
Jeffrey Adams
Hans Adler
Jeremy D. Adler
Judith P. Aikin
Hellmut Ammerlahn
Elizabeth A. Andersen
Linda Archibald
Jeffrey Ashcroft
Michael Bachem
Ulrich Baer
Thomas Baginski
Petra M. Bagley
Timothy Bahti
Claire Baldwin
Andrew Barker
Edward M. Batley
Diana Ipsen Behler
Raimund Belgardt
Stefan Berger
Sigrid Berka
Frederick Betz
Paul Bishop
Peter Boerner
Greg Bond
Ruth B. Bottigheimer
Eoin Bourke
Helga G. Braunbeck

Fritz Breithaupt
Fred Bridgham
Jane K. Brown
Barton W. Browning
Marcus Bullock
Barbara Burns
Anthony Bushell
Helen Cafferty
Salvatore Calomino
Mark Chinca
Albrecht Classen
Sarah Colvin
Jean E. Conacher
Robert Conard
Roger F. Cook
Carol Anne Costabile-Heming
Anthony Coulson
W.A. Coupe
David N. Coury
Sebastian Coxon
Charlotte M. Craig
Ruth P. Dawson
Sheila Janet Dickson
Carol Diethe
Irene Stocksieker Di Maio
David Dollenmayer
William Collins Donahue
Bruce Duncan
Graeme Dunphy
Volker Dürr
Glenn Ehrstine
Friederike Eigler
Rosemarie Elliott
Peter C. Erb
Matthew Erlin
Tamara S. Evans
Helen Fehervary
Bernhard Fetz
Barbara Fischer
Bernd Fischer
Sabine Fischer
Rod Fisher
Heather Fleming
John L. Flood
Thomas C. Fox
Shelley Frisch
Kerstin Gaddy
Howard Gaskill
Francis G. Gentry
Marion E. Gibbs
Jill Gillespie
Robert Gillett
Jeffrey Gould
Peter J. Graves
Sabine Gross
Christian Gundermann
Susan E. Gustafson
Barbara Hahn
Jennifer Ham
Anthony J. Harper
Nigel Harris
Robert E. Helbling
Reinhold Heller
Charles H. Helmetag
Wolfgang Hempel
Astrid Herhoffer
Hillary Hope Herzog
David Hill
Murray Hill
Gerd Hillen
Ingeborg Hoesterey
Malcolm Humble
Irmgard Hunt
Bernd Hüppauf
Peter Hutchinson
Kristen Hylenski
Noah Isenberg
Calvin N. Jones
David H.R. Jones
Michael T. Jones
Martin Kagel
Martin Kane
Brian Keith-Smith
Hans-Wilhelm Kelling
Rolf Kieser
Ian King
Suzanne Kirkbright
Thomas W. Kniesche
Clayton Koelb
Wulf Koepke
Katrin Kohl
Kathleen L. Komar
Todd Kontje
Delia Caparoso Konzett
Matthias Konzett
Barbara Kosta
Helga W. Kraft
Bruce Krajewski
Hannes Krauss
Margarete Lamb-Faffelberger
Alan Lareau
Duncan Large
Edward T. Larkin
Dan Latimer
Steven W. Lawrie
Henry A. Lea
Leo A. Lensing
Ward B. Lewis
Karl Leydecker
Richard Littlejohns
Ladislaus Löb
Elizabeth Loentz
Dagmar C.G. Lorenz
Christoph Lorey
Frederick A. Lubich
Helga Stipa Madland
Donald Marshall
Bernhard R. Martin
Eve Mason
Warren R. Maurer

Winder McConnell
John McCumber
Moray McGowan
Alastair McLeish
Karin M.D. McPherson
Charlotte Melin
Alan Menhennet
Erika A. Metzger
Michael M. Metzger
Franziska Meyer
David Midgley
Michael Mitchell
Ben Morgan
Agnes C. Mueller
Kenneth E. Munn
Brian Murdoch
Kamakshi P. Murti
Wolfgang Nehring
Don Nelson
Maike Oergel
James C. O'Flaherty
Stefanie Ohnesorg
John Osborne
John Roger Paas
Stuart Parkes
Holger A. Pausch
Malcolm Pender
Helmut F. Pfanner
Anthony Phelan
Gertud Bauer Pickar
Burton Pike
Julian Preece
Peter Prochnik
Judith Purver
Helena Ragg-Kirkby
Hermann Rasche
Malcolm Read
Jennifer Redmann
Gertrud Reershemius
J. H. Reid
Max Reinhart
Paul B. Reitter
Nicholas Rennie
Laurence A. Rickels
Hugh Ridley
J. M. Ritchie
Steve Rizza
David Robb
Ian F. Roe
Christian Rogowski
Hugh Rorrison
Herbert Rowland
Inca Rumold
Judith Ryan
Eda Sagarra
Jeffrey L. Sammons
Stephan K. Schindler
Gerd K. Schneider
Eric J. Schwab
Christoph E. Schweitzer
Marilyn Scott Linton
Lesley Sharpe
Timothy Shipe
Robert K. Shirer
Ellis Shookman
Hinrich Siefken
Lisa Silverman
Sunka Simon
Peter Skrine
Duncan Smith
Luke Springman
Patricia H. Stanley
H. Stern
Mary E. Stewart
Alexander Stillmark
Michelle Stott
Arrigo V. Subiotto
John E. Tailby
Rodney Taylor
J.K.A. Thomaneck
Istvan Varkonyi
Nicholas Vazsonyi
Robert Vilain
Hans Wagener
Richard Ernest Walker
Ian Wallace
Ingeborg Walther
Robert Weninger
Peter Werres
Jonathan West
Brett R. Wheeler
Alfred D. White
I.A. White
J.J. White
William Whobrey
Christopher J. Wickham
Juliet Wigmore
Rhys W. Williams
Michael Winkler
Geoffrey Winthrop-Young
Gregory H. Wolf
Harry Zohn

ALPHABETICAL LIST OF ENTRIES

ALPHABETICAL LIST OF WORKS

A

Theodor W. Adorno 1903–1969

Theodor Wiesengrund Adorno is together with Walter Benjamin the most famous figure of the Frankfurt School. Adorno is even infamous for his downbeat readings of mass cultural phenomena, which his critics would like to dismiss as Eurocentric phobicity toward the innovations of popular multicultures. It is indicative (if not symptomatic) of his strong ties with Freud's science that (not unlike Jacques Lacan at the same time) he should have taken on the thought-driving position of negative-transference object. His well-known pronouncements on art and "the culture industry" (mass media culture by another name) are always at some gut level strategically and provocatively unpopular.

Adorno led the way in turning critical attention away from the focus on the rise of National Socialism, which was in a sense behind him, to address related problems within the new setting of exile. The group psychology of Nazi Germany had a global future, if not in the same place then in the new place, as part of the program of the U.S. culture industry. In *Das Unbehagen in der Kultur* (1930; *Civilization and Its Discontents*), Freud performed this about face when he pointed to the cultural state of America to illustrate his words of caution regarding the dangers to civilization posed by group formations based exclusively on mutual identification. Thus both National Socialism and the culture industry were seen to function as fateful misreadings of psychoanalysis, the science or discourse at the same time reshelved, implicitly, as owner's manual to our technological era. Both phrases or phases of this misreading amounted to "psychoanalysis in reverse." While this slogan remains hard or even impossible to pin down to one source (some say Adorno, others say Leo Lowenthal), even so, or even more so, it is the formula that keeps current as perhaps the most influential "conspiracy theory" put forward by the Frankfurt School. It moreover gives the bottom line of Adorno's negative or ambivalent dialectics.

Adorno was born and raised the only child of Oskar Wiesengrund, a wealthy and assimilated Jew, and Maria Calvelli-Adorno, a Roman Catholic of Italian descent. He dropped, or rather incorporated, the patronymic Wiesengrund at the start of his exile from Nazi Germany, and he then put in its place his mother's family name. It was also the name of his mother's unmarried sister, Agathe, who lived as part of the Wiesengrund household and who, together with mother Maria, was Adorno's initiator into the world of music. Why did he change his name when he changed it? Hannah Arendt gives a ruthless reading of the act as one of (unconscious?) collaboration. Martin Jay sees the change as representing Adorno's lasting wish that, still in the 1930s, he could somehow remain within the German-language world. Indeed, he was at Oxford University at the time of his name change only because his application to transfer his *venia legendi* from Frankfurt to Vienna had been turned down. And yet, seen from the side of his inevitable emigration to a new world order of English only, "Adorno" could also be seen as the more functional sound-shape for a world not of his making or liking, which he was nevertheless forced to enter, given the ego's drive to survive.

This survivalist—ego-libidinal or narcissistic—impulse folded into the constitution of the psyche (according to Freud) was also central to Adorno's negative or ambivalent dialectic of Enlightenment, in other words, of our own once and future "Western" culture or discourse. Adorno made the name change at the same time that Freud published *Der Mann Moses* (1939; *Moses and Monotheism*), in which Freud reconstructed the man Moses, who led the Jews out of exile into the promised land of a new identity, as an Egyptian nobleman who borrowed the Jewish people to serve as rescue-carrier of the failed experiment in monotheism that had originally been made in Egypt (under Ikhnaton). Adorno's dismantling of his Jewish identity at the time of crisis shares the same setting (which could be defined, tentatively, as the refusal to receive the crisis as one of identity) with Freud's rereading of Moses. This is not the only note of ambiguity in the work or life of Theodor Adorno that achieves at least the clarity of ambivalence through a restoration of the context he shared with Freud's science. While Gillian Rose rightly associates Adorno's self-reflexively immanent style of inversion with Nietzsche (certainly Adorno advertised as much in his *Minima Moralia* [1951; *Minima Moralia*]), Jürgen Habermas rejects Adorno's "dark" or "postmodern" inclinations as the legacy of Nietzsche. But how is that legacy not mediated by Freud (especially given the transferential medium within which Habermas must judge his former mentor)? At the time of Adorno's name change, the establishment of eclectic psychotherapy in Nazi Germany, which included psychoanalysis (by any other name) as a substantial component in the mix, made regular use of Nietzsche's name when Freud's was being censored. That the end of World War II marked a return of psychoanalysis to West Germany only in name was nevertheless witnessed by Habermas in his commentary on the 1956 conference on Freud, which was cosponsored by the Institut für Sozialforschung in Frankfurt (Adorno was codirector of the Institut at the time): "'Freud in the Present' was the first opportunity for young German academics to learn about the simple fact that Sigmund Freud was the founding father of a living scientific and intellectual tradition" (1980). What was in a name change, therefore, were two or three fundamental aspects of Adorno's thought: the dismantling of identity, often in association with or recognition of the fundamental "perversity" of the ego; the melancholic relationship to an absent culture of the individual, represented as the legacy of a missing father; and—perhaps in sum, perhaps in other words—the Freudian "ambivalence" that informs Adorno's "immanent," "ironic," "negative," and "dialectical" mode of argument, one that does not stop short of reading any word as name and name as word, even or especially his own.

If, at least chronologically, Adorno's first love was music, then his second love was philosophy (at the age of 15, Adorno was introduced to philosophy, in particular Kant's first *Critique,* by Siegfried Kracauer, a friend of the family, who was engaged by Adorno's parents as their son's tutor). Adorno enrolled as a student of philosophy at the Johann Wolfgang Goethe University in Frankfurt, earning his doctorate after three years of study with a thesis on the phenomenology of Edmund Husserl. He first met Max Horkheimer during this course of study in a seminar on Husserl that both attended. Both students seemed to have spent as much time attending psychology seminars as seminars in their declared field of study, philosophy. While the psychology seminars offered at the university prove that the young men were exposed to Gestaltism, the onset of Freud's influence cannot be located in the record of Adorno's studies. Jay suggests that Adorno first came into contact with psychoanalysis while in Vienna or on subsequent trips to Berlin.

The hard-to-place origin of contact does allow for an overlap not only with his second love but with the first one, too. Following a performance he attended in Frankfurt of excerpts from Alban Berg's *Wozzeck,* Adorno was inspired to contact the composer and persuade him to accept him as his student in Vienna. He thus shifted the scene of his studies to the capital of the "new music," which also happened to be the hometown of psychoanalysis. While in Vienna, Adorno wrote his Habilitation thesis on Kant and Freud. For reasons that are only up for speculation, Adorno's advisor Hans Cornelius rejected "The Concept of the Unconscious in the Transcendental Theory of Mind," and the young author, without protest or attempted revision, promptly withdrew his application. What interested Adorno during his stay in Vienna was how psychoanalytic theory founded an empirical science of the unconscious upon a notion (the unconscious) that was itself not empirical.

Having assigned this study of the unconscious to a place in his ongoing work that might be called, in association both with the unconscious or the uncanny, one of unpublication, Adorno commenced a new project, "Kierkegaard: Construction of the Aesthetic," with which he earned his Habilitation in 1933, on the very day Hitler came to power. In this work Adorno for the first time focuses critically on some of the implications and exclusions in Martin Heidegger's settling of metaphysical accounts, and this focus on margins followed from Freud's elaboration of the unconscious and repression. The dispute with Heidegger would be one more lasting main theme in Adorno's work. *Jargon der Eigentlichkeit: Zur deutschen Ideologie* (1965; *The Jargon of Authenticity*), for example, was intended originally as part of *Negative Dialektik* (1966; *Negative Dialectics*). Heidegger's philosophy, according to Adorno, just does not see that the mind is at work in the meanings that confront it; however, the mind also does not constitute such meanings by itself. But Heidegger's philosophy nevertheless provided, by absence and metonymy, good social critique: the absence of any theory of action in this philosophy corresponded to the real social impotence of the individual in society. According to Jay, "although Adorno emphasized the dialectical relationship between history and philosophy, his own thought remained surprisingly constant for virtually all of his mature life." What frames this object constancy in Adorno's thought is his abandoned, deferred, and often split-off investment in psychoanalysis.

Peter Hohendahl links and limits Adorno's investment in Freud's thought to its application for didactic purposes in certain texts, principally the ones concerning mass-media cultures. At the same time, however, this suggests that psychoanalysis serves as the owner's manual shared by the in-group and the outsiders, that it is the happy medium between what the consumers already know, what they get with their programming, and Adorno's immanent critique. It is hard to imagine what Adorno's regular inclusion of social context signifies if not, at least at the same time, some station in the crossing of culture with industry. Rose thus rightly points out that from a Marxist point of view Adorno's neglect of "those social forms on which the analogy of cultural form depends is serious." Because Adorno neglects the full context of Marxian theory, Rose continues, "the process of production is emphasised as all-powerful, and reification becomes a synonym for the principle of power which is universal but unlocatable, and which affects everyone equally." But what if the theoretical frame that holds Adorno accountable belonged as much to psychoanalysis as to Marxism? Certainly some arrangement or coupling between the two superdiscourses was one of the obsessions of the Frankfurt School. But in the couple's theoretical setting, it is hard to imagine a union with psychoanalysis that would not ultimately lead to a rereading of the partner discourse, in this case Marxism, along Freudian lines. Adorno's focus on reification and personification, for example, is mediated—even or especially when it goes without saying—both by psychoanalytic theory and by that theory's analogical or "endopsychic" hookup with the media of mass culture. What makes Adorno's writing so difficult is that he leaves his reading in unprotected association with all that counts as mediation or medium, including his own ambivalence, and thus also his projective involvement, with the objects and objections of his critique. Adorno's writing, because it is always difficult, is also precisely just for that reason invariably didactic. Especially if a point isn't being readily made, demanding discourse teaches thinking.

Adorno taught nonidentity thinking. One of the organizing metaphors of Adorno's performative style, borrowed from Walter Benjamin, was the "constellation," the practice of nonphobic juxtaposition of whatever comes already associated but nonsuperimposed in the reception area of the object or topic under investigation, which in turn can thus be situated and characterized without implying or requiring that the concepts in use are identical with their objects. Nonidentity thinking is also allegorical or mournful (again in association with Benjamin, specifically with his *Der Ursprung des deutschen Trauerspiels* [1925; *The Origin of German Tragic Drama*]), inasmuch as the autonomy thought thus attains is not outside the disintegrative social process but is or performs that process. Nonidentity thinking as the truth of identity thinking reveals the underlying processes as well as the utopian possibilities or impossibilities otherwise covered up through reification, standardization, personalization, or fetishism. The reified concepts of identity thinking describe social phenomena, the appearances of society, as if these in fact had the properties to which the concepts refer. In other words, identity thinking is a norm that has, by default, become either utopian or reified. In society, present tense, the concept cannot identify its true object. The consciousness that recognizes this is, in sum, nonidentity thinking (or negative dialectics).

While excluding it from the present social context, Adorno implies the existence (once upon a time, the best time that never was) of a utopian condition or state of interpersonal mutuality that would supersede intrapsychic self-difference. But according to Freud, this fundamental sexual difference is a given for everyone, even for the most perfect psychopath, on account of "primal repression," the repression of the mother's body whereby the object of desire is secured only as off-limits object, a limit or division that cuts across each individual psyche. Adorno's analyzes the narcissism, self-contradiction, and perversity *constitutive* of the ego (according to Freud) as the socially conditioning medium that is at the same time specific to these social conditions. Thus, the "perversion" arises whereby people accept any ideology that is contrary to their rational interests as long as it is adapted to "reality." As a consequence, Adorno still employs "perversion" not only as his regularly conjured diagnosis of social or cultural ills but as the measure of a secondary or socially fixed and therefore transient degeneration of the natural norm. Thus, the autonomy of the individual is also the (socially determining and determined) ego's loss. The notion of social integration is deemed problematic by Adorno precisely because in this society we cannot but accessorize with the matching ego, an ego that is both opponent of repression on the conscious side and, on the unconscious side, the repressive agency itself. Freud, by contrast, saw human society, which is always organized around violence control or identification, as always meeting in the ego its match and maker. That Adorno at one point could write that psychoanalysis shared with the homosexual a certain cold detachment from the evidence of sexual difference and a perverse reduction of this difference to the same difference, that of narcissistic or mutual identification, should come as no surprise if we consider the social or interpersonal adjustments Adorno was always trying to make in his applications of Freud's science. But the links and the limits all fall down within psychoanalysis. The intellectual-historical parameters that date Adorno's thought, such as his emphatic concept of truth or his metaphysics of modernist art (which bore the corollary, however, that metaphysical experience was no longer available), would regain their staying power if realigned, respectively, with the unconscious or with the tension in psychoanalysis between the shorthand of the theory (of the unconscious) and the in-session materiality of the transference, an "experience" for which it is hard to find the words, in theory, whether they are the same or other words. Thus, we are back inside the dynamic Adorno worked out for his deferred and perpetual Freud thesis, the frame, if by many other names and concepts, for his own projects: the tension, once again, between the nonempirical notion of the unconscious and the foundation and functioning of an empirical science on the basis of this same notion.

Nonidentity thinking does not evacuate or resolve the conceptual blocks or blockages of the philosophical tradition, but it takes them allegorically. According to Adorno, for instance, epistemology is both inherently self-contradictory and nevertheless necessary because it holds the place of an illusion—the socially produced illusion of the subject—and thus its inclusion gives nonidentity thinking greater accuracy than any so-called new philosophy that would abandon altogether the notion of the subject. The future of Adorno's reception lies in the opening up of the intersection of his thought with that of Jacques Derrida. This opening act appears especially pressing given the ways in which American deconstruction (the school of Paul de Man) has succeeded in favoring Benjamin by excluding Adorno, a splitting internal to the reception of Benjamin's thought as devoid of Freudian influence.

LAURENCE A. RICKELS

See also Frankfurt School

Biography

Born in Frankfurt, 11 September 1903. Studied at the University of Frankfurt, Ph.D. 1924; studied music in Vienna with Alban Berg, 1925–28; joined the Institut für Sozialforschung in New York, 1938; head of music study, Institut für Sozialforschung, Institute Office of Radio Research, Princeton, New Jersey, 1938–41; in California with the Institut für Sozialforschung, 1941–49; assistant director, 1950–55, codirector, 1955–58, and director of the Institut für Sozialforschung, in Frankfurt, 1958–69; philosophy and sociology professor, University of Frankfurt, 1958–69. Arnold Schönberg Medal, 1954; Critics' Prize for Literature, 1959; Goethe Medal, Frankfurt, 1963. Died in Frankfurt, 6 August 1969.

Selected Works

Collections

Gesammelte Werke, edited by Rolf Tiedemann, Frankfurt, Suhrkamp, 23 vols., 1970–

Nonfiction

Kierkegaard: Konstruktion des Ästhetischen, 1933
Memorandum: Music in Radio, 1938
Philosophische Fragmente, with Max Horkheimer, 1944; revised as *Dialektik der Aufklärung: Philosophische Fragmente,* 1947; as *Dialectic of Enlightenment,* 1972
Philosophie der neuen Musik, 1949; as *Philosophy of Modern Music,* 1973
The Authoritarian Personality, with others, 1950
Minima Moralia: Reflexionen aus dem beschädigten Leben, 1951; as *Minima Moralia: Reflections from Damaged Life,* 1974
Versuch über Wagner, 1952; as *In Search of Wagner,* 1981
Die gegängelte Musik: Bemerkungen über die Musikpolitik der Ostblockstaaten, 1954
Prismen: Kulturkritik und Gesellschaft, 1955; as *Prisms,* 1967
Dissonanzen: Musik in der verwalteten Welt, 1956
Zur Metakritik der Erkenntnistheorie: Studien über Husserl und die phänomenologischen Antinomien, 1956; as *Against Epistemology: A Metacritique,* 1983
Aspekte der Hegelschen Philosophie, 1957
Die Funktion des Kontrapunkts in der neuen Musik, 1957
Noten zur Literatur, 4 vols., 1958–74

Musikalische Schriften: Klangfiguren [vol. 1]; *Quasi una fantasia* [vol. 2], 1959–63
Mahler: Eine musikalische Physiognomik, 1960
Einleitung in die Musiksoziologie, 1962; as *Introduction to the Sociology of Music*, 1976
Drei Studien zu Hegel, 1963
Eingriffe: Neun kritische Modelle, 1963
Der getreue Korrepetitor: Lehrschriften zur musikalischen Praxis, 1963
Moments musicaux: Neu gedruckte Aufsätze, 1928–1962, 1964
Jargon der Eigentlichkeit: Zur deutschen Ideologie, 1965; as *The Jargon of Authenticity*, 1973
Negative Dialektik, 1966; as *Negative Dialectics*, 1973
Ohne Leitbild: Parva Aesthetica, 1967
Über einige Relationen zwischen Musik and Malerei: Die Kunst und die Künste, 1967
Berg: Der Meister des kleinsten Übergangs, 1968
Impromptus: Zweite Folge neu gedruckter musikalischer Aufsätze, 1968
Über Walter Benjamin, 1968
Komposition für den Film, with Hanns Eisler, 1969; as *Composing for the Films*, 1971
Stichworte: Kritische Modelle 2, 1969
Nervenpunkte der neuen Musik, 1969
Aesthetische Theorie, edited by Gretel Adorno and Rolf Tiedemann, 1970; as *Aesthetic Theory*, 1983
Aufsätze zur Gesellschaftstheorie und Methodologie, 1970
Erziehung zur Mündigkeit: Vortäge und Gespräche mit Helmut Becker, 1959–69, edited by Gerd Kadelbach, 1970
Vorlesungen zur Ästhetik, edited by Christof Subik, 1970
Theodor W. Adorno: Eine Auswahl, edited by Rolf Tiedemann, 1971
Kritik: Kleine Schriften zur Gesellschaft, edited by Rolf Tiedemann, 1971
Aufsätze zur Literatur des 20. Jahrhunderts: Versuch, das Endspiel zu verstehen [vol. 1]; *Zur Dialektik des Engagements* [vol. 2], 1973
Vorlesungen zur Ästhetik 1967–1968, 1973
Vorlesung zur Einleitung in die Soziologie, 1973
Vorlesung zur Einleitung in die Erkenntnistheorie, 1973
Philosophische Terminologie: Zur Einleitung, edited by Rudolf zur Lippe, 1973
Gesellschaftstheorie und Kulturkritik, 1975
Against Epistemology (translated from the German), 1980

Other
Briefwechsel: Theodor W. Adorno und Ernst Krenek, edited by Wolfgang Rogge, 1974

Edited Works
with Gretel Adorno, *Walter Benjamin: Schriften*, 2 vols., 1955
with Gershom Scholem, *Walter Benjamin: Briefe*, 2 vols., 1966

Further Reading

Buck-Morss, Susan, *The Origin of Negative Dialectics: Theodor W. Adorno, Walter Benjamin, and the Frankfurt Institute*, New York: Free Press, 1977
Habermas, Jürgen, "Psycho Thermidor and the Rebirth of Rebellious Subjectivity," *Berkeley Journal of Sociology* 25 (1980)
———, *Der philsophische Diskurs der Moderne*, Frankfurt: Suhrkamp, 1985; as *The Philosophical Discourse of Modernity*, Cambridge, Massachusetts: MIT Press, 1987
Hohendahl, Peter Uwe, *Prismatic Thought: Theodor W. Adorno*, Lincoln: University of Nebraska Press, 1995
Jameson, Fredric, *Marxism and Form: Twentieth-Century Dialectical Theories of Literature*, Princeton, New Jersey: Princeton University Press, 1971
Jay, Martin, *Adorno*, Cambridge, Massachusetts: Harvard University Press, 1984
Rickels, Laurence, *The Case of California*, Baltimore, Maryland, and London: Johns Hopkins University Press, 1991
Rose, Gillian, *The Melancholy Science: An Introduction to the Thought of Theodor W. Adorno*, London: Macmillan, and New York: Columbia University Press, 1978

Aestheticization of Politics

In 1936, Walter Benjamin concluded his essay "Das Kunstwerk im Zeitalter seiner technischen Reproduzierbarkeit" with the notion of aestheticization of politics (versus politicization of art), a notion that was in turn designed, or so it might seem, for its reproducibility. (The standard title of Benjamin's essay in English, "The Work of Art in the Age of Mechanical Reproduction," misrepresents the "age" designated in German as one of "technological reproducibility.") Throughout the essay, as in his follow-up essay, "Über einige Motive in Baudelaire" (1939; "On Some Motifs in Baudelaire"), Benjamin explores what follows from the pressures of technologization and mass formation. Specifically, he argues that the reception of our cultural traditions has been radically altered—rewired—through the advent of photography and film: "The instant the criterion of authenticity ceases to be applicable to artistic production, the total function of art is reversed. Instead of being based on ritual, it begins to be based on another practice—politics." We shift thus from a theatrical or interpersonal stage of representation to the intrapsychic lab space of moviemaking:

> The camera that presents the performance of the film actor to the public need not respect the performance as an integral whole. Guided by the cameraman, the camera continually changes its position with respect to the performance. The sequence of positional views which the editor composes from the material supplied him constitutes the completed film. It comprises certain factors of movement which are in reality those of the camera. . . . Hence, the performance of the actor is subjected to a series of optical tests. . . . Also, the film actor lacks the opportunity of the stage actor to adjust to the audience during his performance, since he does not present his performance to the audience in person. This permits the audience to take the position of a critic, without experiencing any personal

> contact with the actor. The audience's identification with the actor is really an identification with the camera. Consequently the audience takes the position of the camera; its approach is that of testing.

This perspective is internally driven by the need for proximity to all objects in the new visual field of reduction, a reduction of everything, including invisibility, to utter visibility. Participation in technological reproduction or replication, in the reduction of whatever is out there, even or especially if it is out of sight, to visibility leads automatically both to a new perspective of testing, expertise, participation, and distraction, and at the same time to a new immediacy. Our environment is so saturated with technology that we enter directly into this visual field, this new reality, the way a surgeon skips the personal relationship with the patient to penetrate directly into the internal anatomy of the body. The reaction against these inevitable changes takes the form of a "retrenchment" of all the old values of our cultural tradition, those of presence or aura, via the aestheticization of political reality. To clarify this process of retrenchment, Benjamin introduces another distinction: "All efforts to render politics aesthetic culminate in one thing: war." Through war, technological progress can be mobilized without disturbing the traditional property system. But war, less an intention or option than a structure, was there first: our media extensions and inventions were all tried out first under the pressure of war. In the era of total or suicidal warfare, which has also been the era of greatest technical progress, the so-called beginning of war is also the end; thus the new mode of war is one of preparedness, like the shock absorption or inoculation Benjamin otherwise attributes to the mass response to the shock of new technologies.

Typical of the division of labor written into the marriage contract between psychoanalysis and Marxism negotiated by the Frankfurt School, Benjamin owes his account of our mass-technological conditioning to and through shock to Freud's post–World War I investigations of anxiety as defense, but he drops that context of thinking when it comes time to address mass formation on its own (at least in the epilogue, which is organized around the political opposition between fascism and communism). Rather than continue to analyze the formation of the masses, following Freud, as group psychology, and thus as compatible with technology, Benjamin switches registers:

> The growing proletarianization of modern man and the increasing formation of masses are two aspects of the same process. Fascism attempts to organize the newly created proletarian masses without affecting the property structure which the masses strive to eliminate. Fascism sees its salvation in giving these masses not their right, but instead a chance to express themselves. The masses have a right to change property relations; fascism seeks to give them an expression while preserving property. The logical result of fascism is the introduction of aesthetics into political life.

By implication or exclusion, Benjamin gives the fascists credit for a grasp of what Freud diagnosed in the psychology of groups that seems more firm and informed than the understanding he demonstrates at this juncture.

Benjamin's upbeat faith in the future of positive social changes brought about through technology and the formation of masses provoked a rebuttal from Adorno, for example, in "Über den Fetischcharakter der Musik" (1938; "On the Fetish Character in Music"). In a long letter dated 18 March 1936, Adorno criticized Benjamin's use of dialectical materialism in his essay on mass culture as metaphorical and, in terms of historical context, unmediated. The dispute largely observes the dynamic of their relationship, what Adorno refers to as their "philosophical friendship"—one regrettably triangulated, he felt, by Bertolt Brecht's influence. The concluding sentence of Adorno's essay on fetishism and regression in the musical culture industry is thus addressed to Benjamin, reminding him, individual to individual, of the primacy of their friendship: "Collective powers are liquidating an individuality past saving, but against them only individuals are capable of consciously representing the aims of collectivity." We owe to the dispute between friends the two versions of Benjamin's "The Work of Art in the Age of Mechanical Reproduction." The first version, which was published in 1936 in Pierre Klossowsky's French translation (there are a few differences, however, suggesting that the "original" was not exactly the version used for the translation), is more psychoanalytic or even therapeutic in its treatment of crowd responses. For example, Benjamin considers the laughter induced by such modern mascot figures of cinema as Mickey Mouse as mass-media-administered inoculations against the mass psychosis that could result from the pressures of technology or living in groups. Benjamin's positive reading of Mickey Mouse blasted Adorno's sense of proportion or standards. The ensuing struggle over the meaning of Mickey Mouse summons now Marx and Freud, now Benjamin and Adorno, as the partners in this attempted couples therapy or theory. One duo dynamic cannot be superimposed onto the other. Adorno's push toward proper Marxism reflects the pull he was countering and projecting of Brecht's vulgar Marxism. It is hard to imagine a study of mass culture more indebted to Freud's group psychology than Adorno's "On the Fetish Character in Music." And with every cut Adorno makes between the lines of Benjamin's reading he cuts into his own flesh, the body of music he adored.

Even in the epilogue of political opposition, Benjamin had never really left the Freudian perspective outside. Thus he specifies the kind of war that the fascist aestheticization of politics must lead to: mankind's "self-alienation has reached such a degree that it can experience its own destruction as an aesthetic pleasure of the first order." The fascist thus manipulates Freud's insights into group psychology only to the point of his own group membership in a psychotic state, the vanishing point of paranoid projection. The fascist does not see his side of the group relationship, the suicide side. Benjamin's closing sentence, "Communism responds by politicizing art," puts extra pressure on his notion of aestheticization of politics by conjuring up the new horizon of an alternative approach. Adorno took this as a reproach, or as a confusion, regarding his own sponsorship of the contemporary art of suspended reference, as exemplified by Arnold Schönberg and Kafka. This high art of asceticism and rigor, precisely through its user unfriendliness, offered, according to Adorno, the only critique possible in mass consumer society. Adorno's point that there are situations in which only elitism can be truly radical is well taken, but Benjamin of course did not have socialist realism in mind but rather a film such as Chaplin's *Modern Times*. By politicization of art, Benjamin could only have meant—by the testimony of his own discourse, performance, and inside-out concern with allegory—art in which reference is not suspended but rather thematized as problem. Schönberg and Kafka, in this view, are in Chaplin's good company. Benjamin thus anticipated later debates in cultural criticism on the distinction to be awarded modernism versus post-modernism.

The inoculations of mass-media technology are not necessarily proof against fascism. Even when the fascist has the look of bad Nietzscheanism, it is still Benjamin's gadget lover (who comes complete with an owner's manual issued by psychoanalysis) who is looking out of the look. The fascists gave their gadget-loving audience a degree of sexual expression, along group-psychological and thus homoerotic or unisexual lines, while representing and repressing homosexual identification as boundary concept.

Benjamin's contrast between two modes of the production of reception has been lumped together with the long-standing epigonal self-reflection that Germany had never opened up or entered a political forum in the arts: there is no German social novel, to give the usual example. Siegfried Kracauer's *From Caligari to Hitler* (1947) makes of Fritz Lang's addition of a narrative frame to the original story of *The Cabinet of Dr. Caligari* a primal scene. The kind of framing or aestheticizing displacement whereby Lang changed the direct impact of the original story of political oppression and resistance rehearsed or repeated a whole history of projection: in the meantime, the Germans kept their blinders on as they marched not in step with political realities but to the different beat of the phantom dictator. However, Lang's addition can also be seen as having made the concept or device of framing, whether as the closure of the Oedipus complex or as the framing of institutions, the far-reaching concern of the film. Which is the more politically astute version?

According to Phillippe Lacoue-Labarthe and Jean-Luc Nancy, "Germany" was itself, from the beginning, a late construct or artifact removed from political, cultural, or social reality:

> The drama of Germany was also that it suffered an imitation twice removed, and saw itself obliged to imitate the imitation of antiquity that France did not cease to export for at least two centuries. Germany, in other words, was not only missing an identity but also lacked ownership of its means of identification.

"Germany" can thus be seen as staggered by an excess of original imitation—an imitation of an imitation that can never be imitation—a double command given to induce psychotic breakdown as in the individual cases of Hölderlin or Nietzsche. Hence the success of Nazi aestheticization, "the construction, the formation, and the production of the German people in, through, and as a work of art" (Lacoue-Labarthe and Nancy).

In *Buch der Könige* (1991, 1994; *Book of Kings*), the multivolume study still in progress, Klaus Theweleit extracted another genealogy from the boundary blending of Benjamin's points of contrast: Is it state of the art or art of the state? According to Theweleit, artists have established with and for their work "artist states" that run parallel to the political states with which they must negotiate their own diplomatic status and immunity. The diplomatic affiliations that artist-thinkers invent and enter into are not on the same continuum of meaning and decision-making as in stateside politics. In the art-promotional setting, one wing of oppositional politics is also always the other or either wing. Returning to Benjamin, but without taking sides, Theweleit examines how the artist state, as a special-interest group psychology, promotes, once on the diplomatically secured inside, new modes of compatibility with technology.

LAURENCE A. RICKELS

See also Walter Benjamin; Frankfurt School

Further Reading

Adorno, Theodor, "On the Fetish Character of Music," in *The Essential Frankfurt School Reader,* edited by Andrew Arato and Eike Gebhardt, New York: Urizen, 1977; Oxford: Blackwell, 1978

Benjamin, Walter, "The Work of Art in the Age of Mechanical Reproduction," in *Illuminations,* edited by Hannah Arendt, New York: Harcourt, Brace, 1968

Buck-Morss, Susan, *The Dialectics of Seeing: Walter Benjamin and the Arcades Project,* Cambridge, Massachusetts: MIT Press, 1989

Lacoue-Labarthe, Phillippe, and Jean-Luc Nancy, "The Nazi Myth," translated by Brian Holmes, *Critical Inquiry* 16 (1990)

Aesthetics

Although the term *Aesthetik* (Neo-Latin *aesthetica,* English *aesthetics*) was not used before 1735, when it was coined by Alexander Gottlieb Baumgarten (1714–62) in his *Meditationes Philosophicae de Nonullis ad Poema Pertinentibis* (*Philosophical Meditations Concerning Several Matters Pertaining to Poetry*), treatment of matters pertaining to aesthetics occurred as early as the beginning of the 13th century in, for example, the explicit meditations on aesthetic issues in Wolfram's *Parzifal* or the self-conscious concern with the art of poetry in Walther. But by far the most noted among these earlier works is that of Martin Opitz (1597–1639). In his *Buch von der deutschen Poeterey* (1624; Book on German Poetics), Opitz not only reformulates well-known neoclassical doctrines found in Scaliger and Ronsard, but he also urges the development of a native German poetic discourse. While he strongly recommended the imitation of classical models and produced many translations of ancient verse, he declared the primacy of stress-based meter for German poetry, rejecting the syllable-counting systems of the Romance languages. He understood poetry as a kind of "hidden theology" that is both intimately connected to the divine and committed to the transmission of wisdom. In his interest in earlier native verse, his desire for a German national literature, and his sense of the divine mission of the poet, Opitz anticipates important aesthetic issues that are elaborated in the influential writings of the 18th century.

Another important reformulation of neoclassical ideas is Johann Christoph Gottsched's (1700–1766) *Versuch einer critischen Dichtkunst* (1730; *Attempt at a Critical Poetics for Germans*), a magisterial volume insisting on the superiority of French models. He prefers imitation of the French twelve-syllable Alexandrine verse, for example, to the stress-based rhythms championed by Opitz, and insists on adherence to the "rules" of dramatic composition derived from Aristotle and Horace. In spite of the scholarly weight behind these views, energetic opposition to Gottsched appeared almost immediately with the publication of a rival *Critische Dichtkunst* (1740; Critical Poetics) by the Swiss critics Johann Jakob Bodmer (1698–1783) and Johann Jakob Breitinger (1701–76). Bodmer also was an importer of ideas, but he was far more interested in English than in French thought, offering his own translation of Milton's *Paradise Lost*, old English ballads, and other British works. He also appreciated the legacy of medieval German poetry, publishing editions of Wolfram's *Parizifal,* the *Niebelungenlied,* and the Minnesänger. Bodmer and Breitinger thought of art not as secondary to philosophy or theology but as a creative act analogous to the divine creation of the world. Poets imitated nature's creative power, not simply the appearance of natural objects and occurrences.

Baumgarten himself, the founder and namer of the field, produced an aesthetic theory that was far less influential than his coinage of a useful new word. His *Aesthetica* of 1750, although based on the central notion that art is a special form of cognition, finally proposes that art is essentially a kind of analogue of reason that is ultimately inferior to philosophy and rational thought. Three other works of the mid-18th century had far greater impact on aesthetics than anything Baumgarten produced. These were Johann Joachim Winckelmann's *Gedanken über die Nachahmung der griechischen Werke in der Malerei und Bildhauerkunst* (1755; *Reflections on the Imitation of Greek Works in Painting and Sculpture*), Johann Georg Hamann's *Aesthetica in nuce* (1762; *Aesthetics in a Nutshell*), and Gotthold-Ephraim Lessing's *Laokoon* (1766; *Laocoön*).

In his *Reflections on the Imitation of Greek Works in Painting and Sculpture,* Winckelmann (1717–68) created an image of ancient Greece that seized the European imagination almost immediately and that has held it ever since. In recommending that contemporary artists should imitate the statues of antiquity rather than the modern living human form, Winckelmann drew upon his notion of Greek antiquity as a kind of aesthetic Eden, a beautiful, sunny landscape inhabited by young, sleek, athletic—and mostly naked—human bodies. The contemporary artist, he claimed, was at a great disadvantage compared with the sculptor of antiquity, who had far greater opportunity to observe the nude body and far better bodies to observe. Even the body depicted in the most severe stress, as in the famous statue of the Trojan priest Laocoon being crushed to death by monstrous serpents, displays what Winckelmann called "edle Einfalt und stille Größe," a noble simplicity and quiet grandeur. He found the source of these qualities not so much in the matter of the representation as in the spirit (*Geist*) of the artist, who himself had to possess the nobility and greatness of soul exhibited in his work. In thus locating artistic success in a combination of access to nature and inward spiritual greatness, Winckelmann set the outline for much of what was to come in aesthetic theory.

Hamann (1730–88), the "Magus of the north," wrote his aesthetic theory in a somewhat eccentric and at times baffling style (he called it a "rhapsody in cabalistic prose"), but the principal elements of his *Aesthetics in a Nutshell* found their way into the mainstream of romantic thought by way of Herder and Goethe. Hamann mostly was concerned with poetry, and in particular with its reform and renovation. He claims at the outset of his essay that poetry is not something arcane and artificial but rather "the mother tongue of the human race." It is altogether natural for mankind to think poetically, since images are the basic form of all perception. His fundamental idea is closely akin to Baumgarten's, but unlike Baumgarten he unflinchingly carries it through to its conclusion. Instead of subordinating poetry to rational thought, Hamann equates poetry with nature and with Holy Scripture, both of which are forms of God's word made visible to man. Rational thinking is not the goal toward which poetry aims; it is rather poetry's mortal enemy, the deadly letter that kills the divine spirit. Like Winckelmann, he stresses the importance of both the artistic spirit and access to nature: "Nature and Scripture," he claims, are the material out of which a "beautiful spirit . . . creates and imitates."

Lessing (1729–81) responds in his *Laocoon* (1766; *Laocoön*) to Winckelmann's discussion of the famous ancient statue and takes matters in an important new direction. He argues that the tranquil grandeur of the statue comes less from the spirit of the Greek artist and more from the nature of the medium of representation. Statues don't cry out in pain, though Greek heroes often do in literature (Lessing cites Sophocles's depiction of the wounded Philoctetes). Lessing built an aesthetic theory out of the opposition of the graphic and plastic arts, which offer representations that extend in space but not in time, to literature, which offers representations that extend in time but not in space. Poetry is thus primarily a narrative medium, unfolding in history, while sculpture and painting are spatial media that represent a single instant in time. Lessing argues that poetry works best when it deals with linear, historical material, offering the famous example of the description of Achilles' shield in Homer's *Iliad*. Homer's description works well, Lessing explains, because the poet transforms his description of the artifact into a story of how that artifact was made, thus turning a static object unsuitable to representation in poetry into a history ideally suited to that medium. Lessing's insistence on matching the nature of the object represented with that of the medium used to represent it is based on a semiotic theory requiring that "the signs used must have a definite relation to the thing signified." Thus events are properly represented in a medium that is itself an event (poetry), and objects are most correctly signified by other objects (paintings and statues).

Lessing's contribution to aesthetic theory has been frequently praised, amended, criticized, and reconsidered in the two and a half centuries since its appearance. It remains one of the most important discussions of the relation of poetry to the other arts in all of European literature, and its central argument about the appropriateness of the medium of representation to the nature of the represented object continues to provoke productive discussion.

The figure who bridges the apparent gulf between mid-18th-century German aesthetics and the Romantic revolution is Johann Gottfried Herder (1744–1803). One finds traces of Hamann's influence in Herder's work, particularly in his views on language and nature.

Herder thought that language came about as the expression of the most fundamental human experiences and was in its earliest form essentially song. The question of the origin of language coincides with that of the origin of poetry, Herder believed, since in the earliest times the two were the same. Herder thus placed an especially high value on poetry that came from the earliest times, on folk songs, ballads, and oral epics that seemed to him to express directly the experience of a culture in its infancy. People in such a young culture also would be closer to nature and thus better able than modern, urbanized Europeans to have unmediated, genuine experiences. Herder taught his younger friends, Goethe and his contemporaries, to value Shakespeare as the poet of nature ("Shakespeare," 1773). The very thing that had seemed such a great fault to Shakespeare's detractors—that he lacked "art"—was to Herder his greatest virtue. Shakespeare's dramas seemed to him devoid of artifice and full of "authenticity, truth, and historical creativity"—thus far more interesting and moving than anything produced by the French with their "stuffed likeness of the Greek theater."

In Herder it is possible to see clearly the beginnings of the coming aesthetic revolution: the rejection of artifice in favor of the "natural," the view of the poet as a genius in intimate contact with the deepest feelings of his community, and the preference for organic form over neoclassical regularity. These would become central tenets of the Romantic movement that emerged from Germany and swept through Europe and its colonies, a movement whose effects extended through the 19th and well into the late 20th century.

Although German literary historians generally distinguish *Klassik* from *Romantik,* there is good reason, especially when considering the history of aesthetics, to understand German classicism (as well as the so-called Sturm und Drang) as part of a larger movement conveniently termed Romanticism. For the purposes of this discussion, the designation *Romantic* will be used for the aesthetic regime that developed and flourished in Germany in the late 18th and early 19th centuries, replacing neoclassicism as the dominant European conception of art. Goethe, Schiller, Kant, and others not normally called Romantics in the standard handbooks will therefore be considered so here.

One of the most influential documents on aesthetics from this or any period is the *Critik der Urteilskraft* (1790; *Critique of Judgment*), the third of the great works of critical philosophy composed by Immanuel Kant (1724–1804). Among the many important ideas in Kant's third critique is the famous proposition that enjoyment of beauty, whether in art or in nature, occurs "apart from any interest" in the beautiful object. Kant uses "interest" here in the sense common today in legal discourse: that is, a concern for the object as it exists in the real world. Kant claims that when we consider something beautiful, we are utterly indifferent to its real existence and care only about the pleasurable effect its representation has on us. Our "interest" in beauty is therefore always "disinterested" because we have no real-world stake in the existence of the object of our delight. Thus, when Hamlet asks, "What is Hecuba to me, or I to Hecuba, that I should weep for her?" he is remarking on the fact that, though he has an enormous emotional reaction to the plight of this fictional heroine, he has no real interest in her existence (or lack of it).

Kant does not limit his discussion to questions of beauty, but (following earlier British philosophers) goes on to delineate a second class of aesthetic objects, the sublime. He distinguishes the sublime from the beautiful in that beauty offers a *positive* pleasure, the sublime a *negative* pleasure. Beauty, Kant claims, is "attended with a feeling of the furtherance of life," while the sublime involves a sense of at least a momentary hindrance to life, a sense not of charm and delight but of awe and respect. Kant cites "threatening rocks, thunderclouds," volcanoes, hurricanes, and high waterfalls as objects that may, "provided our own position is secure," cause us to have feelings of sublime awe and give us "courage to measure ourselves against the seeming omnipotence of nature."

Kant's division of aesthetic objects into the beautiful and the sublime may seem strained and unnecessary outside the context of his system of thought, but it was extremely useful in helping to understand the differences between the tastes of an earlier, largely neoclassical age and those of the contemporary, largely romantic audience. The tastes of the older generation could be seen as directed toward the beautiful, while those of the younger could readily be understood as directed more often toward the sublime. Both old and young appreciated nature, but the former liked charming gardens while the latter preferred the rugged landscapes of the wilderness. Kant did not take sides, but attempted to explain how both sorts of taste could be understood as arising out of the same basic aesthetic principles.

One of Kant's most devoted readers was also one of Germany's greatest poets, Friedrich Schiller (1759–1805). In 1795–96, Schiller published one of the most brilliant essays on aesthetics to come out of that brilliant period, the treatise *Über naïve und sentimentalische Dichtung* (*On the Naive and Sentimental in Literature*). Essentially an analysis of the artistic temperament, Schiller's essay exemplifies the Romantic emphasis on the artist's soul as the locus of artistic creation and the source of aesthetic value. At the same time, he relates all his ideas to a grand conception of nature, upon which all his notions about poetry and poets are based. This idea of nature owes something to Winckelmann as well as to Kant, for it clearly shows the traces of the ideal, Edenic nature depicted in Winckelmann's portrait of ancient Greece. It is not so much nature as we see it in our ordinary experience as it is nature refined and perfected under the most favorable conditions. Schiller proposes that all poets stand in one of two possible relations to nature thus understood: either they are at one with nature, or they are apart from it and seek it. The former Schiller calls *naïve* poets; the latter he refers to as *sentimental.* The ancient Greeks themselves were the best examples of the naïve type, while modern writers tend on the whole toward the sentimental. And, although he does not explicitly mention it, he clearly intends to suggest that among contemporary poets Goethe stands with the naïve and Schiller himself with the sentimental sort.

Schiller wrote other works on aesthetics, among them *Über das Erhabene* (1793; *On the Sublime*), a pivotal work that uses Kant's notion of the sublime to develop an understanding of the aesthetics of tragedy. Kant had focused attention on what he called the confrontation of freedom and necessity in the sublime moment, as when the traveler looks up at the mountain waterfall and compares himself to it. Such a traveler has a feeling of sublimity in that he recognizes the waterfall's physical and his own spiritual freedom, at the same time that he realizes the waterfall's spiritual and his own physical limitations. Schiller uses this idea to solve the ancient problem of the origin of tragic pleasure, proposing that the audience of tragedy experiences an exactly analogous confrontation of freedom and necessity in the fate of the tragic hero. This idea was later taken up by August Wilhelm Schlegel (1767–1845) in his *Vorlesungen über dramatische Kunst und Literatur* (1809–11; *Lectures on Dramatic Art and Literature*) and became a cornerstone of his theory of tragedy and similar theories produced by his successors. It was a crucial notion, for it allowed a theoretical justification for considering Shakespeare's tragic dramas as true tragedies comparable to those of ancient Greece.

It was Shakespeare more than any other writer who seemed to the poets and philosophers of this period the embodiment of great art. Indeed it was Shakespeare (not themselves) whom they first characterized as "romantic." Herder had written about him with passionate admiration in 1773, and Johann Wolfgang von Goethe (1749–1832) not only wrote an enthusiastic encomium "Zum Shakespeares Tag" (1771; "On Shakespeare's Day") but proclaimed late in life (1820): "Euch verdank ich, was ich bin" ("What I am I owe to you"), wherein the addressee is both his beloved and Shakespeare. Furthermore, one of the most remarkable pieces of literary criticism of its time occurs in Goethe's novel *Wilhelm Meisters Lehrjahre* (1795–96; *Wilhelm Meister's Apprenticeship*), when the young Wilhelm, having taken up with a traveling theater troupe, keeps returning to a proposal that they should perform *Hamlet.* Wilhelm explains the play entirely in terms of the character of the Prince. The power of the play derives from the tragedy of "a great action laid upon a soul unfit for the performance of it." Wilhelm's depiction of Hamlet as "an oak tree planted in a costly jar . . . ; the roots expand, the jar is shivered" set the paradigm for decades of Shakespeare criticism to follow. Here again we detect an aesthetic close to that of Kant and Schiller, a sensitivity to the sublime moment arising from the confrontation of spiritual greatness with physical weakness.

Another feature of Kant's theory of the sublime is its sense of infinity. He claims that nature has the quality of the sublime "in such of its phenomena as in their intuition convey the idea of their infinity." This property of nature is characteristic of Romantic thought. Neoclassical writers had valued nature, too, but their nature was understood as a comprehensible system, rational and finite. The nature we find in Kant and the Romantic generation is unending both in its extent and in its progressive movement. The Romantics shared the time-honored idea that art is an imitation of nature, but their nature was quite different from that envisioned by Gottsched or even Lessing. And the literature that sprang from such a notion of nature was strikingly different as well.

Nowhere is the new aesthetic with its new emphasis on infinite progression more forcefully championed than in the aphoristic and deliberately fragmentary writings of Friedrich Schlegel (1772–1829). Schlegel notoriously defined Romantic poetry as "a progressive, universal poetry" in one of his *Athenäums Fragmente* (1798; *Athenaeum Fragments*). He claims that other forms of poetry are completed, but that Romantic poetry is still in a state of becoming. In fact, Romantic poetry is defined by being unfinished, never perfected, and always in motion. From this point of view, all Romantic poems are fragments that can by definition never be finished. Given this idea of Romantic literature, it is easy to see why Schlegel chose as his own characteristic form of expression the brief, allusive (and often illusive) fragment. Such a literature imitates what for Schlegel and his fellows was the most interesting and important characteristic of nature.

For similar reasons Schlegel was particularly fond of irony, a mode of expression he identified as a kind of "permanent parabasis." In Attic comedy, the Parabasis was the part of the play in which the chorus came forward to discourse on matters important to the playwright but not necessarily germane to the plot. It was an interruption of the story built in to the structure of the comic form. Schlegel's notion of irony asserts that this sort of authorial interruption can be made a permanent part of the rhetorical structure of a literary work. His prime example of this sort of rhetoric at work was Goethe's *Wilhelm Meister,* a novel Schlegel claimed in his essay "Über Goethes *Meister*" (1798; "On Goethe's *Meister*") was "absolutely new and unique." Goethe creates the permanent parabasis Schlegel values by being serious and playful at the same time, by "seeming to smile down from the heights of his intellect upon his work," a work which is absolutely important to him at the same time that it is a vast joke. This sort of irony, which came to be called "romantic irony" by later critics, allows the author to be in his action and apart from it at the same time. It is in this sense a permanent parabasis, for it is both a peripheral digression and the center of the artist's concern.

Irony is central to the aesthetic theory of all the later German Romantics. We find it prominently in the work of Karl Solger (1780–1819), whose *Erwin* (1816) proclaims irony to be "the perfect fruit of artistic intelligence." Ludwig Tieck (1773–1835), Solger's friend, considered irony "that final touch which brings a poetic work to perfection" (1793–96, Preface to *Wilhelm Lovell*). Jean Paul Richter (1763–1825) takes this same notion of irony, renames it "humor," and puts it at the heart of his theory of Romantic poetry, calling it a kind of "inverted sublime" in his *Vorschule der Ästhetik* (1804; *School for Aesthetics*).

Similar ideas about the importance to art of the contrast of the finite with the infinite appear in the work of one of Kant's most brilliant successors, the philosopher Johann Gottlieb Fichte (1762–1814). His series of letters on aesthetics *Über Geist und Buchstab in der Philosophie* (1794; *On the Spirit and the Letter in Philosophy*) attempts to define the "vitalizing force in a work of art we call 'spirit'" in terms that will by now be familiar. Spirit, Fichte says, enters a sphere where there are no limits; it "passes into the infinite." Equal in importance to the contrast between finitude and infinity is that between the living spirit and the dead letter. Fichte says that the artist has "lent his soul to dead matter so that it could communicate itself to us." This idea also can be traced back through Kant and Herder to Hamann, who uses almost exactly the same metaphor.

Fichte's colleague at Jena, Friedrich Wilhelm Joseph von Schelling (1775–1854), was an idealist philosopher who considered aesthetic expression equal to philosophy in its ability to express the truth. In his oration of 1807, *Über das Verhältnis der bildenden Künste zur Natur* (*Concerning the Relation of the Plastic Arts to Nature*), he argues that the successful artist imitates not natural objects but "the spirit of nature, which is at work in the core of things." This notion carries forward the earlier ideas of Bodmer and Breitinger as well as those of Fichte and the other Romantics. Schelling argues that art has the ability to take the object it represents out of time and show it "in its pure being, in the eternity of its life." Art is thus not an idealization of nature but rather a way of locating the essential and presenting it in a permanent form to the senses.

A prominent opponent of Fichte and Schelling was Arthur Schopenhauer (1788–1860), a philosopher who thought of himself as the one true successor to Kant. A significant portion of his magnum opus, *Die Welt als Wille und Vorstellung* (vol. 1, 1819; vol. 2, 1842; *The World as Will and Representation*), is devoted to aesthetics. The aesthetic was important to Schopenhauer primarily because it afforded a kind of temporary escape for individuals chained to the service of an implacable force he called the will, the "ground of all being," the determining force behind all existence. Human beings supplied with an excess of will are able to produce objects which, though ultimately created by the force of the will, are able to escape its contingent necessities. The object of art is therefore "an *Idea,* in Plato's sense, and absolutely nothing else." Such an idea "is drawn only from life itself, from nature, from the world, and only by genuine genius."

Perhaps the most influential of all the philosophers of the early 19th century was Georg Wilhelm Friedrich Hegel (1770–1831), who, like previous Romantic thinkers, was centrally concerned with aesthetics. The clearest exposition of his thinking about art is contained in a set of lectures published posthumously and based on notes both by Hegel and by students in his courses. These *Vorlesungen über die Aesthetik* (written 1823–29; published 1835; *Aesthetics: Lectures on Fine Art*) show many affinities with—but also an essential divergence from—the mainstream of Romantic aesthetics. He understands art as the creation of *Geist* (spirit), but not its most mature and refined form. Hegel understands the world historically, and the history of *Geist* moves through a dialectical progression from art to religion and thence to philosophy, its highest expression. Hegel's view of art thus places it in a far less important position than did earlier Romantic theories.

Hegel was a systematic philosopher, and his conception of art is systematized into a set of hierarchies or progressions. At the high point of aesthetic development stand the Greeks; at the high point of Greek art is tragedy; and at the high point of tragedy is Sophocles' *Antigone,* in Hegel's view the best work of art that has ever been produced. It is also the best work of art that is ever likely to be produced, since the development of Geist since the time of the Greeks has passed the artistic stage, and art in general has declined. Hegel thus returns to a view similar to that of Winckelmann: that the Edenic perfection of Greek art was an apogee that can never be reached again, let alone surpassed.

The Greece of Winckelmann, the historical perspective of Hegel, the pessimism of Schopenhauer—all these elements converge in the work of Friedrich Nietzsche (1844–1900), the last and by far the most controversial of all the 19th-century aesthetic thinkers. His first major publication, *Die Geburt der Tragödie aus dem Geiste der Musik* (1872; *The Birth of Tragedy out of the Spirit of Music*), not only revisits one of the great questions of literary history, but it also proposes aesthetics as the one possible justification for a world that is otherwise unjustifiable. Nietzsche's most famous contribution to the theory of art is his opposition of *das Apollinische* (the Apollonian) with *das Dionysische* (the Dionysian). Apollonian art partakes of the spirit of the god Apollo. It loves the light, seeks clarity and beauty of form, prefers the individual to the collective, and strives for sober reason. Dionysian art, on the other hand, is filled with the spirit of the wine god. It dwells in the darkness, prefers intoxication to sobriety, longs for union with the body of the other, and is tinged with pain and death. It knows the dangers and attractions of the abyss and is familiar with the wisdom of Silenus: that the best fate for a mortal man would be never to have been born, the second best to die quickly. Tragedy arose out of the Dionysian celebration at Athens, with its choral odes and its themes of death and danger, but reached its peak when the representative of the Apollonian—the actor—arrived to balance with individual reason the collective intuition of the chorus.

Few theories of art have had so wide and so deep an impact as Nietzsche's. Although his theory of the origin of Greek tragedy has won few supporters among classical scholars, his conception of art as a confrontation between Apollo and Dionysus has informed the thinking of nearly every later writer on art and indeed many artists as well. The fiction of Thomas Mann and Hermann Hesse, to name just two prominent examples, owes an enormous debt to Nietzsche's Apollo-Dionysus opposition. And much contemporary discussion of the relation of power to art, as in the widely influential writings of Michel Foucault, is explicitly derived from a similar line of thinking in various of Nietzsche's works.

One of Nietzsche's most distinguished, and most controversial, readers in the 20th century was the philosopher Martin Heidegger (1889–1976). Although best known for his great work of existential philosophy *Sein und Zeit* (1927; *Being and Time*), Heidegger was deeply interested in language and poetry, especially the poetry of Hölderlin, as becomes particularly evident in his later writings. Heidegger was notorious for such gnomic utterances as "die Sprache spricht" ("language speaks") and for a writing style deeply dependant on the etymological resources of the German language. Although many of his ideas clearly derive from his deep interest in Nietzsche, his stance toward poetry is fundamentally in keeping with Romantic notions of the origins of all language in poetic discourse. Heidegger became the target of severe criticism from the political Left, not only for his apparent willingness to participate, at least for a time, in National Socialism, but also for the lack of any attention to social-political issues in his work.

On other side of the political spectrum were Walter Benjamin (1892–1940) and Bertolt Brecht (1898–1956), for a short time friends in exile, and both deeply committed to a Marxist view of history. Benjamin's late work *Das Kunstwerk im Zeitalter seiner technischen Reproduzierbarkeit* (1936; *The Work of Art in the Age of Mechanical Reproduction*), primarily a study of photography and film, warns against the possibility of an "aestheticization" of politics that is possible with the technical means available in the 20th century. This essay has become one of the most widely read works of German aesthetics in late-20th-century North America. It is understood as a paradigmatic example of cultural criticism in a mode favored by New Historicist critics.

Even more widely read, however, has been the aesthetic theory of Bertolt Brecht. His *Kleines Organon für das Theater* (1949; *Short Organum for the Theater*) and other writings on the theory of the drama have made terms such as *Verfremdungseffekt* (alienation effect) as common in playhouses as "stage left." Brecht sought to change the theater as completely as he wished the theater to change society. To be an effective instrument of change, he believed, the drama must give up its traditional interest in creating empathy and instead constantly remind the playgoer that what is shown on the stage is not real life. The world should be shown as alterable, and the theater audience should leave the theater wishing to alter it. The famous alienation effect, whereby the audience is reminded by devices such as songs, direct addresses by the actors, projections, placards, and the like, that the play is only a play, intends ultimately to keep the audience intellectually rather than emotionally engaged with the material presented. The play should entertain, to be sure, but ultimately it must move the spectator to political action.

The success of Benjamin's and Brecht's ideas about the relation of the political to art might seem almost to have effaced Heidegger's legacy, but one form of recent aesthetic theory clearly carries that legacy forward. This is the so-called *Rezeptionsästhetik* (aesthetics of reception) of Hans Robert Jauß (1921–). Between Jauß and Heidegger stands Hans-Georg Gadamer (1900–1997), who took the central idea of *Being and Time*—that is, historicity as the central fact of human existence—and applied it to the problem of interpretation. Gadamer's major work, ironically titled *Wahrheit und Methode* (1960; *Truth and Method*), proposes that understanding is always a temporal phenomenon involving a *Horizontverschmelzung* (fusing of horizons), in which the perspective of one temporal moment comes together, however imperfectly, with that of another. Jauß applies this notion to art, proposing that a proper aesthetics needs to take into account the historicity of experience. His lecture/essay *Literaturgeschichte als Provokation* (delivered 1967; published 1970; *Literary History as a Challenge to Literary Theory*) offers the notion of an *Erwartungshorizont* (horizon of expectations) within which every work of art is produced and received. Such a notion would allow the history of a work of art to be understood as a kind of succession of horizons, each differing from all the others, even if only slightly.

Today the field of aesthetics in Germany is dominated by questions raised earlier in the century about the relation of art to politics, society, and history. It seems almost certain that these issues will carry forward into the new millennium.

CLAYTON KOELB

See also Criticism; Jean Paul; Immanuel Kant; Friedrich Schlegel

Further Reading

Abrams, M.H., *The Mirror and the Lamp: Romantic Theory and the Critical Tradition*, New York: Oxford University Press, 1953

Brecht, Bertolt, *Brecht on Theatre: The Development of an Aesthetic*, edited and translated by John Willett, New York: Hill and Wang, and London: Eyre Metheun, 1964

Chytry, Josef, *The Aesthetic State: A Quest in Modern German Thought*, Berkeley: University of California Press, 1989

Holub, Robert, *Reception Theory: A Critical Introduction*, London and New York: Methuen, 1984

MacLeod, Catriona, *Embodying Ambiguity: Androgyny and Aesthetics from Winckelmann to Keller*, Detroit, Michigan: Wayne State University Press, 1998

Nisbet, H.B., editor, *German Aesthetic and Literary Criticism: Winckelmann, Lessing, Hamann, Herder, Schiller and Goethe*, Cambridge and New York: Cambridge University Press, 1985

Richter, Simon, *Laocoon's Body and the Aesthetics of Pain: Winckelmann, Lessing, Herder, Moritz, Goethe*, Detroit, Michigan: Wayne State University Press, 1992

Simpson, David, editor, *German Aesthetic and Literary Criticism: Kant, Fichte, Schelling, Schopenhauer, Hegel*, Cambridge and New York: Cambridge University Press, 1984

Wheeler, Kathleen, editor, *German Aesthetic and Literary Criticism: The Romantic Ironists and Goethe*, Cambridge and New York: Cambridge University Press, 1984

Ilse Aichinger 1921–

Aichinger's first book, for which she is most famous, the novel *Die größere Hoffnung* (1948; *Herod's Children*), contains *in nuce* the motivations and themes of her later writings. At first, critical reactions were mixed, mainly because it did not break away from the events of the Third Reich. Not easy to read, it was praised by professional critics, especially in its translated form in Britain and the United States, moving between dream and reality, a Jewish Child's renunciation, final acceptance of a "greater hope," and destruction by an exploding grenade. Aichinger's attempt to reach the United States and escape an environment of hatred and fear is recorded in scenes with a group of young friends, linked by the leitmotifs of fear, visas, freezing and the multifaceted star symbol. Her naïveté, clear-sightedness, and sheer courage established for Aichinger the importance of the child-figure for her work. Childhood is presented as a state of lost innocence, a mirror to the false values of adult life. Already the intensity of the inner monologue and the direct or indirect speech count more than fullness of epic detail. The need to create language with a return to its original expressive sources dominates Aichinger's later works. In her early short stories, she examines loss of expression when facing anxieties, nightmares, and fantasies. These stories were seen in parallel to Kafka's work at a time when he was hardly known, and this comparison suggested that Aichinger showed signs of developing into an important writer.

Direct speech is, significantly, almost entirely absent from the famous *Spiegelgeschichte* (1979; Story of the Mirror), where, by interweaving three different narrative threads, Aichinger uses a metaphor (the mirror) to intensify a paradox based on Hegel's dialectic of transience and immortality. In this work, a young woman reexperiences her life as if she were watching the accelerating playback of a film. For her, time runs backward; for those who watch her delirious approach to death, time runs forward. The central event of an abortion is fitted into a tripartite structure: death and suffering set against a backdrop of the sky, despair at parting and the excitement of first love set against the sea, and finally, the years of childhood and infancy back to her mother's womb set against a tranquil river. A kinship of opposites is revealed, and the mirroring comes to its focal point exactly at the center of the text, figured in the blind mirror at the abortionist's. This point in the narrative, when the baby's death and the woman's rebirth coincide, is then followed by the momentum of self-reflection. The innocence of love leads to the destruction of its child, which results in recollections that reach back into the mother's own childhood, recollections of birth and premonitions of death. The blind mirror allows the mother to forget the past as the reevaluation of life proceeds. The mirror becomes a metaphor for death but, paradoxically, offers an opening toward a new, unknown possible existence. Typical of Aichinger's stories is the opening phrase, which describes, like Kafka, a totally new situation with a mysterious metaphor—in this case, the green sky reflecting the green sea. Green is later associated with illness and death, so that on second reading a metaphorical subtext emerges. Rereading is the reader's equivalent to the young woman's recollecting her life. The surface simplicity and underlying complexity of *Spiegelgeschichte* won the work the prize of the Gruppe 47 in 1952.

Successful use of reversal of perspectives inspired Aichinger in the 1960s to linguistic experiments, surrealistic visions, and dream sequences. In these experiments, language is gradually removed from its normal associations, and it becomes the theme of her later texts. In the definitive essay *Meine Sprache und ich* (1978; My Language and I), she claims that she no longer talks with her language, as she has no more to say to it, but emphasizes the exploratory function of her dialogues, which often highlight misunderstandings. Such resignation would lead in the 1970s volume *Schlechte Wörter* (1976; Bad Words) to total rejection of coherent, logical word patterns; she replaces them with word fragments to produce what she termed *Ausfälle,* or new strings of associations triggered by single words or phrases. The collection as a whole represents in literary terms what Kleist first posited in his essay *Über das Marionettentheater* (On Puppetshows): the expression of a subconscious psychic level that is freed from both time and place. The Expressionist metaphoric fervor of the early works was reduced to the barest essentials. Each of her short texts became a linguistic world of its own, no longer referring to or criticizing reality but created solely of the words themselves and their applications.

Aichinger's place in recent literary history has been less prominent than that of her husband, poet Günter Eich. While sharing with him a deep concern for the deadening of language in common use, her poems in particular have developed a minimalist use of words, simple in themselves but referring to the presence of another dimension in life. Her reception has suffered from the esoteric quality of her writing, yet among academics, her fondness for experimentation and attempts to provide texts that are deliberately open to multiple layers of interpretation have made her work an intriguing challenge. Dagmar Lorenz's monograph has confirmed these texts' complexities, and recent research has emphasized Aichinger's use of black comedy, paradox, and dialogues to force readers to rethink their priorities. The ambivalent dimensions opened up in the final sections of her stories and short plays reveal a basic unease in the writer, another reason for her work's appeal to the connoisseur rather than the general reader.

BRIAN KEITH-SMITH

Biography

Born in Vienna, Austria, 1 November 1921. Studied at the University of Vienna, 1945–48; reader for S. Fischer, publisher, Frankfurt, East Germany, and Vienna, 1949–50; assistant to the founder, Inge Scholl, of the Hochschule für Gestaltung, Ulm; member, Gruppe 47, from 1951; married the poet and writer Günter Eich, 1953. Gruppe 47 Prize, 1952; Austrian State Prize, 1952; City of Bremen Prize, 1955; Immermann Prize, 1955; Bavarian Academy of Fine Arts Prize, 1961, 1991; Wildgans Prize, 1969; Nelly Sachs Prize, 1971; City of Vienna Prize, 1974; City of Dortmund Prize, 1975; Georg Trakl Prize, 1979; Petrarca Prize, 1982; Belgian Europe Festival Prize, 1987; Weilheim Prize, 1987; Town of Solothurn Prize, 1991; Roswitha Medal. Currently lives in Frankfurt.

Selected Works

Fiction

Die größere Hoffnung, 1948; as *Herod's Children,* 1963
Rede unter dem Galgen, 1952; as *Der Gefesselte,* 1953; as *The Bound Man and Other Stories,* 1955
Eliza, Eliza, 1965
Selected Short Stories and Dialogue (in German), edited by James C. Alldridge, 1966
Nachricht vom Tag: Erzählungen, 1970
Schlechte Wörter (includes radio plays), 1976
Meine Sprache und ich: Erzählungen, 1978
Spiegelgeschichte: Erzählungen und Dialoge, 1979

Plays

Zu keiner Stunde (dialogues), 1957; enlarged edition, 1980
Besuch im Pfarrhaus: Ein Hörspiel, Drei Dialoge, 1961
Auckland: 4 Hörspiele (radio plays), 1969
Knöpfe (radio play), published in *Hörspiele,* 1978
Weisse Chrysanthemum, published in *Kurzhörspiele,* 1979

Poetry

Verschenkter Rat, 1978

Other

Wo ich wohne: Erzählungen, Gedichte, Dialoge (includes stories, poems, dialogues), 1963
Dialoge, Erzählungen, Gedichte (includes dialogues, stories, poems), 1971
Gedichte und Prosa, 1980
Selected Poetry and Prose of Ilse Aichinger, translated by Allen H. Chappel, 1983
Grimmige Märchen, with Martin Walser, edited by Wolfgang Mieder, 1986
Kleist, Moos, Fasane, 1987
Gesammelte Werke, edited by Richard Reichensperger, 8 vols., 1991

Edited Work

Günther Eich, *Gedichte,* 1973

Further Reading

Allridge, James C., *Ilse Aichinger,* London: Wolff, and Chester Springs, Pennsylvania: Dufour, 1969
Bedwell, Carol B., "Who Is the Bound Man? Towards an Interpretation of Ilse Aichinger's *Der Gefesselte,*" *German Quarterly* 38 (1965)
———, "The Ambivalent Image in Aichinger's *Spiegelgeschichte,*" *Revue des Langues Vivantes* 33 (1967)
Eggers, Werner, "Ilse Aichinger," in *Deutsche Literatur seit 1945,* edited by Dietrich Weber, Stuttgart: Kröner, 1970
Endres, E., "Ilse Aichinger," in *Neue Literatur der Frauen: Deutschsprachige Autoruinen der Gegenwart,* edited by Heinz Puknus, Munich: Beck, 1980
Fried, Erich, "Über Gedichte Ilse Aichingers," *Neue Rundschau* 92 (1981)

Gerresheim, Helga-Maleen, "Ilse Aichinger," in *Deutsche Dichter der Gegenwart: Ihr Leben und Werk,* edited by Benno von Wiese, Berlin: Schmidt, 1973

Hildebrand, Alexander, "Zu Ilse Aichingers Gedichten," *Literatur und Kritik* 23 (1968)

Hoffer, K., "Die Räuberin: Zu Ilse Aichingers *Schlechte Wörter,*" *Neue Rundschau* 92 (1981)

Keith-Smith, Brian, "Recent Works by Ilse Aichinger," *German Life and Letters* 91, no. 4 (1988)

Kleiber, Carine, *Ilse Aichinger: Leben und Werk,* Bern, Frankfurt, and New York: Lang, 1984

Lindemann, Gisela, *Ilse Aichinger,* Munich: Beck, 1988

Lorenz, Dagmar C.G., *Ilse Aichinger,* Königstein/Taunus: Athenäum, 1981

Lübbren, Rainer, "Die Sprache der Bilder: Zu Ilse Aichingers Erzählung *Eliza Eliza,*" *Neue Rundschau* 76 (1965)

Moser, Samuel, "Auf Dover zu: Reflexionen über Ilse Aichinger," *Neue Rundschau* 92 (1981)

Rothmann, K., "Ilse Aichinger," in *Deutschsprachige Schriftsteller seit 1945 in Einzeldarstellungen,* edited by Kurt Rothmann, Stuttgart: Reclam, 1985

Schafroth, H.F., "Hinter Prizwalk und Privas: Die Topographie des Privaten im Werke Ilse Aichingers," *Schweizer Monatshefte* 61 (1981)

———, "Ich und Jetzt: Zu Ilse Aichingers Gedichten," in *Frauenliteratur in Österreich von 1945 bis heute,* edited by Carine Kleiber and Erika Tunner, Bern and Frankfurt: Lang, 1986

Spiel, Hilde, "Eh' die Träume rosten und brechen: Ilse Aichingers Gedichte," in *In meinem Garten schlendernd: Essays,* Munich: Nymphenburger, 1981

Tunner, Erika, "Ilse Aichinger: Der Gang über die grüne Grenze," in *Frauenliteratur: Autorinnen, Perspektiven, Konzepte,* edited by Manfred Jurgensen, Bern: Lang, 1983

Weigel, Sigrid, "Schreibarbeit und Phantasie: Ilse Aichinger," in *Frauenliteratur ohne Tradition? Neun Autorinnenporträts,* edited by Inge Stephan et al., Frankfurt: Fischer Taschenbuch, 1986

Peter Altenberg (Richard Engländer) 1859–1919

In an essay from 1912, the Danish literary historian Georg Brandes referred to Peter Altenberg as "a little genius." Arthur Schnitzler, a fellow member of the Jung Wien movement, characterized him as a "geistreicher Sonderling" (witty oddity) and as something of a professional neurotic. Robert Musil went so far as to find it difficult to decide who was the greater writer: Goethe or Altenberg. Each of these descriptions reveal some truth about this complex individual, who came to represent the essence of the Vienna's fin de siècle culture. Peter Altenberg, the man and writer, can best be described as an individual of dichotomies: an antimodern modernist, a misogynistic feminist, an anti-Semitic Jew, and a drug-addicted health fanatic. During his lifetime, Altenberg was as much known for his eccentricity as his writings. While a connoisseur of Egyptian tobacco, he at times adhered to bizarre health diets of milk products and raw eggs. Similarly, his very disdain for his real name, Richard Engländer, and his subsequent adoption of Peter Altenberg both reveal a complex and ambivalent attitude toward his Jewish and sexual identity.

Altenberg, known for his unbridled ways, took it upon himself to parody the artist as an outsider rather than to hide behind the protective guise of Vienna's bourgeois class. For Altenberg, the boundary separating his creative work and his persona did not exist. He consciously cultivated and projected his nonconformist lifestyle into his oeuvre. The eldest among the Jung Wien literary circle, Altenberg, perhaps more than the others, came to represent the decadent milieu of late 19th-century Vienna. Living without any financial stability and unable to maintain living quarters for any extended period, Altenberg set up his "home" in the Café Central in Vienna's Herrengasse, where he spent the better part of each day—he even had his mail delivered there. While Altenberg was viewed by contemporary authors outside of Austria as somewhat of an anomaly, in Vienna his literary production, as well as his colorful persona, influenced and inspired some of the most talented individuals of his age in various artistic disciplines. Among these were Adolf Loos, Oskar Kokoschka, Alban Berg, Arthur Schnitzler, Franz Kafka, and Robert Musil.

Signs of Altenberg's eccentricities were already apparent in his early adulthood. Unable to complete his medical studies in Vienna, or his law studies in Graz, because of his diagnosed psychological condition of "overexcitability of the nervous system," Altenberg "retired" to Vienna's coffeehouse culture at the prime age of 25. But it would take another ten years or so before he would make his mark as a writer. The name Peter Altenberg made its first official appearance in 1896, when he published his best-known work, *Wie ich es sehe* (1896; How I View It). In this collection of literary sketches and "impressions" of life in fin de siècle Vienna, Altenberg took his cues from J.-K. Huysmans's novel *A rebours* (1884; *Against Nature*) by prefacing his book in French and by giving the views on the prose poem that had been articulated by Huysmans's main character in the novel, Des Esseintes. By quoting extensively from Huysmans, Altenberg attempted to project his work beyond the narrow literary sphere of Vienna of his time into a broader European tradition, as well as to call attention to a new form of reading by using prose poems and sketches.

Altenberg's favorite literary medium was the prose poem, as well as the prose sketch, both of which he appropriated as his very own. For his critics, however, his use of the prose sketch helped to increase their disdain for Altenberg, since many believed that no respectable writer would cultivate this low form of narrative style, which was used only by those writing trivial or light entertainment literature. While Altenberg excelled as a writer of prose poems, it would be a disservice to judge his overall accomplishments without considering his many sketches, anecdotes, and aphorisms. Egon Friedell noted that it is precisely in Altenberg's terseness that his qualities as an author emerge. In his writings Altenberg's objective was not so much dictated by any prevailing aesthetics as much as by being as precise and concise as possible. Altenberg himself often referred to his literary pieces as *Skizzen* (sketches) and *Studien* (studies). These classifications of his literary work and the influences they had on Viennese modernism are perhaps better understood when they are viewed in the context of other art forms of the time. Karl Kraus points out that in 1910 and 1911 Arnold Schoenberg composed many of his miniatures while under the spell of Altenberg's aesthetic minimalism.

Just a brief eight years after his death, the German writer Erich Mühsam, who hailed Altenberg as the essence of Vienna in both its negative and positive aspects, was already concerned with Altenberg slowly being forgotten. Aspects of Altenberg's personal behavior and sexual eccentricities did very little to help him maintain a respectable position among critics and literary scholars. In the past 20 years, however, literary historians have been successful in deflating some of the legends that have obscured Altenberg's real achievements. By contextualizing Altenberg's literary oeuvre in Vienna's fin de siècle milieu, recent literary scholars have elevated him back to his rightful position in German letters.

ISTVAN VARKONYI

Biography

Born in Vienna, 3 March 1859. Son of a wealthy merchant; some studied in law and medicine; met up with authors of Jung Wien, 1890s; helped by Karl Kraus to get *Wie ich es sehe* published, 1896; worked as a critic of caberet and variety shows; repeated stays in sanatoriums. Died on 8 January 1919, in Vienna.

Selected Works

Wie ich es sehe, 1896
Ashantee, 1897
Was der Tag mir zuträgt, 1901
Pròdromos, 1905
Märchen des Lebens, 1908
Die Auswahl aus meinen Büchern, 1908
Bilderbögen des kleinen Lebens, 1909
Neues Altes, 1911
Semmering, 1912, 1913
Fechsung, 1915
Nachfechsung, 1916
Vita Ipsa, 1918
Mein Lebensabend, 1919
Das Altenbergbuch, 1921
Der Nachlass, 1925
Nachlese, 1930

Further Reading

Barker, Andrew, "Peter Altenberg's Literary Catalysis," in *From Vormärz to Fin de Siècle: Essays in Nineteenth-Century Austrian Literature*, edited by Mark G. Ward, Blairgowrie: Lochee, 1986
———, "The Persona of Peter Altenberg: 'Frauenkult,' Misogyny, and Jewish Self-Hatred," in *Studies in German and Scandinavian Literature after 1500*, edited by James A. Parente and Richard E. Schade, Columbia, South Carolina: Camden House, 1993
———, *Telegrams from the Soul: Peter A1tenberg and the Culture of Fin-de-siècle Vienna*, Columbia, South Carolina: Camden House, 1996
Barker, Andrew, and Leo A. Lensing, *Peter Altenberg: Rezept die Welt zu sehen*, Vienna: Braumüller, 1995
Lensing, Leo A., "Literature and Photography: Practical and Theoretical Observations on Their Interaction in Modem Vienna," in *Intertextuality: German Literature and Visual Art from the Renaissance to the Twentieth Century*, edited by Ingeborg Hoesterey and Ulrich Weisstein, Columbia, South Carolina: Camden House, 1993
Nienhaus, Stefan, *Das Prosagedicht in Wien der Jahrhundertwende: Altenberg-Hofmannsthal-Polgar*, Berlin: de Gruyter, 1986
Randak, Ernst, editor, *Peter Altenberg oder das Genie ohne Fähigkeiten*, Graz: Stiasny, 1961
Saur, Pamela S., "Peter Altenberg: The 'Radical Bachelor'," in *Joinings and Disjoinings: The Significance of Marital Status in Literature*, edited by JoAnna Stephens Mink and Janet Doubler Ward, Bowling Green, Ohio: Bowling Green State University Popular Press, 1991

Anacreontic Poetry

Anacreontic poetry accompanied the resurgence of the bourgeoisie that occurred during the 18th century. The Thirty Years' War (1618–48) had had a devastating impact on the cities of Germany, destroying the commercial centers and urban culture that had thrived there during the 16th century and leaving a largely courtly society and culture in its place. Over the next 100 years, the middle class again ascended to economic, if not political, dominance and assumed leadership in the cultural sphere as well. While developing its own literary genres, drawing chiefly on England and France for inspiration, the German middle class also adopted forms and motifs more typical of the aristocracy. Anacreontic poetry reflects this phenomenon, for its reveals an appreciation of aesthetic values, sophisticated forms of sensual pleasure, and conviviality formerly considered the preserve of the nobility.

It is scarcely an oversimplification to say that the thematic range of Anacreontic poetry is limited to wine, women, and song, for it displays an endless variety of lyrics and verse tales praising love or the beloved, the fruit of the vine, and merrymaking; these poems thus evince a worldly wisdom decidedly Epicurean in nature. Typically, these texts are set in a bucolic landscape peopled by figures in pastoral garb that bear names drawn from the literature and mythology of classical antiquity. Influenced in motif and mood by French rococo painting and itself representing the German rococo, Anacreontic poetry is predominantly pastel in tone, lightly elegant and flirtatiously erotic. Anacreontic poets often utilized traditional song forms such as the quatrain, which is comprised of iambic or trochaic tetrameter and/or trimeter lines with alternating or brace rhyme. More typical is the freer madrigal, a song form imported from Italy, which exhibits unstrophied or irregularly grouped lines of from two to six iambs that rhyme freely and often contain "orphans," or unrhymed endings. Most characteristic is rhymeless verse of various kinds, ranging from Greek ode forms to traditional meters with or without strophic division and lacking end rhyme. One may ascribe the departure from native rhymed strophes in part to one "enlightened" concern of a rationalist age: that end rhyme detracts from the meaning of words and can force the poet to stray from his intended statement. Indeed, Anacreontic poetry is ultimately "constructed," or contrived, and thus intellectual rather than experiential. More important, however, was the related, massive spread of French neoclassicism throughout Germany during the period.

Anacreontic poetry had its origin in the Anacreontea, a collection of 60 Greek songs written not by Anacreon (sixth century B.C.), as was long believed, but rather by late Greek epigones, who probably lived in the Byzantine Empire during the first centuries of the Christian era. The collection was published by Henri Estienne in 1554 in France, and it found its way through translation and imitation, especially in French (the *Pléiade*) and in English (Ben Jonson, Robert Herrick, Abraham Cowley, and others), into the Germany of the early 18th century. Later, the authentic Anacreon as well as kindred works by Horace and Catullus exerted an influence. German poets of the previous century such as Georg Weckherlin, Martin Opitz, and Paul Fleming had tried their hand at the genre in a broad sense. It was Friedrich von Hagedorn, however, who first cultivated the style extensively and whose work, beginning in 1729, opened the way for German Anacreontic poetry in the strict sense.

German Anacreonticism emerged from the broadly collaborative efforts of three students at the University of Halle during the later 1730s and early 1740s: Johann Wilhelm Ludwig Gleim, Johann Peter Uz, and Johann Nikolaus Götz. The older Gleim introduced Uz and Götz to the works of the ancients, as well as to contemporaries such as Hagedorn, and mentored their translations of Homer, Pindar, and, most significantly, (the pseudo) Anacreon. After Uz made literal translations of the Greek texts, Götz rendered them into verse that was influenced both by the originals and earlier translations of three poems by Johann Christoph Gottsched, the leading literary theoretician and philologist of the time. Gleim published their version of the Anacreontea (unbeknownst to them) in 1746 under the title *Die Oden Anakreons in reimlosen Versen: Nebst einigen andern Gedichten* (*The Odes of Anacreon in Unrhymed Verses: In Addition to Some Other Poems*). He had already proffered a volume of his own work in the manner of the Greek in 1744–45 (*Versuch in scherzhaften Liedern* [*Sampling of Playful Songs*]), and Götz and Uz soon followed suit. Götz's *Versuch eines Wormsers in Gedichten* (*Poetic Attempt of a Citizen of Worms*) appeared in 1746, while Uz's *Lyrische Gedichte* (*Lyric Poems*) came out in 1749. Dissatisfied with the state of the translations upon publication and following lengthy complications, Götz issued a complete revision, together with renderings of Sappho, as *Die Gedichte Anakreons und der Sappho Oden* (*The Poems of Anacreon and the Odes of Sappho*) in 1760. This version of the Anacreontea has been called the linguistic high point of the Enlightenment in Germany and the standard for later Anacreontic poetry. In any case, the efforts of the so-called Halle Circle bore fruit for some 30 years. Anacreontic poetry was cultivated by virtually every poet of note into the 1770s, including Gotthold Ephraim Lessing, Friedrich Klopstock, and the young Johann Wolfgang Goethe.

By the early 1770s, English sentimentalism had begun to permeate poetry, especially lyric poetry, and a short-lived but emotionally charged movement known as the Sturm und Drang (Storm and Stress) had begun to impact poetry and drama alike. Due in part to their Protestant-pietistic heritage and the political fragmentation of Germany, young poets placed a high premium on middle-class values such as feeling, interiority, and individualism and sought a national cultural identity in the German and Germanic past. In this climate, an aristocratic lyric beholden to antiquity could no longer thrive. As if to underscore the transition, Goethe's "Mit einem gemalten Band" ("With a Colored Ribbon") of 1771 metamorphoses a common prop of Anacreontic dalliance into a strong emotional bond, thereby transforming the ethos of the genre.

HERBERT ROWLAND

Further Reading

Browning, Robert Marcellus, *German Poetry in the Age of the Enlightenment: From Brockes to Klopstock,* University Park: Pennsylvania State University Press, 1978

Neuber, Wolfgang, "Johann Nikolaus Götz zum 200. Todestag: Versuch zur Kenntlichmachung eines Paradigmas," *Blätter der Carl-Zuckmayer-Gesellschaft* 7 (1981)

Perels, Christoph, *Studien zur Aufnahme und Kritik der Rokokolyrik zwischen 1740 und 1760,* Göttingen: Vandenhoeck und Ruprecht, 1974

Riedel, Volker, *Der Aufklärer Gleim heute,* Stendal: Winckelmann-Gesellschaft, 1987

Ritchie, J.M., "The German Anacreontic Poets: Gleim, Uz, Götz," in *German Men of Letters,* vol. 6, edited by Alex Natan and Brian Keith-Smith, London: Wolff, 1972

Warde, Newell E., *Johann Peter Uz and German Anacreonticism: The Emancipation of the Aesthetic,* Frankfurt, Bern, and Las Vegas, Nevada: Lang, 1978

Zeman, Herbert, *Die deutsche anakreontische Dichtung: Ein Versuch zur Erfassung ihrer ästhetischen und literarhistorischen Erscheinungsformen im 18. Jahrhundert,* Stuttgart: Metzler, 1972

———, "Friedrich von Hagedorn, Johann Wilhelm Ludwig Gleim, Johann Peter Uz, Johann Nikolaus Götz," in *Deutsche Dichter des 18. Jahrhunderts: Ihr Leben und Werk,* edited by Benno von Wiese, Berlin: Schmidt, 1977

Alfred Andersch 1914–1980

Following the events of 1989, leading German critics have diagnosed the end of *Nachkriegsliteratur* (postwar literature). Their understanding is not simply that the two traditions of East and West Germany had to become one, but, more important, that the concerns that sustained the flourishing intellectual and literary life of the postwar period and that sprang from the burden of German history in the 20th century, together with their unifying aesthetic positions, have finally become irrelevant. Such a diagnosis has finally sealed the revaluation of the work of the Federal Republic's canonical writers and, in particular, of Alfred Andersch.

From the very beginning of the postwar period, Andersch was at the center of the founding activities of West German literature. With Hans-Werner Richter and others, Andersch edited the short-lived periodical *Der Ruf* and its successor *Der Skorpion*—the whole enterprise starting in the *locus classicus* of what was presented as a Phoenix-like rebirth from the ashes, in an American prison camp. Andersch was also instrumental in founding and giving force to the Gruppe 47: his identification with the reemergence of post-fascist literature in the Federal Republic was exemplary, and his past in Dachau and his idealistic participation in the communist youth movement at the end of the Weimar Republic offered outstanding credentials. For two generations, his work represented a typical voice of the literature of the young Republic; indeed (as Heidelberger-Leonard notes), he was a moral authority.

For many readers the entry to Andersch's work was provided by the novel *Sansibar oder der letzte Grund* (1957; *Flight to Afar*), which—once again—is a typical product of its time. The novel uses some obvious techniques of that modernism from which Germany was allegedly cut off during the fascist period. In particular, appropriating strategies from William Faulkner's novel *As I Lay Dying* helped Andersch to mobilize various voices in the telling of a story that, in the spirit of Albert Camus's *La Peste* (1947; *The Plague*), argued for an existential commitment to the fight against the evil represented by fascism. Subsequently Andersch explored with increasing sophistication the positions laid down by French existentialism, in particular those of Jean-Paul Sartre. Andersch's increasing distance from a dogmatic communism (itself, of course, an undertaking absolutely typical of the early FRG), which emerged in fictional form in the figure of Gregor in *Flight to Afar*, had been celebrated in the autobiographical *Bericht* (report) titled *Die Kirschen der Freiheit* (The Cherries of Freedom), which was initially serialized in 1950 and then published in book form in 1952. These political concerns and their relationship to existentialist positions were then discussed in relation to the changing context of postwar developments in the shorter novels *Die Rote* (1960; *The Redhead*) and *Efraim* (1967; *Efraim's Book*), the latter a text that bravely attempts to explore the experience of anti-Semitism. Andersch's exemplary importance for postwar literature is emphasized by the major part he played—through his extensive work for West German radio in the 1950s—in communicating to a wider public an understanding of the literary and philosophical developments that had led to European modernism.

Winterspelt, his most extensive novel, published in 1974, showed that Andersch's concerns remained constant. It concerns the attempt of a German officer, Major Dincklage, to surrender his battalion to the American army in the winter of 1944 and thus to prevent unnecessary loss of life. The novel—despite its fictional character—illustrates in its style aspects of the movement toward the documentary style made popular in the 1960s by Alexander Kluge, among others, but the story also allows the important issues associated with Andersch's early texts to emerge still more clearly. Despite its fast-moving plot, *Winterspelt* contains, no less strongly than before, preeminently aesthetic themes—especially in discussions of a famous modernist painting by Paul Klee, "Polyphon umfaßtes Weiß." The novel thus amounts to a further discussion of the aestheticism that had marked Andersch's work from the start. Central to this evolving discussion is the relationship of aestheticism to the political concerns that had been its constant companion; in *Winterspelt* this discussion is again contextualized against the background of fascism. In some earlier works, aestheticism had been seen as a central element of the resistance to fascism, and the aesthetic theory of Theodor W. Adorno—to which Andersch's work was close—extended this view into a belief in the power of art to resist the pressures of normalization and conformism in all modern state systems, including a capitalist democracy such as the FRG.

In *Flight to Afar,* art (in the shape of an Expressionist woodcarving) is presented as the inspiration of political action, not merely by the characters but—by means of a clear analogy—by the readers of the 1950s. In a phrase that Peter Weiss was to establish, this is the aesthetics of resistance. In other texts—notably in *Die Kirschen der Freiheit*—art appears simply as a retreat from totalitarian politics into an almost pathological form of introspection. In the years of the Federal Republic, the problematic nature of this aesthetic position was less clearly identified, for Andersch was praised as an artist who was committed to democracy and critical citizenship. Further, since his portrayal of characters' retreat from political engagement invariably took the form of a desertion from the conformist majority of the fascist state, no one thought to question the seriousness of Andersch's commitment to West German democracy. When the focus of West German criticism shifted from an affirmation of the new literature of the FRG as an achievement of democracy or as a justification of the new Republic (the phrase under which all writers of the Gruppe 47 both flourished and suffered was that they represented "the conscience of the nation"), Andersch's reception became subject to two different pressures. First, critics increasingly suspected presentations of the idea that German literature itself had passed through the so-called *Stunde Null* (zero hour). Part of this concern was a general awareness that intellectual and literary life does not fit exactly into the tight chronology of the years of fascism, but follows its own logic and chronology. (Hans Dieter Schäfer's presentations of the Hitler years, both culturally and socially, pointed strongly in this direction—this view is by now a commonplace of postwar historiography.)

Second, as literary historians came to focus on the continuities with the past and not just the continuities represented by the suspect figures of the Right (the message that Heinrich Böll and Peter Weiss concentrated upon in the late 1950s and 1960s and that was made more relevant by the Auschwitz trials of the early 1960s), Andersch's biography came to be more critically examined. By this time the achievements of the Federal Republic—specifically, the Adenauer years and the Economic Miracle—were open to question. Andersch himself had offered a damning critique of the West German state, notably in occasional writings in the 1970s and most aggressively in the poem "Artikel 3[3]," a sweeping denunciation of the repressive measures of that period such as the *Berufsverbot* (the legislation introduced in January 1972 debarring the Left from employment in the public service and "strategic professions"), which Andersch saw as a clear violation of Article 3.3 of the Basic Law and a continuation of fascist practices. Paradoxically, however, the very radicalism of this critique threw into question certain elements of Andersch's own early reception, as the real nature of the commitment to democracy and the aesthetic concerns in the Gruppe 47 came into question. If these were generalized concerns focused on Andersch's generation, other criticisms were personalized. Readers became suspicious of a cult of authenticity that was postulated on an incomplete truthfulness in personal biography. A more denunciatory tone came into play, concerning both details of Andersch's biography and an awareness of his, albeit very limited, publishing activities during the Third Reich—a fact that suggested compromise, if not opportunism. It emerged that Andersch, too, had come into the Federal Republic with a less than open past. So Andersch became a thorn in the flesh of the conservative affirmers of the FRG, a disappointment to the New Left, and a symptom of the unresolved problems of his whole artistic generation.

More generally, however, the controversies marked the end of the *Gesinnungsästhetik,* the essentially moral-ideological approach to aesthetics that had underscored not only the attempt of GDR writers to overcome fascism (not dissimilar to the moral positions adopted by literature in the GDR) but the whole claim to moral high ground implicit in the view of the Gruppe 47 as the conscience of the nation. Andersch could not sustain this either in his biography or in his own aesthetic position. So his life and works throw into question the starting point of *Nachkriegsliteratur* and highlight the elitism, the aestheticism, and the fundamental opposition between this writer and the newly created West German democracy. With hindsight, it emerged that the basis of Andersch's early texts was far from the democratic socialism of *littérature engagée,* as desired by cultural politicians and reeducators after 1945. Instead, Andersch's work testifies to a more free-floating aestheticism, which included tolerance for and was itself close to the position associated with such figures as Gottfried Benn and Ernst Jünger, whose compromises with fascism had been factually touched up and aesthetically improved for consumption in the postwar years—a process that had made them the natural enemies of the Gruppe 47. So Andersch's work, for all its continuing fascination and compelling engagement with the issues of our century, not only exemplifies the demise of a committed literature of the postwar period but throws into question the existence and self-understanding of that generation.

HUGH RIDLEY

See also Gruppe 47; Der Ruf

Biography

Born in Munich, 4 February 1914. Apprenticed in the book trade; organized a communist youth association in Bavaria, 1932; three-month arrest in the concentration camp Dachau, 1933; worked as an employee until 1940; drafted to the military and deserted; editorial jobs at *Neue Zeitung,* Munich, and at the Frankfurt and Süddeutsche broadcasting companies; editor of the book series *studio frankfurt* (1952–53), *Claassen Cargo* (1965–67), and the magazines *Der Ruf* (1948–1958) and *Texte und Zeichen* (1955–58); moved to Berzona, Switzerland, 1958. Died in Berzona, 21 February 1980.

Selected Works

Collections

Bericht—Roman—Erzählungen, 1971
Gesammelte Erzählungen, 1971
Norden Süden rechts und links: Reiseberichte 1951–71, 1971
empört euch der himmel ist blau: Gedichte 1946–77, 1977
Studienausgabe, 15 vols., 1979
Neue Hörspiele, 1978
Sämtliche Erzählungen, 1983
Errinnerte Gestalten: Frühe Erzählungen, 1986
Sämtliche Romane, 4 vols., 1988
Das Alfred Andersch Lesebuch, 1989
Gedichte und Nachdichtungen 1946–1977, 1990
Gesammelte Erzählungen, 1990

Fiction

Sansibar oder der letzte Grund, 1957; as *Flight to Afar,* translated by Michael Bullock, 1958
Geister und Leute, 1958; as *The Night of the Giraffe and Other Stories,* translated by Christa Armstrong, 1964
Die Rote, 1960; as *Redhead,* translated by Michael Bullock, 1961
Ein Liebhaber des Halbschattens, 1963
Efraim, 1967; as *Efraim's Book,* translated by Ralph Manheim, 1970
Tochter, 1970
Mein Verschwinden in Providence, 1971; as *My Disappearance in Providence, and Other Stories,* translated by Ralph Manheim, 1978
Winterspelt, 1974; translated by Richard and Clara Winston, 1978
Der Vater eines Mörders, 1980; as *The Father of a Murderer,* translated by Leila Vennewitz, 1994

Essays and Travel Writing

Deutsche Literatur in der Entscheidung, 1948
Europäische Avantgarde, 1948
Die Kirschen der Freiheit, 1952
Piazza San Gaetano, 1957
Paris ist eine ernste Stadt, 1961
Wanderungen im Norden, 1962
Die Blindheit des Kunstwerks und andere Aufsätze, 1965
Öffentlicher Brief an einen sowjetischen Schriftsteller, 1977
Weltreise auf deutsche Art, 1977
Mein Lesebuch der Beschreibungen, 1978
Flucht in Etrurien, 1981
Hohe Breitengrade, 1984
Aus einem römischen Winter, 1988

Radio Plays

Fahrerflucht, 1958
Der Tod des James Dean, 1960

Further Reading

Heidelberger-Leonard, Irene, *Alfred Andersch: Die ästhetische Position als politisches Gewissen: Zu den Wechselbeziehungen zwischen Kunst und Wirklichkeit in den Romanen,* Frankfurt and New York: Lang, 1986

Jendricke, Bernhard, *Alfred Andersch mit Selbstzeugnissen und Bilddokumenten,* Reinbek bei Hamburg: Rowohlt, 1988
Littler, Margaret, *Alfred Andersch (1914–1980) and the Reception of French Thought in the Federal Republic of Germany,* Lewiston, New York: Mellen Press, 1991
Schütz, Erhard, *Alfred Andersch,* Munich: Beck, 1980
Stephan, Reinhardt, *Alfred Andersch: Eine Biographie,* Zurich: Diogenes, 1990
Wehdeking, Volker, *Alfred Andersch,* Stuttgart: Metzler, 1983

Lou Andreas-Salomé 1861–1937

Lou Andreas-Salomé is the author of numerous literary works (more than ten novels and collections of stories); book-length critical studies of Ibsen, Nietzsche, and Rilke; and essays on diverse topics such as religion, Russia, literature and the arts, women and sexuality, and psychoanalysis. While her frequent travels brought her in contact with representatives of the main literary and intellectual circles in Munich, Vienna, Berlin, and Paris, Andreas-Salomé's works resist easy categorization within the established literary movements around 1900. Andreas-Salomé contributed, for instance, to the newly founded journal of the naturalists, *Die freie Bühne* (The Free Theater), in Berlin, and she published a long essay about Ibsen, generally considered the "father" of naturalism, but her own literary works cannot be described as naturalist; they display aspects of a number of literary styles such as naturalism and its presumed countermovements, including the Viennese literary decadence. Furthermore, Andreas-Salomé's writings were not limited to the literary realm but extended to a variety of disciplines and text genres in the course of her long writing career. In the early 1890s, she penned theater and book reviews as well as critical studies of Ibsen and Nietzsche; around 1900, she wrote mostly fiction; after participating in the 1911 Psychoanalytic Convention, Andreas-Salomé became preoccupied with psychoanalysis for the remaining 25 years of her life, practicing as a lay analyst and contributing to the journal *Imago,* which was edited by Freud; and late in her life, Andreas-Salomé wrote about Rilke and Freud as well as her autobiography (which remained unfinished at the time of her death in 1937).

Andreas-Salomé published her first novel, *Im Kampf um Gott* (1885), at the age of 24 under a male pseudonym (Henri Lou). This work adopts the perspective of the male protagonist while her subsequent works (published under her own name) focus on female characters (e.g., the novel *Ruth,* 1895; the collections of stories *Menschenkinder* [Children], 1899, and *Im Zwischenland* [The Land Between], 1902; and her two best-known stories, *Fenitschka* and *Eine Ausschweifung* [Deviations], 1898). In different ways, many of these earlier narratives deal with women trying unsuccessfully to negotiate their attraction to idealized men and with the assertion of their own identities. The stories "Fenitschka" and "Eine Ausschweifung," for instance, portray women's independence and sexual fulfillment as being mutually exclusive because of prevailing social norms and because of women's internalization of these norms. Most of Andreas-Salomé's fiction of this period illustrates women's search for new gender identities in the era of rapid social change around 1900. By contrast, the three novels that she wrote in the early 1900s, *Ma* (1902; Mom), *Das Haus* (1919; The House), and *Ródinka* (1923), tend to idealize family and rural life and portray women who have resolved the conflicts that plague the protagonists in her earlier fiction. The literary works Andreas-Salomé wrote later in her life return to her preoccupation with childhood and adolescence but are now informed by her studies in psychoanalysis (i.e., the drama *Der Teufel und seine Großmutter* [The Devil and his Grandmother], 1922, and the stories collected in *Die Stunde ohne Gott* [The Hour without God], 1922).

Many of the themes that recur in Andreas-Salomé's fiction correspond with experiences discussed in her posthumously published autobiography *Lebensrückblick* (1951): these include a girlhood marked by religious devotion to a father figure and wrought with unfulfilled sexual desire, the complicated position of women claiming independence, and the significance of Russia as the premodern and uncorrupted "other" of European civilization. Based in part on these thematic links between her autobiography and her other works, most earlier critics—continuing a pervasive trend in the reception of women authors—approached Andreas-Salomé's works as an extension of her biography and of her friendships with famous men such as Nietzsche, Rilke, and Freud (e.g., Binion, 1968; Guery, 1879; Peters, 1962; and Sorell, 1975, among others). More recent research explores Andreas-Salomé's work on its own terms, discusses it in the context of turn-of-the-century culture, or charts its implications for the discourse on "Woman and Modernity."

In addition to her success as a writer of fiction, Andreas-Salomé participated actively in the reception of Nietzsche's philosophy and in the formation of Freudian psychoanalysis. According to Biddy Martin, Andreas-Salomé was able to contribute to these and other discourses not only because she lead an unusually independent life for a woman of her social class and generation—but also, ironically, because she adopted traditional notions of femininity both in her self-representation and in the representation of gender roles in her work. By embracing femininity as positive and self-sufficient, she did not challenge or threaten the dominant notions of masculinity in any direct sense, but she created a subject position from which she could participate in major intellectual debates of her time. For instance, Andreas-Salomé balanced "female" admiration against "male" challenge in her relationship to Freud and to psychoanalysis. On the one hand, she admired Freud as a scientist and humanist (1931; *Mein Dank an Freud*) and defended him against his competitors and critics Alfred Adler and C.G. Jung. On the other hand, she consistently transformed psychoanalytic concepts according to her own philosophical views in her contributions to the psychoanalytic journal *Imago*. In her most obvious challenge to Freud, Andreas-Salomé advocated a concept of the unconscious that is not exclusively the result of repression but that is rooted in a primordial stage and plays a positive role in sexual experiences and in creative activities. In contrast to the respect that she gained from Freud and others for her contributions to psychoanalytic theory, her study of Nietzsche—the first comprehensive assessment of his work—was widely ignored. This lack of response to Andreas-Salomé's *Friedrich Nietzsche in seinen Werken* (1894; *Nietzsche*) arguably resulted because she transgressed the socially acceptable role of feminine admirer and adopted instead the position of critical interpreter (Martin).

Despite Andreas-Salomé's intellectual independence, her traditional notion of gender roles put her at odds with both the progressive and the conservative factions of the women's movement. Adopting a position of resistance from within dominant discourses, she promoted essentialist explanations of gender difference but disagreed with male critics who used essentialism to argue for women's "natural" inferiority (most notoriously Otto Weininger in his 1903 *Geschlecht und Charakter* [Sex and Character]). By contrast, Andreas-Salomé maintained that women are different but not inferior or complementary to men. She developed this emancipatory dimension of her essentialist notion of femininity in the book *Henrik Ibsens Frauengestalten* (1892; *Ibsen's Heroines*), one of the earliest studies of Ibsen outside of Scandinavia, and in her essays on women and on sexuality (*Die Erotik* [1910; Eroticism]). Andreas-Salomé strongly encouraged women to pursue their lives beyond mere devotion to someone else or to a career, but in *Die Erotik* she was critical of feminists who idealized maternal qualities and of equal rights activists who advocated competition with men. While Andreas-Salomé's independence served as an example for the "new woman," some feminists (most notably Hedwig Dohm) have criticized Andreas-Salomé's individualistic approach to gender issues and her disregard for the social advancement of women less privileged than herself.

FRIEDERIKE EIGLER

Biography

Born in St. Petersburg, Russia, 12 February 1861. Private instruction in theology and philosophy from her mentor, Hendrik Gillot; studied theology and art history, University of Zurich, 1880–81; contracted tuberculosis; traveled to Italy, 1881–82, and met Malwida von Meysenbug, Paul Rée, and Friedrich Nietzsche; traveled to Russia with Rilke, 1899–1900; participated in a psychoanalytic research colloquia with Sigmund Freud; lay analyst in Königsberg and Göttingen. Died 5 February 1937.

Selected Works

Fiction

Im Kampf um Gott [published under the pseudonym Henri Lou], 1885
Ruth: Erzählung, 1895
Aus fremder Seele: Eine Spätherbstgeschichte, 1896
Fenitschka. Eine Ausschweifung: Zwei Erzählungen, 1898; as *Fenitschka. Deviations: Two Novellas*, translated and with an introduction by Dorothee Einstein Krahn, 1990
Menschenkinder: Novellensammlung, 1899
Ma: Ein Porträt, 1902
Im Zwischenland: Fünf Geschichten aus dem Seelenleben halbwüchsiger Mädchen, 1902
Das Haus: Eine Familiengeschichte vom Ende des vorigen Jahrhunderts, 1919
Die Stunde ohne Gott und andere Kindergeschichten, 1922
Ródinka: Eine russische Erinnerung, 1923
Amor. Jutta. Die Tarnkappe: Drei Dichtungen, edited by Ernst Pfeiffer, 1981

Play

Der Teufel und seine Großmutter: Traumspiel, 1922

Essays

Die Erotik: Vier Aufsätze, 1910
Drei Briefe an einen Knaben, 1917
Das 'zweideutige' Lächen der Erotik: Texte zur Psychoanalyse, edited and with an introduction by Inge Weber and Brigitte Rempp, 1990

Other

Henrik Ibsens Frauengestalten, 1892; as *Ibsen's Heroines*, edited, translated, and with an introduction by Siegried Mandel, 1985
Friedrich Nietzsche in seinen Werken, 1894; as *Nietzsche*, edited, translated, and with an introduction by Siegried Mandel, 1988
Rainer Maria Rilke: Buch des Gedenkens, 1928
Mein Dank an Freud: Offener Brief an Professor Freud zu seinem fünfundsiebzigsten Geburtstag, 1931
Lebensrückblick. Grundriß einiger Lebenserinnerungen, edited by Ernst Pfeiffer, 1951; as *Looking Back: Memoirs*, translated by Breon Mitchell, 1991
In der Schule bei Freud: Tagebuch eines Jahres, 1912/13, edited by Ernst Pfeiffer, 1958

Further Reading

Kreide, Caroline, *Lou Andreas-Salomé: Feministin oder Antifeministin? Eine Standortbestimmung zur wilhelminischen Frauenbewegung*, New York: Lang, 1996
Haines, Brigid, "Lou Andreas-Salomé's *Fenitschka*: A Feminist Reading," *German Life and Letters* 44, no. 5 (1991)
Martin, Biddy, *Woman and Modernity: The Life(Styles) of Lou Andreas-Salomé*, Milwaukee: University of Wisconsin-Milwaukee, 1986
Müller-Loreck, Leonie, *Die erzählende Dichtung Lou Andreas-Salomés und ihr Zusammenhang mit der Literatur um 1900*, Stuttgart: Heinz, 1976
Lou Andreas-Salomé: Blätter der Rilke-Gesellschaft, 1986
Salber, Linde, *Lou Andreas-Salomé: mit Selbstzeugnissen und Bilddokumenten*, Reinbek bei Hamburg: Rowohlt, 1990
Schultz, Karla, "In Defense of Narcissus: Lou Andreas-Salomé and Julia Kristeva," *German Quarterly* 67, no. 2 (1994)
Welsch, Ursula, and Michaela Wiesner, *Lou Andreas-Salomé: Vom 'Lebensurgrund' zur Psychoanalyse*, Munich: Verlag Internationale Psychoanalyse, 1988

Annolied ca. 1080
Religious Poem

It is no coincidence that the Early Middle High German *Annolied* should receive such intense scholarly attention: it is a work of formidable complexity and in many respects unique. Written between 1077 and 1081 in Rhenish-Franconian by a monk at Siegburg, it combines an unusual dualistic history of the world with a biography of Archbishop Anno II of Cologne (ca. 1010–1075). It is in fact a panegyric on the archbishop. Its apparent program was to justify him in the face of widespread criticism and, by theologically significant association, to reinforce his political position and perhaps to campaign for his veneration: he was canonized in 1183.

The 878 lines of the poem are arranged in 49 strophes. Structurally, the *Annolied* falls into three sections: strophes 1–7, a history of the sacred world; strophes 8–33, a history of the secular world; and strophes 34–49, a life of Anno. Each of the historical sections runs in a linear form from the beginnings (the creation, the foundation of civilization) to Anno, while the third presents the archbishop in an idealized form: the poem thus contains three concentric circles (Ittenbach) with Anno as their common center point. This already complex structure is underpinned by an intricate network of numerological patterns of a kind typical of other works of the Salian period (e.g., *Ezzosgesang* [before 1065; Ezzo's Hymn]). Most obviously, we see that Anno appears as the culmination of history in the symbolic strophes 7 and 33. Thus, although the life of Anno fills only 16 of the *Annolied*'s 49 strophes, the main thrust of the entire work is clearly hagiographical. This subordination of history to another purpose is a particularly unusual feature.

The first section of the poem records biblical and ecclesiastical history and the stories of saints beginning with Adam, reaching a climax in Jesus Christ, and proceeding to a resolution in the person of Anno; as Adam is the most significant theological type of Christ in the Old Testament, the symmetry of the passage forces the reader to see Anno as the most significant *imitatio Christi,* who is of greater consequence than the saints who are named before him. Thus, a theological context is established for a claim of Anno's exceptional piety. In a similar but far more complex way, the second section establishes Anno's standing as a secular ruler. Ancient history is presented using the familiar schema of the four empires from Daniel's dream: Babylon, Persia, Greece, and Rome. Then, by a sophisticated application of the *translatio imperii* doctrine, these empires are linked with the foremost Germanic peoples, the Swabians, Bavarians, Saxons, and Franks, respectively. Thus, the priority that Rome enjoys over its predecessors in traditional historiography is transformed into a claim of Frankish supremacy. Likewise, the position of the city of Rome within the Roman Empire is aligned with the position of Cologne to transform the latter into the center of the Franconian realm. Just as we have had the pattern Adam-Christ-Anno, so we now find Jerusalem-Rome-Cologne. By these and other correlations, the archbishop and his diocese are implicitly or explicitly associated with the most momentous events of the past. The impression is given that all prior world history was a preparation for Anno's ministry. From here the poet can lead very naturally into the third section, which is almost a set-piece *vita.* We read of Anno's holiness, the monasteries he founded (principally Siegburg), his political disputes, the theophany that preceded his death, and a miracle in which a certain knavish Volpreht loses his sight when he mocks the dead archbishop but is healed after praying at his grave.

The poet's political agenda has several facets that are still the subject of scholarly debate. As an electoral bishop, Anno had been a major player in imperial politics, controversial particularly in the regency years 1062–64, but he had mixed success in municipal politics (in 1074, he banished the merchants from Cologne but had to ask them to return on their own terms when the local economy collapsed). The poet stresses Anno's unshakable allegiance to the emperor, overlooking the rift that appeared between them later in his life, and depicts those who opposed him as jealous and ungodly. He also appears to take the side of the emperor in the Saxon war of 1075, in which Anno had attempted to mediate. The choice of German rather than Latin indicates a desire to speak to the secular world; the message would appear to be an apologia for Anno's activities and, more generally, an assertion of the role of *Reichsbischöfe* (imperial bishops) in German politics, which the poem combines with a powerful sense of local patriotism.

The *Annolied* is also of interest for a number of unusual incidental features. Being the first serious attempt to trace the rise of the German nation historically, it contains the earliest known reference in the German language to Germany as a geographical unit: *Diutischemi lande*. The material on Julius Caesar is marked by a striking shift whereby the *Bellum Gallicum* takes place in Germany, and the Germans as Caesar's allies help win the *Bellum civile*. There is an account of the origins of *pluralis majestetis* and what appears to be by far the earliest reference to the Crimean Goths. As the poem was a source for the *Gesta Treverorum* (late 11th century; History of Trier) and the *Kaiserchronik* (before 1150; Chronicle of Emperors), some of these motifs were passed on to later historical literature, which in turn comprises the best evidence of the reception of the *Annolied* in the Middle Ages.

Besides the hermeneutical questions that have been mentioned, contemporary scholarly debate on the *Annolied* has focused on the question of genre. The work is the first world chronicle in the German language and, as such, is a predecessor to the series of large-scale chronicles that began with the *Kaiserchronik* and continued into the 15th century. The *Annolied*'s separation of sacred and secular history suggests a historiographical approach that is otherwise unknown in the major German vernacular chronicles, so that the historical sections of the poem are already a difficult form to define. It is the combination of these sections with the biography in the final section, however, that poses the greatest interpretive difficulties. If we take the poem as a chronicle with an appendix, we do not do justice to the hagiographical element, but if we regard it primarily as a saint's life with a historical preamble, we underestimate the extent to which the chronicle section (two-thirds of the poem) has independent statements to make. The three sections are too fully integrated to be treated in isolation, yet together they defy any simple classification. The *Annolied* is something of a medieval curiosity.

GRAEME DUNPHY

See also Martin Opitz

Editions

Das Annolied: Rhythmus de S. Annone Coloniensi archiepiscopo, edited by Martin Opitz, Danzig, 1639

Das Annolied, edited by Max Roediger, in *Monumenta Germaniae Historica: Deutsche Chroniken* I, 1895

Das Annolied, edited by Friedrich Maurer, in *Die religiösen Dichtungen des 11. und 12. Jahrhunderts,* vol. 2, Tübingen: Niemeyer, 1965

Das Annolied, edited by Eberhard Nellmann, Stuttgart: Reclam, 1975

Further Reading

Haverkamp, Anselm, *Typik und Politik im Annolied,* Stuttgart: Metzler, 1979

Heinz, Thomas, "Bemerkungen zu Datierung, Gestalt und Gehalt des Annoliedes," *Zeitschrift für deutsche Philologie* 96 (1977)

Ittenbach, Max, "Aus der Frühzeit rheinischer Dichtung: Das Annolied," *Euphorion* 39 (1938)

Knab, Doris, *Das Annolied: Probleme seiner literarischen Einordnung,* Tübingen: Niemeyer, 1962

Knoch, Peter, "Untersuchungen zum Ideengehalt und zur Datierung des Annoliedes," *Zeitschrift für deutsche Philologie* 83 (1963)

Liebertz-Grun, Ursula, "Zum Annolied: Atypische Struktur und singulare politische Konzeption," *Euphorion* 74 (1980)

Schwarz, Eberhard, "Neue Uberlegungen zur Entstehung des Annoliedes," *Wirkendes Wort* 40, no. 3 (1990)

Thurlow, P.A., "Augustine's City of God, Pagan History and the Unity of the *Annolied,*" *Reading Medieval Studies* 6 (1980)

Antifascist Literature

With the polarization of politics in the closing years of the Weimar Republic came the corresponding division of politically committed literature (institutionally represented by the Nazi Kampfbund für Deutsche Kultur (Militant League for German Culture) and the Communist Bund Proletarisch-Revolutionärer Schriftsteller [BPRS; League of Proletarian-Revolutionary Writers]). Yet when Hitler became chancellor on 30 January 1933, antifascist writers were ill prepared for what was to come: the dissolution of their organizations, the banning of the Communist and Trade Union press, the book burnings on 10 May 1933, and other measures, which appeared to confirm Goebbels's later judgment that antifascist writers were "corpses on leave." Many emigrated at the first opportunity, while some of those who stayed were arrested and imprisoned. Others remained under cover and engaged in clandestine activities, including members of the Berlin branch of the now illegal BPRS, who, until stopped by the Gestapo in 1935, issued a magazine *Hieb und Stich,* produced stickers and flyers, and smuggled out information for exile publications such as *Neue Deutsche Blätter,* edited in Prague (60 reports under the title "Die Stimme aus Deutschland"); *Internationale Literatur,* edited in Moscow by Johannes R. Becher (with its section "Stimme der Illegalen"); and the BPRS account of repression, *Hirne hinter Stacheldraht,* which appeared in 1934 in Switzerland. Exiles sent subversive literature into Germany disguised as innocuous items (so-called *Tarnschriften*), including Brecht's essay "Fünf Schwierigkeiten beim Schreiben der Wahrheit," which appeared in the form of practical directions for first aid. *Neue Deutsche Blätter* appeared from September 1933 to August 1935, edited by Anna Seghers, O.M. Graf, W. Herzfelde, and an anonymous figure who represented the internal opposition in Germany. The last of these, Jan Petersen, made a dramatic appearance in dark shades at the first Internationaler Schriftstellerkongreß zur Verteidigung der Kultur in Paris in 1935. His contributions to *Hieb und Stich,* which formed a chronicle of Nazi measures as they affected a typical street in Berlin-Charlottenburg, were eventually collected under the title *Unsere Straße* (Our Street) and appeared in Paris in 1935, Bern and Moscow in 1936, and London in 1938.

Accounts of the early concentration camps, written by political prisoners after their flight, also soon reached the outside world. These include Hans Beimler's *Im Mörderlager Dachau* (1933; In the Murder Camp Dachau), Willi Bredel's *Die Prüfung* (1934; The Test), Gerhart Seger's *Oranienburg* (1934), Wolfgang Langhoff's *Die Moorsoldaten* (1934; Die Moorsoldaten; also the title of a song that eventually found its way into one of the scenes of Brecht's *Furcht und Elend des Dritten Reiches*), *Dachau* by Walter Hornung (pseudonym of Julius Zerfaß) (1936; Internee 880), *Schutzhäftling 880* by Paul Massing (pseudonym of Karl Billinger) (1935), and the title piece in the anthology *Mord im Lager Hohenstein: Berichte aus dem Dritten Reich* (Murder in Camp Hohenstein: Reports from the Third Reich), which appeared in Moscow in 1933. Despite the conditions under which they worked, inmates of the camps were able on occasion to produce literature for their own individual and collective self-definition and for the maintenance of morale: besides Langhoff's story about the "Zirkus Konzentrazani," which ends with the chorus singing the song mentioned above, there were performances in Dachau of a satire on Hitler in the disguise of a medieval romp, *Die Blutnacht auf dem Schreckenstein* (Night of Blood at Schreckenstein), and of a version of *Faust I* in Sachsenhausen. Works conceived and written in imprisonment include Albrecht Haushofer's *Moabiter Sonette* (Sonnets from Moabit Prison), found in his hands by his brother after his execution by the SS on 23 April 1945; Bruno Apitz's story *Esther,* written in Buchenwald in 1944, which tells of the love between a Jewish inmate (the title figure) and a Kapo; and Werner Krauss's *PLN: Die Passionen der halykonischen Seele* (The Postcode: The Passions of the Halyconian Soul), written with bound hands in 1943–44 in Berlin's Plötzensee prison and then smuggled out. The last of these, eventually published in 1946 (Frankfurt/Main) and 1948 (Potsdam), is the most elaborate piece of writing in the Aesopian style to emerge from the Third Reich, a roman à clef in which a mythical empire led by the Großlenker Mufti has been engaged in seven years of war. At the center stands the figure of von Schnipfmeier, who as post minister introduces the post code; as an uncommitted figure, however, he is used by the regime as window dressing, becomes disillusioned, gains contact with a group of dissidents (Bund der unentwegten Lebensfreude), suffers imprisonment, and finally shows signs of a change of heart. The element of wish-fulfillment is clear; the importance of the text lies in the originality of its satire and in its private morale-boosting function. Krauss, however, also manages to convey insights into the links between the regime and big business, the role of ideology, especially racism, the passivity of the silent majority—its cultivation of the "Reich der schönen Seele" is clearly a dig at "Innerlichkeit"—and the role of propaganda. All these texts can be defined as antifascist in the narrow sense, even those—mainly poems that represent personal reactions to an unimaginable situation—that were not communicated even to other camp inmates or fellow conspirators, although most of their authors must have hoped that they would survive as a record and statement for posterity.

With literature published (and not always banned) in the Third Reich, we enter what has been described as the "thicket" (Reinhold Grimm) of the inner emigration, part of the large body of work that was neither anti-Nazi nor pro-Nazi, as defined and recognized by the authorities. The term *inner emigration,* if it implies a disguised antifascist stance, must exclude the work in traditional genres by a host of now forgotten writers, many of whom started their careers during the Weimar Republic and continued them after 1945. Their role can be defined as similar to that of film directors who produced comedies and musicals devoid of explicit political content throughout the Nazi years. Similarly, it must exclude the apprentice work of young writers who made important careers after 1945 with writing that contributed to the progress toward a democratic and open society in the Federal Republic (Marie Luise Kaschnitz, Günter Eich, Alfred Andersch, and Wolfgang Koeppen, among others). As such an option could not be entertained except in private, even by those (such as Andersch) who had had contact with the Left before 1933; this literature was formally conservative; its setting was socially, historically, and geographically undefined; and its atmosphere, suffused by an existential melancholy that continued to mark West German literature after 1945, indeed allowed an easy accommodation with the international avant-garde (e.g., Sartre, Camus, and Hemingway) when it became accessible. The preferred genres were the story, the radio play, the essay, the travel sketch, the diary, and the poem (especially the sonnet), short forms that nevertheless allowed scope for allegory and metaphysical speculation.

Even after these exclusions, inner emigration remains a gray area and raises fundamental questions of intention and reception: were texts conceived to satisfy two distinct readerships, the party faithful and their organs of control, and the "common reader" with a neutral attitude to political issues who was inclined to support the status quo? In appealing to the latter, were the authors intending merely to confirm their attitudes or, in relation to a few matters at least, to change them?

The dual strategy was most successfully followed by Adam Kuckhoff in *Der Deutsche von Bayencourt* (1937; The German from Bayencourt), the first part of a planned trilogy, in which a farmer of German birth who has become a naturalized Frenchman helps German troops during World War I and is then executed. The simple plot line ensured acceptance by the authorities, but Kuckhoff offered no character whose views—whether chauvinist, pacifist, or socialist—are privileged or can be identified with those of the author. Kuckhoff's impeccable antifascist credentials—he later joined the Schulze-Boysen/Harnack espionage organization, was arrested in September 1942 and was tortured and executed in August 1943—have ensured him a place alongside Werner Krauss (also associated with the "Rote Kapelle"), and if he had been able continue the trilogy to completion, a clearer standpoint would no doubt have emerged. Nonetheless, even from the conversation at the center of the novel between the title figure Sommer and the laborer Barnabas, who voices revolutionary sentiments, it is not possible to extract more than a debate on the issues of patriotism in the context of an earlier conflict. A third member of the organization, Günther Weisenborn, survived arrest and imprisonment to write *Die Illegalen* (The Clandestine Fighters), a resistance play performed in 1946, and to complete Ricarda Huch's survey of the resistance, *Der lautlose Aufstand* (1954; The Silent Uprising).

The Christian authors of the inner emigration produced historical novels that were in some cases conceived before the Third Reich began. When completed and published in the regime's early years, they were then seen by their authors—and no doubt by most of their readers—as having an antifascist dimension. The later activities and eventual fates of these writers demonstrate that they were not armchair Christians. The subject of Jochen Klepper's *Der Vater* (1937; The Father), King Friedrich Wilhelm I of Prussia, was more than acceptable to official opinion, but the spirit in which the novel was written was far from that which inspired the Hohenzollern cult perpetuated by the Nazis, and this spirit is expressed in the tormented piety that the author singles out as the King's principal characteristic. Werner Bergengruen's *Der Großtyrann und das Gericht* (1935; The Tyrant and the Court of Law) and *Am Himmel wie auf Erden* (published in 1940, but banned in the following year; On Earth as it Is in Heaven) are inspired by a Catholicism that structures the plot of the former according to the sequence of temptation, guilt, self-sacrifice by the guilty person or another, confession, and grace, while in the latter the fear of the population of Berlin induced by the prophecy of a flood in 1524 tests the faith of the principal figures and their power to accept the inevitable. Reinhold Schneider's *Las Casas vor Karl V* (1938; Las Casas before Charles V), in its portrayal of the protest of the Dominican against the genocide of the Indians by the 16th-century Spanish colonizers in South America, comes closer to a clear challenge to Nazi racism. In Ernst Wiechert's *Das einfache Leben* (1939; The Simple Life), the simple life of the title represents "Innerlichkeit" as a refuge. The same author's *Der weiße Büffel* (The White Buffalo) is more explicitly antifascist and is, indeed, the boldest example of Aesopian style for public consumption, but it only appeared in print in 1946 (readings having been banned earlier), as did a year earlier *Der Totenwald* (The Forest of the Dead), the report of Wiechert's imprisonment in Buchenwald from May to August 1938. Ricarda Huch made her position clear in her refusal to remain a member of the restructured literary section of the Prussian Akademy of Arts and in her commemoration of the resistance, which was left incomplete on her death; during the years of the Third Reich, however, she remained silent but for a few poems. Works by other Christian writers, including Gertrud von Le Fort, (*Die magdeburgische Hochzeit* [1938; The Wedding in Magdeburg]), Stefan Andres (*El Greco malt den Großinquisitor* [1936; El Greco Paints the Grand Inquisitor]), and Elisabeth Langgässer (*Das unauslöschliche Siegel* [1946; The Inextinguishable Seal] and *Märkische Argonautenfahrt* [1950; Journey of the Argonauts in the Marshes]), can be compared with those of the Christian converts in exile, Alfred Döblin and Franz Werfel.

With Ernst Jünger's *Auf den Marmorklippen* (1939; *On the Marble Cliffs*), however, we enter a more problematic area. The daredevil courage of the war texts has here been replaced by an elitist stoicism designed to console readers with similar attitudes, but it offers no spur to action. In its advocacy of "machtgeschützte Innerlichkeit," the book can be compared to Friedrich Percyval Reck-Malleczewen's *Bockelson: Geschichte eines Massenwahns* (1937; Bockelson: History of a Mass Delusion), a historical study, which, in the guise of a novel, passed the censor but was banned later. Frank Thieß, who later claimed to have coined the term *innere Emigration,* wrote *Das Reich der Dämonen* (published 1941 and then banned; The Empire of the Demons), which condemns all tyranny in a broad view of the empires of Hellas, Rome, and Byzantium and of the clash of pagan cults with Christianity.

None of these are *Schlüsselromane* (romans á clef), although figures in *On the Marble Cliffs* do bear some resemblance to members of the Nazi elite (but not Hitler). For clearer models one must turn to the satirical novels of the exiles, especially Feuchtwanger's *Der falsche Nero* (1936; *The Pretender*) and Brecht's *Der aufhaltsame Aufstieg des Arturo Ui* (written 1941; published 1957; first performed 1958; *The Resistable Rise of Arturo Ui*). Most exile literature can be defined as antifascist, whether it has a contemporary or a historical setting, but certain works are worth singling out for their impact on opinion outside Germany, especially plays such as Ferdinand Bruckner's *Die Rassen* (1933; The Races), Friedrich Wolf's *Professor Mamlock* (1933), above all, Brecht's *Furcht und Elend des Dritten Reiches* (first performed in part in Paris in 1938, published complete in 1945; translated as *The Private Life of the Master Race* and *Fear and Misery in the Third Reich*), and Anna Seghers's novel *Das siebte Kreuz* (1942; *The Seventh Cross*), which was almost immediately filmed in Hollywood. At the same time, Brecht, Walter Benjamin, Ernst Bloch, and others contributed to a theoretical understanding of fascism among emigrants.

In a number of less significant works, one can trace a developing strategy to ensure that satire reached a wider audience both inside and outside Germany and the occupied areas of the continent. Those that appeared initially in exile periodicals aimed to boost morale in the exile community by drawing on the classical and German literary canon, such as Dosio Koffler's *Die Liebesinsel* (1938; The Island of Love) and *Die deutsche Walpurgisnacht* (1941; The German Walpurgis Night), while later pieces, directed—sometimes via radio—at a mass audience in allied countries or at ordinary soldiers at the front, devised more accessible forms of satire, especially Schweikian humor, as in Robert Lucas's *Briefe des Gefreiten Hirnschal* (1945; Letters of Lance Corporal Hirnschal).

The poets of the inner emigration, because their work is above all consolatory and written in traditional forms, now receives little attention, but whether by the Christians Werner Bergengruen, *Der ewige Kaiser* (1937, confiscated by the Nazis; The Eternal Emperor) or *Dies irae* (1945); Reinhold Schneider, *Sonette* (1939); Oskar Loerke (poems that appeared as "Die Jahre des Unheils" in the first issue [1949] of the GDR periodical *Sinn und Form*); or by writers steeped in the humanism of German bildung, such as Haushofer and Rudolf Hagelstange (*Venezianisches Credo* [1948, but written in 1944; Venetian Creed]), such work achieved a significant impact. There is a tendency in these poems to view Nazism as a divine test or as a necessary scourge that will induce expiation and a change of heart. The events of the Third Reich are also seen as part of the eternal battle between God and Satan, and because specific guilt is dissolved in original sin, one may doubt whether this poetry is antifascist in a political sense. The vitriolic *Jamben* (1967; Iambs) of Rudolf Borchardt and *Die Gasgesellschaft* (1969; The Gas Company) of Georg Kaiser are of greater interest now, but although their authors were emigrants, these collections remained unknown to contemporaries. When F.G. Jünger's elegy *Der Mohn* (1934; The Poppy) appeared, it was understood as an attack on National Socialism, but from an elitist, nonpolitical point of view comparable to that of the author's brother Ernst. Gottfried Benn, after his brief public endorsement of the regime, vented his disillusionment in the essays "Zum Thema Geschichte" (1943; On the Subject of History) and "Kunst und Drittes Reich" (1941; Art and the Third Reich) and the poems "General" (1938) and "Monolog" (1941).

The literature of both postwar German states (and to a lesser but significant extent Austria) since 1945 has been deeply involved in the process of *Bewältigung der Vergangenheit* (coming to terms with the Nazi past), which no major author has entirely ignored. Especially those old enough to have experienced the Third Reich directly (including Hans Werner Richter, Alfred Andersch, Heinrich Böll, Günter Grass, Heinar Kipphardt, Siegfried Lenz, and Christa Wolf) determined to free themselves from the tradition of *deutsche Innerlichkeit,* which had allowed large sections of the German educated middle class to avoid a clear stand. Writers of an older generation, whether or not they were emigrants (e.g., Thomas Mann, Hermann Broch, Alfred Döblin, and Wolfgang Koeppen), felt obliged to place it at the center of highly personal debates with their own and Germany's past. From all the *Bewältigungsliteratur,* which continues unabated to the present, one work stands out on account of its scale, depth, and range: Peter Weiss's *Die Ästhetik des Widerstands* (1971–81; *The Aesthetics of Resistance*). It focuses on the antifascist struggle of a tiny embattled minority, commemorates its heroism, introduces real historical figures beside the fictional characters at its center, and above all, reflects on the actual and potential role of committed art under all forms of political oppression.

Just as the poetry of concentration camp inmates (e.g., Hermann Adler, Else Dormitzer, Karl Adolf Gross, Edgar Kupfer-Koberwitz, Gerty Spies, Ilse Blumenthal-Weiß, Gertrud Kantorowicz, Ilse Weber, Adam Kuckhoff, Harro Schulze-Boysen, Dietrich Bonhoeffer, Hans Lorbeer, Hasso Grabner, and Karl Schnog), written largely in traditional forms by persons who had published little or nothing when free, cannot compare with the work of Paul Celan and Nelly Sachs (who did not experience the camps directly), so there is a deep qualitative gulf between the writing of antifascists who actively engaged in resistance and the professionals who examined the Third Reich in retrospect. Yet the former deserve more than commemoration for their courage; their work has an authenticity that allows the reader to view events without any hindsight in the form of history in the making.

MALCOLM HUMBLE

See also Fascism and Literature

Further Reading

Bock, Sigrid, and Manfred Hahn, editors, *Erfahrung Nazideutschland: Romane in Deutschland, 1933–1945: Analysen,* Berlin: Aufbau, 1987

Brekle, Wolfgang, "Die antifaschistische Literatur in Deutschland (1933–1945): Probleme der inneren Emigration am Beispiel deutscher Erzähler (Krauss, Kuckhoff, Petersen, Huch, Barlach, Wiechert u.a.)," *Weimarer Beiträge* 16 (1970)

———, *Schriftsteller im antifaschistischen Widerstand 1933–1945 in Deutschland,* Berlin: Aufbau, 1985

Emmerich, Wolfgang, "Die Literatur des antifaschistischen Widerstandes in Deutschland," in *Die deutsche Literatur im Dritten Reich: Themen, Traditionen, Wirkungen,* edited by Horst Denkler and Karl Prümm, Stuttgart: Reclam, 1976

Frühwald, Wolfgang, and Heinz Hürten, editors, *Christliches Exil und christlicher Widerstand: Ein Symposion an der Katholischen Universität Eichstätt, 1985,* Regensburg: Pustet, 1987

Grimm, Reinhold, and Jost Hermand, editors, *Exil und Innere Emigration, Third Wisconsin Workshop,* Frankfurt: Athenäum, 1972

Hoffmann, Charles W., *Opposition Poetry in Nazi Germany,* Berkeley and Los Angeles: University of California Press, 1962

Hohendahl, Peter Uwe, and Egon Schwarz, editors, *Exil und Innere Emigration II: Internationale Tagung in St. Louis,* Frankfurt: Athenäum, 1973

Humble, Malcolm, "Anti-Nazi Satire by German-Speaking Exiles: Developing Strategies in the Practice of a Problematic Genre," *Forum for Modern Language Studies* 30 (1994)

Klieneberger, H.R., *The Christian Writers of the Inner Emigration,* The Hague and Paris: Mouton, 1968

Krohn, Claus-Dieter, editor, *Aspekte der künstlerischen Inneren Emigration, 1933–1945,* Exilforschung, vol. 12, Munich: Text und Kritik, 1994

Moll, Michael, *Lyrik in einer entmenschlichten Welt: Interpretationsversuche zu deutschsprachigen Gedichten aus nationalsozialistischen Gefängnissen, Ghettos, und KZs,* Frankfurt: Fischer, 1988

Osterle, Heinz D., "The Other Germany: Resistance to the Third Reich in German Literature," *German Quarterly* 41 (1968)

Prümm, Karl, "'Die Zukunft ist vergeßlich': Der antifaschistische Widerstand in der deutschen Literatur nach 1945," in *Gegenwartsliteratur und Drittes Reich: Deutsche Autoren in der Auseinandersetzung mit der Vergangenheit,* edited by Hans Wagener, Stuttgart: Reclam, 1977

Reiter, Andrea, *"Auf daß sie entsteigen der Dunkelheit": Die literariche Bewältigung von KZ-Erfahrung,* Vienna: Löcker, 1995

Schäfer, Hans Dieter, "Die nichtfaschistische Literatur der 'jungen Generation' im nationalsozialistischen Deutschland," in *Die deutsche Literatur im Dritten Reich: Themen, Traditionen, Wirkungen,* edited by Horst Denkler and Karl Prümm, Stuttgart: Reclam, 1976

Schnell, Ralf, *Literarische Innere Enigration, 1933–1945,* Stuttgart: Metzler, 1976

Wirth, Günther, "Über politische Dimensionen der literarischen 'inneren Emigration'," *Weimarer Beiträge* 29 (1983)

Hannah Arendt 1906–1975

Hannah Arendt launched her distinguished career as a political thinker in the early 1950s. Arendt's first major work, *The Origins of Totalitarianism* (1951), was acclaimed as a significant introduction to the conceptual elements of totalitarian rule. Arendt's analysis of Nazi and Stalinist systems was sharpened by her Jewish identity. Her imperative was to clarify Jewish suffering from culturally and ideologically motivated anti-Semitism. Arendt's method of "conceptual analysis" (Young-Bruehl) perplexed her critics, since her abstract approach of isolating concepts and tracing their historical roots was considered inaccurate. Strictly speaking, *The Origins* failed to identify the direct causes of totalitarianism. Nonetheless, Arendt's survey of its disturbing effects was firmly embedded in her personal experiences.

In 1933, Arendt confronted the rise of Nazi power when she was arrested in Berlin for assisting the Zionist leader Kurt Blumenfeld. Miraculously, Arendt was released, and she immediately fled to Paris. In the spring of 1941, Arendt and her husband, Heinrich Blücher, emigrated to the United States, where Arendt held various academic posts—at Chicago's Committee for Social Thought (from 1963) and at New York's New School for Social Research (from 1968). Among Arendt's many professional accolades were numerous honorary doctorates, most notably from Yale. In 1959, Arendt became the first woman professor at Princeton University.

Arendt's post-totalitarian study, *The Human Condition* (1958), is a critique of Marx's historical materialism. Arendt's retrospective survey champions the Greek model of the *polis,* an expression of her idealistic approach to political activity (*vita activa*). The "morphology" of the *polis* remained a central pillar of Arendt's political theory, and in this work it serves as a pivotal connection between the contemporary age's technical skill for "action," "work," and "labor" and the ancient love of ideas (*vita contemplativa*). Similarly, Arendt defends her devotion to "lofty principles" in *Between Past and Future* (1961); she argues that it is not idealistic theorizing but an exercise in learning to practice accountability and political maturity. However, Arendt never entirely abandoned the mental rigors of the training that she received as a pupil of Martin Heidegger and Karl Jaspers. Arendt acknowledged her debt to both 20th-century representatives of Germany's philosophical tradition, but Karl Jaspers provided vital moral support throughout the bitter controversy over Arendt's *Eichmann in Jerusalem: A Report on the Banality of Evil* (1963).

Apart from her academic works, Arendt wrote accomplished commentaries on Jewish affairs. From the mid-1940s, she published numerous articles in the U.S. and Jewish press about the future security of the Jewish state, and her perceptiveness on this matter is rekindled in *The Jew as Pariah* (1978). In 1961, Arendt attended the Eichmann trial as court reporter for *The New Yorker* magazine, but she went, too, because she felt an obligation to her own past. Arendt's report was meant for a lay audience, but her ironic narrative lapsed into high-minded rhetorical flourishes, which offended representatives from all quarters. Her Jewish critics were particularly stunned at her implication that Jewish Councils (*Judenräte*) could have established a principle of "nonparticipation" with Nazi plans for the so-called Final Solution. Arendt regarded Jewish attacks on her scholarly credentials as "a political campaign." Yet her fierce exchange of letters with Gershom Scholem proved that the campaign was highly personal: Scholem publicly broke ranks with Arendt for her lack of "Love of the Jewish people."

Arendt's comment on Eichmann's "banality" markedly revised her earlier conclusion that evil could be rationalized, in Kant's terms, as "radical evil." Arendt's altered opinion allowed her to disentangle the Holocaust from Germany's Enlightenment tradition. In fact, Arendt persistently honored the German intellectual tradition, and it is not surprising that, in her acceptance speech for the Lessing Prize in 1959, Arendt introduced Lessing as humanity's light in *Von der Menschlichkeit in finsteren Zeiten: Gedanken zu Lessing* (1960; translated in *Men in Dark Times,* 1968). What Arendt witnessed in Eichmann was the pathetic face of an inhuman system that was exceptional for fostering an inability to think. Arendt's reflections on surviving this brutal system echoed ideas that she developed in her biography entitled *Rahel Varnhagen* (1958), a critical study of Romanticism, which Arendt completed in 1938, while in exile from Nazi terror. Arendt depicts Rahel as a "parvenu," assimilated by her marriage to 19th-century German society, and as a "pariah"; Rahel is an outsider, imprisoned within salon society.

Arendt's poignant portrayal of the depths of Rahel's dilemma as a German Jewess developed a yardstick for her later commentaries on the Jewish position. Arendt's unspoken ideal remained the "conscious pariah," an objective position that Arendt claimed for herself as an independent observer of the Eichmann trial. While Arendt concentrated on other projects, her study *On Revolution* (1963) was largely obscured by the continuing furor over *Eichmann.* Further studies, *On Violence* (1970) and *Crises of the Republic* (1972), reflected Arendt's deep concern for democratic freedom and stability, but these works, too, remained overshadowed by personal loss.

In 1969, Karl Jaspers died. The death of Arendt's friend and mentor was followed only a year later by the death of Heinrich Blücher. Arendt withdrew into the privacy that she found essential to the thinking that was the preliminary subject of an ambitious three-part project for the Gifford Lectures at the University of Aberdeen in 1973–74. Arendt's last public appearance for these lectures led to the posthumous publication *The Life of the Mind* (1978), edited by Mary McCarthy, in two volumes, *Thinking* and *Willing.* This work rekindles the purely philosophical perspective that Arendt adopted in her doctoral thesis on St. Augustine. Curiously, however, Arendt's late philosophical undertaking profoundly supports her achievement in the field of political science, for Arendt openly criticizes Heidegger, who failed, in her view, to convey the will for political action. Arendt's *Lectures on Kant's Political Philosophy* (1982) sketches the outline she planned for the third volume of her late project, *Judging.* On 4 December 1975, however, Arendt suffered a fatal heart attack at her Riverside Drive apartment. Mary McCarthy recalled in her eulogy Arendt's uncanny gift for "enacting a drama of mind."

SUZANNE KIRKBRIGHT

See also Holocaust (Shoah) Literature

Biography

Born in Hannover, 14 October 1906. Studied at Königsberg University, B.A. 1924; further study at University of Marburg, University of Freiburg, and Heidelberg University; Ph.D. at Heidelberg under Karl Jaspers, 1928; worked with the Young Aliyah, Paris, 1934–40; emigrated to United States, 1941; research director, Conference on Jewish Relations, New York, 1944–46; chief editor, Schocken Books, New York, 1946–48; executive director, Jewish Cultural Reconstruction, New York, 1949–52; naturalized U.S. citizen, 1950; professor, Committee on Social Thought, University of Chicago, 1963–67; professor, graduate faculty, New School for Social Research, New York 1967–75; visiting professor, University of California, Berkeley, 1955, Princeton University, 1959, Columbia University and Brooklyn College, 1960. Guggenheim Fellowship, 1952–54; National Institute of Arts and Letters Award, 1954; Lessing Prize, Hamburg, 1959; Rockefeller Fellowship, 1959–60, 1969–70; Freud Prize, Deutsche Akademie für Sprache und Dichtung, 1967; Sonning Prize for Contributions to European Civilization, Denmark, 1975; numerous honorary doctorates. Died in New York, 4 December 1975.

Selected Works

Nonfiction

Der Liebesbegriff bei Augustin: Versuch einer philosophischen Interpretation, 1929

Sechs Essays, 1948

The Origins of Totalitarianism, 1951; in the United Kingdom as *The Burden of Our Time,* 1951; enlarged edition, 1958

The Human Condition, 1958

Karl Jaspers: Reden zur Verleihung des Friedenpreises des Deutschen Buchhandels, 1958; translated by Clara and Richard Winston in *Men in Dark Times,* 1968

Rahel Varnhagen: The Life of a Jewess, 1958; in the United States as *Rahel Varnhagen: The Life of a Jewish Woman,* 1974

Die Ungarische Revolution und der totalitäre Imperialismus, 1958

Von der Menschlichkeit in finsteren Zeiten: Gedanken zu Lessing, 1960; translated by Clara and Richard Winston in *Men in Dark Times,* 1968

Between Past and Future: Six Exercises in Political Thought, 1961; enlarged edition as *Between Past and Future: Eight Exercises in Political Thought,* 1968

Eichmann in Jerusalem: A Report on the Banality of Evil, 1963; revised edition, 1964

On Revolution, 1963

Men in Dark Times, translated by Clara and Richard Winston, 1968

On Violence, 1970

Crises of the Republic, 1972

Die Verborgene Tradition: Acht Essays, 1976

The Jew as Pariah: Jewish Identity and Politics in the Modern Age, edited by Ron H. Feldman, 1978

The Life of the Mind, edited by Mary McCarthy, 2 vols., 1978

Lectures on Kant's Political Philosophy, edited and with an interpretative essay by Ronald Beiner, 1982

Letters

Hannah Arendt/Karl Jaspers Briefwechsel, 1926–1969, edited by Lotte Köhler and Hans Saner, 1985; as *Hannah Arendt/Karl Jaspers*

Correspondence, 1926–1969, translated by Robert and Rita Kimber, 1992
Between Friends: The Correspondence of Hannah Arendt and Mary McCarthy, 1949–1975, edited by Carol Brightman, 1995
Hannah Arendt/Martin Heidegger, Briefe 1925–75, edited by Ursula Ludz, 1998

Edited Works
Bernard Lazare, *Job's Dungheap: Essays on Jewish Nationalism and Social Revolution,* 1948
Franz Kafka, *Diaries,* with Martin Greenberg, vol. 2, 1949
Hermann Broch, *Dichten und Erkennen* and *Essays,* 1955
Karl Jaspers, *The Great Philosophers,* translated by Ralph Manheim, 2 vols., 1962–66
Walter Benjamin, *Illuminations,* translated by Harry Zohn, 1968

Further Reading
Barnouw, Dagmar, *Visible Spaces: Hannah Arendt and the German-Jewish Experience,* Baltimore, Maryland and London: Johns Hopkins University Press, 1990
Canovan, Margaret, *Hannah Arendt: A Reinterpretation of Her Political Thought,* Cambridge and New York: Cambridge University Press, 1992
Elon, Amos, "The Case of Hannah Arendt," *New York Review,* 6 November 1997
Ettinger, Elzbieta, *Hannah Arendt/Martin Heidegger,* New Haven, Connecticut: Yale University Press, 1995
Ludz, Ursula, editor, *Ich Will Verstehen,* Munich: Piper, 1996
Young-Bruehl, Elisabeth, *Hannah Arendt: For Love of the World,* New Haven, Connecticut: Yale University Press, 1982

Eichmann in Jerusalem 1963

Essay by Hannah Arendt

When in 1960 Israel announced the sensational capture and impending trial in Jerusalem of the Nazi war criminal Adolf Eichmann, Hannah Arendt abruptly canceled her teaching and research plans and approached the *New Yorker* with an offer to report on the trial's proceedings. The five-part trial report, entitled "Eichmann in Jerusalem," appeared in weekly installments during the months of February and March in 1963, nearly one year after Eichmann's death sentence had been carried out. Even before its appearance in the *New Yorker,* Arendt's report was the source of much speculation and heated debate. The publication of the book version in May of that year—now bearing the controversial subtitle "A Report on the Banality of Evil"—sparked extraordinary responses both within and outside the Jewish community, which have continued almost unabated to this day.

Immediately following the report's book publication, eminent Jewish thinkers around the world publicly castigated Arendt as an irresponsible, unsympathetic, and self-hating Jew. Her accusations that Jewish leaders and institutions played a significant role in Germany's extermination of European Jewry and that Israel had attempted to stage a show trial in order to legitimate itself as a national Jewish state were seen as offensive and unfounded. Above all, Arendt was taken to task for belittling the Holocaust with her key thesis, the "banality of evil," which was embodied by Eichmann's comic mediocrity and "thoughtlessness." In a now famous exchange of letters, Gershom Sholem labeled Arendt's thesis as an empty "catchword" or "slogan." With its raising of substantial moral, legal, and national issues, Arendt's report also had a significant impact on contemporary sociopolitical concerns that exceeded Jewish history. Political activists of the 1960s used the report, for example, to point out the United States's fascist qualities, and sociologists applied it to describe the deficits of mass culture. Since the mid-1970s and beyond, during the still-ongoing attempts to work through the legacy of World War II, Arendt's report has become, according to Dan Diner, a "cipher for the historical and moral evaluation of National Socialist crimes," which articulates the universal "possibility of systematic mass murder in the modern era." To be sure, notes Diner, Arendt's once-vilified slogan "now constitutes a career in itself" in academia and public debate. These extreme receptions of Arendt's work point not only to her deliberately provocative stance and to her position as a conscious pariah within Jewish communities but also to a larger ongoing cultural and national politics surrounding fascism and post-Shoah Jewish and German identities. They also suggest the increasing sensationalism and mass commodification of representations of the Holocaust and the Nazi era, which reveals a problematic fascination with fascist culture and its legacies of power and domination (Sontag).

With the publication in 1951 of her monumental work *The Origins of Totalitarianism,* which traces 20th-century totalitarianism from its roots in 19th-century anti-Semitism and imperialism, Arendt established herself as one of the West's most significant political and philosophical thinkers. When the trial report appeared more than a decade later, many believed, as Sholem had charged, that Arendt had revised her earlier thesis of "radical evil," which in *Origins* had been embodied by the incomprehensible crimes of Nazi Germany. As more recent criticism notes, however, Arendt is attempting in her concept of the banality of evil to articulate and refine a critique of fascism that examines its everyday manifestations in modern mass bureaucracy. Her report demonstrates how Germany's institutionalization of fascist ideology brought about the moral failure of an entire civic society, in which deportation, mass murder, and the systematic extermination of peoples came to be perceived as ordinary affairs.

Although this type of evil is by no means banal in its consequences, claims Arendt, it is banal in its efficient outlook and in the routine and "thoughtless" manner in which it carries out its goals. As the embodiment of bureaucratic "thoughtlessness," Eichmann was not a traditional villain in the grand manner of Iago, Macbeth, or Richard III. He was instead, she argues, a mediocre and unimaginative desk murderer with poor language and social skills; his only exceptional quality was "his extraordinary diligence in looking out for his personal advancement." "It was sheer thoughtlessness," not evil intent, writes Arendt, "that predisposed him to become one of the greatest criminals of that period." Arendt's report focuses precisely on the type of institutional and state-administered violence suggested by Eichmann's trial and the fundamental challenges this form of violence poses to the West's judicial, moral, and political codes.

In viewing the phenomenon of fascism as carried out by a system supported by the civic masses and not simply a ruling elite of Nazis, Arendt challenges the seemingly self-propelled apparatus of totalitarian power, as may be implied by Adorno and Horkheimer's analysis of fascism. According to Arendt, fascism was thus not beyond the comprehension of people caught in an infernal machine of oppression; nor was it carried out by a small group in power. Instead, Arendt seeks the agency for this oppressive regime in the petty ranks of administrative bureaucracy and in the professional zeal of ordinary citizens to obey the system's demands. Her portrayal of Eichmann as an ordinary citizen and murderer also works to counter the prosecution's charge that he was the diabolical mastermind of the Final Solution and to suggest that Israel's political motive to establish itself as the national homeland of a persecuted people lay behind its overstated case.

Arendt's civil critique also extends problematically to include the victims of the Holocaust. The uncomfortable truth about the Jewish councils, according to Arendt, was their initial cooperation (before the Final Solution) in systematically locating and delivering otherwise elusive Jews to the German system of persecution. Germany's so-called ruthless toughness in implementing its goal of cleaning Europe of its Jews fell apart when met by resistance such as that found in Denmark, Sweden, Bulgaria, and Italy. It may be argued that, in blurring the status between perpetrator and victim, Arendt stresses active agency and complicity in order to avoid an argument of historical determinism in which Jewish history is understood as an unfolding teleology of persecution. Her functionalist argument points here to the hegemony of modern systems of bureaucracy that require the participation of their victims. However, Arendt's argument also runs the dangerous risk of making banal not only the everyday sorts of fascism in such a system but, ultimately, the suffering of their victims. In doing so, Arendt exchanges the teleology of persecution for that of an abstract systemic logic that no longer distinguishes sufficiently between victimizers and victims. Voiced at a time when Germany was still haltingly confronting its past and when the world, including Jewish communities, was just beginning to understand the extent of Nazi crimes, Arendt's provocative arguments were premature, arguably reckless, and, as a consequence, liable to conflicting interpretations and violent reactions. Nevertheless, Arendt's line of thought has radically shaped and refined the ongoing and evolving discussion of the legacies of fascism.

DELIA CAPAROSO KONZETT

Editions

First edition: *Eichmann in Jerusalem: A Report on the Banality of Evil,* New York: Viking Press, 1963; revised and enlarged edition, New York: Viking Press, 1964

Further Reading

Ainsztein, Reuben, *Jewish Resistance in Nazi-Occupied Eastern Europe,* London: Elek, 1974; New York: Harper and Row, 1975

Arendt, Hannah, "The Concentration Camps," *Partisan Review* 15, no. 7 (1948)

———, *The Origins of Totalitarianism,* New York: Harcourt, Brace, 1951

Arendt, Hannah, and Gershom Scholem, "*Eichmann in Jerusalem:* Exchange of Letters between Gershom Scholem and Hannah Arendt," *Encounter* 22, no. 1 (1964)

Bernstein, Richard J., *Hannah Arendt and the Jewish Question,* Cambridge: Polity Press, and Cambridge, Massachusetts: MIT Press, 1996

Dawidowicz, Lucy S., *The Holocaust and the Historians,* Cambridge, Massachusetts: Harvard University Press, 1981

Diner, Dan, "Hannah Arendt Reconsidered: On the Banal and the Evil in Her Holocaust Narrative," *New German Critique* 70 (Spring 1997)

Hilberg, Raul, *The Destruction of the European Jews,* Chicago: Quadrangle Books, and London: Allen, 1961

Krummacher, F.A., editor, *Die Kontroverse: Hannah Arendt, Eichmann, und die Juden,* Munich: Nymphenburger, 1964

Mann, Golo, "*Eichmann in Jerusalem,*" *Die Neue Rundschau* 4 (1963)

Mommsen, Hans, "Hannah Arendt und der Prozess gegen Adolf Eichmann," in *Eichmann in Jerusalem: Ein Bericht von der Banalität des Bösen,* translated by Brigitte Granzow, Munich: Piper, 1986

Robinson, Jacob, *And the Crooked Shall Be Made Straight: The Eichmann Trial, the Jewish Catastrophe, and Hannah Arendt's Narrative,* New York: Macmillan, 1965

Sontag, Susan, "Fascinating Fascism," in *Under the Sign of Saturn,* New York: Farrar, Straus and Giroux, 1980

Trunk, Isaiah, *Judenrat: The Jewish Councils in Eastern Europe under Nazi Occupation,* Lincoln: University of Nebraska Press, 1972

Achim von Arnim 1781–1831

Achim von Arnim belongs to the second generation of German Romantics, although certain of his later works anticipate poetic realism. He stood at the center of German intellectual life during the Napoleonic Wars and the European Restoration, a position that he derived not only from his many writings but also from his marriage to Bettina Brentano, his accomplishments as a physicist, and his close relationships with major figures such as Clemens Brentano, Goethe, the brothers Grimm, Heinrich von Kleist, Friedrich von Savigny, and Ludwig Tieck. His family's aristocratic standing also afforded him a role in discussions about the great Prussian reforms of the period. In contrast to this early prominence, Arnim's subsequent reputation has suffered extended intervals of neglect. Heinrich Heine, Friedrich Hebbel, Hugo von Hofmannsthal, André Breton, and others have periodically emerged to champion his cause, but they are the exceptions. He has until recently typically been ignored or, worse, unfairly tarred with the brush of reaction and extreme anti-Semitism.

Within the last several decades, however, German and North American scholars have arrived at a new appreciation of Arnim's character and artistic achievement. They have produced the first critical edition of his complete works, established an International Arnim Society, and made a museum of his estate in Wiepersdorf, 40 miles outside of Berlin. More important, they have demonstrated in a variety of studies that Arnim's political thought differs from that of the stereotypical *Junker* and that especially his prose fiction reflects highly modern sensibilities.

For Arnim, politics and literature were inseparable. Even the work for which he is best remembered, *Des Knaben Wunderhorn* (1805–8; *The Boy's Magic Horn*), the enormously popular collection of folk songs that he and Clemens Brentano published, was originally intended to awaken a sense of German nationhood among all classes and regions. The search for unity that underlies all of his texts goes well beyond the notion of political boundaries, however. Typically, the protagonists of his plays, novels, and short fiction find themselves at a turning point in history, torn between a dimly perceived verity grounded in national tradition and the illusory gratifications of fashion or transitory pleasure. One of Arnim's best-known novellas, *Isabella von Ägypten* (1812; *Isabella of Egypt*), offers a good example. In it, the historical Charles V tragically misses the opportunity to bring about a kind of golden age in Europe. Instead of recognizing the historical continuity and genuine love offered by the Gypsy princess Isabella, the emperor succumbs to the soulless lust and greed embodied in three mythical figures: a golem, a bearskinner, and a mandrake.

This story contains many of the features that typify Arnim's works: a willful mixture of historical fact and fantasy, interwoven genres, shifting planes of reality, folk motifs, multifaceted polarities, contrapuntal narrative techniques, grotesque configurations, and broad humor. As in so many of his other works, most of the novella's figures are led astray by false differentiations that are brought about by pecuniary interest, intolerance, voguish enthusiasms, or the reliance on empirical fact. Only occasionally does some figure, usually an idealized woman, rise above these false distinctions to achieve a symbolically presented synthesis.

To contemporaries who were disturbed by his works' eccentricities, Arnim replied that he intended a mythical, poetic truth that transcended mere fact or convention and allowed his readers a view of history's more profound continuities. But few people before the middle of the 20th century saw his writings as anything other than willful pastiches. In her study of Romanticism (*Blüthezeit der Romantik,* 1899), Ricarda Huch spoke for most critics in dismissing Arnim's prose narratives as not being works of art; at the most, she asserted, they provided the raw materials out of which readers could themselves create such works. But this very quality, so damning to sensibilities of the 19th century, proved intriguing to the 20th. The surrealists, for example, delighted in the apparent spontaneity of Arnim's associative structures, and they helped to bring about a new appreciation of works such as *Isabella,* which Breton translated into French. In the 1960s, a growing group of critics began to dedicate itself to the tasks of making Arnim's works more available, of defining their historical contexts more accurately, and of analyzing the narrative strategies that they employ. These studies have demonstrated that Arnim's associative structures do reveal artistic purpose, especially when viewed within the context of reader-response theory.

BRUCE DUNCAN

Biography

Born in Berlin, 26 January 1781. Attended Joachimsthaler Gymnasium, 1793–98; attended Universities at Halle and Göttingen, 1793–98; published a *Theory of Electrical Phenomena*, began to contribute regularly to Germany's most important scientific journal (Gilbert's *Annalen der Physik;* Annals of Physics), 1799; began first novel, 1801; undertook grand tour of Europe, 1801–4; friendship with Clemans Brentano; started work with Brentano on *Des knaben Wunderhorn*, 1804; years of writing and travel within Germany. Published a short-lived *Zeitung für Einsiedler* (Gazette for Hermits), 1808; co-founded the *Christlich-Deutsche Tischgesellschaft* (Christian-German Table Society), which included many of Berlin's most influential men and excluded "Jews and philistines," 1811; married Bettina Brentano, Clemens's younger sister, with whom he eventually had seven children; managed his heavily-mortgaged family estate at Wiepersdorf, eventually clearing its encumbrances, while still writing fiction, book reviews, and articles on politics, science, and agriculture, from 1814; Bettina and the children moved to Berlin, where he visited regularly, 1816. Died suddenly of a stroke in Wiepersdorf, 21 January 1831.

Selected Works

Collections

Werke und Briefwechsel. Historische-kritische Ausgabe, edited by Roswitha Burwick et al., 2000–

Werke in sechs Bänden, edited by Roswitha Burwick et al., 1989–94

Dramas

Halle und Jerusalem, 1811

Der Auerhahn, 1813

Folksong Collection

Des Knaben Wunderhorn, edited with Clemens Brentano, 3 vols., 1805–8; selections as *The Boy's Magic Horn,* translated by Margarete Münsterberg, 1913

Novels

Hollins Liebeleben, 1802

Ariels Offenbarungen, 1804

Armuth, Reichtum, Schuld, und Buße der Gräfin Dolores, 1810

Die Kronenwächter, 1817; second volume (incomplete), 1854

Novella Collections

Der Wintergarten, 1809

Novellensammlung, 1812; as *The Novellas of 1812,* translated by Bruce Duncan, 1997

Landhausleben, 1826

Novellas

Isabella von Ägypten, 1812; as *Isabella of Egypt,* translated by Bruce Duncan in *The Novellas of 1812,* 1997

Die Majoratsherren, 1819; as *Gentry by Entailment,* 1990

Owen Tudor, 1821

Die Kirchenordnung, 1822

Raphael und seine Nachbarinnen, 1824

Der tolle Invalide auf dem Fort Ratonneau, 1835; as *The Mad Veteran of Fort Ratonneau,* translated by William Metcalf, 1946; translated by Helene Scher, 1975; translated by Siegfried Weing, 1997

Further Reading

Bonfiglio, Thomas Paul, *Achim von Arnim's Novellensammlung 1812: Balance and Meditation,* New York: Lang, 1987

Burwick, Roswitha, "Physiology of Perception: Achim von Arnim's Practical and Historical Aesthetics," in *The Romantic Imagination: Literature and Art in England and Germany,* edited by Frederick Burwick and Jürgen Klein, Amsterdam and Atlanta, Georgia: Rodopi, 1996

Duncan, Bruce, "Werke von und über Achim von Arnim seit Volker Hoffmanns 'Die Arnim-Forschung 1945–1972,'" in *Neue Tendenzen der Arnim-Forschung: Edition, Biographie, Interpretation, mit*

unbekannten Dokumenten, edited by Roswitha Burwick and Bernd Fischer, Bern and New York: Lang, 1990
Fischer, Bernd, "Achim von Arnim (1781–1831)," in *German Writers in the Age of Goethe, 1789–1832,* edited by James Hardin and Christoph Schweitzer, Dictionary of Literary Biography, vol. 90, Detroit, Michigan: Gale Research, 1989
Hoermann, Roland, *Achim von Arnim,* Boston: Twayne, 1984
Liedke, Herbert R., *Literary Criticism and Romantic Theory in the Works of Achim von Arnim,* New York: Columbia University Press, 1937
Lokke, Kari E., "Achim von Arnim and the Romantic Grotesque," *Germanic Review* 58 (1983)
Kastinger Riley, Helene M., *Achim von Arnim in Selbstzeugnissen und Bilddokumenten,* Hamburg: Rowohlt, 1979
Weiss, Hermann F., "The Use of the Leitmotif in Achim von Arnim's Stories," *German Quarterly* 42 (1969)
Ziegler, Vickie L., *Bending the Frame in the German Cyclical Narrative: Achim von Arnim's "Der Wintergarten" and E.T.A. Hoffmann's "Die Serapionsbruder,"* Washington, D.C.: Catholic University of America Press, 1991

Bettina von Arnim 1785–1859

Bettina von Arnim was acclaimed for her artistic works and her politically and socially engaged later works, as much as for her cosmopolitan salon, which flourished in Berlin during the 1830s. Bettina's literary notoriety was assured when, cultivating a correspondence with Goethe, she translated their letters into her first epistolary novel, *Goethes Briefwechsel mit einem Kinde* (1835; *Goethe's Correspondence with a Child*). As a fantasy, which included imaginary conversations of Goethe's mother, Frau Rath, Bettina's original interweaving of epistolary and Romantic fiction enhanced her reputation as an associate member of Clemens Brentano's literary set. The Brentanos' intimate circle of poets included, among others, Bettina's husband, Achim von Arnim, and Jacob and Wilhelm Grimm. Her ordination as "the high-priestess of Romanticism" (Püschel) was 19th-century historian Heinrich von Treitschke's response to her artistic portrait, which led to a "cult" of Goethe after his death.

Her preferred name, Bettine, underlined her self-stylizing and her natural claim to a poetic signature. Bettina translated into her art a growing disapproval of repression and censorship, which intensified in the politicized atmosphere of the *Vormärz,* which in turn culminated in Germany's 1848 revolution. Family commitments, as a mother of seven, did not prevent Bettina from inspiring Berlin's youth, who increasingly attached their revolutionary aspirations, as representatives of *Jung Deutschland,* to Bettina's literary art and thriving Berlin salon. By dedicating *Die Günderode* (1840; *Correspondence of Fräulein Günderode and Bettine von Arnim*) to Berlin students such as Philipp Nathusius and Julius Döring, Bettina turned her letters to Karoline von Günderrode into an epistolary epitaph, an act of overcoming her personal grief at her friend's suicide. In 1806, Karoline von Günderrode inflicted a fatal wound to her heart, a tragic response to the death of her intimate friend, Georg Friedrich Creuzer. Günderrode's death became Romantic folklore that was fatally revived by Heinrich von Kleist's suicide in 1811, the same year that Bettina and Achim von Arnim secretly married.

In *Die Günderode,* recollections of Romantic loss are connected to the early death of Bettina's mother, Maximiliane von Brentano, who died when Bettina was only eight years old. A different sense of loss, however, is implied by the opening line of Bettina's 1821 letter to Goethe: "Mit Dir hab' ich zu sprechen!" ("With you, I have to speak!") Bettina implored Goethe to repair the breakdown of their friendship, which occurred after Goethe heard of her reported effrontery, in a public gallery, of his wife, Christiane. An endeavor to mediate her own friendship with Goethe was as unsuccessful as her introducing Goethe to Beethoven. Although a meeting occurred in 1812, Goethe did not requite Bettina's love of Beethoven's genius.

As the pressure of domestic life at Arnim's country estate, Wiepersdorf, became too difficult, Bettina relocated with her family to Berlin's Unter den Linden in 1823. Arnim's untimely death, in 1831, awakened Bettina's determination to oversee a complete edition of his works, notably, *Des Knaben Wunderhorn* (1806; The Boy's Magic Horn). Among the various assistants enlisted for this project was Wilhelm Grimm, whose *Kinder- und Hausmärchen* (1812; *Grimms' Fairy Tales*) were dedicated to Bettina. A fairy-tale idyll, or an introspective view of life that is considered typical of the *Biedermeier* era, is the undertone of *Clemens Brentanos Frühlingskranz* (1844; Clemens Brentano's Wreath of Spring). The letters of the Brentano siblings are Bettina's way of revisiting the idyll of their mutual dependency during childhood. Whatever the *Biedermeier* characteristics of this work, however, Bettina's mature interest was in politics.

In 1837, the suspension of the Hannoverian constitution led to the dismissal of seven distinguished professors, among them the Grimm brothers, who signed a scholarly protest against the constitutional breakdown. *Ilius Pamphilius und die Ambrosia* (1847–48) contained Bettina's virtually unedited letters to Philipp Nathusius. The project dated from 1839, when the plan was to publish her letters to Nathusius and Döring in order to agitate for the reinstatement of the *Göttinger Sieben.* In 1840, however, Frederick William IV secured the reinstatement of Jacob and Wilhelm Grimm, who obtained posts in Berlin. Bettina regarded this as a vindication of her correspondence, through Alexander von Humboldt, with crown prince Frederick William, who ascended the Prussian throne in 1840. Her letters to the King of Prussia were translated into reflections on the ideal monarchy, a loyal project that informed the political message of *Dies Buch gehört dem König* (1843; This Book Belongs to the King). Having secured the King's permission to dedicate this work to him, Bettina directly confronted the newly crowned sovereign with the needs of his people and the growing desire for liberal reform.

The so-called *Polenbroschüre,* a pamphleteering address entitled *An die aufgelöste Preussische National-Versammlung. Stimmen aus Paris* (1848; To the Dissolved Prussian Assembly), underlined Bettina's interest in liberal revolution. Her pamphlet, published under the pseudonym St. Albin, with a deliberately misleading dedication to herself, was not merely an attempt to foil the censors, but a criticism of the Assembly in Frankfurt and Berlin for voting to incorporate Posen into the German Federation. With the dissolution of the Assembly, however, this pamphlet of support for Mieroslaswki and Polish autonomy was overtaken by events. Similarly, the intimation by Prussian ministers that the uprising of the Silesian Weavers in 1844 was incited by Bettina's *Armenbuch* (1844; Paupers' Book) was incorrect. Fearing censorship, Bettina withdrew her work, an incomplete, although telling document to the poverty of the Silesian weavers.

Interest in the political status of Bettina's work revived in the 1980s, especially with 200th birthday editions, but also with Christa Wolf's narrative of Bettina and Karoline von Günderrode's friendship, *Kein Ort. Nirgends* (1979). Wolf concentrated on Bettina's Romantic portrait, *Die Günderode,* to underscore the work's political overtones, situated as it was between the 1830 and 1848 revolutions. Wolf's attempt to rehabilitate Bettina's poetic politics implicitly accentuates the varied elements of the latter's Romantic repertoire. The stylizing of her family heritage, beginning with the discovery of her grandmother Sophie von La Roche's correspondence to Goethe, is as typical of Bettina as her clandestine marriage to Arnim. Bettina was irrevocably linked to an aristocratic world, the literary elite from Goethe to Rahel Varnhagen, and the higher echelons of the Prussian diplomatic service from Savigny to Humboldt. By the conversational tone and epistolary quality of her art, Bettina von Arnim's reputation as a Romantic poetess remains unique insofar as she interpreted the political agendas of a turbulent era.

SUZANNE KIRKBRIGHT

Biography

Born in Frankfurt, 4 April 1785. Granddaughter of the author Sophie von La Roche; sister of the author Clemens Brentano; met Goethe in 1807; settled in Berlin, 1817; in literary circles that included Friedrich Jacobi, L. Tieck, F. Schleiermacher, the Grimm brothers, and the Humboldt brothers; began her writing career in the 1830s. Died in Berlin, 20 January 1859.

Selected Works

Collections

Sämtliche Schriften, 11 vols., 1853
Sämtliche Werke, edited by Waldemar Oehlke, 7 vols., 1920–22
Werke und Briefe, edited by Gustav Konrad and Joachim Müller, 5 vols., 1959–63
"Die Sehnsucht hat allemal Recht": Gedichte, Prosa, Briefe, edited by Gerhard Wolf, 1984
Werke, edited by Heinz Härtl, 1986–
Werke und Briefe, 3 vols., edited by Walter Schmitz and Sibylle von Steinsdorff, 1986–
Bettina von Arnim: ein Lesebuch, edited by Christa Bürger and Birgitt Diefenbach, 1987

Fiction

Goethes Briefwechsel mit einem Kinde. Seinem Denkmal, 1835; as *Goethe's Correspondence with a Child: For His Monument,* translated in part by the author, 1837; book 3 translated as *The Diary of a Child,* 1838; translated in *German Classics of the Nineteenth and Twentieth Centuries,* vol. 7, by Wallace Smith Murray, 1913
Die Günderode, 1840; as *Miss Günderode,* translated (incomplete) by Margaret Fuller, 1842; as *Correspondence of Fräulein Günderode and Bettine von Arnim,* complete translation by Minna Wesselhöft and Margaret Fuller, 1861
Clemens Brentanos Frühlingskranz. Aus Jugendbriefen ihm geflochten, wie er selbst schriftlich verlangte, 1844
Das Armenbuch, 1844; edited by Werner Vordtriede, 1969
Ilius Pamphilius und die Ambrosia, 1847–48
Das Leben der Hochgräfin Gritta von Rattenzuhausebeiuns, with Gisela von Arnim, edited by Shawn C. Jarvis and Herman Grimm, 1986

Other

Dédié à Spontini, 1843
Dies Buch gehört dem König, 2 vols., 1843
An die aufgelöste Preussische National-Versammlung. Stimmen aus Paris (political pamphlet), 1848; as *Polenbroschüre,* edited by Ursula Püschel, 1954
Gespräche mit Daemonen. Des Königsbuches zweiter Band, 1852
Bettine von Arnim und Friedrich Wilhelm IV (correspondence), edited by Ludwig Geiger, 1902
Goethes Mutter in ihren Briefen und in den Erzählungen der Bettina Brentano, edited by Kate Tischendorf, 1914
Bettines Leben und Briefwechsel mit Goethe: aufgrund ihres handschriftlichen Nachlasses nebst zeitgenössischen Dokumenten über ihr persönliches Verhältnis zu Goethe, edited by Reinhold Steig, 1922; revised edition, edited by Fritz Bergemann, 1927
Bettina von Arnim und Rudolf Baier (correspondence), edited by Kurt Gassen, 1937
Die Andacht zum Menschenbild. Unbekannte Briefe von Bettine Brentano (correspondence with Carl von Savigny), edited by Wilhelm Schellberg and Friedrich Fuchs, 1942
Achim und Bettina in ihren Briefen: Briefwechsel Achim von Arnim und Bettina Brentano, edited by Werner Vordtriede, 2 vols., 1961
Der Briefwechsel zwischen Bettine Brentano und Max Prokop von Freyberg, edited by Sybille von Steinsdorff, 1972
Der Briefwechsel Bettine von Arnims mit dem Brüdern Grimm 1838–1841, edited by Hartwig Schultz, 1985
Bettine und Arnim. Briefe der Freundschaft und Liebe, edited by Otto Betz and Veronika Straub, 2 vols., 1986–87
". . . und mehr als einmal nachts im Thiergarten." Bettina von Arnim und Heinrich Bernhard Oppenheim. Briefe 1841–1849, edited by Ursula Püschel, 1990

Edited Works

Ludwig Achim von Arnim, *Sämtliche Werke,* edited with Wilhelm Grimm and Karl August Varnhagen von Ense, 2 vols., 1853–56; revised edition, 21 vols., 1857; reprint, 1982

Further Reading

Bäumer, Konstanze, and Hartwig Schultz, *Bettina von Arnim,* Stuttgart: Metzler, 1995
Baumgart, Hildegard, *Bettine Brentano und Achim von Arnim: Lehrjahre einer Liebe,* Berlin: Berlin Verlag, 1999
Daley, Margaretmary, *Women of Letters: A Study of Self and Genre in the Personal Writing of Caroline Schlegel-Schelling, Rahel Levin Varnhagen, and Bettina von Arnim,* Columbia, South Carolina: Camden House, 1998
Drewitz, Ingeborg, *Bettine von Arnim: Romantik, Revolution, Utopie,* Düsseldorf: Claasen, 1984
Hirsch, Helmut, *Bettine von Arnim: mit Selbstzeugnissen und Bilddokumenten,* Reinbek bei Hamburg: Rowohlt, 1987
Huch, Ricarda, "Brentano," in *Ausbreitung und Verfall der Romantik,* Die Romantik, vol. 2, Leipzig: Haessel, 1908

Lindner, Gabriele, "Natürlich geht das nächste Leben heute an Wortmeldung zu Christa Wolfs Brief über die Bettine," *Weimarer Beiträge* 9 (1982)
Püschel, Ursula, "Weibliches und Unweibliches der Bettina von Arnim," in *"Wider die Philister und die bleierne Zeit": Untersuchungen, Essays, Aufsätze über Bettina von Arnim,* Berlin: Seifert, 1996
Susman, Margarete, "Bettina," in *Frauen der Romantik,* Jena: Diederichs, 1929; Frankfurt: Insel, 1996
Wolf, Christa, *Kein Ort. Nirgends,* Darmstadt: Luchterhand, 1979; Munich: Deutscher Taschenbuch, 1994
———, "Nun ja! Das nächste Leben geht aber heute an," *Sinn und Form* 2 (1980)

Arthurian Romance

The reception of the Arthurian legend in the medieval German-speaking world, mediated predominantly through Old French sources, extends from the last decades of the 12th century to the 16th century. It would seem that, in the earliest period of this reception, influential secular princes, impressed by the culture of the French courts with whom they had social and political contact, were responsible for the transmission of the source manuscripts. The German poets adapted and elaborated these sources creatively, accommodating and reflecting the different cultural, social, and political circumstances of the courts for whom they were writing.

The earliest German Arthurian romance is Hartmann von Aue's *Erec* (ca. 1180), which, together with his later romance *Iwein* (ca. 1200), was seminal in the development of the German tradition. In his adaptation of Chrétien de Troyes's romances (the French poet who shaped the Arthurian material into the literary form that was to have an enduring influence on the development of European narrative literature), Hartmann invites the reader to assess the conduct of the hero knight within the context of the chivalric code as practiced at the court of King Arthur. Central themes in the romances (the balance between the needs of the individual and those of society, love and marriage, service and reward, and adventure as a means of self-aggrandizement and altruistic duty to others) are illuminated through parallel, contrastive, and analogical episodes, which are arranged within the framework of a double-cycle model. Various levels of reality are fused in the narrative: contemporary court life, the magical world of the fairy tale, myth, and salvation history.

In his completion of Chrétien's tale of Perceval, the Grail winner, Wolfram von Eschenbach utilizes the narrative principle of the double cycle model to relativize, although not to devalue, Arthurian chivalry. The Christian pattern of transgression, penance, grace, and redemption inherent in Hartmann's romances are preeminent in *Parzival* (ca. 1200). Where Hartmann had focused on a circumscribed, critical period in the life of his hero knight, Wolfram works with a much broader canvas, drawing on a wide range of literary and nonliterary sources. The biography of Parzival is embedded in a greater historical context, which is defined by his kinship with King Arthur through his father and with the family of Grail keepers through his mother. Wolfram's romance became fundamental to the subsequent development of the "postclassical" German Arthurian romance, particularly with regard to the reception of the Grail legend. Gottfried von Strassburg must be ranked with Hartmann and Wolfram as the greatest German romancers. Gottfried's rendering of the Tristan legend, however, has no connection with the Arthurian world, and the other German Tristan romances have only tenuous links.

In 13th century France, prose and anonymity became the hallmarks of those Old French romances that incorporated the chronicle tradition of Arthurian history, the tales of individual knights, and the history of the Grail. The earliest fragments of the translation into German of the great *Lancelot en prose* (ca. 1225) have been dated to ca. 1250. The prose romance did not take root in the German tradition, however, and the *Prosa-Lancelot* remained an isolated example of its type. Although the figure of Lancelot had been introduced early to German readers in Ulrich von Zatzikhoven's *Lanzelet* (ca. 1194–1205), it did not spark the same degree of interest as Perceval and Tristan, for Chrétien's tale of Lancelot's adulterous relationship with Guinevere (there is no hint of this aspect of the legend in Ulrich's biographical romance) was never adapted into German.

In its negative portrayal of both the efficacy of the secular chivalric ethic and the spiritual inferiority of the Arthurian world to the Grail Kingdom, Albrecht's voluminous *Jüngerer Titurel* (ca. 1270; The Young Titurel) may be regarded as the counterpart to the *Lancelot en prose* in German literature. Albrecht (often identified as Albrecht von Scharfenberg) worked Wolfram's two *Titurel* fragments into an expansive account of the tragic love story of Tschionatulander and Sigune and set it against the eschatological and typological history of the Holy Grail. The surpassing of Arthur's court had already occurred earlier in Wirnt von Grafenberg's *Wigalois* (ca. 1210–15). In this tale of Gawan's son, the focus of interest centers on the concept of an explicitly Christian kingship firmly based in medieval moral theology and realized in the unproblematic and exemplary Wigalois. In Heinrich von dem Türlin's highly eclectic and lengthy romance *Diu Crône* (ca. 1230; *The Crown*), the *roi fainéant* of the classical Arthurian romance is transmuted into an Arthur who has a more central and active role to play, perhaps reflecting the new contemporary ideal of *rex et miles* (king and knight). Indeed, Heinrich declares Arthur to be the subject of the romance, although, as the narrative progresses, it becomes clear that it is in fact Gawan's romance.

In the 13th century, German romancers, despite their claims that they followed a (French) source, drew predominantly on the German tradition and a variety of other literary and nonliterary sources. This is particularly evident in the precourtly world depicted in Der Stricker's romance *Daniel von dem blühenden Tal* (ca. 1220–30; Daniel of the Flowering Valley). In this work, the concept of courtly love is of no consequence, Arthur becomes another Charlemagne, and the pre-courtly ideal of vassalage, familiar from the heroic epic, is exalted. One of the characteristic features of German Arthurian romance from its inception is its intertextuality. Der Pleier conceives his *Garel von dem blühenden Tal* as a corrective to Der Stricker's romance. Together with his *Meleranz* and *Tandareis und Flordibel*, *Garel* (ca. 1240–70) promotes classical courtly ideals, portraying Arthur and his court as chivalric models, which also serve as a contrast to the mores of Der Pleier's own day.

After the 13th century, there are no further shifts in the paradigm of the German Arthurian romance, but rather the compiling, reworking, and recasting of older material: *Der nüwe Parzefal* (1331–36; The New Parzifal) by Philip Colin and Claus Wisse, Ulrich Fuetrer's *Prosaroman von Lanzelot* (ca. 1476; Prose Romance of Lancelot), *Das Buch der Abenteuer* (1473–83; The Book of Adventures), *Der strophische Lanzelot* (ca. 1487; The Strophic Lancelot), and the popular prose chapbooks of the 16th century.

ELIZABETH A. ANDERSEN

See also Hartmann von Aue; Wolfram von Eschenbach

Further Reading

Brogsitter, Karl Otto, *Artusepik*, Stuttgart: Metzler, 1965; 2nd edition, 1971
Emmel, Hildegard, *Formprobleme des Artusromans und der Graldichtung: Die Bedeutung des Artuskreises für das Gefüge des Romans im 12. und 13. Jahrhundert in Frankreich, Deutschland, und den Niederlanden*, Bern: Francke, 1951
Gottzmann, Carola L., *Artusdichtung*, Stuttgart: Metzler, 1989
Gürttler, Karin, *"Künec Artûs der guote": Das Artusbild der höfischen Epik des 12. und 13. Jahrhunderts*, Bonn: Bouvier, 1976
Jackson, William H., and Silvia Ranawake, editors, *The Arthur of the Germans*, Cardiff: University of Wales Press, 2000
Johnson, L. Peter, *Die höfische Literatur der Blütezeit*, Geschichte der deutschen Literatur von den Anfängen bis zum Beginn der Neuzeit, vol. 2, Tübingen: Niemeyer, 1998
Lacy, Norris J., and Geoffrey Ashe, *The New Arthurian Encyclopedia*, Chicago and London: St. James Press, 1991
Mertens, Volker, *Der deutsche Artusroman*, Stuttgart: Reclam, 1998
Schultz, James A., *The Shape of the Round Table: Structures of Middle High German Arthurian Romance*, Toronto and Buffalo, New York: University of Toronto Press, 1983
Thomas, Neil, *The Defence of Camelot: Ideology and Intertextuality in the "Post-Classical" German Romances of the Matter of Britain Cycle*, Bern and New York: Lang, 1992

Art Nouveau *see* Jugendstil

Louise Aston 1814–1871

Louise Aston (née Hoche) had made a name for herself as an enfant terrible before she even published a line. Soon after she moved to Berlin in 1844, she became known as a radical feminist who wore men's clothes, smoked cigars, advocated free love, had numerous lovers, led a sinful life, and had no moral sense whatsoever. These clichés along with the depiction of Aston as a *polterndes Mannweib* (blustering virago)—a common description of her in the contemporary press—have for a long time shaped and dominated the reception of her work. In order to get beyond this facade, it is important to take a closer look at Aston's life and works.

Louise Aston was born in Gröningen near Halberstadt in 1814 as the youngest daughter of Dr. Johann Gottfried Hoche, a senior pastor, and his wife Louise Charlotte Berning Hoche. Compared to other young women of her time, she received a fairly good education, especially in literature and music. In 1835 she married Samuel Aston, an English industrialist who was 24 years her senior and owned a factory in Magdeburg. It is not known whether this was an arranged marriage; what is known, however, is that it was an unhappy relationship that led to divorce in 1838, remarriage in 1841, and a second divorce in 1844. Aston's life changed immensely after her second divorce. She moved to Berlin to connect with intellectual circles and to start a career as a writer.

The years between 1844 and 1855 were turbulent ones for Aston; they were marked by political activism and her involvement in the events surrounding the 1848 revolution. Public attention focused on her unconventional lifestyle, her association with intellectual circles that usually excluded women, and the "blasphemous ideas" that she promoted through her writing. This time was also the most productive in Aston's life: all of the works published during her lifetime were brought out between 1846 and 1850. In the fall of 1848, she was the editor of the weekly revolutionary journal *Der Freischärler* (The Volunteer), which was outlawed in December 1848.

The period between 1845 and 1855 is well documented by her contemporaries: police and newspaper reports in particular give the modern reader an insightful picture of the life of a political activist who fought for the democratization of society, was concerned with the deplorable situation of the working class, and fought vehemently for a woman's right to be considered an equal member of society and—if she chose—to be allowed to live the life of an intellectual. All of these concerns are broadly addressed in her poems—*Wilde Rosen* (1846; Wild Roses) and *Freischärler-Reminiscenzen* (1850; Reminiscences of the Volunteers)—in her novels—*Aus dem Leben einer Frau* (1847; From a Woman's Life), *Lydia* (1848), and *Revolution und Contrerevolution* (1849; Revolution and Counterrevolution)—and in *Meine Emancipation, Verweisung und Rechtfertigung* (1846; My Emancipation, Expulsion, and Vindication), an autobiographic commentary in which she tells her side of the story surrounding her first expulsion from Berlin in 1846. The latter can only be understood in connection with Aston's biography: she was banned from Berlin primarily because her "immoral lifestyle" supposedly posed a threat to social morale, and she decided to address these accusations and the resulting repercussions in order to develop a public forum. Her belief in the power of the press, as well as her social and political activism, places her in a direct context with the Junge Deutschland (Young Germany). Just like the Young Germans, she promoted and fought for political and social concepts that were highly unpopular with the authorities of her day.

Previous attempts to reconstruct even more biographical details based on *Aus dem Leben einer Frau* were not successful: they not only hindered the interpretation of this novel but also led to mistakes regarding her biography, which in turn were corrected by Marilyn Eschinger Carico (1977) and Germaine Goetzinger (1983).

Two topics that dominate Aston's writing are her conviction that women—just like men—have the inalienable right to a free development of their personality and her belief that arranged marriages violate this right by pretending to sanctify a relationship as *Seelenbund* (a union of kindred souls), while in fact it is nothing but a *Seelenhandel* (trade in souls) based on economic and status-related interests, with the woman as a commodity that is sold to the "highest bidder."

In all of her novels, Aston links her criticism of marriage and the search for new concepts of femininity to her political convictions. By shedding light on the deplorable situation of the working class in *Aus dem Leben einer Frau* and in *Revolution und Contrerevolution,* Aston underlines that society as a whole needs to change, that it is women who have to emancipate themselves, even though there is also an urgent need for a redistribution of wealth and for social reform.

With regard to the development of new concepts of femininity, *Lydia* and *Revolution und Contrerevolution* contain the most far-reaching and thought-provoking models. While the same female characters, Lydia von Dornthal and Alice von Rosen, appear in both novels, Aston clearly favors Alice, an emancipated and independent woman who challenges established gender roles. In fact, there are many elements in the depiction of Alice that clearly evoke Aston's own behavior and appearance: she is a strong character who is politically active, wears men's clothes, smokes cigars, and believes in free love as well as in the equality of men and women.

Johanna, the protagonist from Aston's first novel, *Aus dem Leben einer Frau,* is portrayed quite differently. She is introduced as a woman who believes in traditional values and undergoes an awakening process. Forced into an arranged marriage, she remains faithful to her husband until he plans to prostitute her to an aristocrat in exchange for a business loan.

Aston started and ended her career as a writer with the publication of collections of poems, *Wilde Rosen* and *Freischärler-Reminiscenzen,* each containing 12 poems. Most of the poems in *Freischärler-Reminiscenzen* were published first in *Der Freischärler.* The first seven poems of this collection depict the events of the 1848 revolution, and most of the others suggest disappointment with the outcome of the revolutionary events. The remaining five poems focus mainly on women's issues and the need for change. In contrast, the poems in *Wilde Rosen* are more personal: after comparing marriage to a prison or a funeral and so forth in the first five poems, she evokes, in the remaining seven poems, images of happiness and self-assurance and celebrates the idea of being a free woman. The seventh poem in this collection is dedicated to George Sand. Aston was a great admirer of Sand and she most likely took it as a great compliment that her contemporaries referred to her a "German George Sand."

With the publication of *Freischärler-Reminiscenzen,* Louise Aston's career as a writer ended. During the following years, she gradually withdrew from the public sphere. Even though the police surveillance that had started in September 1845 continued until 1867 (1845–67 in Berlin; 1850–56 in Bremen), there is relatively little that is known about the last 20 years of her life. What is known is that following her second expulsion from Berlin in December 1848, Aston traveled a good deal. When she was also expelled from Hamburg, Leipzig, and Breslau, she finally settled in Bremen in 1849, where she married Dr. Daniel Eduard Meier at the end of 1850. The marriage had a major impact on Meier's career as a head physician of a hospital in Bremen: he lost his job because of the reputation of his wife.

Aston and Meier continued to believe in the need for a democratization of society; they became members of the Demokratische Verein (Democratic Association) and kept an association with the Central-Comité für europäische Demokratie (Ligue des Peuples) (Central Committee for a European Democracy; League of the People) in London. Especially in 1851 and 1852, they were repeatedly harassed by the police because of their involvement with these associations. The couple eventually left Germany; Aston followed her husband, who accepted assignments in Russia, the Ukraine, Hungary, and Austria. They returned to Germany in 1871, and Aston died later that year in Wangen. The posthumous publication of an excerpt of her novella *Trop tard* (1885; Too Late) and knowledge of the existence of a novella entitled *Nebelbilder* (Foggy Images) suggest that Aston might not have given up writing completely during the last 20 years of her life.

Aston's feminist contemporaries resented her attitudes toward sexuality and her rejection of marriage: for most women within the early German women's movement, the institution of marriage remained unquestioned. Aston herself took issue with the bourgeois women's movement of her time in her poem "Den Frauen" (To Women), published in *Freischärler-Reminiscenzen.* Claudia von Alemann reflects these tensions and frictions well in her documentary on the early German women's movement, *Das nächste Jahrhundert wird uns gehören* (1987; The Next Century Will Be Ours). Not all of Aston's contemporaries resented her, however: there were also writers and social and political activists—among them Rudolf von Gottschall, Varnhagen von

Ense, Otto von Corvin, Carlos von Gagern, and Karl Frenzel—who looked favorably upon her works and accepted her as a "free thinker." Yet, Aston virtually disappeared from social and literary histories after the mid-1850s. Her works were only rediscovered and reevaluated in the context of modern feminist scholarship.

STEFANIE OHNESORG

Biography

Born in Gröningen near Halberstadt, 26 November 1814. Married English factory owner Samuel Aston, 1835; divorced, 1838; remarried Aston, 1841; divorced him a second time, 1844; became radicalized in views of workers' rights and gender equality, from 1844; lived in Berlin, 1841–46; exiled from Berlin as "staatsgefährliche Person," charged with seeking contact with extremist writers, and her "immoral lifestyle"; returned to Berlin and fought on barricades during revolution, 1848; published the weekly revolutionary journal *Der Freischärler* until forbidden by censors, November through December 1848; second expulsion from Berlin, 1848; settled in Bremen, 1849; married Dr. Daniel Eduard Meier, 1850; lived in Russia, Ukraine, Hungary, Austria, from 1855; returned to Germany, 1871. Died in Wangen/Allgäu, 21 December 1871.

Selected Works

Poetry

Wilde Rosen: Zwölf Gedichte, 1846

Freischärler-Reminiscenzen: Zwölf Gedichte, 1850

Fiction

Aus dem Leben einer Frau, 1847; reprint, edited by Karlheinz Fingerhut, 1982

Lydia, 1848

Revolution und Contrerevolution, 2 vols., 1849

Trop tard [excerpts from a novella from her unpublished works], in volume 1 of *Deutsche Dichterinnen und Schriftstellerinnen in Wort und Bild,* edited by Heinrich Groß, 3 vols., 1885

Other

Meine Emancipation, Verweisung und Rechtfertigung, 1846

Ein Lesebuch: Gedichte, Romane, Schriften in Auswahl, 1846–1849, edited by Karlheinz Fingerhut, 1983

Further Reading

Carico, Marilyn Eschinger, "The Life and Works of Louise Aston-Meier," Ph.D. dissertation, University of Tennessee, Knoxville, 1977

Cyrus, Hannelore, "Von erlaubter und unerlaubter Frauenart, um Freiheit zu kämpfen - Freiheitskämpferinnen im 19. Jahrhundert und die Freie Hansestadt Bremen," in *Grenzgängerinnen: Revolutionäre Frauen im 18. und 19. Jahrhundert: Weibliche Wirklichkeit und männlichen Phantasien,* edited by Helga Grubitzsch, Hannelore Cyrus, and Elke Haarbusch, Düsseldorf: Schwann, 1985

Fingerhut, Karlheinz, " Das Proletariat im bürgerlichen Unterhaltungsroman: Über Louise Aston (1814–1871)," *Die Horen* 30 (1985)

Geiger, Ruth-Esther, "Louise Aston," in *Frauen: Porträts aus zwei Jahrhunderten,* edited by Hans-Jürgen Schultz, Stuttgart: Kreuz, 1981

Goetzinger, Germaine, *Für die Selbstverwirklichung der Frau: Louise Aston: In Selbstzeugnissen und Dokumenten,* Frankfurt: Fischer, 1983

———, "'Allein das Bewußtsein dieses Befreienkönnens ist schon erhebend': Emanzipation und Politik in Publizistik und Roman des Vormärz," in *Deutsche Literatur von Frauen, II: 19. und 20. Jahrhundert,* edited by Gisela Brinker-Gabler, Munich: Beck, 1988

Goodman, Katherine Ramsey, "German Women and Autobiography in the Nineteenth Century: Louise Aston, Fanny Lewald, Malwida von Meysenbug, and Marie von Ebner-Eschenbach," Ph.D. dissertation, University of Wisconsin, Madison, 1977

Grant, Alyth F., "Louise Astons *Lydia:* Ein Beispiel subversiven Umgangs mit literarischen Bildern," *Carleton Germanic Papers* 20 (1992)

Henckmann, Gisela, *Werde, die du bist! Zwischen Anpassung und Selbstbestimmung: Texte deutschsprachiger Schriftstellerinnen des 19. Jahrhunderts,* Munich: Goldmann, 1993

Hulsbergen, Henrike, *Stadtbild und Frauenleben: Berlin im Spiegel von 16 Frauenporträts,* Berlin: Historische Kommission zu Berlin, Stapp, 1997

Möhrmann, Renate, *Die andere Frau: Emanzipationsansätze deutscher Schriftstellerinnen im Vorfeld der Achtundvierziger-Revolution,* Stuttgart: Metzler, 1977

Möhrmann, Renate, editor, *Emanzipation im Vormärz: Texte und Dokumente,* Stuttgart: Reclam, 1978

Müller, Christine von, "Wenn mich der Liebe Flammen heiß umsprühn: Die erotische Rebellion der Louise Aston," *Journal für Geschichte* 4, no. 5 (1982)

Peterson, Uta, "Louise Aston (1814–1871)," in *Women Writers in German-Speaking Countries: A Bio-Bibliographical Critical Sourcebook,* edited by Elke P. Frederiksen and Elizabeth G. Ametsbichler, Westport, Connecticut: Greenwood Press, 1998

Wimmer, Barbara, *Die Vormärzschriftstellerin Louise Aston: Selbst- und Zeiterfahrung,* Frankfurt: Lang, 1993

Athenäum

Of the numerous literary and critical journals that sprouted in Germany toward the end of the 18th century, no other has achieved the renown of the *Athenäum.* Founded and edited by the brothers August Wilhelm and Friedrich Schlegel, it appeared biannually during the years 1798–1800 for a mere total of six issues. Yet its brevity contributes to its reputation as having brought together for one productive moment the leading creative and critical minds that became known as the Jena or "early Romantic" group, the founders of the European literary movement known as Romanticism: the Schlegels, their friends Friedrich Schleiermacher and Friedrich von Hardenberg (Novalis), and their wives Caroline and Dorothea Schlegel.

Following in the footsteps of Maurice Blanchot, Philippe Lacoue-Labarthe and Jean-Luc Nancy have produced an anthology and commentary for French readers, whose English version has served as an introduction into Jena Romanticism for observers of the contemporary theoretical scene. They openly state their views of the movement's current relevance: Jena Romanticism, centered in these years and in this journal, was the first avant-garde group, our birthplace; it initiated the "era of the Subject" that is still our own.

Their high praise should be tempered in two respects: around half of the texts they discuss were not published in the journal; furthermore, if one looks at the journal itself, a good deal of its actual content has dropped from critical view. Moreover, whatever the status of its "modernity," the journal is foremost a product of its historical moment: a moment of fertile reaction to a new European intellectual situation as defined by the French Revolution and the challenge of (Kantian) transcendental philosophy. Thus, Fichte's philosophy was a touchstone for the two friends who led early Romanticism, Novalis and Friedrich Schlegel, while a second point of reference for them was the brightest literary light of the moment, Goethe. While Novalis and Schlegel are often viewed together, as in Walter Benjamin's pathbreaking dissertation, a closer analysis reveals wide differences.

Programmatic for the journal's founding by chief editor Friedrich Schlegel were notions of the sociability of the group, the collective salon-like wit and intellectuality ("symphilosophy") of its members (which included women), and the ideal of anonymous authorship. The appropriate form of writing for this ideal was to be the fragment, a brief prose piece on any topic that could incite further thought without shouldering a burden of discursive proof. Yet the journal also includes essays, letters, dialogues, and poetry. The first issue contained critical pieces by August Wilhelm, the more historically minded of the brothers, along with translations from the Greek by the Schlegels and the first fragment collection entitled *Blüthenstaub* (*Grains of Pollen*) by Novalis, whose friendship with Friedrich did not prevent the latter's editorial insertions and rearrangements. The fragments treat philosophical, religious, aesthetic, scientific, and political themes in tandem, so that the reader could recognize and construct connections. The last fragment expresses the hope that some of the grains of pollen will find a fertile field.

With the second issue of 1798, the journal published pieces that led to its current fame; it contains the 451 fragments later known by the name of the journal, published anonymously but almost all by Friedrich, as was the concluding essay, *Über Goethes Meister* (*On Goethe's Meister*). Among the multitude of themes, innovations in philosophy and literature stand out, along with opinions regarding wit, the social role of women, and literary reviewing and criticism. While religious and political remarks are rare, a famous fragment links the French Revolution with Fichte's philosophy and Goethe's *Wilhelm Meister.* In the area of philosophy, the systematic roles of logic and the principle of contradiction are renounced, and the mind is urged to decide that it must and must not have a system, a typically paradoxical formulation. Fragment 238 (the numbering system was added later) places transcendental philosophy in a parallel with a new form of literature to be called transcendental poetry. Doubtlessly, the most famous conceptual innovation is that of irony. Understanding this concept, however, requires familiarity with the group of fragments Friedrich had already published elsewhere in 1797. The "Socratic irony" described there and elaborated in the fragments reveals once more its Fichtean origins as a point of indifference between self-creation and self-destruction "to the point of irony." These thoughts culminate in fragment 116, the most concise definition of "Romantic poetry," which is seen as both progressive and universal, mixing genres, hovering on the wings of poetic reflection, and forever in a state of becoming and never perfected. This ironic hovering in an "ether of joy" is then discovered in Goethe's *Wilhelm Meister,* a novel described, to its author's approval, as not requiring critical judgment because, with its constant reflective and ironic stance, it judges itself. This self-reflective, self-commenting quality that Friedrich found in the work is for contemporary critics a kind of touchstone of "modernity" and was conceptualized, ironically enough, in a "review" or critical essay that judged a novel about which it claimed that the novel judged itself.

Given the journal's reputation, the paucity of memorable contributions from 1799 is notable. Only Friedrich's letter *Über die Philosophie; an Dorothea* (*On Philosophy: to Dorothea*) is more widely known for its thesis that women should be able to study philosophy; it is a kind of introduction to Friedrich's novel of that year, *Lucinde*. Two lengthy pieces by August address the visual arts; this aspect of the journal is only of historical interest, as are the poetic tribute to Goethe and the brief reviews. The first issue of 1800 brings two central pieces: Friedrich's second collection of fragments, called *Ideen* (*Ideas*), where a turn toward religion, mediated by his friend Schleiermacher, is very noticeable; and the first installment of a Socratic dialogue modeled on the *Symposium* and entitled *Gespräch über die Poesie* (*Dialogue on Poetry*), the most sustained presentation of the early Romantic aesthetic.

The *Dialogue,* which was completed in the journal's final issue, consists of comments by a narrative voice, along with conversations among participants modeled on the early Romantic circle (including the philosopher Schelling), which are in turn interspersed with four longer essays "read" by different members. Of these, the most influential are the "Speech on Mythology," which calls for the creation of a new mythology to replace the culturally uniting force of the ancient one, and the "Letter on the Novel," in which the novel becomes the universal genre that encapsulates the others. The last issue contains arguably the only "literary work" of the journal: Novalis's rhapsodic prose piece *Hymnen an die Nacht* (*Hymns to the Night*), some poetry by Friedrich and August Wilhelm, diverse reviews, and a remarkable swan song, Friedrich's essay *Über die Unverständlichkeit* (*On Incomprehensibility*). An ironic tour de force, Friedrich bids his readers farewell by mocking the infamous incomprehensibility of his journal and by offering a pseudophilosophical categorization of the various kinds of irony until author and reader can no longer find a path out of an irony run amok.

Michael T. Jones

See also Journals; August Wilhelm Schlegel; Friedrich Schlegel

Further Reading

Behler, Ernst, *Irony and the Discourse of Modernity,* Seattle and London: University of Washington Press, 1990

——, *German Romantic Literary Theory,* Cambridge and New York: Cambridge University Press, 1993

Benjamin, Walter, *Der Begriff der Kunstkritik in der deutschen Romantik,* Frankfurt: Suhrkamp, 1973; as "The Concept of Criticism in German Romanticism," in *Selected Writings,* vol. 1, Cambridge, Massachusetts: Harvard University Press, 1996

Blanchot, Maurice, "The Athenäum," *Studies in Romanticism* 22, no. 2 (1983)
Bowie, Andrew, *From Romanticism to Critical Theory: The Philosophy of German Literary Theory,* London and New York: Routledge, 1997
Brown, Marshall, *The Shape of German Romanticism,* Ithaca, New York: Cornell University Press, 1979
Eichner, Hans, *Friedrich Schlegel,* New York: Twayne, 1970
Lacoue-Labarthe, Philippe, and Jean-Luc Nancy, *The Literary Absolute: The Theory of Literature in German Romanticism,* Albany: State University of New York Press, 1988
Schlegel, August Wilhelm, and Friedrich Schlegel, editors, *Athenäum: Eine Zeitschrift,* Photomechanical Reproduction, Darmstadt: Wissenschaftliche Buchgesellschaft, 1983
Schulte-Sasse, Jochen, and Haynes Horne, editors, *Theory as Practice: A Critical Anthology of Early German Romantic Writings,* Minneapolis: University of Minnesota Press, 1997
Seyhan, Azade, *Representation and Its Discontents: The Critical Legacy of German Romanticism,* Berkeley: University of California Press, 1992
Stoljar, Margaret, *Athenaeum: A Critical Commentary,* Bern: Lang, 1973
Wheeler, Kathleen, editor, *The Romantic Ironists and Goethe,* German Aesthetic and Literary Criticism, vol. 2, Cambridge and New York: Cambridge University Press, 1984
Willson, A. Leslie, editor, *German Romantic Criticism,* New York: Continuum, 1982

Aue, Hartmann von, *see* Hartmann von Aue

Aufklärung

There is little consensus on the meaning of the term *Aufklärung* (enlightenment). In its most sweeping and frequent usage, it designates a broad philosophical tradition of antidogmatic intellectual inquiry. Restricting the term's scope to a specific school of German or, for that matter, European thought is problematic. While critics of Eurocentric historiography often employ the term synonymously with Western or European thought, this approach may itself be informed by a Eurocentric fixation. Evidence suggests that all the cultures of which we have sufficient knowledge display periods or movements of enlightenment in their historical developments. In other words, enlightenment can hardly be understood in the terminology of a simplified model of rationalist Eurocentrism or male logocentrism. The European tradition of enlightenment itself can be traced back to the North African and Iberian Middle Ages. Its religious and philosophical foundations reach, of course, even further back, and so do many of its political principles.

Using the term *Enlightenment,* in spite of its transhistorical and transcultural connotations, to name a particular period of German literature can only be justified because this, too, has its own tradition. On the one hand, a number of 18th-century authors professed that their work adhered to a way of thought that they themselves referred to as enlightenment. On the other hand, 19th- and 20th-century literary historians qualified much of the 18th century as the period of the Enlightenment as a means of historicizing and thus containing the political and philosophical demands of enlightened thought. These historians also sought refuge from the taxing claims of enlightened rationality by putting much energy into the construction of a number of "irrational" countermovements such as sentimentalism and Sturm und Drang (Storm and Stress), which, in the historical trajectory of these scholars, exposed the Enlightenment as a mere aberration of the supposedly antirational core of the German mind. Only recently have literary historians begun to interpret these "antirational" aesthetic movements as integral parts of the dialectics associated with the process of enlightenment. However, a number of obstacles still remain before the German literary period of the Enlightenment will be understood as a complex, divergent, and yet complementary process of rational and emotional innovation. Many of these obstacles can be traced back to constructions of a negative teleology of the dialectics of Enlightenment or, more recently, to postmodern inclinations.

Literary histories most often place the period of the German Enlightenment between the years of 1720 and 1785. Some of its philosophical and aesthetic foundations reach back into the 17th century, and it is followed by a decade of the so-called Late Enlightenment. In the shadow of Classicism and Romanticism, this decade of Late Enlightenment has received comparatively little attention. Other literary historians divide the period of German Enlightenment into three phases: rationalism (1680 to 1740), empiricism (1740 to 1780), and criticism (1780 to 1795). Part of the difficulty of structuring the Enlightenment has to do with scholarly economy, as the Enlightenment is the last literary period that spans nearly a whole century. The conventionally established periods that follow the Enlightenment tend to cover no more than 10 or 20 years.

Employing the philosophical term *Enlightenment* with some rigor to the understanding of 18th-century German literature demands that one concentrate on the analysis of the literary effects and aesthetic consequences of Enlightenment ideas and principles. It is, indeed, hardly possible to understand and appreciate Enlightenment literature without, at least, a basic familiarity with the ideas of René Descartes, Baruch Spinoza, Gottfried Wilhelm Leibniz, Christian Wolff, Christian Thomasius, John Locke, David Hume, Charles Montesquieu, Jean Jacques Rousseau, Moses Mendelssohn, Voltaire, Immanuel Kant, and others.

A broad concept of secularization is often used to link the literary production and aesthetic shifts of the period to larger intellectual developments. Enlightenment literature is, indeed, not fully comprehensible without taking its contemporary contexts of theological debate and partisanship into account (including deism, monism, pantheism, natural theology, Pietism, etc.). Perhaps more important, 18th-century literature and thought share many elements that are implied in the term *secularization,* such as the revision of orthodox interpretations of religious revelation, theological norms, and structures. Other elements include, conversely, the centering of the individual and his/her pursuit of subjective, earthly happiness; the quest for universal (natural) human rights; rational conceptualizations of state and community (separation of powers, constitutionalism); the emerging predominance of the third estate; empirical and anthropological psychology, with new analytical and educational impetus; public communication; the vernacular as philosophical and literary language; the quest for universal religious and ethical principles; the separation of state and church; and the call for tolerance.

The German Enlightenment is subliminally Spinozist, but Spinoza is not openly endorsed and his texts are translated less than in other European countries. Primarily influenced by the rationalist alternative to Spinoza, namely by Leibniz's and Wolff's theodicy and monadology, German Enlightenment was, from the outset and with few exceptions, limited to the idea of an ultimate harmony between reason and virtue and to a belief in the status quo. According to Leibniz and Wolff, virtue is the source of all happiness, and mankind's mission is the sovereign development of human reason. God is the creator of the best of all possible worlds. There is no need for any further interference; nature follows its own internal laws that are principally accessible to human reason, albeit not on the surface of empirical inquiry.

The German Enlightenment was closely linked to the economic and cultural rise of the bourgeoisie and its specific ethical and political demands. During the course of the 18th century, the cultural centers moved from the court to the city, especially to Berlin, Hamburg, Zürich, Leipzig, Göttingen, and Halle. The principal intellects of Enlightenment philosophy and culture were members of the third estate, theologians, administrators, and academics. The audience, too, belonged, by and large, to the emerging middle class. This cultural shift from the ruling estates to the third estate was based on a sharp increase in book and journal production and a growing readership. Of particular importance for the cultivation of such a reading (to a large extent female) public were the numerous weekly journals designed after the British *Tatler, Guardian,* and *Spectator,* such as Johann Christoph Gottsched's *Der Biedermann* (1727–29; The Good Fellow) and *Die vernünftigen Tadlerinnen* (1725–27; The Reasonable Tatlers), and Barthold Heinrich Brockes's *Der Patriot* (1724; The Patriot). These journals tend to discuss questions of moral and practical life in the form of short, entertaining, or devotional treatises. From the 1730s to the end of the century, a large number of critical journals offered an innovative public forum for the discussion of philosophical, moral, and religious questions and for regular book reviews. The most important of these journals were *Briefe, die neueste Literatur betreffend* (1759–65; Letters concerning the Newest Literature), edited by Friedrich Nicolai in collaboration with Mendelssohn, Gotthold Ephraim Lessing, and Thomas Abbt; *Allgemeine deutsche Bibliothek* (1765–92; General German Library), edited by Nicolai in collaboration with Johann Gottfried Herder, Abbt, Christian Gottlob Heyne, Joachim Heinrich Campe, Mendelssohn, and Karl Friedrich Zelter, continued as *Neue allgemeine deutsche Bibliothek* (1773–1805; New General German Library); and *Der deutsche Merkur,* edited by Christoph Martin Wieland (1773–89; The German Mercury), continued by Karl August Böttiger as *Der neue deutsche Merkur* (1790–1810; The New German Mercury).

The practical principles, demands, and consequences of enlightenment are perhaps best expressed in Kant's and Mendelssohn's alternative answers to the question posed in the *Berlinische Monatsschrift* in 1783: "What is Enlightenment?" Kant's answer—*sapere aude,* humankind's emergence out of its self-inflicted immaturity—is radical in making the individual the master of his/her own fate and in implicitly demanding and expecting a political development that would allow for such individuality, rationality, and freedom. Mendelssohn had already pondered the question of the relationship of such an independently thinking, autonomous, and self-responsible individual to his/her culturally determined heritage community. Somewhat simplified, one could state that his solution is dialectical. The opposite forces of enlightened reason and inherited culture are mediated by *Bildung,* which attempts to analyze and understand the principles and limits of both inherited cultural practice and freewheeling, autonomous reason. Thus, Mendelssohn already wrestled with a concept of acculturation that is ultimately emancipatory and yet knows of its political and moral responsibilities. One of the cornerstone problems within this paradigm, which in one way or another occupied nearly all 18th-century intellectuals, was the concept of a universal religion of reason and its relationship to the various stories and traditions of religious revelation. Only a common ground in ethical and religious assumptions that could be deducted and formulated by universal reason, it seemed, could guarantee lasting tolerance for alternative religious traditions and practices.

This is the topic of Gotthold Ephraim Lessing's masterwork *Nathan der Weise* (1779; *Nathan the Wise*), which was in part written as a reply to the orthodox criticism of Lessing's main adversary, the Hamburg pastor Melchior Goetz. Lessing's main character, the Jerusalem Jew Nathan (modeled after Lessing's friend Mendelssohn), solves the religious and political tensions between Christianity, Islam, and Judaism by employing the tolerant, ethical principles of humanist reason. Tellingly, the play's central parable of the three rings—a symbol for each religion's particular way to an ultimately universal ethic and truth—is adapted from the Jewish and Arabic Enlightenment of 11th-century Spain. Occupying a new place between tragedy and comedy, the play's form, too, was radically innovative and would remain exceptional for many decades.

German drama had come a long way before Lessing's last play became possible. Gottsched, a student of Wolff and the leading theoretician and playwright of the first half of the German Enlightenment, reconceptualized German drama following the examples of French Classicism. Beginning in 1727 in close collaboration with the ensemble of Karoline and Johann Neuber, he attempted to purge the tragedy of improvised comical interludes and to close the gap between the purified popular performances of traveling theater troupes and the theater of the court. His most important theoretical works are *Versuch einer critischen Dichtkunst vor die Deutschen* (1729; Attempt at a Critical Poetics for Germans) and *Deutsche Schaubühne nach den Regeln und Exempeln der alten Griechen und Römer* (1741–45; German Theater according to the Rules and Examples of the Ancient Greeks and Romans). His exemplary tragedy is *Sterbender Cato* (1732; Dying Cato). In a spectacular allegorical performance, the Harlequin, a symbol of Italian and English folk theater, was driven off the Leipzig stage in 1737.

The first critical reassessment of Gottsched's exclusive orientation toward French Classicism and its grave, static style of declamation came from one of his former students, Johann Elias Schlegel. In his critical piece *Die Aufnahme des dänischen Theaters* (1747; The Reception of the Danish Theatre), Schlegel argued that each culture and nation would have to realize its own individual and independent form of drama and that Shakespeare might be closer to the German national theater than Racine. It was, however, left to Lessing to overcome the limits of Gottsched's particular brand of normative classicism. In his *Hamburgische Dramaturgie* (1767–69; *Hamburg Dramaturgy*), written in close collaboration with Johann Friedrich Löwen, who was the principal force behind an innovative national theater house in Hamburg (partly financed by the city's patricians), Lessing based the catharsis of the Aristotelian tragedy on pity and fear. Influenced by sensualist aesthetics (for instance, Mendelssohn's 1755 *Briefe über die Empfindungen* [Letters on Sensations]) and the emerging theories of bourgeois tragedy, Lessing rejected the common translation of *phobos* as terror or fear of the hero (as preferred in French Classicism) and translated it as fear for the fate of the hero, who is no longer the distant aristocrat engaged in a struggle for power that is meant to evoke admiration and not pity. Rather, the hero's fate is now conceived of as an expression of a universal human possibility, a fate that could potentially be the audience's own. The hero could no longer be the representative of immoral aristocratic politics and power but had to become an object of moral middle-class identification. Lessing also rejected the narrow interpretation of the three dramatic unities of place, time, and plot and insisted only on the consistency of the dramatic plot.

With *Miss Sara Sampson* (1755), he introduced the bourgeois tragedy to the German stage; this work was followed by *Emilia Galotti* (1772). As would become the standard of the German bourgeois tragedy (from Sturm und Drang deep into the 19th century), center stage of both plays is taken by the heart and virtue of the middle-class daughter, who is torn between the love and seduction of her powerful suitor and the moral expectations of her middle-class father.

In his theory of comedy, Lessing breaks with the estate clause, which barred the upper estates from being made objects of ridicule. With *Minna von Barnhelm* (1767), Lessing accomplished one of the few lasting German comedies of the 18th century. The play overcomes the so-called Saxon comedy of types, which had been emphasized by Gottsched and his wife—for instance, her comedy *Die Pietisterei im Fischbeinrock* (1736; Pietism in a Crinoline)—and achieves what may be called the comedy of individual character.

In *Laokoon; oder, Über die Grenzen der Malerei und Poesie* (1766; *Laokoön: An Essay on the Limits of Painting and Poetry*), Lessing introduced a very influential aesthetic theory that points toward the interdependency of the arts' materialities and their possibilities of expression. Partly building on the poetic theories of Johann Jacob Bodmer (*Critische Abhandlung von dem Wunderbaren in der Poesie* [1740; Critical Essay on the Miraculous in Poetry]) and Johann Jakob Breitinger (*Critische Dichtkunst* [1740]), Lessing revisits Johann Joachim Winckelmann's theory of classical art, devises a separate aesthetic realm for literature, and frees it from Horace's dictum "ut pictura poesis," which had justified the dominance of painting and sculpture in aesthetic theory.

Gottsched considered the didactic fable the most advanced prose form. Among the many prose genres that blossomed in the 18th century, however, the novel ultimately experienced the most significant development and growth. Friedrich von Blanckenburg's theory of the novel (*Versuch über den Roman,* 1774), written under the impression of Christoph Martin Wieland's *Die Geschichte des Agathon* (1766–67; *History of Agathon*), was the first comprehensive attempt to explain the novel's importance for the overall development of poetic genres and aesthetic theory. By the end of the century, Friedrich Schlegel would posit the novel as the poetic form par excellence. The German novel of the second and third quarters of the 18th century was strongly influenced by the sentimental and humorist novels of Samuel Richardson, Laurence Sterne, and Henry Fielding and the adventure novels of Daniel Defoe. Traditions and new variations of the so-called gallant and state novel, as well as the picaresque novel, continued to be felt. Hardly any novels from this time have survived in today's canon of German literature. However, many of these works had considerable influence on the novels of German Classicism and Romanticism. Johann Gottfried Schnabel's *Insel Felsenburg* (1731–43; Rock Castle Island) combines the adventure of *Robinson Crusoe* (1719) with the utopia of Thomas More and a new perception of nature, which had been most prominently exemplified in Albrecht von Haller's poem *Die Alpen* of 1728–29.

The heroine of Christian Fürchtegott Gellert's *Das Leben der schwedischen Gräfin von G . . .* (1747–48; The Life of the Swedish Countess of G . . .) marries the best friend of her husband, who himself is presumed killed in battle. When her first husband returns from Russian captivity, reason dictates that she continue the marriage with him. After his death, she is supposed to continue the second marriage. However, shortly after the death of her first husband, her second husband also dies, sparing her of her duties altogether. At least on the surface, this unusual novel exemplifies the strength of individual character that can overcome undeserved twists of fate as well as personal desire. The novel's dialogues and letters are colored with Pietist phrases and pedagogical intent. As in the bourgeois tragedy, it is the heart and desire of the virtuous woman that is sacrificed for the new morals of middle-class relations.

From the 1760s onward, Wieland emerged as the most important German prose writer of his time. *Der Sieg über die*

Schwärmerei; oder, Die Abenteuer des Don Sylvio von Rosalva (1764; The Adventures of Don Sylvio of Rosalva) is a homage to *Don Quixote*. Wieland's Don Sylvio lives in the dreamy world of fairy tales and searches for the mysteries of supernatural love—his lover has been transformed into a butterfly. What he ultimately finds is true earthly love and natural explanations for all the wonders and enigmas he encounters. *Die Geschichte des Agathon* negotiates the genres of the picaresque novel, the educational journal, and the philosophical autobiography. After an adventurous and eventful journey that confronts him with heroism, exile, piracy, and slavery, Agathon, a young contemporary of Plato, achieves a humanist outlook on life and undergoes an aesthetic education. Often considered the first German bildungsroman, the novel remained influential for Goethe's *Wilhelm Meisters Lehrjahre* (1795–1821), Gottfried Keller's *Der grüne Heinrich* (1853–55), and numerous lesser examples of the genre. In many ways, it can also be regarded as a precursor of German Classicism. Wieland's *Die Abderiten, eine sehr wahrscheinliche Geschichte* (part 1, 1774; part 2 1779–80; The Abderites, a Very Probable Story) groups humorous anecdotes and stories around an autobiographical take on the figure of the philosopher Democritus. Narrow-minded citizens of Swiss and Saxon cities are confronted with enlightened and humanist figures of classical Greece: Democritus, Hippocrates, and Euripides. The novel's lighthearted mixture of humor, irony, and humanist tolerance had a great influence on Keller and Jean Paul.

The ubiquitous conflict between Enlightenment authors and the religious orthodoxy was of particular importance to members of the Berlin Enlightenment and Haskala, who gathered around Mendelssohn and Nicolai, the premier publisher and editor of Enlightenment literature. Nicolai himself offers a vivid portrayal of this antagonism in his novel *Das Leben und die Meinungen des Herrn Magister Sebaldus Nothanker* (1773–76; The Life and the Opinions of Master Sebaldus Nothanker).

The poetry of the period is decidedly worldly, sometimes anacreontic in the tradition of Horace, or humorous-ironic, frivolous, and playful, such as the genres of the so-called rococo (associated with the young Lessing, Johann Wilhelm Ludwig Gleim, Christian Fürchtegott Gellert, Salomon Geßner, Ewald von Kleist, Johann Elias Schlegel, and the young Goethe). Influenced by Alexander Pope and James Thomson and informed by Descartes, Leibniz, and Wolff, philosophical and educational poetry also gained in popularity. Often written in Alexandrine meters, these poems introduced and deliberated religious, philosophical, and scientific themes often with a clear didactic impetus (in works by Haller, Kleist, Friedrich von Hagedorn, and the young Wieland). The same philosophical-educational interest helped fables, satires, epigrams, and verse epics to new popularity (such as in works by Lessing, Gottsched, Gellert, Haller, Hagedorn, and Christian Wernicke).

One of the most influential verse epics was Wieland's *Oberon* (first published in *Teutscher Merkur;* book publication in 1796). Wieland transformed the heroic epic into an epic poem of humanist sacrifice and individual love. Huon's and Rezia's uncompromising love and faithfulness for each other educates Oberon, the king of the elves, who finds his way back to his wife, Titania.

A few examples of Enlightenment poetry will have to suffice. Barthold Heinrich Brockes's *Irdisches Vergnügen in Gott* (1721–48; Earthly Happiness in God) is a collection of scientific and moral poems. Brockes's covertly Spinozist poems present nature in all its aspects, small and large, physical and spiritual. God is experienced through the beauty and reason of his creation.

Haller's *Versuch schweizerischer Gedichten* (1732; Attempt of Swiss Poems) offers the first poetic presentation of the sublime beauty of the landscapes and peasant culture in the Swiss Alps. Several poems—most prominently *Die Alpen*—favorably juxtapose rural piety, austerity, and simplicity against the moral and cultural temptations of the city. But the collection also includes philosophical poems on reason, belief, prejudice, virtue, evil, and scientific observation.

Gleim's *Preußische Kriegslieder in den Feldzügen 1756 und 1757, von einem Grenadier* (1758; Prussian War-Songs in the Battles of 1756 and 1757, by a Grenadier) initiated a wave of patriotic poetry. Breaking with the classical ode and employing popular folk rhythms and rhymes, Gleim incorporated many realistic details of warfare and transposed classical models of heroism to contemporary militarism.

Anna Luise Karsch's poems (collection in 1792) were widely celebrated as ingenious folk art. The poems of this autodidactic author were less influenced by classical patterns and norms than by the poetry of her learned male colleagues. Her talent included both private, intimate poems and official heroic songs that gained her the Prussian king's patronage.

The philosophical and educational poetry of the German Enlightenment, however, was soon overshadowed by Friedrich Gottlieb Klopstock (*Der Messias;* 1748–73) and other poets of the so-called Empfindsamkeit (sensibility) on the one hand and the poetry of the young Goethe and other poets of the Sturm und Drang movement on the other hand. The innovative, emphatic, and lyrical voices of these poets have often been characterized as anti-Enlightenment. More recent scholarship, however, no longer hesitates to point to the interconnectedness of enlightened philosophical, political, and psychological ideas with these poets' celebration of individuality, friendship, nature, beauty, patriotism, and ingenuity.

Of greatest importance were the numerous treatises, essays, letters, and memoranda that document the Enlightenment's influence on institutional and political reform and change. The topics reached from religious emancipation to political constitutionalism and the discovery of the rights of women and the fourth estate. Some of the most important political writings are Christian Wilhelm Dohm's *Ueber die bürgerliche Verbesserung der Juden* (1781; On the Improvement of the Civil Status of the Jews), Mendelssohn's *Jerusalem; oder, Über religiöse Macht und Judentum* (1783; Jerusalem; or, Religious Power and Judaism), Theodor Gottlieb von Hippel's *Lebensläufe nach aufsteigender Linie* (1778–81; Biographies in an Ascending Line) and *Über die Ehe* (1774; On Marriage), and Johann Georg Foster's *Reise um die Welt* (1778–80; Travels around the World) and *Ansichten vom Niederrhein* (1791; Views of the Lower Rhine), among many others.

BERND FISCHER

See also Empfindsamkeit; Johann Christoph Gottsched; Immanuel Kant; Gotthold-Ephraim Lessing; Moses Mendelssohn

Further Reading

Alt, Peter-André, *Aufklärung,* Stuttgart: Metzler, 1996

Blumenberg, Hans, *Die Legitimität der Neuzeit,* Frankfurt: Suhrkamp, 1966; revised edition, 1988

Ciafardone, Raffaele, *Die Philosophie der deutschen Aufklärung: Texte und Darstellung,* Stuttgart: Reclam, 1990

Guthke, Karl S., *Das deutsche bürgerliche Trauerspiel,* Stuttgart: Metzler, 1972; revised edition, 1994

Kaiser, Gerhard, *Aufklärung, Empfindsamkeit, Sturm und Drang,* Munich: Francke, 1976

Kimpel, Dieter, *Der Roman der Aufklärung,* Stuttgart: Metzler, 1967

Kondyles, Panagiotis, *Die Aufklärung im Rahmen des neuzeitlichen Rationalismus,* Munich: Deutscher Taschenbuchverlag, 1986

Koselleck, Reinhart, *Critique and Crisis: Enlightenment and the Pathogenesis of Modern Society,* Oxford: Berg, and Cambridge, Massachusetts: MIT Press, 1988

Michelsen, Peter, *Der unruhige Bürger: Studien zu Lessing und zur Literatur des 18. Jahrhunderts,* Würzburg: Königshausen and Neumann, 1990

Mönch, Cornelia, *Abschrecken oder Mitleiden: Das deutsche bürgerliche Trauerspiel im 18. Jahrhundert, Versuch einer Typologie,* Tübingen: Niemeyer, 1993

Porter, Roy, *Kleine Geschichte der Aufklärung,* Berlin: Wagenbach, 1991

Rüsen, Jörn, et al., editors, *Die Zukunft der Aufklärung,* Frankfurt: Suhrkamp, 1988

Schings, Hans-Jürgen, editor, *Der ganze Mensch: Anthropologie und Literatur im 18. Jahrhundert, DFG-Symposion,* Stuttgart: Metzler, 1994

Schmidt, James, editor, *What Is Enlightenment? Eighteenth-Century Answers and Twentieth-Century Questions,* Berkeley: University of California Press, 1996

Schmidt, Jochen, editor, *Aufklärung und Gegenaufklärung in der Europäischen Literatur, Philosophie, und Poetik von der Antike bis zur Gegenwart,* Darmstadt: Wissenschaftliche Buchgesellschaft, 1989

Spies, Bernhard, *Politische Kritik, psychologische Hermeneutik, ästhetischer Blick: Die Entwicklung bürgerlicher Subjektivität im Roman des 18. Jahrhunderts,* Stuttgart: Metzler, 1992

Rose Ausländer 1907–1988

Rose Ausländer's life was representative of many Jewish writers of her generation; it began with an early idyll in Czernowitz, with its natural beauty and rich cultural heritage, and continued amid the brutality of fascist destruction of Jewish communities, exile to the United States, and her eventual return to postwar Germany. She lived for 16 years in the Nelly-Sachs house of the Jewish community in Düsseldorf. During the last ten years, she was confined to her bed and lived for writing poetry, which suggests a gradual shutting out of the world and a closing in on herself. In fact, many of her later poems were a response to the widespread fame and affection she won from countless admirers of her published works. The thousands of letters that she received prove that her poetry was among the most read in the German-speaking world.

Her first volume of poems, *Der Regenbogen* (The Rainbow), appeared in Czernowitz in 1939 and was received with enthusiasm, but its remaining copies were destroyed by the fascists who took over Romania in 1941. Not until 1965, with *Blinder Sommer* (Blind Summer), did her work appear again in book form. After three more short volumes and the publication in 1976 of her *Gesammelte Gedichte* (collected poems), her work began to attract general attention. Before this success, reviews and appreciations of her work emphasized the sincerity, directness, and suffering of a voice haunted by persecution, loneliness, the destruction of personal potential, and the shattering of a cultural world. For some critics, however, her early work was too close to the poetry of Rainer Maria Rilke, Hugo von Hofmannsthal, or Georg Heym; this work was replaced in the 1920s by a style that aped Neue Sachlichkeit. From 1916 until 1957, her poems were rhymed (from 1948 to 1956, she wrote about 30 poems exclusively in English; a fine and chilling unrhymed example is "After the world was atombombed"). In 1957 she met Paul Celan again in Paris; she had been one of the first while still in the Czernowitz ghetto to recognize his potential 20 years earlier. At that time, he had introduced her to the possibilities of modern, unrhymed German poetry written in free rhythms and close to everyday speech. This opened up a new world in which she could create poems that enabled her to express memories and in time overcome them. Poetry was henceforth to become a means of survival. Gradually, she eliminated all but the kernel of direct statements about the past (see 36 *Gerechte*); her lifelong involvement with the thought of Spinoza, Plato, Freud, and, especially, Constantin Brunner (whose work she actively supported in study groups and who had a major influence on her work and life); her interaction with certain landscapes and towns (especially Italy and Venice); and, above all, her direct dialogue with other people.

Many of her poems begin with the word *Ich* but often develop into declarations of sympathy or love for a *Du* figure. From the purely descriptive style of her earlier work and in later poems, often of under a dozen lines, she developed a preoccupation with the word's creative power over her. Sometimes she continued to work for over 20 years on the potentials of a poetic idea, often at first in prose sketches, before it reached its final form; yet the outcome would be a few simple words with direct statements that reveal both fascination for their power and a feeling for the self-discipline they demanded from her. The Passion of her life was to be overcome by her personal commitment to the poetry in which she found a meaning to existence.

The apparent simplicity of her poems and the publication of her collected works (from 1984 on) brought Ausländer a wide general readership, although academic approval has been confined to a few admirers. Many academic critics have concentrated on single poems, and their interest in her work has been overshadowed by the more complex creativity and individuality they see in Paul Celan's poetry. The contrast between past horrors and present mourning and her love of flowers as significant message bearers emerge in her famous lines on Paul Celan's grave: "Keine Blumen gepflanzt / das sei überflüssig / Nichts Überflüssiges / nur / wilder Klatsch-Mohn / schwarzzüngig / ruft uns ins Gedächtnis / wer unter ihm / blühte." This example of her "Balkan melancholy" (Marie Luise Kaschnitz) contrasts with the more prosaic "Briefe II": "Jeden Tag / kommt der Briefträger / und bringt mir / ein Stückchen Welt / Viele Unbekannte / erzählen mir / ihr Geschichten / schenken mir / Freundschaft und Liebe / Ihre Worte umarmen / meine Worte." Some of her poems playfully register simple statements about poetry, including "Raum II": "Noch ist Raum / für ein Gedicht / Noch ist das Gedicht / ein Raum / wo man atmen kann." Longer examples, especially from her earlier period, evoke landscapes from her U.S. exile. Such variety, which reflects a ceaseless enquiry into the possibilities of language despite its recall of oppression, encompasses several sets of tensions such as love and departure, homesickness and longing for the unknown future, pain and joy, and destruction and resurrection. Beatrice Eichmann-Leutenegger rightly interprets this as resolution in a *coincidentia oppositorum* (coincidence of opposites).

Indeed, it is only when all Rose Ausländer's poems are read that the range of her achievement can be assessed. The poetry of her U.S. exile (1921–26 and 1946–61, with a final six-month stay in 1968) owes much to the works of Georg Trakl, Friedrich Hölderlin, Rilke, Else Lasker-Schüler, and Gottfried Benn and was received favorably by Manfred Hausmann and Arnold Zweig in particular. Her later works, in which she developed her own independent style, should be seen also as a poetic answer to the "stultifying silence" through which language had to go after the death camps (Paul Celan's speech *Der Meridian* [1960; *The Meridian*]). The final epigrammatic poems have been criticized for their loss of clarity, yet they, too, belonged to "one of the greatest lyric outputs of the century" (Walther Kummerow). Perhaps the title poem of the collection *Mutterland* (1978; Motherland) sums up best her fate and her poetry: "Mein Vaterland ist tot / sie haben es begraben / im Feuer / Ich lebe / in meinem Mutterland / Wort."' (My fatherland is dead / They have buried it / in Fire / I live / in my motherland / word). Despite the biographical essay by Helmut Braun (1991), much research remains to be done on her life—Braun has, for instance, pointed to the role played by the U.S. poet Marianne Moore in persuading Ausländer in the early 1960s to start writing again in German. A comprehensive appraisal of her 2,500 poems, several short prose pieces, essays, and journalistic pieces has yet to be written. Some 1,500 unfinished drafts are now housed with other material in the Rose-Ausländer-Dokumentationszentrum in Üxheim/Eifel. Most of the secondary literature consists of articles and reviews in newspapers and in general reference works. The fullest list is in Braun (1991).

BRIAN KEITH-SMITH

Biography

Born in Czernowitz/Bukowina, 11 May 1907. Studied literature and philosophy, Czernowitz University; emigrated to the United States, 1921; in New York, 1923; visited Constantin Brunner in Berlin, 1928; editorial work for Czernowitz newspapers, 1931–; taught English and worked as secretary in a chemical factory; escaped deportation from ghetto by working in a library; in New York as correspondent and translator, 1946; regained U.S. citizenship, 1948; settled in Düsseldorf, 1965. Droste-Hülshoff Prize, 1967; Andreas Gryphius Prize, 1977; Ida Dehmel Prize, 1977; Gandersheim Literature Prize, 1980; Bavarian Academy of Fine Arts Prize, 1984. Died in Düsseldorf, 3 January 1988.

Selected Works

Collections
Gesammelte Werke, edited by Helmut Braun, 8 vols., 1984–90

Poetry
Der Regenbogen, 1939
Blinder Sommer, 1965
Invertar, 1972
Andere Zeichen, 1974
36 Gerechte, 1975
Noch ist Raum, 1976
Aschensommer, 1977
Doppelspiel, 1977
Es ist alles anders, 1977
Selected Poems, translated by Ewald Osers, 1977
Mutterland, 1978
Es bleibt noch viel zu sagen, 1978
Ein Stück weiter, 1979
Im Atemhaus wohnen, 1979
Einen Drachen reiten, 1980
Einverständnis, 1980
Mein Atem heisst jetzt, 1981
Südlich wartet ein wärmeres Land, 1982
Mein Venedig versinkt nicht, 1982
Ich zähl die Sterne meiner Worte, 1983
Festtag in Manhattan, 1985
Ich spiele noch, 1987
Freundschafte mit der Mondin, 1987
Der Traum hat offene Augen: Unveröffentlichte Gedichte 1965–78, 1987
Wir ziehen mit den dunklen Flüssen, 1993
Denn wo ist Heimat, 1994
Der Mohn ist noch nicht rot, 1994
The Forbidden Tree: English Gedichte, 1995

Further Reading

Beil, Claudia, *Sprache als Heimat: Jüdische Tradition und Exilerfahrung in der Lyrik von Nelly Sachs und Rose Ausländer,* Munich: tuduv, 1991
Braun, Helmut, "Anmerkungen des Herausgebers," in *Rose Ausländer: Gesammelte Werke in sieben Bänden,* Frankfurt: Fischer, 1988–
———, "Rose Ausländer," in *Hauptwerke der deutschen Literature,* vol. 2, Munich: Kindler, 1994
Braun, Helmut, editor, *Rose Ausländer: Materialien zu Leben und Werk,* Frankfurt: Fischer Taschenbuch, 1991
Eichmann-Leutenegger, Beatrice, "'Ich möchte mich ins wahre Leben schreiben . . .': Zum Leben der Dichterin Rose Ausländer, 1901–1988," *Orientierung* 52, no. 8 (1988)
Glenn, Jerry, "Blumenworte/Kriegsgestammel: The Poetry of Rose Ausländer," *Modern Austrian Literature* 12, no. 3/4 (1979)
Helfrich, Cilly, *"Es ist ein Aschensommer in der Welt": Rose Ausländer, Biographie,* Weinheim: Beltz Quadriga, 1995
Keith-Smith, Brian, "Rose Ausländer," in *An Encyclopedia of German Women Writers 1900–1933*, vol. 1, Lewiston, New York: Mellen, 1997

Köhl, Gabriele, *Die Bedeutung der Sprache in der Lyrik Rose Ausländers,* Pfaffenweiler: Centaurus, 1993
Kruse, J.A., editor, *Rose Ausländer: Eine Ausstellung im Heinrich–Heine–Institut Düsseldorf 4. Mai – 5. Juni 1977,* Düsseldorf, 1977
Kummerow, Walther, "Rose Ausländer," in *Bertelsmann Lexikon Deutsche Autoren: Vom Mittelalter bis zur Gegenwart,* vol. 1, edited by Walther Killy, Gütersloh: Bertelsmann, 1994
Rose-Ausländer-Gesellschaft, editors, *Mutterland Wort: Rose Ausländer 1901–1988,* Uexheim/Eifel: Rose Ausländer Dokumentationszentrum, 1996
Wallmann, Jürgen P., "'Ich will wohnen im Menschenwort': Die Lyrik von Rose Ausländer," *Literatur und Kritik* 15, no. 142 (1980)
Weissenberger, Klaus, "Rose Ausländer," in *Deutschsprachige Exilliteratur seit 1933,* vol. 2, edited by John M. Spalek and Joseph Strelka, Bern and New York: Francke, 1989
Werner-Birkenbach, Sabine, "'Durch Zeitgeräusch wandern von Stimme zu Stimme . . .': Die Lyrikerin Rose Ausländer," *German Life and Letters* 45, no. 4 (1992)
Zimmer-Winkel, Rainer, editor, *Worte: Stark wie der Atem der Erde: Beiträge zu Leben und Werk der jüdischen Dichterin Rose Ausländer (1901–1988),* Trier: Kulturverein AphorismA, 1994

Austria: Late Habsburg Literature in Vienna

As the Habsburg Empire entered its final years, it enjoyed a cultural renaissance that saw German writing from Austria take center stage for the first time since the Middle Ages. With figures such as Arthur Schnitzler, Hugo von Hofmannsthal, and Karl Kraus, a consciously "Austrian" voice grew increasingly audible, and it continues to be heard up to the present day. Although Austrian, and especially Viennese, intellectual life around 1900 was noteworthy for the massive contribution made by figures of Jewish descent (e.g., Gustav Mahler, Arnold Schoenberg, Sigmund Freud, and Theodor Herzl), it would be wrong to assume that it was primarily Jews who stamped their genius onto this culture: Gustav Klimt, Oskar Kokoschka, and Egon Schiele were not Jewish, nor were Adolf Loos, Alban Berg, and Anton Webern.

Viennese writing in the 1890s was stimulated by the rejection of naturalism spearheaded by a coterie of writers in the Cafe Griensteidl. In an ironic reference to the revolutionary "Jung Deutschland" writers of the 1840s, these writers were soon dubbed "Jung Wien" ("Young Vienna"). The coterie was led by Hermann Bahr; Hofmannsthal and Schnitzler were key figures in the group, along with Peter Altenberg, Leopold von Andrian, Richard Beer-Hofmann, and Felix Salten. They remained a loosely-knit group, however; Beer-Hofmann claimed that they only consorted together because it stopped them feeling anxious. The revolution wrought by the "Young Viennese" was primarily an artistic one, for in contrast with the naturalists, their writing rarely confronted the burning political and social realities of a society under terminal stress. They preferred to concentrate instead on psychological and aesthetic issues (e.g., von Andrian, *Der Garten der Erkenntis* [1895; The Garden of Knowledge]; Beer-Hofmann, *Der Tod Georgs* [1900; Georg's Death]). It may be recalled, however, that Theodor Herzl, the founder of Zionism who wrote *Der Judenstaat* (1896; *The Jewish State*), was himself a product of that same coffeehouse culture. Although the "Young Viennese" were preponderantly Jewish, the reaction against naturalism was not an exclusively Jewish-Viennese phenomenon. Its theorist and prophet Hermann Bahr was a gentile, while across in Munich, the very non-Jewish Stefan George was producing his own exquisitely mannered verse in defiant contrast to the naturalists' prosaic formula that "Art = Nature – x." It was, however, in Vienna that the clearest overall picture emerged of the literature that both stemmed from and countered naturalism. Some of the labels liberally and loosely attached to this post-naturalist writing include aestheticism, *l'art pour l'art,* decadence, Impressionism, symbolism, Jugendstil, and neo-Romanticism.

Unlike Germany, there had been no naturalist movement to speak of in Austria, where in the 1870s and 1880s the literary landscape was relatively bland compared with the one in Bismarck's new Reich. Among the significant writers in Austria at that time were the realists Ludwig Anzengruber, Marie von Ebner-Eschenbach, and Ferdinand von Saar. In music, things were very different: Johannes Brahms, Anton Bruckner and Hugo Wolf were all at their peak, and Gustav Mahler was emerging as a great composer. The literary explosion in Vienna was heralded by Bahr's theoretical essays, first collected in *Die Überwindung des Naturalismus* (1891; Overcoming Naturalism), and by the child prodigy Hofmannsthal, known initially only under the pseudonym Loris. His uncannily mature and formally perfect poetry and verse dramas such as *Der Tor und der Tod* (1893; Death and the Fool) owed nothing to naturalism but much to the lyric traditions of France, Germany, England, and Italy. Significantly, Vienna's favorite naturalist was not Gerhart Hauptmann but Henrik Ibsen, the complex psychology of whose characters fascinated Viennese writers more than his social message.

The young Hofmannsthal's work reflected astonishing erudition in a range of languages other than German. Living in a multicultural empire, having roots in Italy and the Slavic countries as well as the German-speaking world, and already fluent in French, English, and Italian, Hofmannsthal reflects literary currents in those countries far more than those in Wilhelminian Germany. By the age of 25, however, his vein of lyric inspiration dried up, and the ensuing crisis in his literary productivity was recorded in one of the most significant literary documents of the early 20th-century, *Ein Brief* (1902; *The Letter of Lord Chandos*). In this invented letter from Philip, Lord Chandos, who never existed, to Francis Bacon (1561–1626), Hofmannsthal captures not only the desperation of his own language crisis but the panic of a sophisticated culture that had suddenly lost confidence in reality itself. For Hofmannsthal/

Chandos, like T.S. Eliot a little later, the center no longer held. Accompanying the disintegration of reality, words disintegrated in his mouth "like moldy fungi" ("die Worte zerfielen mir im Munde wie modrige Pilze"). That this supreme expression of despair about the communicative capacity of language should be expressed in prose of consummate richness and flexibility is not the least ironic feature of this text. First published in *Der Tag*, one of Germany's biggest daily newspapers, its influence can be directly felt in contemporary Austrian novels such as Robert Musil's *Die Verwirrungen des Zöglings Törleß* (1906; *Young Törless*) and Rainer Maria Rilke's *Die Aufzeichnungen des Malte Laurids Brigge* (1910; *The Notebooks of Malte Laurids Brigge*). In its extreme skepticism, the Chandos letter is a classic of early modernism; it also, however, represents the diametric opposite of the modernist undertaking of other Viennese figures such as Karl Kraus, Adolf Loos, and Arnold Schoenberg. Their vision, owing much to Kraus, is grounded upon the conviction that in an increasingly complex and uncertain world, meaning and communication through language are essential and attainable. Faced with doubts about his own lyric gifts, by contrast, Hofmannsthal turned to social art forms such as the theater and to cooperation with other artists. His international fame today rests chiefly upon his work as Richard Strauss's librettist for such operas as *Elektra* (1909), *Der Rosenkavalier* (1911), *Ariadne auf Naxos* (1912), and *Die Frau ohne Schatten* (1919). After the collapse of the empire, and appalled by the carnage of World War I, which he, like the vast majority of Austrian artists and writers, had loyally supported, Hofmannsthal was instrumental along with Max Reinhardt in helping to found the Salzburg Festival, which they hoped would stress the common cultural links binding European civilization together.

The turn to lyricism in verse, prose, and drama was a common feature of Viennese literature of the 1890s. Not all of its practitioners, however, shared Hofmannsthal's genius: Felix Dörmann, a far lesser writer, nevertheless epitomizes the literary decadence that also emerged from naturalism and whose expression is particularly marked in some of Thomas Mann's early writing. The naturalists' concern for people who suffer because of environment and heredity rapidly modified into a typical fin de siècle fascination with disease and death. This morbidity is particularly marked in Dörmann, an accomplished translator and follower of Charles Baudelaire, who ended up writing librettos for operettas. Dörmann's opulent diction and imagery, and the proximity of his writing to Jugendstil art with its intense floral decoration and love of erotic/exotic subjects, were typical features of an age that led the architect and essayist Adolf Loos to proclaim that ornamentation for its own sake was nothing less than criminal (*Ornament und Verbrechen* [1911; *Ornament and Crime*]). That puritan streak in Viennese Modernism, shared by Kraus, Schoenberg, and, later, Ludwig Wittgenstein, must be seen in the context of a poem such as Dörmann's "Was ich liebe" (1892; "What I Love"), whose astonishing last stanza shows why such literature was dubbed "Neo-Romantic" as well as decadent. In reaction to the naturalists' claims to scientific objectivity and rationalism, the subjectivity of Romanticism is taken here to extremes.

That not all literature dealing with extreme subjectivity needs to be like Dörmann's is exemplified by Arthur Schnitzler's work. A trained doctor who had the clinical detachment that medicine requires, Schnitzler ranks alongside Kraus as the great literary diagnostician of late-Imperial Austria. Schnitzler is often regarded as a literary counterpart to Sigmund Freud, and the two had the utmost respect for each other but only met a couple of times. Perhaps they were too close for comfort. Schnitzler's pioneering story, *Leutnant Gustl* (1900; *Lieutenant Gustl*), was the first truly successful application of the interior monologue technique; along with its later companion piece *Fräulein Else* (1924; *Fraülein Else*), this story often reads like one of Freud's psychoanalytic case studies. Freud's resort to literature to explain his scientific discoveries (e.g., the Oedipus complex), along with his narrative analyses of Viennese men and women, further underlines the affinities between these two great Viennese Jewish figures. Like Freud, whose *Traumdeutung* (*The Interpretation of Dreams*) appeared in 1900, Schnitzler viewed sexuality as the prime mover in human behavior. His most radical exploration of sexuality was *Reigen* (1897; *La Ronde*). This drama was only properly published and performed in the 1920s, and performances in Vienna and Berlin unleashed anti-Semitic demonstrations and denunciations of Schnitzler as a pornographer. In ten linked scenes, ten different characters, from a prostitute to an aristocrat, are seen as linked through sexual congress. With astonishing frankness, Schnitzler insists that the force that transcends all class barriers and structures is the libido. As with Hofmannsthal, however, Schnitzler's work seldom provides a direct reflection of a nation riven with tension and gradually breaking up under its own structural ineptitude and the pressures from mass movements such as socialism and nationalism. Schnitzler only grapples gradually and nonconfrontationally with the Austrian anti-Semitism that was articulated in the extreme-right Viennese political groupings in which Hitler first learned his politics. When he does confront these ideas, as in *Professor Bernhardi* (1912), we find a searing indictment of a Catholic establishment unwilling and unable to come to terms with the Jewish presence in it. Here, Schnitzler's full stature emerges as he integrates the social realism of naturalism with the psychological insights of a contemporary of Freud.

Typifying the divisions and conflicts that rent the last years of Imperial Austria, the preeminent satirist Karl Kraus despised the works of "Young Viennese" such as Hofmannsthal, Bahr, and Salten, who achieved international fame as the author of *Bambi* (1923). In his satire, *Die demolierte Literatur* (1897; Literature Demolished), written to celebrate the ripping-down of the Cafe Griensteidl, Kraus drew hilariously malevolent sketches of the "Young Viennese"— from Hofmannsthal ("Goethe at his school-desk") to Bahr ("the gentleman from Linz"), who indicated genius by letting a lock of hair dangle over his brow. The only figure missing from Kraus's hit list was Peter Altenberg, later described as "Ein Narr, der uns Normen gab" ("A fool who gave us norms"). Similar to Schnitzler, the obsessive miniaturist Altenberg is often regarded as an Impressionist—thanks to his awareness of the impact of the fleeting and cursory, the sensual and the instinctive in human life. In some respects, he mediates between and synthesizes Hofmannsthal's lyricism and Schnitzler's psychological portraits. More than either of them, however, Altenberg is a radical experimenter not just with literary forms, but also with the very notion of what constitutes the artistic self.

Initially regarded as a "Young Viennese," the unstable Altenberg was radically different from bourgeois figures such as Hofmannsthal, Andrian, and Schnitzler. One of Baudelaire's tribe of "poètes maudits," he epitomizes the ambiguities of identity that assailed Jews seeking an entrée into Austro-German society through the medium of art. Peter Altenberg was actually born Richard Engländer, which, ironically, had a very Jewish ring. Yet as soon as a Jewish artist adopted a non-Jewish pseudonym (Dörmann, Reinhardt, and Salten were also *noms de plume*), the clear implication conveyed was of role-playing and disingenuousness. In this metamorphosis, with its psychological as well as cultural roots, Altenberg is revealed as one of the most symptomatic writers in Vienna around 1900. Unsure of both his ethnic and sexual identity, he took the name Altenberg from a village just outside Vienna. In this village lived a girl called Bertha, forced by her brothers to act the role of manservant and given the name Peter. Richard Engländer adopted his gentile-sounding pseudonym both to betoken his identification with an exploited segment of society and to acknowledge the feminine component in his own psyche. Both Freud and the anti-Semitic, misogynist Jewish philosopher Otto Weininger, whose *Geschlecht und Charakter* (1903; *Sex and Character*) made great waves in Vienna, insisted that male and female are ideal categories and that bisexuality is the norm, albeit at a level generally unrealized or repressed. Weininger was still being quoted in the 1950s and 60s by the novelists Heimito von Doderer and Günther Grass.

Altenberg's vignettes and prose poems depict life from the perspective of Baudelaire's "flâneur," the wandering observer of city life who turns the urban experience into art. An alcoholic and drug addict who befriended pimps and prostitutes, Altenberg spent years in mental hospitals, which did not stop him preaching *mens sana in sano corpore*. Nor did conventional propriety prevent him from bestowing his affections on girls on the cusp of maturity. Today, he would be considered a potential pedophile, yet in a society where the age of consent was 14 years, and when puberty came later than nowadays, his behavior was not considered illegal (which is not to say that eyebrows were not raised). A similar view was probably taken in Victorian Britain regarding Lewis Carroll and his fascination with girls like Alice.

The recurring problems of personal identity worked through in turn-of-the-century Viennese literature, psychology, and philosophy seem mirrored in the face of the city itself in the period, whose grandiose Ringstraße was the product of a huge urban building program from the mid 1850s onward. The great ceremonial buildings were all pastiche, anachronistic imitations of diverse architectural styles and included a Greek classical parliament, a huge mock-Gothic church, and a Flemish town hall. Already assailed by doubts about their identity, many sensitive Viennese felt like bit-part players on a huge theatrical set, leading their lives against the backdrop of an unreal city. This feeling further reinforced the impression of a world where reality was a shifting commodity, where the genuine had to be sought out from behind an illusory surface. In short, it was the everyday confrontation that German Romantics such as E.T.A. Hoffmann had depicted between two worlds: one real, one false. But how did one tell what was real and what was merely a facade?

As an artist, Altenberg's formal range was narrow—unlike Hofmannsthal and Schnitzler, he wrote no dramas or novels to set alongside the myriad of impressions. Ironically, he appealed to Kraus because in a culture reeking of falseness, the satirist found Altenberg genuine. Through his journal *Die Fackel* (The Torch), produced mostly single-handed from 1899 until his death in 1936, Kraus pilloried the pretensions of Viennese literature and the venalities of metropolitan society. Obsessed with restoring the purity of a German language, which he thought had been defiled in equal measure by "Young Vienna" and the news media, Kraus championed the Viennese farceur Johann Nestroy and the poets Georg Trakl and Else Lasker-Schüler.

The world Kraus loved to hate ended abruptly with the outbreak of war in 1914. From that point forward, his satire took on a different form as he turned his mordant wit onto the war itself and the host of writers and intellectuals such as Bahr and Hofmannsthal who supported it with their pens. His technique often consisted of direct quotations from newspapers and books, through which he contended that the age condemned itself out of its own mouth. In a celebrated phrase, Austria appeared to him like a laboratory for world destruction. The summation of Kraus's quotation technique appears in the gigantic play *Die letzten Tage der Menschheit* (1919; *The Last Days of Mankind*), one of the greatest of all antiwar documents, published only after the empire that had been instrumental in sowing the winds of war had reaped the whirlwind. In essence, however, Kraus's position had not changed from the period in late 1914 when he published his seminal essay *In dieser großen Zeit* (*In These Great Times*). In this essay, he maintains that war is the catastrophic proof of a failure of the imagination, "for if we could imagine it, it wouldn't happen." Kraus's essay refrains from blaming the military or the state itself, preferring to excoriate newspapers grown fat on the profits made from death. As an analysis of 20th-century civilization and its discontents, it is as valid today as ever, for the despairing satirist had been quick to spot that humanity had been reduced to the status of consumer—"Menschheit ist Kundschaft" ("to be human is to be a customer"). Appalled by the German bombardment of Rheims Cathedral, Kraus recognized that "culture" is an early victim of a world motivated by profit and propagated via the rotary press. When, he asks, with an unanswered demand still reverberating at the dawn of a new millennium, "will the greater age of war break, when cathedrals make war on people!"

ANDREW BARKER

See also Decadence; Jung Wien; Vienna

Further Reading

Barker, Andrew, *Telegrams from the Soul: Peter Altenberg and the Culture of Fin-de-Siècle Vienna,* Columbia, South Carolina: Camden House, 1996

Barker, Andrew, and Leo A. Lensing, *Peter Altenberg: Rezept die Welt zu sehen: Kritische Essays, Briefe an Karl Kraus, Dokumente zur Rezeption, Titelregister der Bücher,* Vienna: Braumüller, 1995

Daviau, Donald G., editor, *Major Figures of Turn-of-the-Century Austrian Literature,* Riverside, California: Ariadne Press, 1991

Janik, Allan, and Stephen Toulmin, *Wittgenstein's Vienna,* New York: Simon and Schuster, 1973

Le Rider, Jacques, *Modernity and Crises of Identity: Culture and Society in Fin-de-Siècle Vienna,* translated by Rosemary Morris, Cambridge: Polity, and New York: Continuum, 1993

———, *Hugo von Hofmannsthal: Historicisme et modernité,* Paris: Presses universitaries de France, 1995

Lorenz, Dagmar, *Wiener Moderne,* Stuttgart: Metzler, 1995

Schorske, Carl E., *Fin-de-Siècle Vienna: Politics and Culture,* New York: Knopf, 1979

Swales, Martin, *Arthur Schnitzler: A Critical Study,* Oxford: Clarendon Press, 1971

Thompson, Bruce, *Schnitzler's Vienna: Image of a Society,* London and New York: Routledge, 1990

Timms, Edward, *Karl Kraus, Apocalyptic Satirist: Culture and Catastrophe in Habsburg Vienna,* New Haven, Connecticut: Yale University Press, 1986

Wistrich, Robert S., *The Jews of Vienna in the Age of Franz Joseph,* Oxford and New York: Oxford University Press, 1989

Yates, W.E., *Schnitzler, Hofmannsthal, and the Austrian Theatre,* New Haven, Connecticut: Yale University Press, 1992

Austria: Interwar

The cultural production of interwar Vienna reflects the issues and debates of the first Austrian republic, whose major phases consisted of the immediate post–World War I era, "Red" Vienna (i.e., Social Democrat Vienna, 1920–27), the 1927 riots and the increasing power of conservative and right-wing forces until the attempted Nazi coup in 1934, Austro-Fascism, and the annexation by Nazi Germany in 1938.

Prior to World War I, the collapse of the multinational Habsburg Empire was imminent. The reforms initiated by the last emperor, Karl I, came too late to neutralize the nationalist paradigms that formed in the 19th century. The reorganization of Central and Eastern Europe after the defeat of imperial Germany and Austro-Hungary reflected these national interests. Central and Eastern Europe were transformed into a conglomerate of nation states. Although the attempts to establish a German-Austrian republic failed, the idea of unification persisted. The first Austrian republic, founded in 1919, did not comprise all German-speaking territories of the former monarchy and, with its off-center capital Vienna, it was perceived as too top-heavy and too weak to exist on its own. Moreover, democracy as a system of government was viewed with widespread skepticism. The First Republic was unpopular with large parts of the population, including German nationalists, monarchists, and communists. When on 24 March 1938 Nazi German troops invaded Vienna, they were hailed by the masses. At the time of annexation (*Anschluß*), Austria had already ceased to be a democracy. For some four years it had been ruled by a repressive Catholic government, the Austro-Fascist *Ständestaat,* into which National Socialism, although formally outlawed, had made significant inroads.

The beginnings of the First Republic were overshadowed by the trauma of unprecedented destruction and the nostalgic memory of past greatness, both of which are articulated in autobiographical texts well into the 1980s, such as Elisabeth Freundlich's *Der Seelenvogel* (1986; *The Soul Bird*) and Hilde Spiel's *Die hellen und die finsteren Zeiten* (1989: *The Bright and the Dark Times*). Authors who identified with the aristocratic and haute bourgeois lifestyle of the empire experienced the demise of that grand, cosmopolitan, and somewhat decadent world as a personal tragedy. The 1918 deaths of the painter Gustav Klimt, the designer Otto Wagner (the architect of modern avenues, public facilities, residences, and monuments in Vienna and all across Europe), the designer Kolo Moser, and the painter Egon Schiele, foremost representatives of fin de siècle and early 20th-century culture mark the end of an era. The works of these artists associated with the Secession and the Vienna Workshops were of a supranational significance that the production of the interwar period, less grandiose, more matter-of-fact and regional, did not achieve. Authors engaged in forging a new Austrian discourse focused on more immediate concerns from a social critical perspective (such as the dramatist Ödön von Horváth in *Geschichten aus dem Wiener Wald* [1931; *Tales from the Vienna Woods*]) and from a feminist perspective (such as Mela Hartwig in *Ekstasen* [1928; *Ecstasies*]).

Writing about the values and lifestyle of the prewar era was one way of resisting the new social order, which many authors experienced as threatening and inhospitable. Arthur Schnitzler's prose and dramas, for example, continued to thematize duels and casual romances. However, his later texts, including *Fräulein Else* (1924) or *Traumnovelle* (1926; *Dream Story*) are more sober, cynical, and critical. They lack the flirtatiousness of his earlier work. The wartime trauma found its most shocking expression in the monumental pacifist drama *Die letzten Tage der Menschheit* (1919; *The Last Days of Mankind*) by the satirist and language critic Karl Kraus, editor of the journal *Die Fackel.* Kraus remained in the forefront of Vienna intellectual life, thereby carrying prewar values and aesthetics into the republic of whose social and literary trends he was highly critical. Like other intellectuals of his time, Kraus was an elitist and was skeptical of the Social Democratic leadership, which, he feared, was unable to prevent cultural and moral disintegration. Equally reluctant, Hugo von Hofmannsthal voiced his reservations in the drama *Der Schwierige* (1921; *The Difficult Man*), thematizing the destructive long-range effects of the world war: alienation, social displacement, and loss of identity. Hofmannsthal characterizes the postwar era as irreverent and fundamentally un-Austrian.

In later texts, the disintegration of traditional values and cultural decline are often linked with modern mass culture, nationalism, and socialism, and, by extension, they are viewed as major aspects of totalitarianism and state terrorism. These concepts are invoked, for example, in Stefan Zweig's exile works *Schachnovelle* (1941; *The Royal Game*) and *Die Welt von Gestern* (1942; *The World of Yesterday*) to explain the triumph of National Socialism. Robert Musil, who already in his novella *Die Verwirrungen des Zöglings Törleß* (1906; *Young Törleß*) had exposed deep-seated problems in the education at elite academies, revealed the incompatibility of the old and the new, pointing to the absurdity of a hierarchy void of meaning. The fictitious land of Kakanien in his novel *Der Mann ohne Eigenschaften* (1930–43; *The Man without Qualities*) represents Austria. Hermann Broch also thematizes the erosion of the spiritual and intellectual superstructures. His trilogy *Die Schlafwandler* (1931–32; *The Sleepwalkers*) and his studies on mass psychology revolve around the threat of totalitarianism within what appeared to Broch as the chaos of modern society. Broch's fascination with mass phenomena was shared by other intellectuals; Elias Canetti's monumental study *Masse und Macht* (1960; *Crowds and Power*), inspired in part by the 1927 riots, received vital impulses from the works of Kraus and Broch.

In view of the gradual radicalization of the public sphere and the troubled economy, even the outlook of authors who had initially welcomed a state that promised equal chances for oppressed groups such as Jews—including Eastern European Jews, the focus of Joseph Roth's *Juden auf Wanderschaft* (1927; *Flight without End*)—women, and the proletariat. Faced with racial anti-Semitism, many Jewish authors came to regard the Hapsburg Empire, notably its long-lived monarch Franz Joseph, as emblems of a fairer, more cosmopolitan form of government under which they had been protected as one of the monarchy's numerous nations. Idealized royalist sympathies can be identified in Roth's *Radetzkymarsch* (1932) and *Die Legende vom Heiligen Trinker* (1939; *The Legend of the Holy Drinker*), as well as in Spiel and Zweig.

More optimistic and forward-looking individuals and groups shaped the cultural trends that reflected the new developments specific to interwar Vienna. Many intellectuals active in the cultural production of "Red Vienna" placed high hopes in the democratic system, modern technology, and the reform of urban life. Nowhere was change more manifest than in Vienna, the capital and until 1927 a Social Democratic stronghold. Women had achieved active and passive suffrage and were represented in parliament; Jews, for the first time in Austrian history, had achieved equal access to state offices. Feminists, such as Rosa Mayreder, author of *Geschlecht und Kultur* (1923; *Sex and Culture*), continued to criticize traditional gender roles and the marginality of women in public life. However, career opportunities for women opened up more than ever before. At the same time a Jewish culture of great diversity blossomed that included, among others, Reform Judaism and Jewish orthodoxy, Socialist and Marxist groups, and assimilationism and Jewish Nationalism. Jakob Wassermann, in his autobiographical *Mein Weg als Deutscher und Jude* (1921; *My Life as German and Jew*) gave a vivid, albeit critical, account of Vienna's Jewish subculture. Workers organized themselves in trade unions and cooperative societies, which by 1930 published more than 100 newspapers and journals, of which *Die Arbeiter-Zeitung* (*The Workers' Paper*), *Der Sozialist* (*The Socialist*), and *Der Vertrauensmann* (*The Shop Stewart*) played a key role in public discourse. The *Arbeiterinnen-Zeitung* (1892–1923; *The Working Women's Paper*) reflected the interests of women workers. In 1926 *Die Unzufriedene* (*The Dissatisfied Woman*) took its place. Women were represented in all forms of writing and publishing: Bertha Zuckerkandl Szeps and Alice Schalek worked as high-profile journalists; Veza Canetti, among others, wrote social critical literature for *Die Arbeiter-Zeitung*; and Paula Ludwig authored lyric poetry dealing with the woman's experience.

The social democratic establishment addressed the issues of welfare and public health care, and it subsidized housing in all parts of the city. The most notable project was the Karl-Marx-Hof in Heiligenstadt, built between 1927 and 1930, a fortress-like compound designed to withstand the attacks of right-wing militia. Alternative cultural programs were an integral part of "Red Vienna," whose leadership was highly ambivalent toward the traditional elite culture and rejected popular entertainment, including mass tourism and show business such as the circus, *variété,* and cinema. To the numerous immigrants, the educational and leisure time activities organized by the Social Democratic Party and its affiliated organizations, including continuing education courses, public lectures (such as the ones at the Urania), concerts, theater performances, sports activities and festivals, dances, and political events, provided them access to mainstream society. The extensive public library system encouraged literary and academic pursuits, the creation of public spaces such as parks and bath facilities advanced public health and safety.

As far as popular culture was concerned, cinema and filmmaking were important aspects of interwar Vienna cultural life. Fritz Kortner, Marlene Dietrich, Peter Lorre, and Greta Garbo, and producers such as Billy Wilder, Fred Zinnemann, Fritz Lang, Michael Curtiz, Otto Preminger, and Alexander Korda took part in Viennese film productions. In addition to German-language films, Vienna film studios produced Yiddish films of high caliber. Like the film, minimal art (*Kleinkunst*) such as the cabaret, including the literary cabaret, the *variété,* and experimental theater groups, was not part of the literary establishment. The writers and artists active in these art forms belonged, just as many journalists did, to Vienna's extensive *bohème.* They belonged to a network of coffeehouse circles, a semiprivate, semipublic sphere in which artists and intellectuals of different social background, caliber, and outlook met to exchange ideas, programs, and manifestos. Elias Canetti's autobiography, *Die Fackel im Ohr* (1980; *The Torch in My Ear*), and Friedrich Torberg's *Auch das war Wien* (1984, written in 1939; *Also This Was Vienna*) and *Die Tante Jolesch* (1975; *Aunt Jolesch*), convey an impression of this vibrant yet vulnerable universe that continued to maintain close ties with the other capitals of the former Austro-Hungarian monarchy.

Nationalist and extreme right-wing opposition to the republic existed from the start. In the course of time, conflicts between the militia of the Großdeutsche Volkspartei (Greater German People's Party), the Heimwehr (Home Front), and the Republikanischer Schutzbund (Republican Protection Alliance) of the Social Democratic Party were on the rise, as were politically and racially motivated hate crimes, including the murder of the Jewish author Hugo Bettauer by a right-wing extremist in 1925, less than three years after the publication of his novel *Die Stadt ohne Juden* (1922; *City without Jews*), a work in which the author satirized anti-Semitism and asserted that the Jewish presence contributed significantly to Vienna's prosperity. The riots of 1927 and the burning of the Palace of Justice, which were represented by the political right as a Jewish or Communist plot, the worldwide economic crisis, and rising unemployment prompted growing support for the political right, including the National

Socialists, whose Blut und Boden (blood and soil) ideology appealed not only to provincial Austria but to the academic elite (including German literary scholars such as Heinz Kindermann, Herbert Cysarz, and Josef Nadler). Various kinds of nationalist, racialist, and fascist views are also expressed by numerous literary authors, Nazi sympathizers, or members of the Nazi party (such as Mirko Jelusich, Heimito von Doderer, and Josef Weinheber), and anti-Semitic, ethnocentric, and racist ideas were spread by the active right-wing press.

Klaus Amann (1988) observes that the majority of Austrians rejected authors such as Schnitzler, Kraus, Musil, and Werfel, who were regarded as proper representatives of the Austrian spirit. The invectives against Freud, the controversies involving Schnitzler's drama *Reigen* (1900; *La Ronde*), pervasive anti-Semitism, and fear of technology are indicative of the reactionary undercurrents that inspired the foundation of the *Kampfbund für deutsche Literatur* (Defense Association of German Literature) in 1927 and a celebration of provincial literature sponsored by the *Vaterländische Front* (Patriotic Front) in 1936. These tendencies are recorded in Kraus's *Dritte Walpurgisnacht* (1952, written 1933; *The Third Walpurgisnight*), and their origins are analyzed in Wilhelm Reich's *Massenpsychologie des Faschismus* (1933; *Mass Psychology of Fascism*).

After 1933–34 the participation of leftist and progressive intellectuals in cultural life declined sharply. Even the *Arbeiter-Zeitung,* in fear of an anti-Semitic backlash, laid off Jewish contributors, many of whom were already publishing under neutral-sounding names. Elias Canetti's *Die Blendung* (1935; *Auto-da-Fé*) was ignored, and like all literature by Jewish authors, it was taken out of print when the Nuremberg Laws took effect in 1938. Interwar Austria ended with the mass exodus of dissenters and Jews; however, some of its culture survived in exile, thanks to the activities of cabarettists such as Hermann Leopoldi and Leon Askin and writers and poets such as Theodor Kramer, Berthold Viertel, Albert Drach, and Vicki Baum. Authors who like Torberg and Spiel returned to Vienna established links between the culture of the First and the Second Austrian Republic.

DAGMAR C.G. LORENZ

Further Reading

Amann, Klaus, *Der Anschluss österreichischer Schriftsteller an das Dritte Reich: Institutionelle und bewusstseinsgeschichtliche Aspekte*, Frankfurt: Athenäum, 1988

Amann, Klaus, and Albert Berger, editors, *Österreichische Literatur der dreissiger Jahre: Ideologische Verhältnisse, institutionelle Voraussetzungen, Fallstudien*, Vienna: H. Böhlaus Nachf., 1985

Beckermann, Ruth, and Hermann Teifer, editors, *Die Mazzesinsel: Juden in der Wiener Leopoldstadt 1918–1938,* Vienna: Löcker, 1984

Daviau, Donald G., editor, *Austrian Writers and the Anschluss: Understanding the Past—Overcoming the Past*, Riverside, California: Ariadne Press, 1991

———, *Major Figures of Austrian Literature: The Interwar Years 1918–1938,* Riverside, California: Ariadne Press, 1995

Don, Yehudah, and Viktor Karády, editors, *A Social and Economic History of Central European Jewry,* New Brunswick, New Jersey: Transaction Publishers, 1990

Freidenreich, Harriet Pass, *Jewish Politics in Vienna, 1918–1938,* Bloomington: Indiana University Press, 1991

Gruber, Helmut, *Red Vienna: Experiment in Working-Class Culture, 1919–1934,* New York: Oxford University Press, 1991

Hamann, Brigitte, *Hitlers Wien: Lehrjahre eines Diktators,* Munich: Piper, 1996

Hofmann, Paul, *The Viennese: Splendor, Twilight, and Exile,* New York: Anchor Press, 1988

Oxaal, Ivar, Michael Pollak, and Gerhard Botz, editors, *Jews, Antisemitism, and Culture in Vienna*, London and New York: Routledge and Kegan Paul, 1987

Spiel, Hilde, *Glanz und Untergang: Wien 1866–1938,* Munich: Deutscher Taschenbuch Verlag, 1994

Stieg, Gerald, *Frucht des Feuers: Canetti, Doderer, Kraus, und der Justizpalastbrand,* Vienna: Edition Falter im ÖBV, 1990

Veigl, Hans, editor, *Luftmenschen spielen Theater: Jüdisches Kabarett in Wien,* 1890–1938, Himberg bei Wien: Kremayr and Scheriau, 1992

Wistrich, Robert S., editor, *Austrians and Jews in the Twentieth Century: From Franz Joseph to Waldheim,* New York: St. Martin's Press, 1992

Witek, Hans, and Hans Safrian, editors, *Und keiner war dabei: Dokumente des alltäglichen Antisemitismus in Wien 1938,* Vienna: Picus, 1988

Austria: Post 1945

Austria's post–World War II literature and culture is marked by the ambivalent construction of a distinct national identity intended to distance itself from the greater nationalism of the Third Reich and its pan-Germanic culture, to which Austrians had once more or less willingly subscribed. This reconstruction of a society marked by a separate national identity appears at first as a contradictory enterprise. On the one hand, the retrieval of the Habsburg era, in which a peaceful coexistence of diverse cultures was possible, although these cultures were now no longer copresent to the same degree, seems nostalgic and illusory. On the other hand, with regard to Austria's postimperial history, one must confront a problematic landscape of intense political polarization that led Austria into civil war and the subsequent dictatorship of its corporate state (1934–38). The attempt to revive Austria's national identity in the postwar era is ultimately a revival ex nihilo based on no applicable prior model in Austrian history.

As critics have pointed out, the revival of a national identity is largely inspired by the pragmatic need to emphasize Austria's difference to and noncomplicity with Nazi Germany. For example, Barbara Kaindl-Widhalm discerns in Austria's postwar history no endemic process of democratization but one that is simply administered from above and contingent on the defeat of the Third Reich: "The foreign political military defeat set the conditions for the internal political changes." Austria's national identity thus appears to younger writers and intellectuals as an insidious ideological device covering up its problematic past rather than as a positive set of national and constitutional tenets presumably shared by its citizens. For example, the young Peter Handke expresses his doubts and reservations at the very beginning of Austria's postwar republic, which was inaugurated with the withdrawal of the occupation forces in 1955: "As nothing had changed except for the introduction of a national holiday, and we still heard that we are now free, I gradually understood the expression 'free' and 'unfree' as games of language."

The struggle to let the full truth appear about Austria's complicity with the Nazi genocide and its totalitarian oppression circumscribes the various epochs and shifts of literary trends in Austria's postwar cultural landscape. Beginning with the partial restoration of Austria's Jewish Habsburg legacy and the recovery of the critical vocabularies of modernism (Expressionism, Surrealism, and Dadaism), Austrian literature eventually produces increasingly louder voices of dissent (Bachmann, Bernhard, Handke, Roth, and Jelinek) that penetrate deeper into the internalized patterns of fascist socialization. With the affair surrounding the election of the alleged Nazi war criminal Kurt Waldheim in 1986 to the post of president, the confrontation with Austria's past is finally brought to a head in a public protest by leading Austrian artists and intellectuals. The 1990s brought forth a strong revival of Jewish writing in Austria (Tabori, Jelinek, Schindel, Menasse, Rabinovici, Beckermann, Kerschbaumer, Heller, and Seelich) that attests more to a critical culture than to the belated apologies by the Austrian government. Despite this seeming success story of truth, frequent regressive and reactionary trends have likewise shaped the Austrian cultural landscape. Most recently, the disturbing popularity of Austria's xenophobic Freedom Party, which demands severe restrictions on immigration, causes reason for continued concern and reflects a hard core of unrepenting protofascist sentiment that seems to survive unchallenged in a society that still lags behind the insights of its critical minority of artists and intellectuals.

Austria's immediate postwar literature is undeniably marked by an effort of restoration that relegated questions concerning the past to secondary status. Cultural self-critique offered by Austria's progressive elements appears, in hindsight, partial and incomplete and was more or less entirely repressed in conservative circles. A significant contribution to a new and tentatively critical beginning can be seen in the literary magazine *Der Plan* (1945–48). Otto Basil, *Der Plan*'s editor, insisted on a democratic outlook that had had only a short-lived precedence in Austria's first republic (1919–34) and a cosmopolitan and European orientation that had characterized the Habsburg Empire's supranational culture. The magazine openly discussed the cases of prominent Austrian Nazi proponents in literature (Nadler and Weinheber) and allowed the voices of a younger generation of writers to come to the fore (Aichinger, Mayröcker, Eisenreich, Dor, Celan, and Fried). *Der Plan* also reintroduced the works of Kafka, Rilke, Musil, Broch, and Kraus to its readers, thus partially restoring the innovative and critical voices of the Habsburg era. The revival of Kraus's journalistic legacy, with its relentless style of cultural critique, seemed especially appropriate for a new beginning but found its true echo only in later writers, such as Bachmann, Bernhard, and Jelinek.

On the conservative spectrum, the figures of Hans Weigel, Heimito von Doderer, and Fritz Hochwälder took center stage, distancing themselves from social reform and other left-leaning legacies in their insistence on aesthetic autonomy and tradition. In conservative fashion, their attempt was to restore a lost humanity and morality that the positive sciences had apparently suppressed, leading to the dehumanization of culture. For example, Doderer makes a plea for indirection in language in his dubiously titled *Von der Unschuld im Indirekten* (1947; Of Innocence in Indirection) in opposition to his German contemporary Wolfgang Borchert, who, in his *Manifest* (1947), demands the dismantlement of literary formalism. Similarly, Fritz Hochwälder's *Das heilige Experiment,* which premiered at the Burgtheater in 1947 with great success, portrays the dismantlement of a Jesuit state in Paraguay built on the principles of socialism in favor of a return to more orthodox Christian teachings. However, according to Wendelin Schmidt-Dengler, the play's success depended not exclusively on its restorative and conservative political message but also on its skillful use of dialogue and dramatic action. Indeed, in subsequent writers the conservative tradition of aesthetics, upheld by the likes of Doderer and Hochwälder, would increasingly mix with progressive politics, thereby producing a postideological writing typical of Austria. However, the reappearance of Jewish writing and other suppressed traditions of the avant-garde was required first.

Of interest here is that exile writing had little or a belated effect (Hermann Broch, Elias Canetti, Albert Drach, and Jakov Lind) on the formation of Austria's postwar literature. The few writers who chose to return to a less-than-hospitable Austria often found themselves out of touch with the prevailing literary trends that had been set in the meantime by a younger generation. Thus, it is not surprising that the works of Ilse Aichinger and Paul Celan had a deeper effect than those of older Jewish writers caught up, like their other Austrian contemporaries, in the receding heritage of Habsburg Austria. Aichinger's *Die größere Hoffnung* (1948; *The Greater Hope*) produces an Austrian equivalent of *Trümmerliteratur* (literature of rubble), narrating the story of the original victims of the war rather than the fate of disillusioned *Heimkehrer* (soldiers returning from the war) and displaced Germans assuming themselves the role of victims. Ellen, the Jewish child-protagonist, finds herself amid war, persecution, and despair and yet manages, in imagined scenarios of an escape to Palestine, to survive in an otherwise hopeless situation. Ironically, on the eve of truce she is torn apart by a grenade but has come to accept death without fear. In addition, the novel marks the return of Expressionism in Austrian writing with its largely anonymous and historically nonspecific portrayal of humanity's ethical and existential boundary situations. In the poetry of Celan, especially his widely known "Todesfuge," this Expressionistic effect was heightened in the tensions of surrealist blendings of the banal with nightmarish visions, thereby instilling an even greater discomfort in the reader. Thus, Austria's literature betrays little of the realist tradition that was to define Germany's postwar writings, such as its *Trümmerliteratur* and its ensuing sociodescriptive works by writers of the Gruppe 47.

A more concrete historical setting was offered in Doderer's *Strudlhofstiege* (1951; The Strudlhof Steps), which created a bridge to Austria's post-Habsburg period, allowing a restorative vision of Austrian culture in a prolongation of the Habsburg myth into the near present, as outlined in Claudio Magris's classic study of 1966. Such an evasion of historical responsibility seemed especially attractive in light of Austria's revisionist claim of being a victim of Nazi Germany, a version of history that was embraced to speed up normalization and economic aid and ultimately to restore Austrian sovereignty in 1955. Politically, this brought a greater need for cooperation between the formerly hostile camps of Christian Democrats and Socialists. In what has since been identified as a thoroughgoing political and cultural aesthetic of social partnership undermining democratic decision making (Menasse), a parity commission was set up to settle debates on wage and labor demands beforehand, thereby guaranteeing Austria's social stability. Social partnership, the pillar of Austria's Second Republic, soon informed also a pervasive consensus mentality in which all disagreements were forever harmonized for the sake of promoting a pragmatic politics of economic recovery at the expense of cultural memory. Such a politics clearly pulled Austria into the Western Hemisphere and prevented it from becoming another Soviet satellite state, but it did so at the expense of an inner democratization that had quickly assimilated former Nazis and opponents of fascism into a homogeneous mass of Austrians.

What looked like a promising start in *Wiederaufarbeitung* (working through the past) had quickly become ossified by the 1950s, an era bent on duplicating Germany's economic miracle. The currency reform of 1947 also did much damage to Austrian publishing houses and forced Austrian writers once again to look to Germany for support. Nevertheless, this need for extraterritorial support also brought forth in Austrian writers their cosmopolitan and transnational legacies that had been obliterated by post-Habsburg pan-Germanicism and National Socialism. Ingeborg Bachmann was the first writer to demonstrate that this heritage had not been entirely lost. Unlike Doderer, who in his *Strudlhofstiege* nostalgically portrays the last vestiges of Austria's Habsburg cultural relations with its former Eastern European and southern territories as well as the former Ottoman Empire, Bachmann had the difficult task of reviving a cosmopolitan legacy that was severely eroded in Austria's linguistically and culturally contained postwar republic.

However, the restoration of cosmopolitan and transnational perspectives in Bachmann, who lived most of her life outside Austria (Rome), was not an attempt to recover the lost grandeur of Austria's imperial heritage, as had been the case in numerous Austrian *Heimatfilm* productions of the 1950s. Instead, this perspective is brought into accord with the experience of émigrés and exiles to capture their special and critical vantage point of Austrian and European culture. In her famous story "Drei Wege zum See" (*Simultan,* 1972; *Three Paths to the Lake*), Bachmann depicts in the figure of Franz Joseph Trotta, a descendant of Joseph Roth's prototypical Habsburg state servant family in *Der Radetzkymarsch* (1932; *The Radetzky March*), an Austrian exile critically assessing contemporary culture and its journalistic fetishism with the Algerian war of decolonization and the Hungarian uprising of 1956 against Soviet hegemony. Tutoring the heroine Elisabeth in a cultural politics that respects the unrepresentable of violence and horror, Trotta voices the views of Jean Améry, a real-life Austrian exile and survivor. In his *Jenseits von Schuld und Sühne* (1966; *At the Mind's Limit*) and its chapter on torture, Améry attempts to convey the utter dehumanization, as well as the ultimate unrepresentability, of these horrific experiences suffered under the totalitarian rule of fascism. In pleading to preserve the humanity and integrity of victims, Bachmann's story takes a similarly critical view of Austria's superficial solidarity with victims during the protest era of the 1960s.

Bachmann's critical perspective of a dubious harmonization in a seemingly liberal postwar culture announces itself already earlier in her *Das dreißigste Jahr* (1961; *The Thirtieth Year*), a collection of stories documenting the continuities of fascism in the oppressive political climate of the 1950s. For example, the story "Unter Mördern und Irren" (Among Murderers and Madmen) depicts an evening gathering of male friends (*Stammtisch*) in which former Nazis and Jewish survivors gloss over their past in an attempt to preserve the seemingly harmonious cultural climate of the present. The story ends hauntingly when someone parodies an adjoining gathering of former war comrades and is brutally murdered to the horror of those who wanted to put the past behind them. It is this schizoid and belittling relation to power that Bachmann similarly exposes in her feminist writings—most notably in her incomplete *Todesartenzyklus,* which comprises the novels *Malina* (1971; *Malina*), *Der Fall Franza* (1979; The Case of Franza), and *Requiem für Fanny Goldmann* (1979; Requiem for Fanny Goldmann)—in which her heroines are often complicitous with their own victimization by upholding the male status quo.

Another trajectory of critical thinking can be found in Austria's tradition of language criticism that had its origins in the turn-of-the-century writers Hugo von Hofmannsthal, Fritz Mauthner, and Ludwig Wittgenstein. Especially Wittgenstein's skeptical philosophy of language had a deep effect on Austrian writers, such as the Wiener Gruppe of the 1950s and the Forum Stadtpark in Graz of the 1960s. Bernhard, Handke, and Jelinek, Austria's internationally acclaimed triumvirate of contemporary German literature, directly or indirectly developed their innovative styles around the premises of the avant-garde advances built on the legacy of Wittgenstein. In the 1950s, the Wiener Gruppe (Gerhard Rühm, Friedrich Achleitner, Oswald Wiener, Konrad Bayer, H.C. Artmann, and Andreas Okopenko) rebelled largely against latent ideologies of authoritarianism and fascism that were couched in everyday language and in the elevated styles of bourgeois art. Radically reinventing conventional orthography and grammar and using language in shocking ways, these writers challenged the restorative ambition of the petty bourgeois and drew a larger awareness to the hidden political dimension of language and art. Ernst Jandl, loosely associated with the Wiener Gruppe, produced sound and visual poetry reminiscent of the iconoclastic Dadaist experiments of the 1920s in which society's underlying violence was brought to the fore in syntactic and onomatopoeic depiction as given, for example, in his poem "schtzngrmm," which evoked acoustically the sounds of war and gunfire. These avant-garde endeavors also spilled over into the visual arts, in which Austria's version of surrealism, magic realism (Ernst Fuchs, Arik Brauer, and Rudolf Hausner), was quickly replaced by the more radical performances of the Wiener Aktionismus (Günther Brus, Otto Mühl, Hermann Nitsch, and Rudolf Schwarzkogler). These performances included pathological self-mutilations and stagings of victimizations that evoked the repressed memory of the Holocaust but also appeared to wrest the status of victimhood away from the original victims.

This defiant anti-institutional stance also marks much of the early writings by Thomas Bernhard, whose novels (*Frost,* 1963; *Verstörung,* 1967) are replete with estranged characters and severely isolated individuals bent on self-destructive behavior as a form of pathological dissent. Similarly, Peter Handke's *Publikumsbeschimpfung* (1966; *Offending the Audience*) challenges the complacent conventions of bourgeois theater with its performative staging of language, abandoning the code of character altogether. Likewise, Handke's novel *Die Angst des Tormanns beim Elfmeter* (1970; *The Anxiety of the Goalie at the Penalty Kick*) depicts a pathological murderer overwhelmed by the semiotic suggestions of society that have apparently prodded him to his crime. Parallel to French structuralism and the emergence of the *nouveau roman,* the thematics of language figures predominantly in Austrian writing since the 1960s. The Forum Stadtpark, which under the direction of Alfred Kolleritsch edited the literary magazine *manuscripte,* has made a substantial contribution in introducing young authors (Gert Jonke, Klaus Hoffer, Barbara Frischmuth, Peter Rosei, Julian Schutting, and Wolfgang Bauer) to a sociolinguistic analysis of culture, thereby recovering the earlier experiments of the Wiener Gruppe for a larger mainstream reading audience.

With the advance of the 1970s, the social protest model that directly or indirectly embraced a critique of society through a critique of language had lost much of its force. Avant-garde endeavors seemed remote, austere, and hermetic in light of the changing consumer landscape of Austria that had slowly turned into a tourist and leisure culture. While politically Austria's beloved Socialist chancellor Dr. Bruno Kreisky (1970–83) made significant changes in the educational and social welfare system, Austrian literature increasingly turned to the private realm as a heretofore undiscovered political arena. What is commonly called the New Subjectivity found its first strong proponent in Peter Handke, whose narratives focused on the seemingly unremarkable experience of the everyday. His *Wunschloses Unglück* (1973; *A Sorrow beyond Dreams*), depicting the life of his mother and the tragic circumstances of her suicide, offers an acute sociocultural analysis of everyday histories that had shaped the private experiences of his mother during the era of fascism and postwar reconstruction. Likewise, women writers (Barbara Frischmuth, Brigitte Schwaiger, and Anna Mitgutsch), with Ingeborg Bachmann at the vanguard, discovered in their private lives the political scenarios from within which they attempted to achieve emancipation. Similarly, regional writing focused on traumatic experiences of socialization and produced an Austrian version of the critical *Heimatroman* in the works of Franz Innerhofer, Josef Winkler, and Peter Turrini.

By the 1980s, Austrian writing had thoroughly installed itself on the German literary scene with many of its authors producing their works in major German publishing houses. With the premature death of Ingeborg Bachmann in 1973, the legacy of Austrian literature passed into the hands of Thomas Bernhard and Peter Handke, who dominated the literary market of the 1980s. As productive playwrights and through film adaptations (Handke), they also found further avenues to reach a wider public. In the context of the 1980s, Klaus Zeyringer speaks of a reorientation toward a literary public sphere gradually replacing the earlier literature of interiority. This work in the public arena saw the rise of another major Austrian writer, Elfriede Jelinek, who, in her relentless portrayal of a thoroughly commodified cultural landscape, manages to go beyond the vitriolic criticism that had become the trademark of Bernhard. Her iconoclastic novels *Die Klavierspielerin* (1983; *The Piano Player*) and *Lust* (1987; *Lust*) set new, provocative standards for feminism by implicating women to a greater degree in the maintenance of a conservative social fabric.

With the election of the alleged Nazi war criminal Kurt Waldheim to the post of president, Austria's political landscape was once again haunted by ghosts that it wanted to forget. In reaction to this persistence of amnesia exhibited in Austria's collective memory, the late 1980s and 1990s bring forth an abundance of works that reassess Austria's fascist past and its hidden continuities in the present. Thomas Bernhard's play *Heldenplatz* (1988; Heroes Square) premiered at the 50th anniversary of Austria's annexation and, to the chagrin of many, depicted Austria's unrepenting attitude that had never resulted in any admission of guilt, remittance, or formal apology. Jelinek's subsequent play *Totenauberg* (1991), which likewise premiered at the prestigious national Burgtheater, underscored the latent continuities of fascism in the marketing of native and indigenous culture as a tourist commodity and the simultaneous promotion of immigration restrictions after the opening of the Iron Curtain. Her play, a linguistic scenario harkening back to the avant-garde of the 1950s and 1960s, examines cultural discourses in the new light of the clashing ideologies of belonging and displacement that define the present problematics surrounding citizenship and nationality.

The 1990s post–Cold War era has brought forth further dramatic changes in Austria's literary landscape. We presently witness the emergence of a Jewish literature, taking a much more open critical tone and a less conciliatory attitude in the works of Georg Tabori, Elfriede Jelinek, Robert Schindel, Robert Menasse, Doron Rabinovici, and Marie-Therese Kerschbaumer. Nevertheless, it would be wrong to speak of a sharply defined ethnic literature in the case of these authors, who map out complex transnational identities. In addition, Austrian literature continues to show remarkable international success. Robert Schindel's novel *Gebürtig* (1992; *Born Where?*), Christoph Ransmayr's *Die letzte Welt* (1988; *The Last World*), and Marlene Streeruwitz's *Verführungen* (1996; *Seductions*) stand out as the most prominent novels of recent years. Gerhard Roth's prose cycle *Archive des Schweigens* (1991; Archives of Silence), Elisabeth Reichart's *Februarschatten* (1989; February's Shadows), and Doron Rabinovici's *Suche nach M.* (1997; *Search for M.*) offer incisive internal critique and analysis of Austria's fascist past and its legacies for second-born generations (*Nachgeborene*).

It is yet unclear to what degree European unification will affect literary production other than in the already noted significance of the rethinking of national and cultural affiliations and boundaries that had begun with the opening of the Iron Curtain. This focus on nationhood and citizenship might well bring back a revival of the negotiation of regional and cosmopolitan identities that have given so much force to the literature of fin de siècle Vienna as a valuable model for the present transnational and multicultural reconfiguration of Europe.

MATTHIAS KONZETT

Further Reading

Aspetsberger, Friedbert, et al., editors, *Literatur der Nachkriegszeit und der fünfziger Jahre in Österreich,* Vienna: Österreichischer Bundesverlag, 1984

Aspetsberger, Friedbert, and Hubert Lengauer, *Zeit ohne Manifeste? Zur Literatur der siebziger Jahre in Österreich,* Vienna: Österreichischer Bundesverlag, 1987

Bartsch Kurt, et al., editors, *Für und wider eine österreichische Literatur,* Königstein: Athenäum, 1982

Best, Alan, and Hans Wolfschütz, editors, *Modern Austrian Writing: Literature and Society after 1945,* London: Wolf, and Totowa, New Jersey: Barnes and Noble, 1980
Daviau, Donald G., editor, *Major Figures of Contemporary Austrian Literature,* New York: Lang, 1987
Demetz, Peter, *After the Fires: Recent Writing in the Germanies, Austria, and Switzerland,* San Diego, California: Harcourt, Brace, Jovanovich, 1986
Dor, Milo, editor, *Die Leiche im Keller: Dokumente des Widerstands gegen Dr. Kurt Waldheim,* Vienna: Picus, 1988
Greiner, Ulrich, *Der Tod des Nachsommers: Aufsätze, Porträts, Kritiken zur österreichischen Gegenwartsliteratur,* Munich and Vienna: Hanser, 1979
Magris, Claudio, *Der habsburgische Mythos in der österreichischen Literatur,* Salzburg: Müller, 1966
McGowan, Moray, and Ricarda Schmidt, editors, *From High Priests to Desecrators: Contemporary Austrian Writers,* Sheffield: Sheffield Academic Press, 1993
Menasse, Robert, *Die sozialpartnerschaftliche Ästhetik: Essays zum österreichischen Geist,* Vienna: Sonderzahl, 1990
Schmidt-Dengler, Wendelin, *Bruchlinien: Vorlesungen zur österreichischen Literatur 1945 bis 1990,* Salzburg: Residenz, 1995
Schmölzer, Hilde, *Frau sein und schreiben: Österreichische Schriftstellerinnen definieren sich selbst,* Vienna: Österreichische Bundesverlag, 1982
Spiel, Hilde, editor, *Die zeitgenössische Literatur Österreichs,* Zurich and Munich: Kindler, 1976
Zeyringer, Klaus, *Innerlichkeit und Öffentlichkeit: Österreichische Literatur der achtziger Jahre,* Tübingen: Francke, 1992

Autobiography

Autobiography, as its Greek roots imply, stands for life writing. The term *autobiography* was first published in 1786, with the term *Selbstbiographie* first appearing in the late 18th century (slightly before the advent of Romanticism). According to Robert Folkenflik, in German, the designation may be seen first in Christian Friedrich Daniel Schubart's *Leben und Gesinnungen* (1791; Life and Ideologies). Fundamental to autobiography is the retrospective portrayal of the self and the reflection of an author's spiritual, artistic, or psychological development. Autobiographies have no formal structure, and autobiographical expression enjoys a host of forms that range from the confession to poetic autobiography. Generally, autobiographies are written by those who bear the same name as the protagonist of the narrative. Classically understood, autobiography is an authentic, candid representation of personal experiences in which the uniqueness of the individual is showcased. It functions as a testimony of the creative development of the subject (Goethe, Rousseau). As a genre, autobiography prescribes to be the most intimate, self-reflexive representation of life experience in which a writer, traditionally male, retrospectively plots his life story to create a unified self—beginning with childhood and working chronologically into the autobiographer's present. The autobiographical act thus entails an author selectively structuring his/her life story and organizing it into various phases in order to produce a coherent narrative of the self, as well as to explore the formation of a subject and the interaction between the subject and the sociohistorical context. Yet the understanding of identity, the self, or subjectivity is historically bound and relational, and autobiographical writing and the relationship to the subject has evolved with the changing view of self and authorship.

The late 18th century marks the beginning of a surge of autobiographical writing and an increased recognition of the genre's significance. In fact, the term *autobiography* is intricately bound to a Western post-Enlightenment construction of the self that is rational, self-determining, and unitary and that undergoes a linear, progressive development toward enlightenment. Critic Georg Misch in his extensive 1951 study on autobiography, *History of Autobiography in Antiquity,* saw in the portrayal of public, representative lives in autobiography documents of the progressive unfolding of Western history. The subject, no longer recognized as static, was understood as engaging in a process. The appearance of autobiographies in the 18th century, often referred to as the classical age of autobiography, mirrors an important development in the self-awareness of the European middle class, which set itself apart from the lifestyles and values of the aristocracy and prided itself on its own moral values. At the same time, this "new" subject of autobiography was an exemplary middle-class subject with a moral conscience, undoubtedly conceived as patriarchal and universal, which asserted itself as the moral standard and social norm. It is interesting to note that construction of modern masculinity was closely linked to the new bourgeois society of this time and that "autobiography" became one of men's important areas for self-reflection. Many of the early religious autobiographies, enlargements of confessions that retained the form's properties, are introspective revelations (confessions) of a pious self, such as in the meticulous recordings of Pietists Heinrich Jung-Stilling, *Lebensgeschichte* (1777; Life Story), and Karl Philipp Mortiz, *Anton Reiser* (1785–90), a psychogram of growing up in an abusive, Pietistic household, which was modeled largely on Rousseau's *Confessions* (1781–88). The "I" in many of these early narratives derives its value through its religious affiliation. Different in terms of its more secular framework, Goethe's *Aus meinem Leben: Dichtung und Wahrheit* (completed in 1831; translated as *Memoirs of Goethe; Written by Himself, The Autobiography of Goethe,* and *From My Life*) traces his development as an author and the formation of the self in relationship to his interaction with the outer world. Even though *Dichtung und Wahrheit* subscribes to the traditional teleological narrative of the development of a cohesive self, the title alludes to the theoretical conundrum of self-representation. Moreover, the insight into the function of memory and the blurred boundary between fiction and fact are both intimated in this title.

Regarded as subordinate to literature, autobiography has traditionally received little critical attention. Only within the last few decades has it gained recognition as a historical document as well as a creative, literary product. Consequently, an expansive body of autobiography criticism has moved autobiography from the margins to the center and, in doing so, has expanded the repertoire of voices to include those groups traditionally marginalized. The slipperiness of autobiography as a genre with strict stylistic properties is also made apparent because autobiography's various forms of self-narration, such as letters, diaries, journals, and protocols, stretch its generic boundaries and extend its analytical reach. For example, the letters of writers of the Romantic period—Bettina von Arnim, Karoline von Günderrode, and Rahel Varnhagen—have been recognized as a vital forum for the production of a female subject within a historical framework that restricted female literary contributions.

Recent autobiography criticism has shifted from an interest in representations of individualism as objective testimonies of historical processes and personal development to an interest in subjective interpretations of life and the relationship between the public and private spheres. This shift has lent autobiography a new emphasis. The focus has centered on subjective renderings of personal histories so that the borders once drawn between life and text, documentary and fiction, and between the public and private sphere, in addition to the divisions commonly set between autobiographical and biographical expression, all become indistinct. Influenced by poststructuralism, feminism, and culture studies, the relationship between autobiography and life has become less causal than in past centuries. Veracity has succumbed to interpretation and construal, and referentiality to construct. Traditional assumptions underlying authorship, identity, the autobiographical subject, and referentiality have thus come under suspicion. The "I" of autobiography, as structuralists and poststructuralists radically insist, elides referentiality and is merely an effect of language. Despite different approaches to reading autobiography, critics agree that it has abdicated its function as a storehouse of truth. Instead, autobiography is widely regarded as a strategic act of self-invention and self-enactment. It is the site of constructing a self in order to reflect upon personal history and identity; it emerges as an interplay of imagination, desire, and memory. Based on a reading of the autobiographer's own life, only one among the many versions of the self is produced, and this version is guided by unconscious desires as much as by conscious interpretive strategies of self-portraiture. Self-representation, as contemporary critics have pointed out, demands selecting from a wealth of experiences and facts, identifying key events, and reproducing personal legends that shape the self and constitute self-knowledge. Since contemporary autobiography calls into question the factors that constitute subjectivity, history, and even reference, it also challenges the concepts of authority and uniqueness, a challenge that accelerated during the 1960s with the student movement and feminism. Autobiography showcases a constructed identity that is not fixed but in process, and that is defined through the myriad of experiences and markers of identity such as class, race, gender, ethnicity, sexual preference, and national identity, which all produce subjectivity and self-understanding. Autobiographies reveal more about the present in which the author reflects upon his/her life story than the past. In *Kindheitsmuster* (1976; *Patterns of Childhood*), for example, Christa Wolf contemplates both the possibility of an accurate or authentic recapitulation of the past and the inevitable interference of present needs in processes of memory, and she also acknowledges the unbridgeable fissure between life and text.

Characterized by plurality and by the multiplicity of contributing voices to culture, the postmodern era delivers a new understanding of the subject of autobiography. It is a self intersubjectively constituted, constantly in a state of change, and constantly in dialogue with the outer world. It is a subject-in-process whose identity must be continually assumed and then called into question, evading any ideological unity. Even though autobiography is usually written in old age, or at least in midlife, it may be written by the young. Often it is the product of a time of crisis. For instance, the crisis of individuality during the early part of the 20th century precipitated an observable increase in autobiographical expression. Similarly, the overwhelming presence of autobiographical expression throughout the 1970s and 1980s in German literature, written by postwar authors, reveals a period of crisis and the need to work through the production of subjectivity in a climate that was witnessing dramatic conceptual upheavals and perspectival shifts. The tendency in literature that has been called the New Subjectivity, which became shorthand for a literature of self-discovery and analysis, serves as an example (see Peter Handke, *Wunschloses Unglück: Erzählung,* [1972; *A Sorrow beyond Dreams*]). The plethora of self-searching narratives of the 1970s and 1980s often focus on the legacy of Germany's fascist past and the inevitable mingling of biography and autobiography. A model of this type of narrative is Bernard Vesper's *Die Reise: Romanessay* (1971; The Trip). The autobiographies written in Germany at this time also largely responded to the widespread effort to confront Germany history and work through the intersection of history and daily life. Autobiography, for many of its authors, served as the site for mourning Germany's past and its legacy in the private and public spheres, as well as a means of challenging standard versions of history. In the early 1980s, a "literature of the fathers" emerged as a subset of autobiographical writing in which sons and daughters took their fathers to task: this subset of the genre includes works such as Elisabeth Plessen's *Mitteilung an den Adel* (1977; *Such Sad Tidings*), Christoph Meckel's *Suchbild: Über meinen Vater* (1980; Image for Investigation: About My Father), Sigfrid Gauch's *Vaterspuren* (1979; Traces of Father), Jutta Schütting's *Der Vater* (1980, The Father), Heinrich Wiesner's *Der Riese am Tisch* (1979; The Giant at the Table), Peter Härtling's *Nachgetragene Liebe* (1980; Love in the Aftermath), Ruth Rehmann's *Der Mann auf der Kanzel* (1980; *The Man in the Pulpit*), and Brigitte Schwaiger's *Lange Abwesenheit* (1983; Long Absence). Dealing with Germany's fascist past from the viewpoint of survivors of the Holocaust or subsequent generations, a number of autobiographies bear witness to the atrocities of the Third Reich and the experience of persecution and exclusion, including Ruth Klüger's *weiter leben* (1989; Continuing On) and Cordelia Edvardson's *A Burned Child Seeks the Fire* (1987).

The destabilization of monolithic notions of self and author as authoritative originators and proprietors of texts allowed for the inclusion of heterogeneous voices. In the early 1970s, in both West and East Germany, many women explored their gendered and national identities, opening up a genre that had been representative predominantly of a male subject (Verena Stefan, *Häutungen* [1975; *Shedding*]). Critical interest in women's writing inspired a debate on the use of the term *autobiography* and the crafting of such neologisms as *The Female Autograph* (Domna Stanton) or *Autobiographics* (Leigh Gilmore, 1994), which expressed the resistance toward a signifier that codified a traditional concept of identity. With the advent of the 1980s, the emergent actors of autobiography included minorities in Germany. These narratives further challenged the dominant profile of the autobiographical subject and normative discourses of identity. They include differentiated life experiences from a variety of backgrounds and reflect identities that are neither fixed nor homogeneous but rather fragmented and heterogeneous. These new narratives include works by May Opitz, et. al, *Farbe Bekennen* (1986; *Showing Our Colors: Afro-German Women Speak Out*); Barbara Honigmann, *Roman von einem Kinde* (1986; Novel from a Child); Emine Svengi Özdamar, *Die Brücke vom Goldenen Horn* (1997; The Bridge of the Golden Horn); Esther Dischereit, *Joëmis Tisch*; *Eine jüdische Geschichte* (1988; Joëmis Table: A Jewish Story); and Lea Fleischmann, *Dies ist nicht mein Land: Eine Jüdin verläßt die Bundesrepublik* (1980; *This Is Not My Country: A Jewish Woman Leaves the Federal Republic*).

In recent years, the autobiographical enterprise has ventured into filmic representations of self-exploration such as Jutta Brückner's *Hungerjahre* (1980; *Years of Hunger*), Helma Sanders-Brahms's *Deutschland, bleiche Mutter* (1980; *Germany, Pale Mother*), Jeanine Meerapfel's *Malou* (1980), and Seyhan Derin's *Ben Annemin Kirziyim* (1996; *I'm My Mother's Daughter*).

Both authors and filmmakers in Germany have begun to stage the dramas of identity at a time when the exploration of subjectivity constitutes a vital defining element in the politics of identity.

BARBARA KOSTA

Further Reading

Folkenflik, Robert, editor, *The Culture of Autobiography*, Stanford, California: Stanford University Press, 1993

Goodman, Katherine, *Dis/Closures: Women's Autobiography in Germany between 1790 and 1914*, New York: Lang, 1986

Kosta, Barbara, *Recasting Autobiography: Women's Counterfictions in Contemporary German Literature and Film*, Ithaca, New York: Cornell University Press, 1994

Lejeune, Phillippe, *On Autobiography*, edited by Paul John Eakin, Minneapolis: University of Minnesota Press, 1989

Linville, Susan E., *Feminism, Film, Fascism: Women's Auto/biographical Film in Postwar Germany*, Austin: University of Texas Press, 1998

Misch, Georg, *A History of Autobiography in Antiquity*, translated by E.W. Dickes, Cambridge, Massachusetts: Harvard University Press, 1951

Smith, Sidonie, and Julia Watson, editors, *De/Colonizing the Subject: The Politics of Gender in Women's Autobiography*, Minneapolis: University of Minnesota Press, 1992

Stanton, Domna C., *The Female Autograph: Theory and Practice of Autobiography from the Tenth to the Twentieth Century*, Chicago: University of Chicago Press, 1987

Avant-Garde

Derived from the French military term for the forward troops, or vanguard, of an advancing army, the noun *avant-garde* was already being used figuratively in a number of contexts by the beginning of the 19th century. In the aftermath of the French Revolution, it enjoyed wide circulation as a metaphor for situating progressive political and social thinkers and radical thought and was favored especially by the Saint-Simonists. The term reached what Jost Hermand calls its "erster Höhepunkt" (first height/climax) during the events of 1848, when it was being applied not only to left-wing sociopolitical positions but also to forms of literature in sympathy with such progressive thinking. Even at this early stage, the term's rhetorically advantageous imprecision meant that a diverse spectrum of political scientists and social reformers could appropriate it without thereby subscribing to a common program or shared ideology. In the 19th century, the term frequently served as little more than a badge of honor or as part of a strategy of self-aggrandizement (as in its positive function in the pages of Kropotkin's anarchist publication *L'Avantgarde*), although reactionary circles used it pejoratively to characterize the excesses of fanatical extremists. By the end of the 19th century, the concept was being employed mainly in a depoliticized sense to refer to the work and attitudes of various groups of artists and writers considered—or considering themselves—to be significantly ahead of their time. To be part of the avant-garde or even simply to display tendencies that could be considered avant-gardist was to be associated with radical aesthetics and extreme innovativeness; the term no longer implied a progressive political position, any more than *modernism* did. However, in the 20th century the political and aesthetic connotations of *avant-garde* once more seemed to have merged in a number of areas (e.g., Soviet agitprop, the German political theater of the Weimar Republic, and political cabaret).

Although considerable historical disagreement has always existed about precisely which writers and movements can be assigned to the avant-garde and on the question of whether avant-garde works share certain definable stylistic and thematic features, the term,whether used as a noun or as an adjective, invariably retains three principal associations from its original military context. First, there is the idea of being among culture's attacking troops. In contexts in which belonging to the avant-garde signified commitment to accelerating the processes of cultural change by aggressively challenging and ultimately displacing the traditional, the connotation of fighting for the modern against the apologists of what the futurists called "passéism" enjoyed a powerful appeal. Although in such a perception, representatives of the avant-garde viewed themselves as the shock troops in ultramodernism's battle with the debilitating inheritance of past culture, what this specifically implied could differ radically from country to country and from context to context. A further complicating factor is the extent to which this antagonistic connotation of *avant-garde* often sat uneasily between literal and figurative senses or between an explicit prescriptive program and mere manifesto rhetoric. Aggressive metaphors festooned the language of early avant-garde manifestos and aesthetic programs: "Set fire to the library shelves! Divert the canals to flood the museums . . . Oh, the joy of seeing the glorious old canvasses bobbing up and down in the water, discolored and in shreds"; "we must spit on the Altar of Art"; "jettison Pushkin, Dostoevsky, Tolstoy"; "today we spit out the past that has stuck to our teeth"; "we throw down the gauntlet to the Cubo-Futurists"; "Go to Hell!"; and "Blast!" Not surprisingly, such aggressive rhetoric both reflected and aggravated a climate of irrationality and violence in which audience baiting, heckling, fighting with one's opponents (whether in print or in public places), and organized campaigns against the bourgeoisie became an important ingredient of the cultural polemics of many early historical avant-gardes. Point Ten of Marinetti's 1909 founding futurist manifesto stridently called for the destruction of "museums, libraries and academies of every kind" and identified museums with cemeteries, yet this particular avant-garde's supporters hardly ever engaged in direct acts of cultural iconoclasm. Similarly, the Russian cubofuturists saw themselves as administering a much-needed but merely figurative "slap in the face of public taste" (the title of a key manifesto of 1912 by David Burliuk et al.), and Mayakovsky urged his contemporaries to "toss the old masters overboard from the [metaphorical] ship of modernity," yet again even these avant-garde provocational strategies were essentially a matter of bombast or hostility directed mainly against the bourgeoisie. Although the status of art did undergo a process of what Benjamin later termed *Entauratisierung* (disappearance of aura) in the first quarter of the 20th century, displays of hostility to bourgeois notions of what constituted art or beauty were usually confined to symbolic gesturing (e.g., in Oberdada Johannes Baader and Raoul Hausmann's stochastic collage readings from Gottfried Keller's novel *Der grüne Heinrich* or in the overpainting of the Mona Lisa in Marcel Duchamp's *L.A.O.O.Q.*). What Hans Richter termed Dada "anti-art" was more a provocation of the bourgeoisie than an attempt to move the avant-garde in a direction that would have involved literal acts of cultural vandalism. In their rejection of previous styles and conventions, the avant-garde tended to see and present themselves as engaged in a battle for the new, which inevitably required the rejection of the old. In this sense, being avant-garde was easily reconcilable in German literary circles with Nietzschean metaphors of destroying in order to create and with the bohemian tactics of *épater le bourgeois.*

The second military connotation retained by the term *avant-garde* implies being a small elite group out ahead of the main fighting force. Just as the vanguard of an army reconnoiters well in advance of the main body of troops, so the literary avant-garde was prone to think of itself as being, in Calvin Tomkins's words, "ahead of the game" or standing, as Marinetti puts it, "like proud beacons or forward sentries against an army of hostile stars glaring down at us from their celestial encampments." To be out in front (as on a promontory or the bridge of a ship) was a popular figure of speech for a position of strength, a token of confidence in one's preparatory role as bearer of a new sensibility and in one's vision of the future. (It has even been suggested that the term *avant-garde* was preferred to *die Moderne,* its obvious rival in German-speaking contexts, because of this emphasis on being in an adversarial position of strength.) In some versions of the metaphor, the emphasis is simply on the conflict between the new and the old (as if in some variant on the *querelle des anciens et modernes* in 18th-century France). Here one finds a provocatively simple contrast between old and new, anachronistic art and that responding to its time. In other usages, the more important aspect is the teleological association of spearheading an attack on tradition specifically to prepare the way for a culture more appropriate to generations not yet born. As Lawton, Perloff, and others have argued, the artistic manifesto, setting out of the principles of a new art that was still only in the making and its use of theory to prophesy a new sensibility that was only gradually being evolved, was a genre as characteristic of the avant-garde mind-set as any of its other accomplishments.

One of the more problematic corollaries of the avant-garde's self-understanding in this respect was its widespread but naive equation of technical innovation with aesthetic progress. Many of the international rivalries between various forms of avant-garde, such as between Italian futurists and French cubists and orphists or between Marinetti and the English vorticists, centered on issues of priority and intellectual copyright; to have been the first to engage in a particular experiment (reducing or even destroying the hold of conventional syntax on poetic language, working with montage structures, or incorporating objets trouvés into works) or to set the agenda by introducing new themes into literature (the beauty of machines or the exhilarating experience of combat) was often vital to the credentials of individual avant-garde groupings. The unquestioning cult of innovation for its own sake nurtured the twin fallacious assumptions that the new was axiomatically better than the old and consequently that to have taken literature or painting as far as possible in a new direction should not ideally lead to cultural pluralism but to a situation in which each new avant-garde could be considered successful only if it replaced both passéist assumptions and all previous avant-gardes.

The third and arguably most obvious association retained from the original military context of the term is the idea of the avant-garde as a collective with a common goal and an esprit de corps, hence the importance of various theatrical and literary groupings within the avant-garde (e.g., Die Elf Scharfrichter, the Sturmkreis, the Cabaret Voltaire, Der Neue Club, the Wiener Gruppe, and the Living Theater). The avant-garde cannot be equated with any one specific literary or artistic movement, although Peter Bürger has presented an extremely influential case for seeing in surrealism and Dada paradigmatic manifestations of the early historical avant-garde. Although the early avant-garde can be associated especially with specific historical movements (futurism, cubism, orphism, some branches of Expressionism, vorticism, Dadaism, and surrealism), it cannot be regarded as synonymous with any one of these. Above all, this is because the term refers mainly to an attitude to tradition—to a series of shared assumptions about the aesthetic importance of innovation—and implies a stance toward the bourgeoisie rather than to a specific aesthetic program or a series of historically defining aesthetic characteristics, be they innovative features or the privileging of certain modernist aspects of content. Even a cursory examination of the salient features of the main historical avant-gardes of the early 20th century reveals as many stylistic and thematic elements of heterogeneity in method or content as similarities. Whereas Italian futurism and Russian cubofuturism were preoccupied with experimenting creatively with various forms of asyntactical language, neologism, telegraphic idiom, and poetic morphology, the language of vorticism and Dadaism tended to remain more within the bounds of conventional grammar. Whereas Russian futurism and German Dadaism worked with radical modes of typographical liberation, the typography and layout of other literary avant-gardes, including Expressionism, conformed to more conventional codes. The machine worship and the cult of war that became the hallmark of early Italian futurism found no equivalent in either Russian futurism or German Expressionism, and the importance attached to the unconscious by the surrealists (e.g., in Breton's "Manifeste du surréalisme," 1924) was seldom in evidence in other early avant-garde contexts. Moreover, the significance of collage and montage principles characteristic of Dadaism and surrealism is not echoed to the same extent in either vorticism or Expressionism. Even the cult of the abstract sound-poem (e.g., Hugo Ball's "Wolken") and of nonsense forms (e.g., Hans Arp's "kaspar ist tot") that played such a major role in Zürich Dadaism was not replicated to any significant extent in the more politically oriented Berlin Dadaism. Even the particular genres favored by the different early avant-gardes (visual collage, "Simultangedicht," cabaret performance, happening, and concrete poetry) differ substantially from country to country and from grouping to grouping. If the term *avant-garde* signals certain common attitudes to tradition, experimentation, the art of the future, and the bourgeoisie, the forms that these assumptions take are far from homogeneous.

Whereas the early, so-called heroic avant-gardes of the first quarter of the 20th century often stood in some direct or indirect relationship to World War I—there was a strong interventionist strain to Italian futurism in the period 1914–15, and both Expressionist drama and Dadaism had important pacifist impulses—a more radical repoliticization of the avant-garde took place only in the wake of 1918 with the Sovietized form of Russian futurism that gave rise to the Left Front of the Artists (Lef), the agitprop cultural campaigns of the 1920s, and the theater of Meyerhold and Mayakovsky. That revolutionary socialists and avant-garde writers and artists could work hand in hand was not merely the short-lived dream of certain constructivists and late futurists in the Soviet Union who initially did try to bring the revolution in society into contact with revolutionary aesthetics; it was also the stimulus to Piscator and Brecht's experimental political theater and elements within surrealism. When Aragon, Breton, Eluard, and Soupault changed the title of their journal *La Révolution surréaliste* to *Surréalisme au service de la révolution,* this was intended to give a clear signal that once more the political and aesthetic tendencies of the avant-garde were coming together with a common purpose. However, this was happening not only on the Left Wing: Mussolini's Italian fascism was for a while extremely sympathetic to futurist avant-gardism, and the feeling was reciprocated, not least by Marinetti himself. In Germany, a number of avant-garde and modernist writers of the Weimar period, including Hanns Johst and Gottfried Benn, gravitated toward National Socialism while their Expressionist contemporaries Herwarth Walden and Johannes R. Becher sought refuge in communism. For a while in the 1930s, the avant-garde and various totalitarianisms of the Left and the Right seemed able to accommodate one another, although eventually cultural clampdowns declared the avant-garde incompatible with either Zhdanovite socialist realism or with the Nazis' *völkisch* cultural program. Much of the German avant-garde from Expressionism onward was officially denigrated as "degenerate" in the official 1937 *Entartete Kunst* exhibition; at the same time, in the Soviet Union and in Marxist intellectual circles elsewhere, the avant-garde was gradually becoming equated with formalism, cosmopolitanism, and subjectivism. After 1945, arguments that already had been brought to bear against the avant-garde in the so-called *Expressionismusdebatte* (debate on expressionism), conducted in 1938 between Ernst Bloch and Georg Lukács in the pages of the Moscow exile magazine *Das Wort,* were revived in another guise in Lukács's polemics in *Wider den mißverstandenen Realismus* (1958; *The Meaning of Contemporary Realism*) and in the German Democratic Republic's pillorying of Brecht, Dessau, Eisler, and the Berliner Ensemble in the Cold War period. On the other hand, in the pluralist West the concept of the avant-garde—now more usually encountered in the form "neo-avant-garde"—remained either value free or largely positive.

As terms such as *Wiener Gruppe* and *Grazer Gruppe* suggest, the avant-garde had often become more parochial and marginalized in the decades since 1945. Although these are the two most important postwar avant-garde groups in Austrian literature, counting among their number such writers as Achleitner, Artmann, Bayer, Rühm, Wiener, the early Handke, and Frischmuth, they have enjoyed less international prominence than the groupings of the historical avant-garde. And like the experimental writers associated in the 1960s and 1970s with the Neues Hörspiel and with computer-generated permutational literature (influenced especially by the aesthetic theory of Max Bense and Elisabeth Walther and the experiments of the Ouvroir pour la Littérature Potentielle in Paris), their effect was short-lived. Arguably, some of the most significant postwar writers of the avant-garde, including Gomringer, Heißenbüttel, Jandl, Kriwet, Mayröcker, Mon, and Schmidt, worked independently of any avant-garde grouping, a situation that Lüdke refers to as "einen Avantgardismus der einzelnen" (avant-gardism of individuals). However, the picture is not simply one of fragmentation. A number of developments outside Germany—the *nouveau roman,* the methods of the Brazilian Noigandres concrete poets, pop art, neo-Dadaism, fluxus, and mixed-media happenings—all had a considerable influence on the directions taken by the avant-garde in German-speaking countries. Some of the most significant recent developments have been technical: the importance of stereophony for the experimental radio play, possibilities opened up by virtual reality for newer forms of concrete poetry, and hypertext in permutational literature (e.g., the 1998 CD-ROM version of Okopenko's *Lexikonroman*).

The further one moves into the 20th century, the more disputes over demarcation and questions of taxonomy have become important in discussions of the avant-garde. In the case of the early 20th-century avant-gardes, the main area of demarcation has been between the avant-garde and modernism. Although many commentators have tended to use the terms synonymously (Weightman's *The Concept of the Avant-Garde* is subtitled *Explorations in Modernism,* and Christopher Butler's account of *Early Modernism* [1994] uses *avant-garde* interchangeably with *modernist*), both Bürger and Huyssen have set out detailed arguments for not treating the two terms as if they were isomorphic. Murphy's *Theorizing the Avant-Garde* (1999) offers the most detailed critique to date of the applicability of Bürger's ideas to German literature

Whereas for Bürger modernism continues the myth of art's autonomous status within the aestheticist tradition of *l'art pour l'art,* the historical avant-gardes of the early 20th century are claimed to question the very institution of art, being in essence an "Angriff auf den Status der Kunst in der bürgerlichen Gesellschaft" (attack on the status of art within bourgeois society). Those who do not share Bürger's material aesthetic approach and see the connections posited between certain avant-garde techniques (above all, collage and montage) are dismissed as asking the wrong questions about the avant-garde: "Wo die Bedeutung der durch die historischen Avantgardebewegungen provozierten Zäsur in der Entwicklung der Kunst nicht im Angriff auf die Institution Kunst gesehen wird, rückt die Formfrage (organisches versus nicht-organisches Werk) notwendig ins Zentrum der Betrachtung" (Where the significance of the break in the development of art as caused by the historical avant-garde movements is not seen in the attack on art as an institution, the formal problem [organic versus non-organic work] necessarily comes to occupy the center of reflection). That the avant-garde must be seen historically as an exemplary challenge to the bourgeois "Institution Kunst" is clearly an assumption that endeared *Theorie der Avantgarde* to the 1968 generation of avant-garde scholars. Schulte-Sasse's claim that "the success of any theory of the avant-garde can be measured by how convincingly it can anchor the avant-garde formal principle of collage and montage" is self-validating as Bürger sees these two devices epitomizing the avant-garde's attempt to break down the barriers between art and life and to intervene in social reality. Even if misgivings have been voiced about the assumption that surrealism must be read as the paradigmatic manifestation of avant-garde, and concerning the extent to which other early avant-gardes shared surrealism's agenda, the issues that *Theorie der Avantgarde* raises are vital. Avant-gardes seldom restricted their attention to matters of aesthetic innovation; rather, they aimed at changing both sensibility and society. The main problem left unresolved by approaching the avant-garde through French surrealism—of whether avant-gardes are both part of a *Kunstrevolution* and at the same time essentially *Revolutionskunst*—is, historically speaking, too limiting a dichotomy. Some features of certain avant-gardes can certainly be interpreted using Bürger's model, but closer analysis of individual early avant-gardes or of avant-garde elements in post-1945 experimental literature would suggest that the phenomenon is more elusive than the proposed model.

J. J. WHITE

See also Der Blaue Reiter; Dadaism; Die Moderne

Further Reading

Bayerische Akademie der Schönen Künste, editors, *Avantgarde: Geschichte und Krise einer Idee,* Munich: Oldenbourg, 1966

Böhringer, H., "Avantgarde: Geschichten einer Metapher," *Archiv für Begriffsgeschichte* 122 (1978)

Bürger, Peter, *Theorie der Avantgarde,* Frankfurt: Suhrkamp, 1974; as *Theory of the Avant-Garde,* translated by Michael Shaw, Minneapolis: University of Minnesota Press, 1984

Calinescu, Matei, *Faces of Modernity: Avant-Garde, Decadence, Kitsch,* Bloomington: Indiana University Press, 1987

De Micheli, Mario, *Le avanguardie artistiche del Novocento,* Milan: Feltrinelli, 1966

Egbert, Donald D., "The Idea of 'Avant-Garde' in Art and Politics," *American Historical Review* 73 (1967)

Enzensberger, Hans Magnus, "Die Aporien der Avantgarde," *Einzelheiten II: Poesie und Politik,* Frankfurt: Suhrkamp, 1964; as "The Aporia of the Avant-Garde," translated by John Simon, in *The Consciousness Industry: On Literature, Politics, and the Media,* edited by Michael Roloff, New York: Continuum, 1974

Hermand, Jost, "Das Konzept 'Avantgarde'," in *Faschismus und Avantgarde,* edited by Reinhold Grimm and Jost Hermand, Königstein: Athenäum, 1980

Huyssen, Andreas, *After the Great Divide: Modernism, Mass Culture, Postmodernism,* Bloomington: Indiana University Press, 1986; Basingstoke: Macmillan, 1987

Lohner, Edgar, "Die Problematik des Begriffes der Avantgarde," in *Herkommen und Erneuerung,* edited by Gerald Gillespie and Edgar Lohner, Tübingen: Niemeyer, 1976; also in *Literarische Avantgarden,* edited by Manfred Hardt, Darmstadt: Wissenschaftliche Buchgesellschaft, 1989

Lüdke, W. Martin, editor, *"Theorie der Avantgarde": Antworten auf Peter Bürgers Bestimmung von Kunst und bürgerlicher Gesellschaft,* Frankfurt: Suhrkamp, 1976

Murphy, Richard, *Theorizing the Avant-Garde: Modernism, Expressionism, and the Problems of Postmodernity,* Cambridge and New York: Cambridge University Press, 1999

Poggioli, Renato, *Teoria dell'arte d'avanguardia,* Bologna: Società editrice il Mulino, 1962; as *The Theory of the Avant-Garde,* translated by Gerald Fitzgerald, Cambridge, Massachusetts: Belknap Press of Harvard University Press, 1968

Schulte-Sasse, Jochen, "Foreword: Theory of Modernism versus Theory of the Avant-Garde," in *Theory of the Avant-Garde,* by Peter Bürger, translated by Michael Shaw, Minneapolis: University of Minnesota Press, 1984

Szabolcsi, Miklos, *L'avant-garde littéraire et artistique comme phénomène international,* Amsterdam: Rodopi, 1969

———, "Avant-Garde, Neo-Avant-Garde, Modernism: Questions and Suggestions," *New Literary History* 3, no. 1 (1971)

Tomkins, Calvin, *Ahead of the Game: Four Versions of the Avant-Garde,* Harmondsworth: Penguin, 1965

Weightman, John, *The Concept of the Avant-Garde: Explorations in Modernism,* London: Alcove Press, and La Salle, Illinois: Library Press, 1973

Weisstein, Ulrich, "Le terme et le concept de l'avantgarde en Allemagne," *Revue de l'Université de Bruxelles* 1 (1975)

White, John J., *Literary Futurism: Aspects of the First Avant-Garde,* Oxford: Clarendon Press, and New York: Oxford University Press, 1990

Zima, Peter V., and Johann Strutz, editors, *Europäische Avantgarde,* Frankfurt and New York: Lang, 1987

May Ayim 1960–1996

May Ayim's name will be remembered as that of a writer who had the audacity not only to challenge the German literary canon but to force it to recognize and accept into its annals a term that goes against the self-understanding of Germans: Afro-German. As Ann Adams, the translator of *Farbe bekennen* (1986; *Showing Our Colors*), explains in the afterword to her translation, the name *Afro-German* "designates a population *native* to Germany, raised and acculturated as Germans, with little or no actual contact with their African cultural heritage." This name is thus distinguished from the names "Black French women or men," "Black Britons," and "African Americans," all of which pertain to overseas citizenship or transplanted populations and their descendants. The documented presence of Afro-Germans goes back to the 12th century. Nevertheless, the term evokes disbelief among white Germans and pain in Afro-Germans—the pain of having to live a difference that has no name. Like other members of the African diaspora, they are a hyphenated people.

The ambivalence contained in the hyphen expresses the need for a redefinition of a national German consciousness—a need that found expression in *Showing Our Colors*, the first book to be published in Germany dealing with Afro-Germans as a national entity. Ayim was a coeditor and coauthor of the book. It appeared in German in 1986, and it was followed by an English translation in 1992. The subtitle of the German edition reflects more accurately Ayim's lifelong concerns: "Afro-deutsche Frauen auf den Spuren ihrer Geschichte" (Afro-German Women in Search of Their History). Literature was thus a political tool for Ayim, a tool that she used to make Germans of color visible. As Audre Lorde underscores in her foreword to "Showing Our Colors," many Afro-Germans have "grown into Blackness in the almost total absence of a Black Community." Tortured by the fact that Afro-Germans were and are defined negatively in their own country because of an unacknowledged racism, Ayim forced herself to become an indomitable spokesperson. She bore this burden valiantly at first, but she ultimately broke down under the enormous pressure of combating a racism and sexism that accompanied her every breath, her every move.

A third of the book *Showing Our Colors* is based on Ayim's research into the history of people of African descent in Germany since the 12th century. This research led to the establishment of the Initiative Schwarzer Deutscher (Initiative of Black Germans) organization in 1985, which was the initial spark that ignited the black movement in Germany. In 1989, she cofounded LiteraturFrauen, an association aimed at furthering black and migrant female writers in Germany. Ayim's essay on racism and sexism in *Showing Our Colors* discusses how pseudoscientific literature and myths naturalize and universalize the understanding of blackness as negative and evil. Such an understanding coincided—very conveniently—with the colonial agenda of many European nations during the 19th century by justifying the oppression of blacks. As Ayim stresses, *negro* became a German concept in the 18th century, replacing the less differentiated term *moor* and signifying the ideological separation of Africa into white and black regions during the increasing colonization of the continent.

Consistent with the self-reflexive and polemical nature of her prose writings, Ayim's poetry is characterized by an uncompromisingly honest language. The lines "My fatherland is Ghana / my mother-tongue is German / I carry my homeland in my shoes" mirror her steadfast refusal to categorize or be categorized. She counters the image of a homogeneous monocultural Germany with her blackness and her Germanness. In *blues in schwarz weiss* (1995; Blues in Black White), she challenges with an honesty tempered by elegance and lyrical beauty the hypocritical belief in white homogeneity. The poem "aufbruch" (breaking out) reveals with startling clarity her indefatigable attempts to experience openness, friendliness, and unquestioned acceptance from within the darkness imposed on her and other Afro-Germans by the dominant German culture: "die sterne / in meiner nacht / sind silberne lachtränen / zu allem bereit" (the stars / in my night / are silver laughter-tears / open to everything).

Ayim's writings cross many boundaries by virtue of their sensitivity, humor, and political incisiveness. Although she focuses on the interdependency of racism and sexism in many of her poems, she vehemently refuses to portray herself as a hapless victim of such bigotry: "I wasn't broken by my experiences; instead I gained strength and a certain kind of knowledge from them. The situation of not being able to be integrated forced me to the active struggle which I no longer regard as a burden, but rather as a special challenge for honesty." The question that she heard all her life, "Where do you come from?" followed by the inevitable "When are you going back?" forced her to create an idiom within the dominant language that allowed her to survive. It was the source of her strength. She called this instinct for survival "grenzenlos und unverschämt" (boundless and audacious), which is the title of her book published posthumously in 1997. It is a "gedicht gegen die deutsche sch-einheit" (poem against the German sham-unity). This line shows the extraordinary power of Ayim's language, a language that permits meaning on various levels but does not lend itself easily to translation: a multilayered language not unlike that of a Lasker-Schüler or a Celan. Here, she combines the words "schein" (appearance, illusion) with "einheit" (unity), thus suggesting a word that gives the lie to homogeneity in Germany.

The language available to her could not and would not reflect her own lived experiences. Hence, other cultures and other languages needed to be explored in order to fill this lacuna. She explores yet another literary tool in the form of symbols and idioms from Ghana, her father's birthplace. Using "Adinkra" motifs, she problematizes notions of mortality prevalent in Christian Europe. Rather than accepting voicelessly the living death that is the lot of the black community, she finds new life in the wisdom of the Ashanti. According to the Ashanti, the soul of a dead person goes into the nonmaterial world of the ancestors but also remains in contact with the world of the living. Death is celebrated as eternal life. This belief finds expression in the Akan maxim "onwame nwu nu mawu" (when God dies, I die as well—but since God does not die, neither do I). Shortly before her own death in August 1996, Ayim wrote the poem "abschied" (farewell), in which she shares this celebratory and joyous vision of death with her readers. In this work, she questions the finality of death, seeking instead to dissolve all polarities, to subvert the perception of life and death as oppositional terms. This Nietzschean vision of a point beyond duality lends an incredible, almost magical hope to her poetry: "auf den weg zu mir

/ auf den weg zu dir" (on the way to me / on the way to you). It is true that the deep despondency that she felt about her personal life and a disturbing and depressing German present led to her death. But the word that she chose to describe her death—*Freitod* (free death)—contains Ayim's willingness to embrace death as a new beginning, whereas the term *suicide* carries with it all the ballast of endless despair. Through her texts, she has charged the black community in Germany and German society as a whole to indict a system that continues to permit and encourage racial purity and discrimination.

KAMAKSHI P. MURTI

See also Minority Literatures

Biography

Born as Afro-German (father from Ghana) in Hamburg, 1960. Since 1984, lived and worked in Berlin as a pedagogue and speech therapist; co-founded the Initiative Schwarze Deutsche, 1985, and LiteraturFrauen, 1989, associations aiming to further black and migrant female authors in Germany; her poems have appeared in numerous journals and anthologies. Died 9 August 1996.

Selected Works

Poetry
blues in schwarz weiß, 1995
nachtgesang, 1997

Other
contributions to *Farbe bekennen: Afro-deutsche Frauen auf den Spuren ihrer Geschichte*, 1986; as *Showing Our Colors*, translated by Ann Adams, 1992
contributions to *Entfernte Verbindungen. Rassismus, Antisemitismus, Klassenunterdrückung*, 1993

Further Reading

Gilman, Sander L., *On Blackness without Blacks: Essays on the Image of the Black in Germany*, Boston: Hall, 1982
Grimm, Reinhold, and Jost Hermand, editors, *Blacks and German Culture*, Madison: University of Wisconsin Press, 1986
Kron, Stefanie, *Fürchte dich nicht, Bleichgesicht!: Perspektivenwechsel zur Literatur afro-deutscher Frauen*, Münster: Unrast, 1996

B

Ingeborg Bachmann 1926–1973

A good ten years before the social revolution of the 1960s brought on a new wave of feminism, Ingeborg Bachmann expressed most of its major themes, yet so subtly as to remain unseen and unsung at first. Her uniquely unconditional stance and radically critical thinking, conveyed in highly artistic, sophisticated ways, were recognized by the reading public and the scholarly world largely only after her death. Today, Bachmann stands as an icon of early postwar feminist writing; indeed, she was an isolated voice at a time when the new feminism was neither defined nor fashionable. Bachmann's creative work emerged alongside studies and research in philosophy that culminated in a dissertation (1949) on Martin Heidegger. In this work, she attempted to refute the philosopher—and with him an entire world of thought in male-conceived paradigms. At the same time, however, she realized the sheer impossibility of such an undertaking, for language, itself part of the established system, cannot express what is in need of being expressed. This is the problematic of much of the author's writing.

Her earliest publications of prose and poetry date from 1946. These works set the theme and tone for the author's work throughout; that is, alienation from sensory reality resulting from a male-defined, set system. The main body of Bachmann's later work demonstrates that the thoughts of even the most distinguished male writers among her contemporaries do not pass her scrutiny. Not only is a healthy relationship between the sexes as it ought to be lastly impossible for Bachmann, the male-female duality and tension as manifested in all facets of life inform her art, constituting its genesis and rich content, and at the same time rendering it desperate because of the ultimate impossibility of its expression. Nevertheless, Bachmann became firmly established among postwar writers of the German language, representing an altogether different voice from that of Heinrich Böll, Günter Grass, Uwe Johnson, or Max Frisch, all of whom she knew well. In Gruppe 47, where she had her beginnings, the only other woman writer to gain renown was Ilse Aichinger, who did not eventually match Bachmann's degree of radical thought or productivity.

For Gruppe 47 members and critics of that era, Ingeborg Bachmann was first and foremost a lyric poet; in fact, the male literary establishment of the time insisted on that label for Bachmann even when her first volume of prose appeared in 1961, which many judged a failure (e.g., R. Hartung, 1961). It took another generation of critics, the development of feminist criticism, and the establishment of women critics before Bachmann was fully recognized as a giant among women writers of prose fiction. Circumspect as to her personal life, Bachmann quotes were sometimes exploited by the popular press (e.g., the spurious "Kaiser Interviews" in *Süddeutsche Ztg. Magazine*). While this may have gained Bachmann a wider audience, it did injustice to one of the greatest minds of the 20th century who, at a very young age, was to become the first lecturer to occupy the prestigious, newly created chair for Poetics at the University of Frankfurt in 1959–60. It would be easy to condemn male critics and the popular press for mistaken directions in Bachmann reception, but misrepresentation and even falsification occurred as well in Elfriede Jelinek's adaptation of the first and last novel that Bachmann published during her lifetime, *Malina* (1971), as a film script. The resulting film by Werner Schroeter (1991) simplifies the highly complex existence of a writing woman (and her female or male aspects), situated between father, partner, lover (and their male or female aspects), and other representatives of patriarchy, as a mere treatment of the relationship between the sexes. *Malina,* however, is much more—it is about violence and physical as well as mental torture in human relationships, set in the historical context of fascism and its aftermath. As Alice Schwarzer put it, ten years after the novel, it was being interpreted to death, and another ten years later, it was being filmed to death (*Die Zeit,* 25 January 1991). On the whole, Bachmann criticism, whether feminist, antifeminist, postfeminist, or other brands, has not come to consensus; controversy continues. The Bachmann oeuvre may lastly defy "definitive" interpretation, but the open questions that remain may best be answered by being asked anew in artistic forms such as *Ingeborg Bachmann—wer?,* a text collage for the stage by Claus Peymann (1995); Christa Wolf's integration of Bachmann's poem "Erklär mir, Liebe" (Explain to Me, Love), in the fourth part of *Voraussetzungen einer Erzählung: Kassandra* (1983; Conditions of a Narrative: Cassandra); or Karin Struck's novel *Ingeborg B.* (1993). Titles and treatises such as these hint at the mystery surrounding not only the person but also the work of the author thematized here. These treatments see the Bachmann oeuvre as better understood through artistic transformation and adaptation rather than through critical analysis.

Compared to contemporary criticism of Bachmann's prose and the general reception of her work, criticism of Bachmann's early lyric poetry appears to be relatively unified as to its artistic worth. *Die gestundete Zeit* (1953; Time Measured in Hours) and *Anrufung des Großen Bären* (1956; Invocation of the Great Bear) were immediately recognized as the work of a radically new voice within postwar poetry in the German language. Given the political and literary history immediately preceding these works, National Socialism and the ensuing *Trümmerliteratur* (literature of rubble, literature among the ruins), Bachmann's poems were a sensation in German-speaking countries, much like those of Paul Celan. In its insistence on radical truth rather than high aestheticism, this poetry hit the nerve of the "lost generation." These lyrics exercised fascination because of an obvious consciousness of historical process, which made them realistic, a certain enigmatic style, and a utopian dimension, which surpassed the passivity of earlier writers who produced poetry of lament and reckoning. In such poems as "Alle Tage" (Every Day) or "Früher Mittag" (Early Noon) in her first volume, Bachmann communicates new signs of reality, which she recognizes as a continuation of the war in the patriarchal society and politics of the 1950s. The attempts at depoliticizing Bachmann's poetry was made repeatedly early on, a mistake amply rectified in criticism of the late 1980s and 1990s. The poetry of the second volume, especially, has seen diverse interpretations, including mythological, theological, existential, and psychoanalytical readings, yet almost all of it takes into account Bachmann's more-or-less hidden political agenda of explaining an uneven world that all but incapacitates the female side of art and life.

Although Ingeborg Bachmann did not write drama for the theater stage, the genre is present in her oeuvre in the form of radio plays and librettos. Of the five radio plays from 1952 to 1958, the last one, *Der gute Gott von Manhattan* (The Good God of Manhattan), is the best known. At a time when radio plays reached their greatest popularity, in part because of the lack of other media, Bachmann was present in that literary genre alongside Günter Eich, Ilse Aichinger, Heinrich Böll, and Alfred Andersch. Similar to her earliest radio play and to some measure *Die Zikaden* (1955; Cicadas), with its conflict between dream and reality, the last play has at its theme the dream of absolute love and freedom; the "Good God" constitutes the patriarchal principle in society that opposes those absolutes.

The three texts for music by Hans Werner Henze attest to Bachmann's affinity to music. The 1960 libretto for an opera by Henze is not a mere adaptation of Heinrich von Kleist's play, *Prinz Friedrich von Homburg* (1811) but stands as a text in its own right. In a considerably tightened version, the title figure in *Der Prinz von Homburg,* agonizing over his role and capability as statesman, now appears as the definite protagonist and the center of dramatic action while his antagonist blends into the group of courtiers around him.

Bachmann's plays did not achieve the critical acclaim of the poetry, but the prose was yet to surpass the latter. From today's perspective, seen through the criticism, which has grown vast, Ingeborg Bachmann's prose works are of greater and more lasting significance than either her poetry or plays. Her first collection of short stories, *Das dreißigste Jahr* (1961; *The Thirtieth Year*), caused a rash of comments to the effect that the lyric poet ought to stick to poetry and that the stories were not rationally conceived. This stereotyping of the female voice as being better suited to poetry than prose, however, was dispelled over time. Nevertheless, Bachmann did receive a literary prize for the collection. The title story appears as the most weighty because of its length and the complexity of the main character. The existential crisis of the 30 year old is made visible almost as if he is a model case; a definite turning point in his life shows the loss of a stable, reliable reality as the central experience of modern human beings. The male hero of this story sees his existence as previously known crumble; he tries to flee from the expectations of bourgeois society by way of travel but meets with a car accident that shocks him into the realization that he must redefine himself and his life. His nonfunctioning part, his alter ego, dies at the wheel; the new person survives, having passed a test of life and realizing that a new language and a new existence can and must be found. The individual recognizes his will and his potential to win in a society that violates his freedom.

The story of this anonymous, faceless individual, however, remains inconsequential when compared to the societal problematic in "Unter Mördern und Irren" (Among Murderers and Madmen) in the same collection. In this text from the late 1950s, Bachmann clearly establishes a world divided into executioners and victims, masters and slaves, and colonizers and the colonized, giving an illustration of the continuation of war in so-called peace times in the form of unreflected, unreformed, and dominating maleness. Resembling madmen, a group of drinking veterans relive, amid bursts of laughter, wartime tales of killing; another gathering nearby is heard to be screaming soldiers' songs, and an anonymous stranger who is critical of these groups—while telling of his own inability to shoot on the front lines and his subsequent confinement to a mental institution during war—is murdered by a madman at the pub. Although Bachmann gave this story a male narrator, the author's specific view of a world forever divided in maleness and femaleness shines through. The Jewish characters in the story are the put-upon figures, and the presumed mental case is the victim. Society itself, the author-narrator states, is the greatest and most frequent site and scene of murder (*Mordschauplatz*), and peace is a continuation of war in the form of patriarchy.

The last entry in this collection, "Undine geht" ("Undine Departs"), is Bachmann's best-known and most frequently reprinted story to date. A female voice is delivering a speech on the subject of a misguided, wrong, and divided world, heaping criticism, scorn, and unconditional rejection upon bourgeois society. According to this speech, men have caused society to go wrong, and their conventional, subservient female partners in bourgeois marriage support this mistaken system. Yet the speaker Undine, from her perspective of an otherworldly being, is able to convey hope for rectification and for a better future relationship between the sexes. The dream of absolute love as thematized in earlier poetry is transformed here into a utopian dream of a perfect society at the end of this story, which oscillates between poetic prose and rational argumentation in rhetorical style. The open-ended story dissolves into lyric lines of invitation, longing, and hope, thus constituting one of Bachmann's most optimistic pieces of writing.

"Undine Departs" would seem to be a literary illustration of what Bachmann originally intended to do with her dissertation in philosophy in 1949. According to her own statement, she tried, without success at the time, to refute Martin Heidegger in this scholarly endeavor; yet in her art, she was able to counter and even to contradict with poetic but nevertheless unmistakable language some of the statements in the philosopher's treatises. Furthermore, "Undine Departs" is a key work to the intellectual and political culture of its time, discussing the essential problematic of the women's movement, its anthropological sting, and necessary societal affront.

Bachmann continued writing short stories throughout the 1960s, publishing a collection of five stories under the title of *Simultan* (*Three Paths to the Lake*) in 1972. One of these stories, "Das Gebell" (Dog Barking), presents a plot and characters that appear again in the posthumously published fragmentary novel *Der Fall Franza.* An old mother living alone has hallucinations about dog barking. Allowing herself to be dominated by her son, she had had to give away the dog he hated but she loved. This proves her false love and obedience toward her son, a famous psychiatrist and author on the lecture circuit, who exploits both her and his wife for his self-esteem, vanity, and power. The women's lives are destroyed in subtle ways, but this is shown only metaphorically in this and the other stories. None of these women are able to escape, articulate, or even recognize the destructions of their lives. Even as professionals they still function as catalysts, mediators, and helpers in the lives of men. Their names are frequently in the diminutive, which expresses their diminished standing and underling role.

Der Fall Franza (1979; The Case of Franza) revives Franziska, the psychiatrist Dr. Jordan, and his mother of "Dog Barking." This time, however, female destruction, self-destruction, and suicide are developed with greater complexity and shown directly rather than symbolically. Christa Wolf pointed out the colonization factor in all of Bachmann's novels. These novels were published first in *Werke* (1978; *Collected Works*) and as the *Todesarten-Zyklus* (1979; Ways of Dying), which contains the fragments *Der Fall Franza, Requiem für Fanny Goldmann*, and the completed novel *Malina.* The white male has colonized not only peoples of other races and cultures but women everywhere.

> He has robbed me of my goods. My laughter, my tenderness, my ability for joy, my compassion, my ability to help, my radiance, he has stepped on each of these until they were no longer able to appear. But why does somebody do that, I don't understand . . .

Franza's last words are a curse on the white race, in which "die Weißen" certainly means the white male, the colonizer and master of the colonized.

Bachmann's only finished novel published during her lifetime is *Malina.* It has been called both a love story and a murder mystery. There is a love triangle with a difference: the narrator is an unnamed woman writer who has a male lover, Ivan, and a male alter ego, Malina, perhaps the male side of the narrator's self. The middle part of the book refers to the 1949 Carol Reed film *The Third Man* and explores in dream sequences how racism prevails after 1945 in the form of patriarchy. *Heimat* is a place that contains the cemetery of the murdered daughters. National identity is a theme throughout the novel, with Germanic, Hungarian, and Slavic elements, but the political alliances have been transformed into components of human relationships. Most of all, however, *Malina* is a novel about the obstacles in the process of writing. At the center of the novel lies the difficulty, anguish, and torture of asserting a female voice and self. According to an interview with the author, the woman attempting to write a book has been symbolically murdered several times over, but she has not taken the final disappearing step. She is so damaged that she is no longer useful in life, and she dies, at the very end of the novel, by disappearing into a wall. The final line, "It was murder," sounds like an indictment.

The continuous suppression and destruction of the female, whether daughter, lover, writer, or other in patriarchal society, is captured in the lines spoken to Malina by the female narrator: "Es ist immer Krieg. Hier ist immer Gewalt. Hier ist immer Kampf. Es ist der ewige Krieg." (It's always war. Here there is always violence. Here there is always struggle. It is the eternal war.)

Elfriede Jelinek learned from Ingeborg Bachmann's work, and both writers say that fascism is not a temporary madness but is always ever present. It can appear in the relationship between parents and children, men and women, those in authority and those without, and (mental) colonizers and the colonized. *Malina* carries out the further development of Bachmann's theme from the beginning: that patriarchal fascism is in slow and secret ways just as destructive as murder, with the difference that it entails a long torture in the form of mental cruelty. The female characters in this fiction lose in a male-conceived system. They are and will be the objects of male dominance.

The strong impact and high artistic worth of Ingeborg Bachmann's writing is confirmed in recent criticism that was written 50 years after the genesis and conception of the first set of stories. While the latest controversy also surrounds methodological questions, it primarily represents generational and, above all, gender differences in reception, differences that may remain just as irreconcilable as the ones that Bachmann herself had seen in society. The story "Undine Departs" is once again the subject in an article by Susanne Baackmann, who concludes that this story redefines the ancient structures of desire between the sexes and suggests the possibility of quite a different meeting between men and women. Because the old pattern of the one predesigning and predefining the other does not work, it must be given up for a painful but radical demystifying and demythologizing of the traditional, male-conceived Undine, or female, or Other; only then will a just relationship between the sexes be possible. After Baackmann's publication of her new findings, renewed scholarly controversy about the work of Ingeborg Bachmann ensued and continues today.

IRMGARD HUNT

Biography

Born in Klagenfurt, Austria, 25 June 1926. Studied at the universities of Graz, Innsbruck, and Vienna; Ph.D. in philosophy, 1950; lived with the composer Hans Werner Henze, 1953–56; lived with the writer Max Frisch, 1958–62; worked as a script writer and editor, Rot-Weiss-Rot radio station, Vienna, 1951–53; worked as a freelance writer in Ischia, Naples, Rome, and Munich, 1953–57; in the United States, 1955; in Rome and Zurich, 1958–62; in West Berlin, 1963–65; in Rome from 1965; visiting lecturer on poetics, Frankfurt University, 1959–60. Gruppe 47 Prize, 1953; Culture Circle of German Industry Literature Award, 1955; Bremen Prize, 1957; Association of German Critics Literary Award, 1961; Büchner Prize, 1964; Great Austrian State Prize, 1968; Wildgans Prize, 1971. Died 17 October 1973.

Selected Works

Collections
Werke, edited by Christine Koschel, Inge von Weidenbaum, and Clemens Münster, 4 vols., 1978
Sämtliche Erzählungen, 1980
Sämtliche Gedichte, 1983
In the Storm of Roses: Selected Poems, edited and translated by Mark Anderson, 1986

Poetry
Die gestundete Zeit, 1953
Anrufung des Großen Bären, 1956
Gedichte: Eine Auswahl, 1966
Die Gedichte, 1980

Fiction
Das dreißigste Jahr (stories), 1961; revised edition, 1966; as *The Thirtieth Year,* translated by Michael Bullock, 1964
Malina, 1971; as *Malina,* translated by Philip Boehm, 1990
Simultan (stories), 1972; as *Three Paths to the Lake,* translated by Mary Fran Gilbert, 1989
Undine geht: Erzählungen, 1973; as "Undine Departs," translated by Cedric Hentschel, in *German Short Stories,* 1975
Meisterzählungen, 1974
Der Tag des Friedens, 1976
Der Fall Franza, 1979
Requiem für Fanny Goldman, 1979
Die Fähre, 1982

Plays
Ein Geschäft mit Träumen (radio play), 1952
Das Herrschaftshaus (radio play), 1952
Herrenhaus (radio play), 1954
Die Zikaden (radio play), 1955
Der Idiot, music by Hans Werner Henze (produced 1952), 1955
Der gute Gott von Manhattan (radio play), 1958
Der Prinz von Homburg (opera libretto), music by Hans Werner Henze (from the play by Heinrich von Kleist) (produced 1960), 1960
Der junge Lord (opera libretto), music by Hans Werner Henze (produced 1965), 1965; as *The Young Milord,* translated by Eugene Walter, 1967
Die Hörspiele (radio plays; includes *Ein Geschäft mit Träumen; Die Zikaden; Der gute Gott von Manhattan*), 1976

Other
Jugend in einer österreichischen Stadt (memoir), 1961
Gedichte, Erzählungen, Hörspiele, Essays, 1964
Ein Ort für Zufälle, 1965
Frankfurter Vorlesungen: Probleme zeitgenössischer Dichtung, 1980
Die Wahrheit ist dem Menschen zumutbar: Essays, Reden, kleinere Schriften, 1981
Das Honditschkreuz, 1983
Wir müssen wahre Sätze finden: Gespräche und Interviews, edited by Christine Koschel and Inge von Weidenbaum, 1983
Liebe: Dunkler Erdteil: Gedichte aus den Jahren 1942–1967, 1984
Anrufung der grossen Dichterin (essays), 1984

Translations
Giuseppe Ungaretti, *Gedichte: Italienisch und deutsch,* 1961
Italienische Lyrik des 20. Jahrhunderts, edited by Christine Wolter, translated by Bachmann et al., 1971
Freude der Schiffbrüche, edited by Christine Wolter, translated by Bachmann et al., 1977

Further Reading

Achberger, Karen, "Das alltägliche Unerhörte: Ingeborg Bachmann's Modernist Novellas," in *Neues zu Altem: Novellen der Vergangenheit und der Gegenwart,"* edited by Sabine Cramer, Munich: Fink, 1996
Baackmann, Susanne, "'Beinahe mörderisch wahr': Die neue Stimme der Undine: Zum Mythos von Weiblichkeit und Liebe in Ingeborg Bachmanns "Undine geht,'" *German Quarterly* 68, no. 1 (1995)
Bartsch, Kurt, *Ingeborg Bachmann,* Stuttgart: Metzler, 1988
Beicken, Peter, *Ingeborg Bachmann,* Munich: Beck, 1988; 2nd revised edition, 1992
Höller, Hans, editor, *"Der dunkle Schatten, dem ich schon seit Anfang folge": Ingeborg Bachmann: Vorschläge zu einer neuen Lektüre des Werks,* Vienna: Löcker, 1982
Hunt, Irmgard, "Bemerkungen über Lichtung, Erleuchtung, Epiphanie" (Ingeborg Bachmann wider Martin Heidegger), *Sprache im technischen Zeitalter* 28, no. 113 (1990)
Special Ingeborg Bachmann Issue, *Modern Australian Literature* 18, no. 3/4 (1985)

Malina 1971

Novel by Ingeborg Bachmann

First published in 1971, *Malina* is usually considered to be Ingeborg Bachmann's most significant work of fiction. Originally conceived as one of a series of works under the heading *Todesarten* (Death Styles), *Malina* is the only novel that Bachmann completed, although sufficient material from a second novel, *Der Fall Franza* (1979), exists for meaningful comparisons to be made. As with much of Bachmann's later work, *Malina* first came to be properly appreciated after the development of feminist approaches to her work in the late 1970s. Since then it has it has provided the substance for many different analyses, which have shown the complexity and ambivalence of the novel.

The initial reception of *Malina* was mixed. While some critics still lamented Bachmann's departure from poetry into fiction and regarded the novel as a failed lyric, most reacted more positively, usually interpreting it at first as a love story. Varying degrees of importance were attached to elements that were considered autobiographical; little was known or mentioned about the fact that it was planned as part of a cycle of works (Borhau). Male critics in particular referred to Bachmann's biography, while female critics, who tended to regard the novel more positively, were—then as now—divided as to how far it should be regarded as a feminist work.

More fundamental analyses were developed in the late 1970s. Ellen Summerfield's thesis (1976) first revealed the multilayered quality of the text. Summerfield suggests that the main figures in the novel are to be interpreted as dimensions of the narrator herself, and she sees this "dissolution" of the female narrator ("Auflösung der Figur") as a structuring device in the novel. Since then, it has been generally accepted that the figures exist on various planes of consciousness and in certain respects complement each other. The figure of the narrator has been variously interpreted as breaking down into—or, alternatively, as being constituted only by—different aspects of the narrative, including both the other characters and the social and historical context of Austria.

The structure of the novel initially proved perplexing. A stream-of-consciousness mode predominates and allows breaks in the time sequence to occur. Events from an indeterminate past are brought into present focus on the narrator's *Gedankenbühne* (mental stage). An allusive prologue, at times abstract and philosophical, introduces the characters and the setting: "Vienna," "Today." Three further chapters concentrate on different dimensions of the nameless "Ich" (I) who narrates. "Glücklich mit Ivan" ("Happy with Ivan") depicts the joyful aspect of her life, when the narrator participates in activities in the external world. The second chapter, "Der dritte Mann" (The Third Man), throws the outside world into dark relief, as the narrator experiences an internal world of dreams, which place the individual present into the perspective of a wider historical and social dimension. The final chapter, "Von letzten Dingen" (Last Things), shows the narrator in conflict with the man called Malina; she eventually retreats and disappears "into the wall," a highly problematic conclusion to the novel.

A crucial issue involves this question: who is Malina, and why does the novel take its title from him? Many indications suggest that, if Ivan represents the narrator's emotional needs, Malina embodies her intellectualism and her rational side. A criticism levelled at *Malina,* particularly by feminist critics, is that the contrast between Malina's rationality and the emotional female narrator suggests a conventional view of male and female roles. Bachmann herself declared that that she was only able to write the novel after she discovered the figure of Malina, a male figure, to form the focus of the text, which draws attention to the fact that at one level *Malina* depicts the struggle and fate of a woman writer who can be interpreted as seeking wholeness by integrating her rational and emotional dimensions. While the narrator's relationship with Ivan endures, she is creative. At his behest, she ceases writing the work she had planned, with the ominous title "Todesarten," an ironic self-referential gesture on Bachmann's part. She turns instead to writing an optimistic tale. The fragments of this story, the "Prinzessin von Kagran," suggest a utopian vision in which an ideal past, not yet beset with national boundaries or local languages, will be reflected in an ideal future in which the women will "have shining eyes." With the decline of her relationship with Ivan, the narrator's creativity declines, and the utopian vision of wholeness is lost, as she departs and leaves Malina's voice as the only one to be heard.

Critical attention to the social concerns expressed in *Malina* has developed more recently and has focused on the central chapter, "Der dritte Mann." The narrator's dreams about a father figure, who is at once "her" father and a representative of the generation who supported Nazism, imply a correlation between "fascism" in the political context and at the personal level, which in turn suggests a metaphor for the oppression of women in the family. This aspect has a parallel in *Der Fall Franza,* where the mental violation and rape of the individual woman, Franza, are reflected in ideas about colonial exploitation. Bachmann's treatment of the idea of "fascism" at the private level—as a parallel to, or a metaphor for, political exploitation—has been taken up by her successors, who use terms that sometimes echo *Malina,* as seen especially in the work of Austrian women writers, including Elfriede Jelinek and Elisabeth Reichart.

A film based on *Malina* (directed by Werner Schroeter from a script by Elfriede Jelinek) concentrates on the father figure's Nazism and interweaves elements from the novel with aspects of Bachmann's biography. Thus, instead of disappearing into the wall at the end of the film, the writer is consumed by flames, which parallels Bachmann's own death in a house fire. Recent intertextual approaches reveal that *Malina* has inspired many writers of fiction; they also point to Bachmann's own fruitful use of material from many sources, including music (Achberger).

JULIET WIGMORE

Editions

First Edition: *Malina,* Frankfurt: Suhrkamp, 1971
Critical edition: *"Todesarten"-Projekt,* vol. 3.1–3.2, *Malina,* edited by Monika Albrecht and Dirk Göttsche, Munich: Piper, 1995
Translation: *Malina,* translated by Philip Boehm, New York: Holmes and Meier, 1990

Further Reading

Achberger, Karen, *Understanding Ingeborg Bachmann,* Columbia: University of South Carolina Press, 1995
Boa, Elizabeth, "Women Writing about Women Writing and Ingeborg Bachmann's *Malina,"* in *New Ways in Germanistik,* edited by Richard Sheppard, Oxford: Oxford University Press, and New York: Berg, 1990
Borhau, Heidi, *Ingeborg Bachmanns "Malina": Eine Provokation?* Würzburg: Königshausen und Neumann, 1994
Duffaut, Rhonda, "Ingeborg Bachmann's 'Alternative States': Rethinking Nationhood in *Malina," Modern Austrian Literature* 29, no. 3/4 (1996)
Eifler, Margret, "Ingeborg Bachmann: *Malina," Modern Austrian Literature* 12, no. 3–4 (1979)
Ezergailis, Inta, *Women Writers—The Divided Self,* Bonn: Bouvier, 1982
Gürtler, Christa, *Schreiben Frauen Anders? Untersuchungen zu Ingeborg Bachmann und Barbara Frischmuth,* Stuttgart: Heinz, 1983
Jelinek, Elfriede, *Isabelle Huppert in "Malina": Ein Filmbuch, nach dem Roman von Ingeborg Bachmann,* Frankfurt: Suhrkamp, 1991
Koch-Klenske, Eva, "Die vollkommene Vergeudung: Eine Leseart des Romans *Malina* von Ingeborg Bachmann," in *Die Sprache des Vaters im Körper der Mutter,* edited by Rolf Haubl et al., Giessen: Anabas, 1984
Steiger, Robert, *"Malina": Versuch einer Interpretation des Romans von Ingeborg Bachmann,* Heidelberg: Winter, 1978
Stoll, Andrea, *Ingeborg Bachmanns "Malina,"* Frankfurt: Suhrkamp, 1992
Summerfield, Ellen, *Ingeborg Bachmann: Die Auflösung der Figur in ihrem Roman "Malina,"* Bonn: Bouvier, 1976
Wigmore, Juliet, "Ingeborg Bachmann," in *The Modern German Novel,* edited by Keith Bullivant, Leamington Spa and New York: Berg, 1987

Simultan 1972

Short Stories by Ingeborg Bachmann

Simultan (1972; *Three Paths to the Lake*) was the last major work by Ingeborg Bachmann published during her lifetime. The five stories contained in the collection were composed simultaneously with *Malina,* and many characters, incidents, and locations overlap with those described in the novel. In an interview, Bachmann implied that the stories were written as "light relief" from *Malina,* and some stories give an impression of lightness, even triviality—something for which Bachmann was initially reproached by certain critics, despite an otherwise positive reception. Approaches to *Simultan* have undergone various phases, which largely correspond to changing perspectives on Bachmann's work as a whole. Thus, the initial concentration on her treatment of language as a thematic element ("Simultan") was later overtaken by interpretations that treated the stories particularly in relation to their depiction of women's position in society and other social concerns (seen in "Simultan," "Probleme, Probleme," and "Ihr glücklichen Augen"; "Words for Words," "Problems, Problems," and "Eyes to Wonder"). Later interpretations place increasing emphasis upon the social and political concerns of Bachmann's stories (exemplified in "Drei Wege zum See" and "Das Gebell"; "Three Paths to the Lake" and "The Barking") and foreground their links with *Malina* and Bachmann's incomplete novel *Der Fall Franza* (1979).

Interest in *Simultan* was stimulated particularly by feminist readings from the mid-1970s. Concerns about women's role in society were perceived to be a latent preoccupation of much of Bachmann's work, and these concerns emerge most explicitly in this collection and in *Malina.* All five stories of *Simultan* focus on a female protagonist. Two of these figures, Nadja in "Simultan" and Elisabeth Matrei in "Drei Wege zum See," are successful professional women, while the main characters in the other stories have largely withdrawn from social interaction. Common to all these women is a sense of isolation and a lack of satisfaction with their lives. In the title story, Nadja has become increasingly aware that her existential problems derive from her profession as an interpreter; she is like a machine, a vehicle for other people's words, who rarely expresses her own needs or speaks her own language. When she is eventually faced with a text that she is unable to translate, a passage from the New Testament that is symbolic of the meaning of life, she is forced to realize her own limitations. This *Grenzerlebnis* (threshold experience), paradoxically, brings a sense of relief, as she realizes that she is not merely a perfect mechanism. The inadequacy of language also symbolizes her failed relationships with men, who neither literally nor metaphorically "speak her language." The outer plot of the story depicts Nadja taking a short holiday with a fellow Viennese, with whom, unusually, she is able to speak her native dialect; yet she is nevertheless unable to develop a meaningful relationship with him. This causes her to realize that she has hitherto placed too great a trust in the power of language. Nadja, whose name is a Russian diminutive of the word for "hope," finally returns to her working life feeling more optimistic, because the doubt that has been cast on language has opened up new possibilities for her.

In the centrally placed story, "Ihr glücklichen Augen," the limited perspective of the protagonist, Miranda, is expressed through the image of shortsightedness. Miranda's myopia is a self-induced condition; she constantly loses or breaks her glasses, despite knowing that she is dependent upon them, as she prefers to withdraw from the outside world. Deliberately overlooking her lover's imminent departure from her life, she colludes in her own deception by pretending that the situation suits her. Miranda's self-inflicted isolation and dependency has a parallel in "Probleme, Probleme," where the protagonist, Beatrix, believes herself to be independent, because she has no need to work, while actually living at others' expense. Her freedom, however, is shown to be easily disrupted. From the angle of feminist interpretations particularly, the lightness of tone evident in these two stories proves to be deceptive and to underscore the fact that the protagonists collude in their own oppression. In "Das Gebell," too, the elderly Frau Jordan and her daughter-in-law Franziska (the Franza figure in *Der Fall Franza*) collude in denying the oppression practiced by her son and Franziska's husband, Leo Jordan. While Frau Jordan takes refuge in senility, Franziska discovers too late the penalty for failing to confront the truth about her husband. Furthermore, the despicable truth about the character of Leo Jordan is rooted in his attitude toward Austrian history, especially guilt and denial relating to the National Socialist period, which lends the story a wider dimension.

"Drei Wege zum See," the long final story of the collection, has acquired special significance ever since critics began to emphasize Bachmann's concern with Austrian social and historical issues. Elisabeth Matrei, a photographic journalist, who has escaped the confines of her Austrian "Heimat" and who mixes in famous circles abroad, returns to visit her elderly father in Klagenfurt. The precise topography of the story's setting is emphasized by Elisabeth's attempts to reach a lake by following a map that proves to be unreliable; it has been rendered obsolete by the building of a new highway. The three "paths" that prove to be dead ends have parallels in other tripartite structures in the story, notably Elisabeth's three abortive relationships with men who shared the surname "Trotta." This name, which is redolent of Austrian history and literature, reveals Bachmann's use of intertextual material as a means of broadening the framework of her writing. Bachmann's overlapping concerns with women's roles and the state of the world is evident in the outcome of this story: Elisabeth, who had been persuaded previously both by her editor and her lover not to endanger her life by going to Algeria to report on the war raging there, finally decides to abandon her relationship with Philippe and to accept a commission to report on the war in Vietnam. She sets off for Saigon, optimistic about her prospects for survival. In "Drei Wege zum See," critics have noted Bachmann's concern with a specifically Austrian tradition. The country's status as the amputated rump of the Habsburg Empire is echoed mainly in the story's language and names, but also mirrored in concerns of Bachmann's own time, especially the bloody end to imperialism in Africa and Asia. This aspect also suggests a close link to the subject matter of *Der Fall Franza,* in which political perspectives and the oppression of women come together.

JULIET WIGMORE

Editions

First Edition: *Simultan,* Munich: Piper, 1972

Critical edition: *"Todesarten"-Projekt,* vol. 4, *Der "Simultan"-Band und andere späte Erzählungen,* edited by Monika Albrecht and Dirk Göttsche, Munich: Piper, 1995

Translation: *Three Paths to the Lake,* translated by Mary Fran Gilbert, with an introduction by Mark Anderson, New York and London: Holmes and Meier, 1989

Further Reading

Achberger, Karen, *Understanding Ingeborg Bachmann,* Columbia: University of South Carolina Press, 1995

Bahrawy, Lise de Serbine, *The Voice of History: An Exegesis of Selected Short Stories from Ingeborg Bachmann's "Das dreißigste Jahr" and "Simultan" from the Perspective of Austrian History,* New York: Lang, 1989

Brokoph-Mauch, Gudrun, "Österreich als Fiktion und Geschichte in der Prosa Ingeborg Bachmanns," *Modern Austrian Literature* 30, no. 3/4 (1997)

Dusar, Ingeborg, *Choreographien der Differenz: Ingeborg Bachmanns Prosaband "Simultan,"* Cologne: Böhlau, 1994

Hotho-Jackson, Sabine, "Subversiveness in Ingeborg Bachmann's Later Prose," *New German Studies* 18, no. 1/2 (1994)

Nutting, Peter West, "'Ein Stück wenig realisiertes Österreich': The Narrative Topography of Ingeborg Bachmann's *Drei Wege zum See,*" *Modern Austrian Literature* 18, no. 3/4 (1985)

Schmidt, Tanja, "Beraubung des Eigenen: Zur Darstellung geschichtlicher Erfahrung im Erzählzyklus *Simultan* von Ingeborg Bachmann," in *Kein objektives Urteil—Nur ein lebendiges: Texte und Werke von Ingeborg Bachmann,* edited by Christine Koschel and Inge von Weidenbaum, Munich: Piper, 1989

Schmidt-Bortenschlager, Sigrid, "Frauen als Opfer—Gesellschaftliche Realität und literarisches Modell: Zu Ingeborg Bachmanns Erzählband *Simultan,*" in *Der dunkle Schatten, dem ich schon seit Anfang folge: Ingeborg Bachmann, Vorschläge zu einer neuen Lektüre des Werks,* edited by Hans Höller, Vienna: Locker, 1982

Poetry

Ingeborg Bachmann's lyrics belong almost exclusively to the 1950s. They first attracted critical attention with the prize of the Gruppe 47 in 1953 and were mainly collected in two volumes, *Die gestundete Zeit* (1953; Time Measured in Hours) and *Anrufung des Großen Bären* (1956; Invocation of the Great Bear). While German writers struggled to escape from memories of the immediate Nazi past, her new poetic voice, Austrian and provincial, together with those of Ilse Aichinger and Paul Celan, effectively answered Theodor Adorno's claim that poetry could no longer be written after Auschwitz. The entrance in 1938 of Nazi troops into her hometown Klagenfurt was the key experience of Bachmann's life, motivating her work, which she once summed up in the phrase "Utopia is a direction not a place." The relationship between herself, language, and objects in the world around her was expressed in metaphors of skepticism (see "Alle Tage"). This relationship supported a new poetic medium that would replace the *Kahlschlag* style of German literature that predominated immediately after World War II.

With its references back to the recent past, the first collection, *Die gestundete Zeit,* lives up to its title, suggesting a stopping of time by such horrors. The collection also includes metaphors that were attempts to reach forward again and give new hope. The emphasis in these poems on departure, time running out, and personal and universal transience is all the more poignant because of the attractiveness of the life and land of her childhood, which was destroyed by National Socialism and is now to be left behind. The message of her poetry had instant appeal to a postwar generation that was struggling to find new values, but it was to become the focus of mainly academic interest in more recent years. This work also found acclaim with feminist writers, who nevertheless saw it as too vague and benign, and aesthetically too pleasing. Bachmann herself was aware of these dangers and used ironic double meanings to foreground the self-criticism built into each poem or cluster of poems.

The second collection, *Anrufung des Großen Bären,* usually considered as superior in technique, insight, and creativity, celebrates the powers of poetry and love to console and provide new challenges and hope. The diction is simpler, the militant tone has disappeared (Svandrlik), and the fondness for daring genitive metaphors has gone (Bartsch). The poems, however, call for a departure from the overcivilized north and a return to the original lands of civilization in the south, where musical and literary memories no longer cloud and distort and where a cult of the sun and of primitive living offers an intensity of existence and of self-expression. Light is opposed to darkness (see "Mein Vogel" and "Landnahme"), and the most famous poem, "Anrufung des Großen Bären," offers multiple levels of meaning without an explicit escape into a new utopia. The broken symbolism makes the reader aware of the nuts and bolts of each verse before interrelating them and coming to an overall interpretation. As with Kafka's deliberate ambivalent use of names, referred to in Bachmann's lectures, poetry can reconstruct new worlds, extend our vision, and present the possibility of change. In a phrase from her first lecture on poetry, she reveals her pacifist intention: "If we had the word, if we had language, we should not need weapons." Hans Höller has shown how Bachmann often evoked the lost paradise of her childhood home, while recognizing the experience of love as an attractive but insufficient answer to the problems of existence. The contrast between the language of existential discourse and that of a make-believe world of advertising and commerce becomes both the theme of "Reklame," "Rede und Nachrede," and "Ihr Worte" and an essential ingredient of her later works.

Bachmann's poems reveal a character seeking for roots, faced by the apparently harsh and meaningless landscape of life. Her seemingly unsophisticated images grow into webs of metaphoric expression, often set within a tripartite structure. She was hostile to some of the Italian landscapes in which she later lived, yet their warmth, color, and sensuality inform her work, where the elements of fire, earth, and air, not to mention the sun, all play significant parts. Whereas literature has produced worlds of allusions that have removed man from the presence and time in which he actually lives, for Bachmann time could become a dimension offering endless extension and experience (see "Herbstmanöver"). Her poems often express both the attractions of flight and its restrictions, which can often imply irresponsibility, an act of bad faith, or self-deceit. Using syntheses of various levels of culture, she presents problematic situations and often insists on accepting their existential implications (see the 15 poems of the cycle *Lieder auf der Flucht*).

As with all her writing, her poetry is marked by her lack of illusions about life and her sharp critical intellect. By overcoming sentimentality and resignation, she avoided despair and melancholy, but she never allowed herself the comfort of faith in some fixed utopia. In her challenges to fate she explored the edges of personal existential abysses, and with her powers of suggestion she spoke to various generations of readers. Despite pessimistically forecasting the end of a materialist society, she declared that there is nothing more wonderful than to be alive, because life offers endless possibilities and the freedom to reject formal codes of values. This idea is often expressed in flowing rhythms that break through strict rhyme schemes. In her late poems (e.g., "Kleine Delikatessen" and "Enigma"), some critics have seen her writing off lyrical poetry (Oelmann), whereas Bartsch interprets these works primarily as a break with the central traditions of classical and Romantic poetry and reads "Enigma" as a realignment toward a complete, universal language, and thus, a utopian moment. Her imagery, with strong contrasts between idyllic, rhapsodic sections and harshly reasoned general abstract statements, includes not only natural landscape but also the worlds of myth and fairy tale. Her final poem, "Böhmen liegt am Meer," set mostly in alexandrines and written at the same time as her unfinished cycle of novels "Todesarten," represents a spiritual journey, a frontier land, and hence, as she claimed in an interview, a sign of hope for everyone.

BRIAN KEITH-SMITH

Editions

First editions: *Die gestundete Zeit,* Frankfurt: Frankfurter Verlagsanstalt, 1953; *Anrufung des Großen Bären,* Munich: Piper, 1956

Critical edition: in *Werke,* vol. 1, *Gedichte/Hörspiele/Libretti/Übersetzungen,* edited by Christine Koschel, Inge von Weidenbaum, and Clemens Münster, Munich and Zurich: Piper, 1978

Translations: Selections in *New Young German Poets,* edited by Jerome Rothenberg, San Francisco: City Lights, 1959; *Twentieth-Century German Verse,* edited by Patrick Bridgwater, Harmondsworth and Baltimore: Penguin, 1963; *Modern German Poetry 1910–1960,* edited by Michael Hamburger, London: MacGibbon and Kee, and New York: Grove Press, 1962

Further Reading

Bartsch, Kurt, *Ingeborg Bachmann,* Stuttgart: Metzler, 1988

Bothner, Susanne, *Ingeborg Bachmann, Der janusköpfige Tod: Versuch der literaturpsychologischen Deutung eines Grenzgebiets der Lyrik, unter Einbeziehung des Nachlasses,* Bern, Frankfurt, and New York: Lang, 1986

Heselhaus, Clemens, "Ingeborg Bachmanns gebrochene Symbolik," in *Deutsche Lyrik der Moderne: Von Nietzsche bis Yvan Goll, die Rückkehr zur Bildlichkeit der Sprache,* Düsseldorf: Bagel, 1961

Höller, Hans, "*Die gestundete Zeit* und *Anrufung des Großen Bären:* Vorschläge zu einem neuen Verständnis," in *"Der dunkle Schatten, dem ich schon seit Anfang folge": Ingeborg Bachmann: Vorschläge zu einer neuen Lektüre des Werks,* Vienna: Löcker, 1982

———, *Ingeborg Bachmann: Das Werk: Von den frühesten Gedichten bis zum 'Todesarten'-Zyklus,* Frankfurt: Athenäum, 1987

Holthusen, Hans Egon, "Kämpfender Sprachgeist: Die Lyrik Ingeborg Bachmanns," in *Das Schöne und das Wahre: Neue Studien zur modernen Literatur,* Munich: Piper, 1958

Jurgensen, Manfred, *Ingeborg Bachmann: Die neue Sprache,* Bern, Frankfurt, and Las Vegas, Nevada: Lang, 1981

Kaulen, Heinrich, "Zwischen Engagement und Kunstautonomie: Ingeborg Bachmanns letzter Gedichtyzklus *Vier Gedichte* (1968)," *Deutsche Vierteljahrschrift fur Literaturwissenschaft und Geistegeschichte* 65 (1991)

Mauser, Wolfram, "Ingeborg Bachmann: Flucht-Linien ihrer Lyrik," in *Formen der Lyrik in der österreichischen Gegewartsliteratur,* edited by Wendelin Schmidt-Dengler, Vienna: Österreichischer Bundesverlag, 1981

Oberle, Mechthild, *Liebe als Sprache und Sprache als Liebe: Die sprachutopische Poetologie der Liebeslyrik Ingeborg Bachmans,* Frankfurt, Bern, and New York: Lang, 1990

Oelmann, Ute Maria, *Deutsche poetologische Lyrik nach 1945: Ingeborg Bachmann, Günter Eich, Paul Celan,* Stuttgart: Heinz, 1980

Pichl, Robert, and Alexander Stillmark, editors, *Kritische Wege der Landnahme: Ingeborg Bachmann im Blickfeld der neunziger Jahre,* Vienna: Hora, 1994

Svandrlik, S., "Ästhetizierung und Ästhetikkritik in der Lyrik Ingeborg Bachmanns," in *Ingeborg Bachmann,* edited by Heinz Ludwig Arnold, Munich: Edition Text und Kritik, 1984

Hermann Bahr 1863–1934

With the possible exception of his elegant salon comedy, *Das Konzert* (1909; *The Concert*), which he dedicated to Richard Strauss, Hermann Bahr's work as a creative writer of novels and plays has not withstood the test of time. His reputation has also been adversely affected by his notorious and long-running feud with Karl Kraus. That satirist's contemptuous dismissal of his detested adversary has had a lasting impact on Bahr's reception—both as a man and as a writer. Following Kraus in dismissing Bahr as an illiterate and dishonest buffoon, however, misses out on the wider picture. Bahr may have been a less than great writer, but the self-styled *Mann von Übermorgen* (man of the future), with his perceptive awareness of and generous responses to international literary developments, exerted a powerful influence upon the great literary florescence in Vienna at the end of the 19th century. Bahr was a critic and popularizer of flair and insight, who, thanks to his close contacts with the publisher Samuel Fischer in Berlin, became the wheeler-dealer of Viennese literary life in the 1890s. Hofmannsthal, Schnitzler, Beer-Hofmann, and Andrian, leading lights in that loose grouping of writers known as Jung Wien, who met in the Café Griensteidl until its demolition in 1897, had much to thank Bahr for.

In his book *Zur Kritik der Moderne* (1890; Toward a Critique of Modernism), which collected a series of influential essays written between 1887 and 1890 on such subjects as Ibsen's dramas and the future of modern literature, Bahr cast doubt on the then-dominant mode of literary naturalism and pointed the way forward to a way of writing that would emphasize the subjective and the poetic at the expense of the objective and scientific. Referring to works as yet unwritten, he predicted that they would represent a literature that would explore the psyche and feelings, utilizing the techniques of naturalism to examine the workings of the reality within. Although he did not actually coin the term *die Moderne* (this had come from Eugen Wolff at a meeting of the literary society Durch in 1886), Bahr had certainly made it a term of common currency by the early 1890s. In the essay "Henrik Ibsen," written in Berlin in 1887 and published in the Vienna-based *Deutsche Worte* in the same year, Bahr declared that literary naturalism was merely the precursor of the truly modern, which would consist of a synthesis of Romanticism and naturalism. The function of modern literature was to bring about this synthesis. Thus, well before the performance of the first German Naturalist play of stature, Gerhart Hauptmann's *Vor Sonnenaufgang* (1889; *Before Daybreak*), Bahr had already declared the end of naturalism. As Gotthart Wunberg has persuasively argued, it is in Bahr's original sense of dissatisfaction with literary naturalism, first expressed in his Ibsen essay, that we can find the original stimulus for the post-naturalist literature that emerged in Vienna in the last decade of the 19th century.

Bahr's prediction in *Die Überwindung des Naturalismus* (1891; The Overcoming of Naturalism) that it would be something *Lachendes, Eilendes, Leichtfüßiges* (laughing, scampering, light-footed), however, may have fallen slightly short of the mark.

It is also clear that the literature written in Vienna under the stimulus of Bahr's essays in *Zur Kritik der Moderne* and *Die Überwindung des Naturalismus* had many features that reflected Bahr's enthusiasm for French symbolist literature. This was first acquired during his sojourn in Paris between November 1888 and August 1889. The open-minded response to foreign writing in Vienna was no doubt a reflection of the cultural multiplicity that was a defining feature of the Austro-Hungarian Empire itself. At a time when German nationalism, both cultural and political, was an ever-strengthening force not only in the Wilhelminian Reich, but within the Habsburg realms themselves, however, the internationalism of the Jung Wien writers clearly marked them as unsympathetic to any narrowly parochial view of "German" culture. Initially, the Jung Wiener felt little need to distinguish themselves in any taxonomic way from others writing in German. It was left to Hermann Bahr, the "seismograph," to develop an idea first mooted by Grillparzer in his 1837 essay "Worin unterscheiden sich die österreichischen Dichter von den übrigen?" (In What Ways Are Austrian Writers Different from the Others?). Reviewing Nagl's and Zeidler's *Deutsch-Österreichische Literaturgeschichte* (1897), in which the authors argue that writing in Germany and Austria was growing ever closer together in spirit and substance, Bahr proposed that the opposite was the case. His growing support for the notion of a distinctive Austrian literature was to be taken up with especial enthusiasm by Hugo von Hofmannsthal, one of several Jung Wiener who were glad to accept Bahr's support while harboring major doubts about both his prolix writing and his ever-shifting views. Over the years, Bahr would move from the extreme German Nationalism and Marxism of his younger years to an old age in which he professed allegiance to Austria and Roman Catholicism.

The ideas underscoring the way in which Hofmannsthal and Max Reinhardt founded the Salzburg Festival as the manifestation of the international spirit of Austrian culture also owe much to notions first propounded by Bahr. Yet rarely, if at all, is he remembered as one of the founding fathers of this enduring cultural spectacle. Despite the best efforts of Gotthart Wunberg and Donald Daviau in particular to give a more objective picture of his life and work, Bahr probably still remains best-known as Karl Kraus's *der Herr aus Linz* (the gentleman from Linz), who indicated his own genius by letting a lock of hair dangle across his forehead, and whose major achievement—in the eyes of the satirist, at least—was to seduce a whole generation of young Viennese authors into writing bad German.

ANDREW BARKER

See also Jung Wien

Biography

Born in Linz, Austria, 19 July 1863. Studied economics, law, and classical philology in Vienna, 1881–83; expelled from University of Vienna for political speech, 1883; further study in Graz, Czernowitz, and Berlin, from 1883; received no degree; worked as journalist and reader for S. Fischer Verlag in Berlin, 1884–87; co-founded weekly newspaper, *Die Zeit,* edited feuilleton section, 1894–99; theater critic for *Neues Wiener Tageblatt,* from 1899; for *Neues Wiener Journal,* from 1908; director at Deutsches Theater in Berlin, 1906–7; moved to Salzburg, 1912; dramatic advisor (*Dramaturg*) at Burgtheater in Vienna, 1918; lived in Munich, from 1922. Died in Munich 15 January 1934.

Selected Works

Essays and Reviews

Henrik Ibsen, 1887
Zur Kritik der Moderne, 1890
Die Überwindung des Naturalismus, 1891
Der Antisemitismus, 1893
Der neue Stil, 1893
Wiener Theater, 1892–1898, 1899
Secession, 1900
Rede über Klimt, 1901
Rezensionen (Wiener Theater, 1901–1903), 1903
Gegen Klimt, 1903
Austriaca, 1911
Expressionismus, 1916; as *Expressionism,* 1925
Selbstbildnis, 1923

Plays

Die neuen Menschen (produced 1891), 1887
Die große Sünde, 1889
Die Mutter, 1891
Das Tschaperl, 1898; as *The Poor Fool,* 1938
Wienerinnen, 1900
Das Konzert, 1909; as *The Concert,* 1921
Spielerei, 1920
Ehelei, 1920

Fiction

Theater, 1897
Drut, 1909
O Mensch, 1910
Himmelfahrt, 1916
Die Rotte Korahs, 1918

Further Reading

Barker, Andrew W., "'Der große Überwinder': Hermann Bahr and the Rejection of Naturalism," *Modern Language Review* 78, no. 3 (1983)

Daviau, Donald G., *Hermann Bahr,* New York: Twayne, 1985

de Mendelssohn, Peter, *S. Fischer und sein Verlag,* Frankfurt: Fischer, 1970

Wunberg, Gotthart, editor, *Das Junge Wien: Österreichische Literatur- und Kunstkritik 1887–1902,* vol. 1, Tübingen: Niemeyer, 1976

Hugo Ball 1886–1927

Although he is best known as one of the two primary founders (with Tristan Tzara) of the Dada movement, Hugo Ball's direct involvement in Dada was remarkably brief, lasting little more than a year. Indeed, Ball's entire literary career lasted only 22 years, from his first poems written in 1905 to his final biographical and autobiographical works of 1927. During this brief time, Ball's artistic, intellectual, and spiritual concerns underwent numerous changes, from the youthful romanticism of his early nature poetry, through his Expressionist and Dada periods and a brief involvement with moderate-left politics, to the Catholic mysticism of his final years. Early critical and biographical writing on Ball tended to focus almost exclusively either on his involvement with the Cabaret Voltaire and Zurich Dada or on his development as a Christian writer and thinker. More recent work has increasingly attempted to present a balanced view of his entire career and oeuvre.

Ball's earliest surviving work is a series of lyric nature poems set in the Palatine Forest and published, appropriately enough, in the regionalist journal *Der Pfälzerwald.* His first major literary effort was a dissertation begun in 1909 and abandoned along with his academic studies at the University of Munich. The surviving draft, *Nietzsche in Basel,* was published in 1978. While neither the early poems nor the Nietzsche dissertation rank among Ball's major works, they anticipate several aspects of his later writings, such as the fascination with the magical/mystical properties of language and the influence of Nietzsche.

Following his departure from the University in 1910, Ball began a period of intense involvement with the theater in Berlin, Munich, and elsewhere. From 1910 to 1914 he was active as an actor, director, dramaturge, and playwright with strong ties to the Expressionist movement. Particularly important for Ball during this period was the influence of Russian painter and writer Wassily Kandinsky, whom he met in 1914. Kandinsky's conception of a total theater, in which text, movement, costume, stage design and decor, and music held equal status, struck a chord. Ball and Kandinsky planned an ambitious collaboration, with the promised participation of such figures as Arnold Schönberg, Paul Klee, and Franz Marc. Their project for a *Künstlertheater* (artists' theater) in Munich was cut short by the onset of World War I, but some of its elements were realized two years later in the Zurich Dada performances. Ball's role in the immediate prewar German theater world was prominent, but his own plays of this period—including *Die Nase des Michelangelo* (1911; Michelangelo's Nose) and *Der Henker von Brescia* (1914, complete version published 1992; The Executioner of Brescia)—were not produced.

Another product of the prewar period was a series of poems published in a number of Expressionist periodicals. The best-known (and most notorious) of these, "Der Henker" (1913; "The Executioner"), led to the confiscation, on grounds of obscenity, of the first number of *Revolution,* the short-lived periodical in which it appeared. Portraying, in highly convoluted language, an encounter between a prostitute and her client, the poem equates the sexual act with a brutal execution, while at the same time attributing to orgasm overtones of religious ecstasy and even redemption and innocence. The apparent biblical references were certainly a factor in the banning of the poem; but in the end, a court determined that "Der Henker" was too obscure to be obscene. In addition to the Expressionist poems published under his own name, Ball wrote seven poems in collaboration with his close friend Hans Leybold, published mostly in *Die Aktion* under the pseudonym Ha Hu Baley, as well as three in collaboration with Klabund and Marietta di Monaco under the name Klarinetta Klaball.

After the onset of the war, Ball volunteered for military service, but was rejected for health reasons. A brief visit to the western front in late summer of 1914 transformed his enthusiasm into vehement opposition to the war. Resettling in Berlin, Ball worked as a journalist and critic while organizing, in collaboration with Richard Huelsenbeck, a series of lectures and readings with strong pacifist overtones. His position in Berlin soon became untenable, and in May 1915 Ball emigrated to Zurich, in neutral Switzerland, with his companion, Emmy Hennings.

Living in poverty and in frequent trouble with the local police, Ball spent several months playing piano and writing sketches for a cabaret company of ill repute, the Maxim Ensemble. In February 1916, working with a diverse group of expatriate writers and artists from many parts of Europe, Ball and Hennings established the Cabaret Voltaire. It was home to an eclectic array of artistic performances and other activities that soon developed into the Dada movement.

Ball's connection with the movement was very brief, but his contributions provided some of the defining moments of Zurich Dada. He participated as a piano accompanist, lecturer, and writer. Prominent in the initial Cabaret Voltaire performances was his bitterly sarcastic poem "Totentanz 1916" (Dance of Death 1916), cast in the voice of soldiers engaged in an erotic dance of mutual slaughter as they thank the Kaiser for the privilege of dying.

The best-known product of Ball's brief Dada period is the series of six *Lautgedichte* (sound poems) written and performed in 1916. While "Totentanz 1916" parodies the patriotic rhetoric of a military marching song, Ball's sound poems reject outright the language that Ball and other Dadaists felt was the underpinning of the corrupt civilization that had led inevitably to the massive carnage of the war. Although Ball's sound poems are an attempt to realize Kandinsky's conception of an abstract poetry, they are not wholly devoid of verbal meaning. Composed largely of apparently meaningless syllables strung together to create an effect that is more musical than lexical, the poems do contain meaningful utterances in the form of onomatopoeia, indirect allusions to words in various European languages, and, in all but one instance, titles in German that provide a frame of reference. Thus, in his most famous poem, "Karawane" ("Caravan"), Ball suggests through his title and through the first word "jolifanto" a caravan of elephants, and this suggestion is reinforced by onomatopoeic phrases alluding to the elephants' trumpeting ("ü üü ü") and their heavy footsteps ("tumba ba-umf"). In its published version (1920), "Karawane" utilizes wildly varied typography to reinforce its rejection of conventional language. But the sound poems were first and foremost performance pieces. Indeed, the archetypal image of Zurich Dada is a photograph of Ball reciting one of the poems while dressed in an outlandish costume suggesting a mechanical bishop.

The other major products of Ball's Zurich Dada period are the play *Simultan Krippenspiel* (1986; translated as *A Nativity Play* and *A Bruitist Nativity Play*), and the novel *Flametti* (1918). *Simultan Krippenspiel* is a performance piece consisting of a variety of sounds produced by human voices and by props, tied together by a fairly conventional Christmas narrative. *Flametti* portrays life among a somewhat disreputable cabaret group in Zurich and is based loosely on the author's experiences with the Maxim Ensemble and the Dada group.

Ball's other novel, *Tenderenda der Phantast* (1967; *Tenderenda the Fantast*), was written from 1914 to 1920 and treats in a magical-allegorical fashion elements of Ball's life during this seven-year period, from his prewar journalism through the Dada period to the beginning phases of his return to Catholicism. Dada plays a central role in the work and is anthropomorphized as a heroic character of miraculous birth; two of Ball's sound poems are incorporated into the novel.

Following his definitive break with the Dadaists, Ball worked intermittently for the moderate-left Bern newspaper *Die Freie Zeitung* from 1917 until 1920. The articles he wrote during this period deal with political and cultural topics, with a heavy emphasis on German responsibility for the war and on the bourgeois "Prussian" culture that he blamed for Germany's downfall. Ball's opposition to this culture evolved from the nihilistic anarchist attacks epitomized by Dada to a more expository critique of German civilization in the *Freie Zeitung* articles. In his prose work *Zur Kritik der deutschen Intelligenz* (1919; *Critique of the German Intelligentsia*), Ball traces the militaristic Prussian-German Protestant culture back to Martin Luther's victory over Thomas Müntzer in the Peasants' War and proposes as models for a new German intelligentsia the political and philosophical ideals of the French Revolution and Russian anarchist thought.

This emphasis quickly changed as Ball converted back to the Catholicism of his youth and shifted to theological writing. Retreating with Emmy Hennings into near-total isolation in Ticino, Ball devoted himself to Christian mysticism and an almost monastic discipline. He took a strong interest in early Christianity and Gnosticism, resulting in *Byzantinisches Christentum* (1923; Byzantine Christianity), a book on the lives of three of the Desert Fathers, early Christian ascetics of the fourth through seventh centuries. Ball saw in the asceticism of Pseudo-Dionysius, John Climacus, and Simeon Stylites a remedy for the ills of modern civilization (no longer limited to Germany). A year later, Ball revised *Critique of the German Intelligentsia* under the title *Die Folgen der Reformation* (1924; The Consequences of the Reformation) to bring the work in line with his increasingly orthodox Roman Catholicism. His earlier admiration for the democratic ideals of the French Revolution and for Russian anarchist philosophy was supplanted by advocacy of a rigidly hierarchical theocracy as a model for human government.

Ball's last two books were *Hermann Hesse, sein Leben und sein Werk* (1927; Hermann Hesse: His Life and His Work), the first biography of the already well-known German writer, and *Die Flucht aus der Zeit* (1927; *Flight out of Time*), an autobiographical work based on Ball's diaries of 1913 to 1921. Although the latter work is widely regarded as one of the source documents of Zurich Dada, it is actually an edited version of the diaries, intended to show, in retrospect, Ball's evolution away from chaos and toward his re-embracing of the Catholic faith. To what extent the book deviates from the original diaries is unknown, as the manuscripts are not extant. Ironically, Ball's theological writings were not well-received in Catholic intellectual circles, and he continues to be best remembered as a founder of the Dada movement that he so quickly repudiated.

Timothy Shipe

See also Dadasim

Biography

Born in Pirmasens, 22 February 1886. Grew up in a Catholic household; studied philosophy and sociology in Munich, then in Heidelberg and Basel, 1906–10; disappointed with academic life, he never completed his dissertation on Nietzsche; changed to a career in drama, 1910, and trained under Max Reinhardt in Berlin; worked at theaters in Plauen and Munich, 1910–14; furthered the work of the Expressionist playwright Frank Wedekind; contact with the circle of artists of the Blaue Reiter; worked as editor and theater critic for weekly *Zeit im Bild* in Berlin, 1914–15; moved to Switzerland, 1915, and became an outspoken pacifist; founded the Cabaret Voltaire, 1916, and the Galerie Dada, 1917, seminal places for the Dadaist movement; worked as contributor and editor for *Die Freie Zeitung* in Bern, 1917–20; friendship with Hermann Hesse in an otherwise withdrawn existence during the last years of his life. Died in Sant' Abbondio, Switzerland, 14 September 1927.

Selected Works

Collections
Briefe 1911–1927, 1957
Gesammelte Gedichte, 1963
Damals in Zürich: Briefe aus den Jahren 1915–17, 1978
Der Künstler und die Zeitkrankheit: Ausgewählte Schriften, 1984
Die nichtgesammelten Gedichte, 1996

Fiction
Flametti; oder, Vom Dandysmus der Armen, 1918
Tenderenda der Phantast: Roman, 1967; as "Tenderenda the Fantast," translated by Malcolm Green in *Blago Bung, Blago Bung, Bosso Fataka!: First Texts of German Dada*, 1995

Drama
Die Nase des Michelangelo: Tragikomödie, 1911
Nero: Tragödie in fünf Aufzügen, 1985
Simultan Krippenspiel, 1986; as "Nativity Play," partially translated in *Dada Performance*, 1987
Der Henker von Brescia: Drei Akte der Not und Ekstase, 1992 (act 1 published in 1914)

Nonfiction Prose
Zur Kritik der deutschen Intelligenz, 1919; as *Critique of the German Intelligentsia*, translated by Brian L. Harris, 1993
Byzantinisches Christentum: Drei Heiligenleben, 1923
Die Folgen der Reformation, 1924
Die Flucht aus der Zeit, 1927; as *Flight out of Time*, translated by Ann Raimes, 1974
Hermann Hesse: Sein Leben und sein Werk, 1927

Edited Work
Almanach der Freien Zeitung, 1917–18

Further Reading

Egger, Eugen, *Hugo Ball: Ein Weg aus dem Chaos*, Olten: Walter, 1951
Hennings, Emmy, *Hugo Ball: Sein Leben in Briefen und Gedichten*, Berlin: Fischer, 1929
———, *Hugo Balls Weg zu Gott: Ein Buch der Erinnerung*, Munich: Kösel und Pustet, 1931
———, *Ruf und Echo: Mein Leben mit Hugo Ball*, Einsiedeln: Benziger, 1953

Last, Rex William, *German Dadaist Literature: Kurt Schwitters, Hugo Ball, Hans Arp,* New York: Twayne, 1973
Mann, Philip, *Hugo Ball: An Intellectual Biography,* London: Institute of Germanic Studies, University of London, 1987
Stein, Gerd, *Die Inflation der Sprache: Dadaistische Rebellion und mystische Versenkung bei Hugo Ball,* Frankfurt: Athenaion, 1975
Steinbrenner, Manfred, *"Flucht aus der Zeit?": Anarchismus, Kulturkritik, und christliche Mystik: Hugo Balls "Konversionen,"* Frankfurt and New York: Lang, 1985
Steinke, Gerhardt, *The Life and Work of Hugo Ball, Founder of Dadaism,* The Hague: Mouton, 1967
Teubner, Ernst, *Hugo Ball: Eine Bibliographie,* Mainz: Hase und Koehler, 1992
Teubner, Ernst, editor, *Hugo Ball 1886–1986: Leben und Werk,* Berlin: Publica, 1986
——, editor, *Hugo Ball Almanach,* Pirmasens: Stadt Pirmasens, 1977–
White, Erdmute Wenzel, *The Magic Bishop: Hugo Ball, Dada Poet,* Columbia, South Carolina: Camden House, 1998

Baroque

The German Baroque is often thought of as a period of churchly and courtly preciosity, a preciosity like the Portuguese *baroco* shell from which it derived its name, or of bombast, and it is indiscriminately identified with the 17th century as a whole. The reasons go back to the 18th century, when the term *Baroque* was imported from abroad and applied to literature and, by analogy, to art. The hostile opposition articulated by French encyclopedists of the mid–18th century between the aesthetic ideal of *simplicité* and the unnatural *formes Baroques* of the preceding era of Italian sculpture and architecture (Giovanni Bernini, Francesco Borromini) provided a timely definition for German rationalist Francophiles such as Johann Christoph Gottsched, who were seeking terms of disparagement for the allegorical political dramas and sensuous Italianate verse of the later 17th century. In 1764, the art historian Johann Winckelmann asserted a similar opposition between the beautiful simplicity of nature in antiquity and the ugly mutations of 17th-century Italian art; the literature, too, according to Winckelmann, oozed with the decadence of the obscurantist *concetto* style of Giambattista Marino. Simultaneously, a budding German Romanticism gave rise to three negative tendencies, all epitomized in Johann Gottfried Herder, that would produce ideological barriers to a proper appreciation of German Baroque culture until the 20th century: anticourtly sentiment, an aversion to academic learning, and an organicist anthropology that rejected the foreign strain. The image of the supplicatory polymath grinding out panegyric distichs for a petty prince smelling of the latest French or Spanish perfume owes to this distorted reception of the historical Baroque.

Nineteenth-century dualism pitted "Baroque" against "Renaissance." Jacob Burckhardt's perceptive view in his *Cicerone* (1855) of the relationship between the two concepts as that between a pure language and a crude dialect of it might have offered an alternative to either/or thinking, but once again an antithetical model prevailed. Heinrich Wölfflin's *Renaissance und Barock* (1888) only widened the ideological fault line by contributing exploitable categories for historicist and racial speculations (modern versus medieval; Germanic versus Italian). A science of German Baroque literature dates only from the 1920s; it abandoned typological schemes and concentrated instead on questions of expression and genre within an epochal framework. For a time under National Socialism, "Baroque" became the conceptual darling of an arrogant *Geistesgeschichte* (the view of history as a series of supplantations of weaker by more powerful intellectual forces), which valorized Baroque as a strong "Germanic" or "Gothic" quality (expressive, manly, subjective, bold) as against the weak "un-Germanic" quality of "Renaissance."

After World War II, the late 19th-century view of Mannerism—the effective, decorative style (contorted, uncomfortable, strange) of post-Renaissance art—was revived by Ernst Robert Curtius, a scholar of Romance literatures, as the prototypically avant-garde style of all anticlassical moments in art or literary history. This explanation, first suggested by Nietzsche, would become the vanishing point for the Baroque/Renaissance duality. Curtius's penetrating but ahistorical insight, that much of what had previously gone under the rubric Baroque ought to be called Mannerist, unexpectedly inspired his student Gustav René Hocke to a revolutionary historical thesis: Mannerism is the epochal expression of a modern crisis that can be understood as a clash of centripetal and centrifugal forces. Hocke found Mannerism's German origins between 1520 and 1650, the epoch created by the big bang of the Reformation and shaped by more than 100 years of confessional wars and territorial struggles. The 1960s ramified the crisis/restoration or disorder/reorder thesis sociopolitically, confessionally, intellectually, aesthetically, and institutionally, demonstrating that elements of crisis, tradition, reform, and stability were all present simultaneously in divided 17th-century Germany and combusted to produce the extreme or unusual kinds of language and thought variously called Baroque or Mannerist. Investigations into the rhetorical discourses, intellectual traditions, and phenomena of German literary reception throughout Europe set trends in motion that would dominate research for the remainder of the 20th century. A third and even a fourth foundational pillar of 17th-century culture, in addition to the familiar ones of *Hof* (court) and *Kirche* (church), were uncovered between the late 1960s and early 1990s: *Schule* (universities and intellectual societies, as well as book production) and *Gesellschaft und Politik* (society and politics). Since the early 1990s, an interdisciplinary methodology has been at pains to understand Baroque complexities in terms of combinational logic, as the complex interplay of texts (intertextuality), media (intermediality), or other simultaneously expressive forces, crises, or pathologies, whether national, regional, urban, or individual. The influence of the French *Annales* school has resulted in a preference for regional and localized, often microhistorical studies of previously marginalized subjects (e.g., women, village government, witchcraft, sexuality, and folk medicine).

At millennium's end, Baroque as a metaphor for 17th-century literature in toto is all but dead, although it is still found as a pragmatic category in bibliographical description and college course titles. It is more common now to treat Baroque in one of two ways: as a name for the movement running on a discrete track throughout the 17th century from Martin Opitz to Justus Georg Schottel to Christian Weise that explicitly promoted literary and linguistic reform; or as a category for restorationist, synthesizing, representational, or legitimating projects. Often, Baroque is replaced altogether by the less problematic adjective "17th-century."

Locating the Baroque on a time line is difficult and depends on how it is distinguished from what came before. In Hocke's scheme of things, the restoration of European order following the Peace of Westphalia (1648) marks the onset of the Baroque proper. This crude generalization at least has utility as a principle: the entire age was the child of crisis (Mannerism) and came to maturity in search of stability (Baroque). It is therefore possible to establish the beginnings of the Baroque as early as the last quarter of the 16th century (ca. 1572), when late humanists began to strike the themes and styles that would be the subject of reform in the next century, and its end about a generation into the 18th century (ca. 1740), which saw the rise of the Enlightenment. A narrower range may be established between 1624 (the first German poetics handbook) and 1700 (a spate of anti-Baroque writings).

Germany's belated entry after 1600 into the movement of national vernacular literatures saw a European canon of genres, themes, and rhetorical models already firmly in existence. Did this delay mean that Germany had no Renaissance of its own? Perhaps, insofar as the 16th-century cult of *imitatio antiquitatis* did not take place in the German language and as most indigenous forms were rejected as crude and inflexible in comparison with foreign sophistication. If we include the stream of Latin composition and academic culture that flourished in Germany throughout the 16th century, however, the question may be answered differently. The Germans who comprised the learned elite maintained intimate communications in Latin with their peers across Europe in the so-called Republic of Letters, a republic in name only that included all humanist scholars and writers, including the great literary names of Renaissance Italy, Spain, France, Holland, and England. This neo-Latin current ensured the cultivation in politically and confessionally fragmented Germany of the classical forms. Consequently, when Martin Opitz sounded the call for a national vernacular literature in his *Aristarchus sive de contemptu linguae teutonicae* (1617; Aristarchus; or, On Contempt for the German Language), the formal vehicles stood ready. Seven years later Opitz himself presented for emulation his own German translations of models from ancient, Renaissance, and contemporary foreign poets—especially French (Pierre Ronsard) and Dutch (Daniel Heinsius)—in a thin volume entitled *Buch von der Deutschen Poeterey* (1624; Handbook of German Poetics), and refined German composition subsequently sprang Minerva-like into existence. Not surprisingly, the expressivity of the new literary language did not at first match the formal sophistication of the genres themselves, an incongruity that accounts for the hollow effect of so much early-Baroque poetry in German. The poets were not unaware of this imperfection and strove to overcome it by slavish adherence to established rules of prosody and also by the translation and imitation of foreign masterpieces.

Literary reform in 17th-century Germany—an amalgam of free imperial cities and more than 100 independent territorial states with no dominant political and cultural center—spread via multiple urban and courtly centers. Retracing these paths yields important demographic information about the religious and social connections of the poets and their sponsors: for one thing, the reform was almost exclusively a Protestant (mainly Calvinist and Reformed) affair; for another, the patrons came from noble ranks, while the writers were mostly university-trained doctors, lawyers, and civil or courtly servants. The definitive transition from Latin-based late humanism to the vernacular literary reform can first be witnessed about 1620 at the Calvinist court of Frederick V at Heidelberg, where Opitz was in residence and composed his first collections of poems in the new style. Aesthetic and confessional affinities become immediately visible in Lutheran Strasbourg on the Upper Rhine and at the court of Prince Ludwig of Anhalt-Köthen in Middle Germany, where Germany's most important *Sprachgesellschaft* (language and literary society), the Fruchtbringende Gesellschaft (Fruit-Bearing Society), had been founded in 1617. The latter's aristocratic membership, mostly of the Reformed confession with close ties to Calvinism, adopted the Opitzian literary reform program and recommended it to other cultural centers within the considerable scope of its influence. From these initial centers, the new style spread to other courts, cities, academies, and universities and prompted the founding of further *Sprachgesellschaften* such as the Kürbishütte (Pumpkin Cottage, 1620s in Königsberg); the Aufrichtige Tannengesellschaft (Honorable Society of the Pines, 1633 in Strasbourg); the Teutschgesinnete Genossenschaft (Germanophile Brotherhood, 1642 in Hamburg); and the Pegnesischer Blumenorden (Flower Order on the Pegnitz, 1644 in Nuremberg). In all cases linguistic and literary reform went hand in hand with the propagation of an irenicist (pacifist) doctrine that was aimed at a tolerant, ecumenical solution to the confessional conflicts in Germany and abroad.

In order to properly appreciate the dedication and efficiency of these early literary reformers, one must remember that they carried out their work in the very teeth of the Thirty Years' War (1618–48), one of the longest and most devastating wars in European history. Overrun by foreign armies, crushed by widespread poverty and a useless currency, devoured by disease, and without a national army of its own with which to acquit itself, Germany was, in the words of one of its greatest poets, Andreas Gryphius, "ein Wohnhauß grimmer Schmertzen" (a room of hideous suffering). It is a curious fortuity, then, that the experience of war, with its chaotic offering of horror and hope, eventually forced writers to the self-discovery out of which a distinctively German style of expression emerged. For instance, it is possible on one level to read Hans Jakob Christoph von Grimmelshausen's lengthy *Simplicissimus* (1669; Simplicissimus; or, The Adventures of a Simpleton) as an allegory for the maturation of poetic Germany: at the beginning the young hero Simplex can do no more than stupidly repeat crude phrases he has heard; at the end, as an elderly hermit, he is capable of profound spiritual articulation.

If the grim but often comic language of people and countries at war was one of Simplex's tutors, the other was the language of spirituality, as we are reminded by the lyrical beauty of the song he learns in Book 1 of *Simplicissimus,* which begins "Komm Trost der Nacht, o Nachtigall" (Come, solace of night, O nightingale). The origins of Baroque spiritual poetry were twofold: the church hymns of the Protestant Reformation and the mystical lyrics of late 16th-century Catholic Spain (Teresa of Avila, Juan de la Cruz), both of which were loaded in the 17th century with new content in response to the continuing religious crisis. On the Protestant side, the early-Baroque attempts at writing hymns (Melissus-Schede, Ambrosius Lobwasser) were marred by a too-strict imitation of the French Calvinist models of Clément Marot and Theodore de Beze; but the golden age of Protestant hymnody soon dawned in the songs—many of which are still sung today—of Philipp Nicolai, Simon Dach, Johann Rist, and, most notably, Paul Gerhardt. Others such as Philipp von Zesen, Catharina von Greiffenberg, Johann Klaj, and Andreas Gryphius contributed significantly to the spiritualist lyric of the mature Baroque, though less as hymn writers per se. Although the 17th-century Protestant hymn was rooted in a more indigenous culture than other lyrical forms, it, too, reflects conscious aestheticization and formalization that was in keeping with the principles of literary reform. The widespread influence of Spanish spiritualism affected Catholics and Protestants alike. Its intimate expressions of love achieve special poignancy in works that present Jesus as a tender shepherd and the soul as his bride, as in Friedrich von Spee's *Trutznachtigal* (1649; Defiant Nightingale) or the musical pastorals of the Capucian poet Johann Martin (a.k.a. Laurentius von Schnüffis). In the *Cherubinischer Wandersmann* (1657, 1675; Cherubinic Wanderer) of the mystic Johann Scheffler (a.k.a. Angelus Silesius), a quixotic contemplation of the unions and disjunctions between humanity and divinity is articulated in frequently perplexing epigrams. The most talented lyricist in Catholic Germany was Jakob Balde, although he composed only in Latin.

Some German writers sought to work out a theory of creative imitation that encouraged independence from the method of direct borrowing. As the Nuremberg patrician poet Georg Philipp Harsdörffer explained, the original could be "besser gemacht" (improved upon) through more effective use of rhetorical color and moral clarity and the expansion of themes suitable to the German experience. Therein lies the key to understanding mature Baroque verse. The sonnet, the epigram, the ode, and the eclogue—all are faithfully rehearsed as prescribed in the *Buch von der Deutschen Poeterey*. But with what different results, particularly as the century moved past its midpoint and a more self-confident generation began to free itself from its classical moorings! Gryphius abandons the sonnet's amorous coquetry for existentialist musings on the suffering and vanity of man; the six-foot iambic alexandrine line recommended by Opitz fails to contain the metaphorical exuberance of the exiled Austrian Protestant von Greiffenberg; the erotic and philosophical paradoxes of the young Leipzig poet Paul Fleming strain impatiently against the expressive limits of the ode; allegorical Christian figures drive the mythological characters of classical eclogue from the stage of the spiritual eclogues of the Nuremberg pastoral poet Sigmund von Birken; and the ecstatic sonnets of the Silesian religious fanatic Quirinus Kuhlmann consist of tropological devices thrown together in such idiosyncratic combinations as to render the traditional genre all but unrecognizable. Much poetic activity went into mixed forms that do not fit readily into classical molds: figure-poems in the shape of a horse or an hourglass; riddle epigrams; poems torn into parts and scattered about a book, to be reassembled by the reader; multilingual verse; numerological, cabalistic, or hieroglyphic puzzles; *Klangmalerei* (sound painting); and, everywhere, emblems and emblematic narratives after Horace's axiom "ut pictura poesis" (poetry is like a picture). The dithyrambic declamatory oration invented by Klaj is just one example of the many ephemeral genres created in the heady experimental atmosphere of the 17th century that did not survive into the modern age. The practice of composing poems for special social occasions (*Gelegenheitsdichtung*) flourished as never before or since. Then there were the lyricists of the "Second Silesian School" who defiantly elected to return to Italian concettism or Spanish "Gongorism" (after Luis de Góngora). The à la mode erotic lyrics of Hofmann von Hofmannswaldau, which often employ the stony, provocative imagery of Petrarch's sonnets to the untouchable Laura—"zwo brüste, wo rubin durch alabaster bricht" (two breasts, where ruby gleams through alabaster)—were vilified by the early figures of the Enlightenment as irremediably distasteful.

Beginning with the Dresden court production in 1627 of Ottavio Rinuccini's opera *Dafne,* translated by Opitz and set to music by Heinrich Schütz, Italian forms of spectacle (drama, masque, carnival, procession, opera, and ballet) dominated the stage in Germany. Opitz's German translations of Seneca's *Trojan Women* (1625) and Sophocles' *Antigone* (1636), similar to almost everything he wrote or translated, were intended only to provide models for more serious emulation. The lack of a national center, however, restricted secular theater to comparatively intimate halls. Even the ambitious political and metaphysical plays of the later Baroque could find few venues more public than training academies (*Gymnasien*), universities, and small courts; often they functioned simply as dramatic books for private reading or educational purposes. As a consequence, the plays of the Silesians Andreas Gryphius and Daniel Casper von Lohenstein rapidly fell into oblivion and were not revived on stage until the 20th century. Gryphius's tragedies in particular have received in-depth analysis since their revival and are revealing of the rapid change in the German attitude toward sovereignty at the critical midpoint of the 17th century. *Carolus Stuardus* (drafted 1649) demonstrates royalist sympathies for the executed Charles I and antipathy for the rebellious Puritans; this position was consistent with the prevailing Lutheran attitude of obeisance before *Obrigkeit* (secular authority). Ten years later, *Papinianus* (1659) presents anti-Stuart republican preferences in the figure of Papinian, who is cast in the heroic humanist mold of the great Florentine statesmen Coluccio Salutati and Leonardo Bruni. The Turkish (*Ibrahim Sultan*, 1673), African (*Cleopatra*, 1661), and Roman (*Sophonisbe*, 1680) plays by Lohenstein still await exhaustive analysis. They present complex political and psychological allegories that are rendered all the more difficult by layers of intrigues and personal abnormalities that late 20th-century readers find particularly compelling.

Religious drama in the 17th century was primarily the domain of the Jesuits, for it was a component in the continuing educational enterprise of the Counter Reformation. Its impression on the wider theater culture, however, can hardly be overestimated. Above all, it was the magnificent universal stage, with its cosmic divisions into heaven, earth, and hell, that appealed so irresistibly to the spiritual imagination. The most famous example,

Jakob Biedermann's psychomachia *Cenodoxus* (1602), portrays a Faust-like scholar whose learning and ethical life avail his soul nothing in the end before the flames of hell. Although the Jesuits remained largely unaffected by secular trends in dramatology, Biedermann's successors Jakob Balde and Nicolaus von Avancini did experiment successfully with political themes.

As was the case for both the lyric and the drama, no suitable indigenous models existed for an aesthetic prose in 17th-century Germany, and early-Baroque poetics are silent on the novel. Again, the process began in imitation and translation of European masterpieces, and, again, the initiator was Opitz (who translated John Barclay's *Argenis* [1626–31] and Philip Sidney's *Arcadia* [1638]). Inspired by his example, the *Sprachgesellschaften* encouraged the practice of prose translation. The Anhaltian diplomat Diederich von dem Werder conceived his translation of Torquato Tasso's *Gerusalemme Liberata* (1626; *Das Erlösete Jerusalem*) as a model for an independent German epic, and he followed this with portions of Ludovico Ariosto's *Orlando Furioso* (1632–36). Zesen's *Ibrahims Wunder-Geschichte* (1645; Sultan Ibrahim's Wondrous Story) is a translation of the French novel by Madeleine de Scudéry, which was based on one of the most notorious figures in contemporary Europe (see Lohenstein's drama by the same name); in 1646, Harsdörffer completed the translation, begun in 1619 by the Austrian aristocrat Hanns Ludwig von Kuffstein, of the popular Spanish pastoral novel *Diana* by Jorge de Montemayor. In these and many other prose translations, the principle of creative imitation was effectively applied, with the result that the 17th century was exceptionally rich in original novelists, not only in the late-century picaresque and courtly types, which are fairly well known, but in pastoral forms as well, which have received less attention. It was through the medium of prose that problems of more immediate concern to German readers could be addressed.

Two types of pastoral prose were cultivated in the Baroque. The pastoral novel proper owed directly to the southern European tradition of Jacopo Sannazaro (*Arcadia*) and Montemayor (*Diana*) but also to Sidney in England (*Arcadia*) and Honoré d'Urfé in France (*L'Astrée*). In this self-reflective genre, the disaffected landed gentry laments the war's destruction of rural property and values and the passing of a privileged way of life. The ethic of resignation in *Die verwüstete und verödete Schäferey* (anonymous, 1642; The Devastated and Desolate Pastoral) and Johann Thomas's *Damon und Lisille* (1663) anticipates Goethe's pastoral epic *Hermann und Dorothea* (1798). By contrast, the half-prose, half-verse *Prosaekloge* (prose eclogue), invented by Opitz (in his *Schäferey von der Nimpfen Hercinie* [1630; Pastoral of the Nymph Hercinie]) by combining the traditions of pastoral novel and eclogue, was mainly the pursuit of learned bourgeois poets in urban centers such as Nuremberg. Long disparaged in literary history as a bagatelle, prose eclogue is now recognized as having been a key instrument not only of ludic experimentation but of learned self-reflection and even serious social criticism as well.

Grimmelshausen's *Simplicissimus* is a *Schelmenroman* (picaresque novel). Having evolved in 16th-century Spain (*La vida de Lazarillo de Tormes, Don Quixote*) as a knightly travesty of the medieval epic in the high courtly style, the genre was imported into Germany around 1600 through the translation by the Bavarian libertine Ägidius Albertinus of Mateo Aleman's *Gusman de Alfarache*. The eyewitness fiction of an antihero narrator, combined with an adventurous linear structure, was the ideal vehicle for a realistic portrayal of war and human comedy. Christian Reuter's *Schelmuffsky* (1696) and the novels of Johann Beer, especially *Teutsche Winter-Nächte* (1682; German Winter Nights), can still be read with pleasure.

The German novel of state (*Staatsroman*), an extrapolation in the age of absolutism of the 15th- and 16th-century Spanish courtly novel *Amadís de Gaula,* consists of a roster of characters that reaches into the hundreds with a correspondingly labyrinthine plot. Consigned for 300 years to the rarities cabinet, the novels of state by Lohenstein (*Arminius* [1689–90]) and Duke Anton Ulrich of Braunschweig-Lüneburg (*Aramena* [1669–73] and the unfinished *Octavia* [1677–1707]) are now more accessible and their purpose better understood owing to new critical editions and basic changes in scholarly assumptions about the authors' political and philosophical views. Based on what has been learned from the manuscript drafts that Anton Ulrich made for completing *Octavia,* it appears that he intended to bring the work to a great final act of ecumenical peace—by analogy to the harmonious theodicy of his philosopher friend Gottfried Wilhelm Leibniz—thereby offering a model for the resolution of the debilitating confessional conflicts of the age. Lohenstein's *Arminius* entertains a similarly utopian hope. Reinvoking the ancient spirit of Arminius, the tribal leader praised by Tacitus for leading a unified Germanic force to an unprecedented victory over Rome's occupational legions, Lohenstein envisions the renewal of German national unity under one mighty emperor against the intimidating expansionism of Louis XIV.

These two monumental themes, religious peace and national renewal, were sounded at the threshold of the century of Enlightenment and would continue to inspire German idealism as late as Immanuel Kant and Friedrich Schiller. That they existed together already in the 17th century attests both to the modern thrust of the Baroque and to the continuing vitality of the idea, articulated 400 years earlier by Dante and regularly reinvoked in Renaissance and humanist writings straight through the Baroque, of the possibility of a modern renewal of ancient greatness.

MAX REINHART

See also Andreas Gryphius

Further Reading

Aikin, Judith P., *German Baroque Drama,* Boston: Twayne, 1982
Alewyn, Richard, *Deutsche Barockforschung: Dokumentation einer Epoche,* Cologne: Kiepenheuer, 1965; 4th edition, 1970
———, *Das grosse Welttheater: Die Epoche der höfischen Feste,* Munich: Beck, 1985
Barner, Wilfried, *Barockrhetorik: Untersuchungen zu ihren geschichtlichen Grundlagen,* Tübingen: Niemeyer, 1970
———, editor, *Der literarische Barockbegriff,* Darmstadt: Wissenschaftliche Buchgesellschaft, 1975
Conrady, Karl Otto, *Lateinische Dichtungstradition und deutsche Lyrik des 17. Jahrhunderts,* Bonn: Bouvier, 1962
Curtius, Ernst Robert, *Europäische Literatur und Lateinisches Mittelalter,* Bern: Francke, 1948; as *European Literature and the Latin Middle Ages,* translated by Willard Trask, Princeton, New Jersey: Princeton University Press, 1952; 7th edition, 1990
Dyck, Joachim, *Ticht-Kunst: Deutsche Barockpoetik und rhetorische Tradition,* Bad Homburg: Gehlen, 1966; 3rd edition, Tübingen: Niemeyer, 1991

Garber, Klaus, *Martin Opitz, "der Vater der deutschen Dichtung": Eine kritische Studie zur Wissenschaftsgeschichte der Germanistik,* Stuttgart: Metzler, 1976
Hardin, James, editor, *German Baroque Writers,* 2 vols., Dictionary of Literary Biography, vols. 164 and 168, Detroit, Michigan: Gale Research, 1996
Hocke, Gustav René, *Die Welt als Labyrinth: Manierismus in der europäischen Kunst und Literatur,* edited by Curt Grützmacher, Reinbek bei Hamburg: Rowohlt, 1987
Hoffmeister, Gerhart, editor, *German Baroque Literature: The European Perspective,* New York: Ungar, 1983
Kühlmann, Wilhelm, *Gelehrtenrepublik und Fürstenstaat: Entwicklung und Kritik des deutschen Späthumanismus in der Literatur des Barockzeitalters,* Tübingen: Niemeyer, 1982
Kühlmann, Wilhelm, and Wolfgang Neuber, editors, *Intertextualität in der frühen Neuzeit: Studien zu ihren theoretischen und praktischen Perspektiven,* Frankfurt and New York: Lang, 1994
Pascal, Roy, *German Literature in the Sixteenth and Seventeenth Centuries: Renaissance, Reformation, Baroque,* New York: Barnes and Noble, and London: Cresset Press, 1968
Powell, Hugh, *Trammels of Tradition: Aspects of German Life and Culture in the Seventeenth Century and Their Impact on the Contemporary Literature,* Tübingen: Niemeyer, 1988
Reinhart, Max, editor, *Infinite Boundaries: Order, Disorder, and Reorder in Early Modern German Culture,* Kirksville, Missouri: Sixteenth Century Journal Publishers, 1998
Schöne, Albrecht, editor, *Emblematik und Drama im Zeitalter des Barock,* Munich: Beck, 1954; 3rd edition, 1993
Steinhagen, Harald, editor, *Zwischen Gegenreformation und Frühaufklärung: Späthumanismus, Barock (1572–1740),* Reinbek bei Hamburg: Rowohlt, 1985
Szyrocki, Marian, *Die deutsche Literatur des Barock: Eine Einführung,* Reinbek bei Hamburg: Rowohlt Taschenbuch, 1968

Johannes R. Becher 1891–1958

Throughout much of the 20th century, the name of Johannes R. Becher elicited strong reactions: he was a gifted Expressionist poet or a dangerous but largely incoherent pacifist; he was a tool of Moscow willing to betray the Weimar Republic or an example of an artist who transcended his class and served the proletariat; he was a degenerate enemy of the Third Reich or a hero of the *Volkfront;* his was a strong voice for the survival of German culture in the dark years or the timid voice of a survivor of Stalin's blood purges; he was a heroic pioneer for cultural renewal in the fledgling German socialist state or a vain, grasping functionary who betrayed his friends to retain his own tenuous position. Any of these views can be found in writings about Becher, both during and after his lifetime, and there is doubtless a kernel of truth in most of them.

Johannes R. Becher, the son of a judge in Munich, began writing poetry early. He idolized Dehmel, Hölderlin, and Kleist. An adolescent love affair with a young woman named Fanny Fuss ended in a self-consciously Kleistian suicide pact on Easter Sunday, 1910. Becher shot Fanny and then himself in the chest; she died, and he survived. Images of death, martyrdom, sin, and redemption filled Becher's earliest published works—his Kleist hymn, *Der Ringende* (1911); his first poems, *Die Gnade eines Frühlings* (1912); the novel *Erde* (1912); and *De profundis domine* (1913)—and reflected his struggles with this terrible event.

Becher moved between Berlin and Munich in the years before the war. Ostensibly a student, he wrote, helped with his friend Bachmair's publishing venture, and became a part of the literary café scene in both cities. He also developed a serious morphine addiction that plagued him for the remainder of the decade. In *Verfall und Triumph* (1914), he juxtaposes images of society's outsiders—prostitutes, criminals, the sick, and the impoverished—with visions of apocalyptic change, which he brought forth through the power of the poetic word.

Becher was horrified by the outbreak of the war in 1914 and by the deaths of many of his contemporaries. The imagery of his poetry became more extreme, his syntax became more radical, and his work, with titles such as *An Europa* (1916), *Paän gegen die Zeit* (1918), and *Verbrüderung* (1916), became a series of manifestos for revolution and cultural upheaval. Becher conjured visions of armies of social outcasts rising up to exorcise the horrors of society and offered images of an ill-defined utopia born of this revolution. Becher joined the Spartakists in 1917 and wrote a poem celebrating the birth of the Soviet Union, but not until 1924 did he become an active member of the Communist Party of Germany (KPD).

The intervening years, which brought the end of the war and the failure of the radical revolution Becher had anticipated, also included personal changes for Becher. Since 1916 Katherina Kippenberg of the *Insel Verlag* and Harry Graf Kessler had supported Becher financially and morally, and with their help he slowly weaned himself of his drug addiction. He studied medicine briefly, married and divorced, and had several love affairs. His poetry turned toward a religious utopia in volumes such as *Um Gott* (1921), *Verklärung* (1922), and *Hymnen* (1924).

During the early 1920s, however, Becher involved himself in KPD activities and began to study Marxism. While *Maschinenrhythmen* (written in 1922, published in 1926) combines his old Expressionist imagery with his new communist zeal, *Der Leichnam auf dem Thron* (1925) marked his emergence as an agitational communist poet. Past extremes of image and form yielded to simplicity and directness. This volume and the 1925 novel *(CH Cl=CH)3* (*Levisite*) (1926) resulted in Becher's prosecution for high treason, which caused international protests and established him as an important literary voice for the KPD. In 1928 Becher became the leader of the League of Proletarian-Revolutionary Writers (Bund proletarisch-revolutionärer Schriftsteller) and an editor of its journal, *Die Linkskurve.* He had made the first of several trips to the Soviet Union in 1927 and in 1931 published his dramatic poem *Der grosse Plan,* a celebration of the first Five Year Plan, which was performed by the Neue Volksbühne in Berlin in 1932.

When the Nazis came to power in 1933, Becher was forced into exile, first in Vienna and Prague and then in the Soviet Union. He went to Paris in 1934 and 1935 and helped organize a *Volksfront* of intellectuals that came together at the International Writers' Conference in Defense of Culture in June 1935. He returned to Moscow where he assumed the editorship of the important exile journal *Internationale Literatur: Deutsche Blätter.* In 1936 the pace of Stalin's purges intensified, and many of Becher's closest associates were arrested and perished. By many accounts, Becher was often in peril, but he avoided arrest and survived his own suicidal depressions. He turned his attention as a writer inward; in his poems he reflected on the Germany lost and what it could be. *Der Glücksucher und die sieben Lasten* (1938) evokes the south German landscapes Becher loved and found resonance with such luminaries as Thomas and Heinrich Mann. Becher also wrote an autobiographical novel, *Abschied* (1940), which shows the idealized development of a bourgeois youth toward socialism.

The Hitler-Stalin pact of 1939 struck a blow to the surviving German Communists in Moscow, but the invasion of the Soviet Union was devastating. Becher, like most of the others, was evacuated to Tashkent. His stature as a cultural-political figure allowed an early recall to Moscow in January 1942, where he became part of the propaganda war against the Nazis. He spoke frequently on the radio, and, later in the war, visited prisoner-of-war camps as part of the Nationalkomitee "Freies Deutschland."

Becher returned to Germany in 1945 as a key member of the KPD team in the Soviet Occupation Zone. He founded the Kulturbund for the "renewal of German culture" and helped to found the Aufbau publishing house and the journals *Aufbau* and *Sinn und Form.* He collaborated with Hanns Eisler to write the national anthem for the new German Democratic Republic and in 1953 became the state's first culture minister. He published poetry, a diary, and several volumes of reflective prose, and he edited and revised his earlier work. By 1956, when Stalin's crimes were acknowledged in the Soviet Union, Becher's health had begun to fail and his influence had weakened. He did not move to help several of his closest associates who fell victim to repressive cultural policies in late 1956 and 1957. Although Becher retained his position as minister until his death in 1958, his power had dissipated. After his death, he became an icon of the state, "the poet of the socialist nation," and only with the passing of the GDR has it been possible to begin the process of reassessing Becher's literary achievements and his political significance.

ROBERT K. SHIRER

Biography

Born in Munich, 22 May 1891. Studied philology, philosophy, and medicine in Munich, Jena, and Berlin; cofounded in 1928 the Association of Proletarian-Revolutionary Writers (Bund proletarisch-revolutionäter Schriftsteller); emigrated to the Soviet Union, 1933, where he edited *Internationale Literatur-Deutsche Blätter,* 1935–45; member of the central committee of exiled Communist Party members of Germany; founder and president of the *Kulturbund zur demokratischen Erneuerung Deutschlands;* cofounder of the Aufbau Verlag; founder of the literary magazine *Sinn und Form,* 1949; cultural minister of the GDR from 1954–58. Died 19 November 1958 in East Berlin.

Selected Works

Collections

Das neue Gedicht. Auswahl 1912–1918, 1918
Ein Mensch unserer Zeit. Gesammelte Gedichte, 1929
Der Welt-Entdecker. Ausgewählte Gedichte, 1912–1937, 1938
Gedichte, 1943
Dichtung. Auswahl aus den Jahren 1939-43, 1944
Ein Mensch unserer Zeit in seinen Gedichten, 1911-1951, 1951
Auswahl. 6 Bände, 1952
Vom Anderswerden, 1955
Ein Staat wie unserer Staat, 1959
Becher. Ein Lesebuch für unsere Zeit, 1960
Über Literatur und Kunst, 1962
Gesammelte Werke, 18 Bände, 1966-81
Werke, 3 Bände, 1971
Gedichte, 1975
Becher und die Insel: Brief und Dichtungen, 1916–1954, 1981
Den ganzen Menschen wollen wir erfassen, 1981
Metamorphosen eines Dichters. Gedichte, Briefe, Dokumente 1909–1945, 1992
Der gespaltene Dichter, 1945-58, 1991
Briefe, 1909–1958, 2 vols., 1993

Poetry

Der Ringende, 1911
Die Gnade eines Frühlings, 1912
De profundis Domine, 1913
Verfall und Triumph, 1914
An Europa, 1916
Verbrüderung, 1916
Päan gegen die Zeit, 1918
Die heilige Schar, 1918
Gedichte für ein Volk, 1919
Gedichte um Lotte, 1919
An Alle! 1919
Ewig im Aufruhr, 1920
Zion, 1920
Der Gestorbene, 1921
Um Gott, 1921
Verklärung: Hymne, 1922
Drei Hymnen, 1923
Hymnen, 1924
Der Leichnam auf dem Thron, 1925
Maschinenrhythmen, 1926
Die hungrige Stadt, 1927
Im Schatten der Berge, 1928
Graue Kolonnen, 1930
Der große Plan, 1931
Der Mann, der in der Reihe geht, 1932
An die Wand zu kleben, 1932
Deutscher Totentanz, 1933
Es wird Zeit, 1933
Deutschland, 1934
Der Mann, der alles glaubte, 1935
Der Glücksucher und die sieben Lasten, 1938
Gewißheit des Sieges und Sicht auf große Tage, 1939
Wiedergeburt, 1940
Deutschland ruft, 1942
Dank an Stalingrad, 1943
Die hohe Warte, 1944
Heimkehr, 1946
Volk im Dunkel wandelnd, 1948
Die Faust, 1949
Glück der Ferne — leuchtend nah, 1951
Schritt der Jahrhundertmitte, 1958

Prose, Drama, and Essays
Erde, 1912
*Verfall und Triumph, Band 2,*1914
Vorwärts, du rote Front! 1924
(CH Cl=CH)3 (Levisite); oder, Der einzig gerechte Krieg, 1926
Der Bankier reitet über das Schlachtfeld, 1926
Der verwandelte Platz, 1934
Abschied: Einer deutschen Tragödie erster Teil 1900–1914, 1940; as *Farewell,* translated by Joan Becker, 1970
Deutsche Sendung, 1943
Deutsche Bekenntnis, 1943
Erziehung zur Freiheit, 1946
Wir, Volk der Deutschen, 1947
Vom Willen zum Frieden, 1947
Wir wollen Frieden, 1949
Befreiung, 1949
Auf andere Art so große Hoffnung, Tagebücher, 1951
Verteidigung der Poesie, 1952
Poetische Konfession, 1954
Macht der Poesie, 1955
Von der Größe unserer Literatur, 1956
Das poetische Prinzip, 1957
Walter Ulbricht. Ein deutscher Arbeitersohn, 1958
Die sozialistische Literatur und ihre nationale Bedeutung, 1958
Der Aufstand im Menschen, 1983

Further Reading

Barck, Simone, *Johannes R. Bechers Publizistik in der Sowjetunion, 1933–1945,* Berlin: Akademie, 1976
Dwars, Jens-Fietje, *Abgrund des Widerspruchs: Das Leben des Johannes R. Becher,* Berlin: Aufbau, 1998
Haase, Horst, *Johannes R. Becher: Leben und Werk,* Berlin: Volk und Wissen, 1981
Rohrwasser, Michael, *Der Weg nach Oben: Politiken des Schreibens,* Basel: Stroemfeld, and Frankfurt: Roter Stern, 1980
Stephan, Alexander, "Johannes R. Becher and the Cultural Development in the GDR" *New German Critique* 1, no. 2 (1974)
Weiss, Edgar, *Johannes R. Becher und die sowjetsiche Literaturentwicklung, 1917–1933,* Berlin: Akademie, 1971

Jurek Becker 1937–1997

Jurek Becker achieved international fame with the publication of his first novel, *Jakob der Lügner* (1969; *Jakob the Liar*), which deals with the travails of Polish Jews in a Nazi ghetto during World War II. The novel irrevocably established Becker with the public as a Jewish writer. Yet in his life and work, Becker had numerous conflicting identities to negotiate. He was born a Polish Jew and spent the first nine years of his life in ghettos and concentration camps. He was raised an East German socialist, only to leave East Germany for political reasons in 1977. He spent the remainder of his life in capitalist West Germany. Despite the public perception of him, however, Becker was never quite certain that he was Jewish.

Jakob the Liar presents an extended musing on the possibilities and limits of storytelling; the story is also a metaphor for literature in general. Imprisoned in a ghetto in Nazi-occupied Poland, the Jewish protagonist Jakob pretends ownership of a radio and supplies his fellow Jews with fictional reports on the advance of the Red Army. But Jakob's Scheherazade imitation fails; at the novel's conclusion, the Nazis transport the Jews to a killing center. One can interpret the novel within the strictures of conventional East German antifascist discourse: by supplying false hope, Jakob prevents the Jews from taking up arms against the Germans. But one can also read the text as a subtle reordering of the terms of resistance, as a rejection of the clichéd bathos used to depict the communist heroes of socialist realist prose.

Becker's second novel, *Irreführung der Behörden* (1973; Leading the Authorities Astray), describes the adventures of putative law student and would-be writer Gregor Bienek in East Germany. Bienek appears rather more interested in experiencing life and telling stories than in writing them down, but when a film script is accepted, he is confronted with the compromises (including censorship) success entails. In his following novel, *Der Boxer* (1976; The Boxer), Becker continues his previous investigations into the Holocaust, narration, and the limits of representation. An East German gentile interviews Holocaust survivor Arno Blank in an attempt to construct the latter's biography. The narrator sees Arno as a Jew; the latter is less convinced. Similar to Becker in essays and interviews, Blank argues that the children of Christian parents can decide whether they are Christian; he complains that society denies children of Jewish parents that right. Similar to Max Frisch's play *Andorra* (1961; *Andorra*), *Der Boxer* takes as its starting point Sartre's dictum that a Jew is someone society considers a Jew.

In 1976, the East German government expatriated critic and songwriter Wolf Biermann, causing numerous leading artists and intellectuals to compose and circulate a letter of protest. Becker was among the 12 original signatories. He then wrote *Schlaflose Tage* (1978; *Sleepless Days*), which intensifies his examination, begun in *Irreführung der Behörden,* of the individual in society. In this novel, the East German teacher Simrock begins to take the lofty phrases of the ruling Socialist Unity Party literally, which brings him trouble. His political problems multiply and the school suspends him from his post. Simrock's intransigence is strengthened by the fact that his girlfriend was arrested and imprisoned for trying to cross the iron curtain during a vacation in Hungary.

Sleepless Days presents Becker's angry, defiant, and disappointed reckoning with his country, where the book could not be published. He left East Germany in late 1978. As a visiting writer at Oberlin College, Ohio, he wrote many of the stories contained in the collection *Nach der ersten Zukunft* (1980; After the First Future). The stories reflect some of Becker's earlier preoccupations (Jewish children in a Nazi ghetto, the process of storytelling, and criticism of East German society), as well as his impressions of the United States. In 1982, he published *Aller Welt Freund* (Friend of All the World), his first novel written in the West. Acknowledging its formal and thematic indebtedness to Raymond Chandler's *The Long Goodbye,* Becker's novel describes in a humorously ironic fashion episodes from the life of Kilian, a news editor who has unsuccessfully tried to take his life. Perhaps in an attempt to reach a larger and more general audience, the novel includes mention of several global issues. As opposed to *Irreführung der Behörden, Nach der ersten Zukunft,* and especially *Sleepless Days,* the social context is left purposefully vague.

Becker returns to his earlier strengths in *Bronsteins Kinder* (1986; *Bronstein's Children*), a novel concerning a Jewish family in East Germany. In this work, Hans Bronstein discovers that his father, a concentration camp survivor, has captured a former Nazi camp guard and is torturing him. Similarly to *Der Boxer,* to which there are several intertextual references, the novel asks both what it means to be Jewish and to what extent Jewish survivors could be integrated into (East) German society. Arno Bronstein and his Jewish accomplices refer to East Germany as enemy territory and see no fundamental difference between East and West Germany. For the victims, at least, the past is not past: there are no good Germans. More generally, the novel treats the subject of Jews in socialism; Bronstein, a name mentioned in the title but not in the text, was Trotsky's bourgeois name.

In the 1990s, Becker published *Die beliebteste Familiengeschichte und andere Erzählungen* (1991; The Favorite Family Story and Other Stories) and *Amanda Herzlos* (1992; Amanda Heartless), a novel in which an East German woman is described by three of her lovers. Feuilletonists were divided on the novel's merits, with some complaining that Becker had omitted serious mention of the East German state's abusive nature. Others suggested that in Becker's detailed description of the East German quotidian, with its bureaucracy and stultifying mediocrity, lies an exact account of East German life.

Becker collaborated on over 20 television or feature films, including adaptations of *Jakob the Liar* (1974), *Der Boxer* (1979), *Schlaflose Tage* (1982), and *Bronstein's Children* (1990). In the 1980s and 1990s, he attained considerable popular success writing scripts for the television series *Liebling Kreuzberg* (Attorney Liebling of Berlin-Kreuzberg) and *Wir sind auch nur ein Volk* (We Are Also Only a People), a satirical look at the East German–West German tensions and misunderstandings that resulted from unification. Both series featured Becker's friend Manfred Krug, who had also left East Germany following the Biermann scandal.

THOMAS C. FOX

Biography

Born in Lodz, 30 September 1937. In Ravensbrück and Sachsenhausen concentration camps, World War II; studied at Humboldt University, Berlin, 1957–60, and Filmhochschule, Potsdam-Babelsberg; member of the Socialist Unity Party, 1957 (expelled 1976); writer-in-residence at Oberlin College, Oberlin, Ohio, 1978, Cornell University, Ithaca, New York, 1984, and the University of Texas, Austin, 1987; visiting professor at the University of Essen, 1978; and the University of Augsburg, 1982–83; resident writer, Bergen-Enkheim, 1987; member of the German Academy for Languages and Literature, 1983–97, and the Academy of Arts, Berlin, 1990. Heinrich Mann Prize, 1971; Veillon Prize (Switzerland), 1971; West Berlin Film Festival Silver Bear Award, 1974; City of Bremen Prize, 1974; National Prize for Literature, 1975; Grimme Prize, 1988; Fallada Prize, 1990; Bayerische Prize, 1990; Bundesfilmpreis, 1991. Died on 14 March 1997.

Selected Works

Fiction

Jakob der Lügner, 1969; as *Jacob the Liar,* 1975; as *Jakob the Liar,* 1990
Irreführung der Behörden, 1973
Der Boxer, 1976
Schlaflose Tage, 1978; as *Sleepless Days,* 1979
Nach der ersten Zukunft, 1980
Aller Welt Freund, 1982
Bronsteins Kinder, 1986; as *Bronstein's Children,* 1988
Erzählungen, 1986
Die beliebteste Familiengeschichte und andere Erzählungen, 1991
Amanda Herzlos, 1992

Screenplays

Jakob der Lügner, 1974
Liebling Kreuzberg (television screenplay), 1986, 1988, 1990
Neuner (screenplay), 1991
Wir sind auch nur ein Volk (television screenplay), 1994–95

Other

Warnung vor dem Schriftsteller, 1990

Further Reading

Arnold, Heinz Ludwig, editor, "Jurek Becker," *Text und Kritik* 116 (1992)
Fox, Thomas C., *Border Crossings: An Introduction to East German Prose,* Ann Arbor: University of Michigan Press, 1993
Heidelberger-Leonard, Irene, editor, *Jurek Becker,* Frankfurt: Suhrkamp, 1992
Johnson, Susan, *The Works of Jurek Becker: A Thematic Analysis,* New York: Lang, 1988
Kane, Martin, editor, *Socialism and the Literary Imagination: Essays on East German Writers,* New York: Berg, 1991; distributed in United States by St. Martin's Press
Wetzel, Heinz, editor, "Moral Issues in Jurek Becker's *Jakob der Lügner:* Contributions to a Symposium," *Seminar* 19, no. 4 (1983)
Zipser, Richard, "Interview with Jurek Becker (May, 1978—Oberlin, Ohio)," *Dimension* 11, no. 3 (1978)
———, "Jurek Becker: A Writer with a Cause," *Dimension* 11, no. 3 (1978)

Richard Beer-Hofmann 1866–1945

Richard Beer-Hofmann was born in Vienna one year before imperial Austria would enter into the great Compromise of 1867, the final attempt of the ruling Habsburg dynasty to salvage its political power by forming the multiethnic Austro-Hungarian Empire. During the 1860s, the Habsburg monarchy, faithfully supported by the aristocracy, the bureaucracy, and the military, appeared to be impervious to any threats of disarray or decline. The ethos of the period was marked by an enlightened liberalism. The liberals, who came to power as a result of the Compromise of 1867, helped bring about significant changes in social, economic, and educational matters. While Vienna's liberal bourgeoisie was able to maintain some semblance of tolerance and openness during the following two decades, those liberal values, which they were so eager to embrace earlier, had by the 1890s been emptied of the last vestiges of social and moral commitment. The contradiction between the former social awareness and the growing possessive individualism became more and more apparent in an uneasy nervousness that manifested itself in a self-indulging, self-centered hedonism. It was in this climate that Vienna's liberal bourgeoisie engaged in the construction of the Ringstrasse. Splendid ceremonial displays abounded, and monumental architecture accentuated the fin de siècle culture of the 1890s. Glittering pomp and pageantry became substitutes for any genuine concerns about a social order that was quickly unraveling.

No one had more to lose in the defeat of liberalism than the assimilated, urban Jews of the Austro-Hungarian monarchy. In the brief span of one generation (from 1849, when Jews received the right to vote, to 1867, when they obtained complete emancipation), they had achieved great advances in the arenas of commerce and finance, and in law, medicine, and science. The rapid improvements among the monarchy's urban Jewish population, however, should not be seen as a sign that the monarchy was free of anti-Semitic sentiments. On the contrary, even during the era of bourgeois liberalism there existed a pervasive, yet contained, form of anti-Semitism. As the political power of the liberals began to wane and that of the Christian Socialists and Pan-Germans escalated, the doors of advancements became harder and harder to open.

Another important factor concerning upward mobility among Vienna's Jews had to do with the changing attitudes toward assimilation and having a "respectable" profession. In the generation of Beer-Hofmann's grandparents, assimilation had occurred primarily through economic activity or religious secularization. The fathers of Beer-Hofmann's generation, who already enjoyed a measure of economic success, were glad to finance their sons' university education, which would assure them social mobility and an entry into higher society. Many of the sons, however, were more interested in the arts. As with Beer-Hofmann, many of these young men were motivated by their own aesthetic sensibilities. Reared in well-to-do circumstances by genteel parents, they were, in essence, groomed for the arts. It was in the context of this milieu that the leading literary and artistic figures of the group Young Vienna emerged.

In 1890, when Beer-Hofmann completed his legal studies at the University of Vienna, an important event would prove to have a profound and lasting influence on his life: meeting Arthur Schnitzler. A close friendship quickly flourished and lasted a lifetime. It was through this friendship that the young Beer-Hofmann soon became known in the literary circles of Vienna, although he had not yet begun to write. It was in the exuberant literary ambience of Vienna's Café Griensteidl, surrounded by budding young authors such as Schnitzler, Hugo von Hofmannsthal, Jakob Wassermann, Felix Salten, and Peter Altenberg, that Beer-Hofmann (at the constant prodding of Schnitzler) penned his first prose work.

Beer-Hofmann turned initially to writing short prose works: *Camelias* (1891) and *Das Kind* (1893; The Child). Later, he wrote perhaps his best-known works, the novel *Der Tod Georgs* (1900; The Death of Georg), and *Paula, ein Fragment* (published posthumously in its entirety in 1949). Beer-Hofmann's *Camelias* and *Das Kind* can be best characterized as youthful experiments in which the young author was developing his artistic skills. His attempts, however, were very epigonic, mimicking both the style and plot of the Viennese Decadence. In each narrative the protagonist is a well-to-do young "dandy" who languishes in his daily affairs, falling in and out of unscrupulous relationships and unable to find meaning in his life. In contrast to *Camelias,* however, *Das Kind* shows promising signs of originality. In the latter work, Beer-Hofmann succeeds in creating a better defined protagonist, as well as more dialogue, and introduces a problem to which he returns more fully in his later biblical dramas, namely, the problem of the existence of suffering and evil in the world.

Beer-Hofmann's novel *Der Tod Georgs* reflects a mature literary sophistication and an original imprint on the literature of fin de siècle Vienna. In terms of language, style, and motifs the novel is most often categorized as being quintessentially part of the Jugendstil, or art nouveau movement. While critics, in general, will agree with this, there is nonetheless one significant difference. The image of death at the end of the novel is recast by Beer-Hofmann to represent not the Jugendstil attitude of longing for escape from the suffering and ugliness of life, but rather the culmination of a pilgrimage or journey.

With the success of his novel, Beer-Hofmann turned his attention to drama and delved deeper into the artistic and religious concerns that preoccupied him throughout his entire life. These were the representation of a just and meaningful universal order, despite human suffering and evil in the world; the problem of being an artist and the purpose and process of artistic creation; and the renewal of literary language and the revitalization of the drama. With his attention focused on theater, Beer-Hofmann's friendships with Hugo von Hofmannsthal, Max Reinhardt, and Leopold von Adrian also flourished. Three dramatic works stand out as among Beer-Hofmann's best: *Der Graf von Charolais* (1904; The Count of Charolais), the pantomime *Das goldene Pferd* (published posthumously in 1955; The Golden Horse), and the biblical cycle fragment, *Die Historie von König David* (1905; The History of King David). In each of these plays, Beer-Hofmann returns to the issue of evil and suffering. His objective is to reconcile his personal understanding of the just nature of God and the universal order with the suffering and injustice that he witnessed in the world. No other literary work was to achieve this reconciliation as well as his King David cycle, which Beer-Hofmann envisioned to be his greatest literary achievement. Of the five plays in the cycle, only three exist in their finished form: *Jaákobs Traum* (1918; Jacob's Dream), *Der junge David* (1933; The Young David), and *Vorspiel auf dem Theater zu König David* (1936; Prelude to King David). *König David* (King David) and *Davids Tod* (1936; David's Death) were never completed.

Like many of his contemporaries, Richard Beer-Hofmann was quite conscious of the fact that he stood at the close of an era. His greatest fears, however, were not centered in the certainty of an ending age, but rather in the uncertainty of the one yet to come. Rapid industrialization, the rise of nationalism and militarism, the advance of technology, the ascendance of psychology, and the decline of religion—all helped to shaped Beer-Hofmann's prevailing concerns as a writer.

ISTVAN VARKONYI

Biography

Born in Vienna, 11 July 1866. Early years spent in the Moravian city of Brno; in 1880 the family moved to Vienna, where he completed his schooling at the Akademisches Gymnasium; law degree, University of Vienna, 1890; summer trips to Salzburg, Dolomites, and to Southern Tyrol, 1900–1910; in 1901 moved with family to Rodaun and became Hugo von Hofmannsthal's neighbor; in 1903 took an extensive trip to Italy with family; spent the fall of 1904 in Berlin with Max Reinhardt preparing the premiere of *The Count from Charolais;* directed Goethe's *Iphigenie* in 1928 at the Theater in der Josefstadt; all his work banned in Nazi Germany, 1933; trip to Palestine, 1936; left Vienna for the United States via Switzerland, 1939, where his wife died; continued his emigration alone and arrived in New York in November, 1939; in New York, 1940–44; became U.S. citizen, 1945. Nestroy Prize, Vienna, 1921; Distinguished Achievements Award from the National Institute of the American Academy of Arts and Letters, 1945. Died in New York, 26 September 1945.

Selected Works

Collections
Gesammelte Werke, 1963

Fiction
Novellen, 1893
Der Tod Georgs, 1900

Plays
Der Graf von Charolais, 1904
Jaákobs Traum, 1918; as *Jacob's Dream,* translated by Ida Bension Wynn, 1946
Der junge David, 1933
Vorspiel auf dem Theater zu König David, 1936
Das goldene Pferd, 1955

Poetry
Schlaflied für Mirjam, 1919
Verse, 1941

Nonfiction
Gedenkrede aus Wolfgang Amade Mozart, 1906; as *Memorial Oration on Wolfgang Amadeus Mozart,* in *Heart of Europe,* translated by Samuel R. Wachtell, 1943
Paula, ein Fragment, edited by Otto Kallir, 1949

Further Reading

Bunzel, Matti, "The Poetics of Politics and the Politics of Poetics: Richard Beer-Haofmann and Theodor Herzl Reconsidered," *German Quarterly* 69, no. 3 (1996)
Elstun, Esther N., *Richard Beer-Hofmann: His Life and Work,* University Park: Pennsylvania State University Press, 1983
Elstun, Esther N., "Einsamkeit und Isolation in den Werken Arthur Schnitzlers und Richard Beer-Hofmanns," *Modern Austrian Literature* 19, nos. 3, 4 (1986)
Kosenina, Alexander, "' . . . was wir Juden tun, vollzieht sich auf einer Bühne—unser Los hat sie gezimmert': Richard Beer-Hofmanns Briefwechsel mit Martin Buber (1910–1936)," *Modern Austrian Literature* 29, no. 2 (1996)
Neumann, Hans-Gerhard, *Richard Beer-Hofmann,* Munich: Fink, 1972
Oberholzer, Otto, *Richard Beer-Hofmann: Werk und Weltbild des Dichters,* Bern: Francke, 1947
Scherer, Stefan, *Richard Beer-Hofmann und die Wiener Moderne,* Tübingen: Niemeyer Verlag, 1993
Steck-Meier, Esther, "Richard Beer-Hofmann: Der Tod Georgs (1900)," in *Erzählkunst der Moderne,* Bern: Lang, 1996
Weber, Eugene, "Richard Beer-Hofmann," in *Deutschsprachinge Exilliteratur seit 1933,* vol. 2, edited by John M. Spaleck and Joseph Strelka, Bern: Francke Verlag, 1989
Zohn, Harry, ". . . *ich bin ein Sohn der deutschen Sprache nur . . .": Jüdisches Erbe in der österreichischen Literatur,* Vienna: Amalthea, 1986

Walter Benjamin 1892–1940

Walter Benjamin's achievements have contributed substantially to the reconstituted place of criticism as a genre in modern culture. Nonetheless, while one thinks of the critic's task as mediating between artistic expression and a contemporary audience, Benjamin accomplished this task only to a limited extent. At the end of the 20th century, the authority of his critical perspectives has established him as a paramount figure, yet this posthumous reception has followed a strikingly different course from the constant setbacks that plagued his life story. During his lifetime, his work attracted only a meager readership, although he was recognized by many outstanding individuals of his generation, among them Theodor Adorno, Ernst Bloch, Hannah Arendt, Siegfried Kracauer, and Bertold Brecht. In 1922, after some early forays into theory and philosophy, he completed the first work that made good on his ambitions as a critic: a long and brilliantly original essay on Goethe's *Die Wahlverwandtschaften* (*Elective Affinities*), in which he boldly attacked Friedrich Gundolf, then the reigning authority among Goethe commentators. Hugo von Hofmannsthal accepted the essay with great enthusiasm for the journal *Neue deutsche Beiträge,* and Benjamin felt confident that this prestigious platform would make it impossible for Gundolf's partisans in the George Circle to ignore his challenge, yet it was passed over in silence.

Toward the end of his career, Benjamin published the essay that has since become one of the most widely read and frequently quoted texts on the work of art under modern conditions, "Das Kunstwerk im Zeitalter seiner technischen Reproduzierbarkeit" (1936; "The Work of Art in the Age of Mechanical

Reproduction"). He wrote it for the Frankfurt School's journal, *Die Zeitschrift für Sozialforschung,* completing the first version by the close of 1935, writing a second version in 1936, and making further revisions until 1939. Presenting the richly suggestive theory that the work of art has undergone a "loss of aura" through the dissemination of representations in the modern media, this account has been widely accepted as a defining vision for our relations with the great achievements of the past. Moreover, Benjamin's enthusiastic prognosis for the future role of the new media as he knew them in the 1930s, most especially film, has come to stand as a founding statement for film aesthetics. Passages in this essay assert that film exercises an inherent tendency to move its audiences away from fascism and toward an emancipated, materialist consciousness. Long after Benjamin's death, when scholars began to expand academic interest in popular culture, claims to politically progressive functions for their various disciplines have been frequently argued from those assertions. Yet this essay ran into heavy skepticism from the editors of *Die Zeitschrift für Sozialforschung.* They found both that its thesis rested on an inadequate attempt to embrace Marxist terminology and that its reasoning, "lacking mediation" according to Adorno, arrived at an implausible conclusion on mass-media aesthetics. Brecht, although generally well-disposed to Benjamin and his writing, noted in 1938 that the essay was mystical in its outlook despite its antimystical posture and described it as "gräßlich" (wretched).

Nonetheless, the decades from the 1950s onward, during which Benjamin's work has begun to circulate in new editions, have seen his influence grow irresistibly in many diverse fields of intellectual and creative endeavor. Quotations from his writing have now come to anchor positions in historiography, sociology, political theory, aesthetics, cultural criticism, and literary studies. Both in depth and breadth, this reception attests richly to the power of Benjamin's talent, as well as to an intriguing match between the forms of critical language that he developed and the concerns of our own time. The diversity of approaches in which his writing has been taken up also indicates the internal complications of his thought. To understand his thinking means to understand first and foremost why it is so difficult to reduce his perspective to a single position. Even though his work passed through distinct phases in which particular ideas came to the fore, his unique emphasis on critique never permitted him to take up any conviction except as a means to dialectical movement toward a future that the resources of the present are inadequate to represent with more than provisional security.

Benjamin was born into a prosperous Jewish family in Berlin. His early speculative writings reflect his participation in the pre–World War I youth movement; he was an intellectual leader of the independent student group devoted to the idealist teachings of Gustav Wyneken. When in 1915 Wyneken embraced the war effort on the grounds that it embodied the ideals of spiritual renewal, Benjamin broke with him irrevocably. Looking back from the perspective of middle life on his early devotion to this cause, Benjamin reflected that the conditions of their class had misled the group into a conviction that they could remake the spirit of a culture without changing its concrete conditions. For the next ten years, however, he would pass through many attempts to replace the lost focus in his thinking and in his social existence. He responded first by more urgently pursuing his studies in philosophy. Evading war service on medical grounds, he took up his doctoral studies at Bern. In 1919 he completed a dissertation on the early German Romantics' concept of art criticism. In this work, he established himself as an independent thinker and also encountered a realm of ideas that energetically upheld the significance of criticism vis-à-vis all other modes of expression. The effects of that early encounter clearly persisted until 1940 with the critical function of materialist historiography in "Über den Begriff der Geschichte" ("Theses on the Philosophy of History").

In 1921 he turned to the questions of political theory and action. With "Zur Kritik der Gewalt" ("Critique of Violence"), he took a position that combined anarcho-syndicalism, borrowed from Georges Sorel, with theories of meaning derived from Jewish theology. He had developed these concerns with a messianic theology of language in earlier essays but also brought them to a higher level of maturity in 1921 with "Die Aufgabe des Übersetzers" ("The Task of the Translator"), written as the introduction for his translations of Baudelaire's poetry. In 1924–25, partly inspired by his relationship with a woman revolutionary named Asja Lacis, he declared himself a communist. This did not lead him either to join the Communist Party or, at first, to adopt a rigorous Marxist theory of history in his writing; it did lead him, however, to produce a series of penetrating fragmentary observations or aphorisms published in 1928 under the title *Einbahnstraße* (*One-Way Street*). Benjamin's technique in this book is to represent dialectical images or isolated experiences and then compress them into fragmentary visions of society trembling at the brink of dissolution. The year 1925 also saw an end to his hopes of securing an academic career when his habilitation thesis, published as *Der Ursprung des deutschen Trauerspiels* (*The Origin of German Tragic Drama*), was rejected by Frankfurt University. The scholars on his committee found his argument in that work impenetrable, and, indeed, his monumental intellectual effort to revise the critical view of the Baroque period and the allegorical forms employed in that period is couched in terms that interweave profundity and obscurity.

After this rebuff, he turned instead to literary journalism, publishing a large number of essays, reviews, commentaries on the times, and observations from his travels, which included a journey in 1926–27 to visit Asja Lacis in Moscow. The many articles he produced during this period, such as an essay on the revolutionary potential of surrealism, identified him as a vehement voice on the left, albeit one without any organized affiliation. Under National Socialism, Benjamin was among the first group of intellectuals driven into exile. Cut off from Berlin, the milieu most conducive to his work, he attempted to reestablish himself in Paris, intermittently leaving in the hopeless search for some situation where he could reconcile the needs of his material existence and the conditions necessary for his intellectual labors. Henceforward, the difficulties he experienced in supporting himself changed from annoyances to severe insecurities. The impact of this change can be discerned in the 1934 essay "Der Autor als Produzent" ("The Author as Producer"), in which he develops the thesis that, when the conditions of intellectual labor begin to emulate those of proletarian production, the contradiction between the bourgeois origins of a writer and his revolutionary commitment will be resolved.

The largest enterprise among the tasks he labored to continue during this exile, his great study of capitalist culture in 19th-century Paris, known as *Das Passagen-Werk* (*The Arcades Project*), remained unfinished. The research and thought for this undertaking did result in smaller complete works, including important essays on Baudelaire. The work on Baudelaire elaborates some of Benjamin's most thought-provoking efforts to link evolving forms of literary culture with the material circumstances that capitalist conditions impose on the writer. Although scholars still hotly dispute which period brought about the best or most genuine expression of Benjamin's thinking, these years did result in a series of especially well-focused and self-contained studies on different aspects of an evolving modernity, notably "Franz Kafka" (1934; "Franz Kafka"), "Der Erzähler" (1936; "The Storyteller") and "Eduard Fuchs, der Sammler und Historiker" (1937; "Edward Fuchs, the Collector and Historian"), as well as the mechanical reproduction essay and "Theses on the Philosophy of History."

Benjamin died in 1940, committing suicide while in the custody of Spanish border authorities after attempting to escape from German-occupied France without an entry visa. The suitcase he carried with him most probably contained a more complete version of the *Passagen-Werk,* but it was lost without trace after his death.

In the atmosphere of crisis that constantly revisited Europe after World War I, Benjamin's unwillingness to rest within the bounds of any contemporary programmatic formula of redemption left even those groups and interests to which he stood closest uncertain about his place; this robbed him of a solid readership. The difficulties he presented his contemporaries even affected the two friends and supporters, Gershom Scholem and Theodor Adorno, who became his literary executors and who published the posthumous editions that began the remarkable reassessment that has brought him such fame today. Although Benjamin's thinking had absorbed an essential component of Jewish theology and made emphatic use of messianic and apocalyptic terms, he could not restrict himself to any form of Jewish exclusivity or to the Zionism that attracted many Jews of his generation, including Scholem. Although the core of his talent embraces a mastery of abstract philosophical construction, tensions between him and Adorno reveal Benjamin's conscious unwillingness to let that talent dictate a particular mode of thought whose values he could wholeheartedly support.

The emphasis in his mature writing invites the reader to conclude that he derived the strongest body of his ideas from Marxism, yet he clearly adopts the Marxist inheritance in order to subject other dimensions of his thinking to their most rigorous test. For all the weight he gives historical materialism during the 1930s, however, the most thorough readings of his work show that he never simply adopted this theory as a decisive replacement for his earlier views. More accurately, he found this theory of history and political relations indispensable for the radical rethinking of his earlier concerns.

Yet if these complexities in Benjamin's thinking worked against his finding a secure niche during his lifetime in the period before World War II, the same qualities have made him the ancestor of choice for several generations of intellectuals in the second half of the 20th century. This process began vividly with the German student movement of the 1960s, which took him up as a brilliantly intense revolutionary voice that had spoken without any burden of debt to a party machine. In the 1970s, post-structuralism also found attractive echoes of itself in the sheer power of an imagination that could master the fragments of modernist culture and demonstrate their maneuverability amid the fields of so many forces. His intense critical penetration of mass-produced artifacts continues to arouse great interest in the area of cultural studies. Reception in the English-speaking world began in earnest in 1968 with a collection of his essays entitled *Illuminations,* edited with a lengthy introductory commentary by Hannah Arendt. Despite her explicit effort to center his work in his speculations on language and metaphysics and to identify a kinship between Benjamin and Heidegger, anglophone readers have generally followed the lead of younger German scholars, reading him as an associate of the Frankfurt School who was concerned with the sociology of culture. Since that time, increased attention has also been paid to Jewish elements in his writing.

MARCUS BULLOCK

See also Aestheticization of Politics

Biography

Born in Berlin, 15 July 1892. Met Gustav Wyneken at the Haubinda boarding school, 1905–6, and later became a disciple of Wyneken in the youth movement until 1915; studied at the University of Freiburg, 1912, the University of Berlin, 1913, the University of Munich, 1915–17, and the University of Bern, where he received a Ph.D. in 1919; declared himself a communist, 1924; travel to Moscow in 1926–27; in Paris, 1927; met Bertolt Brecht, 1929; exiled from Germany, 1933–; lived primarily in Paris. Died (suicide) while attempting to escape from occupied France, in Port Bou, Spain, 26 September 1940.

Selected Works

Collections

Schriften, 2 vols., edited by T.W. Adorno and Gretel Adorno, 1955
Illuminationen: Ausgewählte Schriften, edited by Siegfried Unseld, 1961; as *Illuminations,* edited and with an introduction by Hannah Arendt, translated by Harry Zohn, 1968
Gesammelte Schriften, edited by Rolf Tiedemann and Hermann Schweppenhäuser, 7 vols., 1972–89
Reflections: Essays, Aphorisms, Autobiographical Writings, translated by Edmund Jephcott, edited and with an introduction by Peter Demetz, 1978
One-Way Street and Other Writings, translated by Edmund Jephcott and Kingsley Shorter, with an introduction by Susan Sontag, 1979
Selected Writings, vol. 1, *1913–1926,* various translators, edited by Marcus Bullock and Michael Jennings, 1996

Criticism

"Metaphysik der Jugend," 1914; as "Metaphysics of Youth," translated by Rodney Livingstone, 1996
"Zwei Gedichte von Friedrich Hölderlin," 1915; as "Two Poems by Friedrich Hölderlin," translated by Stanley Corngold, 1996
"Über Sprache überhaupt und über die Sprache des Menschen," 1916; as "On Language as Such and the Language of Man," translated by Edmund Jephcott, 1978
Der Begriff der Kunstkritik in der deutschen Romantik, 1919; as *The Concept of Criticism in German Romanticism,* translated by David Lachterman, Howard Eiland, and Ian Balfour, 1996
"Die Aufgabe Übersetzers," 1921; as "The Task of the Translator," translated by Harry Zohn, 1968
"Zur Kritik der Gewalt," 1921; as "Critique of Violence," translated by Edmund Jephcott, 1978
"Goethes Wahlverwandtschaften," 1922; as "Goethe's Elective Affinities," translated by Stanley Corngold, 1996
Der Ursprung des deutschen Trauerspiels, 1925; as *The Origin of German Tragic Drama,* translated by John Osborne, 1977

Einbahnstraße, 1926; as *One-Way Street,* translated by Edmund Jephcott, 1978
"Moskauer Tagebuch," 1927; as *Moscow Diary,* translated by Richard Sieburth, 1986
"Der Sürrealismus," 1929; as "Surrealism," translated by Edmund Jephcott, 1978
"Zum Bilde Prousts," 1929; as "The Image of Proust," translated by Harry Zohn, 1968
"Theorien des deutschen Faschismus," 1930; as "Theories of German Fascism: On the Collection of Essays 'War and Warriors,'" edited by Ernst Jünger, translated by Jerolf Wikoff, 1979
"Karl Kraus," 1931; translated by Harry Zohn, 1968
"Kleine Geschichte der Photographie," 1931; as "A Small History of Photography," translated by Edmund Jephcott and Kingsley Shorter, 1979
"Berliner Chronik," 1932; as "Berlin Chronicle," translated by Edmund Jephcott, 1978
"Der Autor als Produzent," 1934; as "The Author as Producer," translated by Edmund Jephcott, 1978
"Franz Kafka," 1934; translated by Harry Zohn, 1968
"Das Kunstwerk im Zeitalter seiner technischen Reproduzierbarkeit [erste fassung]," 1936; as "The Work of Art in the Age of Mechanical Reproduction," translated by Harry Zohn, 1968
"Paris, die Hauptstadt des XIX. Jahrhunderts," 1935; as "Paris: Capital of the Nineteenth Century," translated by Edmund Jephcott, 1978
"Der Erzähler," 1936; as "The Story-Teller: Reflections on the Work of Nicolai Leskov," translated by Harry Zohn, 1962
"Eduard Fuchs, der Sammler und der Historiker," 1937; as "Eduard Fuchs, the Collector and Historian," translated by Edmund Jephcott, 1978
"Berliner Kindheit um Neunzehnhundert," 1938
"Das Paris des Second Empire bei Baudelaire," 1938; as "Paris of the Second Empire in Baudelaire," translated by Harry Zohn and Quintin Hoare, 1973
"Über einige Motive bei Baudelaire," 1939; as "On Some Motifs in Baudelaire," translated by Harry Zohn, 1968
"Was ist das epische Theater?" 1939; as "What Is Epic Theater?" translated by Harry Zohn, 1968
"Zentralpark," 1939; as "Central Park," translated by Lloyd Spencer with Mark Harrington, 1985
"Über den Begriff der Geschichte," 1940; as "Theses on the Philosophy of History," translated by Harry Zohn, 1968

Further Reading

Benjamin, Andrew, and Peter Osborne, editors, *Walter Benjamin's Philosophy: Destruction and Experience,* London and New York: Routledge, 1994
Brodersen, Momme, *Walter Benjamin: A Biography,* London and New York: Verso, 1996
Cohen, Margaret, *Profane Illumination: Walter Benjamin and the Paris of Surrealist Revolution,* Berkeley: University of California Press, 1993; London: University of California Press, 1995
Hanssen, Beatrice, *Walter Benjamin's Other History: Of Stones, Animals, Human Beings, and Angels,* Berkeley: University of California Press, 1998
McCole, John, *Walter Benjamin and the Antinomies of Tradition,* Ithaca, New York: Cornell University Press, 1993
Nägele, Rainer, editor, *Benjamin's Ground: New Readings of Walter Benjamin,* Detroit, Michigan: Wayne State University Press, 1988
Scholem, Gershom, *Walter Benjamin: The Story of a Friendship,* Philadelphia, Pennsylvania: Jewish Publication Society of America, 1981; London: Faber and Faber, 1982
Smith, Gary, editor, *On Walter Benjamin: Critical Essays and Recollections,* Cambridge, Massachusetts: MIT Press, 1988

Das Kunstwerk im Zeitalter seiner technischen Reproduzierbarkeit 1936

Essay by Walter Benjamin

Walter Benjamin's essay first appeared in 1936 in a French translation; the German original exists in two versions, the first corresponding to the French publication. In its analysis of traditional and modern art forms, of the constitutive role that uniqueness plays in the former and that mechanical reproducibility plays in the latter, and of the far-reaching consequences for the audience that this technical alteration introduces, the essay is one of the 20th century's most influential speculations on art and society. It is also taken, albeit only half correctly, to correspond to Benjamin's social-historical and Marxist-influenced work of the 1930s, and it is his most extended treatment of the medium of film, at the time still relatively new and underanalyzed by art theorists. The apparent correspondence of the essay to other politically engaged writing from the 1930s by Brecht, Lukács, and many others, together with the vagaries of Benjamin's rediscovery and wide reception during the self-consciously politicized 1960s and 1970s, have led to the "Work of Art" essay becoming perhaps Benjamin's single best-known piece of work, anthologized and cited in many different contexts but most often used to represent a Marxist and politicized version of Benjamin. This narrow understanding neglects some of the essay's more enduring points.

The essay is composed of 15 numbered sections, framed by a preface and an epilogue. The framing pieces open and close the essay symmetrically with their appeals to fascism's dangers and communism's response. Benjamin's preface invokes Marx and claims that changes in the "superstructure" of culture are manifesting changes in the substructure of "the conditions of production" that occurred more than half a century earlier. This alleged fact calls for changes in our concepts of art, for "outmoded concepts" could only "lead to a processing of data in the Fascist sense," while he wishes to assist "the formulation of revolutionary demands in the politics of art." The opposition of fascism and communism returns in the epilogue in the especially memorable form of a chiasmus, a figure of speech that twists a parallel structure into one of inverted contrast: "[Mankind's] self-alienation has reached such a degree that it can experience its own destruction as an aesthetic pleasure of the first order. This is the situation of politics which Fascism is rendering aesthetic. Communism responds by politicizing art." The aestheticization of politics is answered, chiastically, by the politicization of art.

In between these politically urgent appeals, arising amid the increasingly desperate atmosphere of Europe in the 1930s (Benjamin wrote the essay in Paris during his exile from Nazi Germany), is a searching analysis of the history and structure of European art that owes more to the reflections of the French poet and aesthetician Paul Valéry, the Austrian art historian Alois Riegl, and the German sociologist Georg Simmel than to the work of Marx and Brecht. Benjamin argues that, from lithography to photography to film, art has increasingly introduced the means of technical reproduction into the very conception and constitution of the work of art itself. This means that the concept of the "original" has come to fall by the wayside. The "unique existence of the work of art determined the history to which it was subject . . . the presence of the original [was] the prerequisite to the concept of authenticity." By contrast, "technical reproduction can put the copy of the original into situations that would be out of reach for the original itself." This shift, viewed from what Benjamin, after Hegel, calls "the perspective of world history," leads to consequences that he analyzes in terms of three related sets of concepts.

The first is the loss of what Benjamin calls "aura." Aura, which he famously defines as "the unique phenomenon of a distance, however close [an object] may be," is what "withers in the age of mechanical reproduction," for the reproduced work of art can be brought "closer spatially and humanly," thereby "overcoming the uniqueness of every reality by accepting its reproduction." "Uniqueness and permanence" thus give way to "transitoriness and reproducibility." What is ultimately at stake is tradition itself, "the essence of all that is transmissible from [an original object's] beginning, ranging from its substantive duration to its testimony to the history that it has experienced."

In keeping with the revolutionary impulse that frames the essay, Benjamin celebrates this loss, but in keeping with his own deeply conservative attitudes toward high art, he is simultaneously ambivalent: the processes of detachment from tradition and substitution of "a plurality of copies for a unique existence . . . lead to a tremendous shattering of tradition that is the obverse of the contemporary crisis and renewal of mankind." Shattering and renewal are the two sides of a coin that Benjamin hopes to see turning right-side-up in history's hands. However, this comes at a cost: "Its most positive [significance] is inconceivable without its destructive, cathartic aspect, that is, the liquidation of the traditional value of the cultural heritage."

His second set of analytic and evaluative terms is more unilinear and less ambivalent: cult value and exhibition value. Anticipating Horkheimer and Adorno's argument in their *Dialectic of Enlightenment* (Benjamin's essay was commissioned by, and published in the journal of, their Institute for Social Research), Benjamin links the aura of the work of art and its integration in tradition with art's original "cult" function, a ritual function that was first magical, then religious. By way of the transitional "secularized ritual" of the cult of beauty during the Renaissance, art is finally "emancipate[d] . . . from its parasitical dependence on ritual" by mechanical reproduction. Cult value is replaced, first in photography and then massively in film, by exhibition value, which Benjamin also confusingly associates with politics.

In the third of his sets of interpretive terms, Benjamin accents the mass character of the work of art's exhibition value. As he inquires into the changes that occur when art detaches from cultic or religious tradition and distance and enters into mass consumption, he asserts that the masses identify with imagery of reality by way of the segmented, disassembled-and-reassembled character of experience that mechanical reproducibility introduces into film. However, once again this is a source of ambivalence for Benjamin. Of the photographic portrait, "a last refuge for the cult value of the picture," he writes, "For the last time the aura emanates . . . in the fleeting expression of a human face. This is what constitutes their melancholy, incomparable beauty." Similarly, in terms that are fraught with the rhetoric of alienation and fragmentation in modern life, the mass audience identifies with the "segmented performances of the individual" film actor by way of adopting the camera's mechanical position and point of view. On the one hand this fulfills "modern man's legitimate claim to being reproduced," but on the other hand it multiplies "the estrangement felt before one's own image in the mirror." Benjamin explicitly notes a sleight of hand at work in film and evaluates it nostalgically: "the representation of reality by the film . . . offers, precisely because of the thoroughgoing permeation of reality with mechanical equipment, an aspect of reality that is free of all equipment. And this is what one is entitled to ask from a work of art."

The mass audience of film, Benjamin believes, mixes enjoyment with a critical, "expert" orientation because film, with its techniques of the close-up and slow motion, expands space and extends movement. However, instead of contemplation and concentration, which imply an absorption *by* the work of art, the film audience is distracted, and this is instead an absorption *of* the work of art. Benjamin evaluates this positively, for it is therapeutic: "The film is the art form that is in keeping with the increased threat to his life that modern man has to face. Man's need to expose himself to shock effects is his adjustment to the dangers threatening him." Distraction becomes appropriation by habit, and "the film with its shock effect meets this mode of reception halfway."

Benjamin's "Work of Art" essay influenced Adorno mostly negatively in that Adorno's analysis of the "culture industry" is far more critical—and prescient—of the manipulative, normalizing, nonrevolutionary effects of film and other popular arts that rely on mechanical reproducibility. Its influence on Malraux's interpretation of art in his *Voices of Silence* and on Gadamer's aesthetics of "the classic" in his *Truth and Method* is extensive but unacknowledged. Its claims for film's revolutionary potential to empower the masses cognitively and politically have gone unanswered by reality, just as its Marxist framework has been liquidated by history. However, its powerful introduction of the categories of aura and mechanical reproducibility into wide use in film theory and the history of art and culture remain of enduring and by now traditional, high-intellectual value.

TIMOTHY BAHTI

Editions

First edition: "Das Kunstwerk im Zeitalter seiner technischen Reproduzierbarkeit" appeared first in a French translation, "L'oeuvre d'art à l'époque de sa reproduction mécanisée," translated by Pierre Klossowski, in *Zeitschrift für Sozialforschung* 5 (1936)

Critical edition: "Das Kunstwerk im Zeitalter seiner technischen Reproduzierbarkeit," in *Gesammelte Schriften,* edited by Rolf Tiedemann and Hermann Schweppenhäuser, vol. 1, Frankfurt: Suhrkamp, 1974

Translation: "The Work of Art in the Age of Mechanical Reproduction," in *Illuminations,* translated by Harry Zohn, New York: Harcourt Brace, 1968

Further Reading

Arendt, Hannah, "Introduction," in Walter Benjamin, *Illuminations,* translated by Harry Zohn, New York: Harcourt, Brace, 1968

Geulen, Eva, "Zeit zur Darstellung: Walter Benjamins *Das Kunstwerk im Zeitalter seiner technischen Reproduzierbarkeit,*" in *Modern Language Notes* 107 (1992)

Jameson, Fredric, *Marxism and Form: Twentieth-Century Dialectical Theories of Literature,* Princeton, New Jersey: Princeton University Press, 1971

Tiedemann, Rolf, and Hermann Schweppenhäuser, "Anmerkungen der Herausgeber," in Walter Benjamin, *Gesammelte Schriften,* vol. 1, Frankfurt: Suhrkamp, 1974

Das Passagen-Werk 1982

Essay by Walter Benjamin

It is truly regrettable that the introduction to *Das Passagen-Werk* (*The Arcades Project*)—a visual contemplation of cultural phenomena—which the "materialist historian" Walter Benjamin promised to provide, is missing. Consisting of materials gathered between 1927 and 1940, the year of Benjamin's self-inflicted death, the project never achieved completion as the magnum opus that it was intended to be. The materials were kept in files of considerable size and in 1982 were published in two extensive volumes as part 5 of Benjamin's *Gesammelte Schriften* (1982). They represent vast quantities of commentaries, notes, excerpted passages, illustrations, quotes, brief reflections, and citations—roughly 15,000 items on 19th-century industrial culture as it took form in Paris—that can be arranged and rearranged in innumerable different constellations of meaning. Only the project's outline is believed to be decipherable. Yet in spite of its fragmentary state, this compilation of materials is considered to be one of the most important documentations of modernity in the frameworks of postmodern cultural and literary theory, philosophy, and sociology of art and literature. The project's leitmotif is the role that the fetish character of commodity has played in history—as seen in the context of the intellectual traditions that influenced Benjamin, including neo-Platonism, neo-Kantianism, early Romanticism, the Kabbalah, Goethe's aesthetics, surrealism, Marxism, and Freudian thought.

In 1927, the concept for *The Arcades Project,* a "materialist philosophy of history" (Benjamin), was first explored in Benjamin's essay "Passagen" for the journal *Der Querschnitt,* later to be called—on the basis of the work sketched in a 1935 essay—*Paris, Capital of the Nineteenth Century.* His decision to write the encyclopedic work came after readings of Louis Aragon's *Le Paysan de Paris* in 1926 and André Breton's *Nadja.* Aragon provided him with the metaphor of the arcade as an image of things past and forgotten, the no-longer fashionable, which at one time had caught and held social attention.

The Arcades Project develops a unique method of historical analysis, which is informed by the imagist theories of Aragon, Breton, and Freud. It can be described as a "dialectics of seeing" (Buck-Morss), which examines debris of mass culture such as gambling, mirrors, street signs, souvenirs, hashish, wax figures, and panoramas as sources of philosophical truth. It was Benjamin's opinion that this work, his most daring intellectual project, represented a "Copernican revolution" in the practice of history writing. It employed his theory of the dialectical image as a vehicle for gaining knowledge. This theory, which deliberately avoids the academic methodologies of hermeneutics, is significantly indebted to the work of the German cultural historian Ludwig Klages. Rejecting the Hegelian affirmation of history as meaningful, Benjamin challenges traditional historiography in his presentation and rejects the conventional philosophical narrative.

Arranged under the headings of key words and using alphabetical uppercase and lowercase ordering sequences, Benjamin set up an extensive filing system for his almost compulsively gathered collection of materials and labored on the files with various degrees of intensity for 13 years. In these files, or *Konvolute* (36 altogether), he systematically organized his notes and excerpts under headings such as "Arcades," "Fashion," "Haussmannization, Barricade Fighting," "The Collector," "Baudelaire," "Epistemology, Theory of Progress," "Prostitution, Gambling," and "Technologies of Reproduction, Lithography," to name but a few. Benjamin discussed in detail the arrangement of the book project for which he had gathered these materials with Max Horkheimer, Theodor Adorno, Gershom Scholem, and Bertolt Brecht. In a 1935 exposé, Benjamin described six provisional chapters, each of which were to deal with a historical phenomenon in relationship to a respective historical figure: 1. Fourier or the Arcades; 2. Daguerre or the Dioramas; 3. Grandville or the World Expositions; 4. Louis Philippe or the Interior; 5. Baudelaire or the Streets of Paris; 6. Haussmann or the Barricades. His plan was to present a collective history of life in 19th-century Paris—not as it was remembered in historiographical discourse, but as it has been forgotten.

The concept of "dialectical images" or the "dialectics of seeing" was intended to serve as the analytical tool of *The Arcades Project.* This cognitive methodology was designed to explain the form of cultural phenomena in terms of the consequences and reactions triggered by the dynamics of those phenomena's social, technological, or economic environments. But these relations between appearance and context, which are understood as the real conditions and explanatory factors of the specifics of cultural forms, are not visible. Hidden under a haze of mythologies, dreams of the collective consciousness, and social utopias, they must first be uncovered in order to be recognizable. Concealed as a language of cultural signs, they leave their traces "in a thousand configurations of life, from permanent buildings to ephemeral fashions." Benjamin had intended in this project to use the materialist perspective that Marx had employed to illuminate the cultural superstructure of capitalism rather than its economic base.

The Arcades Project is fundamentally concerned with unmasking the mythical conditions of cultural history, among them especially the myths of historical progress, development, and natural selection, because, according to Benjamin, there is nothing natural about the path that history takes in comparison with the path of nature, which is, indeed, historical. All such ideologically conditioned cultural mythologies are liquidated by means of "dialectical images" in which the reality of industrial capitalism is made manifest. Examples of such images include fashions that cover up the conditions of reality; the image of the railroad as a signifier of historical progress; the addiction of the upper classes to boredom as a state of existential, immutable paralysis, which in turn is fashionably modeled after the gloomy routine of mass production in factories; the transformation of literary works into commodities, which is caused by the technology of rapid printing and the mass media requirements of journalism; the prostitute as an image of the commodity form; and wax figures as emblems of history's motionlessness. All such cultural phenomena, according to Benjamin, are broken down by history—not into the narratives that are expressed through the fictions of conventional history writing, but into images that the dialectical gaze needs to read in order to decipher their true significance.

The theoretical demands required to comprehend Benjamin's conception of the dialectical image are extensive and complex, especially considering the Hegelian and Marxian tradition that informed his work. The need to read an image dialectically (e.g., an iron construction, a mirror, or a doll) is based on the fact that a cultural phenomenon that functions as a sign (in the Saussurean sense) conceals its true nature; this is comparable, for example, to the true nature of the production of goods, which is concealed by its fetish character. All these forgotten data and facts in their totality, which are obscured and buried in the text of cultural signs in 19th-century Paris, constitute the collective dream of the previous century, which Benjamin wanted to describe in his *Arcades Project*. Thus, the theoretical and descriptive intentions of *The Arcades Project* can be regarded as a "secular, sociopsychological theory of modernity as a dreamworld" (Buck-Morss), and the concept of a collective awakening from that dreamworld as a revolutionary gesture.

HOLGER A. PAUSCH

Editions

First edition: The material constituting the *Passagen-Werk* is in vol. 5 of the *Gesammelte Schriften,* edited by Rolf Tiedemann and Hermann Schweppenhäuser, Frankfurt: Suhrkamp, 1982

Translations: selections in English in Buck-Morss, below; *The Arcades Project,* translated by Howard Eland and Kevin McLaughlin, Cambridge, Massachusetts: Belknap Press, 1999

Further Reading

Buck-Morss, Susan, *The Dialectics of Seeing: Walter Benjamin and the Arcades Project,* Cambridge, Massachusetts: MIT Press, 1989

Markner, Reinhard, and Thomas Weber, editors, *Literatur über Walter Benjamin: Kommentierte Bibliographie 1983–92,* Hamburg: Argument, 1993

Smith, Gary, editor, *Benjamin: Philosophy, Aesthetics, History,* Chicago and London: University of Chicago Press, 1983

Steinberg, Michael P., editor, *Walter Benjamin and the Demands of History,* Ithaca, New York and London: Cornell University Press, 1996

Weigel, Sigrid, *Body- and Image-Space: Re-Reading Walter Benjamin,* London and New York: Routledge, 1996

Wismann, Heinz, and Miguel Abensour, editors, *Walter Benjamin et Paris: Colloque international 27–29 Juin 1983,* Paris: Cerf, 1986

Witte, Bernd, *Walter Benjamin: An Intellectual Biography,* Detroit, Michigan: Wayne State University, 1991

Gottfried Benn 1886–1956

Morgue und andere Gedichte (Morgue and Other Poems), a 50-pfennig pamphlet containing nine short poems, became an overnight succès de scandale in 1912, launching the "double life" (*Doppelleben*—the title of Benn's 1950 autobiography) of the newly qualified doctor and leading exponent of the new "Expressionism." Notoriety of a different kind resulted from his brief but all-too-public infatuation with the heroic rhetoric of regeneration in 1933. After retreating into the army medical corps, controversy again surrounded his extraordinary *Come-back* (his word), when the most prominent (and almost only) survivor of the Expressionist decade demonstrated to a younger generation how it was possible still to write poetry "after Auschwitz" (Adorno), and whose *Kulturpessimismus* (cultural pessimism) stood in a curiously symbiotic relationship with the zeitgeist, eclipsing the legacy of George, Hofmannsthal, and, above all, Rilke. Nor has his posthumous reputation ceased to fluctuate between aversion and fascination, often, since the 1960s, in juxtaposition with that of Bertolt Brecht, his perceived antipode.

First came the "incomparably unsavory" images that caused such revulsion. They were new to German lyric poetry, which had largely escaped the crasser manifestations of naturalism, but the eruptive, elemental force with which the macabre visions of this "infernal Breughel" surfaced, or rather broke through surface appearances (*Zusammenhangsdurchstoßung*), were a far cry from objective autopsy reports. Cast in a tone of ironic detachment—in stark contrast to the Liliencron-inspired Impressionism of *Rauhreif* (1910; Hoarfrost) and *Herbst* (1912; Fall)—*Morgue* was as radical a *Durchbruch* (breakthrough—the fashionable term soon to acquire additional military currency) as Kafka's *Das Urteil* (*The Judgment*) and Schönberg's *Pierrot lunaire,* which were written in the same annus mirabilis of 1912. Superficially, Rilke's *Morgue* poem from *Neue Gedichte* (1907; *New Poems*), reflecting the gruesome fin de siècle appeal of the Paris morgue, set a precedent. But whereas the similes of the last *"Wie"-Dichter* ("as-if" poet, as Benn called Rilke) conjure up some vaguely humanizing activity that links the anonymous corpses, the male and female bodies thrown together on the dissecting slab in Benn's *Requiem* lie "kreuzweis. Nah, nackt, und dennoch ohne Qual" (crosswise. Near, naked, yet untormented) in a scurrilous biblical travesty, a posthumous crucifixion providing redemption from the Strindbergian agony of sexual intimacy. Bodies give birth to their own organs, brain, and testicles; "Gottes Tempel und des Teufels Stall" (God's temple and the devil's sty) meet in the bottom of a bucket.

In *Kreislauf* (Circulation), a morgue attendant returns a prostitute's gold filling into circulation—only earth need return to earth. In *Kleine Aster* (Little Aster), the flower jokingly placed between a corpse's teeth is exhorted to rest in peace. In *Negerbraut* (Negro Bride), it is the surgeon's knife that robs a Desdemona figure of her virginity. Even more subversive of traditional expectations, the title *Schöne Jugend* (Beautiful Youth) refers to a family of young rats to which all sentiment is directed, rather than to the drowned girl whose corpse nourishes them. The Ophelia theme echoes Georg Heym's adaptation (1910) of Rimbaud's *Ophélie,* itself echoing Rimbaud's first "*voyant,*" Baudelaire, and the aesthetic of, for instance, *Une charogne* (Carrion), which embraces both the ugliness of putrefaction and its artistic transmutation. With *Mann und Frau gehn durch die Krebsbaracke* (Cancer Ward), one senses, as did Ernst Stadler, that such cynicism might mask "a despairing protest against the tragic nature of life" as that poem's moving coda shifts from the cancerous bodies to their dissolution: "Fleisch ebnet sich zu Land. Glut gibt sich fort. / Saft schickt sich an zu rinnen. Erde ruft." (Flesh flattens down to land. Warmth passes on. / Sap prepares to flow. Earth calls.) Similarly, in the poignant Passion poem *Saal der kreißenden Frauen* (Labor Ward), the dehumanizing jargon of a doctor peremptorily inducing labor only intensifies the epiphany of the ensuing birth, and a vision of this modern Christ-child's final agony is offset by the 12 other newborn infants waiting to take its place.

Over the next decade Benn nevertheless continued to shock the bourgeoisie with ever shriller evocations of Berlin's low life, casting a jaundiced eye on their seedy couplings ("Hurenkreuzzug. Syphilisquadrille" [Whores' crusade, syphilis quadrille], *Ball,* 1917). Exclamatory sequences of nouns (an extensive pathologist's lexis) predominate; few verbs and even fewer adjectives weaken the *Wallungswert* (emotional impact) of this Expressionist *Telegrammstil* (telegraphic style), from the *Nachtcafé* (Night Café) sequence (1912–17; this work prompted friend Georg Grosz's 1918 drawing *Dr Benns Nachtcafé*) to *Fleisch* (1917; Flesh), *Der Psychiater* (1917; The Psychiatrist), *Das Instrument* (1917; The Tool), *Notturno* (1917; Nocturne), *Innerlich* (1921; Inward), and *Tripper* (1922; Gonorrhea). Nor were his own (multiple) liaisons exempt. Yet the provocation of a line such as "Eine Frau ist etwas für eine Nacht" (A woman is good for one night only) is consistently offset by a withdrawal into the solitude of an imagination that ultimately affords him (or his poetic persona, or both) more authentic fulfillment. This gulf between self and world—a solipsism most infamously expressed in the ironically titled poem *Synthese* (1917; Synthesis): "Auch was sich noch der Frau gewährt, / Ist dunkle süße Onanie" (Even what is rendered to woman / Is dark sweet masturbation)—is central to the whole life and work of a self-confessed *Antisynthetiker,* who maintained to the end, "ich bin Isolationist, mein Name ist Monroe" (I am an isolationist, my name is Monroe).

In counterpoint to Dr. Benn's bleak diagnoses, which excoriate "die Krone der Schöpfung, das Schwein, der Mensch" (the crown of creation, that bastard, man—*Der Arzt* [1917; The Doctor]), are his visionary prescriptions involving escapes to some archaic, Mediterranean utopia through self-generated Dionysian ecstasy. Fundamental to the "thalassale Regression" (back to the sea [*Regressiv,* 1927]) of these travel-poster reveries is "das Südwort schlechthin" (a word that epitomizes the South), namely, the color blue. But this mythical *Süd-Komplex* soon climaxes in "das entstirnte Blut" (the "deforeheaded" blood) of an ecstatically suicidal Icarus (*Ikarus* [1915]), and in the caryatid (*Karyatide* [1916]) who is exhorted to unbend her knee in a bacchanalian dance and liberation from her stone prison (also, implicitly, from the soaring aspiration of medieval masons in Rilke's early cathedral poems), only to "bloom to death" (*zerblühe dich*).

The key to these regressive fantasies is a morbidly rapturous *nostalgie de la boue,* a literal longing for mindlessness: "O daß wir unsere Urahnen wären. / Ein Klümpchen Schleim in einem warmen Moor" (Oh that we were our primal ancestors. / A lump of slime in some tepid swamp—*Gesänge* [1913; Songs]). For Benn, the brain and consciousness, the *principium individuationis* of Schopenhauer and Nietzsche, are a source only of pain, and progress, development, and "ascent" are bought at too high a price. At best, each man is an island with "no verticals," and "only disconnect" is the ultimate wisdom (*Reise* [1916; Journey]). In the words of Dr Rönne, Benn's alter ego in the dramatic sketch *Ithaka* (1914): "Das Gehirn ist ein Irrweg. Ein Bluff für den Mittelstand" (The brain is the wrong path. A bluff for the middle classes). Fueling such frenetic loathing for knowledge (*Erkenntnisekel*) and mockery of the two months longer *Frau Meier* might live as a result of two centuries of scientific research is an irrational yearning for positivism's odyssey of deferred gratification to come to an end: "Wir wollen den Traum. Wir wollen den Rausch. Wir rufen Dionysos und Ithaka!" (We want dreams. We want rapture. We summon Dionysus and Ithaca!) The professorial representative of Northern logic and progress (whom they attack with their foreheads!) is nevertheless permitted an uncanny prediction of what lies in store for such sub-Nietzschean iconoclasts and would-be lotus eaters: "Ihr trübes Morgenrot! Ihr werdet verbluten, und der Mob feiert über eurem Blut ein Frühstück mit Prost und Vivat!" (You bleak dawn! You will bleed to death, and the mob will breakfast on your blood and cry Cheers!)

While posted to a venereal clinic in occupied Brussels (1915–17), Benn was to experience a clinical *Depersonalisation,* a crumbling of selfhood under bombardment from the sheer plethora of contingent things, which he projects (long before Sartre's 1938 *La Nausée*), together with the alternating phases of detached exhilaration, into five short pieces—*Gehirne* (Minds), *Die Eroberung* (The Conquest), *Die Reise* (The Journey), *Die Insel* (The Island), and *Der Geburtstag* (The Birthday)—and into *Diesterweg,* whose protagonist, like Benn himself, is invalided home to Berlin. This thin corpus of Expressionist prose, 60 pages in all, written in the spring of 1916, is a worthy companion to the intense, similarly elliptic, and innovative "absolute prose" of Sternheim (*Napoleon,* 1915; *Busekow,* 1914) and Carl Einstein (*Bebuquin,* 1912)—who were, coincidentally, Benn's acquaintances in Brussels.

Poems such as *O, Nacht* (1916; Oh, Night), *Cocain* (1917), and the cycle *Betäubung* I–V (1925; Anaesthetic) make explicit another occasional source of euphoria: a drug-induced dissolution of the self ("Ich-Zerfall"), although the "word-cloudbursts" that now celebrate this synesthetic state are—paradoxically, yet characteristically—sculpted into regular rhyming stanzas. Whether prompted by obsessional neuroses, "because the pressure we are under is great" ("sind es Zwangsgedanken, / ist der Zwang doch groß-Grenzenlos" [1925; Boundless]), or stimulated by the cataracts of words themselves—that most potent of hallucinogens ("Das Wort ist der Phallus des Geistes, zentral verwurzelt" [The word is the mind's phallus, centrally rooted] [*Probleme der Lyrik,* 1951])—Benn's creativity is not easily reduced to T.S. Eliot's distinction between the man who suffers and the mind that creates. As the *Epilog* to a first collected works suggests in 1922—"total erledigt. Ich schreibe nichts mehr" (totally washed up. I will write no more)—it was a mind at the end of its tether.

The 50-odd poems that he nevertheless produced in the 1920s are formally distinctive: up to six stanzas in length, each has eight short lines that alternate masculine and feminine rhymes and are imbued with an elegiac sense of finality and a falling rhythm to match (reflected in the many jazz settings). The utilitarianism of *homo faber* gets short shrift, as does Weber's Protestant work ethic (*Grenzenlos*). Hegel's progressive dialectic ("from Hellesponts to Hoboken Quay . . . what's the sense of it all, who knows?" [*Qui Sait,* 1927]) and a mechanistic, onward-and-upward determinism attributed to Darwin both collapse before the utter contingency of events ("Waterloo: Bonaparte's saddle didn't fit" [*Chaos,* 1923]), the unfathomability of existence. History consists of eternally recurrent "pathological case histories" ("die Krankengeschichte von Irren" [*Zum Thema Geschichte,* 1929]). In a feverish gallop ("fiebernde Galoppade" [*Spuk*, 1922]), whole civilizations pass in cursory kaleidoscopic review, "flowers of the desert" now vanished without trace (*Der späte Mensch* [1922; Late Man]); these civilizations are contrasted to such timeless, primitive, South Seas island cultures as *Palau* (1922). At best, some overwhelming urge to create form ("Riesenformungszwang") produces mysterious artifacts—the Easter Island statues (*Osterinsel,* 1927) or the gargoyles on Notre Dame, chimeras of infinity amid cosmic isolation (*Verlorenes Ich* [1943; Lost Self]).

The venereal diseases that Benn treated in his failing practice left more overt traces in his work ("sinnlose Phallen schneuzen / sich ins Antlitz der Welt" [senseless phalluses snort into the world's face] [*Banane,* 1925]) than world war, revolution, and hyperinflation. Nor, when good times came to his beloved Berlin, was the hedonistic new Babylon's exhilaration reflected in his poetry. Instead, "der Schöpfungsstunde / traumbeladenes Wort" (the hour of creation's dream-laden words) came in the darkened backroom of his surgery or was sparked by random browsing in the National Library. The catacombs of this "Satzbordell" (sentence-bordello) and "Fieberparadies" (fever-paradise) "glühn im Wortvibrier" (glow as the words vibrate [*Staatsbibliothek,* 1925]); even histories of art and atlases transport the imagination ("Überbesetzung seiner / mittels Geographie"—*Ostafrika* [1925; East Africa]).

Into each montage the poet weaves what the programmatic *Der Sänger* (1925; The Singer), another ironic archaism, calls "seine schweren Substanzen" (his weighty essences), as the poem moves slowly and mysteriously "ins Nichts" (into nothingness). Benn's nihilism will remain all-pervasive, but its artistic exploitation ("die artistische Ausnutzung des Nihilismus") as a powerful inducement to create form ("die formfordernede Gewalt des Nichts") is also a source of joy ("Nihilismus ist ein Glücksgefühl"), creativity's transcendent bliss ("die Transcendenz der schöpferischen Lust") having replaced religious transcendence within European nihilism: according to Benn, God is a bad stylistic principle ("Gott ist ein schlechtes Stilprinzip"). Nietzsche's legacy is palpable—primarily the Nietzsche who "from the chaos within gave birth to a dancing star," proclaiming art to be the last metaphysical activity after the collapse of Western values. Benn the self-styled *Prismatiker* aligns his own creed of *Ausdruckskunst* (i.e., Expressionism) with the perspectivism Nietzsche substituted for the search for "truth": "die Bruchflächen funkeln zu lassen . . . der Drang, sich auszudrücken, zu formulieren, zu blenden, zu funkeln" (to make the fractured edges glitter . . . the compulsion to express oneself, to formulate, dazzle, sparkle [*Nietzsche—nach fünfzig Jahren,* 1950]).

Flattered by election to the Preußische Akademie der Künste in 1932, soon replacing Heinrich Mann, whom he venerated, as the provisional head of its literary section, Benn found himself calling for suspension of all political activity by its members "unter Anerkennung der veränderten geschichtlichen Lage" (in view of the altered historical situation). His public response to Klaus Mann's still conciliatory private reproach to *his* erstwhile hero was the infamous March 1933 *Antwort an die literarischen Emigranten* (Answer to the Literary Émigrés), which cited "the perhaps tragic, but certainly fated task of history, replete with images" ("die Geschichte, bilderbeladen bei ihrer vielleicht tragischen, aber jedenfalls schicksalbestimmten Arbeit")—images that the Nazi *Gesamtkunstwerk* readily supplied. The irony of the situation was not lost on Thomas Mann, whose *Betrachtungen eines Unpolitischen* (1918; *Reflections of an Unpolitical Man*) had also defended the indefensible by "aestheticizing politics" in line with Nietzsche's maxim that life can only be justified as an aesthetic phenomenon.

But as the academy emptied and an auto-da-fé of literary modernism took place outside, Benn's Expressionist past weighed heavier than his defense of the conservative revolution and "the new biological type" in, for example, his April 1933 broadcast *Der neue Staat und die Intellektuellen* (The New State and the Intellectuals). His spirited November 1933 *Bekenntnis zum Expressionismus* (Commitment to Expressionism) was his nemesis, for by naively attempting to define the Nazis themselves as "Expressionists" in his sense, he provoked further accusations of *Kulturbolschewismus* (cultural bolshevism) and more questions about his racial origins. Several much-discussed poems put a brave face on what already seems to be recognition of his *Irrnis* (erring): "nur nicht fragen, / nur nicht verstehn" (don't ask, don't try to understand), simply accept the fleeting "Rausch aus Schweigen" (silent intoxication) and impending tragedy. But even heroic pessimism was a dangerously *défaitiste* sentiment: "nur diese Stunde / ihr Sagenlicht / und dann die Wunde, / mehr gibt es nicht" (this hour alone / its mythical light / and then the wound, / that's all there is—*Durch jede Stunde* [1933; Through Every Hour]). A Nietzschean *amor fati* is even more pronounced in *Dennoch die Schwerter halten* (1933; Hands on Swords Nevertheless), but the melancholy resignation of *Am Brückenwehr* (1934; At the Fortified Bridge) is already that of the lonely thinker whose thought has been betrayed. Reenlistment as an army doctor in 1935 provided timely refuge against attacks in the Nazi press on his *Ferkeleien* (filth), while the eventual *Schreibverbot* (ban on writing) in 1938 ensured that all further lyrics were "for the bottom drawer" (*Schubladenliteratur*)—in practice, an archive established by Benn's patrician, Hanseatic patron and confidant, Friedrich Wilhelm Oelze.

Postings in Hanover, Berlin, and in 1943–45, Landsberg an der Warthe, near the eastern front, supplied copious "evidence of victory from the Reich *you* represent" ("Siegsbeweise / aus dem von dir vertretenen Reich"—*Einsamer nie* [1936; Never More Lonesome]). These "victories of the spirit" and other poems accumulated during ten years of silence found a public thirsty for his unique blend of rhapsodic nihilism and nonchalance, of hard-edged sentimentality and slang. Even returning émigrés acknowledged the preeminence of the poetry, reserving their criticism for Benn the man—*Schuft* (blackguard—Alfred Döblin), *Opportunist* (Johannes R. Becher), *moralischer Versager* (moral reprobate—Klaus Mann)—notably after his somewhat self-serving autobiography *Doppelleben* drew attention to his own dictum that "the army is the aristocratic form of emigration." Like Heidegger, an admirer of his poetry, Benn failed to show sufficiently unambiguous contrition.

Benn thought the 44 *Statische Gedichte* (1948; Static Poems), which were first published in Switzerland, inferior to his new prose works, especially *Der Ptolemäer* (1949; The Ptolemy—also suggesting an imperturbably "static," pre-Copernican or ahistorical, mandarin stance), but it was the new poetry's "süße, fast schluchzende Sangbarkeit" (sweet, almost sobbing singability—Friedrich Sieburg), together with the older favorites contained in the *Trunkene Flut* (Drunken Flood) anthology, which had such sensational resonance in 1949. Literary prizes and public acclaim followed. *Probleme der Lyrik,* a lecture delivered in Darmstadt in 1951, was an accessible and highly influential poetics, which insisted on the all-importance of form, including "das Sakrale des Reims" (the sacred quality of rhyme—when not used to shock, unlike "Gotts . . . Odds" [1924]), especially his own now preferred lyrical form of three four-line stanzas: "diese faszinieren kraft ihrer Form das Jahrhundert" (thanks to their form, these fascinate the century). In Benn's 327 poems, twice that many allusions to flowers, trees, or gardens have been counted (to his chagrin, his wife banned further mention of roses), but such subject matter is at best contingent to "das absolute Gedicht, das Gedicht ohne Glauben, das Gedicht ohne Hoffnung, das Gedicht an niemanden gerichtet, das Gedicht aus Worten, die Sie faszinierend montieren" (the absolute poem, the poem without faith, without hope, addressed to no one, made of words assembled in a fascinating way). The naming of things retains its magic generative power—but equally words (especially nouns: Substantive!) are keys unlocking ancient memories (Plato's amanuensis) and repositories of infinite suggestive reach ("Sichel-Sehnsucht," "Rosenhirn," and "Marmorlicht"). In one superb example of this credo in "Ein Wort" (1941)—that in the beginning was the word—the creative process is itself enacted (cf. Joshua 10: 12–13), its *paroles essentielles* (Mallarmé) evolving toward ultimate hermetic self-sufficiency:

> A word, a clause—: from ciphers, life,
> its sense, is suddenly laid bare,
> the sun stands still, the spheres fall silent
> and all things merge into the word.
> A word—a gleam, a flight, a fire,
> a shooting flame, a streaking star—
> then dark again, ineffable,
> in empty space round world and me.

If truth and beauty finally parted company with Mallarmé, it is precisely the "truth" of Benn's poetry, and its premise, "Stil ist der Wahrheit überlegen" (style is superior to truth), that critics from Michael Hamburger to Jürgen Habermas have questioned. "Rather a stimulating charlatan than a *petit-bourgeois* emitting 'moods'" is one of Benn's typically defiant responses to such criticisms (letter to his daughter, 30 July 1949). Torn as his dreamlike melodies are between cerebral and archaic forces—solipsistic rather than humanitarian, esoterically suggestive flotsam and jetsam rather than logically coherent images—their seductive, melancholy musicality nevertheless exercises a perennial spell. And if susceptibility to parody is a reliable indicator of durability, Benn's place on Parnassus seems secure:

> The most beautiful verses of men
> —now *you* try and find a rhyme!—
> are those of Gottfried Benn:
> Brain, Lernaean lime—
> The Soviet Zone's not immune to it
> Roses, phylum and cortex.
> Epigones play a tune to it—
> Benn's sweet engrammatic vortex.
> (from Peter Rühmkorf, *Lied der Benn-Epigonen* [Song of the Benn Imitators], 1959)

FRED BRIDGHAM

See also Fascism and Literature

Biography

Born in Mansfeld, 2 May 1886. Philology and theology student, University of Marburg, 1903–4; medical student, University of Berlin, 1905–10; Ph.D. from Kaiser Wilhelm Academy, 1912; military service, 1912; service in the army medical corps, 1914–17, and 1935–45; received the Iron Cross, second class, 1914; assistant at the Pathological Institute, Westend Hospital, 1912–13; ship's physician, 1913; specialist in skin disease and sexually transmitted diseases, 1917–35; embraced, 1932–34, and then renounced, 1934, National Socialism; acting chairman of the literary division of the Prussian Academy of Art, 1933; private medical practice in West Berlin, from 1945. Büchner prize, 1951; Order of Merit, first class, Federal Republic of Germany, 1952. Died 7 July 1956.

Selected Works

Collections

Gesammelte Werke, edited by Dieter Wellershoff, 4 vols., 1958–61
Primäre Tage: Gedichte und Fragmente aus dem Nachlass, edited by Dieter Wellershoff, 1958
Medizinische Schriften, edited by Werner Rübe, 1965
*Späte Gedichte: Fragmente, Destillationen, Apr*è*slude,* 1965
Poems, translated by Michael Lebeck, 1967
Selected Poems, edited by Friedrich Wilhelm Wodtke, 1970
Sämtliche Erzählungen, 1970
Gesammelte Werke in der Fassung der Erstdrucke, edited by B. Hillebrand, 1982–
Sämtliche Werke, edited by Gerhard Schuster, 4 vols., 1986–89
Prose, Essays, Poems, edited by Volkmar Sandor, 1987
Poems 1937–1947, translated by Simona Dradhici, 1991

Poetry

Morgue und andere Gedichte, 1912
Söhne, 1913
Fleisch, 1917
Schutt, 1924
Betäubung, 1925
Spaltung, 1925
Die Dänin, 1925
Gesammelte Gedichte, 1927
Ausgewählte Gedichte: 1911–1936, 1936
Zweiundzwanzig Gedichte: 1936–1943, 1943
Statische Gedichte, 1948
Trunkene Flut: Ausgewählte Gedichte, 1949
Fragmente, 1951
Destillationen, 1953
*Apr*è*slude,* 1955
Gesammelte Gedichte 1912–1956, 1956
Lyrik: Auswahl letzter Hand, 1956

Plays

Ithaka, 1914
Etappe, 1919
Der Vermessungsdirigent, 1919
Das Unaufhörliche (oratorio), music by Paul Hindemith (produced 1931), 1931
Die Stimme hinter dem Vorhang (radio play), 1952

Fiction

Gehirne, 1916
Diesterweg, 1918
Die gesammelten Schriften, 1922
Der Ptolemäer, 1949
Dr. Rönne: Frühe Prosa, edited by Ernst Neff, 1957
Roman des Phänotyp: Landsberger Fragment, 1944, 1961
Weinhaus Wolf und andere Prosa, 1967

Other
Das moderne Ich, 1920
Gesammelte Prosa, 1928
Fazit der Perspektiven, 1930
Nach dem Nihilismus (essays), 1932
Der neue Staat und die Intellektuellen (essays), 1933
Kunst und Macht (essays), 1934
Ausdruckswelt: Essays and Aphorismen, 1949
Drei alte Männer (dialogues), 1949
Goethe und die Naturwissenschaften, 1949
Doppelleben; Zwei Selbstdarstellungen (autobiography), 1950
Frühe Prosa und Reden, 1950
Essays, 1951
Probleme der Lyrik (speech), 1951
Frühe Lyrik und Dramen, 1952
Monologische Kunst: ein Briefwechsel zwischen Alexander Lernet-Holenia und Gottfried Benn, 1953
Altern als Problem für Künstler, 1954
Provoziertes Leben: Eine Auswahl aus den Prosaschriften, 1955
Reden, 1955
Soll die Dichtung das Leben bessern?, with Reinhold Schneider, 1956
Über mich selbst: 1886–1956, 1956
Ausgewählte Briefe, 1957
Briefe an Carl Werckshagen, 1958
Das gezeichnete Ich: Briefe aus den Jahren 1900–1956, 1962
Briefe an F.W. Oelze, edited by Harald Steinhagen and Jürgen Schröder, 3 vols., 1977–80
Briefwechsel mit Paul Hindemith, edited by Ann Clark Fehn, 1978
Gottfried Benn, Max Rychner: Briefwechsel 1930–1956. edited by Gerhard Schuster, 1986
Briefe an Tilly Wedekind 1939–1955, 1986
Briefe an Elinor Büller 1930–1937, 1992

Edited Work
Lyrik des Expressionistischen Jahrzehnts, 1955

Further Reading

Alter, Reinhard, *Gottfried Benn: The Artist and Politics (1910–1934),* Bern: Lang, 1976
Brode, Hanspeter, *Benn-Chronik: Daten zu Leben und Werk,* Munich and Vienna: Hanser, 1978
Casey, Paul F., and Timothy Joseph, editors, *Gottfried Benn: The Galway Symposium,* Galway: Galway University Press, 1990
Dierick, Augustinus Petrus, *Gottfried Benn and His Critics: Major Interpretations, 1912–1992,* Columbia, South Carolina: Camden, 1992
Greve, Ludwig, *Gottfried Benn, 1886–1956* (illustrated exhibition catalog), Marbach: Deutsche Schillergesellschaft, 1986
Hamburger, Michael, *The Truth of Poetry,* London: Weidenfeld and Nicholson, 1968
Hillebrand, Bruno, *Benn,* Frankfurt: Fischer, 1984
Hillebrand, Bruno, editor, *Über Gottfried Benn: Kritische Stimmen,* 2 vols., Frankfurt: Fischer Taschenbuch, 1987
Holthusen, Hans Egon, *Gottfried Benn: Leben, Werk, Widerspruch, 1886–1922,* Stuttgart: Klett-Cotta, 1986
Reininger, Anton, "Regressive Sehnsucht und ihre sprachliche Manipulation: Benns Lyrik der zwanziger Jahre," *Annali: Sezione Germanica, Studi Tedeschi* 27 (1984)
Ridley, Hugh, *Gottfried Benn: Ein Schriftsteller zwischen Erneuerung und Reaktion,* Opladen: Westdeutscher Verlag, 1990
Rübe, Werner, *Provoziertes Leben: Gottfried Benn,* Stuttgart: Klett-Cotta, 1993
Schröder, Jürgen, *Gottfried Benn: Poesie und Sozialisation,* Stuttgart: Kohlhammer, 1978
Steinhagen, Harald, *Die Statischen Gedichte von Gottfried Benn: Die Vollendung seiner expressionistischen Lyrik,* Stuttgart: Klett, 1969
Wodtke, Friedrich Wilhelm, *Gottfried Benn,* Stuttgart: Metzler, 1962; revised edition, 1970

Berlin

Like no other city, Berlin embodies the contradictions of German history and culture. The various meanings of historical Berlin are contested in political discourse, reinvented by popular culture, and reformulated by the tourist industry. The city's territorial expansion, its political consolidation with Prussia, and its growth as the capital of an empire are all linked to the names of margraves, electors, and kings. By contrast, the gradual, contested integration of diverse groups of immigrants into a population of self-defined Berliners—Jews, Huguenots, Poles, and Turks, to name just a few—also has helped to mold Berlin's unique identity. The center of revolutionary struggle, liberation movements, and harsh repression, the city has experienced alternating periods of freedom and censorship in the arts. Industrialization and modernity came late to Berlin but then exploded in exponential growth. All are factors in the cultural dynamism that made Berlin a magnet for writers and other artists in the 20th century.

Berlin is a young city in comparison with cities colonized by the Romans in the west. It was mentioned first in 1237 as Berlin-Cölln, which corresponds to the names of the twin villages on the river Spree. During this medieval period, the population consisted of a mixture of Germanic and Slavic peoples. Jews are mentioned for the first time in 1317, when they were given protection in return for money. From this point, Berlin's Jewish community would grow, and persecution would be followed by periods of relative lenience. A part of the original center of medieval Berlin, the *Nikolaiviertel,* was rebuilt by the East Germans and is all that is left of the early city.

From the 15th century onward, the city would be associated with the Hohenzollern dynasty. During the Age of the Reformation, Protestantism inspired the beginnings of a cultural life in the city as the Electors (*Kurfürsten*) continued to consolidate their power in the Mark Brandenburg. The artist Lucas Cranach painted in the city in 1528, the city's first theater premier took place in 1541, and Paul Gerhardt's Protestant hymns mark the high point of the period's literary achievement. Berlin's first newspaper was founded early in the next century, but it was soon unable to publish without agreeing to censorship in 1632. By then, the Thirty Years' War (1618–48) had begun to take its toll; at the end of the war, the city's population had decreased to 6,000 from a previous high of 12,000–14,000. Cultural and commercial renewal came to the city when the Great Elector (ruled 1640–88) granted more Jews permission to reside there and issued the Edict of Potsdam (1685), which allowed Huguenots exiled from France to settle in Berlin. The Huguenots' presence also had an impact on cultural life and taste. French began to enter the vocabulary of common Berliners at that time and was to become an integral part of the urban *Platt* dialect that is still spoken by many Berliners. In the final quarter of the 17th century, the architect and sculptor Andreas Schlueter designed the Arsenal (*Zeughaus*), which still stands at *Unter den Linden,* and the palace in the old city center, which existed in various forms until it was damaged during World War II and then finally destroyed by the East German government.

The 18th century began with another step in Berlin's consolidation with Prussia, when Frederick III (ruled 1688–1713), the son of the Grand Elector, took the title of King of Prussia in 1701. His son, King Frederick William I (ruled 1713–40), the "soldier king," placed exclusive emphasis on the military and set the tone for a Spartan Berlin. In the first census of the city in 1719, Berlin was reported to have 64,000 inhabitants, 20 percent of which were Huguenots. Later, under Frederick II, known as Frederick the Great (ruled 1740–86), cultural life would bloom during the Enlightenment (*Berliner Aufklärung*). Already in 1706, Berlin had been called "*Spree- Athen*" for the first time, a name that has come to be associated with the Age of Reason in Berlin. Frederick resided mostly in Potsdam, his "Versailles," but commissioned several buildings designed by Hans Georg von Knobelsdorff, including the *Palais,* now the seat of the Humboldt University, and the state opera house at *Unter den Linden,* which was the first opera house anywhere to be constructed as a freestanding building. The increasingly prosperous middle classes were admitted to the king's opera, but they also began to cultivate their own taste in art. Daniel Chodowiecki's depictions of middle-class Berlin street scenes present a counterpoint to the portraits of the French-born court painter, Antoine Pesne. Although Frederick was a passionate Francophile and a great admirer of Voltaire, whom he attracted to the court for a short period, his liberalizing of censorship enabled German to gain ground as a literary language among the rising middle classes. Newspapers, books, and journals flourished. Despite Frederick's reputation for enlightened despotism and his advocacy of religious tolerance, he did maintain strict limitations on the Jews' economic and civil rights. At the same time, Moses Mendelsohn, the great Jewish Enlightenment thinker, challenged bigotry by his very being and promulgated the view that religion's worth lay in its moral influence on human affairs. Gotthold Ephraim Lessing is the pivotal figure. In his theoretical works, he championed Shakespeare against prevailing French conventions as a means to create a national German drama. His great comedy *Minna von Barnhelm* (1768) was a popular success with Berliners because of its contemporary setting in Berlin against the background of the Seven Years' War. Its premier in the theater in the *Behrenstrasse* was followed by other commercial successes, among them Goethe's *Götz von Berlichingen* in 1774 and Schiller's *Die Räuber* (*The Robbers*) in 1783. A German national theater had established itself in Berlin, and, by the end of the century, middle-class writers were writing increasingly for the middle classes.

Berlin's architectural landscape was lent its neoclassic cast under Frederick William II (ruled 1786–97) and Frederick William III (ruled 1797–1840). The Brandenburg Gate, the monument that would become Germany's most enduring symbol, was designed by Carl Gotthard Langhans and erected in 1791. Two years later, Johann Gottfried Schadow's sculpture the "Quadriga" was placed on top. At the same time, a new Romantic school was beginning to reject the classicism of the Enlightenment; they instead found inspiration in an idealized German medieval past and emphasized individuality, subjectivity, emotion, and the freedom of expression. Karl Friedrich Schinkel, the great architect of several neoclassic buildings in the heart of Berlin (*Schauspielhaus, Neue Wache,* and *Altes Museum*), also created paintings and stage sets that responded to the Romanticism of the new age, and the paintings of Caspar David Friedrich were exhibited in the Academy of Arts. Despite flourishing Romantic schools in Jena, Heidelberg, and Dresden, Berlin remained a magnet for Romanticism during the Napoleonic age (1806–14). The Berliners Ludwig Tieck and Wilhelm Wackenroder, along with the Brothers Schlegel, were early leaders of the Romantic movement at the turn of the century. At this time, women played an increasingly influential role in intellectual and creative spheres, strengthening the argument for greater participation by women in public life. Literary salons hosted by Henriette Herz and Rahel Levin Varnhagen von Emse were centers for artistic and political discussions. Bettina von Arnim is a stellar name in this regard, both for her social engagement and her literary creativity. Johann Gottlieb Fichte, the first philosophy professor at the University of Berlin, cofounded in 1810 by Alexander von Humboldt, led the way to a radical subjective Romanticism and an anti-Napoleonic German nationalism. Berlin continued to attract writers, among them Achim von Arnim, de la Motte Fouque, Chamisso, and Heinrich von Kleist. Somewhat later, E.T.A. Hoffmann and Eichendorff made Berlin their own.

After Napoleon's defeat in 1814, there emerged simultaneously a strong nationalist desire for German national unity and a longing for a liberal democratic *Rechtsstaat.* Although Frederick Wilhelm had promised liberalization in exchange for victory, he did not deliver. The first drive for liberalization came from a student movement, the *Burschenschaften.* "Turnvater" Friedrich Ludwig Jahn, a founder and supporter of the youth movement, ran his gymnastics school in the *Hasenheide,* then on the outskirts of Berlin, and represented a contradictory mixture of chauvinistic nationalism and democratic fervor. The revolt, however, resulted in harsh repression and censorship (including the Carlsbad Decrees of 1819 and the Vienna "Final Act" of 1820). The period thereafter leading up to the March Revolution of 1848 in Berlin is known as both the Restoration and the pre-revolutionary *Vormärz.* At the Berlin University, Professor of Philosophy Georg Wilhelm Friedrich Hegel was teaching a conservative view of the state but spawned both conservative Old Hegelian and progressive New Hegelian schools of thought. Karl Marx was associated with the latter. Heinrich Heine, the brilliant Jewish poet and political satirist, had to leave Berlin for Paris; the progressive *Junges Deutschland* movement and exponents of women's rights were persecuted. Outside of Felix Mendelssohn-Bartholdy's musical triumphs, cultural life in the city languished under censorship. However, the political drive toward democracy culminated in March 1848, as crowds advanced toward the palace, where a battle ensued that left 200 citizens dead. Frederick William IV (ruled 1840–61) promised to lift all harsh measures and grant civil liberties, but in the end he was not forced to make good on his promise.

At this time, Berlin was a conservative and somewhat provincial place in comparison to other great European cities; however, it was rapidly growing into a center of commerce and scientific and technical expertise. In 1815, Berlin had 200,000 inhabitants, a number that would double by 1850 as a result of the industrial revolution. By 1870, the population had grown to 800,000; by 1890, to 1.5 million. Immigrants from the eastern provinces came in droves to find work as new classes consisting of capitalist entrepreneurs and the urban proletariat emerged. The latter lived in stark poverty in the *Mietskasernen* (workers' tenement blocks). European revolutionaries also made their way to the city, which, by the turn of the century, had a burgeoning workers' movement and was known as "Red Berlin." When William I (ruled 1861–88) came to power, however, it was neither liberal democracy nor revolutionary socialist ideas that triumphed but rather German unification; the Empire was achieved in 1871 by Otto von Bismarck's policy of force, *Blut und Eisen* (blood and iron).

Wilhelminian Berlin of the Second Empire takes its name from Wilhelm II, who ruled as Kaiser from 1888–1918. German colonies were established in Africa and the Pacific, while at home in Berlin, civic and commercial construction boomed. Buildings as diverse as the *Bode Museum,* the *Anhalter Bahnhof,* the Reichstag, and Wertheim's department store came into being. The cathedral (*Berliner Dom*) and the *Kaiser-Wilhelm-Gedächtniskirche* were part of Wilhelm's conservative drive to build churches, while S-Bahn and railway connections to the city were expanded. Berlin was now compared to Chicago rather than to Athens. Realism gained ascendancy in the arts along with middle-class financial dominance. Friedrich Spielhagen and Wilhelm Raabe produced novels inspired by Berlin, and the most famous of Berlin novelists, Theodor Fontane, wrote his greatest works in the 1890s. Naturalism reached its pinnacle in the same decade with the dramas of Gerhart Hauptmann. The *Freie Bühne* was founded privately to avoid royal censorship and conservative taste. The *Volksbühne* movement was launched in 1891 by the Social Democrats to provide theater to a proletarian audience. The greatest painter of the time was the realist Adolph Menzel. Yet, the reaction against realism in the arts was already underway; the Berlin Secession, led by the painter Max Liebermann, introduced Impressionism and the works of Edvard Munch to the city. Käthe Kollwitz, known for her unique combination of Expressionist and urban realist styles, began to portray the poor in Berlin, and the drawings of Heinrich Zille portrayed the popular image of working-class Berlin.

Expressionist painting also had its debut as the painters of *Die Brücke* (The Bridge) moved to Berlin in 1910. The expressionist journal *Der Sturm* (The Storm), edited by Herwath Walden, broke the boundaries between literary and fine arts. During this decade of World War I, the lyric poet Else Lasker-Schüler lived as a bohemian in the city, and Gottfried Benn wrote his early Expressionist poems there. Expressionist evocations of the modern metropolis were included in the famous anthology of poetry, *Menscheitsdämmerung* (1920; Twilight of Man), edited by Kurt Pinthius.

As Germany faced defeat in 1918, the Kaiser was forced to abdicate, which ended the reign of the Hohenzollern. After the ensuing Spartacus uprising was quashed, the leaders of the communist movement, Karl Liebknecht and Rosa Luxemburg, were murdered by the Right Wing. Although a democratic Weimar Republic had been installed by the Social Democrats, the government would be forever plagued by a bitter legacy of political polarization. Berlin's most famous decade began in 1920 with the unification of the loosely linked towns and localities into a greater metropolis. The devastating conditions after the war and the inflation of 1923 gave way to unparalleled prosperity, and *Groß- Berlin* built the largest community transportation system in the world. The city became motion personified; Ernst Ludwig Kirchner, Max Beckmann, Otto Dix, and Georg Grosz painted the horror of war and the city's booming recovery. Berlin became a crossroads for modernism, the European avant-garde, and the artistic world. Fascination with the machine, the masses, and the urban experience, for example, informed the photo montage and collage techniques of Berlin Dadaists such as John Heartfield and Hannah Höch. During this period, Kurt Tucholsky and Carl von Ossietzky were associated with the left-wing journal *Die Weltbühne.* At the same time, Berlin became the center of a gay and lesbian subculture, which organized politically for the decriminalization of homosexuality under the leadership of Magnus Hirschfeld, the first modern researcher in the field of human sexuality.

The heady intensity of Expressionism and postwar protest were replaced by *Neue Sachlichkeit* (New Objectivity) in the mid–1920s. The functionalism of the *Bauhaus* under the leadership of Walter Gropius set the pace in architectural design, while the city's some 50 theaters produced a wide variety of theatrical offerings. The first modern opera, Alban Berg's *Wozzeck,* premiered in 1925, the same year that Arnold Schoenberg joined the Berlin academy. Max Reinhardt continued to mount his lavish productions, Erwin Piscator's proletarian theater performed "epic theater" and *agitprop* for working-class audiences, and *Die Volksbühne* mounted the dramas of Ernst Toller, the poet revolutionary, who had by then become a world celebrity. Bertolt Brecht and his musical collaborator Kurt Weill achieved international reputations with the success of *Die Dreigroschenoper* (1928; *Threepenny Opera*). Carl Zuckmeyer's satire on militarism, *Der Hauptmann von Köpenick* (*Captain of Koepenick*), was performed in 1931. Berlin novels include Hans Fallada's *Kleiner Mann, was nun?* (1932; *What Now, Little Man?*) and Alfred Döblin's *Berlin Alexanderplatz* (1929; *Alexanderplatz, Berlin*). Irmgard Keun wrote about the "new woman" and sexual freedom in her popular novels. It is not surprising that studios in Berlin and its immediate surroundings dominated the production of film, the most modern of all media. The city itself also served as the setting for diverse films by the great directors Fritz Lang, G.W. Pabst, Friedrich Murnau, and Piel Jutzi. These works range from Expressionist evocations of the dangers of the city to its documentary celebration, which is represented by Walter Ruttmann's *Berlin: Sinfonie einer Großstadt* (1927; *Symphony of a Great City*). A burst of great early sound films were produced at the end of the era, among them G.W. Pabst's *Die Dreigroschenoper* (1931; *The Threepenny Opera*), Leontine Sagan's *Mädchen in Uniform* (1931; *Girls in Uniform*), and the most famous one, Joseph von Sternberg's *Der blaue Engel* (1930; *The Blue Angel*), which made Marlene Dietrich an international star. In addition, we associate female cabaret performers and celebrity names such as Dietrich, Greta Garbo, Josephine Baker, Anita Berber, and Lotta Lenya with Berlin in the 1920s. American popular perceptions of the city in the 1920s also have been influenced by Bob Fosse's film *Cabaret* (1972), which was based on Christopher Isherwood's *Berlin Stories* (1935).

The National Socialists were a growing presence in the city from the mid-1920s, when Joseph Goebbels was made party boss (*Gauleiter*) of Berlin. After Moscow, Berlin was the strongest communist stronghold in the world. With the crash in 1929, however, unemployment rose tenfold. Theater scandals were staged by the Nazis and bullying tactics were put into force. Street fighting between communists and Nazis were common in the last years of the Republic, and although Hitler never received a majority in "Red Berlin," Berlin became the capital of the infamous Third Reich after Hitler came to power in 1933. Under the Nazis, the cultural life of Berlin collapsed. Over 1,300 writers alone, plus countless performers, composers, musicians, and other artists, were forced into exile. The Reichstag fire of 1933 also was used as a pretext to arrest left-wing intellectuals. A ceremonial burning of books took place in front of the university library and included works by Heine, Freud, Heinrich Mann, Kurt Tucholsky, Ernst Toller, and many others. At the beginning of the Nazi period, there were 200,000 Jews in the city; at its end, only 5,000 were left. Jews, who enjoyed full civil rights in the Weimar Republic, lost everything with the Nüremberg Laws and the infamous Kristalnacht in 1938. Many, including the young poet Gertrud Kolmar, died in camps as victims of the Nazi genocide. Another Berlin poet, Nelly Sachs, who went into exile, won the Nobel Prize for her poetry on the Holocaust. Some writers such as the famous Gottfried Benn first supported the Nazis but soon became disillusioned. Others remained and attempted to keep some independence. The bitter tension between this latter group, called the "Inner Emigration," and those artists who went into exile would dominate cultural debate in the aftermath of the war.

Nazi aesthetics espoused a classicist celebration of premodern values—icons included the powerful and dominating nude male warrior, and the female figure as rural mother. Essentially, all the great works of modern art produced during the decade were pronounced *entartet* (decadent). They were either destroyed, confiscated for the infamous art exhibition *Entartete Kunst,* or sold on the international black market. Modernity and its capital Berlin, despite Hitler's dependence on the modern industry for his war effort, was declared "un-German." Hitler's distaste for Berlin is suggested by his commissioning the architect Albert Speer to redesign the city incorporating monumental parade boulevards and by his intention to rename it *Germania.* Problematic artistic achievements of the period are Leni Riefenstal's propaganda film *Triumph des Willens* (1935; *Triumph of the Will*) and her film *Olympiade.* The latter depicts the 1936 Olympics, which were held in the stadium that is still used for sports events today.

By the end of the war (1939–45), Berlin lay in ruins. The city was divided into four allied sectors and governed by the Four Powers agreement. As cold war tensions between the Western allies and the Soviet Union became increasingly virulent, the American, British, and French sectors were soon known as "West Berlin"; the Russian sector, which included the city center, was "East Berlin." When in 1948 the Western allies instituted a currency reform that divided the city economically, the Soviets answered with a blockade of West Berlin. The Allies response was a successful airlift that kept the Western part of the city alive and in Western hands. Censorship prevailed on both sides during the first decade after the war, with a gradual lifting in the West. Complicated and contradictory cultural policies by the Four Powers toward those who had participated in the arts under Nazism also had a strong impact on cultural life. Wolfgang Staudte, who had worked in the Nazi film industry, lived in the West but could not at first work there. He directed the first German film made after the war for DEFA, in the East German film studios that newly inhabited the former UFA buildings in Babelsberg. *Die Mörder sind unter uns* (1946; *The Murderers Are Among Us*) was shot in the ruins of the city. After the founding of the Federal Republic of Germany in 1949, East Germany followed suit by becoming the German Democratic Republic. East Berlin became its official capital, "Berlin Hauptstadt der DDR." Economic problems led to an uprising on 17 June 1953 in East Berlin, and despite efforts to shore up the communist economy, a "brain drain" of well-educated professionals from East to West, particularly across the border in Berlin, led on 13 August 1961 to the erection of the Berlin Wall, which would seal the border to Western emigration for 28 years.

Berlin East and Berlin West were twin cities again, this time teeming with spies, competing as showcases of capitalism and communism, and shadowing each other in literature, theater, opera, music, cinema, and art. New theaters and opera and concert halls were constructed in West Berlin, and the Free University was founded as a counterpart to the Humboldt University in the East. Of the older generation of postwar writers, the Berliner Wolfdietrich Schnurre stands out for his *Kahlschlag* lyrics and his short stories, while Arno Schmidt and Uwe Johnson wrote Berlin novels that addressed the division of the city. West Berlin artistic and business activity was heavily subsidized, and other measures were taken to make the "island city" attractive; for example, Berlin's citizens were not subject to the draft. Many disaffected young artists made their way to West Berlin, which took on a special character, when Munich, Cologne, and Hamburg also became cultural centers within the Federal Republic. Berlin was the city of spontaneous "art happenings," left-wing students, and "independent," but subsidized filmmaking. Peter Schneider's *Lenz* (1973), based on Büchner's novella, captured the spirit of students in the aftermath of the 1968 movement. Helke Sander, who broke with the Marxist SDS (German Socialist Student Alliance) because of its refusal to address gender inequalities, founded the feminist journal *Frauen und Film* in an attempt to break ground for women filmmakers. Her *Redupers* (1977; *The All-Round Reduced Personality*), which is part documentary and part autobiography, depicts the Berlin of the 1970s. Peter Schneider's novel *Der Mauerspringer* (1982; *The Wall Jumper*) captures both the malaise of the Wall and the mentality of the *Grenzgänger* who refuses the identities offered by the two German states. By the 1980s, the Western side of the Wall had become a giant easel, upon which professional and unprofessional artists alike painted ironic expressions of protest. Wim Wenders, associated with the New German Cinema, returned from filmmaking in the United States to make *Himmel über Berlin* (1988; *Wings of Desire*), the last great work devoted to the divided city.

East Berlin was the indisputable cultural center of East Germany. Most exiles who returned to the GDR after World War II settled there, as well as almost all of the writers and artists who were known in the West. Bertolt Brecht, and later his wife, the great actress Helene Weigel, directed the Berliner Ensemble in world famous productions of his masterworks. The East German regime, led by the SED (Socialist Unity Party) and following the Soviets, imposed socialist realism in the arts and attempted to steer "cultural production" in order to help build socialism while controlling the opposition through regulation and surveillance by the Stasi (State Security Organization). *Kulturpolitik* (cultural policy) under Walter Ulbricht or, subsequently, Erich Honecker ushered in periods of freezing and thawing in censorship and control. In a society without freedom of the press or expression, literature increasingly took on a substitute role, and "reading between the lines" became a communicative strategy for readers and authors alike. This was particularly true of GDR women's literature. Writers such as Irmtraud Morgner, Helga Königsdorf, Helga Schubert, Maxi Wander, and Christa Wolf expressed the gap between public claims and private experience. In this setting, various shades of opposition emerged, but most East German writers and other artists were neither pro-West nor opposed to socialism as such, but were against the repressiveness of the regime. Figures from the older generation, including Stephan Hermlin and Stefan Heym, as well as a younger generation consisting of Wolf, Heiner Müller, Günter Kunert, Sarah Kirsch, and Christoph Hein attempted to do a balancing act. Wolf's *Der geteilte Himmel* (1963; *Divided Heaven*) and *Nachdenken über Christa T.* (1968; *The Quest for Christa T.*) were attempts to challenge the status quo and to redefine the limits of socialist realism. Ulrich Plenzdorf's work *Die neuen Leiden des jungen W.* (1973; *The New Sorrows of Young W.*), along with Volker Braun's *Unvollendete Geschichte* (1975, 1989; Unfinished Story), addressed the increasing problems of youth. In 1976, Wolf Biermann, the popular *enfant terrible* and songwriter, was expatriated by the East German government while performing in the West. Most writers signed protests about this act and ran afoul of the authorities. There followed an enormous exodus of East German writers to the West, including Jurek Becker, the author of *Jakob der Lügner* (1968; *Jacob the Liar*), and Reiner Kunze (1976; *Die wunderbaren Jahre*). The two most prominent writers who remained were Wolf and Müller, both of whom gained international reputations during the 1980s. A final prophetic work was Helke Misselwitz's documentary film *Winter Adé* (1988; Farewell, Winter), which showed women speaking openly about their problems.

The Wall fell in 1989, with writers and other artists agitating for a new beginning. The GDR, which had presented itself as having one of the world's leading economies, was found to have an increasingly obsolete one, and in the first free elections held in 40 years, the people voted overwhelmingly for Chancellor Kohl's Christian Democratic Union and for unification with the Federal Republic. This occurred on 3 October 1990, less than a year after the Wall had come down. A period of great turmoil followed for the East. Under the terms of the unification contract, property was to be returned to original owners or their heirs. Industries were privatized, or, if no longer economically viable, dissolved. Much unemployment and make-work programs ensued in the transitional economic vacuum. As cultural institutions came under the scrutiny of commissions, university departments were dissolved and the organization of education in the East was made to conform to that in the West. The upheavals created great resentment, misunderstanding, and mistrust between *Ossis* and *Wessis*, soon to be dubbed *Besserwessis* and *Jammerossis*, and these phenomena were generally referred to as *Die Mauer im Kopf*. Nowhere was this more virulent than in discussions about joining formerly separate institutions such as the PEN Club or the Academy of Arts. For instance, it was revealed that the leader of a nonconformist alternative literary culture in Prenzlauer Berg, Sascha Anderson, had been hired and supported by the Stasi. Further revelations of various kinds of collaboration with the Stasi shook Berlin. Squabbling and finger-pointing between those who had left the GDR before the Wall came down and those who stayed were as vehement as arguments between Easterners and Westerners. At the same time, Berlin became a center for organizations that were founded to recognize the citizenship status of *Ausländer* as well as for those unrecognized German minorities such as Turks and African-Germans. Post-Wall Berlin also became synonymous with youth culture, techno, and the love parade. New Berlin novels have appeared: Günter Grass, a long-time resident of West Berlin, published his Berlin novel *Ein weites Feld* (1995; A Big Subject). Thomas Brussig's satiric novel on the Wall's opening, *Helden wie wir* (1996; Heroes Like Us) hit the best-sellers' list and has played to full houses in a dramatic adaptation.

More than any other place in Germany, Berlin has had to come to terms with unification. It is the only one among the German *Länder* (states) to be composed of a former Eastern and a former Western part. Decisions still come highly politicized, including renaming streets in East Berlin, the issue about what to do with the empty East German Palace of the Republic, and the question of whether to rebuild the Hohenzollern palace. The culture wars were most virulent in Berlin, but in 1999, as the government prepared to move to its new capital, the two sides of the city appeared to unite against the privileges of the newcomers. Christo wrapped the old Reichstag in 1994 in a Berliner Volksfest atmosphere, and a newly designed Reichstag opened in 1999. The film *Das Leben ist eine Baustelle* (1997; Life is a Construction Site), directed by Wolfgang Becker, has garnered a persistent following and shows the poorer regentrifying neighborhoods without regard to East or West. As the new millennium approached, the former death strip was full of cranes; Berlin was the largest construction site in the world.

HELEN CAFFERTY

See also Berliner Ensemble; Weimar Republic

Further Reading

Albertz, Heinrich, *Die Chronik Berlins*, Dortmund: Chronik Verlag, 1986; 2nd edition, 1991

Ankum, Katharina von, editor, *Women in the Metropolis: Gender and Modernity in Weimar Culture*, Berkeley: University of California Press, 1997

Becker-Cantarino, Barbara, editor, *Berlin in Focus: Cultural Transformations in Germany*, Westport, Connecticut: Praeger, 1996

McShine, Kynaston, editor, *Berlinart 1961–1987*, New York: Museum of Modern Art, 1987

Bullivant, Keith, *The Future of German Literature*, Oxford and Providence, Rhode Island: Berg, 1994

Eckardt, Wolf von, and Sander L. Gilman, *Bertolt Brecht's Berlin: A Scrapbook of the Twenties*, Garden City, New York: Anchor Press, 1975; London: Abelard, 1976

Eldorado: Homosexuelle Frauen und Männer in Berlin, 1850–1950: Geschichte, Alltag und Kultur, Berlin: Frölich und Kaufmann, 1984

Emmerich, Wolfgang, *Kleine Literaturgeschichte der DDR: Erweiterte Neuausgabe*, Leipzig: Kiepenheuer, 1996; 2nd edition, 1997

Friedrich, Otto, *Before the Deluge: A Portrait of Berlin in the 1920's*, New York: Harper and Row, 1972; London: Joseph, 1974

Fries, Marilyn Sibley, *The Changing Consciousness of Reality: The Image of Berlin in Selected German Novels from Raabe to Döblin*, Bonn: Bouvier, 1980

Glass, Derek, Dietmar Rösler, and John J. White, editors, *Berlin: Literary Images of a City-Eine Großstadt im Spiegel der Literatur*, Berlin: Schmidt, 1989

Gleber, Anke, *The Art of Taking a Walk: Flanerie, Literature, and Film in Weimar Culture*, Princeton, New Jersey: Princeton Unversity Press, 1999

Kaes, Anton, Martin Jay, and Edward Dimendberg, *The Weimar Republic Sourcebook,* Berkeley: University of California Press, 1994
Kracauer, Siegfried, *From Caligari to Hitler: A Psychological History of the German Film,* Princeton, New Jersey: Princeton University Press, and London: Dobson, 1947
Ladd, Brian, *The Ghosts of Berlin: Confronting German History in the Urban Landscape,* Chicago: University of Chicago Press, 1997
Richie, Alexandra, *Faust's Metropolis: A History of Berlin,* New York: Carroll and Graf, and London: HarperCollins, 1998
Rollka, Bodo, Volker Spiess, and Bernhard Thieme, editors, *Berliner Biographisches Lexikon,* Berlin: Haude and Spener, 1993
Roters, Eberhard, *Berlin, 1910–1933,* New York: Rizzoli, 1982
Taylor, Ronald, *Berlin and Its Culture: A Historical Portrait,* New Haven, Connecticut: Yale University Press, 1997

Berliner Ensemble

The Berliner Ensemble has established itself as one of the most respected and influential theaters in the world. It was founded by Bertolt Brecht and Helene Weigel when they returned to East Berlin after their many years in exile. Following much tenacious lobbying and the widely acclaimed production of *Mutter Courage und ihre Kinder* (produced 1939; *Mother Courage and Her Children*), the company was set up with the approval of the Sozialistische Einheitspartei Deutschlands (SED) on 1 September 1949. Initially, the Berliner Ensemble performed at Wolfgang Langhoff's Deutsches Theater in East Berlin, where Brecht's *Trommeln in der Nacht* (1922; *Drums in the Night*) had been put on during the Weimar Republic. The Ensemble debuted in November 1949 with a production of *Herr Puntila und sein Knecht Matti* (produced 1941; *Mr. Puntila and His Man Matti*). Enjoying the luxury of a state-subsidized company, Brecht set about staging the plays written during his long years in exile as well as adaptations of works by Shakespeare, Sophocles, and J.M.R. Lenz. Brecht had always favored a cooperative approach. He now gathered around himself a collective of collaborators, and many of the famous names in German theater have been or are associated with the Berliner Ensemble.

In March 1954, the company moved to the Theater am Schiffbauerdamm, situated at the heart of Berlin not far from the Friedrichstraße and Unter den Linden. It is a theater whose unassuming—or even drab—exterior provides a striking contrast to its magnificent neo-Baroque interior. The Theater am Schiffbauerdamm was already familiar to Brecht from the prewar years, as the premiere of his immensely successful *Die Dreigroschenoper* (1929; *The Threepenny Opera*) in 1928 had taken place there.

In July 1954, the Ensemble embarked on its first international tour to Paris where its production of *Mother Courage and Her Children* caused a sensation and established the reputation of both the Berliner Ensemble and Brecht as a director; the production also generated interest in the techniques of Brecht's anti-illusionistic Epic Theater. The Ensemble also helped to promote a positive image of the GDR abroad, but this did not prevent friction between Brecht and the SED regime, which resulted from the contradiction between Brecht's Epic Theater and the official doctrine of Socialist Realism. Brecht's form of drama was attacked by the writer Friedrich Wolf and the critic Fritz Erpenbeck, both of whom toed the party line, accusing Brecht of "formalism."

The official East German press tended simply to ignore productions. A high point for the Ensemble was the staging of *Der kaukasische Kreidekreis* (1949; *The Caucasian Chalk Circle*) in 1954, but this was ignored by the most important newspaper in the East, *Neues Deutschland,* until the play's huge success in Paris, after which Brecht's form of theater was paraded as evidence of the tolerance and multiplicity of the GDR.

Following Brecht's death in 1956, his widow, Helene Weigel, retained her role as theater manager and upheld a strict Brechtian tradition until her death in 1971. The fame of the company was cemented with productions such as *Der aufhaltsame Aufstieg des Arturo Ui* (produced 1941; *The Resistible Rise of Arturo Ui*), which had Ekkehard Schall in the leading role. Weigel, a noted actress, also contributed to the Ensemble's reputation with performances in Brecht's adaptation *Coriolan* (produced 1952 and 1956; *Coriolanus*) and *Die Mutter* (produced 1931; *The Mother*).

Under Weigel's leadership, the Berliner Ensemble had essentially remained a Brecht theater, but when Ruth Berghaus became director in the 1970s, she embarked on a program of political and artistic renewal. For instance, she staged works by Heiner Müller, who had incurred the wrath of the East German state and whose works had been blacklisted. Berghaus was supported in her endeavors at innovation by the younger directors B.K. Tragelehn and Einar Schleef. The changes did not meet with official approval, and she was replaced by the Brecht disciple Manfred Wekwerth in 1977. Even then, however, the Ensemble did not restrict itself exclusively to Brecht's dramas.

Since German unification, the Berliner Ensemble has found itself in a state of flux and, frequently, artistic and financial crisis. In 1991, Matthias Langhoff, Fritz Marquardt, Heiner Müller, Peter Palitzsch, and Peter Zadek assumed the artistic management of the Ensemble, and it became a limited company, while nevertheless continuing to rely on financial support from the Berlin city government. Largely as a result of personality clashes, however, the collective leadership experiment failed, and Müller in effect became the sole artistic director until his death in December 1995. Formerly a protégé of Brecht, Müller was acknowledged by many as the greatest dramatist since Brecht and as his rightful successor.

Under Müller's influence the theater concentrated on works by Brecht, Müller, and Shakespeare, but it is unclear whether this focus will be maintained. Claus Peymann, currently with the Vienna Burgtheater, is due to take over the management of the Berliner Ensemble in 1999. It remains to be seen which artistic direction the theater will take under Peymann's leadership and whether he will be able to breathe new life into the Ensemble despite dwindling financial support. An additional uncertainty is caused by the aspirations of other protagonists on the cultural scene. The Ilse-Holzapfel-Stiftung, inaugurated in 1993 by the dramatist Rolf Hochhuth, is now the owner of the theater building, and Hochhuth has made no secret of his wish to see the Ensemble fulfill a dual role: on the one hand performing his own plays and on the other hand perpetuating its GDR tradition as a Brechtian theater, and here he has the support of Brecht's heirs.

The Berliner Ensemble has recently attempted to raise its profile with centenary productions and with the world premiere of Brecht's *Die Maßnahme* (1930; *The Measures Taken*). Despite recent successes with *The Resistible Rise of Arturo Ui* and *Mr. Puntila and His Man Matti,* however, the Ensemble still lacks a sense of direction. The financial turmoil and political and cultural upheaval of the Federal Republic since unification have been reflected in the situation of the Berliner Ensemble. Currently, the Ensemble is pinning its hopes on Peymann, whose leadership will determine the future of the Ensemble 40 years after its inception.

STEVEN W. LAWRIE

See also Berlin; Bertolt Brecht

Further Reading

Brecht, Bertolt, *Arbeitsjournal,* 2 vols., Frankfurt: Suhrkamp, 1973

Fuegi, John, *Brecht and Company: Sex, Politics, and the Making of Modern Drama,* New York: Grove Press, 1994

Hecht, Werner, *Brecht Chronik: 1898–1956,* Frankfurt: Suhrkamp, 1997

Jendreiek, Helmut, *Bertolt Brecht: Drama der Veränderung,* Düsseldorf: Bagel, 1969

Knopf, Jan, *Brecht-Handbuch: Theater: Eine Ästhetik der Widersprüche,* Stuttgart: Metzler, 1980; special edition, 1986

Mittenzwei, Werner, *Der Realismus-Streit um Brecht: Grundriß der Brecht-Rezeption in der DDR, 1945–1975,* Berlin and Weimar: Aufbau, 1978

Monk, Egon, *Auf dem Platz neben Brecht: Erinnerungen an die ersten Jahre des Berliner Ensembles,* Berlin: Parthas, 1998

Subiotto, Arrigo V., *Bertolt Brecht's Adaptations for the Berliner Ensemble,* London: Modern Humanities Research Association, 1975

Thomson, Peter, and Glendyr Sacks, editors, *The Cambridge Companion to Brecht,* Cambridge and New York: Cambridge University Press, 1994

Wekwerth, Manfred, *Schriften: Arbeit mit Brecht,* Berlin: Henschelverlag Kunst und Gesellschaft, 1975

Willet, John, *The Theatre of Bertolt Brecht: A Study from Eight Aspects,* London: Methuen, 1959; 4th edition, 1967

Thomas Bernhard 1931–1989

Thomas Bernhard emerged in the 1960s as one of Austria's major writers alongside Ingeborg Bachmann and Peter Handke, challenging the popularity of such established writers as Heinrich Böll and Günther Grass on the German literary scene. Bernhard's idiosyncratic prose style, with its highly ironized and hyperbolic invectives against culture, tradition, and society, stood in stark contrast to the Enlightenment ethos of Germany's liberal writers (most notably represented by the Gruppe 47) and an equally complacent literary avant-garde with its derivative revivals of the classical avant-garde of the 1920s. Combining mainstream and avant-garde techniques in a manner that avoided self-congratulatory statements of social revolt and politically slanted criticism, Bernhard attracted an audience that had grown tired of ideological instruction and what came to be seen as radical posturing.

Along with his novels and plays, which contributed quickly to Bernhard's public notoriety, the author made himself a name as a skillful impresario of public scandals. His histrionic verbal assaults on the institutional complicity of state and culture have earned him the epithets of *Übertreibungskünstler* (artist of exaggeration) and *Nestbeschmutzer* (one who befouls the nest). However, Bernhard's public provocations are not a mere by-product of his literary work but in fact provide the key to understanding his work. As a relentless cultural critic in the manner of Karl Kraus and Theodor Adorno, Bernhard consciously stages his provocations in the public sphere to explode the safe confines of liberal ideology, its consensus mentality, and its seemingly enlightened perspectives.

The early works of Bernhard offer a dissonant mixture of pathologically estranged expressionist prose and a dark parody of the idyllic *Heimatsroman* (folkloric novel). For example, *Frost* (1963) depicts the fate of the painter Strauch, whose monologues on death and the failure of art indicate a growing descent toward madness and suicide in a rural setting that is hostile to any form of creativity. Similarly, *Verstörung* (1967; *Gargoyles*) offers a case study of cultural decline and ensuing madness in the character of Prince Saurau, who has succumbed to the weight of his heritage and fortune, which he believes his son will systematically destroy. By the 1970s, Bernhard's prose had obsessively recast these stock scenarios of cultural despair in such novels as *Das Kalkwerk* (1970; *The Lime Works*) and *Korrektur* (1975; *Correction*). Alongside its Gothic thematics, Bernhard's works developed complex epistemic patterns of second- and third-hand narration, casting even more doubt on the narrator's reliability and the possibility of unmediated experience. The portrayal of schizoid characters from the vantage point of a skeptical epistemology of refracted and fragmented realities lends Bernhard's early novels a haunting atmosphere of radical ambivalence. Thus, a socially oppressive climate is heightened by the persistent failure of metaphysical foundations.

In his subsequent autobiographical childhood narratives (*Die Ursache, Der Keller, Der Atem, Die Kälte,* and *Ein Kind,* together translated as *Gathering Evidence*), which were published between 1975 and 1982, Bernhard's misanthropic prose finally begins to relax and show more openly its human and social concerns. The increased comical stance adopted by the author in his late works of the 1980s allowed him to develop more consistently the stance of a critic aware that he himself is guilty of all the charges he makes. *Wittgensteins Neffe* (1982; *Wittgenstein's Nephew*) began a series of late novels in which Bernhard explores art and its relation to the public sphere, subjecting them both comically and tragically to the scrutiny of a sobered criticism. For example, the tragic nephew of Wittgenstein, a remnant of the bourgeois cultural heritage, finds himself increasingly out of touch with the contemporary cultural industry in which the musical and marketing genius of Herbert von Karajan represents a new corporate prototype of the artist. Likewise, in *Holzfällen* (1984; *Woodcutters*), the avant-garde is dismissed as a petty bourgeois clique indulging in calculated scandals and pseudorebellions while entertaining a tacit reverence for the high arts as represented by the *Burgschauspieler* (actor from Austria's national theater) who is the honorary guest of their *künstlerisches Abendessen* (artistic soirée). *Alte Meister* (1985; *Old Masters*) can be read as Bernhard's adaptation of Adorno's dictum that "Kitsch lurks beneath every work of art." Canonical art is exposed by the novel's spokesperson, the critic Reger, as complicit with national self-aggrandizement and cultural arrogance. The entire novel, offering humorous tirades against established cultural icons, is nevertheless a serious attempt to point to the social contradictions that surround art as a vehicle for dubious mainstream ideologies. *Auslöschung* (1986; *Extinction*), Bernhard's last novel, makes these ideologies more explicit by focusing on the insidious Nazi past that haunts Austrian history. In an unorthodox move, Bernhard's hero donates the entire estate and inheritance of his Nazi parents to the Jewish community in Vienna as a belated gesture of remittance and acknowledgment of guilt.

It is not surprising that Bernhard's theatrical writing style culminated in a play titled *Heldenplatz* (1988; Heroes Square, where Hitler's annexation speech was cheered by the Viennese), which, on its premiere, turned the entire country of Austria into a "Bernhardesque Staatstheater," as one critic put it. The play, which premiered at the prestigious Burgtheater (Austria's national theater), triggered an embarrassing display of falsely wounded national pride in which both left- and right-wing politicians objected to the negative representation of Austria by the two Jewish main characters in the play. Bernhard's plays, which have often been seen as mere dramatic vehicles for the prototypical Bernhardesque misanthrope (e.g., *Minetti,* 1976), have all along been highly confrontational in their treatment of the Nazi era. For example, *Vor dem Ruhestand: Eine Komödie von deutscher Seele* (1979; *Eve of Retirement*) premiered in Stuttgart during the affair of Minister President Filbinger (indirectly portrayed in the figure of Justice Rudolf Höller), who had eagerly passed down death sentences as a naval judge in the Third Reich. Bernhard's equally confrontational *Heldenplatz* led the way for a reassessment of Austria's hegemonic postwar culture, which tolerated no dissent from its official standpoint. In the wake of the Waldheim affair, the play asserted a provocative Jewish point of view of Austrian affairs and helped bring public attention to Jewish writers such Robert Menasse, Elfriede Jelinek, Robert Schindel, and Doron Rabinovici and their disagreement with a culture marked by persistent amnesia and strategic harmonization of all conflicts.

MATTHIAS KONZETT

Biography

Born in Heerlen, the Netherlands, 10 February 1931. Lived in Austria from 1932; gave up school in 1947 and took up a commerical apprenticeship; contracted tuberculosis and spent two years in convalescence, 1951–52; attended the Viennese Academy of Music and Drama, 1947–51; worked as a freelance writer and court reporter for the *Demokratisches Volksblatt,* a socialist newspaper in Salzburg, from 1952; contributed to *Die Furche,* 1953–57; studied at the Mozarteum, Salzburg, 1955–57; traveled to Italy and Yugoslavia, 1953–57, London, 1960, and Poland, 1962–63; settled on a farm in Ohlsdorf, Upper Austria, 1965. Died 12 February 1989, leaving a contested will that prohibits publication and performance of his work in Austria.

Selected Works

Novels and Prose Works

Frost, 1963
Amras, 1964
Ungenach: Erzählung, 1968
An der Baumgrenze, 1969
Verstörung, 1967; as *Gargoyles,* 1970
Prosa, 1967
Watten: Ein Nachlass, 1969
An der Baumgrenze, 1969
Das Kalkwerk, 1970; as *The Lime Works,* translated by Sophie Wilkins, 1973
Gehen, 1971
Midland in Stilf: Drei Erzählungen, 1971
Der Italiener, 1971
Der Kulterer, 1974
Die Ursache, 1975; as *An Indication of the Cause,* translated by David McLintock, in *Gathering Evidence,* 1985
Korrektur, 1975; as *Correction,* translated by Sophie Wilkins, 1979
Der Wetterfleck, 1976
Der Keller, 1976; as *The Cellar,* translated by David McLintock, in *Gathering Evidence,* 1985
Der Atem, 1978; as *Breath,* translated by David McLintock, in *Gathering Evidence,* 1985
Der Stimmenimitator, 1979; as *The Voice-Imitator,* translated by Kenneth J. Northcott, 1997
Ja, 1978; as *Yes,* translated by Ewald Osers, 1991
Die Erzählungen, 1979
Die Billigesser, 1980; as *The Cheap-Eaters,* translated by Ewald Osers, 1990
Die Kälte, 1981; as *In the Cold,* translated by David McLintock, in *Gathering Evidence,* 1985
Ein Kind, 1982; as *The Child,* translated by David McLintock, in *Gathering Evidence,* 1985
Wittgensteins Neffe: Eine Freundschaft, 1982; as *Wittgenstein's Nephew,* translated by David McLintock, 1989
Beton, 1982; as *Concrete,* translated by David McLintock, 1984
Der Untergeher, 1983; as *The Loser,* translated by Jack Dawson, 1991
Holzfällen: Eine Erregung, 1984; as *Woodcutters,* translated by David McLintock, 1987; as *Cutting Timber,* translated by Ewald Osers, 1988
Alte Meister: Komödie, 1985; as *Old Masters,* translated by Ewald Osers, 1989
Auslöschung: Ein Zerfall, 1986; as *Extinction,* translated by David McLintock, 1995

Plays

Ein Fest für Boris, 1970; as *A Party for Boris,* translated by Kenneth J. Northcott and Peter Jansen, in *Histrionics: Three Plays,* 1990
Der Ignorant und der Wahnsinnige, 1972
Die Jagdgesellschaft, 1974; as *The Hunting Party,* in *Performing Arts Journal* 5 (1980)

Die Macht der Gewohnheit, 1974; as *The Force of Habit,* 1976
Der Präsident, 1975; as *The President,* 1982
Die Berühmten, 1976
Minetti: Portrait des Künstlers als alter Mann, 1976
Immanuel Kant, 1978
Vor dem Ruhestand: Ein Komödie von deutscher Seele, 1979; as *Eve of Retirement,* 1982
Der Weltverbesserer, 1980
Am Ziel, 1981
Der deutsche Mittagstisch, 1981; as *The German Lunch Table,* in *Performing Arts Journal* 6 (1981/82)
Über allen Gipfeln ist Ruh, 1981
Der Schein trügt, 1983; as *Appearances Are Deceiving,* in *Theater* 15 (1983)
Der Theatermacher, 1984; as *Histrionics,* translated by Kenneth J. Northcott and Peter Jansen, in *Histrionics: Three Plays,* 1990
Ritter, Dene, Voss, 1984; as *Ritter, Dene, Voss,* translated by Kenneth J. Northcott and Peter Jansen, in *Histrionics: Three Plays,* 1990
Einfach kompliziert, 1986
Elisabeth II., 1987
Heldenplatz, 1988
Claus Peymann kauft sich eine Hose und geht mit mir essen, 1990

Further Reading

Daviau, Donald, "Thomas Bernhard's *Heldenplatz,*" *Monatshefte* 83, no. 1 (1991)
Demetz, Peter, *After the Fires: Recent Writing in the Germanies, Austria, and Switzerland,* San Diego, California: Harcourt Brace Jovanovich, 1986
Dittmar, Jens, *Thomas Bernhard: Werkgeschichte,* Frankfurt: Suhrkamp, 1981; 2nd edition, 1990
Dowden, Stephen D., *Understanding Thomas Bernhard,* Columbia: University of South Carolina Press, 1991
Hoesterey, Ingeborg, "Postmoderner Blick auf die österreichische Literatur," *Modern Austrian Literature* 23, no. 3/4 (1990)
Konzett, Matthias, "*Publikumsbeschimpfung:* Thomas Bernhard's Provocations of the Austrian Public Sphere," *The German Quarterly* 68, no. 3 (Summer 1995)
Schmidt-Dengler, Wendelin, *Der Übertreibungskünstler: Studien zu Thomas Bernhard,* Vienna: Sonderzahl, 1986; 3rd edition, 1997

Frost 1963

Novel by Thomas Bernhard

Frost is the first of a series of long prose texts, often referred to as novels, that appeared in rapid succession and led to *Auslöschung* (1986; *Extinction*), Thomas Bernhard's longest text, which was followed by three years of writing dramas and autobiographical texts. Many themes and narrative structures of his later texts are already present or prefigured in *Frost,* despite its being a text that still retains aspects of more conventional narratives. As in many other texts by Bernhard, *Frost* is characterized by pushing narration to extremes, radical exaggeration, reduction and repetition rather than diversity and change, and a fascination with madness, death, and destruction. Its literary precursors are the experimental prose works of the early 20th century and Romanticism. Bernhard was soon recognized as a new and powerful voice in German and Austrian literature. But wide recognition and praise for his virtuosity and uncompromising independence came only after two more "novels" had been published (*Verstörung* [1967; *Gargoyles*] and *Das Kalkwerk* [1970; *The Lime Works*]). Confined, remote, and lurid sites cut off from the world characterize the space of these texts. The plot is reduced to a bare minimum, often centered around two figures, and based on long monologues and brief passages of description. Its constricted, bleak, and narrow sites signify an absence of meaning and, despite their remoteness and isolation, are in many ways representative of the world. It has been argued that Bernhard's later texts (after *The Lime Works*), while being more witty and amusing, are in danger of losing their suggestive power and of turning his startling monomania into sterile obsession and compulsive linguistic ritual. While in earlier texts the grotesque is disquieting, it has a tendency in his later works to lapse into mannerism and monotony.

Frost is situated in a loathsome space, which is connoted by a low-grade country inn, a meager village, and a dark forest that has been exploited and destroyed by the pulp industry. The people inhabiting this area are poor, ill, uneducated, and alarmingly narrow-minded. While Austria is referred to, no pretense at a realistic representation of political or social reality is made. Place and constellations of personnel are fantastic constructions. They are observed with a pathological obsession devoid of empathy or of hope for an improvement of the general misery. Strauch, the main character, is a poor painter who has not painted a picture for a long time. Having fled the world and retreated to this forlorn place, he leads a miserable and lonely life, wandering around observing a reality he deeply detests. His brother, with whom he has had no contact for 20 years, pays a student to spy on the painter and report on him. Posing as a law student, this student of medicine spends 26 days with the painter. Everything we know about Strauch and his world is filtered through the perception of this informant, the narrating "I" recording the painter's long monologues about the village and life in general and referring to his observations as "labor." The narrative perspective is highly complicated, however, as it continuously jumps from direct to indirect speech, and as it is recorded in the subjunctive but often slips into the indicative mode, or into descriptions in the observer's own words. It is never made clear whether the informant's report is reliable or to what degree his image of the painter's life and the reporting of his utterances are true representations. As the text is predicated on a skepticism concerning the possibility of understanding the world and the other in general, the reader is left in a state of insecurity and with an apparently highly subjective account based upon a dubious source of information. In the end, the student leaves and a few days later reads in the paper that the painter has disappeared in a snowstorm and his body has not been found.

While Strauch, like other characters in Bernhard's texts, is a central figure for the narrative, he is not an active and self-determined subject but rather a function of a situation that he is unable to control or change. He is condemned to life and confined to the restrictions of the narrative structure. Throughout the text, reality is reduced to images that are processed through the painter's mind and reported by the observer, who is paid for his service and, toward the end, realizes that he is being "forced" into Strauch's orbit and observes, "I am no longer I." The painter's mind emerges as saturated with images. His mind is not open, is no longer concerned with perceiving and exploring the world, but only with repeating what is known to him beyond doubt. What produces this closure is neither religious dogma nor political ideology or ignorance (which is at the root of the villagers' closed minds) but his "knowledge" of life as a catastrophe that stretches from birth to death.

This foregone conclusion leads to the closure of his mind and determines his apodictic reactions to the violations inflicted on the subject by the violence of the catastrophic world. Strauch has liberated himself from this world and is "free" to an astonishing degree, but at the price of complete isolation, inertia, and an extreme closure of mind that is an anticipation of death. He is past the point of skepticism that poses the question as to whether anything about the world can be known and whether true communication is possible. He has no doubt but knows the answers to all questions. Therefore, it is permissible—and even necessary—to create a world of his own that no longer requires observation and that leaves no questions open. Strauch is completely assured of what he says and, therefore, shuns doubt and self-reflexivity. The ensuing coherence is not a source of pleasure; on the contrary, it is born of despair.

No attempt is made to determine whether Strauch's world is real, a distortion of reality, or mere fantasia. These distinctions lose their significance and are superseded by a rhetoric of cohesion, which emerges from a feeling of despair from his "knowledge" of life as a catastrophe beyond comprehension. A nauseating disgust of the world leads to aversion and closure. The very possibility of an openness of the mind, necessary for understanding the world and for love or erotic relationships, is excluded from the start (love is sex, and sex is the brute realization of physical drives combined with lust for power). The text has gone full circle from modern skepticism to dogmatism. It is solely based on one individual's authority to determine what reality is, without making a universal truth claim. The meaninglessness of Strauch's world creates no desire for understanding and needs no interpretation. Strauch's world is coherent, shows no cracks or contradictions. However, the narration leaves no doubt that this is the real problem. As the real world is incomprehensible, the painter's closed construction makes it coherent, and the question emerges as to the delusion of this reality: is the world in the head a product of madness or, alternatively, is the mad world in need of a reconstruction that does not ignore its catastrophic character but rather associates it with an order that makes it fit for narration?

BERND HÜPPAUF

Editions

First edition: *Frost,* Frankfurt: Insel-Verlag, 1963

Further Reading

Beutner, Eduard, "Körperlicher Schmerz: Zur Darstellbarkeit einer Grenzerfahrung, am Beispiel von Thomas Bernhards *Frost,* Waltraut Anna Mitgutschs *Die Züchtigung* und Gustav Ernst," in *Literaturkritik und erzählerische Praxis: Deutschsprachige Erzähler der Gegenwart,* edited by Herbert Herzmann, Tübingen: Stauffenberg, 1995

Eben, Michael C., "Thomas Bernhard's *Frost*: Early Indications of an Austrian Demise," *Neophilologus* 69 (1985)

Gößling, Andreas, *Thomas Bernhards frühe Prosakunst: Entfaltung und Zerfall seines ästhetischen Verfahrens in den Romanen,* Berlin and New York: de Gruyter, 1987

Mittermayer, Manfred, "Strauch im Winter: Thomas Bernhards *Frost* als Inszenierung eines Ichzerfalls," *Modern Austrian Literature* 21 (1988)

——, *Thomas Bernhard,* Stuttgart: Metzler, 1995

Mixner, Manfred, "'Wie das Gehirn plötzlich nur mehr Maschine ist . . .': Der Roman *Frost* von Thomas Bernhard," in *In Sachen Thomas Bernhard,* edited by Kurt Bartsch et al., Königstein: Athenäum, 1983

Heldenplatz 1988

Play by Thomas Bernhard

Anniversaries are for remembering and, usually, for celebrating. In 1988, the Burgtheater in Vienna, acknowledged as the leading stage throughout the entire German-speaking world, celebrated its foundation a century earlier. In a city where art, enjoying vast state subsidies, often dominates newspaper front pages, and where cultural tourism is a major factor in the national economy, the event should have been the occasion for much joy and self-congratulation, for postwar Austria had secured a level of prosperity outstripping that of most other European states.

It was natural that the Burgtheater should want to commission a work by a prominent Austrian dramatist to mark that anniversary. It was unfortunate for those wishing to see the event as the highlight of the cultural calendar that 1988 also marked a second anniversary and that the commissioned writer was Thomas Bernhard. That second anniversary was Hitler's jubilant reception in Vienna 50 years earlier in 1938 following the unresisted takeover of the country by the German army. History books show Hitler addressing ecstatic throngs of Austrian Nazi supporters in the Heldenplatz (Heroes Square). As one writer has described it, the occupation was "rape by consent."

In 1988, Thomas Bernhard's play returned—quite literarally—to this very spot. In its staging and setting, *Heldenplatz* could be described as a modest chamber work. It consists of three scenes and has almost no external action and very little visible dramatic movement. Its cast is also modest in number and well below the natural capacity of such a grand stage as the Burgtheater. The first and third scenes are set in an apartment next to the Heldenplatz in the very heart of Vienna, and the second scene is played in the nearby Volksgarten with the Burgtheater visible in the background; this device obliges the audience to be aware that it is looking at itself and is therefore part of the play.

Today it is difficult to decide which was the more theatrical event: the play taking place on the stage of the Burgtheater or the fury it unleashed well before the first performance, for the play leaves not a single aspect of the Austrian state unscathed. Bernhard's notorious and characteristic trademark of unrelieved tirades upon Austria and the Austrians unleashed apoplexies of rage among prominent and ordinary citizens alike. In what appears to have been an orchestrated maneuvre by the popular press to whip up opposition to state-subsidized art, Bernhard and his German-born director at the Burgtheater, Claus Peymann, provided ideal targets. The expectation in some quarters that mass demonstrations would prevent the premiere taking place was unfulfilled. Instead, the work was celebrated as a coup de théâtre, and, if not always acclaimed critically as one of Bernhard's greatest works for the theater, the play can now be seen as something far more differentiated than a bad-mouthing of the Austrian state.

The plot of *Heldenplatz* is uncomplicated in the extreme. A Jewish intellectual and distinguished academic, Professor Josef Schuster, has committed suicide by leaping from the window of his Viennese apartment. As a young man, he along with his brother had fled from Austria as Hitler occupied the country and had joined that band of distinguished Jewish émigrés who graced British and U.S. universities. After the war Josef Schuster was induced by the city fathers in Vienna to return and teach at the university, an outward gesture of reconciliation and Austria's return to civilized values.

Although Josef is dead when the stage curtain rises, it is his voice and the suggestion of his presence that dominates much of the play, for most of the dialogue consists of the various characters remembering and repeating verbatim the Professor's unremittingly negative and caustic comments on his native Austria and his regret at ever having returned from Oxford.

In his great historical drama *König Ottokars Glück und Ende* (1825), which celebrates the establishment of the house of Habsburg, Austria's national poet Franz Grillparzer sings a paean to his homeland: "It is a goodly land . . . Where lies a land that can compare?" Bernhard's play is the reply, destroying mercilessly every aspect of national life, every institution, and every political office. The stupidity of life in the nation's capital is eclipsed only by the even greater boorishness of life in its provinces. In a country whose nerves were already in shreds following the international criticism of President Waldheim's election, Bernhard's attack could not have found a more sensitive spot. His most painful assault on national sensitivity is spoken by Schuster's daughter, Anna, in her very simple utterance: "Conditions today are really just as they were in thirty-eight." The cryptic shorthand of the reference holds for the Austrian state the unbearable charge that this modern, democratic, and flourishing country is no better than when the citizens of the first Austrian Republic gave Hitler a hero's welcome in 1938. Bernhard's accusation is brutally clear: this land and its citizens have not changed one iota since they handed themselves over willingly to the author of the Holocaust.

Understandably, the play's attack on the nation's honor has dominated discussion of *Heldenplatz,* but there are timely reminders that the work goes beyond this issue to suggest the decline of all of Western culture (Konzett). Josef Schuster chooses death while his brother is portrayed as having chosen resignation and a superficial assimilation that could be revoked by the assimilators at any time. The play ends with the growing sound of hysterical crowds offstage, an unmistakable reference to the greeting of Hitler by the Viennese. In shock, the Professor's widow collapses facedown into her meal at the funeral wake, and the final words are spoken by the brother: "It was an absurd idea to return to Vienna. But then the world is made up of absurd ideas." In outward appearance the play might, indeed, have drawn on elements from the theater of the absurd; in intention, however, it came uncomfortably close to social realism.

ANTHONY BUSHELL

Editions

First edition: *Heldenplatz,* Frankfurt: Suhrkamp, 1988

Further Reading

Dowdon, Steve, "Thomas Bernhard's Austria," *Partisan Review* 61 (1994)

Eisner, Nicholas, "*Theatertheater/Theaterspiele:* The Plays of Thomas Bernhard," *Modern Drama* 30 (1987)

Konzett, Matthias, "*Publikumsbeschimpfung:* Thomas Bernhard's Provocations of the Austrian Public Sphere," *German Quarterly* 68, no. 3 (Summer 1995)

Kiebuzinska, Christine, "The Scandal Maker: Thomas Bernhard and the Reception of *Heldenplatz,*" *Modern Drama* 38 (1995)

Wittgensteins Neffe 1982

Novel by Thomas Bernhard

Wittgensteins Neffe (*Wittgenstein's Nephew*) is Bernhard's first novel that deals directly with the cultural public sphere, drawing largely on the fame and shadow surrounding the industrialist family of the Wittgensteins with its patronage of the arts (e.g., Klimt), its philosophical genius Ludwig Wittgenstein, and its extreme domestic tragedies (three suicides among Ludwig's siblings). The protagonist of Bernhard's narration, the real-life and widely known Viennese public figure Paul Wittgenstein (Ludwig's nephew) can be seen as the last embodiment of an elite bourgeois acquisition of culture, with its implicit purpose of legitimating its own economic ascent against the fading feudal order of Habsburg Austria. The confrontation between this aesthetic heritage of bourgeois culture and its modern counterpart in consumer society is the central theme of novel.

The semi-autobiographical novel, which recounts the author's and Wittgenstein's friendship, begins in the remote locale of adjoining lung and mental sanatoria where both Bernhard and Wittgenstein meet after having suffered, respectively, a severe physical and a mental breakdown. What unfolds is the story of two social misfits who, because of their misunderstood enthusiasm for the arts and their own unsparing preoccupation with them, suffer periodically from mental and physical exhaustion. This fateful encounter and friendship contribute eventually to the partial recovery of the author-narrator, for whom Wittgenstein's colorful life, its relation to the arts, and its tragic end carry the significance of his own emerging critical perspective of culture. Wittgenstein is not presented as merely another example of Bernhard's severely estranged and self-destructive characters that had become the trademark of his earlier works. Instead, Bernhard undertakes in this novel a more extensive critical case study of the consumptive relation between the arts and its consumer audience.

Wittgenstein initially embodies the decline of the bourgeois public sphere and its dubious self-legitimation through the conspicuous consumption of art. However, his dissenting spirit, especially as manifested in his later life, recalls as well the idealized, early revolutionary stages of the public sphere envisioned as an alternative and nonconformist social space. Wittgenstein's initial appearance in the role of the *Kunstrichter* (art critic), serving as the model for Bernhard's own critical self-definition, is marked by an uncritical genius and social complacency. Here Wittgenstein's unshaken confidence and vitality reign supreme in his pursuit of culture, representing a vulgar form of what Kant defined as the genius' apodictic judgment. For example, he elevates himself to an unchallenged critical authority at the Vienna State Opera, where he becomes a feared "Premieremacher," deciding quite arbitrarily either the failure or success of a particular performance through his undaunted booing or cheering. Wittgenstein, in fact, bears not so much the trait of the genius as that of the dandy-comedian who, through provocative and gratuitously self-referential gestures, mocks and unmasks society's cultural pretensions. In this activity, however, he becomes an idiosyncratic cultural fanatic who nevertheless remains enslaved to the institutions surrounding culture. Traveling addictively around the world to visit all the opera houses, he returns to Vienna's conservative establishment, embracing it all the more in his typical idiosyncratic fashion: "The Met is nothing. Covent Garden is nothing. None of them were anything next to Vienna. *But of course*, he said, *the Vienna Opera is really good only once a year.*"

Wittgenstein, whose willful judgment of taste appears to sway an audience temporarily, remains ultimately ineffective in subverting the social order dominating the arts. Even within his domain as *Kunstrichter,* he loses out to the impeccable judgment of an even greater fanatic than himself, the unerring musical and self-promoting genius Herbert von Karajan: "The genius of Karajan was too great as to be even irritated by Paul." As the towering figure in Austria's culture and the international music world, Karajan reflects not only the problematic triumph of artistic will but also the transition from the traditional bourgeois artist to the self-promoting genius on the commodity market of mass consumerism. Comparatively, a lesser genius such as Paul Wittgenstein, incapable of fully modernizing himself, is reduced to a slave of his own image as a fashionable social singularity and as one of the vanishing executors of Austria's traditional cultural heritage. Bernhard, who sees in Karajan "the first of all the music workers in the world," advances here, albeit uncritically, a principle of productivity over the mere passivity and apathy of consumerism, as embodied by Wittgenstein reduced to private connoisseurship and to vicarious pleasures of dreaming up scenarios that cannot be realized.

Wittgenstein's persistence in art, at a time when it no longer secures any social privilege for him, constitutes ultimately an indirect criticism of Karajan as a cultural and economic institution. Surrounded by personal tragedy—Wittgenstein's lifelong companion dies, and he is cut off from financial support by the family—the portrait of the hero in Bernhard's novel matures to that of the tragic comedian who has learned to endure in the face of adversity. Mortally ill, Wittgenstein still manages to last through a six-hour performance of Wagner's *Tristan und Isolde* on a cheap standing-room ticket. The late Wittgenstein begins to resemble Walter Benjamin's positive reconstruction of the dandy in the figure of the *flaneur* who meanders among the vestiges of a dying bourgeois culture. As with Benjamin's *flaneur,* Wittgenstein betrays neither the anonymous face of the mass individual (as with the myth of Karajan and the anonymous institutional powers supporting his success) nor the concealed gaze of the private individual or self-appointed genius. Instead, in animated cultural conversations and visits to the opera and the *Musikverein,* he shows himself to be a *Kulturmensch* bent on sharing his vision of art with others.

In *Wittgenstein's Nephew,* which indicates a major departure from Bernhard's earlier work, the author recasts through Wittgenstein his active position within the Austrian cultural sphere. By confronting himself critically in his double, he breaks with the alienated bourgeois cultural heritage that had haunted his earlier work and recovers the constructive and intersubjective aspects that propelled the traditional bourgeois public sphere forward into an era of mass culture. The novel demonstrates that mass culture is capable of internal critique and a renewed communicative focus once it comes to terms with its bourgeois legacy and its own ideological will toward collective assertion. The novel triggered a final period in Bernhard's writings that brought his cultural critique to bear on Austria in a more provocative and constructive sense.

MATTHIAS KONZETT

Editions

First edition: *Wittgensteins Neffe: Eine Freundschaft,* Frankfurt: Suhrkamp, 1982

Translation: *Wittgenstein's Nephew: A Friendship,* translated by David McLintock, New York: Knopf, 1989

Further Reading

Daviau, Donald, "The Reception of Thomas Bernhard in the United States," *Modern Austrian Literature* 21, no. 3/4 (1988)

Fetz, Gerald, "Thomas Bernhard and the 'Modern Novel'," in *The Modern German Novel,* edited by Keith Bullivant, Leamington Spa and New York: Berg, 1987

Honegger, Gitta, "Wittgenstein's Children: The Writings of Thomas Bernhard," *Theater* 15 (1983)

Konzett, Matthias, "*Publikumsbeschimpfung*: Thomas Bernhard's Provocations of the Austrian Public Sphere," *German Quarterly* 68, no. 3 (Summer 1995)

Schlaes, Amity, "Thomas Bernhard and the German Literary Scene," *New Criterion* 5 (January 1982)

Schmidt-Dengler, Wendelin, and Martin Huber, editors, *Statt Bernhard: Über Misanthropie im Werk Thomas Bernhards,* Vienna: Edition S, 1987

Updike, John, "Ungreat Lives," *New Yorker,* 4 February 1985

———, "Studies in Post-Hitlerian Self-Condemnation in Germany and Austria," *New Yorker,* 9 October 1989

Weber, Albrecht, "Wittgensteins Gestalt und Theorie und ihre Wirkung im Werk Thomas Bernhards," *Österreich in Geschichte und Literatur* 25 (1981)

Biblical Drama

Dramatizations of the Bible in the German language were an important element of religious culture from the 13th to the 17th centuries. They were a means, along with sermons, creeds, and the visual arts, of allowing the laity access to the contents of the Bible and to the tenets of Christian faith. The Bible of the medieval church was in Latin, and texts of the complete Scriptures were rarely encountered outside theological faculties; the Reformation encouraged vernacular translations of the Bible, and printing made them more widely available, but high illiteracy rates meant that there continued to be a need for communication modes that also reached the common people. Nevertheless, the Reformation altered the content, context, and function of biblical drama so completely that it will be treated separately from the medieval period in this article.

German biblical drama of the Middle Ages, similar to all medieval religious drama, originated in church liturgy, specifically in embellishments of the Easter and Christmas liturgies, which took the form of sung evocations of the visit to Christ's empty tomb or the adoration of the infant Jesus. These embellishments, or "tropes," are known as *Quem queritis* tropes after the Latin question ("Whom do you seek?") with which they begin. This question is posed by an angel either to the women who have come to the tomb to anoint Christ's body or to the shepherds at the manger. The dialogue in the tropes does not correspond exactly to the letter of the gospel; the drama that developed out of these liturgical embellishments also maintained a fairly loose relation to the scriptural text and drew freely on nonscriptural sources such as theological treatises, hagiography, and liturgy. *Quem queritis* tropes appeared in the German-speaking world from around the 10th century, at the same time as Latin offices (music dramas performed within the framework of the liturgy) and plays; the earliest surviving vernacular plays are from the 13th century. It is important not to impose an evolutionary schema on these facts; later forms do not supplant earlier ones (Latin offices continued into the 18th century, long after the vernacular tradition of biblical drama had expired), and there is no clear and unidirectional development from simple to complex forms, or from fully liturgical to fully dramatic compositions (the distinction between offices and plays in Latin is particularly fluid).

The earliest surviving biblical dramas to make use of German date from the first half of the 13th century. The appearance of vernacular drama around this time reflects the more intensive evangelization of the laity encouraged by the Lateran Council of the Church of 1215; the plays also responded to and encouraged a new tone in lay piety, which placed greater emphasis on Christ's humanity and suffering. A particularly interesting play in this regard is the Benediktbeuern Passion play. The play, which possibly dates from the beginning of the 13th century, is mainly in Latin, but three characters are given speeches in German: Mary Magdalene, the Virgin Mary, and Longinus, the centurion who pierced the crucified Christ's side with his lance and was cured of his blindness. The choice is significant: the speeches of these characters focus on the themes of sin, repentance, and redemption through Christ's sacrifice on the cross; thus, they communicate a key doctrinal messsage to the laity and at the same time afford an opportunity for emotional involvement in Christ's suffering. From around 1250, we have plays in which all of the action is in German; the high point of medieval biblical drama in German was reached in the 15th and early 16th centuries, when the towns where most of the plays were performed were at the peak of their prosperity and political importance. The extant plays come predominantly from towns in Hesse and the Frankish Rhineland, the Tyrol, Swabia and Switzerland, Austria and Bavaria, and the East Central German regions. The surviving play texts by no means give the complete picture; performance records show that almost every town in Germany and German-speaking central Europe had a tradition of biblical drama.

Around 150 German or mixed German-Latin biblical plays survive from the 13th to the 16th centuries. Plays for the Easter season are by far the most numerous in this corpus: these are chiefly Passion plays, Easter plays (in theory, only the latter dramatize the resurrection), and *planctus* plays (dramatizations of the Virgin's lament beneath the cross); there are also plays that concentrate on individual scenes from the Easter story. A smaller number of plays are connected with the Christmas season: nativity plays, prophet plays, and plays of the annunciation and the purification of the Virgin. In addition, there are doomsday plays and Corpus Christi plays (similar to Passion plays in content, but performed on the feast of Corpus Christi), *sponsus* plays (dramatizations of the parable of the wise and foolish virgins), an Antichrist play, and a very few dramatizations of Old Testament narratives.

Staging a play in a late medieval town typically involved collaboration between the church, the town council, and the citizens. Clerics wrote the play text, directed the performance, and also acted some of the parts. The council sanctioned the performance, made arrangements for public order and safety, and sometimes contributed money toward the production and, especially, the construction of the stage. Male citizens, chiefly from the mercantile and artisan classes, acted the parts that were not taken by clerics. Women actors were a very rare exception; female roles were normally played by men. Sometimes the actors were involved in the play through their membership of craft guilds; sometimes there existed fraternities for the specific purpose of financing and performing a play. The length of performance could vary tremendously, from a few hours to several days (in 1514, the Bozen Passion play was performed over seven feast days, from Palm Sunday to Easter Day). Dialogue was chanted in a kind of recitative that was more audible than normal speech, especially when the performance took place out of doors.

Plays were performed both indoors, usually in churches, and outdoors, on the town square or marketplace. The staging was either "successive" or "simultaneous." Successive staging was the norm for Corpus Christi plays, which typically consisted of a procession of tableaux. With simultaneous staging, the acting area (Latin *platea* [street]) accommodated all of the scenes (Latin *mansiones* [houses], or *loca* [stations]) of the action, which were simultaneously visible to the audience. At the beginning of the performance, the actors took up their positions on their respective *loca* and remained there for the entire duration, making their "entrances" by standing up and their "exits" by sitting down at the end of their scene. For some Passion and Easter plays of the 15th and 16th centuries, we have contemporary plans or descriptions of the simultaneous stage; although their relation to the texts of the plays is sometimes problematic, they give us precious information about the physical configuration of the acting area and its symbolic dimension. The *loca* for Passion plays comprise both the "historical" scenes of the gospel narrative (for example, Gethsemane or Calvary) and the "transcendent" scenes of heaven and hell, represented by a scaffold surmounted by God's throne and a gaping jaw that has swallowed the souls of the dead, respectively. The stage therefore places human life and actions on this earth under the watchful gaze of God and the devil: God, who will sentence humans to one or other of the eternal destinations according to their "performance" on earth, and the devil, who is always tempting humans into sin in order to swell the population of hell.

This spatial symbolism reveals one of the functions of biblical drama: to make the invisible (but nonetheless real) transcendent order of the cosmos visible to the spectators. Symbolism of this kind worked together with the sermonizing rhetoric of the plays to inculcate and orchestrate in the audience sentiments of Christian piety, compassion, and remorse; it was not unusual for performances to conclude with the singing of hymns by the actors and the public, priestly benedictions, the celebration of mass, or even the sale of indulgences. Alongside these religious functions, lay participants could sometimes introduce other, quite profane motives of their own. For example, the Nördlingen archives for the early 16th century record on several occasions that men who played the devils in the Corpus Christi procession were disciplined by the council for behaving in a lewd and offensive way toward women spectators. Incidents such as these, when actors exceeded what was regarded as acceptable license, have nothing to do with the "official" purpose of the plays; nevertheless, they are important because they show how plays could provide an "unofficial" outlet for behavior that tested the limits of secular propriety.

The Reformation put an end to the medieval tradition of biblical drama, but it also fostered a new kind of Bible play. Luther stated in the preface to his New Testament translation of 1521 that the true knowledge of the gospel consists in understanding the message of salvation by grace alone and not in knowing the life and works of Christ—precisely the things that Passion plays and Easter plays threatened to foreground in the minds of their spectators. Accordingly, performances of these plays ceased in towns and regions that became Protestant, although they continued to be performed in Catholic areas into the 17th century; indeed, in Luzern they reached their apogee under the direction of Renwart Cysat (1545–1614). By contrast, Protestant reformers encouraged biblical drama as a means of spreading the new doctrine and, especially, as a vehicle for the moral instruction of the young; a great deal of Protestant biblical drama was written for performance by schoolboys, although it was sometimes acted by the wider community as well, especially in regions with an established tradition of civic performance, such as Switzerland.

Whereas most of the authors of medieval plays remained anonymous, Protestant dramatists are known by name. The most important are: Burkhard Waldis (1490–1555), Paul Rebhun (1500–1546), Sixt Birk (1501–54), Thiebolt Gart (ca. 1540), Jakob Ruoff (d. 1558), Hans von Rüte (d. 1558), Jörg Wickram (ca. 1500–1562), Andreas Pfeilschmidt (ca. 1555), Jos Murer (1530–80), Thomas Brunner (ca. 1535–71), Georg Rollenhagen (1542–1609), and Nikodemus Frischlin (1547–90). Some of these authors wrote plays in Latin as well as German; Birk, for example, wrote German plays for the citizens of Basle and Latin ones, some of which were adaptations of his Basle productions, for the pupils of the St. Anna Gymnasium in Augsburg, of which he became headmaster in 1536. The humanist background of many of the authors reveals itself in their imitation of classical rhetoric and dramatic structure; these influences are strongest in the Latin plays but are also carried over into the vernacular. Rebhun's *Susanna* (1535), for instance, is divided into five acts, each ending in a chorus.

Protestant Bible dramatists kept closer to Scripture than their medieval predecessors and drew their material from the Old Testament and Apocrypha far more than from the New Testament. Luther himself remarked in the preface to his 1534 Apocrypha translation that the stories of Judith and Tobias would make a fine tragedy and a good comedy, respectively; these narratives, along with those of Joseph and Susanna, became staples of Protestant plays. Among the favored New Testament themes for these plays were the story of Lazarus and the parable of the prodigal son. The choice of subject matter was determined by the need to avoid direct representation of Christ's Passion and Resurrection (this was a taboo for many Lutherans). Luther advocated dramatic performances in schools as a means of inculcating morality and social discipline; accordingly, Protestant Bible plays offer moral teaching about obedience to parents, the dangers of bad company, and the female virtues of purity and subservience in marriage.

In the late 16th and early 17th centuries, cultural, social, and political changes conspired to bring about the end of the tradition of regular performances of biblical drama in German. The stage became professionalized and took up new themes introduced by strolling players from England; at the same time, towns declined in political influence and ceded their cultural position to the courts. In areas of the Catholic Counter Reformation, biblical drama was cultivated by the Jesuits, but this tradition, which continued into the 18th century, was entirely Latin. The most famous biblical drama still performed regularly in German today, the Oberammergau Passion play, has only a very attenuated connection with the medieval tradition. The play was first performed in 1634 using an adapted 15th-century Augsburg text that underwent several further transformations in the course of the 17th and 18th centuries; the version now in use is essentially a creation of the 19th century.

MARK CHINCA

See also Religion and Literature

Further Reading

Axton, Richard, *European Drama of the Early Middle Ages,* London: Hutchinson, 1974; Pittsburgh, Pennsylvania: University of Pittsburgh Press, 1975

Bergmann, Rolf, "Spiele, mittelalterliche geistliche," in *Reallexikon der deutschen Literaturgeschichte,* 2nd edition, vol. 4, Berlin and New York: de Gruyter, 1979

———, *Katalog der deutschsprachigen geistlichen Spiele und Marienklagen des Mittelalters,* Munich: Beck, 1986

Chambers, E.K., *The Medieval Stage,* Oxford: Clarendon Press, 1903

Linke, Hansjürgen, "Das volkssprachige Drama und Theater im deutschen und niederländischen Sprachbereich," in *Europäisches Spätmittelalter,* edited by Willi Erzgräber, Wiesbaden: Athenaion, 1978

———, "Vom Sakrament bis zum Exkrement: Ein Überblick über Drama und Theater des deutschen Mittelalters," in *Theaterwesen und dramatische Literatur: Beiträge zur Geschichte des Theaters,* edited by Günter Holtus, Tübingen: Francke, 1987

Mehler, Ulrich, et al., editors, *Mittelalterliches Schauspiel,* Amsterdam and Atlanta, Georgia: Rodopi, 1994

Meredith, Peter, and John E. Tailby, editors, *The Staging of Religious Drama in Europe in the Later Middle Ages: Texts and Documents in English Translation,* Kalamazoo: Western Michigan University, Medieval Institute Publications, 1983

Mezger, Werner, "Quem quaeritis—wen suchen ihr hie? Zur Dynamik der Volkskultur im Mittelalter am Beispiel des liturgischen Dramas," in *Modernes Mittelalter: Neue Bilder einer populären Epoche,* edited by Joachim Heinzle, Frankfurt: Insel, 1994

Muir, Lynette R., *The Biblical Drama of Medieval Europe,* Cambridge and New York: Cambridge University Press, 1995

Neumann, Bernd, *Geistliches Schauspiel im Zeugnis der Zeit,* Munich: Artemis, 1987
Parente, James A., Jr., *Religious Drama and the Humanist Tradition: Christian Theater in Germany and in the Netherlands, 1500–1680,* Leiden and New York: Brill, 1987
Roloff, Hans-Gert, "Reformationsliteratur," in *Reallexikon der deutschen Literaturgeschichte,* 2nd edition, vol. 3, Berlin and New York: de Gruyter, 1977
Simon, Eckehard, editor, *The Theatre of Medieval Europe: New Research in Early Drama,* Cambridge and New York: Cambridge University Press, 1991
van Abbé, Derek, *Drama in Renaissance Germany and Switzerland,* Melbourne: Melbourne University Press, 1961
Walz, Herbert, *Deutsche Literatur der Reformationszeit: Eine Einführung,* Darmstadt: Wissenschaftliche Buchgesellschaft, 1988
Wickham, Glynne, *The Medieval Theatre,* London: Weidenfeld and Nicolson, 1974; 3rd edition, Cambridge and New York: Cambridge University Press, 1987; distributed in United States by St. Martin's Press
Young, Karl, *The Drama of the Medieval Church,* Oxford: Clarendon Press, 1933; reprinted 1967

Biedermeier Period

The term *Biedermeier* has been used to define the period of German literature from the restoration of the old order following the defeat of Napoléon in 1815 to the revolutions of 1848, but of the many terms used to categorize periods of literary history, *Biedermeier* is undoubtedly one of the most controversial, with much debate surrounding its suitability and with many critics arguing that it may at most be used to describe certain types of writing within that period. The origins of the term are to be found in the name Gottlieb Biedermaier, the fictitious author of exaggeratedly naive poems that appeared in the Munich journal *Fliegende Blätter* from 1855 onward. In the early 1900s, it served to describe a style of solid but uninspiring furniture from the first half of the previous century, and then the term gradually began to be applied to the literature and overall ethos of the three decades preceding the revolutions of 1848. Scholarly use of the term became established, if by no means generally accepted, in the 1930s through the critical writings of Wilhelm Bietak, Günther Weydt, and Paul Kluckhohn. Kluckhohn identified an attitude of resignation that was common to many writers after the Congress of Vienna and that served to distinguish them from the earlier Romantic generation. Weydt emphasized themes of quiet domesticity and a bourgeois interest in "Sammeln und Hegen," the collecting and cherishing of material possessions, as evidenced in works such as Stifter's *Der Nachsommer* (1857; *Indian Summer*). Other qualities that were seen as typical of the Biedermeier ethos were moderation; the love of the simple life, especially in rural surroundings; and a nostalgic interest in the past or in childhood. Writers whose work could be seen in such terms were claimed as representatives of the movement: Droste-Hülshoff, Mörike, Gotthelf, but in particular, and as a consequence of Bietak's 1931 monograph, Austrian writers such as Grillparzer, Lenau, Raimund, and Stifter. When in 1935 Kluckhohn chose to devote his journal *Deutsche Vierteljahrsschrift* to a detailed discussion and analysis of Biedermeier and its connotations, opinion became divided between the pioneers of the scholarly use of the term, who emphasized the cautious, conservative aspects of the period; critics in the more militantly National Socialist journal *Dichtung und Volkstum,* who sought heroic and vibrant elements in the Biedermeier; and those who attacked the "Biedermeier psychosis" of the time and insisted that the term should only be used for third-rate authors (Backmann).

The immediate postwar period saw what was perhaps an inevitable harking back to the perceived safe domesticity of the Biedermeier—in the most cautious and conservative sense of the term as a euphemism for the "good old days"—but interest soon became marginalized either by the suspicion of all literary periods that was prevalent in the 1960s and 1970s or by an emphasis on progressive and revolutionary aspects of the pre-1848 period that was encapsulated in the newly fashionable term *Vormärz.* Debate was resuscitated by Friedrich Sengle's monumental trilogy on the *Biedermeierzeit* (1971–80), which sought to rehabilitate the term as a global description of the period's literature. Sengle could not disguise the problems inherent in the term, however, and himself felt constrained to distinguish between *Biedermeierzeit* as a term for the period as a whole, in which he included liberal writers such as Büchner and Heine and incorporated the mood of "Zerrissenheit und Weltschmerz" (rupture and melancholy), and Biedermeier as a description of the period's more conservative authors and themes. For many reviewers and later critics (e.g., Neubuhr), such distinctions were problematic or simply untenable, as the conservative connotations acknowledged by Sengle were seen to inevitably color any use of the term. For Richard Brinkmann, Biedermeier could not be neutralized as "only a name," as Sengle had sought to argue, and it was best not used if adequate account was to be given of the full spectrum of views and styles found during the period in question. Since Sengle, the term *Biedermeier* has at least remained in the critical consciousness but has continued to provoke debate and sometimes rejection in favor of any one of a variety of alternatives, whether *Vormärz, Restaurationszeit,* or *Frührealismus.* Recent literary histories reveal an inconsistent picture: some devote individual chapters to the Biedermeier, and others refer only to *Restaurationszeit* and make no mention of Biedermeier. Particularly interesting are the various editions of the *Deutsche Literaturgeschichte* by Wolfgang Beutin, published by Metzler. The first edition (1979) only uses the term *Vormärz*; the second edition (1984) adds almost a full page, highlighted by italics and the use of a semitabular layout, to explain its rejection of the term *Biedermeier* as "an inadmissible generalisation of only *one* aspect of a very complex epoch" and to suggest (somewhat inaccurately) that *Biedermeier* is only used in older accounts of literary history despite Sengle's attempts to justify its use. The third edition of 1989 retains this section but removes the italics and other highlighting features; subsequent editions make no further changes.

The delineation of the Biedermeier has been and remains problematic in a number of ways. Is it a period, a mentality, or a style? Is it, above all, a chronological period clearly defined by political events (1815–48) and characterized by the restrictions of post-Napoleonic conservatism? In this case, a number of works that most would argue merit inclusion (many of Stifter's) would have to be excluded. Is it a mental attitude and approach to life that one might describe as cautious, conservative, with a certain bourgeois pride in accumulating material possessions, emphasizing lasting moral values, and idealizing a group of concepts associated with home, the region, and the family? Such a mentality is indicated by the importance at the time of the salon and the small literary or musical gathering, which is exemplified by Schubert's circle of friends; it also underpins the more popular or trivial literary manifestations of the Biedermeier such as the almanac, pocketbook, or *Stammbuch* (family album). Or is the Biedermeier to be seen as a stylistic tendency: traditional in its choice of literary forms, realistic, even to the point of naturalism, but selective in its choice of often rural subjects, while at the same time avoiding the irony and social comment that enable us to categorize Keller as a post-1848 realist, despite what look like many Biedermeier features in his work.

Arguably the most satisfactory approach is to see the Biedermeier first and foremost as a mentality, typical in turn of a particular historical period and frequently expressed through certain stylistic features. Inherent in all three approaches is a further important question: which authors are Biedermeier? Few would fully agree with Sengle's linguistic sleight of hand that allows for the inclusion of liberal writers such as Heine and Büchner, but modern research has found new depths of complexity, whether political or psychological, in certain works that might also disqualify authors originally included (Grillparzer and Nestroy being the most obvious examples). Conversely, one may espy distinctly Biedermeier features in authors usually traditionally allocated to other periods (including Eichendorff and Keller). For those critics unashamed to use a term that others see as something of an insult—indicative of cosy, parochial conservatism—there is some measure of agreement on the inclusion of Droste, Gotthelf, Raimund, Lenau, Mörike, and Stifter. It has become fashionable, however, to legitimize the use of the term *Biedermeier* by espousing the implications in the subtitle to Heinz Politzer's controversial 1972 monograph *Grillparzer: Das abgründige Biedermeier,* which, loosely translated, suggests hidden depths or dark secrets beneath the surface. How "abgründig" a writer's work can be before they cease to be Biedermeier or the term loses all coherent meaning is a difficult question to answer. The discovery of repressed sexual desires in the priest in Stifter's *Kalkstein* (*Limestone*) may simply add an extra facet to his character; the many layers of psychological and political complexity in Grillparzer's works should arguably have long since disqualified him. Admittedly, the words spoken by Rustan at the end of *Der Traum ein Leben* (1834; *A Dream Is Life*) are a veritable Biedermeier manifesto, but it is doubtful whether they reflect Grillparzer's views: "One thing brings happiness in this life, one thing alone: quiet peace of mind and a heart free of guilt. Greatness is dangerous, fame a meaningless game."

Leaving aside those writers that, Sengle notwithstanding, are more usually considered too overtly liberal in their attitudes to merit the designation Biedermeier, one may see the typical Biedermeier literary genres as lyric poetry (from authors such as Mörike, Droste, and Lenau) and, especially, as short prose fiction (from authors such as Gotthelf, Stifter, Mörike, and Droste). In an age that saw the innovative drama of Büchner and Grabbe and the unconventionally ironic lyrics and travel journals of Heine, the Biedermeier writers clung to traditional literary forms. Central to any delineation of Biedermeier prose is the work of Stifter, with its fascination with the world of nature; these works provide meticulous descriptions of geological forms and changing weather, as in the thunderstorm in *Limestone* or the snowstorm in *Bergkristall* (*Rock Crystal*). Human beings pale into insignificance alongside the wonders of nature, and those aspects of human life that are emphasized are the unchanging or cyclical features. Stifter's famous preface to *Bunte Steine* (1853), the collection of stories that includes *Limestone* and *Rock Crystal,* can be seen as a quintessentially Biedermeier statement; in what was intended as a rebuttal of Hebbel's claim that he could not depict greatness and heroism, Stifter challenges the traditional notions of great and insignificant. Rather than sudden outbursts of violent activity, whether in nature or in man, the permanence in nature or a lifetime of peaceful activity are what Stifter considers great.

The emphasis on lasting values in Stifter's work is typical of many writers of the period, including Mörike, Gotthelf, Raimund, and Grillparzer. Implicitly or explicitly, these values are derived from Goethe or from Enlightenment ideas of humanity and morality that were filtered through the works of German classicism, while the subjectivity and individualism of more recent Romantic philosophy is rejected. A didactic intention is often not far from the surface, and it is more overt in Gotthelf's stories such as *Die schwarze Spinne* (1842; *The Black Spider*), which warns readers of the dangers of evil and godlessness. The power and danger of evil is an important aspect of Droste-Hülshoff's famous novella *Die Judenbuche* (1842; *The Jew's Beech Tree*), although this is a psychologically complex work that leaves its meaning unclear and unresolved. Nevertheless, Droste-Hülshoff, not least in her poetry, presents an essentially conservative, religious weltanschauung that reflects her aristocratic background. Mörike's excellently crafted poetry seems to shy away from strong passion, to preach modesty and an acceptance of God's will, and to convey a sense of renunciation and isolation. The poem "Verborgenheit" (1838; Seclusion) asks the world to leave him alone with his bliss and his suffering and not to tempt him with gifts of love. Mörike's poems, often set in the evening or at midnight, convey senses of time passing, fleeting hours ("flüchtige Stunden"), and the end of the day or, perhaps, the end of an age. Similar to Stifter, Mörike often gives a precise image of nature that is very different from the nebulous Romantic moods in Eichendorff's poems, although some of the mystery of nature has remained. The feeling of understatement that characterizes Mörike's lyric output is also found in his most famous prose work. *Mozart auf der Reise nach Prag* (1855; *Mozart on*

His Way to Prague), which, despite making frequent reference to musical genius and giving a genuine sense of the demonic power of the conclusion to *Don Giovanni,* seeks to portray Mozart as an ordinary fallible human being, walking in the forests with his wife, guiltily facing up to the consequences after he has absent-mindedly plucked a prize pomegranate off a tree, or enjoying an evening of music and anecdotes in the midst of an admiring aristocratic gathering.

The significance of drama in the period is mainly confined to Austria and, more particularly, to popular comedy, which, for practical reasons of financing and avoiding expensive delays, could not risk problems with the censor. Johann Nestroy's frequent brushes with authority illustrate the problem but also question his credentials as a Biedermeier author; more typical is Ferdinand Raimund, whose plays are deeply rooted in popular traditions of farce and magic play and in particular continue to draw on the popularity of the *Besserungsstück,* or play of improvement. Self-awareness and contentment with one's lot is the message preached in the conclusions of Raimund's best plays, although the line "Zufrieden muss man sein" (one *must* be content) in *Der Verschwender* (1837 [produced 1834]; The Spendthrift) seems to underline the forced nature of the various happy endings that provide only a partial answer to the questions posed. The depiction of Rappelkopf's self-hatred and split personality in *Der Alpenkönig und der Menschenfeind* (1837 [produced 1828]; *The King of the Alps*) is also surprisingly modern and unsettling within the conventional comic framework. As with other writers of the period, the conservative moral message that justifies the label *Biedermeier* is relativized by modern complexities beneath the surface, complexities that may have eluded the authors themselves.

IAN F. ROE

See also Franz Grillparzer; Adalbert Stifter

Further Reading

Backmann, Reinhold, "Grillparzer und die heutige Biedermeier-Psychose," *Jahrbuch der Grillparzer-Gesellschaft* 33 (1935)

Beutin, Wolfgang, et al., editors, *Deutsche Literaturgeschichte: Von den Anfängen bis zur Gegenwart,* 5th edition, Stuttgart: Metzler, 1994

Bietak, Wilhelm, *Das Lebensgefühl des "Biedermeier" in der österreichischen Dichtung,* Vienna: Braumüller, 1931

Boden, Petra, "Im Käfig des Paradigmas: Biedermeierforschung 1928–1945 und in der Nachkriegszeit," *Euphorion* 90 (1996)

Brinkmann, Richard, "Gedanken über einige Kategorien der Literaturgeschichtsschreibung," *Euphorion* 69 (1975)

Hermand, Jost, *Die literarische Formenwelt des Biedermeiers,* Giessen: Schmitz, 1958

Jennings, Lee, "Biedermeier," in *A Concise History of German Literature to 1900,* edited by Kim Vivian, Columbia, South Carolina: Camden House, 1992

Kluckhohn, Paul, "Biedermeier als literarische Epochenbezeichnung," *Deutsche Vierteljahrsschrift* 13 (1935); reprinted in *Begriffsbestimmung des literarischen Biedermeier,* edited by Elfriede Neubuhr, Darmstadt: Wissenschaftliche Buchgesellschaft, 1974

Neubuhr, Elfriede, editor, *Begriffsbestimmung des literarischen Biedermeier,* Darmstadt: Wissenschaftliche Buchgesellschaft, 1974

Roe, Ian F., and John Warren, editors, *The Biedermeier and Beyond,* Bern and New York: Lang, 1999

Sengle, Friedrich, *Biedermeierzeit: Deutsche Literatur im Spannungsfeld zwischen Restauration und Revolution, 1815–1848,* 3 vols., Stuttgart: Metzler, 1971–80

Weydt, Günther, "Literarisches Biedermeier," *Deutsche Vierteljahrsschrift* 9 (1931); reprinted in *Begriffsbestimmung des literarischen Biedermeier,* edited by Elfriede Neubuhr, Darmstadt: Wissenschaftliche Buchgesellschaft, 1974

Wolf Biermann 1936–

In Germany, where, perhaps more than in any other country, music and literature have tended to cross-pollinate or even be inextricably intertwined, a reliance on minimal forms of literary expression involving music, as in popular songs, has a long tradition. In the late 1960s and early 1970s, several German political songwriters, riding the wave of widespread student rebellion, became household names in political communes and communities far beyond German-speaking countries. Whereas some critics see the very existence of polit-bards with string instruments as a living anachronism, others take a different view. In a time of gigantic multimedia hype, the single man or woman with a guitar conjures up, in the minds of the discontented, a modern-day David confronting Goliath, and this image evokes sympathies for the issues raised by the polit-bard.

Wolf Biermann, the most popular among German songwriters, has been writing poetry and songs for nearly four decades. Before any other singer, he began calling himself a *Liedermacher,* a term decidedly reminiscent of Brecht's *Stückeschreiber,* which in turn is derived from the English term *playwright.* Because the etymology of the latter points to *Stückemacher* rather than to *Stückeschreiber,* the new term *Liedermacher* exposes some old roots not only in terminology but in literary traditions as well. These traditions in German-speaking countries alone allow us to trace Biermann's cultural ancestors as far back as Walther von der Vogelweide and to include Heinrich Heine among his forerunners. Biermann calls the latter his "frecher Cousin," or his "Meister"; he has definitely mastered Heine's calculated simplicities. Naturally, the forerunners also include Brecht, who is simply referred to as "Meister" throughout Biermann's oeuvre. In German-speaking countries, poets such as Biermann might also be referred to as *Dichtersänger,* German for the term most commonly used for the representatives of this genre in France. After initial reservations on part of the literary establishment and after receiving only minor literary awards, in 1989 Biermann was awarded the Hölderlin Prize and thereafter virtually all the most prestigious German literary awards.

Biermann's constant references to natural patterns give his poetry and songs a catchy, compelling quality. Nature serves as a reminder that things are continually changing, forever in flux. At his best, Biermann not only points to synchronous motions of natural rhythms and political developments but also allows them to flow together, creating a genuine amalgam of society and nature. Synchronizing the motions and the dialectics of nature with developments in society has been considered an important hallmark of German political poetry from Walther von der Vogelweide to Brecht. Like Brecht, Biermann, refusing to embrace the customary cynicism of his age, derives great joy from the stoic calm and relaxed beauty of nature in the face of hectic and often futile, absurd, or outright destructive human activity.

Early on, Biermann contrasted the calm beauty of landscapes with the sterility of a dogmatic Communist Party bureaucracy enforcing policies contradicted by daily reality. According to the *Liedermacher,* nature does not tell lies in the way that the unnatural Party apparatus or the media in the East used to twist the truth. Naturally, from the very beginning the German Democratic Republic (GDR) cultural bureaucracy wanted none of this, and as early as 1965, it condemned all such tendencies as anarchistic, individualistic, and threatening to public order. The dissident singer was soon considered the number one taboo in his country of choice, where in 1976 he made history by becoming the first publicly known person ever to be stripped of GDR citizenship. This watershed event in GDR cultural policy polarized cultural life in the GDR and made the front pages of many Western newspapers. Many critics now actually consider his expatriation the beginning of the end of the GDR. In the fall of 1989, Biermann himself became an agent of change in the GDR when he performed before large audiences in Leipzig and East Berlin, events that were broadcast on both West and East German television. Thereafter, the *Liedermacher* witnessed the concrete-reinforced GDR collapse like a house of cards.

Biermann's path—from naive Communist cadre to the GDR's enfant terrible and international cause célèbre and finally, after 1989, to his metamorphosis into a poet laureate (often described as displaying a neoconservative bent), a media celebrity, and darling of the liberal and, with reservations, even of the conservative press—is well documentable, as is his gradual shift of focus from political songwriter to political essayist. In the latter function, he continues to needle his former followers on the Left, as is manifest in his contributions to the smart *Frankfurter Allgemeine Zeitung.* (Especially noteworthy among these essays is his 1994 obituary for Erich Honecker, longtime leader of the erstwhile GDR, in which Biermann, somewhat arrogantly and also self-referentially, reinterprets historical dimensions: "Honecker ist eine historische Mücke, unsterblich eingeschlossen im Bernstein meiner Ballade"—"Historically speaking, Honecker is a fly, immortally preserved in the amber of my ballad.") In the eyes of most contemporary left-leaning German journalists, their fallen idol was simply unable to resist the temptations of the marketplace and the lure of the limelight. The critic Reich-Ranicki stated it with customary precision: "Da steht er nun, Wolf Biermann, der gescheiterte Revolutionär, der siegreiche Poet" (There he stands, Wolf Biermann, the failed revolutionary, the victorious poet).

Among the issues now raised by Biermann are the persistent threat of a nuclear Armageddon, pressing environmental issues, and the GDR's past. In the paradoxical fashion he is so fond of, Biermann maintains that progress is the result of personal initiative and individual responsibility rather than the inevitability of historical processes. But increasingly, and in the quasi-algebraic stylistic means that he loves to employ, Biermann expresses a general loss of belief in future dialectical progress. Presently, he often shows a virtual obsession with self-annihilating mirror opposites and chiastic reversals, revealing a fascination with static antagonisms unable to release their dialectical tension and thus their formative potential.

Over the last four decades, the singer Biermann has turned into a cultural philosopher with his finger on society's pulse and has thus managed to establish the political song as an important medium of political discourse and a literary subgenre in its own right. Yet, most important, in writing his songs, this *Liedermacher* has played and still plays his part in assuring an uneasy world that the nightmare of a German Europe is, among German intellectuals, gradually being replaced by the dream of a European Germany. In doing so, the polit-bard has himself inevitably become part of the long and proud transcultural tradition of political songwriting.

PETER WERRES

See also Liedermacher

Biography

Born in Hamburg, 15 November 1936. Moved to East Germany, 1953; studied at Humboldt University, Berlin, 1959–63; singer, composer, and guitar virtuoso; stage assistant at Bertolt Brecht's Berliner Ensemble, 1957–59; candidate for the Socialist Unity party; forbidden to perform or be published, East Germany, 1965–76; East German citizenship revoked as a result of a concert given in Cologne, 1976; East German citizenship reinstated, 1989. Fontane Prize, 1969; Offenbach Prize, 1974; German Record Award, 1975, 1977; Deutscher Kleinkunstpreis, 1979; Hölderlin Award, 1989; Mörike Prize, 1991; Büchner Prize, 1991; Heine Prize, 1993; Nationalpreis, 1998. Currently lives in Hamburg Altona.

Selected Works

Poetry

Die Drahtharfe: Balladen, Gedichte, Lieder, 1965; as *The Wire Harp,* translated by Eric Bentley, 1968
Mit Marx- und Engelszungen: Gedichte, Balladen, Lieder, 1968
Vier neue Lieder, 1968
Für meine Genossen: Hetzlieder, Balladen, Gedichte, 1972
Deutschland: Ein Wintermärchen, 1972
Nachlaß I (songs), 1977
Wolf Biermann: Poems and Ballads, translated by Steve Gooch, 1977
Loblieder und Haßgesänge, edited by Andreas M. Reinhard, 1977
Preußischer Ikarus: Lieder, Balladen, Gedichte, Prosa, 1978
Verdrehte Welt—das seh' ich gerne, 1982
Und als ich von Deutschland nach Deutschland: Lieder mit Noten, Gedichte, Balladen aus dem Osten, aus dem Westen, 1984
Three Contemporary German Poets: Wolf Biermann, Sarah Kirsch, Reiner Kunze, edited by Peter J. Graves, 1985
Affenfels und Barrikade: Gedichte, Lieder, Balladen, 1986
Alle Lieder, 1991

Wolf Biermann: Ein deutsch-deutscher Liedermacher/A Political Songwriter between East and West (dual language anthology), 1992
Alle Gedichte, 1995
Süßes Leben, Saures Leben, 1996

Fiction
Das Märchen vom kleinen Herrn Moritz, 1972
Das Märchen von dem Mädchen mit dem Holzbein: Ein Bilderbuch, 1979

Play
Der Dra-Dra: Die grosse Drachentöterschau in 8 Akten mit Musik (produced 1971), 1970

Essays
Klartexte im Getümmel: 13 Jahre im Westen, 1990
Über das Geld und andere Herzensdinge: 5 prosaische Versuche über Deutschland, 1991
Ich hatte viel Bekümmernis: Meditation zur Kantate Nr. 21 von J.S. Bach, 1991
Der Sturz des Dädalus, 1992
Wie Man Verse macht und Lieder (Heine Vorlesungen), 1997

Translations
Daniel Julij, *Berichte aus dem sozialistischen Lager,* 1972
Jizchak Katzenelson, *Das Lied vom ausgerotteten jüdischen Volk,* 1994

Further Reading

Antes, Klaus, et al., *Wolf Biermann,* Munich: Edition Text und Kritik, 1975
Berbig, Roland, et al., editors, *In Sachen Biermann: Protokolle, Berichte, und Briefe zu den Folgen einer Ausbürgerung,* Berlin: Links, 1994
Hammer, Jean-Pierre, "Wolf Biermann, Poète maudit?" *Les langues modernes* 62 (1968)
Hermand, Jost, "Wolf Biermanns Dilemma," *Basis* 4 (1974)
Ketelsen, Uwe K., "Reformkommunismus, Wolf Biermann, sozialistischer Realismus," *Akzente* 5 (1971)
Kloehn, Ekkehard, "Die Lyrik Wolf Biermanns," *Der Deutschunterricht* 21 (1969)
Koch, Christoph, "Der Liedermacher Wolf Biermann," *Europäische Begegnung* 6 (1966)
Meier-Lenz, D.P., *Heinrich Heine—Wolf Biermann: Deutschland, Zwei Wintermärchen—ein Werkvergleich,* Bonn: Bouvier, 1985
Raddatz, Fritz J., "Wolf Biermann, Günter Kunert," in *ZEIT-Gespräche 2,* Frankfurt: Suhrkamp, 1982
Reich-Ranicki, Marcel, "Wolf Biermann und die SED," in *Wer schreibt provoziert,* Munich: Deutscher Taschenbuch, 1966
Rosellini, Jay, *Wolf Biermann,* Munich: Beck, 1992
Rothschild, Thomas, editor, *Wolf Biermann: Liedermacher und Sozialist,* Reinbek bei Hamburg: Rowohlt, 1976
———, "Wolf Biermann," in *Liedermacher: 23 Porträts,* Frankfurt: Fischer, 1980
Schwarzkopf, Oliver, et al., editors, *Wolf Biermann: Ausgebürgert,* Berlin: Schwarzkopf und Schwarzkopf, 1997
Werres, Peter, *Die Liedermacher Biermann und Degenhardt, 1960–1976: Eine Zwischenbilanz,* New York: Goldstein and Schatz, 1990
———, "Lea Fleischmann and Wolf Biermann: Like Strangers in Their Own House," in *Insiders and Outsiders: Jewish and Gentile Culture in Germany and Austria,* edited by Dagmar Lorenz and Gabriele Weinberger, Detroit, Michigan: Wayne State University Press, 1994
———, "Wolf Biermann und Brechts Dialektik," *Brechtjahrbuch* 21 (1996)

Bildung

If 19th-century Germany was the battleground for the political self-assertion of the bourgeoisie, the 18th century had been the terrain on which the bourgeoisie mustered its moral and ethical strength. Along with the developing notion of *Kultur,* no concept was more crucial for this preparatory stage than that of *Bildung.* Distinct from *Erziehung,* which was nominally less associated with the immanent development of the individual, *Bildung* was a concept of the external facilitation of individual development, which had the express goal of realizing the individual's latent and unique potential, which, in turn, was defined in terms of reason, expression, and will. Solidifying and expanding its etymological ground, which encompassed both the idea of image and form (*Bild*) as well as the idea of formation and creation (*bilden*), *Bildung* during the German Enlightenment became formulated as an educational imperative to develop universal faculties of reason, will, and taste to the point that individual subjects were capable of autonomously forming themselves in their own image, within and without.

Historically, the concept of *Bildung* represented the confluence of a secularized version of the Pietist conception of man as a creation in the image of God with the universalist understanding of the human agent as a subject who was regulated by innate, rational capacities. The political task implied in the ideals of *Bildung* in the late 18th century was, therefore, to reform the state-citizen relation in such a way that the state's primary purpose would be to provide the conditions for the full self-realization and freedom of its citizens, who, in turn, would serve the state as free subjects. *Bildung* was at its origin thus deeply implicated in the broader republican ideals of the Enlightenment and reflected a profound faith in the harmonious reciprocity of individual and collective self-legislation.

However universalist its aspirations, *Bildung* remained, both politically and pedagogically, a thoroughly bourgeois category. As embodied in the protagonist of Johann Wolfgang Goethe's *Wilhelm Meister's Apprenticeship* (1795), itself the artistic apotheosis of a new genre of the novel called the bildungsroman,

Bildung was secured neither from above nor from the status of birth, but through the activation of one's unique character and the capacity to communicate this uniqueness to others. Rational capacities, the formation of desire, and the means to construct a meaningful reality: these constitutive elements of autonomy were all developed in opposition to the heteronomy of state interests, as well as to the tastes and ideals derived from a particular social standing. Hence, *Bildung* clearly became not only a goal for individuals but, by the 1770s, a project for the emerging middle classes that shared a common ethical value system (*gesitteten Mittelstand*).

Defined in Immanuel Kant's terms as a collection of agents who are ends in themselves rather than means to an end, the educated middle class (*Bildungsbürgertum*) insisted on a state conceptualized in republican terms, which embodied a dialectical reciprocity between individual and collective autonomy. With communal well-being seen as dependent on bourgeois (*bürgerliche*) values, which, in turn, were dependent on public education, there was a clear imperative for the kinds of educational and political reforms carried out by Humboldt and Freiherr von Stein in the early 19th century. At the same time, however, the liberal political aspirations of *Bildung* never ventured far from the real and ideal struggles of the German nation. Following Kant's universal-historical trajectory, Johann Gottfried Herder insisted that the way in which humans come to recognize and cultivate their godlike status as an end in themselves was profoundly determined by historical context, climate, and personal and collective needs. *Bildung* of the individual and the public must be closely tied to and must serve to foster the cultural particularity of the nation that provides the substantive horizon to reason.

The political developments of the early 19th century vastly increased the specifically national demands on public education. The considerable reforms undertaken by the state, especially in Prussia, required far greater participation by the educated classes in the affairs of state and, moreover, raised the expectations of these educated classes with regard to their role in politics. Both as an exponent of a limited state and the reformer of its educational institutions, Humboldt insisted that the state should provide institutional opportunities in public schools for the full cultivation of its citizens. For Humboldt, in spaces set aside from the heteronomous imperatives of political reality, schools of higher learning should secure for citizens the opportunity to develop those innate capacities of reason, which would lead toward the autonomous agency that is the precondition for full and productive contribution to society.

Animated debates turned on whether education should be seen primarily in terms of its use-value for the state or, as in Humboldt's or Johann Heinrich Pestalozzi's model, whether the state should exist primarily in order to facilitate the education of citizens, who were its true constituents. It was Germany's defeat by Napoleon, however, that generated a truly national deliberation on the meaning of *Bildung*. In his *Addresses to the German Nation* (1808), Johann Gottlieb Fichte permanently transformed the universalist, republican concept of education into a specifically *German* education (*Deutsche Nationalbildung*). In the face of defeat, Fichte insisted that Germans should not focus on that which makes them humans but on that which makes them German. *Bildung* thus became a means to cultivate national cohesion rather than individual autonomy.

With the conservative restoration after 1815 and with the defeat of the educated classes and their liberal-republican ideals by conservative forces in 1848, both the cosmopolitan and the nationally productive potency of *Bildung* were on the wane. Liberal voices from Georg Gottfried Gervinus to Robert von Mohl and Karl Rotteck continued to have faith in the liberal promise of *Bildung*; moreover, Lorenz von Stein and Karl Marx could still implicitly agree at mid-century that the universalist impulses of *Bildung* did play an important role in leveling class distinctions. For the most part, however, the distance between educational reality and the emancipatory origins of *Bildung* only grew larger. By the 1870s, the *Bildungsbürger* had been reduced, in Friedrich Nietzsche's celebrated parlance, to a meek and degenerate philistine (*Bildungsphilister*); *Bildung* became the mere cultural capital of "respectable society," something one owned and acquired as a fashionable sign (*schöngeistig*) of class status or, more likely, class pretenses. Furthermore, the institutions of public education (*Bildungswesen*) had, by the end of the 19th century, become instrumentalized structures of educational administration that were guided by the strategy of policy imperatives rather than by the ideals of a cosmopolitan human community.

In the course of the 19th century, moreover, the very concept of *Bildung* had lost cohesion. Already in the 1820s, and certainly by the time that the Grimms included the term in their dictionary in 1860, its irreducibly dispersed uses precluded *Bildung* from being formulated in any coherently compelling way. By the early 20th century, the concept was actively shunned by the same educated elites that had developed it into the centerpiece of an emancipated German cultural nation over a century before. Intellectual figures from Thomas Mann to Karl Jaspers saw in the mandarin culture and the *Bildungsbürgertum* symbols of political, social, and cultural quietism and an apology for decline. Robbed of the liberal, humanist society it had once promised, *Bildung* in the 20th century remained inextricably bound up with the fate of the German nation and its dangerously ambiguous relation to the universalist, cosmopolitan ideal that for Germany could never become an autochthonous reality.

BRETT R. WHEELER

Further Reading

Elias, Norbert, *The Civilizing Process,* translated by Edmund Jephcott, New York: Urizen, 1978; in 2 vols., Oxford: Blackwell, 1978–82

Geuss, Raymond, "Kultur, Bildung, Geist," *History and Theory* 35 (May 1996)

Holborn, Hajo, "Der deutsche Idealismus in sozialgeschichtlicher Beleuchtung," in *Moderne deutsche Sozialgeschichte,* edited by Hans-Ulrich Wehler, Cologne: Kiepenheuer and Witsch, 1976

Mosse, George, *Confronting the Nation: Jewish and Western Nationalism,* Hanover, New Hampshire: University Press of New England, 1993

Rauhut, Franz, and Ilse Schaarschmidt, *Beiträge zur Geschichte des Bildungsbegriffs,* Weinheim: Beltz, 1965

Sheehan, James J., *German Liberalism in the Nineteenth Century,* Chicago: University of Chicago Press, 1978

Vierhaus, Rudolf, "Bildung," in *Geschichtliche Grundbegriffe: Historisches Lexikon zur politisch-sozialen Sprache in Deutschland,* vol. 1, edited by Otto Brunner et al., Stuttgart: Klett, 1972

Weil, Hans, *Die Entstehung des deutschen Bildungsprinzips,* Bonn: Cohen, 1930

Bildungsroman

The bildungsroman (novel of education, formation) typically tells the story of a young man's maturation to adulthood. Most critics distinguish between the broader term *Entwicklungsroman* (novel of development), which has been applied to narratives of personal growth from Wolfram von Eschenbach's *Parzival* (ca. 1210) to the present, and the more specific term *bildungsroman,* which arose only in the late 18th century. Although the term was coined by Karl Morgenstern in the first decades of the 19th century, it did not come into general usage until around 1900, largely because of the influence of Wilhelm Dilthey. The delay between the adoption of the critical term *bildungsroman* and the writing of the novels it purports to describe has been the source of persistent skepticism regarding the term's usefulness, a skepticism that is exacerbated by the fact that many of the novels generally considered of the bildungsroman genre lack the optimism that was emphasized in early definitions of the genre. The result has been a paradoxical situation in which critical studies of the bildungsroman abound while the status of individual examples of the genre has remained open to question. Some critics have gone so far as to declare the genre itself a phantom (Sammons, Redfield), yet it remains a fixture of contemporary critical discourse.

The bildungsroman arose together with modern individualism out of the breakdown of the authority of church and state in the course of the 18th century. Reacting against the rationalism of the early Enlightenment, writers such as Samuel Richardson in England and Jean-Jacques Rousseau in France began to explore human passions in their work. The bourgeois nuclear family took shape, characterized by a new emphasis on love and companionship in marriage, increased attention to children, and the growing conviction that only men should enter public life while women fulfilled their destiny in the home. Authors broke away from their former dependence on aristocratic patronage to write for a rapidly expanding audience of bourgeois readers who found new models of sentiment in the novels of the period. The German Pietist movement also helped pave the way for a newly introspective literature, encouraging individuals to look within themselves for evidence of their salvation and to write about their personal religious experiences. By the end of the century, it seemed to many individuals that they were living in an era of unprecedented historical change in which the only certainty was that their world would be different from that of their parents. Rocked by the cataclysmic events of the French Revolution, guided by sentiment, and steeped in the latest literature, authors began to write the narratives of personal development that have come to be called the bildungsroman.

Early examples of the genre in Germany include Christoph Martin Wieland's *Die Geschichte des Agathon* (1766–67; translated as *Agathon* and *The History of Agathon*), Sophie von La Roche's *Geschichte des Fräuleins von Sternheim* (1771; *The History of Lady Sophie Sternheim*), and Karl Philipp Moritz's *Anton Reiser* (1785–90). Goethe gave the genre its definitive form with *Wilhelm Meisters Lehrjahre* (1795–96; *Wilhelm Meister's Apprenticeship*), writing of a young man who rejects his middle-class upbringing to seek adventure in the theater. Meister eventually leaves the theater, becomes engaged, and discovers that he is the father of a child from an earlier romantic affair. In the final chapters of the novel, he is taken in by the members of a secret society dedicated to a progressive fusion of aristocratic and bourgeois values. Assessments of the novel have varied widely since its first appearance, some heralding it as a profound expression of the humanism of Weimar classicism and others denouncing it as politically conservative and hostile to the spirit of poetry.

Chief among the latter was the early Romantic writer Novalis (Friedrich von Hardenberg), who composed his *Heinrich von Ofterdingen* (1802; *Henry von Ofterdingen*) in deliberate opposition to what he felt was Goethe's increasingly prosaic text. Other German Romantic "brothers" of Wilhelm Meister (cf. Jacobs) include Ludwig Tieck's *Franz Sternbalds Wanderungen* (1798), Joseph Freiherr von Eichendorff's *Ahnung und Gegenwart* (1815), and E.T.A. Hoffmann's parodic *Lebensansichten des Katers Murr* (1820–22). Less easy to categorize but also influenced by Goethe and associated with the bildungsroman tradition are Friedrich Hölderlin's *Hyperion* (1797–99) and the novels of Jean Paul Friedrich Richter. Late in life, Goethe published an unconventional sequel to the *Lehrjahre, Wilhelm Meisters Wanderjahre* (1821–29; *Wilhelm Meister's Journeyman Years*), which brings to a close the heyday of the German bildungsroman.

The rise of the historical and social novel in the 1820s and 1830s, coupled with the death of Goethe and his contemporaries, signaled what Heinrich Heine would term the "end of the Goethean period of art." A genre linked, however problematically, to the ideals of German humanism and the spirit of the late Enlightenment became increasingly difficult to sustain in an era of Schopenhauerian pessimism and Marxian materialism. Perhaps symptomatically, the most prominent examples of the German-language bildungsroman in the 19th century were not written by Germans at all. These include the Swiss Gottfried Keller's *Der grüne Heinrich* (1854–55, revised 1879–80; *Green Henry*) and the Austrian Adalbert Stifter's *Der Nachsommer* (1857; *Indian Summer*). With the advent of 20th-century modernism, conditions for the continuation of the bildungsroman would seem still less propitious, yet novels by Hermann Hesse and Thomas Mann's magisterial *Der Zauberberg* (1924; *The Magic Mountain*) participate self-consciously, if often ironically, in the bildungsroman tradition. Hitler's rise to power and Germany's defeat in World War II would seem to have eradicated any vestiges of the optimism originally associated with the genre, and yet again the bildungsroman form structures literary attempts to come to terms with German fascism, such as Thomas Mann's *Doktor Faustus* (1947) and Günter Grass's *Die Blechtrommel* (1959; *The Tin Drum*). More recently, Botho Strauß's *Der junge Mann* (1984; *The Young Man*) could be seen as a postmodern adaptation of elements of the classical and Romantic bildungsroman.

Critics continue to debate whether the term can be applied to other European literatures or whether it is a peculiarly German genre. Late 19th-century German critics maintained that the bildungsroman expressed "typically German" characteristics of inwardness and self-reflection. Increasingly, nationalist German literary historians in the early 20th century drew parallels between the hero's maturation in the bildungsroman and Germany's rise to economic and military power (Kontje, 1993). Skepticism on the part of many postwar German critics derives in part from the ideological abuses to which the genre was subject in the years before 1945. Non-German critics, on the other hand, have not hesitated to discuss novels by Jane Austen, George Eliot, Gustav Flaubert, and many others as examples of the bildungsroman (Moretti, Redfield).

Another bone of contention in bildungsroman criticism has been the question of whether the genre should be restricted to works by and about men or whether one can speak productively of a "female bildungsroman." Some argue that the genre's origins are closely tied to the gender polarities arising in the late 18th century that restricted women to the private sphere and thus that it is an implicitly masculine genre (Smith); others contend that the term can be employed for fruitful discussions of novels that portray female development both in Germany and beyond (Abel et al., Blackwell, Fuderer).

Finally, critics have begun to consider the bildungsroman the representative genre of Western aesthetic ideology in implicit opposition to non-Western cultures (Redfield). As Edward Said argued in *Orientalism,* the West has defined the "Orient" as a passive Other incapable of development (*Bildung*). As the narrative of white, European, and predominantly male subject formation, the bildungsroman is thus closely tied to the economic, imperialist, and racist domination of Western society over "the rest of the world." Future studies of the bildungsroman might focus on the link between culture and imperialism in the canonical texts of the Western tradition while exploring the extent to which subaltern cultures have appropriated or subverted the conventions of the bildungsroman.

TODD KONTJE

See also Epistolary Novel; Goethe, Wilhelm Meisters Lehrjahre; Wieland, Geschichte des Agathon

Further Reading

Abel, Elizabeth, et al., editors, *The Voyage In: Fictions of Female Development,* Hanover, New Hampshire and London: University Press of New England, 1983

Beddow, Michael, *The Fiction of Humanity: Studies in the Bildungsroman from Wieland to Thomas Mann,* Cambridge and New York: Cambridge University Press, 1982

Blackwell, Jeannine, "*Bildungsroman Mit Dame:* The Heroine in the German *Bildungsroman* from 1770 to 1900," Ph.D. diss., Indiana University, 1982

Fuderer, Laura Sue, *The Female Bildungsroman in English: An Annotated Bibliography of Criticism,* New York: Modern Language Association of America, 1990

Gerhard, Melitta, *Der deutsche Entwicklungsroman bis zu Goethes "Wilhelm Meister,"* Halle: Niemyer, 1926; reprinted Bern and Munich: Francke, 1968

Hardin, James N., editor, *Reflection and Action: Essays on the Bildungsroman,* Columbia: University of South Carolina Press, 1991

Hörisch, Jochen, *Gott, Geld, und Glück: Zur Logik der Liebe in den Bildungsromanen Goethes, Kellers, und Thomas Manns,* Frankfurt: Suhrkamp, 1983

Jacobs, Jürgen, *Wilhelm Meister und seine Brüder: Untersuchungen zum deutschen Bildungsroman,* Munich: Fink, 1972

Jacobs, Jürgen, and Markus Krause, *Der deutsche Bildungsroman: Gattungsgeschichte vom 18. bis zum 20. Jahrhundert,* Munich: Beck, 1989

Kontje, Todd, *Private Lives in the Public Sphere: The German "Bildungsroman" as Metafiction,* University Park: Pennsylvania State University Press, 1992

———, *The German Bildungsroman: History of a National Genre,* Columbia, South Carolina: Camden House, 1993

Mayer, Gerhart, *Der deutsche Bildungsroman: Von der Aufklärung bis zur Gegenwart,* Stuttgart: Metzler, 1992

Miles, David H., "The Picaro's Journey to the Confessional: The Changing Image of the Hero in the German *Bildungsroman,*" *PMLA* 89 (1974)

Minden, Michael, *The German Bildungsroman: Incest and Inheritance,* Cambridge and New York: Cambridge University Press, 1997

Moretti, Franco, *The Way of the World: The Bildungsroman in European Culture,* London: Verso, 1987

Redfield, Marc, *Phantom Formations: Aesthetic Ideology and the Bildungsroman,* Ithaca, New York: Cornell University Press, 1996

Sammons, Jeffrey L., "The Mystery of the Missing *Bildungsroman,* or: What Happened to Wilhelm Meister's Legacy?" *Genre* 14 (1981)

Selbmann, Rolf, *Der deutsche Bildungsroman,* Stuttgart: Metzler, 1984

Smith, John H., "Sexual Difference, *Bildung,* and the *Bildungsroman,*" *Michigan Germanic Studies* 13 (1987)

Swales, Martin, *The German Bildungsroman from Wieland to Hesse,* Princeton, New Jersey: Princeton University Press, 1978

Maxim Biller 1960–

Already known in Germany as a journalist and columnist, Maxim Biller exploded onto the literary scene in 1990 with his first collection of short stories, *Wenn ich einmal reich und tot bin* (If I Were Rich and Dead). With this debut, Biller was heralded as one of the new, young Jewish writers of the postwar generation, along with authors such as Robert Schindel and Barbara Honigmann. Biller's extreme realism and autobiographical tendencies, however, stand in contrast to the more academic, often abstract style common to much of German postwar literature. Biller has been openly critical of the literary marketplace in Germany and has voiced his criticisms in several of his essays and journalistic pieces.

Born in Prague as the son of Russian Jews, Biller's fiction centers around Jews, Germans, and their relationship in a post-Holocaust society. Whether his characters are immigrants, emigrants, or Jewish and non-Jewish Germans who were born and raised in Germany, all are influenced in some way by Germany's history. The issues Biller confronts in his writing are emotionally laden, and it is therefore not surprising that his writing has received a controversial reception. Biller is praised for the black humor through which he critically represents society. Sander Gilman has proclaimed him the enfant terrible of the younger generation, and he has often been compared to Jewish-American authors such as Philip Roth and Saul Bellow. Biller, however, has also been criticized for the rawness of his writing, his sometimes undifferentiated criticisms, and his often negative portrayal of the Jewish community.

Biller's social and cultural criticisms are not only evident in his fiction, but also in his essays, where his direct polemic style has made him many enemies and earned him many admirers. In *Die Tempojahre* (1991; The Tempo Years), a collection of essays and interviews, he makes his voice heard in the public sphere by commenting on the social, political, and cultural life in contemporary Germany. His essays tackle a variety of topics, including politics, film, television, and literature. Biller does not support a particular ideology; he instead maintains a critical distance from all points of view in his analyses. Many of the essays in this collection criticize the bourgeois complacency of modern society, the lack of a young, critical intelligentsia to regenerate public life in Europe, and the stagnant cultural and political scene in Germany, which he argues is under the control of antiquated politicians, publishers, and the proverbial ivory tower of German academia. Nobody is immune to Biller's criticism—not even himself. His apparent arrogance is mitigated by an element of self-irony.

In his two collections of short stories, *Wenn ich einmal reich und tot bin* and *Land der Väter und Verräter* (1994; Land of the Fathers and Traitors), Biller shows how perpetrators, victims, and their descendants continue to live in the shadow of the Holocaust. Biller effectively utilizes stereotypes to reveal prejudices and to provoke the reader to reexamine his or her own standpoint. Many of his stories deal with the irreparable gap between those who lived through World War II and their descendants, who are unable to understand fully the experience of their parents and grandparents. His characters try to negotiate life in the present in light of the past, and in their attempts they reveal that the *Vergangenheitsbewältigung* (confrontation of the past) that has supposedly happened in Germany has not occurred to the extent that people assume.

Guilt is a central concept for many of Biller's characters. The children of the perpetrators still experience feelings of guilt, and many compensate for these with philo-Semitism, which Biller portrays as merely yet another form of anti-Semitism. The survivors suffer from guilt complexes as well. Some feel guilty because they were simply lucky enough to survive. Many of Biller's characters, however, secured their survival through the betrayal of family, friends, and fellow Jews. Rather than universally condemning these characters, Biller puts them in a moral gray zone, where their deeds, although not condoned, are made relative by the historical situation, and where their inability to escape their memories evokes sympathy on the part of the reader.

Jews who betray other Jews, Jews who calculatedly profit in the aftermath of the Holocaust, and Germans' problems dealing with their living Jewish citizens (as opposed to the "toten, zu denen man rückwirkend so nett sein kann, ohne daß es wirklich weh tut" [the dead, to whom one can be retroactively nice without incurring pain], *Wenn ich einmal reich und tot bin*): all of these explosive themes have remained largely taboo in literature. Biller consciously breaks these taboos, thereby bringing these themes to discussion in the public sphere. He complicates these issues by juxtaposing them with questions of Jewish identity, the problematic of Jewish self-hate, and the self-imposed "ghettoization" by those who choose to isolate themselves from the larger public discourse

Both of Biller's collections of short stories deal with similar themes, but in *Land der Väter und Verräter,* the malaise experienced by exiles of Eastern European communist regimes is emphasized as well. Similar to Biller's own biography, many of his characters were forced to flee after the Prague Spring. For many of the "fathers" in this collection, the terrors of fascism collide with the terrors of Stalinism to create an even more enigmatic emotional combination. In these stories, Biller addresses the complications that arise in situations of exile, where issues of Jewish identity impinge upon issues of national identity and language.

Biller, who writes with brutal honesty, reveals his aesthetic program in his stories and essays: to create literature that has a soul—living literature that represents life experiences in all their complexities and subtleties. In many of his stories, Biller achieves this element of reality through the strong presence of a subjective first-person narrator, whose voice is often difficult to distinguish from that of the author. After two collections of short stories and a collection of essays, Biller has not exhausted his exploration of Jewish life after the Holocaust, nor has he exhausted his critical voice. He continues to be active as an award-winning journalist and writer, and he will undoubtedly continue to shake up the German literary scene with his future endeavors.

KRISTEN HYLENSKI

Biography

Born in Prague, Czechoslovakia, 1960. Moved with his family to Germany in 1970; freelance writer and journalist; editor of the magazine *Tempo;* published his stories, columns, and critical essays in *Der Spiegel, Süddeutsche Zeitung,* and *Weltwoche.* Tukan-Prize (for his short story collection *Land der Väter und Verräter*); Otto Stoessel Prize, 1996; Preis des Europäischen Feuilletons, 1996. Currently lives in Munich.

Selected Works

Stories

Wenn ich einmal reich und tot bin: Erzählungen, 1990
Land der Väter und Verräter: Erzählungen, 1994

Essays and Interviews

Die Tempojahre, 1991
Aufbruch nach Deutschland: Sechzehn Foto-Essays, edited by Sibylle Bergemann et al., 1993
Brauchen wir eine neue Gruppe 47? Interviews mit Joachim Kaiser und Maxim Biller: 55 Fragebögen zur deutschen Literatur, edited by Joachim Leser and Georg Guntermann, 1995

Edited Work
with others, *Forum Allmende,* 1990

Further Reading
Feinberg, Anat, "Abiding in a Haunted Land: The Issue of *Heimat* in Contemporary German-Jewish Writing," *New German Critique* 70 (1997)
Gilman, Sander L., *Jews in Today's German Culture,* Bloomington: Indiana University Press, 1995
Köppen, Manuel, "Auschwitz im Blick der zweiten Generation: Tendenzen der Gegenwartsprosa (Biller, Grossman, Schindel)," in *Kunst und Literatur nach Auschwitz,* Berlin: Schmidt, 1993
Nolden, Thomas, "Contemporary German Jewish Literature," *German Life and Letters* 47, no. 1 (1994)
———, *Junge jüdische Literatur: Konzentrisches Schreiben in der Gegenwart,* Würzburg: Königshausen und Neumann, 1995

Bingen, Hildegard von, *see* Hildegard von Bingen

Franco Biondi 1947–

Franco Biondi is one of the most important representatives of current migrant literature in Germany. Through his literary texts, his theoretical essays, and his activities as a publisher, he has had a significant influence on the development of this literary phenomenon.

Biondi started his literary career at the beginning of the 1970s. The author, who first saw his literary achievements as a part of a European workers' literature, soon joined the Werkkreis Literatur der Arbeitswelt (Literature Workshop for Workers). As he did not feel that the interests of the labor immigrants were fully represented there, he became involved in ALFA (Associazione Letteraria e Faccoltà Artistiche), the first organization of migrant writers in the Federal Republic of Germany, which was formed in 1975. Many of his early poems and narratives were published in *Il Mulino,* a literary magazine that was founded by members of this group. ALFA saw itself as a representative of the Italian immigrants and enhanced the publication of texts in the Italian language. The writing that was promoted by the group could often be characterized as therapeutic. In many cases it was motivated by homesickness. It mirrored the authors' idealized images of their home country and their illusory dreams of a successful and happy return. By that time, however, the population of labor migrants in Germany had already become a multinational phenomenon and German had become a lingua franca among the workers. Many of them had given up hopes of return and started to settle down in the foreign country.

As a consequence of these changes, Biondi soon distanced himself from ALFA's regressive concept. In 1980, along with writers from 12 different countries, he founded the Polynationaler Literatur- und Kunstverein (PoLiKunst; Polynational Literature and Art Association). He also was the cofounder of the multinational publishing collective Südwind (Southern Wind). Within the framework of these groups, he formulated—in cooperation with Rafik Schami—the first program of a multinational literature movement that was set up by members of ethnic minorities in Germany. In their essay *Literatur der Betroffenheit* (1981; Literature of Involvement), Biondi and Schami insisted upon the expression *Gastarbeiterliteratur* (Literature of Labor Immigrants) to characterize their literary and political activities. The authors deliberately chose this term in order to turn a word that was used to discriminate against these workers into a weapon of their own and to classify their writing as a political act. *Gastarbeiterliteratur* was described as a means of creating a feeling of unity among the various ethnic minority groups. It also aimed to enforce political change by informing the German public about the reality of ethnic minorities in their society and by evoking their emotional and political involvement. During the 1980s, Biondi coedited several anthologies by Südwind and PoLiKunst, which were distributed by alternative publishing houses and which helped increase the German readership's awareness of writing by ethnic minorities. Unfortunately, these publications also contributed to the pejorative reception of this literature as a homogenous phenomenon that should be valued mainly as a reflection of *Gastarbeiter* reality. The failure of the *Gastarbeiterliteratur*-concept soon became evident. In 1985, PoLiKunst disbanded. Biondi, like other writers, spoke out for an individualization of immigrant literature and for a stronger emphasis on aesthetic forms.

Biondi's literary work highlights the different stages in the development of immigrant experience. His early writing is dedicated to the problems of first-generation labor immigrants. Their alienation from their native countries and their marginalized existence in Germany are the main themes of his prose and poetry. Biondi's narrative *Passavantis Rückkehr* (1982; Passavanti's Return), which was first published in Italian in 1976, features an immigrant who tries to return to his village in southern Italy after having lost his job in Germany. However, Passavanti's dreams of a smooth return are doomed to failure. He is mocked by his former friends because of his lack of success. In addition, the idealized image of his home that he cherished during his stay in Germany does not stand up to reality. After a tragic incident during a drinking competition at the village pub, he is definitively expelled from the community and returns to Germany—this time for good, he says. The protagonist's name "Passavanti" means "the one who moves forward." Paradoxically, Passavanti's progress lies in his return to Germany—in his turning away from his illusionary dreams.

A particular emphasis in Biondi's early poetry is placed upon the struggle of the labor immigrants with the German language and the disparagement by the Germans of the *Gastarbeiterdeutsch* (the German spoken by foreign workers). The author often includes this language variety into his texts, thereby turning a discriminated means of expression into an art form. His poem *Nicht nur Gastarbeiterdeutsch* (1979; Not Only Gastarbeiterdeutsch) follows an immigrant's attempts to express his anger about discrimination and his demands for equality in the German language. Like Passavanti, the protagonist of this poem progresses. His linguistic confidence gradually grows and so does his political conscience.

In his novella *Abschied der zerschellten Jahre* (1984; Farewell of the Shattered Years), Biondi concentrates on the situation of third-generation immigrants who were born in Germany and often define themselves as Germans, but are excluded from their native country by a rigid law on aliens. His protagonist, Mamo, is threatened with extradition. He barricades himself in his flat with a weapon in order to fight for his right to stay. The real reason for his act of rebellion is his objection to the *Gastarbeiter* stereotypes that are common in German society. Mamo does not want to identify with the images of the fatalistic or homesick labor migrant. For Mario, they apply to his father's generation. Nevertheless, those images are constantly forced on him and cut back his possibilities of constructing his own identity.

In his novels *Die Unversöhnlichen: Im Labyrinth der Herkunft* (1991; The Irreconcilables: In the Maze of Origin) and *In deutschen Küchen* (1997; In German Kitchens), Biondi again returns to the condition of first-generation immigrants. Both texts focus on the idea that former labor migrants have established themselves as members of ethnic minorities in Germany. They feel the urge to appraise their past in order to come to terms with the fragmentations of their identity, which happened in the different stages of their migrant life. Looking back on his early years as a *Gastarbeiter*, the protagonist of *In deutschen Küchen* reaffirms Passavanti's cognition, that emigration is a final decision. It does not allow the possibility for return.

SABINE FISCHER

Biography

Born in Forli, Italy, 8 August 1947. Trained as a welder; emigrated to Germany, 1965; worked in various factory and assembly line jobs, 1965–75; attended evening school, from 1971, and eventually received the German Abitur, or high school diploma; studied psychology, 1976–82; currently director of a social and pedagogical counseling center in Hanau, near Frankfurt; published his first poems in the Italian immigrant journal *Il Mulino;* cofounded an editorial series for migrant literature, *Südwind Gastarbeiterdeutsch,* with Jusuf Naoum, Suleman Taufiq, and Rafik Schami, 1980, as well as the Polynationale Literatur- und Kunstverein, a transnational forum for literature and the arts. Adelbert von Chamisso Prize, with Gino Chiellino, 1987.

Selected Works

Fiction

Passavantis Rückkehr. Erzählungen, 1982
Abschied der zerschellten Jahre: Novelle, 1984
Die Unversöhnlichen, oder, Im Labyrinth der Herkunft, 1991
In deutschen Küchen, 1997

Poetry

Nicht nur Gastarbeiterdeutsch: Gedichte, 1979
Ode an die Fremde: Gedichte, 1973–93, 1995

Essays

Literatur der Betroffenheit, 1981
"Über den literarischen Umgang mit der Gastarbeiteridentität," with Rafik Schami, in *Ein Gastarbeiter ist ein Türke,* 1983
Von den Tränen zu den Bürgerrechten: Italienische Emigrantenliteratur in der Bundesrepublik, 1984
Das Fremde wohnt in der Sprache, 1986

Edited Work

Zwischen Fabrik und Bahnhof: Prosa, Lyrik und Grafiken aus dem Gastarbeiteralltag, 1981

Further Reading

Fischer, Sabine, and Moray McGowan, "From *Pappkoffer* to Pluralism: Migrant Writing in the German Federal Republic," in *Writing Across Worlds: Literature and Migration,* edited by Russell King, et al., London and New York: Routledge, 1995
Möhrle, Katja, "Franco Biondi: Ein literarischer Spurensucher," in *Letteratura de-centrata: Italienische Autorinnen und Autoren in Deutschland,* edited by Caroline Lüderssen and Salvatore A. Sanna, Frankfurt: Diesterweg, 1995
Krechel, Rüdiger, and Ulrike Reeg, editors, *Werkheft Literatur: Franco Biondi,* Munich: Iudicium, 1989
Reeg, Ulrike, *Schreiben in der Fremde: Literatur nationaler Minderheiten in der Bundesrepublik Deutschland,* Essen: Klartext, 1988
Rösch, Heidi, *Migrationsliteratur im interkulturellen Kontext: Eine didaktische Studie zur Literatur von Aras Ören, Aysel Özakin, Franco Biondi, und Rafik Schami,* Frankfurt: Verlag für Interkulturelle Kommunikation, 1992

Bismarck Era

On 30 September 1862, shortly after his appointment as chancellor, Bismarck made the declaration for which he is best known: that political problems are not to be solved by speeches and majority decisions, but "durch Eisen und Blut" (by blood and iron). Having been appointed to resolve the constitutional conflict between government and parliament, which had arisen over the proposed army reform, he was viewed with deep distrust by the educated middle classes, whose political orientation was predominantly National-Liberal. Bismarck responded to the problems at home with a skillful but aggressive foreign policy that led to the wars of 1864, 1866, and 1870–71, in which Prussia, at first alone and then in alliance with the rest of Germany, including Bavaria and the southern states, secured a spectacular series of military victories that culminated in the proclamation of the Second Empire in occupied Versailles in 1871. These events were seen to vindicate the chancellor, for they led to that unity to which the National Liberals had long vainly aspired. From 1866, the Liberals therefore undertook a process of self-criticism that led to a compromise with Bismarck and their support for the chancellor until the swing to the right at the end of the decade, which saw Liberalism supplanted as an integrating force by a conservative agrarian-industrial coalition.

While welcoming Bismarck's major unifying achievement, representative Liberal figures such as the novelist Gustav Freytag and the aesthetician Friedrich Theodor von Vischer had, from the outset, expressed reservations that national unity should have been imposed from above, under Prussian leadership, rather than emerging organically through a gradual cultural process (bildung) within the nation as a whole. It is symptomatic that Freytag's cycle of historical novels, *Die Ahnen* (1872–80; The Ancestors), which provides an idealized, but partial prehistory of the unified state, is broken off at 1848, the year of the failed democratic revolution. Others, however, responded to the new situation by seeking to appropriate the victories, declaring them to be a victory for German culture, or, more specifically, for German National-Liberal, Protestant culture; the Battle of Königgrätz (1866), it was famously said, had been won by the Prussian schoolmaster. At the time, the lone voice of Nietzsche was raised scornfully against this claim in the *Unzeitgemäße Betrachtungen* (1873–76; *Thoughts out of Season*).

The founding years of the Second Empire, the *Gründerzeit,* saw a widespread expression of assent to the newly constituted state, beginning with the triumphal entry of the victorious armies in Paris and Berlin in 1871 and followed by the erection or completion of great national monuments: the *Siegessäule* in Berlin, the *Niederwalddenkmal* overlooking the Rhine at Rüdesheim, the *Hermannsdenkmal* at Detmold, and Cologne Cathedral. All of this took traditional, even archaic form, for the victors, not disposed to take artistic lessons from the vanquished, were inclined to dismiss as signs of decadence the first stirrings of literary and artistic modernism that were already evident in the France of Flaubert, Zola, Rimbaud, Manet, and the Impressionists. A particularly favored genre was the national epic in verse or prose, which provided legitimization in the form of a historical pedigree and contained forerunners and prophets such as Arminius, Barbarossa, Luther, and Hutten, and prefigurations such as the Reformation and the Wars of Liberation. The representative public culture, like the neofeudal political structures of the Bismarckian constitution, was thus strangely at odds with the infrastructure of the dynamic modern industrial state that was emerging in the Germany of the 1870s. The imposing facade, still to be encountered in the anachronistically historicist architecture of the railway stations, bridges, and banks that have survived from this period, was its characteristic form of expression; it was an image that would be critically explored in Thomas Mann's *Buddenbrooks* (1901; *Buddenbrooks*) and his brother Heinrich's *Der Untertan* (1917; *The Loyal Subject*).

As a result, there was, for the years 1860–90, a greater-than-usual discrepancy between what was regarded as important literature at the time and what has secured a place in the literary canon. The former is represented by the work of writers such as Paul Heyse, the first German to be awarded the Nobel Prize for literature (1910), Emanuel Geibel, Felix Dahn, and Ernst von Wildenbruch; the latter by Theodor Fontane, Theodor Storm, Wilhelm Raabe, and the Swiss, Conrad Ferdinand Meyer.

To begin with, the educated middle classes took on with enthusiasm their role in the cultural reinforcement of political unification at home: the *Kulturkampf,* the anti-Catholic policy pursued during the 1870s, is directly reflected in the themes and character stereotypes of the historical novel. At the same time, claims were being staked for a worthy position for German culture on the international stage; certain of the corresponding endeavors, however, rapidly transcended the nationalistic ambitions to which they owed a large part of their initial impetus and ended up leaving an enduring imprint on the development of modern European culture. The most notable examples are in the theater, where the reforms emanating from the Meiningen Court Theatre and disseminated in its European tours (1874–90) laid the basis for modern stage practice, and, above all, in opera, where at the Bayreuth Festival (from 1876) the Wagnerian *Gesamtkunstwerk* was realized, consolidating the already dominant presence of Richard Wagner in European musical life.

In literature, similar aspirations were shared by the journal *Deutsche Rundschau,* founded by Julius Rodenberg in 1874 to provide for Germany an organ with the standing of the English *Quarterly Review* and the French *Revue des deux mondes.* National Liberal in orientation, it immediately established itself as a forum for major writing over a wide cultural spectrum. With few exceptions, the important names in the intellectual life of the time are to be found among its contributors: the historians Theodor Mommsen, Heinrich von Sybel, and Max Lenz; the philosopher Wilhelm Dilthey; the literary critics Georg Brandes, Wilhelm Scherer, and Erich Schmidt; the art historians Carl Justi, Hermann Grimm, and Konrad Fiedler; and the music critic Eduard Hanslick. These are, moreover, not just important names in the context of the Bismarck era; they are at the same time some of the greatest names in the German scholarly tradition. Correspondingly, a large part of the most distinguished writing of this period takes the form of the literary biography or the critical essay.

The combination of the journal's status and the financial benefits of pre-publication in journals enabled Rodenberg also to secure major writers such as Gottfried Keller, Storm, Berthold Auerbach, Meyer, Heyse, Fontane, Louise von François, and Marie von Ebner-Eschenbach as regular contributors of original works; among the important writers of this generation, only Raabe is absent. In this way, the *Deutsche Rundschau* did much to foster the short prose narrative, the *Novelle,* which flourished during these two decades, and which so conveniently matched the practical requirements of a monthly journal.

Heyse was the leading theorist and the acknowledged master of this form, but for more serious engagement with contemporary issues, one has to look at the work of Storm and the slightly younger Meyer. For both the former, already an established writer, and the latter, in his mid-40s but as yet without any significant literary achievement to his name, 1870 brought a visible gain in artistic self-confidence that was expressed in a distinct assertiveness on a thematic level. At the center of their narratives, they regularly placed decisive and effective "Bismarckian" characters such as Hauke Haien in *Der Schimmelreiter* (1888; *The Rider on the White Horse*) and the eponymous hero of *Jürg Jenatsch* (1874), whose actions, nevertheless, are morally questionable and whose motives are subtly laid bare in all their ambivalence.

The concise and dramatic *Novelle* form privileges character over situation, and despite the details of the regional settings that they gave their stories, Meyer and Storm tended to present history in foreshortened manner and, in accordance with the dominant ideology, as the work of great men. With Fontane and Raabe, by contrast, the detail lies in the social rather than the psychological realism, which makes for greater distance and creates a more unambiguous sense of detachment. In the case of Fontane, this led the writer from the conservatism of his middle years, by way of a carefully differentiated account of the wars of unification, to his emergence in his Berlin novels as a restrained but incisive critic of the mores of the imperial capital. At the same time, Fontane contributed to the formal development of the German novel by providing its strongest link with the realist tradition dominant in English, French, and Russian literature during the 19th century. The experiments in perspectivist narrative techniques undertaken by Raabe, Meyer, and Storm are evidence of an increased reflectiveness about formal matters; similar to the symbolist style of Meyer's best poetry, however, they point toward later developments without contributing to subsequent theoretical debates.

The middle decade of the Bismarck era is dominated by writers of the chancellor's own generation. Fontane did not publish his first novel, *Vor dem Sturm* (1878; *Before the Storm*), until he had reached his late 50s, but his formative years go back to the period before the wars. He is virtually alone among older writers in securing the respect of the younger generation that came to maturity in the late 1880s and 1890s; he provides a link with them through the social content of his novels and his theater criticism.

For the younger generation of writers, the last decade of the Bismarck era was a time of theory and preparation. Their efforts were favored by the liberalization throughout Germany of the laws governing the right to practice trade, which permitted rapid growth in the cultural "industries" of publishing, the press, and the theater; they were only ineffectively restrained by the antisocialist legislation of 1878, for this legislation prompted an alliance between the younger intellectuals and organized socialism, although this alliance did not long survive the repeal of these laws after Bismarck's dismissal. Through iconoclastic attacks on prominent figures such as Heyse and Geibel and on commercially successful but lesser figures such as Paul Lindau and Hugo Lubliner, various literary groups sought to introduce European modernism, in the form of naturalism, to Germany. In Munich, Zola was championed by Michael Georg Conrad; in Berlin, Ibsen was championed by Otto Brahm, which heralded a renewal of the dramatic form that had languished since the death of Hebbel.

The early naturalists, although more radical in their artistic aspirations and, at least in the 1880s, in their social commitment and their political sympathies, were no less ambivalent in their attitude to Bismarck and his achievements. They, too, were moved in large part by the same nationalist impulses as their immediate forebears and shared many of the same prejudices against their Latin neighbors. Moreover, it was to the chancellor that the brothers Heinrich and Julius Hart, early pioneers of the naturalist movement in Berlin, expressly appealed for support in an open letter in an early number of their programmatic journal *Kritische Waffengänge* (1882; Critical Battles). Among the close associates of Conrad was the prolific Karl Bleibtreu, son of a patriotic battle painter of the 1860s and 1870s, and himself the author of numerous literary equivalents. Prominent in naturalist literary circles in Berlin was the young Maximilian Harden; he was later to be the editor of *Die Zukunft* and Bismarck's most vociferous supporter in the years following his dismissal.

The early naturalists were nevertheless successful in sweeping away some overblown reputations and opening up literary life and cultural institutions to the innovative tendencies being pursued in other European countries but largely ignored by the *Deutsche Rundschau.* They also began to extend the range of material covered by serious literature so as to embrace the social problems arising from rapid industrial and urban growth and to exploit more consciously the increased opportunities for the dissemination of literature to a new and wider public. Their first successes fall just within the era of Bismarck and mark the beginnings of the process in which German literature, paradoxically held back by political success, finally caught up with developments in other European countries.

JOHN OSBORNE

See also Naturalism

Further Reading

Adorno, Theodor W., *Versuch über Wagner,* Berlin: Suhrkamp, 1952

Bucher, Max, et al., editors, *Realismus und Gründerzeit: Manifeste und Dokumente zur deutschen Literatur 1848–1880,* 2 vols., Stuttgart: Metzler, 1975–

Cowen, Roy C., *Der Naturalismus: Kommentar zu einer Epoche,* Munich: Winkler, 1973

Deuerlein, Ernst, and Theodor Schieder, editors, *Reichsgründung 1870/71: Tatsachen, Kontroversen, Interpretationen,* Stuttgart: Seewald, 1970

Evans, Richard J., editor, *Society and Politics in Wilhelmine Germany,* London: Croom Helm, 1978

Haacke, Wilmont, *Julius Rodenberg und die Deutsche Rundschau: Eine Studie zur Publizistik des deutschen Liberalismus,* Heidelberg: Vowinckel, 1950

Hamann, Richard, and Jost Hermand, *Gründerzeit,* Epochen deutscher Kultur von 1870 bis zur Gegenwart, vol. 1, Munich: Nymphenburger Verlagshandlung, 1971

Hermand, Jost, *Von Mainz nach Weimar (1793–1919): Studien zur deutschen Literatur,* Stuttgart: Metzler, 1969

Hirschmann, Günther, *Der Kulturkampf im historischen Roman der Gründerzeit, 1859–1878,* Munich: Fink, 1978

Just, Klaus Günther, *Von der Gründerzeit bis zur Gegenwart,* Handbuch der deutschen Literaturgeschichte, Abt. 1, Darstellungen, 4, Bern: Francke, 1973

Lenman, Robin, et al., "Imperial Germany: Towards the Commercialization of Culture," in *German Cultural Studies: An Introduction,* edited by R.A. Burns, Oxford and New York: Oxford University Press, 1995

Martini, Fritz, *Deutsche Literatur im bürgerlichen Realismus, 1848–1898,* Stuttgart: Metzler, 1962; 4th revised edition, 1981

Osborne, John, *Vom Nutzen der Geschichte: Studien zum Werk Conrad Ferdinand Meyers,* Paderborn: Igel, 1994

Peschken, Bernd, and Claus-Dieter Krohn, editors, *Der liberale Roman und der preußische Verfassungskonflikt,* Stuttgart: Metzler, 1976

Pflanze, Otto, *Bismarck and the Development of Germany,* 3 vols., Princeton, New Jersey: Princeton University Press, 1963

Reuter, Hans-Heinrich, *Fontane,* 2 vols., Munich: Nymphenburger Verlagshandlung, 1968

Sammons, Jeffrey L., *Wilhelm Raabe: The Fiction of the Alternative Community,* Princeton, New Jersey: Princeton University Press, 1987

Vondung, Klaus, *Das wilhelminische Bildungsbürgertum: Zur Sozialgeschichte seiner Ideen,* Göttingen: Vandenhoeck und Ruprecht, 1976

Der Bitterfelder Weg

Der Bitterfelder Weg (Bitterfeld Way) was an East German literary program founded in 1959 to signal cultural continuities with the early days of the Communist Party (founded in 1916 as the Spartacus Party). The program dealt intensively with the world of work and production and had an underlying goal of encouraging productivity and boosting morale.

The 1950s had witnessed dramatic industrial growth in the German Democratic Republic (GDR). Although the Khrushchevian denunciation of Stalinism was missing in GDR politics, leadership recognized that systemic improvements were necessary to achieve economic stability. The ensuing changes, *Der Bitterfelder Weg* among them, allowed for some expressions of individual initiative and opinion. These changes led to a period known as *Tauwetter* (thaw), which began in 1956–57.

During its 1958 congress, the governing party, the SED (Sozialistische Einheitspartei Deutschlands [the Socialist United Party of Germany]), called for policies that aimed to further the socialist cultural revolution by facilitating the participation of the *Volk* (average citizenry) in the production of cultural goods, thereby dismantling a barrier inherited from capitalist social structures. In 1955, the miners of Nachterstedt wrote an open letter calling for increased resonance between literature and the *Volk* and asserting a desire for more books about workers' lives and their battles to build the new republic. By 1957, the *Nachterstedter Brief* and similar gestures led the secretary general of the SED, Walter Ulbricht, to call for artists to move from the esoteric margins of society. Eventually, such calls encouraged the decision of the fifth congress of the SED in 1958 to eliminate the estrangement between the arts and the working classes.

In the first months of 1959, "Nikolai Mamai," one of the workers' brigades of the Bitterfeld Electrochemical Combine, challenged the other brigades to a writing competition called "Working, learning, living in Socialism." In this competition, workers were encouraged to produce literature that reflected their lives and experiences. The first Bitterfeld Conference was held in 1959, with an aim to establish the program on a national scale. During the conference, Ulbricht urged workers to "storm the heights of culture": they were to develop their talents as producers of high culture by recording their experiences in writing. The conference motto was "Kumpel, greif zur Feder, die sozialistische Nationalkultur braucht Dich!" (Comrade, pick up your pen: the socialist national culture needs you!)

Writing circles were formed at the factories, and a new genre called the *Brigadetagebuch* (brigade diary) was developed. Initially, participation was enthusiastic: workers were eager to take part in these arenas of critical and political expression. The act of engaged criticism quickly became problematic, however, when the leadership sensed that expressions of individual opinion could lead to conflict with the party; the diaries' focus was then shifted from politics to aesthetics. This shift robbed the workers' opinions of any impact, and the demands placed on the journals became unrealistic. The workers were expected to produce high-quality literature, although they lacked the kind of education that professional writers enjoyed. Fearing that its authority might be undermined by critical dissent from the masses, the party crippled a valuable aspect of the program, leaving the writing workers to struggle with the external regulation of their projects instead of allowing them to pursue productive avenues of expression.

Additionally, increases in the production of literature about workers' lives was sought from full-time professional writers. They were to work in the factories and supplement their writing with hands-on experience, an injunction heeded by writers such as Franz Fühmann, whose familiarity with the shipbuilding docks at Rostock was apparent in *Kabelkran und blauer Peter* (1961; Cable-Crane and Blue Peter), and Brigitte Reimann, a schoolteacher who went to work at the soft-coal factory at Hoyerswerda and then wrote *Ankunft im Alltag* (1961; Arrival at the Everyday). While working at a railroad-car factory, Christa Wolf suffered an accident—an incident that she later used in her novel *Der geteilte Himmel* (1963; *Divided Heaven*).

At the second Bitterfeld Conference in 1964, the topic of *Arbeiterdichter* (writing workers) was limited to praising the brigades for successfully establishing a new genre, although the traditional literary forms produced by *Arbeiterdichter* had begun to proliferate. Pre-Bitterfeld works include Willi Bredel's *Maschinenfabrik N & K* (1930; Machine Factory N & K), Erwin Strittmatter's *Tinko* (1954; Tinko), and Hans Marchwitza's *Roheisen* (1955; Crude Iron), but the first conference had prompted contributions such as Erik Neutsch's *Bitterfelder Geschichten* (1961; Bitterfeld Stories) and *Spur der Steine* (1964; Trail of Stones), Karl Heinz Jakobs's *Beschreibungen eines Sommers* (1961; Description of a Summer), and Strittmatter's *Ole Bienkopp* (1963; *Ole Bienkopp*). In these works, the individual is often portrayed as contributing to the common good but facing a problematic situation that can only be rectified by locking horns with authorities. His professional competence and commitment make clear that his political home is in the GDR, yet by challenging the party, he manages to effect change and increase productivity. Another recurring theme is a faith in the values of the republic, which prevails over romantic or familial relationships. In this case, an initial struggle with authorities takes place, but in the end the individual recognizes the rectitude of the party's stance and relinquishes his affections for the welfare of the whole.

Most of the discussions at the second conference revolved around the efforts of professional writers. The level of individual expression and open criticism that had been encouraged at the first conference and tolerated until a short time after the construction of the Berlin Wall in 1961 was now admonished, and the trend toward subjectivity (*Neue Subjektivität*) was seen as a decadent disregard for the travails of the working class. Characteristic of this shift is the fact that, although Neutsch's *Spur der Steine* won the national literature prize in 1964, the film based on the book was banned shortly after its release in 1966.

Der Bitterfelder Weg imposed considerable limitations on artistic license and engendered some discontent among authors. Nevertheless, subjection to norms was at least a demonstration of the party's interest in one's cultural contribution. This interest encouraged many to strive for artistic integrity within the program, which resulted in noteworthy literature.

HEATHER FLEMING

See also German Democratic Republic; Socialist Realism

Further Reading

Emmerich, Wolfgang, *Kleine Literaturgeschichte der DDR,* Darmstadt: Luchterhand, 1989

Eversberg, G., "Die Bewegung schreibender Arbeiter in der DDR," *Ästhetik und Kommunikation* 13 (1973)

Gebhardt, Charlotte Emily Armster, "Bitterfeld and the GDR novel," Ph.D. diss., Stanford University, 1975

Gerlach, Ingeborg, *Bitterfeld: Arbeiterliteratur und Literatur der Arbeitswelt in der DDR,* Kronberg: Scriptor, 1974

Greiner, Bernhard, *Von der Allegorie zur Idylle: Die Literatur der Arbeitswelt in der DDR,* Heidelberg: Quelle und Meyer, 1974

Huebener, Theodore, *The Literature of East Germany,* New York: Ungar, 1970

Jarmatz, Klaus, "Literaturpolitische Probleme der 2. Bitterfelder Konferenz," *Weimarer Beiträge* 3 (1968)

Münz-Koenen, Ingeborg, et al., *Literarisches Leben in der DDR 1945 bis 1960,* East Berlin: Akademie, 1980

Orlow, Peter, *Die Bitterfelder Sackgasse: Literaturpolitik der SED zwischen 1965 und 1969,* Pfaffenhofen/Ilm: Ilmgau, 1970

Röhner, Eberhard, *Arbeiter in der Gegenwartsliteratur,* East Berlin: Dietz, 1967

Rüther, Günther, *"Greif zur Feder, Kumpel": Schriftsteller, Literatur, und Politik in der DDR 1949–1990,* Düsseldorf: Droste, 1991

Trommler, Frank, "DDR-Erzählung und Bitterfelder Weg," *Basis* 3 (1972)

Blätter für die Kunst

First published in Berlin by Stefan George and Carl August Klein (1867–1952), the literary periodical *Blätter für die Kunst* (issued from 1892 to 1919; Leaves for Art) presented original works of art, primarily poetry, and some critical commentary. It emulated such French and Belgian vehicles of symbolist aesthetic doctrine as *La Plume* (1889–1904; The Plume) and *La Wallonie* (1886–92; Wallonia). Beyond the journal's unusually long life, its title under various imprints distinguished George's published works and the poetry and treatises on literature, philosophy, history and the arts, challenging and often controversial, written by his disciples. This Kreis (circle) of men and some women of George's own age, but mainly younger, included poets and scholars who became influential at major universities. Beginning around 1900, they proclaimed George as a seer-poet whose consecrated passion and eloquence would reorient the nation in the spirit of ancient Greece and in the teachings of Nietzsche and thus would lead it toward heroic beauty and the harmony of body and soul. The *Blätter* and the books published under their aegis were the medium of their movement's aristocratic purpose: to redeem Germany from modernity and to restore to its very essence the purity and integrity of former times.

In 1892, George and his associates, chiefly Hugo von Hofmannsthal (1874–1929), meant to propagate a "new art," a "geistige kunst" (spiritual art) or "art for art itself," which was based on symbolist precepts that George had absorbed in France. In this effort, they hoped to undermine neo-Romantic sentimentalism and naturalistic social criticism alike. *Blätter für die Kunst* was intended for an exclusive circle of like-minded readers, but comments in early issues reflect how hard it was to gain even a small audience. Copies were available in one bookstore each in Berlin, Paris, and Vienna. The first number's 32 pages project unmistakably symbolist attitudes on art and life into German poetry, presenting early verses by George, Hofmannsthal's dramatic fragment *Der Tod des Tizian* (1891; The Death of Titian), and some of the latter's most haunting verses.

In all, 12 volumes (*Folgen*) of the journal appeared, the first four containing five separate issues (*Bände*) each: I in 1892–93, II in 1894–95, III in 1896, and IV in 1897 and 1899. The single-volume issues are V, dated 1900–1901; VI, dated 1902–3; VII, dated 1904; VIII, dated 1908–9; IX, dated 1910; X, dated 1914; and XI–XII, dated 1919. All of the volumes were printed in a roman typeface, which was then more common in scientific writing, instead of the conventional "gothic" or "fraktur" characters. Moreover, unless they occurred first in a sentence or verse, all words were printed in lowercase, flouting the rule that German nouns are capitalized. Punctuation followed "natural" cadences rather than grammatical dictates. George wanted to encourage reading the poems aloud to comprehend fully their musical qualities. Using a typeface shared by most other European languages helped to naturalize German poetry into a larger literary community.

George fastidiously cultivated a tradition of the continuity and uniformity of the *Blätter* over the journal's entire life. Books of selected works from each phase of its history appeared in 1899 (1892–98), 1904 (1898–1904), and 1909 (1904–9). The communal project of the Kreis's extensive artistic productivity, academic scholarship, and prescriptive critiques of German culture published under the imprint of the *Blätter für die Kunst* represented for George's followers a legacy second only to the "Master's" works themselves. The subtitle of Friedrich Wolters's account of the *Blätter,* underlining their role as an institution of German culture, claims to present no less than "German intellectual history since 1890."

The evolution of the *Blätter* closely parallels George's creative lifetime. Almost all issues begin with a selection of his most recent poems, often well before they are collected in books. Thus, the *Blätter* indicate more sensitively than the lyrical cycles critical changes in George's outlook. Early numbers emphasize cosmopolitan kinship with symbolists of all nations, presenting translations of Baudelaire, Mallarmé, Verlaine, Swinburne, D'Annunzio, and the Polish Rolicz-Lieder, to name only a few. Well before the turn of the century, however, programmatic commentaries by George and others address the woeful situation of the arts in Germany, and the editors modify substantially their initial aloofness from social and cultural questions. While reproductions of drawings and the scores of musical settings of George's poetry appeared in early volumes, verse subsequently became the dominant medium. The poems and prose of Karl Wolfskehl (1869–1948) and Ludwig Klages (1872–1956) typically imparted a sense of chiliastic doom that came to transcend artistic concerns.

In their shared pessimism about the state of German society and culture, especially following World War I, members of the Kreis persisted in believing that the nation must seek redemption in the edifying forms and eternal truths that great poetry teaches, however tragic those truths might be. The *Blätter* came to reject the subjective individualism of symbolism and Expressionism in favor of works that idealize in history and myth those who subordinate their own interests to a higher common good. Such poetry, like George's itself, takes on a character sometimes regarded as excessively "historicizing" and "monumental." Dante and Shakespeare, whose works George and Friedrich Gundolf (1880–1931) translated extensively, exemplify the ideal poet whose art expresses his people's highest goals and inspires their realization. The Kreis's sense of itself as a community expressing as a single voice the vision of its prophetic "Master" is best conveyed by the fact that the younger poets whose verses appear in the final three volumes of the *Blätter* are not named.

Among the 55 artists and writers who contributed to the *Blätter,* many achieved lasting distinction in the cultural context of their age and beyond, especially Hofmannsthal, Wolfskehl, Klages, Gundolf, Ernst Bertram, and Karl Gustav Vollmoeller. The journal's values and artistic aims are today generally regarded as overly aesthetic, elitist, and driven by conservative, indeed, reactionary social and political interests. Nonetheless, the *Blätter für die Kunst* and the works resulting from George's leadership are documents that are indispensable to understanding the art and ideology of Germany and its complex interactions with the cultural community of Europe.

MICHAEL M. METZGER

See also Stefan George; Journals

Further Reading

Alt, Peter-André, "Hofmannsthal und die 'Blätter für die Kunst,'" in *Wahrnehmungen im poetischen All: Festschrift für Alfred Behrmann,* edited by Klaus Deterding, Heidelberg: Winter, 1993
Boehringer, Robert, *Mein Bild von Stefan George,* Munich: Bondi, 1951; 2nd, enlarged edition, Düsseldorf: Küpper, 1968
Breuer, Stefan, *Ästhetischer Fundamentalismus: Stefan George und der deutsche Antimodernismus,* Darmstadt: Wissenschaftliche Buchgesellschaft, 1995
Goldsmith, Ulrich K., *Stefan George,* New York: Columbia University Press, 1970
Kluncker, Karlhans, *"Blätter für die Kunst": Zeitschrift der Dichterschule Stefan Georges,* Frankfurt: Klostermann, 1974
Landfried, Klaus, *Stefan George: Politik des Unpolitischen,* Heidelberg: Stiehm, 1975
Landmann, Georg Peter, *Stefan George und sein Kreis: Eine Bibliographie,* Hamburg: Hauswedell, 1960; 2nd, enlarged edition, 1976
Metzger, Michael M., and Erika A. Metzger, *Stefan George,* New York: Twayne, 1972
Rieckmann, Jens, *Hugo von Hofmannsthal und Stefan George: Signifikanz einer 'Episode' aus der Jahrhundertwende,* Tübingen: Francke, 1997
Winkler, Michael, *Stefan George,* Stuttgart: Metzler, 1970
———, *George-Kreis,* Stuttgart: Metzler, 1972
Wolters, Friedrich, *Stefan George und die "Blätter für die Kunst": Deutsche Geistesgeschichte seit 1890,* Berlin: Bondi, 1930

Der Blaue Reiter

Although often identified generally as the manifestation of German Expressionism in the visual arts in Munich, or even more comprehensively as the second major group, alongside Dresden's *Brücke,* of early Expressionist artists, *Der Blaue Reiter* consisted fundamentally of two artists, Wassily Kandinsky and Franz Marc. Rather than as a group of artists working, exhibiting, and living together, in the manner of *Brücke,* they conceived of their partnership as editorial, because it was formed in 1911 specifically to compile the almanac *Der Blaue Reiter,* published in May 1912 by Piper Verlag, and as organizational, because it also conceived and realized two Munich exhibitions devoted to "the secret connection of new artistic production" that was appearing in "all corners of Europe." One of these exhibitions was of paintings at the Moderne Galerie Heinrich Thannhauser in December 1911, and a second was devoted to prints, watercolors, and drawings at the Art Gallery Hans Goltz from February to April of 1912. Together, the *Almanac* and the exhibitions were fundamental pioneering formulations of an aesthetics of Expressionism and of the principles of modernism in Germany.

When asked about the founding of the *Blaue Reiter* in 1930, Kandinsky offered a mundane, almost simplistic recollection that belied the exhilaration and utopian ambitions that accompanied his and Marc's plans in 1911: "We invented the name '*Der Blaue Reiter*' at the coffee table in the garden pavilion at Sindelsdorf [the small Bavarian town where Marc lived]. We both liked blue; Marc—horses, me—riders. Thus the name came of its own accord. And we appreciated Frau Maria Marc's magical coffee all the more." Kandinsky initiated plans for "a sort of almanac" that would discuss current exhibition and provide critical essays written by artists during the summer of 1911, and he wrote Marc that the volume should "mirror the entire year, and a chain to the past and a beam of light into the future must inject the fullness of life into this mirror." The initial proposed title, *The Chain,* was soon replaced by *The Blue Rider.* Not an arbitrarily selected figure, the horse and rider whose stylized form would appear on the *Almanac* cover took their inspiration from images of St. George, the patron saint of the Bavarian Lower Alpine town Murnau, where Kandinsky's companion, the painter Gabriele Münter, owned a summer home, and also the patron saint of Moscow. Just as the saint was depicted as overcoming evil in the shape of a dragon and thereby rescuing a princess, the endangered personification of goodness, as well as an entire city, so the artists viewed themselves as the embattled heroes of a new art who sought to overcome the limits of traditional illusionism, with its dependence on the visual material world, and to replace it with a purified art, spiritual in its essence, in order to prepare for a radically reformed future. "We wander onward in new realms," Marc observed, "and have the startling experience of that everything being untrodden, unsaid, unspoiled and unexplored. The world lies pure before us . . . [and] is giving birth to a new era." Kandinsky identified the coming new era as "the great age of the Spiritual" and for that age prepared an art that would address its viewers synesthetically, enabling them to "hear forms and taste colors." Content should be transmitted not by the logical or contemplative identification of recognizable objects in a visually narrative sequence, but by a "commanding inner necessity," which viewers should comprehend, not understand rationally, and with which they should identify.

To communicate and propagate this aesthetic, the *Blaue Reiter* almanac and exhibitions were organized, but they also signified a major split in the group of progressive artists who were then active in Munich. In 1909, they organized, under Kandinsky's leadership, as the New Artists Association Munich (Neue Künstler-Vereinigung München, frequently identified solely by its initials, NKVM). In addition to Kandinsky, the major members included Gabriele Münter, Alexei Jawlensky, Marianne Werefkin, and Alfred Kubin; Franz Marc joined in 1911. Controversy and division emerged within the Association around the person, ideas, and art of Kandinsky, however, and in 1912 the exhibition jury refused to hang his abstract painting, *Composition V.* In response, Kandinsky, Münter, Marc, and Kubin resigned from the Association, and since plans for the *Almanac* were already in progress, Kandinsky and Marc as its editors immediately organized a counter-exhibition of their own works and of the other artists who had left the NKVM, as well as paintings by August Macke, Heinrich Campendonck, and Arnold Schoenberg; from Paris, they also brought works by Robert Delaunay and Henri Rousseau. Together, these paintings proclaimed a modernist program that extended from Kandinsky's efforts at a new visual vocabulary that was not dependent on the givens of common visual experience to the naive realism of the Douanier Rousseau, with the subjectively Expressionist compositions of Münter, Marc, Macke, and the others ranged between the two extremes.

Kandinsky justified such a multiplicity of formal expression in his essay "Concerning the Question of Form" in the *Almanac,* which postulated that "the combination of abstraction with representation, the choice between the infinity of abstract forms or from objectified material, i.e. the choice from the individual means within both areas, is and remains the domain of the artist's inner desire." According to Kandinsky, any external imposition of methods, means, or content must be avoided in order to maintain the freedom of the artist, who in turn should emulate the unspoiled practice of children whose drawings fulfill only the purposes they themselves impose on them and are free of the artifices of established artistic practice. The goals of the new art movement should then be "the replacement of the soulless-material life of the 19th century" and the "construction of the soulfilled-spiritual life of the 20th century, which we experience and which already manifests and embodies itself in strong, expressive and determined forms."

Franz Marc echoed these thoughts in his essay, "The 'Wild Men' of Germany," which similarly argued that "art concerns the most profound things, that the renewal [of art] may not be formal in character, but rather must represent a renaissance of thought itself." The goal should be "to produce through their works *Symbols* that have their proper place on the altars of the coming spiritual religion and behind which the technical creator will disappear."

The *Almanac,* however, was not limited to such discussions of the programs and issues of a new visual art. An innovative selection of illustrations juxtaposed modern works with children's drawings and African and South American masks, Japanese woodcuts and Egyptian shadow puppets, Bavarian and Russian folk art, and medieval sculpture. The eclectic mixture stipulated a linkage—Kandinsky's "chain"—between these diverse objects from geographically and temporally widely separated cultures and made possible a synthetic comparison, through which each work's "inner necessity" or its correspondence to the demands of its time, place, and creator would be made manifest, a historically apparent visual similarity. The picture selection established a discourse that complemented the choice of texts. Although most of the essays—not only Kandinsky's and Marc's, but others by August Macke, the Russian artist David Burliuk, and the French poet Roger Allard—concentrated on the visual arts, in emulation of Enlightenment and Romantic almanacs, the collage of the *Almanac's* content incorporated musical scores by Schönberg, Alban Berg, and Anton von Webern; essays on music theory and music criticism; and poetry and an experimental play by Kandinsky, *The Yellow Sound.* Conceptually, within the covers of the *Almanac,* a modernist *Gesamtkunstwerk* was therefore composed and presented as both a document of contemporary efforts and a prototype for future development and further realization.

Like the *Almanac* itself, Kandinsky's play offered an innovative fusion of otherwise disparate arts. Rather than "drama," Kandinsky described it as "a stage composition," which referred to its lack of action or plot, the lack of true dialogue, and the replacement of personal characters by the unexplained, depersonalized presences of five giants, "vague creatures," a child, a man, and people in loose garments or in tights, accompanied offstage by a choir and a tenor. The figures' placement in stage compositions in conjunction with the effects of light, color, and the music of the Russian composer Thomas von Hartmann provide the fundamental emotive content of the piece. Words, insofar as they are used, are "totally unclear words," invented conjunctions of sounds, or single verses whose phrases are suggestive but lacking in meaningful coherence:

Die Blumen bedecken alles, bedecken alles, bedecken alles.
Schließ die Augen! Schließ die Augen!
Wir schauen. Wir schauen.
Bedecken mit Unschuld die Empfängnis.
Öffne die Augen! Öffne die Augen!
Vorbei. Vorbei.

(All is covered by flowers, all is covered, all is covered.
Close your eyes! Close your eyes!
We gaze. We gaze.
With innocence we cover conception.
Open your eyes! Open your eyes!
Gone. Gone.)

Kandinsky's play, with its nontemporal scenes and depersonalized *Bewegungsgestalten,* has its roots in symbolist theater, notably the plays of Maurice Maeterlinck and the works of Paul Scheerbart, as well as the plays and theories of contemporary revolutionary Russian dramatists such as Nicolaj Evreinoff. It also continues Kandinsky's earlier experiments in sound poetry, which were published as *Klänge* in 1912, but it is best characterized as a projection of the realm of his abstract paintings onto the stage. The colors and forms here are fused with word, tone, and movement, and the pictorial space is made transversable to offer a new linkage to the world beyond them in a perhaps unrealizable, utopian Expressionist *Gesamtkunstwerk.*

In 1914, Kandinsky joined with Hugo Ball to plan a grandiose production of *The Yellow Sound,* but the play was not performed as the plans were curtailed by the outbreak of World War I. A second edition as well as a second volume of the *Almanac* likewise fell victim to the war. With his publications—the *Almanac,* the theoretical tract *Über das Geistige in der Kunst* (1911–12), and his autobiographical essay *Rückblicke* (1913)—Kandinsky promulgated the premises of a new anti-naturalistic aesthetic and art that the artists represented in the *Almanac* and the two *Blaue Reiter* exhibitions were developing. The first, pioneering exhibition traveled in 1912 first to Cologne and then formed the basis of the exhibition *Blauer Reiter, Franz Flaum, Oskar Kokoschka, Expressionisten* at Herward Walden's Berlin gallery *Der Sturm.* In these and other exhibitions in Germany, Switzerland, and Scandinavia, the art of the *Blaue Reiter*—embracing Alexei Jawlensky and Marianne Werefkin now, as well as Paul Klee—was presented to an international public and propagated as the radical but consequential manifestation of a new age, a new sensibility, and a new, transformed future during 1912–14. The utopian effort collapsed with the outbreak of World War I, however, and its artists were dispersed: Kandinsky returned to Russia, Münter left for Sweden to await him there, Jawlensky and Werefkin escaped to Switzerland, and Marc and Macke were activated by the German Imperial Army and died on the Western Front. Although the surviving artists returned to Germany after the war, no effort to revive the *Blaue Reiter* and its ambitious, optimistic program was made.

Reinhold Heller

See also Avant-Garde; Expressionism; Die Moderne

Further Reading

Buchheim, Lothar Günther, *Der Blaue Reiter und die "Neue Künstlervereinigung München,"* Feldafing: Buchheim Verlag, 1959
Friedel, Helmut, and Annegret Hoberg, *The Blue Rider in the Lenbachhaus Munich,* Munich: Prestel, 2000
Hüneke, Andreas, editor, *Der Blaue Reiter: Dokumente einer geistigen Bewegung,* Leipzig: Reclam, 1989; 3rd edition, 1991
Kandinsky, Wassily, *Kandinsky: Complete Writings on Art,* edited by Kenneth C. Lindsay and Peter Vergo, Boston: Hall, 1982
Kandinsky, Vassily, and Franz Marc, *Briefwechsel, mit Briefen von und an Gabriele Münter und Maria Marc,* edited by Klaus Lankheit, Munich: Piper, 1983
Kandinsky, Vassily, and Franz Marc, editors, *Der Blaue Reiter,* Munich: Piper, 1914; new documentary edition as *The Blaue Reiter Almanac,* edited by Klaus Lankheit, London: Thames and Hudson, and New York: Viking Press, 1974; reprint, New York: Da Capo Press, 1989

Johannes Bobrowski 1917–1965

When Johannes Bobrowski died on 2 September 1965 at the age of 48, a lengthy obituary by the East German critic Günter Hartung pointed out that nobody at the time was in a position to assess the loss to German literature that had occurred due to Bobrowski's death. Hartung argued that such an assessment was made all the more difficult because Bobrowski's oeuvre was very small indeed and because his work had met with little understanding, even though it had been treated with much respect. It is true that Bobrowski's work comprises no more than two slender volumes of poetry, two novels, a few small volumes of short stories, and other prose writings. All of this was published between 1961 and the time of the author's death. A further volume of poetry was published posthumously. Bobrowski was translated into English (with little impact), and Reclam incorporated a selection of his short stories into their Universalbibliothek series. The East German film industry, moreover, made an excellent film of his novel *Levins Mühle*. Nevertheless, Bobrowski has remained an author of limited public appeal. He has become at best an insider tip among literary scholars. Within the much wider context of the question of what will and should remain of East German literature, however, a strong case has to be made for a continued interest in Bobrowski and for his permanent inclusion in the pantheon of great German writers. This case rests upon Bobrowski's innovative and creative use of the German language, his explosion of the confines of traditional regional literature, and his treatment of the historical theme of the Germans and their Eastern neighbors, which are all of timeless relevance.

To understand Bobrowski's work, we must be aware of his geographical origins in the Lithuanian border regions. The population mix of Germans, Lithuanians, Poles, Gypsies, and Jews provided an experiential background to virtually all of Bobrowski's writing. He started his writing career as a lyric poet during his time as a German soldier in occupied Soviet territories: "I started writing on Lake Ilmen in 1941, about the Russian landscape, but as a foreigner, a German. That developed into a theme, roughly: the Germans and Eastern Europe."

After Bobrowski and his family settled in East Berlin after World War II, he devoted his writing to this theme. His lyric poetry is full of yearning for the land of his childhood and youth. But Bobrowski is not a regional writer (*Heimatdichter*) in any traditional sense; he explodes this traditional genre. His evocations of the people in the landscape are depicted within the context of his main theme of the Germans and the peoples of Eastern Europe. He describes his writing as "an attempt to express the unfortunate and culpable relationship of the German people towards her eastern neighboring people up until the most recent past, and thus make a contribution towards overcoming revanchist tendencies." Bobrowski, then, is a regional writer, but he is at the same time a political writer with a clear-cut didactic purpose: to make transparent the historical past, the German guilt, and to force people think about this past with a view to counteract revanchist xenophobic nationalism. Bobrowski is very much a writer of *Vergangenheitsbewältigung* (coming to terms with the past).

In short-story form, Bobrowski illustrates his task as a writer in "Betrachtung eines Bildes" (1965; "Looking at a Picture"), published in the collection *Der Mahner* (1967; *The Admonisher*). Ostensibly, this story is the description of a picture that comes to life in the figure of a man who erects crosses as reminders against heedless forgetfulness. Shörij, the man in the story, and Bobrowski, the writer, have the task to record, remind, and warn present and future generations. His attempt to make the guilt of the Germans visible is poignantly illustrated in his short story "Rainfarn" (1964; "Tansy"), published in the collection *Böhlendorff und Mäusefest* (1965; *Boehlendorff and the Dance of the Mice*). This story starts off like a sight-seeing trip through the town of Tilsit by a narrator who has become invisible by utilizing the magic powers of the tansy. The story takes place during the Third Reich just before the unification of the Memel area with Germany in 1938, and it presents the exodus of German Jews to Lithuania with a scene on the bridge across the Memel River. The narrator feels that the best he can do is to counteract the taunts of German officials, but he realizes that he is invisible, and he concludes that it is useless to be an observer, for an observer does not see anything. Only by being seen does one see. Only then can one make a stand. The narrator concludes that we did not do that. We remained invisible, and therefore did not see; this notion, in turn, summarizes the guilt of the German ordinary people. The short story "Lipmanns Leib" (1962; "Lipmann's Body") in the same collection tries to trace individual guilt and its psychology in a border hamlet. It deals with the ritualistic murder of a Jew based on the ritual of baptism. As a story it is an outright condemnation of sordid "small-town" xenophobic nationalism, and it is as relevant today as when it was written.

Bobrowski's two great novels, *Levins Mühle: 34 Sätze über meinen Gro(vater* (1964; *Levin's Mill: 34 Statements about My Grandfather*) and *Litauische Claviere* (1966; Lithuanian Pianos), deal with the same major themes. Apart from the fact that *Levin's Mill* contains one of the greatest love scenes in world literature, these novels establish Bobrowski as one of the most accomplished raconteurs of the 20 century, ranking easily with his very distant relative Günther Grass, the Brazilian novelist Jorge Amado, and Gabriel García Márquez. Bobrowski's style and narrative technique, although unmistakably his own, share many features with these other storytellers.

When Bobrowski said that he wanted to make German guilt visible by utilizing very concrete and very simple matters, his statement also serves to explain his literary technique. His situations are always seemingly very simple and everyday, and his lyric and narrative style seems naive and straightforward. He says about his short story "Mäusefest" ("Dance of Mice"): "It started as all my stories start: without a plan and without preconceptions, simply with an interplay of light and shadow." His style seems to be rambling and aimless, interspersed with addresses and questions to the reader, but it is in fact poignantly and progressively hermeneutical. Bobrowski himself acknowledges the influence of Gustave Flaubert and Anton Chekhov as storytellers who rejected the extraordinary and sensational as subject matter in order to illustrate the human condition. Bobrowski writes about small, simple, and even idyllic things, but he depicts tragic and broken idylls in the context of panoramic historical situations. For Bobrowski, this is the only path that helps us comprehend the monstrous events of history such as the genocide of Jews, Poles, Gypsies, and others.

J.K.A. THOMANECK

Biography

Born in Tilsit, East Prussia (now Sovetsk, CIS), 9 April 1917. Studied art history at the University of Berlin, 1937–41, but interrupted by national service; army service, 1939–45; prisoner of war, Russia, 1945–49; editor for Lucie Groszer, children's book publishers, Berlin, 1950–59; editor, Union Verlag, East Berlin, 1959. Gruppe 47 Prize, 1962; Alma König Prize, 1962; Heinrich Mann Prize, 1965; Veillon Prize (Switzerland), 1965; Weiskopf Prize, 1967 (posthumous). Died 2 September 1965.

Selected Works

Collections

Gesammelte Werke, edited by Eberhard Haufe, 3 vols., 1987
Shadow Land: Selected Poems (includes the collections *Shadow Land*

and *From the Rivers* and other poems), translated by Ruth and Matthew Mead, 1984

Poetry
Sarmatische Zeit, 1961
Schattenland Ströme, 1962
Wetterzeichen, 1966
Shadow Land, translated by Ruth and Matthew Mead, 1966
Im Windgesträuch, edited by Eberhard Haufe, 1970
Selected Poems: Johannes Bobrowski, Horst Bienek, translated by Ruth and Matthew Mead, 1971
From the Rivers, translated by Ruth and Matthew Mead, 1975
Literarisches Klima: Ganz neue Xenien, doppelte Ausführung, 1978
Yesterday I Was Leaving, translated by Rich Ives, 1986

Fiction
Levins Mühle: 34 Sätze über meinen Großvater, 1964; as *Levin's Mill: 34 Statements about My Grandfather,* translated by Janet Cropper, 1970
Böhlendorff und Mäusefest, 1965
Litauische Claviere, 1966
Der Mahner: Erzählungen und andere Prosa, 1967
Drei Erzählungen, 1970
Taste Bitterness (stories), translated by Marc Linder, 1970
Böhlendorff: A Short Story and Seven Poems, translated by Francis Golffing, 1989

Other
Nachbarschaft: Neun Gedichte; Drei Erzählungen; Zwei Interviews; Zwei Grabreden: Zwei Schallplatten; Lebensdaten, 1967

Translation
Boris Pasternak, *Initialen der Leidenschaft,* translated with Günther Deicke, 1969

Edited Works
Gustav Schwab, *Die schönsten Sagen des klassischen Altertums,* 1954
Hans Clauert, *Der märkische Eulenspiegel,* 1956
Jean Paul, *Leben Fibels,* 1963
Wer mich und Ilse sieht im Grase: Deutsche Poeten des 18. Jahrhunderts über die Liebe und das Frauenzimmer, 1964
Gustav Schwab, *Die Sagen von Troja und von der Irrfahrt und Heimkehr des Odysseus,* 1965

Further Reading

Dehn, Mechthild, and William Dehn, *Johannes Bobrowski: Prosa, Interpretationen,* Munich: Oldenburg, 1972
Müller, Joachim, "Der Lyriker Johannes Bobrowski: Dichtung unserer Zeit," *Universitas* 23 (1968)
Scrase, David, *Understanding Johannes Bobrowski,* Columbia: University of South Carolina Press, 1995
Thomaneck, J.K.A., "DDR-Literatur in englischer Übersetzung: Seghers und Bobrowski," *zeitschrift für germanistik* 3 (1983)

Johann Jakob Bodmer 1698–1783

Johann Jakob Bodmer, one of the most productive and influential writers of the German Enlightenment, is primarily known today for his writings on aesthetics and poetics. He is viewed, along with Johann Jakob Breitinger, his friend, collaborator, and partner in much of his work, within the context of the quarrel that arose between them and Johann Christoph Gottsched regarding the nature and standards of quality literature (commonly referred to as the "Leipzig-Zürich Literaturstreit"). This conflict is credited with having weakened the dominance that Gottsched's narrowly rationalist, normative poetics exercised on German-language literature and criticism from the publication of his *Critische Dichtkunst* in 1730 through the work's fourth edition in 1751. Although Bodmer was influenced by the rationalist philosophy of Christian Wolff and Gottfried Wilhelm Leibniz and used similar analytic categories to those employed by Gottsched, there is a marked change of emphasis in the way he used those categories. He showed an interest in the critical and skeptical thought of Pierre Bayle and the British sensualist John Locke, and he critically engaged sensualist thinkers on issues in poetics (most notably in his *Brief-Wechsel* with Calepio). Bodmer and Breitinger's "victory" is seen as having opened the door to aesthetic considerations that led to the literary movements of Sentimentality (1740–80), the late Enlightenment movement of the Storm and Stress (1770–81), and even to German classicism (1786–1805) and Romanticism (1795–1830).

Bodmer was very active as a philologist, translator (most important, Milton's *Paradise Lost* and a two-volume edition of Homer's works), editor, historian, and contributor to several of the period's journals. Through his various efforts, he participated in contemporary discussions on historical, political, educational, and theological issues. He was one of the first scholars to turn his attention to Medieval German literature (most important, the "Nibelungenlied" and the German minnesinger) at a time when British and French culture dominated in European literary discourse.

In 1720, Bodmer cofounded the language society Die Gesellschaft der Mahler, and between 1721 and 1723, he coedited its periodical, *Die Discourse der Mahlern* (*Die Mahler der Sitten* in the revised and expanded 1746 edition). The periodical was inspired by Joseph Addison and Richard Steele's English moral weekly the *Spectator,* with which, in a French translation, Bodmer became familiar while he was in Lugano. Although some of the other members of the society contributed to the journal, Bodmer and Breitinger authored an overwhelming number of the articles. In addition to aesthetic and poetological issues, they also discussed problems in moral philosophy, affect psychology, conduct, gender relations, and pedagogy. Discourse five is particularly noteworthy, for in that text Bodmer introduced historical pragmatism to Switzerland. In his brief discussion of types of historiography, he emphasizes the importance of contextualizing historical events and figures against the background of the culture's ethics, mores, and customs. This was to have a profound influence on their view of literature. Among the other important periodical publications to which Bodmer contributed were the *Sammlung Critischer, Poetischer, und andrer geistvollen Schriften, Zur Verbesserung des Urtheils und des Wizes in den Wercken der Wohlredenheit und der Poesie; Critische Briefe; Neue Critische Briefe;* and *Freymütige Nachrichten.*

In his *Critische Abhandlung von dem Wunderbaren in der Poesie und dessen Verbindung mit dem Wahrscheinlichen* (1740; Critical Treatment of the Fantastic in Poetry and Its Relation to Verisimilitude), Bodmer counters Voltaire's and Constantin de Magny's criticisms of Milton's *Paradise Lost,* which alleged that the poem inappropriately handled its classical and biblical material through its allegorical interweaving of angels, devils, and other supernatural powers. Bodmer's defense is based on his assertion that the represented figures are artistically genuine and convincing and that the crucial point is whether they arouse, touch, and stimulate the reader, not just whether they correspond to the logical categories of the intellect. It is with this assertion that Bodmer is considered by many to have initiated a line of argument that subsequently asserted the autonomy of the work of art, although he certainly does not make this assertion himself. In this work, Bodmer also negotiates between the rationalist critique of the pompous and ornate style of the late Baroque (a criticism that he harbors against Lohenstein's work in particular) and his belief that the use of figurative language and the representation of sublime topics powerfully affect the reader and are thus essential to literature. Bodmer concludes that, if figurative language is used as means to an acceptable end and not as an end in itself, it should not be rejected out of hand.

In 1741, Bodmer wrote what is considered to be his most important poetological work: the *Critische Betrachtungen über die poetischen Gemählde der Dichter* (Critical Observations Concerning the Poetic Paintings of the Poets) Here he discusses the affective qualities of a work, stylistics, the relations between literature and the visual arts, imagination, and the criteria for the selection of sublime topics. His conception of the imagination in this work is no longer strictly limited to logical intellectual operations, as it was in his earlier writings (e.g., *Von dem Einfluß und Gebrauche der Einbildungs-Kraft* [1727; Concerning the Influence and Use of the Imagination]). Here it is an important aesthetic and productive capacity. He asserts that literature is similar to painting in that both represent images to the recipient (an assertion that Lessing later criticizes in his *Laokoon*), but that literature is superior because it also represents the invisible, whereas the visual arts cannot. Although these ideas allow the imagination a much greater role in the production of literature, Bodmer is far from disregarding verisimilitude as a limiting force on literary representation. Nonetheless, he broadens the concept of verisimilitude by allowing that the possible world created in the imagination of the author establishes the criteria by which probability is to be judged and that these criteria might be other than those that operate in the logically conceived and empirically visible, that is, "real" world.

Bodmer's own attempts at literature in the 1750s through the 1770s have never been well received. The plots, or the lack thereof, are a main focus of the criticism. His literary works are important, however, in that they are his attempt to realize his poetological principles. In his *Brief-Wechsel von der Natur des poetischen Geschmackes* (1736; Correspondence on the Nature of Poetic Taste), Bodmer clearly privileges the representation of characters over action. Consistent with the French neoclassical tradition of Corneille, he argues that the effect of a work proceeds from the virtue of its characters. He correspondingly represents defenders of political and religious freedoms, representatives of sensibilities with moral integrity, and great figures of antiquity, biblical times, and national history; he also depicts negative contrasts to these positive characters in order to provide political instruction to his readers. We also see his attempt to select "patriotic" themes and characters from Swiss and German history in order to develop a "national" literature. Bodmer wrote heroic epics, patriotic and historical dramas, and parodies and satires, all of which can be roughly organized into four groups. These groups are defined by the historical tradition from which the material was selected: Greek and Roman history, English or Italian history and literature, Swiss and German history, or the Bible.

Kenneth E. Munn

Biography

Born in Greifensee, Switzerland, 1698. An official in Zurich, 1720; professor of history and politics at Zurich grammar school, 1725–75; city councillor, Zurich, 1737; with J.J. Breitinger, founded the journal *Die Discourse der Mahlern,* 1721–23. Died in Schönenberg, near Zurich, 1783.

Selected Works

Collections

Schriften, 1938

Treatises

Critische Abhandlung von dem Wunderbaren in der Poesie, 1740
Critische Betrachtungen über die poetischen Gemählde der Dichter, 1741

Poetry

Noah (religious epic), 1750; as *Noah,* translated by Joseph Collyer, 1767
Jakob und Joseph (religious epic), 1751
Die Synd-Flut (religious epic), 1751
Jakob und Rachel (religious epic), 1752
Conradin von Schwaben (historic epic), 1771

Plays

Electra, 1760
Ulysses, 1760
Julius Caesar, 1763

Translation

Der Verlust des Paradieses, prose translation of Milton, *Paradise Lost,* 1732; verse translation, 1742; revised translation, 1754

Further Reading

Bender, Wolfgang, "J.J. Bodmer und Johann Miltons 'Verlohrnes Paradies,'" *Jahrbuch der deutschen Schillergesellschaft* 11 (1967)
———, *Johann Jakob Bodmer und Johann Jakob Breitinger,* Stuttgart: Metzler, 1973
———, "Rhetorische Tradition und Ästhetik im 18. Jahrjundert: Baumgarten, Meier, und Breitinger," *Zeitschrift für deutsche Philologie* 99 (1980)
Bing, Susi, *Die Naturnachahmungstheorie bei Gottsched und den Schweizern und ihre Beziehung zu der Dichtungstheorie der Zeit,* Würzburg: Triltsch, 1934
Brandes, Helga, *Die Gesellschaft der Maler und ihr literarischer Beitrag zur Aufklärung: Eine Untersuchung zur Publizistik des 18. Jahrhunderts,* Bremen: Schünemann, 1974

Brown, F. Andrew, "Locke's 'Essay' and Bodmer and Breitinger," *Modern Language Quarterly* 10 (1949)
Herrmann, Hans Peter, *Naturnachahmung und Einbildungskraft: Zur Entwicklung der deutschen Poetik von 1670 bis 1740*, Bad Homburg: Gehlen, 1970
Müller, Jan-Dirk, "J.J. Bodmer's Poetik und die Wiederentdeckung mittlehochdeutscher Epen," *Euphorion* 71 (1977)
Preisendanz, Wolfgang, "Mimesis und Poiesis in der deutschen Dichtungstheorie des 18. Jahrhunderts," in *Rezeption und Produktion zwischen 1570 und 1730*, edited by Wolfdietrich Rasch et al., Bern: Francke, 1972
Scherpe, Klaus R., *Gattungspoetik im 18. Jahrhundert: Historische Entwicklung von Gottsched bis Herder*, Stuttgart: Metzler, 1968
Schmidt, Horst-Michael, *Sinnlichkeit und Verstand: Zur philosophischen und poetologischen Begründung von Erfahrung und Urteil in der deutschen Aufklärung (Leibniz, Wolff, Gottsched, Bodmer und Breitinger, Baumgarten)*, Munich: Fink, 1982
Stahl, Karl Heinz, *Das Wunderbare als Problem und Gegenstand der deutschen Poetik des 17. und 18. Jahrhunderts*, Frankfurt: Athenaion, 1975
Torbruegge, Marilyn K., "Bodmer and Longinus," *Monatshefte* 63 (1971)
Wehrli, Max, *Johann Jakob Bodmer und die Geschichte der Literatur*, Frauenfeld and Leipzig: Huber, 1936
Wetterer, Angelika, *Publikumsbezug und Wahrheitsanspruch: Der Widerspruch zwischen rhetorischem Ansatz und philosophischem Anspruch bei Gottsched und den Schweizern*, Tübingen: Niemeyer, 1981

Helene Böhlau 1859–1940

Helene Böhlau's long writing career produced many short stories and novels, but her reputation is grounded—perhaps unjustifiably (Becker)—in her contribution to feminist literature of the late 19th century. Indeed, before the turn of the century, she was one of the most widely read women writers alongside Gabriele Reuter, although her reputation as a serious writer later declined.

Although never herself politically active, Helene Böhlau reflected the thinking of the moderate middle-class women's movement of her day. Her first works, collected in *Novellen* (1882), in the anecdotal mode of a Paul Heyse, seem pleasant and unthreatening, similar to the very popular *Ratsmädelgeschichten* (1888; *Ratsmädel-Stories*). Yet even these charming tales, which draw on Böhlau's intimate knowledge of her birthplace Weimar and its history, focus on women's lives and their struggles with the limitations set upon their emotional and intellectual development. Her first major novel, *Der Rangierbahnhof* (1896; The Marshalling Yard), subsequently fully revealed her awareness of contemporary literary movements and contemporary gender issues.

The oppressive city setting of this novel, contrasted with its alpine opening, owes a debt to the naturalists, although it lacks their minutely detailed observation. The central figure Olly (Olga) Kovalski reveals already in her nickname the fate awaiting women: trivialization, both of their creative and emotional needs. Olly's aspirations as a painter conflict with the submission required of her as a married woman needing security, yet there is no stereotypical opposition of repressive male and victimized woman. One man at least, the painter Köppert, models the ideal understanding of both artist and woman; equally, Olly's problems are partially self-created. Her sense of her artistry is still predicated on a male concept of genius that conflicts with her own internalized sense of her "natural" female role as wife and mother. Yet the novel's feminist agenda is not unambiguous. The absolutist view of the artist as genius deriving from Schopenhauer (Brinker-Gabler) sets unachievable standards; the reassuringly strong figure of Anne, the husband's cousin, seems to celebrate traditional female virtues; and Olly's slightly sentimentalized, early death preempts extended debate on gender issues. Despite this, however, the novel as a whole represents an implicit challenge to men to combine the nurturing and self-sacrifice normally expected of women, as a first step toward rethinking gender roles.

In her next novel, *Das Recht der Mutter* (1896; A Mother's Right), Böhlau issues a more explicit challenge: to the discriminatory law on unmarried mothers. Where moderate feminists of the time were mainly concerned with education and professional life, this novel demands a freer legal code that would legimitize all mother-child bonds; these demands also implicitly attack romantic love and champion women's ability and right to combine work and emotional fulfillment. In *Halbtier!* (1899; Semi-Animal!), the provocation is stronger still, as the protagonist Isolde Frey finally kills the man who abuses her. For Brinker-Gabler, this is one of the most striking novels of the period because of its insight into the way in which women are denied autonomous subjectivity and its mix of naturalistic detail and metaphor, which draw upon both Schopenhauerian and Buddhist thought on overcoming one's self through pain. Despite its powerful portrayal of the brutal reductiveness under which women labored, however, the novel lacks an understanding of female sexuality comparable to that in works by Lou Andreas-Salome or Laura Marholm.

This lack constituted a major point of critical attack after the turn of the century: for Carl Bleibtreu in 1912, Helene Böhlau was already "ma(los überschätzt" (largely overestimated) and lacking "das absolut Erotische" (the absolute erotic). After 1900, in fact, her emancipatory energy flagged noticeably and virtually disappeared after 1914, when she turned to historical subjects or depicted clichéd figures such as brave soldiers and staunch women. Nationalistic elements crept in, although there is no evidence to suggest she supported Nazism. She continued to write lighter fiction into the late 1930s.

Viewed historically against the wider fight for women's rights, Helene Böhlau may seem tame; one might argue that after 1900 she failed to challenge the sharpening antagonism toward women or to explore the female psyche in all its facets. Yet one can also argue (Singer) that the seemingly clichéd tragic endings of her novels represent a challenge to the tradition in women's literature of harmonizing material and are a realistic marker of women's frustrations. She was certainly not a great writer, but she offers valuable insights into her time.

MARY E. STEWART

Biography

Born in Weimar, Germany, 22 November 1859. Privately educated because of ill-health, but made cultural visits abroad with parents; married in Turkey to the writer and philosopher Friedrich Arndt, 1886, who converted to Islam to divorce his first wife (some of Helen Böhlau's subsequent novels give her name as Frau Omar Al Raschid Bey); lived in Constantinople, 1886–88, and later Ingolstadt and Munich; continued to write prolifically with the support of her husband; after her husband's death in 1911, edited his philosophical works for publication; never an overt supporter of fascism but resisted hints that her husband might have been Jewish; on son, a doctor, gave up Turkish citizenship to fight in World War I and became an active Nazi. Ebner Prize for literature, 1905. Died in Widdersberg, near Herrsching, on the Ammersee, south of Munich, 26 March 1940.

Selected Works

Collections
Gesammelte Werke, 9 vols., 1927–29

Novels
Novellen, 1882
Der Rangierbahnhof, 1896
Das Recht der Mutter, 1896
Schlimme Flitterwochen: Novellen, 1898
Das Halbtier! 1899
Die Ratsmädchen laufen einem Herzog in die Arme, 1905
Eine zärtliche Seele, 1929

Stories
Ratsmädelgeschichten, 1888
Ein Sommerbuch, 1903

Further Reading

Becker, Josef, *Helene Böhlau: Leben und Werk,* Ph.D. dissertation, Universität Zürich, 1988
Brinker-Gabler, Gisela, *Deutsche Literatur von Frauen,* vol. 2, Munich: Beck, 1988
Diethe, Carol, *Towards Emancipation: German Women Writers of the Nineteenth Century,* Oxford: Berghahn, 1998
Kübler, Gunhild, *Die soziale Aufsteigerin: Wandlungen einer geschlechtsspezifischen Rollenzuschreibung im deutschen Roman, 1870–1900,* Bonn: Bouvier, 1982
Singer, Sandra L., *Free Soul, Free Woman? A Study of Selected Fictional Works by Hedwig Dohm, Isolde Kurz, and Helene Böhlau,* New York: Lang, 1995

Jakob Böhme 1575–1624

According to an early biographer and disciple, Jakob Böhme experienced the first of a number of spiritual visions late in 1600 when he saw a reflection of himself in a pewter bowl. On the basis of this episode, his thought as a whole developed, and his continuing concern over the problem of theodicy was solved: his "spirit saw immediately in all and through all creatures, knew God in plant and grass, who He was and what His will was," and came to understand how the contradictions evident everywhere in the created world could be integrated into a holistic view of the creation. For Böhme, the divine being, the Nothingness or *Ungrund* (the Abyss, associated with God the Father), reaches to Something (associated with the divine person of the Son) as a burning love, and as Holy Spirit enlightens the human spirit, itself originally created in and by that love. The individual is to find fulfillment in a mystical love union, often described by Böhme as marriage with the divine Sophia, Wisdom, "God in His depths, the Holy Spirit's corporality." Placing strong emphasis on the freedom of the human will, Böhme taught that the male fire raging within individuals can be overcome by the mediation of the divine Sophia's female love light, received through faith in Christ and the birth of God in the individual's soul.

Böhme depicts this theosophy and the devotional life patterned on it in a range of ways, making wide use of various cabalistic and alchemical images, as well as of traditional Christian language, influenced as he was by Theophrast Bombast von Hohenheim, Paracelsus, Valentin Weigel, Renaissance Neoplatonism, and 16th-century mystical spiritualism. His first published piece, *Morgenröte im Aufgang* (1612; *Aurora*), clearly marks his hermetic and pansophistic interests and reflects the way style and thought are integrally linked throughout his work. In the *Aurora* he initially formulates his theory of *Natursprache,* the original language of Adam and the root or mother of all human speech "in which arises the complete and perfect experiential knowledge of all things." This language of the totality of nature is known to no one, resting as it does in divine mystery, but, Böhme claims, was communicated to him spiritually through the grace of God. The theory explains much of Böhme's style, which is complex in its very simplicity.

A strikingly direct writer, an autodidact unencumbered in any way by academic style, Böhme extended the meanings of root German and Latin words to serve him as technical terms, peculiar to his own system, and at the same time delighted in formulating new etymologies. Thus, *Lust* and *Essenz* serve in a wide range of contexts to link various aspects of his thought in single words that defy simple translation; the same is true of *Qualität,* which Boehme relates to both *Quelle* (source) and *Qual* (torment), as he links the "fel" in *Teufel* (devil) to *Fall* (the fall). Language, thought, and reality as a whole are thus closely bound together; the discovery of "the signature of things" is in large part the discovery of things themselves in their essence. Thus, the subtitle of his *De Signatura Rerum* of 1622 reads "The signature of all things, showing the sign and signification of the several forms and shapes in the creation, and what the beginning, ruin, and cure of everything is. It proceeds out of eternity into time, and again out of time into eternity, and comprises all mysteries." This program he develops to its fullest in the *Mysterium Magnum* of 1623, the largest of his works, an extended exegesis and exposition of Genesis, treating, as he tells his readers, "the manifestation or revelation of the divine Word . . . expounding the kingdom of nature and the kingdom of grace." Human beings speak, write, and understand, according to Böhme, by the power of the Word of God, incorporated and formed in them at creation. This ability carries with it great responsibility: as the name of God, the Word must not be abused, on the pain of eternal punishment.

Böhme's writings and spiritual insights had a striking influence throughout Europe immediately following his death and well into the 19th century. His own followers, particularly Abraham von Franckenburg and Johann Theodor von Tesch, were active missionaries, transmitting his works to Quietist writers in the Lowlands (Antoinette Bourignon and Pierre Poiret) through German Philadelphians such as Johann Wilhelm Petersen and their English followers, Jane Leade and John Pordage. In Holland, Böhme's works were edited and published as a collection by his greatest disciple, Johann Conrad Gichtel, and in printed form had a significant impact on German Baroque poets such as Angelus Silesius and Quirinus Kuhlmann, on German Pietism initiated by Philipp Jacob Spener in 1675, and above all on the radical wing of that movement in figures such as Gottfried Arnold. The German Romantics, above all Friedrich Wilhelm Joseph von Schelling and Georg Wilhelm Friedrich Hegel, did much to popularize Böhme's work in the 19th century, and its effect continued to be noted in the works of Roman Catholic writers such as Franz von Baader. In 17th-century England, Böhme's works were translated by John Sparrow, influenced such diverse figures as the poet John Milton, the Cambridge Platonist Benjamin Whichcote, and the physicist Isaac Newton, and were edited as a whole and popularized by William Law. They also played an important role in the development of the poetry of William Blake and the thought of Samuel Taylor Coleridge.

PETER C. ERB

See also Mysticism

Biography

Little is known of Böhme's life until he became a citizen in Görlitz in 1599. Active in business in the city as a shoemaker; he wrote his *Aurora,* 1612, outlining his theosophical positions, but the work fell afoul of Gregory Richter, the Orthodox Lutheran pastor in the city, and Böhme ceased to publish for some seven years; controversy grew again from 1618 when he began to publish once more and continued to the close of his life when he was exiled for a short time, although he returned to Görlitz, where he received the sacrament a few days before his death, 17 November 1624.

Selected Works

Collections

Theosophia Revelata, edited by Johann George Gichtel and Johann Wilhelm Ueberfeld, 1730; facsimile reprint as *Sämtliche Schriften,* edited by Will-Erich Peuckert, 11 vols., 1955–61
The Works of Jacob Behmen, the Teutonic Theosopher, translated by John Sparrow and others, 4 vols., 1764–81
Die Urschriften, edited by Werner Buddecke, 2 vols., 1963–66

Theosophical Writing

Morgenröte im Aufgang, 1612; as *The Aurora,* translated by John Sparrow, 1656; in volume 1 of *The Works of Jacob Behmen*
Theosophische Sendbriefe, 1618–24; edited by Gerhard Wehr, 2 vols., 1979; as *Theosophick Letters,* translated by John Sparrow, 1661
Beschreibung der drei Principien Göttliches Wesen, 1619; as *Description of the Three Principles of Divine Essence,* translated by John Sparrow, 1648; in volume 1 of *The Works of Jacob Behmen*
Von dreifachen Leben des Menschen, 1620; as *The High and Deep Searching out of the Threefold Life of Man,* translated by John Sparrow, 1650; in volume 2 of *The Works of Jacob Behmen*
Viertzig Fragen von der Seelen, 1620; as *The Forty Questions of the Soul,* translated by John Sparrow, 1647; in volume 2 of *The Works of Jacob Behmen*
Von der Menschwerdung Jesu Christi, 1620; as *Of the Becoming Man, or Treatise of the Incarnation,* translated by John Sparrow, 1659; in volume 2 of *The Works of Jacob Behmen*
Von sechs theosophischen Puncten, 1620; as *A Book of the Great Six Points,* translated by John Sparrow, 1661; in *Six Theosophic Points and Other Writings,* translated by John Rolleston Earle, 1919
Kurtze Erklärung von sechs mystischen Puncten, 1620
Gründlicher Bericht vom Irdischen und Himmlischen Mysterio, 1620
Unterricht von den letzten Zeiten, 1620
Schutz-Schriften wieder Balthasar Tilken, 1621; as *Apology to Balthazar Tylcken,* translated by John Sparrow, 1661
Bedencken über Esaiä Stiefels Büchlein, 1621/1622; as *A Consideration Upon the Book of Esaias Stiefel,* 1653
Der Weg zu Christo, 1622; as *The Way to Christ Discovered,* translated by John Sparrow, 1648; as *The Way to Christ,* translated by John Joseph Stoudt, 1947
De Signatura Rerum, 1622; as *Signatura Rerum; or, The Signature of All Things,* 1651; in volume 4 of *The Works of Jacob Behmen*
Von der Gnadenwahl, 1623; as *Concerning the Election of Grace,* translated by John Sparrow, 1655; in volume 4 of *The Works of Jacob Behmen*
Mysterium Magnum, 1623; as *Mysterium Magnum,* translated by John Sparrow, 1654; in volume 3 of *The Works of Jacob Behmen*
Von Christi Testamenten, 1624; as *Of Christ's Testaments,* translated by John Sparrow, 1652; in volume 4 of *The Works of Jacob Behmen*
Betrachtung Göttlicher Offenbahrung, 1624
Schutz-Rede wieder Gregorium Richter, 1624; as *A Defence [Directed Against] Gregory Rickter . . . ,* translated by John Sparrow, 1661
Clavis, 1624; as *The Clavis, or Key,* translated by John Sparrow, 1647
Six Theosophic Points and Other Writings, translated by John Rolleston Earle, 1919; new edition, with introductory essay by Nicolas Berdyaev, 1958

Further Reading

Benz, Ernst, *Der vollkommene Mensch nach Jacob Boehme,* Stuttgart: Kohlhammer, 1937
Berdyaev, Nicolas, "Unground and Freedom," in *Jakob Böhme, Six Theosophic Points and Other Writings,* translated by John Rolleston Earle, Ann Arbor: University of Michigan Press, 1958
Elert, Werner, *Die voluntarische Mystik Jacob Boehmes,* Berlin: Trowitzsch, 1913
Konopacki, Stephen A., *The Descent into Words: Jacob Boehme's Transcendental Linguistics,* Ann Arbor, Michigan: Karoma, 1979
Koyré, Alexandre, *La philosophie de Jacob Boehme,* Paris: Vrin, 1929
Miller, Arlene A., *Jacob Boehme: From Orthodoxy to Enlightenment,* Ph.D. dissertation, Stanford University, 1971
Peuckert, Will-Erich, *Das Leben Jacob Böhmes,* in volume 10 of the *Sämtliche Schriften,* Stuttgart: Frommann, 1961

Stoudt, John Joseph, *Jacob Boehme: His Life and Thought*, New York: Seabury, 1957

Thune, Nils, *The Boehmenists and the Philadelphians: A Contribution to the Study of English Mysticism in the 17th and 18th Centuries*, Uppsala: Almqvist and Wiksells, 1948

Walsh, David, *The Mysticism of Innerworldly Fulfilment: A Study of Jacob Boehme*, Gainsville: University Presses of Florida, 1983

Weeks, Andrew, *Boehme: An Intellectual Biography of the Seventeenth-Century Philosopher and Mystic*, Albany: State University of New York Press, 1991

Heinrich Böll 1917–1985

Heinrich Böll started writing as early as 1937, but his first publications were in the postwar era. He was then perceived mainly as a pacifist chronicler of the absurdity of war and, after the currency reform of 1948, as an outspoken, religiously motivated critic of the conservative restoration of the Federal Republic and its pseudo-respectable establishment, its media, and its obsession with economic success and social conformity—with forging ahead while burying the past. His reputation rested initially on carefully crafted radio plays and short stories, a favorite form in which he excelled with many masterpieces. His career began to take off when the Gruppe 47 awarded him its prize for one such story in 1951, the year of his first published novel, *Wo warst du, Adam?* (translated as *Adam, Where Art Thou?* and *And Where Were You, Adam?*), which, however, took several years to sell the 3,000 copies printed. From about 1953 onward, after the relative success of his second novel, *Haus ohne Hüter* which was reprinted within the same year (1954; translated as *Tomorrow and Yesterday* and *The Unguarded House*), he became increasingly known as a novelist of great popularity and considerable skill. His two attempts at writing for the stage (*Ein Schluck Erde* [1961; A Mouthful of Earth] and *Aussatz* [1970; Leprosy]), were not successful. The apparent realism of his contemporary and provincial fiction, using various locations in and near Cologne (which is never mentioned by name), was misread as a relatively unsophisticated reflection of social reality. However, the naively used labels *Trümmerliteratur* (literature of ruins) and *Waschküchenliteratur* (literature of the wash house), which were applied to the fiction of his early years, did catch an essential aspect of his whole oeuvre. The very setting in the social reality of *einfache Leute* (ordinary people), characteristic of the earlier works, indicates Böll's distrust of conformist careerism and social success. The origin of his continued interest in the collapse of bourgeois society, that "Urthema der Literatur" (original theme of all literature), as he later said in 1975, predates the war: it helped him grasp the rise of National Socialism, to understand the effect of the world war and of its aftermath, and to shed light on the German normality, apparently restored thanks to the economic miracle that quickly obliterated the memories of the past. The insecurity it produced is behind the alienation and distrust—behind the obsession with security and political correctness of thought and action—that are at the center of his work of the 1970s and 1980s. The threat to human society, which prides itself on its Christian heritage but betrays its meaning, results from the disintegration of once-shared assumptions about individual and communal fulfillment. It is tangibly and audibly present in the linguistic dissimulations and distortions of a language that can no longer be trusted.

Böll insisted that his work was at all stages an attempted approximation to the unexplored riddles of recent German history ("lauter Annäherungsversuche an die Unerklärlichkeiten der jüngeren deutschen Geschichte"). He believed passionately in his role as *leidenschaftlicher Zeitgenosse* (impassioned contemorary) (1975), and in the relevance for his work of contemporary events and their origins, which must not be forgotten. His output, both in his fiction and in many public speeches, reviews, essays, and interviews (at home and abroad), became more and more forthright in his defense of a language that retains and protects human values ("eine bewohnbare Sprache") and in his satirical or critical exploration of the destructive power of conformist clichés. This made him a controversial, even persecuted, public figure in his own country in times of dramatic social and political change, from the debate about German rearmament under Adenauer, to Chancellor Brandt's socialism and his *Ostpolitik* (which Böll supported), to the fierce debate about emergency laws curtailing basic human rights suspended in the interest of security and public safety, and to the antinuclear protests against the stationing of cruise missiles. Böll's deep-seated distrust of the simplistic imposition of law and order that kills off all genuine striving after justice and human development ("Der Schrei nach 'Ruhe und Ordnung' ist der Schrei nach dem Tod," he argued in 1969) is at the heart of all the games he plays with social reality and its language in his fiction.

At times of public hysteria, he was both accused of subversive left-wing anarchic tendencies (*Böllschewismus* was a cunning label) and venerated as the good man from Cologne (*der gute Mensch zu Köln*) or even as the conscience of the nation. Much of the public debate over the merits of his work was colored by this; even the award of the prestigious Nobel Prize in 1972 was seen by some as a recognition of his national and international advocacy of reconciliation, patience, and forgiveness rather than as an accolade for the literary quality of his writing. Through the critical reception of his work runs the continuing suspicion that he was, at his best, telling tales in the traditional mode; his more ambitious modernism and stylistic complexity, which became more pronounced with *Billard um halbzehn* (1959; *Billiards at Half-Past Nine*) and eventually took him to the experimental work *Frauen vor Flußlandschaft* (completed before his death and published posthumously in 1985; *Women in a River Landscape*), have remained controversial. Their extensive demands on the creative and investigative imagination of the reader have too often been judged as flawed authorial control, as dubiously fashionable modernism, and toward the end of his life, simply as signs of failing control and advancing senility.

Böll rejected the clichéd public images of himself as subversive villain or superhuman authority as neither deserved nor desirable. The reception of his work by enthusiastic readers, in both East and West Germany (he was the most frequently published and most widely read West German author in the German Democratic Republic), as well as abroad in translation in many languages, was largely unaffected by the controversies surrounding his public role and his literary merit. Many of his novels were serialized in major national papers; some were also transformed into films: *Das Brot der frühen Jahre,* by H. Vesely (1962); *Nicht versöhnt* (based on *Billard um halbzehn*), by J.M. Straub (1965); *Ansichten eines Clowns,* by V. Jasny (1975); and, most successfully of all, *Die verlorene Ehre der Katharina Blum,* by Volker Schlöndorff (1977). In fact, any Böll reader will be aware of the way in which his characters might see experience, past or future, as a film sequence running in their heads. When Böll died, his books had sold more than 35 million copies worldwide, more than half of them in translation.

A more objective, informed, and comprehensive critical view of his achievement is beginning to emerge, now that work on his literary estate and preparations for a great critical edition have begun. Böll insisted that all his writing—in fact, all his literary activity as a reviewer, translator, editor, speaker, essayist, poet, playwright, writer, and novelist—had been a single, virtually uninterrupted process of writing, a "Fortschreibungsprozeß" (1966, 1971). He saw himself not as a realist (and claimed to be incapable of understanding what realism might be) but as someone whose greatest joy was writing, experimenting with a set of characters who come into our view by the language they use.

What changed were the dominant themes and historical settings of his texts, which moved from the helpless victims trapped in war and its immediate effects (*Der Zug war pünktlich* [1949; *The Train Was on Time*] and *And Where Were You Adam* [1951]), to the postwar Germany of ruins and the black market (*Und sagte kein einziges Wort* [1953; translated as *Acquainted with the Night* and *And Never Said a Word*]; *The Unguarded House* [1954]; and *Das Brot der frühen Jahre* [1955; translated as *The Bread of Our Early Years* and *The Bread of Those Early Years*]), to the outsiders in the successful society of the Federal Republic of the economic miracle (*Billiards at Half-Past Nine* [1959] and *Ansichten eines Clowns* [1963; *The Clown*]), and to the great attacks on the absurd obsession of German society, humorously or satirically exposed, which is fed by a manipulative press claiming to advocate law and order (*Ende einer Dienstfahrt* [1966; *The End of a Mission*]; *Die verlorene Ehre der Katharina Blum* [1974; *The Lost Honor of Katharina Blum*]; *Berichte zur Gesinnungslage der Nation* [1975]; *Fürsorgliche Belagerung* [1979; *The Safety Net*]; and *Women in a River Landscape* [1985]). At the center of this oeuvre is *Gruppenbild mit Dame* (1971; *Group Portrait with Lady*), one of his finest and most sophisticated novels, which shares many features with the others, above all the provocative "combination of marriage, sex, love and religion" (1968) Böll had identified publicly as one of the driving forces behind all his writing: his personal theology of the sacrament of love. For Böll, writing was "one of the few available possibilities to have a life and to protect and hold on to life" (1956); the deeply religious hidden motivation, which questions and transcends institutionalized Christianity, occasionally comes to the fore in attempts to make his interviewer understand. (The early influence of the writers of the French *renouveau catholique* and other outsiders to the establishment, such as Theodor Haecker, makes itself felt here and deserves investigation.) Turning the labeling of much early German postwar writing as *Versehrtenliteratur* (1969) into an appropriate metaphor for a dominant characteristic, both of himself as an author and of his figures, Böll had drawn attention to the obvious vulnerability of the sensitive personal response that does not hide behind the accepted consensus.

However, for a fuller understanding of Böll's oeuvre, more significant than the themes and settings and the qualities of the characters is his belief that reality is not something that can easily be found and then depicted as if reflected in a mirror and, similarly, that a reliable and trustworthy form of language must, in a process of *Sprachfindung* (1964), be searched for because the true utterance of genuine human sensibility is buried under a heap of clichéd phrases ("*Floskelmüll,*" 1985).

In his last novel (1985), Böll has a character reflect that human sensibility can be killed off by "Angst, Phantasie und Apathie." Deep anxiety is at the heart of the experience of many of his characters, who have enough imagination to read their situation and discover its true reality but are up against the thoughtless apathy that they share with others. When the author told his interviewer in 1975 that it is impossible to recognize reality without sufficient imagination ("*kann man ohne Phantasie die Wirklichkeit garnicht erkennen*"), he was reiterating his plea of 1961 (*Der Zeitgenosse und die Wirklichkeit* [Reality and Its Contemporaries]) that the facts and actual details will never reveal the true reality that only our imagination, capable of remembering the past encrypted in the facts (*Erinnerung*) and of grieving over these reminders (*Trauer*), can decode. Decoding the facts to discover the hidden reality, the true *Wirklichkeit,* is compared by Böll to accepting and opening a letter addressed to us that we, however, might simply ignore. The role of the writer, Böll argued in his *Frankfurter Vorlesungen* (1966; Frankfurt Lectures) and in an interview in 1969, is therefore to create reality out of some given data—to transform them into something ("geschaffene Wirklichkeit") that will have consequences in opening up the buried significance of human life. Again, the ultimately theological derivation of this conception of the artist and his or her motivation requires further critical exploration.

On a more immediately accessible level, the writer combines creative imagination with well-founded knowledge and political insight. Literature must communicate matters that are more subtle than those that the fixed, often opaque, and sometimes rigid vocabulary of scholarly investigation, ecclesiastical pronouncement, or political debate can handle (1967, 1969). The games the author plays are language games—montages of linguistic utterance that invite the reader either to see through their distorting implications or to accept them as genuine. Language is brimful of "particularly tricky material" ("besonders heikle Objekte," 1968) that threatens to extinguish the spark of life. The vocabulary of contemporary language is riddled with the detritus of questionable attitudes unthinkingly transported. Getting us as readers to question the words we hear and to subvert the images they conjure up is the writer's task, in much the same way in which the young Böll was taught by the German master of his traditional *Gymnasium* in Cologne to reduce the chaotic language of Hitler's *Mein Kampf* to some tangible content and meaning ("dieses ganze Sprachgewirr zu reduzieren auf eine Art Inhalt und eine Art Aussage," 1975). Such experimental tests of the linguistic reliability of common parlance will demonstrate how little of it stands up to carefully considered scrutiny (1975). One of the characters in *And Never Said a Word* complains that ever since the war his head has been full of superfluous verbiage and that the sermons of the local bishop owe their vocabulary to an index of theology: the resulting ennui has displaced the chance of finding a challenging truth. If the writer succeeds in breaking open the shells of these words—if the reader is able to respond to the challenge posed by the experiment of the game that the author invites him to share—the text might have far-reaching consequences. Looked at from this point of view, Böll's texts are of a linguistic subtlety that is frequently missed and that might require a fine ear for tones that are constantly shifting.

Therefore, it is especially striking, as J.H. Reid has convincingly argued (1987), that from the beginning Böll employs multiple internal focalizers, a number of first-person narrators, or a profusion of narrative levels, finally arriving at a point at which the text pretends to stem from a process of research, resulting in a reportage or a reconstructed account. The unreliable version of events deliberately invites the reader to complete the true story; in the radical experiment of *Women in a River Landscape,* the reader is only offered dialogue and monologue.

To a large extent, Böll's short stories, stories, novels, and radio plays share in these experimental qualities, which extend a few minutes, hours, or days, through time remembered and anticipated, into a complex web of human interaction in which silent gestures ultimately might be more trustworthy and reliable than most of the words spoken. The reality created in the games that Böll plays with his characters and their language is essentially, often subversively, seen through their eyes and articulated in the imperfect linguistic fashion that they themselves might have come to distrust. Four of Böll's finest novels provide good examples: *And Where Were You Adam?* (see separate entry), *Billiards at Half-Past Nine, The Clown,* and *Group Portrait with Lady.* In these, as in almost all his work, the fictional reality is located in the immediate present yet is continually juxtaposed with glimpses of the past.

The last three of these novels use a narrowly circumscribed situation in which the game that the author plays with us through language creates the fictional reality. The first of these is set on 6 September 1958 but creates a multifaceted reflection of German history over three generations with the help of ten focalizers, moving easily between direct and indirect interior monologue and direct speech. Typically, Böll's most sympathetic characters are misfits in their society who are turned into rejects by their stubborn refusal to go with the latest fashion in accepted opinion and attitude. Considered as rejects and fallen from the grace of social approval, they form the "wichtigste Gegenstand der Literatur" (1975): never fixed and frozen into rigid attitudes, they can remain truly alive.

The second of these novels uses as the narrator and focalizer just such an outsider, rejected as *Abfall* (waste) by his family and the social world into which he was born, who is trapped in his flat in Bonn for a few hours on an evening in March 1962. His only contacts with the outside world are the voices of those he tries to contact by telephone and whose language vividly reminds him of the mostly detestable attitudes that have made him what he now is: an embittered, hurt, vulnerable clown who collects significant *Augenblicke.* Taken literally, *Augenblick* suggests the pregnant moment, but the word also strongly connotes the penetrating glance of the eye that is not blind to what it perceives. For him, the secret of what terrifies him is encapsulated in the detail that haunts him. The burden of the past remembered, with all its personal grief over love betrayed—by his mother, by his "wife" Marie, and by the Church, which has substituted an institution of marriage for the sacrament of love—renders him unfit for good German society. The outcast quietly and bitterly subverts superficial perceptions of reality and reveals a truer picture to the reader, who must piece together the complex mosaic of impressions, memories, voices, and attitudes.

The last example presents the reader with the assumption that an unnamed researcher working in 1970–71 has attempted to reconstruct the life—in fact, the personality—of the "lady" at the heart of the novel. Forty-eight-year-old Leni exists for the reader only in the reflection of her exceptional qualities in the memories and stories of others, in the researcher's interviews with those who knew her. It is striking that in all these cases the invitation to the reader to become an imaginative creator is the real challenge. An apparently very narrowly defined situation progressively opens up a whole vista of contradictory and conflicting pieces of evidence, scattered over and gathered from decades of history. In all cases, the tone and sound of language and the language of direct or indirect monologue—of words read, spoken, and overheard—are used to locate the figures in our imagination as we are forced to judge their reality against the utopian and the homeless, values ultimately implied by the author who recedes more and more from the texts.

Böll has always been considered a master in the observation of detail, yet he insisted that he required very little reality for his fiction. What he did need to find, again and again, was the fictional constellation that would provide him with an imaginative way into the creation of a reality that would become transparent for the reader who has eyes to see and ears to hear.

Hinrich Siefken

Biography

Born in Cologne, 21 December 1917. Studied at the University of Cologne; worked as a joiner and in the book trade; served in the German army, 1939–45; married Annemarie Cech, 1942; prisoner of war, 1945; career as a writer from 1946; member, German Academy for Language and Literature, 1953; coeditor of *Labyrinth,* 1960–61; of *L,* 1976–; guest professor at Frankfurt University, 1963/64; president of PEN International, 1971–74. Resigned from Catholic Church, 1979. Prize of Gruppe 47, 1951; Rene Schickele Prize, 1952; Deutscher Kritikerpreis, 1953; Charles-Veillon-Prize, 1960; Georg Büchner Prize, 1967; Nobel Prize for Literature, 1972; medal of the International League for Human Rights, 1974. Died in Bornheim-Merten, 16 July 1985.

Selected Works

Collections

Werke, edited by Bernd Balzer, 10 vols., 1977–78
In eigener und anderer Sache: Schriften und Reden, 1952–85, 9 vols., 1988

Fiction

Der Zug war pünktlich, 1949; as *The Train Was on Time,* translated by Richard Graves, 1956; translated by Leila Vennewitz, 1973

Wanderer, kommst du nach Spa . . ., 1950; as *Traveller, If You Come to Spa . . .*, translated by Mervyn Savill, 1956
Die schwarzen Schafe, 1951
Wo warst du, Adam? 1951; as *Adam, Where Art Thou?* translated by Mervyn Savill, 1955; as *And Where Were You, Adam?* translated by Leila Vennewitz, 1974
Nicht nur zur Weihnachtszeit, 1952
Und sagte kein einziges Wort, 1953; as *Acquainted with the Night*, translated by Richard Graves, 1954; as *And Never Said a Word*, translated by Leila Vennewitz, 1978
Haus ohne Hüter, 1954; as *Tomorrow and Yesterday*, translated by Mervyn Savill, 1957; as *The Unguarded House*, translated by Mervyn Savill, 1957
Das Brot der frühen Jahre, 1955; as *The Bread of Our Early Years*, translated by Mervyn Savill, 1957; as *The Bread of Those Early Years*, translated by Leila Vennewitz, 1976
So ward Abend und Morgen, 1955
Unberechenbare Gäste: Heitere Erzählungen, 1956
Im Tal der donnernden Hufe, 1957
Doktor Murkes gesammelte Schweigen und andere Satiren, 1958
Der Mann mit den Messern, 1958
Die Waage der Baleks und andere Erzählungen, 1958
Der Bahnhof von Zimpren, 1959
Billard um halb zehn, 1959; as *Billiards at Half-Past Nine*, translated by Patrick Bowles, 1961
Als der Krieg ausbrach, Als der Krieg zu Ende war, 1962; as *Enter and Exit*, translated by Leila Vennewitz, in *Absent without Leave: Two Novellas*, 1965
Ansichten eines Clowns, 1963; as *The Clown*, translated by Leila Vennewitz, 1965
Entfernung von der Truppe, 1964; as *Absent without Leave*, translated by Leila Vennewitz, in *Absent without Leave: Two Novellas*, 1965
Ende einer Dienstfahrt, 1966; as *The End of a Mission*, translated by Leila Vennewitz, 1968
Eighteen Stories, translated by Leila Vennewitz, 1966
Absent Without Leave and Other Stories, translated by Leila Vennewitz, 1967
Geschichten aus zwölf Jahren, 1969
Children Are Civilians Too (stories), translated by Leila Vennewitz, 1970
Gruppenbild mit Dame, 1971; as *Group Portrait with Lady*, translated by Leila Vennewitz, 1973
Der Mann mit den Messern: Erzählungen (selection), 1972
Die verlorene Ehre der Katharina Blum, 1974; as *The Lost Honor of Katharina Blum*, translated by Leila Vennewitz, 1975
Berichte zur Gesinnungslage der Nation, 1975
Fürsorgliche Belagerung, 1979; as *The Safety Net*, translated by Leila Vennewitz, 1982
Du fährst zu oft nach Heidelberg und andere Erzählungen, 1979
Gesammelte Erzählungen, 2 vols., 1981
Das Vermächtnis, 1982; as *A Soldier's Legacy*, translated by Leila Vennewitz, 1985
Die Verwundung und andere frühe Erzählungen, 1983; as *The Casualty*, translated by Leila Vennewitz, 1986
Der Angriff: Erzählungen 1947–1949, 1983
Veränderungen in Staeck: Erzählungen 1962–1980, 1984
Mein trauriges Gesicht: Erzählungen, 1984
Frauen vor Flußlandschaft: Roman in Dialogen und Selbstgesprächen, 1985; as *Women in a River Landscape: A Novel in Dialogues and Soliloquies*, translated by David McLintock, 1988
Stories, translated by Leila Vennewitz, 1986
Der Engel schwieg, 1992
Erzählungen, 1994

Plays
Die Brücke von Berczaba (broadcast 1952); in *Zauberei auf dem Sender und andere Hörspiele*, 1962
Der Heilige und der Räuber (broadcast 1953); in *Hörspielbuch des Nordwestdeutschen und Süddeutshen Rundfunks*, vol. 4, 1953; as *Mönch und Räuber*, in *Erzählungen, Hörspiele, Aufsätze*, 1961
Ein Tag wie sonst (broadcast 1953), 1980
Zum Tee bei Dr. Borsig (broadcast 1955); in *Erzählungen, Hörspiele, Aufsätze*, 1961
Anita und das Existenzminimum (broadcast 1955)
Eine Stunde Aufenthalt (broadcast 1958); in *Erzählungen, Hörspiele, Aufsätze*, 1961
Die Spurlosen (broadcast 1957), 1957
Bilanz (broadcast 1957); with *Klopfzeichen*, 1961
Die Stunde der Wahrheit (broadcast 1958)
Klopfzeichen (broadcast 1960); with *Bilanz*, 1961
Ein Schluck Erde (produced 1961), 1962
Zum Tee bei Dr. Borsig (includes *Mönch und Räuber; Eine Stunde Aufenthalt; Bilanz; Die Spurlosen; Klopfzeichen; Sprechanlage; Konzert für vier Stimmen)*, 1964
Hausfriedensbruch (broadcast 1969); with *Aussatz*, 1969
Aussatz (produced 1970); with *Hausfriedensbruch*, 1969

Poetry
Gedichte, 1972
Wir kommen weit her: Gedichte, 1986

Other
Bekenntnis zur Trümmerliteratur, 1952
Irisches Tagebuch, 1957; as *Irish Journal*, translated by Leila Vennewitz, 1967
Im Ruhrgebiet, photographs by Karl Hargesheimer, 1958
Unter Krahnenbäumen, photographs by Karl Hargesheimer, 1958
Menschen am Rhein, photographs by Karl Hargesheimer, 1960
Brief an einen jungen Katholiken, 1961
Erzählungen, Hörspiele, Aufsätze, 1961
Assisi, 1962
Hierzulande, 1963
Frankfurter Vorlesungen, 1966
Aufsätze, Kritiken, Reden, 1967
Leben im Zustand des Frevels, 1969
Neue politische und literarische Schriften, 1973
Politische Meditationen zu Glück und Vergeblichkeit, with Dorothee Sölle, 1973
Der Lorbeer ist immer noch bitter: Literarische Schriften, 1974
Drei Tage in März, with Christian Linder, 1975
Der Fall Staeck; oder, Wie politisch darf die Kunst sein? with others, 1975
Briefe zur Verteidigung der Republik, with Freimut Duve and Klaus Staeck, 1977
Einmischung erwünscht: Schriften zur Zeit, 1977
Missing Persons and Other Essays, translated by Leila Vennewitz, 1977
Querschnitte: Aus Interviews, Aufsätzen, und Reden, edited by Viktor Böll and Renate Matthaei, 1977
Warum haben wir aufeinander geschossen? with Lew Koplew, 1981
Rendezvous mit Margaret. Liebesgeschichten, 1981
Was soll aus dem Jungen bloss werden?; oder, Irgendwas mit Büchern, 1981; as *What's to Become of the Boy?; or, Something to Do with Books* (memoir), translated by Leila Vennewitz, 1984
Der Autor ist immer noch versteckt, 1981
Vermintes Gelände: Essayistische Schriften 1977–1981, 1982
Antikommunismus in Ost und West, 1982
Ich hau dem Mädche nix jedonn, ich han et bloss ens kräje. Texte, Bilder, Dokumente zur Verleihung des Ehrenbürgerrechts der Stadt Köln, 29 April 1983, 1983

Ein- und Zusprüche: Schriften, Reden und Prosa 1981–83, 1984
Weil die Stadt so fremd geworden ist, 1985
Bild-Bonn-Boenisch, 1984
Die Fähigkeit zu trauern: Schriften und Reden 1983–1985, 1986
Denken mit Heinrich Böll, 1986
Rom auf den ersten Blick: Landschaften, Städte, Reisen, 1987
Die Hoffnung ist wie ein wildes Tier: Der Briefwechsel zwischen Heinrich Böll und Ernst-Adolf Kunz, 1945–53, edited by Herbert Hoven, 1994

Translations
(all with Annemarie Böll)
Kay Cicellis, *Kein Name bei den Leuten,* 1953
Adriaan Morriën, *Ein unordentlicher Mensch,* 1955
Kay Cicellis, *Tod einer Stadt,* 1956
Paul Horgan, *Weihnachtsabend in San Cristobal,* 1956
Patrick White, *Zur Ruhe kam der Baum des Menschen nie,* 1957
Paul Horgan, *Der Teufel in der Wüste,* 1958
Brendan Behan, *Die Geisel,* 1958
Brendan Behan, *Der Mann von morgen früh,* 1958
J.M. Synge, *Ein wahrer Held,* 1960
Tomás O'Crohan, *Die Boote fahren nicht mehr aus,* 1960
Paul Horgan, *Eine Rose zur Weihnachtszeit,* 1960
Bernard Malamud, *Der Gehilfe,* 1960
J.D. Salinger, *Kurz vor dem Krieg gegen die Eskimos,* 1961
Bernard Malamud, *Das Zauberfass,* 1962
J.D. Salinger, *Der Fänger im Roggen,* 1962
Brendan Behan, *Ein Gutshaus in Irland,* in *Stücke,* 1962
J.D. Salinger, *Franny und Zooey,* 1963
Eilís Dillon, *Die Insel der Pferde,* 1964
J.D. Sallinger, *Hebt den Dachbalken hoch, Zimmerleute; Seymour wird vorgestellt,* 1965
G.B. Shaw, *Caesar und Cleopatra,* 1965
Brendan Behan, *Die Spanner,* 1966
Eilís Dillon, *Die Insel des grossen John,* 1966
Flann O'Brien, *Das harte Leben,* 1966
J.D. Salinger, *Neun Erzählungen,* 1966
Eilís Dillon, *Die schwarzen Füchse,* 1967
Eilís Dillon, *Die Irrfahrt der Santa Maria,* 1968
Eilís Dillon, *Die Springflut,* 1969
Eilís Dillon, *Seehunde SOS,* 1970
Anne Moody, *Erwachen in Mississippi,* 1970
G.B. Shaw, *Candida, Der Kaiser von Amerika, Mensch und Übermensch,* 1970
G.B. Shaw, *Handbuch des Revolutionärs,* 1972

Edited Works
with Erick Kock, *Unfertig ist der Mensch,* 1967
with Freimut Duve and Klaus Staeck, *Verantwortlich für Polen?* 1982

Further Reading

Balzer, Bernd, editor, *Heinrich Böll, 1917–1985, zum 75. Geburtstag,* Bern and New York: Lang, 1992
Butler, Michael, editor, *The Narrative Fiction of Heinrich Böll,* Cambridge and New York: Cambridge University Press, 1994
Conard, Robert C., *Heinrich Böll,* Boston: Twayne, 1981
——, *Understanding Heinrich Böll,* Columbia: University of South Carolina Press, 1992
Finley, Frank, *On the Rationality of Poetry: Heinrich Böll's Aesthetic Thinking,* Amsterdam and Atlanta, Georgia: Rodopi, 1996
Huber, Lothar, and Robert C. Conard, editors, *Heinrich Böll on Page and Screen: The London Symposium,* London: University of London, Institute of Germanic Studies, 1997
Reid, J.H., "Heinrich Böll: From Modernism to Post-Modernism and Beyond," in *The Modern German Novel,* edited by Keith Bullivant, Leamington Spa and New York: Berg, 1987
——, *Heinrich Böll: A German for His Time,* Oxford: Wolff, and Oxford and New York: Berg, 1988
Sowinski, Bernhard, *Heinrich Böll,* Stuttgart: Metzler, 1993
Vogt, Jochen, *Heinrich Böll,* Munich: Beck, 1978; 2nd edition, 1987

Ansichten eines Clowns 1963

Novel by Heinrich Böll

When Heinrich Böll's novel *Ansichten eines Clowns* (*The Clown*) appeared in 1963 at the end of the Adenauer era, West Germany was enjoying its economic miracle, its status as a new democracy, and its membership in NATO. All in all, it was a prospering self-satisfied nation, feeling free of its past and looking forward to the future. These achievements in economics and politics, however, had in large part been accomplished by the integration of ex-Nazis into all aspects of public and private life and by a willful forgetting about Germany's recent crimes against humanity. Böll's novel focuses on these negative aspects of the German recovery. Böll's book, however, was not the only work published that year to do so. Rolf Hochhuth's play *Der Stellvertreter* (1964; *The Deputy*) and Carl Amery's sociological study *Die Kapitulation oder deutscher Katholizismus heute* (1967; *The Capitulation: The Lesson of German Catholicism*) also appeared in that year. To the latter, Böll contributed an important epilogue that complemented the social critique of his novel.

When one considers the unpopular social message of *The Clown,* which is set in the milieu of West German politics, it is remarkable that this book has become Böll's most widely read novel. In 1981, a German poll of "best books" ranked *The Clown* 16th, three places behind Goethe's *Faust* and far ahead of Böll's other works. Today, this novel still enjoys success unanticipated by critics in 1963. At that time it was generally agreed that a work so closely tied to the politics of an era would not survive changing historical conditions, as Hochhuth's drama has not. *The Clown* is, indeed, very parochial in many ways, treating primarily the alliance between the Catholic Church and the Bonn government from 1949 to 1960, the hypocrisy and opportunism of former Nazis, the restoration of prewar materialistic values in a rush to consumption, and above all, the nation's acute loss of memory regarding the war.

Surprisingly, the book did miss much of the important political discourse of the time—such as the remilitarization of Germany, unification politics, and the anticommunist hysteria created by the Cold War. Nonetheless, the book still caused a furor and divided German critical opinion.

Understandably, the Catholic press unanimously rejected the novel as outrageously unfair in its depiction of the church. But the secular press was not much kinder. Eight reviews by prominent intellectuals appeared in *Die Zeit* in May and June 1963, and they typify the controversy surrounding the novel. In summary, these reviewers concluded that the narrator, the atheistic clown, was an unbelievable character obsessed about things

Catholic, that his naïveté was an inappropriate vehicle for the book's social criticism, that the remaining characters were mere semblances of real people, that the simplistic depiction of the rich as negative and the poor as positive was an affront to reality, and that the book should be dismissed merely as an expression of the author's political resentment.

Nonetheless, the novel also had its supporters among the critics in *Die Zeit*. They praised the narrator for his intelligent, insightful observations on the church, the state, and society. They found that his language was consistent with his character, education, and class, that his social criticism flowed directly from his querulent personality, and that his critique of the collusion of church and state, his suspicion of the convenient conversion of Nazis to democracy, and his censure of the nation's eagerness to forget the past were all justified by reality. They also lauded the strategies Böll employed to integrate the theme of the book into its structure, especially the way in which he reduced the present to a brief period of about three hours. During this time, the narrator broods in his apartment berating friends and enemies by phone as he recalls the last 20 years of German history—Böll also successfully used this structural device of shortening the narrated time and expanding the narrative time in other works of the 1950s and 1960s. One aspect of the novel that the majority of the critics commended, however, was the tragic love story of Hans Schnier, the clown, and Marie Derkum, his common-law wife.

In 1970, an unsuccessful dramatic version of *The Clown* directed by Alfred Radok opened in Düsseldorf. But a film version made six years later for German television by the Czech filmmaker Vojtech Jasny and starring Helmut Griem had a modest success. Böll himself collaborated on both the German scripts. These adaptations of *The Clown* proved that there was a continuing interest in this story that the critics had not foreseen in 1963. When the novel appeared in English in 1965, reviewers in the United States immediately noted a similarity between the outsider Hans Schnier and the social misfit Holden Caulfield in J.D. Salinger's *The Catcher in the Rye* (1951)—a book that Böll had in fact translated with his wife while he was writing *The Clown*. Readers in the East and the West were beginning to see that the novel had at its core universal themes that transcended the limits of German politics. First and foremost, they responded to the love story and the struggle of a hapless anarchist who longs for a better world. They recognized that the political hypocrisy and opportunism the clown so hated were common to all political systems, and they saw that his perception that West Germany was developing into a one-party democracy through the blurring of party differences was a trend in many Western democracies. After the war in Vietnam, perceptive readers in the United States realized that the clown's complaint about the failure of the German people to deal with their nation's criminal past also applied to them. Moreover, readers came to see that the clown's protest against the religious and state control of marriage and his pleading for an anthropological understanding of human love anticipated widespread social changes. Also foresighted were Hans Schnier's arguments against "abstract money"—that money not spent on necessities and pleasures but used only for creating more money and power—arguments that became a hallmark of leftist social criticism in the 1970s. Readers saw the clown more and more as an example of a powerless individual struggling for autonomy in a world that depersonalized the individual by numbers and statistics. Critics also began to recognize the clown as an artist, a court jester, and a speaker of unpopular truth (well illustrated in the novel by the clown's performances in East Germany). Some critics also started to understand that this vision of the artist as critic was tied to Böll's Jean-Paulian concept of humor, the process of exalting the lowly and chastising the elevated, a theory that Böll explained in his *Frankfurter Vorlesungen* (Frankfurt Lectures) in 1966. Hence, critics began to read the novel for its satiric quality and explicate the work in relation to theories by Schiller, Hegel, Jean Paul, and Bakhtin.

Subsequent responses to the novel, however, were not universally positive. Feminists castigated the presence of male chauvinism in Hans's treatment of Marie and stereotypical characterizations of women by the author. However positively or negatively one now reads the novel, it has become clear that Böll wrote a revolutionary book in 1963, one that embodied what now is known as the spirit of the 1960s.

ROBERT CONARD

Editions

First edition: *Ansichten eines Clowns,* Cologne: Kiepenheuer und Witsch, 1963

Critical edition: *Ansichten eines Clowns: Roman mit Materialien und einem Nachwort des Autors,* Cologne: Kiepenheuer und Witsch, 1985

Translation: *The Clown,* translated by Leila Vennewitz, New York: McGraw-Hill, 1965

Further Reading

Balzer, Bernd, *Heinrich Böll: "Ansichten eines Clowns,"* Frankfurt: Diesterweg, 1988

Beck, Evelyn T., "A Feminist Critique of Böll's *Ansichten eines Clowns," University of Dayton Review* 12, no. 2 (1976)

Bernhard, Hans-Joachim, *Die Romane Heinrich Bölls: Gesellschaftskritik und Gemeinschaftsutopie,* Berlin: Rütten und Loening, 1970; 2nd edition, 1973

Butler, Michael, *Understanding Heinrich Böll,* Columbia: University of South Carolina Press, 1992

———, "*Ansichten eines Clowns:* The Fool and the Labyrinth," in *The Narrative Fiction of Heinrich Böll,* edited by Michael Butler, Cambridge and New York: Cambridge University Press, 1994

Götze, Karl-Heinz, *Heinrich Böll: "Ansichten eines Clowns,"* Munich: Fink, 1985

Leiser, Peter, *Heinrich Böll: "Das Brot der frühen Jahre," "Ansichten eines Clowns,"* Hollfeld: Beyer, 1974

Müller, Rolf, *Clowneske Wirklichkeit: Eine Untersuchung der clowneske Elemente in Heinrich Bölls Roman "Ansichten eines Clowns,"* 8th edition, Hollfeld: Bange, 1991

Römhild, Dorothee, *Die Ehre der Frau ist unantastbar: Das Bild der Frau im Werk Heinrich Bölls,* Pfaffenweiler: Centarus-Verlagsgesellschaft, 1991

Wo warst du, Adam? 1951

Novel by Heinrich Böll

Heinrich Böll's first published novel *Wo warst du, Adam?* (1951; *And Where Were You, Adam?*) was largely ignored at the time; 3,000 copies took six or seven years to sell. It was the author's own favorite among his works, however; its penultimate chapter was recast by him as the radio play *Die Brücke von Berczaba*

(The Bridge of Berczaba; broadcast in 1952). In its subject matter and its proximity to the immediate present of the early 1950s, it is characteristic of Böll's fiction, particularly that of his early years. It deals with individuals caught in the inglorious and chaotic retreat of the German army from the eastern front in Romania and Hungary in 1944–45, all the way back to the U.S. lines advancing into Germany from the west. It ends with the absurd death of soldier Feinhals (the one character making an appearance in most chapters) by friendly fire in front of his parents' house. Feinhals is discharged from his unit with orders to regroup in the Ruhr area, but he goes home in civilian clothes, absent without leave. The last of seven token shots, usually carefully directed away from the U.S. lines whose superior firepower must not be engaged, aimed on this day by a fanatic German at houses flying the flags of surrender, kills Feinhals. The characters in the novel are all, to varying degrees, largely helpless pawns in a man-made catastrophe over which they have no control; they have lost, or lose, any belief in the cause for which they have been, or have, enlisted.

The novel is built up of chapters that each give a separate aspect of this retreat. They pick out individuals whose paths accidentally cross, without establishing a coherent narrative, using the fragmentation of the supposedly common cause and the vulnerability of these characters to suggest to the reader that these inglorious, pathetic, as well as tragic individual snapshots have to function as a substitute for the impossible overall picture. Each chapter juxtaposes the immediate present of the war with information about the prewar past of the relevant character, thus allowing us to perceive—through reflection, flashback, memories, or authorial intrusion—the complex reality beneath the surface appearance. This brings the novel's strategies close to the techniques (such as abrupt openings and closures, the emphasis on closely observed detail, and the restricted point of view) that Böll was using to great effect in the short stories with which he made his reputation in those years, without reducing his first novel to a collage of short stories.

Böll was a voracious reader throughout his life, which is evident in a number of influences on *Wo warst du, Adam?* The novel owes its title to the secret diaries of the dissident Catholic writer Theodor Haecker, the *Tag- und Nachtbücher, 1939–1945,* which were posthumously published in 1947 and widely praised in reviews as the unheard voice of the other Germany. Haecker's intention had been to preserve for posterity, lest we forget, sub specie aeterni the significance of the historical events. Haecker had written that this significance would not be captured by professional historians and suggested that an outsider such as himself was required for the task, someone who would not be subject to obligations of any official status. By 1947, Böll had experienced, as his letters to Ernst-Adolf Kunz show, the increasing reluctance of publishers to give the public anything other than the sweet entertainment ("Pralinen," said Böll) they craved. The passage the novel quotes from Haecker's diaries emphasizes the alibi function of a world war: Adam, who has eaten of the forbidden fruit, conscious of good and evil, excuses himself by referring to his unwanted part in the catastrophe. A second motto, taken from Antoine de Saint-Exupery's account of the exciting life of a pilot, *Flight to Arras* (1942), available in a German translation at the time, offers the perspective of war as ersatz adventure, as a disease like typhoid that no individual victim can stop.

The specific way in which Böll writes a pacifist war novel flows from all these points. His novel is neither an adventure yarn nor a tale dominated by the mythical "Frontgeist" (war spirit), which turns boys into men. The reader encounters the vulnerability of privates and officers, soldiers and civilians, and men and women; Germans, Romanians, Hungarians, and Jews; and Nazis, agnostics, and Christians. Seen through the eyes of the Hungarian Frau Susan (chapter 8), war appears as the ridiculous and disgusting activity of men, who are paid large amounts of money and who travel into foreign countries to do nothing useful in particular. To the men, it is a "Scheißkrieg," in which nothing works any more; it is also a war that cannot be won, an unpracticed exercise in disorganized retreat, in which the high-ranking officers and civilians use their position to get out of danger first.

By contrast, real courage, and often insubordination and criminal neglect of regulations, are shown by ordinary soldiers. Schneider stays with the seriously wounded as the hospital is overrun by Russian tanks and dies in pointless fire, which is triggered by his stepping on an unexploded dud with which nobody could be bothered. Feinhals shares a rare moment of transient love with Ilona, a Jewish teacher of German who was brought up by nuns in Szentgyörgy. She disappears in the ghetto and is taken to an extermination camp while he waits for her and is brought back to the front line; he cannot forget her words that prayer is all about consoling God. Greck, physically unfit for the action that eventually engulfs and kills him, has sold a pair of trousers to a Jewish tailor and begins to realize the extent of the corrupt dealings between army personnel and local people (which the reader encounters repeatedly). Finck ends up dying while carrying a suitcase of wine at the front line, so that his boss will not lose a bet in the officers' mess. Bauer refuses to play the heroic role demanded of him, complete with tin hat, to shore up the collapsing line of organized retreat; the brain injury he sustains as he falls off his motorbike, however, turns him into a casualty, and he repeats at regular intervals the word "Bjeljogorsche" while facing courtmartial for self-immolation. Böll ensures that the reader sees enough of the civilian background of these figures to grasp the various forms of the conflict between human individuality, in all its frailty, and the uniform military roles none of these characters can, or want to, satisfy. Even Filskeit, the commander of the concentration camp, has a private agenda. Since he is obsessed with choral singing, a niche in the system was initially guaranteed for him as a choirmaster and as an expert in organizing choruses rather than as a member of the active service. Neither his physical appearance nor his inability to kill, until Ilona's perfect singing of a litany provokes him to uncontrollable rage, fit the reader's clichéd expectations about a man in his position.

There are some weaknesses in the handling of the point of view, but overall the novel has gained rather than lost with the passage of time, with some of the finest passages devoted to the observation of physical detail (a flowerpot disintegrating in flight behind the car at which it was aimed) and to the tender sacrament of love.

HINRICH SIEFKEN

Editions

First edition: *Wo warst du, Adam?* Opladen: Friedrich Middelhauve, 1951

Translation: *And Where Were You, Adam?* translated by Leila Vennewitz, London: Secker and Warburg, 1974

Further Reading

Bance, Alan, "Heinrich Böll's 'Wo warst du, Adam?': National Identity and German War Writing; Reunification as the Return of the Repressed?" *Forum for Modern Language Studies* 29 (1993)
Bernhard, Hans Joachim, *Die Romane Heinrich Bölls: Gesellschaftskritik und Gemeinschaftsutopie,* Berlin: Rütten und Loening, 1970; 2nd edition, 1973
Durzak, Manfred, "Die problematische Wiedereinsetzung des Erzählers: Heinrich Bölls Romane," in *Gespräche über den Roman,* Frankfurt: Suhrkamp, 1976
Jeziorkowski, Klaus, "Heinrich Böll: Wo warst du, Adam? (1951)," in *Deutsche Romane des 20. Jahrhunderts: Neue Interpretationen,* edited by Paul Michael Lützeler, Königstein: Athenäum, 1983
Vogt, Jochen, *Heinrich Böll,* Munich: Beck, 1978; 2nd edition, 1987
White, John J., "War, Dissidence, and Protest in Böll's Early Fiction," in *Heinrich Böll on Page and Screen: The London Symposium,* edited by Lothar Huber and Robert C. Conard, London: University of London, Institute of Germanic Studies, 1997

Ludwig Börne 1786–1837

In the first two decades following the defeat of Napoléon and the restoration of authoritarian government in Germany by the Congress of Vienna in 1815, the most effective and articulate voice of resistance and opposition came to be that of Ludwig Börne, a relentless and increasingly radical journalist, essayist, and satirist. He was a painful thorn in the side of the Metternichian system. By the end of his life, he had earned the hostile rage of the rulers and the privileged classes but the respect and admiration of the majority of German liberals and dissidents.

Börne was born as Juda Löw Baruch in Germany's most important ghetto, which was cramped and teeming before French revolutionary artillery brought down its walls in 1796, but which was vibrant and full of potential. His father was a banker and the representative of the ghetto to the emperor, the alleged protector of the Jews. The young man began to study medicine, as that was the only course of study open to Jews, but in Heidelberg and Giessen, under Napoleonic occupation, he was able to switch to administrative science, receiving a doctorate with a dissertation on the condition of the Frankfurt Jewish community. In 1811, he obtained a position as a police official but lost it after the restoration of Jewish disabilities in 1815; he managed, however, to negotiate a small pension. He gradually found his way to his real calling as an acerbic commentator on public affairs. In 1817, he made the acquaintance of Jeanette Wohl, a woman of lively cultural and political interests who was to be his friend and encourager for the rest of his life. In the following year, he converted to Protestantism and was baptized as Carl Ludwig Börne. Immediately thereafter, he began to publish an irregularly appearing periodical, *Die Wage: Eine Zeitschrift für Bürgerleben, Wissenschaft, und Kunst* (1818–20; The Scale: A Journal for Civic Life, Learning, and Art). This was the first of several efforts to create a medium for progressive ideas; the periodical was constantly hounded by the increasingly strict censorship of the times, but Börne countered that censorship with such agility that he sometimes drove the censors quite crazy. Since direct political commentary was not permissible, he coded many of his arguments in theater reviews and drama criticism. He was not much interested in the theater, which had become a kind of circus that substituted for a public sphere and that generated gossip about stars; he employed this empty discourse as a pretext for allusions to the misrule of the age and used a slashing wit that became a stylistic model for a whole oppositional generation. His ability to talk about one thing while discoursing about another became quite refined. For example, his popular *Monographie der deutschen Postschnecke* (1821; Monograph on the German Mail Snail) reads as an amusing account of the tedium of a stagecoach journey, but it is actually about the backwardness and immobility of the oppressed German states. He was demanding about the responsibility of writers and intellectuals to apply their expressive skills to the cause of freedom; he grew particularly acrimonious about Goethe's failure to do this, charging that the author had withdrawn into aesthetic indifference. Börne also dismissed Schiller, who was regarded by many as the poet of freedom, as an irrelevant philistine.

Börne edited various newspapers one after the other in a struggle with the censorship; having visited Paris in 1819, he was arrested in the following year but released for lack of evidence. He returned to Paris, publishing a series of reports in Baron Johann Friedrich von Cotta's *Morgenblatt für gebildete Stände* (Morning Paper for Educated Classes) from 1822 to 1824. The skill of his pen even attracted the interest of Metternich; Börne horrified his father by refusing to have anything to do with this opportunity for advancement among the powerful. In 1828, he moved for a time to Berlin; in the following year he made the acquaintance of Heine's publisher, Julius Campe, who began publishing Börne's collected works. Soon after the French revolution of 1830, he moved to Paris, where he was to live for the rest of his life. There, he wrote a series of *Briefe aus Paris* (1831–34; Letters from Paris), which eventually reached six volumes; he also came to be sarcastically critical of the July Monarchy and ever more of a republican, commenting ferociously on the oppressive conditions in Germany as well. Further, he published political and cultural commentary in French periodicals. For a working-class readership, he translated into German the protosocialist tract of the defrocked radical priest Félicité de Lamennais, *Paroles d'un croyant* (1834; *Words of a Believer*). When Heine and the Young Germans were banned in 1835, Börne was left out of the decree, probably because he could not have been charged, as the others were, with lasciviousness and blasphemy. Nevertheless, he savaged the critic Wolfgang Menzel, recently turned reactionary and anti-Semitic, who was regarded as the instigator of the ban, with a last polemic, *Menzel der Franzosenfresser* (1837; Menzel the French-Eater).

He became, if anything, more famous posthumously than he had been during his lifetime. He figured as a model and inspiration for a whole generation of liberals and dissidents, the majority of whom esteemed him above Heine on grounds of character and fidelity. Börne and Heine had got along reasonably well before 1830, and Börne hoped that Heine would be his ally and collaborator when he came to Paris. But Heine brushed him off, regarding him as a puritanical and untimely radical and laughing at both his revolutionary expectations and his entourage of petty-bourgeois artisans and working men. Börne, in turn, criticized Heine in print as a dandy and aesthete who was betraying the progressive cause. Three years after Börne's death, in 1840, Heine struck back with an ingenious but ill-considered book, asserting his superior vision along with indecorous, wholly fabricated insinuations concerning Börne's relationship to Jeanette Wohl and her husband. The book damaged Heine's standing with his public for a long time. With the rehabilitation of Heine after World War II, however, the judgment was reversed; critics began to accept Heine's estimate of his superior revolutionary vision and a repressive, myopic Börne, whose reputation went into eclipse. Conversely, in more recent years, a fairer and discriminating view of Börne has begun to emerge, and he may yet regain his seat among the German champions of liberty and equality.

JEFFREY L. SAMMONS

Biography

Born in Frankfurt am Main, ?6 May 1786. Studied medicine, University of Halle, 1804–6, and administrative science, University of Heidelberg, 1807–8, and University of Giessen, 1808; Dr. Phil. Police official, Frankfurt, 1811–15; editor, essayist, and journalist, Frankfurt, 1818–21, Paris, 1822–24, Frankfurt and Berlin, 1824–30, and Paris, 1830–37. Died in Paris, 12 February 1837.

Selected Works

Collections
Gesammelte Schriften, 8 vols., 1829–34
Gesammelte Schriften, 17 vols., 1835–47
Nachgelassene Schriften, 6 vols., 1844–50
Sämtliche Schriften, edited by Inge and Peter Rippmann, 5 vols., 1964–68

Essays and Reportage
Für die Juden, 1816
Der ewige Jude, 1821
Denkrede auf Jean Paul, 1826
Briefe aus Paris, 1831–34
Menzel der Franzosenfresser, 1837
Ludwig Börne's Urtheil über H. Heine: Ungedruckte Stellen aus den Pariser Briefen, edited by Jeanette Wohl, 1840

Translation
Worte des Glaubens von Abbé de La Mennais, 1834

Further Reading

Anderson, Mark, "Ludwig Börne Begins His Professional Career as a Freelance German Journalist and Editor of *Die Wage,*" in *Yale Companion to Jewish Writing and Thought in German Culture 1096–1996,* edited by Sander L. Gilman and Jack Zipes, New Haven, Connecticut and London: Yale University Press, 1997
Bock, Helmut, *Ludwig Börne: Vom Gettojuden zum Nationalschriftsteller,* Berlin: Rütten und Loening, 1962
Estermann, Alfred, editor, *Ludwig Börne, 1786–1837,* Frankfurt: Buchhändler-Vereinigung, 1986
Gesellschaft der Freunde der Stadt- und Universitätsbibliothek Frankfurt am Main, *Ludwig Börne und Frankfurt am Main: Vorträge zur zweihundertsten Wiederkehr seines Geburtstages am 6. Mai 1986,* Frankfurt: Klostermann, 1987
Hardin, James, "Ludwig Börne," in *German Writers in the Age of Goethe, 1789–1832,* Dictionary of Literary Biography, edited by James Hardin and Christoph E. Schweitzer, vol. 90, Detroit, Michigan: Gale Research, 1989
Hinderer, Walter, "Ludwig Börne, der Apostel der Freiheit," in *Über deutsche Literatur und Rede,* Munich: Fink, 1981
Jasper, Willi, *Keinem Vaterland geboren: Ludwig Börne, Eine Biographie,* Hamburg: Hoffmann und Campe, 1989
Labuhn, Wolfgang, "Ludwig Börne als politischer Publizist, 1818–1837," in *Juden im Vormärz und in der Revolution von 1848,* edited by Walter Grab, et al., Stuttgart: Burg, 1983
Marcuse, Ludwig, *Revolutionär und Patriot: Das Leben Ludwig Börnes,* Leipzig: List, 1929; as *Börne: Aus der Frühzeit der deutschen Demokratie,* Rothenburg ob der Tauber: Peter, 1968
Oellers, Norbert, "Ludwig Börne," in *Deutsche Dichter des 19. Jahrhunderts,* edited by Benno von Wiese, Berlin: Schmidt, 1969
Oesterle, Ingrid, "Bewegung und Metropole: Ludwig Börne, 'der gegenwärtigste aller Menschen, die sich je in den Straßen von Paris herumgetrieben haben?'" in *Vormärzliteratur in europäischer Perspektive,* vol. 2, edited by Martina Lauster and Günter Oesterle, Bielefeld: Aisthesis, 1998
Rippmann, Inge, and Wolfgang Labuhn, editors, *"Die Kunst — eine Tochter der Zeit": Neue Studien zu Ludwig Börne,* Bielefeld: Aisthesis, 1988

Bourgeois Tragedy

Traditional heroic tragedy, advocated primarily in Germany by Johann Christoph Gottsched, who believed that German theater should imitate French classicism and provided a model in his *Der sterbende Cato* (1732; Cato Dying), did not grant the bourgeoisie representation on the stage. Heroic tragedy was concerned with the fate and struggles of kings and heroes; the conflicts experienced by the middle class in its daily life were left to comedy. Gradually, however, as the middle class gained economic strength and became the primary consumer of art, a change occurred. Bourgeois writers began to treat the moral principles and conflicts of the newly self-confident middle class in a serious manner, as tragedy rather than as comedy.

Precursors of the *bürgerliches Trauerspiel,* or bourgeois tragedy (sometimes translated as domestic tragedy) were Andreas Gryphius's *Cardenio und Celinde* (1648; Cardenio and Celinde) and the prose, lyrics, and drama of the educator Christian Weise. His didactic drama *Der gründenden Jugend überflüssige Gedanken* (1668; Superfluous Thoughts of Flourishing Youths), for example, was concerned with moral and practical education. These dramas, however, had no emulators until the middle of the 18th century.

By this time, dramas were being written in England and France that had a commanding impact on the German theater. Pierre de Marivaux and Philippe Destouches wrote "serious comedy" (*comédie larmoynate* [tearful], *comédie psychologique*). In Germany, the genre was adopted by Christian Fürchtegott Gellert, whose *weinerliche Lustspiele* (tearful comedies [the term is Lessing's]), *Die Betschwester* (1745; *The Prayer Sister*), *Das Los in der Lotterie* (1746; The Ticket in the Lottery), and *Die zärtlichen Schwestern* (1947; *Tender Sisters*) were precursors of German bourgeois drama. Developments in France led to the theory and practice of Denis Diderot, who challenged "eternal aesthetic verities" and argued that drama should be realistic and have psychological depth. According to Diderot, characters on the stage in the new *tragédie domestique et bourgeoise* should be representatives of the middle class. Diderot's *Le fils naturel* (1757; The Natural Son) and *Pére de famille* (1758; *The Father*), written after the publication of Germany's first bourgeois tragedy, *Miß Sara Sampson* (1755; *Miss Sara Sampson*), were translated into German by *Sara*'s author, Gotthold Ephraim Lessing. That the development toward bourgeois tragedy was a European phenomenon, with writers greatly interested in each others' work, is further evidenced by the fact that Diderot translated Lessing's *Sara* into French.

Meanwhile, from across the channel, new currents affected Germany. Already in 1731, George Lillo had written a play that was completely opposed to the fashionable drama in London. *The London Merchant; or, the History of George Barnwell* is a prose tragedy with a domestic setting. Derived from an old ballad, it tells the story of George Barnwell, and honest and hard-working businessman who falls prey to a representative of dissipated and decadent "high" society. He is seduced by Millwood and commits robbery—he steals from his employer—at her instigation. His death on the gallows is almost that of a martyr.

Barnwell, who represents bourgeois values of hard work, honesty, virtue, and sensitivity, falls because of the scheming and manipulative Millwood. A critique of the dissipated upper classes and a celebration of bourgeois values are exemplified in this play. It is generally believed that this drama was the primary influence on Lessing, although a case can be made that inspiration also came from proto-bourgeois dramas such as Thomas Shadwell's *The Squire of Alsatia* (1688), Susannah Centlivre's *The Perjur'd Husband* (1700), and Charles Johnson's *Caelia* (1733). The sentimental novels of Samuel Richardson were also influential on the continent. *Pamela* (1740) and *Clarissa Harlowe* (1749) were translated into numerous languages and found avid readers in Germany. In these complicated and emotional novels, Richardson outlines new paradigms for family relationships, for interactions between men and women and husbands and wives. Dispensing with the marriage of convenience, marriage is henceforth to be based on love and friendship. This required an entirely new attitude toward the family. In this new social vision, the bourgeois male negotiates a "sexual contract" with the bourgeois female in which the wife subordinates herself to the husband in economic and political matters and stays out of the public sphere but is put in charge of the emotional well-being of the family in the private sphere.

The greater self-confidence of England's middle class permitted bourgeois tragedy to develop earlier than in Germany. In Germany, one cannot really speak of a self-aware and self-conscious bourgeois culture, and a concentration of bourgeois writers and artists, until the middle of the 18th century. Lessing's *Miss Sara Sampson* was immediately well received on the German stage, and until 1772 it found many imitators, but it was later superseded by other bourgeois tragedies, particularly by Lessing's *Emilia Galotti.* As his setting for this first attempt at a drama consciously directed at the middle class, Lessing chose England, which became a metaphor for democracy and liberty in many other 18th-century German texts.

Central to the genre is the father-daughter relationship. The patriarchal father adores his daughter and engages in a life and death struggle with an aristocratic seducer who is determined to wrest his daughter away from him. The seducer is either villainous or less so but is always portrayed as self-indulgent and weak. The virtuous daughter, torn between love for her father and for her lover, is destroyed in the ensuing struggle for her possession. The mother, if one appears in the play, is portrayed as frivolous and foolish, particularly from the father's point of view, because she does not reject the aristocrat's advances toward her daughter.

The dramas also feature an aristocratic female competitor for the aristocrat's affections and a villainous bourgeois male rival for the daughter. Not all of the characters in a bourgeois tragedy are members of the middle class, but the values under consideration are, so the plays focus on the increasingly emotional and sentimental relations of the evolving bourgeois (nuclear) family.

Structurally, bourgeois tragedy retained many features of classical drama. Lessing believed that a drama should consist of one carefully interconnected action. Unlike Aristotle, however, Lessing placed emphasis on the dramatic hero, not on the action. Here he was innovative because he argued for a mixed dramatic figure, one representing an individual who was neither completely good nor completely evil—in other words, a character with whom the bourgeois audience could identify. Lessing also favored a more "natural" language than that preferred by classical tragedy. He discussed his theory of tragedy in his *Briefe, die neueste Literatur betreffend* (1759–65; Letters Concerning the Newest Literature) and his *Hamburgische Dramaturgie* (1767–69; *Hamburg Dramaturgy*).

The plot of *Miss Sara Sampson,* which premiered in Frankfurt an der Oder in 1775, already encompasses all of the stock characters of bourgeois tragedy. Mellefont, who has seduced Sara Sampson, takes her to the countryside, where the couple spends nine weeks at an inn. Even though Mellefont professes to love Sara, he is not eager to marry, because from his aristocratic perspective marriage would destroy romantic love. This is an impossible situation for the bourgeois Sara, who falls ill and languishes in bed. Mellefont's former lover, Marwood, appears and brings along their daughter Arabella. She has also alerted Sara's father, Sir William Sampson, to his daughter's whereabouts. It is Marwood's distinct purpose to regain Mellefont for herself. Mellefont swears that he will never return to Marwood, but he fails to prevent her from having the personal meeting with Sara that she insists upon. During this encounter, Marwood reveals her identity and mixes poison into Sara's medication. Sir William, who has forgiven Sara, enters as she lies dying. The generous Sara forgives Marwood. Mellefont is so moved by Sir William's and Sara's generosity that he is neither able to forgive himself nor accept Sir William's offer to accept him as a son. Mellefont commits suicide, and Sir William accepts responsibility for the care of Arabella.

The plot of Lessing's more famous and influential bourgeois tragedy, *Emilia Galotti* (1772), is more complex inasmuch as it not only delineates newly emerging family relations but more precisely addresses the growing conflict between the bourgeoisie and the aristocracy. It is partially based on a frequently dramatized motif that originated with the Roman historian Livius, who writes of the Roman citizen Virginius killing his young and innocent daughter Virginia in order to save her from the pursuits of Appius Claudius. Premiered in Brunswick in 1772, the play is set in Italy, giving Lessing an opportunity to criticize severely an aristocratic ruler without risking censorship. In the play, the prince of Gustalla, a frivolous and self-indulgent young man, falls in love with the portrait of Emilia, who is about to be married. He attempts to delay the marriage by offering to send the bridegroom, Count Appiani, abroad. The young man, who shares the dislike of Emilia's father, Odoardo, for the court, declines the offer and the marriage plans proceed. The prince now relies on the assistance of his scheming and ignoble chamberlain, Marinelli, who plots to have Emilia kidnapped on her way to the country. During the kidnapping, Appiani is killed and Emilia is taken to the prince's pleasure palace, the castle Dosalo. Gradually, all of the principal characters gather at the castle. The first to arrive is Emilia's distraught mother, who had been responsible for Emilia's exposure to life and education in the city, over the objection of the father. Then a furious Odoardo appears, followed shortly thereafter by the furious former lover of the prince, Countess Orsina. The countess carries a dagger, with which she hopes Odoardo will kill the prince. Instead, Odoardo kills his daughter.

Emilia Galotti and Schiller's *Kabale und Liebe* (*Intrigue and Love;* original title, *Luise Millerin,* premiered 12 years later in 1784 in Frankfurt), are the 18th-century's most significant bourgeois tragedies. Schiller's play is again concerned with both political and familial situations. The poor musician Miller is devoted to his daughter Luise and concerned about her romantic involvement (largely welcomed by his wife but not by him) with Ferdinand, the son of the president. As the action unfolds, Luise's predicament, her loyalty to her father, and her new loyalty to her lover are particularly developed. Ultimately, she chooses her family. After her parents have been jailed by Ferdinand's father, who wants him to marry Lady Milford and not the bourgeois Luise, Luise is told by the villainous presidential secretary Wurm that she can save her parents only by writing a love letter to the Lord Chamberlain von Kalb. Wurm, who has his own designs on the young woman, forces Luise to swear that the letter is hers. This intrigue, designed to prevent Ferdinand's marriage to Luise, ends in death. Ferdinand accuses her of betrayal, and Luise, who has sworn an oath, does not defend herself. Ferdinand poisons her, and only when she realizes she is dying, does she reveal the truth. The theme of forgiveness, familiar from *Sara Sampson,* here reasserts itself. Luise forgives Ferdinand who, as he also dies, forgives his father. Giuseppe Verdi based his 1849 opera *Luise Miller* on this drama.

There are numerous lesser known 18th-century bourgeois tragedies, some of which deserve mention. Kristiane Karoline Schlegel's *Düval und Charmille* (1778) and Johann Gottlob Benjamin Pfeil's *Lucie Woodvil* (1756) are essentially plays about gender relations. Their authors are extremely critical of bourgeois morality and depict the damage caused by male libertinism. The wife in *Düval,* the fiancée in *Lucie,* and the inamoratas of the men involved suffer because of male unfaithfulness. The women are not self-assured aristocrats but bourgeois women who already in these early depictions of family life are enmeshed in the well-known double standard for male and female sexual behavior. The new concepts of sentimental or erotic love, a pressing topic at a time when the marriage of convenience was rapidly falling into disfavor, also appear in Eleonore Thon's *Adelheit von Rastenberg* (1788) and Sophie Albrecht's *Theresgen* (1791). In the latter play, the heroine drowns herself because she is in love with Count Adolf but has been ordered by her father to marry her middle-class suitor.

The conventional plot structure of bourgeois tragedy—seduction of the bourgeois daughter by an aristocrat, raging anger by her overly protective father, and the death of the daughter—undergoes a transformation in several Sturm und Drang (Storm and Stress) dramas. Most prominent of these plays are Jakob Michael Reinhold Lenz's *Der Hofmeister* (1774; *The Tutor*) and *Die Soldaten* (1776; *The Soldiers*) and Heinrich Leopold Wagner's *Die Kindsmörderin* (1776; The Child Murderess). In these dramas, which feature themes and characters similar to those in bourgeois tragedy, the central female characters do not do not die and fathers and daughters are reconciled. Women, who have largely disappeared in traditional bourgeois tragedy, remain a part of the family, although, as in *The Tutor,* it turns out to be a patched up family rather than the harmonious, sentimental one envisioned by bourgeois ideology.

Two further late 18th-century bourgeois tragedies that avoid tragic outcomes are Victoria von Rupp's *Jenny; oder, Die Uneingennützigkeit* (1777; Jenny; or, Unselfishness) and Marianne Ehrmann's *Leichtsinn und gutes Herz; oder, Die Folgen der Erziehung* (1786; Frivolity and a Good Heart; or, The Consequences of Education). Ehrmann shares Sturm und Drang preoccupations with social reform, and sometimes its style. Her bourgeois heroine, Lottchen, believes social rank to be an accident of birth and, without anyone's guidance or assistance, insists that the count, who seduced her, marry her, which he does.

The last well-known German bourgeois tragedy is Friedrich Hebbel's *Maria Magdalena* (1843). Here, the action takes place in a completely bourgeois world, although social status does become an issue. Hebbel depicts the middle class as hypocritical and intolerant, particularly in the figure of the self-righteous father, whose rigid attitudes destroy his daughter and his son. After this, the term *bürgerliches Trauerspiel* begins to fall out of use, to be replaced by social drama.

Scholarly interpretations of bourgeois tragedy are manifold. One conventional reading of the genre suggests that it represents the politically impotent bourgeoisie's literary, cultural, moral, and political attack on the aristocracy. The new cultural production of the bourgeoisie, focusing largely on itself, is seen as a declaration by the middle class that it will no longer tolerate aristocratic oppression. The destructive nature of strict class boundaries is illustrated by the death of the bourgeois heroine. A related political reading, particularly of Lessing's *Emilia Galotti,* which is the most frequently interpreted bourgeois tragedy, suggests that Lessing is also criticizing the bourgeoisie for its passivity vis à vis the aristocracy. Odoardo's dagger, intended for the prince, is turned against his own daughter because he finds himself incapable of raising his hand against the ruler. The association in the bourgeois mind between God and secular rulers is a factor here. In addition to political interpretations and, of course, formal interpretations as the locus classicus of bourgeois tragedy, *Emilia* has seen numerous psychological, sociological, and religious interpretations. Emilia's guilt is the major preoccupation: why she has to die is the most frequently asked question. One answer is that Emilia recognizes that she is capable of letting herself be seduced and chooses death over moral culpability. As it gained economic and cultural, if not political, power, the middle class sought to differentiate its identity from that of the aristocracy. Middle-class values and ideology placed primary emphasis on moral virtue and particularly stressed the sexual purity of bourgeois women. The middle class regarded itself superior to the aristocracy in the moral realm. Emilia's action, her choice of death to avoid moral and sexual transgressions, distinguishes her as an ideal bourgeois woman.

More recent interpretations of bourgeois tragedy focus on family structure and gender relations. The majority of scholars argue that bourgeois tragedy reinforces existing yet changing patriarchal structures. In these plays, the bourgeois male, himself uncertain about his public identity because of his lack of a political voice, assumes an increasingly powerful role in the family. The new "sentimental family father" absorbs the mother inasmuch as he also becomes the emotional center of the family. The father's love, however, is tyrannical, self-serving, and oppressive. Dissenting opinions hold that the genre depicts a patriarchy in crisis rather than one in the process of being reconfirmed and therefore presents sentimental bourgeois fathers, who compensate for their lack of a public role by taking control of the practical and the emotional life of their families.

A growing number of scholars are becoming interested in bourgeois tragedy's representation of mothers, and several fine studies have been written on this topic. In bourgeois tragedy, the mother is either absent—that is, she has died before the action begins, as in *Miss Sara Sampson*—or she is represented as shallow, thoughtless, and even stupid, as in *Emilia Galotti* and *Intrigue and Love.* A number of scholarly explanations have been given for the mother's "absence" and her insignificant role in the plot in addition to the argument that the father is usurping the emotional realm. For instance, some have argued that mothers and daughters are eliminated to preserve sole male control over the terms of culture and subject formation. For the masculine imagination, in this critical view, mothers and their bodies (and daughters capable of becoming mothers) represent disorder and are a threat to culture and its ideal of a unified, autonomous, and rational male subjectivity. Women are therefore repressed; only men, the foundation of family renewal, and sometimes girls such as Arabella in *Sara Sampson,* who will be educated by Sir William and his male servant, remain. Sole control by men over the education of their children is also given as a reason for the absence of mothers. Another is the diminished social status assigned to housewives and mothers. An argument could also be made that, because mothers in bourgeois tragedy promote their daughters' possible marriages to aristocrats and prefer life in the city and court to being relegated to the house, they resist the new passive domestic roles designed for women by patriarchal society and therefore must be eliminated to make room for the new bourgeois woman, the figure later idealized as the angel in the house.

Hebbel's *Maria Magdalena,* with which the genre comes to its conclusion, portrays a failed bourgeois family. The mother, irrelevant to the socialization of her children, worships her son, rejects her daughter, and retreats into religion. Mother and daughter die, the son leaves, and unlike 18th-century bourgeois tragedy where the spectator is included to sympathize with the father, no one feels sympathy for this father, who is left alone.

Another contemporary approach to bourgeois tragedy is the reevaluation, mostly by feminist scholars, of the *Machtweib.* The term, which means "power(ful) woman," has conventionally been assigned to Marwood, Orsina, possibly Lady Milford, although her character becomes transformed, and similar figures in 18th-century German drama. Traditionally, the *Machtweib* has been interpreted very negatively, as the representation of irrationality and chaos. More recent scholarship focuses on the intelligence, independence, and willingness to act of these female characters. The aristocratic *Machtweib* is an "uppity woman"; she belongs to the social class that mothers in bourgeois tragedy crave for their daughters. This figure's negative representation and interpretation is undoubtedly linked to the mother's absence from that genre.

Bourgeois tragedy continues to be read and studied because, as the first genre devoted to the middle class, it represents a new aesthetic, one that challenges the norms of classical heroic tragedy. At the same time, it illuminates bourgeois problems and values. Its juxtaposed depiction of political conflicts with domestic life allows for a broad range of interpretations, which reflect changing historical conditions and scholarly preoccupations. Many of the plays, particularly *Emilia Galotti* and *Intrigue and Love,* are regularly performed in Germany, where they are produced in both conventional and experimental versions.

HELGA STIPA MADLAND

See also Gotthold-Ephraim Lessing

Further Reading

Barry, Thomas F., "Love and the Politics of Paternalism: Images of the Father in Schiller's *Kabale und Liebe,*" *Colloquia Germanica* 22, no. 1 (1989)

Brown, Francis Andrew, *G.E. Lessing,* New York: Twayne, 1971

Daunicht, Richard, *Die Entstehung des bürgerlichen Trauerspiels in Deutschland,* Berlin: de Gruyter, 1963; 2nd edition, 1965

Gustafson, Susan E., *Absent Mothers and Orphaned Fathers: Narcissism and Abjection in Lessing's Aesthetic and Dramatic Production,* Detroit, Michigan: Wayne State University Press, 1995

Guthke, Karl Siegfried, *Das deutsche bürgerliche Trauerspiel,* Stuttgart: Metzler, 1972; 5th edition, 1994

Hart, Gail Kathleen, *Tragedy in Paradise: Family and Gender Politics in German Bourgeouis Tragedy 1750–1850,* Columbia, South Carolina: Camden House, 1996

Jonnes, Dennis, "Solche Wäter: The Sentimental Family Paradigm in Lessing's Drama," *Lessing Yearbook* 12 (1980)

Mathäs, Alexander, "Between Self-Assertion and Self-Denial: Gender and Ideology in Eighteenth-Century Domestic Tragedy," *Lessing Yearbook* 27 (1995)
McInnes, Edward, "Maria Magdalena and the Bürgerliches Trauerspiel," *Orbis Litterarum* 28 (1973)
——, "'Eine bürgerliche Virginia?' Lessing's *Emilia Galotti* and the Development of the Bürgerliches Trauerspiel," *Orbis Litteratum* 39, no. 4 (1984)
Mönch, Cornelia, *Abschrecken oder Mitleiden: Das deutsche bürgerliche Trauerspiel im 18. Jahrhundert: Versuch einer Typologie,* Tübingen: Niemeyer, 1993
Prutti, Brigitte, "*Coup de Théatre—Coup de Femme* or: What is Lessing's Emilia Galotti Dying From?" *Lessing Yearbook* 26 (1994)
Saße, Günter, *Die aufgeklärte Familie: Untersuchungen zur Genese, Funktion, und Realitätsbezogenheit des familialen Wertsystems im Drama der Aufklärung,* Tübingen: Niemeyer, 1988
Sharpe, Lesley, *Friedrich Schiller: Drama, Thought, and Politics,* Cambridge and New York: Cambridge University Press, 1991
Sørensen, Bengt Algot, *Herrschaft und Zärtlichkeit: Der Patriarchalismus und das Drama im 18. Jahrhundert,* Munich: Beck, 1984
Stephan, Inge, "'So ist die Tugend ein Gespenst': Frauenbild und Tugendbegriff im bürgerlichen Trauerspiel bei Lessing und Schiller," *Lessing Yearbook* 17 (1985)
Szondi, Peter, *Die Theorie des bürgerlishen Trauerspiels im 18. Jahrhundert,* Frankfurt: Suhrkamp, 1973; 4th edition, 1979
Walsøe-Engel, Ingrid, *Fathers and Daughters: Patterns of Seduction in Tragedies by Gryphius, Lessing, Hebbel, and Kroetz,* Columbia, South Carolina: Camden House, 1993
Wurst, Karin A., *Familiale Liebe ist die 'wahre Gewalt': Die Repräsentation der Familie in G.E. Lessings Dramatischem Werk,* Amsterdam: Rodopi, 1988
——, "Abwesenheit-Schweigen-Tötung: Die Möglichkeit der Frau? Lessings Funktionalisierung literarischer Klischees," *Orbis Litteratum* 45 (1990)

Sebastian Brant 1457–1521

Sebastian Brant spent nearly all of his life in either Strasbourg or Basle, two cities that, during this period, combined strong ecclesiastical and mercantile traditions with an openness to the spirit of intellectual inquiry and moral renewal that characterized German Christian Humanism. Brant himself was closely involved with humanist culture, not least through his associations with the relatively new University of Basle (founded in 1460), the distinguished scholar Jakob Wimpfeling and preacher Johann Geiler von Kaysersberg in Strasbourg, and the leading printers of both towns.

His own career was exceptionally varied. He was a lawyer, academic, local politician, and imperial adviser, as well as being an important literary figure in the broadest sense of the term. He worked as an editor for numerous printers, selecting works for publication, providing introductory or elucidative material as required, and frequently supervising the work of illustrators. He translated into German a number of Latin works, principally of a religious or didactic character; and he was comparably prominent as a publicist who issued broadsheets in both Latin and German on subjects ranging from legal, political, and moral questions to the most sensational happenings of his day. In his capacity of town clerk of Strasbourg, Brant was also responsible for some noted historical writings, in which pride in his region and in the empire as a whole is much in evidence. He was, moreover, a celebrated writer on jurisprudence, evincing a particular interest in Roman law and a desire for its propagation. Last but not least, he was a lyric poet, composing Latin verse on a variety of religious subjects, as well as eulogies of past heroes, his own friends, and—inevitably, given both his nationalistic bent and his personal acquaintance with the emperor—Maximilian I.

In spite of these multifarious activities, however, Brant is known today almost exclusively as the author of *Das Narrenschiff* (*The Ship of Fools*), a didactic-satirical poem in German verse, which first appeared in 1494. *The Ship of Fools* is divided into some 112 short chapters, in which Brant excoriates countless manifestations of folly that he believed to be prevalent in his day. These range from the superficially trivial (such as dancing, hunting, behaving inappropriately in church, and following the latest sartorial fashions) through the unequivocally sinful (such as lust, avarice, and the other Deadly Sins) to the downright unpardonable (such as heresy, suicide, and the murder of children). All of Brant's many fools do, however, share certain common characteristics: they behave selfishly, compulsively, immoderately, and without regard for their eternal destiny; and they do this above all because they do not truly know themselves.

Accurate self-knowledge is, in Brant's eyes, the key to overcoming folly, and it is specifically such self-knowledge that *The Ship of Fools* sets out to promote. At the beginning and end of the work, Brant likens his work to a mirror into which a fool may look, recognize himself, and, as a consequence, be empowered to amend his life.

This mirror can, in principle, also be used by illiterate fools. Each chapter of *The Ship of Fools* is illustrated by a substantial woodcut, and Brant implies in his prologue that the essence of the work as a whole may be culled by perusing these woodcuts alone. Certainly they are of generally excellent quality (probably more than half are by the young Albrecht Dürer), and they often reinforce both tellingly and entertainingly the didactic message of the chapters they accompany. This is far from invariably the case, however (for instance, some seven woodcuts are used to illustrate more than one chapter); ultimately, one suspects that Brant's claim that the woodcuts alone suffice for the communication of his message was no more than a pious (or disingenuous) hope.

Nevertheless, the presence of lively woodcuts, along with the simplicity of the work's language, was no doubt one of the reasons why, in Brant's lifetime and throughout the 16th century, *The Ship of Fools* met with extraordinary success in terms of both sales and influence—indeed, it has become something of a scholarly commonplace to hail it as the most successful book in

German before Goethe's *Werther.* Some 16 German editions of Brant's poem had appeared by 1519, and it was translated into Latin (by Jakob Locher) in 1497, and then from the Latin into French, Dutch, and English (the versions of Alexander Barclay and Henry Watson both date from 1509). Moreover, *The Ship of Fools* was used or imitated by such diverse authors as Johann Geiler von Kayserberg, Thomas Murner, Erasmus of Rotterdam, Hermann Bote, and Hans Sachs, and it can be said to have initiated a whole new genre of "folly literature."

Many of its modern readers, however, have charged the poem with mediocrity of content and incoherence of form and thus have found its success difficult to comprehend. A series of influential studies by Ulrich Gaier has suggested that this view may be attributable, at least in part, to modern readers' failure to recognize various structural patterns and rhetorical techniques characteristic of ancient Roman satire, which were more easily discerned and appreciated by Brant's humanist contemporaries. The gulf that has at times existed between 16th- and 20th-century assessments of the work is, however, surely primarily attributable to the fact that it struck a chord with many of Brant's contemporaries, one that no longer resonates so powerfully today. *The Ship of Fools* was plainly seen as both reflecting and helping to explain the realities of a society in turbulent transition. The poem itself is very much a product of its time, combining as it does late-medieval elements (such as its quintessentially Middle High German verse form, its manifest indebtedness to 15th-century "estates" satires, and its in many respects deeply conservative worldview) with aspects that bespeak the influence of Renaissance humanism (such as its enthusiastic espousal of both classical rhetoric and the Virgilian concept of the wise man and its typically humanist bent toward nationalism and anticlericalism). *The Ship of Fools* does not, however, merely reflect trends present in late 15th- and early 16th-century society, but it also seeks both to diagnose and cure society's ills. These ills, it suggests, can be reduced to a single common denominator, namely folly; and folly, ultimately, is curable. To that extent at least, *The Ship of Fools* is an optimistic, even comforting work; the fact that Brant's nostrum does not involve the Church and its sacraments but rather the acquisition of individual self-knowledge must also have struck his contemporaries as both challenging and liberating.

NIGEL HARRIS

See also Humanism

Biography

Born in Strasbourg, 1457. Baccalaureate in law from the University of Basle, 1477; licenciate 1483–84; lecturer in canon law, civil law, and poetry, University of Basle, 1484–1500; doctor of law, 1489; dean of law faculty, 1492, and professor of Roman and canon law, University of Basle, 1496; returned to Strasbourg, 1500; became legal adviser to city council, 1501, and town clerk, 1503; for most of his career, active as lawyer, editor, and author; from 1502, adviser to Emperor Maximilian I. Died in Strasbourg, 10 May 1521.

Selected Works

German Verse

Das Narrenschiff, 1494; edited by Friedrich Zarncke, 1854; also edited by H.A. Junghans (modern German translation, with interpretative material), 1966, and by Manfred Lemmer, 1968; as *The Ship of Fools of the World,* translated by Alexander Barclay (based on the Latin version by Jakob Locher), 1509; translated by Henry Watson (also based on Locher), 1509; as *The Ship of Fools,* translated by Edwin H. Zeydel, 1944; translated by William Gillis, 1971

Latin Verse

Rosarium ex floribus vitae passionisque domini nostri Jesu Christi consertum, 1492
In laudem gloriose virginis Mariae multorumque sanctorum varii generis carmina, 1494
Varia carmina, 1498

Legal Writing

Expositiones sive declarationes omnium titulorum iuris, 1490

Historical Writing

Uszugk einer Stadt Straszburg alt harchomen und bestetigten freyheiten, 1520
Chronik über Deutschland, zuvor des lands Elsaß und der löblichen statt Straßburg (unfinished, published posthumously)

Other

Von der wunderbaren geburd des kinds bey wurmbs, 1495
Von der wunderlichen zamefügung der öbersten Planeten, 1504
Von dem anfang und Wesen der statt Jerusalem, 1518

Translations

Phagifacetus seu de moribus et facetiis mensae, 1490
Liber faceti, 1496
Disticha Catonis, 1498

Edited Works

St. Augustine, *De civitate Dei,* 1489
St. Ambrose, *Opera,* 1492
Decretum Gratiani, 1493
Christopher Columbus, *De insulis in mari Indico nuper inventis,* 1494
Jakob Locher, *Theologica emphasis,* 1496
Johannes Reuchlin, *Scenica Progymnasmata,* 1498
Der heilgen Leben, 1502
Virgil, *Opera,* 1502
Freidank, *Bescheidenheit,* 1508
Ulrich Tengler, *Layenspiegel,* 1509
Petrarch, *Von der Artzney beyder Glück,* 1532

Further Reading

Bernstein, Eckhard, *German Humanism,* Boston: Twayne, 1983
Fink, Gonthier-Louis, editor, *Sebastian Brant, seine Zeit und "Das Narrenschiff": Actes du Colloque international,* Strasbourg: Université des Sciences Humaines, 1995
Gaier, Ulrich, *Studien zu Sebastian Brants "Narrenschiff,"* Tübingen: Niemeyer, 1966
———, "Sebastian Brant's *Narrenschiff* and the Humanists," *PMLA* 83 (1968)
Könneker, Barbara, "'Eyn wis man sich do heym behalt': Zur Interpretation von Sebastian Brants *Narrenschiff,*" *Germanisch-Romanische Monatsschrift* 45 (1964)
———, *Satire im 16.Jahrhundert: Epoche, Werke, Wirkungt,* Munich: Beck, 1991
Manger, Klaus, *"Das Narrenschiff": Entstehung, Wirkung, und Deutung,* Darmstadt: Wissenschaftliche Buchgesellschaft, 1983
Van Cleve, John, *The Problem of Wealth in the Literature of Luther's Germany,* Columbia, South Carolina: Camden House, 1991
———, *Sebastian Brant's "The Ship of Fools" in Critical Perspective, 1800–1991,* Columbia, South Carolina: Camden House, 1993

Volker Braun 1939–

Volker Braun has a place at the forefront of the "middle generation" of writers who first came to prominence in the German Democratic Republic (GDR) in the 1960s. These writers replaced the literature written in exile by former émigrés from Nazi Germany and the largely undistinguished works of socialist realism that characterized the previous decade with texts that established the distinctive new voice of a literature rooted in GDR experiences. Whether in his poetry, prose, drama, or theoretical statements, Braun's work expresses the excitement, the frustration, and—ultimately—the deep disappointment of participating in an experiment in socialism that was to fail. Although always loyal to the GDR, he became a thorn in the side of officialdom through his increasingly radical criticism of the yawning gap between socialist ideals and GDR reality. Consequently, publication of his work was frequently delayed by the censor, sometimes for many years.

The early work (1959–74) demonstrates a firm commitment to the GDR, but this is by no means uncritical. Although his first volume of poetry, *Provokation für mich* (1965; Provocations for Me), expresses youthful enthusiasm for the construction of socialism, his impatience at the shortcomings in the process is already clear. Similarly, the play *Die Kipper* (written in 1965; first performed and published in 1972; The Tippers) and the prose texts in *Das ungezwungne Leben Kasts* (1972; Kast's Unconstrained Life) focus on problems inherent in socialist production and socialist democracy. Braun's belief that literature must involve itself in the political process rather than pursue the illusion of autonomy is argued in "Politik und Poesie" (1971; Politics and Poetry).

From the early 1970s, Braun became palpably disillusioned with the GDR's "really existing socialism." This is evident in prose works such as *Unvollendete Geschichte* (1977; Unfinished Story) and *Hinze-Kunze-Roman* (1985; Hinze-Kunze-Novel), both of which had particular difficulties passing the censor. At the same time his concerns widened perceptibly to embrace not only the problems of socialism generally (as reflected in plays on historical themes focusing on problems of the socialist revolution such as *Großer Frieden* [1976; first performed in 1979; *The Great Peace*]) but also global issues such as the ecological crisis. He remained loyal, however, to an ideal of socialism that showed striking similarities to the ideas of Ernst Bloch and Rudolf Bahro. His play *Die Übergangsgesellschaft* (1988; The Society in Transition) follows Bloch in debating the nature of socialism by working with the conflicting concepts of order and freedom. The play's preoccupation with the theme of "crossing the border" marks a decisive stage in Braun's gradual but inevitable break with "really existing socialism" and its ossified ideology. Disillusioned by the development of socialism in the GDR, his work on the history of the socialist revolution in the Soviet Union, and the ecological devastation caused by technological civilization, he began to see history not as following an ascertainable and definable pattern but as a process that is open and unknowable in advance.

At the beginning of the 1980s, Braun became the target of a new generation of GDR poets, who criticized him as a representative of those writers who, despite their disaffection with "really existing socialism," continued to espouse the socialist ideal of undogmatic Marxism. This conflict coincided with Braun's reassessment of his position through an intensive engagement with the life and work of Rimbaud. The result was *Rimbaud: Ein Psalm der Aktualität* (1984; *Rimbaud: A Topical Psalm*), a key work in which Braun developed a new approach to literature based on the primary importance of the author's own subjectivity. Breaking radically with the increasingly discredited aesthetics of official GDR discourse, he embraced modernism, which had long been rejected in the GDR as an expression of Western decadence and alienation. Intertextuality now became a key feature of his work as, influenced by Peter Weiss, he developed a new "poetics of resistance" (Grauert) in the name of emancipated labor, emancipated sexual relations, and democracy. The poem "Das innerste Afrika" (1984; "The Innermost Africa") represents the first and perhaps most striking example of this new direction in Braun's writing.

From the early 1980s, the main impulse behind his work increasingly became a critique not just of socialism but of the destructive direction taken by modern technological civilization, which he saw as a threat to the very survival of the human species. With its unsparing exposure of the shortsighted industrial policy that sacrificed a village and its natural landscape to the supposed requirements of technologically advanced socialism, *Bodenloser Satz* (1988; Bottomless Sentence) represented a fundamental critique of the failure of GDR socialism, and it has been widely seen as an anticipation of the GDR's demise.

Braun shared the keen disappointment of many German literary intellectuals at the collapse of the GDR, and his poem "Das Eigentum" ("The Property") has become a classic expression of that widely shared reaction: "Da bin ich noch: mein Land geht in den Westen" (Here I am still: my land has gone west). In his view, the Stalinism of the East had been succeeded by a Western brand, and this meant that it remained literature's duty to offer underground resistance to the arrogance of power. Such resistance to the West's "Stalinism of money" is evident in the prose text *Der Wendehals* (1995; The Turncoat); this text is also, however, an attack on the spineless alacrity with which many from the East caved in to the requirements of capitalism. The text's apparent playfulness of tone, with its insistent exploration of the nature of freedom and genuine experience, barely conceals the underlying sense of despair. The eponymous heroine of the play *Iphigenie in Freiheit* (1992; Iphigenia in Freedom)—a work that deals metaphorically with the end of the GDR and that deplores the effects of Germany's unification—embodies the same melancholy felt by many socialist intellectuals since 1990. A programmatic statement in the important poem "Benjamin in den Pyrenäen" ("Benjamin in the Pyrenees") articulates the implications for Braun's work today: "Ich habe nichts zu sagen. Nur zu zeigen." ("I have nothing to say. Only to show.")

Ian Wallace

Biography

Born in Dresden, 7 May 1939. Studied at the University of Leipzig, 1960–64; worked as machine operator and construction worker; in Siberia, 1964, France, 1971; reader or assistant director for the Berliner Ensemble, 1965–66 and 1977–90, and the Deutsches Theater in Berlin, 1972–77; in Cuba, Peru, and Italy, 1976; in the United Kingdom, 1980;

in China, 1988; in the United States, 1990. Heine Prize, 1971; Heinrich Mann Prize, 1980; Lessing Prize, 1981; City of Bremen Prize, 1986; GDR National Prize, 1988; Berlin Prize, 1989; Schiller Prize, 1992; member of the Academy of Arts, Berlin. Currently lives in Berlin.

Selected Works

Plays

Die Kipper (produced 1972), 1972
Guevara; oder, Der Sonnenstaat (produced 1977), 1977
Großer Frieden (produced 1979), 1976; as *The Great Peace* (produced 1983)
Stücke, 2 vols. (includes *Die Kipper; Hinze und Kunze; Schmitten; Tinka; Guevara oder Der Sonnenstaat; Großer Frieden; Simplex Deutsch; Dimitri; Des Eisenwagen; Lenins Tod; T.; Totleben; Die Übergangsgesellschaft; Siegfried Frauenprotokolle Deutscher Furor; Transit Europa; Der Ausflug der Toten*), 1983–89
Siegfried Frauenprotokolle Deutscher Furor (produced 1986), 1987
Die Übergangsgesellschaft (produced 1987), 1988
Transit Europa (after the novel *Transit* by Anna Seghers) (produced 1988), 1987
Lenins Tod (produced 1988), 1988
Böhmen am Meer (produced 1992), 1992
Iphigenie in Freiheit (produced 1992), 1992

Poetry

Provokation für mich, 1965
Wir und nicht sie, 1970
Gegen die symmetrische Welt, 1974
Training des aufrechten Gangs, 1979
Langsamer knirschender Morgen, 1987
Der Stoff zum Leben 1–3, 1990
Die Zickzackbrücke: Ein Abrißkalender, 1992
Lustgarten. Preußen (Ausgewählte Gedichte), 1996
Tumulus, 1999

Fiction

Das ungezwungne Leben Kasts: Drei Berichte, 1972; enlarged edition, 1979
Unvollendete Geschichte, 1977
Berichte von Hinze und Kunze, 1983
Hinze-Kunze-Roman, 1985
Bodenloser Satz (first published in *Sinn und Form*) 1990
Wie es gekommen ist, 1993
Das Nichtgelebte, 1995
Der Wendehals, 1995
Die vier Werkzeugmacher, 1996
Die Unvollendete Geschichte und ihr Ende, 1998

Other

Es genügt nicht die einfache Wahrheit: Notate, 1975
Verheerende Folgen mangelnden Anscheins innerbetrieblicher Demokratie: Schriften, 1988
Wir befinden uns soweit wohl. Wir sind erst einmal am Ende. Äußerungen, 1998
Texte in zeitlicher Folge, 10 vols., 1989–93

Further Reading

Cosentino, Christine, and Wolfgang Ertl, *Zur Lyrik Volker Brauns*, Königstein: Forum Academicum, 1984
Grauert, Wilfried, *Ästhetische Modernisierung bei Volker Braun: Studien zu Texten aus den achtziger Jahren*, Würzburg: Königshausen und Neumann, 1995
Jucker, Rolf, editor, *Volker Braun*, Cardiff: University of Wales Press, 1995
Profitlich, Ulrich, *Volker Braun: Studien zu seinem dramatischen und erzählerischen Werk*, Munich: Fink, 1985
Rosellini, Jay, *Volker Braun*, Munich: Beck and Edition Text und Kritik, 1983
Wallace, Ian, *Volker Braun: Forschungsbericht*, Amsterdam: Rodopi, 1986

Bertolt Brecht 1898–1956

One of the most intellectual, experimental, and antitraditional of all modern writers, Brecht exerted a decisive influence on the development of 20th-century theater, dramatic theory, and styles of acting. He was also a significant poet and was active in film and fiction. From very early in his career, Brecht was determined to unsettle his public, and he was especially concerned to elicit a rational response from readers and spectators. This urge in part explains the constant "improvements" to which he subjected his work: he revised his plays more than any other dramatist in literary history as he attempted to sharpen the ideological or political effect, to accommodate a changed point of view, or to correct what he saw as misplaced audience reaction. He drew many ideas from his intimate involvement with the production of his own plays and especially from his constant discussion with others, relying on collaborators and assistants to a far greater extent that any other major writer as well as on older works from a variety of cultures that he often radically adapted for the modern stage. Music played a part in virtually all his plays, and here too he depended on collaboration with like-minded, antitraditional figures who could compose "gestic" music, the kind capable of conveying particular attitudes. Yet Brecht was a difficult man with whom to work—selfish, self-important, and often ruthlessly pragmatic—and the human, socialist ideals he advocated in his later works are rarely evident in his dealings with his collaborators.

Brecht's refusal to draw firm conclusions, his preference for ambiguity, for vagueness in location and time, and especially his ability to arouse ambivalent emotions toward his characters has resulted in different societies and new generations being able to interpret his works afresh. In recent years, lively debate has centered on questions surrounding Brecht's life and his collaboration with figures who decisively influenced his practice of writing, for example, the musicians Kurt Weill and Hanns Eisler, as well as devoted and selfless lovers such as Elisabeth Hauptmann and Margarete Steffin, whose contribution was substantial but only minimally or temporarily acknowledged. There has also been revived interest in his debt to the work of his predecessors and a greater focus on the nature of his verse. Although the collapse of the German Democratic Republic (GDR) led to a slight reduction in critical attention, the centenary of his birth (1998) has witnessed a powerful resurgence of interest.

Brecht began writing toward the end of World War I, reacting against the Expressionist tendencies that then dominated the theater: the techniques of abstraction, the "telegram" style of dialogue, the emphasis on "vision" and idealism, etc. Throughout his life, he was to reject what he considered artificial or escapist, and although his first major play, *Baal* (first version 1918, rewritten many times), debunked aspects of the Expressionist mode, it actually contains numerous features of the Expressionists' general attack on naturalism (and on the tradition of verisimilitude), which Brecht adapted for his own purposes. Although such elements were only to be formalized in theoretical writing some ten years later, the principal features associated with Brechtian theater are already evident: no traditional exposition and development, no denouement, little plot, undeveloping and often contradictory characters, events likely to shock the bourgeois (together with general questioning of the presuppositions of bourgeois society), vagueness in location and time scale, and poems and songs. These features were to recur in his following plays of the 1920s, which saw the development of a theme that was to remain constant throughout his career: the conflict between characters' reason and their natural instincts as they struggled for survival in a transient, capitalist world.

Despite the strong socialist currents in postwar German society, Brecht remained essentially a cynical, anticapitalist rebel until he decided to study Marxism to develop his play *Joe Fleischhacker* (1926). Thereafter, socialist philosophy increasingly began to shape his view of the world. However, although there were sharp anticapitalist thrusts in late 1920s plays such as *Die Dreigroschenoper* (produced 1928; published 1928; *The Threepenny Opera*), a clear message, either social or political, was lacking; a more consistent edge is not evident until the "learning plays" of the early 1930s, notably *Die Maßnahme* (produced 1930; *The Measures Taken*) and *Die Ausnahme und die Regel* (written 1930, published 1937; *The Exception and the Rule*), in which capitalist society is analyzed with a clarity and consistency that the author was never to reemploy. Social situation, already important in the early plays, takes precedence over psychology.

These latter plays bear the heavy imprint of Brecht's theory of theater. Always ready to formulate a view on literature, preferably a provocative one, and quite untroubled by whether it contradicted an earlier statement, Brecht had from the start shown an inclination not to encourage empathy or to "carry away" his spectators in the typically classical manner. He consistently emphasized the importance of critical distance and the intellectual power of the theater: for him the medium represented an instrument of social change. His views were given their most famous formalized presentation in the "Notes" to *Aufstieg und Fall der Stadt Mahagonny* (1930; *The Rise and Fall of the City of Mahagonny*), in which the difference between his own and traditional theater is presented in antithetical, tabular form: the famous concept of Brechtian "Epic" Theater (sometimes referred to as "non-Aristotelian") is set against traditional "dramatic" theater (sometimes referred to as "Aristotelian" or "culinary"); the table concludes with the opposition of "feelings" and "reason." For Brecht, the creation of a new relationship between spectator and stage aims to encourage audiences to reflect critically, to recognize social forces, and to arouse the desire for change. The concept of *Verfremdung* (making strange) is central, embracing the idea of preventing traditional empathy but also forcing a fresh perspective on what is familiar yet what nevertheless needs to be questioned. Over the years, critics have regularly pointed out the inconsistencies in Brecht's stream of pronouncements about theatrical performance. His final major (and only sustained systematic) statement, "Kleines Organon für das Theater" (1948; "Short Organum for the Theatre"), reveals a considerable shift from his earlier views on the question of audience "enjoyment," but his views on nonmimetic performance and critical distance remain constant. These views are reflected most clearly in his consistent employment of "anti-illusion" devices such as a bare stage with crude backdrop; when employed, any stage apparatus is prominent; there is music, often songs that provide a form of commentary on the action; placards signal events to come, thus reducing suspense; the language is often nonrealistic; and the style of acting draws attention to the very process of acting. The application of these "epic" principles is at its most severe in Brecht's middle period.

The pieces written between 1929 and 1933 are concerned largely with aspects of communism, and Brecht left Germany as soon as Hitler came to power. Despite being without a theater in which he could be wholeheartedly involved in rehearsals (which led to constant reshaping of the plays as he emphasized to actors the importance of positioning, gesture, and visual expression), Brecht continued writing. His plays ranged from those directed against the Nazis, notably *99%* (1938, later as *Furcht und Elend des III. Reiches* [1945, *Fear and Misery in the Third Reich*]), to the major plays on which his reputation now rests, especially *Mutter Courage und ihre Kinder* (produced 1941; *Mother Courage and Her Children*), *Der gute Mensch von Sezuan* (produced 1943; *The Good Woman of Setzuan*), and *Galileo* (produced 1943; subsequently *The Life of Galileo*). These later works all rely on much greater character delineation and exposure of human conflicts both between and within characters than in the earlier period, but the dark humor is maintained.

Brecht left U.S. exile in 1947 and returned to East Berlin in 1948. His final years represent an anticlimax. He enjoyed control of a theater, the Berliner Ensemble, where he could devote much of his time to directing and producing, but security, celebration, and semiclassical status did not inspire the quality of writing that the pressures of exile had done; and although he outwardly embraced the socialist aims of the GDR and was feted there, he was occasionally subjected to considerable criticism and forced to adapt certain plays in ways that conflicted with his wishes. His relationship to communism remains a source of debate. The GDR's regime was embarrassed by his rejection of empathy and of "positive heroes," cornerstones of socialist writing. Many of his earlier plays were considered ideologically unsound.

The most significant publication of the late period is actually a small verse collection, *Buckower Elegien* (1953; *Buckow Elegies*), which comprise stark, "minimal" poems, their brevity the natural conclusion to the author's frequently concise style and his preference for a rhythm that deliberately unsettles. From the start of his career as a poet, Brecht had rejected classical verse as well as that of the Expressionists, whose pathos he regarded as false. He advocated a more confrontational form of poetry, one that would challenge the intellect—verse that was "useful," had a social value, and that thus matched the force of his dramas. Brecht's strong originality, his antitraditional method of composing, and his constant questioning of prevailing attitudes and beliefs, together with his delight in surprising or disturbing his reader, produce constantly changing lines in which a form of *Verfremdung* is as common as in the drama; the emotions raised are "productive" in the sense of arousing us to insight and possible social protest. The first main collection, *Hauspostille* (1927; *Manual of Piety*), regularly surprises in its choice of material (anarchic, antisocial themes are common in the early years); there are also shifts in register, deviation from orthodox grammar and diction, slang, a generally sullen attitude, and verse that seems to question its validity as verse. The title of the collection is heavily ironic, yet Brecht regularly exploited the Bible for language and ideas. In this early period, there is a considerable mixture of styles as well as the clear influence of various popular forms and of such diverse figures as Rudyard Kipling and François Villon. Some poems are nihilistic or anarchical; others reveal an acute social conscience. There is parody, travesty, and sometimes plagiarism, though at times complete originality.

The study of Marx led to more serious poetry with a changed tone, to more openly didactic and rhetorical verse, and often to more antiliterary forms, as the poet with a social conscience began to speak more loudly. National Socialism, Hitler, and the threat of war were to inspire a large number of poems, many satirical as much as reflective. The major collection of exile, and the peak of Brecht's poetic maturity, is the *Svendborger Gedichte* (1939; Svendborg Poems, i.e., pieces for the most part written near Svendborg, Denmark). Its most famous inclusion, "An die Nachgeborenen" ("To Those Born Later"), contains Brecht's most quoted lines, those that suggest that a conversation about trees (i.e., about things of beauty) is almost a crime because it implies a silence over the many horrors that are taking place. All the best poems of this period are in "rhymeless verse with irregular rhythms" (the title of a major essay on aspects of verse), one of the most striking features of which is a disruption of rhythm to create tension or to throw a particular word into relief; there is constant variation not only of rhythm but also of idea and tone as Brecht gently probes, questions, and doubts. The encounter with Chinese poetry (through the medium of English) led to increasing compression and greater exploitation of simple detail. Brecht was as prolific a poet as a playwright (almost 2,500 poems), but in all his work, whether poetry, drama, or prose, he was distinctly uneven. His weaker poems (and there are many) tend to follow more traditional patterns.

Since Brecht's death, practically every major dramatist has needed to engage with his controversial legacy, and his plays themselves remain among the most widely produced in the world.

PETER HUTCHINSON

See also Berliner Ensemble; Episches Theater

Biography

Born in Augsburg, 10 February 1898. Studied at the University of Munich, 1917–18, 1919; medical orderly during World War I; drama critic for *Der Volkswille,* Augsburg, 1919–21; dramaturge, Munich Kammerspiele, 1923–24; in Berlin, 1924–33; dramaturge, Deutsches Theater; left Germany upon Hitler's assumption of power, 1933; in Denmark, 1933–39; lost German citizenship, 1935; editor, with Lion Feuchtwanger and Willi Bredel, of *Das Wort,* Moscow, 1936–39; in Sweden, 1939; fled Sweden, 1941; in California, United States, 1941–47; called before the House Un-American Activities Committee, 1947; back in Switzerland, 1947–49; Austrian citizen, 1950; in East Berlin after 1949; artistic adviser to the Berliner Ensemble, 1949–56; Kleist Prize, 1922; Stalin Peace Prize, 1954. Died 14 August 1956.

Selected Works

Collections

Gesammelte Werke, 2 vols., 1938
Gesammelte Werke, 1953–
Gesammelte Werke (Stücke, Gedichte, Prosa, Schriften), 20 vols., 1967; supplemented with *Texte für Filme,* 2 vols., 1969, *Arbeitsjournal,* 2 vols., 1974, and *Gedichte aus dem Nachlass,* 2 vols., 1982
Collected Plays, edited by John Willett and Ralph Manheim, 1970–
Poems 1913–1956, edited and translated by John Willett and Ralph Manheim, 3 vols., 1976
Collected Short Stories: 1921–1946, edited by John Willett and Ralph Manheim, translated by Yvonne Kapp, Hugh Rorrison, and Anthony Tatlow, 1983
Werke: Grosse kommentierte Berliner und Frankfurter Ausgabe, edited by Werner Hecht et al., 1988–

Plays

Baal (produced 1922; revised version 1926), 1922; revised version in *Stücke,* vol. 1, 1955; edited by Dieter Schmidt, 1968; translated by Eric Bentley, in *Baal; A Man's a Man; The Elephant Calf,* 1964; translated by Peter Tegel, in *Collected Plays,* 1970
Trommeln in der Nacht (produced 1922), 1922; as *Drums in the Night,* translated by Frank Jones, in *Jungle of Cities and Other Plays,* 1966; also translated by John Willett, in *Collected Plays,* vol. 1, 1970
Im Dickicht der Städte (as *Im Dickicht,* produced 1923; revised version 1927), 1927; edited by Gisela E. Bahr, 1968; as *In the Jungle of Cities,* translated by Gerhard Nellhaus, 1957; as *Jungle of Cities,* translated by Anselm Hollo, in *Jungle of Cities and Other Plays,* 1966
Pastor Ephraim Magnus, with Arnolt Bronnen (from the play by Hans Henny Jahn) (produced 1923)
Leben Eduards des Zweiten von England, with Lion Feuchtwanger (from the play by Christopher Marlowe) (produced 1924); edited by Reinhold Grimm, 1968; as *Edward II,* translated by Eric Bentley, 1966; as *The Life of Edward II of England,* translated by Jean Benedetti, in *Collected Plays,* vol. 1, 1970
Die Kleinbürgerhochzeit (as *Die Hochzeit,* produced 1926), 1966; as *A Respectable Wedding,* translated by Jean Benedetti, in *Collected Plays,* vol. 1, 1970
Mann ist Mann, with others (produced 1926), 1927; as *Man Equals Man,* translated by Eric Bentley, in *Seven Plays,* 1961; translated by Gerhard Nellhaus, in *Collected Plays,* vol. 2, 1979; as *A Man's a Man,* translated by Eric Bentley, in *Baal; A Man's a Man, The Elephant Calf,* 1964
Das Elefantenkalb, with *Mann ist Mann,* 1927; as *The Elephant Calf,* translated by Eric Bentley, in *Baal; A Man's a Man; The Elephant Calf,* 1964; translated by Gerhard Nellhaus, in *Collected Plays,* vol. 2, 1979
Kalkutta 4. Mai (with Lion Feuchtwanger, from a play by Feuchtwanger in *Drei Angelsächsische Stücke*), 1927; translated as *Warren Hastings,* in *Two Anglo-Saxon Plays,* 1928
Die Dreigroschenoper, music by Kurt Weill (from the play by John Gay) (produced 1928), 1928; as *The Threepenny Opera,* translated by Desmond Vesey and Eric Bentley, 1964; translated by Hugh MacDiarmid, 1973; translated by Ralph Manheim and John Willett, in *Collected Plays,* vol. 2, 1979

Happy End, with Elisabeth Hauptmann, music by Kurt Weill (produced 1929); translated and adapted by Michael Feingold, 1982

Lindberghflug, music by Kurt Weill and Paul Hindemith (produced 1929), 1929; retitled *Der Ozeanflug*

Aufstieg und Fall der Stadt Mahagonny, music by Kurt Weill (produced 1930), 1929; as *The Rise and Fall of the City of Mahagonny,* translated by W.H. Auden and Chester Kallman, 1976

Das Badener Lehrstück vom Einverständnis, music by Paul Hindemith (produced 1929), in *Versuche,* vol. 2, 1930; as *The Didactic Play of Baden-Baden on Consent,* in *Tulane Drama Review,* May 1960

Der Jasager/Der Neinsager, music by Kurt Weill (produced 1930), in *Versuche,* vol. 4, 1931; edited by Peter Szondi, 1966; as *He Who Said Yes; He Who Said No,* translated by Wolfgang Sauerlander, in *The Measures Taken and Other Lehrstücke,* 1977

Die Maßnahme, music by Hanns Eisler (produced 1930), in *Versuche,* vol. 4, 1931; edited by Reiner Steinweg, 1972; as *The Measures Taken,* translated by Eric Bentley, in *The Modern Theatre,* vol. 6, edited by Eric Bentley, 1960; in *The Jewish Wife and Other Short Plays,* 1965; translated by Carl R. Müller, in *The Measures Taken and Other Lehrstücke,* 1977

Versuche, vols. 1–7, 9–15, 1930–57

Die heilige Johanna der Schlachthöfe (broadcast 1932; produced 1959), in *Versuche,* vol. 5, 1932; edited by Gisela E. Bahr, 1971; as *Saint Joan of the Stockyards,* translated by Frank Jones, in *From the Modern Repertoire,* series 3, edited by Eric Bentley, 1956; translated by Ralph Manheim, in *Collected Plays,* vol. 3, 1991

Die Mutter, music by Hanns Eisler (from the novel by Maksim Gor'kii), in *Versuche,* vol. 7, 1932; edited by W. Hecht, 1969; as *The Mother,* translated by Lee Baxandall, 1965; translated by Steve Gooch, 1978

Die Sieben Todsünden der Kleinbürger, music by Kurt Weill (produced 1933), 1959; as *The Seven Deadly Sins of the Petty Bourgeoisie,* in *Collected Plays,* vol. 2/3, 1979

Die Rundköpfe und die Spitzköpfe, music by Hanns Eisler (produced 1936), in *Gesammelte Werke,* vol. 2, 1938; as *Roundheads and Peakheads,* translated by N. Goold-Verschoyle, in *Jungle of Cities and Other Plays,* 1966

Die Gewehre der Frau Carrar (produced 1937), 1938; as *The Guns of Carrar,* 1971; as *Señora Carrar's Rifles,* in *Collected Plays,* vol. 4, 1983

Furcht und Elend des III. Reiches (produced as *99%,* 1938), 1945; as *The Private Life of the Master Race,* translated by Eric Bentley, 1944; as *Fear and Misery in the Third Reich,* in *Collected Plays,* vol. 4, 1983

Die Ausnahme und die Regel, music by Paul Dessau (produced 1937), in *Gesammelte Werke,* vol. 2, 1938; as *The Exception and the Rule,* translated by Eric Bentley, in *The Jewish Wife and Other Short Plays,* 1965; translated by Ralph Manheim, 1977

Die Horatier und die Kuriatier, music by Kurt Schwän (produced 1958), in *Gesammelte Werke,* vol. 2, 1938; as *The Horatians and the Curatians,* in *Accent,* 1947

Das Verhör des Lukullus (broadcast 1940; revised version, music by Paul Dessau, produced 1951), 1951; as *The Trial of Lucullus,* translated by H.R. Hays, 1943; translated in *Plays,* vol. 1, 1960

Mutter Courage und ihre Kinder: Eine Chronik aus dem Dreßigjährigen Krieg (produced 1941), 1949; in *Versuche,* vol. 9, 1949; 2nd revised edition, 1950; edited by W. Hecht, 1964; as *Mother Courage and Her Children: A Chronicle of the Thirty Years War,* translated by H.R. Hays, 1941; translated by Eric Bentley, in *Seven Plays,* 1961, and *Collected Plays,* vol. 2, 1962; translated by John Willett, in *Collected Plays,* vol. 5, 1980; 6th edition, 1990

Der gute Mensch von Sezuan (produced 1943), in *Versuche,* vol. 12, 1953; revised edition, 1958; edited by W. Hecht, 1968; as *The Good Woman of Setzuan,* translated by Eric Bentley, in *Parables for the Theatre,* 1948; as *The Good Person of Szechwan,* translated by John Willett, in *Plays,* vol. 2, 1962; as *The Good Person of Sichuan,* translated by Michael Hofmann, 1989

Galileo (produced 1943; revised version, with Charles Laughton, produced 1947; revised version, as *Leben des Galilei,* produced 1955), 1955; edited by W. Hecht, 1963; as *Galileo,* translated by Brecht and Charles Laughton, in *From the Modern Repertoire,* series 2, edited by Eric Bentley, 1953; as *The Life of Galileo,* translated by Desmond I. Vesey, 1960; translated by John Willett in *Collected Plays,* vol. 5, 1980

Der kaukasische Kreidekreis (produced 1948), in *Sinn und Form—Sonderheft,* 1949; as *The Caucasian Chalk Circle,* translated by Eric Bentley, in *Parables for the Theatre,*1948; translated by James and Tania Stern, with W.H. Auden, in *Collected Plays,* vol. 7, 1960

Herr Puntila und sein Knecht Matti (produced 1948), in *Versuche,* vol. 10, 1950; as *Mr. Puntila and His Man Matti,* translated by John Willett, in *Collected Plays,* vol. 6, 1977

Die Antigone des Sophokles (from Hölderlin's translation of Sophocles) (produced 1948), 1955; translated as *Antigone,* 1989

Der Hofmeister (from the play by J.M.R. Lenz) (produced 1950), in *Versuche,* vol. 11, 1951; as *The Tutor,* in *Collected Plays,* vol. 9, 1973; translated and adapted by Pip Broughton, 1988

Herrnburger Bericht, music by Paul Dessau (produced 1951), 1951

Der Prozess der Jeanne d'Arc zu Rouen 1431 (from his radio play; produced 1952), in *Stücke,* vol. 12, 1959; as *The Trial of Joan of Arc,* in *Collected Plays,* vol. 9, 1973

Don Juan (from the play by Molière) (produced 1953), in *Stücke,* vol. 12, 1959; as *Don Juan,* in *Collected Plays,* vol. 9, 1973

Die Gesichte der Simone Machard, with Lion Feuchtwanger (produced 1957), in *Sinn und Form,* vols. 5–6, 1956; as *The Visions of Simone Machard,* translated by Hugh and Ellen Rank, in *Collected Plays,* vol. 7, 1976

Die Tage der Kommune, music by Hanns Eisler (produced 1956), in *Versuche,* vol. 15, and *Stücke,* vol. 10, both 1957; as *The Days of the Commune,* in *Dunster Drama Review,* 1971; translated by Clive Barker and Arno Reinfrank, 1978

Pauken und Trompeten, with Elisabeth Hauptmann and Benno Besson, music by Rudolf Wagner-Regeny (from a play by George Farquhar) (produced 1956), in *Stücke,* vol. 12, 1959; as *Trumpets and Drums,* in *Collected Plays,* vol. 9, 1973

Der aufhaltsame Aufstieg des Arturo Ui (produced 1958), in *Stücke,* vol. 9, 1957; as *The Resistible Rise of Arturo Ui,* translated by Ralph Manheim, in *Collected Plays,* vol. 6, 1976

Schweyk im zweiten Weltkrieg, music by Hanns Eisler (produced 1957), in *Stücke,* vol. 10, 1957; edited by Herbert Knust, 1974; as *Schweik in the Second World War,* translated by William Rowlinson, in *Collected Plays,* vol. 7, 1976

Coriolan (from the play by William Shakespeare) (produced 1962), in *Stücke,* vol. 11, 1959; as *Coriolanus,* in *Collected Plays,* vol. 9, 1973

Seven Plays (includes *Jungle of Cities; Man Equals Man; St. Joan of the Stockyards; Mother Courage and Her Children; Galileo; The Good Woman of Setzuan; The Caucasian Chalk Circle*), edited and translated by Eric Bentley, 1961

Der Bettler; oder, Der tote Hund, in *Stücke,* vol. 13, 1966; as *The Beggar; or, The Dead Dog,* translated by Michael Hamburger, in *Collected Plays,* vol. 1, 1970

Er treibt den Teufel aus, in *Stücke,* vol. 13, 1966; as *Driving Out a Devil,* translated by Richard Greenburger, in *Collected Plays,* vol. 1, 1970

Lux in Tenebris, in *Stücke,* vol. 13, 1966; as *Lux in Tenebris,* translated by Eva Geisel and Ernest Borneman, in *Collected Plays,* vol. 1, 1970

Der Fischzug, in *Stücke,* vol. 13, 1966; as *The Catch,* translated by John Willett, in *Collected Plays,* vol. 1, 1970

Jungle of Cities and Other Plays (includes *Jungle of Cities; Drums in the Night; Roundheads and Peakheads*), translated by Anselm Hollo et al., 1966

Turandot; oder, Der Kongress der Weisswäscher, music by Hanns Eisler (produced 1969), in *Gesammelte Werke,* 1967

Der Brotladen (produced 1967), 1969

Screenplays

Kuhle Wampe, with others, 1932; published as *Kuhle Wampe: Protokoll des Films und Materialien,* edited by W. Gersch and W. Hecht, 1969

Hangmen Also Die, with John Wexley and Fritz Lang, 1943

Fiction

Der Dreigroschenroman, 1934; as *A Penny for the Poor,* translated by Desmond I. Vesey and Christopher Isherwood, 1937; as *Threepenny Novel,* translated by Desmond I. Vesey and Christopher Isherwood, 1956

Kalendergeschichten, 1948; as *Tales from the Calendar,* translated by Yvonne Kapp and Michael Hamburger, 1961

Die Geschäfte des Herrn Julius Cäsar, 1957

Poetry

Taschenpostille, 1926

Hauspostille, 1927; as *Manual of Piety,* translated by Eric Bentley, 1966

Lieder Gedichte Chöre, with Hanns Eisler, 1934

Svendborger Gedichte, 1939

Selected Poems, 1947

Die Erziehung der Hirse, 1951

Hundert Gedichte, 1951

Gedichte, edited by S. Streller, 1955

Gedichte und Lieder, edited by P. Suhrkamp, 1956

Selected Poems, translated by H.R. Hays, 1959

Poems on the Theatre, translated by John Berger and Anna Bostock, 1961

Gedichte aus dem Nachlass, edited by Herta Ramthun, 2 vols., 1982

Poems and Songs from the Plays, translated by John Willett, 1990

Other

Theaterarbeit, with others, 1952

Kriegsfibel, 1955

Schriften zum Theater, 1957; as *Brecht on Theater,* edited and translated by John Willett, 1964

Flüchtlingsgespräche, 1961

Dialoge aus dem Messingkauf, 1964; as *The Messingkauf Dialogues,* translated by John Willett, 1965

Arbeitsjournal, edited by Werner Hecht, 2 vols., 1973; as *Journals, 1934–1955,* edited by John Willett, translated by Hugh Rorrison, 1993

Autobiographische Aufzeichungen 1920–1954, Tagebücher 1920–22, edited by Herta Ramthun, 1975; *Tagebücher* as *Diaries 1920–22,* translated by John Willett, 1979

Briefe, edited by Günter Gläser, 2 vols., 1981

Über die bildenden Künste, edited by Jost Hermand, 1983

Letters 1913–1956, edited by John Willett, translated by Ralph Manheim, 1990

Translation

Martin Andersen-Nexö, *Die Kindheit,* translated with Margarete Steffin, 1945

Further Reading

Fuegi, John, *Bertolt Brecht: Chaos, According to Plan,* Cambridge and New York: Cambridge University Press, 1987

———, *Brecht and Company: Sex, Politics, and the Making of the Modern Drama,* New York: Grove Press, 1994

Hecht, Werner, *Brecht Chronik: 1898–1956,* Frankfurt: Suhrkamp, 1997

Knopf, Jan, *Brecht-Handbuch,* 2 vols., Stuttgart: Metzler, 1980; special edition, 1996

Thomson, Peter, and Glendyr Sacks, *The Cambridge Companion to Brecht,* Cambridge and New York: Cambridge University Press, 1994

Thomson, Philip J., *The Poetry of Brecht: Seven Studies,* Chapel Hill: University of North Carolina Press, 1989

Willett, John, *Brecht in Context: Comparative Approaches,* London and New York: Methuen, 1994; revised edition, 1998

Die Dreigroschenoper 1928

Play by Bertolt Brecht, music by Kurt Weill

The immediate and phenomenal success of Bertolt Brecht's most popular play, *Die Dreigroschenoper* (*The Threepenny Opera*), has been attributed to a variety of social and aesthetic factors operating at the height of the Weimar Republic. The work was clearly in part a fascination, the first major and consistent example of Brechtian "epic theater," and it thus represented a form of novelty in its revolt against the "well-made play," accepted styles of acting, and pleasure-seeking theatergoers themselves. The play subverted other traditional categories, however, not least in its substantial musical dimension—the racy songs that frequently interrupt its incredible plot (a good number drawing on poems by François Villon) and above all the anti-Wagnerian, experimental compositions of Kurt Weill (which bear marked influences of jazz and modern dance rhythms).

In the many songs we find a mood that all critics agree fits the period: a light-hearted, sarcastic rejection of traditional form and harmony, frequently sharpened by aggressive discord. The appeal is no less in that these songs are full of surprises, in their content (lugubrious scenes of death, murder, prostitution), form (regularly inverting expectations), language (which is full of colloquial, inappropriate words and phrases), and logic—or the lack of it. The songs are antitraditional, and they are severely critical of social behavior, yet despite the fact that they frequently present uncomfortable questions on various aspects of social existence, we are barely able to reflect on them before being transported into a completely different mood. Although much of the critique of capitalist decadence is directed at the theatergoer, it is constantly shifting and is never presented too seriously; it is often dissipated by the music, which is attacking a different aspect of tradition.

Some prominent early critics (Ernst Bloch, Theodor Adorno) thought that the public enjoyed the work for the wrong reasons, that they "misunderstood" it and failed to see that its critique of corruption, decadence, and capitalist values was directed at them rather than the Victorian England in which the drama is set. In addition, audiences enjoyed the catchy tunes rather than recognizing their subversive intent. Although the latter point may hold true, the former is now held to be unlikely, although Brecht himself was certainly uneasy about the reception of particular aspects of his play, especially the public's identification with the villainous "hero." Brecht's firm shift to Marxism (which closely followed the premiere of *Die Dreigroschenoper*) led to a sociopolitical revision of the play and an appendix of "notes" that outlined aspects of "epic theater" and forced a communist reading of the text (1931). Through occasionally crass insertions into the dialogue, the central characters became more bourgeois and ruthlessly capitalist. Thrusts at capitalism became more direct, such as "What is the difference between a skeleton key and a share? . . . What is the difference between killing a man and employing a man?" Nevertheless, all the songs, the cornerstone of the play's success, remained: the shameless, Villon-inspired celebration of good living, "Die Ballade vom angenehmen Leben" ("Ballad of the Pleasant Life"), the Kipling-inspired nostalgia for colonial expansion, "Der Kanonen-Song" ("Cannon Song"), and the famous, gloriously self-indulgent aperçu, "Erst kommt das Fressen, dann kommt die Moral" ("Grub First, Morals After," for years considered by Brecht to be the best line he had ever written). The combination of such praise of materialism, individualism, and sensuality with blunt anticapitalist fanfares renders the moral of the play even more unclear than it was in the first version. Nevertheless, critics have moved to the view that much of the fascination of *Die Dreigroschenoper* lies precisely in the fact that the work is such a patchwork of ambiguous, sometimes contradictory themes, unsettling questions, ridiculous comedy, illogical progression, and frequently shocking vulgarity.

Besides the revised version of the play, Brecht also undertook a film adaptation, *Die Beule* (1931; The Bruise), directed by G.W. Pabst, which led to a court case as a result of the author's determination to emphasize political elements far beyond the wishes of the producer (Brecht lost the case but made the circumstances the subject of an extended sociocultural essay). He also completed a novel, *Der Dreigroschenroman* (1934; *Threepenny Novel*), in which he attempted to sharpen the political message even further. Neither recaptured the force of the original, although the film is now recognized as a classic.

Some studies of the play have emphasized the importance of the attack on traditional opera and operetta and the significance of this for an age that enjoyed satire and cabaret. Brecht had a low view of opera: it exemplified that type of art that he was to label "culinary." In *Die Dreigroschenoper,* the ridiculousness of the operatic aria is suggested initially by the effects that accompany each song: excessive lighting to achieve "emotional" effect (in mockery of the style of Max Reinhardt), which is followed not by a "sentimental dream" but antisentimental, often vulgar language reinforced by such unoperatic instruments as saxophone, barrel organ, or waa-waa mute on the trumpet. The "orchestra" is prominently in view. Much of our enjoyment thus lies in the parody of the operatic mode.

More recent views of the play have highlighted the nature of Brecht's heavy debt to others: to the Augustan source on which the plot draws heavily (John Gay, *The Beggar's Opera*); to several other aspects of Gay's work that are taken over by Brecht (such as cynical views on mankind, exploitative social structures, and the constant sexual banter); to the role played by Brecht's collaborator Elisabeth Hauptmann, who translated the original Gay into German and worked tirelessly on the adaptation; to the assistance of numerous other figures in Brecht's circle. Above all, however, recent approaches have emphasized the vital role of Kurt Weill (seen most clearly in Stephen Hinton's outstanding collection of essays, in which the composer is given titular prominence). Music plays a role in almost every one of Brecht's plays, but here the parody of traditional, and especially of sentimental, tunes combined with innovative use of instrument, chord, and phrasing was vital in establishing the basis for the playwright's, as much as the composer's, international fame.

PETER HUTCHINSON

Editions

First edition: *Die Dreigroschenoper ("The Beggar's Opera"): Ein Stück mit Musik in einem Vorspiel und acht Bildern nach dem Englischen des John Gay,* Berlin: Felix Bloch Erben and Vienna: Universal Edition, 1928

Critical edition: in *Werke: Große kommentierte Berliner und Frankfurter Ausgabe,* vol. 2, edited by Jürgen Schebera, Berlin and Weimar: Aufbau, and Frankfurt: Suhrkamp, 1988

Translations: *The Threepenny Opera,* translated by Desmond Vesey and Eric Bentley, New York: Grove Press, 1964; translated by Hugh MacDiarmid, London: Eyre Methuen, 1973; these earlier translations have been superseded by Ralph Manheim and John Willett, in *Collected Plays,* vol. 2, London: Eyre Methuen, 1979

Further Reading

Giles, Steve, "Rewriting Brecht: *Die Dreigroschenoper* 1928–1931," *Literaturwissenschaftliches Jahrbuch* 30 (1989)

Hinton, Stephen, editor, *Kurt Weill: "The Threepenny Opera,"* Cambridge and New York: Cambridge University Press, 1990

McNeff, Stephen, "The Threepenny Opera," in *The Cambridge Companion to Brecht,* edited by Peter Thomson and Glendyr Sacks, Cambridge and New York: Cambridge University Press, 1994

Unseld, Siegfried, editor, *Bertolt Brechts "Dreigroschenbuch": Texte, Materialien, Dokumente,* Frankfurt: Suhrkamp, 1960

Weisstein, Ulrich, "Brecht's Victorian Version of Gay: Imitation and Originality in the *Dreigroschenoper,*" in *Critical Essays on Bertolt Brecht,* edited by Siegfried Mews, Boston, Massachusetts: G.K. Hall, 1989

Mutter Courage 1949

Play by Bertolt Brecht

Mutter Courage und ihre Kinder: Eine Chronik aus dem Dreißigjährigen Krieg (1949; *Mother Courage and Her Children: A Chronicle of the Thirty Years War*) is one of the best-known plays by the leading 20th-century German playwright Bertolt Brecht. It was written shortly after the outbreak of World War II, between late September and early November 1939 in Sweden, where Brecht and his family were living in exile. The play was written in part to warn the Scandinavian countries that they could not hope to profit from trade with Hitler's Germany without themselves becoming victims of Nazi aggression. Brecht had already expressed similar sentiments in his one-act plays *Dansen* (1939; *Dansen*) and *Was kostet das Eisen?* (1939; *What's the Price of Iron?*). Although the play was directly stimulated by the situation in Europe, however, it nevertheless transcends the realms of historical events and retains a general validity today as an analysis of the phenomenon of war.

Brecht chose to distance the action by locating it within the historical framework of the Thirty Years' War (1618–48). As he had done before with plays such as *Die Dreigroschenoper* (1928; *The Threepenny Opera*), *Der Jasager/Der Neinsager* (1930; *He Who Said Yes/He Who Said No*), and *Die Mutter* (1932; *The Mother*), Brecht drew on the work of another writer—in this case taking inspiration from H.J.C. Grimmelshausen's *Trutz Simplex; oder, Ausführliche und wunderseltzame Lebensbeschreibung der Ertzbetrügerin und Landstörtzerin Courasche* (1670; *The Runagate Courage*). Beyond the name and Courage's occupation as tradeswoman, however, comparatively little of the original novel remains in Brecht's play. During his exile years, Brecht often campaigned unsuccessfully for performances of his work, but *Mother Courage* was staged in Zurich in April 1941. Brecht, however, objected to the misinterpretation of his work by both the audience and critics. The character of Mutter Courage was seen as a victim and was compared to Niobe, the suffering mother figure in Greek mythology.

Disappointed by the reception of the Zurich performance, Brecht made numerous changes for his own production of the play at the Deutsches Theater in Berlin in January 1949, which he directed together with Erich Engel. He strove to put the character Mutter Courage in an even more negative light and to stifle audience sympathy for the character. Mutter Courage was not to be seen as a victim; her vain desire to profit from war is directly responsible for the death of her children. Like the millions of fellow travelers who had hoped to survive the Nazi regime, her "Grand Capitulation" is a conscious decision motivated by the misguided self-interest that formed a prerequisite for those who engineered and profited from the war.

Despite its success, Brecht's play was criticized in East Germany from the official standpoint of Socialist Realism, which demanded the audience be given a clear indication of the appropriate manner of behavior. The figure of Mutter Courage, however, learns nothing from her experiences and still hopes to profit from war, despite all that has befallen her. By failing to appreciate the value of a negative example, critics in the East demonstrated how little they understood Brecht's dramatic technique. Epic Theater aims not to draw the audience into the action but to encourage critical distance, as if the audience were observing an experiment. Brecht attempted to counter criticisms of his work by comparing the figure of Mutter Courage to a guinea pig in an experiment. Just as the guinea pig learns nothing about biology, Mutter Courage learns nothing from the catastrophic events. What mattered, Brecht felt, was that the audience drew the appropriate conclusions. Additionally, Brecht does include the figure of the dumb Kattrin, who demonstrates an alternative response in her resistance to the horrors of war. Those socialist critics who approved of the play did so by drawing direct parallels from *Mother Courage* to the experience of World War II and by emphasizing the importance of Kattrin as the "soul of the people," silenced or killed by Hitler.

Audiences in West Germany, made up of those who had survived the Nazi years, tended to identify with the Courage figure, seeing her as a sly individual capable of surviving a situation over which she had no control. The interpretation corresponded to the prevailing view in the West that the individual could not be held responsible for the rise of fascism. This widespread attitude, which was supposedly supported by Brecht's play, formed the basis in 1955 for the Swiss dramatist Friedrich Dürrenmatt's theory of drama—in which he rejected tragedy in favor of comedy because of the absence in tragedy of a sense of individual responsibility.

Brecht provides a Marxist interpretation of war, and, despite the play's historical setting, it serves as a commentary upon modern capitalism. War is presented as the continuation of business by other means, with the Church providing an ideological foundation for the military. The audience is given a worm's eye view of events, with the major protagonists in the conflict remaining in the background. Those who do indeed profit from war remain out of sight while it is the "little people" who foot the bill, irrespective of victory or defeat. Brecht's analysis of war quite clearly has revolutionary implications.

Mother Courage is one of the best examples of Epic Theater. The action, which is episodic, is explained in advance of each scene so that the interest lies not in what happens, but rather in how it happens. Brecht's alienation effect is in evidence in the "double scenes" in which two sets of action take place simultaneously on stage, thus reminding the audience that it is watching a play. The songs are also an important part of Epic Theater. Music for the play was composed in 1946 by Paul Dessau, who later worked on other plays with Brecht. Despite the apparent relevance of the songs within their respective context, they disrupt the progress of the plot, provide contradictions and broader insights, and thereby encourage a critical attitude in the audience. The play, which is an important example of Brecht's later, mature work, continues to fascinate audiences today and is performed frequently on stages throughout the world.

STEVEN W. LAWRIE

Editions

First edition: *Mutter Courage und ihre Kinder: Eine Chronik aus dem Dreißigjährigen Krieg,* in *Versuche,* vol. 9, Berlin and Frankfurt: Suhrkamp, 1949; 2nd revised edition, 1950 (Brecht considered the second, revised edition to be authoritative)

Critical edition: in *Werke: Große kommentierte Berliner und Frankfurter Ausgabe,* edited by Werner Hecht et al., vol. 6, Berlin and Weimar: Aufbau, and Frankfurt: Suhrkamp, 1988–

Translation: *Mother Courage and Her Children: A Chronicle of the Thirty Years War,* translated by John Willett, in *Collected Plays,* vol. 5, London: Methuen 1980; 6th edition, 1990

Further Reading

Brecht, Bertolt, "Anmerkungen zur Oper *Aufstieg und Fall der Stadt Mahagonny,*" in *Werke: Große kommentierte Berliner und Frankfurter Ausgabe,* vol. 24, edited by Werner Hecht et al., Berlin and Weimar: Aufbau, and Frankfurt: Suhrkamp, 1988–

——, "Zu *Mutter Courage und ihre Kinder,*" in *Bertolt Brecht: Werke, Große kommentierte Berliner und Frankfurter Ausgabe,* vol. 24, edited by Werner Hecht et al., Berlin and Weimar: Aufbau, and Frankfurt: Suhrkamp, 1988–

Hinck, Walter, "*Mutter Courage und ihre Kinder:* Ein kritisches Volksstück," in *Brechts Dramen: Neue Interpretationen,* edited by Walter Hinderer, Stuttgart: Reclam, 1984

Knopf, Jan, *Brecht-Handbuch: Theater, Eine Ästhetik der Widersprüche,* Stuttgart: Metzler, 1980; special edition 1986

Leiser, Peter, *Bertolt Brecht: "Mutter Courage und ihre Kinder," "Der kaukasische Kreidekreis,"* Hollfeld: Beyer, 1973

Müller, Klaus-Detlef, editor, *Brechts "Mutter Courage und ihre Kinder": Materialien,* Frankfurt: Suhrkamp, 1982

White, Alfred D., *Bertolt Brecht's Great Plays,* London, Basingstoke, and New York: Macmillan, 1978

Johann Jakob Breitinger 1701–1776

Johann Jakob Breitinger, a significant figure of the Enlightenment in the German-speaking world, was active as an editor, literary critic, educator, and theologian. He contributed many articles to periodicals and was a member of various literary and patriotic societies. Breitinger is known primarily for his writings on aesthetics and poetics, and he is viewed—along with Johann Jakob Bodmer, his friend and collaborator in much of his work—within the context of the quarrel that arose between them and Johann Christoph Gottsched, which is commonly referred to as the "Leipzig-Zürich Literaturstreit." This conflict is credited with having weakened the dominance that Gottsched's narrowly rationalist, normative poetics exercised on German-language literature and criticism from the publication of his *Critische Dichtkunst* in 1730 through the work's fourth edition in 1751. Bodmer and Breitinger's "victory" is seen as having opened the door to aesthetic considerations that led to the literary movements of Sentimentality (1740–80), the late-Enlightenment movement of the Storm and Stress (1770–81), and even to German classicism (1786–1805) and Romanticism (1795–1830).

Although influenced by rationalist principles derived from the philosophy of Christian Wolff and Gottfried Wilhelm Leibniz—in this respect he is similar to Gottsched—Breitinger interprets these categories very differently, with a marked change in emphasis. Most important, he particularizes the central concept of mimesis by drawing attention to the perspectival nature of all perception and, consequently, all representation; by allowing more freedom to the imagination; and by insisting on the indispensability of figurative language—notions that Gottsched viewed with suspicion, if not outright rejection. It is also important to note that Breitinger critically engaged and borrowed ideas from sensualist thinkers in his reflections on literature and language—in particular the thought of John Locke (1632–1704), Jean-Baptiste Du Bos (1670–1742), and Ludovico Antonio Muratori (1672–1750).

The most important of the journals to which Breitinger contributed was *Die Discourse der Mahlern* (in the second, expanded, 1746 edition, *Die Mahler der Sitten*). This periodical was the publication of Breitinger and Bodmer's language society, Die Gesellschaft der Mahlern, and it was modeled after Joseph Addison and Richard Steele's English moral weekly, the *Spectator*. Although this periodical had contributions by other members of the society, Breitinger and Bodmer wrote the majority of articles. They primarily discussed moral and social issues, offering practical advice and guidance to their readers. Among the other important periodical publications to which Breitinger contributed were the *Neue Zeitungen aus der gelehrten Welt: Zur Beleuchtung der Historie der Gelehrsamkeit;* the *Sammlung Critischer, Poetischer, und andrer geistvollen Schriften, Zur Verbesserung des Urtheils und des Wizes in den Wercken der Wohlredenheit und der Poesie;* and the *Freymütige Nachrichten von neuen Büchern, und andern zur Gelehrtheit gehörigen Sachen.*

In his *Critische Abhandlung von der Natur, den Absichten und dem Gebrauche der Gleichnisse* (1740; Critical Treatment of the Nature, Goals, and Use of Parables), Breitinger proposes the concept of the logic of the imagination as the important criterion of verisimilitude, thereby expanding the concept of mimesis. He argues that the goal of literature is to affect the reader's heart and to elevate the soul and that powerful and beautiful images are the best way to achieve this end. These images provide the reader with a lively representation, whereby the soul is touched and the affect inflamed. According to Breitinger, the problem with Baroque writers is not that they use such images (Gottsched's position), but that they use them incorrectly and to the wrong ends. The text was not well received, although Gottsched remarked on it with distanced approval in a letter before the beginning of the conflict.

Breitinger's signature work is his two-volume *Critische Dichtkunst* (1741; Critical Poetics). While reasserting the contemporary commonplace that the primary goal of art is the imitation of nature, he particularizes the notion of mimesis by noting that the author represents a perspective on nature in an imagined possible world and that this effort rather than the universal, logical criteria of the real world sets the standard by which verisimilitude is to be judged. Breitinger goes even further, arguing that the pleasing qualities of an artistic work are more important than its didactic content because these qualities are truly aesthetic, whereas a text's usefulness is a quality shared by all textual types. Furthermore, he claims that new materials can most successfully produce enjoyment, along with the usual materials that evidence the beautiful, the great, and the marvelous.

With these assertions, Breitinger (re)opened the door to innovation and creation in literature, but it must be remembered that he also carefully places limitations on literature's imaginative and emotional dimensions by asserting that the element of design is essential to the work of art. Breitinger's emphasis on figurative language also has innovative moments, alongside its often tiresome and pedantic attention to detail. In addition, we see his distance from conventional rationalist positions in his criticism of the overly ornate style of late Baroque literature. He attacks Baroque writers for their rigid adherence to classical rhetoric and for not having the stimulation of the reader's fantasy as their primary goal.

Breitinger's work is organized by a concern for the role of literature in a republican society. He has often been considered merely a transitional figure from the rigid rationalist poetics of Gottsched to the *Genieästhetik* of the Storm and Stress and the subjectivist poetics of Romanticism. Recent scholarship, however, has turned its attention to a reconstruction of his poetics within the broader context of developments in European poetics, historiography, and philosophy from the late 17th to the mid–18th centuries. This reconstruction has provided us with a more accurate understanding of his significance for his time and for the history of German-language culture.

Kenneth E. Munn

Biography

Born in Zurich, 1701. Attended the Collegium Carolinum, 1715–20, where he met Johann Jakob Bodmer; ordained as a Protestant minister, 1720; editor of the *Neue Zeitungen aus der gelehrten Welt: Zur Beleuchtung der Historie der Gelehrsamkeit,* 1725; employed as a private tutor by J.J. Leu and the former mayor of Zurich, Hans Kaspar Escher; professor of Hebrew at the Collegium Humanitatis and acting professor of Hebrew, Collegium Carolinium, Zurich, 1731; co-edited a critical edition of the Septuagint, 1730–32; co-edited with Bodmer the *Helvetische Bibliothek*, 1735–41; position as professor at the Collegium Carolinum made permanent, 1740, where he began lectures in logic and rhetoric; named professor of Greek literature at the Collegium Carolinum and canon of the seminary at Großmünster, 1745; co-edited with Bodmer a two volume edition of Minnesinger poets, 1758–59; cofounder of the Asketische Gesellschaft junger Geistlicher, a society for the discussion of pastoral issues, 1768; rector of the Zurich secondary school, 1772–75. Died in Zurich, December 1776.

Selected Works

Nonfiction

Die Discourse der Mahlern, 4 vols., edited with Johann Jakob Bodmer, 1721–23
Critische Dichtkunst, 2 vols., 1740
Zuverlässige Nachricht und Untersuchung von dem Alterthum der Stadt Zürich und von einer neuen Entdeckung merkwürdiger Antiquitäten einer bisher unbekannten Stadt in der Herrschafft Knonau, 1741

Edited Works

Helvetische Bibliothek, bestehend in historischen, politischen, und critischen Beyträgen zu dem Geschichten des Schweitzerlands, 6 vols., edited with Johann Jakob Bodmer, 1735–41
Lauffer, Historische und Critische Beyträge zu der Historie der Eidsgenossen, 4 vols., edited with Johann Jakob Bodmer, 1739
Sammlung critischer, poetischer, und andrer geistvollen Schriften, zur Verbesserung des Urtheils und des Wizes in den Wercken der Wolredenheit und der Poesie, 5 vols., edited with Johann Jakob Bodmer, 1741–44
Verteidigung der Schweitzerischen Muse, Herrn D. Albrecht Hallers, 1744
with Johann Jakob Bodmer, *Critische Briefe*, 1746
Der Mahler der Sitten: Von neuem übersehen und starck vermehret, 2 vols., edited with Johann Jakob Bodmer, 1746
Museum Helveticum, 7 vols., edited with Jakob Zimmermann, 1746–53
Proben der alten schwäbischen Poesie des dreyzehnten Jahrhunderts: Aus der Maneßischen Sammlung, edited with Johann Jakob Bodmer, 1748
Sammlung von Minnesingern aus dem schwaebischen Zeitpunct CXL Dichter enthaltend, edited with Johann Jakob Bodmer, 1758–59

Further Reading

Bender, Wolfgang, *Johann Jakob Bodmer und Johann Jakob Breitinger*, Stuttgart: Metzler, 1973
———, "Rhetorische Tradition und Ästhetik im 18. Jahrhundert: Baumgarten, Meier, und Breitinger," *Zeitschrift für deutsche Philologie* 99 (1980)
Bing, Susi, *Die Naturnachahmungstheorie bei Gottsched und den Schweizern und ihre Beziehung zu der Dichtungstheorie der Zeit*, Würzburg: Triltsch, 1934
Brandes, Helga, *Die Gesellschaft der Maler und ihr literarischer Beitrag zur Aufklärung: Eine Untersuchung zur Publizistik des 18. Jahrhunderts*, Bremen: Schünemann, 1974
Brown, F. Andrew, "Locke's 'Essay' and Bodmer and Breitinger," *Modern Language Quarterly* 10 (1949)
Herrmann, Hans Peter, *Naturnachahmung und Einbildungskraft: Zur Entwicklung der deutschen Poetik von 1670 bis 1740*, Bad Homburg: Gehlen, 1970
Kowalik, Jill Anne, *The Poetics of Historical Perspectivism: Breitinger's "Critische Dichtkunst" and the Neoclassic Tradition*, Chapel Hill: University of North Carolina Press, 1992
Martinson, Steven D., *On Imitation, Imagination, and Beauty: A Critical Reassessment of the Concept of the Literary Artist during the Early German "Aufklärung,"* Bonn: Bouvier, 1977
Möller, Uwe, *Rhetorische Überlieferung und Dichtungstheorie im frühen 18. Jahrhundert: Studien zu Gottsched, Breitinger, und G.Fr. Meier*, Munich: Fink, 1983
Müller, Jan-Dirk, "J.J. Bodmer's Poetik und die Wiederentdeckung mittelhochdeutscher Epen," *Euphorion* 71 (1977)
Preisendanz, Wolfgang, "Mimesis und Poiesis in der deutschen Dichtungstheorie des 18. Jahrhunderts," in *Rezeption und Produktion zwischen 1570 und 1730*, edited by Wolfdietrich Rasch et al., Bern: Francke, 1972
Scherpe, Klaus R., *Gattungspoetik im 18. Jahrhundert: Historische Entwicklung von Gottsched bis Herder*, Stuttgart: Metzler, 1968
Schmidt, Horst-Michael, *Sinnlichkeit und Verstand: Zur philosophischen und poetologischen Begründung von Erfahrung und Urteil in der deutschen Aufkärung (Leibniz, Wolff, Gottsched, Bodmer und Breitinger, Baumgarten)*, Munich: Fink, 1982
Stahl, Karl Heinz, *Das Wunderbare als Problem und Gegenstand der deutschen Poetik des 17. und 18. Jahrhunderts*, Frankfurt: Athenaion, 1975
Wetterer, Angelika, *Publikumsbezug und Wahrheitsanspruch: Der Widerspruch zwischen rhetorischem Ansatz und philosophischem Anspruch bei Gottsched und den Schweizern*, Tübingen: Niemeyer, 1981

Clemens Brentano 1778–1842

Clemens Brentano, a writer of novels, novellas, and dramas, is a major representative of German Romanticism and indeed popular religious writings in the first half of the 19th century. Although his death in 1842 barely aroused the attention of the literary world of the time, his lyric poetry spanning over 40 years captured the hearts of German-speaking peoples and served as a basis for German lyric poetry throughout the century. The tumultuous historical epoch, stretching from the rise of Napoléon's dictatorship and the German wars of liberation and through the period of restoration, reflected his chaotic personal life and diverse literary production.

Born into a wealthy, educated family, his grandmother was the writer Sophie La Roche. Brentano moved to Jena in 1798. It was in this city, then the center of early Romanticism, that the young Brentano entered literary circles that included August Wilhelm and Friedrich Schlegel, Dorothea Veit, and Ludwig Tieck and began his life as a writer defending the Romantic spirit. Throughout his oeuvre, his internal struggle with simplicity and modernity is present. While idealizing the past, Brentano explores how German literary and historical traditions can renew the present. Poesy was not only the ultimate expression of the unencumbered self, free from the constraints of a society of philistines, but it rejuvenated humankind as well.

While in Jena, Brentano published his first work, *Gustav Wasa* (1800; Gustav Wasa), in which he ardently defended the Romantic poetic program. The satire, which reveals a strong influence from Tieck, ridicules traditional writers, in this case August von Kotzebue, and their outdated modes of expression. In 1801–2, he published the novel *Godwi; oder, Das steinerne bild der Mutter: Ein verwilderte Roman* (Godwi; or, The Stone Statue of the Mother: A Novel Grown Wild), a bildungsroman that was his greatest contribution to the Romantics' notion of a modern form of prose. Following the lead of Tieck's *Franz Sternbalds Wanderungen* (1798; Franz Sternbald's Wanderings), Friedrich Schlegel's *Lucinde* (1799), and later Novalis's *Heinrich von Ofterdingen* (1802), Brentano offered an alternative to Goethe's classical bildungsroman, *Wilhelm Meisters Lehrjahre* (1795–96; *Wilhelm Meister's Apprenticeship*). The two-volume work narrates the nonlinear development of Godwi's highly subjective existence through a series of erotic wanderings and pleasures. Godwi's development, his amoral life, and his search for entertainment reflect the Romantics' notion of experience as a totality of being and existence.

Brentano's works for the stage reveal his belief that art has a mystical power to redefine not only humankind but history as well. The libretto *Die lustigen Musikanten* (1803; The Merry Minstrels), set to music by E.T.A. Hoffmann in 1805, thematizes the tensions between art and life. To survive, a group of singers perform and display their creativity, but this form of art is shown in stark ironic contrast to their terrible living conditions. In the commedia dell'arte and Shakespearean traditions, *Ponce de Leon* (1804) is a comedy that demonstrates Brentano's mastery of language. In the drama, which is poorly suited for performance because of its difficult language, characters' identities are concealed by disguises and costumes; tragedy is avoided only by an unbelievable "happy-end" solution brought about by a father figure. These dramas appeared during Brentano's tumultuous marriage to the author Sophie Mereau, who died in 1806. While living in Bohemia, Brentano began *Die Gründung Prags: Ein historisches-romantisches Drama* (1815; The Founding of Prague: A Historical-Romantic Drama), in which the mystical Czech history gives way to a modern, lyrical, Christian present.

When Brentano met Achim von Arnim in 1801 in Göttingen, his life was changed forever. They soon struck up a close friendship; in fact, Clemens's sister Bettina married Achim in 1811. Living in Heidelberg, the locus of Romanticism in its second phase, Brentano and Arnim published in 1805 the first volume of *Des Knaben Wunderhorn* (*The Boy's Magic Horn*), which would turn out to be their most influential work; volumes II and III followed in 1807 and 1808. Typical for the Romantics' interest in historical German literature, the two young authors collected and edited German folk songs and poems. They avoided literal transcription of the poems and instead opted for modern versions that captured the spirit of the times as well as folk ideas and language. The work was well received, even by those who had earlier denounced Romanticism, and helped foster an awareness of German identity during a period when German states were under French rule. With Arnim and Joseph von Görres, Brentano cofounded and coedited the Romantic journal *Zeitung für Einsiedler* (Newspaper for Hermits), later *Tröst Einsamkeit* (Comfort Loneliness).

The production of lyric poetry is the most consistent aspect of Brentano's life, which is characterized by its inconsistencies. His poetry appeared rarely by itself but was embedded in his prose and dramatic works as well as in personal correspondence. Although his poetry was influential and acclaimed, a collection of only his poetry appeared only in 1852, ten years after his death. His poems include some of the most recognizable in German literary history, such as "Sprich aus der Ferne," "Ein Fischer saß in Kahne," "Am Rhein schweb ich her und hin," "Der Spinnerin Nachtlied," and "Lore Lay." The themes of romantic longing and harmony between nature and humankind are evident throughout his oeuvre, but his rhythmic, songlike poetry also reveals tensions between subjective existence and terrorizing reality. The haunting search for an artistic muse, so often found in Brentano's poetry, underscores his lifelong fear of losing his poetic inspiration.

For many Romantic authors, the *Märchen* was the apotheosis of Romantic poetics and enabled authors to create a fantastic, believable reality. Characterized by a desire to recapture and reestablish a lost innocence, simplicity, and piety, Brentano's *Märchen* and short prose intertwine mysterious events and natural phenomena with folk-peasant rationalizations. After a period of limited literary production, Brentano published three of his most well known and unusual short prose pieces in 1817. *Die mehreren Wehmüller und ungarischen Nationalgesichter* (The Many Wehmüllers and Hungarian National Faces), a fantastic grotesque, consists of four individual narratives connected by an overarching framed story. The painter Wehmüller discovers that nature is not so creative as one thinks, and there are only 39 different national faces, differentiated only by scars and facial hair. While on the border between Croatia and Hungary, he discovers that his doppelgänger has mastered his artistic technique. This leads to the other narratives, even more fantastic, that evoke images of Hoffmannesque tales. In *Die drei Nüße* (The Three Nuts), Brentano demonstrates his artistic breadth by writing an early detective story that involves the attempt to solve a murder committed out of jealousy. Brentano harkens back to the Loreley theme of the potentially dangerous power of beauty and couples it with incestuous love between brother and sister. The lyrical, romantic novella *Geschichte vom braven Kasperl und dem schönen Annerl* (1817; translated as *Honor; or, The Story of Brave Caspar and the Fair Annerl* and *The Story of Just Caspar and Fair Annie*) is a melancholic story about suicide, execution, infanticide, and honor. When the petty officer Kasperl discovers that his father is a criminal, he commits suicide while his lover, Annerl, is hanged for killing her illegitimate child, a product of her seduction by a nobleman. With several twists, the fate of Kasperl and Annerl are brought together by an 80-year-old grandmother, who appeals to the reigning duke for a monument to be erected at the grave site of the two. The grandmother, intervening as narrator, explains the notion of honor that each had and differentiates between a positive, religiously based sense of honor and a dangerous, egotistical form.

In 1817, Brentano, whose works had previously revealed his interest in a form of modern mysticism and Catholicism, publicly accepted the Catholic faith after he moved to Berlin in 1814 and became acquainted with a group of evangelical Catholics.

Despite critics' claims that he was indentured to his Catholic causes, Brentano occasionally wrote in the Romantic style that he helped create, but most of his writings were dedicated to Catholicism. Isolating himself from society, he published his most widely read work in 1833, *Das bittere Leiden unseres Herrn Jesu Christi: Nach den Betrachtungen der gottseligen Anna Katharina Emmerich* (1914; *The Passions of Our Lord Jesus Christ according to the Revelations of Anna Catharina Emmerich*), in which he recorded the visions of the stigmatized nun Anna Katherina Emmerich. Alienated and completely withdrawn from society, Brentano died in 1842 as a forgotten poet.

GREGORY H. WOLF

Biography

Born in Ehrenbreitstein, 9 September 1778. Grandson of author Sophie von La Roche; brother of author Bettina von Arnim; studied at the University of Bonn, 1794; at Halle University, 1797; studied medicine at the University of Jena, 1798–1800; met Achim von Arnim in Göttingen, 1801; married Sophie Mereau, 1803 (died 1806); married Auguste Bußmann, 1807 (divorced 1812); associated with the Heidelberg group of Romantics; founding editor with von Arnim, *Zeitung für Einsiedler;* in Bohemia, 1811–13; in Vienna, 1813–14; in Berlin, 1817–42; secretary and copyist for the nun Anna Katharina Emmerich, 1817–24. Died in Aschaffenburg, 28 July 1842.

Selected Works

Collections

Gesammelte Schriften, edited by Christian Brentano, 9 vols., 1852–55
Werke, edited by Wolfgang Frühwald, 4 vols., 1963–68
Werke, edited by Max Preitz, 3 vols., 1974
Sämtliche Werke und Briefe, edited by Jürgen Behrens, Wolfgang Frühwald, and Detlev Lüders, 6 vols., 1975–86

Novel

Godwi; oder, Das steinerne bild der Mutter: Ein verwilderte Roman, 2 vols., 1801–2

Plays

Satiren und poetische Spiele. Gustav Wasa, 1800
Die lustigen Musikanten: Singspiel (opera libretto), music by E.T.A. Hoffmann (produced 1805), 1803
Ponce de Leon: Ein Lustspiel, 1804
Die Gründung Prags: Ein historisches-romantisches Drama, 1815

Poetry and Folksongs

Des Knaben Wunderhorn: Alte deutsche Lieder, edited with Achim von Arnim, 3 vols., 1805–8; selections as *The Boy's Magic Horn,* translated by Margarete Münsterberg, 1913
Gedichte, edited by Wolfgang Frühwald, 1968

Short Fiction

Die drei Nüße, 1817
Geschichte vom braven Kasperl und dem schönen Annerl, 1817; as *Honor; or, The Story of Brave Caspar and the Fair Annerl,* translated by T.W. Appell, 1847; as *The Story of Just Casper and Fair Annie,* translated by Helene Scher, 1975
Die mehreren Wehmüller und ungarischen Nationalgesichter: Erzählung, 1817
Gockel, Hinkel, und Gackeleia: Märchen wiedererzählt, 1838; as *The Wondrous Tale of Cocky, Clucky, and Cackle,* translated by C.W. Heckethorn, 1889; as *The Tale of Gockel, Hinkel, and Gackeliah,* translated by Doris Orgel, 1961
Fairy Tales from Brentano, translated by Kate Freiligrath Kroeker, 1885
New Fairy Tales from Brentano, translated by Kate Freiligrath Kroeker, 1888

Nonfiction

Das bittere Leiden unseres Hernn Jesu Christi: Nach den Betrachtungen der gottseligen Anna Katharina Emmerich, Augustinerin des Klosters Agnetenberg zu Dülmen, 1833; as *The Passions of Our Lord Jesus Christ according to the Revelations of Anne Catharina Emmerich,* 1914

Further Reading

Birrell, Gordon, "Paternal Order and Disorder in Brentano's 'Kasperl und Annerl'," *Monatshefte* 88 (1996)
Brandstetter, Gabriele, *Erotik und Religiosität: Eine Studie zur Lyrik Clemens Brentanos,* Munich: Fink, 1986
Fetzer, John F., *Clemens Brentano*, Boston: Twayne, 1981
Frühwald, Wolfgang, "Clemens Brentano," in *Deutsche Dichter der Romantik*, edited by Benno von Wiese, Berlin: Schmidt, 1971; 2nd edition, 1983
——, *Das Spätwerk Clemens Brentanos (1815–1842): Romantik im Zeitalter der Metternich'schen Restauration,* Tübingen: Niemeyer, 1977
Frye, Lawrence O., *Poetic Wreaths: Art, Death, and Narration in the Märchen of Clemens Brentano,* Heidelberg: Winter, 1989
Hoffmann, Werner, *Clemens Brentano: Leben und Werk,* Bern and Munich: Francke, 1966
Kastinger Riley, Helene M., *Clemens Brentano,* Stuttgart: Metzler, 1985
Lubkoll, Christine, "Männlicher Gesang und Weiblicher Text? Das Verwirrspiel der Autorschaft in Clemens Brentanos 'Der Sänger'," in *Autorschaft: Genus und Genie in der Zeit um 1800,* edited by Ina Schabert and Barbara Schaff, Berlin: Schmidt, 1994
Müller-Seidel, Walter, "Brentanos naive und sentimentalische Poesie," *Jahrbuch der deutschen Schillergesellschaft* 18 (1974)
Neumann, Gerhard, "Der Schreiber und die alte Frau: Weibliche und männliche Autorschaft in Brentanos 'Geschichten des braven Kasperl und dem schönen Annerl'," in *Autorschaft: Genus und Genie in der Zeit um 1800*, edited by Ina Schabert and Barbara Schaff, Berlin: Schmidt, 1994
Regener, Ursula, "Arabesker Godwi: Immanente Kunsttheorie und Gestaltreflexion in Brentanos Roman," *Modern Language Notes* 103 (1988)
Reifenberg, Bernd, *Die "schöne Ordnung" in Clemens Brentanos Godwi und Ponce de Leon,* Göttingen: Vandenhoeck und Ruprecht, 1990
Zierden, Josef, *Das Zeitproblem im Erzählwerk Clemens Brentanos,* Frankfurt and New York: Lang, 1985

Hermann Broch 1886–1951

Hermann Broch's decisive turn to writing came in the late 1920s. Over the next two decades he was to produce three major novels, the trilogy *Die Schlafwandler* (1931–32; *The Sleepwalkers*), *Der Tod des Vergil* (1945; *The Death of Virgil*), and the incomplete and posthumous *Die Verzauberung* (1976; *The Spell*), as well as stories, critical essays, philosophical and sociopolitical writings, and a corpus of poetry. Toward the end of his life, when he was primarily preoccupied with his psychology of mass hysteria, Broch lost his faith in the potential ethical and cognitive insights that he had initially hoped literature would be able to deliver. For this reason, Hannah Arendt, who only knew him during his final American years, referred to him as a "reluctant writer." Yet Broch had turned to creative writing in a spirit of hope after his disappointment in what he saw as the lamentable state of current philosophy, which he had experienced at first hand while studying under the leading logical positivists of the Vienna Circle. At the end of the 1920s, at the time of work on *The Sleepwalkers,* Broch expressed his conviction that "the new form of the novel has taken over the task of absorbing the parts of philosophy which . . . correspond to metaphysical needs but which are today reckoned . . . to be either 'non-scientific' or, in Wittgenstein's words, 'mystical.'" Literature, he believed, not only responded more adequately to mankind's metaphysical needs, but it could also give the ethical impetus that had been rigorously excluded from contemporary philosophy. Broch's thinking by then owed too much to Kant, Schopenhauer, and Hegel for him to be able to regard philosophy and literature as simple alternatives. The philosophy with which he specifically contrasted creative writing (*Dichtung*) was logical positivism, and the kind of literature that he saw as the antidote to contemporary philosophy's dereliction of responsibility was above all a new form of philosophical (or "polyhistorical") novel, which was able to synthesize psychological fiction with the philosophy of history.

What was to become Broch's lifelong, theory-based, experimental approach to fiction is already well in evidence in his first substantial piece: "Eine methodologische Novelle" (A Methodological Novelle). This was later to appear in revised form with the even more revealing title of "Methodisch konstruiert" in the posthumously published Novelle-novel *Die Schuldlosen* (1950; *The Guiltless*). The method employed here, one clearly indebted to Zola's notion of the "experimental novel," is to erect a series of theoretical premises, creative hypotheses, and notions of probable development that guide the course of the narrative and guarantee the typicality of the caricatured philistine mind-set. The extent to which every component of Broch's fiction has a logical justification and an exemplifying function invariably tends to move the resultant material in the direction of allegorized philosophy. In the case of his methodological Novelle, Broch worked deductively from theory to narrative exemplification; in *The Sleepwalkers,* on the other hand, he appears to be moving inductively in the other direction, from fictive illustration that delineates a theory, which is able to account for the material's significance. Yet despite this impression, it is not insignificant that Broch began work on the trilogy by first drafting the last novel, *Huguenau; oder, Die Sachlichkeit* (*The Realist*), which was to contain the diagnostic and explanatory "Disintegration of Values" chapters. In fact, throughout the next two decades, Broch's fiction was to display a marked tendency to be theory-driven, the major difference being between the early works, where theory is often a highly prominent and explicit component, and the later ones, where the underlying rationale remains implicit and the requisite theoretical context is more likely to be found in separately published essays.

Although his long contextualizing essay *Hofmannsthal und seine Zeit* (1974; *Hugo von Hofmannsthal and His Time*) and the novel *The Spell,* set in a fictionalized version of the region around Alt-Aussee in Styria, show that Broch was not averse to setting works in his native Austria, he chose to situate the *Sleepwalkers* trilogy in Wilhelmine Germany. No doubt this afforded the necessary distance and objectivity to analyze the vast gallery of victims of the modern disintegration of values seen in *Pasenow, Esch,* and *Huguenau.* A further possible factor could be the suggestion that the process of disintegration was at the time more advanced in Germany than in Austria. In any case, the degree of abstraction in the depiction of the shifting milieus (imperial Berlin, the *Junker* estates of West Prussia, and the Rhineland and Moselle regions) did not require a high degree of local color; instead, it was the psychological dislocations experienced by modernity's victims and the survival strategies that they adopted that were the main foci of interest. The concepts of "romanticism," "anarchy," and "realism," which Broch's novel employs in its diagnosis of a fragmented contemporary world, may seem disarmingly idiosyncratic (although each is explained in the work's theoretical chapters), but the sense of "sleepwalking"—leaving behind the reassuringly circumscribed realm of reason, order, and shared values—is powerfully communicated even in the first relatively conventional volume in the series. Both the novel's paradigmatic illustrations and its diagnosis present us with a picture of a world of loneliness, where individuals seek refuge in private value systems or attempt to return to the securities of the past, although they do not find an adequate solution to the modern predicament. The rational "partial value-systems" depicted in *The Sleepwalkers* demonstrate at what cost the absolute realm of the irrational (for which Broch used the code phrase "the Christian-Platonic Idea") is ignored. At the end of the process of disintegration, we are shown the "value-free" amoralism and the eventual anarchy of the deserter, confidence trickster, murderer, and rapist Huguenau. Alongside his automatic response to the loss of a coherent, absolute value-system, we witness the pathetic attempts of other figures to turn the clock back by variously putting their faith in sectarian Christian mysticism, preparing the way for the advent of some unspecified messiah; reasserting the world's lost moral coherence by imposing bookkeeping principles of credit, debit, and balance; or acting on the belief that some form of sacrifice will put things right. Although overrigid reason and nebulous irrationality both assume a series of suspect forms in *The Sleepwalkers,* the novel's main charge is clearly that myopic "partial value-systems" have played a major role in insulating people from the need to acknowledge their metaphysical loss.

Broch's next novel, *Die unbekannte Größe* (1933; *The Unknown Quantity*), can be read as a coda to *The Sleepwalkers* inasmuch as it is the story of how the unworldly mathematician

Richard Hieck is forced to rethink his philosophy as a result of both the death of his younger brother and falling unexpectedly in love with one of his female colleagues. The "unknown quantity" of love and his newfound sense of mortality are presented as transforming experiences for Hieck, even if the novel does not follow him beyond their impact. Broch's rewriting of this rather predictable story as a screenplay and its serialized prepublication in a German newspaper are both early indications of his recurrent problem concerning how many concessions to make or whether he should not compromise himself by writing with an eye to a middlebrow readership. After *The Unknown Quantity,* he was never to compromise his standards to the same extent again.

In 1936, Broch completed the first version of his so-called "Mountain Novel," published posthumously, first by Rhein-Verlag under the title *Der Versucher* (1953), then as *The Spell.* Reminiscent in some respects of Thomas Mann's *Mario and the Magician,* it is the story of a mystical demagogue's attempt to keep his hold over a mountain community and win the villagers over to his brand of false nature mysticism. The intruder, Marius Ratti, gradually seduces most of the community with his talk of a new mythical union between man and nature, his diatribes against modern technology, and his preaching of the need for scapegoats and a sacrificial victim—who is duly killed as a ritual purification of the village. Like the storyteller in Mann's *Mario,* the first-person narrator, the country doctor, is not fully immune to the leader figure's fascinating appeal, although he is more sympathetic to the demagogue's main adversary: Mutter Gisson, a Jungian Earth Mother figure whose gnostic utterances and cryptic folk wisdom hardly come across as an adequate response to the fascist threat that the figures of Ratti and his dwarf accomplice Wenzel are intended to represent.

In 1937 Broch abandoned work on a second version of *The Spell.* Responding to the increasingly threatening political climate (the Abyssinian War, Hitler's expansionist threats, the Spanish Civil War, and the growing threat to Austria's own national integrity), he turned from literature to political involvement, drafting a "Resolution" to the supine League of Nations and developing an antifascist "theory of humanity." Although ineffective at the time, these activities laid the foundations for a number of Broch's major nonliterary projects during his years of exile in the United States: his theories of law and politics, and his *Völkerbundtheorie* (Theory of the League of Nations). Less immediately, this change of direction would also be of great significance for his uncompleted but substantial theory of mass hysteria: *Massenwahntheorie.* In America he would also write *The Death of Virgil* and, on the insistence of his European publishers, set about completing *The Guiltless* and, unsuccessfully, the third version of *The Spell,* as well as writing *Hugo von Hofmannsthal and His Time* for the Bollingen Series.

The Death of Virgil represents the peak of Broch's engagement with myth, mythology, and Jungian archetypes. In "Die mythische Erbschaft der Dichtung" (1945; The Mythical Heritage of Literature) and "The Style of the Mythical Age" (1947; published originally in English), Broch pleaded for a literary return to myth, not so much as a mythological scaffold superimposed on modernity in the manner of Joyce's *Ulysses,* but as a "new myth" that he felt Kafka's novels embodied. In the case of *The Death of Virgil,* however, he still attempted to create a new myth out of the building blocks of two earlier mythological sources: Virgil's own *Aeneid* and the New Testament. Writing of the story "Die Heimkehr des Vergil," the seed of his later Virgil novel, Broch notes:

> it did not require much reflection to recall the parallels between the first century BC and our own world—civil war, dictatorship, a dying off of old religious forms; . . . I knew of a legend in which Virgil had wanted to burn the *Aeneid* and—accepting the legend—I could assume that a mind such as Virgil's could hardly have been driven to such an act of despair by trivial reasons, but rather that the entire historical and metaphysical content of the epoch had played its part in the decision.

In other words, within the space of an account of the last 24 hours of the Latin poet's life, the novel would be required to indicate a cultural diagnosis similar in scope to that in *The Sleepwalkers*: to suggest parallels between a fictive pre-Christian world and contemporary European politics on a scale comparable to those attempted in *The Spell,* to suggest analogies between the Roman poet's sense of a new savior's imminence and comparable motifs in Virgil's *Eclogues,* and to relate one man's mythical journey by water to the harbor at Brundisium (a symbolic birth) to an eventual death, which is figured as a replica of the Book of Genesis in reverse. Built into the question of why, or even whether, the fictive Virgil should want to have the *Aeneid* destroyed were to be Broch's own misgivings about the poet as an ivory-tower figure (Virgil spends his dying hours in a tower and runs the gauntlet of the mob-like *Volk* while being borne on a litter to his deathbed). This problem of the poet's status in the people's eyes is compounded by Virgil's equivalent of Broch's own misgivings about poetry's epistemological inadequacies. The resultant work, although multilayered and rich in mythological and historical associations, is first and foremost a lyrical *pièce de résistance.* It is with respect to the language chosen to convey Virgil's feverish interior monologues and his strangely hallucinatory conversations with Caesar Augustus, his friends, and attendants that opinions are wont to differ. Aldous Huxley advised Broch to break up the interminably complex, disorienting sentences, but their author was intransigent. According to his English translator, Broch claimed that the rhythms of the novel came to him while in a Nazi prison in the form of "long, wavelike sentences, mounting slowly to a peak and receding, their crescendos and diminuendos following each other like the oceanic surge of an incoming tide." The work's challenging style makes few concessions to the reader, but for those hardy enough to immerse themselves in its unrelenting syntax, complex mythicizing structures, and high degree of cross-cultural intertextuality, *The Death of Virgil* brings many rewards.

Most of Broch's published work between 1945 and his death in 1951 was undertaken on commission and partly with a view to reestablishing his reputation in Europe. When the German publisher Willi Weismann sent him the unsolicited proofs of some of his earlier *Novellen,* he rewrote them, adding further stories and a series of lyrical bridging passages. The result became *The Guiltless.* The theme of political guilt is symbolically transposed to a modern reworking of Mozart's *Don Giovanni* (interpreted within the framework of Kierkegaard's *Either/Or*), but just as *The Spell*'s translation of the rise of fascism to a parabolic mountain community is not without its drawbacks, so here the equation of private relations with recent politics lacks the historicity of Mann's *Doctor Faustus.* Broch's greatest postwar achievement, his *Massenwahntheorie,* had to wait until 1979 before it appeared in the critical edition; it has yet to receive the scholarly attention it deserves.

J. J. WHITE

Biography

Born in Vienna, Austria, 1 November 1886. Studied at the Technical College for Textile Manufacture, Vienna, 1904–6, and the Spinning and Weaving College, Mülhausen, 1906–7; administrator for the Red Cross, Austria, during World War I; managed his family's factory, Teesdorf, 1907–27; reviewer for *Moderne Welt,* Vienna, 1919; studied mathematics, philosophy, and psychology, Vienna University, 1926–30; writer; arrested and detained by the Nazis, 1938; in London, 1938; in the United States involved in refugee work, from 1940; became U.S. citizen, 1944; fellow at Saybrook College, Yale University, New Haven, Connecticut, 1949. Guggenheim fellowship, 1941; member of the American Academy, 1942. Died 30 May 1951.

Selected Works

Collections

Gesammelte Werke, edited by Felix Stössinger, et al., 10 vols., 1953–61
Kommentierte Werkausgabe, edited by Paul Michael Lützeler, 13 vols., 1974–81

Fiction

Die Schlafwandler: Eine Romantrilogie, 1931–32; as *The Sleepwalkers: A Trilogy,* translated by Edwin and Willa Muir, 1932; new edition, with introduction and notes by John J. White, 2000
Pasenow; oder, Die Romantik, 1888, 1931
Esch; oder, Die Anarchie, 1903, 1931
Huguenau; oder, Die Sachlichkeit, 1918, 1932
Die unbekannte Größe, 1933; as *The Unknown Quantity,* translated by Edwin and Willa Muir, 1935
Der Tod des Vergil, 1945; as *The Death of Virgil,* translated by Jean Starr Untermeyer, 1945
Die Schuldlosen, 1950; as *The Guiltless,* translated by Ralph Manheim, 1974
Der Versucher, edited by Felix Stössinger; in *Gesammelte Werke,* vol. 4, 1953
Der Bergroman, edited by Frank Kress and Hans Albert Maier, 4 vols., 1969
Barbara und andere Novellen, edited by Paul Michael Lützeler, 1973
Die Verzauberung, edited by Paul Michael Lützeler, 1976; as *The Spell,* translated by H.F. Broch de Rothermann, 1987

Plays

Die Entsühnung (produced 1934)
Aus der Luft gegriffen; oder, die Geschäfte des Baron Laborde (produced 1981)

Other

Zur Universitätsreform, edited by Götz Wienold, 1969
Gedanken zur Politik, edited by Dieter Hildebrand, 1970
Briefwechsel 1930–1951, with Daniel Brody, edited by Bertold Hack and Marietta Kleiss, 1971
Völkerbund-Resolution, edited by Paul Michael Lützeler, 1973
Hofmannsthal und seine Zeit: Eine Studie, 1974; as *Hugo von Hofmannsthal and His Time: The European Imagination 1860–1920,* edited and translated by Michael P. Steinberg, 1984
Menschenrecht und Demokratie: Politische Schriften, edited by Paul Michael Lützeler, 1978
Briefe über Deutschland, 1945–1949: Die Korrespondenz mit Volkmar von Zühlsdorff, edited by Paul Michael Lützeler, 1986
Das Teesdorfer Tagebuch für Ea von Allesch, edited by Paul Michael Lützeler, 1995
Hannah Arendt–Hermann Broch Briefwechsel, 1946–51, edited by Paul Michael Lützeler, 1996
Psychische Selbstbiographie, edited by Paul Michael Lützeler, 1999

Further Reading

Arendt, Hannah, *Men in Dark Times,* New York: Harcourt, Brace, 1968
Dowden, Stephen D., editor, *Hermann Broch: Literature, Philosophy, Politics: The Yale Broch Symposium 1986,* Columbia, South Carolina: Camden House, 1988
Durzak, Manfred, *Hermann Broch,* Stuttgart: Metzler, 1967
———, *Hermann Broch: Der Dichter und seine Zeit,* Stuttgart: Kohlhammer, 1968
Durzak, Manfred, editor, *Hermann Broch: Perspektiven der Forschung,* Munich: Fink, 1972
Lützeler, Paul Michael, *Hermann Broch: Eine Biographie,* Frankfurt: Suhrkamp, 1985; as *Hermann Broch: A Biography,* translated by Janice Furness, London: Quartet Books, 1987
Schlant, Ernestine, *Hermann Broch,* Boston: Twayne, 1978
Strelka, Joseph, editor, *Broch heute,* Frankfurt: Suhrkamp, 1977
Ziolkowski, Theodore, *Hermann Broch,* New York: Columbia University Press, 1964

Die Schlafwandler 1931–1932

Novel by Hermann Broch

Although the English translation of the work appears as a single volume, the individual novels comprising Broch's *Schlafwandler* trilogy (1931–32; *The Sleepwalkers*) were first published separately in German. Each title indicates the specific year in which events take place, as well as identifying the central character and the style of thinking or stage within the progressive disintegration of values that he epitomizes: *Pasenow; oder, Die Romantik, 1888; Esch; oder, Die Anarchie, 1903;* and *Huguenau; oder, Die Sachlichkeit, 1918.* Broch confessed that he would have ideally liked to call the project simply "Historical Novel," but he appreciated that such a generic abstraction would have been detrimental to sales of a work that was, in any case, challengingly philosophical. He thus chose instead to center the trilogy on the sleepwalking image, with its association of people moving in a dreamlike state of semi-awareness from a world of hitherto protectively ordered codes of behavior and ethical norms to an alternative reality whose essence they could not yet comprehend. In order to illustrate this shift, the narrative approach combines depth psychology with philosophy of history. "With the collapse of traditional cultural fictions," Broch declared in a draft "Methodological Prospectus," "the dreamlike element (das Traumhafte) is progressively set free."

Sleepwalking, in Broch's idiosyncratic symbolism, is an experience that manifests itself in a wide variety of diverse forms: eccentric rationalizations, the failure to stay within the rigid behavior patterns defined by one's social background or profession, sectarian mysticism, the erotic, the pseudo-messianic, the amoral, and directionless anarchic outbursts. The extent to which Broch's trilogy is primarily (or even exclusively) a diagnosis of the modern world's "atomization of values" and spiritual fragmentation—or points the way toward a possible transcendence of the predicament exemplified by virtually all the characters in *Pasenow, Esch,* and *Huguenau*—has remained a matter of scholarly dispute. The final volume, and in particular the trilogy's "Epilogue," has played a major role in the case for and against this idea.

Broch's *magnum opus* is predicated on the assumption that the ethically and epistemologically disintegrating world that it depicts is the culmination of a 400-year process of secularization. As a result of this process, the Christian-Platonic absolute (Broch's hyphenated term) that once gave meaning to all ideas, values, and actions has been replaced by a series of mere "partial value systems" or "private theologies." As a consequence of what the novel calls "the unleashing of logic," moreover, the 20th century has lost the coherence of a world whose "whole system of values was subordinated to the living value of faith." Where once God was the central point of reference (or "point of plausibility") giving absolute meaning to all value systems, these have now become autonomous, each one being espoused by a different kind of person: "like strangers they exist side by side, an economic value-system of 'good business' next to an aesthetic one of *l'art pour l'art,* a military code of values side by side with a technical or an aesthetic one." This "disintegration of values," one of the trilogy's central concepts, is presented as a largely negative phenomenon, not just on account of the loss of spiritual coherence, but because the various coexisting surrogate "partial value-systems" compete for hegemony both within the individual and within society. And in Broch's eyes, "when the secular exalts itself as the absolute, the result is always romanticism." The trilogy's governing antitheses of order and chaos, reason and the irrational, and the material and the spiritual are already present in the way in which the first volume treats the destabilizing experiences of a member of the officer caste (Pasenow), and the pattern finds its nadir in the manner in which the final novel, set in 1918, chronicles the human loss exacted by World War I, an event that is presented more as a symptom than an ultimate cause of the loss of absolutes, which is the trilogy's main theme. Each novel in the trilogy reflects the process of disintegration by being written in a different style and displaying a symptomatic "style of thought." *Pasenow* still retains vestiges of Fontane's world, which supported largely shared social codes and values. By contrast, the final novel, with its mixture of contrapuntally arranged subplots, theoretical chapters, lyrical episodes, and changing styles, represents a unique experimental vehicle for evoking the period of extreme disintegration, even if it does display some similarities with such multistranded narratives as Gide's *The Counterfeiters* and Huxley's *Point Counter Point* and the stylistic pluralism of Joyce's *Ulysses.* Although Broch's trilogy clearly belongs to the body of intellectual romans-fleuves diagnosing the state of the Western European culture that emerged during the interwar years (works including Mann's *Magic Mountain,* Musil's *Man without Qualities, Ulysses,* and *The Counterfeiters*), there are certain key respects in which the author's claim that his work is a radical innovation ("ein Novum") nevertheless rings true. The ingenious fusion of the trilogy format with stylistic experimentation makes it strikingly different from all of the canonical "encyclopedic" or "polyhistorical" works, as Broch called them, with which it is usually compared. By offering cross sections of three social microcosms (*Junker*-dominated, agrarian West Prussia; the petit bourgeois commercial world of the Rhineland; and the middle-class, small-town world of the Moselle), Broch is able to dissect the process of disintegration at three different junctures and thus make the unfolding historical process both dramatic and vivid.

The Sleepwalkers is that rare thing in 20th-century fiction: an intellectual novel without intellectual protagonists. Deliberately rejecting what he saw as the contrived way in which Mann, Musil, and Huxley handled the novel of ideas—by resorting to the strategy of having inordinately verbose intellectuals and artists engage in contrived philosophical discussions within the narrative—Broch boldly inserts the theory underlying the whole trilogy in discursive form in the concluding *Huguenau* novel. This "Disintegration of Values" essay offers a retrospective theoretical framework for the understanding of the various characters, events, and symbols that make up the entire trilogy. And since this section, rather than being superimposed, grows out of the fictive elements, its author was unwilling to allow the "Disintegration of Values" material to be published separately. Not only is the theoretical diagnosis presented as if it was in part derived inductively from the plot's examples, it also forms part of the elaborate "architectonic" or "polyphonic" (Broch's terms) contrapuntal structure of *Huguenau.* It thus has the double function of offering the theory behind the fiction as well as representing the most rational of analytical discourses within a stylistic spectrum ranging from the abstract and diagnostic to the lyrical and irrational. By this strategy, Broch hoped the novel would be able to reinstate concerns about ethics and the spirit—the loss of which he saw as one of the primary symptoms of the disintegration of the values presented in *The Sleepwalkers.*

J. J. WHITE

Editions

First edition: *Die Schlafwandler: Eine Romantrilogie,* 3 vols., Munich: Rhein-Verlag, 1931–32

Critical edition: in *Kommentierte Werkausgabe,* vol. 1, edited by Paul Michael Lützeler, Frankfurt: Suhrkamp, 1974

Translation: *The Sleepwalkers: A Trilogy,* translated by Edwin and Willa Muir, London: Secker and Warburg, and New York: Little Brown, 1932; new edition, with introduction and notes by John J. White, London: Penguin, 2000

Further Reading

Brude-Firnau, Gisela, *Materialien zu Hermann Brochs Die Schlafwandler,* Frankfurt: Suhrkamp, 1972

Cohn, Dorrit C., *The Sleepwalkers: Elucidations of Hermann Broch's Trilogy,* The Hague: Mouton, 1966

Geissler, Rolf, *Möglichkeiten des modernen deutschen Romans: Analysen und Interpretationsgrundlagen zu Romanen von Thomas Mann, Alfred Döblin, Hermann Broch, Gerd Gaiser, Max Frisch, Alfred Andersch und Heinrich Böll,* Frankfurt: Diesterweg, 1962

Hatfield, Henry, *Crisis and Continuity in Modern German Fiction,* Ithaca, New York: Cornell University Press, 1969

Kreutzer, Leo, *Erkenntnistheorie und Prophetie: Hermann Brochs Romantrilogie Die Schlafwandler,* Tübingen: Niemeyer, 1966

Kundera, Milan, *The Art of the Novel,* New York: Grove Press, 1988; London: Picador, 1990

Lützeler, Paul Michael, *Hermann Broch: Ethik und Politik: Studien zum Frühwerk und zur Romantrilogie Die Schlafwandler,* Munich: Winkler, 1973

Steinecke, Hartmut, *Hermann Broch und der polyhistorische Roman: Studien zur Theorie und Technik eines Romantyps der Moderne,* Bonn: Bouvier, 1968

Stevens, Adrian, et al., editors, *Hermann Broch: Modernismus, Kulturkrise und Hitlerzeit,* London: Institute of Germanic Studies, 1994

Vollhardt, Friedrich, *Hermann Brochs geschichtliche Stellung: Studien zum philosophischen Frühwerk und zur Romantrilogie "Die Schlafwandler" (1914–1932),* Tübingen: Niemeyer, 1986

Ziolkowski, Theodore, "Hermann Broch and Relativity in Fiction," *Wisconsin Studies in Comparative Literature* 3 (1967)

———, *Dimensions of the Modern Novel: German Texts and European Contexts,* Princeton, New Jersey: Princeton University Press, 1969

Georg Büchner 1813–1837

Universally considered one of the greatest German writers of the 19th century, Georg Büchner left behind only a small literary oeuvre upon his death at the age of 24. Numerous performances of Büchner's plays are now held every year throughout Europe and North America. The atechtonic or open-ended structure of his dramatic works later influenced such German-speaking dramatists as Wedekind, Brecht, and Dürrenmatt. Moreover, Büchner's prescient, sometimes apocalyptic depiction of the victimization of the individual by society and the state deeply affected the spiritual weltanschauung of German Expressionism. Likewise, Büchner's incisive portrayal of the tormented, alienated subjectivity of his characters exerted a profound impact on 20th-century existentialist drama in all its forms, including theater of the absurd. An important opera based on his play *Woyzeck* (written 1835–37, first published 1879, first produced 1913) was composed by Alban Berg (*Wozzeck,* first performed in 1925). A film version of the same work, directed by Werner Herzog, appeared in 1979. *The Serpent's Egg* (1977), a film by the Swedish director Ingmar Bergman, manifests the influence of Büchner on this artist's dark aesthetic. Never an adherent of such movements as literary realism or left Hegelianism, Büchner's so-called realist aesthetics focus on historical and societal collisions that evince, ultimately, arcane metaphysical implications.

In the wake of German Idealism, the contradictions and collisions portrayed in Büchner's literary works render highly problematic the monumental philosophical syntheses envisaged by the great Romantic Idealists Goethe, Fichte, Hegel, and Novalis. For example, in *Dantons Tod* (1835, first performed 1902; *Danton's Death*), Büchner depicts how a powerful revolutionary dictator—whose persona is based on the historical figure, Louis de Saint-Just—transmogrifies Fichte's utopian dialectics of historical evolution into a chilling justification of mass murder. Büchner's works encompass multifarious dimensions of significance, one of which involves his anti-Hegelian refusal to sublate, and therefore to resolve, the complex dissonances and shattering negations that he incorporates into his dramas. Scholarly efforts to explicate these works thus exhibit anything but a harmonious consensus as to the "meaning" of a particular text. Notwithstanding their complexity, however, Büchner's writings are increasingly gaining wide popular recognition outside of Germany as literary masterpieces having particular resonance with readers and audiences at the close of the 20th century.

Büchner's first published piece was a privately printed political leaflet written in 1834, entitled *Der hessische Landbote* (1834; translated as *The Hessian Courier* and *The Hessian Messenger*). Appalled by the powerlessness and despair of the impoverished proletariat in the grand duchy of Hesse, Büchner seeks to bring readers of his leaflet to a full awareness of the reality of their situation. He asserts that the grand duchy exists only to benefit the wealthy; the latter therefore have a vested interest in perpetuating the stagnant feudal order that is the foundation of their power. Furthermore, Büchner claims that the merciless exploitation and immiseration of the many by the few in Germany is indeed sanctioned by the political and religious status quo predominating in the land. Büchner's arguments in *The Hessian Messenger* clearly demonstrate his wish to demythologize the traditional notion of the feudal hierarchy as an institution decreed by God. He therefore exposes this theocratic order as an authoritarian glorification of inequality.

Between October 1834 and January 1835, Büchner composed one of the supreme masterpieces of world literature. A historical drama of the French Revolution, *Danton's Death* portrays a dynamic convergence of supraindividual historical forces and human subjectivity. This problematic convergence is particularly evident in the persona of Danton himself: a figure based on the historical revolutionary Georges Danton. At the outset of the Reign of Terror, Büchner's character is tortured in conscience because of his recent involvement in the infamous September Massacres of 1792. Danton's internal anguish is so profound that he longs for death. Tempted to flee personal responsibility in a Fichtean fantasy of historical determinism, Danton nevertheless defends his decision to order the slaughter that inaugurated the Terror, for among the victims of "September" were many powerful counterrevolutionary factions bent on restoring the ancient feudal regime (Büchner, 1986). This system had for centuries destroyed the lives of untold millions of the poor and disenfranchised. Assuming full existential responsibility for his revolutionary actions, Danton curses the awful historical Necessity—that of blood-letting—entailed by his assumption of this responsibility: "It must—it was this 'must' . . . Who has spoken this 'must,' who?" In this context, Danton utters his contempt for Jesus Christ, blasphemously accusing the latter of having "made it easy for himself" by fleeing the terrible necessity involved in authentic revolutionary struggle (Büchner, 1986). Danton's view is that in the apotheosis of his crucifixion and death, Christ eluded the inevitable moral, existential, and historical implications of revolution. Repudiating Christ, Danton affirms his own revolutionary striving as having been guided by the purpose of bringing real (i.e., *this-worldly*) salvation to suffering humanity.

Büchner's novella, *Lenz* (1839; *Lenz*), displays his nature-mysticism. Like Danton, Büchner's character Lenz is based on a historical personage, the poet Jakob Michael Reinhold Lenz. Lenz's rapturous descriptions of nature in Büchner's story are inspired by the philosopher Spinoza. Identifying the universe with God, this thinker defines nature as a dynamic totality of unlimited creative power. Each "mode" brought forth in the flow of nature's sempiternal duration is ensouled. Thus, in Spinoza's pantheistic view, all modal individuals, from leopard frogs to galaxies, are thinking and extended mirrors of God's *perfectio,* or unrestricted power-to-be. For Büchner's Lenz, the supreme source of joy attainable by humans lies in poetically intuiting the monistic life force of the *natura naturans* (God) as it is expressed in its creatures: "He believed it must be boundless ecstasy to be touched . . . by the unique life of every form; to commune with rocks . . . and plants; to assimilate each being in nature as in a dream" (Büchner, 1986). In the momentary exaltation of his Spinozan vision, Lenz admires the simple beauty and nobility of the common people. He also theorizes that true art can be created only by those whose genius, like that of the 17th-century Dutch painters, allows them to penetrate the veil of the Many to enter into mystic communion with the One, which is the ultimate source of life: "Only this abides: Infinite Beauty, . . . unfolding itself in eternal metamorphosis" (Büchner, 1992). However, throughout his narrative, Büchner contraposes Lenz's beatific adoration of nature to his description of the progressive deterioration of the latter's psyche into a dark nightmarish schizophrenia. Thus, his illness precipitates Lenz's tragic alienation from the divinity he worships.

Echoes of Büchner's critique of feudalism in *The Hessian Messenger* occur in his comedy *Leonce und Lena* (first published 1842, first produced 1895; *Leonce and Lena*). In this drama, Büchner assails the mystique of royalty by portraying his monarch figure, King Peter, as a megalomaniacal buffoon. In like fashion, he depicts members of the aristocracy as idle parasites who live off the impoverished laboring classes. The sociocritical impetus of *Leonce and Lena* reaches its consummation in Büchner's final work, a fragmentary play entitled *Woyzeck*. In this masterpiece of social drama, society is described as a living hell: a place of torture and enslavement for the working poor. Lenz's Spinozan affirmation of the irreducible dignity belonging to all human beings is thus shown, in *Woyzeck,* to be nullified by societal oppression.

Woyzeck, the title character of Büchner's play, ekes out a meager existence as an army barber. His wife, Marie, and their newly born child are the only sources of meaning and beauty in Woyzeck's world. Driven to near insanity by the degradation of his societal circumstances, Woyzeck breaks down upon learning of Marie's unfaithfulness with a petty officer, the Drum Major. In despair, he murders Marie. This horrible act mirrors the cruelty pervading Woyzeck's social environment, where he is systematically dehumanized. Viewed as a soulless automaton by the sadistic Doctor, Woyzeck becomes a guinea pig for the latter's scientific experiments. The Doctor's cold ruthlessness is paralleled by two other representations of bourgeois society: the Captain and the Professor. In *Woyzeck* Büchner thus depicts how the undivided affirmation of being embodied in Woyzeck's love for Marie is distorted into a hideous act of murder. But the "efficient cause" of this evil does not lie in Woyzeck's tormented consciousness alone. Instead, Büchner's play powerfully indicts a society that enslaves the workers and the poor as bearing ultimate responsibility for his character's act.

Like her husband, Marie is portrayed as a subject mercilessly degraded to the status of an object. Her treatment by the Drum Major is analogous to the Doctor's behavior toward Woyzeck, for Marie's brutish lover desires only to exploit her body. On the other hand, Marie's willingness to prostitute herself results from her desperation, the terrible corollary of her impoverished life. She therefore seeks to use the Drum Major, whose social status is higher than her husband's, to extricate herself and her child from the self-perpetuating hopelessness of their situation. Given her own status in society, this effort is destined to be a futile one. In effect, Büchner represents both Woyzeck and Marie as victims of a society founded on the insane notion that human beings, especially those occupying the lowest social strata, possess no intrinsic worth but are merely vehicles meant to serve purposes imposed from without.

RODNEY TAYLOR

Biography

Born in Goddelau, Duchy of Hesse Darmstadt, 17 October 1813. Medical student, University of Strasbourg, 1831–33, and University of Giessen, 1833–34; doctorate in biology, University of Zurich, 1836; founder of the political organization Gesellschaft der Menschenrechte, 1834; fled Germany to avoid arrest for sedition, 1835; lecturer in comparative anatomy, University of Zurich, 1836–37. Died 19 February 1837.

Selected Works

Collections

Nachgelassene Schriften, edited by Ludwig Büchner, 1850
Sämmtliche Werke und handschriftlicher Nachlass, edited by K.E. Franzos, 1879
Gesammelte Werke und Briefe, edited by Fritz Bergemann, 1922
Complete Plays and Prose, translated by Carl Richard Mueller, 1963
Sämtliche Werke und Briefe, edited by Werner R. Lehmann, 2 vols., 1967–71
Plays, translated by Victor Price, 1971; translated by Michael Hamburger, 1972
Complete Works and Letters, edited by Walter Hinderer, translated by Henry J. Schmidt, 1986
Complete Plays, edited by Michael Patterson, translated by John MacKendrick, 1987
Werke und Briefe, edited by Karl Pörnbacher, 1988
Sämtliche Werke, Briefe, und Dokumente, edited by Henri Poschmann, 1992–
Complete Plays, Lenz and Other Writings, edited and translated by John Reddick, 1993

Plays

Dantons Tod: Dramatische Bilder aus Frankreichs Schreckensherrschaft (produced 1902), 1835 (incomplete version); complete version in *Nachgelassene Schriften,* 1850; as *Danton's Death,* translated by Stephen Spender and Goronwy Rees, 1939; translated by T.H. Lustig, in *Classical German Drama,* edited by Lustig, 1963; translated by James Maxwell, 1968; translated by Victor Price, 1971; translated by Jane Fry and Howard Brenton, 1982; translated by John

MacKendrick, 1987; translated by John Reddick in *Complete Plays, Lenz and Other Writings,* 1993

Leonce und Lena (produced 1895); in *Mosaik, Novellen, und Skizzen,* edited by K. Gutzkow, 1842; as *Leonce and Lena,* translated by Eric Bentley, in *From Modern Repertoire,* vol. 3, 1956; also translated by Victor Price, 1971; translated by John Reddick in *Complete Plays, Lenz and Other Writings,* 1993

Woyzeck (produced 1913), 1879; as *Wozzeck,* in *Sämtliche Werke,* 1879; edited bo John Buthrie, 1988; as *Woyzeck,* translated by Theodore Hoffmann, in *The Modern Theatre,* vol. 1, edited by Eric Bentley, 1955; translated by Carl Richard Mueller, in *Complete Plays and Prose,* 1963; translated by Henry J. Schmidt, 1969; translated by Victor Price, 1971; translated by Michael Hamburger, 1972; translated by John MacKendrick, 1979; translated by John Reddick, in *Complete Plays, Lenz and Other Writings,* 1993

Fiction

Lenz, in *Telegraph für Deutschland,* January 1839; as *Lenz,* translated by Carl Richard Mueller, in *Complete Plays and Prose,* 1963; translated by Michael Hamburger, in *Three German Classics,* edited by Ronald Taylor, 1966; translated by F.J. Lamport, in *The Penguin Book of Short Stories,* 1974; translated by John MacKendrick in *Complete Plays,* 1987; translated by John Reddick in *Complete Plays, Lenz and Other Writings,* 1993

Other

Der hessische Landbote, with Pastor Weidig (pamphlet), 1834; as *The Hessian Courier,* translated by John MacKendrick, in *Complete Plays,* 1987; as *The Hessian Messenger,* translated by Henry J. Schmidt, in *Complete Works and Letters,* 1987; translated by John Reddick in *Complete Plays, Lenz and Other Writings,* 1993

Further Reading

Benn, Maurice B., *The Drama of Revolt: A Critical Study of Georg Büchner,* Cambridge and New York: Cambridge University Press, 1976

Hauschild, Jan-Christoph, *Georg Büchner: Biographie,* Stuttgart: Metzler, 1993

Knapp, Gerhard P., *Georg Büchner,* Stuttgart: Metzler, 1977; 2nd edition, 1984

Kobel, Erwin, *Georg Büchner: Das Dichter,* Berlin and New York: de Gruyter, 1974

Mayer, Hans, *Georg Büchner und seine Zeit,* Wiesbaden: Limes-Verlag, 1946; 4th edition, Frankfurt: Suhrkamp, 1980

Reddick, John, *Georg Büchner: The Shattered Whole,* Oxford: Clarendon Press, and New York: Oxford University Press, 1994

Sengle, Friedrich, *Biedermeierzeit,* vol. 3, *Die Dichter,* Stuttgart: Metzler, 1980

Taylor, Rodney, "History and the Transcendence of Subjectivity in Büchner's Robespierre," *Neophilologus* 72 (1988)

Whitinger, Raleigh, "Echoes of Novalis and Tieck in Büchner's *Lenz,*" *Seminar* 25 (1989)

Dantons Tod 1835

Play by Georg Büchner

One of the supreme achievements of 19th-century European literature, Georg Büchner's *Dantons Tod* (*Danton's Death*) is a historical drama encompassing multiple layers of meaning, which extend from issues concerning freedom and historical determinism to the existential significance of death. Approximately one-sixth of the drama consists of quotations from documents written during the French Revolution; the work also contains excerpts from a variety of historical studies. Likewise, *Danton's Death* incorporates occult references to philosophical works by Leibniz, Herder, and Fichte.

A dominant theme of Büchner's play lies in his depiction of a complex interrelationship between supraindividual historical forces and the subjective volitions—and psychic anguish—embodied in the great leaders of the French Revolution. Danton's tormented persona incarnates the collision between a darkly irrational historical necessity and the humane goals for the revolution that he originally projected for this movement. In opposition to his colleague, Robespierre, Danton perceives that the Reign of Terror signifies the failure of the revolution to bring an egalitarian democracy into existence.

As Danton is portrayed in the play, his revolutionary humanism does not prevent his decision to initiate the so-called September Massacres of 1792, which was, in his retrospective view, a pragmatic decision. Danton's purpose was to save the revolution from counterrevolutionary monarchist powers that were bent on its destruction. In a conversation with Julie, his wife, Danton maintains that his sanctioning of bloody purges on a massive scale was necessitated by his duty to the people:

> We fought them and won, that wasn't murder, it was . . . self-defense, we had to do it . . . it's the "must" [*Muß*] that did it. Who'd ever curse the hand on whom the curse of the "must" has fallen? Who spoke the curse, who?

Because of the torments inflicted upon him by his conscience, however, Danton yearns for death. His ultimate resolution to die exemplifies Büchner's ingenious portrayal, throughout his drama, of the *spiritual implications* of volitions, actions, and events taking place in the "external" domain of revolutionary history.

Indeed, Büchner powerfully articulates the magnitude of Danton's internal torment by raising this agony of conscience to the level of speculative metaphysics. Following their imprisonment by the Jacobins, Danton and his fellow revolutionaries engage in a bizarre discussion on the topic of death. Philippeau, Büchner's personification of cosmic optimism, assures Danton that human existence is immortal, analogizing the vital entelechy to a flower, the autumn crocus. Philippeau prophesies that the eventual withering of this flower's blossom must inevitably be succeeded by its miraculous reappearance. Similarly, death does not doom the monadic human persona to extinction. As do Leibniz and Jesus Christ, Büchner's character avers that the phenomenon of death is akin to sleep. More specifically, Philippeau likens death to the mere winter slumber of an autumn-flowering herb. Hence, following the demise of each one of its ephemeral bodies, the soul enters into a period of tranquil dormancy. When the preordained season of its "winter sleep" has elapsed, the soul is newly reborn "in the eternally blossoming garden of Time." For Philippeau, the human entelechy's endless cycle of death and rebirth corresponds to a preestablished divine order. Moreover, his quasi-Leibnizian metaphysic of immortality implies that throughout its series of reincarnations the soul ascends into progressively higher planes of mystic enlightenment.

Danton, however, impugns his friend's philosophical epiphany. Dismayed by this response, Philippeau asks Danton what he wishes for in death. "Peace" is the latter's reply. Danton asserts that real tranquillity can be found only in nothingness. Death, he hopes, will offer him the oblivion of eternal sleep, effecting the disintegration of his self-conscious *Ich* (Ego). Death will, consequently, annihilate his memory (*Gedächtnis*), thus disburdening him of all future awareness of the perdurability of his subjective identity in the stream of time. Danton views the dissolution of his subjectivity as tantamount to his *salvation,* his liberation from the incessant turmoil of his conscience: "[The grave] will annihilate my memory." Tragically, this turmoil has long since coalesced with Danton's inmost sense of personal identity. But his anguish is so great as to cause him to fear that the freedom for which he longs is a delusion born of unfounded desire. Despairingly acceding to Philippeau's doctrine of palingenesis, Danton bitterly—and satirically—contemplates the future agonies he is condemned to suffer as a result of his sempiternal personhood:

> What an edifying prospect! From one dung-heap to the other. So that's divine progression, is it? . . . I'm sick of school benches, I've sat on them so long my backside's as bare as a baboon's.

Thus, Danton's dark irony, reminiscent of Voltaire, transmogrifies Philippeau's sanguine theory of immortality into a disturbing expression of his psychic pain.

The convergence of internal subjectivity and historical actuality embodied in Büchner's Danton is likewise exemplified in Robespierre. In an angry confrontation with Danton, the latter defends the necessity of continuing the Terror, arguing that the ultimate aim of this phase of history is the creation of a socialist state. Following Danton's departure, however, Robespierre, alone in the darkness, encounters a nightmare apparition of his imagination: the personification of his tortured conscience. The horrifying guilt he suffers in ordering multitudes to the guillotine assumes a wraith-like form out of whose finger, pointed at the dictator, effuses an unstanchable flow of blood:

> Why can't I drive the thought from my mind? With bloody finger it points and points. I swathe it in layer upon layer of rags, but always the blood comes bursting through.

Similar to Danton, his former colleague, Robespierre's revolutionary goals and aspirations confront him with the awful necessity of causing blood to be shed for the sake of salvaging the revolution. Robespierre affirms the revolution as an event ordained by divine Providence to liberate the oppressed masses of the poor from their life of servitude to corrupt hierarchies of power. To accomplish the purpose of saving humankind from its perennial state of degradation, Robespierre is willing, indeed, to take upon himself the burden of being a "Messiah of Blood" (*Blutmessias*), the appalling designation given him by his onetime friend, Camille Desmoulins. Robespierre views his grim "messianic" vocation as destined, after a necessary period of travail, to usher in a millennial new age of Rousseauean virtue and spiritual *perfectibilitas.* The leader of the Terror therefore asserts his historical role as, in effect, superseding the reign of Jesus Christ. For Robespierre, the eschatological Kingdom promised by Christ was an illusion that perpetuated the this-worldly impuissance of Occidental humanity by positing a transcendent heaven as the goal of true salvation. But Büchner portrays his *Blutmessias* as a figure tragically doomed to become a victim of his own chiliastic visions. The historical prototype of Büchner's character was toppled from power shortly after Danton's execution: Robespierre mounted the scaffold of the guillotine on 28 July 1794. As Büchner was aware from his historical sources, members of the crowd witnessing Robespierre's execution made hushed comparisons of the event to the crucifixion of Christ. *Danton's Death* thus shows Büchner to be one of only two writers in the entire 19th century (the other was Thomas Carlyle) to appreciate the paradoxical yet tragic *greatness* of the historical Robespierre, who was called by the people *l'Incorruptible.*

RODNEY TAYLOR

Editions

First edition: *Dantons Tod: Dramatische Bilder aus Frankreichs Schreckensherrschaft,* Frankfurt: Sauerländer, 1835

Critical edition: in *Sämtliche Werke, Briefe, und Dokumente,* edited by Henri Poschmann, Frankfurt: Deutscher Klassiker Verlag, 1992

Translation: *Danton's Death,* in *Complete Plays, Lenz and Other Writings,* translated by John Reddick, London and New York: Penguin, 1993

Further Reading

Adolph, Winnifred R., *Disintegrating Myths: A Study of Georg Büchner,* New York: Lang, 1996

Behrmann, Alfred, and Joachim Wohlleben, *Büchner: Dantons Tod: Eine Dramenanalyse,* Stuttgart: Klett-Cotta, 1980

Georg Büchner: Dantons Tod, Lenz, Leonce und Lena, Woyzeck, Stuttgart: Reclam, 1990

Grimm, Reinhold, *Love, Lust, and Rebellion: New Approaches to Georg Büchner,* Madison: University of Wisconsin Press, 1985

Hilton, Julian, *Georg Büchner,* New York: Grove Press, and London: Macmillan, 1982

Jancke, Gerhard, *Georg Büchner: Genese und Aktualität seines Werkes,* Kronberg: Scriptor, 1975

Knapp, Gerhard P., *Georg Büchner: Dantons Tod,* Frankfurt: Diesterweg, 1983

Poschmann, Henri, *Georg Büchner: Dichtung der Revolution und Revolution der Dichtung,* Berlin: Aufbau, 1983

Reddick, John, "Georg Büchner and the Agony of Authenticity," *Forum for Modern Language Studies* 23 (October 1987)

Rey, William H., *Georg Büchners "Dantons Tod": Revolutionstragödie und Mysterienspiel,* Bern and Las Vegas, Nevada: Lang, 1982

Taylor, Rodney, *History and the Paradoxes of Metaphysics in "Dantons Tod,"* New York: Lang, 1990

——, "Saint-Just's Theodicy of History in *Dantons Tod,*" *Michigan Germanic Studies* 23, no. 1 (Spring 1997)

Wittkowski, Wolfgang, *Georg Büchner: Persönlichkeit, Weltbild, Werk,* Heidelberg: Winter, 1978

Woyzeck 1879

Play by Georg Büchner

Büchner began work on *Woyzeck* in 1835 in Strasbourg, where he took refuge after fleeing from Hesse to avoid imprisonment for his revolutionary activities. When he died in 1837 at the age of 23 in Zurich, where he had taken up a university lectureship in comparative anatomy, he left drafts of 32 scenes and a fair copy of 16. The scenes are not numbered, there is no overall plan, and the handwriting is hard to decipher. Consequently, the printed versions vary according to editors' conjectures as to the intended final version. The first edition appeared in 1879, with numerous errors, including the incorrect title (*Wozzek*), which was adopted by Alban Berg for his opera *Wozzeck* (written in 1917–21, but not staged till 1925). The first performance took place in Munich on 8 November 1913; it was directed by Eugen Kilian with Albert Steinrück as Woyzeck. Other important productions—by Victor Barnowski (again with Steinrück), Max Reinhardt (with Eugen Klöpfer), and Jürgen Fehling (with Walter Franck)—followed in Berlin in 1913, 1921, and 1947, respectively. Werner Herzog's film, with Klaus Kinski in the title role, was released in 1979. Despite its incompleteness, *Woyzeck* is one of the outstanding masterpieces of the German theater. Its more limited success in English-speaking countries stems mainly from the difficulties of translation.

The play is set in early 19th-century provincial Germany. Franz Woyzeck struggles to support his mistress, Marie, and their illegitimate child on the pittance that he earns as a soldier, barber, and medical guinea pig. When Marie deceives him with a drum major, he buys a knife and kills her. He then either drowns himself or is arrested. Similar to Büchner's first play, *Dantons Tod* (written and published in 1835; *Danton's Death*), *Woyzeck* is based on documentary material, in particular, two studies by a Dr. J.C.A. Clarus that argue that the historical Woyzeck—who was publicly beheaded in Leipzig in 1824—had been responsible for his actions. Apart from reducing Woyzeck's age, substituting the young Marie for the middle-aged widow killed by Woyzeck, and attributing to Marie Woyzeck's child by yet another woman, Büchner adhered closely to the events reported in his sources. At the same time, he created the first and most powerful European tragedy of proletarian life.

In politics, Büchner anticipated socialism, believing that only violent revolution could improve the lot of the masses but despairing of its immediate prospects. In philosophy, he rejected idealism in favor of positivist determinism. In aesthetics, he condemned classical approaches and pioneered realism. Carrying the methods of "Storm and Stress" and domestic tragedy one step further and echoing German folklore, the Bible, and Shakespeare, *Woyzeck* has influenced all the major modern movements in drama: naturalism, Expressionism, Epic Theater, documentary theater, and the theater of the absurd.

Technically, *Woyzeck* is a magnificent example of the "open" form. Concealing extreme sophistication behind a seemingly simple story and achieving the greatest impact through the greatest economy of means, it conveys an overwhelming impression of metaphysical disorientation through its fragmented structure. The action proceeds through short, stark episodes, highlighting the decisive moments and leaving the rest to the spectator's imagination. The characters—with the exception of Woyzeck, who is presented from a variety of angles—take the shape of concise sketches or grotesque caricatures. The dialogue, which deliberately lacks grammatical or logical coherence and often disintegrates into silence, is interspersed with snatches of song and is colored by dialect, slang, and literary allusions. Defying intellectual comprehension, recurrent key words, interrelated images, and ironic double meanings form a complex network of associations, themes, and moods that operate simultaneously on many different levels of significance.

Despite sharing many ideas with Büchner's radical pamphlet *Der hessische Landbote* (1834; *The Hessian Messenger*), the play goes far beyond social criticism. The Captain, who patronizes and bullies Woyzeck, belies his strident middle-class morality by his existential fear and boredom, while the Doctor, who misuses Woyzeck for his experiments, combines a false scientific materialism with an equally false philosophical idealism. In one digression, a fairground showman reveals the animal in humanity, ridiculing all notions of dignity, reason, and freedom; in another, a grandmother's fairy tale about a lost orphan reflects the desolation of all human beings in a world without purpose.

The plight of Woyzeck—and to some extent Marie—provides the most moving representation of human beings at the mercy not only of social circumstances but also of physiological and psychological compulsions that they can neither control nor comprehend. Büchner's portrayal of these compulsions corresponds to his realistic conception of the ineluctable forces of nature, but it also carries an atmosphere of supernatural fate. Marie cannot withstand the attraction of the brutally virile drum major but is nevertheless haunted by a sense of sin. Woyzeck is as irresistibly drawn to Marie as he is driven, in a fit of jealousy, to murder her. Exploited and degraded by his superiors, mocked by his successful rival, betrayed by the one person he trusted, lonely, frightened, and sick in body and mind, he can be regarded as the product of everyday social, economic, and medical factors. At the same time, however, his hallucinations suggest transcendental visions of apocalypse and chaos. The inarticulate and confused outcast who strains in vain to understand his suffering becomes the epitome of alienated man, facing the mysteries of an indifferent or hostile universe.

In a famous letter to his fiancee in 1834, Büchner describes his awareness of a "ghastly uniformity in human nature" and an "inescapable force in human conditions," ending with the agonized question: "What is it in us that lies, murders, steals?" In the unfinished story *Lenz* (probably begun in 1835), he declares that the writer "must love humanity in order to penetrate the peculiar nature of each individual," and he considers none "too low" or "too ugly" for his attention. The same fundamental questions about the human predicament and the same unconditional love of humanity underlie his sympathetic account of his tormented, innocently guilty antihero. Although it offers no answers and no hope of redemption, *Woyzeck* gives an exhilarating demonstration of Büchner's compassion, intellectual courage, and unique artistic talent.

LADISLAUS LÖB

Editions

First edition: *Wozzek*, in *Sämmtliche Werke und handschriftlicher Nachlass*, edited by K.E. Franzos, Frankfurt am Main: Sauerländer, 1879

Critical edition: *Woyzeck*, edited by John Guthrie, Oxford and New York: Blackwell, 1988

Translation: *Woyzeck*, in *Complete Plays, Lenz and Other Writings*, translated by John Reddick, London and New York: Penguin, 1993

Further Reading

Arnold, Heinz Ludwig, editor, *Georg Büchner I/II* and *Georg Büchner III*, Munich: Text und Kritik, 1979, 1981

Benn, Maurice B., *The Drama of Revolt: A Critical Study of Georg Büchner*, Cambridge and New York: Cambridge University Press, 1976

Bornscheuer, Lothar, editor, *Georg Büchner: Woyzeck*, Stuttgart: Reclam, 1972

Buch, Wilfried, *Woyzeck: Fassungen und Wandlungen*, Dortmund: Crüwell, 1970

Dedner, Burghard, "Die Handlung des *Woyzeck:* Wechselnde Orte—'geschlossene Form'," *Georg Büchner Jahrbuch* 7 (1988–89)
Glück, Alfons, "Der 'ökonomische Tod': Armut und Arbeit in Georg Büchners *Woyzeck,*" *Georg Büchner Jahrbuch* 4 (1984)
Goltschnigg, Dietmar, *Rezeptions- und Wirkungsgeschichte Georg Büchners,* Kronberg: Scriptor, 1975
Gray, Richard T., "The Dialectic of Enlightenment in Büchners *Woyzeck,*" *German Quarterly* 61 (1988)
Hauser, Ronald, *Georg Büchner,* New York: Twayne, 1974
Hilton, Julian, *Georg Büchner,* London: Macmillan, and New York: Grove Press, 1982
Hinderer, Walter, *Büchner: Kommentare zum dichterischen Werk,* Munich: Winkler, 1977
Kanzog, Klaus, "Wozzeck, Woyzeck, und kein Ende: Zur Standortbestimmung der Editionsphilologie," *DVLG* 47 (1973)
Knight, Arthur Harold John, *Georg Büchner,* Oxford: Blackwell, 1951; New York: Barnes and Noble, 1974
Lindenberger, Herbert Samuel, *Georg Büchner,* Carbondale: Southern Illinois University Press, 1964
Martens, Wolfgang, "Zum Menschenbild Georg Büchners: *Woyzeck* und die Marionszene in *Dantons Tod,*" *Wirkendes Wort* 8 (1957/58)
Martens, Wolfgang, editor, *Georg Büchner,* Darmstadt: Wissenschaftliche Buchgesellschaft, 1965; 3rd edition, 1973
Mautner, Franz H., "Wortgewebe, Sinngefüge, und 'Idee' in Büchners *Woyzeck,*" *Deutsche Vierteljahrsschrift für Literaturwissenschaft und Geistesgeschichte* 35 (1961)
May, Kurt, "Büchner's *Woyzeck,*" *Die Sammlung* 5 (1950)
Mayer, Hans, *Georg Büchner und seine Zeit,* Wiesbaden: Limes-Verlag, 1946; 4th edition, Frankfurt: Suhrkamp, 1980
Paulus, Ursula, "Georg Büchners *Woyzeck:* Eine kritische Betrachtung zu der Edition Fritz Bergemanns," *Jahrbuch der deutschen Schiller-Gesellschaft* 8 (1964)
Pongs, Hermann, "Büchners *Woyzeck,*" in *Das Bild in der Dichtung,* Marburg: Elwert, 1927
Poschmann, Henri, *Georg Büchner: Dichtung der Revolution und Revolution der Dichtung,* Berlin: Aufbau, 1983; 3rd edition, 1988
Reddick, John, *Georg Büchner: The Shattered Whole,* Oxford: Clarendon Press, and New York: Oxford University Press, 1994
Richards, David Gleyre, *Georg Büchners Woyzeck: Interpretation und Textgestaltung,* Bonn: Bouvier, 1975
——, *Georg Büchner and the Birth of the Modern Drama,* Albany: State University of New York Press, 1977
Schmidt, Henry J., *Satire, Caricature, and Perspectivism in the Works of Georg Büchner,* The Hague: Mouton, 1970
Ullman, Bo, *Die sozialkritische Thematik im Werk Georg Büchners und ihre Entfaltung im 'Woyzeck,'* Stockholm: Almqvist und Wiksell, 1972
Werner, Hans-Georg, "Büchners *Woyzeck:* Dichtungssprache als Analyseobjekt," *Weimarer Beiträge* 12 (1981)
Wittkowski, Wolfgang, *Georg Büchner: Persönlichkeit, Weltbild, Werk,* Heidelberg: Winter, 1978

Bundesrepublic Deutschland *see* Federal Republic of Germany

Gottfried August Bürger 1747–1794

Bürger is best known for his poetry, which represents an important contribution to the attempt of German literature in the last third of the 18th century to free itself from preordained norms and "rules" and to respond more directly to the lived experience of ordinary people and, in particular, to less rational realms of experience. He belongs to no one literary-historical grouping: the rococo gestures to be found in some of his earlier poetry soon gave way to a new intensity of expression, and he developed connections with the *Hainbund* in Göttingen and published in the *Göttinger Musenalmanach.*

Bürger's enthusiasm for folk poetry and Shakespeare and his attempt to use poetry to convey the rawness of experience, however, mean that he had more in common with the Sturm und Drang. He seems to have discovered his gift for extended narrative poems in the folk style during 1773. While composing his *Lenore* (1773), he was encouraged by reading Herder's essay on Ossian and Goethe's *Götz von Berlichingen* (translated as *Goetz of Berlichingen with the Iron Hand* and *Ironhand*), because both authors shared his impulse to develop a new kind of literature that eschewed academicism and drew on popular traditions. Bürger's ballads, including *Der wilde Jäger* (1785; *The Wild Huntsman's Chase*), *Des armen Suschens Traum* (1774; Poor Suschen's Dream), and *Des Pfarrers Tochter von Taubenheim* (1781; *The Lass of Fair Wone*), have a vividness and directness that belie both the care with which they were composed and Bürger's command of classical techniques. They also frequently draw on popular superstitions involving the supernatural, ghosts, and retributions, which add a note of horror and mystery but also hint at psychological complexities. The use of direct speech enhances the dramatic qualities, and insistently recurring rhythms and motifs and the subordination of description and reflection to the dynamic of the narrative all produce the energy that made these poems, especially *Lenore,* celebrated throughout Europe.

Working as a rural magistrate, Bürger had considerable practical knowledge of country life and country attitudes. This knowledge is evident from the ballads, but they also suggest a strong sense of justice. He himself felt hounded by his superiors and frustrated by his circumstances, and his ballads often criticize the abuse of power. This sense of defiance in the face of injustice and inhumanity is seen most strongly in Bürger's explicitly political poems, such as *Der Bauer: An seinen Durchlauchtigen Tyrannen* (1776; The Peasant to His Most Illustrious Tyrant), which formulate complex political arguments with a simplicity and force of moral pathos that in turn look forward to Brecht. This spirit continues into later poems, such as *Die Tode* (1793; Death), which criticize the reactionary responses to the French Revolution in Germany.

It is a sign of the directness of Bürger's poetry that critics have often been drawn to make moral judgments on his life—either seeing him as a man of the people who neglected the privileges he enjoyed or condemning him for his love for Molly, his first wife's sister. This troubled, illicit relationship produced a love poetry that is strikingly direct and unsentimental in its unflinching acknowledgment of pain. This poetry presents love as a natural force that is neither good nor bad, but necessary. Among these poems are examples of the sonnet, which, with his protégé August Wilhelm Schlegel, Bürger reintroduced into German literature. In his ballads, political poetry, and, perhaps most effectively of all, love poems such as *An die Menschengesichter* (In People's Eyes) or *An das Herz* (To My Heart), Bürger is able to convey the impression of experiences that—through references to the supernatural, justice, and the overwhelming power of love—transcend the everyday, but he does this without diminishing or denying the ultimate reality of the everyday.

Bürger is also well known today because of his reworking of the humorously improbable anecdotes of Baron von Münchhausen, *Wunderbare Reisen zu Wasser und Lande, Feldzüge und lustige Abentheuer des Freyherrn von Münchhausen* (1786; *Baron Münchhausen's Miraculous Adventures on Land*). Bürger's version, based on the English of Rudolf Erich Raspe, contains several episodes of Bürger's own invention and has become the standard source of many later versions.

Bürger's creative nature was perhaps best suited to short forms such as poems or even the episodes that make up the Münchhausen story, and the pressures of his life meant that he left many longer projects unfinished, such as a translation of the *Iliad*. He did, however, intervene in contemporary debates on a wide range of topics, including the question of the appropriate meter for translating classical Greek verse into German and issues relating to German style and the reform of German orthography. In later life, he lectured on stylistics, aesthetics, and philosophy. He was one of the first to lecture on Kant, but his most important discursive writing concerned his ideal of popular literature. In the prefaces to editions of his poems and in some rather disjointed, rhapsodic essays such as "Aus Daniel Wunderlichs Buch" (1776; From Daniel Wunderlich's Book) and *Von der Popularität der Poesie* (posthumous; On the Popularity of Poetry), Bürger developed an important conception of a literature that would adopt the clarity and vigor of folk poetry so as to become a literature for the people as a whole, not just for the learned: "Popularität eines poetischen Werkes ist das Siegel seiner Vollkommenheit" (The popularity of a poetic work is the mark of its perfection). In 1791, this view of literature was subjected to a devastating and hurtful attack by Schiller in his essay *Über Bürgers Gedichte* (*On Bürger's Poems*). But although Schiller deplored the accessibility and directness of Bürger's poetry, regarding it as a compromise with the idealist aesthetic that he himself had recently come to espouse, it is precisely these qualities that have guaranteed the survival of Bürger's poems.

DAVID HILL

Biography

Born in Molmerswende in the Harz, 31 December 1747. Studied theology at Halle, 1764–67, and law at Göttingen, 1768–72; magistrate in Gelliehausen near Göttingen, 1772–84; married Dorette Leonhart, 1774 (died 1784); married Dorette's sister Molly, 1785 (died 1786); edited *Göttinger Musen-Almanach*, 1779–94; lecturer and later professor at the University of Göttingen, 1784–94; married Elise Hahn, 1790 (divorced 1792); criticism of his poems by Schiller, 1791. Died in Göttingen, 8 June 1794.

Selected Works

Collections

Sämtliche Werke, edited by K. Reinhard, 4 vols., 1796–1802

Fiction

"Aus Daniel Wunderlichs Buch," *Deutsches Museum*, 1776

Wunderbare Reisen zu Wasser und Lande, Feldzüge und lustige Abentheuer des Freyherrn von Münchhausen, 1786; as *Baron Munchausen's Miraculous Adventures on Land*, translated by Ulrich Steindorff, 1933

Poetry

Gedichte, 2 vols., 1778–89

Further Reading

Beutin, Wolfgang, and Thomas Bütow, editors, *Gottfried August Bürger (1747–1794)*, Frankfurt and New York: Lang, 1994

Carrdus, Anna, *Classical Rhetoric and the German Poet 1620 to the Present: A Study of Opitz, Bürger, and Eichendorff*, Oxford: European Humanities Research Centre, 1996

Häntzschel, Günter, *Gottfried August Bürger*, Munich: Beck, 1988

Häntzschel, Günter, and Hiltrud Häntzschel, editors, *Gottfried August Bürger, 1747–1794: Sämtliche Werke*, Munich and Vienna: Hanser, 1987

Kaim-Kloock, Lore, *Gottfried August Bürger: Zum Problem der Volkstümlichkeit in der Lyrik*, Berlin: Rütten und Loening, 1963

Kertscher, Hans-Joachim, editor, *G.A. Bürger und J.W.L. Gleim*, Tübingen: Niemeyer, 1996

Kluge, Gerhard, "Gottfried August Bürger," in *Deutsche Dichter des 18. Jahrhunderts: Ihr Leben und Werk*, edited by Benno von Wiese, Berlin: Schmidt, 1977

Little, William A., *Gottfried August Bürger*, New York: Twayne, 1974

Scherer, Helmut, *Lange schon in manchem Sturm und Drange: Gottfried August Bürger, der Dichter des Münchhausen, Eine Biographie*, Berlin: Scherer, 1995

Schöne, Albrecht, *Säkularisation als sprachbildende Kraft: Studien zur Dichtung deutscher Pfarrersöhne*, Göttingen: Vandenhoeck und Ruprecht, 1958

Strodtmann, Adolf, editor, *Briefe von und an Gottfried August Bürger: Ein Beitrag zu Literaturgeschichte seiner Zeit*, 4 vols., Berlin: Paetel, 1874

C

Cabaret

An artistic forum that has fostered lively exchange, cabaret (German: *Kabarett*) is rich in connotations and variations. In the most simple sense of the word, a cabaret is a performing space. The French term signifies a pub—in the narrower sense since the late 19th century, a pub or intimate restaurant with a podium or a small stage, which in German is called a *Brettl,* the "little board." Here, composers, actors, singers, and dancers can present their works to a paying bourgeois audience; in the least formal manifestations, spectators are also welcome to join the performance. Another meaning of the word defines a theatrical form and refers to a divided serving platter offering small amounts of many different items. As a performance art, in fact, cabaret is a program of distinct numbers in a variety of miniature forms: songs (often called *Chansons,* implying a more literary tone), monologues, sketches and one-act plays, improvisational dances, puppet shows, shadow plays, and even short films. A German synonym for cabaret is therefore *Kleinkunst:* small art, a miniature chamber art of intimacy and concentration. Such cabaret programs can have a disjointed character that verges on montage; until the middle of the 20th century, the performances were traditionally connected by a *Conférenciér* or master of ceremonies, who provided a witty, running commentary on the act, often spiced with references to current events. In its broadest sense, *Kabarett* and its adjectival form *kabarettistisch* are used to characterize satirical poetry, songs, and topical performance art with an informal, ironic, or slightly literary tone. Thus, modern German usage distinguishes between *Kabarett,* which implies an intellectual, critical performance, and *Cabaret,* which is used for purely entertainment-based shows, especially of an erotic nature.

Recent scholarship (especially that of Klaus Budzinski) postulates three major periods and forms of German cabaret: the "literary cabaret" of the late Wilhelmine Empire (1901–18), the "literary-political cabaret" of the Weimar Republic (1918–33), and "political-satirical cabaret" in post–World War II Germany. These categories call our attention to important shifts in the cabaret's character over its century-long development, although they tend to overstate its political or resistance value and to obscure its artistic and ideological variety by foregrounding its textual and satirical elements.

The early German cabaret was in part inspired by its Parisian predecessors of the 1880s and 1890s: the Montmartre artists' pubs, theaters such as Rodolphe Salis's Chat Noir (Black Cat) or Aristide Bruant's Mirliton (Whistle), and the sensational café-concert singer Yvette Guilbert. At the same time, however, the German artists followed a vision of a "literary music hall" that would address the entertainment needs of an urbane metropolitan audience without compromising artistic quality. In this spirit, poet Otto Julius Bierbaum introduced a best-selling collection of *Deutsche Chansons* (German Songs) in 1900 and called for an "applied poetry" that synthesized literature and entertainment. In January 1901, Ernst von Wolzogen opened his Buntes Theater (Colorful Theater) in Berlin, which was nicknamed the *Überbrettl* in playful allusion to Nietzsche's *Übermensch.* Featuring elegantly costumed and staged *Chansons* along with pantomimes, parodies, one acts, folk songs, and dances, this stylish theater (which was anything but intimate: it seated 650 and, in its new house opened that same year, 800) promised an ennoblement of entertainment and was an overnight sensation. Among the more prominent authors featured here were Detlev von Liliencron, Christian Morgenstern, Ludwig Thoma, Hanns Heinz Ewers, Bierbaum, and Wolzogen—although for the most part, their works were performed by professional actors and singers, not by the poets themselves. Soon Berlin was filled with imitation *Überbrettls* and cabaret theaters; their repertoire was dominated not by the literary pretenses that launched the cabaret movement but rather by pandering, sentimental, and silly operetta and music-hall fare. For all its sensation, Wolzogen's original stage quickly degenerated and closed in 1902.

An alternative model of the cabaret, closer to the French version, developed simultaneously in Munich, where in April 1901 a group of bohemian artists opened the Elf Scharfrichter (Eleven Executioners) in a Schwabing pub and declared their intention to "execute" the enemies of the times in their performances, which mocked reactionary and Philistine tendencies in current politics and culture. On this stage, playwright Frank Wedekind also sang his disrespectful, often shocking verses to his own lute accompaniment. Although folk songs, parodies, and conventional *Überbrettl* fare filled these programs as well, the tone was more intimate and impudent than that of Wolzogen's stage. Numerous such artists' pubs or *Künstlerkneipen* opened in Berlin as well, offering a bohemian subculture at once nonconformist and romantic in the locales of poets such as Peter Hille, Danny Gürtler, and Hans Hyan, or the painter Max Tilke. The Elf Scharfrichter, by contrast, quickly wearied under the constant pressure to produce successful new shows and closed in 1904. The leading artists of this stage moved to Vienna and were instrumental in founding a vital cabaret tradition there; a pinnacle of this new tradition was the designer cabaret Fledermaus (Bat), founded in 1907, which featured the groundbreaking work of the Wiener Werkstätte. Such locales and troupes were typically short-lived; their sensation derived from their novelty and youthful energy. Routine, ever-changing fashions, and the tensions between artistic aspirations and the pressure for commercial success generally brought a swift demise to these establishments. Some survived by changing their form: Max Reinhardt's Schall und Rauch (Noise and Smoke), founded in Berlin in 1901, for instance, became an intimate one-act theater where he launched his career as a director of international renown. By 1910, little remained of the artistic and cultural impetus of the *Kleinkunst* stage. What survived were for the most part stylish wine bars with cabarets that featured off-color songs, although their best manifestations, including the singer Claire Waldoff or the composer Rudolf Nelson, offered clever wit and tunes with a cheeky, topical flair.

The cabaret's intimacy and improvisational character still offered promise to young, avant-garde artists. The Berlin Expressionists, including Kurt Hiller, Jakob van Hoddis, and Georg Heym, founded the experimental podiums Neopathetisches Cabaret (Cabaret Neopathos) and Gnu in 1910 and 1911, respectively, although their programs resembled literary salon evenings more than the conventional entertainment *Brettl* of the day. In the midst of World War I, an international group of young artists around the German expatriate Hugo Ball opened the Cabaret Voltaire (1916) in Zurich. Their performances of shockingly modern art, including abstract dances, phonetic poetry, simultaneous recitations in multiple languages, and contemporary music, soon went under the name of Dada. This anti-art of nonsense and rebellion against the artistic and cultural establishment continued in a series of salons and gallery performances after the cabaret closed down. In the 1920s, Dadaism grew into an international art movement with centers in Berlin, Paris, Hanover, and New York.

The Weimar Republic was a high point of the cabaret. This was due in part to the end of censorship, which had severely limited the critical potential of the stage. The conflicts and changes in the political, social, cultural, and moral spheres during this troubled era also offered the cabaret, which has always seen itself as an ironic mirror of its times, a wealth of material to lampoon. During the first years after World War I, the cabaret's artistic scope was enriched by the participation of a number of young authors who brought trenchant cultural and political critiques and innovative literary techniques inspired by Expressionism, Dadaism, futurism, and the growing movement of "new sobriety." Klabund, Walter Mehring, Ferdinand Hardekopf, Kurt Tucholsky, and others wrote for the stages Schall und Rauch, Größenwahn (Megalomania), and Wilde Bühne (Wild Stage). In the latter theater, soubrette Trude Hesterberg combined text, music, costumes, and staging into an integrated, multidimensional performance that would make modern literature accessible to a new audience. Bertolt Brecht performed his own songs here in 1923 and was booed off the stage: his lyrics and performance style were still too harsh and strange for the pleasure-hungry cabaret audience. By the mid-1920s, however, lighter entertainment had again supplanted the critical tone of the inflation years, and lyricists such as Marcellus Schiffer and author-composer Friedrich Hollaender turned their energies to intimate topical revues as well as the huge variety-theater styled Kabarett der Komiker (Comedians' Cabaret) in Berlin. The economic collapse of 1929 and the resulting radicalization in the political arena were accompanied by the growth of small, informal ensembles of young actors; some had a sharp political edge, including Werner Finck's Katakombe (Catacombs).

Many cabaret artists were Jewish and/or leftists and fled Germany when the Nazis came to power. Some of these performers were active in troupes that attacked the new regime from the vantage point of exile, such as Erika Mann's Pfeffermühle (Peppermill) in Zurich (and later New York), the Laterndl (Little Lantern) in London, or the Arche (Ark) in New York. Although these shows were of great importance to the identity and self-worth of the émigrés, their political resonance was minimal. Other performers stayed in Germany, hoping to adapt to the new conditions, but the Nazis had little tolerance for satire, and cabaret artists ran the constant risk of arrest. In particular, Finck repeatedly tested the limits with his suggestive political allusions, which were spoken only between the lines. The last vestiges of liberal Weimar-era *Kleinkunst,* the theaters Katakombe and TingelTangel, were closed down in 1935. Humorous, topical entertainment—albeit of a milder, more conformist tone—continued in locales such as the now Aryanized Kabarett der Komiker. Even in the concentration camps, interned performers entertained one another with cabaret shows that expressed their despair but held out the promise of hope. By 1941, freedom of expression had been severely curtailed by order of Goebbels, and in August 1944, the remaining cabarets and entertainment stages were closed down.

Thanks to their flexibility and modest technical requirements, but also owing to their talent for addressing the emotional and cultural concerns of the day, cabarets were among the first entertainments to spring up in the ruins after the war. In Munich, Erich Kästner and others revived the style of topical, literary cabaret of the Weimar era in the Schaubude (1945; Show-Booth) and the Kleine Freiheit (1951; Little Freedom), while Günter Neumann produced Berlin revues that held up a critical mirror to current events and trends, such as *Schwarzer Jahrmarkt* (1947; Black Market). Neumann founded a hit radio cabaret in West Berlin in December 1948: the Insulaner (Islanders) attacked the communist regime that had instituted the Berlin Blockade, and the troupe continued to propagandize against the GDR until 1968. In the Western zones and later Federal Republic, the Kom(m)ödchen (Little Comedy/Commode) of Kay and Lore Lorentz, founded in 1947 in Dusseldorf, and the Münchner Lach- und Schießgesellschaft, founded in 1956 in Munich, with Dieter Hildebrandt, attacked restorative tendencies in Adenauer's republic, while East German troupes such as Die Distel (Thistle), founded in Berlin in 1953, and Die Pfeffermühle, begun in Leipzig in 1954, put their "positive satire" clearly in the service of the GDR regime, despite occasional tones of criticism that gave rise to political difficulties and even repression. On the whole, post–World War II cabaret was more oriented toward texts and satire than musical and theatrical presentation, and shows generally had a strong ensemble character without the connecting *Conférenciér.* With the student movement and the rise of political radicalism in the 1960s and 1970s, troupes of students and young intellectuals such as Hannelore Kaub's

Bügelbrett (Ironing Board), founded in Heidelberg in 1959 and continued in Berlin in 1965, or the Munich Rationaltheater (1965) leveled fundamental systemic attacks on West German politics and social institutions, while other, less oppositional ensembles found their way into the mass media of television, which often entailed political compromises if not downright censorship. In subsequent debates surrounding the function of cabaret, radical thinkers mistrusted its entertainment value and accused it of supporting the status quo by venting frustration through harmless laughter and providing politicians with an alibi of tolerance toward the modern court jesters, whose criticisms were consumed with delight but never taken seriously. Floh de Cologne, founded in Cologne in 1966, therefore abandoned the cabaret form altogether and became a political rock band in order to reach a young audience who had the potential to implement cultural change.

Many performers established themselves with satirical solo programs, such as Dietrich Kittner and Werner Schneyder, as had previously Hanns Dieter Hüsch, Wolfgang Neuss, and the multitalented Austrian Georg Kreisler. The rise of the *Liedermacher,* the satirical singing bard, was linked to the revival of the critical songs and cabaret culture of the day as well. The 1980s saw the growth of less political cabaret entertainers—the *Blödelbarden* or nonsense poets and singers, or the drag acts of *Travestie* artists—as well as troupes directed to special interests: feminist troupes, foreign worker cabarets, and an ensemble of the physically handicapped. Many cabarets of the former GDR were forced to close or redefine themselves after reunification in 1989–90.

Jürgen Henningsen's 1967 *Theorie des Kabaretts* (Theory of the Cabaret) identifies a series of literary and theatrical devices used by the cabaret to promote critical thought and change in its audience. His image of the cabaret as an instrument of sociopolitical consciousness and enlightenment is surely idealistic and downplays the entertainment and artistic values of *Kleinkunst,* but his theoretical model of "playing with the audience's acquired context of knowledge" draws attention to the dynamics of communication between cabaret performers and their audience: a dialogic and creative process that goes far beyond traditional theater. Typical techniques of the cabaret include plays on language and punning, jarring juxtapositions of styles and topics, deceptions that unmask audience expectations, and omissions that require the viewer to make an unstated connection. As the cabaret has limited technical means at its disposal, it depends on suggestion, improvisation, and the power of language for its effects. Cabaret performance is thus nonrealistic or anti-illusionist and offers direct contact between the stage and the audience. The cabaret performer is engaged in a complex negotiation of simultaneous roles but is never wholly absorbed by a dramatic figure; the performer remains conspicuously an actor playing or demonstrating a character. These stylistic features bring the cabaret into the realm of Brechtian theater, with its destruction of theatrical illusion and dissociation of the actor and the dramatic role. Typically, the satirical performer teases and mocks the audience, even to the point of shock and direct insult, exploring the borders of taboos, prejudices, and intolerance.

The connections between the cabaret and innovations in literature and the theater were strongest in the period up until 1933. During this time, important artists and designers also turned to the cabaret as a forum for new ideas and forms. August Endell designed a fanciful *Jugendstil* theater for Wolzogen; Josef Hoffmann and his Viennese colleagues created not only the performance space and costumes of the Fledermaus but all the accessories down to the silverware; George Grosz and John Heartfield created savage Dadaist puppets for Schall und Rauch in 1919. The Russian émigré cabaret Der Blaue Vogel (The Blue Bird), founded in Berlin in 1921, featured stunning sets and costumes with Expressionist and futurist touches that were the talk of Europe. In music as well, the cabaret both provided and received important impulses. The earliest cabaret composers came largely from a classical background; Oscar Straus and Walter Kollo were noted for their operettas, and even Arnold Schoenberg worked briefly for Wolzogen and wrote several *Brettl-Lieder* (with one exception, unperformed). With the rise of commercial entertainment music through gramophones, sheet music, and the radio, cabaret music became ever more closely linked to the popular song. In the 1920s, dance music and jazz set the tone. The leading composers included Rudolf Nelson, Friedrich Hollaender, Mischa Spoliansky, and Werner Richard Heymann, the latter three of whom soon achieved fame as film composers. Kurt Weill, who composed the music for Brecht works including *Die Dreigroschenoper* (1928; *The Threepenny Opera*), was not a cabaret composer, but his so-called *Songs* were influenced by the genre and its mediation between entertainment, cliché, and critical unmasking. Above all, Hollaender's cabaret songs for Marlene Dietrich in *The Blue Angel* (1929) brilliantly re-created the atmosphere of a seedy honky-tonk or *Tingeltangel* and became a symbol of an era of radical social and moral change. He further built on this tradition in his songs for the film *A Foreign Affair* (1947), which included the bitterly ironic "Black Market" (again sung by Dietrich).

ALAN LAREAU

See also Karl Valentin; Weimar Republic

Further Reading

Appignanesi, Lisa, *Cabaret,* New York: Grove Press, revised edition, 1984

Budzinski, Klaus, *Pfeffer ins Getriebe: So ist und wurde das Kabarett,* Munich: Universitas, 1982

Budzinski, Klaus, editor, *So weit die scharfe Zunge reicht: Die Anthologie des deutschsprachigen Cabarets,* Munich: Scherz, 1964

Budzinski, Klaus, and Reinhard Hippen, *Metzler Kabarett Lexikon,* Stuttgart: Metzler, 1996

Henningsen, Jürgen, *Theorie des Kabaretts,* Ratingen: Henn, 1967

Jelavich, Peter, *Munich and Theatrical Modernism: Politics, Playwriting, and Performance, 1890–1914,* Cambridge, Massachusetts: Harvard University Press, 1985

———, *Berlin Cabaret,* Cambridge, Massachusetts: Harvard University Press, 1993

Kirchhof, Peter K., editor, *"Ein Spaß braucht keinen": Kabarett in Deutschland,* special issue of *Die Horen* 40, no. 1 (1995)

Kühn, Volker, editor, *Kleinkunststücke,* 5 vols., Weinheim: Quadriga, 1987–94

———, *Die zehnte Muse: 111 Jahre Kabarett,* Cologne: VGS, 1993

Lareau, Alan, *The Wild Stage: Literary Cabarets of the Weimar Republic,* Columbia, South Carolina: Camden House, 1995

Rösler, Walter, *Das Chanson im deutschen Kabarett, 1901–1933,* Berlin: Henschelverlag, 1980

Segel, Harold B., *Turn-of-the-Century Cabaret,* New York: Columbia University Press, 1987

Senelick, Laurence, editor, *Cabaret Performance,* 2 vols., New York: PAJ, 1989–; Baltimore, Maryland, and London: Johns Hopkins University Press, 1993

Elias Canetti 1905–1994

Elias Canetti's life and work span the better part of the 20th century. Influenced by intellectuals and artists associated with turn-of-the-century Vienna and shaped by major events of the 20th century, Canetti developed a poetics that resists easy categorization. His work includes diverse genres, both fictional and nonfictional, all of which are marked by a remarkable clarity in style and language.

In the early 1930s, Canetti wrote his only novel, *Die Blendung* (1935; *Auto-da-Fé*), and two dramas, *Hochzeit* (1932; *The Wedding*) and *Komödie der Eitelkeit* (1950; *Comedy of Vanity*). The only other literary texts that he published were a third drama, *Die Befristeten* (1964; translated as *Life-Terms* and *The Numbered*), and a collection of 50 imaginary character studies, *Der Ohrenzeuge* (1974; *Earwitness*). During and after World War II, Canetti conducted massive research for his anthropological study *Masse und Macht* (*Crowds and Power*), which appeared in 1960. Many of his subsequent texts comment on the genesis of his previous works and elaborate on the issues raised in them. This extensive self-commentary includes several volumes of notes and aphorisms and a three-volume autobiography, which captures the first 30 years of his life. Other important publications during the last three decades of his life include a long and insightful essay on Kafka, *Der andere Prozess: Kafkas Briefe an Felice* (1969; *Kafka's Other Trial: The Letters to Felice*), and an account of his trip to Morocco, *Die Stimmen von Marrakesch* (1968; *The Voices of Marrakesh*).

A sephardic Jew who was born in Bulgaria and spent his youth in several different countries, Canetti was exposed to multiple languages early on—German being the fifth language that he had learned by the age of eight. He has thus been called a truly European writer. Yet despite his exile to England in 1938, which remained his major domicile after World War II, he continued to write in German and to feel indebted to his Austrian cultural heritage. As his autobiography details, his life and work were shaped by the intellectual climate of the 1920s and 1930s, namely, by the formative years he spent in Vienna, where he met Robert Musil, Hermann Broch, and Karl Kraus, among others, and by his extended stays in Berlin, where he encountered Wieland Herzfelde, Bertolt Brecht, George Grosz, and Isaac Babel. Canetti has been influential, in turn, for a number of contemporary writers—among them authors of such diverse backgrounds as Salman Rushdie, Siegfried Lenz, Erich Fried, Martin Walser, and Günter Grass.

Canetti rarely made any public appearances, except for occasional interviews and readings from his works; he was never actively involved in any literary group or association; and he refrained from making statements on political or social issues. Yet his work can hardly be considered nonpolitical or aloof from social problems. Indeed, his lifelong preoccupations have been with phenomena that are central to 20th-century history and politics: phenomena such as the individual and the crowd, and power and death. Disregarding the postmodern problematization of the humanist tradition, Canetti's work insists upon a humanistic and profoundly moral definition of the role of the writer. His is a humanism that is extremely conscious of the catastrophic failure of Western civilization in the 20th century and that asserts the value of every single being despite these failures.

In a speech that Canetti gave at the occasion of Hermann Broch's 50th birthday (1936), he maintained that the modern writer assumes the roles that philosophy and religion can no longer fulfill: namely, striving toward universal knowledge (*Erkenntnis*) and grappling with the problem of death. In an oft-quoted phrase, he states "so lange es den Tod gibt, ist jeder Spruch ein Widerspruch" (as long as there is death, every word is a protest against death). Forty years later, Canetti confirmed this stance in his 1976 Munich speech "Der Beruf des Dichters" (The Profession of the Writer). Emblematic of Canetti's outsider position within the intellectual discourse of the mid-1970s, this speech affirms the moral responsibility of the writer and flatly rejects the nihilism that Canetti sees in both contemporary literature and proclamations of the "death of literature." In the speech, he also evokes a figure that is central to his poetics and to his anthropology: namely, the notion of *Verwandlung* (transformation or metamorphosis). According to Canetti, the potential of the artist or storyteller to enact and preserve via *Verwandlung* the multiplicity, changeability, and the specificity of (human) life is the only way to counter the pervasive accumulation of power and the homogenizing forces in (post)modern society. When he envisions the writer as "Hüter der Verwandlungen" (guardian of metamorphoses), he has in mind writers such as Franz Kafka and Stendhal, but it is also the model that he sought to emulate in his own writings. Although not without its blind spots and contradictions, this poetic and anthropological notion of *Verwandlung* can be best witnessed in Canetti's notes and aphorisms, as well as in *The Voices of Marrakesh,* texts that embody his fascination with and respect for the integrity of other cultures and other beings (humans and animals).

Canetti started writing in his mid-20s, but he remained relatively unknown until he was almost 60 years of age: subsequent to the publication of *Crowds and Power* in 1960, his previous works were reissued and successfully promoted by Hanser, which became Canetti's exclusive publisher. In the late 1960s, Canetti started to receive a number of prestigious literary prizes in Germany and elsewhere. Beginning in the 1970s, Canetti's work received increasing attention among international scholars and, after he received the Nobel Prize in 1981, there were regular symposia and book publications dealing with his work. Canetti's popularity in the general reading public rose considerably with the publication of the first volume of his autobiography, *Die gerettete Zunge* (1977; *The Tongue Set Free*), but he was still relatively little known when he received the Nobel Prize for literature in 1981. Canetti lived long enough to see both the translation of his works into many different languages and wide recognition among scholars and the general reading public.

The reasons for the considerable delay in the reception of his works are in part political, most notably the rise of National Socialism, which curtailed the reception of his debut novel and his early dramas. Other reasons for the delay are his relative isolation during his prolonged exile in England and his general reluctance to participate in contemporary literary trends or intellectual debates. But in part this late reception can also be attributed to the nature of his works, some of which transgress traditional disciplinary boundaries (e.g., *Crowds and Power*), and others of which stretch accepted standards of literary "taste" (e.g., the novel and his dramas).

Canetti completed his first and only novel, *Auto-da-Fé,* in 1931 at the age of 26. According to Canetti's own accounts, his original outline in the "Comédie humaine an Irren" (The Human Comedy of the Insane), inspired by the caricaturist George Grosz, called for eight different protagonists, each of them a satirically conceived figure. The paranoid scholar Kien was the only figure Canetti developed into the protagonist of a full-scale novel. Many have read this grotesque novel, which depicts the downfall and ultimate self-destruction of Kien (he sets himself on fire with his library), as a foreshadowing of the intellectual's failures and/or fate during fascism. The novel continues to provoke a wide range of interpretations, which see in it everything from a misogynist account of the battle of the sexes to a narrative about the embattled and ultimately disintegrating position of the individual in modern society.

The novel's reception was not only hampered by the political situation in the mid-1930s but also by the conservative political climate in the postwar years. In the late-1940s, the novel received far more attention in its translated versions in England and France. *Auto-da-Fé* did not receive wider attention in Germany until its third publication in 1963 (by Hanser), more than 30 years after it was written.

Canetti's dramatic work includes two early dramas (*The Wedding* and *Comedy of Vanity*), written in Vienna, and a third drama (*Life-Terms*), written in London while he was still working on *Crowds and Power*. Canetti coined the term *Akustische Masken* (acoustic masks) for employing language, specifically various Viennese dialects and sociolects, as the central means of characterization. The earlier dramas' relentless social criticisms (e.g., of a society driven by greed and sexual appetites in *The Wedding*) are indebted to the satirical tradition of Johann Nestroy and Karl Kraus. His last play dramatizes in a highly stylized manner an idea central to *Crowds and Power:* Canetti's critique of the apparent acceptance of death in modern societies.

Similar to the novel, it took several decades before the early dramas received some attention. The premiere theatrical performances of *The Wedding* and the *Comedy of Vanity* in the early 1960s in Braunschweig provoked scandals—the language and content of these plays were deemed offensive. The productions by Hans Hollmann in 1978 (Vienna) and 1985 (Basel), by contrast, were quite successful.

Canetti spent several decades working on his study *Crowds and Power,* a work that can be considered his response to the catastrophic results of 20th-century ideologies—specifically World War II and the Holocaust—despite its relative lack of explicit references to contemporary history. Instead, Canetti bases his central arguments on a vast range of mythological, ethnographic, historical, and religious sources—all of which he seeks to present in an unmediated manner. *Crowds and Power* complements his early novel in many ways. While *Auto-da-Fé* deals with the disintegration of the individual, the anthropological study traces the psychology of the crowd and the transformation of the individual in the crowd throughout human history. The study also presents a phenomenology of the *Machthaber* (dictator) who, Canetti argues, through his absolute control over crowds of people seeks to negate the finality of life. Canetti's persistent *Tod-Feindschaft* (fight against death), one of the most noted aspects of his works, is best understood as a critique of the pervasive human ambition for power and domination.

Similar to his previous works but for different reasons, *Crowds and Power* received little attention when it was published in 1960. The initial lack of reception was probably due both to the interdisciplinary nature of his study and to Canetti's idiosyncratic approach: deliberately ignoring any established system of thought, most notably Marxism and psychoanalysis, he claimed to be the first to take seriously the materiality and multiplicity of the phenomena he studied. Adorno's inability or unwillingness (in a 1962 discussion) to engage in any serious debate with Canetti is emblematic of the difficulties his monumental study faced in the intellectual climate of the 1960s.

In the 1970s, critics began to recognize the importance of *Crowds and Power.* While this study initially received attention mainly from literary scholars, since the late 1980s there has been some productive cross-disciplinary exchanges (see Pattilo-Hess and Benedikt). An early example for *Crowds and Power*'s impact outside of literary studies is Klaus Theweleit's study of fascist ideology, *Männerphantasien* (1977–78; *Male Fantasies*), which draws heavily on Canetti's book.

In his three-volume autobiography, Canetti reconstructs the biographical and historical circumstances within which his two major works, *Auto-da-Fé* and *Crowds and Power,* emerged. Canetti's carefully crafted life story is directed toward the telos of becoming a writer and posits the author's own written cosmos against the catastrophic events of 20th-century history and politics. In contrast to many (post)modern autobiographies, which scrutinize the very process of remembering and which question traditional notions of the subject and language, Canetti's autobiography is marked by an unshattered sense of identity and by an unequivocal belief in the revitalizing power of language and narration. These aspects have contributed to the popularity of his autobiography. The picture would be incomplete, however, without considering the very different kind of self-presentation that Canetti practices in his five volumes of notes and aphorisms. He started writing these brief prose texts in the late 1940s because, as he put it rather bluntly, the exclusive focus on *Crowds and Power* became "suffocating"; he continued writing and publishing them until the end of his life. In contrast to the teleological organization of the autobiography, the open-ended structure of the notes allows for comments that demonstrate both the unusual breadth of Canetti's readings and interests and the insistence with which he revisits and challenges some of his own long-held convictions.

FRIEDERIKE EIGLER

Biography

Born in Ruse (Rustschuk), Bulgaria, 25 July 1905. Ph.D. in chemistry from the University of Vienna, 1929; full-time writer; lived in England from 1938; Foreign Book Prize (France), 1949; Vienna Prize, 1966; Critics Prize (Germany), 1967; Great Austrian State Prize, 1967; Büchner Prize, 1972; Nelly Sachs Prize, 1975; Franz Nabl Prize (Graz), 1975; Keller Prize, 1977; Order of Merit (Bonn), 1979; Europa Prato Prize (Italy), 1980; Order of Merit (Germany), 1980; Hebbel Prize, 1980; Nobel Prize for literature, 1981; Kafka Prize, 1981; Great Service Cross (Germany), 1983; honorary doctorates from the University of Manchester, 1975, and the University of Munich, 1976. Died 14 August 1994.

Selected Works

Collections
Gesammelte Werke in 9 Bänden, 1995

Fiction
Die Blendung, 1935; as *Auto-da-Fé,* translated by C.V. Wedgwood, 1946 (also published as *The Tower of Babel,* 1947)
Der Ohrenzeuge: 50 Charaktere, 1974; as *Earwitness: Fifty Characters,* translated by Joachim Neugroschel, 1979
Die Schildkröten: Roman, 1999

Plays
Hochzeit (produced 1965), 1932; as *The Wedding,* 1986
Komödie der Eitelkeit (produced 1965), 1950; as *Comedy of Vanity,* translated by Gitta Honegger, with *Life-Terms,* 1982
Die Befristeten (produced 1967), in *Dramen,* 1964; as *Life-Terms,* translated by Gitta Honegger, with *Comedy of Vanity,* 1982; as *The Numbered,* translated by Carol Stewart, 1984
Dramen (includes *Hochzeit; Komödie der Eitelkeit; Die Befristeten*), 1964

Other
Masse und Macht, 1960; as *Crowds and Power,* translated by Carol Stewart, 1962
Die Stimmen von Marrakesch: Aufzeichnungen nach einer Reise, 1967; as *The Voices of Marrakesh,* translated by J.A. Underwood, 1978
Der andere Prozess: Kafkas Briefe an Felice, 1969; as *Kafka's Other Trial: The Letters to Felice,* translated by Christopher Middleton, 1974
Die gespaltene Zukunft: Aufsätze und Gespräche, 1972
Die Provinz des Menschen: Aufzeichnungen 1942–1972, 1973; as *The Human Province,* translated by Joachim Neugroschel, 1978
Das Gewissen der Worte: Essays, 1975; second, expanded edition, 1976; as *The Conscience of Words,* translated by Joachim Neugroschel, 1979
Die gerettete Zunge: Geschichte einer Jugend, 1977; as *The Tongue Set Free: Remembrance of a European Childhood,* translated by Joachim Neugroschel, 1979; in *The Memoirs of Elias Canetti,* 1999
Die Fackel im Ohr: Lebensgeschichte 1921–1931, 1980; as *The Torch in My Ear,* translated by Joachim Neugroschel, 1982; in *The Memoirs of Elias Canetti,* 1999
Das Augenspiel: Lebensgeschichte 1931–1937, 1985; as *The Play of the Eyes,* translated by Ralph Manheim, 1986; in *The Memoirs of Elias Canetti,* 1999
Das Geheimherz der Uhr: Aufzeichnungen 1973–1985, 1987; as *The Secret Heart of the Clock: Notes, Aphorisms, Fragments 1973–1985,* translated by Joel Agee, 1989
Die Fliegenpein: Aufzeichnungen, 1992; as *The Agony of Flies: Notes and Notations,* translated by H.F. Broch de Rotherman, 1994
Aufzeichnungen, 1992–1993, 1996
Nachträge aus Hampstead: Aus den Aufzeichnungen 1954–71, 1994; as *Notes from Hampstead: The Writer's Notes, 1954–1971,* translated by John Hargraves, 1998

Translations
Upton Sinclair, *Leidweg der Liebe,* 1930
Upton Sinclair, *Das Geld schreibt: Eine Studie über die amerikanische Literatur,* 1930
Upton Sinclair, *Alkohol,* 1932

Further Reading

Arnold, Heinz Ludwig, editor, *Elias Canetti,* Munich: Boorberg, 1973; 3rd expanded edition, Munich: Edition Text und Kritik, 1982
Barnouw, Dagmar, *Elias Canetti zur Einführung,* Hamburg: Junius, 1996
Bartsch, Kurt, and Gerhard Melzer, editors, *Elias Canetti: Experte der Macht,* Graz: Droschl, 1985
Eigler, Friederike, *Das autobiographische Werk von Elias Canetti,* Tübingen: Stauffenburg, 1988
Falk, Thomas H., *Elias Canetti,* New York: Twayne, and Toronto: Maxwell Macmillan Canada, 1993
Hennighaus, Lothar, *Tod und Verwandlung: Elias Canettis poetische Anthropologie aus der Kritik der Psychoanalyse,* Frankfurt and New York: Lang, 1984
Pattilo-Hess, John, and Michael Benedikt, editors, *Der Stachel des Befehls: IV. Canetti Symposium,* Vienna: Löcker, 1992
Ruppel, Ursula, *Der Tod und Canetti: Essay,* Hamburg: Europäische Verlagsanstalt, 1995

Die Blendung 1935

Novel by Elias Canetti

Written in the space of one year (1930–31), *Die Blendung* (1935; translated as *Auto-da-Fé* and *The Tower of Babel*) represents Elias Canetti's highly critical, often hilarious, and sometimes bitter reckoning with Weimar-era culture. Similar to Thomas Mann's *Magic Mountain,* Canetti's novel inquires into the continued relevance of high culture to the modern world. If the descent of Mann's hero into the "world" just at the point of the outbreak of World War I leaves us with a tragic sense of the superfluity of culture, the message of *Auto-da-Fé* is no less bleak, perhaps even more radically skeptical: "Culture" in this novel makes its appearance as a pedant's questionable fortress against the onslaughts of the material (read: modern) world. The novel's preeminent evocation of this siege mentality is the protagonist's private library, the windows of which have been walled up to keep the world at a safe—which is to say, scholarly—distance. It is no exaggeration to suggest that the beleaguered hero, Peter Kien, wraps himself in German *Bildung* and *Kultur* in order to ward off a menacing modernity: before embarking on his daily constitutional, Kien arms himself with several carefully selected volumes from his library, which he believes will function as a prophylactic against the seductions of the city. When Therese evicts him from his actual library, he takes refuge in his imaginary *Kopfbibliothek* (library in the head).

As a self-proclaimed leading scholar, the *Privatgelehrter* Kien evokes both the positivism that still dominated in the natural sciences (even after the pathbreaking discoveries of Albert Einstein and Werner Heisenberg), as well as the Weimar-era neo-Kantianism that sought to provide a fresh philosophical grounding for the humanities in the wake of their marginalization and declining prestige. Kien's ill-conceived solution is to graft the methods of the former onto the spirit of the latter. As a master philologist—the world's greatest living Sinologist, as he continually asserts—he is endowed with the authoritative ability to reconstruct whole cultures from scant and fragmented texts. His assertion of learned "objectivity," however, is undermined in the course of the novel as we discover that his primary hermeneutic impulse derives from the hatred he bears toward his housekeeper, Therese, whom he marries because of her solicitous treatment of his library. Each of his grandiose theories, such as his *Philoso-*

phie der Blindheit (philosophy of blindness) and, later, his sudden conversion to a revolutionary view of historical change, turns out to be rooted in petty personal matters. Kien himself claims that his philological prowess qualifies him to interpret authoritatively his wife's ontological status. At the police inquiry (in the chapter entitled *Privateigentum* [Private Property], often held to be the novel's best), Kien, believing and ardently wishing himself guilty of Therese's murder, launches into an extended self-defense, the high point of which is his declaration that the woman standing directly behind him and very much alive is in fact a mere hallucination, a *Schein-Therese*. This humorous unmasking of positivism's "will to power" reveals the influence of Nietzsche even as it anticipates the analysis of Foucault.

This in itself would amount to a delicious satire on the misappropriation of "culture," an unforgettable academic parody of positivist hubris. But Canetti deepens and complicates his critique by replicating in the reader the same errors that we so readily detect in the novel's characters. Again and again, we catch these figures in the act of projecting their own desires onto others; we even witness them reconfiguring the world around them (as in Kien's erasure of Therese) to fit their own idiosyncratic needs. In Book 3, it is our turn. After depriving the reader for over 400 pages of any kind of figure with whom to identify—*Auto-da-Fé* is peopled by Hobbesian louts—Canetti introduces the likable and handsome Georg, Kien's winsome younger brother. Falling for Georg's own insistence that he is his brother's polar opposite, readers have tended to turn to him as the beacon of hope in an otherwise cheerless narrative world. Although this sanguine view of Georg is not borne out by the novel, this 11th-hour gambit does powerfully bring home to the reader the novel's epistemological critique—that knowing is saturated by desire—which heretofore had been trained solely upon the comic figures.

Reacting in part to the primacy of scientific positivism prized by the naturalists, literary modernism espoused an "inward turning," an increased valuation of the subjective, and a fascination with the "fragmented self." In *Auto-da-Fé,* it is Georg who is above all affiliated with this antipositivistic posture; and in this he is, indeed, diametrically opposed to Kien. Nowhere is this more apparent than in his adoration of the "gorilla man," who inspires Georg's "conversion" from gynecology to psychiatry. The novel pillories this kind of primitivist retreat from modernity, which was widespread in the early part of the century, and went in the Germanophone countries by the name of *Lebensphilosophie* ("life philosophy"). Although Georg reinvents himself as a multiple, mercurial self—a self-styled anti-authoritarian "walking wax-tablet" who takes on the persona dictated by the needs of his patients—he remains at root as will-dominated as his elder brother.

Canetti's satiric stance toward this most cherished item of literary modernism—fragmented subjectivity—may be explained by his acute awareness that some political selves showed no sign of losing their resiliency, psychological and literary trends notwithstanding. In his autobiography as well as in the essay "Das erste Buch" (1975; The First Book), Canetti relates the deep impression left by the brutal police massacre perpetrated upon unarmed civilians as a reprisal for the burning of the Viennese Palace of Justice in 1927. As a witness to such episodes of social upheaval, and, of course, as a Jew, Canetti was keenly aware—perhaps more so than many of his modernist colleagues—of what was at stake in the uncritical depiction of unstable, fragmented identities.

By the time of its publication in 1935, *Auto-da-Fé* was, as the modernist work of a Jew, already sealed off from the larger and more lucrative German book market. Three years later, with the annexation of Austria, the novel was lost to German readers entirely until 1963, when it reappeared in the wake of Canetti's other major work, the anthropological study *Masse und Macht* (1960; *Crowds and Power*). Inevitably, but not always persuasively, *Crowds and Power* has been held to provide the hermeneutic key to the novel. Generally known in England and the United States by the title *Auto-da-Fé* (which is unfortunate in that some readers still do not recognize the title as referring to an English text), the same translation made a brief appearance under the title *Tower of Babel*.

Although history is to some extent responsible for the novel's belated reception, the matter is more complex than that. Because *Auto-da-Fé* challenges some of high modernism's most basic assumptions—even while it enacts similar formal experimentation and takes up classic modernist themes—the novel was never fully integrated into the modernist canon. Postwar New Criticism, with its sometimes lugubrious existentialist bent and apolitical orientation, was simply not poised to acknowledge a comic modernist novel with such obvious social concerns. For in satirizing the escapist positions occupied by *both* brothers Kien, *Auto-da-Fé* laments the loss of the social. The novel's evanescent depiction of Vienna, for example, presents a "privatized" cityscape that is shorn of its ability to provide communal orientation. In the figure of Siegfried Fischerle, a grotesque amalgam of contemporaneous anti-Jewish stereotypes who plays a key role in the second and longest of the novel's books, *Auto-da-Fé* confronts the abdication of universality in German humanist *Kultur,* which is most evident in its failure effectively to oppose racial anti-Semitism. Once again, "culture" is powerless, perhaps even frivolous, in the face of politics. In the penultimate chapter of the novel, Kien, prodded by Georg, mounts a long-winded survey of Western culture that is intended to prove the inferiority of women. The sheer quantity and range of texts from which Kien is able to quote so readily—from Homer to the *Nibelungenlied* to Thomas Aquinas and beyond—leave the reader feeling that this misogyny is not merely an idiosyncratic distortion but a disturbing attribute of culture itself.

Although Kien commits suicide at the novel's end, Canetti may be seen to redeem his *Büchermensch* (book man), the term he later used to refer to his protagonist, with the publication of *Crowds and Power*. Here, the armchair academic, a kind of "anti-Kien" and presumably Canetti himself, moves beyond the "Orientalist" prejudices and perversions of his fictional predecessor, leading the reader through a labyrinth of largely non-European myth and folklore in search of transformative sources for human society. Canetti's two great life works, then, stand in a relationship of question and answer: the novel's merciless negations lead to the tentative and hard-won possibility of *Verwandlung* (metamorphosis) proposed in the final sections of *Crowds and Power.*

WILLIAM COLLINS DONAHUE

Editions

First edition: *Die Blendung,* Vienna: Herbert Reichner, 1935. Although the copyright is 1935, the novel was not actually issued until 1936.

Translation: *Auto-da-Fé,* translated by C.V. Wedgwood, London: Cape, 1946; New York: Seabury Press, 1974; this same translation also appeared in the United States as *The Tower of Babel,* New York: Knopf, 1947

Further Reading

Barnouw, Dagmar, *Elias Canetti,* Stuttgart: Metzler, 1979

Canetti, Elias, "Das erste Buch: *Die Blendung,*" in *Das Gewissen der Worte,* Munich and Vienna: Hanser, 1975; 2nd revised edition, 1976

———, *Die Fackel im Ohr: Lebensgeschichte 1921–1931,* Munich and Vienna: Hanser, 1980; as *The Torch in My Ear,* translated by Joachim Neugroschel, 1982; in *The Memoirs of Elias Canetti,* 1999

———, *Das Augenspiel: Lebensgeschichte 1931–1937,* Munich: Hanser, 1985; as *The Play of the Eyes,* translated by Ralph Manheim, 1986; in *The Memoirs of Elias Canetti,* 1999

Darby, David, *Structures of Disintegration: Narrative Strategies in Elias Canetti's "Die Blendung,"* Riverside, California: Ariadne Press, 1992

Donahue, William Collins, "'Eigentlich bist du eine Frau. Du bestehst aus Sensationen': Misogyny as Cultural Critique in Elias Canetti's *Die Blendung,*" *Deutsche Vierteljahrsschrift für Literatur und Geistesgeschichte* 71, no. 4 (1997)

Essays in Honor of Elias Canetti, translated by Michael Hulse, New York: Farrar, Straus, and Giroux, 1987

Göpfert, Herbert, *Canetti lesen: Erfahrungen mit seinen Büchern,* Munich: Hanser, 1975

Lawson, Richard H., *Understanding Elias Canetti,* Columbia: University of South Carolina Press, 1991

Sokel, Walter H., "The Ambiguity of Madness: Elias Canetti's Novel *Die Blendung,*" in *Views and Reviews of Modern German Literature: Festschrift for Adolf D. Klarmann,* edited by Karl S. Weimar, Munich: Delp, 1974

———, "Zum Verhältnis von Autobiographie und Roman bei Elias Canetti," in *Ist Wahrheit ein Meer von Grashalmen? Zum Werk Elias Canettis,* edited by Joseph P. Strelka and Zsuzsa Széll, Bern: Lang, 1993

Die Fackel im Ohr 1980

Essay by Elias Canetti

Die Fackel im Ohr (*The Torch in My Ear*) is the second volume of Elias Canetti's memoirs. It deals with the author/narrator's formative experiences in interwar Germany and Austria, and it features Vienna, the capital of the first Austrian Republic, as its geographical and cultural focal point. Canetti, however, is not concerned with the political culture of "Red Vienna" and its socialist government. A Sephardic Jew from rural Bulgaria who made German his literary medium, Canetti's autobiographical voice is the product of a productive marginality: he is just enough of an outsider not to be drawn into the mass movements of the time, either fascist or socialist. A polyglot who spent part of his childhood in Vienna, he is, however, also enough of an insider to listen closely and understand those around him and to assess critically the society around him. Still under the influence of his most recent literary encounters, Aristophanes and Gilgamesch, he takes up residence together with his brother in Vienna's traditional immigrant's neighborhood, the Second District. He does not blend in with the Ashkenazim from Eastern Europe, however; rather, he positions himself within a smaller network of people: some intellectuals, and some occasional acquaintances. Of equal importance are his reading and his own fast-evolving ideas. Contrary to the majority of Jewish writers of East European background such as Friedrich Torberg, Karl Kraus, and Joseph Roth, Canetti examines Vienna's volatile society after the collapse of the Austro-Hungarian Empire from the perspective of an interested but personally uninvolved observer. He remains unaffiliated with any political party, and his views are seemingly unaffected by those of the mainstream. Canetti receives inspiration from unlikely places such as the psychiatric hospital Am Steinhof next to which his later suburban apartment is located, street scenes, individuals that strike his curiosity, and, finally, the citywide riots of 27 July 1927, which fascinate him as do all mass events.

The words *Die Fackel* (the torch) in the title of Canetti's autobiography alludes to the well-known journal published and largely written by Karl Kraus, a famous Viennese journalist who inspired Canetti's unqualified admiration because of his satirical genius, uncompromising moral and linguistic standards, and eccentric personality. Over time Canetti becomes increasingly aware of his idol's limitations, and his adoration falters. This process parallels Canetti's withdrawal from his mother and is symptomatic of his own growing independence. The intellectual struggle with Kraus as well as the life-and-death conflict with his mother in conjunction with his intensifying friendship with Veza, his future wife, signify the autobiographer's coming of age. The term *Ohr* (ear) refers to the sense organ that dominates the text and to the youthful narrator's predominantly receptive mode: he listens to the voices, dialects, and conversations around him while shaping his own mind. The concept of the "speech mask," used as a literary device in Canetti's dramas as well as his novel *Die Blendung* (1935, *Auto-da-Fé*), was derived from these intense listening experiences. Style and speech, rather than psychology, in fact, have remained foremost in Canetti's characterization of groups and individuals.

Despite the seemingly random choice of motifs and encounters, *The Torch in My Ear* is designed to foreground the formative events in the author's life in front of a larger historical panorama. Canetti's notebooks reveal how deliberately he constructed his memoirs as a coherent, teleological narrative. Canetti took issue with critics who commented on what they perceived as a lack of spontaneity. Arguing that life is future-directed, he defended his comprehensive self-narrative and the omniscient narrator, asserting that at the age of 80 it is impossible to write as if one had committed suicide at the age of 40 (*Aufzeichnungen 1942–1985*). Indeed, the vast temporal distance between the actual events and the time of narration is quite apparent. On the basis of later experiences, Canetti allows his profoundly subjective persona to make apodictic pronouncements on literature, moral issues, and personalities and to trace his changing attitudes to the world around him. Public developments receive the same weight as private events, including the narrator's first encounter with his future wife at one of Kraus's readings, and the emotional conflicts with his more-than-life-size mother whom he loves, dreads, respects, and abhors. In an intense psychological power struggle, Mrs. Canetti is finally defeated by Veza Taubner-Calderon, a woman of learning, wit, and critical judgment, the "beautiful raven lady," as Canetti calls her. Veza is a writer associated with the Viennese and Berlin avantgarde and gradually replaces Canetti's mother as his primary critic. As his advisor she comes to play a key role in building his career. Significantly, *The Torch in My Ear* ends with a project description of Canetti's first novel.

The dominant narrative in *The Torch in My Ear* is an autobiographical bildungsroman (educational novel) about Canetti's path in becoming an intellectual pioneer and the author of the foremost analysis of the mass events of his age: throughout the narrative Canetti underscores his independence from the leading theories of his time, psychoanalysis and Marxism. Events and personalities are subordinated to the major plot. The crumbling structures of the erstwhile Habsburg monarchy, encounters with kindred spirits such as Hermann Broch and eccentrics such as the self-styled Viennese Buddhist Fredl Waldinger, or those with fascinating and repulsive intellectual adversaries such as George Grosz and Bert Brecht—all of these are devices to showcase views and attitudes adopted or rejected by Canetti. This process of comparison and opposition brings the narrator's uniqueness to light. Canetti characterizes himself as a radical individualist, a loner, driven by the desire to excel.

The event that many writers and critics have described as the ultimate cataclysm of the era, the burning of Vienna's Palace of Justice in 1927, brings this segment of Canetti's life in Vienna to a close. The following brief episode in Berlin and his disillusionment with the German avant-garde express *in nuce* the tenuousness of an era of social experimentation. With the realization that Berlin, with its worldly and intellectual temptations, offers no viable alternative to his chosen path, the narrator emerges intellectually stabilized, ready to confront and bear witness to the following momentous decades.

DAGMAR C.G. LORENZ

Editions

First edition: *Die Fackel im Ohr: Lebensgeschichte 1921–1931,* Munich and Vienna: Hanser, 1980.

Translation: *The Torch in My Ear,* translated by Joachim Neugroschel, New York: Farrar Straus, and Giroux, 1982; in *The Memoirs of Elias Canetti,* New York: Farrar, Straus, and Giroux, 1999 (contains *The Tongue Set Free, The Torch in My Ear,* and *The Play of the Eyes*).

Further Reading

Beller, Manfred, "The Fire of Prometheus and the Theme of Progress in Goethe, Nietzsche, Kafka, and Canetti," *Colloquia Germanica* 17, no. 1/2 (1984)

Boyers, Robert, et al., "Remembering Elias Canetti," *Salmagundi* 104–5 (1994)

Cohen, Yaier, "Elias Canetti: Exile and the German Language," *German Life and Letters* 42, no. 1 (1988)

Darby, David, "A Literary Life: The Textuality of Elias Canetti's Autobiography," *Modern Austrian Literature* 25, no. 2 (1992)

Doppler, Alfred, "Gestalten und Figuren als Elemente der Zeit- und Lebensgeschichte: Canettis autobiographische Bücher," in *Autobiographien in der österreichischen Literatur: Von Franz Grillparzer bis Thomas Bernhard,* edited by Klaus Amann and Karl Wagner, Innsbruck: Studien Verlag, 1998

Eigler, Friederike, *Das autobiographische Werk von Elias Canetti,* Tübingen: Stauffenburg, 1988

Elbaz, Robert, *Elias Canetti: or, The Failing of the Novel,* New York: Lang, 1995

Foell, Kristie A., "July 15, 1927: The Vienna Palace of Justice Is Burned in a Mass Uprising of Viennese Workers, a Central Experience in the Life and Work of Elias Canetti," in *Yale Companion to Jewish Writing and Thought in German Culture, 1096–1996,* edited by Sander L. Gilman and Jack Zipes, New Haven, Connecticut: Yale University Press, 1997

Greif, Hans Jürgen, "Masse und Tod in Canettis *Die Fackel im Ohr,*" *Etudes Germaniques* 39, no. 1 (1984)

Handel, Amos, and Howard E. Gruber, "Formative Encounters in Early Adulthood: Mentoring Relationships in a Writer's Autobiographical Reconstruction of His Past Self," *Human Development* 33, no. 4/5 (1990)

Hulse, Michael, editor, *Essays in Honor of Elias Canetti,* New York: Farrar, Straus, and Giroux, 1987

Kimball, Roger, "Becoming Elias Canetti," *New Criterion* 5, no. 1 (1986)

Lawson, Richard H., *Understanding Elias Canetti,* Columbia: University of South Carolina Press, 1991

Modern Austrian Literature 16, no. 3/4 (1983), special Elias Canetti issue, edited by Donald G. Daviau

Piel, Edgar, *Wenn Dichter lügen: Literatur als Menschenforschung,* Zurich: Interfrom, 1988

Reiss, Hans, "The Writer's Task: Some Reflections on Elias Canetti's Autobiography," in *Elias Canetti: Londoner Symposium,* edited by Adrian Stevens and Fred Wagner, Stuttgart: Heinz, 1991

Rosenfeld, Sidney, "1981 Nobel Laureate Elias Canetti: A Writer," *World Literature Today* 56, no. 1 (1982)

Schieth, Lydia, "Europa-Erinnerung als Rekonstruktion: Autobiographien europäischen Lebens: Elias Canetti und Manes Sperber," in *Suchbild Europa: Künstlerische Konzepte der Moderne,* edited by Jürgen Wertheimer, Amsterdam: Rodopi, 1995

Seidler, Ingo, "Who Is Elias Canetti?" *Cross Currents: A Yearbook of Central European Culture* 2 (1982)

Trautwein, Ralf, *Die Literarisierung des Lebens in Elias Canettis Autobiographie,* Berlin: Galda und Wilch, 1997

Masse und Macht 1960

Essay by Elias Canetti

At least 30 years in the making, this ambitious study ultimately seeks to comprehend what may come to be seen as the 20th century's two greatest disasters, Nazism and the Cold War. Elias Canetti asserts that the modern masses, although not without analogous historical prototypes, are the phenomenon *par excellence* of the contemporary era; as such, they are the primary unit of analysis in this eclectic and far-flung study. Based upon wide-ranging investigations (mainly in anthropology, mythology, and folklore, but also in psychology and history), Canetti posits certain synchronic and cross-cultural propensities for crowd formation, as well as a given set of power behaviors. By acknowledging these strictures, Canetti suggests, we can discover not just our limitations, but also a modicum of freedom that can redirect the destructive course of history. In the end, *Masse und Macht* (*Crowds and Power*) proffers a hard-won and qualified optimism: Hitler and nuclear annihilation are ominous, but not inevitable, phenomena. The only hope of avoiding further catastrophe lies in finding more humane ways of managing our crowd and power needs and in practicing the uniquely human trait of "transformation" (*Verwandlung*).

Contrary to prevalent and largely negative conceptions of the crowd, Canetti demonstrates that destructiveness, although undeniable and at times obscenely violent, is a secondary trait associated with the crowd's need to expand. Indeed, Canetti first introduces us to the crowd in its most positive of manifestations, as exemplified in its ability to provide a sense of "release" (*Entladung*) from the pressures of overdeveloped individuation. The crowd offers an experience of equality (*Gleichheit*) and connectedness that effectively counteracts the individual's experience of isolation, distance, and social stratification. But the crowd is essentially labile, and even in its most positive aspect poses a threat. The prospect of egalitarian release simultaneously offers the prospect of respite to individuals constrained to subordinate themselves to another's power. In this way, a vulnerability to crowd formation builds up in individuals who are burdened by an accumulation of authoritarian "commands" (*Befehle;* see below). Thus, while crowds are essentially anterior to, and in no way a mere function of, leaders (the chief point of contrast with Freud's conception of crowds), they can easily fall prey to an unscrupulous *Führer*—a term Canetti pointedly employs in this postwar context.

If crowds are, fundamentally, "beyond good and evil," power, as Canetti describes it, clearly is not. Canetti locates power in diverse activities ranging from the very immediate and physical act of grasping and destroying an animal of prey, to the asking of probing analytical questions, to the unacknowledged joy we experience in surviving the dead. At the heart of his conception of power, however, is the "command." Derived from the "fight or flight" instinct, all other commands retain to some extent the death threat of the original. Each command leaves behind in the recipient a "thorn" (*Stachel*), which retains the precise character of the original command. At times, Canetti speaks of these thorns as having a memory, if not a mind, of their own. The build-up and discharge of such thorns (no less a hydraulic model than Freud's famed "principle of constancy") form the basis of Canetti's anthropology and the kernel of his moral exhortations. We must find ways to interdict the command at the point of entry, he admonishes, for an individual encumbered by an abundance of thorns quickly becomes susceptible to acts of inhumanity. Children overburdened by commands (and the residual thorns) will spend their adulthood attempting to discharge them without ever fully grasping what is driving their lives.

This rather literal notion of an individual's "economy of commands" (*der Befehlshaushalt des Menschen*), which uncharacteristically veers toward a deterministic view, must be judged against its intended explanatory power. For it enables Canetti to show why those who carry out orders, obliged to harbor that "foreign body" (*fremde Instanz*) which even when discharged leaves behind a scar, inevitably see themselves as the principal victim: "One perceives *oneself* to be its [the thorn's] victim, and therefore has no feeling for the actual and true victim." Palpably present as the *telos* motivating the entire project, Nazism emerges explicitly at key moments in this work. Indeed, when Canetti presents his culminating case study of the ultimate paranoid potentate, a magisterial two-part analysis of Daniel Paul Schreber's *Denkwürdigkeiten eines Nervenkranken* (1903; *Memoirs of My Nervous Illness*), he defends his selection of this potentially anomalous case on the grounds that it serves to illustrate all the salient aspects of power presented thus far in this study—providing a profile of the "'ideal' power-wielder" (*der 'ideale' Machthaber*)—and, more specifically, that it illuminates the career of Adolf Hitler. Canetti links the Holocaust (although the Nazi genocide against European Jewry was not yet known as such) to the great inflation of the 1920s, which he treats not primarily as an economic event, but as a crowd phenomenon. Canetti's animus toward traditional historiography, as well as his insistence on universal (if open-ended) categories, prevented him from seeing the Holocaust in its historical specificity.

The enduring appeal of *Crowds and Power,* however, will probably not be its specific account of Nazism and the Holocaust, but its richly diverse, unorthodox, and ebullient method of inquiry. By assembling and commenting upon a vast collection of largely non-European myth and folklore, in addition to a riveting set of anthropological reports and local histories, Canetti seeks to convince us of the legitimacy and universality of his categories. One is tempted to view this method as structuralist, but Canetti abjured both the structuralists' comparative rigor as well as their assumption that cultural practices tend to obscure deeper social truths. Canetti typically chooses to read *with* rather than against the grain of his sources, although he does so selectively. Adorno worried that Canetti was confusing "representation" with underlying "reality," and, predictably, distanced himself from the study's consistently ahistorical approach; he was more enthusiastic about the study's sweeping indictment of power. As in all grand and radical social theories, Canetti employs the factors he has established as primary and determinative—crowds and power—to explain "surface" phenomena as diverse as war, the rise and fall of world religions, mass murder, inflation, national symbols, mental illness, morality, and even politics itself. If, in the process, he lays himself open to the charge of reductionism, this may simply inhere in the nature of the project. Canetti systematically reveals the contemporary "psychic repertoire" (*der seelische Haushalt des Menschen*) as replete with vestiges of primitive ritual and biologically programmed behavior, yet he is ultimately committed to the prospect of positive transformation. Paradoxically, the animal kingdom is something humans both evolve *from* and develop *toward:* the very skill of "Verwandlung" is grounded in the human potential to imitate and modify animal behavior.

Cautious optimism is a crucial aspect of the book's original appeal. Published during the height of the Cold War, Canetti's analysis seemed to offer a way of transcending the political deadlock. First, the East-West divide is revealed to be a manifestation of the age-old "double crowd" (*Doppelmasse*), new only in the alarming nuclear technology at its disposal. Secondly, Canetti identifies the real threat in both capitalist and socialist societies as the unfettered drive toward industrialized mass production, itself a crowd phenomenon rendered more menacing by the available technology. In locating this common denominator beyond surface political differences, Canetti appeared, at least at the level of analysis, to have cut the Gordian knot. He was hailed as being above ideology.

Canetti's attraction to readers is certainly also due to his narrative sovereignty and to the extraordinary range of his topics. Indeed, the very qualities that have frustrated his reception by social scientists—his rejection of established academic methods and disciplinary boundaries, his refusal to place himself in the context of other social theorists, and his almost whimsical juxtaposition of topics—endear him to readers of a less systematic bent. Although it has inspired similarly eclectic work such as Klaus Theweleit's *Männerphantasien* (1977–78; *Male Fantasies*), *Crowds and Power* remains the province, principally, of literary critics who believe this study holds the interpretive key to the author's fictional output. Canetti's virtuoso skill as a storyteller at times threatens to overwhelm his own analytical agenda. In this respect, Canetti himself may be the essential topic of *Crowds and Power:* in his unexpected leaps of logic and insight, and in the creative connections he makes between apparently disparate material, he affirms our drive to make sense of a world whose increasing complexity threatens to elude our grasp. Although clearly possessed of an uncommon talent and breadth of learning, Canetti, as an amateur armchair anthropologist and cultural observer, simultaneously embodies the generalist reader's own intellectual ambition.

This celebration of the Western "universal scholar" is qualified, however, in two important ways. First, Canetti pointedly includes intellectual inquiry itself within his indictment of power. Second, he explicitly takes European cultural imperialism to task: this vaunted cultural achievement did not prevent the barbarism of World War II, Canetti reminds his target European audience. While the substance of *Crowds and Power* offers an important corrective to European ethnocentrism, however, it is not likely that the "primitive peoples" (*Naturvölker*)—upon whose stories and cultural practices Canetti lavishes so much attention in this study—will delight in their portrayal here. Although *Crowds and Power* takes a substantive step toward eradicating the "Orientalist" prejudice toward non-European cultures, which Canetti first pilloried in the Weimar-era novel *Die Blendung* (1931; *Auto-da-Fé*), this study is by no means free of a distinctly Western orientation. But neither does Canetti seek to deny this perspective, a point reflected perhaps most memorably in his lyrical travel memoir *Die Stimmen von Marrakesch* (1967; *The Voices of Marrakesh*); here, as in *Crowds and Power,* Canetti suggests that facing up to a particular subject position, even embracing one's status as outsider, may be the absolute prerequisite to any meaningful cross-cultural understanding.

William Collins Donahue

See also Fascism and Literature

Editions

First edition: *Masse und Macht,* Hamburg: Claassen, 1960

Translation: *Crowds and Power,* translated by Carol Stewart, London: Gollancz, and New York: Viking Press, 1962

Further Reading

Barnouw, Dagmar, *Elias Canetti,* Stuttgart: Metzler, 1979

"Elias Canetti: Discussion with Theodor W. Adorno," translated by David Roberts, *Thesis Eleven* 45 (1996)

Essays in Honor of Elias Canetti, translated by Michael Hulse, New York: Farrar, Straus, and Giroux, 1987

Göpfert, Herbert G., *Canetti lesen: Erfahrungen mit seinen Büchern,* Munich: Hanser, 1975

Lawson, Richard H., *Understanding Elias Canetti,* Columbia: University of South Carolina Press, 1991

McClelland, John, "The Place of Canetti's *Crowds and Power* in the History of Western Social and Political Thought," *Thesis Eleven* 45 (1996)

Roberts, David, "Crowds and Power or the Natural History of Modernity: Horkheimer, Adorno, Canetti, Arendt," *Thesis Eleven* 45 (1996)

Robertson, Ritchie, "Canetti as Anthropologist," in *Elias Canetti: Londoner Symposium,* edited by Adrian Stevens and Fred Wagner, Stuttgart: Heinz, 1991

Tönnies, Sibylle, "Die Klagemeute: Warum sich Deutsche den Opfern aufdrängen," *Frankfurter Allgemeine Zeitung,* 23 April 1996

Veza Canetti 1897–1963

Until the posthumous publication of three works of fiction—the episodic novel *Die gelbe Straße* (1990; *Yellow Street*), the short-story collection *Geduld bringt Rosen* (1992; Patience Brings Roses), and the novel *Die Schildkröten* (1999; The Tortoises)—and the play *Der Oger* (1991; The Ogre), Veza Canetti was known for the loving portrait painted of her by her husband, the Nobel laureate Elias Canetti, in the second volume of his autobiography, *Die Fackel im Ohr* (1980; *The Torch in My Ear*). While he expresses a great emotional and intellectual debt to the English-speaking young woman that he met at one of the public readings given by the great Viennese satirist Karl Kraus, presenting her as a strong-minded, independent individual, Canetti leaves the impression that her main achievement lay in rescuing him from the clutches of his overbearing mother. He does not mention that she, some eight years his senior, began to write her own stories at the same time he commenced his first masterpiece, *Die Blendung* (1936; *Auto-da-Fe*), and enjoyed arguably greater success than he did in prewar Vienna before they both fled Austria after the Nazi takeover. Elias Canetti also does not say that his wife of 30 years had a withered arm, which restricted her movement, caused her great embarrassment, and perhaps helps explain her interest in the cripple "die Runkel" (*Die gelbe Straße*), one of her most memorable grotesques, and her sympathy for others who suffered physical disadvantage.

Born Venetiana Taubner-Calderon, Canetti was politically on the left after 1918, an allegiance reflected especially in the stories published in *Geduld bringt Rosen,* most of which first appeared in the renowned *Arbeiter-Zeitung,* edited by the Marxist Ernst Fischer, between 1932 and 1933. Fischer recalled finding refuge in the Canettis' Vienna flat during the street fighting in February 1934. He describes her as "modest" but "proud," believing her "goodness" to be "the distillation of a dark, smouldering passion." Yet "the choice of name [Magd (Maid)] was in keeping with her nature," since she set out to serve humanity—and her husband. Elias Canetti hints, too, in his introduction to *Die gelbe Straße,* that she subordinated herself and her work to him, which on her rediscovery enhanced her interest to feminists.

Veza Canetti published under a variety of revealing pseudonyms, including Veza Magd and the even more brutal sounding Veronika Knecht (servant or slave). After she won a prize in a short-story competition organized by the *Arbeiter-Zeitung* for "Der Zwinger" (The Fixter), which became the last chapter of

Die gelbe Straße, Wieland Herzfelde included "Geduld bringt Rosen" in an anthology published by his famous Malik publishing house. She was clearly at the beginning of a promising career when the fascist coup in Austria made further publication impossible for a Jewish socialist and feminist.

She continued to write for the next 20 years, however: a novel entitled *Die Schildkröten* (The Tortoises), which addresses the subject of emigration with emotional rawness and immediacy, was accepted by publishers in London on the eve of World War II, but the outbreak of war prevented its publication. Veza Canetti's 1947 translation of Graham Greene's *The Power and the Glory* was thereafter her only book to find its way into print during her lifetime despite her and her husband's best efforts. She mentions two other novels, *Die Geniesser* (The Enjoyers) and a version of the Kaspar Hauser story, both of which are lost to posterity: she destroyed most of her manuscripts in despair at failing to interest publishers in 1956. All that survived is what her husband managed to save.

Veza Canetti died unsung and unknown in the obscurity of British exile, mourned by her husband and a small circle of friends, including Helga Michie, sister of Ilse Aichinger, and the novelists Rudolf Nassauer and Bernice Rubens. While there are signs that she sacrificed her talent to Elias Canetti as the superior talent in their partnership, it was only thanks to him that her books, which now sit on library shelves as nagging postscripts to his voluminous writings, were finally published at all. Veza Canetti's biography is ultimately a distraction, however instructive it may be for our understanding of women writers in general and left-wing Jewish women writers under National Socialism in particular. She claims her place in literary history for her vivid descriptions of Viennese working-class milieus, her satirical humor and gentle didacticism, her ability to address social and moral issues delicately yet powerfully, and her unsentimental picture of 1920s Vienna. Her narrative analysis of social behavior invariably focuses on the victims of class or gender exploitation, and she succeeds in presenting the motivation and the thoughts of the disadvantaged and showing, too, that those in power rarely act out of malice or spite. In this economically harsh world, the fate of a person can depend on an employer's whim ("Der Sieger" [The Victor], in *Geduld bringt Rosen*), and the loss of a job can spell destitution ("Geduld bringt Rosen" [Patience Brings Roses]). If there is a unifying theme in her work, it is the effects of economic, emotional, or psychological power on its victims, including the disabled, children with or without families, wives in unequal marriages, widows left to fend for themselves, employees in service or in industry, the unemployed, the insane, and the incarcerated. Veza Canetti must also count as one of the first women writers to show the unwitting complicity of oppressed women in their oppression (*Der Oger*). In "Der Tiger," chapter four of *Die gelbe Straße,* of which there is a dramatic version in Elias Canetti's *Nachlaß,* she balances this portrait by showing a woman who is triumphant in a battle of wits with a powerful male.

The loss of her other post-1934 work is one of the many literary tragedies wrought by National Socialism.

Julian Preece

Biography

Born in Vienna, 21 November 1897. Frequent visits to England, where her half-brother Maurice Calderon lived, until the outbreak of World War I; after 1918, worked as a translator and as a teacher in a private school; met Elias Canetti, 1924; stories published in the *Arbeiter-Zeitung,* 1932–33; married Elias Canetti, 1934; emigration to Paris, November 1938, and to London, January 1939, where she and Elias lived in Hampstead; destroyed most of her unpublished work, 1956. Died 1 May 1963.

Selected Works

Fiction

Die gelbe Straße: Roman, 1990; as *Yellow Street,* translated by Ian Mitchell, 1990

Geduld bringt Rosen: Erzählungen, 1992

Play

Der Oger, 1991

Translation

Graham Greene, *Die Kraft und die Herrlichkeit,* 1951

Further Reading

Canetti, Elias, *Die Fackel im Ohr: Lebensgeschichte 1921–1931,* Vienna and Munich: Hanser, 1981

Fischer, Ernst, *Erinnerungen und Reflexionen,* Reinbek bei Hamburg: Rowohlt, 1969

Göbel, Helmut, 'Nachwort' to *Die gelbe Straße,* Munich and Vienna: Hanser, 1990

Lorenz, Dagmar C.G., "Feminism and Socialism in Vienna (Veza Canetti)," in *Keepers of the Motherland: German Texts by Jewish Women Writers,* Lincoln and London: University of Nebraska Press, 1997

Meidl, Eva, "Die gelbe Straße, Parallelstraße zur 'Ehrlichstraße'? Außenseiter in Veza Canettis Roman *Die gelbe Straße* und Elias Canettis Roman *Die Blendung,*" *Modern Austrian Literature* 28, no. 2 (1995)

Preece, Julian, "The Rediscovered Writings of Veza Magd-Canetti: On the Pyschology of Subservience," *Modern Austrian Literature* 28, no. 2 (1995)

Carolingian Period

The Carolingian period is associated with the reign of the Frankish King Karl, best known by the title Charlemagne, Charles the Great, who became king of the dominant Germanic tribe, the Franks, in 768 and who gradually consolidated his rule over a large area of what is now Germany, the Low Countries, France, and part of Italy. He was crowned emperor in Rome on Christmas Day, 800, as the head of what was proclaimed as a new and (since it was Christian) Holy Roman Empire. Where the Carolingian period ends is more difficult. An optimist might claim 1919 and the abdication of the last Austrian emperor; a pessimist would say (with far more justification) that it ended with Charlemagne's own death in 814. Charlemagne was indeed a dominant and forceful personality, and in his lifetime he held together a large area of modern Europe. However, Charlemagne's immediate family ruled in Germany (which was separated from what we would now term France as early as 842) until the beginning of the tenth century, and even thereafter cultural developments continued that had begun in the reign of Charlemagne himself.

Charlemagne became king of the Franks in 768 and, after the death of his brother in 771, was sole ruler over territories that stretched from the river Saale in eastern Germany to Frisia, and which covered most of France right down to the Pyrenees plus what is now Holland, Belgium, and Switzerland. In the course of his reign, he conquered Lombardy and soon controlled much of Italy, using his excellent relations with the papacy. He subsumed Bavaria/Austria into his territories, and after a series of campaigns that lasted for decades, he even managed to convert and bring under his rule the intransigent Saxons. He made some forays into Spain against the Saracen rulers there, but the former Roman province of Hispania was one of the few areas of the old Western Roman Empire that he did not control.

The lands that Charlemagne ruled were very extensive indeed, and he managed to protect his borders against outside forces, such as the Slavs, Avars (White Huns), and Vikings. His own territory was kept relatively stable by the efforts of able administrators and *missi dominici* (royal envoys) who passed on his commands, and he held annual general assemblies at different royal centers. In terms of external diplomacy, he maintained relations with the Anglo-Saxons in England, corresponded with King Offa, and took England's greatest scholar, Alcuin (735–804), from York to his palace school in Aachen. After a somewhat uneasy truce with the Arab rulers in Spain, Charlemagne eventually made a peace treaty in 810 with the Caliph of Cordoba, and in the same year he established a pact with the Vikings. On a larger scale, he established cordial relations with the Byzantine Empire, with the Caliphate of Baghdad (he corresponded with Harun al Rashid), and most important, with the papacy. As a result of his support for Pope Leo III, he was crowned emperor by him in Rome and was thus able to speak of a *renovatio imperii,* a renewal of the Roman Empire, now transferred to the Franks. Charlemagne saw himself very much as the heir to the Roman emperors. When he died in 814, however, his rule continued on a broad basis only for one more generation. After the death in 840 of his son, known as Lewis the Pious, family strife led to the breakup of the empire into what would become the ancestors of the modern Western European states. By 911, his last ruling descendant in Germany, Lewis the Child, died without a successor.

Even though the Carolingian Empire did not really survive for long after the loss of the dominant figure of Charlemagne himself, the cultural achievements of the Carolingian period were enormous. The term *renaissance* is sometimes used, and there was indeed under Charlemagne a flowering of literature and the encouragement of an educational and religious policy. It has to be stressed, however, that Carolingian literature is almost exclusively Latin; nevertheless it is in the period of Charlemagne and his successors that we see the first writings in German: the birth of vernacular literature in Old High German, the earliest stage of German language. Throughout this period, writing in German is extremely limited, and compared with Latin writings, it is almost insignificant. It is, however, a beginning, and there are some enormously important documents from this period for the later history of German culture. For the most part, these German writings are fragments, depending almost exclusively (although with one or two important exceptions) on Latin literature and culture; without exception, however, we owe the fact that German was written down at all at this stage to Christian monks.

Charlemagne's court, based at Aachen, was a cultural and literary center, and he built up under Alcuin's supervision a palace school (*academy* might be a better word), which gave consideration to the standardizing of canon law, the monastic rule of St. Benedict, the liturgy, and the Bible itself. The school produced educational texts on rhetoric, grammar and dialectic, astronomy, arithmetic, music, and geometry. The Carolingian period also saw the writing of numerous annals, historical and biographical writings in prose and verse, saints' lives, theology and biblical commentary (these were especially numerous), political and philosophical writings, hymns and other verse of all kinds, and epistolary, nature, commemorative, and panegyric writings, sometimes based on the classics. Charlemagne himself was concerned that Latin should be understood properly by the clergy at least, and in the Carolingian period, important classical and postclassical works were preserved. It cannot be stressed enough that Carolingian literary culture was a Latin culture, and that however interesting it may be to us, the new writing in German is both very small in substance and far from independent. Much of it, too, has survived by accident, preserved on the occasional blank pages of Latin manuscripts and sometimes at the edges and in the margins of Latin works. In addition, the laws that Charlemagne continued to standardize were a mixture of Roman law and German tribal custom, and some of the texts contain German words for specifically Germanic practices.

Latin writers in the Carolingian period (taken in its broadest sense) included not only Alcuin but also Hrabanus Maurus (784–856), abbot of the important monastery of Fulda and later archbishop of Mainz, who wrote a large number of biblical commentaries and encyclopedic theological works as well as poems. The monastery school at Fulda produced a number of other scholar-writers, including Einhard, the biographer of Charlemagne. Under the tutelage of Hrabanus, who was enormously influential as a teacher, came writers such as Servatus Lupus of Ferrières (ca. 805–62), who was eventually the abbot of a French monastery and was much involved with the preservation of the classics, and who was, incidentally, interested in the German language. The same school educated the poet Walahfrid Strabo (ca. 808–49) and also the first named German poet, Otfrid, later of the monastery at Weissenburg. Elsewhere in the empire of Charlemagne and his successors, Latin letters also flourished, and the wife of an official of Charlemagne's son Lewis the Pious, the lady Dhuoda, wrote in 841 an interesting book of advice to her son about how to behave, both at court and in general moral terms.

Charlemagne strengthened greatly the Christianity already established in German territories (other than Saxony) in the wake of Irish and Anglo-Saxon missions. The cultural centers were the monasteries, and under Charlemagne's rule, although these were still distanced from each other without easy communication, they became very important throughout his lands and produced a great deal of writing, almost as the equivalent of the modern universities. Many of the earlier monasteries of the south of Germany had been Irish foundations, but these were now gradually regularized under the Benedictine Rule. St. Gallen, for example, became a royal monastery of some importance, and the imperial foundation at the Reichenau on Lake Constance was similar, as was Murbach in Alsace. Bavarian monasteries included Freising, Wessobrunn, and St. Emmeram at Regensburg. Most of these monasteries had scriptoria and libraries containing the works of the church fathers plus those of Isidore of Seville, Boethius, Bede, Alcuin, Hrabanus, and usually some Christian-Latin poetry.

It was in Charlemagne's reign that German was first committed to writing in the monasteries, using the (not entirely suitable) Latin alphabet; Charlemagne's reforms had provided a unified, neat, and legible lettering based on classical models, called Carolingian minuscule. He was interested in German and apparently collected epic poems (which have not survived, and which his son stopped because he thought they were unchristian). Charlemagne's reforms must not be exaggerated as far as the German language is concerned, but he did call for dissemination of the Creed, the Pater noster, and the professions of faith to be available in translation.

The first writings in German are very much in the service of Christianity. There are early translations of the Pater noster and of the Creed, and formulas of renunciation of pagan gods, of course—the standard material required for a country in which Christianity still requires consolidation and in some areas actual conversion. As far as more developed writings are concerned, however, from the end of the eighth century onward, the relationship to Latin and the pedagogical intent remains clear. The monasteries engaged greatly in the practice of glossing, of adding German words to Latin writings to assist their understanding. Works of all kinds were glossed, and this was a practice that continued throughout the Middle Ages. Besides the glosses, however, the reign of Charlemagne and his successors saw translations of theological writings: the careful early version in Old High German of Isidore of Seville's *Adversus Judaeos* provided a useful text for basic theological discussion, for example. Somewhat later, closer to the middle of the ninth century, came a translation of a different kind (that is, adhering more closely to the Latin original and thus faithful in the religious sense) of the Gospel-Harmony compiled originally in Greek by Tatian(os) in the second century and translated into Latin.

Glosses and translation clearly depend on Latin originals. As far as the original German writings of the Carolingian period are concerned, we have a variety of types, if not a large amount. The total of original writings in German in the period would not fill much more than a single large volume. While all of the material is Christian in that it was written down by monks (and even material that is pre-Christian has usually been adapted), there are a few relics preserved of pre-Christian German literature. The Old High German charms, pronouncements designed to cure or ameliorate a medical condition of some sort (such as a cut or a sprain), show their antiquity by referring in one or two cases (such as the *Merseburger Zaubersprüche*) to Germanic gods. However, all have been Christianized by the addition of prayers, and most of them are completely Christian. One work, the *Hildebrandslied* (Lay of Hildebrand), is clearly pre-Christian in content, set in the world of the Goths, naming actual fifth- and sixth-century figures, and showing a heroic conflict between a father and son. The work is written in the Germanic style, using alliterative long-lines of the sort found in Old Norse and Old English poetry. It is written in a Christian manuscript and has been slightly adapted to make reference to God, but its antiquity is clear: it is a throwback even among what we have of Old High German, and there is no explanation for why it was written down, except perhaps antiquarian interest on the part of the monks.

Other Germanic heroic works have not survived in the vernacular from this period, although there must have been an oral tradition. We do have, however, stories from the history of early Germanic tribes preserved in languages such as Anglo-Saxon or Old Norse, and indeed in Latin, as in the case of the poem of *Waltharius,* perhaps from the tenth century, which depicts Attila the Hun as well as Burgundian and Visigothic rulers. The (very much adapted) tale of one of Charlemagne's own battles, the attack in 778 on his luggage train in the pass of Roncesvalles in the Pyrenees, is referred to in Latin writings, and there is a famous poem, the *Chanson de Roland* (*Song of Roland*) in French, but a German version came only very much later. Finally, we have evidence of far later works, such as the *Nibelungenlied* (*Fall of the Nibelungs*), written in the 13th century but using far older material.

As far as German literature goes, the most important figure of the Carolingian age as a whole is Otfrid von Weissenburg. Otfrid was a monk who had been at Fulda and who became the master of the school at Weissenburg, now Wissembourg in French Alsace. His achievement is to have composed (ca. 860) in German rhymed verse a Gospel-poem, a mixture of biblical narrative and commentary to which an entire manuscript is devoted. The work (of over 7,000 lines) is accompanied by German verse dedicatory letters and a Latin letter addressed to Liutbert, Otfrid's superior and the successor to his old teacher, Hrabanus, at the see of Mainz. The letter is significant, as it makes a careful case to justify what Otfrid was doing. Clearly, he felt the work needed explanation, namely, for writing it in German, for which he apologizes, as German is a "barbaric and uncultivated language." However, he still composed in German, and the manuscript (now in Vienna) that Otfrid himself corrected was even copied several times. German is afforded some status, but it was still dependent on Latin. There had been an earlier Carolingian Gospel poem, the Old Saxon *Heliand,* but that was in alliterative verse. Otfrid used rhymed long-lines, based probably on Latin hymns, and his work has Latin chapter heads. Moreover, his whole style (and this is true of the *He-*

liand as well to a very large extent) reflects the biblical commentary of the time, which would present the text of the Bible not only in its literal sense but also by drawing allegorical connections between the Old and New Testaments, seeing it as containing prophecies of the end of the world and using it to preach general morals. Otfrid does all these things in his Gospel-narrative.

The chronology of the Old High German texts is difficult to determine, but none of the other survivals is as important as Otfrid's far larger-scale effort. Possibly predating Otfrid are alliterative pieces on the beginning of the world (the so-called *Wessobrunn Creation*) and the last judgment (a work known as *Muspilli,* which also contains rhymes). In Otfrid's wake came smaller biblical pieces, such as an adaptation in verse of one of the Psalms and a little hymn to St. Peter. There is a very badly copied poem on the life of St. George, and it is an indication of the status of German that an earlier German poem about St. Gall, the missionary, has survived only in a Latin translation.

One further work requires special mention, namely, the *Ludwigslied* (Lay of Louis). This poem is in what is clearly Otfridian rhymed verse, using the same kind of strophes (Otfrid grouped two long-lines together; this poem sometimes groups three). It tells the story of a battle over the Vikings won by Charlemagne's great-grandson, who was, however, king of what we would call France, and it was recorded in German in a French monastery in a manuscript that contains mainly Latin but also one of the earliest Old French texts known. This last reminder of the extent of Charlemagne's original empire is a carefully constructed song of praise for the victorious king as well as a piece of propaganda for his slightly shaky throne (although in fact he died not long after), but it both describes events and interprets them in a theological manner.

Beyond these writings in German, there is very little more in the Carolingian period or even from the reigns of the succeeding Saxon emperors. Collected editions of Old High German monuments include, it is true, all kinds of fragments, even single lines of text written by scribes as practice in the margins or at the end of manuscripts. However, the proportions of Carolingian literature must always be born in mind. For the most part it is in Latin, and with very few exceptions, what German there is is thinkable only within that Latin culture. The *Hildebrandslied,* it is true, stands out as a work of a different type, but it is a random survival only, and the Germanic alliterative style in which it is written was not used much more in written German. What survived was the end rhyme used by Otfrid, and the copying and transmission of his work is far more significant. He, too, was aware that writing in German was unusual, and he felt the need to justify it. The trickle of German did increase in size after the Carolingian period, slowly at least, as vernacular literature moved away from the monasteries into the hands of secular priests attached to cathedrals, for example, but as late as the 11th century, another German monk, Notker of St. Gallen, known as "the German," also felt the need to justify the fact that he was using German in his teaching. It would be another century, and well beyond the Carolingians, before German became a fully established literary language.

BRIAN MURDOCH

Further Reading

Bertau, Karl, *Deutsche Literatur im europäischen Mittelalter,* Munich: Beck, 1972–73

Bostock, John Knight, *A Handbook on Old High German Literature,* Oxford: Clarendon Press, 1955; 2nd edition revised by K.C. King and D.R. McLintock, 1976

Braune, Wilhelm, editor, *Althochdeutsches Lesebuch,* 16th edition revised by Ernst A. Ebbinghaus, Tübingen: Niemeyer, 1979

Braunfels, Wolfgang, editor, *Karl der Größe: Lebenswerk und Nachleben,* 5 vols., Düsseldorf: Schwann, 1965–68

Curtius, Ernst Robert, *Europäische Literatur und lateinisches Mittelalter,* Bern: Francke, 1948; 11th edition, 1993; translated by Willard R. Trask: *European Literature and the Latin Middle Ages,* New York: Pantheon Books, 1952; London: Routledge and Kegan Paul, 1953

Duckett, Eleanor Shipley, *Carolingian Portraits: A Study in the Ninth Century,* Ann Arbor: University of Michigan Press, 1962

Dutton, Paul Edward, editor, *Carolingian Civilization: A Reader,* Peterborough, Ontario: Broadview Press, 1993

Godman, Peter, *Poetry of the Carolingian Renaissance,* London: Duckworth, and Norman: University of Oklahoma Press, 1985

———, *Poets and Emperors: Frankish Politics and Carolingian Poetry,* Oxford: Clarendon Press, and New York: Oxford University Press, 1986

Groseclose, J. Sidney, and Murdoch, Brian, *Die althochdeutschen poetischen Denkmäler,* Stuttgart: Metzler, 1976

Heinzle, Joachim, editor, *Geschichte der deutschen Literatur von den Anfängen bis zum Beginn der Neuzeit*: I/i: Wolfgang Haubrichs, *Die Anfänge,* Frankfurt: Athenäum, 1988 and I/ii: Gisela Vollmann-Profe, *Von den Anfängen bis zum hohen Mittelalter,* Königstein: Athenäum, 1986

King, K.C., "The Earliest German Monasteries," in *Selected Essays on Medieval German Literature,* edited by John L. Flood, A.T. Hatto, and K.C. King, London: University of London, Institute of Germanic Studies, 1975

Laistner, M.L.W., *Thought and Letters in Western Europe, A.D. 500 to 900,* London: Methuen, 1931; 2nd edition, London: Methuen, and Ithaca, New York: Cornell University Press, 1957

Manitius, Max, and Paul Lehmann, *Geschichte der lateinischen Literatur des Mittelalters,* Munich: Beck, 1911–31; reprint, 1964–65

McKitterick, Rosamond, *The Frankish Kingdoms under the Carolingians 751–987,* London and New York: Longman, 1983

———, *The Carolingians and the Written Word,* Cambridge and New York: Cambridge University Press, 1989

Murdoch, Brian, *Old High German Literature,* Boston: Twayne, 1983

Schlosser, Horst Dieter, editor, *Althochdeutsche Literatur,* Frankfurt and Hamburg: Fischer, 1970; revised edition, 1989

Sonderegger, Stefan, *Althochdeutsche Sprache und Literatur,* Berlin and New York: de Gruyter, 1974

Steinmeyer, Elias von, editor, *Die kleineren althochdeutschen Sprachdenkmäler,* 1916; reprinted as 2nd edition, Berlin: Weidmann, 1963

Wipf, Karl A., editor, *Althochdeutsche poetische Texte,* Stuttgart: Reclam, 1992

Catharina Regina von Greiffenberg *see* Greiffenberg, Catharina Regina

---

Paul Celan 1920–1970

Paul Celan's poetry is surely the most remarkable of all German-language attempts to give expression in lyric form to the Holocaust and its psychological consequences. Born in Romania as Paul Antschel (his pseudonym, Celan, is an inversion of "Antschel"), he grew up with German as his mother tongue and began to write his first poems as a teenager. In 1942, his parents were deported to a forced-labor camp in Ukraine, where they both perished; he himself spent time in one or more labor camps in Romania during the same period. Alongside numerous translations from English and French, these years saw the beginnings of his serious poetry: he began to put together a first volume upon his release from labor camp in early 1944.

The extent to which the Holocaust experience permeated his poetry was initially greatly underestimated by most critics and scholars. Although his first published poem, *Todesfuge* (first published 1948, but retracted; published again in 1952; *Death Fugue*) clearly referred to the Nazi death camps, it seemed to early readers to occupy an isolated position among his works. *Death Fugue* rapidly became a cultural icon in the German attempt to come to terms with National Socialism and the Third Reich. Widely anthologized and much studied, the poem describes how concentration camp prisoners are forced to sing and play music while their fellow internees dig graves for those who have been shot by the Nazi guards. Yet even this unequivocal depiction of National Socialist abominations has been subjected to criticism in the course of the prolonged debate, initiated by Theodor W. Adorno, about whether lyric poetry "after Auschwitz" might not itself be a barbaric phenomenon. Some readers found the poem, with its imitation of musical form, too aesthetic to provide an appropriate response to the Nazi crimes. Yet the grating contrast the poem sets up between its aesthetic form and the horrendous events it describes is a crucial part of its effect.

Although formally very different from most of Celan's other poetry, *Death Fugue* is in fact no exception thematically. Celan's first two volumes of poetry, *Der Sand aus den Urnen* (1948; The Sand from the Urns) and *Mohn und Gedächtnis* (1952; Poppy and Remembrance), announce in their very titles the motifs of death and remembrance common to Celan's work as a whole. Night, ashes, forgetfulness, the bitterness of time, and a weeping eye are all recurrent images in this first phase of his writing. In the poetry of his mature period, represented by *Sprachgitter* (1959; Speech-Grille) and *Die Niemandsrose* (1963; The No-Man's Rose), the problematic nature of linguistic expression becomes increasingly urgent. Celan's language in this phase is elliptical, allusive, and dazzlingly polysemous. Hesitance, stuttering, syntactical gaps, parenthetical phrases, obscure compound words, and disturbing word breaks at the ends of lines are distinctive features of Celan's mature style.

Celan's engagements with Martin Buber's concept of "I and Thou" and with Mandel'shtam's notion of poetry as dialogue are crucial ingredients in this phase. Celan's brief speech in acceptance of the Bremen Prize for Literature in 1958 develops the image of poetry as a "message in a bottle," a message that does not know where it will be washed up on land or who will extract it from the bottle, but which aims to speak to this unknown person all the same. "Poems have, in this sense, embarked on a journey: they are steering toward something," he writes in this speech. The poems of *Sprachgitter* and *Die Niemandsrose* enact this conception of "open dialogicity." Celan's late volumes, *Atemwende* (1967; Breath-turn), *Fadensonnen* (1968; Threadsuns) and *Lichtzwang* (1970; Light-Compulsion), are radically reduced to their basic elements. Some of these poems, such as the much-studied seven-line "Fadensonnen," present themselves as miniatures in which words seem to huddle together in cryptic combinations. Celan's last volume, *Schneepart* (1971; Snow Part), published posthumously after his suicide in the Seine, continues this condensed and elliptical mode. The French student uprising of 1968, which he supported, and the end of the Prague Spring later in the same year, which shocked him profoundly, resonate with Celan's recollections of Romania under Nazism in some of these late poems. The motif of a "breath-turn" is increasingly enacted in the splitting of words over two lines; speech is increasingly fragmentary, constantly threatening to be reduced to a mere stream of air across the "open glottis." The world is frequently depicted as a wasteland, a minefield, or a swamp.

Despite the manifold difficulties that his texts present, Celan was adamant in declaring his poetry "not at all hermetic." He believed that his poetry was quite transparent, but only if readers were willing to see it the right way. This discrepancy between Celan's own view of his poetry and that of most critics at the time can be explained, in part, by the deep suspicions of aestheticism held by the influential Gruppe 47, which had worked hard to make modernist techniques again function in the service of a new social and political engagement appropriate to the postwar period. Celan's difficult, compressed poetry appeared to these writers to be a return to French symbolism, especially the self-reflexive poetry of Mallarmé. Certainly, Celan's poetry is deeply influenced by French symbolism; it also owes a great deal to the French surrealists, as well as to certain previously unknown poems by Rilke that were published for the first time in the six-volume edition of 1966. This mixture of impulses made Celan's poetry appear in a distinctly formalist light.

In fact, however, Celan's poems were from beginning to end an intense engagement with the Holocaust and with the postwar world, which he saw as permanently "wounded" by this sequence of events. In this world, the speaking subject has become fractured, and its relationship even with the most intimate other (the "Du" [thou] that figures in so many of Celan's poems) is precarious and fragile. In sharp distinction to the nebulous and associative style of symbolism, Celan's texts aim for the greatest precision possible in a language that was sullied by its uses under National Socialism. At times, language breaks down almost entirely. At other times, it is marked by rifts that cannot be smoothed over. Counterbalancing these effects is Celan's use of special terms from botany, geology, and other special fields of knowledge. Words that critics first took to be neologisms that appealed to the reader's creative intuitions have since been revealed to be unusual, but very precise, terms that can be found in larger German dictionaries such as that of the Grimms. In addition to these technical terms, Celan's poems are constantly invaded by words and phrases from Hebrew, as well as by allusions to Kabbala and Jewish mysticism. In this way, his poetry insists on the particularity of Jewish experience by inserting into German texts fragmentary elements from the culture that Nazism had tried to eradicate. Celan's writing thus forms a sustained response to Adorno's claim that it would be barbarous to write poetry after Auschwitz.

The tension created by this position became especially evident in Celan's relation to the philosopher Martin Heidegger, who had been rector of Freiburg University in 1933–34 and a loyal member of the Nazi party until the end of the war. Celan's poem "Todtnauberg" (the name of a mountain in the Black Forest) recounts his meeting with Heidegger in 1967. Celan had hoped that Heidegger would express remorse for his involvement with National Socialism—indeed, when he composed the poem a week after this visit, Celan still believed there would be "a coming word in the heart" of the philosopher. Celan was bitterly disappointed by Heidegger's failure to break his silence about his guilt. Even the gift of a bibliophile edition of "Todtnauberg" did not elicit an apology from the philosopher.

Celan's frustration over this exchange compounded his distress over critics' continuing charges that his poetry was hermetic. Psychologically fragile, Celan had already been laboring under a plagiarism charge that had been brought in 1953 and again in 1960 by Claire Goll, who believed that Celan had illicitly borrowed from the work of her late husband, Yvan Goll. Although the chronology of Celan's writing did not support Claire Goll's claims, Celan felt helpless in the face of what he saw as her relentless persecution. Against this backdrop, Celan reacted with increasing agitation to reviewers' complaints about his poetry's obscurity. He felt that the German critical establishment was set upon occluding the message that he was trying to send about the Holocaust and its consequences. Even when he received the prestigious Georg Büchner Prize in 1960, he was not convinced that his poetry had been understood. His acceptance speech, "Der Meridian" (The Meridian) is, if anything, even more elliptical and difficult than his poetry. It is also a response to the charge of obscurity. Arguing against the notion of absolute poetry, Celan sees the poem as the site for a meeting of minds: "The poem desires to reach an Other, it needs this Other, it needs a partner. It seeks this Other out, it addresses it." The prize speech insists upon the communicative function of poetry and also upon poetry's essential political involvement and implications.

Recent scholarship has been more attentive to the complex layering of meanings in Celan's poetry. The decline of *werkimmanente Interpretation* (the German equivalent of New Criticism) and a return to a more contextualized reading of texts has cleared away much of what at first appeared to be the nebulosity of Celan's texts. New understandings of intertextual relations have helped to clarify Celan's elaborate citational and allusive practices. Over the past 15 years, scholars have energetically brought to bear upon their readings of Celan's poems biographical and historical facts, special meanings of words, references to Jewish texts and religious beliefs, and allusions to other poetry in various languages. Celan's prolific reading and his many translations from works by Shakespeare, Mandel'shtam, Rimbaud, Valéry, Michaux, Supervielle, Ungaretti, and others have been increasingly taken into account in scholarly studies of his writing. The publication of his collected works in 1983 provided an important tool for this work. Although much still remains to be done, some of the most important barriers to understanding Celan's poetry have now been removed. Rather than attempting to unlock his writing by meditating on the texts in a vacuum, scholars now recognize that painstaking work on Celan's special vocabulary and range of reference is essential. His poetry will never lose its enigmatic quality, but it is now understood as an enigma whose secrets can be unlocked.

JUDITH RYAN

Biography

Born in Czernowitz, Bukovina, Romania, 23 November 1920. Studied at the University of Tours, France, 1938–39; at the University of Czernowitz, 1939–41; studied for a Licence-ès-Lettres in Paris, 1950; imprisoned in a forced-labor camp during World War II; emigrated to Vienna, 1947; in Paris, 1948; language teacher and translator in Paris, 1950–70. Bremen Prize for Literature, 1958; Büchner Prize, 1960. Died (suicide) in Paris, 20 April 1970.

Selected Works

Collections

Gedichte, 2 vols., 1975
Poems, translated by Michael Hamburger, 1980
Gesammelte Werke, edited by Beda Allemann, Stefan Reichert, and Rolf Bücher, 5 vols., 1983; vol. 3 as *Collected Prose,* translated by Rosemarie Waldrop, 1986
Gedichte 1938–1944, 1985

Poetry

Der Sand aus den Urnen, 1948
Mohn und Gedächtnis, 1952
Von Schwelle zu Schwelle, 1955
Sprachgitter, 1959
Die Niemandsrose, 1963
Atemwende, 1967
Todtnauberg, 1968
Fadensonnen, 1968
Lichtzwang, 1970
Speech-Grille and Selected Poems, translated by Joachim Neugroschel, 1971
Schneepart, 1971
Selected Poems, translated by Michael Hamburger and Christopher Middleton, 1972
Nineteen Poems, translated by Michael Hamburger, 1972

Zeitgehöft: Späte Gedichte aus dem Nachlass, 1976
Thirty-Two Poems, translated by Michael Hamburger, 1985
Sixty-Five Poems, translated by Brian Lynch and Peter Jankowsky, 1985
Last Poems, translated by Katherine Washburn and Margaret Guillemin, 1986

Other
Edgar Jené und der Traum vom Traume, 1948
Der Meridian, 1961

Translations
Anton Chekhov, *Taranii* (into Romanian), 1946
Mikhail Lermontov, *Un eroual timpalu* (into Romanian), 1946
Konstantin Simonov, *Chestinnea Rusa* (into Romanian), 1947
E.M. Cioran, *Lehre vom Zerfall,* 1953
Aleksandr Blok, *Die Zwölf,* 1958
Arthur Rimbaud, *Das trunkene Schiff,* 1958
Osip Mandel'shtam, *Gedichte,* 1959
Paul Valéry, *Die junge Parze,* 1960
Sergei Esenin, *Gedichte,* 1961
Jean Cayrol, *Im Bereich einer Nacht,* 1961
Georges Simenon, *Maigret und die schrecklichen Kinder,* 1955
Georges Simenon, *Hier irrt Maigret,* 1955
Henri Michaux, *Dichtungen,* 1966
William Shakespeare, *Einundzwanzig Sonette,* 1967
Jules Supervielle, *Gedichte,* 1968
André du Bouchet, *Vakante Glut: Gedichte,* 1968
Giuseppe Ungaretti, *Das verheissene Land,* 1968
Alexander Blok, Osip Mandel'shtam, and Sergei Esenin, *Übertragungen aus dem Russischen,* 1986

Further Reading

Block, Haskell M., editor, *The Poetry of Paul Celan: Papers from the Conference at the State University of New York at Binghamton, October 28–29, 1988,* New York: Lang, 1991
Colin, Amy, *Paul Celan: Holograms of Darkness,* Bloomington: Indiana University Press, 1991
Colin, Amy, editor, *Argumentum e Silentio/International Paul Celan Symposium,* Berlin and New York: de Gruyter, 1987
Felstiner, John, *Paul Celan: Poet, Survivor, Jew,* New Haven, Connecticut: Yale University Press, 1995
Glenn, Jerry, *Paul Celan,* New York: Twayne, 1973
Meinecke, Dietlind, editor, *Über Paul Celan,* Frankfurt: Suhrkamp, 1970
Menninghaus, Wilfried, *Paul Celan: Magie der Form,* Frankfurt: Suhrkamp, 1980
Nägele, Rainer, "Paul Celan: Configurations of Freud," in *Reading After Freud: Essays on Goethe, Hölderin, Habermas, Nietzsche, Brecht, Celan, and Freud,* New York: Columbia University Press, 1987
Neumann, Gerhard, "Die 'absolute' Metapher: Ein Abgrenzungsversuch am Beispiel Stéphane Mallarmés und Paul Celans," *Poetica* 3 (1970)
Strelka, Joseph P., editor, *Psalm und Hawdalah: Zum Werk Paul Celans: Akten des Internationalen Paul Celan-Kolloquiums, New York, 1985,* Bern and New York: Lang, 1987

Todesfuge 1948

Poem by Paul Celan

Paul Celan's haunting *Todesfuge* (written in 1944; first published in *Der Sand aus den Urnen,* 1948, but retracted; published again in *Mohn und Gedächtnis,* 1952; *Death Fugue*) anchors his status as the major postwar poet in the German language. In *Death Fugue,* the genocide of the European Jews, which had been carried out by Germans, finds expression in the perpetrators' language. Before the end of the war, and thus long before the German literary scene regained its breath or before its survivors returned from exile, Celan's darkly mesmerizing poem emerged as the ethical and aesthetic standard by which the literary responses to the catastrophe are still measured today. Much of the acclaim of Celan's poem rests on his decision to cast the horrors of a death camp in a metrical setting that recalls a musical fugue. The reception of *Death Fugue,* Celan's most explicit poem about the Holocaust, is also representative of more general debates in postwar Germany regarding the relation between art and suffering, literature and history, and "pure" and "engaged" poetry.

Death Fugue was originally written in Romanian in 1944 in Celan's native Czernowitz after the poet had returned from a Nazi labor camp and his parents had been murdered by the Germans. Celan shaped facts from oral and written accounts by survivors of Poland's death camps into searing surrealist images. In the poem, a blue-eyed German camp commander spends his evenings writing love letters to a golden-haired "Margarete" in Germany after days of torturing and killing "his Jews"—among them an ashen-haired "Shulamith"—for sport. Celan manipulates rhetorical conventions and images from older poetry to forge a powerful dirge for the murdered Jews. In his cynical characterizations of death in the camps as "a master from Germany" and of the Jews as finding a "grave in the air," Celan subverts both the Nazi ideology that built a "master race" from a tradition of cultural excellence, and the benign Yiddish term for Jews as *luftmenschen,* or "air-beings," who end up as smoke above the crematoria of the camps. By casting the horrific interactions between Jewish inmates and their German torturers in incantatory rhythms, Celan shows that in the camps, horrors that had formerly been largely restricted to the realm of the imagination were literalized. Although metrically and verbally close to late symbolist verse, *Death Fugue* skirts the elegiac and escapist aspects found in much of the poetry written in the camps.

When Celan read *Death Fugue* at the 1952 meeting of Gruppe 47, some of the fellow poets were moved by his unflinching and yet distanced depiction of the Shoah, while others took issue with what they considered his undue aestheticization of the Shoah. Subsequent reviews of the poem generally tended to follow one of these two views. Some critics viewed the poem as a first step in a "labor of mourning" and as exemplary of art's capacity to transcend and sublimate tremendous injustice and suffering. Failing to recognize the poem's biting critique of the notion of "mastery" or overcoming, these critics regarded the poem as the optimistic affirmation of a possible reconciliation between Jewish victims and German perpetrators. *Death Fugue* became required reading in many German high schools, and when teachers' manuals addressed the poem's explicit theme at all, they suggested that the murdered Jews in Celan's poem had transcended death itself. At the same time, other critics charged Celan with an excessive reliance on metaphors and angrily, and often self-righteously, faulted *Death Fugue* with veiling the horrors of the Shoah through its musicality. Reviewers raised the question of whether Celan had the right to write a poem about an event that they located, and frequently seemed to prefer to leave, in the realm of the "unspeakable."

Death Fugue was widely anthologized and translated, and its popularity and notoriety all but overshadowed Celan's achievement of developing an unmistakably singular voice in his later collections. By the late 1950s, Celan objected to the canonization of *Death Fugue* and prohibited further reprintings. He refused requests to read the poem in public and, in 1958, wrote a remarkable palinode entitled "Engführung" ("Straitening"), where he alludes to the musical term for a "narrow passage" that occurs at the point in a musical fugue when a theme is altered. The elliptical, dense "Straitening" is more representative of Celan's overall achievement and undoes, in abstracted language, some of the gripping images of *Death Fugue* and, in particular, the strong sense of place that was evoked as a residual Romantic topos in the earlier poem. In spite of frequent allusions to the images and rhythms of *Death Fugue* in his later work, however, Celan disputed that these allusions constituted a retraction of *Death Fugue.*

Over the last three decades, Celan's popularity as the author of *Death Fugue* grew while critics tried to show that his achievement reached beyond that early poem. During the 1970s and 1980s, Celan scholarship became a subindustry of *Germanistik,* and the genre of Holocaust literature has achieved an unexpected afterlife. More recent interpretations of *Death Fugue* have situated the poem within the contexts of Celan's life and other writings, the growing body of Holocaust literature, and other poetic traditions. Critics now read the poem mostly as an indictment for an unforgivable crime and an instance of a survivor's complex refusal to be deprived of the right for expression and to yield his language to the perpetrators. The poem's rhetorical dimensions are now viewed in light of more recent insights into the relation between the nature of traumatic survival, testimony, and collective history. With growing interest in Celan's position as the last poet of the tradition of the modern European lyric, *Death Fugue* is no longer seen as his sole achievement, and Celan's work is less frequently reduced as an allegory of the conscience of postwar Germany, or as an ultimate expression of Jewish suffering.

This more nuanced critical understanding has not prevented truncated lines of the poem from becoming instrumentalized in German cultural discourse. Quotes torn from *Death Fugue* adorn artistically insignificant but successful canvasses by painters such as Anselm Kiefer, and *Death Fugue* is often recited during public events in order to promote Germany's acknowledgment of its responsibility for the past and to serve as evidence of the country's contrition. *Death Fugue* has been set to music, and television documentaries rely on the poem for a dose of legitimacy and highbrow verbiage. Even if Celan's poem itself refuted Adorno's maxim about poetry after Auschwitz, *Death Fugue* has not withstood the culture industry's capacity to turn the artistic expression of irremediable suffering and loss into banality and kitsch. While *Death Fugue* proved not immune to its lessening into cliché, the poem opens, for all of literature, the possibility of speaking in the face of overwhelming loss.

ULRICH BAER

Editions

First edition: *Todesfuge,* in *Der Sand aus den Urnen,* Vienna: Sexl, 1948 (retracted); published again in *Mohn und Gedächtnis,* Stuttgart: Deutsche Verlags-Anstalt, 1952

Critical edition: in *Gesammelte Werke,* edited by Beda Allemann, Stefan Reichert, and Rolf Bücher, Frankfurt: Suhrkamp, 1983

Translation: *Death Fugue,* translated by Michael Hamburger, in *Poems of Paul Celan,* New York: Persea, 1980

Further Reading

Buck, Theo, "Lyrik nach Auschwitz," in *Datum und Zitat bei Paul Celan: Akten des Internationalen Paul Celan-Colloquiums Haifa 1986,* edited by Chaim Shoham and Bernd Witte, Bern and New York: Lang, 1987

Felman, Shoshana, *Testimony: Crises of Witnessing in Literature, Psychoanalysis, and History,* London and New York: Routledge, 1992

Felstiner, John, "A Fugue after Auschwitz," in *Paul Celan: Poet, Survivor, Jew,* New Haven, Connecticut: Yale University Press, 1995

Janz, Marlies, *Vom Engagement absoluter Poesie: Zur Lyrik und Ästhetik Paul Celans,* Frankfurt: Syndikat, 1976

Meinecke, Dietlind, *Wort und Name bei Paul Celan: Zur Widerruflichkeit des Gedichts,* Bad Homburg: Gehlen, 1970

Olschner, Leonard, "Fugal Provocation in Paul Celan's *Todesfuge* and *Engführung,*" *German Life and Letters* 43, no. 1 (October 1989)

Stiehler, Heinrich, "Die Zeit der *Todesfuge:* Zu den Anfängen Paul Celans," *Akzente* 1 (1972)

Adelbert von Chamisso 1781–1838

The son of a noble family from the Champagne region of France, Louis Charles Adélaïde de Chamisso was driven from his home at the age of 11 by the consequences of the French Revolution. After traveling through the Netherlands, Luxembourg, Trier, Liège, the Hague, Düsseldorf, Würzburg, and Bayreuth, the family came to Berlin, where Louis, now Adelbert, trained as a painter of porcelain and became a page to Queen Friederike Luise. Already a soldier in the Götze regiment at age 17, Chamisso advanced his education—begun with private tutors in France and continued at the French *Gymnasium* in Berlin—by copious reading in the barrack and watch-rooms. French Enlightenment authors (Voltaire, Diderot, Rousseau), German Romantics (Novalis, A.W. Schlegel, the authors published in Tieck's *Musenalmanach für das Jahr 1802*), Goethe and the ideals of Weimar classicism, and the Greek classics led Chamisso to an aesthetic idealism, which he shared with his circle of close friends (from 1803). Chamisso, Karl August Varnhagen von Ense, Wilhelm Neumann, and Julius Eduard Hitzig formed the "Nordsternbund" (North Star Alliance) with David Ferdinand Koreff, Julius Klaproth, August Neander (David Mendel), Louis de la Foye, Ludwig Friedrich Franz Theremin, Ludwig Robert (Levin), Georg Andreas Riemer, and August Ferdinand Bernhardi to pursue the search for knowledge and truth through science and letters. With Varnhagen and Neumann, Chamisso edited three volumes of the *Musenalmanach* (1804, 1805, 1806); he began work on a Faust scene (*Faust: Ein Versuch*, 1803; *Faust: A Dramatic Sketch*), in which an aging, truth-seeking Faust determines by the force of his own will to overcome doubt and uncertainty ("Der Zweifel ist menschlichen Wissens Grenze" [Doubt sets the limit of human knowledge]). By taking his own life, Faust performs the act of will that is answer to the ultimate question ("Vielleicht Vernichtung nur, vielleicht Erkenntnis, Gewißheit doch" [Perhaps merely annihilation, perhaps knowledge, in any even certainty]).

The question of human will (vs. fate) lies at the center also of *Adelberts Fabel* (1806), a simple allegorical tale in which Adelbert discovers, through dreamlike experience, that life's path is determined by a synthesis of will and necessity. In accordance with principles of early Romantic dramatic theory, Chamisso's dramatic adaptation of material from the medieval (1509) chapbook *Fortunati Glücksäckel und Wunschhütlein* (1806; Fortunatus's Lucky Purse and Wishing Hat) combines elements of the comic and tragic and explores the binary tension in Chamisso's own being between wanderlust and the quest for a place of belonging. This crisis of belonging reached a head as, under Napoleon, the Germany Chamisso loved no longer existed and the France of his youth was its enemy ("wo auch ich sei, entbehr' ich des Vaterlandes" [Wherever I may be I have no fatherland). A close relationship with Helmine von Chézy, with whom he translated A.W. Schlegel's Viennese lectures on literature into French, brought him into Mme de Staël's circle. During a 14-month stay (March 1811–May 1812) at her retreat in Coppet, near Geneva, Chamisso received his introduction to botany through long field trips with Auguste de Staël. During this time, he also laid the foundation for the training he would need for his world voyage as he immersed himself in travelogues and the study of English and Spanish.

In the fall of 1812, he returned to Berlin to begin to study medicine. When the Wars of Independence against Napoleon broke out, Chamisso withdrew to the Itzenplitz estate near Kunersdorf (Oderbruch). A children's tale begun there for Hitzig's children became *Peter Schlemihls wundersame Geschichte* (completed 1813; *The Wonderful History of Peter Schlemihl*), the narrative of a young man who sells his shadow for unlimited wealth, only to find that in doing so he has forfeited social acceptance. Schlemihl ultimately finds redemption in the selfless life of the roving naturalist. The underlying philosophy of *Adelberts Fabel* permeates *Peter Schlemihl:* Peter's successful overcoming of life's adversity rests in his exercise of free will to accept his condition and to proceed using the resources available to him. At a critical juncture, the shadowless Peter turns from being an aimless victim of circumstances and his own failings to an agent of his own destiny. Natural science, which gives the fictional Schlemihl a purpose in life, became the anchor of Chamisso's own existence two years later. Chamisso's Romantic fascination with philosophical speculation, the supernatural elements of folktales, the metaphysical battle between right and wrong, and the social question of belonging yielded in the middle of the decade to a dedication to empirical science.

Through Hitzig's mediation, Chamisso was accepted in 1815 as ship's naturalist on the Russian brig *Rurik* for a voyage to the Pacific in search of the Northwest Passage. Chamisso published two records of this voyage around the world: a rigorously scientific account of geological, topographical, botanical, zoological, ethnographic, navigational, historical, and linguistic information ("Bemerkungen und Ansichten" [notes and opinions]), which was included with Captain Otto von Kotzebue's official account of the trip (1821), and a more anecdotal narrative ("Tagebuch" [journal]), written informally as if told to friends (1836). The personal reflections of the "Tagebuch," while not free of an idealized, Rousseau-inspired view of indigenous populations, anticipate many of the consequences of American and European missionary activity, mercantilism, and power politics in the region. The voyage directly contributed little to Chamisso's literary output ("Aus der Beeringstraße [im Sommer 1816]" (From the Bering Straight [Summer 1816]) "Bei der Rückkehr [Swinemünde im Oktober 1818]" (On My Return [Swinemünde, October 1818]) "Salas y Gomez" [1830]), though his sustained interest in Pacific lore led to a small number of poems based on tales and legends. On the other hand, the many plant specimens collected on this voyage provided much of the raw material for two decades of scientific publication. Chamisso's appointment as first assistant at the Botanical Garden in Schöneberg and as second curator of the Royal Herbarium (under D.F.L. Schlechtendal) in 1819 enabled him to publish naming articles for 763 plant species and 37 new genera, and to contribute to the scientific literature on salps (sea worms), coral reefs, peat moors, and the flora of North Germany. In 1837, on the recommendation of Alexander von Humboldt, he was elected to the Berlin Academy of Sciences, where he presented his treatise "Über die Hawaiische Sprache" (1837; On the Hawaiian Language).

In 1819, an honorary doctorate from the University of Berlin, employment, and a happy marriage to Antonie Piaste allowed Chamisso to settle into harmonious domesticity. His poetry became the occupation of his leisure time; his botany earned his livelihood. Opposed to the reactionary politics of 1820s Europe, Chamisso used social and political criticism as a motivator for many of his poems of that decade and voiced support for the July Revolution in Paris (1830). However, in the years following 1831 his tone became less radical and more supportive of the economic and social status quo. An uncompromising opponent of what he saw as the amorality of das Junge Deutschland, Chamisso nevertheless stimulated the development of the social and political direction in Vormärz writing. He favored Heine and was an early advocate of Freiligrath.

Chamisso's verse rarely emerged directly from his personal experience; he processed topoi, themes, and subject matter culled from the lore and literature of many cultures. He composed German poetry using the traditions of Lithuania, Denmark, Russia, Greece, Arabia, China, and the South Seas, and translated poems and songs by Béranger. From 1833 until his death, he edited the *Deutscher Musenalmanach* with Gustav Schwab. He elevated the art of the tercet to a new level ("Salas y Gomez"). The strong narrative element of his lyricism found continuation in the works of Gottfried Keller, Theodor Fontane, and Wilhelm

Raabe and the 19th-century ballad. Robert Schumann ("Frauenliebe und -Leben"), Friedrich Silcher, Edvard Grieg, and Karl Loewe set his poems to music, and until World War I anthologists included his poems in collections for their solid 19th-century values. Many of his botanical names and the supporting classification work remain in use, but with the exception of *Peter Schlemihl,* his literary work has been ignored for most of the 20th century.

His name survives in the Adelbert von Chamisso Prize, which is awarded annually to a German writer whose native language is not German.

Christopher J. Wickham

Biography

Born in Boncourt, France, January 1781. Emigrated to Prussia to escape the French Revolution, 1792; in the Hague, Düsseldorf, Würzburg, and Bayreuth; in Berlin, from 1796; studied medicine, University of Berlin, 1812–13; attendant to Queen Friederike Luise, 1796; ensign in the Prussian army, 1798; lieutenant, 1801; active service in Hameln, 1806; discharged 1808; cofounder of the literary club Nordsternbund, 1803; in France and Switzerland, 1806–12; naturalist accompanying Otto von Kotzebue to the South Seas and Northern Pacific, 1815–18; curator, Berlin Botanical Gardens, 1819; co-editor, with Gustav Schwab, *Deutscher Musenalmanach,* Berlin, 1833–38. Member of the Berlin Academy of Sciences; honorary doctorate, University of Berlin, 1819. Died 21 August 1838.

Selected Works

Collections

Werke, 6 vols., vols. 5–6 edited by Julius Eduard Hitzig, 1836–39
Poetische Werke, 1868
Aus Chamissos Frühzeit: Ungedruckte Briefe nebst Studien, edited by Ludwig Geiger, 1905
Sämtliche Werke, edited by Ludwig Geiger, 4 vols., 1907
Werke, edited by Hermann Tardel, 8 vols., 1907–8
Werke, edited by Peter Wersig, 1967
Sämtliche Werke, edited by Jost Perfahl and Volker Hoffmann, 2 vols., 1975

Fiction

Peter Schlemihls wundersame Geschichte, edited by Friedrich de la Motte Fouqué, 1814; revised edition, 1827; as "Zauberposse," 1817; as *Peter Schlemihl,* translated by John Bowring, 1823; translated by Leopold von Löwenstein-Wertheim, 1957; as *The Wonderful History of Peter Schlemihl,* translated by William Howitt, 1843; translated by Frederic Henry Hedge, 1899; translated by Theodore Bolton, 1923; translated by Peter Rudland, 1954; as *The Shadowless Man; or, The Wonderful History of Peter Schlemihl,* 1845
Erzählungen, 1947

Poetry

Gedichte, 1831
Zwei Gedichte (ein altes und ein neues): Zum Besten der alten Waschfrau, 1838
Frauen-Liebe und Leben: Ein Lieder-Cyklus, 1879; as *Women's Love and Life: A Cycle of Song,* translated by Frank V. Macdonald, 1881
The Castle of Boncourt and Other Poems, translated by Alfred Baskerville, in *German Classics of the Nineteenth and Twentieth Centuries,* vol. 5, 1913

Plays

Faust, 1803; in *Musenalmanach auf das Jahr 1804,* edited by Chamisso and Karl August Varnhagen von Ense, 1804; as *Faust: A Dramatic Sketch,* translated by Henry Phillips, Jr., 1881
Die Wunderkur (completed 1825)
Der Wunder-Doktor, from a play by Molière, 1828
Fortunati Glückseckel und Wunschhütlein, edited by E.F. Kossmann, 1895

Other

De animalibus quibusdam e classe Vermium Linnaeana in circumnavigatione terrae auspicate comite N. Romannzoff, duce Ottone de Kotzebue annis 1815. ad 1818, 1819
"Bemerkungen und Ansichten auf einer Entdeckungs-Reise, unternommen in den Jahren 1815–1818 . . . ," in *Entdeckungsreise in die Südsee und nach der Berrings-Strasse zur Erforschung einer nordöstlichen Durchfahrt unternommen in den Jahren 1815–1818,* by Otto von Kotzebue, vol. 3, 1821; as "Remarks and Opinions of the Naturalist of the Expedition," translated by H.E. Lloyd, in *A Voyage of Discovery into the South Sea and Beering's Straits, for the Purpose of Exploring a North-east Passage, Undertaken under the Command of the Lieutenant in the Russian Imperial Navy, Otto von Kotzebue,* 1821
Cetaceorum maris Kamtschatici imagines, ab Aleutis e ligno fictas, 1825
Übersicht der nutzbarsten und der schädlichsten Gewächse, welche wild oder angebaut in Norddeutschland vorkommen: Nebst Ansichten von der Pflanzenkunde und dem Pflanzenreiche, 1827
Salas y Gomez, 1830; in Karl Lentzner, *Chamisso: A Sketch of His Life and Work with Specimens of His Poetry and an Edition of the Original Text of "Salas y Gomez,"* 1893
Plantae Ecklonianae Gentianearum et rosacearum novearum descriptiones fusiorea, 1833
Reise um die Welt mit der Romanzoffischen Entdeckungs Expedition in den Jahren 1815–1818, 1836; as *A Voyage around the World with the Romanzov Exploring Expedition in the Years 1815–1818 in the Brig Rurik,* edited and translated by Henry Kratz, 1986; as *The Alaska Diary of Adelbert von Chamisso Naturalist on the Kotzebue Voyage 1815–1818,* translated in part by Robert Fortuine, 1986
Über die Hawaiische Sprache: Versuch einer Grammatik der Sprache der Sandwich-Inseln, 1837
Leben und Briefe, edited by Julius Eduard Hitzig, 1839; revised edition, 1842
Adelbert von Chamisso und Helmina von Chézy: Bruchstücke ihres Briefwechsels, edited by Julius Petersen and Helmuth Rogge, 1923

Translation

Bérangers Lieder, with Pierre Jean de Béranger, edited with Franz Gaudy, 1838

Edited Works

Musenalmanach auf das Jahr 1804 [1805, 1806], with Karl August Varnhagen von Ense, 3 vols., 1803–5
Deutscher Musenalmanach für das Jahr 1833 [1834, 1835, 1836, 1837, 1838], with Gustav Schwab, 6 vols., 1833–38
Deutscher Musenalmanach für das Jahr 1839, with Franz Gaudy, 1839

Further Reading

Atkins, Stuart, "Peter Schlemihl in Relation to the Popular Novel of the Romantic Period," *Germanic Review* 21 (1946)
Brockhagen, Dörte, "Adelbert von Chamisso," in *Literatur in der sozialen Bewegung,* edited by Alberto Martino, Tübingen: Niemeyer, 1977
du Bois-Reymond, Emil Heinrich, "Adelbert Chamisso as a Naturalist," *Popular Science Monthly* 38 (1890–91)
Feudel, Werner, *Adelbert von Chamisso: Leben und Werk,* Leipzig: Reclam, 1971
Fulda, Karl, *Chamisso und seine Zeit,* Leipzig: Reißner, 1881
Kuzniar, Alice, "'Spurlos verschwunden': Peter Schlemihl und sein Schatten," *Aurora* 45 (1985)

Lahnstein, Peter, *Adelbert von Chamisso: Der Preuße aus Frankreich*, Munich: List, 1984
Liebersohn, Harry, "Discovering Indigenous Nobility: Tocqueville, Chamisso, and Romantic Travel Writing," *American Historical Review* 99 (1994)
Menza, Gisela, *Adelbert von Chamissos "Reise um die Welt mit der Romanzoffischen Entdeckungsexpedition in den Jahren 1815–1818": Versuch einer Bestimmung des Werkes als Dokument des Überganges von der Spätromantik zur vorrealistischen Biedermeierzeit*, Frankfurt and Las Vegas, Nevada: Lang, 1978
Mornin, Edward, "Zur Behandlung fremdsprachiger Stoffe in den Gedichten Adelbert von Chamissos," in *Begegnungen mit dem "Fremden": Akten des VIII. Internationalen Germanistenkongresses, Tokyo 1990*, Munich: Iudicium, 1991
———, "'Wie verzweifelnd die Indianer pflegen': American Indians in Chamisso's Poetry," *Seminar* 33 (1997)
———, "'. . . viele Städte der Menschen gesehen und Sitten gelernt': Observations on Chamisso's Cosmopolitan Verse," *Colloquia Germanica* 31 (1998)
———, "Adelbert von Chamisso: A German Poet-Naturalist and His Visit to California," *California History* 78 (1999)
Neumarkt, Paul, "Chamisso's *Peter Schlemihl*: A Literary Approach in Terms of Analytical Psychology," *Literature and Psychology* 17 (1967)
Renner, Rolf Günter, "Schrift der Natur und Zeichen des Selbst: *Peter Schlemihls wundersame Geschichte* im Zusammenhang von Chamissos Texten," *Deutsche Vierteljahrsschrift* 65 (1991)
Schneebeli-Graf, Ruth, editor, *Adelbert von Chamisso . . . und lassen gelten, was ich beobachtet habe: Naturwissenschaftliche Schriften mit Zeichnungen des Autors*, Berlin: Reimer, 1983
Schulz, Franz, "Die erzählerische Funktion des Motivs vom verlorenen Schatten in Chamissos *Peter Schlemihl*," *German Quarterly* 45 (1972)
Schweizer, Niklaus, *A Poet among Explorers: Chamisso in the South Seas*, Bern and Frankfurt: Lang, 1973
Wallach, Dagmar, "Adelbert von Chamisso: *Peter Schlemihls wundersame Geschichte*," in *Interpretationen*, Erzählungen und Novellen des 19. Jahrhunderts, vol. 1, Stuttgart: Reclam, 1988
Wambach, Annemarie, "'Fortunati Wünschhütlein und Glückssäckel' in neuem Gewand: Adelbert von Chamissos *Peter Schlemihl*," *German Quarterly* 67 (1994)

Gino Chiellino 1946–

Gino Chiellino is an award-winning Italian poet and essayist and a preeminent theoretician, critic, and promoter of the literature written by national and ethnic minorities in Germany. He emigrated to the Federal Republic of Germany (FRG) in 1970 at a time when its government actively recruited guest workers (1957–73) in southern Europe and North Africa to boost the industrial and service-sector workforce of West Germany's burgeoning postwar economy. Whereas the life and writings of many first-generation minority writers were shaped by their experience as immigrant laborers, Chiellino's personal and poetic experience is marked by his university studies in Germany and his subsequent 20-year-long employment as professor of Italian language and literature at the University of Augsburg.

Until 1980, Chiellino and other writers and artists of diverse national and ethnic backgrounds had no access to the general German reading public, since German publishing houses, newspapers, and the media—in deliberate and often cynical disregard—excluded their literary works and art from publication. In 1980, to break down the establishment's "wall of silence" erected against minorities and for their literary voices to be heard, Chiellino cofounded the Polynationaler Literatur- und Kunstverein (Polynational Literature and Art Association), as whose first president he served from 1981 to 1984. Financially and editorially independent from the German literary and media establishment, this association promoted the literary and cultural endeavors of all minority groups. It published their art and writings—uncontrolled, unmediated, and uncensored by German publishers, editors, and scholars. In 1983, the authors Chiellino, Franco Biondi, Rafik Schami, Jusuf Naoum, and Suleman Taufiq founded the editorial team Südwind Literatur (Southern Wind Literature), under whose editorship, for the first time, the literature of the "writers of emigration" entered into the consciousness of the general German reading public and of popular and academic critics.

The author of three highly touted collections of poetry thus far, Chiellino composes his poems directly in German, a language that is not his own. His preference for German over his native Italian grows out of his intent to enter into dialogue not only with a broad German readership but also with the multinational and multilinguistic minority population in Germany and with contemporary German writers and intellectuals. His work tries to foster in the reader values of enlightenment: critical openness, tolerance, acceptance of diversity, and respect for others. Thus, the point of departure for his poetry is the self-imposed mandate to enlighten his German audience and to raise its awareness of the plight of foreigners, who are still in large measure excluded from political, cultural, and everyday life within a hostile dominant culture. Chiellino's poetry adopts an oppositional stance and consciously employs a terse and unadorned poetic style that harks back to the tradition of poetic realism and is undergirded by a socially and politically activist agenda. He assumes a point of view "from the outside," not unlike that adopted by the German poets Paul Celan, Rose Ausländer, Bertolt Brecht, and Friedrich Hölderlin, to whom some of his poems are dedicated and with whose poetry he carries on a lyrical discourse.

The poems in his first collection, *Mein fremder Alltag* (1984; My Strange Everyday Life), center around the emigrant's arrival and initial orientation in the foreign host society. They explore the interactions, feelings, sorrows, and irritations that a foreigner is likely to experience in a new culture: feelings of loneliness and isolation stemming from a lack of human contact and from the inability to communicate in the foreign language; the awareness of one's otherness and difference; the loss of a sense of belonging; the exploited, marginalized, and silenced existence of foreigners; the discriminating and dehumanizing treatment by citizens and authorities of the foreign society; the search for a new personal and cultural identity; the call for political and emotional solidarity across all minority enclaves in Germany; and the hope for stability in the face of an ever-present threat of deportation.

In his second collection of poems, *Sehnsucht nach Sprache* (1987; Yearning for Language) Chiellino explores the social and historical reasons leading people to emigration, which, for him, is never based on free will but is instead forced on the impoverished Italian industrial and agrarian working class. He retrospectively examines the cultural and linguistic multidimensionality of his own background. Some of his poems are written in three languages: in his native Calabrian dialect, in Italian, and in German. Estranged not only from his Italian "home" but also from the German host society and alienated from both the Italian language of his youth and the ethnocentricity of the German language, which is incapable of rendering the essence of foreignness, his poetry speaks both of the impossibility of ever returning "home" and of ever "arriving" in the new culture.

Chiellino's theoretical and aesthetic core belief is the idea that a minority writer's perception of the new reality is not a holistic one that can be expressed in perfect poetic visions synthesizing poetic form and content and time and space. As a result of the minority writer's existential experience of homelessness, his or her perception of reality remains ruptured, fragmentary, and myopic. It is this reality, the "in-between-spaces-and-times," as Chiellino calls it, that he tries to capture in his poetry. To this end, the German language, as it exists, is unusable for Chiellino, as it is estranged from his outsider experience. With its inherently Germanocentric worldview, the language is laden with unexamined clichés, stereotypes, and discriminations clothed in euphemisms to describe the outsider. The German language, mirroring the institutionalized system of domination, is a mechanism of thought and behavior control that keeps the cultural outsider at a distance. And yet, Chiellino wants to find a lyrical "home" in the German language and express his "difference," which is the source of his inspiration and creativity. Treading new linguistic territory, his poems are attempts to break up the ethnocentricity of German, to be "different" in German, and to create an "other" German language.

In his third collection of poems, *Sich die Fremde nehmen* (1992; Stripping Oneself of Foreignness), Chiellino challenges Germans to rethink their outdated notions of cultural and national identity that are still restricted to establishing and protecting a common and "homogeneous" culture, language, and creed. His political activism is directed against the xenophobic *Ausländergesetz* (Foreigners Act), which, granting the immigrant only a temporary and provisional status, denies the immigrant all citizen rights and excludes him or her from political and cultural participation. The latest poems lay out the vision of mutual recognition and political partnership in an open society characterized by ethnic and cultural pluralism.

Perhaps because of the still-pervasive assumption that the production of literature of high quality remains the prerogative of ethnic German writers, Chiellino's demanding and enigmatic poems have received no serious critical attention to date. Whenever his poetry and the texts written by minorities in general are discussed, critics point out that migrants' literature is valuable primarily for its accomplishments in the area of social documentation. Thus, a serious appreciation of the extraordinary literary and aesthetic quality of Chiellino's work is yet to be realized.

THOMAS BAGINSKI

Biography

Born in Carlopoli, Italy, 11 July 1946. Educated at seminary school in Santa Maria a Vico, near Naples, 1959–61; at seminary school in Florence, 1961–63; at high schools in Salerno, 1963–64, and in Cosenza, 1964–66. Studied sociology and Italian in Rome, 1966–70; taught elementary school for Italian children in Mannheim, 1970–72; lecturer in Italian at the university in Gießen, 1974–76; Ph.D. in comparative literature, 1976; professor of Italian at the university in Augsburg, from 1978; co-founded *PoLiKunst*, 1980; acted as its first president, 1981–84; co-edited 12 literary anthologies, from 1983. TV movie *Felice heißt der Glückliche* (1984; The Fortunate Man's Name Is Felice) by Hilde Bechert and Klaus Dexel, is based on poems by Chiellino. Adelbert von Chamisso Prize for best creative writing by a foreign author, *ex aequo* with Franco Biondi, 1987; Writer-in-Residence at the University of Pittsburgh, 1998.

Selected Works

Poetry
Mein fremder Alltag, 1984
Sehnsucht nach Sprache, 1987
Hommage à Augsburg, 1991
Equilibri estranei, 1991
Sich die Fremde nehmen, 1992

Treatises
Die Futurismusdebatte: Zur Bestimmung des futuristischen Einflusses in Deutschland, 1978
Die Reise hält an: Ausländische Künstler in der Bundesrepublik, 1988
Literatur und Identität in der Fremde: Zur Literatur italienischer Autoren in der Bundesrepublik, 1989
Am Ufer der Fremde: Literatur und Arbeitsemigration, 1870–1991, 1995

Other
Kleines Italien-Lexikon: Wissenswertes über Land und Leute, 1981/83

Further Reading

Biondi, Franco, "Von den Tränen zu den Bürgerrechten: Ein Einblick in die italienische Emigrantenliteratur," *Zeitschrift für Literaturwissenschaft und Linguistik* 14 (1984)
Borries, Mechthild, and Hartmut Retzlaff, editors, *Gino Chiellino: Werkheft Literatur,* Munich: Iudicium, 1992
Chiellino, Gino, "Una letteratura del Sud che nasce al Nord: Betrachtungen zur Literatur italienischer Autoren in der Bundesrepublik," *Italienisch* 19 (1988)
———, *Fremde: A Discourse of the Foreign,* Toronto: Guernica, 1995

Reeg, Ulrike, *Schreiben in der Fremde: Literatur nationaler Minderheiten in der Bundesrepublik Deutschland,* Essen: Klartext, 1988

———, "Die 'andere' Sprache: Zur Lyrik zweier italienischer Autoren in der Bundesrepublik Deutschland," *Italienisch* 21 (1989)

Röhrig, Johannes W., *Begegnung über Grenzen hinweg: Italienische Emigrantenlyrik in der Bundesrepublik Deutschland und ihre Traditionen,* Gerbrunn: Lehmann, 1989

———, *Worte in der Fremde: Gespräche mit italienischen Autoren in Deutschland,* Gerbrunn: Lehmann, 1992

Children's Literature

German children's literature technically begins with the *Abrogans* (eighth century), whose glosses served students in their Latin studies. German juvenile literature from the Middle Ages to the Early Modern period was thoroughly propadeutic; it was also mostly ecclesiastical, written in Latin, European in distribution, and thus not bound to a specific national tradition. As trade, courtly life, and state bureaucracy developed, the educational needs of lay, largely noble society increasingly expanded to include instruction in technical and worldly knowledge, as well as in proper moral and civil behavior and manners.

The age of humanism and the Reformation, with the help of the printing press, produced a large and richly variegated body of juvenile literature, a trend that endured until the Thirty Years' War (1618–48). The expansion of education beyond the noble and ecclesiastical estates, however, prompted no less luminary figures than Erasmus of Rotterdam, Martin Luther, and Johannes Reuchlin to publish works for young people.

Protestant education instilled a sense of duty to one's calling in life and led to training for one's future predetermined place in society, where work was the external expression of charity. Further, according to Luther, the family should supplant the church as the location of elementary religious instruction. Luther intended his *Der Kleine Catechismus/Fuer die gemeyne Pfarherr vnd Prediger* (1529; *The Little Catechism/For the Common Pastor and Preacher*) for just such home instruction, even though the title suggests that the book is for preachers. But it was Lukas von Prag's *Ain schoene frag Vnd Antwurt den Jungen kündern* (1522; *A Nice Question and Answer for Young Children*) that set an important precedent for what became the standard question-answer format for Protestant education.

Humanism held language study, especially the Latin of Cicero and Quintilian, to be the key to and basis for all other study. An important early text, *Adolescentia* (1500), by Jakob Wimpfeling, contains a mosaic of classic, medieval, and humanistic texts, and it emphasizes both rules for virtuous living and the importance of correct Latin. For his *Colloquia familiaria* (1518–33), Disiderius Erasmus collected 70 conversations (along with Aesop's fables, Odyssian sagas, songs, and farces) that he had based on school life, and with these he painted a lively picture of the politics, religion, and morality of the times, partly in a satirical mode. Erasmus's most famous juvenile tract, *De civilitate morum pueriium* (1530; *A Lytell Booke of Good Maners for Chyldren*), was also one of his most widely published works and became the model for all *Anstandsliteratur,* a genre based on the classical Latin model that espouses the humanistic virtues of dignity, generosity, self-confidence, and resolve. But this text is most remarkable in its position that youth is capable of self-determination and is able to develop a sense of judgment and reason on its own, a position that anticipated the philanthropic philosophy of the Enlightenment. School textbooks in the early 16th century also evinced an emerging emphasis on German identity. Johannes Cochlaeus's *Breuis Gemanie descriptio* (1512) represented the first geography and history of Germany described by a German and was the first to describe Germanic tribes as aboriginal to Germany (scholars in the Middle Ages held that Germans descended from the ancient Trojans). Moreover, Valentin Ickelsamer produced the first formal grammar on the German language for use in schools, *Die rechte weis aufs kuortzist lesen zu lernen* (1527; *The Correct Way to Learn to Read in the Shortest Time*).

By the second half of the 17th century, four major developments were already underway, which have traditionally been regarded as innovations of the Enlightenment: the development of practical education, with importance placed on technical expertise and knowledge of nature and the world; the intensified employment of illustrations and pictures in teaching; the adaptation of material to the level of children's ability to conceive and assimilate knowledge, from simpler to more complicated levels; and a growing market for profane, nonpedagogical texts in German for leisure reading.

The new pedagogical direction that emphasized teaching according to age levels inspired a wealth of new approaches to children's books. The richly illustrated first reader by Johannes Buno, *Neues ABC- und Lesebuechlein* (1650; *New ABC and Reader*), used sophisticated pneumonic pictorial devices to teach phonics and the alphabet, thereby applying the concept that play is critical for children's learning. Also in line with this idea, Melchior Mattsperger produced *Geistliche Herzens-Einbildungen* (1684–92; *Religious Images from the Heart*), the foundation work for a whole genre of biblical hieroglyphic and pictographic religious texts. Works in this genre replace individual words with tiny illustrations (not a rebus), a method still used today for teaching reading to young children. Perhaps the grandest juvenile literary creation from this period is Johann Amos Comenius's *Orbis sensualium pictus* (1658; *The Visible World; or, The Chief Things Therein Drawn in Pictures*), often referred to as the *Orbis pictus.* Besides introducing reading through pictures, it contains dual-language texts (Latin-German) and presents the first children's encyclopedia, which covers topics such as plants, moral codes, the role of the citizen and the state, the nature of God, and much more. Comenius intended this book for all reading levels, and even pre-reading children were to be inspired to learn by looking at the pictures. Finally, Christian Weise was one of the most significant authors for more mature youth, especially with books such as his *Politische Fragen* (1690; *Political Questions*) and *Ausfuehrliche Fragen / über die Tugend-Lehre* (1696; *Thorough Questions on Lessons of Virtue*). Weise, who also published many textbooks on rhetoric and school dramas, documented the political thinking of the late 17th century by conceiving politics in terms of techniques of power and by orienting his thoughts on the pragmatic modern idea of absolutist political authority.

The late 18th century is so important that German children's literary histories often begin with the Enlightenment, which is also known as the Age of Pedagogy. The reasons for this strategy lie partly in the traditional periodization of German literary history and partly in a historical understanding of the embourgeoisement of German society in the 1700s. On the one hand, literary histories often place the origins and flowering of a modern, specifically German national literature in the last third of the 18th century; hence, by association, the study of German children's literature looks to the same years for the blossoming of youth culture. On the other hand, transformations in the middle class included new standards in schooling and child rearing, based on Enlightenment philosophy, for the growing segment of the population who served as the state's functional elite and the carriers of German culture. Therefore, a demonstrable proliferation of juvenile literature during the Enlightenment, which fulfilled a great demand for education, edification, and entertainment, certainly marks an important juncture, if not the starting point for this literary field.

Two conflicting philosophical works influenced children's literature and education in the Enlightenment: John Locke's prephilanthropic *Thoughts on Education* (1693) proposed that children are essentially irrational beings who should be educated to reason; Jean Jacques Rousseau's *Emile* (1762) declared that children live in their own world and should not be corrupted with strenuous study before their natural relationship to nature and the world has unfolded on its own. *Emile* inspired the two most well-known Enlightenment children's authors: Christian Felix Weiße and Joachim Heinrich Campe. The publications of these two authors encompass all the important genres for juvenile literature that proliferated in this time: the children's magazine, moral-didactic literature, the Robinsonade, travelogues, family parlor games, and fact books (on science, nature study, history, geography, and philosophy). Weiße published the most famous of the many children's periodicals that began appearing in this age of the moral weeklies: *Der Kinderfreund* (1776–82; *The Child's Friend*), which was intended for children of both genders between the ages of five and 12. From his work on *Der Kinderfreund,* Weiße spun off numerous publications in a variety of genres, including *Lieder für Kinder* (1767; *Songs for Children*); *Schauspiele für Kinder* (1792; Plays for Children); and *Neues A, B, C, Buch* (1773; *The New ABC Book*). By contrast, Campe distinguished himself as the great encyclopedist for children and sought to combine knowledge of the world with moral instructions on commitment to the family and home in the most entertaining fashion possible. His 12-volume *Kleine Kinderbibliothek* (1778–84; *Little Children's Library*) became a standard work for the school and in the homes of the educated elite. Clearly, however, his most popular and much-imitated book was *Robinson der Jüngere* (1779–80; *Robinson Junior*). Campe based this loose adaptation of Defoe's novel on Rousseau's *Emile,* emphasizing the natural, undisturbed unfolding of youth's inborn nature. The framing of the story is all-important: the father, with family and friends gathered in the house's garden, narrates the story of Robinson (a German youth from Hamburg). This story is interpolated with the father's questions and answers on its moral and practical lessons. Campe also wrote travelogues in which he couched lessons on geography, cosmography, nature, other peoples and societies, and economics and trade in the adventure of discovery. That the young male was Campe's intended reader is clear from his book on manners and civility, *Theophron* (1790).

Young women occupied a separate public sphere, and most of the period's moral and educational literature prepared female bourgeois youth for the triadic role of housewife, spouse, and mother. One notable magazine for girls, *Für deutsche Mädchen* (1781–82; *For German Girls*), underscored this family-bound role by representing spousal relationships based on rational rather than sentimental love. Also typical in philanthropic literature were the warnings against higher learning and frivolous reading for women. Sophie von La Roche's *Briefe an Lina* (1785; *Letters to Lina*) deviates a little from this restricted view of women's role in society. La Roche addressed her letters to a 15-year-old girl and offered advice intended to prepare the girl for her future duties as a grown woman. The author's instructions in practical and ethical matters combined philanthropic ideas with sentimentality and stressed that, although women have the same abilities as men, the moral necessity of class and gender determines that the woman be satisfied with her role as the ennobler of the man.

In the first third of the 19th century, book production increased at a dramatic rate; during this period, one can begin speaking of a specific juvenile literature for private and family reading that is clearly distinguished from school texts. Further, children's literature became less a part of a pedagogical program and more closely associated with Romantic authors, including E.T.A. Hoffmann and Clemens Brentano, who also wrote for children. The philanthropic movement did continue, and moral-ethical educational literature comprised the largest number of new titles. But the great wealth of morality tracts, plays, epistolary texts, handbooks, parables, and fables produced in Germany between 1800 and 1860 failed to survive; these texts remain memorable largely due to the elaborate and masterful illustrations that graced them.

As Germany entered this period of turmoil, from the Napoleonic wars to the rise of Prussia, with the economic strife that attended early industrialization, an escapist drive toward holistic idealism found expression in poeticized conceptions of children and childhood, especially in the märchen and sagas that have become world classics. Romantic idealism held that the figure of the child represented integrity, unity, harmony, and perfection in nature. The spontaneity of young fantasy contained the spirit of art, religion, and the miraculous. The child also embodied the concept of a lost golden age—Novalis (Friedrich von Hardenberg) envisioned this age within the Christian Middle Ages. The popular children's book *Die Ostereier* (1816; *The Easter Eggs*) by Christoph von Schmid literally frames stories in medieval knightly narratives from the Christian age; in this work, small things become intensified and miraculous in order to support the belief in benevolent fate, nature's mercy, and human constancy and faith. The child's "heile Welt" (wholesome world) offers a sense of succor while simultaneously presenting childhood as a tender, vulnerable realm that needs protection from polarities (such as sexual difference) and strife. Such wholesomeness expresses itself in the penchant toward idyllic animal fairy tales and in tableaux of familial bliss (often in bucolic settings). In its own subdued way, the family idyll in particular also fit well in the later Biedermeier milieu. Here, the influence of Rousseau was still relevant, but in Germany the stronger resonance from the Enlightenment came from Johann Gottfried Herder. As general superintendent of schools in Weimar, Herder had in 1786 undertaken significant reforms, applying his theories that children occupy a separate world of their own and that learning must be connected to play and pleasure. Herder's ideas corresponded to other pedagogical trends, including Pestalozzi's ideal of child rearing in the nuclear family, with the mother at the center of the household as the educator. Herder's theory was also compatible with Friedrich Fröbel's ideas, which drove the kindergarten movement; Fröbel's *Mutter und Kose-Lieder* (1844; *Mother and Comfort Songs*) represents a unique example of Romantic pedagogy, educational theory, and material for communication between mother and children through songs, rhymes, and games.

The emergence of the children's märchen formed the greatest legacy of early 19th-century German children's literature. Of note is Albert Ludwig Grimm's *Kindermährchen* (1809; *Children's Tales*), but, unquestionably, the best-known work of German juvenile literature in the world remains the *Kinder- und Hausmärchen* (1812–15; *Tales for Children and the Home*) of Jacob and Wilhelm Grimm. The Grimms appropriated stories from the folk traditions, mostly of France and Germany, and constructed moral-pedagogical tales firmly in the Romantic tradition, with the child as the actor who becomes wholesome through proper behavior. Wilhelm Hauff followed the Grimms' success with a series, *Mährchen-Almanach* (1826–28), dedicated specifically *für Söhne und Töchter gebildeter Stände* (For the Sons and Daughters of the Educated Classes). After Grimms' *Märchen,* the most durable work of juvenile literature from the period is Gustav Schwab's (1792–1850) retelling of classic myths and legends, *Die schönsten Sagen des klassischen Alterthums* (1838–40; *The Finest Sagas of Classic Antiquity*).

In stark contrast to the idealism in children's literature of this period, popular literature reflected the influence of the market on literary production. According to critics of the time, opportunistic, mass-producing hack writers were endangering children's wholesomeness. This division between "good" (educational and edifying) literature and literature for consumption set the stage for a controversy that continues today. The lines between good and bad literature, however, were often blurred. For example, *Die Ostereier* started as a popular series of stories in cheap editions and then later appeared in a more respectable format. Perhaps the most notorious of the opportunists was Franz Hoffmann, who became one of most widely read (and denounced) children's authors of the 19th century, especially for the adventure *Ein rechtschaffener Knabe* (1849; *A Righteous Boy*). The mass-market literature also included some overtly racist and anti-Semitic texts, such as Gustav Nieritz's *Die Negersklaven und der Deutsche* (1841; *The Negro Slave and the German*) and Eduard von Ambach's *Der Jude: oder, Neigung und Pflicht* (1850; *The Jew: or, Inclination and Duty*).

For young children, the accidental runaway best seller in this period was the early picture book *Lustige Geschichten und drollige Bilder* (1845; *Humorous Stories and Witty Pictures*), known now as *Struwwelpeter* (*Slovenly Peter*), written and illustrated by the physician Heinrich Hoffmann for his children. This small picture book depicts the painful, even fatal consequences of misbehavior such as playing with matches and thumb sucking. The crude drawings improved in later editions, even if the doggerel verse remained. Still, the pictures became some of the most emblematic and most often parodied in Germany to this day. Later, Wilhelm Busch would also secure his fame by illustrating in drawings and verse the mischievous antics of Max and Moritz in the eponymous book (1865) that became the first successful comic book.

In the period of Germany's rapid industrialization, the sentimental bucolic environment came to represent a healthy refuge from modern urban discord, especially for adolescent girls. Berthold Auerbach (Moses Baruch Auerbacher) established the idyllic village narrative through his *Scharzwälder Dorfgeschichten* (1845; *Black Forest Village Stories*) and novel *Barfüßle* (1856; *Little Barefoot*); the idyllic village narrative as a genre maintained a presence through the 1920s, with authors such as Heinrich Sohnrey. Ottilie Wildermuth's village stories appropriated the country setting for girls' literature and made it the ideal space for girls' education. The most well-known example of pastoral coming-of-age literature are the Heidi novels (1880–81) by the Swiss author Johanna Spyri. Clementine Helm bestowed the name that became synonymous with female adolescence with the novel *Backfischchens Leiden und Freuden* (1863; *Little Baked Fish's Sufferings and Joys*). Henceforth, such girls' books would be known as *Backfisch*-literature, with Emmy von Rhoden's *Der Trotzkopf* (1885; *The Bullheaded Girl*) and Else Ury's *Nesthäckchen und ihre Puppen* (1918; *Fledgling and Her Dolls*) standing out as the most popular among many that continued this trend.

For male German youth, a marked tendency toward historicism and pan-Germanism emerges, mostly in war narratives. Viktor von Scheffel's fictional account of the warrior monk *Ekkehard* (1855) became an early classic during the Foundation years after 1871, and countless imitations followed throughout the Wilhelminian period; Felix Dahn glorified the ascendance of the Germanic tribes in *Kampf um Rom* (1876; *Battle of Rome*), a novel which is still popular today. Hermann Löns, otherwise known for his animal stories, published the "peasant chronicle" *Der Wehrwolf* (*Harm Wulf, A Peasant Chronicle*) in 1910. Set in the Thirty Years' War, Löns's novel maintained its enormous popularity and respect, and it became the model for historical, nationalistic blood-and-soil literature. Among the numerous nature stories of the late 19th century, *Die Biene Maja* (1912; *The Bee Maja*) by Waldemar Bonsels mixes an anthropomorphic märchen with aspects of the war novel; it also became a great best-seller later in the Weimar period. Colonial aspirations of wilhelminian Germany appeared in Gustav Frenssen's political novel *Peter Moors Fahrt in den Südwest* (1906; *Peter Moor's Travels to Southwest Africa*). Vastly more popular and resilient than all other juvenile literature of this period, however, were the adventure novels of Karl May, probably the best-selling German author of all time. In his chauvinistic Wild West and Near East adventures, the German hero vanquishes all foes; even among his allies, the German represents the race of the future that will supersede the declining civilizations of other noble peoples in the world. May designated only a few novels specifically for young people, including *Der Schatz im Silbersee* (1894; *The Treasure in Silver Lake*), but novels such as *Winnetou* (1893) and *Durchs wilde Kurdistan* (1892; *Through Wild Kurdistan*) sat on the bookshelves of almost all adolescent males and are still popular today among all age groups.

The Weimar Republic (1918–33) witnessed a dramatic shift in youth culture with the introduction of film, radio, and mass daily newspapers and periodicals. Conservative suspicions about the new media in Germany's first democracy led to a range of legislation that tightened controls on young people by passing laws controlling cinema and "trash" literature and by keeping radio firmly under the jurisdiction of the postal service, an institution whose bureaucrats suffered little sympathy for the new republic. Young people, however, also acquired more autonomy as consumers and thus became a market factor in their own right, which meant that more writers addressed youth's interests directly, rather than as mediated through parents and teachers. The emphasis on a new immediacy with young readers shifted writers toward a marked realism. Already before the war, a progressive pedagogical movement in Bremen inspired both Heinrich Scharrelmann's *Berni* series (1906–26) and his brother Wilhelm Scharrelmann's stark tale of an orphan's boyhood *Piddl Hundertmark* (1912); later, Carl Dantz's *Peter Stoll* (1925) continued the trend toward an engagement and immediacy with young people and their environment. Also before the war, a socialist children's literature began to take shape. Until the late 1920s, works in this movement generally appropriated the bourgeois märchen as the primary genre, but in so doing they created a form of "reality" märchen that closely addressed the young proletariat in its (usually urban) environment. The socialists, and, later, members of the Proletarian-Revolutionary Writers Union, published such märchen as Hermynia zur Mühlen's *Was Peterchens Freunde erzählen* (1921; *The Stories Little Peter's Friends Told*), Berta Lask's *Auf dem Flügelpferde durch die Zeiten* (1925; *On the Winged Horse of the Ages*), Bela Balázs's *Das richtige Himmelblau* (1925; *The Correct Sky Blue*), and Lisa Tetzner's *Hans Urian* (1929). In the late 1920s, the phenomenal success of Erich Kästner's apolitical realist children's novels *Emil und die Detektive* (1928; *Emil and the Detectives*) and *Pünktchen und Anton* (1931; *Dotty and Anton*) established a paradigm for others. Communist authors such as Alex Wedding (Grete Weiskopf) reacted critically to Kästner and the new realism; Wedding's *Ede und Unku* (1931) and Lisa Tetzner's *Der Fußball* (1932; *The Soccer Ball*) strived for authentic portrayals of working-class children, which the authors offered as a corrective to the bourgeois characters that Kästner created.

The period of National Socialism (1933–45) coordinated juvenile literature under the banner of the Nazi movement. The Nazi classic *Der Hitlerjunge Quex* (1932; *The Hitler Youth Quex*) by Karl Aloys Schenzinger relates the story of a Hitler Youth's heroic martyrdom and was the first and most popular in a line of Hitler Youth novels. Otherwise, the period produced books about sports, adventures, Nazi heroes, and Germanic Volk poetry. The racist element was generally not as strident as one might expect, with rare blatant examples of anti-Semitism such as in the picture book *Der Giftpilz* (1938; *The Poison Mushroom*) by Ernst Hiemer. The German juvenile literary tradition also continued in exile, with notable examples such as Lisa Tetzner's *Die Kinder aus Nr. 67* (1933–49; *The Children from Apartment Block 67*) and Kurt Held's (Kurt Kläber) *Die rote Zora* (1941; *The Red Zora*).

After World War II, the division of Germany established two courses for children's literature: one in the Federal Republic of Germany (FRG) and the Republic of Austria, and the other in the German Democratic Republic (GDR). In both the East and West, in different ways, an institutionalization and internationalization of juvenile literature emerged. The institutions in the FRG reflect the international character of postwar juvenile literature with the establishment of the International Youth Library in 1948 in Munich, followed by the creation of the International Board on Books for Young People in 1953. The West was also quick to impose legal controls, with West Germany passing a law in 1953 that created a review board to protect children from "dangerous" literature (*jugendgefährdende Schriften*); conservative groups argued that comic books and television damaged healthy emotional and intellectual growth and required strict controls. On the positive side, Germany began awarding national prizes in 1956; the winners have included a number of non-German authors. Moreover, since 1963, the Research Institute for Juvenile Literature in Frankfurt am Main has contributed greatly to the academic and historical scholarship in juvenile literature and media studies. By contrast to developments in the West, East Germany adapted the Soviet institutional model, with the establishment of official publishing houses for young people's literature (Verlag Neues Leben and Der Kinderbuchverlag). The creation of these institutions was thoroughly coordinated with an entire apparatus for production, criticism and evaluation, prizes, and education. Still, East German juvenile literature should in no way be regarded as a monolithic imitation of a Soviet ideal; similar to the early years in the West, many of the early translations came from Scandinavian and Anglo-American authors. East Germany developed an independent tradition inherited from the Weimar period and evolved through its own phases a distinct and complex idiom.

The Soviet Zone and, later, the German Democratic Republic did consciously derive its juvenile literary heritage from the socialist tradition of the Weimar Republic, reprinting books such as Wedding's *Ede und Unku* and publishing new works by Weimar authors, such as *Geschichten aus der Murkelei* (1947; *Stories from Murkel-Land*) by Hans Fallada (Rudolf Ditzen) and *Trini* (1954) by Ludwig Renn (Arnold Friedrich Vieth von Golßenau). As in the West, children's literature in the GDR at first avoided immediate social and political problems and conflicts and never addressed the National Socialist past. *Tinko* (1954), Erwin Strittmatter's story of a boy's developing socialist consciousness in a country village represents the outstanding classic juvenile book of this period. Otherwise, Benno Plundra exemplifies the affirmative socialist spirit, evident in the title *Ein Mädchen, fünf Jungen und sechs Traktoren* (1951; *One Girl, Five Boys, and Six Tractors*); Horst Beseler deals with the moral lapses of the West in *Die Moorbande* (1952; *The Swamp Gang*), which is a story of West German children who protest against military escalation in their country. Brigitte Reimann was one of the first to break from the exclusively positive treatment of life and to confront the personal and political problems in socialist reality in her novel *Ankunft im Alltag* (1961; *Arrival in Real Life*). From this time, authors increasingly expressed sensitivity to discords and injuries of society, exemplified by Plundra's *Lütt Matten und die Weiße Muschel* (1963; *Little Matt and the White Mussels*) and *Das Herz des Piraten* (1985; *The Heart of the Pirate*).

The constraints of writing in the GDR inspired some of its richest contributions to juvenile literature, which took the form of stories of other lands and historical narratives. In these works, writers maintained the realist mode and adhered to a socialist prerogative, while also integrating fantasy and adventure. Using Ludwig Renn as a case in point, *Trini* (1954) relates the struggles of a Mexican Indian boy during the early 20th-century revolutions. In *Der Neger Nobi* (1955; *The Negro Nobi*), a boy and his animal friends help drive out the white oppressors. The novels *Herniu und der blinde Asni* (1956; *Herniu and the Blind Asni*) and *Herniu und Armin* (1958) challenge the right-wing nationalist cult of the ancient Germanic legends. Many others contributed to the children's historical literature of the GDR, from Alex Wedding, in *Söldner ohne Sold* (1948; *Mercenary without Pay*, after 1951 entitled *Das große Abenteuer des Kasper Schmeck* [*The Great Adventure of Kasper Schmeck*]), which is about a youth in the American Revolution, to Werner Heiduczek, in *Die seltsamen Abenteuer des Parzival* (1974; *The Strange Adventures of Parzival*), which gives a Marxist slant to the medieval epic.

Immediately from the postwar period to the present, the genres of children's poetry and theater have flourished. In the GDR, Bertolt Brecht's "Kinderhymne" (1950; *Children's Hymn*) stands out as the great children's anthem. GDR children's verse includes a great variety of themes, from Peter Hacks's praise of rural life to the love poems by Gisela Steineckert in the cycle *Erkundung zu Zweit* (1974; *Reconnaissance Together*). In the West, Josef Guggenmos and James Krüss stand out as the great children's lyricists. East and West Germany have also both expended generous resources to promote children's theater. In 1963, the GDR required all theaters, especially in cities without a specific children's theater program, to produce at least two children's plays each season. In the West, children's theater is ubiquitous, and the Grips Theater in Berlin in particular has acquired international acclaim.

West German juvenile literature began, as in the GDR, with a long period of apolitical, affirmative, and escapist forms. Similar to trends in the East, West Germany published an unprecedented amount of children's literature in translation, less Russian than in the East, but a great deal more from English, Scandinavian, and other languages, with Astrid Lindgren's *Pippi Longstocking* (1949) as the period's benchmark. The connection to the Weimar Republic was not as well nurtured as in the East; Erich Kästner remained influential with books such as *Das doppelte Lottchen* (1949; *Lisa and Lotte*) and *Die Konferenz der Tiere* (1949; *The Conference of the Animals*), but the initiative belonged to the new escapism in West German children's writing, seen in works such as James Krüss' Helgioland stories, the fairy stories of Otfried Preußler, and Michael Ende's *Jim Knopf und Lukas der Lokomotivführer* (1960; *Jim Button and Lukas the Locomotive Engineer*). The mid-1950s witnessed the beginning of a massive advance in German children's writing in general, which quickly made up for the century or so when most children's literature was considered trivial, substandard, and even dangerous. The immense output of new titles by German and Austrian authors continues unabated to the present.

Only gradually in the early 1960s did West German juvenile literature begin to correct the overwhelming retreat from political and private dissonances. The emergence of children's books dealing with the Nazi past offers an idea of how juvenile literature began confronting other hard issues such as sexuality, divorce, injustice, and death. Clara Asscher-Pinkof's novel about Jewish children in hiding, *Sternkinder* (1961; Netherlands 1946; *Star Children*), received the German National Book Award in 1962; Ursula Wölfl narrated the Nazi persecution of Roma in *Mond, Mond, Mond* (1962; *Moon, Moon, Moon*); and the Austrian Winfried Bruckner published the harrowing fictional account of children in the Warsaw Ghetto, *Die toten Engel* (*The Dead Angels*), in 1963. Later notable examples include *Wie war das eigentlich?* (1979; *What Was It Really Like?*) by Max von der Grün and *Reise im August* (1992; *The Trip in August*) by Gudrun Pausewang. The number of German juvenile books on Nazism and the Holocaust, and, for that matter, children's literature on racism and intercultural understanding, was and continues to be small; the amount tends to rise and fall in waves in response to major events such as war crimes trials. And many of the books dealing with the Nazi past, including Hans Peter Richter's *Damals war es Friedrich* (1961; *Back Then It Was Friedrich*), have received criticism for concealed apologetics, sympathy for the oppressors, downplaying the tragedies, and blatant distortions.

The watershed year 1968, the year of the student movement, was revolutionary in many ways in West German cultural history; it also ushered in an unprecedented candor in dealing with young people's existential crises. In the antiauthoritarian wave, children received an exalted status as equals with or even superior to adults, and children were expected to deal with real life and stand up for their rights. Christine Nöstlinger's *Wir pfeifen auf den Gurkenkönig* (1972; *We Don't Give a Hoot about the Cucumber King*) portrays the resistance of children against adult authority. In the internationally successful novel *Momo* (1973), Michael Ende pits the child Momo and her life-affirming values against the adult "gray men" who rob people of their time and ability to love. The focus on the child's perspective and real-life problems led to two major trends. First, numerous novels since the 1970s deal critically with the faults and problems of adults that affect children. Peter Härtling (1933) has made such critical realism his stock in trade, dealing with topics that include disability (*Das war der Hirbel* [1973; *That Was Hirbel*]), sexuality (*Ben liebt Anna* [1979; *Ben Loves Anna*]), death (*Alter John* [1981; *Old John*]), unemployment (*Fränze* [1989]), and divorce (*Lena auf dem Dach* [1993; *Lena on the Roof*]). Second, many works in this period place the child's subjectivity in the center and explore issues such as introversion, fantasies and dreams, emotional distress, and self-discovery. Nöstlinger's adolescent novel *Spatz in der Hand* (1974; *Sparrow in the Hand*) and the children's story by Kirsten Boie, *Mit Kindern redet ja keiner* (1990; *Nobody Talks to Children*), are commonly cited as texts that focus on the inner world of young people.

In the last decades, German children's literature has continually expanded in the number of original works and translations. Moreover, the authors of juvenile literature have increasingly come to understand themselves as artists and intellectuals on a par with those who write for adults; they have also, in fact, been finding a substantial adult readership. In volume and quality, German children's literature has caught up with Northwest European and North American children's literature and is earning recognition such as it has not enjoyed since the early 19th century.

LUKE SPRINGMAN

See also Fairy Tales

Further Reading

Brüggemann, Theodor, and Otto Brunken, editors, *Handbuch zur Kinder- und Jugendliteratur vom Beginn des Buchdrucks bis 1570,* Stuttgart: Metzler, 1987

Brüggemann, Theodor, and Hans-Heino Ewers, editors, *Handbuch zur Kinder- und Jugendliteratur von 1750 bis 1800,* Stuttgart: Metzler, 1982

Dahrendorf, Malte, *Kinder- und Jugendliteratur im bürgerlichen Zeitalter,* Königstein: Scriptor, 1980

Doderer, Klaus, editor, *Lexikon der Kinder- und Jugendliteratur,* 4 vols., Weinheim: Beltz, 1975–

Dolle-Weinkauff, Bernd, *Comics: Geschichte einer populären Literaturform in Deutschland seit 1945,* Weinheim: Beltz, 1990

Dyhrenfurth-Graebsch, Irene, *Geschichte des deutschen Jugendbuches,* Leipzig: Harrassowitz, 1942

Ewers, Hans-Heino, editor, *Kinder- und Jugendliteratur der Romantik: eine Textsammlung,* Stuttgart: Reclam, 1984

Ewers, Hans-Heino, and Myriam Mieles, editors, *Kinder- und Jugendliteratur: Von der Gründerzeit bis zum Ersten Weltkrieg,* Stuttgart: Reclam, 1994

Ewers, Hans-Heino, and Ernst Seibert, *Geschichte der österreichischen Kinder- und Jugendliteratur vom 18. Jahrhundert bis zur Gegenwart,* Vienna: Buchkultur, 1997

Haas, Gerhard, editor, *Kinder- und Jugendliteratur: Ein Handbuch,* Stuttgart: Reclam, 1984

Hunt, Peter, editor, *International Companion Encyclopedia of Children's Literature,* London and New York: Routledge, 1996

Kamenetsky, Christa, *Children's Literature in Hitler's Germany,* Athens and London: Ohio University Press, 1984

Kaminski, Winfred, *Einführung in die Kinder- und Jugendliteratur: Literarische Phantasie und gesellschaftliche Wirklichkeit,* Weinheim and Munich: Juventa, 1987

Köster, Hermann L., *Geschichte der deutschen Jugendliteratur,* in *Monographien,* Hamburg: Janssen, 1906

Mattenklott, Gundel, *Zauberkreide: Kinderliteratur seit 1945,* Stuttgart: Metzler, 1989

Nassen, Ulrich, *Jugend, Buch, und Konjunktur, 1933–1945,* Munich: Fink, 1987

Wallesch, Friedel, editor, *Sozialistische Kinder- und Jugendliteratur der DDR: Ein Abriß zur Entwicklung von 1945 bis 1975,* East Berlin: Volk und Wissen, 1977

Wegehaupt, Heinz, *Vorstufen und Vorläufer der deutschen Kinder- und Jugendliteratur bis in die Mitte des 18. Jahrhunderts,* Berlin: Kinderbuchverlag, 1977

Wild, Reiner, and Otto Brunken, editors, *Geschichte der deutschen Kinder- und Jugendliteratur,* Stuttgart: Metzler, 1990

Classicism *see* Klassik

Matthias Claudius 1740–1815

Matthias Claudius's career as a writer spans the period from 1763 to 1812, one of the most consequential and productive eras in the sociopolitical and cultural history of Germany. If revolution occurred in France rather than in Germany, its ideals and aftermath had a profound effect on Germans. Claudius experienced and responded to this effect and to developments in philosophy and theology from the early Enlightenment through Kantian rationalism on to its transformation and eclipse in the Romantic philosophers and the young Hegel. In different ways, he participated in and helped define the later phases of the so-called golden age of German literature, from the Sturm und Drang (storm and stress) to Weimar classicism and Romanticism.

Literary histories generally associate Claudius with the Sturm und Drang, and indeed he cherished many of the ideals of this pre-Romantic movement: nature, creative genius, imagination, feeling, and freedom. Herder early called him a genius in the contemporary sense, and he gained widespread recognition as editor of and frequent contributor to the literary page of a highly respected newspaper that published works by many of the Sturm und Drang generation. However, even contemporaries recognized him as an individualist, and he has recently been called an enfant terrible of literary history because of the difficulty of categorizing him adequately.

Ambivalence has characterized the response to Claudius down to the present. Largely for political and religious reasons, he fell into disfavor with many during the 1780s and 1790s, only to win the respect of the Romantics, some of whom considered him a spiritual father. Through all the vagaries of history, he has enjoyed a solid core of admirers that includes figures of the stature of Schopenhauer, Thomas Mann, and Samuel Beckett. He has been especially popular in the educated middle class, especially among Christians. His poetry has inspired some 1,000 musical settings, and his "Abendlied" ("Evening Song") is arguably the most popular poem and song in the German language. The celebration of his 250th birthday in 1990 produced a flurry of activity in both the popular and the academic press. Claudius is probably more "alive" than any other poet of his age except Goethe. However, his popularity rests on a mere handful of the some 750 titles that constitute his work. He is generally considered a minor poet by literary historians and has only recently attracted closer scholarly scrutiny. As recently as 1990, commentators revealed their continuing ambivalence toward him by speaking of both his childlike piety and his atheism.

Claudius's first literary publication, a collection of Anacreontic verse and moral tales titled *Tändeleien und Erzählungen* (1763; Trifles and Tales), met with sharp criticism, but he developed a respectable literary page in the *Hamburgische Adreß-Comptoir-Nachrichten* (1768–70; Hamburg Registry Office News), for which he published a series of satiric treatises criticizing the claims of reason vis-à-vis feeling, a formally original review in praise of the moral affect elicited by Lessing's comedy *Minna von Barnhelm,* and a masterful poem on motherly love, "Ein Wiegenlied bei Mondschein zu singen" ("A Lullaby to Be Sung by Moonlight"). This success led him to the editorship of *Der Wandsbecker Bote* (1771–75; The Wandsbeck Courier), which Claudius elevated to one of the most important literary publications of the day through his own works and those of many of his leading contemporaries.

Following the demise of *Der Wandsbecker Bote,* Claudius published a collection of his contributions to the paper under the striking title *Asmus omnia sua secum portans; oder, Sämmtliche Werke des Wandsbecker Bothen, I. und II. Teil* (1775; Asmus Carrying All His Things; or, Collected Works of the Wandsbeck Courier, Parts I–II), an apparent omnium-gatherum that nonetheless reveals a fine sense of composition of both text and illustration. Here, one finds a multitude of "small" forms—reviews, essays, narratives, epistles, various prose reflections, epigrams, dialogues, verse tales, fables, lyric poetry, and more—as well as a wide range of sacred and profane themes and reverent and satiric tones, all under the watchful eye of "Friend Hain," the friendly Grim Reaper on the frontispiece, whose presence evokes a poignant sense of life in both its fullness and its frailty. In a narrative tour de force titled *Eine Chria,* Claudius uses his naive chief spokesman, Asmus, to travesty rationalist theology in favor of religious experience. In the equally whimsical familiar essay "Über das Genie" (On Genius), he discloses his skepticism toward language that derives from his dualistic view of nature and humanity and his notion of intuitive experience and metaphor as the best, if imperfect, means of resolving the dualism. Although some of the poems criticize abuses of power, such as the Danish slave trade, three death poems—"An - als ihm die - starb" ("To - On the Death of His -"), "Der Tod und das Mädchen" ("Death and the Maiden"), and "Bei dem Grabe meines Vaters" ("At My Father's Grave") show the poet at his best.

Claudius published six additional volumes of *Collected Works* in intervals of three to nine years. Part III (1778) offers much the same formal and thematic range as its predecessor. However, part IV (1783) already evinces a turn toward greater seriousness and a preponderance of prose, and parts V to VIII (1790, 1798, 1803, and 1812) represent generally a discursive attempt to counter the rationalist, republican, and aestheticist tendencies of the time. This work should not be underestimated or ignored. If exercising little influence on the course of theology, Claudius's many religious writings had an immense effect on the history of piety in Germany. His *Paul Erdmanns Fest* (Paul Erdmann's Jubilee, part IV) espouses the practical equivalent of enlightened absolutism, which, although conservative from a European point of view, was relatively progressive within the German context. From a strictly literary standpoint, however, one will likely prefer political verse such as "Eine Fabel" (part VI) and "Urians Nachricht von der neuen Aufklärung" (part VI; "Urian's Report on the Recent Enlightenment") and certainly the lyric poetry. Among the prose pieces of the later volumes, Claudius interspersed poems such as "Evening Song" (part IV), "Kriegslied" (part IV; "Song of War"), "Der Mensch" (part IV; "Man"), "Christiane" (part VI), "Der Tod" (part VI; "Death"), and "Die Sternseherin Lise" (part VII; "The Star Gazer Lisa"), for which he is chiefly remembered today.

Herbert Rowland

Biography

Born in Reinfeld (between Hamburg and Lübeck), 15 August 1740. Studied theology and then law and public administration, University of Jena, 1759–62; lived with parents in Reinfeld, 1762–64; private secretary to a government official in Copenhagen, 1764–65; returned to parents' home, 1765–68; editor of and contributor to the *Hamburgische Adreß-Comptoir-Nachrichten,* 1768–70, and then *Der Wandsbecker Bote,* 1771–75; government official and editor of the *Hessen-Darmstädtische privilegirte Land-Zeitung in Darmstadt,* 1776–77; resided in Wandsbeck, 1777 until his death, living initially on proceeds from works, tutoring, and translating; granted yearly stipend, 1785, and named bank accountant, a virtual sinecure, in Altona, 1788, by Crown Prince Friedrich of Denmark; lived in exile due to Napoleonic Wars, 1813–14. Died 21 January 1815.

Selected Works

Collections

Asmus omnia sua secum portans; oder, Sämtliche Werke des Wandsbecker Bothen, 8 parts in 7 vols., 1775–1812
Werke, edited by Carl Christian Redlich, 10th edition, 2 vols. in 1, 1879
Ausgewählte Werke, edited by Wilhelm Flegler, 1882
Werke, edited by Georg Behrmann, 1907
Ausgewählte Werke, edited by Walter Münz, 1990
Sämtliche Werke, edited by Jost Perfahl, Rolf Siebke, and Hansjörg Platschek, 8th edition, 1996

Further Reading

Berglar, Peter, *Matthias Claudius in Selbstzeugnissen und Bilddokumenten,* Hamburg: Rowohlt, 1972
Görisch, Reinhard, *Matthias Claudius oder Leben als Hauptberuf,* Hamburg: Wittig, 1985

Herbst, Wilhelm, *Matthias Claudius der Wandsbecker Bote: Ein deutsches Stillleben,* 3rd edition, Gotha: Perthes, 1863; 4th edition, 1878
Kranefuss, Annelen, *Die Gedichte des Wandsbecker Boten,* Göttingen: Vandenhoeck und Ruprecht, 1973
Roedl, Urban, *Matthias Claudius: Sein Weg und seine Welt,* Berlin: K. Wölff, 1934; 3rd edition, Hamburg: Wittig, 1969
Rowland, Herbert, *Matthias Claudius,* Boston: Twayne, 1983
——, *Matthias Claudius: Language as "Infamous Funnel" and Its Imperatives,* Madison, New Jersey, and London: Fairleigh Dickinson University Press, and Cranbury, New Jersey: Associated University Presses, 1997
Stammler, Wolfgang, *Matthias Claudius der Wandsbecker Bothe: Ein Beitrag zur deutschen Literatur- und Geistesgeschichte,* Halle: Waisenhaus, 1915

Concrete Poetry

The term *concrete poetry* denotes an international literary movement that flourished between the 1950s and the 1970s, continued into the 1990s, and was particularly popular in Germany and Austria. Concrete poems were, according to Eugen Gomringer, intended to be "a reality" in themselves, "and not . . . about something or other" (1956). The factors that gave rise to the style include the rediscovery of the avant-garde in the post–World War II years; the increasing role played by technology, advertising, and the new media in modern life; and contemporary developments in linguistics and philosophy, ranging from semiotics to the theories of Marshall McLuhan. Although the form displays many international constants (Gomringer stresses its "internationalism"), concrete poetry was always shaped by its specific cultural context. In West Germany, it was generally accompanied by fully developed theories and was largely nonpolitical, although its underlying tenor was to provide a fresh start for postwar writing. In East Germany, as in other Eastern European countries and South America, it had more overtly political aims. In Italy, it took on the futurist inheritance; in the United States, it was closer to Fluxus; and in France, practitioners were often aligned with *Tel quel.* The reception has also differed. In Italy and the United States, concrete poetry has been assimilated into the contemporary avant-garde. In the United Kingdom and Eastern Europe, it largely belonged to the countercultural "underground." In West Germany and Austria, however, it has long been treated as a legitimate heir to the first avant-garde, is published by major publishers, and is an accepted feature of the literary establishment.

The genre has its roots in European modernism and, further back, in the long tradition of visual poetry that derives from antiquity. Mallarmé's *Un Coup de dés* (1897; *A Throw of the Dice*), the Futurist "words-in-freedom," Apollinaire's *Calligrammes,* Dadaism, and the *Merzkunst* of Kurt Schwitters all provided important precedents. The term *concrete poetry* itself was first used by Ernest Fenellosa in a 1908 essay (which had a major impact on Ezra Pound). Theo van Doesburg's concept of "concrete painting," formulated in 1930, likewise fed into the form, particularly via Max Bill's definition of "concrete art," which he called the style that "makes abstract ideas visible by means of purely artistic means" (1936). However, notwithstanding forerunners such as Carlo Bellloli (from 1943), concrete poetry proper, its theory, and generically distinct examples did not emerge until after World War II.

Concrete poetry's German-speaking pioneer was a Bolivian-born Swiss, Eugen Gomringer, who worked as Max Bill's secretary in 1954–58. Gomringer wrote his earliest concrete poems, prior to the term's invention, in 1951–52, publishing the first German examples, *konstellationen* (constellations), in 1953. This was also the year that the Swede Öyvind Fahlström published the first *Manifesto for Concrete Poetry.* The year before, the Noigandres Group, taking its name from a word used by Ezra Pound, had convened in Brazil, as had the earliest members of the Vienna Group, comprising at first H.C. Artmann and Konrad Bayer, and later Oswald Wiener, Gerhard Rühm, and Friedrich Achleitner. In 1954, Gomringer published his own manifesto, written programmatically in lowercase letters, *vom vers zur konstellation* (*from verse to constellation*), and by 1956 he had adopted the now-agreed-upon term in his manifesto, *konkrete dichtung.* That year, the Stuttgart group had begun to form around the philosopher Max Bense, whose series *rot* (red), edited with Elisabeth Walther, became a vehicle for the new style. Leading Stuttgart figures included Reinhard Döhl, Klaus Burckhardt, Helmut Heissenbüttel, and the typographer Hansjörg Mayer, who published *An Anthology of Concrete Poetry* (1967). The painter Diter Rot was also associated with them, and belonged to the Material Gruppe, along with Daniel Spoerri and Carlfriedrich Claus. Other significant figures in the first major phase of German concrete poetry included the politically orientated poet Claus Bremer, Ferdinand Kriwet, Franz Mon, and Timm Ulrichs, as well as the Austrian Heinz Gappmayr. It was, however, the Viennese poet Ernst Jandl who became perhaps the best-known German-language practitioner.

In the words of a Brazilian co-founder of the Noigandres group, concrete poetry is "a poetry of things—against expression." The German theory, helpfully collected by Thomas Kopfermann (1974), similarly stresses the concrete "materiality" of language. This can lead both to *visuelle Poesie* (visual poetry), and to *Lautpoesie* (sound poetry). For Max Bense, the major German theoretician, the literary "text" (a preferred term, distinguishing the new writing from "literature" and "poetry") represents an "observable object," existing in the nexus between "self and world" (1971). For Bense, "concrete poetry" arises when "the linguistic elements"—namely "verbal, visual, and vocal"—are used "simultaneously, both semantically and aesthetically," and the "statement" is reflected in the "visual arrangement." Emphasizing another aspect of the new writing, the term *experimentelle poesie* highlights its scientific and innovative approach. Though not a synonym, the term *experimentelle poesie* is often used in association with *konkrete poesie.*

Its materiality lends the language of concrete poetry a validity correlative to that of mathematics or physics. For Franz Mon, materiality includes not only the visible and the acoustic, but syntax, semantic structures, articulation, melody, pitch, and tempo (1970). The analytic physicality of concrete poetry (comparable to physics' concentration on subatomic particles) entails emphasizing both linguistic microstructures and phenomena at the margins of poetry, music, and painting. Hence, Mon argues, by exploiting visible language (the alphabet), a text can also be a picture. New names are often used to designate such poems: Gomringer's "constellations," "ideograms," and "typogrammes," or Mon's "text-figures, reduced to a few basic elements," even to "a single letter," and his *Textgespinste* ("text-webs"). Concrete poetry incorporates fine art, typography, and design into its meaning.

The chief characteristics of the first phase of *konkrete poesie* are exemplified in the visual poems of Gomringer and Rühm. Their poems are objective in character, with no poetic 'ich' ('I'), and have a minimalist style, sometimes consisting of brief statements, or of only a single word or letter. The poems' structure is often geometrical, with an emphasis on "spatialism" (Pierre Garnier's term) and typography, as in Gomringer's rectangular "schweigen" (silence) and "das schwarze geheimnis" (the black secret) dating to 1954, or Rühm's rectangular "du" (you) and "alles" (everything) of the same year. Such pieces illustrate Claus Bremer's theoretical point that in concrete poetry, "the content is pure form" and "the form is pure content." This concordance is reflected in concretism's most common type style, lowercase-only sans serif, with Futura being the most popular typeface. This type style emphasizes concrete poetry's modern, functional, scientific character, and also recalls the Bauhaus, with its emphasis on form, meaning, and craftsmanship. It is a spartan style, denoting a "cool" aesthetic. In other poems, the use of the typewriter is similarly objective and mechanical in its effect.

Much concrete poetry is characterized by mechanical repetitions and permutational techniques. Gomringer's "schweigen" repeats the same word14 times in a block with a space in the center. The poem, in Gomringer's terminology, represents an "ideogram," i.e. a word-image in which the logical structure exactly reflects the single, semantic idea that the poem represents.

"Concreteness" lends the form a self-referentiality which is both tautological and (often) witty. In one rectangle, Rühm arranges the word *leib* (body) in four columns of eight lines, but the pattern breaks in the last line, where the two words are juxtaposed, in a jocular mimicry of bodily contact. Such structures are generally abstract and non-iconic in character, though there are some iconic ones, notably Reinhard Döhl's "Apfel" (Apple) of 1965, made from the repeated word *Apfel* cut into the shape of the fruit, with the word *Wurm* (worm) hidden away in the lower right.

Concrete poetry breaks with traditional grammar, syntax, and linearity, needing to be seen on the page, which itself becomes part of the text, and looked at like a picture. It cannot be read like traditional verse. This can be seen in Max Bense's poem of 1966, in which a sentence that could be read in various ways—for example, "i think is something" or "i is something think"—is presented spatially. In varying Descartes's *cogito ergo sum,* Bense's poem, with its fractured circularity in form, meaning, and reading pattern, draws attention to the material identity of thought, language, and the reading process. The meaning depends on the visual display and is intensely theoretical. The importance of the visual dimension is also apparent in Rot's books of the later 1950s and in Hansjörg Mayer's *alphabetenquadratbuch* (alphabetsquarebook, 1964–65), which contain no words at all, but is composed of artfully arranged letters, sometimes overprinted to the point of illegibility.

A further theoretical dimension is concrete poetry's involvement with semiotics. It often plays on iconicity, or refers to the relation between signifier and signified, as in Timm Ulrich's "bild" (picture), where the word *bild* appears within a rectangular frame, serving both as signifier (language) and signified (visual art). Heinz Gappmayr's work particularly concentrates on the paradoxes inherent in the sign-character of language. In "weiss" (white/know), published in 1962, the one word *weiss* is printed in white on a black rectangle and, beside it, in black on a white rectangle. Such visual punning gives rise to what John Sharkey calls "mindplay" and is a key feature of the genre: the "concrete" language creates a high degree of abstraction.

According to the classification introduced by the English concrete poet Bob Cobbing, such classical concrete poetry may be called "clean." The freer, non-geometrical, mixed-media style, Cobbing calls "dirty." This form abjures the cool, logical stringencies in geometrical design, being less tied to cold type, and is more intuitive and emotional. Preferred media here include collage, pencil, pen-and-ink, painting, photo-poetry, photomontage, stencils, and rubber stamps. Although the geometrical form as practiced by Gomringer was essential to the movement's original self-definition, the "dirty" style is almost as old and was also used by writers of the "clean" form, such as Mon and Rühm. The East German Carlfriedrich Claus, whose watercolors date back to the mid 1940s, evolved his characteristic *sprachblätter* (language pages) in the 1950s and 1960s. These dense, near-illegible psychogrammes, with titles such as "Allegorischer Erinnerungsakt" (1963; Allegorical Act of Memory), rely on Claus's own handwriting as a visual medium: words inscribed with varying degrees of density, from pale gray to deep black, coalesce into abstract patterns, like a magnetic field, or merge with figurative elements such as eyes or hands. In Claus, the concrete method reveals the strange interface of memory, politics, and the unconscious.

Generically, this kind of poetry is close to mixed media. Beginning in 1959, Ferdinand Kriwet produced his first "sehtexte" (texts for seeing), leading to the densely typed "lesebögen" (1960–61) and his "rundscheiben" (round discs) collected in *leserattenfaenge* (bookwormtrap, 1965). In the 1960s, his work extended to "poem-paintings," performances, and multimedia installations, in which words were inscribed on perspex, projected onto screens, and displayed as neon lighting. Similarly, Timm Ulrichs has developed what he calls *Totalkunst* (total art). His poetry borders on other forms such as conceptual art, land art, body art, and performance art. His materials include wood and stone and his own body, as in "Selbst-Signierung" (1962; "Self-Signing,"), which consists of his own signature on his upper arm. If removed from the typographical stringencies typical of "clean" concrete, his work demonstrates the same concern with language as a material. The form's proximity to book art is also often apparent, as in Konrad Balder Schäuffelen's *Lotterie Romane* (lottery novels, 1975) containing upwards of 30,000 rolls of paper stored in wooden boxes to be read at random.

Several major concrete poets from the early phase are best understood today as all-rounders, pursuing a kind of *Gesamtkunst* via various media. Much use has been made in sound poetry of electronics, and sound poetry often overlaps with the *neues Hörspiel* (new radio play) in the electro-acoustic productions of Mon, Rühm, and others, who profited from German radio's openness to experimentation in the 1960s and 1970s. However, Mon also produces collages and semantic texts, and Rühm creates freehand drawings, published in *Zeichnungen* (1987), and performs his work at the piano, while Jandl writes, draws, and performs in a jazz combo. All sound poetry depends on performance, and Jandl is at his most characteristic as a live performer. Although he has written purely visual texts, many of his typewriter poems are essentially scores. A work such as "niagara fälle" (niagara falls), in his punningly entitled collection *laut und luise* (1966; "sound and louisa"/"loud and still"), resembles a waterfall on the page, but it works best when rendered acoustically by the poet himself, resembling what Viktor Shklovski has called "a ballet for the speech organs."

Ironically, it was not before June 1989 that an anthology of East German visual poetry, *wortBILD: Visuelle Poesie in der DDR,* was prepared. It finally appeared in 1990, bringing together figures such as Carlfriedrich Claus and two other longstanding East German outsiders, Ruth and Robert Rehfeld, with many younger figures such as Elke Erb. The mood here merges 1960s radicalism with the punk-style protest of the Prenzlauer Berg. Concrete poetry, like post-war Germany, had come of age.

In recent years, the term *konkrete poesie* has fallen out of use, having been replaced by the more all-embracing *neue poesie,* which also includes work covered by the term *experimentelle poesie.* This reflects a situation in which the innovations achieved by *konkrete poesie* have been integrated into a wider, more plural literary field, the contemporary Avante-Garde. The movement is still shaped by the concrete poets proper and by closely associated figures, such as Helmut Heissenbüttel, whose programmatically entitled *Textbücher* were a landmark of new textual procedures, but it is more plural than before. The work of several intellectually challenging younger writers, such as Schuldt's enigmatic *Leben und Sterben in China* (1983; Life and Death in China), straddles many media, including concrete poetry, objects, installations, radio plays, and experimental texts. Indeed, although concrete techniques have long been used in the novel, from Bayer's *der kopf des vitus bering* (the head of vitus bering, 1965) to Wiener's *die verbesserung von mitteleuropa* (the improvement of middle europe, 1969), and from Heissenbüttel's *D'Alemberts Ende* (D'Alembert's End, 1970) to Gerhard Rühm's *textall* (text-universe, 1993), its methods are becoming more widespread, and more linked with narrative, in the prose of writers such as Friederike Mayröcker and Ludwig Harig. Much innovative writing today explores the interface between experimentalism and more traditional approaches, and a greater stress on the imagination is apparent in the works of writers and poets such as Reinhard Priessnitz and Oskar Pastior. Their work develops the older concern with materiality into new areas, including invented languages, palindromes, anagrams, and lipograms.

JEREMY D. ADLER

Further Reading

Adler, Jeremy, and Ulrich Ernst, *Text als Figur: Visuelle Poesie von der Antike bis zur Moderne,* Weinheim: VCH, 1987

Butler, Michael, "Concrete Poetry and the Crisis of Language," *New German Studies* 1 (1973)

Cobbing, Bob, and Peter Mayer, *Concerning Concrete Poetry,* London: Writers Forum, 1978

Gumpel, Liselotte, *"Concrete" Poetry from East and West Germany: The Language of Exemplarism and Experimentalism,* New Haven, Connecticut: Yale University Press, 1976

Konkrete Poesie, Text und Kritik, vols. 25, 30, Munich: Richard Boorberg Verlag, 1970–71

Jackson, David K., *Experimental - Visual - Concrete: Avant-Garde Poetry since the 1960s,* Amsterdam: Rodopi, 1996

Jandl, Ernst, *Die schöne Kunst des Schreibens,* Darmstadt: Luchterhand, 1976

Kessler, Dieter, *Untersuchungen zur konkreten Dichtung: Vorformen, Theorie, Texte,* Meisenheim am Glan: Hain, 1976

Kopferman, Thomas, editor, *Theoretische Positionen zur Konkreten Poesie,* Tübingen: Niemeyer, 1974

Prawer, Siegbert S., "Some Recent Language Games," in *Essays in German Language, Culture, and Society,* edited by Siegbert S. Prawer, R. Hinton Thomas, and Leonard Forster, London: University of London, Institute of Germanic Studies, 1969

Scholz, Christian, *Untersuchungen zur Geschichte und Typologie der Lautpoesie,* 3 vols., Obermichelbach: Scholz, 1989

Schauber, Cornelius, editor, *Deine Träume - Mein Gedicht: Eugen Gomringer und die konkrete Poesie,* Nördlingen: Greno, 1989

Weaver, Mike, "Concrete Poetry," *Journal of Typographic Research* 1 (1967)

Weiermair, Peter, editor, *Von für über Heinz Gappmayr,* Zirndorf: Verlag für moderne Kunst, 1985

Weiss, Christina, *Seh-Texte: Zur Erweiterung des Textbegriffes in konkreten und nach- Konkreten visuellen Texten,* Zirndorf: Verlag für Moderne Kunst, 1984

Wulff, Michael, *Konkrete poesie und Sprachimmanente Lüge. Von Ernst Jandl zu Ansätzen einer Sprachästhetik,* Stuttgart: Heinz, 1978

Court Culture

"God knows, what the court is . . . a thing of flux and change . . . erratic, never permanently in one place. . . . The court is the same, but its membership changes . . . an unnumbered multitude striving to please one single man—and today we are one multitude, tomorrow a different one . . . a giant with a hundred hands, a hydra of many heads." Walter Map, satirizing the English court in the late 12th century, suggests both its complexity and its fascination as a sociocultural phenomenon. For around 1,000 years, from the 8th to the 18th century, during the monarchical-aristocratic phase of Western European history from the Carolingian Empire through medieval feudalism to Renaissance and Baroque absolutism, the courts of kings and high nobles were the prime centers of power, military might, administration, privileged society, pageantry, art, and literature.

The nucleus of the court, as it took shape in the Middle Ages, was the household of the ruler, his family with its menials and attendants, his permanent staff of professional aides, and the incumbents of high court offices such as chamberlain, steward, cupbearer, and marshal. Clerical aides staffed the court chapel, drafted legal and administrative documents, tutored the noble young, and functioned as diplomats, physicians, and architects. A much larger, fluctuating number of nonresident courtiers came to court on particular missions, performing military service and attending councils, ceremonial occasions, and festivals. During the 12th century, the households of major bishops and princes began to imitate the royal court and replicate these patterns one level lower down the feudal hierarchy.

At every historical stage and institutional level, courts generated forms of culture: material artifacts, customs, social rituals and manners, visual art, music, and literature. The diverse manifestations of court culture all express a sense of hegemony and privilege: they serve the self-display and self-promotion of ruling elites, "represent" and legitimize power, and articulate and justify the ethos of aristocracy.

The material culture of the court displayed its luxurious lifestyle, its exclusivity. Charlemagne's palace and chapel at Aachen (ca. 800) took inspiration and materials—columns and statues—from Italy, so that they physically embodied the "translation of empire" from Rome to Francia. A tendency to build architecturally grand residences was evident by the 12th century in Germany on the part of kings (Frederick Barbarossa at Goslar or Gelnhausen) and princes (Henry the Lion of Saxony at Braunschweig). By the late Middle Ages, Prague and Vienna possessed imposing palaces, and court architecture reached its hypertrophic climax at Baroque Schönbrunn and Rococo Potsdam. From lavish clothes made of exotic fabrics to luxury foods, spices, and wines, from richly worked furniture and tapestries to water supplies and sanitary arrangements, the court fashioned an exclusive style and quality of life. In the Middle Ages and the Renaissance, writings on warfare, architecture, falconry, and tournaments emanated from the material culture of the court, while painting, sculpture, manuscripts, and luxury printed books had, apart from their aesthetic and intellectual value, an appeal as rare and prized material artifacts.

Castles and palaces formed the stage set for a social culture of the court. What began around 800 as the endeavor to socialize a rough warrior caste had, by the 17th century, elaborated itself into rules of etiquette for all occasions, protocols of ceremony and ritual event. From the 12th century to the age of Louis XIV, French aristocratic culture provided the models for Germany. The *hovesprache* of medieval chivalry and key elements of its festive culture—tournament, courtly love song, and the myths of King Arthur—were imported from France. Festivals to mark the climaxes of the Christian year, major political assemblies, and dynastic rites—weddings, the knighting of sons—expressed the "joy of the court," illustrated the élan of nobility (and its taste and capacity for luxury), and bonded the steeply hierarchical aristocratic group in a shared ethos and in common service and allegiance to the ruler. Ceremony and festivity inculcated courtesy and measured and civilized behavior. Refinement of relations between the sexes, played out in polite talk and the elegant body language of dance, came to be a mark of noble society. The socializing, acculturating potential of the court was mediated in the controlled eroticism of courtly love song and by the utopian vision of altruistic chivalry in Arthurian romance.

The literature and visual arts of the court articulated its ideology and social ethos. They celebrated the power and prestige of the prince and presented legitimizing images of political and military projects. Thus, the *Rolandslied,* composed ca. 1170 for Henry the Lion, Duke of Saxony by his court chaplain Conrad, glorifies Henry's Carolingian ancestry, his status as imperial prince, and his achievements as conqueror and Christianizer of the Slavs. The work must also be seen in the wider context of Henry's artistic patronage: the building of a lavish residence, in front of it a lion statue, symbol of the Welf dynasty, and the commissioning of a sumptuous evangeliary, a marble altar, and other treasures for the rebuilt palace church—enterprises that consciously emulated traditional forms of royal patronage. Literature at the courts of the later 12th and 13th centuries—Minnesang and Arthurian romance—reflected courtly aspirations to the refinement of sensibility and behavior in its utopian images of a polite and humane society. It contributed as entertainment to the festive joy of the court, but it was also a vital part of a cultural project that aimed to redefine nobility as a moral and spiritual, as well as merely a genetic, quality. These major medieval poets exploited genres and sources emanating from France. Courtly literature and art in Germany from beginning to end assimilated and disseminated international high culture: in Carolingian times, the traditions of Imperial and Christian Rome; in the Renaissance, classical culture and its Italian rebirth; and in the 17th and 18th centuries, the splendors of the Habsburg Empire and Bourbon France. Although feudalism and absolutism never ceased to appeal to Christian theology for their ideological legitimacy, court culture was also the earliest and most sustained assertion of secularized value structures, in the forms of social interaction and aesthetic expression. The articulation in courtly literature from the 12th to the 17th centuries of the themes of love and marriage, chivalry and lordship, documents a key dialectic of religious and secular ideology and sensibility in European thought and praxis. Although literature was a main form of court culture, it was, however, not invariably the most active or accomplished. Especially from the Renaissance onward, it was rivaled and outstripped in Germany by architecture, painting, sculpture, pageant, opera, and ballet.

From the later eighth and for much of the ninth century, the court of Charlemagne and his descendants, notably Louis the Pious and Charles the Bald, provides a first major example of the cultural role of the royal household. Its products—liturgical, scholarly, and literary manuscripts, and church and secular architecture—were stimulated by Charlemagne's coronation as Roman emperor in 800. Indeed, it illustrates with particular force the connection between court culture and the ideological projects from which it was generated (and which, in turn, are represented and justified in it). The heritage of imperial and Christian Rome is reflected in the palace chapel at Aachen, the monasteries of Lorsch and Fulda, illuminated manuscripts of works of antique learning and Roman liturgy, and artifacts by goldsmiths and ivory carvers. At this earliest date, we already find literature presenting images of the court, its ethos and values: "David [biblical pseudonym for Charlemagne!] loves poets,

David is the poets' glory," sings the Frankish noble and abbot Angilbert. This literature was written by scholarly clerics whose medium was a refurbished neoclassical Latin—the reform of barbarized Latin in church and educational usage was a main thrust of the cultural renewal of *romanitas* in the Frankish Empire. One important genre of court literature, here and in future centuries, was dynastic history, represented here by Einhard's biography of Charlemagne, which was modeled on Suetonius's lives of the Caesars. Alcuin, the Anglo-Saxon monk who became Charlemagne's closest aide, sketches in a verse letter an affectionate picture of the court and its clerical staff: priests and scribes, medics and tutors, and the overseers of the kitchen and the wine cellar, who all minister to the spiritual, intellectual, and convivial needs of the royal household. Theodulf, from Visigothic Spain, also surveys the hierarchy of the court. A flattering tableau of the emperor ("nothing in Charlemagne is not worthy of praise") shows him receiving the tribute of foreign races and simultaneously depicts him as the benevolent *paterfamilias,* flanked by his sons (who divest him of cloak and sword as he rests from his imperial labors) and daughters (who ply him with kisses, roses, nectar, and apples)—although not by his concubines or illegitimate children. Next, his court clerics—pious, learned, and wise—attend him. But Theodulf combines solemnity with an affectionate satire of his courtier colleagues, especially the foibles of their appearance, manners, and appetite (Alcuin spouts words of wisdom while supping alternately from a wineglass and a beer mug).

The prizing of latinity did not exclude German as a language of court culture. Einhard tells how Charlemagne had copies made of "ancient barbarian poems in which were sung the deeds and wars of kings of old." Major texts of Old High German literature in the ninth century—Otfrid's Gospel Harmony or the Old Saxon *Heliand*--came out of a context of Christian humanism, which ultimately emanated from the court. But vernacular literature was not yet prestigious enough to be the vehicle of court learning and civilization.

Court culture in Germany reached its medieval climax in the 12th century. Frederick I, "Barbarossa," embarked in the 1150s on a project to revive his ancestor Charlemagne's conception of the German Empire as a renewed Roman *imperium.* Campaigns to establish military and political domination of Italy and papal Rome went together with administrative and legal reforms aimed at consolidating the emperor's authority. Ideological conviction also generated a cultural energy evident most impressively in this age in literary works of various genres—first in Latin, then in the German vernacular. The main patrons of these works were members of the feudal aristocracy, members of old noble families and "ministerial" knights, whose careers were built on military service of the king and administrative functions at court. Such courtiers might be clerics or laymen; the demarcation was not sharp. Rainald of Dassel, educated in France, was archbishop of Cologne and Barbarossa's imperial chancellor; he also fought and died as a knight and was a patron of secular poetry. Clerics from noble and knightly families benefited in the 12th century from education at the universities of France and Italy; their training opened up careers in the chanceries of kings, bishops, and princes. Their cultural aspirations also led them to commission or themselves produce court literature in a number of forms. Encouraged by Barbarossa himself, Bishop Otto of Freising wrote a political biography of his nephew the emperor, the *Gesta Frederici,* which was modeled on Einhard's life of Charlemagne and classical histories. Historiography became a staple medium at medieval courts; its exponents were often close to the men who made history and had access to diplomatic and legal sources. From France, learned clerics brought the sophisticated Latin verse cultivated in the schools and at the French and Anglo-Norman courts. German reception and imitation of this poetry—moral and social satire, erotic love lyric—is best attested by the anthology known as the *Carmina Burana.* At Barbarossa's court, its prime exponent was the "Archpoet" (*Archipoeta*), pseudonym of a cleric from a knightly family who composed for his patron Archbishop Rainald a panegyric epic on Barbarossa's Italian wars, as well as satires on the contemporary Church and drinking and gambling songs. The transition from clerical Latin to lay vernacular court literature came in the last quarter of the 12th century. Alongside clerics who mediated between Latin and German literary culture, including Heinrich von Veldeke, whose adaptation of Virgil's *Aeneid* was known at the royal court by about 1185, we find literate laymen such as the ministerial knight Friedrich von Hausen and Barbarossa's son, later Emperor Henry VI, composing love songs (Minnesang). Both epic poets and Minnesingers owed cultural debts to the clerical Latin tradition and, above all, to Romance (Northern French and Occitan) models and sources: French court culture provided vital stimulus for Germany. Instrumental in this assimilation of French culture at Barbarossa's court was his second wife, Beatrice of Burgundy, who was the patron of several Occitan troubadours. Great court occasions such as the festival at Mainz in 1184 to mark the knighting of Barbarossa's two eldest sons provided opportunities for such cultural interaction. One measure of this interaction is the high incidence of vocabulary borrowed from French—loan words and semantic loans—in the *hovesprache,* the sociolect and emergent literary language of the court around 1200. This modish lexis of knighthood and tournament, poetry, dance, festivity, luxurious dress, and refined social pastimes rapidly developed into a supple and expressive medium of narrative and lyric poetry, the vehicle of the European cultural project of chivalry.

From about 1180, the cultural example of the royal court was rapidly followed at the courts of major imperial princes, whose growing power and prestige led to their formation of large households "in the royal manner," as the *Historia Welforum* (Chronicle of the Welf Dynasty) tellingly puts it. Literary production was soon evident at these princely courts. Conrad's *Rolandslied* (ca. 1172) is a translation of the Old French *Chanson de Roland,* which was available thanks to the dynastic marriage of Duke Henry of Saxony with Mathilda, daughter of Henry II of England. The *Rolandslied* celebrates Henry's kinship with Charlemagne and provided a historical prototype for his crusading campaigns of colonization in Eastern Europe. This pattern of learned clerics writing courtly history, in German or Latin (the *Historia Welforum* was composed in the same years for Henry's cousin, Welf VI), replicated that already established at the royal court. At the princely courts, too, clerics provided the infrastructure of learning and often mediated the source texts, which allowed chivalric courtiers, often of ministerial status and with a measure of literacy, to evolve a vernacular literary tradition.

In the decades around 1200, the new genres of secular poetry in German—the Arthurian romance, Minnesang, and political and ethical poetry (*Sangspruchlyrik*)—took court literature rapidly to its aesthetic peak. Most of these court poets can be identified as knights: a number of Minnesingers were high-born nobles; others, including the great narrative poets Hartmann von Aue (*Erec, Iwein*) and Wolfram von Eschenbach (*Parzival, Willehalm*), were ministerials or from the lower knighthood. Clerics also composed in German, most notably Gottfried von Strasburg (*Tristan*). Walther von der Vogelweide is the first identifiable professional poet-singer; he provided the court with both Minnesang and songs of political, social, and ethical comment. These court poets produced story and song for courts such as those of Landgrave Hermann of Thuringia, Duke Leopold VI of Austria, and Wolfger, bishop of Passau, later patriarch-archbishop of Aquileia. The courtly orientation of their art is never hard to discern. In the romances of *Erec, Iwein,* and *Parzival,* the court of King Arthur displays a model of wise governance and refined behavior, nurturing chivalry committed to social order and Christian service. These stories of young noblemen learning to subjugate their instincts and ambitions to the disciplines of chivalry and aristocratic marriage delineated models of acculturation and socialization for courtly youth. Minnesang acted out vicarious love experiences, which permitted the courtly audience to identify variously with idyllic erotic fantasies or with the delicate introspections of unrequited lovers, while respecting the constraints and prohibitions that court hierarchies and dynastic marriage rules imposed on the young at court. In the climactic years before and after 1200, this flowering of secular literature was the prime aesthetic expression of court culture. It celebrated princely power and educated aristocratic youth to exercise it, and by propagating a chivalric ethic and a vision of knighthood as a unitary social and cultural ideal for princes and courtiers, it redrew the borders between the secular and the religious consciousness.

Only brief discussion of court culture after the medieval apogee is possible. That choice does not devalue its historical and aesthetic significance, but it reflects the relative unimportance since the Renaissance of courtly literature, which is overshadowed by architecture and the visual arts, and by pageant, opera, and ballet. As the first impact of Italian humanism and Burgundian court art reached Germany in the 15th century, the courts of Countess Mechthild of the Palatinate and Duchess Eleonore of Austria provided patronage for the revival of chivalric literature in the works of Hermann von Sachsenheim (*Die Mörin,* 1453) and Thüring von Ringoltingen (*Melusine,* 1456). Eleonore (daughter of James I of Scotland) was even implausibly credited with the authorship of the prose romance *Pontus und Sidonia.* The court of Emperor Maximilian I (reigned 1486–1519) most fully displayed the early reception of Italian and French Renaissance court culture. Maximilian's literary patronage combined the preservation of medieval poetry and the promotion of Renaissance art and learning—a fusion of conservatism and innovation evident also in his political project, which attempted to revive the medieval status of the empire and to assimilate humanist political theory. In 1504, he commissioned a compendium of medieval German narrative literature, the *Ambraser Heldenbuch.* To Maximilian's prescription, Melchior Pfinzing composed *Teuerdank,* a quasi-allegorical romance around the emperor's journey to the Netherlands to meet his bride, Marie of Burgundy, which was printed with fine woodcuts in 1517. *Der Weißkunig,* conceived and part-dictated by Maximilian, written by his secretary Marx Treitzsauerwein, apotheosizes his youth, wars, and marriage. His essays on horticulture, hunting, and fishing reflect a changing image of the prince as "universal man," who is versed in the practical arts and sciences, in husbandry as well as in chivalric tournament, and in war and statecraft. Maximilian's patronage extended to humanist Latin poets and scholars such as Conrad Celtis, Ulrich von Hutten, and Willibald Pirckheimer, and to Albrecht Dürer, the genius of Renaissance art in Northern Europe.

An adequate account of court culture in the 17th and 18th centuries would require appreciations of many different artistic endeavors: music history from Schütz to Haydn, palace and garden architecture, the genesis of opera and ballet, and the multimedia events of pageant and choreographed festival. Literature in the stricter sense played a modest role in this last phase of the ancien régime. Princes and nobility continued to be patrons of historiography, writings on politics and economics, and science (including the occult). The printing press, the changed conditions of the production and dissemination of books, and the rise of a middle-class reading public and literary aesthetic, however, began to limit the influence of courts on German literature. And in any case, courtly society well into the 18th century denigrated the German language as culturally and socially inferior, a snobbery typified in Voltaire's expression of surprised relief when he found that French was the language of Frederick the Great's court: "Je me trouve içi en France, on ne parle que notre langue!"

The courtly literature of the 16th and 17th centuries was in fact largely written by middle-class novelists such as Jörg Wickram (*Ritter Galmy,* 1539) or Andreas Heinrich Bucholtz (*Hercules und Valiska,* 1659–65). Greater prestige attached to foreign imports: *Amadis de Gaule* (first translation 1569) or Philip Sidney's *Arcadia* (1629). After the Thirty Years' War (1618–48), a resurgence of courtly literature was evident in the novels of Duke Anton Ulrich of Braunschweig-Lüneburg (*Aramena,* 1669–73) and the novels and dramas of Daniel Casper von Lohenstein (*Arminius,* 1683; *Sophonisbe,* 1666). In exotic settings, their heroes and heroines enact triumphs and tragedies of noble virtue. *Hofpoeten* such as Johann von Besser and Benjamin Neukirch also contributed "occasional" verse to grace the ceremonial life of the court. Furthermore, the classic treatises on courtly manners and ethics, such as Castiglione's *Cortegiano,* were translated and imitated. With Georg Philipp Harsdörffer and Christian Thomasius, a German literature of courtesy books was established.

These middle-class writers, however, wrote works that the printing press made available to a readership well beyond the elite court circle. Altogether, the changed nature and economics of the printed book in early modern Germany meant that literature was the first of the courtly arts to broaden its accessibility and democratize its appeal—and thus to lose its function and esteem as an aspect of court culture.

Jeffrey Ashcroft

Further Reading

Bullough, Donald, *The Age of Charlemagne,* London: Elek, 1965; New York: Putnam, 1966

Bumke, Joachim, *Courtly Culture: Literature and Society in the High Middle Ages,* translated by Thomas Dunlap, Berkeley and Oxford: University of California Press, 1991

Dickens, A.G., editor, *The Courts of Europe: Politics, Patronage, and Royalty 1400–1800,* London: Thames and Hudson, and New York: McGraw-Hill, 1977

Elias, Norbert, *The Court Society,* translated by Edmund Jephcott, Oxford: Blackwell, and New York: Pantheon Books, 1983

Fleckenstein, Josef, editor, *Das ritterliche Turnier im Mittelalter: Beiträge zu einer vergleichenden Formen- und Verhaltensgeschichte des Rittertums,* Göttingen: Vandenhoeck und Ruprecht, 1985

———, editor, *Curialitas: Studien zu Grundfragen der höfisch-ritterlichen Kultur,* Göttingen: Vandenhoeck und Ruprecht, 1990

Jaeger, C. Stephen, *The Origins of Courtliness: Civilizing Trends and the Formation of Courtly Ideals, 939–1210,* Philadelphia: University of Pennsylvania Press, 1985

Kaiser, Gert, and Jan-Dirk Müller, editors, *Höfische Literatur, Hofgesellschaft, Höfische Lebensformen um 1200,* Düsseldorf: Droste, 1986

Müller, Jan-Dirk, *Gedechtnus: Literatur und Hofgesellschaft um Maximilian I.,* Munich: Fink, 1982

Müller, Rainer A., *Der Fürstenhof in der frühen Neuzeit,* Enzyklopädie deutscher Geschichte, vol. 33, Munich: Oldenbourg, 1995

Paravicini, Werner, *Die ritterlich-höfische Kultur des Mittelalters,* Enzyklopädie deutscher Geschichte, vol. 32, Munich: Oldenbourg, 1994

Scaglione, Aldo D., *Knights at Court: Courtliness, Chivalry, and Courtesy from Ottonian Germany to the Italian Renaissance,* Berkeley and Oxford: University of California Press, 1991

Strong, Roy C., *Art and Power: Renaissance Festivals, 1450–1650,* Woodbridge: Boydell Press, 1984

Watanabe-O'Kelly, Helen, *Triumphall Shews: Tournaments at German-Speaking Courts in Their European Context, 1560–1730,* Berlin: Gebrüder Mann, 1992

Wenzel, Horst, *Höfische Geschichte: Literarische Tradition und Gegenwartsdeutung in den volkssprachigen Chroniken des hohen und späten Mittelalters,* Bern, Frankfurt, and Las Vegas, Nevada: Lang, 1980

Criticism

While in the English and French tradition *criticism* is used as an umbrella term for the study of literary history, interpretation, and historical scholarship, the English term *literary criticism* denotes two different things, which is reflected in its dual German translation. The term *Literaturwissenschaft* was introduced by Th. Mundt and K. Rosenkranz in the 1840s and stands for literary scholarship in the form of literary theory, poetics, and literary history, while *Literaturkritik/Theaterkritik* is, at least since the 19th century, understood as a "form of journalism, thus excluding rather than including literary theory and academic critics" (Hohendahl). Today, *Literaturkritik* is mainly perceived as feuilleton (the arts feature section) in mass media such as newspapers, magazines, radio, and television that deals with the evaluation of current literature on the basis of contemporary aesthetics (taste) rather than the systematic and historical analysis of texts. While *Literaturwissenschaft* as an academic discipline usually has a greater historical distance to its topics and a more structured discourse, *Literaturkritik* as part of the mass media has to react immediately, *Theaterkritik* sometimes overnight, to new publications and stagings. *Literaturkritik* is usually essayistic and often takes the form of reviews and interviews; its language, unlike the *Fachsprache* of *Literaturwissenschaft,* is geared toward the general public.

Criticism (*Kritik*) and *critic* (*Kritiker*) are derived from the Greek term *krinein* (*to separate, to decide, to judge*). Criticism originally meant to investigate the origin and the accuracy of classical works. The term critic was mainly applied to grammarians, who developed the philological methods to that end. During the time of humanism, philological textual criticism became an important tool for biblical exegesis. Nicholas Boileau in his work *L'art poetique* (1674; *The Art of Poetry*) was the first to detach the term from purely textual criticism and apply it to a work's literary aspects. In this context, literary criticism meant mainly judging texts based on the rules of ancient rhetoric and poetics. The literary works had to conform to the rules established by authorities such as Aristotle, Cicero, and Horace. Poetry was treated within the framework of eloquence and had to follow the rules established by rhetoric (*ars bene dicendi*). In Germany, the debate at the beginning of the 18th century concerning literary taste was the crucial factor that liberated criticism from the dominance of the ancient authorities.

Johann Christoph Gottsched stands at the beginning of modern criticism in Germany. While some of his views on the poet in *Versuch einer critischen Dichtkunst* (1730–51; Attempt at a Critical Poetics) are still based on the rhetorical and poetic traditions of the past, and most of the text creates the impression of a poetry instruction manual, Gottsched also included a chapter on "taste." With this chapter, he goes beyond any older works on poetics and therefore becomes the first critic who shows an intention to provide a philosophical basis for criticism. Gottsched writes in the preface to the second edition:

> Over the last several years, the practice of criticism has become more common in Germany than it had hitherto, thus the true concept of criticism has become more familiar. Today even young people know that a critic or judge of art deals not just with words but also with ideas; not just with syllables and letters but also with the rules underpinning entire arts and art works. It has already become clear that such a critic must be a philosopher and must understand something more than the mere philologists, who only collect variant texts, or assemble vast lists of penmanship and printing errors.

According to Gottsched, each work has to be judged not only on the basis of a set of formalistic rules established by the ancients, but it also has to stand up in the court of reason, thus freeing criticism, at least in part, from the dominance of ancient authorities. Literary criticism, thus, has its place in literary journals designed to educate the general public; it serves the purpose of advancing "the acceptance of German literature and the purification of the taste of his fellow countrymen" (Hohendahl).

Gotthold Ephraim Lessing perceived the role of the *Literaturkritiker* more like the one of a guide who leaves the final judgment to the reader. According to him, instead of the truth the critic provides "food for thought" to the general public, thus promoting the literary debate. Johann Gottfried Herder, on the other hand, saw the critic more on the side of the author as a "congenial" spirit, thus supporting the concept of a cultural elite. At the end of the 18th century, there were two contradicting tendencies in *Literaturkritik*. On the one hand, it became the discussion forum for high-ranking authors appealing mainly to the educated classes; on the other hand, writers such as Friedrich Nicolai, who published the *Allgemeine deutsche Bibliothek,* tried to shape *Literaturkritik* into a means to enlighten the general public.

During the Romantic period in Germany, the formation of cultural elites was enforced. Popular criticism seemed to have favored polemics, while the "productive criticism" of literature was seen by Friedrich Schlegel (*Athenäum*) to be the congenial completion and rejuvenation of high-ranking works of literature. They did not necessarily have to be new publications, but could also be found in the past. During the 19th century, the more theoretically oriented criticism distanced itself from both popular literature and the mass audience and took hold in the universities and their literary journals. With the mass publication of literature and the foundation of many new newspapers and journals, popular criticism, on the other hand, became part of the feuilleton, which influenced its form, content, language, and style. The political agenda of *das Junge Deutschland* and *Vormärz,* which was designed to transcend the distinctions between art and life, literature and politics, also supported the development of a journalistic style in *Literaturkritik*. Prominent writers of the 19th and early 20th century who took the feuilletonistic style of *Literaturkritik* to new heights were Theodore Fontane and Alfred Kerr. Kerr even proposed assigning the status of an independent genre to *Literaturkritik*.

The rise of National Socialism in Germany brought an end to literary criticism as such. The goal of the literary critic was now the destruction of every opinion that diverged from the official party line. The following statement appeared in *Die neue Literatur* in 1932: "We are at war, engaged in the grim defense of our holiest treasures, of the substance and the way of life of our nation. We are confronted . . . by an impertinent, shameless, murderous fellowship of rootless literati and Asians who poison and corrupt everything. And we have no choice but to fight to the destruction of their spirit or ours, their way of life or ours here in Germany." Under the control of Goebbel's *National Ministry for Popular Enlightenment and Propaganda,* undesirable publications were blacklisted and *Literaturkritik,* with the exception of publications in exile, had to support wholeheartedly the cultural program of the Nazis.

After 1945, the press in Germany was controlled by the Allies and had to serve the sole purpose of reeducation. Somewhat surprisingly, *Literaturkritik* did not play a significant role in this process. Only after the reestablishment of a capitalist social and economic system within the framework of a bourgeois democracy did *Literaturkritik* resume its function in the Federal Republic of Germany, although it was initially impaired by the legacy of the past and the resulting ahistorical and apolitical treatment of literature in Germany. In the German Democratic Republic, the role of *Literaturkritik* was curtailed by the creation of a communist state, which largely limited the possibilities of criticism within the framework of a socialist ideology.

The establishment of modern literary criticism is at least in part the result of the expansion of the book market. It also played an important role in the creation of a bourgeois public sphere, a function that contributed to the discreditation of *Literaturkritik* in the 1960s. Today, *Literaturkritik* has to fulfill several cultural functions: it provides information about the ever-increasing number of new publications, and, by means of book reviews, it establishes selection criteria for potential readers as well as library purchases and tries to provide them with the necessary background information to be able to digest the works in question. *Literaturkritik* also points out weaknesses and shortcomings in contemporary literature, thus allowing authors and publishers to improve the quality of their products. It also stimulates the public discussion of literature in general.

BERNHARD R. MARTIN

See also Aesthetics; Hermeneutics

Further Reading

Barner, Wilfried, editor, *Literaturkritik: Anspruch und Wirklichkeit: DFG-Symposion 1989,* Stuttgart: Metzler, 1990

Draeger, Hartmut, *Vom Kulturasketismus zum geistlichen Biedermeier: Protestantisch- konservative Literaturkritik im preussischen Vormärz,* Berlin: Grabner, 1981

Estermann, Alfred Adolph, *Die deutschen Literatur-Zeitschriften, 1815–1850: Bibliographien, Programme, Autoren,* 5 vols., Munich and New York: Saur, 1988–89

Flitner, Christine, *Frauen in der Literaturkritik: Gisela Elsner und Elfriede Jelinek im Feuilleton der Bundesrepublik Deutschland,* Pfaffenweiler: Centaurus-Verlagsgesellschaft, 1995

Frye, Northrop, *Anatomy of Criticism: Four Essays,* Princeton, New Jersey: Princeton University Press, 1957

Geissler, Rolf, *Dekadenz und Heroismus: Zeitroman und völkischnationalsozialistische Literaturkritik,* Stuttgart: Deutsche Verlags-Anstalt, 1964

Getschmann, Dirk, *Zwischen Mauerbau und Wiedervereinigung: Tendenzen der deutschsprachigen journalistischen Literaturkritik, Metakritik und Praxis,* Würzburg: Königshausen and Neumann, 1992

Hinderer, Walter, *Elemente der Literaturkritik,* Kronenberg/Taunus: Scriptor, 1976

Hohendahl, Peter Uwe, *Literaturkritik und Öffentlichkeit,* Munich: Piper, 1974

Hohendahl, Peter Uwe, editor, *A History of German Literary Criticism, 1730–1980,* translated by Franz Blaha et al., Lincoln: University of Nebraska Press, 1988

Jens, Walter, editor, *Literatur und Kritik,* Stuttgart: Deutsche Verlags-Anstalt, 1980

Mayer, Hans, editor, *Deutsche Literaturkritik im zwanzigsten Jahrhunder: Kaiserreich, Erster, Weltkrieg und erste Nachkriegszeit (1889–1933),* Stuttgart: Goverts, 1965

Opitz, Alfred, *Heine und das neue Geschlecht: von der 'Poesie der Lüge' zur 'politischen Satire': die Rezeption von Heines Lyrik in der Literaturkritik der Junghegelianer,* Aalborg: Aalborg universitetforlag, 1981

Papenfuss, Monika, *Die Literaturkritik zu Christa Wolfs Werk im Feuilleton: Eine kritische Studie vor dem Hintergrund des Literaturstreits um den Text "Was bleibt,"* Berlin: Wissenschaftlicher, 1998

Reich-Ranicki, Marcel, *Der romantische Prophet: Anmerkungen zu Friedrich Schlegels Literaturkritik,* Heidelberg: Müller, 1993

Schiller, Dieter, *Der abwesende Lehrer: Georg Lukacs und die Anfänge marxistischer Literaturkritik und Germanistik in der SBZ und frühen DDR,* Berlin: "Helle Panke" zur Förderung von Politik, Bildung und Kultur, 1998

Wellek, René, *A History of Modern Criticism, 1750–1950,* 8 vols., New Haven, Connecticut: Yale University Press, 1955–92

D

Dadaism

The Dada movement began in 1916 in Zurich as a protest against World War I, which was raging beyond the borders of neutral Switzerland, and against the intellectual and cultural conditions that had led to this war. In February of that year, in the *Holländische Meierei* at *Spiegelgasse* 1, a group of young writers and artists, mostly citizens of the warring countries who had taken refuge from military conscription, founded the Cabaret Voltaire, a café/performance space that featured eclectic performances of music, poetry, and dance that represented the major artistic trends of the late 19th and early 20th centuries. Chief among the founders were the German writers Hugo Ball and Richard Huelsenbeck, the Romanians Marcel Janco and Tristan Tzara, and the Alsatian Jean (Hans) Arp. Ball and Huelsenbeck brought a strong German Expressionist flavor to the early days of the movement; the cabaret performances included readings of the works of such German writers as Wedekind, Lasker-Schüler, and von Hoddis. Tzara brought to the mix a strong interest in the techniques of Italian futurism.

The most distinctive elements of the Cabaret Voltaire performances were the chanting of primitivistic incantations such as Tzara's *Chants nègres* (of supposedly African origin) and the recital of Ball's sound poems. Indeed, the most famous image of Zurich Dada is a photograph of Ball reciting one of these poems, while dressed in an outrageous armor-like costume.

Sometime between May and June, the participants in the Cabaret Voltaire began referring to their activities by the name "Dada," which first appeared in print in early June. The origins of the name were much contested among the participants, and in later years Tzara vied with Huelsenbeck over credit for "discovering" the word. The truth will probably never be known. However, the most enduring version of the story—that Tzara discovered the word by randomly opening a German-French dictionary and pointing at the French word for "hobbyhorse"—is almost certainly a fabrication. In any case, "Dada" soon became the name not only of the developing movement, but also of a short-lived gallery and the international journal that Tzara edited in Zurich and later in Paris. The word was rich in overtones for the various participants: it was among the first speech sounds emitted by infants, it meant "yes yes" in many Eastern European languages, and it was even the name of a hair lotion sold in Zurich.

Tensions developed between Ball (who had no interest in making Dada into an artistic movement) and Tzara (who had ambitions for Dada as the latest trend in the international avant-garde). By mid-1917, Ball had definitively broken with Dada, and others were joining the movement. The German artist and filmmaker Hans Richter, the Austrian writer Walter Serner, and the French artist and writer Francis Picabia were among those who became active in the later phases of Dada in Zurich.

Following the end of the war, most of the participants in Zurich Dada left Switzerland, spreading the movement to several of the major cities of Europe. Tzara moved to Paris, where his arrival was eagerly awaited by a group of young French poets, including Louis Aragon, André Breton, and Paul Eluard; the French branch of Dada that these writers established would, by the mid-1920s, develop into the much more long-lived surrealist movement. In Germany, the chief centers of Dada were Berlin, Hanover, and Cologne.

In Berlin, several groups of antiwar activists with strong Expressionist leanings had begun organizing lectures and readings and publishing quasi-underground magazines as early as 1916. Chief among these were the brothers Wieland Herzfelde and John Heartfield, who coopted a dormant student publication, *Neue Jugend* (New Youth), the writers Franz Jung and Raoul Hausmann, editors of *Die Freie Strasse* (The Free Street), the graphic artist and poet George Grosz, and the messianic former architect Johannes Baader. Several of these individuals had experienced the war firsthand as soldiers and had returned to the capital determined to speak out against the conflict. Even earlier, in February 1915, an evening in honor of fallen poets organized by none other than Ball and Huelsenbeck had provocatively included readings of French as well as German soldiers who had died in the war.

When Huelsenbeck returned to Berlin from Switzerland in 1917, he joined forces with this radical antiwar group and began participating in their publications and actions. They, in turn, soon adopted the term "Dada" for their activities and began distancing themselves from Expressionism. In January 1918, Huelsenbeck read his "First Dada Speech in Germany" and announced the founding of the "Club Dada" in Berlin. The first official "Dada Evening" was held in April 1918 in the *Berliner Sezession;* it featured manifestos by Huelsenbeck and Hausmann, who advocated direct political action by artists and attacked the Expressionists, many of whom had become strong supporters of the German war effort. From the outset, Berlin Dada was more overtly political than the original movement in Zurich, and many of the participants were affiliated with the communists. In the immediate postwar period, the Dadaists sided with the German revolution of the Sparticists and opposed the Weimar Republic. Some, including Hausmann, maintained close (if often strained) ties with the *Novembergruppe*. While continuing to hold lectures and performances in formal stage settings, some of the Dadaists—most notably Baader and Hausmann—staged disruptive actions that can be seen as forerunners of the "guerrilla theater" of the 1960s. The most notorious of these actions was Baader's disruption of the inaugural meeting of the new German National Assembly at Weimar in February 1919, when the self-styled *Oberdada* and "ruler of the planet" threw copies of a leaflet proclaiming the "Dadaists against Weimar" onto the heads of the delegates.

The culmination of Berlin Dada was the *Erste Internationale Dada-Messe* (First International Dada Fair), a major exhibition that was held in the summer of 1920 at the *Kunsthandlung Otto Burchard*. Gathering works from the major Dada centers in Europe, the *Dada-Messe* was dominated by Baader's five-story "Great Plasto-Dio-Dada-Drama: Germany's Greatness and Decline," arguably the first "installation" art work.

As in Zurich, a division developed among the Berlin Dadaists. This schism could be loosely described as one between the anarchists and the communists. The former, while aligning themselves with the revolutionary left, were not to be bound by Marxist orthodoxy, and their political activity had a strong element of self-parody. A collective manifesto by Jefim Golyscheff, Hausmann, and Huelsenbeck demanded, on the one hand, the elimination of unemployment and the expropriation of private property and, on the other hand, the recognition of the simultaneous poem as the communist state prayer. At the height of the German revolution, several members of the movement declared an independent Dada Republic in the Nikolassee district. This tongue-in-cheek approach to the revolution could hardly have met with the approval of more orthodox communists such as Grosz, Heartfield, and Herzfelde. While a number of the participants continued to pursue Dadaist activities in Germany and abroad, Berlin Dada can hardly be said to have existed as a movement after 1920.

The most characteristic expressions of Berlin Dada, aside from guerrilla actions and provocative performances, came in its visual arts. The development of the photomontage technique by Heartfield, Hausmann, and Hannah Höch is one of the movement's greatest achievements. Another is the biting, often gruesome satire in the drawings and prints of Grosz, Otto Dix, and Rudolf Schlichter. The literary output of Berlin Dada was perhaps less distinctive. Nevertheless, the Berlin Dadaists produced an impressive array of innovative journals; many of them were produced for only one or two issues before they were banned and replaced by the next journal. Among the titles were *Der blutige Ernst* (Bloody Seriousness), *Der Dada, Der Einzige* (The Only One), *Jeder Mann sein eigner Fussball* (Every Man His Own Football), and *Die Pleite* (Bankruptcy). Grosz, Hausmann, Herzfelde, Huelsenbeck, Jung, and Walter Mehring all published books of fiction or poetry during the Dada period in Berlin. The Malik-Verlag, founded by Herzfelde in 1917, was the publisher of a number of these journals and books; it soon became one of the most important left-wing publishing houses in Weimar Germany.

Dada in Hanover was essentially a one-person movement. The writer and artist Kurt Schwitters was too closely tied to a middle-class lifestyle for the tastes of most of the Berlin Dadaists, and *Merz* (the all-purpose name Schwitters applied to his art, his writings, and the journal that he edited) was never "officially" accepted as part of the Dada movement. Nevertheless, Schwitters's use of collage, found objects, and sound poetry placed him clearly within the spirit of Dada. Furthermore, Schwitters maintained close ties with many of the Dadaists both inside Germany (especially Hausmann and Höch) and abroad, and his journal *Merz* published writings and illustrations by numerous representatives of the international Dada movement. He participated in Dada readings and events in Prague and the Netherlands.

In Cologne, the Dada movement was extremely short-lived, lasting only from 1919 to 1920. Its chief participants were Arp, the artist Max Ernst, the artist-writer Alfred Ferdinand Gruenwald (using the pseudonym Johannes Baargeld), and several less well-known visual artists. Baargeld's immediate postwar activities were closely aligned with those of the Sparticists in Berlin. In February and March of 1919, Baargeld and Ernst published five numbers of *Der Ventilator,* a journal associated with the Independent Socialist Party of Germany (USPD); it bore marked similarities to the publications of the Berlin Dadaists, and it was promptly banned by the British occupation authorities in the Rhineland. During the same period, audience members disrupted an Expressionist reading at the Hotel Disch and a performance of Raoul Konen's pro-monarchist play *Der junge König* (The Young King) at the *Kölner Schauspielhaus;* Max Ernst is known to have been involved in at least the latter action.

In November 1919, under the rubric *Gruppe D,* the first Cologne Dada exhibition was held as part of the fall exhibit of the *Kölnischer Kunstverein.* The Dadaists exhibited in a separate room from the *Gesellschaft der Künste,* which marked the separation of the Dada group from an organization of progressive artists that Ernst had helped found a year earlier. The *Gruppe D* exhibition, whose catalog was published under the title *Bulletin D,* featured works by Baargeld, Ernst, Arp, Angelika and Heinrich Hoerle, and others—alongside found objects, African masks, and works by children and "dilettantes."

The *Gruppe D* established itself as an "official" branch of the international Dada movement under the name *Zentrale W/3.* Arp arrived from Zurich in February 1920 for the first of several brief stays in Cologne, where he collaborated extensively with Ernst, Baargeld, and others on literary and artistic works. *Die Schammade,* the second of the Cologne Dada publications, appeared in April 1920, and it included some of the most important Dada writings of Arp, Baargeld, and Ernst. (The title is an untranslatable coinage with overtones of retreat, capitulation, sham, and charade.) Also in April was the notorious exhibition *Dada-Vorfrühling* (Dada Early Spring), which was held in the courtyard of the Winter Brewery, and which spectators entered via the men's rest room. This exhibition included some highly provocative sculpture-constructions; one of Ernst's contributions incorporated an ax and a text that invited the viewer to destroy the piece. Another characteristic product of this later period of Cologne Dada was a series of collaborative visual and literary collage works by Arp and Ernst known as *Fatagaga* (an acronym for "Fabrication des tableaux gazométriques garantis" [Manufacture of guaranteed gas meter pictures]).

Following the *Dada-Vorfrühling* exhibition, a number of participants split from W/3 and formed a separate group calling itself *Stupid.* When Arp left for France in late 1920, the Dada period in Cologne came to an end, although some of the collaborative work was continued at an international meeting with the Paris Dadaists in the Tirols in the summer of 1921.

While the Dada movement in Germany ended, for all practical purposes, by 1921 at the latest, its participants remained active in the artistic and literary avant-garde for many decades, and many of them continued to produce work in the spirit of Dada. A number of the visual artists were associated with the constructivist movement in the 1920s. The group associated with Herzfelde's Malik-Verlag published work that was closely aligned with the Communist Revolution in Russia, but which incorporated the biting social satire and the collage techniques that characterized much of Berlin Dada. Schwitters created his *Merz* texts, collages, and constructions until his death in 1948. The rise of Nazism made most of the former Dadaists go into exile; for Hitler, Dada represented the epitome of *entartete Kunst* (decadent art). Several Dadaists (including Grosz, Huelsenbeck, and Richter) ended up in New York, where they played a vital role in chronicling the history of Dada when interest in the movement revived in the 1950s and 1960s. The fictional writings of German Dada seem to have little impact on later German literature, but Dada poetry had a strong influence on the development of trends such as concrete poetry. The work of Schwitters and Hausmann was very important for the poets of the Wiener Gruppe, and in the final years of the German Democratic Republic, some members of the emerging Prenzlauer Berg group saw in Dada one of their chief forebears. The influence of Dada on the visual arts since World War II has been considerable; artistic trends such as happenings, fluxus, performance art, and punk have strong roots in French and German Dada.

TIMOTHY SHIPE

See also Avant-Garde; Hugo Ball; Richard Huelsenbeck; Die Moderne; Kurt Schwitters

Further Reading

Ball, Hugo, *Flight Out of Time: A Dada Diary,* translated by Ann Raimes, Berkeley and London: University of California Press, 1996
Ball, Hugo, and Emmy Hennings, *Damals in Zürich: Briefe aus den Jahren 1915–1917,* Zurich: Arche, 1978
Benson, Timothy O., *Raoul Hausmann and Berlin Dada,* Ann Arbor, Michigan: UMI Research Press, 1987
Bergius, Hanne, *Das Lachen Dadas: die Berliner Dadaisten und ihre Aktionen,* Giessen: Anabas, 1989
Bolliger, Hans, et al., *Dada in Zürich,* Zurich: Kunsthaus Zürich, 1985
Dada Artifacts, Iowa City: University of Iowa Museum of Art, 1978
Foster, Stephen C., and Rudolf E. Kuenzli, *Dada Spectrum: The Dialectics of Revolt,* Iowa City: University of Iowa, 1979
Greenberg, Allan C., *Artists and Revolution: Dada and the Bauhaus, 1917–1925,* Ann Arbor, Michigan: UMI Research Press, 1979
Hausmann, Raoul, *Am Anfang war Dada,* Giessen: Anabas, 1972; 3rd revised edition, 1992
Huelsenbeck, Richard, *Memoirs of a Dada Drummer,* translated by Joachim Neugroschel, New York: Viking Press, 1974; Berkeley: University of California Press, 1991
Huelsenbeck, Richard, editor, *The Dada Almanac,* translated by Malcolm Green et al., London: Atlas Press, 1993
Last, Rex William, *German Dadaist Literature: Kurt Schwitters, Hugo Ball, Hans Arp,* New York: Twayne, 1973
Mehring, Walter, *Verrufene Malerei; Berlin Dada: Erinnerungen eines Zeitgenossen und 14 Essais zur Kunst,* Düsseldorf: Claassen, 1983
Motherwell, Robert, editor, *The Dada Painters and Poets: An Anthology,* New York: Wittenborn, Schulz, 1951; 2nd edition, Cambridge, Massachusetts: Belknap Press of Harvard University Press, 1989
Philipp, Eckhard, *Dadaismus: Einführung in den literarischen Dadaismus und die Wortkunst des 'Sturm'-Kreises,* Munich: Fink, 1980
Pichon, Brigitte, et al., editors, *Dada Zurich: A Clown's Game from Nothing,* New York: Hall, and London: Prentice Hall International, 1996
Richter, Hans, *Dada: Art and Anti-Art,* translated by David Britt, London and New York: Thames and Hudson, 1997
Riha, Karl, and Hanne Bergius, editors, *Dada Berlin: Texte, Manifeste, Aktionen,* Stuttgart: Reclam, 1977
Riha, Karl, and Jörgen Schäfer, editors, *Fatagaga-Dada: Max Ernst, Hans Arp, Johannes Theodor Baargeld, und der Kölner Dadaismus,* Giessen: Anabas, 1995
Schäfer, Jörgen, *Dada Köln: Max Ernst, Hans Arp, Johannes Theodor Baargeld und ihre literarischen Zeitschriften,* Wiesbaden: Deutscher Universitäts-Verlag, 1993
———, *Dada in Köln: ein Repertorium,* Frankfurt and New York: Lang, 1995
Schuhmann, Klaus, editor, *Sankt Ziegenzack springt aus dem Ei: Texte, Bilder, und Dokumente zum Dadaismus in Zürich, Berlin, Hannover, und Köln,* Leipzig: Kiepenheuer, 1991
Stokes, Charlotte, and Stephen C. Foster, editors, *Dada Cologne Hanover,* New York: Hall, and London: Prentice Hall International, 1997
Thater-Schulz, Cornelia, editor, *Hannah Höch: Eine Lebenscollage,* Berlin: Argon, 1989
Verkauf, Willy, editor, *Dada: Monograph of a Movement,* New York: Wittenborn, and London: Tiranti, 1957

Decadence

In its most general sense, the term *decadence* signifies a process, condition, or period of deterioration or decline, as in the morals of a whole society or a family, or as in the morals associated with art. In all instances, the underlying meaning suggests a malady or pathological condition resulting from a fundamental imbalance, excess, overrefinement, or disease. In the narrower or more specialized sense, decadence as a term applied to literature is essentially an aesthetic concept that refers to a self-centered aesthetic culture. In the case of the depiction of the decline of a family or an individual member of a family, the accent is on the moral issues, even though the cause of decadence is frequently an aesthetic one, as best exemplified in Thomas Mann's *Buddenbrooks* (1901).

It was the sociocultural sense of decadence that preceded and laid the foundations for the more specialized literary concept. The concept of decadence was probably first introduced by Montesquieu in his *Considérations sur les causes de la grandeur des Romains et de leur décadence* (1734; *Considerations on the Causes of the Grandeur and Decadence of the Romans*), which was an attempt to give a sociological explanation for the fall of the Roman Empire using the scientific method. The fact that this work was followed fairly closely in time by Edward Gibbon's *The Decline and Fall of the Roman Empire* (1776) suggests that Roman civilization became if not the prototype then the classical example of decadence. In its earliest usage, then, the term referred to a defunct entity invested with an aura of grandeur. Rousseau appears to have been the first to apply the term to contemporary culture. He saw the prevalence of an unnatural inequality based on power and wealth as an egregious symptom of corruption in modern society. According to Rousseau, modern conditions constituted a "fall" from original happiness into human misery.

Using the familiar biological analogies of the latter 19th century, the French author Paul Bourget formulated a theory of decadence in his *Essais de psychologie contemporaine* (1883), which brings together cultural and aesthetic strands into a meaningful complex. In this essay, Bourget conceives of society as an organism. In the healthy society, each individual, analogous to the individual cell, works together for the good of the whole. In a decadent society, the cells (individuals) cease to subordinate their energy to the energy of the whole body, which results in anarchy and imbalance. In a decadent society, the individual parts are no longer subordinate to the whole; they are merely subordinate to other parts. In this sense, Gustav Freytag's novel *Soll und Haben* (1855; *Debit and Credit*) constitutes one of the earliest examples of decadence in German literature. In this novel, Baron von Rothsattel, an aristocrat with an illustrious family history, loses his estate through the machinations of a Jewish broker. Freytag, despite his blatant anti-Semitism, is fair enough to inform the reader that the baron himself is partly to blame for his financial ruin because he feels it necessary to maintain his extravagant lifestyle. Anton Wohlfahrt, a middle-class merchant, takes it upon himself to rescue the fallen aristocrat, but he first must listen to a sermon from his supervisor, who is highly critical of the baron.

> The family that exhausts itself in pleasure-seeking activity will sink to the level of folk life in order to give way to new invigorating energies. Every person who seeks to acquire an eternal privilege for himself and his descendants at the expense of the free movement of other people I regard as someone working against the healthy development of our State.

Bourget proceeds to define aesthetic decadence as the analogue to social decadence, arguing that the same basic principle or law governs both society and language. In the classical style, the various parts of a literary work theoretically form an organic whole by being subordinate to that whole, whereas in the decadent style, the parts become independent of the whole. This idea was picked up by Friedrich Nietzsche, who applies it to Wagner's music in his essay *Der Fall Wagner* (1888; *The Case of Wagner*).

> What is the sign of every literary decadence? That life no longer dwells in the whole. The word becomes sovereign and leaps out of the sentence, the sentence reaches out and obscures the meaning of the page, the page gains life at the expense of the whole—the whole is no longer a whole. . . . The whole no longer lives at all: it is composite, calculated, artificial, an artifact.

It is the perception of this basic imbalance, the inordinate importance of the individual word, that became the major symptom of an increasing interest in the precision of physical description in naturalism and of psychological and physiological representation in impressionism. Aesthetic or literary decadence may thus be regarded, at least in part, as an outgrowth of the drive for precision of expression, for the exact nuance, the finely wrought differentiation in the representation of sense-impressions, of feelings and states of mind. In the context of this movement for subtlety and precision of expression, what is distinctive about decadence is that its representations tend to focus more on the morbid, the neurotic, or the artificial.

Nietzsche and Hermann Bahr were the most articulate analysts of decadence in Germany and Austria, respectively. Both drew on French sources. Nietzsche's ideas left their imprint on the concept of decadence in German literature, which acquired a double meaning. In this evolving concept, aesthetic and intellectual overrefinement combine with the idea of physical change. This process, in turn, can be interpreted in two ways: as a decline or degeneration or as the prerequisite for development to a higher plane—a process, essentially, of *regeneration*.

Hermann Bahr came into contact with the lifestyles and literary products of decadence during his stay in Paris (1888–89). He identifies four characteristics of decadence: a "romanticism of the nerves"; a penchant for the artificial; an infatuation with the mystical, that is, the desire to "express the inexpressible"; and an attraction to the immense and the boundless. Bahr also draws a connection between Romanticism and decadence in order to differentiate the latter from naturalism: the object of representation in decadent art is no longer the outside world but the mind and nerves of the artist. This turn inward, however, does not aim at installing the intellect as the absolute or controlling agency; rather, its goal is the subjective rendering of sense-impressions. Modern man is characterized by a nervous sensitivity that is exposed to a constant shift of optical, acoustic, and olfactory sense-impressions. Bahr's theory clearly sees decadence as an outgrowth of impressionism rather than naturalism. Bahr actually began as a naturalist writer, but in 1891, after recognizing the limitations of naturalism, he wrote *Die Überwindung des Naturalismus* (*Surmounting Naturalism*), in which he acknowledges a debt to the style of naturalism insofar as it trained the writer for close observation of detail and precision.

If naturalism shares anything with decadence, it is only that its style also places a high premium on precision. As for subject matter or thematics, the two movements have little if anything in common. It is impressionism that provides a close comparison with decadence. Decadent art was aristocratic, elitist, and narcissistic. The themes of naturalism, by contrast—poverty, the misery and squalor of the proletariat, social and economic injustice, and social activism—were regarded by the countermovements to naturalism as banal and unworthy as objects of artistic representation. The rejection of social and political engagement in impressionism bears the stamp of Nietzschean influence: pity and active politics were seen as deflections from what should be the real concerns of the individualist artist and the aristocrat of the intellect.

Impressionism provided the framework into which the motifs of decadence could easily be accommodated, since there were numerous areas of overlap. In general, impressionism is urban art; it presents the artistic experience of the city and its ephemeral impressions. The major contribution of impressionism to the history of style and artistic representation is the enormous expansion of sense-impressions that it depicts in all their complexity with utmost precision. The impressionist artist is usually a passive spectator, often a bohemian type, who is receptive to the stimuli of the outside world but totally uninvolved with social or political problems. Impressionism and decadence thus both share the trait of a self-centered aesthetic culture. Personal experiences are represented much more often than social experiences. While the concerns of decadence tend to favor experiences of solitude and seclusion, there is also a marked interest in communicating one's own morbid condition to others, as is superbly exemplified by Christian Buddenbrook in Thomas Mann's *Buddenbrooks.*

> Suddenly Christian said: "It's strange . . . sometimes I can't swallow! Now that's nothing to laugh at; it's terribly serious. I get the idea that I won't be able to swallow and then when I try I really can't. The food is lodged way back in my mouth, but the muscles in my throat simply won't function. They no longer obey my will. You see, the thing comes down to this: I don't even dare to want to swallow. . . . In addition to that, it sometimes seems to me that all the nerves on my left side are too short."

Christian Buddenbrook is the typical decadent who relishes describing—much to the chagrin of the other family members—the sensations of overrefined senses and nerves.

Hermann Bahr's short novel *Die gute Schule* (1890; *The Good School*), with the subtitle *Seelische Zustände* (*States of Mind*), is an early example of decadent eroticism. Interestingly, it was first published in the naturalist journal *Freie Bühne* when it aroused attention in Berlin literary circles. The nameless hero is clearly patterned after the French prototype formulated by Bourget and depicted in Huysmans's *A Rebours* (1884; *Against the Grain*). But Bahr gives his story a new twist: the decadent artist, thanks to his work, outgrows his decadence and becomes in the end a complacent bourgeois. Although one might be tempted to interpret this ending as deliberate irony or satire, there is good reason to believe that Bahr meant it to be taken seriously, since shortly afterward he began publishing critical studies of decadence. In *Renaissance: neue Studien zur Kritik der Moderne* (1897; New Studies on the Criticism of Modern Literature), he not only subjects the whole movement of decadence to ridicule, he also attacks Huysmans's *Against the Grain,* which had always been regarded as "the Bible of decadence." Bahr came to see decadence as an escape from life that takes refuge in a world of illusion, a dreamworld in which the artist sinks into self-oblivion. Decadence was thus essentially a movement away from nature, which Bahr sees epitomized in Oscar Wilde's *Decay of Lying* (1889): "Enjoy nature? I am glad to say that I have lost that faculty," says Vivian in a dialogue with Cyril. For Bahr, Wilde's view may be summarized as Art must not follow life. Remote from all reality and with her eyes turned away from the shadows of the cave, art reveals her own perfection.

The Good School is exemplary in that it illustrates how impressionism merges with decadence.

> He felt as if the soles of his feet were being stroked by soft velvety needles in a rhythm that became ever more subtle, more tender, and more rapid. And this indescribable bliss crawled stealthily up his spine; waltzed its way up to his neck and in a movement that became ever more desirous, intense, incessant, it passed its fingernails over his neck and up toward his fearful brain. There, he thought, precisely when it would become the most ecstatic, it would also be fatal. And he listened and listened: a cold saw, it seemed, was cutting into his arteries; it sounded like an exultant screaming violin.

Bahr's portrayal of decadence compares favorably with Stanislaw Przybyszewski's impressionistic depiction of Chopin's music in his essay *On the Psychology of the Individual* (1906).

> It is like the chlorotic color of an anemic person with transparent skin through which the fine veins can be seen. His slender figure with its long legs and arms exhibits in each movement the inimitable grace of degenerated noble races. . . . Chopin's music can be compared to the trembling nervousness of the over-refined, to a constant painful irritability of bare wounds . . . and to the fatigue of a hypersensitive person in whose eyes the sunlight can penetrate only prismatically. . . . On the other hand, this music is also passion, it is the convulsion and agony of the death struggle, it is a flight from oneself, an urge for disintegration, delirium.

Artificiality of style is inherent in decadence particularly in the representation of nature. Artificiality is characteristic of aestheticism and might be called decadent only if cultivated for its own sake. Its motivation is a reaction against the conventional and commonplace descriptions of nature, and as such is part of the antinaturalism movement. An excerpt from Max Dauthendey's short story *Im blauen Licht von Penang* (1915; *In the Blue Light of Penang*) illustrates motifs of seclusion, artificial gardens, and the exotic.

> The courtesan's house was situated like a lonely white room in the depths of a rose garden. Instead of flower beds there stood porcelain vases of a bluish color and tall as a man in long rows along the garden fence; yellow- and red-spotted tiger lilies grew in bouquets in vases. Slender wanderpalms (*Wanderpalmen*) with pitch-black, fan-shaped leaves assumed the boastful posture of sinister peacocks around the white villa. A scarlet electrine tree (*Elektrinenbaum*) spread its foliage across the garden entrance. The red mesentery of the blossoms gave to the air a bloody luster like a butcher's chopping block. The garden in its colors appeared to mirror the inner life of the courtesan. Its artifice of porcelain vases, the somber nature of the wanderpalms, and the inconsiderate lascivious redness of the electrine trees all reminded one of the proprietress.

The passage exhibits features that are only marginally decadent. While there is nothing inherently pathological in the description, we do note a marked interest in the artificial even though, paradoxically, it is nature that is being depicted. The extravagant and the sterile are extolled at the expense of the natural and the vital. The courtesan does not belong to the world of the bourgeois; nor does her garden. Again, we see how decadence is related to the world of the aristocrat; in its very foundations, it is antibourgeois.

Aestheticism as a movement appears to be more at home in Austria than in Germany. A few characteristic motifs of decadence are to be found in the aestheticism of the young Hugo von Hofmannsthal in works such as *Der Tor und der Tod* (1893; *The Fool and Death*), although it would be misleading to define him as a typical representative of decadence. More recent assessments of decadence see artificiality as the weakest and least-widespread motif of decadence.

So far, we have been considering literary decadence as an aesthetic phenomenon involving the individual artist. Decadence, however, also has a broader social and cultural dimension that goes beyond the realm of the individual artist but at the same time suggests a connection with the aesthetic of overrefinement. This variant of decadence figures prominently in the genealogical or family novel and frequently involves the last scion of an illustrious aristocratic or patrician family. Gustav Freytag's *Debit and Credit* has already been mentioned as a prototype. In this novel, the aristocrat has wasted or misused his energy instead of subordinating it to the welfare of the community as a whole. The decadents in such novels show an increasing inability to master life. Decadence enters in Thomas Mann's *Buddenbrooks* because of a hereditary predisposition to the aesthetic and an acquisition of culture. Hanno Buddenbrook, the last scion of a Hanseatic patrician family, succumbs to the seduction of Wagner's music—as does Hans Castorp in Mann's *Der Zauberberg* (1924; *The Magic Mountain*). Gustav Aschenbach's fall and ultimate death in Mann's *Der Tod in Venedig* (1913; *Death in Venice*) is the result of his perception of ultimate beauty and perfection in the androgynous Tadzio. Aschenbach ignores the warning of the encroaching plague in Venice, remains in the city in close pursuit of his idol, and dies there (the composer Richard Wagner, who exerted a powerful influence on Mann, died in Venice as well).

Nearly a decade earlier than *Buddenbrooks,* Ricarda Huch's *Erinnerungen von Ludolf Ursleu dem Jüngeren* (1892; *Memoirs of Ludolf Ursleu, the Younger*) appeared. It is also a genealogical novel dealing with an aristocratic family. The causes of decadence here have no connection with art; rather, the disintegration of the family has more to do with its life of leisure. Individual family members have no serious stake in the welfare of the community and eventually grow weary of their purely formal existence, which is imbued with pleasure seeking. Ludolf, the chronicler of his family history, is paralyzed by pessimism and sees the world as a place where all activity is fleeting and vain. In the true Romantic tradition, he believes that only death can offer true peace.

The atmosphere of culture-weariness also permeates Eduard von Keyserling's decadent novels about aristocratic families, as the following excerpt from *Abendliche Häuser* (1914; *Twilight Houses*) illustrates.

> We have nothing else to do but to sit and wait until one after another has crumbled away. Again they passed meadows over which the fog was hovering; again a nightingale was singing in the elderberry bushes, and the sounds of an accordion were lost in the night, but today all this did not touch Egloff. It moved past him like life which one views through the windows of a train with eyes tired from traveling.

The fact that Bahr's artistic hero in *The Good School* overcomes his decadence illustrates another facet of the phenomenon that was mentioned earlier: namely, that a double perspective grew out of Nietzsche's analyses of decadence. Decadence could be seen as decline or degeneration or as the prerequisite for the development to a higher plane—a process of regeneration. Such a perspective allows for the possibility of overcoming decadence. Examples of this direction of thought are found in novels such as Johannes Schlaf's *Das Dritte Reich* (1900; *The Third Empire*), Kurt Martens's *Roman aus der Decadence* (1898; *A Novel of a Decadent Period*), and Hermann Stehr's *Leonore Griebel* (1900; *Leonore Griebel*). Schlaf considered the emergence of decadence to be a natural phenomenon, but he argued that it would be superseded by a new type of man with physical strength and sound moral character. There are distinct echoes here of Nietzsche's Zarathustra: "Man is something that must be overcome." The characters in these novels do exhibit traits of decadence, but the emphasis is not on the disease but rather the overcoming of the disease. With such a shift in emphasis, the motif of decadence would seem to be of marginal interest.

Literary decadence is a specific form of preoccupation or fascination with disease. In this respect, it differs from the representation of ordinary illness, which can be a staple of almost any literary work. Decadence became pronounced in a particular cultural era during which the members of the aristocracy and the patriciate showed an increasing tendency to question the values of their own class. Added to this was the growing interest in abnormal psychology to which the emerging discourse of psychoanalysis gave a significant impetus.

DON NELSON

See also Austria: Late Habsburg Literature in Vienna; Jugendstil; Jung Wien

Further Reading

Bauer, Roger, "Decadence bei Nietzsche: Versuch einer Bestandsaufnahme," in *Literary Theory and Criticism: Festschrift Presented to Rene Wellek in Honor of His Eightieth Birthday,* edited by Joseph P. Strelka, 2 vols., Bern and New York: Lang, 1984
Bithell, Jethro, *Modern German Literature, 1880–1938,* London: Methuen, 1939
Eickhorst, William, *Decadence in German Fiction,* Denver, Colorado: Swallow, 1953
Helbling, Carl, *Die Gestalt des Künstlers in der neueren Dichtung,* Bern: Seldwyla, 1922
Huysmans, Joris Karl, *Against the Grain,* New York: Hartsdale, 1931
Jacob, Gerhard, "Thomas Mann und Nietzsche: Zum Problem der Dekadenz," Ph.D. diss., Universität Leipzig, 1926
Kafitz, Dieter, editor, *Dekadenz in Deutschland: Beiträge zur Erforschung der Romanliteratur um die Jahrhundertwende,* Frankfurt and New York: Lang, 1987
Kohlschmidt, Werner, et al., editors, *Reallexikon der deutschen Literaturgeschichte,* Berlin: de Gruyter, 1958
Koppen, Erwin, *Dekadenter Wagnerismus: Studien zur europäischen Literatur des Fin de siècle,* Berlin and New York: de Gruyter, 1973
Nietzsche, Friedrich, *The Case of Wagner,* translated by Walter Kaufmann, New York: Vintage Press, 1970
Nordau, Max, *Degeneration,* New York: Appleton, 1912
Rasch, Wolfdietrich, *Die literarische Decadence um 1900,* Munich: Beck, 1986

Deutsche Demokratische Republik *see* German Democratic Republic

Deutsche Demokratische Republik see German Democratic Republic

---

Wilhelm Dilthey 1833–1911

Wilhelm Dilthey's importance lies in his attempt to provide the humanities, or "human studies" *(Geisteswissenschaften)* as Hodges translates the term, with a systematic historical and methodological foundation. Based on an analysis of the common precepts of the individual disciplines, their histories, and their methodologies, Dilthey attempts to elaborate on a nonexisting primary or basic discipline (*Grundwissenschaft*) to create the general theoretical framework for research in the humanities. This goal dominates his work from the first volume of *Einleitung in die Geisteswissenschaften* (1883; *Introduction to the Human Sciences*) to *Der Aufbau der geschichtlichen Welt in den Geisteswissenschaften* (1910; The Construction of the Historical World in the Human Sciences). In Dilthey's view, human studies include, beyond philology and history, the social sciences and encompass all fields that in a broad sense deal with human expression and action. Human studies are defined by their inherent methodological uniqueness that sets them apart from positivistic and metaphysical approaches. Their methodology is based on the "natural" interrelation between the creative and the interpreting mind. According to Dilthey, the human studies strive to understand (*verstehen*) their subject, while the goal of the natural sciences (*Naturwissenschaften*) is to explain it *(erklären)*. Reason alone is considered an insufficient basis for understanding. Understanding, Dilthey claims, must be perceived as an act in which not only intellect but also lived experience and emotions participate; understanding thus requires the "wollend, fühlend, vorstellende Wesen" (willing, sensing, imagining being).

In his hermeneutics, Dilthey declares life itself the decisive agent that melds lived experience, expression, and understanding (*Erleben, Ausdruck, und Verstehen*) into one unified whole. In Dilthey's philosophy, this process of interpretation, by which life is understood through itself, characterizes the human studies as *Lebensphilosophie.*

Besides his theoretical works, Dilthey published biographies and studies in the area of intellectual history. In 1870, the first volume of *Das Leben Schleiermachers* (The Life of Schleiermacher) appeared. He also wrote on Leibnitz, Frederic the Great, and Hegel. His book *Die Jugendgeschichte Hegels* (1905; Hegel's Early Years) gave important new impulses to research on Hegel.

During Dilthey's lifetime, his most influential book was *Das Erlebnis und die Dichtung* (*Poetry and Experience*) published in 1905. Its collection of essays on Lessing, Goethe, Novalis, and Hölderlin became the basis for research focusing on intellectual history (*Geistesgeschichte*) within the field of "human studies." Dilthey's work also proved to be influential on philosophers such as Max Scheler, Edmund Husserl, and Martin Heidegger.

Several factors may account, at least in part, for the decline of Dilthey's influence. First, there was the claim that his hermeneutics would lead to historical relativism with no room for absolute rational truths and ideals (*Historismusverdacht*, Ernst Troeltsch/Heinrich Rickert). Second, Dilthey's search for a general theory of knowledge (*Theorie des Wissens, Grundwissenschaft*) that could overcome the dualism between the sciences and the humanities was replaced by a theory of sciences (*Wissenschaftstheorie*) that is content with the explanation of rules, conventions and procedures of individual disciplines and no longer interested in analysing the prerequisites, validity, and limitations of knowledge. Finally, the dualism between the sciences and the humanities has lost its importance in the current discourse. Contemporary theories rather focus on the difference between the social sciences and the traditional historical and philosophical disciplines, thus placing the rift Dilthey had observed between the sciences and the humanities within the framework of human studies.

Since large parts of Wilhelm Dilthey's writings were unfinished when he died in 1911, the full scope of his work did not become apparent until the posthumous publication of his manuscripts in the *Gesammelte Schriften,* which began in 1914 and is still incomplete. Dilthey's influence on philosophy and literary studies, which only began a few years before his death, peaked in the years between World War I and World War II. During the "Methodenstreit" in the 1960s, Dilthey's theories once again attracted scholarly attention by way of Hans Gadamer's critical discussion of Dilthey's hermeneutics in *Wahrheit und Methode* (1960; *Truth and Method*) and Jürgen Habermas's reaction to it. This renewed interest in Wilhelm Dilthey's work is reflected in the founding of the *Dilthey-Jahrbuch für Philosophie und Geschichte der Geisteswissenschaften* in 1983.

BERNHARD R. MARTIN

See also Hermeneutics

Biography

Born in Biebrich/Rhine, 19 November 1833. Son of a protestant pastor; began study of theology in Heidelberg in accordance with his parents' wishes, 1852; moved to Berlin, continued in theology, but shifted focus to philology, philosophy, and history, 1853; passed the first state's examination in theology, followed by the "Schulamtsprüfung" (state's examination for secondary school teachers), 1856; worked as high school teacher, then entered an academic career; received doctorate, 1864, and became professor of philosophy at Basel, 1867–68; moved to Kiel, 1868, Breslau, 1871, and Berlin, 1883, where he taught until 1908. Died in Seis am Schlern, Southern Tirolia, 1 October 1911.

Selected Works

Collected Works

Gesammelte Schriften, 1914–

The Essence of Philosophy, translated by Stephen A. Emery and William T. Emery, 1954

Selected Writings, edited, translated, and introduced by H.P. Rickman, 1976
Selected Works, various translators, edited by Rudolf A. Makkreel and Frithjof Rodi, 1985–

Philosophical Writing

Das Leben Schleiermachers, 1870
Einleitung in die Geisteswissenschaften, 1883; as *Introduction to the Human Sciences,* translated by Ramon B. Betanzos, 1988; translated and edited by Rudolf A. Makkreel and Frithjof Rodi, in *Selected Works,* vol. 1, 1989
Die Jugendgeschichte Hegels, 1905
Das Erlebnis und die Dichtung, 1905; as *Poetry and Experience,* in *Selected Works,* vol. 5, translated by L. Agosta et al., 1985
Der Aufbau der geschichtlichen Welt in den Geisteswissenschaften, 1910
Dilthey's Philosophy of Existence: Introduction to Weltanschauungslehre (from *Gesammelte Schriften,* vol. 8), translated by William Kluback and Martin Weinbaum, 1957
Meaning in History: W. Dilthey's Thoughts on History and Society (from *Gesammelte Schriften,* vol. 7), translated by H.P. Rickman, 1961; as *Pattern and Meaning in History: Thoughts on History and Society,* 1962
Descriptive Psychology and Historical Understanding (from *Gesammelte Schriften,* vol. 21, translated by Richard M. Zaner and Kenneth L. Heiges, 1977

Further Reading

Albert, Karl, *Lebensphilosophie: Von den Anfängen bei Nietzsche bis zu ihrer Kritik bei Lukacs,* Freiburg: Alber, 1995
Bambach, Charles R., *Heidegger, Dilthey, and the Crisis of Historicism,* Ithaca, New York: Cornell University Press, 1995
Bollnow, Otto Friedrich, *Dilthey: Eine Einführung in seine Philosophie,* Stuttgart: Kohlhammer, 1967
Dilthey-Jahrbuch für Philosophie und Geschichte der Geisteswissenschaften, Göttingen: Vandenhoeck and Ruprecht, 1983– (annual)
Fellmann, Ferdinand, *Symbolischer Pragmatismus: Hermeneutik nach Dilthey,* Reinbek bei Hamburg: Rowohlt Taschenbuch, 1991
Herrmann, Ulrich, *Bibliographie Wilhelm Dilthey: Quellen und Literatur,* Berlin: Beltz, 1969
Hodges, Herbert Arthur, *Wilhelm Dilthey: An Introduction,* London: Paul, Trench, Trubner, and New York: Oxford University Press, 1944
———, *The Philosophy of Wilhelm Dilthey,* London: Routledge, 1952
Hogrebe, Wolfram, *Deutsche Philosophie im XIX. Jahrhundert: Kritik der idealistischen Vernunft: Schelling, Schleiermacher, Schopenhauer, Stirner, Kierkegaard, Engels, Marx, Dilthey, Nietzsche,* Munich: Fink, 1987
Jung, Matthias, *Dilthey zur Einführung,* Hamburg: Junius, 1996
Makkreel, Rudolf A., *Dilthey, Philosopher of the Human Studies,* Princeton, New Jersey: Princeton University Press, 1975
Maraldo, John C., *Der hermeneutische Zirkel: Untersuchungen zu Schleiermacher, Dilthey und Heidegger,* Freiburg: Alber, 1974
Palmer, Richard E., *Hermeneutics: Interpretation Theory in Schleiermacher, Dilthey, Heidegger, and Gadamer,* Evanston, Illinois: Northwestern University Press, 1969
Plantinga, Theodore, *Historical Understanding in the Thought of Wilhelm Dilthey,* Buffalo, New York: 1980
Rickman, Hans Peter, *Dilthey Today: A Critical Appraisal of the Contemporary Relevance of His Work,* New York: Greenwood Press, 1988
Tuttle, Howard N., *The Dawn of Historical Reason: The Historicality of Human Existence in the Thought of Dilthey, Heidegger, and Ortega y Gasset,* New York: Lang, 1994
Zöckler, Christofer, *Dilthey und die Hermeneutik: Diltheys Begründungen der Hermeneutik als Praxiswissenschaft und die Geschichte ihrer Rezeption,* Stuttgart: Metzler, 1975

Alfred Döblin 1878–1957

Alfred Döblin is known to general audiences as the author of *Berlin Alexanderplatz* (1929; *Berlin Alexanderplatz*), which is considered to be the German response to the modernistic narrative techniques of John Dos Passos and James Joyce and one of the outstanding big-city novels of the century, the major novel on Berlin in the 1920s. The novel was first turned into a movie in 1931, and its transformation into a television series (1983) arguably became the major achievement of filmmaker Rainer Werner Fassbinder. Döblin himself, saddened by the lack of success of his other works, attributed the success of *Berlin Alexanderplatz* to a misunderstanding: it was read, he said, solely as a novel on the Berlin underworld.

Döblin must, however, be considered one of the major German-language novelists of the 20th century. His modernist style and technique was nourished by his scientific training, especially in physiology and psychiatry. Döblin's themes were life and death, and, therefore, life-generating forces such as sexuality and destructive forces such as violence. His fearless experimentation with new points of view, different forms, techniques, and styles made him a "proteus," who was always good for surprises and ready to shock readers. Döblin's prose can never be neutral; it never leaves readers indifferent, and it rarely leaves them satisfied.

Döblin was a participant in the avant-garde group around Herwarth Walden, editor of the periodical *Der Sturm,* in the years before World War I. After these Expressionist beginnings, he became a major player in the leftist literary circles in the Berlin of the 1920s, before and after *Berlin Alexanderplatz.* The notoriety of this book embroiled Döblin in literary and political controversies, but he maintained his reputation and visibility during his exile years in France before World War II. Döblin, however, was almost totally isolated in the United States from 1941 to 1945. Finally, his attempts to rebuild German cultural life after 1945 as an officer of the French military government, and to regain his German readership with works written after 1933, were beset by misunderstandings and disappointments on both sides and were largely failures. Therefore, Döblin's career can by no means be reduced to *Berlin Alexanderplatz;* he wrote a dozen major novels. Although he is chiefly remembered as a writer of narrative prose, he also published several plays, a travel account (*Reise in Polen* [1926; *Journey to Poland*]), political commentaries and books, philosophical and religious essays, autobiographical texts, and much literary criticism and book reviews.

Döblin's first significant book was published in 1913 when he was 35 years old. This collection of expressionistic short stories was entitled *Die Ermordung einer Butterblume* (The Assassination of a Dandelion); some of the stories had previously been published in *Der Sturm.* The texts, unusual if not shocking in their content, narrative perspective, and style, deal primarily with sexuality (or the body) and violence and offer endings with no solutions.

Döblin's breakthrough came with his first published novel, *Die drei Sprünge des Wang-lun* (1915; *The Three Leaps of Wang-lun*), subtitled "A Chinese Novel." It takes place in 18th-century China and tells the events around an uprising of an originally nonviolent sect of poor people, which is eventually crushed by the violent measures of the Chinese army. The novel, centering on the problems of violence versus nonviolence and activism versus the passive endurance of one's fate, enfolds an intense and colorful picture of the entire Chinese society—it is especially memorable in its depiction of mass movements, mass hysteria, and mass violence. Although the work takes its title from Wang-lun, its nominal protagonist, the human individual is anything but the center and the agent of events.

The two-volume historical novel *Wallenstein* (1920) once again focuses on mass violence, fanaticism, and senseless greed rather than individuals such as Wallenstein, let alone any "heroes." Out of the violence and savagery emerges the quest for overcoming the cycle of violent chain reactions, embodied in the Emperor Ferdinand II. *Wallenstein* has remained one of Döblin's enduring works. It stands at the foreground of a new type of historical novel in Germany, which is opposed to the popular patriotic *romans fleuves* of the late 19th century, such as Gustav Freytag's *Die Ahnen* and Felix Dahn's *Ein Kampf um Rom.* Döblin, embroiled in the debates about the "end of the novel," called his texts "epics" to distinguish them from psychological novels of the bourgeois class.

Döblin's monumental epic about the future of humankind, *Berge Meere und Giganten* (1924; Mountains, Oceans, and Giants), with its baffling lack of closure, found few enthusiasts, as did his verse epic on Indian mythology, *Manas* (1927), whose rather prosaic verses were nonetheless highly praised by Robert Musil. It was finally with *Berlin Alexanderplatz* that Döblin, now more than 50 years old and still in the avant-garde, matched his modernist style and technique, enriched by montage in the manner of Joyce, with a subject matter to the taste of the German audience: his own city of Berlin, and, more specifically, the proletarian quarters in the East around the Alexanderplatz (including the Jewish Scheunenviertel). The story of Franz Biberkopf, convicted of homicide and trying to remain *anständig* (law abiding), brings the reader into contact with the pulse of the modern city and takes place among the dispossessed and criminals—it is this dimension of the plot of the novel that has ensured its enduring commercial success (Döblin earned more from this novel during the first months of its sale than from all of his previous books combined).

Döblin was always more than merely a "novelist," and in the waning years of the Weimar Republic, the political dimensions of literature and of individual authors' works became dominant. *Berlin Alexanderplatz* provided the opportunity for the communist writers' periodical *Die Linkskurve* to document their ideological separation from other leftist writers, the "fellow travelers." A letter from a student asking Döblin for advice about how intellectuals should act in the present political crisis brought about a series of public letters collected in the book *Wissen und Verändern!* (1931, Knowing and Transforming), which in turn generated more controversy. But all debates and manifestos became meaningless when President Hindenburg appointed Adolf Hitler chancellor of the Reich, on 30 January 1933. Döblin fled to Switzerland, and he then moved to France. For several years, he was active in the movement of Jewish Territorialism, the non-Zionist group that was trying to find a Jewish homeland other than Palestine. In this period, he wrote *Jüdische Erneuerung* (1933; Jewish Renewal) and *Flucht und Sammlung des Judenvolkes* (1935; Flight and Regrouping of the Jewish People).

Döblin's exile narratives should have been more "accessible" to readers, because writing provided his only income in a shrinking market. The only exile novel that shows traces of market considerations, however, is *Pardon wird nicht gegeben* (1935; *Men without Mercy*). It is a Berlin story of mother-son conflicts and the problem of political allegiances, with marked autobiographical elements. Döblin's first exile novel, *Babylonische Wandrung* (1934, Babylonian Migration), has an uncertain plot, a tone of humor and irony, and many grotesque scenes. Considering that this work was Döblin's first response to the shock of the events of 1933 and that his exile was particularly severe since it meant not only the loss of his (linguistic) home base, but also that of his profession as a physician, the novel was as fascinating as it was baffling.

Exile brought Döblin's fundamental criticism of Western imperialism to the fore, and this criticism found its expression in his vast trilogy on the colonization of South America, variably entitled *Amazonas* or *Das Land ohne Tod* (1937–38; The Land without Death). The majority of its second part is devoted to the Jesuit Republic in Paraguay, a Western experiment in nonviolence. In its third part, *Der neue Urwald* (The New Jungle), which takes the action into the present, the restless and greedy white men are finally swallowed by the jungle their ancestors had tried to conquer. Once more, nature is the center, and the human individual is marginalized.

What was it that had gone wrong in German history? *Wissen und Verändern* had tried to give answers, but the immediate decisive event had been the failed revolution of 1918–19 after the end of World War I, which Döblin, like others, considered to be the beginning of the fascist reaction that later threatened the entire continent. The four-volume *Erzählwerk,* a "narrative text" written closely from documents and personal memories, called *November 1918* (1939–50), reflects Döblin's own odyssey and, in general, the exile's plight and disorientation during World War II. Volume 1 had been published in 1939, but the manuscript of volume 2 (later divided in two parts because of its length) was part of Döblin's baggage when he had to flee from Paris in June 1940. His escape caused a severe trauma and his turn to Christianity. In Los Angeles, where he received and reworked the manuscript preserved by a French friend, he converted to Catholicism, which had a decisive impact on the last volume, *Karl und Rosa,* written 1942–43. The entire trilogy/tetralogy was finally published in Germany in 1948–50, with most of the original first volume omitted because of French censorship. Although Döblin's sympathies are clearly with the communist cause of Karl Liebknecht and Rosa Luxemburg, he finally opts for a metapolitical Christian solution to social problems and wars. This serious realization of Christian charity and love is embodied in his protagonist Friedrich Becker who, however, finds out that society is not ready for his message.

When Döblin returned to Germany in the fall of 1945, as an official in the cultural section of the French military government (Döblin was French citizen), he came with the sense of a mission. He wanted to help rebuild German culture from the devastation of the past 12 years, and he wanted to propagate and debate his new Christian beliefs. Christianity and, especially, Catholicism, however, had "conservative" connotations in this period, and Döblin did not fit into this postwar restoration era. At the same time, Germans who remembered Döblin from before 1933, especially *Berlin Alexanderplatz,* were surprised to find this anarchist-socialist now in the Catholic camp. Döblin's Christian narratives and essays, notably *Der Oberst und der Dichter* (1946; The Colonel and the Writer) and *Das unsterbliche Herz* (1946; The Immortal Heart) found ideologically biased readers, a fact that also limited the impact of his autobiographical account *Schicksalsreise* (1949; *Destiny's Journey*), whose most impressive parts deal with the author's escape through France in 1940.

Unfortunately, a combination of circumstances prevented Döblin's last novel, *Hamlet; oder die lange Nacht nimmt ein Ende* (1956; Hamlet; or the Long Night Takes an End), from appearing before the last moments of his life. It was actually put into print by an East German publisher. This complex and rather uneven text has the structure of a cycle of novellas that are told within an overall narrative framework. This narrative framework and the therapeutic telling of the stories uncover the deadly family conflicts to which the seriously injured World War II soldier returns; there are two versions of the ending, which have fundamentally different consequences for the question of whether this "Hamlet" will survive after the destruction of his family.

Döblin's endings for his narratives were never conclusive; they were the beginning of a new round of conflicts and reflections. This is most evident in *Berlin Alexanderplatz* but generally true for all of his works. Döblin's thinking never came to an end, even after his conversion. Therefore, his poetic, political, philosophical, and religious positions seem to shift, and his work cannot be summarized in short statements. Except for his short Expressionist period, he cannot be claimed for any movement or "school," or for any political ideology. His influence in his own generation, however, was considerable. Bertolt Brecht is a case in point. Furthermore, if his impact on German readers after 1945 was minimal, major prose writers still learned from him, including Arno Schmidt, Wolfgang Koeppen, and especially, Günter Grass, who acknowledged his debt in his speech "Über meinen Lehrer Döblin" (About My Teacher Döblin; first published in *Akzente* [1967]), which pointed specifically to *Wallenstein* as a model for his own writing. And there is no doubt about the continuing impact of *Berlin Alexanderplatz.*

WULF KOEPKE

Biography

Born in Stettin, 10 August 1878. Moved to Berlin, 1888; medical student at Berlin University, 1900–1904, and Freiburg University, 1904–5; medical degree, 1905; medical officer in the German army, World War I; worked in a psychiatric hospital, Regensburg; general medical practice, Berlin, 1911–14, and again, 1919–33; member of the Schutzverband deutscher Schriftsteller, 1920, and president, 1924; drama critic for the *Prager Tageblatt,* 1921–24; in Poland, 1924; member, with Bertolt Brecht, of Group 1925; in France to escape the Nazis, 1933; French citizen, 1936; emigrated to the United States, 1940; screenplay writer, Metro Goldwyn Mayer, 1940–41; converted to Roman Catholicism, 1941; returned to Germany, 1945; education officer, Baden-Baden, 1945; editor of *Das Goldene Tor,* 1946–51; cofounder, 1949, and vice president of literature section, 1949–51, Academy for Science and Literature, Mainz; in Paris, 1953; frequent hospital and sanatorium stays, 1954–57. Fontane prize, 1916; member of the Prussian Academy of the Arts, 1928. Died 26 June 1957.

Selected Works

Collections

Ausgewählte Werke in Einzelbänden, edited by Walter Muschg, Heinz Graber, and Anthony W. Riley, 31 vols., 1960–
Die Zeitlupe: Kleine Prosa, edited by Walter Muschg, 1962
Die Vertreibung der Gespenster, edited by Manfred Beyer, 1968
Gesammelte Erzählungen, 1971
Ein Kerl muss eine Meinung haben, edited by Manfred Beyer, 1976

Fiction

Die Ermordung einer Butterblume und andere Erzählungen (stories), 1913
Die drei Sprünge des Wang-lun, 1915; as *The Three Leaps of Wang-lun,* 1991
Die Lobensteiner reisen nach Böhmen (stories), 1917
Wadzeks Kampf mit der Dampfturbine, 1918
Der schwarze Vorhang: Roman von den Worten und Zufällen, 1919
Wallenstein, 2 vols., 1920
Blaubart und Miss Ilsebill, 1923
Berge Meere und Giganten, 1924; revised edition as *Giganten,* 1932
Die beiden Freudinnen und ihr Giftmord, 1925
Feldzeugmeister Cratz, Der Kaplan, Zwei Erzählungen, 1926
Manas: Epische Dichtung, 1927
Berlin Alexanderplatz: Die Geschichte vom Franz Biberkopf, 1929; edited by Werner Stauffacher, 1996; as *Alexanderplatz, Berlin: The Story of Franz Biberkopf,* translated by Eugene Jolas, 1931 (also published as *Berlin Alexanderplatz: The Story of Franz Biberkopf,* 1978)
Babylonische Wandrung; oder, Hochmut kommt vor dem Fall, 1934
Pardon wird nicht gegeben, 1935; as *Men without Mercy,* translated by Trevor and Phyllis Blewitt, 1937
Das Land ohne Tod, 1937–38; as *Amazonas,* edited by Walter Muschg, 1963
Die Fahrt ins Land ohne Tod, 1937
Der blaue Tiger, 1938

Der neue Urwald, 1948
November 1918: Eine deutsche Revolution, 1939–50
Bürger und Soldaten 1918, 1939
Verratenes Volk, 1948; as *A People Betrayed,* translated by John E. Woods, 1983
Heimkehr der Fronttruppen, 1949
Karl und Rosa, 1950; as *Karl and Rosa,* translated by John E. Woods, 1983
Der Oberst und der Dichter; ober, Das menschliche Herz, 1946
Heitere Magie, zwei Erzählungen, 1948
Hamlet; oder, die lange Nacht nimmt ein Ende, 1956

Plays
Lydia und Mäxchen: Tiefe Verbeugung in Einem Akt (produced 1905), 1906
Lusitania (produced 1926), 1920
Die Nonnen von Kemnade (produced 1923), 1923
Die Ehe (produced 1931), 1931

Other
"Gedächtnisstörungen bei der Korsakoffschen Psychose," diss. med. Freiburg/Br., 1905
Gespräche mit Kalypso über die Liebe und die Musik (essays), 1910
Der deutsche Maskenball (essays), 1921
Staat und Schriftsteller, 1921
Reise in Polen, 1926; as *Journey to Poland,* translated by Joachim Neugroschel, 1991
Das Ich über der Natur, 1927
Alfred Döblin. Im Buch—Zu Haus—Auf der Strasse, with Oskar Loerke, 1928
Der Bau des epischen Werkes, 1929
Wissen und Verändern! Offene Briefe an einen jungen Menschen, 1931
Jüdische Erneuerung, 1933
Unser Dasein, 1933
Flucht und Sammlung des Judenvolkes: Aufsätze und Erzählungen, 1935
Der historische Roman und Wir, 1936
Die deutsche Literatur: Ein Dialog zwischen Politik und Kunst, 1938
Der Nürnberger Lehrprozess, 1946
Der unsterbliche Mensch: Ein Religionsgespräch, 1946; with *Der Kampf mit dem Engel: Religionsgerpräch,* 1980
Die literarische Situation, 1947
Unsere Sorge—der Mensch, 1948
Schicksalsreise: Bericht und Bekenntnis, 1949; as *Destiny's Journey,* edited by Edgar Pässler, translated by Edna McCown, 1992
Die Dichtung, ihre Natur und ihre Rolle, 1950

Edited Works
Confucius, *The Living Thoughts of Confucius,* 1940
Arno Holz, *Die Revolution der Lyrik,* 1951
Minotaurus: Dichtung unter den Hufen von Staat und Industrie, 1953

Further Reading
Dollenmayer, David B., *The Berlin Novels of Alfred Döblin,* Berkeley: University of California Press, 1988
Keller, Otto, *Döblins Montageroman als Epos der Moderne,* Munich: Fink, 1980
Kiesel, Helmuth, *Literarische Trauerarbeit: Das Exil- und Spätwerk Alfred Döblins,* Tübingen: Niemeyer, 1986
Kreutzer, Leo, *Alfred Döblin: Sein Werk bis 1933,* Stuttgart: Kohlhammer, 1970
Links, Roland, *Alfred Döblin: Leben und Werk,* East Berlin: Volk und Wissen, 1965
Meyer, Jochen, editor, *Alfred Döblin, 1878–1978: Eine Ausstellung des Deutschen Literaturarchivs im Schiller-Nationalmuseum,* Munich: Kosel, 1978
Müller-Salget, Klaus, *Alfred Döblin: Werk und Entwicklung,* Bonn: Bouvier, 1972; 2nd edition, 1988
Prangel, Matthias, *Alfred Döblin,* Stuttgart: Metzler, 1987
Prangel, Matthias, editor, *Materialien zu Alfred Döblin, "Berlin Alexanderplatz,"* Frankfurt: Suhrkamp, 1975
Schöne, Albrecht, "Berlin Alexanderplatz," in *Der Deutsche Roman: Vom Barock bis zur Gegenwart,* edited by Benno von Wiese, Düsseldorf: Bagel, 1963
Schuster, Ingrid, and Ingrid Hannids-Bode, editors, *Alfred Döblin im Spiegel der zeitgenössischen Kritik,* Bern: Francke, 1973
Tewarson, Heidi Thomann, *Alfred Döblin: Grundlagen seiner Ästhetik und ihre Entwicklung, 1900–1933,* Bern and Las Vegas, Nevada: Lang, 1979
Ziolkowski, Theodore, *Dimensions of the Modern Novel: German Texts and European Contexts,* Princeton, New Jersey: Princeton University Press, 1969

Berlin Alexanderplatz 1929

Novel by Alfred Döblin

Alfred Döblin's only critical and commercial success, as well as his last novel to be published in Germany before Hitler's accession to power, *Berlin Alexanderplatz* remains his acknowledged masterpiece and the greatest *Großstadtroman* in German. A 1930 version for radio (script by Döblin, first broadcast 1963) and a first film version in 1931 (directed by Piel Jutzi, with Heinrich George as Franz Biberkopf and Döblin's collaboration on the script) attest both to the novel's popularity and to the author's interest in these media. Although an early review by Walter Benjamin praised Döblin's radical use of montage to break out of the conventions of bourgeois narration, Marxist critics attacked the work as reactionary because its hero, Franz Biberkopf, is a petty criminal and protofascist rather than a genuine proletarian.

Promptly translated into the major European languages (into English by Eugene Jolas in 1931 as *Alexanderplatz, Berlin* and also published in 1978 as *Berlin Alexanderplatz*), the novel was soon tagged by Anglo-Saxon critics as having been influenced by Joyce's *Ulysses.* Breon Mitchell has shown convincingly that Döblin did in fact change his manuscript after reading a German translation of Joyce's work, and Döblin himself called Joyce "a good wind in my sails." Certainly, the shifting and multifarious narrative modes of *Berlin Alexanderplatz* are more reminiscent of Joyce than of the conventional narrator of Dos Passos's *Manhattan Transfer,* whose influence on *Berlin Alexanderplatz* some scholars have also claimed to discern. However, unlike Dos Passos's parallel narrative strands, *Berlin Alexanderplatz* is focused firmly on its central figure, Franz Biberkopf, an erstwhile furniture mover, ex-convict, street vendor, occasional burglar, and pimp.

At the beginning of the novel, Biberkopf is released from prison after having served time for the manslaughter of his girlfriend, Ida. He now vows to live a decent and orderly life. However, three increasingly harsh mishaps frustrate his resolution.

He is arrested for the murder of his new girlfriend, Mieze, a crime actually committed by his supposed friend and partner in crime, Reinhold, the paragon of "that cold force which nothing in life can change." Biberkopf falls into an almost catatonic state in the prison's psychiatric ward, nearly dies, and emerges from the ordeal somehow purified. In the end, he contents himself with a job as assistant gatekeeper in a "medium-sized factory."

It is Döblin's brilliant use of montage throughout *Berlin Alexanderplatz* that makes of this straightforward plot of fall and redemption one of the greatest novels of German modernism and, incidentally, a documentary view of Berlin in the late 1920s. In some cases, he simply cut text out of a source and pasted it into the manuscript: jumbled together on almost every page are advertising copy, local government announcements, fragments of a potboiler lesbian novel, texts of Tin Pan Alley and patriotic songs, inspirational poetry, and the multitudinous individual voices of the teeming metropolis. Biberkopf and the other characters are immersed in this sea of words, so that it is not always clear whose head they are running through. Yet Döblin's montage is not a random assemblage but a calculated construct that comments on, illuminates, and relativizes Biberkopf's individual fate. In fact, the whole novel can be read as a critique of the idea of tragic fate. This is the import of the ironic comparison of Biberkopf to Orestes at the end of the novel's second book as well as of the stories told by the Hasidic Jew who helps Biberkopf regain his mental equilibrium in book 1. (The assimilated and educated Berlin physician Döblin had rediscovered his spiritual roots in Eastern European Judaism during a trip to Poland in 1924, and passages in his reportage *Reise in Polen* [1924; *Journey to Poland*] anticipate the urban montages in *Berlin Alexanderplatz*.)

As the novel progresses, the montage increasingly includes fragments of the two great stories of faith under duress from the Old Testament: Abraham and Isaac and Job. These, together with the culminating struggle between the great leveler Death and the apocalyptically evil Whore of Babylon over the soul of the catatonic Biberkopf, as well as the hero's eventual purification through suffering, foreshadow Döblin's conversion to Christianity during his exile in California.

However, the novel's deeply ambiguous and open ending leaves the reader uncertain of the identity and political allegiances of the masses whom Biberkopf "coolly" watches march past his factory gatehouse. Whom will he avoid? With whom does he feel the solidarity trumpeted in the last chapter? On the one hand, Biberkopf fits the psychological profile of the petit bourgeois yearners for order to whom Hitler appealed. Early in the novel, he peddles Nazi papers ("He is not against the Jews, but he is for law and order") and gets into a fight with former friends who are Communists; later he goes to anarchist meetings to bait the speakers. On the other hand, Hans-Peter Bayerdörfer has tried to show that, at the end of the novel, Biberkopf has achieved an understanding of the need for solidarity against the false collective that promotes war. Döblin himself acknowledged the dilemma posed by the novel's ending in a letter of 18 September 1931: "A more passive-receptive element with tragic overtones is opposed to an active element that is more optimistic. . . . In *Berlin Alexanderplatz* I definitely wanted to bring Fr. Biberkopf to the second phase—I didn't succeed." During his exile, Döblin continued to explore this central opposition of passive submission versus action in the novels *Pardon wird nicht gegeben* (1935; *Men without Mercy*) and especially the great tetralogy of the failed German revolution, *November 1918* (1939–50). Döblin's conversion in the midst of writing the latter work lends its dilemma explicitly Christian overtones.

In the early 1920s, Brecht acknowledged the influence of Döblin on his theory of Epic Theater, and his friendship with the older writer continued into the years of exile. Postwar writers as diverse as Wolfgang Koeppen, Arno Schmidt, Peter Rühmkorf, and most notably Günter Grass have celebrated Döblin as a mentor, and Rainer Werner Fassbinder's monumental 15-hour film version of *Berlin Alexanderplatz* (1983; with Günter Lamprecht's brilliant interpretation of Franz Biberkopf) both introduced a new generation to Döblin's masterpiece and brought out the homoeroticism implicit in Biberkopf's relationship with Reinhold.

David Dollenmayer

Editions

First edition: *Berlin Alexanderplatz: Die Geschichte vom Franz Biberkopf,* Berlin: S. Fischer, 1929

Critical edition: edited by Werner Stauffacher, Zürich: Walter-Verlag, 1996

Translation: *Alexanderplatz, Berlin: The Story of Franz Biberkopf,* translated by Eugene Jolas, New York: Viking Press, 1931 (also published as *Berlin Alexanderplatz: The Story of Franz Biberkopf,* 1978)

Further Reading

Bayerdörfer, Hans-Peter, "Der Wissende und die Gewalt: Alfred Döblins Theorie des epischen Werkes und der Schluß von *Berlin Alexanderplatz,*" in *Materialien zu Alfred Döblin: "Berlin Alexanderplatz,"* edited by Matthias Prangel, Frankfurt: Suhrkamp, 1975

———, "Berlin Alexanderplatz," in Deutsche Romane des 20. Jahrhunderts, vol. 1, Stuttgart: Reclam, 1993

Becker-Cantarino, Barbara, "Die Hure Babylon: Zur Mythisierung von Gewalt in Döblins *Berlin Alexanderplatz,*" in *Methodische reflektieretes Interpretieren: Festschrift für Hartmut Laufhütte zum 60. Geburtstag,* edited by Hans-Peter Ecker, Passau: Rothe, 1997

Benjamin, Walter, "Krisis des Romans: Zu Döblins *Berlin Alexanderplatz,*" in *Gesammelte Schriften,* edited by Hella Tiedemann-Bartels, vol. 3, Frankfurt: Suhrkamp, 1972

Dollenmayer, David B., *The Berlin Novels of Alfred Döblin,* Berkeley: University of California Press, 1988

Grass, Günter, "Über meinen Lehrer Döblin," in *Über meinen Lehrer Döblin und andere Vorträge,* Berlin: Literarisches Colloquium, 1968

Keller, Otto, *Döblins Montageroman als Epos der Moderne,* Munich: Fink, 1980

Mitchell, Breon, *James Joyce and the German Novel, 1922–1933,* Athens: Ohio University Press, 1976

Reid, James H., "*Berlin Alexanderplatz:* A Political Novel," *German Life and Letters* 21 (1968)

Sander, Gabriele, *Erläuterungen und Dokumente: Alfred Döblin, Berlin Alexanderplatz,* Stuttgart: Reclam, 1998

Sontag, Susan, "Novel into Film," *Vanity Fair* (September 1983)

Tatar, Maria, "'Wie süß ist es, sich zu opfern': Gender, Violence, and Agency in Döblin's *Berlin Alexanderplatz,*" *Deutsch Vierteljahrsschrift* 66 (1992)

Widdig, Bernd, *Männerbünde und Massen: Zur Krise männlicher Identität in der Literatur der Moderne,* Opladen: Westdeutscher Verlag, 1992

Ziolkowski, Theodore, *Dimensions of the Modern Novel: German Texts and European Contexts,* Princeton, New Jersey: Princeton University Press, 1969

Documentary Literature

Documentary literature uses quotations from historical and topical texts systematically, often for political motives, but not for added verisimilitude or aesthetic effects; it remains situation-independent, a free creation of its author. Factual genres (biography, autobiography, or journalistic work) are usually excluded. The earliest documentary work was perhaps Georg Büchner's *Dantons Tod* (1835, produced 1902; *Danton's Death*), which took speeches from historical accounts of the French Revolution. Alfred Döblin's *Berlin Alexanderplatz* (1929; translated as *Berlin, Alexanderplatz* and *Alexanderplatz, Berlin*) stands out among a number of documentary works of the 1920s. Satires by Karl Kraus and others work by juxtaposing documents without overt authorial intervention, as does Alexander Kluge's *Schlachtbeschreibung* (1964; Description of a Battle), where the battle of Stalingrad is narrated through documents.

In the 1960s, West German authors increasingly tried to show political commitment and write operatively; the distinction of literary and factual texts was blurred. Thus, journalistic and biographical texts came in. Günter Wallraff's worm's-eye-view reports on industrial and underclass life, *Wir brauchen dich. Als Arbeiter in deutschen Industriebetrieben* (1966; We Need You. As a Worker in German Industrial Plants) and *13 unerwünschte Reportagen* (1969; 13 Unwelcome Reports), are pure factuality but use a collage of elements more sophisticated than is usual in journalism. Later, Wallraff denied literary pretensions, embedding his writing in practical work to improve social conditions and to unmask business and media practices. Literary status was also claimed for Erika Runge's *Bottroper Protokolle* (1968; Bottrop Transcripts): ordinary folk told their stories, centered on the effects of a mine closure, to the tape recorder; the author put the reminiscences in readable form, but with a covert bias toward radical politics. The product can be thus turned to political use, but it remains a subjective document.

The 1960s also brought the flowering of "Documentary Theatre": a few staged plays with political aims to present a historical truth and thus influence contemporary attitudes. Documentation aided their instrumental function. Opposing what they saw as slanted reporting in the bourgeois media, dramatists created their own publicity and controversy. Mostly they mixed documentary and invented material ("semi-documentary"). Pure factuality was rarely aimed at: it seemed unliterary, impossible, or likely to lose itself in details. For understanding, analysis, and enlightenment, the writer had to choose a theme, select and adapt material, and even invent whole scenes or plots.

"Documentary" was thus largely a marketing term that exploited the postwar public's love of "facts." When historical words were interwoven with free creations, it created the classic "reality" of historical drama, prone to subjective interpretation, even distortion, by historians and playwrights. Television documentary, which also flourished in Germany in the 1960s, had to face similar problems. More positively, documentary fitted a post-1945 tendency to reject poetic style and to concentrate on analyzing and reforming reality by the deconstructive use of reality's own language. Critics and writers wedded to the concept of creativity thought that borrowing words from reality showed a mechanical and functional approach that abandoned poetic truth and vision in favor of factuality and immediate operative effect; the stress on surface reality must hinder the search for viable deeper explanations. Bertolt Brecht used documentary style only in *Furcht und Elend des Dritten Reiches* (1945; translated as *Fear and Misery in the Third Reich* and *The Private Life of the Master Race*); Max Frisch, Friedrich Dürrenmatt, and Martin Walser also rejected documentary theater. Documentary writers, however, were just as aware of the need to instrumentalize their bits of reality and to produce an independent, alternative reality sui generis, coolly (like Brecht) and objectively (in Marx's sense), showing characteristic situations and supraindividual social mechanisms.

The first consistent documentary theater was Erwin Piscator's of the 1920s. Similar to Marxist directors in the Soviet Union, particularly Sergei Tretiakov, Piscator saw authenticity and commitment as inseparable. He liked to connect (imagined) individual fates seen in personal stories enacted on stage with (reproduced) stormy historical backgrounds (often great events such as the Russian Revolution) from film clips and projections, which elucidated the context. Dramas were often rewritten to become epic and semidocumentary and to suit the political agenda. The premiere of Ernst Toller's *Hoppla, wir leben!* (1927; *Hoppla!*) ended with the spontaneous singing of the "Internationale" in the audience.

At the West Berlin *Freie Volksbühne,* Piscator produced Rolf Hochhuth's *Der Stellvertreter* (1963; translated as *The Representative* and *The Deputy*), Heinar Kipphardt's *In der Sache J. Robert Oppenheimer* (1964; In the Matter of J. Robert Oppenheimer), and Peter Weiss's *Die Ermittlung* (1965; *The Investigation*), thus reestablishing documentary, which survived until 1970. The 1960s canon embraces about 14 plays, some with better claims to belonging than others. Epic techniques from Brecht and Piscator—projections, films, recordings, sudden cuts, and characters commenting their own actions and apostrophizing the audience—were commonly used.

Hochhuth's *Deputy* has a fictional plot: a young priest tries to force Pope Pius XII to protest publicly against the genocide in 1943. This play touches historical reality only occasionally; no authentic dialogue is used. It relies on general facts to reinforce its basically emotional effect; it is not led by specific documentary evidence. His dramaturgy here is untypical of documentary writing, for it stresses our free will in making moral decisions rather than the social conditioning of ethos; he insists on his own dramatic freedom to idealize—any newsreel can better portray raw concrete reality. In this play, Hochhuth combines historical and invented figures in a Schillerian psychological drama, trying to prove that Pius XII was inadequate; but he does not send the audience out to prove that one can react more adequately to the situation of the 1960s.

Its acceptance as the first example of documentary theater was an accident. Piscator's influential foreword to the book set it in a Schillerian tradition of historical drama, but he also stressed the factual elements; Hochhuth claimed to be the mouthpiece of history, providing a long appendix of *Historische Streiflichter* (Historical Sidelights) that dealt with his historical investigations. The attack on Pius XII's silence brought about international controversy in which the play was treated as history. Documents published as a consequence of this controversy shed doubt on some of Hochhuth's views; but despite aesthetic and historiographical failings, Hochhuth showed that live theater could still shake the world.

Hochhuth's *Soldaten: Nekrolog auf Genf* (1967; *Soldiers*), with many historical notes in the stage directions, was another occasion for public outrage. It presents Winston Churchill during the war as committing mass murder through the policy of bombing German cities and as the murderer of the Free Polish leader General Sikorski. Hochhuth carefully studied the bombing policy, which was topical because of the Vietnam War, and personally campaigned to outlaw bombing of civilian populations. But he lost two libel cases in Britain for the lack of available documents condemning Churchill. Hochhuth's Churchill, forced to choose between two equally destructive courses of action (destroying the Polish government on whose behalf Great Britain originally declared war or risking the loss of the vital Soviet alliance), becomes a tragic hero. Hochhuth's *Guerillas* (1970; Guerrillas) has an invented plot and characters; its documentary element consists of references, notes on facts, and the overall political aim.

Peter Weiss rose to fame with *Die Verfolgung und Ermordung Jean Paul Marats dargestellt durch die Schauspielgruppe des Hospizes zu Charenton unter Anleitung des Herrn de Sade* (1963; *The Persecution and Assassination of Jean Paul Marat . . .*). *Marat/Sade* is certainly a political play with two fairly balanced contenders: Sade represents political quietism and the belief in autonomous self-development, and Marat embodies values of social justice and solidarity. Virtuoso games with time, and with the lunatic asylum inmates and the obsessions of the characters they play, show an avant-garde creative project rather than the cool use of documented fact.

The Investigation consists largely of adapted and rearranged excerpts from the proceedings of the Frankfurt trial of warders from Auschwitz. The lengthy, diffuse trial is condensed into a short text, made abstract (a reality sui generis) and amenable to a cool rational analysis by the spectator. Weiss believed that Auschwitz was relevant to the 1960s, that crimes of the same nature were still being committed, and that our guilt could be assuaged—in Enlightenment fashion—only by understanding the state of the world and changing it. In the play, victims and persecutors in the camps are not groups separated by immutable fate, but are products of the same capitalist-fascist system; according to this view, a bureaucratic mass murder could happen again in any system that taps our latent asocial elements. Weiss's witnesses are not individuals but represent particular workings of social pressures; anything personal, emotional, or shocking is toned down.

His *Gesang vom lusitanischen Popanz* (1967; Song of the Lusitanian Bogeyman) tries to tell in 11 tableaux the story of Portuguese colonialism in Angola. The inhuman international colonialist and capitalist system, the object of Weiss's attack, is symbolically represented on stage by the eponymous bogeyman, a huge figure of scrap iron. Its language is a distillation of the clichés of authoritarianism with religious underpinnings; but nobody claims that the speeches were actually made by any Portuguese ruler. At first no theater in West Germany would touch this one-sided, undramatic play, which pleaded for Eastern bloc socialism. Again, its roles are depersonalized: individuals are made into oppressed or oppressors by the system, regardless of personality. In this play, Weiss avoids illusionism and empathy; the language with its varying rhythms fulfills a distancing function.

Another play with a mammoth title, generally abbreviated *Vietnam-Diskurs* (1968; Vietnam Discourse), is again consciously one-sided: it spans thousands of years, and it shows the Vietnamese people's efforts to shake off successive oppressors, concentrating on the then current war by using a mass of quoted material. Simple and monotonous, in rhythmically stylized language, it gives few opportunities for argument or for the audience to make up its own mind. How such a play could make bourgeois audiences act to aid the oppressed is unclear, but it did foster anti–Vietnam War feeling. The play was performed in Frankfurt, but practical corollaries to its radical message, including having a collection in aid of the Viet Cong, were disallowed.

Trotzki im Exil (1970; *Trotsky in Exile*), a biographical play, is factually based on quotations and documents, but its view of Trotsky was found to be too shallow. The play's canter through Russian history from 1900 to 1940 was too full of slogans and short circuits. In this play, Weiss sees politics and artistic endeavor as dual paths to revolutionary change; this view works against a Leninist emphasis on politics. Trotsky fails to come to life as a character because Weiss presents events in arbitrary order, as flashbacks from the aging revolutionary as he sits at his desk. As a whole, the author's interpretation of historical forces remains unclear.

Kipphardt made his mark with *Der Hund des Generals* (1962; The General's Dog). The plot was invented, but the intention of bringing Nazi crimes into public awareness was there; film and projected documents were used to give context. His *In der Sache J. Robert Oppenheimer* notched 27 productions in West Germany in 1964–65. It is based on the record of the U.S. government hearings about whether Oppenheimer, an atomic physicist who had once been in contact with communists and had refused to work on the hydrogen bomb, should be considered a security risk. Kipphardt tried, harder than any other documentary playwright, to stick verbatim to that record, excluding anything nonhistorical and taking a kernel of significance from the mass of material. Similar to Weiss's later work, he telescopes the number of witnesses. Monologues between scenes and an epilogue are invented. Unfortunately, what most interests Kipphardt, the conscience of the physicist, scarcely expressed itself in the hearings. The underlying problem of the physicist's responsibility for the destructive use made of his discoveries is greater than the historical Oppenheimer's personal dilemma. The character instead becomes a typical intellectual-as-hero with a tender conscience. Despite some optimism about the prospects of pure research, the conclusion is really pessimistic: individuals cannot influence what is wrong with our complex and divided world. We see in this play figures who are individuals but dependent on their function in the military-industrial complex, which Kipphardt takes as a given rather than something to be deconstructed.

In *Joel Brand: Die Geschichte eines Geschäfts* (1965; Joel Brand: The Story of a Deal), Kipphardt's aims are further from his documents. The plot turns on Adolf Eichmann's proposal to free 1 million Hungarian Jews if the allies provide 10,000 trucks for the German army. But the allies intern the middleman, Brand, rather than listen to him; Eichmann's speculation with the moral interests of the allies fails; and the Jews of Budapest are taken to Auschwitz. What interests Kipphardt—Eichmann's background and whether anyone, subjected to the same forces, might have become an Eichmann—is remote from the documents, and the Eichmann portrayed is not a historically accurate figure. All the characters, even Eichmann, are only subordinates, victims of fate, with little scope for action in the implicitly accepted, unexplained circumstances. The play is thus a tragedy.

Günter Grass's *Die Plebejer proben den Aufstand* (1966; *The Plebeians Rehearse the Uprising*) is set in the Berliner Ensemble on 17 June 1953, as Bertolt Brecht works out his confused, inadequate response to the East German workers' rising. Interestingly, however, Brecht is referred to as "der Chef" throughout; moreover, the play in rehearsal is not, as in reality, Strittmatter's *Katzgraben,* but Shakespeare's *Coriolanus*. *Plebeians* is as much about the intellectual and politics in general as about Brecht; it diverges greatly from fact (Grass called it a model presentation) and gives little useful analysis of Brecht, who emerges as an aesthete because Grass does not take his politics seriously. Nor does Grass think Brecht could have made a political difference on 17 June even had he wished to do so, which undermines the play.

Tankred Dorst's *Toller* (1968; Toller) uses quotations and documents, not to underline some historical truth inherent in the play, but as particles of reality. Rejecting the claims of documentary drama, Dorst said that he did not write to correct people's view of a historical episode, the Bavarian Räterepublik (Soviet republic) of 1918–19. The events of history have been compressed and dramatized, although realistically presented. The audience can interpret the events, Toller's attitude, and Dorst's view of it at will.

Hans Magnus Enzensberger's *Das Verhör von Habana* (1970; The Havana Hearings) was conceived as reconstructing a revolutionary act, the 1961 hearings of Cubans involved in the Bay of Pigs fiasco, with added scenes from the military action in other parts of the country. Enzensberger claimed that every word of the text had been said in Havana. His aestheticization of the text by selection and stage treatment was supposed to produce an artificial theatrical entity with a functional effect. The theme is the counterrevolutionary, reactionary potential of the frequently unconscious ideology of the middle class. The play shows solidarity with the Cuban revolution and wishes to generalize from it, although what Cuban lessons could be applied to West Germany, or how the German audience could learn them, was unclear. The characters are described as types with whom the audience could identify and whose failure, manifest through the hearings, should make their German counterparts think. But even after listening to the scenes, members of the audience showed typical shortsighted attitudes to problems of trade unionism or land reform.

The purest documentary plays retain dramatic conflict and let the spectator interpret and decide between attitudes, while presenting a left-wing slant backed with evidence. But the movement remained part of the system of capitalist publishing and subsidized theaters, and it filled only the vacuums that the system offered. Its sole political effect was to activate those who were already intellectual and leftward-orientated; it did not directly reach wider audiences. At the Frankfurt premiere of *Popanz,* the play was overtaken from the Left: students occupied the stage demanding that the audience leave the theater and join a demonstration.

ALFRED D. WHITE

See also Socialist Realism

Further Reading

Barton, Brian, *Das Dokumentartheater,* Stuttgart: Metzler, 1987
Blumer, Arnold, *Das dokumentarische Theater der sechziger Jahre in der Bundesrepublik Deutschland,* Meisenheim: Hain, 1977
Subiotto, A.V., *German Documentary Theatre,* Birmingham: University of Birmingham Press, 1972
Zipes, Jack D., "The Aesthetic Dimensions of the German Documentary Drama," *German Life and Letters* 24 (1971)

Heimito von Doderer 1896–1966

Franz Carl Heimito Ritter von Doderer was born in Weidlingau-Hadersdorf, near Vienna. The unusual name Heimito, a diminutive of the Spanish Jaime, seems to have been the choice of his mother, who heard it during a vacation in Spain. Combining it with the archaic Heimo resulted in Heimito. The knighthood (Ritter von) had been bestowed on Doderer's grandfather in recognition of his work as an architect who participated in designing the military arsenal constructed after the revolution of 1848. Heimito, the youngest of six children, graduated from the Gymnasium in 1914 and, after a semester as a student of law at the University of Vienna, joined a cavalry regiment.

The young knight—outfitted with well-tailored uniform, saber, and a fine horse paid for by papa, riding off into the mindless carnage of World War I—represents well the two worlds in which Doderer's life and work are located. For the rest of his life, he combined traditional postures, such as habits of dress and gestures of courtesy, with anything but conforming bourgeois private behavior. The tension between outward control and inner rage characterizes many of Doderer's works, including the grotesquely humorous short stories and novels *Die erleuchteten Fenster* (1950; The Illuminated Windows) and *Die Merowinger* (1962; The Merovingians), as well as in the panoramas of prefacist Austria, such as *Die Dämonen* (1956; *The Demons*).

Doderer's brief military service on the Eastern Front came to an abrupt end when he was captured by the Russians near Olesza in Galicia on 12 July 1916. He then spent four years in Siberian prisoner-of-war (POW) camps. The camaraderie of the camp life, the clash of the forces opposing each other during and after the Russian Revolution, and not least of all, the experience of the vastness of the Russian-Siberian landscape were to be formative and permanent influences. In the summer of 1920, he and seven other POWs left the camp and, as Wolfgang Fleischer describes in his detailed biography, made their way not as escapees but as soldiers returning home, supported and nourished by the local population—in part on train, in part on foot—reaching St. Petersburg and proceeding through the Baltic states to Stettin

(Szczecin) and then by German military transport to Vienna, where he arrived at his parents' house on 14 August 1920.

Having begun to write while on leave in 1916, Doderer continued to compose short prose sketches in POW camp (collected in *Die Sibirische Klarheit* [1993; Siberian Clarity]). Back in Vienna, he decided to "become a writer." His diaries reveal the single-minded determination with which he set to developing his skills, studying history and psychology, writing daily, making long reading lists, and keeping track of works read and those to be reread. Although plagued by self-doubt, he stuck to this goal with amazing tenacity for the rest of his life. Little could he know that more than 30 years and another world war would go by before broad recognition and commercial success would be his. Although he had published articles, essays, stories, and novels, it was not until 1951, with the publication of *Die Strudlhofstiege; oder, Melzer und die Tiefe der Jahre* (1951; The Strudlhof Steps or Melzer and the Depth of Years), that he was finally established and thus rid of constant money worries.

With the public recognition of this novel began the construction of a Doderer myth, contributed to by the author himself, an eager press, and an eager public. He became an Austrian icon, a modern-day Austrian Dostoyevsky, a 20th-century relic of the great 19th-century prose-writing tradition. Public presentations, readings, awards, speeches, and all the trappings of commercial success were showered on Doderer, finally confirming his determination over at least three decades. In 1956, the publication of his magnum opus *The Demons* put the icing on the cake of recognition. His popularity peaked in 1957 with his rakish countenance on the cover of the news magazine *Der Spiegel*. Public hoopla continued until his death. However, by and by, unsavory tidbits of Doderer's life emerged, from his brief membership in the (then) illegal National Socialist Party to his broad-spectrum sexual appetites. The deconstruction of the Doderer myth culminated in 1966 with the publication of the minutely researched biography by Wolfgang Fleischer, Doderer's personal secretary for the last three years of the author's life. What emerges might best be described as a writer whose private behavior was frequently self-serving and who sacrificed virtually everything to his writing.

The novels that established Doderer as a major figure in postwar German literature are distinguished by a truly original voice. In *Die Strudlhofstiege* and *The Demons,* Doderer reaches back to the great humorists Jean Paul and Wilhelm Raabe. Both novels instantly establish a narrative voice that is brimming with comfort and gentle tolerance, clearly omniscient, sharing confidences, including the reader in embracing "we's," and inviting us to be as understanding of human foibles as the narrator himself. Doderer's language, peppered with idiosyncratic but highly apt symbols and metaphors, sparkles with subtlety and originality. His unrelenting focus on the craft of writing and his maniacal insistence on daily practice for nearly four decades result in freshness of language, erudition without pomposity, and an extraordinary suppleness.

Before Doderer achieved a measure of success, he had written short pieces for various Viennese newspapers; a volume of poetry (*Gassen und Landschaft* [1923; Alleys and Landscapes]); a short novel (*Das Geheimnis des Reiches* [1930; The Mystery of the Empire]), partly based on his experiences in Russia; and in 1938, after establishing a connection with the Munich publisher Biederstein (later C.H. Beck), his first substantial novel, *Ein Mord den jeder begeht* (1938; *Every Man a Murderer*). Written in the shadow of horror in Dachau, the provocative title does not point to a connection with the historical realities of Doderer's surroundings. Rather, it is the story of a young man who, as part of a prank, has unwittingly killed a young woman and who spends the rest of the novel first being haunted by the image of the victim and then setting out to find the murderer, only to discover that he did it. The circular pattern of the plot, interwoven with the notion of ineluctable personal destiny, has only the faintest connection with the historical background.

Doderer's next novel, *Ein Umweg* (1940; A Detour), brings together the notion of predetermined fate with the author's penchant for and detailed knowledge of early German history. The novel tells of the fate of the soldier during the Thirty Years' War who is rescued from the gallows by a woman willing to marry him. A young Spanish count enters into the plot, and, in a kind of crossing of fates, the German soldier trying to avoid the gallows ends up being hanged, and the young count, who falls in love with the woman who rescued the rascal, is in the end killed by the soldier. No one seems to be able to extricate himself from his destiny. This second novel, published by Biederstein, still did not gain Doderer much recognition or relief from permanent money worries.

In April 1940, Doderer wrote to the U.S. Consulate General in Vienna to apply for emigration to the United States, converted to Catholicism, and was drafted into the German air force, in which he served until his capture by the British in Norway near the end of the war. Again, Doderer managed to write during his military service and made a point of preserving a private sphere in the midst of the madness of the war. During the enforced absence from Vienna, the image and possible metaphoric significance of the elaborate set of steps known as the *Strudlhofstiege* captured his imagination, and, beginning with his diaries during the war, the breakthrough novel named after these stairs took shape. Postwar poverty and hunger (combined with a brief *Schreibverbot* imposed because of Doderer's membership in the Nazi party) and the effort required to finish the immense undertaking took up the next five years. Success finally came in 1951 with the publication of the novel *Die Strudlhofstiege.*

The set of outdoor steps called *Strudlhofstiege* functions in the novel as a meeting place or, rather, a criss-crossing place for different characters as well as a symbol of Viennese and, by extension, Western civilization. Melzer represents a tentative link to the tradition of the bildungsroman inasmuch as his *Menschwerdung*—his slow maturation and growing understanding of human relationships—forms an important part of the novel. Recent criticism has argued that Melzer moves from immature rigidity to mature flexibility, only to return to fossil status. The phrase "Tiefe der Jahre" points to a very important strategy in almost all Doderer's writing: events are almost always told from considerable historical distance. Doderer avoids writing as a contemporary, and in theoretical writing and diary entries, he argues for the critical importance of memory. A romantic-mystical streak in Doderer places much faith in the operations of the subconscious or emotions recollected in tranquillity.

Doderer's penchant for recollection is especially manifest in his next and second major novel, which ensured his reputation and his finances. *The Demons* (with the same title as the German translation of Dostoyevsky's *The Possessed*), set in the 1920s, aims to give a sense of the dawning Hitler era. A sweeping panorama of life in Vienna, moving with Dickensian inclusiveness through all levels of society, it has as its focal point the burning of the "Justizpalast" on 15 July 1927. Doderer thought that this represented the "Cannae" of Austrian freedom, and he succeeds in portraying the mindless rage and the ominousness of the quasi-criminal behavior of rioters. However, the strongest impressions that the novel leaves are the symbols pointing to the senselessness of violence. During the riots, an innocent woman carrying a pail of milk is killed, and the description of the milk mingling with her blood on the sidewalk remains a haunting image, not coincidentally also pointing to the Austrian colors. In the end, this novel will remain an outstanding achievement in 20th-century German literature because of its encompassing scope, the freshness and beauty of its language, the lucidity of its composition, and its memorable characters.

One aspect of Doderer's work that is easily overlooked is its humor, which is unquenchable and often shading into the grotesque. It is found not only in several exquisite short and "shortest" stories but also in two novels: *Die erleuchteten Fenster* and *Die Merowinger.* The former is at the same time a caricature of the Austrian (or any) petty bureaucrat and the slow process of overcoming the mental rigidity acquired from a lifetime's diet of legalisms and rule books, complete with episodes of fairly harmless voyeurism and a fairy-tale ending reminiscent of Mozart's *Magic Flute.*

Die Merowinger is a grotesque romp satirizing medical, psychological, political, and business institutions. Childerich, a late descendant of the medieval Merovingians, is bent on accumulating a confusion of beard styles and marrying, divorcing, and remarrying with dizzying mindlessness to utterly confuse normal family relationships. In the end, his raging hormones are quieted by surgical castration.

Doderer's last major writing project remained incomplete. Only one of four planned novels subsumed under the code *Roman No. 7* was finished: *Die Wasserfälle von Slunj* (1963; *The Waterfalls of Slunj*). It charts the family history of an English family living and working in Austria in the late 19th to early 20th centuries and explores the contrast between those who can live with and fully accept the way things are, especially the (uncontrollable) powers of nature, and those who are destroyed by the sheer presence of its force, symbolized, among other things, by the waterfalls. The second novel, *Der Grenzwald* (fragment, 1967; The Forest at the Border) returned again to the time in Siberian POW camps during and after World War I. The fragments that do exist allow a glimpse into what would surely have become a work close to Doderer's ideal of what he called the "roman muet" (the quiet novel), in which the narrator and his ideology recede into the background.

In addition to these major works are a series of short stories, an array of theoretical works, and several massive volumes of diaries, almost impenetrable to nonspecialists. A slim volume of aphorisms collected under the Baroque title *Repertorium* (1969) represents a treasure of the wit and flashes of verbal brilliance that are the hallmark of Heimito von Doderer.

MICHAEL BACHEM

Biography

Born in Weidlingau-hadersdorf, Austria, 5 September 1896. Reserve officer, Austrian dragoon regiment, 1915; prisoner of war, Siberia, 1916; Ph.D. in history from the University of Vienna, 1925; drafted into the German Air Force, 1940; examiner of potential Luftwaffe officers, Vienna 1943; prisoner of war, Norway, 1945; member of the Nazi Party, 1933–38; converted to Roman Catholicism, 1940; reader for a publisher, Vienna, 1946; banned from publishing works until 1950. Confederation of German Industry Novelist's prize, 1954; Austrian State Grand Award, 1954; Prikheim Medal of Nuremburg, 1958; Raabe Prize, 1966; ring of Honour of the City of Vienna, 1966; member of the Institute for Research in Austrian History, 1950. Died 23 December 1966.

Selected Works

Collections

Frühe Prosa, edited by Hans Flesch-Brunningen, 1968
Die Erzählungen, edited by Wendelin Schmidt-Dengler, 2 vols., 1973–76
Commentarii: Tagebücher aus dem Nachlass, edited by Wendelin Schmidt-Dengler, 2 vols., 1976–86
Das Doderer-Buch: Eine Auswahl aus dem Werk Heimito von Doderers, edited by Karl Heinz Kramberg, 1976

Fiction

Die Bresche: Ein Vorgang in vierundzwanzig Stunden, 1924
Das Geheimnis des Reichs, 1930
Ein Mord den jeder begeht, 1938; as *Every Man a Murderer,* translated by Richard and Clara Winston, 1964
Ein Umweg, 1940
Die erleuchteten Fenster; oder, Die Menschwerdung des Amtsrates Julius Zihal, 1950
Die Strudlhofstiege; oder, Melzer und die Tiefe der Jahre, 1951
Das letzte Abenteuer, 1953
Die Dämonen, 1956; as *The Demons,* translated by Richard and Clara Winston, 1961
Die Posaunen von Jericho: Neues Divertimento, 1958; as "The Trumpets of Jericho," translated by Vincent Kling, in *Chicago Review* 26, no. 2 (1974)
Die Peinigung der Lederbeutelchen (stories), 1959
Die Merowinger; oder, Die totale Familie, 1962
Roman No. 7:
  Die Wasserfälle von Slunj, 1963; as *The Waterfalls of Slunj,* translated by Eithne Wilkins and Ernst Kaiser, 1966
  Der Grenzwald (fragment), 1967
Unter schwarzen Sternen (stories), 1966
Meine neunzehn Lebensläufe und neun andere Geschichten, 1966
Die Wiederkehr der Drachen: Aufsätze, Traktate, Reden, edited by Wendelin Schmidt-Dengler, 1972
Die Sibirische Klarheit, 1993

Poetry

Gassen und Landschaft, 1923
Ein Weg im Dunklen: Gedichte und epigrammatische Verse, 1957

Other

Der Fall Gütersloh: Ein Schicksal und seine Deutung, 1930
Von der Unschuld des Indirekten, 1947
Grundlagen und Funktion des Romans, 1959; as "Principles and Functions of the Novel," in *30th International Congress of the P.E.N. Clubs,* 1959
Wege und Unwege, edited by Herbert Eisenreich, 1960
Die Ortung des Kritikers, 1960
Albert Paris Gütersloh: Autor und Werk, with others, 1962
Tangenten: Tagebuch eines Schrifstellers 1940–1950 (correspondence), 1964
Mit der Sprache leben, with Herbert Meier and Josef Mühlberger, 1965
Repertorium: Ein Begreifbuch von höheren und niederen Lebens-Sachen, edited by Dietrich Weber, 1969

Briefwechsel 1928–1962, with Albert Paris Gütersloh, edited by Reinhold Treml, 1986

Edited Work

Albert Paris Güterloh, *Gewaltig staunt der Mensch,* 1963

Further Reading

Bachem, Michael, *Heimito von Doderer,* Boston: Twayne, 1981

Barker, Andrew W., "Heimito von Doderers 'Indirekter Weg,'" *Forum for Modern Language Studies* 18, no. 4 (1982)

———, "Heimito von Doderer and National Socialism," *German Life and Letters* 42, no. 2 (1988)

Fleischer, Wolfgang, *Das verleugnete Leben: Die Biographie des Heimito von Doderer,* Vienna: Kremayr und Scheriau, 1996

Hopf, Karl, "Die Funktion der Tagebücher Heimito von Doderers," *Modern Austrian Literature* 24, no. 1 (1991)

Jones, David, "Heimito von Doderer and Man's Existential Fear," *Papers on Languages and Literature: A Journal for Scholars and Critics of Language and Literature* 20, no. 2 (1984)

Loew-Cadonna, Martin, "Suspense in Doderers Erzählen," *Sprachkunst: Beiträge zur Literaturwissenschaft* 21, no. 2 (1990)

Luehrs, Kai, "'Fassaden-Architektur': Zur Struktur der Wiener Romane Heimito von Doderers," *Zeitschrift für deutsche Philologie* 114, no. 4 (1995)

McInnes, Malcolm, "Doderer versus Hausmeister," *German Life and Letters* 41, no. 2 (1988)

Sommer, Gerald, and Wendelin Schmidt-Dengler, editors, *Erst bricht man Fenster, dann wird man selbst eines: Zum 100. Geburtstag von Heimito von Doderer,* Riverside, California: Ariadne Press, 1997

Trommler, Frank, *Österreich im Roman: Eine Untersuchung zur dargestellten Wirklichkeit bei Joseph Roth, Robert Musil, und Heimito von Doderer,* Munich: 1965

Weber, Dietrich, *Heimito von Doderer,* Munich: Beck, 1987

Die Strudlhofstiege 1951

Novel by Heimito von Doderer

Heimito von Doderer's 909-page novel *Die Strudlhofstiege; oder, Melzer und die Tiefe der Jahre* (1951; The Strudlhof Steps; or, Melzer and the Depth of the Years) brought Doderer the recognition he had labored for since the early 1920s. A big-city novel comparable to Döblin's *Berlin Alexanderplatz* (1929), the work "emerged" in Doderer's diaries during the 1940s while he was an officer in the German air force. Rich in detail, complicated but lucid in its four-part composition, it portrays the lives of a group of friends in the pre–World War I Austro-Hungarian Empire and in Vienna in the 1920s. Doderer traces the development of Lieutenant Melzer, whose first name we never learn, as well as the life of a number of other characters, prominent among them René Stangeler, the author's alter ego; Etelka and Asta, the alter egos of the author's sisters, Astri and Helga; Mary K., the beautiful widow; Rittmeister Eulenfeld, the shady and delightfully sarcastic older gentleman; and a host of characters, some of whom had populated earlier narratives (Zihal) and some of whom will later become key figures in other Doderer novels, for example, Mary K. in *Die Dämonen* (1956; *The Demons*).

The novel has no single story line but rather a series of contiguous plots. If a center exists, it is the protagonist mentioned in the title, whose life is touched or who touches most. At the heart is the gradual maturation of Melzer, who develops from a nice, obedient young man who is essentially always taken along and dropped off somewhere to an equally nice young man who at the moment of a terrible streetcar accident has the presence of mind to save the life of the victim, Mary K. As Gerald Sommer has shown in his analysis of the novel, the streetcar scene reverberates with religious symbols, Melzer holding the wounded Mary K. as if depicting a Pietá and at the same time a moment of mystical change for the protagonist.

The novel also traces the development of a number of other characters, such as Doderer's alter ego, René Stangeler; Doderer's sister Astri is transformed into Asta in the novel, and his real sister, Helga, becomes the tragic suicidal Etelka of the novel. A thin plot involving smuggling Austrian tobacco to Germany, mixing up identical twins, and assorted love affairs contributes to the action.

Very much the work of a mature writer who had been practicing his word craft at least since his days in a Siberian prisoner-of-war camp (1916–20), the novel speaks with the voice of a unique and unmistakable narrator imbued with subtle, colorful, occasionally eccentric, and always entirely apt language. Doderer clearly has found his own voice, which for the first time in his oeuvre is sustained and fully confident. One sign of his consummate mastery is the appearance of an avuncular raconteur masking the painstaking attention to detail, weaving meaning into seemingly insignificant details with ease and comfort. Doderer's compositional skill and his original, highly lyrical language result in one of the most beautiful of German novels.

Tied to the heightened sense of storytelling is the role that memory plays as an organizing principle. The narrator's digressions, interjections, interpolated explanations, and flashbacks—all lucid and purposeful—are held together by the narrative voice, which quickly establishes a conciliatory, friendly-to-confiding tone and in a sense talks. Doderer, from a family of architects, planned this and other large compositions on large drawing boards and developed methods of color coding and his own shorthand to keep track of the composition. As a result, as Dietrich Weber has pointed out, the novel can be compared to an ornament, extraordinarily complicated but transparent in its design.

The staircase, part of the title of the novel, forms its literal and metaphoric center. An elaborate set of divided steps, not far from one of the many domiciles of the author, it is at the same time the place where various characters meet and their paths cross, and it gradually becomes an allegory for urban and urbane civilization. The architectural detail stands for decorum, civility, and manners and contrasts to what Doderer refers to as the chicken coup ladder of directness. In Doderer's language, the staircase constructed on a slope changes an abrupt and straight descent into decorative subdivisions, a simple gesture into an elaborate one. Gradually, this central metaphor begins to stand for civilized behavior itself.

It also serves as a symbol for the endurance of human artifacts and, strange as this might sound, as a metaphor for acceptance or tolerance. Doderer has coined a very apt code word capturing the meaning that he saw in this architectural detail of the city of Vienna: he identifies it as "die Umwegigkeit des Lebens," roughly translatable as "life's tendency to detour [or redirect] us." Doderer, who tried to keep his theorizing and philosophizing out of his novels, wrote repeatedly about the contrast of the direct and the indirect and constructed an elaborate theory defending his view that storytelling is quintessentially metaphoric or indirect.

In the novel, the indirect or "ex-centric" approach might mean beginning a chapter with peripheral details and then gradually moving toward the focus of the plot or the apparently aimless way in which a character such as Melzer develops, lounging on a bearskin and drinking strong coffee. Doderer, who has a streak of the mystic in him, often seems to prefer accidental apperception over conscious efforts to discover. An atmosphere, a scent, a fleeting noise, or glancing at the sky can produce a long chain of associations and in the end lead to more substantial insights than attempts at argumentation or theorizing.

One aspect of this novel might seem puzzling: written during and after Europe's years brimming with horror, virtually no reference is made to historical events or persons. Only the subtlest hints exist, such as when René Stangeler refers to the "Wahnsinn der Zeit" (the madness of the times). Yet, during one of the Turkish coffee-inspired conversations between Stangeler and Melzer, the author reveals what seems to be the reason for this apparent ignoring of "reality." It is tied to another one of Doderer's somewhat esoteric notions, namely, that of the distinction between what he calls "second reality" and "first reality." The former refers to the world as we want it or, more important, as ideologues want it to be at the cost of holocausts; the latter represents what Doderer refers to as the "fester Boden des wirklichen Seins" (firm ground of real being) or attempts to articulate in the aphorism of "lebensgemäß denken, nicht denkensgemäß leben" (thinking in harmony with life, not living according to thought).

In this and other novels, Doderer criticized ideology, but not by way of smuggling philosophizing into his novels in the manner of Thomas Mann but by mostly eliminating any ideology from his own brand of naturalism. Reaching back into the prehistory of the historical events of the 20th century, Doderer worked consciously against the traditional and prevailing trends in German novel writing. He thus ran the risk of being seen as a relic of bygone literary traditions. Not surprisingly, Doderer is often absent in studies of postwar German fiction. Only recently have critics begun to take a broader view and accept Doderer's depiction of pretotalitarian Europe as a legitimate way to grope toward understanding the unavoidable questions raised by Germany's recent history.

MICHAEL BACHEM

Editions

First edition: *Die Strudlhofstiege; oder, Melzer und die Tiefe der Jahre,* Munich: Biederstein, 1951

Further Reading

Achleitner, Friedrich, "Von der Unmöglichkeit, Orte zu beschreiben: Zu Heimito von Doderers *Strudlhofstiege,*" in *"Excentrische Einsätze": Studien und Essays zum Werk Heimito von Doderers,* edited by Kai Luehrs, Berlin and New York: de Gruyter, 1998

Haslinger, Adolf, editor, "Wiederkehr und Variation: Bildkette und Bildgefüge in Doderers Roman *Die Strudlhofstiege,*" in *Sprachkunst als Weltgestaltung: Festschrift für Herbert Seidler,* Salzburg: Pustet, 1966

Hinterhauser, Hans, "Heimito von Doderer und *Die Strudlhofstiege,*" in *Romanistik Integrativ: Festschrift für Wolfgang Pollak,* edited by Robert Tanzmeister, Vienna: Braumüller, 1985

Hirschbach, Frank D., "Heimito von Doderers *Die Strudlhofstiege:* Ein Roman der Zeit," *Papers on Language and Literatures: A Journal for Scholars and Critics of Language and Literature,* no. 3 (1967)

Hopf, Karl, "Von der 'Strudlhofstiege' zum 'Grenzwald': Die Funktion der Topographie in den Romanen Heimito von Doderers," *Österreich in Geschichte und Literatur* 16 (1972)

Luehrs, Kai, "'Fassaden-Architektur': Zur Struktur der Wiener Romane Heimito von Doderers," *Zeitschrift für deutsche Philologie* 114, no. 4 (1995)

Sommer, Gerald, *Vom "Sinn aller Metaphorie": Zur Funktion komplexer Bildgestaltungen in Heimito von Doderers Roman "Die Strudlhofstiege"—Dargestellt anhand einer Interpretation der Entwicklung der Figuren Mary K. und Melzer,* Frankfurt and New York: Lang, 1994

Weber, Dietrich, "Die Köstlichkeit all' ihrer Wegstücke in allen ihren Tagen': *Die Strudlhofstiege,*" in *Heimito von Doderer,* Munich: Beck, 1987

Tankred Dorst 1925–

Tankred Dorst is considered one of the best leading German contemporary authors. Since 1970 he has worked in close cooperation with Ursula Ehler, of whom he said in an interview: "She is a permanent mutual inspiration and a correction [of my ideas]. . . . Ursula also supplies ideas and innovations which merge with the material and enrich it." Dorst is known primarily for his experimental dramas, including theatrical productions for marionettes, and prose works; in both genres he offers various perspectives on postwar German society. His literary output also includes modern versions of plays and prose works, some written originally by Thomas Dekker, Denis Diderot, Hans Fallada, Heinrich Mann, and Ludwig Tieck; his fairy-tale plays; and his translations of Molière and Sean O'Casey.

In his early productions, Dorst uses parables, satires, and parodies in which he criticizes the shortcomings of modern society, especially as they occurred in the time of the *Wirtschaftswunder,* the economic miracle of West Germany. Portrayed in these mostly one-act plays are real estate speculators, as in *Gesellschaft im Herbst* (1960; Party in Autumn), and people making a living from the misfortune of others, as in *Die Kurve* (1962; *The Curve*). Dorst's affinity to Bertolt Brecht can be seen in his eastern parable *Grosse Schmährede an der Stadtmauer* (1961; *Grand Tirade at the Town-Wall*), a play that was performed successfully the same year as the wall was built in Berlin.

The 1960s and 1970s were times of political unrest, and literature was understood as a medium of making people aware of inadequate social and political situations. Writers such as Enzensberger, Grass, Hochhuth, Kipphardt, Scharang, Wallraff, Weiss, and others took issue with the subjective form of reporting present and past events in the mass media, especially television, and they turned to documentary literature in order to stem the *Wirklichkeitsverfälschung* (falsification of reality). Dorst also wrote some documentary works in which he described the psychological effects of external reality on the actions and beliefs of individuals. His best-known and most widely discussed drama is the semidocumentary revue play *Toller* (1968), which is about the Munich Soviet Republic of 1919. Its main character is the Expressionistic dramatist Ernst Toller, who symbolizes the difficult role of the intellectual and artist in the political arena, a problem treated also by other contemporaries of Dorst. This play had an added significance since its staging coincided with the student unrests of the late 1960s and early 1970s. Historical facts were also utilized in Dorst's television play *Sand* (1971), in which a student murders the writer Kotzebue, and in *Eiszeit* (1973; *Ice Age*). In the latter play, Dorst portrays the Nobel laureate Knut Hamsun's last years in a Norwegian old-age home. This play stirred up a controversy because Hamsun, who died in 1952, was a strong supporter of the Third Reich and stuck to his beliefs even after the atrocities of the Nazis became known. Dorst was criticized in Germany, as well as in the United States, for presenting Hamsun as an admirable character and a genius. While *Ice Age* is set in the postwar and postfascist period, his revue *Kleiner Mann—was nun?* (1972; Little Man—What Now?) takes place in the prefascist time of the late 1920s, portraying, according to Dorst, "not ideologies, but people, suffering small perpetrators of their time."

Dorst believes that a literary work benefits greatly from personalized historical experiences, and a large number of subsequent works derive from Dorst's family history. This is the case in his comedy *Auf dem Chimborazo* (1975; On Mount Chimborazo) and the novel *Dorothea Merz* (1976). The latter's life is shown against the cultural, political, and social events of the period between the 1920s and 1930s, reconstructed through diary entries, photographs, and dialogues. Implicit is Dorst's criticism of the middle class, whose members did not recognize the dangers of fascism in 1933. *Klaras Mutter* (1978; Klara's Mother), part of the family saga, contains a very touching mother-daughter relationship, probably the result of Ursula Ehler's collaboration. Set in approximately the same time frame is the prose work *Die Reise nach Stettin* (1984; The Trip to Stettin), which bears witness to the destruction caused by the war and the so-called evacuation of the Jews. All of these works deny the *Stunde Null*, or zero-hour, because past experiences and suffering of the people are seen to be continued into the present and future. This is true for people in the socialist East and the capitalistic West, the latter exemplified in *Mosch* (1978).

In Dorst's plays, characters usually do not succeed in making our world a better one, "in which the spirit shall rule over chaos," as he writes in *Merlin* (1981). With 97 scenes in 375 pages and a seven-hour stage performance, this play is one of the longest texts in German theater. Merlin, a medieval magician and the son of the devil, has good intentions, but these are thwarted by "idealists, the seekers of the Holy Grail, the founders of Round Tables and ideal states, who proclaim new theories and promise salvation and want to bring the great happiness to mankind through new regimes and systems." Neither Merlin nor Percival (in *Parzival*, 1990), the legendary Grail-seeker, turns this imperfect world around; Percival causes destruction wherever he goes, not because he is evil, but because he does not know any better. Christianity, so Dorst seems to be saying, is powerless to govern the conduct of men. This is also the case in *Korbes* (1988; Korbes), whose title character is a monster in human form, and in Dorst's play *Nach Jerusalem* (1994; To Jerusalem), in which six characters, outcasts from society, are in a futile search for happiness, which does not lie in the possession of material goods, as Dorst also shows in his comedy *Wegen Reichtum geschlossen: Eine metaphysische Komödie* (1998; Closed Because of Affluence: A Metaphysical Comedy).

Recurring in many of Dorst's plays is the blending of truth and illusion—on the personal level in *Ich, Feuerbach* (1986; I, Feuerbach) and on the political level in his fragmentary play *Der verbotene Garten* (1988; The Forbidden Garden), in which d'Annunzio tries to force the vision of his invented aestheticized world upon his contemporaries, thereby lending support to Mussolini and the spread of fascism. All of these plays show that truth is subjective and that men and women cannot clearly distinguish between reality and illusion; the subtitle "An Attempt about Truth" that Dorst gave to his play *Fernando Krapp hat mir diesen Brief geschrieben* (1992; Fernando Krapp Wrote Me the Letter) applies to many of his later productions. A further problem for Dorst is that value systems and people change over time, so that a once-recognized truth is not eternal and may be different for different generations. This the case in the play *Die Schattenlinie* (1995; The Shadow Line), in which the son of an enlightened intellectual turns to racism and murder despite his tolerant and enlightened upbringing. Here, Dorst criticizes liberals who fight for peace and solidarity globally but neglect to practice these ideals at home.

It is not surprising that Tankred Dorst is considered one of the most dominant figures on the German literary scene, especially in the theater. He is well received, not only by intellectuals, but also by the general public, which finds his works educational and entertaining. Many of his works have appeared on German television and as radio plays, and he is also known through the many interviews he has given. His works span the period of almost 30 years and show the interfacing of a given sociohistorical development with the problematic nature of man. To him, man is a complex being, made up of rational and irrational elements, who has difficulties distinguishing clearly between reality and illusion and, therefore, makes mistakes. Important, however, is that human beings do not give up their vision, even if it cannot be realized, as is usually the case with Dorst's characters. The common denominator of Dorst's plays is, as he himself stated in a recent interview, the failed utopia: "When I view all of my plays then I see very clearly that they are very similar. . . . The failed utopia is a topic which I have always dealt with."

GERD K. SCHNEIDER

Biography

Born in Oberlind bei Sonneberg, Thüringen, 19 December 1925. Drafted into the military at the age of 16; resumed his study of German literature in 1951 at the University of Bamberg and the University of Munich, where he also studied art history and drama; since the late 1950s Dorst has worked as a freelance playwright; his play *Toller* received international attention, 1968; began collaborating with Ursula Ehler, 1970s. He is one of the most frequently performed playwrights of the contemporary German stage. Prize of the National Theater, Mannheim, 1960; City of Munich Prize, 1964; Hauptmann Prize, Berlin, 1964; City of Florence Prize, 1970; Lisbon Theater Prize, 1970; Dramatist's Prize, Mülheim, 1989; Büchner Prize, 1990; first recipient of the Max Frisch Prize, Zürich, 1998.

Selected Works

Plays
Gesellschaft im Herbst, 1960
Große Schmährede an der Stadtmauer; Freiheit für Clemens; Die Kurve, 1962; as *Three Plays* (includes *Grand Tirade at the Town-Wall; The Curve; A Trumpet for Nap*), translated by Henry Beissel, 1976
Der Kater oder Wie man das Spiel spielt, 1963
Die Mohrin, 1964
Toller: Szenen aus einer deutschen Revolution, 1968
Sand: Ein Szenarium, 1971
Kleiner Mann—was nun? (after Hans Fallada), 1972
Eiszeit, 1973; as *Ice Age*, translated by Peter Sander, 1973
Auf dem Chimborazo, 1975
Goncourt oder Die Abschaffung des Todes, 1977
Mosch: Ein Film, 1978
Villa, 1980
Merlin; oder, Das wüste Land, 1981
Deutsche Stücke: Werkausgabe, 1985
Frühe Stücke, 1986
Ich, Feuerbach, 1986
Der nackte Mann, 1986
Politische Stücke, 1987
Korbes: Ein Drama (radio play), 1988
Der verbotene Garten: Fragmente über d'Annunzio, 1988
Parzival: Ein Szenarium, 1990
Wie im Leben wie im Traum und andere Stücke, 1990
Karlos: Ein Drama, 1990
Fernando Krapp hat mir diesen Brief geschrieben: Ein Versuch über die Wahrheit, 1992
Herr Paul: Ein Stück, 1993
Nach Jerusalem (radio play), 1994
Die Schattenlinie und andere Stücke, 1995
Die Legende vom armen Heinrich, 1996
Was sollen wir tun? Variation über ein Thema von Leo Tolstoi. Der Gott unter dem Ahornbaum. Die halb geöffnete Tür, 1996
Geschichte der Pfeile: Ein Tryptichon, 1996
Harrys Kopf, 1997
Wegen Reichtum geschlossen: Eine metaphysische Komödie, 1998

Essays
Das Geheimnis der Marionette, 1957
Auf kleiner Bühne-Versuche mit Marionetten, 1959
Die Bühne ist der absolute Ort, 1962

Fiction
Dorothea Merz, 1976
Klaras Mutter, 1978
Eisenhans: Ein Szenarium, 1983
Der verbotene Garten: Fragment über D'Annunzio, 1983
Die Reise nach Stettin, 1984
Grindkopf: Libretto für Schauspieler, 1986

Further Reading

Bekes, Peter, "Tankred Dorst," in *Kritisches Lexikon zur deutschsprachigen Gegenwartsliteratur*, edited by Heinz Ludwig Arnold, Munich: Edition Text und Kritik, 1978
Dorst, Tankred, and Markus Desaga, editors, *Auskünfte von und über Tankred Dorst*, Bamberg: Arbeitsbereich des Faches Neuere Deutsche Literaturwissenschaft Universität Bamberg, 1991
Erken, Günther, editor, *Tankred Dorst*, Frankfurt: Suhrkamp, 1989
Hanusch, Gisa, *Stillgestellter Aufbruch: Bilder von Weiblichkeit in den "Deutschen Stücken" von Tankred Dorst und Ursula Ehler*, Frankfurt and New York: Lang, 1996
Heller, Heinz B., "Tankred Dorst," in *Deutsche Literatur der Gegenwartsliteratur in Einzeldarstellungen*, vol. 2, edited by Dietrich Weber, Stuttgart: Kröner, 1977
Hoover, Marjorie L., "Tankred Dorst: *Klaras Mutter*," *World Literature Today* 53, no. 4 (1979)
Kux, Manfred, *Moderne Dichterdramen: Dichter, Dichtung, und Politik in Theaterstücken von Günter Grass, Tankred Dorst, Peter Weiss, und Gaston Salvatore*, Cologne and Vienna: Böhlau, 1980
Laube, Horst, editor, *Werkbuch über Tankred Dorst*, Frankfurt: Suhrkamp, 1974
Rothmann, Kurt, "Tankred Dorst," in *Deutschsprachige Schriftsteller seit 1945 in Einzeldarstellungen*, edited by Kurt Rothmann, Stuttgart: Reclam, 1985
Schneider, Gerd K., "Tankred Dorst," in *Contemporary German Fiction Writers*, edited by Wolfgang Elfe and James N. Hardin, Detroit, Michigan: Gale Research, 1988

Albert Drach 1902–1995

In 1988, Albert Drach received the Büchner Prize, Germany's most distinguished literary award. He was by then far beyond the age of 80. As his books were then republished, a new generation of readers and critics discovered one of the most original and radical writers in German literature since 1945. On several earlier occasions, the literary public sphere had become aware of Drach only to forget him again for decades. In 1968, the *Times Literary Supplement* called Albert Drach and Elias Canetti "the most talented avant-garde writers working in the German tongue." Nevertheless, the novelist and playwright remained an outsider to German literature. This obscurity derives in part from the life and fate of an Austrian Jew who, in 1938, had to leave his country after the so-called annexation of Austria by Nazi Germany.

In contrast to the often moralizing and didactic tone of German literature of the 1950s and 1960s, Drach's confrontation of Austria's fascist corporate state (1934–38), his own exile, and the restorative postwar era exhibits a provocative and cynically satirical style. Drach's unique, detached, and laconic language, his so-called *Protokollstil* (legalese style), became his trademark. While this legalese diction may pretend to render facts objectively, the actual literary protocol of Drach, who was both a lawyer and a Jew, is extremely tendentious and denunciatory: suspicions, slander, accusations, and value judgments are presented in a pseudo-objective manner as truths and facts. Drach borrows heavily from legal discourse and the subjunctive, as well as the complicated syntax of German, to enhance his style. In response to the powers of physical and verbal violence, Drach thus launched a subversive literary discourse that appears to have been assimilated to the bureaucratic and inhumane language of those in power—so as to break it open from within. A further ingredient of his prose is the thematization of sexuality. Since erotic effect and the representation of physical and psychological violence against women cannot be neatly separated in Drach's writings, this has led to characterizations that define his works as either pornographic or emancipatory. With his grotesque exaggerations and his view of language as a medium of manipulation, Drach follows the tradition of Austrian language critique, which reaches from Viennese popular theater of the 18th and 19th centuries through Karl Kraus to the early works of Peter Handke and the present work of Elfriede Jelinek.

Drach's first novel, *Das große Protokoll gegen Zwetschkenbaum* (1964; *The Massive File on Zwetschkenbaum*), was written in French exile in 1939. In this work, the fate of the Eastern European Talmudic scholar Schmul Leib Zwetschkenbaum mirrors the historical sufferings of the Jews. Zwetschkenbaum's legal predicament begins when he eats prunes that do not belong to him while under a prune tree by the same German name (Zwetschkenbaum). What follows is an odyssey through hospitals, mental institutions, and prisons during the era of the declining Habsburg monarchy. The novel is set during and immediately after World War I, and the naive hero becomes increasingly more entangled in the fangs of a malicious anti-Semitic environment whose logic of exclusion he fails to comprehend. Zwetschkenbaum's central problem poses itself as follows: How can understand one's suffering from within divine providence, and how can one take up guilt when one is innocent? The clash between the naive piety of the Talmudic scholar and the hostile anti-Semitic environment ultimately creates the novel's satirical and comical effect. Indeed, Zwetschkenbaum does not merely figure as the victim but also bears prophetic traits that make him appear as an incarnation of a higher being on earth.

Drach's autobiographic works cover the period from 1934 through 1950. *"Z.Z." das ist die Zwischenzeit* (1968; The Interim Era) recounts the increasingly precarious situation of Jews living in Austria's prewar era. The novel's object of inquiry, the son, as the author ironically refers to himself, is confronted with both latent and manifest anti-Semitism during a crucial phase in his search for identity. The responsibility of the father is passed on to the son at a time when political self-determination has lost its legitimation and Austria has turned into a protofascist, corporate state (1934–38). Again, the question of guilt takes up the novel's center. The more that his fellow citizens incriminate themselves in their attitude toward Jews, the more insistent the son becomes in taking up his own individual guilt. The sexual adventures of the hero have often been seen as signs of irresponsibility. The achievement of the novel, however, is the unsparing depiction in which the victim reclaims the right of the perpetrator. Imprisoned in historical accounts that distinguish only between victims and demonic perpetrators, survivors of the Holocaust often seem to have been deprived of their authorship of history. Drach's blatant disregard toward the victims has to be understood as an act of liberation. As such, Drach's perspective did not fit neatly into official postwar accounts, which contributed to the author's marginalization.

Unsentimentale Reise: Ein Bericht (1966; *Unsentimental Journey: A Report*) was written between 1945 and 1947, immediately after the author's return from his French exile. The novel, offering an ironic reply to Laurence Sterne's *A Sentimental Journey through France and Italy,* is indebted to the tradition of the German developmental novel, which is patterned after Goethe's *Wilhelm Meister.* In the style of the picaresque novel of the 17th and 18th centuries, Peter Kucku, the novel's hero and the author's alter ego, survives a series of dangerous incidents and amorous adventures. He repeatedly manages to escape capture by the Vichy authorities by means of deceit, lies, erratic flight, and cold-blooded composure at crucial moments of crisis. In one such instance, his Viennese identity papers bearing the abbreviation I.C.C. (Israelite Cultural Community) are translated as "In the Catholic Creed." Survival for Drach often bears the quality of a cynical joke. After internment in several French camps, Kucku reaches a mountain village in the backwoods of Nice, escaping the authorities once again under absurd circumstances. As a supposed non-Jew, who was not drafted to military service but finds himself in the middle of the war in Southern France, he appears equally suspicious to both locals and Nazi authorities. In his diary entries, published as *Das Beileid* (1993; Condolences), Drach depicts his own difficult and tedious return from Nice to the demoralized postwar Austria. For many years he had to battle with authorities to reclaim his former property.

In *Untersuchung an Mädeln: Kriminalprotokoll* (1971; Inquiry of Young Girls), Drach displays once again the strength of his protocol style. Two girls become the victims of a male chauvinist assembly comprised of legal officials, jurors, and a surrounding rural population, which is deeply rooted in the ideology of National Socialism. The novel likewise expresses the rebellious youth of Austria's 1960s, and it was adapted into a film in 1998. Drach's novels, narrations, and plays display the conflicting spirits of the Enlightenment, the libertin, and the pornographer the Marquis de Sade. It is no accident that his most well known play is entitled *Marquis de Sade* (1929). Drach's ethical position can be located in his breaking of taboos and in his provocative exposure of the petty criminal bourgeoisie that was largely responsible for the success of the Nazis.

BERNHARD FETZ

Biography

Born in Vienna, 17 December 1902. Studied law in Vienna and resided as a lawyer and writer in Mödling, near Vienna; escaped Nazi persecution, 26 October 1938, and fled to Yugoslavia, Paris, and Southern France; interned several times in France, he miraculously escaped deportation to a concentration camp; survived the war as an ice-skating instructor, mycologist, and translator for the Resistance Movement in the backwoods of Nice; worked as an interpreter for the American occupying forces in Nice; returned to Mödling, 1948, taking up his former profession as lawyer. Died in Drachhof, Mödling, 27 March 1995.

Selected Works

Collections
Gesammelte Werke, 5 vols., 1965, 1968

Novels

Das große Protokoll gegen Zwetschkenbaum, 1964, 1989; as *The Massive File on Zwetschkenbaum,* translated by Harry I. Dunkle, 1995

Die kleinen Protokolle und das Goggelbuch: Erzählungen, 1965; as *Ironie vom Glück: Kleine Protokolle und Erzählungen,* 1994; as *Das Goggelbuch,* 1993

Unsentimentale Reise: Ein Bericht, 1966, 1988; as *Unsentimental Journey: A Report,* translated by Harry I. Dunkle, 1992

"Z.Z." Das ist die Zwischenzeit, 1968, 1988

Untersuchung an Mädeln: Kriminalprotokoll, 1971, 1991

In Sachen de Sade: Nach dessen urschriftlichen Texten und seiner Kontaktpersonen, 1974

IA UND NEIN: Drei Fälle, 1992

Das Beileid: Nach Teilen eines Tagebuchs, 1993

O Catilina: Ein Lust- und Schauertraum, 1995

Further Reading

Fetz, Bernhard, editor, *In Sachen Albert Drach,* Vienna: WUV-Universitätsverlag, 1995

Fischer, André, *Inszenierte Naivität: Zur ästhetischen Simulation von Geschichte bei Günter Grass, Albert Drach, und Walter Kempowski,* Munich: Fink, 1992

Fuchs, Anne, "The Labyrinth and Abjection in Albert Drach's *Unsentimentale Reise,*" *Journal of German Life and Letters* 49, no. 2 (April 1996)

Fuchs, Gerhard, and Günter A. Höfler, editors, *Albert Drach,* Graz: Droschl, 1995

Gilman, Sander L., "Albert Drach's *Das große Protokoll gegen Zwetschkenbaum:* Madness and the Discourse of the Jews," *Modern Austrian Literature* 26, no. 2 (1993)

Preisendanz, Wolfgang, "Zum Vorrang des Komischen bei der Darstellung von Geschichtserfahrung in deutschen Romanen unserer Zeit," *Poetik und Hermeneutik* 7 (1976)

Schlant, Ernestine, "An Introduction to the Prose Narratives of Albert Drach," *Modern Austrian Literature* 13, no. 3 (1980)

———, "Albert Drach's *Unsentimentale Reise:* Literature of the Holocaust and the Dance-of-Death," *Modern Austrian Literature* 26, no. 2 (1993)

Annette von Droste-Hülshoff 1797–1848

Acclaimed during her lifetime for her poetry and her writings about Westphalia and celebrated after her death as a regional—and religious—writer by friends and critics in Germany, Annette von Droste-Hülshoff's initial reception was carefully managed by family members and friends who sought to promulgate an image of Droste as a recluse, devoted to her family, supportive of the values of her class and the conservative interests of the nobility, and faithful daughter of the church. More far reaching in impact, however, was the 1862 biographical sketch of Droste by Levin Schücking—her protégé, literary and personal confidant, and erstwhile literary agent. This self-serving portrayal has continued to affect the reception of Droste, her creative process, and her works.

The undeniable quality of her poetry and its nontraditional style and subject matter led early critics, including Schücking, to praise what they perceived to be the masculine nature of her writing. The same qualities gained Droste international recognition, and in 1961 she became the first woman author in the German language to be included in the British series *German Men of Letters.* Over the years critics have treated Droste as a Romantic, a realist, and a political conservative, as well as an associate of the liberal Jungdeutschen (the Young Germany movement); others have noted naturalist, Impressionist, and Expressionist qualities in her writings. While Friedrich Sengle's presentation of Droste as representative of Christian Biedermeier thought and ethics has become the dominant view, the often unconventional style and nature of some of Droste's best works defy simple classification. Her struggle to find her own voice and her rejection of both the kind of poetry associated with women's writing in the 19th century and the more radical and political tone of the liberal activists of her day have brought her in recent years both recognition as a forerunner of women's writing and high acclaim by contemporary German women writers and feminist critics. Throughout the years Droste's most discussed work has remained *Die Judenbuche* (1842; translated as *The Jew's Tree, The Jew's Beech Tree,* and *The Jew's Beech*), although Droste's poetry, particularly her ballads and poems set in the heath, have enjoyed continued popularity and have been anthologized and incorporated in school texts. More recently, attention has been directed to Droste as a woman writer, her friendships with women writers, her sense of self as woman, and the innovative qualities and modernity of her writings. Droste's extensive correspondence, her early and less popular works, and her humor have been addressed as well. The 100th anniversary of her death and the comprehensive historical-critical edition of her works nearing completion have contributed to both wider popular acclaim and increased scholarly interest.

Droste wrote poetry as a child; by her teens her desire for literary expression was a determined resolve. In addition to poetry, she began work in 1813 on *Bertha,* a tragedy, which she left unfinished; this was followed by a verse narrative, *Walter* (1818), and a semiautobiographical prose work, *Ledwina* (begun in 1819, later abandoned). A cycle of religious poetry intended for her grandmother, also begun in 1819, was redefined in subsequent years and later completed as *Das geistliche Jahr* (1851; The Spiritual Year). Following several attempts at publication, Droste published her first book-length collection of poetry in 1838. The 1842 publication of a number of poems in Johann

Friedrich Cotta's *Morgenblatt,* followed by the serial appearance of her Westphalian criminal tale, *The Jew's Tree,* established Droste's fame and position as Germany's foremost woman writer. The 1844 collection of her poetry under her full name cemented her position in the world of letters.

Droste's poetry encompasses highly popular ballads, many written in the early 1840s, such as "Der Schloßelf" (The Castle Elf), "Der Graue" (Waller), "Der Geierpfiff" (The Vulture's Whistle), "Der Tod des Erzbischofs Engelbert von Köln" (The Death of the Archbishop Engelbert of Cologne), and "Der Knabe im Moor" (The Boy in the Moor). She also produced lyric poetry unique in its expressive mode and its diversity, including the evocative imagery of "Haidebilder" (Scenes of the Heath) and the often muted social criticism of "Zeitbilder" (Commentary on the Times). In addition, she wrote poems intensely personal in focus, such as "Am Thurme" (On the Tower), "Mondesaufgang" (Moonrise), "Der Todesengel" (The Angel of Death), "Mein Beruf" (My Calling), and "Der Dichter—Dichters Glück" (The Poet—Poet's Bliss)—poems that also document Droste's growing sense of self and, ultimately, her self-affirmation as a poet. Droste's writing in her last years was hampered by illness, but it includes poems of unrivaled quality: "Die ächzende Kreatur" (Suffering Creation), "Im Grase" (Lying in the Grass), "Durchwachte Nacht" (Wakeful Night), "Die todte Lerche" (The Dead Lark), and "Lebt wohl" (Farewell).

Of her larger poetic works, the Alpine epic *Das Hospiz auf dem Großen St. Bernhard* (1827–37; The Hospice of St. Bernhard) and the historical verse epic *Die Schlacht im Loener Bruch* (1835–38; The Battle of Loener Bruch) received enthusiastic response from contemporaries. But the verse novella *Des Arztes Vermächtnis* (1833–37; The Doctor's Testament) and the verse narrative *Der "Spiritus familiaris" des Roßtäuschers* (1842; The Horse Trader's Demon) most clearly transcend the poetic practices of the 19th century and reveal exciting dimensions of Droste's poetic vision with their power of language, effective manipulation of narrative voice in the portrayal of their protagonists' uncanny experiences, and interplay of subjective and objective reality (features that also mark many of her shorter works). Droste's religious, unconventional *Das geistliche Jahr,* with its intense and often personal soul searching and its occasional note of existential anguish, warrants further critical examination.

Droste's plan for an extensive depiction of the Westphalian countryside and the life and customs of its people, styled in part after Washington Irving, dates to the early 1830s. Although never completed as envisioned, the project led to several prose works of diverse form and style. Central to her fame is the complex novella, referred to both as "A Criminal Story of the Paderborn Region" and as "Friedrich Mergel," published as *Die Judenbuche.* Droste's contribution to the genre of travel literature, *Westphälische Schilderungen* (Depictions of Westphalia; also called *Bilder aus Westfalen*), appeared in 1845 in the *Historisch-politische Blätter für das katholische Deutschland* and evoked regional controversy and familial consternation. The opening chapters of *Bei uns zu Lande auf dem Lande* (At Home in the Country), cast as a fictional diary, were published posthumously. Ironically it was not *The Jew's Tree* but *Westphälische Schilderungen* for which Droste was best known at the time of her death. Plans for a collection of narratives with Elise Rüdiger never materialized, and Droste completed only one portion of a longer narrative set in the Netherlands, the "criminal story" *Joseph* (1886; also published as *Mevrouw van Ginkel*). Noteworthy, too, is Droste's collaboration in the completion of Schücking's project *Malerisches und romantisches Westphalen* (1839; Picturesque and Romantic Westphalia), for which she not only contributed poetic works but also provided historical, anecdotal, and folkloric materials and text.

Droste's only completed drama, the comedy *Perdu! oder, Dichter, Verleger, und Blaustrümpfe* (1860, written in 1840; All's Lost! or, Poets, Publishers, and Bluestockings), is a tongue-in-cheek portrayal of the literary circle in Münster in which Droste participated briefly and is marked by wit, deft portraiture, and humorous dialogue. While she presents the group largely as it was perceived and judged by her family and their friends, the work's playful humor masks critical insights into the male domination of the publication world and the restricted nature of literary expression for women poets.

While filial and familial responsibilities required Droste to conduct extensive correspondence, other letters maintained communication with the outside world. Often gossipy and anecdotal and marked at times by role playing, even subterfuge, her letters reveal a keen sense of humor and a talent for caricature and droll, often playful depictions. Those written to literary-minded friends—Christoph Bernhard Schlüter, Wilhelm Junkmann, Sibylle Mertens, Adele Schopenhauer, and Elise Rüdiger, as well as Schücking—include discussions of literary plays and her creative mode and reveal her determination for publication and her concern with preserving the integrity of her texts. The recent, expanded, and documented edition has brought increased attention to Droste as a correspondent and constitutes a valuable resource.

GERTRUD BAUER PICKAR

Biography

Born in Schloß Hülshoff near Münster, Westphalia, 10 January 1797. Educated with her brothers; independent, extensive reading; interest in geology and natural science, folklore and superstition, and supernatural tales and phenomena; private instruction in singing, piano, and musical composition; in Rüschhaus with her mother and sister after the death of her father, 1826; travel to Cologne, Bonn, Coblenz, Eppishausen (Switzerland), and Meersburg. Died in Meersburg, 24 May 1848.

Selected Works

Collections

Gesammelte Schriften von Annette Freiin von Droste-Hülshoff, edited by Levin Schücking, 3 vols., 1878–79
Sämtliche Werke, edited by Karl Schulte Kemminghausen, 4 vols., 1925
Historisch-kritische Ausgabe, edited by Winfried Woesler, 14 vols., 1978–
Sämtliche Werke in zwei Bänden, edited by Bodo Plachta and Winfried Woesler, 1994

Poetry

Gedichte von Annette Elisabeth von D . . . H . . ., 1838
Gedichte von Annette Freiin von Droste-Hülshoff, 1844
Das geistliche Jahr: Nebst einem Anhang religiöser Gedichte von Annette von Droste-Hülshoff, edited by Christian Bernhard Schülter and Wilhelm Junkmann, 1851

Letzte Gaben: Nachgelassene Blätter von Annette Freiin von Droste-Hülshoff, edited by L. Schücking, 1860
Gedichte von Annette von Droste-Hülshoff, edited by Winfried Woesler, 1978

Fiction
Bei uns zu Lande auf dem Lande, 1860
Die Judenbuche, 1842; as *The Jew's Tree,* translated by Lionel and Doris Thomas, 1958; as *The Jew's Beech Tree,* translated by Michael Bullock, in *Three Eerie Tales from 19th Century German,* 1975; as *The Jew's Beech,* translated by Michael Fleming, in *Eight German Novellas,* 1997
Joseph, 1886
Ledwina, 1886; translated by David Ward, in *Bitter Healing,* 1990
Westphälische Schilderungen aus einer westphälischen Feder, 1845

Play
Perdu! oder, Dichter, Verleger, und Blaustrümpfe, 1860

Other
Briefe von Annette von Droste-Hülshoff und Levin Schücking, edited by Theo[phanie] Schücking, 1893
Briefe der Annette von Droste-Hülshoff und Levin Schücking, edited by Hermann Cardauns, 1909
Die Briefe der Annette von Droste-Hülshoff, edited by Karl Schulte Kemminghausen, 2 vols., 1944

Further Reading

Arend, Angelika, "'Es fehlt mir allerdings nicht an einer humoristischen Ader': Zu einem Aspekt des Briefstils der Annette von Droste-Hülshoff," *Monatshefte* 82 (1990)
———, "Humor and Irony in Annette von Droste-Hülshoff's 'Heidebilder'-Cycle," *German Quarterly* 63 (1990)
Berglar, Peter, *Annette von Droste-Hülshoff in Selbstzeugnissen und Bilddokumenten,* Reinbek bei Hamburg: Rowohlt, 1967
Bernd, Clifford Albrecht, "Clarity and Obscurity in Annette von Droste-Hülshoff's *Judenbuche,*" in *Studies in German Literature of the Nineteenth and Twentieth Centuries: Festschrift for Frederic E. Coenen,* edited by Siegfried Mews, Chapel Hill: University of North Carolina Press, 1970
Frederiksen, Elke, and Monika Shafi, "Annette von Droste-Hülshoff (1797–1848): Konfliktstrukturen im Frühwerk," in *Out of Line/Ausgefallen: The Paradox of Marginality in the Writings of Nineteenth-Century German Women,* edited by Ruth-Ellen Boetcher Joeres and Marianne Burkhard, Amsterdam and Atlanta, Georgia: Rodopi, 1989
Gödden, Walter, *Die andere Annette: Annette von Droste-Hülshoff als Briefschreiberin,* Paderborn: Schöningh, 1991
———, *Annette von Droste-Hülshoff: Leben und Werk, Eine Dichterchronik,* Bern and New York: Lang, 1994
Gössmann, Wilhelm, *Annette von Droste-Hülshoff: Ich und Spiegelbild, Zum Verständnis der Dichterin und ihres Werkes,* Düsseldorf: Droste, 1985
Guthrie, John, *Annette von Droste-Hülshoff: A German Poet between Romanticism and Realism,* Oxford and New York: Berg, 1989
Hallamore, Joyce, "The Reflected Self in Annette von Droste's Work: A Challenge to Self-Discovery," *Monatshefte* 61 (1969)
Heselhaus, Clemens, *Annette von Droste-Hülshoff: Werk und Leben,* Düsseldorf: Bagel, 1971
Morgan, Mary, *Annette von Droste-Hülshoff: A Woman of Letters in a Period of Transition,* Bern and Las Vegas, Nevada: Lang, 1981
Niethammer, Ortrun, and Claudia Belemann, editors, *Ein Gitter aus Musik und Sprache: Feministische Analysen zu Annette von Droste-Hülshoff,* Paderborn: Schöningh, 1992
Peucker, Brigitte, "Droste-Hülshoff's Ophelia and the Recovery of Voice," *Journal of English and German Philology* 82 (1983)
Pickar, Gertrud Bauer, "*Perdu* Relaimed: A Reappraisal of Droste's Comedy," *Monatshefte* 76 (1984)
———, "The Battering and Meta-Battering of Droste's Margreth: Covert Misogyny in *Die Judenbuche*'s Critical Reception," *Women in German Yearbook* 9 (1994)
———, "The 'Bauernhochzeit' in Droste's *Die Judenbuche:* A Contemporary Reading," in *Weltbürger, Textwelten: Helmut Kreuzer zum Dank,* edited by Leslie Bodi et al., Frankfurt and New York: Lang, 1995
———, *Ambivalence Transcended: A Study of the Writings of Annette von Droste-Hülshoff,* Columbia, South Carolina: Camden House, 1997
Plachta, Bodo, *"1000 Schritte von meinem Canapee": Der Aufbruch Annette von Droste-Hülshoffs in die Literatur,* Bielefeld: Aisthesis, 1995
Roebling, Irmgard, "Weibliches Schreiben im 19. Jahrhundert: Untersuchungen zur Naturmetaphorik der Droste," *Deutschunterricht* 38 (1986)
———, "Heraldik des Unheimlichen: Annette von Droste-Hülshoff (1797–1848), Auch ein Porträt," in *Deutsche Literatur von Frauen,* edited by Gisela Brinker-Gabler, vol. 2, Munich: Beck, 1988
Rölleke, Heinz, *Annette von Droste-Hülshoff: "Die Judenbuche,"* Bad Homburg: Gehlen, 1970
Salmen, Monika, *Das Autorbewußtsein Annette von Droste-Hülshoffs,* Frankfurt and New York: Lang, 1985
———, *Annette von Droste-Hülshoff und die moderne Frauenliteratur,* Bensberg: Thomas-Morus-Akademie, 1987
Schatzky, Brigitte E., "Annette von Droste-Hülshoff," in *German Men of Letters,* edited by Alex Natan, London: Wolff, 1961
Schneider, Ronald, *Realismus und Restauration: Untersuchungen zu Poetik und epischem Werk der Annette von Droste-Hülshoff,* Kronberg im Taunus: Scriptor, 1976
———, *Annette von Droste-Hülshoff,* Stuttgart: Metzler, 1977; 2nd edition, 1995
Sengle, Friedrich, *Biedermeierzeit: Deutsche Literatur im Spannungsfeld zwischen Restauration und Revolution, 1815–1848,* 3 vols., Stuttgart: Metzler, 1971–80
———, "Zum geschichtlichen Ort Annettes von Droste-Hülshoff (1797–1848)," in *Sprache und Bekenntnis: Hermann Kunisch zum 70. Geburtstag,* Sonderband des Literaturwissenschaftlichen Jahrbuchs, Berlin: Duncker and Humblot, 1971
Wells, Larry D., "Indeterminance as Provocation: The Reader's Role in Annette von Droste-Hülshoff's *Die Judenbuche,*" *Modern Language Notes* 94 (1979)
Woesler, Winfried, *Modellfall der Rezeptionsforschung: Droste-Rezeption im 19. Jahrhundert,* 2 vols., Frankfurt and Las Vegas, Nevada: Lang, 1980

Friedrich Dürrenmatt 1921–1990

Friedrich Dürrenmatt was a dramatist, prose writer, essayist, amateur painter of pronounced individuality, moralist *ex negativo,* and diagnostician of human dereliction. While his works may have occasional affinities with Kafka, the Epic Theater of Brecht, or existentialism, in his art he was foremost an experimentalist of prodigious imagination. His thought began to revolve early around a dramaturgic credo that he expounded in his *Theaterprobleme* (1955; *Problems of the Theater*), which left its mark on virtually all his works. Crucial to his theory is his notion of the grotesque, which has both stylistic and substantive connotations: our world of brutal enormities defies any reliable standards of moral reason and cannot be represented by the rational teleology of tragedy, but it can be presented with a comedic model of its grotesque distortions. The ensuing aesthetic *Verfremdung* (estrangement) may arouse a critical reevaluation of that world. The dramaturgic paradigm is not self-contained or "modernist"; although its links to reality are not didactically belabored, however, they are made amply manifest in eloquent imagery and episodic material. In his later writings, the image of the labyrinth is central. It implies the bewildering chaos of the human world, which in his plays and stories is underscored by the determining role of irrational chance, *Zufall,* in human destiny.

His early prose sketches and short tales (1942–51), collected in *Die Stadt* (1952; The City), have the character of parables akin to Kafka's and show a penchant for macabre situations and imagery. With two detective novels, *Der Richter und sein Henker* (1950–51; *The Judge and His Hangman*) and *Der Verdacht* (1951–52; *The Quarry*), which, contrary to the traditional *Krimi* (detective story), feature a flawed and scheming police inspector, Dürrenmatt attained popular success. By the 1970s, the printings of *The Judge and His Hangman* reached over 1 million copies. *Das Versprechen: Requiem auf den Kriminalroman* (1958; *The Pledge*) and *Die Panne* (1956; translated as *Traps* and *A Dangerous Game*) added to his reputation as a writer of unusual psychological fiction dealing with crime, guilt, and justice.

Dürrenmatt's nascent international renown, however, is due largely to some of the dramas that he wrote between 1947 and 1961. In the immediate postwar period, drama production in Germany was sparse, and Dürrenmatt, along with his Swiss compatriot Max Frisch, stepped into the breach. After his first drama, *Es steht geschrieben* (1947; It Is Written), which was about the 16th century German Anabaptists and fraught with irreverent burlesque humor, Dürrenmatt found his comedic voice in *Romulus der Große* (1948; translated as *Romulus* and *Romulus the Great*), which portrays the last Roman emperor as an ironic fool who makes sport of his alleged historic mission. Three subsequent plays with clearly aimed grotesque polemics contributed greatly to the author's eventual ranking as a "modern classic." *Die Ehe des Herrn Mississippi* (1952; *The Marriage of Mr. Mississippi*) enacts with many "epic" devices the clash of two prominent Western ideologies—bourgeois Old Testament fundamentalism and Marxism—and contrasts them with religious quietism. All three standard-bearers, however, come to grief in the face of capitalist venality, incarnated in the amoral Anastasia.

The breakthrough to world fame occurred with *Der Besuch der alten Dame* (1956; *The Visit*), a "tragic comedy" which lays bare with acerbic grotesque satire the moral cant and greed of the postwar consumer society. The play was performed all over Europe, East and West, and on Broadway in an adaptation by Maurice Valency in 1958; the play was made into a film in 1964. Eventually, the play was shown in nearly 50 countries and printed in a score of translations. *Die Physiker* (1962; *The Physicists*) focuses on both the threat to human civilization by the advance of science and technology and the moral responsibility of the scientist. Within the structural limits of a classical drama, the world is presented *in nuce* in an insane asylum, where the attempts of a physicist to quash his new and potentially lethal theories are thwarted by the insane resident psychiatrist who, in league with the military-industrial complex, has dreams of world dominion. The drama immediately conquered world stages; even in the 1980s, it still figured among the most often performed plays in Germany. Since their inception, *The Visit* and *The Physicists* enjoyed great popularity in Eastern Europe and Russia, where they were hailed as anti-capitalist manifestos.

The drama *Ein Engel kommt nach Babylon* (1954; *An Angel Comes to Babylon*) brings to the fore Dürrenmatt's notion of the "courageous man" who in outer defeat sets his inner world in order; this notion is a vestige of the tragic outlook that is modulated throughout his dramatic oeuvre. Dürrenmatt's eight radio plays, which were written in the same period, are topically related to the detective novels and some dramas but have suffered from the decline of interest in the genre as such in the late 20th century. From the middle 1960s to the end of his life, his stage plays became more experimental and elicited varying critical responses. In *Der Meteor* (1966; *The Meteor*), the startling resurrection of an immortal writer serves as a foil for the existential failings of the people around him. *Porträt eines Planeten* (1970; Portrait of a Planet) highlights in a series of set pieces a good life on earth as a patently missed opportunity by its denizens, as they face the impending end of the planet in a cosmic conflagration. In his adaptations of two Shakespeare plays, *König Johann* (1968) and *Titus Andronicus* (1970), and a Strindberg drama, *Play Strindberg: Totentanz nach August Strindberg* (1969; *Play Strindberg: The Dance of Death*), Dürrenmatt experimented with the concept of a minimalist drama. His use of a skeletal structure designed to uncover the underlying psychological mechanisms in human affairs led to his own *Der Mitmacher* (1973; The Collaborator), a drama expressing with chilling understatement murderous public collusions in high and low places. The play incurred massive rejection, which promoted his long apologia, *Der Mitmacher: Ein Komplex* (1976).

In his two late novels and his last drama, he reverts to a full range of grotesque stylistic bravura. In *Justiz* (1985; *The Execution of Justice*), he pillories the waywardness of legal justice; *Durcheinandertal* (1989; Pell-Mell Valley) exposes global corruption in a world bereft of even a *deus absconditus. Achterloo* (1984), a play within a play staged in an insane asylum, is a panopticon of anachronisms that suggests the ever renewed senselessness of human history. In *Stoffe I–III, Labyrinth* (1981; Topics, Labyrinth) and *Stoffe IV–IX, Turmbau* (1990; Topics, Tower Construction), Dürrenmatt created a unique genre of writerly autobiography, exemplified by nine pieces of new fiction based on the conception of the world as labyrinth—the Tower of Babel is its vertical image—the labyrinth is also a prominent and multifaceted image in his paintings.

In his many essays and lectures (1969–80), partially stimulated by travels abroad, invitations from universities and international congresses, and responses to the many literary prizes conferred on him, he often looks askance at the meliorative pretenses of ideologists, East and West, the irrational vagaries of the collective mentality, and the ensuing chaos of history. Yet he holds out some fragile hope for the latent moral sensibility in the individual, when kindled by the promptings of art and literature. Dürrenmatt has been taken to task by some critics for merely exposing problems without proposing possible remedies, his stance of skeptical suspense in some sociopolitical matters, and his bleak sense of human history. Other critics recognize that his apparent negativity is but the obverse of a moral revolt that he shares with other writers of grotesques such as Günter Grass, Joseph Heller, and Kurt Vonnegut. Their art often mirrors the very thing it polemicizes: the moral torpor of a proudly enlightened world.

ROBERT E. HELBLING

Biography

Born in Konolfingen, near Bern, Switzerland, 5 January 1921. Studied at the University of Zurich, one term; studied at the University of Bern, 1941–45; drama critic for *Die Weltwoche,* Zurich, 1951–53; codirector, Basle Theaters, 1968–69; co-owner, *Züricher Sonntags-Journal,* 1969–71; writer-in-residence, University of Southern California, Los Angeles, 1981; traveled to the United States and Mexico, 1959, 1969, the Soviet Union, 1964 and 1967, Israel, 1974, Greece and South America, 1983–84, Egypt, 1985. City of Berne prize, 1954; Radio Play prize (Berlin), 1957; Italia prize, 1958; Schiller prize (Mannheim), 1959; New York Drama Critics Circle award, 1959; Schiller prize (Switzerland), 1960; Grillparzer prize, 1968; Kanton Berne prize, 1969; Welsh Arts Council International Writers prize, 1976; Buber-Rosenzweig medal, 1977; Zuckmayer medal, 1984; Austrian State prize, 1984; Bavarian literature prize, 1985; Büchner prize, 1986; Schiller prize (Stuttgart), 1986; Ernst Robert Curtius prize, 1989; numerous honorary doctorates and fellowships. Died 14 December 1990.

Selected Works

Collections

Werkausgabe, 30 vols., 1980–86

Plays

Es steht geschrieben (produced 1947), 1947; revised version, as *Die Wiedertäufer* (produced 1967), 1969
Der Blinde (produced 1948), 1960; revised edition, 1965
Romulus der Grosse (produced 1949), 1956; revised version (produced 1957), 1958; translated as *Romulus,* 1962; as *Romulus the Great,* translated by Gerhard Nellhaus, in *Four Plays,* 1964
Die Ehe des Herrn Mississippi (produced 1952), 1952; revised version, 1957; film version, 1961; as *The Marriage of Mr. Mississippi,* translated by Michael Bullock, in *Four Plays,* 1964
Ein Engel kommt nach Babylon (produced 1953), 1954; revised version (produced 1957), 1958; as *An Angel Comes to Babylon,* translated by William McElwee, in *Four Plays,* 1964
Der Besuch der alten Dame (produced 1956), 1956; film version, 1963; as *The Visit,* translated by Maurice Valency, 1958; translated by Patrick Bowles, 1962
Nächtliches Gespräch mit einem verachteten Menschen (radio play), 1957; as *Conversation at Night with a Despised Character,* n.d.
Komödien I–III, 3 vols., 1957–70
Das Unternehmen der Wega (radio play), 1958
Frank V, music by Paul Burkhard (produced 1959), 1960
Der Prozess um des Esels Schatten (radio play), 1959
Stranitzky und der Nationalheld (radio play), 1959
Abendstunde im Spätherbst (radio play; also produced on stage, 1959), 1959; as *Episode on an Autumn Evening,* translated by Myron B. Gubitz, 1959; as *Incident at Twilight,* in *Postwar German Theatre,* edited by Michael Benedikt and George E. Wellwarth, 1968
Der Doppelgänger (radio play), 1960
Es geschah am hellichten Tag (screenplay), 1960
Herkules und der Stall des Augias (radio play; also produced on stage, 1963), 1960; translated as *Hercules and the Augean Stables,* translated by Agnes Hamilton, 1963
Die Panne, from his own novel (radio play; also televised 1957; produced on stage 1979), 1961; revised version, 1979
Gesammelte Hörspiele (includes *Abenstunde im Spätherbst; Der Doppelgänger; Herkules und der Stall des Augias; Nächtliches Gespräch mit einem verachteten Menschen; Die Panne; Der Prozess um des Esels Schatten; Stranitzky und der Nationalheld; Das Unternehem der Wega*), 1961
Die Physiker (produced 1962), 1962; television version, 1963; as *The Physicists,* translated by James Kirkup, 1964
Four Plays 1957–62 (includes *Romulus the Great; The Marriage of Mr. Mississippi; An Angel Comes to Babylon; The Physicists*), translated by Gerhard Nellhaus et al., 1964
Der Meteor (produced 1966), 1966; as *The Meteor,* translated by James Kirkup, 1973
König Johann (from the play by William Shakespeare) (produced 1968), 1968
Play Strindberg: Totentanz nach August Strindberg (produced 1969), 1969; as *Play Strindberg: The Dance of Death,* translated by James Kirkup, 1972
Titus Andronicus (from the play by William Shakespeare) (produced 1970), 1970
Porträt eines Planeten (produced 1970; revised version produced 1971), 1970
Urfaust (from the play by Johann Wolfgang von Goethe) (produced 1970), 1980
Woyzeck (from the play by Georg Büchner) (produced 1972), 1980
Der Mitmacher (produced 1973), 1973; enlarged edition, *Der Mitmacher—Ein Komplex* (includes notes, essays, narratives), 1976
Die Frist (produced 1977), 1977
Achterloo (produced 1983), 1984
Achterloo IV (produced 1988)

Fiction

Pilatus, 1949
Der Nihilist, 1950; reprinted as *Die Falle*
Der Richter und sein Henker, 1952; as *The Judge and His Hangman,* translated by Cyrus Brooks, 1954
Die Stadt: Prose 1–4, 1952
Das Bild des Sisyphos, 1952
Der Verdacht, 1953; as *The Quarry,* translated by Eva H. Morreale, 1961
Grieche sucht Griechin, 1955; as *Once a Greek . . . ,* translated by Richard and Clara Winston, 1965
Die Panne: Eine noch mögliche Geschichte, 1955; as *Traps,* translated by Richard and Clara Winston, 1960; as *A Dangerous Game,* translated by Richard and Clara Winston, 1960
Der Sturz, 1971
Das Vesprechen: Requiem auf den Kriminalroman, 1958; as *The Pledge,* translated by Richard and Clara Winston, 1959

The Judge and His Hangman; The Quarry: Two Hans Bärlach Mysteries, translated by George Stade, 1983
Minotaurus: Eine Ballade, illustrated by Dürrenmatt, 1985
Dürrenmatt: His Five Novels (includes *The Judge and His Hangman; The Quarry; Once a Greek; A Dangerous Game; The Pledge*), 1985
Justiz, 1985; as *The Execution of Justice,* translated by John E. Woods, 1989
Der Auftrag; oder, Vom Beobachten des Beobachters der Beobachter, 1986; as *The Assignment; or, On Observing of the Observer of the Observers,* translated by Joel Agee, 1988
Durcheinandertal, 1989

Other
Theaterprobleme, 1955; as *Problems of the Theater,* translated by Gerhard Nellhaus, in *Four Plays,* 1964, and with *The Marriage of Mr. Mississippi,* 1966
Friedrich Schiller: Rede (address), 1960
Der Rest ist Dank (addresses), with Werner Weber, 1961
Die Heimat im Plakat: Ein Buch für Schweizer Kinder (drawings), 1963
Theater-Schriften und Reden, edited by Elizabeth Brock-Sulzer, 2 vols., 1966–72; translated in part as *Writings on Theatre and Drama,* edited by H.M. Waidson, 1976
Monstervortrag über Gerechtigkeit und Recht, 1968
Sätze aus Amerika, 1970
Zusammenhänge: Essay über Israel, 1976
Gespräch mit Heinz Ludwig Arnold, 1976
Frankfurter Rede, 1977
Lesebuch, 1978
Bilder und Zeichnungen, edited by Christian Strich, 1978
Albert Einstein: Ein Vortrag, 1979
Stoffe I–III: Labyrinth: Winterkrieg in Tibet, Mondfinsternis, Der Rebell, 1981
Plays and Essays, edited by Volkmar Sander, 1982
Denken mit Dürrenmatt, edited by Daniel Keel, 1982
Die Welt als Labyrinth, 1982
Rollenspiele: Protokoll einer fiktiven Inszenierung und "Achterloo III" (includes text of play *Achterloo III),* 1986
Versuche, 1988
Stoffe IV–IX. Turmbau: Begegnungen, Querfahrt, Die Brücke, Das Haus, Vinter, Das Hirn, 1990
Midas; oder, Die Schwarze Leinwand, 1991
Kants Hoffnung, 1991
Gedankenfuge, 1992
Friedrich Dürrenmatt: Gespräche, 4 vols., 1996

Further Reading
Arnold, Armin, editor, *Zu Friedrich Dürrenmatt,* Stuttgart: Klett, 1982
Bänziger, Hans, *Frisch und Dürrenmatt,* Bern: Francke, 1960; 7th edition, 1976
Federico, Joseph A., "The Political Philosophy of Friedrich Dürrenmatt," *German Studies Review* 12 (1989)
Keel, Daniel, editor, *Herkules und Atlas: Lobreden und andere Versuche über Friedrich Dürrenmatt,* Zürich: Diogenes, 1990
———, editor, *Über Friedrich Dürrenmatt,* Zürich: Diogenes, 1980; 4th edition, 1990
Knapp, Gerhard Peter, *Friedrich Dürrenmatt,* Stuttgart: Metzler, 1980; 2nd edition, 1993
Knapp, Gerhard Peter, and Gerd Labroisse, editors, *Facetten: Studien zum 60. Geburtstag Friedrich Dürrenmatts,* Bern and Las Vegas, Nevada: Lang, 1981
Knapp, Mona, and Gerhard Peter Knapp, "Recht—Gerechtigkeit—Politik: Zur Genese der Begriffe im Werk Friedrich Dürrenmatts," *Text und Kritik* 56 (1977)
Knopf, Jan, *Friedrich Dürrenmatt,* Munich: Beck, 1976; 4th edition, 1988
Lazar, Moshe, editor, *Play Dürrenmatt,* Malibu: Undena, 1983
Sheppard, Vera, "Friedrich Dürrenmatt as a Dramatic Theorist," *Drama Survey* 4 (1965)
Tantow, Lutz, *Friedrich Dürrenmatt: Moralist und Komödiant,* Munich: Heyne, 1992
Whitton, Kenneth S., *Dürrenmatt: Reinterpretation in Retrospect,* New York and Oxford: Wolff, 1990

Die Physiker 1962

Play by Friedrich Dürrenmatt

Friedrich Dürrenmatt's eighth stage play, *Die Physiker* (1962; *The Physicists*), is considered his greatest work apart from *Der Besuch der alten Dame* (1956; *The Visit*). Its high degree of critical and popular acclaim on both sides of the Atlantic was both immediate and enduring, beginning with the play's premiere at the Zurich Schauspielhaus on 20 February 1962. In this first production, Therese Giehse played the part of the megalomaniac psychiatrist Dr. Mathilde von Zahnd; in 1964, she reprised this role for a German television production. Hans-Christian Blech played Möbius, the physicist who, in a noble but ultimately pointless gesture, dons the mask of insanity to forestall the dissemination of his potentially disastrous scientific discovery.

The German premiere in Munich (23 September 1962) was followed by performances in practically every German-speaking theater; the 1598 performances of the play during the 1962–63 season far outnumbered the second most frequently performed play of that season, namely, Max Frisch's *Andorra* (934 performances). That season marked a turn toward political and documentary drama, which provided a refreshing alternative to the bland restagings of older dramas that dominated stages in the early years of the Federal Republic.

The first English-language performance of *The Physicists,* on 9 January 1963 in London, was directed by Peter Brook. Although this premiere was once again hailed by critics and audiences, Dürrenmatt was aghast at the shift of the play's focus from political and ethical commentary to overwrought, farcical whodunit. Beginning with the play's opening on Broadway on 13 October 1964, a cleft between critics and spectators became evident. Critics alleged that the play posed overly high intellectual demands, while audiences applauded the complex structure of the play and made this drama the popular hit of the season—and a popular work throughout the early 1970s. By the latter half of this decade, critics and audiences were tiring of the play's relentless scrutiny of individual and collective responsibility, but *The Physicists* still has a secure place in the repertoire of many German-language theaters.

The Physicists reprises several themes from Dürrenmatt's earlier works, especially the role of personal sacrifice in serving the greater good of the community. This play, however, is guided by a new set of artistic, ethical, and political concerns in its exploration of issues of personal and collective responsibility, and it is marked by Dürrenmatt's growing pessimism regarding the outcome of individual efforts. In the years immediately preceding the composition of this play, Dürrenmatt had taken a highly public stance on the building of the first atom bomb; in a 1956 essay, he condemned the "international elite" of scientists who had acquiesced in the corrupt exploitation of their knowledge by politicians. *The Physicists* premiered during the height of Dürrenmatt's ultimately fruitless campaign to vote down Switzerland's participation in the atomic defense of Europe. The theme of *The Physicists*—man's ability to destroy the universe in the name of scientific progress and our *in*ability to halt such progress—is played out in an insane asylum. Dürrenmatt was forced to acknowledge the limitations of the theater in promoting social and political change, which is evidenced in his poignant notation on *The Physicists:* "A drama can trick spectators into facing reality, but it cannot force them to resist it and most assuredly not to conquer it."

This statement concluded the "21 Points" Dürrenmatt appended to *The Physicists* in order to outline his political and aesthetic concerns. In the "21 Points," Dürrenmatt contends that the collective has replaced the individual in the atomic age and that individual attempts to resolve societal dilemmas are doomed to failure. The pithy aesthetic prescriptions of the "21 Points" have provided critics with ample theoretical fodder with which to interpret *The Physicists*—notwithstanding the playwright's insistence that these theories of drama do not drive his plays. (Dürrenmatt's very first point states: "I proceed not from a thesis but from a story.") His use of the terms "chance" (*Zufall*) and "flash of inspiration" (*Einfall*) to describe the building blocks of this drama have been adopted as part of the standard critical vocabulary for *The Physicists.*

By contrast, Dürrenmatt's use of the word *comedy* in the play's subtitle, "A Comedy in Two Acts," has fueled a controversy among critics, who have sought to establish either that the comic emphasis of Act I or that the predominance of tragic elements in Act II better reflects the play's essence. Ultimately, this controversy turns on a specious dichotomy between tragedy and comedy. In *The Physicists* and other Dürrenmatt plays, however, comedy and tragedy coalesce, not in tragicomedy (which typically culminates in a happy denouement), but in the grotesque. *The Physicists*'s grotesque characters and bizarre plot twists reflect Dürrenmatt's loss of faith in both the moral universe that he considered essential to tragedy and the rational social order that he presumed essential to comedy. His is not the theater of the absurd; *The Physicists*'s tightly knit plot, which resembles the form of his earlier detective novels, paints reality in grotesque strokes—most memorably in the character of Dr. Mathilde von Zahnd, the insane director of the insane asylum, who exploits Möbius's scientific discoveries in an improbable, yet devastatingly real manner.

Dürrenmatt's extensive stage directions, which provide a plethora of historical, architectural, and panoramic descriptions that prove altogether irrelevant to the sealed universe of the mad physicists, specify that this play will respect the "Aristotelian unities" of time, place, and action, because "only classical form is suitable for a plot which takes place among madmen." By inviting comparisons to ancient Greek drama through this structural device, as well as through Dürrenmatt's reference to *Oedipus Rex* in the ninth of his "21 Points," the author establishes a stark contrast between the tragic heroes of yore, who battled fate, and the grotesque challenges of our era, in which chance reigns supreme. The events of the play and, by implication, the planet, are spiraling toward what Dürrenmatt's oft-quoted third point calls "the worst possible turn of events." When the play has reached the direst outcome, with Möbius's recognition that his efforts to nullify his discovery were for naught, the play ends.

In the inevitable comparisons to Brecht that abound in the critical literature, contrasts far outweigh similarities in discussions of characterization, form, and content. Critics have called the play's protagonist Möbius the antithesis of Brecht's Galileo, because Galileo's recantation of his *Discorsi* ultimately serves the cause of science and progress, whereas Möbius's resolution to secrete his insights is in vain. The futility of Möbius's attempt to rescue mankind from the fruits of his own research lends credence to the playwright's pessimistic view that in our era, some scientific discoveries are best retracted. Unlike the expansive epic theater of Brecht, *The Physicists*'s claustrophobic milieu closely resembles Sartre's *Huis Clos* (1945; *No Exit*) and Pirandello's *Enrico IV* (1921; *The Emperor*). And unlike Brecht, Dürrenmatt does not engage in political polemics to advocate or condemn any particular doctrine, but to raise probing questions by portraying characters who look straight into the abyss.

SHELLEY FRISCH

Editions

First edition: *Die Physiker,* Zurich: Verlag der Arche, 1962
Critical edition: in *Werkausgabe,* vol. 7, Zurich: Diogenes Verlag, 1980
Translation: *The Physicists,* translated by James Kirkup, New York: Grove Press, 1964

Further Reading

Kempf, Franz, "Brecht und Dürrenmatt als Dramatiker: Antipoden oder Dioskuren, Versuch einer Bilanz," *Weimarer Beiträge* 37, no. 7 (1991)
Knapp, Gerhard Peter, *Friedrich Dürrenmatt: Die Physiker,* Frankfurt: Diesterweg, 1979
Mayer, Hans, *Über Friedrich Dürrenmatt und Max Frisch,* Pfüllingen: Neske, 1977
Morley, Michael, "Dürrenmatt's Dialogue with Brecht: A Thematic Analysis of *Die Physiker,*" *Modern Drama* 14 (1971)
Taylor, Heimtraud F., "The Question of Responsibility in *The Physicists,*" in *Friedrich Dürrenmatt: A Collection of Critical Essays,* edited by Bodo Fritzen and Heimtraud F. Taylor, Normal, Illinois: Applied Literature Press, 1979
Whitton, Kenneth S., "*Der Besuch der alten Dame*" and "*Die Physiker,*" London: Grant and Cutler, 1994

E

Christine Ebner 1277–1356

At the height of German medieval mysticism in the 13th and 14th centuries, many German nuns in Dominican convents reported religious visions through which they had personal contact with God. Whereas the first major wave of female mysticism from the 11th through the 13th centuries, which produced such famous mystical writers as Hildegard of Bingen, Elisabeth of Schönau, Mechthild von Magdeburg, and Gertrud the Great, affected mostly northern and central Germany, during the early 14th century south German women convents also began to participate in this spiritual and literary movement. Dominicans were especially well-known for their interest in book production, either by copying religious texts or by writing their own accounts. These Dominican mystics, including Anna von Munzingen, Christine Ebner, Margareta Ebner (not related), Elsbeth von Oye, and Elisabeth Stagel, created, on the one hand, so-called sisterbooks (Vitae sororum) in which the mystical visions of many convent women, initially written down in individual documents, were compiled and repeatedly edited in a collective effort. On the other hand, they wrote autobiographical mystical reports reflecting upon their personal visions and experiences.

Christine Ebner was the daughter of a wealthy bourgeois family in Nuremberg and entered the Dominican convent of Engelthal near Nuremberg at the age of 14. Similar to many other religious women of her time, she was a very devout Christian and struggled hard to achieve an ascetic lifestyle by castigating herself for extensive periods. She experienced the first visions in 1291. Reports of visions, if acknowledged by the authorities as authentic (i.e., as being divinely inspired), were quickly proclaimed to be messages from God and so appealed to both the clergy and the laity. Christine's reports, however, first met with criticism from her convent, but soon she was acknowledged as a true mystic. In 1317, at the suggestion of her male confessor, Konrad von Füssen, Christine began to write down her mystical revelations and continued with this work almost until the end of her life. This text is today known as Christine's *Leben und Gesichte* (Life and Visions) and reflects the mystic's great concern to share her religious visions with her contemporaries because these were given to her by the Godhead, as she said, to communicate them to her contemporaries. Parallel to many other female mystics of her time, Christine Ebner understood her role to be God's mouthpiece and to follow in the footsteps of Moses, and she said that she was told that His, Christ's, grace was also put forward to mankind through her. Only the divine authority, however, made it possible for her to proclaim her visions, which were radically contradictory to the dominant attitude by the church, which in turn excluded women from taking any active part in the religious life. Quite typical for many 14th-century women mystics, Christine also used many imageries of child bearing and nursing the Christ child in imitation of the Virgin Mary. In visions that were even more emotional and personal than in Mechthild von Magdeburg's mystical accounts, Christine and other Dominican sisters perceived Christ as their lover, bridegroom, and lord with whom they enjoyed personal, physical, and erotic contact. In addition, this mystical writer described her convent as a family, with the mother superior as their true mother who cares for her children and helps them to receive inspiration to love God with all their heart.

Christine was soon highly acclaimed for being God's beatified vessel and attracted many visitors to her convent. Particularly during the time of the Black Death (1347–51), many people flocked to Engelthal in the hope of receiving salvation through the mystic's divine connections. In 1349, a group of flagellants arrived at the convent, followed by Emperor Charles IV in 1350, who sought her personal blessings.

Mystics such as Christine made many efforts to convey to their contemporaries what they had seen in their visions and often tried to establish personal contacts with similar-minded clerics. Christine enjoyed a particular relationship with the mystically influenced Priest Heinrich of Nördlingen, with whom she exchanged many letters. This correspondence soon included important discussions of mystical experiences by Christine, her religious sisters, and even her confessor Konrad von Füssen. In her *Büchlein von der Genaden Überlast* (Little Book of the Overwhelming Burden of Grace), composed sometime after 1346, Christine recorded the history of her convent and reflected upon the virtues and visions of its past members, who all had supposedly experienced, in one way or the other, direct contact with the Godhead. This *Büchlein* was one example of a whole genre of so-called *Schwesternbücher* or sisterbooks, which were written in a number of southwest German Dominican convents, and which contained stories of the lives and visions of many of the convent's inhabitants. Christine included a chronicle of her convent and close to 50 accounts of fellow sisters who had enjoyed mystical revelations similar to her own. All of the women appear as models of religious obedience, asceticism, devotion to prayer, service for their fellow sisters, and, above all, vessels of God's grace. Christine also referred to many historical events of her times such as the plague, pogroms against the Jews, the rulership of Emperor Charles IV, local events in Nuremberg, and others.

In 1351, the secular itinerant priest Heinrich of Nördlingen (died 1379) visited Christine Ebner, who was 74 years old by then, in her convent to discuss with her the practical implications of her mystical visions. Through his connections Christine got in touch with like-minded mystical writers such as Margareta Ebner in the convent of Medingen near Dillingen in the vicinity of the Danube. Both Heinrich and Christine understood their experiences to be a call from God to develop a form of mystical ministry that circumvented the strict control exerted by the church, which prohibited women from any active involvement in the liturgy and in preaching. The convent of Engelthal offered, similar to many other women's monasteries (including Adelhausen, Unterlinden, Gotteszell, and Kirchberg), a peculiar and powerful framework for women to create a more or less self-contained female community where women could overcome the traditional gender barriers that normally excluded them from the active life in the church and where they could gain direct access to God and, hence, be authorized to preach and write about their visions. Christine Ebner found an important successor in the mystical writer Adelheid Langmann, also a member of the Engelthal cloister.

ALBRECHT CLASSEN

Biography

Born in Nuremberg, 3 March 1277. At the age of 14, joined the Dominican convent in Engelthal; experienced mystical visions from 1291; corresponded with the mystic Heinrich of Nördlingen from 1338; because of her fame as a mystic, she was often visited by high-ranking contemporaries from 1349; visited by Henrich of Nördlingen, 1351. Died in Engelthal, 27 December 1356.

Selected Works

Der Nonne von Engeltal Büchlein von der Genaden Überlast, edited by Karl Schröder, 1871

Leben und Gesichte der Christine Ebnerin, Klosterfrau zu Engelthal, edited by Georg Wolfgang Karl Lochner, 1872

Further Reading

Kramer, Dewey Weiss, "'Arise and Give the Convent Bread': Christine Ebner, the Convent Chronicle of Engelthal, and the Call to Ministry among Fourteenth-Century Religious Women," in *Women as Protagonists and Poets in the German Middle Ages*, edited by Albrecht Classen, Göppingen: Kümmerle, 1991

Lewis, Gertrud Jaron, *By Women, for Women, about Women: The Sister-Books of Fourteenth Century Germany*, Toronto: Pontifical Institute of Mediaeval Studies, 1996

Oehl, Wilhelm, editor and translator, *Das Büchlein von der Gnaden Überlast von Christine Ebner*, Paderborn: Schöningh, 1924

Peters, Ursula, "Nonnenbuch und Gnaden-Vita: mystische Vitenliteratur süddeutscher Dominikanerinnen im 14. Jahrhundert," in *Deutsche Literatur von Frauen*, edited by Gisela Brinker-Gabler, vol. 1, Munich: Beck, 1988

Ringler, Siegfried, "Ebner, Christine," in *Die deutsche Literatur des Mittelalters: Verfasserlexikon*, 2nd revised edition, edited by Kurt Ruh, et al., vol. 2, Berlin and New York: de Gruyter, 1980

Marie von Ebner-Eschenbach 1830–1916

Marie von Ebner-Eschenbach, acclaimed as one of the greatest German-language narrative authors of the 19th century, already showed signs of literary talent as a young girl. Although discouraged by her family from developing these gifts, she was encouraged by the dramatist Franz Grillparzer, with whom she as an adult maintained a close and fruitful friendship. Writing in the style of late 19th century realism, Ebner-Eschenbach is most often grouped with authors such as Wilhelm Raabe, Ferdinand von Saar, Paul Heyse, Theodor Fontane and Gottfried Keller; her work at all times, however, speaks in its own distinctive voice.

In many ways, Ebner-Eschenbach's career as an author was an ongoing struggle to find this voice. German was her third language, after Czech and French; it was largely through the urging of her cousin, and later, husband, Moritz von Ebner-Eschenbach, that she began to focus on German as the language of her literary production. More significantly, Ebner-Eschenbach grappled to find an adequate means of expressing women's perspectives and experience in the language of a highly traditional patriarchal society. Characterized by clarity, grace, and an often epic distance from the passions of her characters, her work was frequently praised by contemporary critics for its "masculine" spirit—its relative freedom from "feminine," that is, ostensibly "sentimental" characteristics and content interesting "only" to women. Ebner-Eschenbach's prose was stereotyped early as being "pedagogical," a fact that in many ways has obscured the true originality, humanity, and depth of her oeuvre.

Although poetry was her first medium of literary expression, Ebner-Eschenbach soon focused her attention on drama. Inspired by her childhood visits to the Viennese Burgtheater and her love for Schiller's dramatic works, Ebner-Eschenbach determined at a young age to become an "Austrian Shakespeare." Although she devoted almost 30 years of her life to this pursuit, success as a dramatic artist remained beyond her grasp. Modern criticism has established that this failure arose from a complex of causes beyond alleged aesthetic and dramatic weakness. These causes included resentment at her intrusion into a domain viewed as the province of men, the misunderstanding of her perspective as a woman and her characterization of strong female characters, the fickle taste of Viennese audiences, stage politics, and the vicious treatment that she received in the press.

It was only when she turned to prose that Ebner-Eschenbach's works began to meet with success. A prolific and disciplined author, she was at home with a number of genres, including novels, novellas, short stories, parables, fairy tales, travel journals, and autobiography. Her aphorisms compete in wit and sagacity with those of Friedrich Nietzsche.

Regardless of the genre, Ebner-Eschenbach is always a skilled storyteller. Although she frequently utilizes a third-person narrator, she at times casts stories into the first person or adopts the form of letters or a "dialogisierte Novelle" (novella in dialogue), which is essentially a one-act play. She exhibits particular dexterity in her use of the *Rahmengeschichte* (frame story), in which some event in the framing story provokes the retelling of the inner narrative. In "Die Reisegefährten" (1901; Fellow Travelers), for example, the doctor finds himself in a train compartment with a young man, to whom he begins to reveal his past. The structure of "Oversberg" (1892) is even more intriguing; here, a first-person narrator recounts his experience at dinner with his colleagues, who listen while the inspector recounts Oversberg's story. Each of the figures at the table has an individual personality, and all interact with each other as they interrupt and comment on the story.

Ebner-Eschenbach's works are characterized by a deep sense of humanity and compassion that frequently erupts into outrage at the abuse of one individual by another and that anguishes with people who, through their pride and weakness, destroy their own happiness and that of those around them. Perhaps most notable is the novel *Das Gemeindekind* (1887; *Their Pavel*), in which the boy Pavel is neglected, exploited, and abused by various members of the community that is responsible for his care. As a challenge to the social determinism of the naturalists, Ebner-Eschenbach chronicles the way in which Pavel thwarts the expectation that he will become a criminal like his parents; instead, he develops into an independent man of integrity who wrangles grudging respect from the community.

No social class is spared Ebner-Eschenbach's biting critique. For example, the story "Er laßt die Hand küssen" (1886; He Sends a Hand Kiss) reveals the violence rampant at all levels of society. The story mercilessly unmasks the arrogance, negligence, and callousness displayed by nobles who arbitrarily impose their will on their subjects without any concern for their effects on individual lives. At the same time, it exposes the tyrannical village father who assuages his own frustrations by beating his wife, enforcing his will on his son through inflicting physical pain, and ruthlessly exploiting his son's money-making ability.

Children as individuals are often ignored in literature, especially within a society that expected children to be completely voiceless and obedient to the will of their parents. In "Der Vorzugsschüler" (1901; The Honor Student), however, Ebner-Eschenbach poignantly brings to life the despair of the child who is driven to suicide by the absolute demands of his father, who is forcing him to be something that it is beyond his capability to become.

Although she never identified herself as a feminist, Ebner-Eschenbach's narratives powerfully illuminate the many facets of women's lives and experience in a patriarchal society that did not value them as individuals. From imperious rulers, femmes fatales, and girls sent into arranged marriages to resigned, silenced wives, the stories vibrate with images of women as they attempt to navigate the circumstances of their lives.

Of all the honors that Ebner-Eschenbach received, perhaps the most revealing was a celebratory document signed by 10,000 Viennese women from all social classes, an enduring tribute to the fact that, with her sharp eye, gentle irony, deep psychological insight, and above all, her compassion, the author gave a voice, and, therefore, a validity, to the experience of the voiceless in society.

MICHELLE STOTT

Biography

Born Marie, Countess Dubsky, in Zdislavic, Moravia, 13 September 1830. Throughout her childhood, spent the summers at Zdislavic, the winters in Vienna; educated privately, directed particularly by the interests of her stepmother; lived in Klosterbruck, Moravia, 1848–56, where her husband taught at a military academy; lived predominantly in Vienna, 1856–; established her reputation as an author when her story "Lotti die Uhrmacherin" appeared in the *Deutsche Rundschau,* 1879; first Austrian woman to receive the Ehrenzeichen für Kunst und Wissenschaft, 1898; first woman to receive an honorary doctorate from the University of Vienna, 1900. Recipient of numerous honors in her last years. Died in Vienna, 12 March 1916.

Selected Works

Collections

Gesammelte Werke in drei Einzelbänden, edited by Johannes Klein, 1956–58
Gesammelte Schriften, 10 vols., 1893–1910
Gesammelte Werke, 9 vols., 1961
Sämtliche Werke, 6 vols., 1920
Seven Stories by Marie von Ebner-Eschenbach, translated by Helga H. Harriman, 1986

Fiction

Aus Franzensbad: Sechs Episteln von keinem Propheten, 1858
Das Gemeindekind, 1887; as *Their Pavel,* translated by Lynne Tatlock, 1996
Der Nachlaß der Marie von Ebner-Eschenbach, 1947
Das Waldfräulein, 1969
Unsühnbar, edited by Burkhard Bittrich, 1978; as *Beyond Atonement,* translated by Vanessa von Ornam, 1997
Bozena, 1980
Ausgewählte Erzählungen, 1981

Other

Marie von Ebner-Eschenbach: Tagebücher, edited by Karl Konrad Polheim and Norbert Gabriel, 5 vols., 1989–96
Aphorisms: Marie von Ebner-Eschenbach, translated by David Scrase and Wolfgang Mieder, 1994
Autobiographische Schriften I. Meine Kinderjahre. Aus meinen Kinder- und Lehrjahren, edited by Christa-Maria Schmidt, 1989
Autobiographische Schriften II. Meine Erinnerungen an Grillparzer, edited by Christa-Maria Schmidt, 1989

Further Reading

Bramkamp, Agatha C., *Marie von Ebner-Eschenbach: The Author, Her Time, and Her Critics,* Bonn: Bouvier, 1990
Harriman, Helga H., "Marie von Ebner-Eschenbach in Feminist Perspective," *Modern Austrian Literature* 18, no. 1 (1985)

Kraus-Worley, Linda, "Reading and Writing Stories/Histories: Marie von Ebner-Eschenbach's 'Er lasst die Hand küssen'," in *Neues zu Altem: Novellen der Vergangenheit und der Gegenwart,* edited by Sabine Cramer, Munich: W. Fink, 1996

Mieder, Wolfgang, "'Ausnahmen können auch die Vorboten einer neuen Regel sein': Marie von Ebner-Eschenbach's Proverbial Aphorisms," *Modern Austrian Literature* 26, no. 1 (1993)

Ockenden, R.C., "Unconscious Poesy? Marie von Ebner-Eschenbach's 'Die Poesie des Unbewussten'," in *Gender and Politics in Austrian Fiction,* edited by Ritchie Robertson and Edward Timms, Edinburgh: Edinburgh University Press, 1996

Pfeiffer, Peter C., "Geschichte, Leidenspathos, feminine Subjektivität: Marie von Ebner-Eschenbachs Autobiographie *Meine Kinderjahre,*" *Monatshefte für Deutschen Unterricht, Deutsche Sprache und Literatur* 87, no. 1 (1995)

Rose, Ferrel V., *The Guises of Modesty: Marie von Ebner-Eschenbach's Female Artists,* Columbia, South Carolina: Camden House, 1994

Steiner, Carl, *Of Reason and Love: The Life and Works of Marie von Ebner-Eschenbach (1830–1916),* Riverside, California: Ariadne Press, 1994

Thum, Reinhard, "Parental Authority and Childhood Trauma: An Analysis of Marie von Ebner-Eschenbach's 'Die erste Beichte'," *Modern Austrian Literature* 19, no. 2 (1986)

———, "Oppressed by Generosity: Dismantling the Gilded Marital Cage in Marie von Ebner-Eschenbach's 'Erste Trennung'," in *Neues zu Altem: Novellen der Vergangenheit und der Gegenwart,* edited by Sabine Cramer, Munich: W. Fink, 1996

Toegel, Edith, "Daughters and Fathers in Marie von Ebner-Eschenbach's Works," *Oxford German Studies* 20/21 (1991–92)

———, "'Entsagungsmut' in Marie von Ebner-Eschenbach's Works: A Female-Male Perspective," *Forum for Modern Language Studies* 28, no. 2 (1992)

———, "The 'Leidensjahre' of Marie von Ebner-Eschenbach: Her Dramatic Works," *German Life and Letters* 46, no. 2 (1993)

Eckhart, Meister, *see* Meister Eckhart

Marianne Ehrmann ca. 1755–1795

Marianne Ehrmann's experience in the theater profoundly influenced her major novel, *Amalie: Eine wahre Geschichte in Briefen* (1788; Amalie: A True Epistolary History), which was reprinted in 1798 as *Antonie von Warnstein* (Antonie of Warnstein). Although Christine Touaillon in her *Der deutsche Frauenroman des 18. Jahrhunderts* (1919; The 18th-Century German Woman's Novel) reads the work as a conventional sentimental epistolary novel, this is not the case. Touaillon, whose broad and seminal study did not have room for nuances, does not take account of the fact that the second part of the novel, entirely devoted to the theater, is the first theater fiction written by a woman. In this work, Ehrmann greatly expands the genre of the sentimental novel inasmuch as her main characters, the two correspondents Amalie and Fanny, discuss broad topics ranging from education to convents, treatment of servants, and theater reform. Maya Widmer, in her afterword to a new edition of *Amalie* (1955), interprets the work as a female bildungsroman, a claim not without merit. While the bildungsroman emerging about this time does not use the epistolary form, however, Ehrmann's work does share many of its characteristics. Her character, Amalie, travels, has adventures, grows, and asserts herself as an individual. The novel, whose two main characters are outspoken, critical, and not at all passive, was well received in the 1780s, but was severely criticized by the 1790s, which probably reflects rapidly shifting attitudes toward women.

In her 1939 study *Das Wirken der Frau im frühen deutschen Zeitschriftenwesen* (The Activity of Women in Early German Journalism), Edith Krull comments on Ehrmann's ironic and provocative style, calling her the only woman whose writing resembles that of the Sturm und Drang (Storm and Stress) and suggesting that her ideas and language may have annoyed some of her contemporaries. Ehrmann was particularly well known as the editor of and a major contributor to the two women's journals she founded, and her work was read well into the 19th century. After a long caesura, she has been rediscovered by feminist scholars, who have been particularly interested in the journals. These scholars stress Ehrmann's ability, shared by her contemporaries, to subvert subtly the emerging order, which required women to devote themselves entirely to domesticity. They de-emphasize Ehrmann's strong voice, which proclaimed that women must think in order to feel, an attitude that at least partially contributed to her dismissal by Cotta as the editor of *Amaliens Erholungsstunden.* The journal was continued as *Flora,* and it was later described as insipid by Friedrich von Schiller.

Ehrmann clearly saw herself as an *Aufklärer* (enlightenment figure) and regarded the education of women as her primary mission. To that end, she wrote moral essays, biographies of admirable women intended as models, sketches, short stories, anecdotes, and aphorisms. Without question, it was Ehrmann's intention to insert her voice in the ongoing gender debate and give it a different slant, stressing reason and emotion as desirable for both women and men. This conviction is also apparent in *Philosophie eines Weibs. Von einer Beobachterin* (1784; Philosophy of a Woman. By a Female Observer). This anonymously published essay is somewhat influenced by Rousseau but does not adopt his ideal of passivity for women. The essay saw two editions, was translated into French, and seems to have been somewhat controversial, since it provoked a response by Ignaz Anton Adam Felner, *Philosophie eines Mannes. Ein Gegenstück zur Philosophie eines Weibes. Von einem Beobachter* (1785; Philosophy of a Man. A Counterpart to Philosophy of a Woman. By a Male Observer), in which the author protested Ehrmann's characterization of men. Primarily, Ehrmann believed men to be fallible human beings who, like women, did not know everything.

Ehrmann's aphorisms, far-ranging, didactic, and humorous, were first published in a women's journal edited by Theophil Ehrmann, *Frauenzimmer-Zeitung* (1787; Women's Journal). They were republished as *Kleine Fragmente für Denkerinnen* (1789; Small Fragments for Women Thinkers; reprinted 1994 as *Ein Weib ein Wort* [A Woman Is as Good as Her Word]). Here, as in all her writings, Ehrmann emerges as a cultural critic. Her insight into human behavior is astute, her critique expedient. She recognized, for example, the motivations of many men's criticism of women as prejudice and the impact of male prejudice on women's intellectual and personal development. When Ehrmann died, she was given a compliment in the influential journal *Allgemeine deutsche Bibliothek* (General German Library), which she might have rejected, for it discredited other women. The reviewer commented that other shallow German women verse makers should have crossed the Styx in her place.

Ehrmann wrote one play, the domestic tragedy *Leichtsinn und gutes Herz oder Die Folgen der Erziehung* (1786; Frivolity and a Good Heart; or, the Consequences of Education). Interestingly, this play ends as a comedy, with a marriage between a commoner and an aristocrat. Ehrmann was well acquainted with domestic tragedy—her character Amalie, for example, performs the role of Lady Milford in Friedrich Schiller's important play belonging to this genre, *Kabale und Liebe* (1783; Intrigue and Love). Her reversal of the conventional death of the seduced bourgeois innocent, who instead marries the aristocrat, illustrates her reformatory spirit, an affinity she had with Sturm und Drang writers such as Jakob Michael Reinhold Lenz.

Ehrmann's early death ended her 11-year publishing career. Her writing is of literary and cultural interest and is invaluable for the study of 18th-century culture. In Switzerland, her work has recently been recognized in an exhibit held in Berne in 1994 and Basel and Zurich in 1995.

HELGA STIPA MADLAND

Biography

Born in Rapperswil, Switzerland, 25 November ca. 1755. Educated by her uncle, Dominicus von Brentano; worked as governess and housekeeper, 1775–77; moved to Vienna, where she became an actress, ca. 1780; moved to Strasbourg, 1785; married Theophil Ehrmann, ca. 1786; moved to Isny, 1787, and to Stuttgart, 1788; edited *Amaliens Erholungsstunden* and *Die Einsiedlerin aus den Alpen* in Stuttgart. Died in Stuttgart, 14 August 1795.

Selected Works

Novels

Amalie: Eine wahre Geschichte in Briefen, 1788; edited by Maya Widmer and Doris Stump, 1995
Graf Bilding: Eine Geschichte aus dem mittleren Zeitalter, 1788
Nina's Briefe an ihren Geliebten, 1788

Play

Leichtsinn und gutes Herz oder die Folgen der Erziehung: Ein Original-Schauspiel in fünf Aufzügen, 1786

Journals

Amaliens Erholungsstunden: Teutschlands Töchtern geweiht, 12 vols., 1790–92
Die Einsiedlerinn aus den Alpen, 8 vols., 1793–94

Essay

Philosophie eines Weibs, 1784

Aphorisms

Kleine Fragmente für Denkerinnen, 1789

Further Reading

Böhmel-Fischera, Ulrike, "'Keine eigentliche Schulgelehrsamkeit': Marianne Ehrmans Begriff der 'Denkerin,'" *Querelles: Jahrbuch für Frauenforschung* 1 (1996)
Brandes, Helga, "Das Frauenzimmer-Journal: Zur Herausbildung einer journalistischen Gattung im 18. Jahrhundert," in *Deutsche Literatur von Frauen,* 2 vols., edited by Gisela Brinker-Gabler, Munich: Beck, 1988
Dawson, Ruth, "'And This Shield Is Called—Self Reliance'—Emerging Feminist Consciousness in the Late Eighteenth Century," in *German Women in the Eighteenth and Nineteenth Centuries,* edited by Ruth-Ellen B. Joeres and Mary Jo Maynes, Bloomington: Indiana University Press, 1986
Herger, Lisbeth, "Frauenpublizistik am Beispiel von Marianne Ehrmann (1755–1795)," in *Alltag in der Schweiz seit 1300,* edited by Bernhard Schneider, Zurich: Chronos, 1991
Kirstein, Britt-Angela, *Marianne Ehrmann: Publizistin und Herausgeberin im ausgehenden 18. Jahrhundert,* Wiesbaden: Deutscher Universitätsverlag, 1997
Madland, Helga Stipa, "An Introduction to the Works and Life of Mariane Ehrmann (1755–95): Writer, Editor, Journalist," *Lessing Yearbook* 21 (1989)
———, "Gender and the German Literary Canon: Marianne Ehrmann's Infanticide Fiction," *Monatshefte* 84, no. 4 (1992)
———, *Marianne Ehrmann: Reason and Emotion in Her Life and Works,* Women in German Literature, vol. 1, edited by Peter D.G. Brown, New York: Lang, 1998
Schumann, Sabine, "Das 'lesende Frauenzimmer': Frauenzeitschriften im 18. Jahrhundert," in *Die Frau von der Reformation zur Romantik,* edited by Barbara Becker-Cantarino, Bonn: Bouvier, 1980
Stump, Doris, "Eine Frau 'von Verstand, Witz, Gefühl, Fantasie und Feuer,' Zu Leben und Werk Marianne Ehrmanns," in *Amalie, eine wahre Geschichte in Briefen,* by Marianne Ehrmann, edited by Maya Widmer and Doris Stump, Bern: Haupt, 1995
Weckel, Ulrike, "Lehrerinnen des weiblichen Geschlechts, die ersten Herausgeberinnen von Frauenzeitschriften und ihr Publikum," in

Geschichte der Mädchen- und Frauenbildung, vol. 1, Frankfurt and New York: Campus, 1996

Widmer, Maya, "Mit spitzer Feder gegen Vorurteile und gallsüchtige Moral—Marianne Ehrmann, geb. von Brentano," in *Und schrieb und schrieb wie ein Tiger aus dem Busch: über Schriftstellerinnen in der deutschsprachigen Schweiz,* edited by Elisabeth Ryter, Zurich: Limmat, 1994

——, "Amalie—eine wahre Geschichte?" afterword, in *Amalie, eine wahre Geschichte in Briefen,* by Marianne Ehrmann, edited by Maya Widmer and Doris Stump, Bern: Haupt, 1995

Wurst, Karin, "Marianne Ehrmann geb. von Brentano (1755–1795)," in *Frauen und Drama im achtzehnten Jahrhundert,* Cologne: Böhlau, 1991

Günter Eich 1907–1972

In 1946, Günter Eich, released from a U.S. prison camp, returned to Greifenhausen to resume his life as a writer, which had been interrupted by war and conscription. A founding member of the Gruppe 47, which soon became immensely important on the literary scene of postwar Germany, he emerged to rank along with Ingeborg Bachmann, Paul Celan, Nelly Sachs, and Marie Luise Kaschnitz as a leading poet and radio dramatist. Postwar readers, still suffering from the inhumanities and language abuses of National Socialism, perceived Eich's early lyric poems as representative of the new "sound" of German poetic expression. On the basis of their calm, unemotional diction, precise and simple imagery, and reflective detachment from the poetic subject, exemplified in his first three rich and powerful collections, *Abgelegene Gehöfte* (1948; Remote Farmsteads), *Untergrundbahn* (1949; Subway), and *Botschaften des Regens* (1955; Messages of the Rain), Eich's poems were regarded as seminal documents of the effort to reconstitute literary language as an instrument of knowledge and truth. In this respect, Hans Magnus Enzensberger, a younger member of that postwar generation of poets, observed that Eich's poems were as quiet as they were radical in combining responsibility and freedom. Peter Bichsel described him as a "silent anarchist."

In 1929, two years after publication of his first poems, Eich was a pioneer of the radio play in Germany, collaborating with Martin Raschke on *Leben und Sterben des Sängers Caruso* (The Life and Death of the Singer Caruso). It was not until the 1950s, the "golden years" of the German radio play, however, that he achieved prominence in this genre. Plays such as *Träume* (first broadcast 1951, published 1953; *Dreams*), *Sabeth, oder Die Gäste im schwarzen Rock* (1951; Sabeth, or The Guests in Black Tails), *Der Tiger Jussuf* (1952; The Tiger Jussuf), *Das Jahr Lazertis* (1953; *The Year Lacertis*), and *Zinngeschrei* (1955; Cry of Tin)—to name but a few of his extensive productions—were either enthusiastically received or fiercely condemned, yet they were never ignored. These years were Eich's most successful as a radio dramatist and poet, a time when he received awards including the very first prize of the Gruppe 47 (1950), the prize of the Academy of Arts in Bavaria (1951), the prize of the "Kriegsblinden" (soldiers blinded in the war) for radio plays (1952), and above all, the eminently important and influential Georg Büchner Prize in 1959. In the reality of cultural politics of the Federal Republic of Germany, this recognition signaled Eich's acceptance as one of the "Olympian" writers of modern German literature, a category that also included figures such as Böll, Dürrenmatt, Frisch, Grass, Lenz, Weiss, Walser, and a few others.

Together with Georg Britting, Wilhelm Lehmann, and Karl Krolow, Eich is considered one of the most prominent representatives of nature poetry, especially because of his poems' tendency to find mysterious signs and structures in the natural world. The influences and discursive links of Eich's brand of nature poetry can be traced back to German Romanticism, his familiarity with Chinese poetry, and the 20th-century European tradition of the so-called hermetic poetry associated with such names as Baudelaire, Mallarmé, Valéry, Ungaretti, Celan, and Mandelstam. Generally, this term—which was defined and analyzed in 1936 by Franceso Flora in *La poesia ermetica*—denotes obscure, difficult poetry with a tendency not only toward a private manner and vocabulary but toward condensation as well. Language and imagery are subjective, and the "sound" and suggestive power of the words are of great importance. Seen in the light of this tradition, Eich's poems make sense not as descriptions of representative components of the world but as linguistic structures with which reality can be experienced. He explained his specific poetological view of the world in 1956 in Vézelay, in his brief contribution during a meeting of French and German writers entitled "Some Remarks on 'Literature and Reality'": "Writing is not only a profession but also a decision to see the world as language. . . . I write poems to orient myself in reality. I view them as trigonometric points or buoys that mark the course in an unknown area. Only through writing do things take on a reality for me."

In the course of the 1960s and 1970s, academic and general reception of Eich had reached its zenith. Numerous editions of his works were printed and reprinted; monographs, dissertations, and an abundance of articles in critical magazines and newspapers on his works were produced; and his poems and radio plays attracted a great many admirers. In spite of all these positive reactions to his works, Eich never sought out the limelight of publicity, and until his death in 1972, he was reluctant to talk about himself or his past. Having become part of the literary canon of modern German literature, his works were taught in public schools and universities. He was also respected as a writer who had lived through National Socialism and endured the war as a soldier without compromising his integrity and humanity. Looking back at the National Socialist past and the way that the German public in the 1960s dealt with its recent history, Eich was aware that he was in part used as an alibi in efforts to soothe the conscience of German society. For this and other reasons—changes in the cultural climate, reactionary politics, and the dehumanizing forces in the modern world—Eich withdrew more and more into the language-oriented universe of his meditative and mysterious late poetry, which includes the collection *Anlässe und Steingärten* (1966; Occasions and Rock Gardens) and the controversial prose poems *Maulwürfe* (1968; Moles). These poems caused a greater stir among the public and his critics than had any of Eich's works since *Dreams*, a radio play first broadcast in April 1951.

Eich's reception started to change in 1979. Critics discussed the problem that writers such as Eich, Peter Huchel, and Wolfgang Koeppen may have been more deeply involved with the National Socialist regime than was previously believed and that their nonparticipation, resistance, and persecution was actually a myth. Such questions gave rise years later to a heated discussion about the role that Eich played in the Third Reich, a controversy that was sparked by Glenn Cuomo's 1989 monograph *Career at the Cost of Compromise: Günter Eich's Life and Work in the Years 1933–1945*. In this monograph, Cuomo describes Eich's work in the radio industry during the Hitler regime, a career that began in 1933 and that resulted in an astonishing amount of almost 160 radio plays. In the light of this engagement, Cuomo comes to the conclusion that Eich chose in those years to pursue a career in an environment where compromise was inevitable.

HOLGER A. PAUSCH

Biography

Born in Lebus/Mecklenburg, 1 February 1907. Studied economics and sinology in Berlin, Leipzig, and Paris; since 1932–33, worked as a freelance writer and author for a broadcasting company in Berlin; drafted and served in the German army, 1939–1945; taken as a prisoner of war by the United States army during World War II; traveled extensively and translated Chinese. Married the writer Ilse Aichinger, 1953. Georg Büchner Prize, 1959. Died in Groß Gmein, Austria, 20 December 1972.

Selected Works

Collections

Fünfzehn Hörspiele, 1966
Gesammelte Maulwürfe, 1972
Ein Lesebuch, 1972
Gedichte, 1973
Gesammelte Werke. 4 Bände, 1973, 1991
Pigeons and Moles: Selected Writings of Günter Eich, translated by Michael Hamburger, 1991

Poems

Gedichte, 1930
Abgelegene Gehöfte: Gedichte, 1948
Untergrundbahn, 1949
Botschaften des Regens, 1955
Ausgewählte Gedichte, 1960
Zu den Akten, 1964
Anlässe und Steingärten, 1966
Nach Seumes Papieren, 1972

Radio Plays and Prose

Der Traum am Edsin-Gol, 1932
Schritte zu Andreas, 1935
Träume, 1953; as *Dreams*, 1990
Die Mädchen aus Viterbo, 1954
Der sechste Traum, 1954
Zinngeschrei, 1955
Die Brandung vor Setúbal, 1957; as *The Rolling Sea at Setubal*, published with *The Year Lacertis* in *Journeys: Two Radio Plays*, translated by Michael Hamburger, 1968
Allah hat 100 Namen, 1957
Stimmen, 1958
Marionettenspiele, 1964
In anderen Sprachen, 1964
Festianus, Märtyrer, 1968
Kulka, Hilpert, Elefanten. Erzählungen, 1968
Maulwürfe: Prosa, 1968
Ein Tibeter in meinem Büro: 49 Maulwürfe, 1970
Katharina: Erzählungen, 1974
Zeit und Kartoffeln, 1973
Der 29. Februar. Erzählung, 1978

Further Reading

Briner, Heinrich Georg, *Naturmystik, biologischer Pessimismus, Ketzertum: Günter Eichs Werk im Spannungsfeld der Theodizee*, Bonn: Bouvier, 1978
Cuomo, Glenn R., *Career at the Cost of Compromise: Günter Eich's Life and Work in the Years 1933–1945*, Amsterdam and Atlanta, Georgia: Rodopi, 1989
Kohlenbach, Michael, *Günter Eichs späte Prosa: Einige Merkmale der "Maulwürfe,"* Bonn: Bouvier, 1982
Krispyn, Egbert, *Günter Eich*, New York: Twayne, 1971
Lieberherr-Kübler, Ruth, *Von der Wortmystik zur Sprachskepsis: Zu Günter Eichs Hörspielen*, Bonn: Bouvier, 1977
Neumann, Peter Horst, *Die Rettung der Poesie im Unsinn: Der Anarchist Günter Eich*, Stuttgart: Klett-Cotta, 1981
Pausch, Holger, and Marianne Herzog, "Vergessene Texte, Schrift, und Sprache: Beobachtungen zur Günter Eich-Kontroverse," *Wirkendes Wort* 45 (1995)
Richardson, Larry L., *Committed Aestheticism: The Poetic Theory and Practice of Günter Eich*, New York and Bern: Lang, 1983
Schafroth, Heinz F., *Günter Eich*, Munich: Beck, 1976
Schulte, Susanne, *Standpunkt Ohnmacht: Studien zur Melancholie bei Günter Eich*, Münster: Literatur Verlag, 1993
Vieregg, Axel J.A., *Der eigenen Fehlbarkeit begegnet: Günter Eichs Realitäten 1933–1945*, Eggingen: Edition Isele, 1993

Joseph Freiherr von Eichendorff 1788–1857

Joseph Freiherr von Eichendorff is the most popular of the German Romantic writers and is best known for his lyrical poetry and his novella *Aus dem Leben eines Taugenichts* (1826; translated as *Memoirs of a Good-for-Nothing, The Happy-Go-Lucky*, and *The Life of a Good-for-Nothing*). His popularity has undoubtedly been enhanced substantially by the fact that many of his poems were set to music. These songs were sung throughout the 19th century up until the 1950s by students and youth groups all over Germany. So popular were the songs based on his poems that they were virtually regarded as folk music. Older generations were required, as an integral part of their school curriculum, to memorize dozens of poems by renowned German poets, principal among them Eichendorff. That tradition is no longer cultivated in modern German educational institutions, and Romantic poems are, consequently, not as well known and cherished by today's young people as they were by their grandparents. Nevertheless, when thinking of Romanticism, some of Eichendorff's poems still immediately bring to mind the typical Eichendorff motifs that are so closely associated with German Romanticism: the rustling of the wind in the forest (*Waldesrauschen*), the moonlit sky with its bright stars, the song of the nightingale, wanderlust, romantic longing, love of God and his creations, and the melancholy tune of violins. These motifs, although limited in number, occur frequently in Eichendorff's best-known poems, many of which are interspersed in his prose writings.

Eichendorff's exuberant celebration of nature as a reflection of God's love for man is considered to be typically Romantic, and this praise is all the more surprising since his own life as a devoted civil servant did not particularly correspond to what is popularly regarded as the "Romantic life." To be sure, the fertile fields of rolling grain, gentle hills, and endless forests surrounding his ancestral country estate, Schloss Lubowitz, in the upper Oder Valley near Ratibor in the southern part of the province of Silesia (now Poland), left a lasting impression on the young man's mind, and that impression was strongly reinforced by the poet's regular and frequent return visits throughout his life. Besides the natural beauty of Upper Silesia, his sojourn as a student in Heidelberg must be regarded as a major contributing factor in Eichendorff's poetic development. The town, nestled in the Neckar valley, with the old stone bridge spanning the river, the partly ruined castle situated high above the town on the wooded hillside, the narrow medieval streets, and the famous university in the center with its perceived tradition of carefree student life, typifies Romanticism more than any other German city. Here, Eichendorff met and associated with other noted authors of the so-called younger Romantic movement: Novalis (*Hymnen an die Nacht, Heinrich von Ofterdingen*), Arnim and Brentano (noted for their famous folk-song collection *Des Knaben Wunderhorn*), and the influential lecturer and essayist Joseph Görres. Arnim and Brentano's folk-song collection, now located in the Heidelberg University Library, served as a rich source of inspiration for Eichendorff.

With his first novel, *Ahnung und Gegenwart* (1815; Premonition and Present Time), Eichendorff continued the tradition of the German bildungsroman, the first major example of which is Goethe's *Wilhelm Meister.* As in his novellas, which he wrote later, his early prose passages are frequently interrupted by lyrical poems, which in turn exemplifies an ideal sought by Romantic writers: the unity of the arts, notably prose and poetry. Both *Ahnung* and his later novel *Dichter und ihre Gesellen* (1834; Poets and Fellows) were of but fleeting interest. Eichendorff's theater productions, moreover, lack dramatic quality and pale in comparison with those of Tieck and others. Only his comedy *Die Freier* (1833; The Suitors) enjoys continued popularity and an occasional performance on the German stage. In noted contrast, his Romantic fairy stories *Die Zauberei im Herbste* (1808; Magic in the Fall), *Das Marmorbild* (1826; *The Marble Statue*), *Eine Meerfahrt* (1835; A Journey on the Sea), *Das Schloss Dürande* (1837; Castle Durande), and *Die Glücksritter* (1841; Knights of Fortune) are charming tales that depict conflicts between sensual temptation and the moral values of the Christian religion. His real genius, however, is revealed in his novellas. *Memoirs of a Good-for-Nothing* remains his best novella and has endured as one of the most popular prose writings in German literature. The "good-for-nothing" miller's son symbolizes the perfect antithesis to the typical "Philister." As God's favorite, he is sent into the "world" to be shown the creator's marvels in nature. Like a migrating bird, singing and playing his violin, Taugenichts's fairy-tale-like adventures take him south, finally to Rome, and then back to a palace near Vienna where, in the end, in typical fairy-tale fashion, he wins the hand in marriage of the "duchess," who, in reality, turns out to be the niece of the porter. As his guardian angel, however, she has faithfully watched over and guided him. While Taugenichts is favored by God and watched over by his "angel," "die Trägen," those who in their moral inertia "lie around at home," fail to be uplifted by God's miracles and remain forever preoccupied with mundane tasks.

Enchanted, the reader is captivated by the carefree life of the antihero who subordinates himself to God's will, his good fortune throughout, the beautiful depiction of nature in all of its glory, and the consoling and soul-soothing assertion: "und es war alles, alles gut."

In this masterful novella, but even more so in his poetry, Eichendorff's absolutely superb genius, his mastery of technical perfection, and his instinct for the synergism of spiritual values is revealed most strikingly. Perfect in language, rhythm, content, and form; rich in musicality; charming in their childlike, naive simplicity; and filled with human warmth and emotion, these poems have created for generations of readers the characteristic Romantic magical mood. They have also defined that mood as set by the depiction of the forest, mountains and valleys, medieval castles, nightingales, soulful tunes of guitars and violins in the distance, eternal jubilant springtime, the longing for "home," and, above all, God's unconditional love for man.

HANS-WILHELM KELLING

Biography

Born in Lubowitz, Silesia, 10 March 1788. Studied at Halle University, 1805–6, and Heidelberg University, 1807–8; studied law in Vienna, 1810–12; served in the volunteer forces in the War of Liberation, 1813–14 and 1815; commissioned, 1813; walking tour through the Harz mountains, 1805; in Paris and Vienna, 1808; in Lubowitz, 1809; in Berlin, 1809–10; dispatch clerk with the War Ministry, Berlin, 1815; civil servant trainee, 1816–19; assessor, 1819–21, for the Prussian Royal Government; government councillor for Danzig, 1821, the Ministry of Education and Cultural Affairs, Berlin, 1823, 1831–44, and Königsberg, 1824. Died 26 November 1857.

Selected Works

Collections

Werke, 4 vols., 1841; revised as *Sämtliche Werke,* 6 vols., 2nd edition, 1864

Vermischte Schriften, 5 vols., 1866–67

Werke, edited by Richard Dietze, 2 vols., 1891

Werke, edited by Ludwig Krähe, 2 vols., 1908

Gedichte, Erzählungen, Biographisches, edited by Max Wehrli, 1945

[Selected Poems], edited by Gerhard Prager, 1946

Neue Gesamtausgabe der Werke und Schriften, edited by Gerhart Baumann and Siegfried Grosse, 4 vols., 1957–58
Werke, edited by jost Perfahl et al., 5 vols., 1970–88
Werke, edited by Wolfgang Frühwald, Brigitte Schillbach, and Hartwig Schultz, 6 vols., 1985–

Fiction
Ahnung und Gegenwart, 1815
Aus dem Leben eines Taugenichts und Das Marmorbild: Zwei Novellen nebst einem Anhange von Liedern und Romanzen, 1826; *Aus dem Leben eines Taugenichts* as *Memoirs of a Good-for-Nothing,* translated by Charles Godfrey Leland, 1866; translated by Bayard Quincy Morgan, 1955; translated by Ronald Taylor, in *German Romantic Stories,* edited by Frank Ryder, 1966; as *The Happy-Go-Lucky,* translated by A.L. Wister, 1906; as *The Life of a Good-for-Nothing,* translated by Michael Glenny, 1966; *Das Marmorbild* as "The Marble Statue," translated by F.E. Pierce, in *Fiction and Fantasy of German Romance,* edited by Pierce and C.F. Schreiber, 1927
Viel Lärmen um Nichts, in *Der Gesellschafter,* edited by C.F. Gubitz, 1832
Dichter und ihre Gesellen, 1834
Das Schloss Dürande, 1837
Die Entführung, 1839
Die Glücksritter, 1841
Libertas und ihr Freier, 1864
Eine Meerfahrt, 1864
Auch ich war in Arkadien, 1866
Novellen, 1927
Erzählungen, 1946
Erzählungen, edited by Werner Bergengruen, 1955
Das Wiedersehen, edited by Hermann Kunisch, 1966

Poetry
Gedichte, 1837; revised edition, 1843
Neue Gedichte, 1847
Julian, 1853
Robert und Guiscard, 1855
Gedichte aus dem Nachlasse, edited by Heinrich Meisner, 1888
Joseph und Wilhelm von Eichendorffs Jugendgedichte, edited by Raimund Pissin, 1906
Eichendorffs Jugendgedichte aus seiner Schulzeit, edited by Hilda Schulhof, 1915
Gedichte, edited by A. Schaeffer, 1919
The Happy Wanderer and Other Poems, translated by Marjorie Rossy, 1925
Gedichte. Ahnung und Gegenwart, edited by Werner Bergengruen, 1955

Plays
Krieg den Philistern! 1824
Meierbeths Glück und Ende, in *Der Gesellschafter,* edited by F.W. Gubitz, 1827
Ezelin von Romano, 1828
Die letzte Held von Marienburg, 1830
Die Freier, 1833
Das Incognito: Ein Puppenspiel: Mit Fragmenten und Entwürfen anderer Dichtungen nach den Handschriften, edited by Konrad Weichberger, 1901; edited by Gerhard Kluge, with *Das Loch; oder, Das wiedergefundene Paradies: Ein Schattenspiel* (by Ludwig Achim von Arnim), 1968

Other
Die Widerherstellung des Schlosses der deutschen Ordensritter zu Marienburg, 1844
Zur Geschichte der neueren romantischen Poesie in Deutschland, 1846
Über die ethische und religiöse Bedeutung der neueren romantischen Poesie in Deutschland, 1847
Die geistliche Poesie Deutschland, 1847
Der deutsche Roman des achtzehnten Jahrhunderts in seinem Verhältnis zum Christenthum, 1851
Zur Geschichte des Dramas, 1854
Geschichte der poetischen Literatur Deutschlands, 2 vols., 1857
Aus dem Nachlass. Briefe und Dichtungen, edited by Wilhelm Kosch, 1906
Fahrten und Wanderungen 1802–1814 der Freiherren Joseph und Wilhelm Eichendorff, edited by Alfons Nowack, 1907
Lubowitzer Tagebuchblätter, edited by Alfons Nowack, 1907
Liederbuch, illustrated by Josua Leander Gampp, 1922
Schlesische Tagebücher (diaries), edited by Alfred Riemen, 1988

Translations
Juan Manuel, *Der Graf Lucanor,* 1840
Pedro Calderón de la Barca, *Geistliche Schauspiele,* 2 vols., 1846–53
Miguel de Cervantes, *Fünf Zwischenspiele,* edited by A. Potthoff, 1924

Edited Work
Gedichte, by Lebrecht Dreves, 1849

Further Reading

Brandenburg, Hans, *Joseph von Eichendorff: Sein Leben und sein Werk,* Munich: Beck, 1922
Kunz, Josef, *Eichendorff: Höhepunkt und Krise der Spätromantik,* Darmstadt: Wissenschaftliche Buchgesellschaft, 1951
Lüthi, Hans Jürg, *Dichtung und Dichter bei Joseph von Eichendorff,* Bern and Munich: Francke, 1966
Seidlin, Oskar, *Versuche über Eichendorff,* Göttingen: Vandenhoeck und Ruprecht, 1964; 3rd edition, 1985
Stöcklein, Paul, editor, *Eichendorff Heute,* Munich: Baierischer Schulbuch-Verlag, 1960; 2nd edition, Darmstadt: Wissenschaftliche Buchgesellschaft, 1966

Aus dem Leben eines Taugenichts 1826

Novella by Joseph Freiherr von Eichendorff

There is something peculiarly local about the reception of Eichendorff's novella *Aus dem Leben eines Taugenichts* (*Memoirs of a Good-for-Nothing*). For both Theodor Fontane and Thomas Mann, Good-for-Nothing represents qualities "exemplarily German" (Mann); he is the representative "type . . . of an entire nation" (Fontane). Why such a subtle and complicated people would see itself embodied in a figure of breathtaking guilelessness and erotic innocence is something of a mystery. The *ingénu,* the "innocent fool," however, is a feature of German literature from Parzival and Simplicissimus to the Grimms' Hans im Glück and Hans Castorp of Mann's *Magic Mountain.* Eichendorff's version of this literary topos has been especially popular, running to almost 100 editions in its first century of existence, and almost 60 more between 1945 and 1954. Other cultures, despite frequent translations, have found the novella difficult to assimilate with the same enthusiasm. Foreigners may be more likely to see the prototypical German embodied in Faust.

Unlike Faust, Good-for-Nothing lacks all elements of the demonic. He is gentle and nonviolent; his story is devoid of the sensational and transgressive. The narration does not froth and foam with titanic desperation. Gentle irony is its most characteristic mood. When Byronic characters do appear, they are treated with disdain. Eckbrecht, Good-for-Nothing's disheveled Roman acquaintance, raves drunkenly of his own genius and alienation from normal life, but our hero only feels horror for such attitudes. His true affinities are with the Wordsworth whose "chosen guide" in the *Prelude* is a wandering cloud. Those who find Eichendorff's book "quintessentially Romantic" are not wrong, if it is understood that in *Memoirs of a Good-for-Nothing* Romanticism is Catholic and Austrian, as opposed to Protestant and Promethean. There is no storming of heaven, ripping of bodices, or Gothic experimentation. When E.T.A. Hoffmann is invoked, it is always with disapproval. For Eichendorff, Hoffmann was a person whose whole life was only "a witty capriccio without actual substance." The earliest manuscripts of *Memoirs of a Good-for-Nothing* date from 1817, which was well within Hoffmann's career. Eichendorff had just given up his carefree student days to work as an employee (*Referendar*) in the Prussian civil service. An impoverished member of the landed gentry, he was beginning the life of monotony and routine that is the lot of the typical middle-class drudge. He had married in 1815. The longing of Good-for-Nothing for the bohemian life of the wandering minstrel and his envy of the uncaged bird both suggest Eichendorff's own nostalgia for an existence irretrievably lost.

His hero is "good for nothing" primarily in the Philistine evaluation. The boy's irritable father needs practical help with the work at his mill and takes offense as our hero stretches comfortably in the sun listening to the yellowhammer's avian arias in praise of idleness. It is not that our hero is lazy. He is intensely alive and energetic and leaps at the stern injunction to go forth into the wide world to seek his fortune. He just loves life too much to waste it in the dreary routine of daily toil. Soon losing the few coins his father gives him, Good-for-Nothing wanders aimlessly and happily, playing his fiddle and singing the lovely Franciscan lyric, "The man who in God's favor stands, / Has His command to wander free." Eventually, he meets any number of other Philistine types: the castle gardener who insists on productivity, the doorman who is disdainful of the hero's violin, and the farmer who cares neither for Italy nor for the *Pomeranzen* supposed to grow there. Complacency is an attitude he occasionally has to fight in himself as well.

The hero's cheerful songs draw the attention of two elegant ladies in a carriage; one of them is plump, aggressive, and cheerful, and the other is pale, distant, and contemplative. Both appeal to him, but he prefers the second. This pair constitutes the bipolar female figure familiar from *Das Marmorbild* (1826; *The Marble Statue*). Both women are thus characters in the story but are types as well. The direct and lively Flora is a type of Venus, while Aurelia, who seldom meets his gaze, is a type of the Virgin Mary. Each is in herself the bearer of a noumenal force, and during his moments of visionary uplift, our hero sees his acquaintances wrapped in the aura of their wider significance. Once, as he rows a party of celebrants that includes Aurelia, she trails a lily in the water of the pond. He looks at her reflection, which is that of an angel floating through the blue sky. Aurelia converts the water to firmament. Later he has a dream under an apple tree during which the same symbolic elements are reversed. It is Sunday, and Aurelia in white seems to float toward him on the wings of ringing chimes. She takes him by the hand, but when he sees her reflection in the water, Venus's element, her eyes turn fixed and hard, the water roils, and his fair lady becomes sinister and frightening. Representatives of Venus repeatedly lay siege to his virtue, but he is so awkward and erotically inept that he escapes unscathed, much to the annoyance of the ladies in question. His fidelity to Aurelia is unshakable and may be the reason for the allusion to the legend of the beautiful Magelone, which is also a story of fidelity rewarded.

A misunderstanding as to Aurelia's marital status leads to his flight to Italy at the same time as Flora and young Count Leonhard elope in disguise in the same direction. Our hero, although oblivious throughout to what is really happening, is of service to the couple in several inadvertent ways. Since Flora is disguised as a man, Good-for-Nothing is taken by spies to be Flora in disguise; they pursue him instead of the fleeing couple. When he returns home to Austria and Aurelia from "deceitful" Italy, there is a burst of patriotic relief. Soon he finds himself caught in a tender trap set by Flora and Leonhard, who have arranged for Aurelia and her faithful troubadour to be married in a double ceremony with themselves. In the garden scene,where all misunderstandings are corrected, we find Aurelia holding a riding crop instead of her usual lily. Flora also manipulates the same instrument, flinging it in the air, her brown locks flying. It is just a hint that the two poles of woman approximate each other at the moment of matrimony; the riding crop may even suggest the taming of men's nondomestic impulses. Leonhard enjoins the couple to "love each other like bunnies" (*Kaninchen*). Such an unsettling injunction is almost forgotten as Good-for-Nothing and his bride sit cracking almonds and dreaming of setting out again for Italy with all their favorite friends.

Dan Latimer

Editions

First edition: *Aus dem Leben eines Taugenichts und Das Marmorbild: Zwei Novellen nebst einem Anhange von Liedern und Romanzen,* Berlin: Vereinsbuchhandlung, 1826

Critical edition: in *Werke,* vol. 2, edited by Jost Perfahl, Munich: Winkler Verlag, 1970

Translations: *Memoirs of a Good-for-Nothing,* translated by Bayard Quincy Morgan, London: Calder, and New York: Ungar, 1955; translated by Ronald Taylor, in *German Romantic Stories,* edited by Frank Ryder, New York: Continuum, 1966

Further Reading

Adorno, Theodor W., "In Memory of Eichendorff," in *Notes to Literature*, 2 vols., edited by Rolf Tiedemann, translated by Shierry Weber Nicholsen, New York: Columbia University Press, 1991

Blackall, Eric A., "Moonlight and Moonshine: A Disquisition on Eichendorff's Novels," *Seminar* 6 (1970)

Bohm, Arnd, "Competing Economies in Eichendorff's *Aus dem Leben eines Taugenichts,*" *German Quarterly* 58 (1985)

Fontane, Theodor, letter to Paul Heyse, 6 January 1857 (quoted in Hughes)

Gould, Chester Nathan, "Literary Satire in Eichendorff's *Aus dem Leben eines Taugenichts,*" *Journal of English and Germanic Philology* 33, no. 2 (1934)

Hughes, Glyn Tegai, *Eichendorff: Aus dem Leben eines Taugenichts,* Great Neck, New York: Barron's Educational Series, and London: Arnold, 1961

Lukács, Georg, *German Realists in the Nineteenth Century,* translated by Jeremy Gaines and Paul Keast, edited by Rodney Livingstone, London: Libris, and Cambridge, Massachusetts: MIT Press, 1993

Mann, Thomas, "Von der Tugend," in *Betrachtungen eines Unpolitischen,* 1918; as "On Virtue," in *Reflections of a Nonpolitical Man,* translated by Walter D. Morris, New York: Ungar, 1983

Radner, Lawrence, *Eichendorff: The Spiritual Geometer,* Lafayette, Indiana: Purdue University Studies, 1970

Schumann, Detlev, "Eichendorff's *Taugenichts* and Romanticism," *German Quarterly* 9, no. 4 (1936)

Seidlin, Oskar, "Eichendorff's Symbolic Landscape," *PMLA* 72 (1957)

Workman, John D., "The Significance of the Taugenichts for Eichendorff," *Monatshefte* 33 (1941)

Carl Einstein 1885–1940

Although it is difficult to categorize Einstein's achievements, a number of common threads run through his multifarious activities: a radical contempt for what he saw as bourgeois values in literature, politics, and art; a tendency to find himself propelled into extreme positions, which he defended tenaciously; and a perennial quest for the transcendental, the "Wunder," the mystical, as a necessary and radical corrective to the rational world of scientific positivism.

Before World War I, he was the first German intellectual to champion cubism. Moreover, he was convinced that the theoretical implications of cubism could be applied to other arts, and he sought to give expression to this conviction in his remarkable prose piece *Bebuquin; oder, Die Dilettanten des Wunders* (1912; Bebuquin; or, The Dilettantes of Miracle). When the outbreak of hostilities threatened a widespread repudiation of French cultural values, Einstein responded by extolling Picasso and by translating from the French the letters of Vincent van Gogh. While 93 German intellectuals signed a manifesto justifying the war as a defense of German values, Einstein published a highly original analysis and justification of African art, a book that was to influence a generation of German writers. Transposing his revolutionary views on art to the political sphere, Einstein, having helped negotiate the withdrawal of German troops from Belgium, then returned to Berlin to take part in the abortive revolution on the side of the Spartakists. Because he elected to exile himself to France, his spiritual home, as early as 1928, Einstein is (like his friend Carl Sternheim) sometimes omitted from the annals of exile writing. When he fought in the Spanish Civil War, Einstein found himself, almost by accident, on the side of the anarchists and syndicalists in Barcelona. This latter activity effectively precluded any escape to Spain and led directly to his death in 1940, when he was, with many German refugees, trapped near the Spanish border.

Bebuquin; oder, Die Dilettanten des Wunders, published in installments in the periodical *Die Aktion* in 1912, was probably conceived in 1906 or 1907, for a short piece, entitled "Herr Giorgio Bebuquin," appeared in a journal edited by Franz Blei, *Die Opale,* in 1907. Both the early version and the final publication, which bears the note that it was "written for André Gide 1906/1909," display an intense involvement with the scientific, philosophical, and aesthetic issues that were stimulated by Einstein's academic studies. Indeed, the final text reflects Einstein's extraordinary capacity to grasp complex arguments and to apply them to literature. His "antinovel" implies a rejection of both the notion of nature as an objective reality and the perceiving subject as an adequate means of gaining access to that reality. Influenced by the physicist Ernst Mach and the art historian Konrad Fiedler, as well as by contemporary writers such as Paul Scheerbart, Einstein produced an antinovel that eschewed psychological verisimilitude in the interest of constituting a metaphysical, quasi-religious reality. Perhaps the clearest indication of Einstein's project emerges in the essays entitled "Totalität" (1914; Totality). Here he argues that art is not mimetic; its objects do not exist in the empirical world but are constituted in the act of seeing. Moreover, art is concerned not with the depiction of objects but with the structuring of a way of seeing. Art thus frees objects from the web of causal connections into which scientific rationality would enclose them and constitutes them as "absolute" objects, objects in their own right. Thus, the totality that comes into being is transcendent. According to Einstein, art embodies a mode of perception in which the traditional distinction between the perceiving subject and the object perceived is broken down; the art object is not a paraphrase, a metaphor, or an example of something else; it constitutes a reality in its own right.

If *Bebuquin* offered a creative illustration of Einstein's radical aesthetic, the theoretical framework was most clearly illustrated by *Negerplastik* (1915; African Art). For Einstein, African art embodied all the features that he had defined in the "Totalität" essays. Its discovery, contemporary with cubism, enabled Western art, according to Einstein, to overcome a loss of three-dimensionality, which had beset it since the Renaissance. The Renaissance had seen the development of perspective and, with it, the identification of the spectator's view with that of the artist, which thereby limited "den kubischen Raum." For Einstein, African art was, above all, religious and transcendent, qualities that precluded tacit collusion between artist and spectator; the religious function of the work further implied that the viewer played no part in determining the meaning. According to Einstein, African art did not present a frontal perspective that combined with a suggestion of depth; rather, through surface distortion, it offered a simultaneity of perspectives that could be apprehended in a single act of perception. The static quality of African statuary, he argued, results from the way that movement, successive variousness, was translated into formal, spatial qualities. Einstein was not concerned about interpreting specific examples of African statuary or masks, viewing the decorative features as mere ornament on utilitarian objects, or setting his chosen examples within a historical context. What he sought was to offer a radically new aesthetic, which, he believed, was exemplified and justified by African art.

It is unclear how much (or how little) Einstein knew of African art in 1915. Certainly, he gave no attributions for the illustrations that he appended to his text, and he appears not to have distinguished between African and Polynesian art, for several of his illustrations are obviously Polynesian. However, his essay had one unexpected consequence: early in 1916, the German military authorities, convinced by the success of the book that they had an expert on Africa on their hands, transferred Einstein to Brussels, where he was employed in the civilian administration of the Colonial Office, which was responsible for the Belgian Congo. It was in Brussels that Einstein began to study more systematically the ethnographic material readily available to him. In 1916, he published "Drei Negerlieder" in the periodical *Die Aktion,* which he described as "Nachdichtungen"; the following year a further three pieces appeared in the same journal; and the journal *Marsyas* published a series of "Negermythen," which were later included in his *Afrikanische Legenden* (1925; African Legends). These works were derived from a series of ethnographic surveys of various Congolese tribes, the *Collections de Monographies ethnographiques,* edited by Cyr. van Overbergh. Six of these myths are simply Einstein's translations from a 1910 study by Emile Torday and Thomas Joyce on the Bakuba and Bushongo tribes; five are from the 1912 companion volume by Robert Schmitz on the Baholoholo. Einstein's failure to give his sources may have buttressed his reputation as an expert on Africa and may have implied that he had more direct access to African culture than was actually the case. But Einstein used his access to the Belgian sources profitably; by 1921, when he published *Afrikanische Plastik* (African Statuary), he was able to supply detailed notes on individual items, precise attributions, and a bibliography of secondary sources.

Einstein's introduction to *Afrikanische Plastik* is far less speculative and theoretical than *Negerplastik.* While he continues to argue in *Afrikanische Plastik* that African sculpture resolves formal problems that the modern artist faces, he seems to have developed a healthy skepticism about "modish ideas of a romantic primitivism." He now insists that the ethnologist's help is essential in classifying the works of different tribes, yet he retains his conviction that African art offers radical cubist solutions to problems faced by modern artists. What his 1921 account gains in precision and circumspection, however, it loses in vigor and enthusiasm. It was precisely Einstein's relative ignorance of the historical, geographical, and ethnological contexts that permitted him in *Negerplastik* to employ African art as a justification of both cubism and his own aesthetic theory and practice. Just how close the similarities are between *Negerplastik* and Einstein's views on cubism emerges from his discussion of cubism in his *Die Kunst des 20. Jahrhunderts* (1926; The Art of the 20th Century), which comprises volume 16 of the *Propyläen Kunstgeschichte.* The cubist revolution is the focal point of Einstein's history, and the terminology that the work employs in writing about cubism makes it clear that the author both endorsed cubism and defined its revolutionary aesthetic in terms strikingly similar to those which he had used in 1915 to define African art. Cubism involved, for Einstein, the presentation of three-dimensional space in two-dimensional form, but without the interference of perspective. The result is "Totalität," a way of seeing that combines different perspectives to create a sense of the wholeness of an object.

The historical context of Einstein's remarks should not be ignored: he was, at an unpromising time, contributing to a fruitful mediation between French (cubist) experiments and a German public that had been encouraged by World War I to view anything French as decadent and subversive. As a regular contributor to the periodical *Die Aktion,* which became a vehicle for radical opposition to the war, Einstein was, through his advocacy of a radical new aesthetic, contributing to that opposition. Nor should the art historical context be ignored. Einstein's work also draws on Wilhelm Worringer's remarkable *Abstraktion und Einfühlung* (1907; *Abstraction and Empathy*), a seminal work for the Expressionist generation. Worringer's thesis was as follows: Graeco-Roman art, together with European art since the Renaissance, is an art of empathy, an art that sets out to maximize through perspective the empathy between the spectator and the work. Against this is set a countertendency in art, an urge to abstraction, an art that actively prevents the anthropocentric identification of viewer and artist in the work and that offers not immanence but transcendence. For Worringer, primitive art, Egyptian art, and early German art share an urge to provide objects that are not metaphors for something in the empirical world but ends in themselves. Einstein, whose eclecticism was notorious, clearly derived his justification for cubism (and the critical terminology that he employs to describe African art) from Worringer. Einstein's theory also had religious implications: his new mode of seeing (which he variously termed "vision," "the miraculous," the "hallucinatory," "totality," "the absolute"—or any tautological combination of these), being intuitive and transcendent, was a much-needed reaction to the process of increasing rationalism that had dominated European culture since the Renaissance. Einstein's cultural pessimism and his repudiation of scientific positivism both involved a positive reappraisal of the primitive and the medieval. The Expressionist generation frequently resorted to religious analogies to convey that "vision which they extolled." What mattered for Einstein was the association of certain formal features with transcendence, leading him to conclude that all African art was essentially religious. It is tempting to speculate that Einstein was, in some attenuated form, seeking a route back to the Jewish faith that his father, Daniel Einstein, head of the "Israelitische Landesstift" in Karlsruhe, had embraced, but that the self-styled prodigal son, Carl, had abandoned.

The experience of war and his involvement in the Soldiers' Council in Brussels in 1919 helped to persuade Einstein that there was a political dimension to African art. In an essay on primitive art in 1919, he redefines it as a "rejection of capitalist tradition," which imbued his theories with his recently acquired political radicalism. Together with this politicization came a more differentiated and historical interpretation of African art: by 1926 Einstein could, in his comments on the reopening of the Berlin Völkerkunde-Museum, remark on African art objects as "symbols of defeated, colonized peoples." Looking back in his volume *Die Kunst des 20. Jahrhunderts,* Einstein felt able to criticize those who (as he had himself done 11 years earlier) used African art merely as an antidote to an overcerebral, overcivilized society, and as a surrogate religion. By 1926 he was aware that African art needed to be viewed in its cultural context. Yet, paradoxically, the extraordinary impact of *Negerplastik* rested precisely on its refusal to explore that context.

By 1926 at the latest, Einstein had developed a more critical view of the Expressionist period. His growing political commitment to Marxist ideas made it clear to him that aesthetic revolution was not congruent with political revolution and could even serve as a substitute to it. After moving to Paris in 1928, Einstein involved himself with the surrealist debate. In *Die Fabrikation der Fiktionen* (The Fabrication of Fictions, written in the early 1930s, but published only in 1973), Einstein, conditioned by the political polarization of the period and alienated by the extreme subjectivity that he detected in surrealism, conducted his own retrospective debate on Expressionism. The key to his disillusionment is found in his diagnosis of the artist intellectual's isolation from the collective, for while he argues that African art is the product of a collective consciousness, he claims that modern art is trapped in its own subjectivity. By the 1930s Einstein had become an outspoken critic of the modernist exploitation of primitivism, an exploitation to which he had, through *Negerplastik,* contributed in no small measure.

While it was fashionable in the three decades after his untimely and tragic death to present Einstein as a forgotten or unjustifiably neglected writer, his career has, with the more recent publication of the five volume *Werke* and with a spate of doctoral dissertations, undergone a renaissance. His eclecticism and experimentation appear far less suspect to a postmodernist generation, and his many and varied contributions to literature, art history, aesthetics, ethnography, and cultural history, and the intellectual verve with which he operated at the interstices of these different fields have all won him a dedicated band of supporters, particularly in France and Germany.

RHYS W. WILLIAMS

Biography

Born in Neuwied am Rhein, 26 April 1885. Studied art history and philosophy, Berlin University, 1904; served on the Western Front, then moved to Brussels as a member of the military government; involved in the Spartakist uprising in Berlin, 1918–19; moved to Paris, 1928; fought in the Spanish Civil War. Died (suicide) near Pau, France, 3 July 1940.

Selected Works

Collections

Gesammelte Werke, edited by Ernst Nef, 1962
Gesammelte Werke in Einzelausgaben: Die Fabrikation der Fiktionen, edited by Sibylle Penkert, 1973
Werke, Band 1 (1908–1918), edited by Rolf-Peter Baacke, 1980
Werke, Band 2 (1919–1928), edited by Marion Schmid, 1981
Werke, Band 3 (1929–1940), edited by Marion Schmid and Liliane Meffre, 1985
Werke, Band 4: Aus dem Nachlaß I, edited by Hermann Haarmann and Klaus Siebenhaar, 1992
Werke, Band 5: Die Kunst des 20, Jahrhunderts, edited by Hermann Haarmann and Klaus Siebenhaar, 1996

Fiction and Nonfiction

Bebuquin; oder, Die Dilettanten des Wunders, 1912
Wilhelm Lehmbrucks graphisches Werk, 1913
Negerplastik, 1915
Anmerkungen, 1916
Der unentwegte Platoniker, 1918
Afrikanische Plastik, 1921
Die schlimme Botschaft, Zwanzig, Szenen, 1921
Der frühere japanische Holzschnitt, 1923
Die Kunst des 20. Jahrhunderts, 1926
Giorgio de Chirico, 1930
Georges Braque, 1934

Edited Works

with Georg Grosz, *Der blutige Ernst,* 1919
Afrikanische Legenden, 1925
with Paul Westheim, *Europa-Almanach,* 1925
Documents, 1929–31

Further Reading

Braun, Christoph, *Carl Einstein: Zwischen Ästhetik und Anarchismus: Zu Leben und Werk eines expressionistischen Schriftstellers,* Munich: Iudicium, 1987
Donahue, Neil, "Analysis and Construction: The Aesthetics of Carl Einstein," *German Quarterly* 61 (1988)
Heissenbuttel, Helmut, editor, *Carl Einstein,* Munich: Edition Text und Kritik, 1987
Heißerer, Dirk, *Negative Dichtung: Zum Verfahren der literarischen Dekomposition bei Carl Einstein,* Munich: Iudicium, 1992
Ihekweazu, Edith, "'Immer ist der Wahnsinn das einzig vermutbare Resultat': Ein Thema des Expressionismus in Carl Einsteins *Bebuquin,*" *Euphorion* 76 (1982)
Kiefer, Klaus H., "Carl Einsteins Negerplastik: Kubismus und Kolonialismus-Kritik," in *Literatur und Kolonialismus,* edited by Wolfgang Bader and Janos Riesz, Frankfurt: Lang, 1983
———, "Carl Einstein and the Revolutionary Soldiers' Councils in Brussels," in *The Ideological Crisis of Expressionism: The Literary and Artistic German War Colony in Belgium 1914–1918,* edited by Rainer Rumold and O. K. Werckmeister, Columbia, South Carolina: Camden House, 1990
Kiefer, Klaus H., editor, *Carl-Einstein-Kolloquium 1986,* Frankfurt and New York: Lang, 1988
———, editor, *Carl-Einstein-Kolloquium 1994,* Frankfurt and New York: Lang, 1996
Kramer, Andreas, *Die 'verfluchte Heredität loswerden': Studie zu Carl Einsteins "Bebuquin,"* Münster: Kleinheinrich, 1990
Meffre, Liliane, *Carl Einstein et la problématique des avant-gardes dans les arts plastiques,* Bern and New York: Lang, 1989
Oehm, Heidemarie, *Die Kunsttheorie Carl Einsteins,* Munich: Fink, 1976
Penkert, Sibylle, *Carl Einstein: Beiträge zu einer Monographie,* Göttingen: Vandenhoeck und Ruprecht, 1969
Schulte-Sasse, Jochen, "Carl Einstein; or, The Postmodern Transformation of Modernism," in *Modernity and the Text,* edited by Andreas Huyssen and David Bathrick, New York: Columbia University Press, 1989
Sorg, Reto, *Aus den 'Gärten der Zeichen': Zu Carl Einsteins "Bebuquin,"* Munich: Fink, 1998
Williams, Rhys W., "Primitivism in the Works of Carl Einstein, Carl Sternheim, and Gottfried Benn," *Journal of European Studies* 13 (1983)

Empfindsamkeit

Empfindsamkeit, or sensibility, designates the aspect of 18th-century culture concerned with feeling. Secondarily, it refers to sentimentality as a cultural phenomenon in later periods. It names neither a period nor a specific movement, but the word suggests a tendency or strand (*Strömung*) of 18th-century culture, and it normally appears in anthologies and literary histories in the constellation "Aufklärung, Empfindsamkeit, Sturm und Drang."

Empfindsamkeit extends the values of the Enlightenment to the realm of the emotions. Empirical examination and analysis, the search for the universal and typical, and tolerance of the eccentric are focused here on the newly emerging interiorized subject of the 18th century. Empfindsamkeit addresses the balance between head and heart—*Zufriedenheit* (contentment)—and, especially, disruptions to it such as passion, enthusiasm, boredom, and melancholy. Most commonly the imbalance appears as an overflowing of emotion. It is identified characteristically in the title of Friedrich Leopold Graf zu Stolberg's influential essay "Über die Fülle des Herzens" (1777; On Fullness of Heart), and it was adopted as the typical emotional stance of the Sturm und Drang. Empfindsamkeit is also concerned with the emotional faculties of imagination and intuition and with the combinations of emotional and rational faculties that result in sympathy, taste, and virtue. These interests were discussed under the rubrics of epistemology, moral philosophy, aesthetics, and literature and constitute an important strand of what the 18th century meant by "humanity." The famous apostrophe to sensibility in Laurence Sterne's *Sentimental Journey* (1768) characterizes the self-consciousness of the period's fascination with both extremes and fine nuances of feeling. This definition of sensibility deals not with feeling per se, but with the subject's observation and analysis of its own vagaries of feeling. In this respect it represents an important step in the gradual emergence of depth psychology by the end of the century. Prior to the 18th century, the discourses of virtue and emotion were still rooted in the religious sphere; by attaching them to the natural human world instead, Empfindsamkeit marked a new level of secularization in European culture.

The concern with emotion and observing the process of emotion was consistently tied to a new notion of nature, which became the carrier of affect previously associated with the supernatural. This new status was expressed in the controversy surrounding the revival of Spinoza's pantheism (the *Spinoza-Streit* of the 1780s unleashed by Friedrich Heinrich Jacobi), descriptions of and apostrophes to Nature, and discussions of the relationship of the picturesque and the sublime in regard to landscape. The English garden, with its apparent informality but careful programming of the visitor's emotional response, superseded the formal garden in this period. In landscape painting, Claude Lorrain was still supreme, but he was valued increasingly as a painter of mood rather than of truth to nature as he had been in the 17th century, and mood, primarily nostalgia, came to the fore in his followers and in Watteau. Even Sir Joshua Reynolds, the leading advocate of neoclassicism in painting, placed his subjects before increasingly emotive landscape backgrounds. Ruins, especially artificial ruins, were a necessary part of the landscape scenario; their literary counterpart was the fragment. The privileged emotions evoked by nature were those connected to memory and loss, whether mourning or nostalgia, which, unlike a similar preoccupation in Baroque culture, were now associated simultaneously with sensations of pleasure. Tears became a central image and arose as frequently from admiration and joy as from grief. Mourning was a much represented activity, and *Hamlet* became Shakespeare's most popular play for the first time in the history of his reception. By making the play's jester his spokesman for sentimentality, Sterne ironically highlighted the importance to the age of Hamlet's second-most-famous line, spoken in the graveyard, "Alas poor Yorick, I knew him, Horatio."

These themes coalesce in the two literary heroes of Empfindsamkeit, Shakespeare and Ossian. Shakespeare was valued for his naturalness and for his profound understanding of human psychology as the 18th century had just discovered it—"Nichts so Natur als Shakespeares Menschen!" (Nothing's so natural as Shakespeare's people!), Goethe cried in his "Rede zum Shakespeares-Tag" (1771, first published 1854; Shakespeare's Day Oration). Ossian, the Irish bard to whom James Macpherson attributed his forged epic of 1765, is the centerpiece of the emotional climax of Goethe's *Die Leiden des jungen Werthers* (1774; translated as *The Sorrows of Werther* and *The Sufferings of Young Werther*), the signature work of German Empfindsamkeit. In a mosaic of laments, the epic details the tragic deaths of its heroes and heroines, so that each segment seems in itself a fragment of some larger world now lost to knowledge. Itself an artificial ruin, *Ossian* reveals the latent connection between the nostalgia of Empfindsamkeit and the emergence of historicism.

Empfindsamkeit was practiced across all genres in Germany. In the drama it can be found in the extreme sensitivity of the title hero in Johann Elias Schlegel's neoclassical tragedy *Canut* (1746) and more obviously in the bourgeois tragedies pioneered by Gotthold Ephraim Lessing with *Miß Sara Sampson* (1755; translated as *Lucy Sampson, or The Unhappy Heiress* and *Miss Sara Sampson*). Its best-known and most influential examples were narrative, particularly Goethe's *Werther,* Johann Martin Miller's *Siegwart, eine Klostergeschichte* (1776; *Siegwart: A Monastic Tale*), and Sophie von La Roche's *Geschichte des Fräuleins von Sternheim* (1771; *The History of Lady Sophia Sternheim*). The effusive journal, similar in tone to Werther's letters, became a new genre in the hands of Johann Jakob Wilhelm Heinse and others. It is typical of the self-consciousness of the movement that *Werther* was both the acme and critique of Empfindsamkeit. Almost as influential and as popular all over Europe were Salomon Geßner's *Idyllen* (1756; translated as *Rural Poems* and *Idyls*) in rhythmic prose, which, unlike the Theocritean and Virgilian texts on which they are otherwise modeled, introduce sentimental family situations among the loves of shepherds. Johann Heinrich Voß's pastoral *Luise* (1795) and Goethe's *Hermann und Dorothea* (1797), which focus entirely on the middle-class family, were the classical heirs of this work. The other crucial narrative in the formation of Empfindsamkeit within Germany was Friedrich Gottlieb Klopstock's *Messias,* which began to appear in 1747. It is difficult to separate the impact of Klopstock's epic from that of his odes and other poems; he was revered in his time and in succeeding generations as the founder of the lyric style associated with Empfindsamkeit and as the enabler of German classical and romantic lyric. Other lyric poets identified with Empfindsamkeit are members of the Göttinger Hain (Göttingen Grove), a group gathered around Heinrich Christian Boie, and the Göttinger Musenalmanach that he founded in 1770. Ludwig Christoph Heinrich Hölty, Friedrich Leopold Graf zu Stolberg, and Voß are the best known poets in the group, while Gottfried August Bürger, Friedrich Daniel Schubart, and Matthias Claudius were associated more loosely with it.

The term *empfindsam* first appears in German in a letter by Luise Adelgunde Gottsched written on 4 September 1757. Lessing claimed to be coining the word when he proposed it to Johann Joachim Christoph Bode in order to translate the title of Laurence Sterne's *Sentimental Journey* in 1768, but it already had sufficient currency that several contemporaries noticed Lessing's error. Bode accepted the suggestion, and the term was rapidly adopted in German. Only in 1773 did *sentimental* appear as a German word rather than an explicit borrowing from French. Both words were connected with moral and physical delicacy and with the themes of friendship, love, and sensual capacity.

In the 1770s and 1780s, the term *Empfindsamkeit* designated the period of its vogue (1740 to the 1780s), and it was often used in combination with Sturm und Drang. This term broadened rapidly, however, to mean the preoccupation with or flaunting of feeling in general (sentimentality). In the late 1770s, a parallel pejorative vocabulary of sensibility emerged (e.g., *Empfindelei*). By 1830, *sentimental* and its derivatives, as well as all derivatives of *empfindsam,* had become pejorative. Empfindsamkeit was reevaluated as a historical phenomenon rather than a pathology at the end of the 19th century; it was identified as the irrational counterpoint to the Enlightenment and, by nationalist scholars, as the beginnings of a specifically German culture. Since World War II, it has increasingly been subsumed as an aspect of 18th-century culture complementary to and entwined with the Enlightenment and the Storm and Stress movement.

The emergence of Empfindsamkeit in Germany was multiply determined. Three significant strands of English influence have been identified: the psychologizing of moral philosophy by Shaftesbury and the school of Cambridge Platonists; the poetry of melancholy and death that was extremely popular in Germany (by Edward Young, Elizabeth Rowe, Thomas Gray, and Oliver Goldsmith); and the sentimental novels of Samuel Richardson, Oliver Goldsmith, and Laurence Sterne. The fact that the word *sentimental* was imported into German from French points to important French impulses as well, most notably from Diderot and the confessions and novels of Rousseau, which follow on a tradition of cultivation of feeling in the novel into the late 17th century.

The importance of Pietism and the emergence of the middle class for the development of Empfindsamkeit have been topics of much debate (summarized in Sauder). From the time that Empfindsamkeit became a subject of historical scrutiny in the mid–19th century, it was considered to have its roots in the rising middle class and in the Pietist movement that reached its height around 1730 and experienced a late flowering in the works of Count Niklaus Ludwig von Zinzendorf. Mystic influences on Empfindsamkeit became the exclusive focus of scholarship on the period at the beginning of the 20th century, and these influences were seen as the beginnings of the German overcoming of Western rationalism in the Nazi period. Since the war, many studies have focused on the complex that links sensibility, the rise of the middle class, and Pietism. It is difficult to determine the precise degree of secularization in the Pietist vocabulary that pervades the language of Empfindsamkeit. It is equally difficult to determine whether the adoption of religious language was motivated by a reaction against the rationalism of the Enlightenment or as a complement to it, especially since recent work by Gerhard Kaiser has pointed to the often cordial relations between leading Pietists and Enlightenment intellectuals. Similarly, it has been difficult to establish whether Empfindsamkeit was a product of the emerging middle class or a vehicle by which that class achieved intellectual respectability. The relationship of Empfindsamkeit to the emergence of the love-based nuclear family has begun to be explored relatively recently. It is emblematic that the term entered the language through Luise Adelgunde Gottsched but that its invention is credited to Lessing: in its concern with the tenderer emotions, Empfindsamkeit arose in women's writing (correspondence) and in plots focused on women (the novels of Richardson and bourgeois tragedy), but its feminine qualities were rapidly taken over by the dominant male culture. Only in La Roche and, since the discovery of her correspondence in 1950, Meta Klopstock has the specifically female voice of German Empfindsamkeit remained audible.

Empfindsamkeit ceased to be a dominant strand in German cultural life in the 1780s, but it never disappeared entirely. It was readily absorbed into the more drastic tones of the Sturm und Drang. While Goethe and Schiller turned away from it in the late 1780s, other writers, most notably Johann Gaudenz Freiherr von Salis-Seewis and Friedrich Matthisson, continued to write poetry in the sentimental mode through the 1790s. The tendency of Empfindsamkeit to self-analysis and the cultivation of feeling grounded the more sophisticated and generally less melancholy psychic practices of German Classicism and Romanticism. Nevertheless, *Ossian* (in Italian translation) and *Werther* remained among Napoléon's favorite books. After the Restoration, Biedermeier-era writers turned consistently to Empfindsamkeit rather than to the more immediately preceding cultural movements for its inspiration. Even Goethe reiterated his devotion to Laurence Sterne in his last years. The lyric of Empfindsamkeit in particular took on new life and popularity in settings of its poems and of Biedermeier imitations of them by major composers of the 19th century such as Schubert, Schumann, and Brahms. German anthologies of poetry through the 19th century also continued to feature the poets of Empfindsamkeit, and their tonalities color the lyrics of early modernist poets such as Georg Trakl. Sentimentality in a less specifically historical sense persists as a central quality in canonical narratives of the 19th century; in popular literature and film it remains a dominant quality even today.

JANE K. BROWN

See also Aufklärung

Further Reading

Brown, Marshall, *Preromanticism,* Stanford, California: Stanford University Press, 1991

Doktor, Wolfgang, and Gerhard Sauder, editors, *Empfindsamkeit: Theoretische und Kritische Texte,* Stuttgart: Reclam, 1976

Hohendahl, Peter Uwe, *Der europäische Roman der Empfindsamkeit,* Wiesbaden: Athenaion, 1977

Kaiser, Gerhard, *Aufklärung, Empfindsamkeit, Sturm und Drang,* Munich: Francke, 1976

Kluckhohn, Paul, *Die Auffassung der Liebe in der Literatur des 18.*

Jahrhunderts und in der deutschen Romantik, Halle: Niemeyer, 1922; 3rd edition, Tübingen: Niemeyer, 1966
Langen, August, *Der Wortschatz des deutschen Pietismus,* Tübingen: Niemeyer, 1954; 2nd edition, 1968
Sauder, Gerhard, *Empfindsamkeit, Band I: Voraussetzungen und Elemente,* Stuttgart: Metzler, 1974
Schulte-Sasse, Jochen, *Literarische Struktur und historisch-sozialer Kontext: Zum Beispiel Lessings Emilia Galotti,* Paderborn: Schöningh, 1975
Trunz, Erich, "Seelische Kultur: Eine Betrachtung über Freundschaft, Liebe und Familiengefühl im Schrifttum der Goethezeit," *Deutsche Vierteljahresschrift* 24 (1950); reprinted in Erich Trunz, *Weltbild und Dichtung im Zeitalter Goethes,* Weimar: H. Böhlaus Nachfolger, 1993

Ems, Rudolf von, *see* Rudolf von Ems

Engels, Friedrich, *see* Marx and Marxism

Engländer, Richard, *see* Peter Altenberg (Richard Engländer)

Enlightenment *see* Aufklärung

Hans Magnus Enzensberger 1929–

Unique among the generation of postwar German authors for the prominent role he has played in the cultural and intellectual debates of the last four decades, Hans Magnus Enzensberger first achieved recognition in the late 1950s and early 1960s for his provocative poetry and essays. His prolific work, however, includes fiction, documentary prose, drama, radio plays, commentaries, edited editions, and translations, as well as many productions in different media (film, textbooks, children's literature, reportage, audio recordings, libretti, and cabaret performance). Enzensberger's writing, which fuses an adroit handling of language with keen analysis, displays a continual, although not always continuous, development that has placed him at the forefront of the major trends that have affected the German literary scene since 1945. The postwar rediscovery of modernism, pivotal social and political crises, and the gradual emergence of a postmodernist sensibility are reflected in his works; issues that have preoccupied him include what constitutes ethically responsible action, whether literature can remain relevant in the electronic media age, and how reflective individuals make sense of events.

Enzensberger gained a broad literary background from studies at universities in Erlangen (where he wrote a dissertation on the Romantic German poet Clemens Brentano), Freiburg (site of a literary circle surrounding Rainer M. Gerhard, a poet and small-press publisher with international contacts), Hamburg, and Paris, at the Sorbonne. Experiences that shaped his career included student theater productions, a stint as a radio program editor in Stuttgart working under the writer Alfred Andersch, a lectureship in Ulm (where he encountered the "Concrete poets" Helmut Heißenbüttel, Eugen Gomringer, and Max Bense), contact with philosopher Theodor Adorno, international travels, and numerous translation projects (especially from English, French, Russian, Swedish, and Spanish). His first three volumes of poetry, *Verteidigung der Wölfe* (1957; Defense of the Wolves), *Landessprache* (1960; Language of the Land), and *Blindenschrift* (1964; Braille), and the essays collected as *Einzelheiten* (two volumes, 1962; revised 1964; Details) and *Politik und Verbrechen* (1964; *Politics and Crime*), established his reputation as one of the "angry young men" of postwar German literature. He had already been awarded the prestigious Büchner Prize in 1963 and held the guest professorship for poetry at the University of Frankfurt am Main in 1964–65. Although somewhat of an outsider at Gruppe 47 meetings and regarded initially by a few critics as tendentious, Enzensberger quickly gained a reputation as a highly original poet of acute intellect. His use of montage, conversational language, far-flung associations, and contemporary topics expanded the repertoire of techniques available to the German lyric genre; his "Fremder Garten" ("Strange Garden," from *Verteidigung der Wölfe*), which anticipates his later writings on environmental issues, is considered one of the first ecological poems.

Stylistically, his verse shows affinities to the poetry of Heinrich Heine, Bertolt Brecht, Gottfried Benn, Günter Eich, William Carlos Williams, and other modernists of the early 20th century. In turning to these literary predecessors, Enzensberger showed a commitment to creating a poetry that could adequately express meaning in the post-Holocaust era, a goal that he pursued both in his own verse and a series of programmatic essays. His influential anthology of international verse, *Museum der modernen Poesie* (1960; Museum of Modern Poetry), encouraged fellow writers to use international literature as a "working annex" for revitalizing German literature. While *Museum* compiled an impressive array of translations by some of the most prominent postwar German poets, essays in the *Einzelheiten* volume subtitled "Poetry and Politics" skeptically criticized experimentation for its own sake and portrayed socially engaged writers as models for German authors. An effective mediator of international literature and perspectives, Enzensberger promoted the work of Lars Gustafsson, Pablo Neruda, Nelly Sachs, and César Vallejo. His 1963 essay "In Search of the Lost Language" summarizes efforts to rebuild German literature, and Enzensberger continued innovative publishing projects as a reader for Suhrkamp (1963–64); he also founded *Kursbuch* (1965–75; Time Table) and *TransAtlantik* (1980–82; Transatlantic), and he was the editor of the book series *Die andere Bibliothek* (1989–; The Other Library).

Another part of *Einzelheiten,* "The Consciousness Industry," considered the postwar transformation of European culture. Building on the theoretical basis laid by the Frankfurt School philosophers Adorno and Max Horkheimer, Enzensberger criticized the power of the mass media, the language of journalism, and growing manifestations of Eurocentric attitudes (especially in tourism). *Einzelheiten* and *Politik und Verbrechen* considered the flawed nature of legal systems internationally, and various journalistic writings throughout the 1960s addressed current discussions of social theory by Hannah Arendt, Jürgen Habermas, and Herbert Marcuse. Enzensberger skillfully brought these matters and discussions to the attention of a broad audience of readers by effectively wielding rhetoric, didactic modes, concrete examples, and shrewd synopsis.

The years 1965 to 1968 are often regarded as marking a turning point in Enzensberger's career; some critics see his work in this period as symptomatic of a stubbornly nonconformist attitude toward political causes while others (Grimm) regard his efforts as part of his long-standing, undogmatic activism and characteristic of his uncanny ability to anticipate events. *Blindenschrift,* which made use of subdued, discursive voice and snapshot-like scenes, contrasted with his previous collections of rhetorically charged verse and appeared to signal a moderation in tone. In response to the growing political unrest in the late 1960s and also prompted by the infringement on civil rights within Germany, the war in Vietnam, and international student political demonstrations, Enzensberger turned his attention to documentary literature and took an increasingly public and often provocative stance on the issues of the day. In 1968 he resigned a position as a visiting fellow at Wesleyan University (Connecticut), using open letters to prominent international newspapers to announce that this move was prompted by the U.S. involvement in Vietnam (a gesture undercut when he traveled to the Far East before going to Cuba, as he implied he would immediately). Recognizing literature's limited practical ability to effect change, he acknowledged that it had in important respects become marginal to contemporary political debates. One important essay for *Kursbuch* ("Berliner Gemeinplätze" [Berlin Commonplaces]) even spoke of the "death of literature," a phrase widely misunderstood at the time as a call for the abandonment of literature altogether. Still, both *Gedichte 1955–1970* (1971; Poems 1955–1970) and *Die Gedichte* (1983; The Poems) give evidence that the author continued to work in the lyric genre during the subsequent decade.

Meanwhile, Enzensberger publicly advocated forms of literature suited to educating the readers politically, and he pursued this with the documentary drama *Das Verhör von Habana* (1970; *The Havana Inquiry*), which was based on testimony given at the trials held in Cuba after the Bay of Pigs invasion; *Freisprüche* (1970; Acquittals), a collection of statements by revolutionaries on trial; *Der kurze Sommer der Anarchie* (1972; The Short Summer of Anarchy), a biography of the Spanish anarchist Buenaventura Durruti; and essays collected in *Palaver* (1974; Palaver). A series of related editions, for which Enzensberger served as editor or commentator, appeared as well: Georg Büchner's *Der Hessische Landbote* (1965; The Hessian Messenger); *Klassenbuch* (1972; Class Book), a political reader; *Kurzgefaßter Bericht von der Verwüstung der Westindischen Länder* (1966; *The Devastation of the Indies*) by Bartolomé de las Casas; and *Gespräche mit Marx und Engels* (1973; Conversations with Marx and Engels). The latter two works were widely translated.

Enzensberger's experiments with diverse primary sources informed his next collection of poetry, *Mausoleum* (1975; *Mausoleum*), a series of ballads about the lives of mostly obscure inventors and historical figures. The poems deconstruct the notion of progress in technology and human history by using ironically montaged quotations gleaned from an encyclopedic array of texts. Its references to French Enlightenment philosophers and other theorists (Roland Barthes, René Descartes, Denis Diderot, Michel Foucault, Jean Jacques Rousseau, and others) were followed in the next two decades by a series of texts inspired by their work: *Der Menschenfeind* (1979; The Misanthrope), *Der Menschenfreund* (1984; The Philanthropist), *Diderot und das dunkle Ei* (1990; Diderot and the Dark Egg), *Diderots Schatten* (1994; Diderot's Shadow), and *Voltaires Neffe* (1996; Voltaire's Nephew).

Poetic sequence form, which structured *Mausoleum,* was further explored in *Der Untergang der Titanic* (1978; *The Sinking of the Titanic*). A highly crafted composition, this epic poem narrates its own history—how it began during Enzensberger's stay in Cuba in the late 1960s and then was lost in the mail, only to be reconstructed and completed in Berlin ten years later. Subsequent reworkings of the *Titanic* material involved a radio play (1979) and a dramatic production staged by Georg Tabori (1980). One of the few successful contemporary long poems in German, and perhaps Enzensberger's most important single work, the *Titanic* juxtaposes fictionalized vignettes set on board the sinking ship against musings about political activism of the late 1960s, and it thus expresses both the activist position Enzensberger once embraced and the mood of resignation in the 1970s. The epic is replete with allusions to literature (Dante, Edgar Allan Poe, Johann Wolfgang von Goethe, and others), art (Brueghel, Casper David Friedrich, and Albrecht Dürer), popular culture (film, souvenirs, songs, and Titanic flotsam), and contemporary events (the oil crisis, immigration issues, and television reports). It concludes with the autobiographically conceived main protagonist remarking, "I continue to wail, and to swim," an affirmation that expresses that, although perhaps little can be done to change the status quo, an individual should nonetheless resist apocalyptic chaos and apathy.

This stance of self-conscious protest continues in Enzensberger's major publications after the *Titanic,* the verse collections *Die Furie des Verschwindens* (1980; The Fury of Disappearance), *Zukunftsmusik* (1991; Music of the Future), and *Kiosk* (1995; *Kiosk*), as well as the essays *Politische Brosamen* (1982; *Political Crumbs*), *Ach Europa!* (1987; *Europe, Europe: Forays into a Continent*), *Mittelmaß und Wahn* (1988; *Mediocrity and Delusion*), *Die Große Wanderung* (1992; The Great Migration), *Aussichten auf den Bürgerkrieg* (1993; *Civil War*), and *Zickzack* (1997; Zigzag). His late verse reflects upon the location of boundaries between public and private domains, a sense of mortality, and the prospect of mass destruction (as in the long poem on the impact of the atomic age, "Die Frösche von Bikini" [The Frogs of Bikini]). Many poems register the intrusion of electronic media, chaos theory, molecular biology, and computer technology upon the "old medium" of poetry.

Enzensberger's essays, by contrast, examine new forms of illiteracy and cultural transformation brought on by the electronic media, pervasive consumerism, and inevitably imperfect governance systems; they use wit, bold formulations, dramatizations, and other descriptive strategies to stir readers. Enzensberger had in important respects given intellectuals on the Continent a voice in matters of international politics, yet his *Civil War* evoked mixed responses because he questioned whether direct action in Bosnia would have the desired results. This cool reception was followed by a period of limited comment on current events on the author's part. Assessments of his work will probably always be tied to the politically controversial stances he has taken, and Enzensberger himself has acknowledged his reputation as a writer who moves rapidly from one position to another, notably in *Der Fliegende Robert* (1989; The Flying Robert), a collection of poetry, scenes, and essays related to this subject.

Recognized as one of Germany's most significant and influential authors since 1945, Enzensberger has achieved an international reputation as a poet and essayist, particularly in Great Britain, the United States, and Scandinavia. His accomplishment lies in his adroit use of the linguistic medium, trenchant argumentation, and consistent resistance to the marginalization of literature in the public sphere. More than most authors, he has been able to absorb international trends productively and to mediate these to others, thus influencing several decades of younger writers who have learned from the ways in which Enzensberger's complex fascination with various experimental, multicultural, and forgotten texts has enriched literary language. As a postwar German author mindful of the painful consequences of Nazism, Enzensberger has continued to write about the contemporary world with a sense that history and the responsibility intellectuals have to society must always be kept in view when creating art. Although the connections between poetry and the temporal events of politics may sometimes develop coincidentally, they are in his view inevitable, a sentiment voiced in the title poem from *Kiosk,* which concludes, "Auch ich kaufe gern / bei den Parzen ein." (I, too, like to shop at the Fates).

CHARLOTTE MELIN

Biography

Born in Kaufbeuren, 11 November 1929. Studied at the universities of Freiburg and Hamburg; Ph.D. from University of Erlangen, 1955; studied at the Sorbonne, University of Paris, 1952–54; served in the Volkssturm, 1944–45; program editor, South German Radio, Stuttgart, 1955–57; guest lecturer, Academy of Design, Ulm, 1956–57; reader for Suhrkamp publishers, Frankfurt, 1960–61; professor of poetry, University of Frankfurt, 1964–65; founder, 1965, and publisher, 1970–90, of *Kursbuch;* founding editor of *TransAtlantik,* 1980–82; publisher of Die Andere Bibliothek book series, from 1985; fellow, Center for Advanced Studies, Wesleyan University, Middletown, Connecticut (resigned 1968), in Norway, 1961–65. Villa Massimo grant, 1959; Jacobi Prize, 1956; Critics Prize (Germany), 1962, 1978; Büchner Prize, 1963; Etna-Taormina Prize, 1967; Nuremberg Cultural Prize, 1967; Pasolini Prize, 1982; Heinrich Böll Prize, 1985; Bavarian Academy of Fine Arts Award, 1987; Currently lives in Frankfurt.

Selected Works

Poetry

Verteidigung der Wölfe, 1957
Landessprache, 1960
Gedichte, 1962
Blindenschrift, 1964
Poems, translated by Michael Hamburger, 1966
Poems for People Who Don't Read Poems, translated by the author, Michael Hamburger, and Jerome Rothenberg, 1968; as *Selected Poems*, 1968
Gedichte 1955–1970, 1971
Mausoleum: 37 Balladen aus der Geschichte des Fortschritts, 1975; in English, translated by Joachim Neugroschel, 1976
Der Untergang der Titanic, 1978; as *The Sinking of the Titanic*, translated by the author, 1980
Beschreibung eines Dickichts, 1979
Die Furie des Verschwindens: Gedichte, 1980
Dreiunddreißig Gedichte, 1981
Die Gedichte, 1983
Hans Magnus Enzensberger, edited by A.V. Subiotto, 1985
Gedichte, 1950–1985, 1986
Zukunftsmusik, 1991
Selected Poems, translated by the author and Michael Hamburger, 1994
Kiosk: Neue Gedichte, 1995; as *Kiosk*, translated by the author and Michael Hamburger, 1997
Gedichte 1950–1995, 1996

Plays

Das Verhör von Habana, 1970; as *The Havana Inquiry*, 1974
El Cimarrón, music by Hans Werner Henze (from a work by Miguel Barnet) (produced 1970), 1971
La Cubana, music by Hans Werner Henze (produced 1975)
Der tote Mann und der Philosoph (radio play), 1978
Der Menschenfeind (from the play *Le Misanthrope*, by Molière (produced 1979), 1979
Der Menschenfreund (produced 1984), 1984
Die Tochter der Luft (produced 1992), 1992
Voltaires Neffe, 1996

Other

Zupp: Eine Geschichte in der sehr viel vorkommt, 1959
Brentanos Poetik, 1961
Einzelheiten, 1962
Einzelheiten II: Poesie und Politik, 1964
Politik und Verbrechen, 1964; as *Politics and Crime*, edited by Michael Roloff, 1974
Politische Kolportagen, 1966
Deutschland, Deutschland unter anderm: Äusserungen zur Politik, 1967
Staatsgefährdende Umtriebe, 1968
Der kurze Sommer der Anarchie, 1972
The Consciousness Industry, edited by Michael Roloff, 1974
Palaver: Politische Überlegungen (1967–1973), 1974
Der Weg ins Freie: Fünf Lebensläufe, 1975
Raids and Reconstructions: Essays on Politics, Crime, and Culture, 1976
Politische Brosamen, 1982; as *Political Crumbs*, 1990
Critical Essays, edited by Reinhold Grimm, 1982
Ach Europa! 1987; as *Europe, Europe: Forays into a Continent*, translated by Martin Chalmers, 1989
Dreamers of the Absolute: Essays on Politics, Crime, and Culture, 1988
Mittelmaß und Wahn: Gesammelte Zerstreuungen, 1988; as *Mediocrity and Delusion*, 1992
Requiem für eine romantische Frau, 1988
Der fliegende Robert: Gedichte, Szenen, Essays, 1989
Diderot und das dunkle Ei: Eine Mystifikation, 1990
Die Große Wanderung, 1992
Aussichten auf den Bürgerkrieg, 1993; as *Civil War*, translated by Piers Spence and Martin Chalmers, 1994
Diderots Schatten, 1994
Zickzack: Aufsätze, 1997
Der Zahlenteufel, 1997; as *The Wizard of Numbers*, translated by Michael Henry Heim, 1998
The European Challenge: Essays on Culture, Value and Policy in a Changing Continent, with others, edited by Kees Paling and Vic Veldheer, 1998

Translations

John Gay, *Die Bettleroper* (in *Dreigroschenbuch*), 1960
Jacques Audiberti, *Quoat-Quoat*, in *Theaterstücke 1*, 1961
William Carlos Williams, *Gedichte*, 1962
César Vallejo, *Gedichte*, 1963
Franco Fortini, *Poesie*, 1963
Lars Gustafsson, *Die Maschinen: Gedichte*, 1967
Pablo Neruda, *Poesie impure: Gedichte*, 1968
Alexander Suchovo-Kobylin, *Der Vampir von St. Petersburg*, 1970
Edward Lear, *Komplette Nonsens*, 1977
Pablo Neruda, *Die Raserei und die Qual: Gedichte*, 1986
Edith Södergran, *Klauenspur: Gedichte und Briefe*, 1990
Lars Gustafsson, *Ein Vormittag in Schweden*, 1998

Edited Works

Clemens Brentano, *Gedichte, Erzählungen, Briefe*, 1958
Museum der modernen Poesie, 1960
Allerleirauh: Viele schöne Kinderreime, 1961
Vorzeichen: Fünf neue deutsche Autoren, 1962
Andreas Gryphius, *Gedichte*, 1962
Gunnar Ekelöf, *Poesie*, translated by Nelly Sachs, 1962
Nelly Sachs, *Ausgewählte Gedichte*, 1963
Georg Büchner, *Der Hessische Landbote*, 1965
Bartolomé de las Casas, *Kurzgefaßter Bericht von der Verwüstung der Westindischen Länder*, 1966; as *The Devastation of the Indies*, 1974
Friedrich Schiller, *Gedichte*, 1966
Heinrich Mann, *Politische Essays*, 1968
Freisprüche: Revolutionäre vor Gericht, 1970
Klassenbuch: Ein Lesebuch zu den Klassenkämpfen in Deutschland 1756–1971, 1972
Gespräche mit Marx und Engels, 1973
Der Weg ins Freie, 1975
Allgemines deutsches Reimlexikon, 1982
Das Wasserzeichen der Poesie, under the pseudonym Andreas Thalmayr, 1985
Ludwig Börne und Heinrich Heine: Ein deutsches Zerwürfnis, 1986
Alexander Herzen, *Die gescheiterte Revolution*, 1988
Stig Dagerman, *Europa in Trümmern: Augenzeugenberichte aus den Jahren 1944–1948*, 1990

Further Reading

Bridgewater, Patrick, "Hans Magnus Enzensberger," in *Essays on Contemporary German Literature*, edited by Brian Keith-Smith, London: Oswald Wolff, 1966
Dietschreit, Frank, and Barbara Heinze-Dietschreit, *Hans Magnus Enzensberger*, Stuttgart: Metzler, 1986

Enzensberger, Hans Magnus, "In Search of the Lost Language," *Encounter* 21, no. 3 (1963)
Fischer, Gerhard, editor, *Debating Enzensberger: "Great Migration" and "Civil War,"* Tübingen: Stauffenburg, 1996
Grimm, Reinhold, "The Commitment and Contradiction of H.M. Enzensberger," *Books Abroad* 47, no. 2 (1973)
———, "Poetic Anarchism? The Case of H.M. Enzensberger," *Modern Language Notes* 97, no. 3 (1982)
———, *Texturen: Essays und anderes zu Hans Magnus Enzensberger*, New York: Lang, 1984
Grimm, Reinhold, editor, *Hans Magnus Enzensberger*, Frankfurt: Suhrkamp, 1984
Korte, Hermann, "Hans Magnus Enzensberger," in *Kritisches Lexikon zur deutschsprachigen Gegenwartsliteratur,* Munich: Edition Text und Kritik, 1997
Melin, Charlotte, "A Look at Enzensberger's America before and after 'On Leaving America'," in *Amerika! New Images in German Literature,* edited by Heinz D. Osterle, New York: Lang, 1989
Monroe, Jonathan, "Swimming and Wailing through History," *Northwest Review* 19, no. 3 (1981)
———, "Between Ideologies and a Hard Place: Hans Magnus Enzensberger's Utopian Pragmatist Poetics," *Studies in Twentieth Century Literature* 21, no. 1 (1997)
Parkes, K. Stuart, *Writers and Politics in West Germany,* New York: St. Martin's Press, and London: Croom Helm, 1986
Schickel, Joachim, editor, *Über Hans Magnus Enzensberger,* Frankfurt: Suhrkamp, 1972; 3rd edition, 1979
Schultz, K. Lydia, "A Conversation with H.M. Enzensberger," *Northwest Review* 21, no. 1 (1983)
———, "Writing as Disappearing: Enzensberger's Negative Utopian Move," *Monatshefte* 78, no. 2 (1986)
Sewell, William Seymour, "H.M. Enzensberger and William Carlos Williams: Economy, Detail, and Suspicion of Doctrine," *German Life and Letters* 32, no. 1 (1978/79)
———, "Doppelgänger Motif and Two-Voiced Poems in the Work of H.M. Enzensberger," *German Quarterly* 52, no. 3 (1979)
Siefken, Hinrich, and J.H. Reid, editors, *"Lektüre—ein anarchischer Akt": A Nottingham Symposium with Hans Magnus Enzensberger,* Nottingham: University of Nottingham, 1990

Episches Theater

The concept of Epic Theater (Episches Theater) as it developed in Germany during the 1920s has a dual lineage. On the one side, it descended from Erwin Piscator's expansion of the stage action by means of film and documentary material, which was intended to represent the decisive historical trends of the time. On the other side, it descended from the analytical approach to the presentation of dramatic action cultivated by the theater director Erich Engel and, subsequently, by Bertolt Brecht.

Piscator exploited the technical facilities available to the modern theater in order to convey a sense of the monumental political developments of the time—whether his subject matter was German history, the Russian Revolution, or the working-class struggle in North America. In this sense of the term, *Epic Theater* contained the notion of establishing a foundation myth for the new age that was anticipated in the wake of World War I. In his public statements of the late 1920s, Brecht supported Piscator's theatrical ventures as a style of theater appropriate to the times, and he evidently learned much from Piscator about the contribution that back projection, moving film, and stage machinery could make to a production. But in his private notes of the time, he was critical of an approach that sought to enthuse theatergoers about the atmosphere of revolution rather than using the opportunities of live theater to revolutionize their thinking.

Engel, who directed several productions of Brecht's plays in the course of the 1920s, including *The Threepenny Opera,* is remembered for a style of interpretation that exposed the dramatic structure of a play, whether traditional or modern, by encouraging the actors to take an intellectual approach to the presentation of their roles and by means of simple gestures and cool, clear diction. His productions also tended to isolate each scene as an entity in itself rather than treating it as contributing toward the impetus and atmosphere of the play as a whole. Brecht explicitly acknowledged Engel's contribution to the techniques of Epic Theater in 1927, and several features of Engel's production style entered into Brecht's later theorization of Epic Theater. In his notes to the opera *Rise and Fall of the City of Mahagonny,* on which he collaborated with the composer Kurt Weill and the stage designer Caspar Neher in 1928–30, Brecht systematizes his thinking about the direction in which he wished to see the theater develop, drawing up a table of distinctions between "epic" and "dramatic" theater. Brecht's use of these terms is strongly mindful of their traditional poetological connotations: "epic" for him implies an act of narration that tells a modern audience what their world is really like—as opposed to presenting them with the illusion of a drama unfolding before their eyes. It is in this context that Brecht emphasizes that audiences should have rational, intellectual responses to theatrical performances; he thus downplays the principle on which Aristotelian theories of drama are based, that audiences should empathize with the plight of characters on stage. At a later date, Brecht illustrated his approach to stage acting by imagining a street scene in which individual bystanders seek to explain to others, by means of words and gestures, how a traffic accident had come about. At a more sophisticated level, he envisaged each scene of a play as embodying what he called a *Gestus,* a demonstration of an aspect of human relations that revealed something about the underlying organization of the society that the play depicted.

Brecht's notes on the Mahagonny opera lay particular emphasis on the "separation of the elements" in a theatrical production: the text, the actions, the music, and the visual effects should not be thought of as combining into an organically integrated whole but as providing contrasting and mutually critical perspectives on each other. His conception of Epic Theater is Marxist, not only in the sense that it is frequently associated with a critique of capitalist society and with the hope for a historical transcendence of that society, but in its explicit emphasis on the susceptibility of the social world to processes of change that derive ultimately from the changing nature of economic production. In Brecht's view, it is a fundamental purpose of Epic Theater to represent the world as changeable. It was on this basis that he developed ideas about techniques of *Verfremdung* (i.e., representing aspects of the familiar world on stage in ways that made them appear strange or remarkable). He wanted Epic Theater to assist the audiences of a "scientific age" in comprehending the complexities of the world in which they lived and to train them in the habits of observation appropriate to that world. It is also clear from Brecht's actual practice in theater, as well as from his later theoretical writings (particularly the 1948 "Short Organum for the Theatre"), however, that the effects of discovery that he wished to offer theater audiences depended as much on judicious combinations of conventional theatrical techniques (including naturalistic ones) as they did on the innovative style of acting that he describes in his early writings. Brecht's conception of Epic Theater became influential in the 1950s and 1960s—when the reputation of the Berliner Ensemble was at its height—not only in the sense that it invited imitation but also that it stimulated writers and directors to develop his ideas in a critical spirit both within the German Democratic Republic (Volker Braun, Peter Hacks, and Heiner Müller) and further afield (Max Frisch, Friedrich Dürrenmatt, Peter Weiss, Edward Bond, and Peter Brook). Since that time, the techniques associated with it have become incorporated into the standard repertoire of effects in international theater.

DAVID MIDGLEY

Further Reading

Benjamin, Walter, *Versuche über Brecht,* Frankfurt: Suhrkamp, 1966; as *Understanding Brecht,* London: New Left Books, 1973

Brauneck, Manfred, editor, *Klassiker der Schauspielregie: Positionen und Kommentare zum Theater im 20. Jahrhundert,* Reinbek bei Hamburg: Rowohlt, 1988

Fuegi, John, *Bertolt Brecht: Chaos, According to Plan,* Cambridge and New York: Cambridge University Press, 1987

Grimm, Reinhold, editor, *Episches Theater,* Cologne and Berlin: Kiepenheuer und Witsch, 1966; 3rd edition, 1972

Innes, C.D., *Erwin Piscator's Political Theatre: The Development of Modern German Drama,* Cambridge: Cambridge University Press, 1972

Knopf, Jan, *Brecht-Handbuch: Theater,* Stuttgart: Metzler, 1980

Speirs, Ronald, *Bertolt Brecht,* Basingstoke: Macmillan, and New York: St. Martin's Press, 1987

Szondi, Peter, *Theorie des modernen Dramas: 1880–1950,* Frankfurt: Suhrkamp, 1956; as *Theory of the Modern Drama,* Cambridge and Oxford: Polity, and Minneapolis: University of Minnesota Press, 1987

Voigts, Manfred, *Brechts Theaterkonzeptionen: Entstehung und Entfaltung bis 1931,* Munich: Fink, 1977

Willett, John, *The Theatre of Erwin Piscator: Half a Century of Politics in the Theatre,* London: Methuen, 1978

Epistolary Novel

Traditional definitions and descriptions of epistolary fiction, and, specifically, the epistolary novel, epitomize the schizophrenic elitism inherent in modern literary criticism. On the one hand, the letter per se, subsumed as a subgenre under autobiographical writings, is valued because it provided the developing modern novel with a naturalized link to historical authenticity. The letter supposedly grounded the novel in empirical reality. For this purpose, 18th-century novels, circumspect for their fictionality and their portrayal of bourgeois interiors that revealed the previously hidden lives of women, often include editorial prefaces that base the novel's existence on the circumstantial discovery of a "bag of mail," as in Christian F. Gellert's *Leben der schwedischen Gräfin von G**** (1750; *Life of the Swedish Countess G****). In such works, the author hides behind the professional objectivity of an editor, simply collecting and sorting an autobiographical narrative rather than inventing it. The result is a "double fictionality," by which one fiction authenticates the other in form of a fiction (H. Brown). In addition, once the 18th-century epistolary writers stripped the letter of most of the classical ideas of rhetoric and style, they raised the aristocratic idea of aesthetic "Natürlichkeit" (naturalness) to the genre's new code (Nickisch, Nies). Due to women's perceived role as mediators between culture and nature, authentic letters by women or letters written as women would have supposedly written them presented a "natural origin," which could then be framed within an authorial narrative. Samuel Richardson professedly based his epistolary novel of morality, *Pamela; or, Virtue Rewarded* (1740), on his model book of letters for educated young women. One of the most famous instances of letters producing a fiction around their author's voice and their historical authenticity are the *Lettres Portugaises* (1669; *Portuguese Letters*), supposedly written by the narrator herself, a young nun; we have recently discovered, however, that the work was written by Claude Barbin himself after all. But even before the authorship was suspect, writing *a la Portugaise* became the *crier dernier* style for a whole generation of amorous correspondences and epistolary novels.

On the other hand, the letter's attraction for expressions of desire, whether in the form of personal confession, scandalous gossip, or political challenge, has also imbued the epistolary novel with a heightened sentimentality, as in Sophie von La Roche's *Geschichte des Fräuleins von Sternheim* (1771; *The History of Lady Sophia Sternheim*) and Johann Wolfgang Goethe's *Die Leiden des jungen Werthers* (1774; translated as *The Sorrows of Young Werther* and *The Sufferings of Young Werther*), which was a vent for excess and licentiousness. Choderlos des Laclos's *Les Liaisons Dangereuses* (1782; *Dangerous Liaisons*) is an example of the latter, so-called extravagant narratives (MacArthur), not only in content but also in form: the rake Marquis de Valmont writes his most famous love letter to virtuous Madame de Tourvel—the letter that finally proves his honorable intentions to her—on the naked back of a prostitute. While the letter form thus imparted its fiction of legitimacy to the new genre, the modern novel, it also imparted to it its incestuous and adulterous desires (also the desire for the transgression of its generic limits, desires that both founded and challenged the novel's status [Tanner]). With Mikhail Bakhtin, one could call the epistolary novel the most obvious expression of polyphonic discourse. Hans Robert Jauss even goes so far as to see a displacement of the sentimental novel of the 18th century by a self-reflective critique of the novel via letters.

In addition to the importance of the epistolary form for the modern novel during the course of its development in the 18th century, authors and scholars in the period conducted their literary theory and philosophy as, not just in form of, epistolary correspondence and thereby, as Habermas (1987) and Heckendorn Cook have argued, expanded their bourgeois private sphere to a literary public. For the German context, Gert Mattenklott explicates how the "longing for autarchic self-creation" reached its high point with the Romantics and their "embracing of theory and novel." As evidenced by Friedrich Schlegel's *Lucinde* (1799) and his *Gespräch über die Poesie* (1800), the Romantic mixture of reflections, letters, and bildungsroman ruptured narrative authority, which in turn structurally shaped the form of the modern novel. According to Karl Heinz Bohrer, Gustav Hillard, and Gottfried Honnefelder, the letter exhausted its special qualities as a dialogic medium in the process. With the discontinuity and dissolution of the individual subject, the letter supposedly lost its ability to communicate and became just another manneristic form of self-reflective narrative.

The critical bias inherent in these dualistic genre definitions marks the history of the epistolary novel and articulates itself in the separation of the letter's "particularity of material existence in a specific historical moment" from its vehicle function for literary or theoretical contents (Kauffmann, 1992). In the wake of positivist science, annotated editions of letters chosen for their autobiographical authenticity and for their historical value exemplify the first extreme. Their role was to supply substantial evidence for the master narratives of literary criticism and historiography. Even today, editions of letters and epistolary novels are chosen according to preexistent biases such as fame, fortune, scandal, literary merit, and historical evidence. With the advance of feminist criticism and social history, new editions reflect a change in focus. The "ordinary" letter has become the center of attention for many period and local studies. Due to the increased availability of these letters, which previously had to be read in libraries and archives, more and more essays about epistolary theory and fiction concentrate on or include the "familiar" letter (Goldsmith). The other extreme includes studies in which letters simply carry out the critic's aesthetic directions (Bohrer). Both extremes of epistolary theory are interested not so much in the letters themselves as in the subjects who wrote the letters and the individual subjects who constitute themselves in and through the letters. For theories based on Gellert's postulation that the letter stands in for oral dialogue, that it is a "direct personal expression of a subject's feelings and intentions," the questioning of these subject positions automatically results in a proportional superfluity of the epistolary novel (Nolden).

With the conventional or imaginary sending of a letter, the activities and personnel involved in writing and reading are separated by time and place and defined accordingly. In addition, a letter, real or metaphorical, is a dispatch, conceived of as a physical object moving through time and space (e.g., a message in a bottle, *Rohrpost,* or *Briefpost*); its very existence as a letter presupposes a detachment from its originating environment (writer, sender, place, and time). But as the discussion about the subject-position should have made clear, it is not just the letter that changes location; the subject itself is dislocated in the process. Jacques Derrida studies this result of the postal system in his theoretical epistolary novel *La Carte Postal* (1980; *The Postcard*). With the advance of mechanically and electronically handled mail, mail-order business transactions, computerized banking, and electronic mail via fax, satellite, or computer, it is understandable that literary scholars find it difficult to sort out their letters. Ivar Ivask and John L. Brown's essays in the special issue of *World Literature Today*: *The Letter: A Dying Art?* (1990) provide an example of this difficulty in their melodramatic accounts of the fate of the letter in a media age. Ivask believes that scholars and readers alike find a respite from "impersonal experimentation for experimentation's sake" in the letter form, which lets them "share in the realities of our common human experience in time and place." Brown states that all agree that "the health of the letter has been dealt a fatal blow by the telephone, the telegram, the cassette, the fax, and other technical innovations that have deprived it of its raison d'être. The authentic 'personal' letter (factitious as this can often be) has been further devaluated by the rise of computerized mail." The insecurity about the "law of genre" also points to the larger problems and challenges for literary criticism today. The complexity of communication forms and their interaction with the epistolary form necessitates interdisciplinary cooperation and a diversity of methodological approaches.

When scholars and writers speak of the trend of modern epistolary fiction toward aesthetic monologization (Bohrer) or even proclaim the end of the letter as a communicative medium and a literary device (Honnefelder), their arguments can only be understood if situated within the anxiety about the fate of art and the subject in our postindustrial age: "[P]ublic discussion increasingly conjured up the end of the letter. Throughout the 20th century the tendencies to declare the death of the letter became stronger. Blamed was the extension of other communication media which let the letter appear as a *curiosum* in the public mind." This tendency, characterized here by Angelika Ebrecht, reflects an uneasy cultural pessimism, which is in turn fueled by a rigidly normative definition of genre. This definition found new nourishment in the modernist crisis of the subject, the subject's dislocation in the technological age, and this self-conscious subject's attempt at expressing its crisis as an inversion of the private/public dichotomy of the Enlightenment: "Now letters should constitute less the public sphere than shelter the private sphere from the transformation through a cultural i.e. social situation conceived as destructive" (Ebrecht). During a time of instability such as the early decades of the 20th century, the letter's major function again became its character as a vehicle, its ephemeral quality, and this inspired Jürgen Habermas (*Wege aus der Moderne,* 1988) to see modernism as an unfinished project: "In the enhanced valuation of the transitory, the liminal, the ephemeral, in the celebration of the dynamic, the longing for an immaculate, pausing presence announces itself. As a self-negating movement, modernism is 'longing for true presence.'"

The very "waywardness" of the letter is invested with the ability to transcend its content and move beyond the limitations of its time and place (H. Brown). In Hugo von Hofmannsthal's *Ein Brief* (1902; translated as *A Letter* or *The Lord Chandos Letter*), which connects this therapeutic function of the letter most notably with the critique of language, the letter ambiguously attests to the impossibility of establishing meaning, while at the same time enabling a transcendence of the hermeneutic crisis. Hans Bemmann's *Erwins Badezimmer; oder, Die Gefährlichkeit der Sprache* (1984; Erwin's Bathroom; or, The Danger of Language) continues Hofmannsthals's tradition by employing the letter form as a means to restore the polysemic potential of language for humanity's and humanism's survival against all odds (Göttsche, Simon). Indeed, the increase in publications of epistolary novels at the end of the 20th century, most noticeable in the internationally popular *Griffin and Sabine* art-book trilogy by Nick Bantok (1991–93), speaks of a desire for simplification and comprehension of communications technology, postindustrial networks, postcolonial liaisons, and hybrid connections (sexual, racial, and cultural). It is as if the letter were sending itself beyond each crisis into a stable universe while taking its participants back toward the Enlightenment idea of an individual existing in a mediated, yet well-temperate harmony with nature. The letter form is deaestheticized to preserve its cognitive potential for the process of aestheticization.

As a sample of the quantity and diversity of contemporary epistolary fiction in Germany, and as a suggestion for further reading, I offer the following titles, although many more could be mentioned: Marga Berck's *Sommer in Lesmona* (1951; A Summer in Lesmona), Christine Brückner's *Ehe die Spuren verwehen* (1954; Before the Traces Disappear) and *Das glückliche Buch der a.p.* (1970; The Happy Book of a.p.), Ingeborg Bachmann's *Malina* (1971; *Malina*), Peter Handke's *Der kurze Brief zum langen Abschied* (1972; *Short Letter Long Farewell*), Ulrich Plenzdorf's *Die neuen Leiden des jungen Werther* (1973; The New Sufferings of Young Werther), Irmtraud Morgner's *Leben und Abenteuer der Trobadora Beatriz nach Zeugnissen ihrer Spielfrau Laura* (1974; Life and Adventures of Trobadora Beatriz), Friederike Mayröcker's *Die Abschiede* (1980; The Farewells), Stefan Heym's *Ahasver* (1981; *The Wandering Jew*), Wolfgang Hildesheimer's *Mitteilungen an Max* (1983; *Missives to Max*), Herbert Rosendorfer's *Briefe in die chinesische Vergangenheit* (1983; *Letters Back to Ancient China*), Natascha Wodin's *Briefe aus Rußland* (1984; Letters from Russia), Hans Bemmann's *Erwin's Badezimmer; oder, Die Gefährlichkeit der Sprache* (1984; Erwin's Bathroom; or, The Danger of Language), Peter-Jürgen Boock/Peter Schneider's *Ratte—tot . . .* (1985; Rat—dead), and Eva Demski's *Hotel Hölle, guten Tag . . .* (1987; Hotel Hell, Good Morning).

SUNKA SIMON

See also Bildungsroman; Goethe, Die Lieden des jungen Werthers; Sophie von La Roche

Further Reading

Altman, Janet Gurkin, *Epistolarity: Approaches to a Form,* Columbus: Ohio State University Press, 1982

Becker-Cantarino, Barbara, "Leben als Text: Briefe als Ausdrucks- und Verständigungsmittel in der Briefkultur und Literatur des 18. Jahrhunderts," in *Frauen, Literatur, Geschichte,* edited by Hiltrud Gnüg and Renate Möhrmann, Stuttgart: Metzler, 1985

Benstock, Shari, "From Letters to Literature: 'La Carte Postale' in the Epistolary Genre," *Genre* 18 (Fall 1985)

Bohrer, Karl Heinz, *Der romantische Brief: Die Entstehung ästhetischer Subjektivität,* Munich: Hanser, 1987

Brown, Homer Obid, "The Errant Letter and the Whispering Gallery," *Genre* 10, no. 4 (Winter 1977)

Brown, John L., "Whatever Happened to Mme. de Sévigné? Reflections on the Fate of the Epistolary Art in a Media Age," *World Literature Today* 64, no. 2 (Spring 1990)

Ebrecht, Angelika, et al., editors, *Brieftheorie des 18. Jahrhunderts: Texte, Kommentare, Essays,* Stuttgart: Metzler, 1990

Favret, Mary A., *Romantic Correspondence: Women, Politics, and the Fiction of Letters,* Cambridge and New York: Cambridge University Press, 1993

French, Lorely, *German Women as Letter Writers, 1750–1850,* Madison, New Jersey: Fairleigh Dickinson University Press, 1996

Goldsmith, Elizabeth C., editor, *Writing the Female Voice: Essays on Epistolary Literature,* Boston: Northeastern University Press, and London: Pinter, 1989

Göttsche, Dirk, *Die Produktivität der Sprachkrise in der modernen Prosa,* Frankfurt: Athenäum, 1987

Heckendorn Cook, Elizabeth, *Epistolary Bodies: Gender and Genre in the Eighteenth-Century Republic of Letters,* Stanford, California: Stanford University Press, 1996

Hillard, Gustav, "Vom Wandel und Verfall des Briefes," *Merkur* 23 (1969)

Honnefelder, Gottfried, *Der Brief im Roman: Untersuchungen zur erzähltechnischen Verwendung des Briefes im deutschen Roman,* Bonn: Bouvier, 1975

Ivask, Ivar, "The Letter: A Dying Art?" *World Literature Today* 64, no. 2 (Spring 1990)

Jauss, Hans Robert, *Question and Answer: Forms of Dialogic Understanding,* Minneapolis: University of Minnesota Press, 1989

Kamuf, Peggy, *Fictions of Feminine Desire: Disclosures of Heloise,* Lincoln: University of Nebraska Press, 1982

Kauffman, Linda S., *Discourses of Desire: Gender, Genre, and Epistolary Fictions,* Ithaca, New York: Cornell University Press, 1986

———, *Special Delivery: Epistolary Modes in Modern Fiction,* Chicago: University of Chicago Press, 1992

MacArthur, Elizabeth Jane, *Extravagant Narratives: Closure and Dynamics in the Epistolary Form,* Princeton, New Jersey: Princeton University Press, 1990

Moravetz, Monika, *Formen der Rezeptionslenkung im Briefroman des 18. Jahrhunderts,* Tübingen: Narr, 1990

Nickisch, Reinhard M.G., *Brief,* Stuttgart: Metzler, 1991

Nies, Fritz, "Un genre féminin," *Revue d'Histoire Litteraire de la France* 78 (1978)

Nolden, Thomas, *An einen jungen Dichter: Studien zur epistolaren Poetik,* Würzburg: Königshausen und Neumann, 1995

Perry, Ruth, *Women, Letters, and the Novel,* New York: AMS Press, 1980

Picard, Hans Rudolf, *Die Illusion der Wirklichkeit im Briefroman des 18. Jahrhunderts,* Heidelberg: Winter, 1971

Runge, Anita, *Literarische Praxis von Frauen um 1800: Briefroman, Autobiographie, Märchen,* Hildesheim: Olms-Weidmann, 1997

Runge, Anita, and Lieselotte Steinbrügge, editors, *Die Frau im Dialog: Studien zu Theorie und Geschichte des Briefes,* Stuttgart: Metzler, 1991

Simon, Sunka, "Contemporary Epistolary Fiction and Theory: A Postmodern Poetics?" Ph.D. dissertation, Johns Hopkins University, 1992

Tanner, Tony, *Adultery in the Novel: Contract and Transgression,* Baltimore, Maryland: Johns Hopkins University Press, 1979

Voßkamp, Wilhelm, "Dialogische Vergegenwärtigung beim Schreiben und Lesen: Zur Poetik des Briefromans im 18. Jahrhundert," *Deutsche Vierteljahrsschrift* (1971)

Eschenbach, Wolfram von, *see* Wolfram von Eschenbach

Exile Literature

The term *exile literature* normally refers to literary works produced in the period 1933–45. Recent research, however, tends to extend these date limitations in both directions. Even before 1933, certain prominent literary figures had chosen to live and work outside Germany and Austria. Joseph Roth and Kurt Tucholsky lived in Paris; Herwarth Walden had left for the Soviet Union; and René Schickele moved to Sanary-sur-Mer in the south of France, which was later to become one of the favored locations for exiles from Germany, although at first many preferred Paris. But exile meant forced departure—not free choice. Those in danger left immediately, including Robert Neumann, Alfred Kerr, Heinrich Mann, and Walter Mehring. Heinrich Mann accepted Czech citizenship but lived in France. His brother, Thomas Mann, continued to have his books published in Germany until November 1936, when he, too, accepted Czech citizenship. He remained a Czech citizen for eight years but lived in Switzerland until he moved to the United States and became an American citizen. Switzerland had offered a refuge for many German-speaking radicals in the 19th century, but by 1933, it had introduced strict immigration laws and excluded more refugees than it admitted. By contrast, Czechoslovakia became the preferred first home for many exile writers and intellectuals. The Netherlands, too, with its long experience of publishing and printing, offered a refuge for those exiles still eager to find outlets for their work. But France, Czechoslovakia, and the Netherlands would all prove short-lived homes for exiled writers as the Nazi war machine overran these countries.

Despite the warning signs in Hitler's *Mein Kampf,* many writers were slow to leave. Some delayed until it was too late, and they were imprisoned and murdered. The case of Carl von Ossietzky was taken up by an international campaign that led to his being awarded the Nobel Peace Prize in 1935, but this did not save him from torture and death in a concentration camp. Writers still inside Germany after January 1933 were soon made fully aware of Nazi intentions when on 10 May, university students, with high-level encouragement, ceremoniously burned the books of all those authors who were deemed opponents of the new regime, especially if they were Jews, communists, or pacifists. So Erich Maria Remarque, author of the war book the Nazis hated, *Im Westen nichts Neues* (1929; *All Quiet on the Western Front*), became an early exile. By the time the Law for the Establishment of the Reich Culture Chamber was brought out on 22 September 1933, over 2,000 writers had emigrated, and there was not a single author of international standing left in Germany.

Although deprived of citizenship and, apparently, of their reading public, exile authors did not lapse into silence. On the contrary, a remarkable range of activity developed in exile: indeed, it could be argued that the only valid German literature produced after 1933 was that produced by the "other Germany" outside the national boundaries. Remarkably, publishers for exile literature were found in Amsterdam, Prague, Vienna, Paris, and Zurich. Soviet Russia, Great Britain, and North and South America became home to exiles fleeing further afield. There, too, publishers were found. Banned journals came to life again, literary organizations and networks were set up, and exile books were collected—as in the German Freedom Library in Paris, which, by the first anniversary of the book burning, had a stock of some 13,000 volumes. Poems continued to be written, novels were published, and in Zurich and Vienna for a time plays could be performed. As a Marxist, Bertolt Brecht had been one of the first to emigrate, and he was lucky enough to have the first productions of his exile plays in Zurich's Schauspielhaus.

Clearly, exile literature had to be different from what was being produced inside Nazi Germany, but the debate revolved around the question of how it could differ. In some important cases there could be no expectation of immediate change. Many major works, such as Robert Musil's *Der Mann ohne Eigenschaften* (*The Man without Qualities*), had been started before the author had had to leave Austria. Despite its great length (three volumes), this work remained unfinished when the author died in exile in Geneva in 1942. Similarly, that other great Austrian writer, Hermann Broch, could not suddenly change direction. From 1934 on, he did attempt work in an anti-Nazi vein, but his most famous novel, *Der Tod des Vergil* (1945; *The Death of Virgil*), written in U.S. exile and published in 1945, seems far removed from such concerns. At the same time, works by such authors, even if continued in exile, could not remain unaffected by the events of the time. The "pressure to be political" was inescapable even for apolitical writers such as Musil, Broch, and Thomas Mann. Aesthetic questions were also important. Would exile literature be a continuation of the difficult, avant-garde trends of the Weimar Republic, or would the year 1933 mark a break with the past and bring a need to confront the problems of the present more directly and accessibly?

Responses to the Nazi seizure of power were in effect bound to be disparate. Writers in exile had only one thing in common: the fact that they had been forced to leave their homeland. Apart from that, they were a mixture of every form of political and aesthetic persuasion. Many (but by no means all) of the exiled authors were Jewish, and even Jewish writers in many cases were so assimilated that only Nazi extremism had forced them to look anew at their forgotten roots. Not surprisingly, there was no such thing as a unified exile community of interest. Writers in exile brought with them many of the best features of the lost homeland but also many of the worst (such as intellectual infighting). In such circumstances, exile literature could never be homogeneous.

To all, exile came as a shock. Although many were convinced that their residence abroad would be of short duration and that the rotten regime would soon collapse, exiles instead saw National Socialism establish itself and gain success in many spheres—from the economic to the military. Some reviewed their position, decided they could not stand an uprooted existence, and returned. The most notorious case of this kind was that of Ernst Glaeser, an established literary figure who went into exile in Switzerland, where he wrote *Der letzte Zivilist* (1936; *The Last Civilian*), a novel charting the rise of National Socialism in a small town. The book became a best-seller that was translated into 25 languages. But by 1939, Glaeser had decided to return and was welcomed back into Nazi Germany. Nevertheless, such renegades were comparatively few. Even the outright monarchists and conservatives among the exiles could not stomach the Nazi regime. The greatest of these was undoubtedly Joseph Roth, an Austrian, who produced a stream of novels from *Flucht ohne Ende* (1927; *Flight without End*) and *Radetzkymarsch* (1932; *Radetzky March*) onward, which marked him out as one of the greatest German prose writers of the age. The author of *Hiob* (1930; *Job*), a parable of the Old Testament Jew, Roth could never be viewed favorably by the anti-Semitic Nazis, and he died in exile in Paris in 1939.

In this connection, it is easy to assume that the novel would prove the preferred genre for writers in exile. Drama needs the technical resources of a modern theater, while poetry is often regarded as the domain of a small, select elite. This view, however, disregards other possibilities. Writers have to survive, and in many cases, this meant writing, as Joseph Roth did, for newspapers and exile journals. Hence, it is not surprising that some journalists were immediately successful while more literary figures took longer to adapt. The newspaper world of the Weimar Republic had been highly developed, and its pressmen and women were soon able to exploit their talents to attack National Socialism with a vigor equal to the venom with which the Nazis had attacked them. Their first impulse was to expose the horrors of the Nazi prisons and concentration camps, and a flood of books for this purpose was soon on the market, such as the *Dungeons of Spandau* (1933), by the famous "raging reporter" Egon Erwin Kisch, followed by similar material put out by the propaganda genius Willi Münzenberg in his Editions du Carrefour. This series included Arthur Koestler's *Black Book on Spain* (1936), which was clearly modeled on Münzenberg's *Brown Book on Reichstag Fire and Hitler Terror* (1933), which in turn had sold some 600,000 copies in some 25 languages by 1935. Eventually, this fierce opponent of National Socialism fell out of favor with Stalin and the Communist Party. Münzenberg died in mysterious circumstances while trying to escape from France. Koestler went on to become one of the most successful of all exiles writing in German. His international standing was confirmed by the appearance of his novel *Darkness at Noon* (1940); it dealt with Russia but was rooted in his experiences in the Spanish Civil War. One of the prodigies of Berlin journalism of the 1920s, Koestler freed himself from the Communist ideology and was henceforth denounced by the faithful as a renegade.

Writers in exile had to tackle the problem of National Socialism, but it was not only in journalistic or historical form that concern over the nature of Germany and the quest for the roots of the tragedy were to be found. Writers also wrote about the experience of exile itself, sometimes exploiting, as Thomas Mann did, the possibilities of the historical novel, as in *Joseph in Ägypten* (1936; *Joseph in Egypt*), which he had been working on in his Joseph series since 1932. In 1936, Mann also started on *Lotte in Weimar*. But the dominant form of the age, apart from the historical novel, was the so-called *Deutschlandroman* (Germany novel). Even before Glaeser, Lion Feuchtwanger, the famous author of *Jud Süß* (1925; *Jew Süß*), had brought out *Die Geschwister Oppenheim* (1933; *The Oppenheims*) in Amsterdam. This novel was part of a trilogy that had started with *Erfolg* (1930; *Success*), a novel about Hitler's beginnings in Bavaria, and that was completed with *Exil* (1939; *Exile*), published in Amsterdam. All three novels were gathered together under the heading "Waiting-Room Trilogy," and they characterized the essential exile experience. What Feuchtwanger, with his focus on the experiences of a middle-class Jewish family, appreciated more than most was the fact that anti-Semitism was at the very heart of the National Socialist program. His model for the *Deutschlandroman* was followed by similar novels by F.C. Weiskopf and Oskar Maria Graf.

Other novelists, besides such radicals, also showed their concern for Germany in the form of the novel, including Heinz Liepmann with *Das Vaterland* (1933; *The Fatherland*) and Arnold Zweig with *Das Beil von Wansbeck* (1947–48; *The Executioner's Axe*), which was not published until after the war. Of all the novels of this type, the most successful was *Das Siebte Kreuz* (1942; *The Seventh Seventh Cross*) by Anna Seghers. She had started writing it in France in 1937, and it began to appear in serial form in the exile journal *Internationale Literatur* in Moscow. It eventually came out as a book in German in Mexico. In English translation it became a Book-of-the-Month Club selection in the United States before being turned into a Hollywood film. With such roots in France, Russia, Mexico, and the United States, it serves as a perfect example of the exile novel. A similar fate awaited Zweig's novel. Based on a story from a Prague newspaper read by Zweig in England, it eventually came out in Hebrew in Israel. After the war, Zweig's novel was published in Sweden and acclaimed in the German Democratic Republic, where it was filmed in 1951. It was then filmed later in the Federal Republic. Both novels give a cross section of life in Nazi Germany, showing how the mass of the people continued to live in a police state in which abnormality had become the norm. The novels written in exile by Irmgard Keun also present a clear picture of life in Nazi Germany—their great merit. The perspective of her novel *Nach Mitternacht* (1937; *After Midnight*) is that of a young girl. She offers no ponderous antifascism, simply the experience of life under a dictatorship expressed with wit and humor. Thomas Mann's son Klaus favorably reviewed Keun's *After Midnight* under the heading "German Reality" and himself went on to publish a series of exile novels, the most successful of which was his roman à clef, *Mephisto* (1936), yet another *Deutschlandroman*. This novel reflects the reality of the Third Reich through the prism of the glamorous world of the theater. This work, too, was later made into a successful film.

Inside Germany, the most popular literary form both with regime-friendly writers and with so-called inner emigrants was the historical novel. As noted, this also proved to be the case with exile authors, to the point where they were accused of a flight from reality. Thomas Mann had shown the way with his cycle of Joseph novels, and Feuchtwanger followed with his Josephus novels, but Heinrich Mann spent years in exile in France expressing his opposition to everything Hitler and National Socialism stood for by writing novels based on the historical figure of Henry IV of France (1935, 1938; *Henri Quatre*). Even Brecht wrote a Julius Caesar novel, and Gustav Regler and others followed in the same vein. Perhaps the most epic of all such historical surveys was delivered by Alfred Döblin with the 2,000 pages of his *November 1918* (completed and published 1948–50), while the most prestigious of all the exercises in the historical form was Thomas Mann's *Doktor Faustus,* first published in 1947 by the firm Bermann-Fischer, which had by then moved from exile in Vienna to Stockholm. Similar to Hermann Hesse's *Glasperlenspiel* (*The Glass Bead Game*), however, this work did not appear until after the war, although its impact was by no means thereby diminished.

In general, most critical attention has been directed to the novels of German literary exile. As far as the drama is concerned, Bertolt Brecht has captured most of the limelight, with the result that many other exile dramatists have slumbered in his shadow. Ferdinand Bruckner, one of the most successful dramatists of the Weimar Republic, did, however, deal directly with the Third Reich in an early play, *Die Rassen* (1934; *Races*), which, as its title indicates, tackles the treatment of Jews. Friedrich Wolf, too, was successful with *Professor Mamlock,* a play on a similar theme, which, after its theatrical premiere in Zurich in 1934, reached an international public through a Russian film adaptation in 1938. Other Weimar dramatists faded in exile. Ödön von Horváth was accidentally killed in Paris; Ernst Toller became one of the many suicides in exile; and only Franz Werfel, with his *Jacobowsky und der Oberst* (1944; *Jacobowsky and the Colonel*), a "comedy of a tragedy" about the fall of France, had a Broadway and Hollywood hit. He also had international success with the film version of his novel *Das Lied von Bernadette* (1941; *The Song of Bernadette*). Of the dramatists, Brecht alone went on to write a series of magnificent plays, although even he never had the Broadway success for which he longed. Since he was a confirmed Marxist, this was an unlikely ambition. His antifascist plays such as *Arturo Ui* would never have been acceptable in such a milieu, but then neither would his parable plays and experiments in epic theater and alienation, which never deal with Germany or the Third Reich directly. Only in *Flüchtlingsgespräche* (*Refugee Conversations*), written in Finland in 1940–41, did Brecht comment on political developments in Germany in order to expose key concepts of the Nazi system.

While it was exile in Finland that gave birth to *Refuge Conversations,* it was exile in Denmark that was the trigger for Brecht's most famous collection of poems, the *Svendborger Gedichte* (1939; *Svendborg Poems*). Brecht thereby established himself not only as the greatest dramatist in exile but also as the greatest German poet in exile. Yet he was by no means the only exile poet. In fact, an incredible amount of poetry was written in exile by many poets of great talent and ability, and they found publishers for their work. Some of them used their lyrical talents to attack National Socialism in various verse forms. In this sphere, Thomas Mann's daughter Erika, with her cabaret *Die Pfeffermühle* (*The Pepper Mill*), was among the most successful. But there were other outlets for exile poetry. Adrienne Ash has discerned three separate literary generations of poets in exile. In her view, the first and older generation was made up of those associated with Expressionism and the avant-garde of the Weimar Republic—Johannes R. Becher, Else Lasker-Schüler, Franz Werfel, Max Herrmann-Neiße, and others. Poets of the second generation were in their 30s and 40s in 1933: writers such as the Austrian Theodor Kramer, who was doomed to spend years in exile in England. Poets of the younger generation had the most difficult time of all. They had no reputation to bring with them into the foreign environment and spent years in exile. One of these poets, Erich Fried, at least shared his exile with later Nobel Prize-winner Elias Canetti. Fried reestablished contact with Germany and Austria after the war, but the work of many poets remained buried in the obscurity of forgotten exile journals. Many poets, such as Fried, were Jewish, and once the horrors perpetrated by the Nazis became known, such poets had particular problems if they wished once again to become part of mainstream German literary culture. Some writers, including Else Lasker-Schüler and Karl Wolfskehl, were by then deeply committed to their Judaic heritage. Lasker-Schüler returned to Palestine; Wolfskehl died in exile in New Zealand. Nelly Sachs lived and worked in the Third Reich, but after seven years she was able to escape. While in exile in Sweden, she published two volumes of poetry for which she was awarded the Nobel Prize.

By 1945, the extent of the Holocaust was known, and many exile writers were reluctant to return. Radical writers, such as Stefan Heym, who returned to the German Democratic Republic, received a warmer welcome than others who returned to the Federal Republic or Austria. Altogether, the period 1933–45 marks a disastrous break in the history of German literature. Many exiles have still not won back their rightful place in the canon of German literature.

J.M. Ritchie

See also Holocaust (Shoah) Literature

Further Reading

Arnold, Heinz Ludwig, editor, *Deutsche Literatur im Exil, 1933–1945,* 2 vols., Frankfurt: Athenäum, 1974

Berendsohn, Walter Arthur, *Die humanistische Front,* 2 vols., Zürich: Europa, 1946

Berglund, Gisela, *Deutsche Opposition gegen Hitler in Presse und Roman des Exils,* Stockholm: Almquist und Wikseel, 1972

Durzak, Manfred, editor, *Die deutsche Exilliteratur 1933–1945,* Stuttgart: Reclam, 1974

Kantorowicz, Alfred, *Politik und Literatur im Exil: Deutschsprachige Schriftsteller im Kampf gegen den Nationalsozialismus,* Hamburg: Christians, 1978

Köpke, Wulf, and Michael Winkler, editors, *Deutschsprachige Exilliteratur: Studien zu ihrer Bestimmung im Kontext der Epoche 1930 bis 1960,* Bonn: Bouvier, 1984

Krispyn, Egbert, *Anti-Nazi Writers in Exile,* Athens: University of Georgia Press, 1978

Loewy, Ernst, et al., editors, *Exil: Literarische und politische Texte aus dem deutschen Exil 1933–1945,* Stuttgart: Metzler, 1979

Ritchie, J.M., *German Literature under National Socialism,* London: Croom Helm, and Totowa, New Jersey: Barnes and Noble, 1983

Schiller, Dieter, et al., editors, *Kunst und Literatur im antifaschistischen Exil 1933–1945,* 7 vols., Frankfurt: Röderberg Verlag, 1978–81

Serke, Jürgen, and Wilfried Bauer, *Die verbrannten Dichter: Berichte, Texte, Bilder einer Zeit,* Weinheim: Beltz und Gelberg, 1977; 3rd edition, 1978

Spalek, John, et al., editors, *Deutsche Exilliteratur seit 1933,* 3 vols., Bern and Munich: Francke, 1976

Stephan, Alexander, *Die deutsche Exilliteratur 1933–1945,* Munich: Beck, 1979
Trapp, Frithjof, *Deutsche Literatur im Exil,* Bern and New York: Lang, 1983
Walter, Hans-Albert, *Deutsche Exilliteratur 1933–1950,* 4 vols., Darmstadt: Luchterhand, 1972–74
Wegner, Matthias, *Exil und Literatur: Deutsche Schriftsteller im Ausland 1933–1945,* Frankfurt: Athenäum, 1967; 2nd edition, 1968
Winckler, Lutz, editor, *Antifaschistische Literatur,* 3 vols., Kronberg: Scriptor-Verlag, 1977

Expressionism

The social background to the Expressionist era was conditioned by the unification and industrialization of the German empire. A new generation born in the rapidly expanding cities was brought up by parents who clung to the inherited values of their own parents, while the economic situation, especially after the collapse in 1873, demanded new ideas and social patterns. The older generation, aware of the collapse of its values but encouraged by a regime that bolstered its image with militarism and discipline, tried to impose on the younger generation precisely those values that were no longer relevant. Conflict between the generations developed, and this particular conflict was given form in Expressionist literature. Escalation of this conflict produced the extreme positions exemplified by Franz Kafka's story *Das Urteil* (1913; *The Judgement*), where the son accepts his father's condemnation and kills himself; Kafka's *Brief an den Vater* (1953; *Dearest Father*), where the father expands into almost mythological proportions; Walter Hasenclever's drama *Der Sohn* (1914; *The Son*), where the son's hatred justifies itself in a call to the brotherhood of all humanity; and Franz Werfel's story *Nicht der Mörder, der Ermordete ist schuldig* (1920; Not the Murderer, the Victim Is Guilty), where the son posits an inexplicable law interfering in the relationship with his father.

Of equal sociological importance for the development of Expressionism was the repressive educational system, which was based on classical studies, positivism, and the insistence of the infallibility of those in authority. Reactionary elements held on to the most oppressive parts of the curriculum—despite attempts at reform in 1892 and 1900—and many high school suicides were triggered by the philistinism of pre-1914 Wilhelmine society. Conformism encouraged a growth in bohemianism, which was marked by radical forms of subjective narcissism, cynicism (Frank Wedekind), or satire (Carl Sternheim). The years 1890 to 1914 was a period of social experiment and searches for new styles; these shifts, in turn, led to extreme characterizations in literature (Wedekind's Marquis von Keith and Heinrich Mann's Diedrich Heßling in *Der Untertan* [1918; *Man of Straw*]). The search was on for new utopias, a search that Ernst Bloch summed up in his *Geist der Utopie* (1918; Spirit of Utopia): "We are the wanderers . . . we are living this age physically and organically either as part of it or overtaking it, leading, plunging into what had not yet really happened, as creative beings." World War I was seen as something abnormal, outside historical reality, for history was understood by the younger generation as an expression of the creative spirit. Frustration and boredom demanded a chance for individual expression and for the birth of a new heroic man, but these hopes were dashed in the slaughter of World War I.

Such a traditional sociological and historical approach also applied to modernism in general. If the more specific term *Expressionism* was used with varying effect and justification, including as a contrast to Impressionism, current usage reflects problems when the movement is seen as a historical process. Fritz Martini's three-phase definition in the *Reallexikon* provides one example. Martini argues that early Expressionism (pre-1914) had a mainly metaphysical or ethical basis. By contrast, according to Martini, revolutionary Expressionism was an antiwar movement during World War I that led to a form of politically and socially aimed literature. An extreme form of this developed under Kurt Hiller from 1915 in a strongly rationalist program known as "Activism."

Late Expressionism, after 1918, Martini suggests, led either into Dadaism and Surrealism; the sober skepticism of *Sachlichkeit* as seen in the early works of Bertolt Brecht; or a new form of verbal absolutism in which all early associations and values were destroyed, as seen in Gottfried Benn's later works. This scheme implies a fusion of two methods of approach: either the terms are used historically (e.g., the phrase "Das expressionistische Jahrzehnt," which was used by Gottfried Benn as a title for an anthology of lyrics), or they signify styles of writing.

The so-called Expressionist generation was aware of the relativization of sensory and psychical processes explored by Ernst Mach and supported early in the 20th century by physicists, sociologists, philosophers, and theologians, yet those Expressionists wished to break free from their immediate spiritual and social heritage. They were denounced by the German establishment in their own time as an embarrassment, by their contemporaries and Dadaists as inadequate, by the activist writers as irrelevant, by the Nazis as decadent, and despite their talk of revolution, by major Marxist critics as unavoidably bourgeois. It was their fate to be seen out of focus, falsely magnified as representatives of the international revolts of a whole generation or shown up as second-rate individuals producing works of ephemeral value. Most of the so-called Expressionists turned away from the styles of their youth to develop different attitudes and forms (e.g., the artists Beckmann, Kandinsky, Kirchner, Kokoschka, and Nolde, and the writers Döblin, Kafka, Kaiser, and Werfel), and most were unhappy with the definition of Expressionism. This suggests that Expressionist attitudes and achievements were a necessary part of youth at that time, a stage in human development that could be registered in literary or artistic form—according to talent, temperament, environment, historical, and social conditions.

The term *Expressionism* was also applied to a range of qualities associated with the new historical situation at the turn of the century. The "discovery" of the subconscious suggested that man could again understand himself as both creator and creature. With this discovery came renewed interest in earlier civilizations, especially in native art. The Expressionist writer found independent sources from which to explore and develop his individual will, so that, ideally, it could create a new world, revolutionary in its radical independence from recent inherited forms and devoid of any self-constricting political or social aims. No longer should the end product be marked with the signature of its creator, but it would be a pure creation with a character of its own, free from traces of inherited aesthetic norms. As such, the newly independent Expressionist product resembled the late fruition of Romantic art theories (e.g., Novalis). Classical aesthetic norms, including the harmonious balance between form and content, the imitative perfection of organic order, and the restraint from purposeful intent extraneous from the object itself, were no longer held to be valid. The freeing of form from imitative patterning implied separation from both tradition and nature itself. Nature was to serve as an inspiration for rather than a controlling force on the artistic will. In Expressionist writings, certain topoi occur repeatedly, not as traditional symbols, but as focusing points of the release from mimetic description (e.g., the crystal, light, the sun, revolution, youth, revelation, war, and utopia). Certain means of expression are radically explored and refashioned, including colors, masks, athematic and atonal structures, syntax, and rhythm.

Overall, most definitions of *Expressionism* suggest either a fusion of separate methods of approach or emphases on a turning point. Thus, Willi Duwe describes three periods: Georg Heym's poetry of "demonic visions," the "breakthrough to community," and the impassioned postwar calls for the "brotherhood of humanity." Kurt Hiller used four key words to define a positive reaction to Impressionism: attitude, will, intensity, and revolution. Such reaction was to be called Expressionism "because of its concentrated and willed production of the essential." Vaguer formulations came from Yvan Goll in 1914. He called Expressionism a "colouring of the soul," a form of experience rather than an art form, which was "lying in the air of our times." Alfred Döblin toned down the definition further: "It was and is a movement, an atmospheric wave, like a moving barometric high or low pressure area. Not a trend, just the opposite: fermentation, no more . . . the whole thing cannot have a name, or at least not yet. If we speak of Expressionism then we are putting the cart before the horse." Gunter Martens isolates vitalism as a force in aspects such as excess, parody, and perversion. The fundamental breakout from classical norms to a new synthesis is also suggested in the composer Arnold Schoenberg's essay *Das Verhältnis zum Text* (1912; Our Relationship to the Text), which represents what in poetic terms the poet Rainer Maria Rilke called *Umschlag* (reversal), a moment at which the poet was ready to be changed from being inarticulate to being capable of almost automatic expression. Carl Sternheim's comedies *Aus dem bürgerlichen Heldenleben* (1911–15; *Scenes from the Heroic Life*) foreshadowed Expressionism by reducing language so that it expressed what characters really thought rather than what society required them to say. Exploration of subjects taboo to Wilhelmine society was another essential aspect of the new attitudes (see Wedekind's Lulu dramas, 1895 and 1903). In more recent definitions, Expressionism is seen as a field of tension that is set between poles of self-dissociation and the renewal of man and that is more radical in its emphasis on self-dissociation than modernism in general (Silvio Vietta).

Expressionist visions for the future, however, were clouded by prophecies and lamentations, so that the same writer or artist could be cast as both a doomsayer and a utopian. The threat of man's destruction through the machine, the sense of the fall of Western man and Western civilization, and a semireligious awareness of the approach of a day of judgment concentrated a whole generation's minds. The call to change was all the more strident because of belief in such prophets as Nietzsche, with his insistence on the need for man to renew himself, and in the action-based cures of the futurists from Italy, especially their leader, Filippo Tommaso Marinetti. Every accepted value was challenged; every limited action implied total reorientation. Literature was to become engaged, and its periodicals and anthologies were given programmatic names that called for social change. Out of the excited pathos of the prewar years grew an almost messianic hope for a new society.

Expressionist literary life from the 1890s onward mainly took place in the cafés of large cities such as Berlin, Munich, Vienna, and Prague, but also in those of smaller towns. The café offered a meeting place in which young people could meet on equal terms to discuss and study new ideas. It offered an escape from the oppression of the family home and a central focus for the lives of young people. Eroticism, dandyism, release of the imagination for creative purposes, and exotic and fantastic visions were frequent topics of discussion; in short, these discussions set up an alternative imaginary world almost as a surrogate for the shortcomings of Wilhelmine life. Without the Neuer Club, set up in March 1909 by Kurt Hiller, and similar institutions, literary Expressionism would have taken a different course. In smaller towns, literary activity centered on plans for the publication of new, often short-lived periodicals and on the search for publishers, especially for contemporary lyric poetry.

All the traditional material used to define Expressionism has tended to obliterate some features essential to the art and writings of the immediate pre–World War I period in Germany, the development of these features during World War I, and the quick demise of Expressionism as a phenomenon after the war. It also does not take into account the enormous influence of Expressionism after World War II. There were, for instance, typical 20th-century experiences that translated into images of self-dissociation, angst, insecurity, and alienation that were central to Expressionism. The more strident critical voices spoke out not just against Wilhelmine society but also against the world of economic progress, the belief in rationality, and the powers of science to change human society. If a strong but loosely programmed interest in anarchism, socialism, pacifism, and psychoanalysis can easily be attributed to Expressionism, however, these interests can also be associated with other contemporary "isms." Furthermore, a more general revolt against Western civilization cannot be subsumed specifically by Expressionism.

The notion that man's creativity is separate from a divinely controlled, permanently set universal order is also essential to understanding the choice of themes by artists and writers in this period. The Expressionists often found inspiration for their aesthetic aims in late German classical, 19th-century, and symbolist writings. Thus, the emphasis on the loosening of bonds between material objects and the means of artistic expression—found in the syntactical freedom expressed within the strict, closed poetic lines and strophe forms of early Expressionist poetry—had already been hinted at by Friedrich Schiller: "The artist can make his form consume the material." This is also seen in Richard Wagner's exploration of the limits of tonality in *Tristan und Isolde* (1859; *Tristan and Isolde*) and in the tone poems of Richard Strauss. In Expressionist theory, Lothar Schreyer was to claim in his essay "Das Wesen des Körperlichen" (1918) that "material does not create form, but form material." Whereas Expressionists sometimes reacted with despair toward their environment and the human condition in general, and they recorded their emotions almost automatically, some of them crafted with care ways toward new worlds. Somber, apparently unfinished works could suggest hopeless despair, yet others seemed to escape this in the discovery and definition of new abstract forms. Artists, composers, and writers gave themselves the task of forming a utopia and presenting a new man. Common to all major art forms in the period, however, were portrayals of man as a victim, and a wide range of negative metaphors was used to portray him as a *Defizienz-Figur* (Wolfgang Rothe). A vocabulary of hostile forces threatened the vacuous center represented by the creature man. Deserted by God because man had rejected him or hopelessly impotent because left to his own devices, the Expressionist antihero either indulged in fruitless self-negating projections of doom or trembled with eager anticipation for the way out of the abyss toward the light of new goals.

Out of the Expressionist feelings of isolation grew an awareness of the dualistic structure of existence, and there are clear links between the literature of Expressionism and negative theology. These are to be seen above all in the use of one central topos: light, which represents the physical presence in this world of an extra dimension. Apparent parallels can be seen in Novalis's statement "Light is the action of the universe" or with Philipp Otto Runge's perception of light in his color theory as a fourth dimension. Yet there is a world of difference between the Romantics' positive extension and allegorization of the natural world, which was designed to reestablish a link between the self and the universe through the medium of light, and the Expressionists' reduction and intensification of light, which was designed to reveal the essence of a natural world that is often independent of the poetic self. Light can suggest change, a state of heightened consciousness, an awareness of an earthly paradise, or a not-too-distant utopia. Blindness, darkness, paleness, and being lost are partly answered by this general topos. It offers man the chance to transcend himself, contains his prophetic utterances that criticize and produce new visions, and directs and inspires the will toward spiritual and even physical action. In Expressionist literature, light is used often as a mirror effect (see the early part of Carl Einstein's novel *Bebuquin* [1912; *Bebuquin*] or Ernst Barlach's drama *Der arme Vetter* [1918; The Poor Cousin]). It was also used by Expressionist stage directors and dramatists (see Georg Kaiser's *Gas-Trilogie* or Ernst Toller's drama *Die Wandlung* [1919; Change]).

Research has also examined Expressionism in terms of its manifestos, by referring to such patterns as suggested by Wilhelm Worringer's claim of a parallelism of the Gothic spirit with that of the new writing and art. Expressionism was a form of total reaction to contemporary society, an artistic and literary counterpart to the philosophical outcries of the *Lebensphilosophen* (Martens): thus, Schoenberg's almost pathological reaction to the bourgeois, or the Dadaists' and surrealists' more radical destruction of bourgeois fantasies. The contrast between mere existence and conscious growth responding to the demands of life is a central feature of Expressionist development. Constraint is opposed to an open-ended involvement with life. Replacement of cozy passivity by a committed expression of artistic will even informs the structure of such works as Carl Sternheim's narrative prose or Georg Kaiser's early dramas. The vision of a new man unencumbered by the blinkered outlook of the bourgeoisie implied harnessing and then releasing spiritual forces.

Expressionist man is above all an isolated figure. Whereas Hofmannsthal's Claudio in *Der Thor und der Tod* (1893; *The Fool and Death*), Gilbert's Bunthorne in *Patience* (1881), and Feuerbach's painting of Iphigenie (1871) represent post-Romantic 19th-century isolation, however, their formulations reflect a veneer of harmony, a lingering on of classical balance and proportion. Their suffering is contained within a formal framework that does not threaten to burst at the seams. In Expressionist examples, such as Munch's *Jealousy* (1897), Strauss's *Elektra* (1903; *Elektra*), or Wedekind's Lulu plays (1895 and 1903), the central characters are, by contrast, imprisoned within a self-consuming set of forces. These works turn the moment of expression from being a statement of final acceptance, where resignation or irony can be used as a form of self-detachment, into a vision of departure toward an inescapable process of self-destruction. Expressionist isolation includes the awful realization that there is no escape, that the course is set. It is full of foreboding for the future, as seen in the self-analytical thought of the theologian Sören Kierkegaard or in Alban Berg's opera on Büchner's *Woyzeck* (1879; *Wozzeck*). The sense of boredom to be found in symbolist, neo-Romantic, and even naturalist writers is replaced by angst.

Expressionism was conditioned by the political and social background of late 19th-century Germany and by the prospect and eventual experience of World War I. A largely middle-class generation revolted against backward-looking imitation of earlier cultural models and belief in a materialist, technically driven society promising increased affluence and imperial grandeur. In place of tradition and belief in institutions, Expressionist writers reasserted the importance of the suffering individual. Out of an awareness of the collapse of civilized values grew hope for new societies based on the brotherhood of man, ecological awareness, and a willingness to experiment. Fear and foreboding were answered by an at times desperate, even frenzied insistence on radical change. Perhaps the most radical subject matter in poetry came in Gottfried Benn's collection *Morgue* (1912; Morgue), the most experimental forms in August Stramm's short visions of death and sex, the most exotic worlds in Else Lasker-Schüler's poetry, the most carefully crafted city poems by Georg Heym, the most frightening, drug-ridden nightmares by Georg Trakl, and the maddest whimsies by Jakob van Hoddis. If one sets aside Kafka's tortured works in clinically sober style, the most extreme example of prose was the later art critic Carl Einstein's novel *Bebuquin; oder, Die Dilettanten des Wunders* (1912), only one step removed from the demonic, surreal world of the illustrator Alfred Kubin's novel *Die andere Seite* (1909; *The Other Side*) Short stories of fantasy by Alfred Döblin, Kasimir Edschmid, Albert Ehrenstein, Gustav Meyrink, Georg Heym, and Paul Scheerbart evoke extraordinary human situations on the edge of everyday experience. Leading dramas include those by the sculptor Ernst Barlach, with their themes of isolation and redemption, the social criticism of Carl Sternheim, the religious and revolutionary works of Ernst Toller, and the wide-ranging experimental application of Strindberg's so-called station or the serial dramas of Georg Kaiser. Many of these works appeared in the major periodicals *Der Sturm, Die Aktion, Die Fackel,* and *Die weißen Blätter* and in the several dozen short-lived minor periodicals that appeared in most German and Austrian towns between 1910 and 1920. Expressionism was at the center of a renaissance of creative spiritual activity that provided a short-lived window of tense hope before militarism, capitalism, Marxism, and other systems subjected the bourgeois ideal dream of peaceful acceptance of the status quo to the harsh realities of a developing world, and where the economic and technological progress of the 20th century was to make ever greater demands on the individual.

Major events in public awareness of Expressionism include the publication of Kurt Pinthus's anthology of lyric poetry *Menschheitsdämmerung* (1920; The Twilight of Mankind), the exhibition "Entartete Kunst" in Munich in 1937, the so-called *Expressionismusdebatte* between leading Marxist thinkers (Ernst Bloch, Georg Lukács, and Anna Seghers) in the late 1930s, the Marbach exhibition in 1960, *Expressionismus: Literatur und Kunst,* the reprint publications of several periodicals and series by Kraus Reprint in the 1970s, and the publication of editions of Expressionist writers, especially during the 1970s and 1980s.

BRIAN KEITH-SMITH

See also Der Blaue Reiter; Georg Trakl

Further Reading

Anz, Thomas, and Michael Stark, editors, *Expressionismus: Manifeste und Dokumente zur deutschen Literatur 1910–1920,* Stuttgart: Metzler, 1981
Behr, Shulamith, et al., editors, *Expressionism Reassessed,* Manchester and New York: Manchester University Press, 1993
Brinkmann, Richard, *Expressionismus: Internationale Forschung zu einem internationalen Phänomen,* Stuttgart: Metzler, 1980
Bronner, Stephen Eric, and Douglas Kellner, editors, *Passion and Rebellion: The Expressionist Heritage,* London: Croom Helm, 1981; South Hadley, Massachusetts: Bergin, 1983
Cardinal, Roger, *Expressionism,* London: Paladin Books, 1984
Dierick, Augustinus Petrus, *German Expressionist Prose: Theory and Practice,* Toronto and Buffalo, New York: University of Toronto Press, 1987
Diethe, Carol, *Aspects of Distorted Sexual Attitudes in German Expressionist Drama with Particular Reference to Wedekind, Kokoschka, and Kaiser,* New York: Lang, 1988
Jones, M.S., *Der Sturm: A Focus of Expressionism,* Columbia, South Carolina: Camden House, 1984
Keith-Smith, Brian, editor, *German Expressionism in the United Kingdom and Ireland,* Bristol: University of Bristol, 1986
Krull, Wilhelm, *Prosa des Expressionismus,* Stuttgart: Metzler, 1984
Kuhns, David F., *German Expressionist Theatre: The Actor and the Stage,* Cambridge and New York: Cambridge University Press, 1997
Paulsen, Wolfgang, *Deutsche Literatur des Expressionismus,* Bern and New York: H. Lang, 1983
Raabe, Paul, and Ingrid Hannich-Bode, *Die Autoren und Bücher des literarischen Expressionismus: Ein bibliographisches Handbuch,* Stuttgart: Metzler, 1985; 2nd edition, 1991
Rumold, Rainer, and O.K. Werckmeister, editors, *The Ideological Crisis of Expressionism: The Literary and Artistic German War Colony in Belgium 1914–1918,* Columbia, South Carolina: Camden House, 1990
Sheppard, Richard, editor, *Expressionism in Focus,* Blairgowrie: Lochee, 1987
Stark, Michael, *Für und wider den Expressionismus: Die Entstehung der Intellektuellendebatte in der deutschen Literaturgeschichte,* Stuttgart: Metzler, 1982
Taylor, Seth, *Left-Wing Nietzscheans: The Politics of German Expressionism, 1910–1920,* Berlin and New York: de Gruyter, 1990
Waller, Christopher, *Expressionist Poetry and Its Critics,* London and Atlantic Highlands, New Jersey: Institute of Germanic Studies, University of London, 1986
Zeller, Bernhard, Paul Raabe, and H.L. Greve, editors, *Expressionismus, Literatur und Kunst, 1910–1923,* Munich: Langen-Müller, 1960

Das Ezzolied 1063

Religious Poem

This religious poem, one of the smaller poetic works of German literature in the Old High German period, exists in two manuscripts, the older dated in the second half of the 11th century (S—Strassburg/Ochsenhausen) in Alemannic dialect and the younger from the 12th century in Bavarian dialect (V—Vorau). The older manuscript (S) contains only seven strophes, two having four rhymed couplets each and five with six rhymed couplets each. The younger manuscript shows emendations and has expanded to 34 strophes (420 verses). The symbolic significance of the number 34 can be inferred from an alternate title for the poem, "Cantilena de Miraculis Christi," or Song about Christ's Miracles.

Ezzos Gesang (Ezzo's Song) is unique among poetic works from this period because of its identification of both its author and the composer of its melody, a certain Wille; the music to the poem, unfortunately, is not extant. The younger manuscript text (V) states in its opening lines that the patron of the poem was Bishop Gunther of Bamberg (active as bishop 1057–65) and that the poem played a certain role in the reform efforts that led to the regularization of secular clergymen, who became monks of the Augustinian Order. The origin of the text, its author, and its subsequent use as a crusading hymn are confirmed in the *Vita* of Altmann, Bishop of Passau (ca. 1130).

Thematically, the poem weaves together an account of world history as a history of events leading to salvation and, as an integral part of that history, to the life and miracles of Jesus Christ. The early imagery of the poem portrays on various levels the struggle between light and darkness. The light imagery culminates with the appearance of the morning star (*morgenstern*), John the Baptist, the forerunner of the true light, and Jesus Christ.

The strophic structure of the poem, setting aside the introductory strophe, corresponds to the 33 years of the life of Christ; the thematic structure, however, is more general. The narrative approach is that of the history or chronicle of the world as a linear concatenation of events from the Creation to the Last Judgment. The textual sources are defined as the books of Genesis and Kings and the four Gospels. The opening verse of John 1:1 (*In principio erat verbum*) introduces the image of the Word and the true Son of God, who is present at and participating in the Creation. This light in the darkness (Jesus Christ) represents, to those who remain steadfast in their belief in him, the promise of Paradise. While no attention is given to the actual creation of the world as narrated in Genesis, the poem provides a detailed description of the eight parts of the creation of man: his flesh from the muddy earth; dew for his sweat; stones for his bones; plants (*Wurzeln*) or roots for veins; grass for his hair; blood from the sea; his spirit from the clouds; and his eyes from the sun. According to the poem, the breath of life comes from God himself. The mythical imagery of this description, as poetic and fanciful as it is, remains within the context of a factual report—as though it were part of the story of Genesis. For Ezzo, Genesis and the miraculous events of the biblical history are factual events that need no theological interpretation to reveal their deeper meanings. Adam's acquiescence to the devil's advice, the subsequent reign of death and darkness over the world, and the burden of that sin on all Adam's descendants are reported in a straightforward way; there is no reference to the role of Eve.

Ezzo maintains the imagery of light to link the Old and New Testaments; God, the central source of all light, dispels the darkness of Adam's fall by sharing his light in the persons of Abel, Enoch, Noah, Abraham, and David. The appearance of John the Baptist then presages the arrival of the true light in human form, Jesus Christ, as the morning star announces the rising of the sun. These events are both the fulfillment of a plan and a guarantee of redemption and salvation for mankind. The words and miraculous works of Jesus Christ are not only expressions of love but signs and examples to be followed.

Ezzo's narrative is orderly, if not strictly chronological. He treats the birth of Christ, the baptism, and several miracles—namely, changing water to wine, raising the dead, feeding the 5,000, and walking on the waters. The final period of Christ's life, the crucifixion, the "Harrowing of Hell," the resurrection, and the ascent into Heaven, are presented as the victory of light over darkness. According to the poem, these events were prefigured by the actions of Abel, Abraham, Moses, and Passover, with the significant effect being that Christ's death was itself the victory over death.

The last five strophes of Ezzo's Song are prayerful, less a narrative directed to others than a personal discourse between the narrator and God. The conclusion uses words and phrases that give the impression of a hymn of thanks and gratitude for release from the oppression of sinfulness, much as the children of Israel were released from oppression of the Pharoah. The fulfillment of the plan, a theme resonating throughout the poem, is reinforced by the certainty of redemption. The assurance of salvation, reaffirmed in the moment of Christ's death, is in Ezzo's view the essence of faith. The last strophe is an acceptance of that assurance, an expression of belief in the power and efficacy of the Holy Trinity, and an acknowledgment that our judgment, the grace of eternal life, was guaranteed by Christ's death.

Ezzo's Song is in several respects a work of transition; the language falls technically under the rubric Old High German, although it leans toward the language of the early Middle High German period. Its theme is not unique, though the treatment stands out among works of this period for its directness of expression, its combination of sober narrative and imaginative turns of phrase, and its movement from a general address to an audience of believers to a personal statement of faith and trust.

Richard Ernest Walker

Further Reading

Groseclose, J. Sidney, and Brian Murdoch, *Die althochdeutschen poetischen Denkmäler,* Stuttgart: Metzler, 1976

Murdoch, Brian, *Old High German Literature,* Boston: Twayne, 1983

Soeteman, Cornelis, *Deutsche geistliche Dichtung des 11. und 12. Jahrhunderts,* Stuttgart: Metzler, 1963; 2nd edition, 1971

F

Fairy Tales

The English term *fairy tales* (*Feenmärche*) initially referred to tales about fairies, but when Wilhelm and Jacob Grimm reconceptualized the genre as "Märchen" in their *Kinder- und Hausmärchen* (1812–1815; *Grimms' Tales*), they meant magic tales, folk tales, etiologies, anecdotes, animal tales, jests, burlesques, and legends rather than tales about fairies. The Grimms's definition, because their collection enjoyed so privileged a position among European intellectuals throughout the 19th and into the 20th centuries, came to characterize the modern genre, which was often called the "Gattung Grimm." The English-language term, however, remained *fairy tales,* which long confused efforts to define the genre, particularly since it was also applied to the Grimms' tales, which contained many Germanically magic creatures but few fairies. Recent anglophone terminological distinctions between "tales about fairies" and "fairy tales" have begun to ease that problem.

German usage distinguishes between fairy tales (*Zaubermärchen*) and folktales (*Volksmärchen*). Fairy tales delineate wish fulfillment and typically culminate in a "happy ending" (the achievement of sufficient food, great wealth, or a royal marriage). The Russian structuralist Vladimir Propp (*Morphology of the Folktale*) characterized a magic tale narrative as the satisfactory passage from "lack" (hunger, poverty, egregious or dangerous position, or powerlessness) to "lack liquidated" (safety, social elevation, or a sufficiency of food or wealth). Since the late 17th century, European fairy tales have been situated typically, although not exclusively, in asocial locations (such as forests or sequestered spaces); their heroes and heroines have faced alien foes (such as witches and wizards, wicked kings, and grasping queens), impossible tasks (such as emptying a lake with a slotted spoon), and character-revealing trials (such as kind or cruel treatment of animals or old people), routinely in triple recurrence. Magic itself forms a central component of fairy tales.

Folktales, in contrast, tend to take place in familiar venues (bedrooms, kitchens, taverns, and villages) and generally offer wryly recounted comic shifts in power relationships that lead to a temporary alleviation of oppressing circumstances. Instead of encountering kings, queens, princes, princesses, fairies, and talking animals, folktale protagonists interact with antagonists, with whom they are closely acquainted and who are typically immediately above or below them on the scale of social power (e.g., servants, day laborers, supervisors, doctors, priests, husbands, and wives). Folktales render the world as it is experienced, but in exaggerated and/or humorous form. Social cunning or plain stupidity, rather than magic, determines tales' outcomes.

Fairy tales are either "literary" or "folk" in style. Literary fairy tales such as the ones published in Europe during the 16th, 17th, and 18th centuries (by authors such as Gianfrancesco Straparola, Giambattista Basile, and Mme d'Aulnoy) are lengthy, with convoluted and intertwining plots and subplots; their language is as richly embroidered as their characters' sumptuous clothing.

As an identifiable literary genre, the rags-to-riches fairy tale is distinctly modern. Its archetypal plot details gaining status through magic agency by wedding a wealthy spouse such as a prince or princess. Although both male and female Cinderella tales existed in the past and still exist today, female ones dominate the modern genre. This both records and mirrors the disproportionate exclusion of women from moneymaking professions in the early modern period in Europe, a condition that left marriage the principal option for achieving financial security.

Before the first rags-to-riches fairy tales emerged in published form in the 1500s, standard collections of brief narratives exhibited a different character. They consisted of jocular tales of scalawags, charlatans, and deceivers. Marital infidelity, a favorite theme, offered rib-splitting variations on standard plots. Tale collections in southern and northern Europe—Boccaccio's *Decameron* in Italy and Chaucer's *Canterbury Tales* in England, as well as numerous other 16th-century Italian, French, and German collections—cheerily recounted raucous sexuality. Chief among those in terms of subsequent influence was Gianfrancesco Straparola's *Piacevoli Notte* (1551; Delightful Nights), which entered the German publishing tradition in the late 1500s.

The first published collection that consisted entirely of fairy tales in the modern sense was Giambattista Basile's *Pentamerone* (2 vols., 1634, 1636). From 1697 until about 1800, the fairy tales of Mme Marie-Catherine d'Aulnoy dominated the French fairy-tale tradition. The style she set in "The Golden Branch," "Finette Cendron," "The Yellow Dwarf," and "The Green Serpent," to name only a few, provided a durable model for literary fairy tales that were frequently simplified and republished in the chapbooks of the *Bibliothèque bleue.* Subsequently translated into German by Friedrich Immanuel Bierling as the nine-volume

Cabinet der Feen (1761; Chamber of Fairies), along with tales by Murat, Lhéritier, la Force, and Auneuil, it predated Friedrich Justin Bertuch's *Blaue Bibliothek aller Nationen* (1790–97; International Blue Book Series) by a generation. Bertuch modeled his *Blaue Bibliothek* on the French *Bibliothèque bleue* and included tales from Mme d'Aulnoy and later French fairy-tale authors, as well as Oriental tales, and, most consequentially for 19th-century Germany, the juvenilized *Contes du temps passé* (1697) by Charles Perrault. In disseminating Perrault's tales to a broad-based German readership, Bertuch, who had written of a worldwide oral "Märchentradition," positioned fairy tales among the folk actually as well as theoretically. French literary fairy tales of the early 18th century thus provided the ultimate source for plot and motif in the German fairy-tale tradition. The forms in which those tales were edited for German consumption, however, ranged from translation (either word-for-word or free) to self-consciously archaized (in order to fit into the notion of folk origins). As Manfred Grätz persuasively demonstrated in *Das Märchen in der deutschen Aufklärung* (1988), much of the German folk fairy-tale tradition was neither "folk" nor "German."

Gottlieb Wilhelm Rabener published the first literary tale about fairies in German in 1755; in 1764, Christoph Martin Wieland inserted fairies into his stories about Don Sylvio de Rosalva; and in 1777, Wilhelm Christhelf Siegmund Mylius retailed three fairy tales by the Comte d'Hamilton in a form and context that promoted a long-lasting belief in folk origins and oral tradition. This tradition was given theoretical form by Johann Gottfried Herder (1744–1803), who celebrated fairy tales as "Volkspoesie," folk art, in 1778. In this spirit, Johann Karl August Musäus published his five-volume *Volksmärchen der Deutschen* (1782–87; Folktales of the German People), which was quickly followed by Christoph Wilhelm Guenther's *Kindermärchen aus mündlichen Erzählungen gesammelt* (1787; Children's Tales Gathered from Oral Tellings) and Benedikte Naubert's *Neue Volksmärchen der Deutschen* (1789–93; New Folktales of the German People). Despite their titles, both Guenther's and Naubert's collections retailed elaborate and elaborated literary fairy tales. Literary fairy tales flourished among Germany's 18th-century leisured women readers, who devoured them in both French and German editions.

Fairy tales have largely depended on the printing press for their spread, an assertion first advanced by Albert Wesselski in *Versuch einer Theorie des Märchens* (1931). The history of a single tale, "Beauty and the Beast," provides a good example. Born in second-century Rome, Apuleius's "Cupid (Amor) and Psyche" was nowhere in evidence during the medieval period, but it reentered Western narrative tradition when it was published in Latin in 1469. Translated into and published in nearly every European language, it took on innumerable local colorations. In Western Europe in the 18th century, one author after another recast "Cupid and Psyche"; its most influential reworking was by Mme Leprince de Beaumont, who placed it among Bible stories and other fairy tales in her *Magasin des enfans* (1756).

Germany's 18th-century educators viewed fairy tales as antipathetic to rational thought and castigated them roundly as a dangerously nonrational counterforce to an enlightened education. Germany's 19th-century response to fairy tales developed among sympathetic writers such as Karl Teuthold Heinze (1765–1813, also known as Christian Traugott), Clemens Brentano (1778–1842), and Achim von Arnim (1781–1831). In this intellectual climate, Jacob and Wilhelm Grimm, similar to many of their countrymen, understood fairy tales as a thoroughgoing folk product.

Literary fairy tales occupied a privileged position in the early decades of 19th-century Germany. Novalis (1772–1801), writing to Friedrich Schlegel in 1800, credited genuine fairy-tale authors with prescience. His contemporaries Ludwig Tieck (1773–1853), Carl Wilhelm Salice Contessa (1777–1825), Friedrich de la Motte Fouqué (1777–1843), E.T.A. Hoffmann (1776–1822), Christian August Vulpius (1762–1827), and even Johann Wolfgang Goethe (1749–1832) composed elaborate literary fairy tales, whose style and content harked back to those of Mme d'Aulnoy. It was a literary tradition that would be continued in the work of Wilhelm Hauff (1802–27), Eduard Mörike (1804–75), and Gottfried Keller (1819–90), as well as in scores of literary annuals.

During the early 19th century, a widely held positivist belief in unbroken chains of tradition encouraged scholars to ascribe fairy tales' simplified plots, as chapbooks had disseminated them to country readers, to the "childhood of humanity" and to view them as the folk equivalent of ancient Greek myth. By positing an unbroken oral tradition, they could substitute for the fragmented Germanies they inhabited a single nation whose unlettered folk's oral tradition linked them to a mythically portrayed, united medieval past.

Persuaded that "Märchen" were a genre of the people, Wilhelm and Jacob Grimm began collecting tales as young men. Initially drawing on tales told by friends and acquaintances in and near Cassel, they published their first volume as *Kinder- und Hausmärchen* in 1812. Volume 2, by contrast, drew heavily on the repertoire of Dorothea Viehmann and was eventually augmented by tales from 16th-, 17th-, 18th-, and 19th-century German tale collections.

Wilhelm carefully shaped the *Kinder- und Hausmärchen* word by word to produce a folk tone (simple sentences joined by coordinate conjunctions in conversational style) that has come to characterize the genre as a whole. Wilhelm's Märchen vocabulary relied on daily usage and favored descriptive adjectives such as "kind," "wicked," "evil," "hardworking," "lazy," "handsome," "beautiful," "ugly," "rich," and "poor." Colors in the tales are similarly limited, with notable groupings of red, white, and black (e.g., Snow White's red lips, white skin, and black hair). "Silver" and "gold" often appear, either in their own right or as descriptors (e.g., for hair color). Jewels are generally restricted to emblematic ones such as diamonds, rubies, and pearls. The simplified vocabulary and referents of the Grimms' tales or Asbjørnsen and Moe's in Norway (which were modeled on *Grimms' Tales*) distinguish them from literary fairy tales.

The Grimms often encountered different versions of the same tale. In editing variant tellings, Wilhelm retained elements that he regarded as German and discarded foreign ones. In trying to account for the evident fact of differing versions, he developed a theory of origins that replaced the idea of a single unbroken chain of oral tradition with a notion that charted multiple chains of oral tradition emanating from a single point of origin (monogenesis). This conceptualization of fairy-tale history encouraged Wilhelm to piece together tale fragments in order to be able to approximate ancient originary narratives from the "childhood of humanity."

Although the Grimms' tales ultimately became the most influential collection of fairy tales in Europe and the world, Ludwig Bechstein's fairy tales (*Deutsche Märchen* [1845; German Tales]; *Neues Deutsches Märchenbuch* [1856; New German Tale Book]) far outsold the Grimms' books during most of the 19th century. Bechstein's playful prose detailed a bourgeois world suffused with Enlightenment ideals, whose child protagonists regarded magic as alien and took independent action to accomplish impossible tasks. In Bechstein's tales female witches and male malefactors existed in equal numbers, but stereotypically wicked stepmothers hardly existed at all. Above all, families reconstituted themselves at a tale's happy conclusion. In humorous language Bechstein poked fun gently at values to which both he and his readers automatically subscribed (social stability, financial caution). In contrast, the Grimms' tales delineate rural proletarian society, where impoverished children wait passively for magic helpers to reward their proven goodness; where girls and women strive and suffer silently; and where female witches far outnumber male ogres. Bechstein's tales dominated 19th-century booksales; the Grimms' tales overwhelmingly prevailed in the 20th century.

The 19th century also witnessed a return of fairy tales to women's pens. Scores of female authors composed fairy tales, beginning with Sophie Mereau-Brentano, Sophie de la Motte Fouqué, Agnes Franz, Caroline Stahl, Amalie Schoppe, and Bettina von Arnim (1785–1859), and continuing with her daughter Gisela, around whom the Berlin Kaffeterkreis developed in 1843.

At the end of the 19th century, a combination of changing language patterns, growing nationalism, and emerging socialist educational theory resulted in the dominance of the Grimms' tales. In the 20th century dissident voices were occasionally raised. Revisionist anti-fairy tales welled up in the Weimar period; during the Allied occupation of Germany after World War II, the Grimms' tales were first removed wholesale from school and public library shelves and then for a brief period banned from republication. Beginning in 1968 and continuing into the 1970s, a second wave of revisionism occurred, when anticapitalist and anti-authoritarian fairy tales came into favor. During the 40-year period of socialist government in Eastern Germany, the brutal conclusions of many of Grimms' tales were softened. For example, in West German editions of "The Goosegirl," the wicked maid who had usurped her mistress's rightful position as royal bride is stripped naked, put into a nail-studded barrel, and pulled to her death by two white horses, whereas in the East German Kinderbuchverlag edition, the wicked maid is simply chased from the country.

The Grimms viewed fairy tales as a set of narratives composed in a simpler age by a simpler people who had passed the stories unchanged from one generation to another in unvarying language. This conceptualization had profound consequences for the subsequent study of the genre. Of all hypotheses of fairy-tale genesis, the Grimms' single-source theory has exerted the greatest influence. It designates fairy tales' form as myth in a crumbled state (i.e., "Cupid and Psyche" becomes "Beauty and the Beast"), and it posits an army of simple oral narrators, wholly outside literate and literary tradition, a postulate that was necessary in order to account for the 1,000-year period during which tales such as "Beauty and the Beast" went undocumented. As a theoretical construct, the Grimms' hypothesis of continuous oral tradition is centrally flawed by the absence of documentary evidence. Despite the logical problems this engendered, the Grimms' theory of continuous oral tradition enjoyed a long success, because it solved four 19th-century problems, which were social, political, intellectual, and literary in nature. It dignified "the folk" socially by attributing to it an ability to recognize verbal art and to pass it on intact. In a politically satisfying manner, the Grimms' theory affirmed the folk as a unitary and unifying entity within the loose confederation of several hundred principalities, bishoprics, free cities, dukedoms, margravates, and counties that then composed "Germany." In intellectual terms, the Grimms' theory was the first to address the fairy-tale phenomenon descriptively. Literarily, the Grimms' theory created a respectable status for fairy tales among later German Romantics, many of whom composed literary fairy tales of strange and compelling beauty.

From 1812 to the 1970s, the Grimms' view of the monogenesis and oral folk dissemination of fairy tales provided a theoretical basis for the most widespread scholarly investigative method, the historico-geographical, or Finnish, school of research, as well as for a multitude of subtheories. The notion of an "unbroken oral tradition" suggested that fairy tales contained surviving fragments of ancient cultural material, while ancillary theories equated "ancient" with "primitive" and "childlike." Related cultural anthropological inquiries suggested that fairy tales verbalized ancient rites of passage, in particular, puberty rites. Other interpreters understood fairy tales as transformed Indo-European, Greek, and Roman myth, an approach embraced by many French and German exegetes. For example, those who adhered to solar myths averred that Red Riding Hood represented sunrise, the wolf variously "light" or "night," and the huntsman a solar deity.

Once fairy tales had been defined as a product of the folk, many interpreters understood "folk" as "people." The slipperiness of the definite and indefinite articles allowed scholars to conflate "a people" or "the people" with "[all] people." From there it was but a short step to asserting a oneness of the meaning and content of fairy tales with the human psyche. Thus, one of the first psychological interpreters of fairy tales, Ludwig Laistner, proposed in 1889 that fairy tales, along with myths and legends, resulted from dreams that expressed basic emotions such as anxiety or hope.

Another psychological approach posited fairy tales as taletellers' (or audiences') projected needs and desires, principal among which were autonomy and sex. Here, the familiar names are those of Franz Riklin (*Wunscherfüllung und Symbolik in Märchen* [1908; Wish Fulfillment and Symbolism in Fairy Tales]), Sigmund Freud, and Bruno Bettelheim (*The Uses of Enchantment,* 1977). With his studies of enduring cultural archetypes, Carl Jung's works encouraged his followers to understand fairy tales as expressions of a collective unconscious.

The fairy tale genre is a troublesome notion. The soldier-poet Giambattista Basile was at home with complex Baroque anagrams and formal poetry based on classical models, but his fairy tales proceeded from the meanest mouths in Naples and, as an antigenre, clearly lay outside the classically determined literary canon of his day. Early scholars of Basile's fairy tales ignored the spellbinding achievement of a sophisticated 17th-century mind, that is, Basile's canonically elaborate prose and carefully constructed plots, and, instead, accepted the tales' surface valuation as a literary satire or as an insipid jumble of meaningless tales.

An anticlassical premise also underlay Charles Perrault's fairy tales, for, to him, fairy tales embodied modern norms and values. But Perrault, unlike Basile, rejected vulgar folk language, chose aristocratic vocabulary and behavior, and dedicated his simple tales to a royal "Mademoiselle," as befitted articulate tales with worldly morals.

German fairy-tale authors of the 19th century followed Perrault in rejecting Greece's and Rome's gods and heroes; they portrayed kings, princesses, fairies, and magic. In espousing a genre that nurtured magic and fantasy and in positing fairy tales as an antirational force, they anticipated 20th-century psychoanalytic interpretations.

RUTH B. BOTTIGHEIMER

See also Children's Literature; Jacob Grimm and Wilhelm Grimm

Further Reading

Bottigheimer, Ruth B., *Grimms' Bad Girls and Bold Boys,* New Haven, Connecticut: Yale University Press, 1987
Enzyklopädie des Märchens, Berlin: de Gruyter, 1977–
Fabula, 1959–
Grätz, Manfred, *Das Märchen in der deutschen Aufklärung,* Stuttgart: Metzler, 1988
Holbek, Bengt, *Interpretation of Fairy Tales,* Folklore Fellows Communications vol. 239, Helsinki: Academia Scientiarum Fennica, 1987
Klotz, Volker, *Das europäische Kunstmärchen: Fünfundzwanzig Kapitel seiner Geschichte von der Renaissance bis zur Moderne,* Stuttgart: Metzler, 1985
Lüthi, Max, *The European Folktale: Form and Nature,* translated by John D. Niles, Philadelphia, Pennsylvania: Institute for the Study of Human Issues, 1982; Bloomington: Indiana University Press, 1986
Marvels and Tales, 1987–
Rölleke, Heinz, *Die Märchen der Brüder Grimm,* Munich: Artemis, 1985
Uther, Hans-Jörg, editor, *Märchen vor Grimm*, Munich: Diederichs, 1990
Wesselski, Albert, *Versuch einer Theorie des Märchens,* Reichenberg i.B.: Kraus, 1931

Hans Fallada 1893–1947

Hans Fallada (whose real name was Rudolf Ditzen) was the slyly authentic chronicler of the two most turbulent periods of modern German history, the Weimar Republic and Nazi rule, which provided the settings and themes for his popular best-sellers. He first gained international acclaim with his downbeat novel of the Great Depression, *Kleiner Mann—was nun?* (1932; *Little Man, What Now?*), whose modest hero Johannes Pinneberg, a Berlin shop assistant, caught the imagination of societies across the industrial world in which ordinary people were struggling to survive in the face of brutal economic circumstances and the consequent political upheaval they caused. Pinneberg stood for millions who, while only seeking a decent life for themselves and their families, were trapped in a crisis beyond their comprehension and thrust down into poverty.

Little Man, What Now? was the fictional counterpart to Siegfried Kracauer's perceptive sociological analysis of the lower middle classes in Germany, *Die Angestellten* (1929; White Collar Workers), which ascribed the uprootedness and insecurity of urban clerks and shop assistants to the acute vagaries and unpredictability of contemporary capitalism. The novel's instant success quickly led to international recognition; indeed, a comparable English novel set in working-class Manchester, *Love on the Dole* by Walter Greenwood, was rejected by the first publisher approached on the grounds that their spring list for 1932 already included "a book on a similar theme"—*Little Man, What Now?*

Fallada caught the atmosphere of life in Berlin with extraordinary accuracy. He had worked there for the publisher Rowohlt for a couple of years without ever participating in the intense intellectual and artistic life of the capital. Fallada was trained in agriculture, and through the 1920s he worked predominantly as a bookkeeper or an agent on various large estates in the east of Germany. His own daily experience fed into his first successful novel, *Bauern, Bonzen, und Bomben* (1931; Peasants, Bosses, and Bombs). The novel was based on his reporting of a trial in Neumünster, and it describes the intricate political intrigues in country areas that helped undermine the Weimar Republic. Here and in later works Fallada showed his skill in filtering large-scale historical events through the unassuming routine of daily provincial life, as Edgar Reitz did later with his film epic *Heimat.*

Fallada was neither a political thinker nor a philosopher; he reacted emotionally to events, and his strength as a writer was a fecund imagination that effortlessly devised a stream of possible situations, which were then executed with realistic detail and dialogue. Although without political affiliations, Fallada was briefly arrested by the Nazis in 1933—he was denounced by a former landlord—but he then withdrew to a smallholding near Feldberg in Mecklenburg. His love for this corner of Germany prevented him later on from going through with a planned emigration. The ambiguous official attitude to this popular writer—the Nazis read *Little Man, What Now?* as a hard-hitting critique of the Weimar Republic but waited in vain for an anti-Jewish novel from Fallada—resulted finally in his being declared "undesirable," although he was not banned from publishing.

A fairly passive anti-Nazi, from his country retreat Fallada continued to produce sharp and readable novels. He drew upon his own immediate experience of imprisonment in the Greifswald and Neumünster gaols—he served two sentences for embezzlement in the 1920s—for *Wer einmal aus dem Blechnapf frißt* (1934; *Who Once Eats out of the Tin Bowl*). This work tells the story of a petty criminal who is marginalized when he tries to reintegrate into society on his release from prison. In this work, Fallada shows his own bitterness and his compassion for the insignificant individual in this indictment of the existing criminal justice system. *Wolf unter Wölfen* (1937; *Wolf among Wolves*) relives the nightmare millions of citizens endured in the turbulent hyperinflation of the early 1920s; the harshness of life in both Berlin and the provinces is vividly evoked, but the realism is marred by the slightly sentimental cozy family scene at the end (a fault found in *Little Man, What Now?* and other books).

Through years of personal troubles (frequently changing jobs, jail, and periods of hospitalization for drug addiction and nervous illness) Fallada always maintained a phenomenal rate of writing. Much of his output was books for children, but in the dark war years he produced two reminiscences of his own life, *Damals bei uns daheim* (1942; The Way Things Were at Home) and *Heute bei uns zu haus* (1943; The Way Things Are Now). Subtitled *Erlebtes, Erfahrenes, und Erfundenes* (What I Experienced, Learned, and Invented), these works are fictionalized manipulations of Fallada's past; they are amusingly bland but unreliable and inaccurate as autobiography. He chronicled in the minutest detail his latter years in Feldberg in the unpublished Farm Diaries, however, and this work is an invaluable social document of day-to-day data.

By a quirk of fate Fallada was appointed mayor of Feldberg by the occupying Soviet forces in 1945; he held this post for only a few months. This was also his time of reckoning with Nazism and the ambiguity of his own earlier political stance. *Der Alpdruck* (1947; The Nightmare) is a fictionalized confessional account of the pusillanimity, compliance, and betrayal of so many Germans—including himself—during the previous 12 years. As a novel it is uneven and patchy, with little narrative coherence; Fallada seems to have hastily scribbled down his immediate experiences in the aftermath of the war, not shunning his increasing alcohol and drug dependency. Earlier, while in hospital in 1944, he had composed in two frenetic weeks his final testimony to his losing battle with alcoholism, *Der Trinker* (1950; *The Drinker*), which he directed should be published posthumously. The upsurge in Fallada's output in these last few years was crowned by the first anti-Nazi postwar novel in Germany, *Jeder stirbt für sich allein* (1947; Every Man Dies Alone), again written at breakneck speed a few months before his death. He derived the story from authentic Gestapo files that came into his hands concerning the case of a modest worker couple who distributed subversive leaflets after their son died at the front, but were then caught and executed. Their futile resistance is heroic in a muted key; although crushed, they yet show that spark of all Fallada's unassuming protagonists, the desire to be "anständig" (decent).

Fallada was frequently caught up in the criminal justice system (his father was a judge, and he himself served prison sentences and was accused of murder), and he attended psychiatric institutions because of his addiction to cocaine, morphine, and alcohol. He was familiar with the world of prostitution, theft, and petty crime, and he used this world vividly in his work. Unlike comparable contemporaries such as Kästner and Döblin, Fallada did not seek to embed an implied message in his stories; there is nothing metaphorical about his narration, which is literal and down-to-earth. His prosaic style employs, in description and dialogue, the exact linguistic registers of his protagonists, and it is accessible in the manner of *Unterhaltungsliteratur* (popular literature). It is Fallada's facility for selecting authentic situations in their minutest everyday detail that enables him to evoke the flavor of a precise time and place and that makes him a seismograph of the vicissitudes of the Germany of his time. Provincial and petty suburban life were his forte, and in this setting power relations were articulated in the course of ordinary life: over the counter, the desk, and the table. They were also articulated between shopkeeper and customer, petty functionary and claimant, manager and employee, and authority and underdog. Human values, social commitment, and sympathy for the victims of society are integral to Fallada's appealing novels.

ARRIGO V. SUBIOTTO

Biography

Born in Greifswald, 21 July 1893. Moved with his family to Berlin, 1899; killed a friend in a duel, attempted suicide, and was admitted to a mental sanatorium, 1911; intermittent posts in agricultural offices and on large estates, 1913–25; imprisoned on embezzlement charges, 1924, 1926; lived near Feldberg, Mecklenburg, from 1933; frequently admitted to institutions for drug and alcohol rehabilitation, 1944–47; appointed mayor of Feldberg by Soviet occupation forces, June to October, 1945. Died in East Berlin, 5 February 1947.

Selected Works

Collections
Werke in zehn Bänden, edited by Günther Caspar, 1962–

Novels
Bauern, Bonzen, und Bomben, 1931
Kleiner Mann—was nun? 1932; as *Little Man, What Now?* translated by Eric Sutton, 1933; translated by Susan Bennett, 1996
Wer einmal aus dem Blechnapf frißt, 1934; as *Who Once Eats out of the Tin Bowl,* translated by Eric Sutton, 1934
Wolf unter Wölfen, 1937; as *Wolf among Wolves,* translated by Philip Owens, 1938
Der Alpdruck, 1947
Jeder stirbt für sich allein, 1947
Der Trinker, 1950; as *The Drinker,* translated by Charlotte and A.L. Lloyd, 1952

Further Reading

Caspar, Günter, *Fallada-Studien,* Berlin and Weimar: Aufbau, 1988
Crepon, Tom, *Leben und Tode des Hans Fallada,* Halle and Leipzig: Mitteldeutscher Verlag, 1978; 9th edition, 1992
Gessler, Alfred, *Hans Fallada: Sein Leben und Werk,* Berlin: Volk und Wissen, 1972; 2nd edition, 1976
Manthey, Jürgen, *Hans Fallada in Selbstzeugnissen und Bilddokumenten,* Reinbek bei Hamburg: Rowohlt, 1963
Reardon, Roy, editor, *Kleiner Mann: Was nun?* London: Methuen, 1987
Schueler, H.J., *Hans Fallada: Humanist and Social Critic,* The Hague: Mouton, 1970
Williams, Jenny, *More Lives than One: A Biography of Hans Fallada,* London: Libris, 1998
Wolff, Rudolf, editor, *Hans Fallada: Werk und Wirkung,* Bonn: Bouvier, 1983

Fascism and Literature

Doubts have been expressed as to whether a fascist literature of real value is possible. As far as Germany is concerned, the fascist literature of the 1930s has disappeared almost without trace, despite the success of certain works at the time, as publication figures show. The literature of the Third Reich, however, had a considerable prehistory. There had long been strong strands of a protofascist, conservative, antiliberal, and antidemocratic literature before 1933. After that date, the government was in a position to eliminate everything it disapproved of—particularly all left-wing, Jewish, or avant-garde works—in order to clear the way for a racially and biologically based literature, which would serve the National Socialist cause. What was felt to be appropriate for the new Germany was a literature of the peasant. For the Nazis, literature of the city was not only decadent and rootless, it inevitably depicted class conflict. Such conflict was to be removed from the literary scene; in its place, literature would present the Germanic ideal of a harmonious society in which there was no longer a middle class, peasants, or workers, but only a folk-community of Germans united by their common race. To this end, the Third Reich attempted to construct a line of descent showing the inevitability of its own creation.

Naturally, the Third Reich claimed descent from the German classics, but there were certainly difficulties. The Jewish protagonist of Gotthold-Ephraim Lessing's *Nathan der Weise* (1779; *Nathan the Wise*) was unacceptable in Nazi Germany. There were equal difficulties with some works by Schiller, and the cosmopolitanism of Goethe could not always be forced into the required mold. German Romanticism seemed more amenable, and Goebbels himself had written a doctoral dissertation on a Romantic topic. In his speech of 15 November 1933 for the opening of the new Reich Literature Chamber, he coined the phrase "steely Romanticism" to formulate that for which the new fascist literature should strive. But the Nazi treatment of the Romantics had to be carefully selective. A post-Romantic such as Richard Wagner was more in line with the Nazi vision. He was "völkisch" enough. He was the ideal combination of spiritual and political leader, and, best of all, he was also an outspoken anti-Semite who presented Germanic heroes, and, according to Arthur Rosenberg, Wagner expressed the Nordic soul, the Nietzschean power of the will, and the struggle for greatness and honor. Among the lesser lights after Wagner who influenced fascist thinking in Germany, Houston Stewart Chamberlain, the author of *Grundlagen des neunzehnten Jahrhunderts* (1899; *Foundations of the Nineteenth Century*), was the closest to the master. It was he who started the cult of Wagner and Bayreuth of which Hitler himself became such a devoted follower. A work of cultural criticism similar to Chamberlain's, which had a vision of a coming dictatorship, was Oswald Spengler's *Untergang des Abendlandes* (1918–22; *Decline of the West*). Goebbels tried to enlist Spengler for National Socialism, but he refused to join the party. More directly exploitable for party purposes was the book with the prophetic title *Das dritte Reich* (1923; *The Third Reich*), by Arthur Moeller van den Bruck.

For more recent literary ancestors, the Nazi ideologues sought their roots in the homeland literature of the turn of the century, such as the works of Johannes Langbehn, Friedrich Lienhard, and Adolf Bartels. Langbehn's *Rembrandt der Erzieher* (1890; *Rembrandt the Educator*) had been an enormously successful work of cultural criticism. According to Langbehn, Bismarck had created in the Second Reich an economic and political triumph, but one that had failed to bring the equivalent cultural success. Langbehn's message was the need to prepare the path for the great German culture to come. The ideal held up was that of the corporate state, with German culture as the model for the whole of Europe. Langbehn's influence can be most clearly observed in Adolf Bartels, whom Adolf Hitler singled out for the highest honor the Nazi Party could bestow. Bartels was noted particularly for his anti-Semitism. His histories of German literature became standard reading in schools in the Third Reich, imparting the message that the Jew was alien to German culture. Heine was a special target for his contempt, but Heine was not alone. Bartels's anti-Semitism was transported into every aspect of German literature. For Bartels (as for Langbehn), the point of departure was the changing cultural situation of the Second Reich. According to such protofascist thinkers, capitalism was changing the world as they knew it and not for the better. But he had a positive message to offer: salvation could be achieved through a return to the old values, to homeland art and regional pride. Bartels put these ideals into his creative writing as well as his essays and histories of German literature. His most popular work, the historical novel *Die Dithmarscher* (1898; *The People of Dithmarsch*), had sold over 200,000 copies by 1928—thereby disproving right-wing claims that the book market was controlled by Jews and left-wingers. And, indeed, there was plenty of evidence in the Weimar Republic that there was a market for protofascist writing of this kind. There were nationalist clubs and literary journals, and writer Friedrich Lienhard became famous not only as an author of regional novels in the Bartels vein but also as a dedicated crusader against big-city decadence and cosmopolitanism. His anti-Berlin appeal was a rallying cry in nationalist circles, and he became, with Bartels, the founder of the so-called Heimatkunstbewegung (Homeland Art Movement).

What all of these protofascist forerunners of National Socialism had in common was a regressive perspective. The modern world was rejected and the preferred vision was in the past. They looked back to German classicism (without the ingredients of humanity and civilization), a selective view of German Romanticism, a selective view of individualism (focusing on the great artist and the great leader), and the postrevolutionary years of the 1850s in which the poetic realism of the regionalist Otto Ludwig was favored. Certain basic elements of this regressive view were to become characteristic features of the coming fascist literature, in particular a pale, easily accessible realism and a classicist monumentalism. Naturalism was taboo. In the literary sphere, as elsewhere, the National Socialists saw themselves as part of a cultural revolution, and some in the movement were tempted for a time to align themselves with the radical avant-garde. Goebbels showed evidence of a weakness for modern art, and for a brief spell there were signs that Expressionism might have the same impact in National Socialist Germany as futurism was having in the new fascist Italy. The party line from Hitler, however, soon became clear. Modernism would not be tolerated. Literature in the Third Reich would be conservative, traditional, and largely regional. Literature of this kind was not the monopoly of Germany at this time, as names such as Giono, Timmermanns, and Maurice Barrès indicate, but it was generally to the Nordic countries that National Socialist Germany was to look for the literature that it could admire. Trygve Gulbrannsen was among the most widely read authors in the Third Reich, although he never declared his allegiance to it. The Icelandic writer Gunnar Gunnarson received rave notices in Germany, especially after 1934, when he came out publicly in favor of the new regime. In 1937, he received the Henrik Steffens Prize from the city of Hamburg; in 1940, after a tour of Germany with the Swedish author Clara Nordstrom and the Dutch author Jo van Ammers-Küller, he was received in Berlin by the Führer. Knut Hamsun was equally active in his support of the Third Reich. He made many public statements in favor of the Third Reich. He even defended the German invasion of Norway, declared Norwegian resistance to be senseless, came out in favor of Quisling, and advocated a Europe under German leadership, which would fight against England. For Will Vesper, the Nazi critic, he was the greatest epic writer of the time.

Such Nordic tales of the homeland were clearly not harmless, and German writers had employed this tradition in the past. Moving back from the city to the land meant by no means a return to a completely idyllic, pastoral, and harmonious age, for it had to be demonstrated that the peasant, like the soldier, had to be prepared to defend himself and his native land—with blood if necessary. The fascist cult of Blut und Boden (blood and soil) was already inherent in this kind of regressive, aggressive literature. The essential elements of blood and soil literature have been described as, first, depictions of settlement and, second, as representations of the defense of that settlement. This is the pattern of the most successful of the prefascist novels, *Der Wehrwolf* (1910; *The Werewolf*) by Hermann Löns. Löns was killed in the early months of World War I, but not before he had launched an appeal for a leader to emerge from the masses, save the German nation, and lead it to triumph. By the end of World War II, his idea of the Werewolf had become a last ditch defense of the homeland against the advancing allied forces. Another writer who saw the title of his most successful novel taken up as a political slogan by the National Socialists was Hans Grimm, whose *Volk ohne Raum* (1926; *People without Space*) had sales that reached the 500,000 before 1938. Apart from the idea of Lebensraum and the novel's militant nationalism, Grimm, although never a party member, came close to the Nazi ideology through his treatment of race, his thoughts about the Jews, and the significance that he gives to Nordic man.

Grimm was still alive and selling well after the end of World War II. Paul Ernst, who did declare himself a National Socialist shortly before he died in 1933, did not have the same mass appeal as Grimm, yet he was recognized by the Nazis and propagandized accordingly. His greatest influence was on the monumental, myth-type drama that the Nazis favored. Even more outspoken on race was Hermann Burte, the author who brought the *Hakenkreuz* (swastika) into his novel *Wiltfeber, der ewige Deutsche* (1912; *Wiltfeber, the Eternal German*). Burte became a leading literary figure during the Nazi regime. However, the absolute nadir in literary anti-Semitism was reached by Artur Dinter in his novel *Die Sünde wider das Blut* (1922; *The Sin against the Blood)*. After 1933, Dinter did not enjoy the literary career he expected. His desire to prove that Christ was Aryan antagonized many, and he fell from favor. However, anti-Semitism and violence continued to be fundamental elements in Nazi literature, as demonstrated by the works of Hans Zöberlein, which included *Der Befehl des Gewissens* (1937; *Conscience Commands*). Zöberlein was in the SA (*Sturmabteilung*, or "Brownshirts") and became a brigade leader and a holder of the Blood Order and the Party's Golden Badge of Honor. In 1948, he was condemned to death for participation in a war crime, but the sentence was commuted. He died in 1964.

It is tempting to assume that all Nazi literature is the product of brutal frontline soldiers such as Zöberlein. Nothing could be further from the truth. The ideology had a far wider appeal. Erwin Guido Kolbenheyer, for example, was a true intellectual who before he gained high office in the party was writing historical-philosophical dramas and novels with Germanic heroes. Another writer as rooted as Kolbenheyer in the cultural traditions of the Austro-Hungarian empire—and one destined to become as much a pan-German nationalist as Kolbenheyer—was the Austrian Josef Weinheber. At first sight, this prophet of pure poetry seems the last person one would expect to find in the company of brown-shirted barbarians, yet he remained right to the end one of the party's most prominent literary figures. Many still think of Weinheber as a real poet. An even greater number of people are convinced that Ernst Jünger was one of the greatest stylists in the German language. Others consider him one of the most dangerous of fascist thinkers. Jünger was an ice-cold intellectual. He may have admired the demagogic magic of Hitler, and he was certainly close to Goebbels, but he never joined the party even though most of his nationalist colleagues did, including Blunck, Johst, Stoffregen, Jungnickel, Müller-Partenkirchen, Steguweit, Beumelburg, Fechter, Schauwecker, and others. Jünger's *Die totale Mobilmachung* (1931; *Total Mobilization*) and *Der Arbeiter* (1932; *The Worker*) may be read as visions of the totalitarian state, but Jünger himself played no part in turning these visions into the reality of the Third Reich. Although he held himself aloof from the practical politics of the time, however, there is no doubt that his famous books, which glorified the frontline experience of World War I, were of great service to the Third Reich.

While Jünger remained on the fringes of the party, there is no doubt that Josef Goebbels was at the very heart of the movement. He, too, had attempted to express himself in literary form, although for copyright and legal reasons most of his literary oeuvre still remains unpublished to this day. One of his literary works is available for study, namely his novel *Michael: Ein deutsches Schicksal in Tagebüchern* (1929; Michael: From the Diary of a German Life). As Stephen Spender recognized, this novel contains in literary guise all the fascist symptoms. Certainly many of the usual ingredients are there: the camaraderie of the frontline fighter, the appeal for sacrifice for the fatherland, and the peasant rooted in the soil, among others. Michael the hero even develops fascist ideas about the role of women in society. The woman's duty is to be lovely and bring children into the world. Not surprisingly, by the end Michael is compounding his own brew of anti-Semitism and anti-Marxism. From specious arguments, Michael arrives at the strange but peculiarly fascist conclusion that the real struggle is between Christ and Marx; for him, Christ represents the principle of love and Marx the (Jewish) principle of hate. All this is argued out in the context of a discussion of Expressionism and modern art.

If the connection between modernist movements and National Socialism is one that the literary efforts of Goebbels force upon the reader, the same might be said of the works of Arnolt Bronnen. Famous in the Expressionistic "Roaring Twenties" through his violent play *Vatermord* (1920; *Patricide*), he moved politically from left to right during this period. Tucholsky denounced his Freikorps novel *O.S.* (*1929*; *Upper Silesia*) as drawing-room fascism. Making sure after 1933 that he could get close to Goebbels, Bronnen exploited his connections with radio and the new medium of television for the benefit of the Nazi party. By the end of the war, he was again on the move politically; after the war he settled in Communist East Germany. Opportunism had permitted Bronnen a modest career under the Nazis and he survived. The other famous member of the Expressionist generation who acclaimed the Nazi accession to power cannot be accused of such opportunism. Gottfried Benn was the apolitical poet of pure poetry, yet he was one of the first to proclaim his allegiance to the Nazi movement. At the invitation of Hanns Johst, his fellow Expressionist, who was to become president of the Nazi Reich Literature Chamber, Benn made a speech about Stefan George, the poet and author of *Das neue Reich* (1928; *The New Reich*), assuming, as many did, that George would be sympathetic to the new regime. But instead, George went into exile in Switzerland. Benn also played an active part in the Nazification of the Prussian Academy of Arts, and a few days after his speech about George, he gave a radio talk in which he welcomed the National Socialist revolution. While so many of Germany's leading writers had been forced to emigrate, it was a sensation when Benn, one of the greatest poets of the period, declared himself in this way. But the Nazis did not welcome avant-garde intellectuals, and by May 1936, he was being attacked in the Nazi press and denied permission to publish. Eventually, in his famous phrase, he emigrated into the army.

Gottfried Benn was a great poet who was partly blinded for a short period. There were, however, countless other poets who were prepared to serve the ideology devotedly, and, at first, poetry was encouraged as a cultural weapon in the formation of a mass party. Such poetry tended to be violent and aggressive. The most famous example is the poem by the Nazi "martyr" Horst Wessel, which Goebbels turned into the party anthem. The party poets who followed, including Heinrich Anacker, Gerhart Schumann, and Baldur von Schirach, were soon occupying official positions within the hierarchy. Not all Nazi poetry, however, is of a crude, warlike kind. In fact, the party also favored poetry of a traditional sort such as ballads and sonnets, poetry that the Reich's leaders could claim was part of the true German cultural heritage and was distinct from the decadent avant-garde. All of this poetry is lost without a trace. Fascist theater was almost equally unsuccessful. It had not had to wait until 1933 to reach the stage in Germany. One year before the takeover, Mussolini's Napoléon play *A Hundred Days* was mounted as a grand theatrical occasion in Weimar. The next large-scale theatrical event was the production of the play by Hanns Johst that was dedicated to Adolf Hitler and devoted to the Nazi "martyr" Leo Schlageter. These high points were followed by a downward trend. The so-called Thing plays, performed with casts of thousands in specially constructed open-air stadiums, proved to be too quasi-religious, allegorical, wordy, and abstract—in other words, too untheatrical. The Thing movement had to be abandoned. Plays modeled on Paul Ernst's work also resulted in monumental failures. Blood and soil dramas proved no more successful. So, despite a great deal of high-level government support, performances in the best theaters, and productions by the best directors, fascist theater in the Nazi vein proved a failure. Like Nazi poetry, it has now disappeared without a trace. Nothing from this period ever enjoys a revival.

Altogether, as far as German literature is concerned, nothing of value was produced. Ernst Jünger and Gottfried Benn are still admired, but they were never real Nazis. Although some of the writers of the Nazi period were still alive and publishing after 1945, their former fame has declined and they are now hardly ever discussed.

J.M. Ritchie

See also Antifascist Literature; National Socialism

Further Reading

Damus, Martin, and Ralf Schnell, editors, *Kunst und Kultur im deutschen Faschismus,* Stuttgart: Metzler, 1978

Denkler, Horst, and Karl Prümm, editors, *Die deutsche Literatur im Dritten Reich: Themen, Traditionen, Wirkungen,* Stuttgart: Reclam, 1976

Gilman, Sander L., editor, *NS-Literaturtheorie: Eine Dokumentation,* Frankfurt: Athenäum, 1971

Hartung, Günter, *Literatur und Ästhetik des deutschen Faschismus,* Berlin: Akademie-Verlag, 1983

Ketelsen, Uwe-Karsten, *Völkisch-nationale und nationalsozialistische Literatur in Deutschland, 1890–1945,* Stuttgart: Metzler, 1976

———, *Literatur und Drittes Reich,* Schernfeld: Süddeutsche Verlag, 1992; 2nd edition, 1994

Loewy, Ernst, and Hans-Jochen Gamm, editors, *Literatur unterm Hakenkreuz: Das dritte Reich und seine Dichtung,* Frankfurt: Europäische Verlagsanstalt, 1966; 3rd edition, 1977

Ritchie, J.M., *German Literature under National Socialism,* London: Croom Helm, and Totowa, New Jersey: Barnes and Noble, 1983

Schäfer, Hans Dieter, *Das gespaltene Bewußtsein: Über deutsche Kultur und Lebenswirklichkeit, 1933–1945,* Munich: Hanser, 1981; 3rd edition, 1983

Schonauer, Franz, *Deutsche Literatur im Dritten Reich: Versuch einer Darstellung in polemisch-didaktischer Absicht,* Freiburg: Walter, 1961

Thunecke, Jörg, editor, *Leid der Worte: Panorama des literarischen Nationalsozialismus,* Bonn: Bouvier, 1987

Vondung, Klaus, *Völkisch-nationale und nationalsozialistische Literaturtheorie,* Munich: List, 1973

Wardetzky, Jutta, *Theaterpolitik im faschistischen Deutschland: Studien und Dokumente,* Berlin: Henschelverlag, 1983

Wulf, Josef, editor, *Literatur und Dichtung im Dritten Reich: Eine Dokumentation,* Gütersloh: Mohn, 1963

Zortman, Bruce, *Hitler's Theater: Ideological Drama in Nazi Germany,* El Paso, Texas: Firestein Books, 1984

Rainer Werner Fassbinder 1945–1982

Almost two decades after his death, Rainer Werner Fassbinder remains the most influential of the German filmmakers and actors whose works formed what came to be called the New German Cinema. His own production includes film and television, theater, radio plays, and essay writing. His lifestyle as well as his internationally recognized artistic talent, made him and his repertoire company famous. His many prizes for his films and television productions were balanced or enhanced by his reputation as the enfant terrible of German culture. He was, especially toward the end of his short life, part of an internationally recognized group of artists and performers who moved with apparent ease between their national homelands and international artistic centers, such as New York in the 1970s and 1980s. At the same time, Fassbinder, unlike Mick Jagger or other international celebrities, remained resolutely a performer of Germanness. His familiar physical presentation included the clothing, attitudes, and manners of what might be called a German grunge style with its insistence on antibourgeois attitudes, the beer belly, and the fulminations against German establishment attitudes and political policies. His films and theater productions often intervene directly in the political and social life of the then West German state, in which he purported to see and to oppose resurgences of fascism, a blindness to history, and enormous greed and corruption. However, his works are not only one-sided ideological portrayals of capitalist social relations. They suggest as well the complicity of all social classes in their own domination and often focus on representations of gender-based personal relations in which the basic elements of oppression are often contained. Pair bonding under the rubric of hetero- or homosexual love was his particular bête noire, and he attacked that powerful set of social conventions within every medium he utilized while continuously experimenting with it in his personal life. He is often today remembered as a gay filmmaker and an outspoken advocate of homosexuality. Films such as *Die bitteren Tränen der Petra von Kant* (1972; *The Bitter Tears of Petra von Kant*), *Querelle* (1982), and *In einem Jahr mit dreizehn Monden* (1978; *In a Year of Thirteen Moons*) are frequently interpreted as works whose focus is entirely on questions of homosexual relations in a homophobic culture, and it is undoubtedly correct to see in these and others of Fassbinder's works his preoccupation with gender and sexuality.

Fassbinder's career began with theater pieces and films that, in part reflecting the political and social upheavals of the late 1960s and early 1970s, tore apart the illusionary fabric of allegedly stable West German society and its economic prosperity, revealing the chaos of personal and political desires lying just below the surface. Although he worked in collective media, theater, film, and television, he was from the start a representative of the authorial practice in which the director, often combining the role with that of screenwriter, producer, actor, editor, and cameraman, tries to stamp each piece with a clearly personal and easily recognizable style. Fassbinder's style quickly betrayed the notion of collectivity as he increasingly dominated the entire undertaking of his production in often tyrannical ways that he himself reveals to his audiences in his films.

An early admirer of Godard, he later became enamored of Douglas Sirk and a proponent of a genre, melodrama, that was otherwise virtually neglected in German media productions. In Sirk's use of melodrama, Fassbinder saw the successful combination of the personal film with commercial appeal. He also recognized in Sirk the same deep suspicion of sexual or romantic love as the most finely tuned instrument of oppression in bourgeois society.

His interventions in German social and political practices and illusions began during his earliest works in the anti-theater in Munich and continued in his early films *Liebe ist kälter als der Tod* (1969; *Love Is Colder than Death*), *Katzelmacher* (1969), *Warum läuft Herr R. Amok?* (1969; *Why Does Mr. R. Run Amok?*), and *Der amerikanische Soldat* (1970; *The American Soldier*). Specific focus on German attitudes toward migrant workers is given in *Angst essen Seele auf* (1973; *Fear Eats the Soul*). "Deviant" social and sexual practices are exposed in *Chinesisches Roulette* (1976; *Chinese Roulette*) and in *Bolwieser* (1977) and *Die dritte Generation* (1979; *The Third Generation*), which highlights a deep attraction among all classes of Germans for the regime of the fathers. These revelations reached a political peak during the crises in Germany following the deaths in the high-security prison of two of the leaders of the Red Army faction. In his contribution to the collective production, *Deutschland im Herbst* (1978; *Germany in Autumn*), Fassbinder relentlessly exposes his own deepening terror about the return to fascism advocated by so many Germans in the wake of the social disturbances of the period. In an especially compelling and typical Fassbinder scene in which he interviews his own mother on her desires, he portrays the complex nature of the desire for fascism, first forcing his mother to reveal her belief that Germans need a strong but benevolent leader while overwhelming her with his own brand of masculine terror, echoing in his behaviors the very leader figure she desires.

Even his most successful theater piece, *Bremer Freiheit* (1971; *Bremen Freedom*), is not as influential as the never publicly performed *Der Müll, die Stadt, und der Tod* (1975; *Garbage, the City, and Death*), arranged for production during his tenure as artistic director of Frankfurt's Theater am Turm. He was fired from his position as a result of the controversies surrounding this piece, in which he outraged virtually all German society by portraying the murder of a prostitute by a rich Jew who uses his victim status as a former prisoner in a concentration camp to legitimate his own practices of terror. The piece was withdrawn from publication in the third volume of his theater pieces and attacked even after Fassbinder's death by West German Chancellor Helmut Kohl on the occasion of a potential performance in 1985. *Garbage, Death, and the City* is, in addition to its provocative elements, also Fassbinder's way of drawing attention to the practice of producing taboos that in turn, though apparently honored, lead to the production of blaming and then repeating the process of "othering" that lies at the heart of all fascisms.

His trilogy of films about the Federal Republic of Germany (FRG)—*Lola* (1981), *Die Ehe der Maria Braun* (1978; *The Marriage of Maria Braun*), *and Die Sehnsucht der Veronika Voss* (1982; *The Longing of Veronika Voss*)—were complemented by films representing several of the classics of German literature, including Fontane's *Effi Briest* (1974) and the television serial film of Döblin's novel *Berlin, Alexanderplatz* (1979–80), one of the most expensive television productions in Germany, testifying materially to Fassbinder's compelling artistic reputation.

At his death in 1982, he had completed the film *Querelle* (1982), based on the work by Jean Genet, and was engaged in numerous future projects, including the film *Rosa L.* as part of his film compendium of German history, *Der Mann Moses,* based on Freud's famous essay, and *Kokain,* based on the work of Pitigrilli. He starred in Wolf Gremm's film *Kamikaze* (Fassbinder had regularly appeared not only in his own films but also in those of many other directors), playing the role of police lieutenant Jansen, a role that many feel is a self-portrait.

Fassbinder was undoubtedly the most famous German artistic talent of the postwar era, for some a shockingly gross version of German culture and for others a kind of "Balzac of the Federal Republic" (Töteberg, 1995). He produced about three films a year, acted and wrote, directed in theaters, and conducted an intense public life that was never separate from his personal life. Since his death, his work, including the previously unknown pieces and fragments, and his person continue to be a locus of both aesthetic and sociopolitical controversy. The celebration of his life and work included the famous if unsuccessful attempt in 1985 to perform *Garbage, the City, and Death,* leading to further protests and virulent controversies still lying at the very heart of then West German and now unified, if not united, German society.

DUNCAN SMITH

See also Film and Literature

Biography

Born in Bad Wörishofen, Bavaria, 31 May 1945. Attended the *Schauspielschule* (drama school) in Munich, 1964–66; worked for the *Büchner Theater* and *the Action Theater;* since 1971, freelance writer, director, and filmmaker; led the *Theater am Turm;* 1974–75, Frankfurt; lived in Paris and Munich. Hauptmann Prize, 1969; numerous film prizes, 1969–82. Died in Munich, 10 June 1982.

Selected Works

Collections
Antiteater. Bd. 1, 1970
Antiteater. Bd. 2, 1972
Antiteater. Bd. 3, 1976
Anarchie in Bayern und andere Stücke, 1985
Rainer Werner Fassbinder—Die Kinofilme. Bd. 1, 1985
Rainer Werner Fassbinder—Die Kinofilme. Bd. 2–4, 1990
Sämtliche Stücke, 1991

Writings
Schatten der Engel, 1976
Das bißchen Realität, das ich brauche: Wie Filme entstehen, 1976
Angst essen Seele auf, 1978
Der Film Berlin Alexanderplatz, 1980
Der Müll, die Stadt und der Tod, 1981
Die bitteren Tränen der Petra von Kant, 1982
Katzelmacher: Preparadise sorry now, 1982
Querelle, 1982
Filme befreien den Kopf, 1984
Die Anarchie der Fantasie: Gespräche und Inteviews, 1986

Films
Die Stadtstreicher, 1965
Das kleine Chaos, 1966
Liebe ist kälter als der Tod (*Love Is Colder than Death*), 1969
Katzelmacher, 1969
Warum läuft Herr R. Amok, 1969
Pioniere in Ingolstadt (based on the play by Marieluise Fleißer), 1970
Der Händler der vier Jahreszeiten, 1971
Die bitteren Tränen der Petra von Kant (*The Bitter Tears of Petra von Kant*), 1972
Wildwechsel (based on the play by Franz Xaver Kroetz), 1972
Angst essen Seele auf (*Fear Eats the Soul*), 1973
Effi Briest (based on the novel by Theodor Fontane), 1974
Faustrecht der Freiheit (*Bremen Freedom*), 1974
Wie ein Vogel auf dem Draht, 1974
Mutter Küster's Fahrt zum Himmel, 1975
Angst vor der Angst, 1975
Ich will doch nur, daß ihr mich liebt, 1976
Satansbraten, 1976
Chinesisches Roulette (*Chinese Roulette*), 1976
Bolwieser (based on Oskar Maria Graf), 1977
Frauen in New York, 1977
Despair - Eine Reise ins Licht, 1977
Deutschland im Herbst (*Germany in Autumn*), 1978
Die Ehe der Maria Braun (*The Marriage of Maria Braun*), 1978
In einem Jahr mit dreizehn Monden (*In a Year of Thirteen Moons*), 1978
Berlin, Alexanderplatz (based on the novel by Alfred Döblin), 1979–80
Die dritte Generation (*The Third Generation*), 1979
Lili Marleen (based on the song sung by Lale Andersen), 1981
Lola, 1981
Die Sehnsucht der Veronika Voss (*The Longing of Veronika Voss*), 1982
Querelle, 1982

Further Reading

Elsaesser, Thomas, *Fassbinder's Germany: History, Identity, Subject,* Amsterdam: Amsterdam University Press, 1996
Hake, Sabine, "Television, Tabloids, and Tears: Fassbinder and Popular Culture by Jane Shattuc," *Historical Journal of Film, Radio, and Television* 16, no. 2 (1996)
Hayman, Ronald, *Fassbinder, Film Maker,* London: Weidenfeld and Nicholson, and New York: Simon and Schuster, 1984
Hoberman, J., "The Rise and Fall and Rise of Rainer Werner Fassbinder," *Village Voice* 42, no. 4 (1997)
Lorenz, Juliane, et al., editors, *Das ganz normale Chaos: Gespräche über Rainer Werner Fassbinder,* Berlin: Henschel, 1995; translated as *Chaos as Usual: Conversations about Rainer Werner Fassbinder,* New York and London: Applause, 1997
Macnab, Geoffrey, "The Merchant of the Four Seasons/Der Handler der vier Jahreszeiten," *Sight and Sound* 7, 11, 62 (1997)
Rayns, Tony, editor, *Fassbinder,* London: British Film Institute, 1976; 2nd revised and expanded edition, 1980
Rentschler, Eric, editor, *West German Filmmakers on Film,* New York: Holmes and Meier, 1988
Shattuc, Jane, "R.W. Fassbinder as a Popular Auteur: The Making of an Authorial Legend," *Journal of Film and Video* 45, no. 1 (1993)
Silverman, Kaja, *Male Subjectivity at the Margins,* New York: Routledge, 1992
Töteberg, Michael, "Rainer Werner Fassbinder," *Kritisches Lexikon zur deutschsprachigen Literaturgeschichte* 54 (1995)
Töteberg, Michael, editor, *Fassbinder,* Munich: Edition Text und Kritik, 1989
Watson, Wallace Steadman, *Understanding Rainer Werner Fassbinder: Film as Private and Public Art,* Columbia: University of South Carolina Press, 1996

Federal Republic of Germany

Although the Federal Republic of Germany did not formally come into existence until 21 September 1949, the date it was recognized by the United States, Britain, and France, its creation was prefigured over a year earlier when, on 20 June 1948, the largely worthless Reichsmark was replaced by the deutsche mark in the Western zones of occupation. This currency reform, which cemented the economic division of Germany, was in turn the result of the failure of the Western Allies to come to any agreement with the Soviet Union about the future political and economic shape of their former common enemy. With the nascent Cold War increasingly being played out on German soil, the division of Germany was to last over 40 years until 3 October 1990. The accession on that date of the German Democratic Republic (GDR), the state that had been set up in eastern Germany on the territory of the Soviet Zone of Occupation on 7 October 1949, to the Federal Republic meant that the latter's political, economic, and social systems were extended eastward to create an entity of 16 Federal States and a population of approximately 80 million people. Once the Berlin Wall had collapsed in 1989, the majority of the citizens of the communist GDR concluded, albeit with encouragement from their powerful neighbor, that they wished to enjoy the benefits that the "German model" had to offer. This was the term that was widely used to underline the success of the West German state that had been established 40 years earlier.

The initial success of the Federal Republic was undoubtedly due to the rapid economic recovery that took place in the 1950s. The introduction of the deutsche mark created the stability for normal economic activity that replaced the chaos associated with the black market of the previous years, when cigarettes provided a currency substitute. The tangible aspect of the reform—that each adult received 40 marks—also created the impression that all were somehow equal at the start of a new era. In fact, those who owned productive capacity then had the chance to put that capacity to good use to earn valuable money, whereas those who had held wealth in the form of money in the bank found that it was now largely devalued. At the time, however, this was less an issue than the need for all groups to work together to rebuild the damage done by Hitler's war.

Other factors that helped the burgeoning economy of the Federal Republic were funds from the American European Recovery Program, frequently referred to as Marshall Aid, and the general boom conditions that accompanied the Korean War. As other states concentrated on military production, the Federal Republic was increasingly able to supply civilian goods to an expanding market both at home and abroad.

The economic system adopted by the Federal Republic became known as the social market economy. In this system, as the term *market economy* implies, the laws of supply and demand, rather than government planning, control economic activity, although there is a role for the state in maintaining competition through the prevention of monopoly. The term *social* implies that the weakest members of society are protected by a welfare system. Another term relevant to the discussion of the German economy is the *magic square*. The Stability Law of 1967 laid down four economic goals: low inflation, full employment, growth, and a positive balance of payments. In many countries, it has proved difficult to achieve all of these goals simultaneously, but not in most years in the pre-1990 Federal Republic. Keeping down inflation was a political and social necessity given German history, and this goal was facilitated by the existence of an independent central bank, the Deutsche Bundesbank, which controlled interest rates and the money supply. The demands of the labor market allowed for the absorption of German refugees from the east and, later, millions of foreign workers into the economy. That healthy levels of growth were achieved was due in part to the demand for German goods abroad, which produced surpluses in the balance of payment account. What was termed in the era of extremely rapid growth in the 1950s the "economic miracle" developed into sustained prosperity.

In tandem with its economic progress, the Federal Republic also attained a high level of political stability. Mindful of the weaknesses of the constitution of the Weimar Republic, those responsible for writing the Federal Republic's Basic Law (*Grundgesetz*), a term used in preference to constitution in order to underline the provisional nature of the state pending German reunification, sought to ensure that governance would proceed in an orderly manner. Executive power was to be firmly in the hands of the federal chancellor, who "determined the guidelines of policy" rather than share power with the president, as in the Weimar system. The federal president, who was not to be directly elected, was reduced to a largely ceremonial role. The Basic Law also made it extremely difficult to dismiss the federal chancellor, something that could only be achieved by a "constructive vote of no confidence." This meant that the lower house of parliament (*Bundestag*) also had to agree on a successor by absolute majority at the same time the existing incumbent was replaced. This proved possible in 1982 when Helmut Kohl became chancellor. With very limited exceptions, there were no provisions for referenda within the Basic Law, arguably the clearest sign that it was designed in the interests of stability.

The Basic Law also referred specifically to the role of parties in the political process, and the establishment of a stable party system undoubtedly helped to consolidate the Federal Republic. Weimar democracy had been dogged by a plethora of parties and, consequently, unstable coalition governments; by the 1960s, however, a three-party system, which was to hold for over 20 years until the success of the ecological Greens, was established in the Federal Republic, at least in terms of parliamentary representation. A tough electoral law that generally restricted parliamentary representation to those gaining at least five percent of the vote consolidated this state of affairs. The three parties consisted of the Christian Democrats (CDU), who were organized in a separate sister party in the state of Bavaria under the name Christian Social Union (CSU), the Social Democrats (SPD), and the much smaller liberal Free Democrats (FDP). Since neither of the major parties has usually been able to gain an overall majority, the FDP has tended to determine, through its choice of partner, which party leads the ruling coalition. In 1969, it made possible the election of the Social Democrat Willy Brandt to the post of chancellor; since 1982, however, it has supported the Christian Democrats, as it did at the inception of the Federal Republic.

The federal nature of the new state created in the west of Germany in 1949 is undoubtedly another part of the German model. A system based on decentralization reflects not only the fear of the kind of centralization practiced by the Nazis but also historical German traditions of particularism. Even if some of the federal states (*Bundesländer*) that came into being after 1949 did not correspond to former boundaries, they offered a point of identification, especially when German nationalism had been besmirched by Nazism. In direct political terms, the states do not possess great power, except in the areas of education and broadcasting; however, they have a major influence on legislation passed by the Federal Parliament. Representatives of state governments make up the upper house (*Bundesrat*), which has wide powers to delay and even block parliamentary bills. Accordingly, federalism acts as a check on executive power. This is also one of the functions of the Federal Constitutional Court (*Bundesverfassungsgericht*), which determines what may be considered as in accordance with the constitution. In the 1950s, it gained prominence by banning extremist parties as undemocratic and, therefore, unconstitutional (it banned the communists in 1956); subsequently, however, the court has used its powers, often controversially, both to block legislation such as the abortion law reform in the 1970s and to sanction planned government actions, including the deployment of troops outside the NATO area in the 1990s.

Finally, in the area of politics, it is necessary to mention the foreign policy of the Federal Republic. From the outset, the aim was to overcome the legacy of the German past through integration with the West. This took the form of participation in Western supranational organizations, that is to say, all bodies aimed to promote European integration including the European Coal and Steel Community and, from 1956 on, NATO. As a member of these institutions, the Federal Republic sought to prove itself a reliable partner in international affairs. In addition, it sought in particular accommodation with its former enemy France, something that found expression in the Franco-German Friendship Treaty of 1963. By the end of the 1980s, the Federal Republic had achieved sufficient international standing, at least with its major ally, the United States, for there to be no effective opposition to German unification, regardless of the memories of the past.

Despite these achievements, it would be hard to maintain that the preunification Federal Republic was a society at ease with itself, at least in the early years of its existence. A variety of concerns found expression, especially in the literature of the time. The major one was undoubtedly the Nazi past, which cast its shadow over most areas of society. An immediate concern was the continued presence of former National Socialists in positions of power and influence. Especially controversial was the leading civil servant in the office of Chancellor Adenauer, Hans Globke, who had been the coauthor of the commentary to the 1935 Nuremberg laws that stripped Jews of their rights. In the area of justice, there was not only continuity of personnel but also the failure to prosecute those who had passed grotesque sentences, including the judges who had imposed the death penalty for telling anti-Nazi jokes. No judge was ever brought to trial for his Nazi past. Where there were prosecutions for war crimes, these did not appear to be pursued with particular vigor, at least until the trial of Auschwitz guards in the 1960s.

Behind worries about failures to address the Nazi legacy was concern about a revival of past attitudes. The decision to create an army in the early 1950s less than a decade after the Nazi defeat led to widespread public protest, based on a fear of a rebirth of militarism. Also feared was right-wing extremism, whether it surfaced in the shape of desecration of Jewish cemeteries or in the more organized form of political parties. In any event, the society of the Federal Republic did not revert to traditional patterns, in part because of the culture of protest. The army never reestablished its previous prestige, and successes for extremists at the ballot box proved short-lived. The Adenauer government did agree to compensate Israel, and the integration of former Nazis into society can be viewed in retrospect as an achievement that helped to maintain the stability of the Federal Republic.

If the Federal Republic was itself a product of the Cold War, then its ruling elite undoubtedly embraced the Western standpoint in that conflict. The anticommunism of the Federal Republic did, however, create a degree of concern, particularly among intellectuals, because it was seen as an unreflecting continuation of Nazi propaganda. They feared the argument that, if the enemy of the Nazis was still today's enemy, then Nazism was in part justified. Moreover, Adenauer's "policy of strength," through which he hoped to extract concessions from the East, appeared to have failed with the building of the Berlin Wall. Accordingly, the abandonment of this policy by the Brandt government in favor of détente met with approval by intellectuals and, indeed, by large parts of the population, who now favored dialogue as a means of reducing tension and alleviating conditions for Germans in the East.

The economic success of the Federal Republic created a materialistic society. As prosperity increased, it became fashionable to speak of "waves," beginning with the "eating wave," during which people satisfied their postwar hunger; this wave was followed by the clothes and travel waves. For social critics, the almost exclusive pursuit of material goals was a distortion of human values, especially given recent history. Paradoxically, these pursuits took place in a society that preached Christian morality and in which the doctrines of the church, especially those of the Catholic Church, influenced many aspects of life. Homosexuality, for example, remained outlawed until the late 1960s, while abortion remains until the present, at least technically, against the law.

In the early years of the Federal Republic, a mixture of clerical and traditional German authoritarianism certainly created an illiberal climate. A major worry was that the Federal Republic would never be anything more than a token democracy. Such fears were not immediately banished by the advent of a Social Democratic government. It, too, was accused of authoritarian methods for its attempts to rid the public service of political extremists and for the measures it took to combat terrorism. Many writers were concerned that the law designed to stop the promotion of violence would inhibit its presentation in works of literature.

Despite all the fears, the Federal Republic did become an increasingly liberal society. The rhetoric of the early years of the Kohl government concerning an intellectual and moral change did not amount to much in reality. By the time of unification, the Federal Republic was in nearly every respect a success. The economy, despite occasional recessions, had become by far the most powerful and successful one in Europe, political institutions were stable, and membership of NATO and the European Community appeared to bring many advantages. Even those who had been prone to criticize in the past, namely, writers and intellectuals, began to express positive views. The Federal Republic had brought the kind of freedom that had been unknown in previous German states. The younger generation, especially, had accepted the Westernization of society and largely abandoned dreams of German unity. In short, Germany, or at least its Western part, had become something like a "normal democracy," not just in terms of institutions but also in the positive attitude of the population toward liberal democracy. It was, therefore, no wonder that most Germans in the East wanted to join what, by comparison, seemed an earthly paradise.

The issue that now arises is the extent to which unification has changed the Federal Republic. At the level of institutions the answer is clear: very little. The former German Democratic Republic was absorbed into the existing framework with minimal constitutional changes. Similarly, the existing political parties have moved eastward, albeit with varying degrees of success. Nevertheless, enough questions have arisen to make talk of a German model much more questionable than before.

In the economic field, it has not been possible, since the end of the postunification boom, to speak of the "magic square." Whereas inflation has been kept low, growth has been sluggish, there have been balance of payments deficits, and most significantly, unemployment has rocketed, reaching well over 4 million. One major reason given for these trends has been the German economy's lack of competitiveness in an age of a globalized economy. As a result of the years of prosperity, critics claimed, Germans worked the shortest hours and enjoyed the longest holidays and some of the highest wages of workers in any comparable country. This could no longer be made up for by higher productivity or superior goods that remained attractive, even if expensive. A further burden for employers was the high contributions that had to be made to social welfare, especially to pensions and health care. The solutions generally offered to these problems include greater flexibility of labor markets, deregulation, and lower taxes. What has undoubtedly happened since unification is that many companies, especially in the East, have withdrawn from national or regional pay agreements and sought to pay what they felt they could afford. Thus, one aspect of the German model of "social partnership" between employers and trade unions, binding agreements on wages and hours, has diminished in significance. There has also been a growth of part-time jobs up to the limit at which no contributions have to be made to social welfare.

Although the economy began to grow again in 1998, there is likely to be continuing pressure to follow the Anglo-Saxon economic model of freer markets and less generous social welfare. What is not in doubt is that the economy will continue to be burdened by the costs of rebuilding in the East, especially as the economic recovery seems likely to be restricted largely to the West. By the time of unification, industry in the GDR was in a state of increasing decay, while the introduction of the deutsche mark at a generous rate took no account of the economic reality of traditional Eastern markets. The result was a mass closure of factories and widespread unemployment, which were major contributory factors to discontent in the East that was only slightly mitigated by job creation schemes. On the positive side, a few pockets of modern industry such as the Opel works at Eisenach have been created, while the amount spent on general renovation has changed the physical appearance of formerly dilapidated cities and towns.

Dissatisfaction in the East is also visible in the world of politics. Although the CDU/FDP coalition was able to continue after the two postunification elections of 1990 and 1994, by the second election it was clear that two-party systems had developed in the two sections of the country. In the Western states, the old four-party system, which now includes the Greens, remains. In the East, two of these parties are of little significance. The liberal Free Democrats can gain little support where there is as yet no prosperous middle class favoring reduced taxes and free market economics, and ecological issues remain a low priority in an area ravaged by deindustrialization. The Eastern allies of the Greens, the former civil rights activists whose aim is a democratic GDR, have lost significance in united Germany, even if their name is now incorporated in the party's title, Alliance 90/The Greens (*Bündnis 90/Die Grünen*). There is now also a specifically Eastern party, the Party of Democratic Socialism (PDS), seen as the successor party to the former ruling communists. This party appeals to some of those who feel disadvantaged by German unity, in particular those who enjoyed status in the GDR state apparatus or universities but who have now lost their previous positions. Others who feel to have lost from unity have turned to right-wing extremist parties.

The disenchantment felt in the East is one of the major problems of the post-1990 Federal Republic. It is not a simple case of material deprivation through unemployment, higher prices for rents, transport, and the like. In many ways, as in car ownership, East Germans are far better off than before. The problem is rather a sense that they do not have a contribution to make to postunification Germany on the basis of their previous experience under communism—in other words, that they are second-class citizens. Many feel that they have been taken over in the way that the few attractive parts of GDR industry were largely taken over by Western interests during the privatization process. The situation can be illustrated further with reference to literature. Whereas parts of GDR literature were valued throughout Germany as an expression of dissidence, it is now claimed in some quarters that nearly all GDR writers were in fact close to the state, especially the many who had relations with the State Security Service (Stasi). GDR citizens feel they are viewed in the same light by Westerners, as conformists who refused to rebel against their dictatorial masters. Moreover, they lack the social refinements that have come with economic prosperity. What is undoubtedly true is that what has been called "internal unity" is going to take a long time to achieve.

Alongside the dichotomy between East and West, the other major concern about unified Germany is whether the previous ethos of democracy at home and partnership in foreign policy is giving way to increased nationalism. The most shocking events of the early 1990s were undoubtedly the various attacks that took place on non-Germans. In the East, there were attacks on hostels housing asylum seekers with bystanders showing approval; in at least one case, in Rostock, the police more or less stood idly by. Arson attacks on the homes of immigrants in the Western towns of Mölln and Solingen followed, and these occasions had fatal consequences. These incidents, together with a degree of electoral success for right-wing neofascist parties, do suggest a growth in nationalist extremism.

There has also been increased discussion of issues relating to the nation at an intellectual level. One person in the foreground of this debate has been the editor of the periodical *Merkur,* Karl Heinz Bohrer. At the time of the Falklands War, he praised the action of the British, comparing it with the trivial, unheroic concerns of the Germans. At the time of unity, he attacked German provincialism, in which category he included the false cosmopolitanism of those who avoided all identification with their native country. For him, the nation-state was still the main agent of history. A phrase that entered public discussion at this time was the "self-confident nation" (*Die selbstbewußte Nation*), which reflected the views of certain young intellectuals that, 50 years after World War II, it was time for Germany to cease national self-deprecation. Issues came to a head with the 50th anniversary of the end of the war in 1995, with more nationalistic groupings rejecting the idea that the end of Nazism should be viewed as liberation rather than capitulation. As a major rally planned to present this view flopped, it can be claimed that the New Right lost this particular argument.

This is not to say that the left-liberal attitudes often associated with the literary Gruppe 47, which came to dominate intellectual life in the Federal Republic, have remained unchallenged. Following the student movement of the late 1960s, there was talk of a change of prevailing attitudes, a phenomenon that came to be known as the *Tendenzwende* (change of direction). This certainly occurred in the field of education, where progressive theories and, in higher education, student participation gave way to more traditional approaches. In literary and intellectual life, questions of German unity came to the fore in the 1980s and are reflected in the works of Günter Grass, Peter Schneider, and Martin Walser. Since unity, the most contentious debates have centered around Botho Strauß's critique of the pluralist society and his praise of traditional values, including those associated with the military, in his 1993 essay "Anschwellender Bocksgesang" ("Impending Tragedy").

Questions relating to war and defense have become leading issues in the postunification Federal Republic. The outbreak of the Gulf War led to major soul-searching, which produced a split between "pacifists" and "bellicists." Whereas many young people opposed the war—at universities, debates about the issues replaced normal classes—and a number of writers produced a volume with the emotional title *Ich will reden von der Angst meines Herzens* (I Wish to Speak of my Heart's Fear), others saw the measures taken by the United States and its allies as fully justified. For Hans Magnus Enzensberger, Saddam Hussein was a reincarnation of Hitler, while Wolf Biermann stressed the threat to Israel, a point of special poignancy in Germany.

During the Gulf War, the only direct military German involvement was the sending of air force units to Turkey, a member of NATO that was felt to be under threat from Iraq. Otherwise, the support given was financial, since it appeared that the Basic Law did not allow military operations outside the NATO area. After the war, the question arose about whether this was, indeed, the case. When the Constitutional Court ruled that "out-of-area" operations were permissible on the basis of a parliamentary majority, this majority was easily achieved in the case of Bosnia, and some of the Green parliament members were even willing to accept that German troops were needed in this particular operation. Support for German involvement was also given by the philosopher Jürgen Habermas, which he justified by referring to the need to fight fascism in former Yugoslavia. In March 1999 German troops were involved in the Kosovo operation, taking part in military action for the first time since 1945.

The overall question that arises is whether Germany is turning, albeit slowly, into a society of bellicose nationalists. On the question of Yugoslavia, it can be argued that the catastrophe was exacerbated by the premature recognition of Croatia and Slovenia in 1991 by the European Community, which occurred under pressure from the German Foreign Ministry. In 1998, German demands for a reduction to its financial contributions to Europe became particularly vocal. In domestic politics, some of the major pieces of legislation in the early 1990s were the measures taken to reduce the number of people seeking asylum. At the same time, no efforts were made to reform immigration and nationality laws. German nationality laws, based on the concept of jus sanguinis, which makes descent or blood the determining factor in questions of nationality rather than place of birth (jus soli), mean that third-generation inhabitants of, for example, Turkish origin have no automatic right to German citizenship. At the same time, ethnic Germans whose forebears settled in Romania or Russia centuries ago have a more-or-less automatic right to citizenship, of which many have made use since the fall of communism. In the case of those viewed as foreigners, the problem is compounded by the common refusal to accept that Germany is a country of immigration. This idea is underlined by the term first used to describe the foreign workers who arrived in the prosperous 1960s: "guest workers" (*Gastarbeiter*). Although there have always been tension between these workers and certain sections of the indigenous population, the situation has deteriorated since unification and economic crisis. As long as they lack full civil rights as a result of what can be seen as an atavistic concept of nationality, this situation is likely to continue.

If there are signs that the Federal Republic has changed since unification, there are equal indications of continuity. Despite public disquiet, the Kohl government accepted and even pressed for the Single European Currency. The advent of this new currency in 2002 will mean the final disappearance of the deutsche mark, the symbol of postwar prosperity. The introduction of fixed exchange rates, on 1 January 1999, the first part of the "Euro project," did not create any particular tensions. Indeed, European unity was always the priority of Chancellor Kohl, a member of the generation that remains aware of the catastrophes wrought by European division. Nationalism and bellicosity, moreover, do not seem to be the major characteristic of most Germans. If there are young German males who espouse neo-Nazism, there are also increasing numbers who refuse compulsory military service, preferring the longer alternative of some form of social service. Youth culture, too, remains dominated by American and British influences in such areas as music and colloquial speech. In the world of literature, best-seller lists are dominated by translations—again, hardly a sign that Germany is becoming a chauvinistic country.

In 1997, a leading language institute chose *Reformstau* (reform blockage) as its word of the year. Specifically, this word refers to the failure of the political class to address the economic and social issues facing the Federal Republic. If such a diagnosis was correct, it could be attributed to the approaching 1998 election and the parliamentary stalemate created by the ability of the Social Democrats to block legislation because of their majority in the *Bundesrat*. The Social Democrat/Green coalition that gained power in 1998 is now in a better position to instigate reforms, although its first measures (including the reform of the nationality laws) have been beset by problems. What the term *Reformstau* also suggests is that unification has challenged the previous "German model" and rendered change necessary, particularly in the economic sphere. Indeed, there can be no doubt that the incorporation of 16 million new inhabitants and the creation of a larger and potentially more powerful entity in the center of Europe are bound to have consequences.

Given German history, the changes of 1989–90 were bound to raise disquiet, which has been increased by certain subsequent events. On the other hand, there are still many grounds for regarding the postunification Federal Republic as a "normal" state. The overcoming of division ended an artificial situation, and, unlike its historical predecessors, the Federal Republic now has no territorial disputes with its neighbors. The major question posed by Goethe of where Germany "lies" is therefore solved, even if the related one of "who is a German?" is not. Most important, the vast majority of Germans have accepted democracy, no longer seeing it as an alien Western concept. Indeed, in most respects, the Federal Republic is thoroughly Westernized. It also remains, despite recent problems, highly prosperous.

Nevertheless, it would be wrong to end on a note of complacency. Similar to all comparable countries, the Federal Republic has to adapt to rapid technological and economic change. It has to do this while integrating new territory with a very different political and social legacy. Both challenges will require a quickness of reaction and sensitivity that have as yet not always been displayed. The other challenge is, of course, the past, which continues to cast a shadow over German identity. At the moment, there seems scant chance of a return of traditional nationalism. Recent debates, however, suggest that national issues are again on the agenda. Whereas it can be argued that a degree of healthy patriotism is preferable to a vague internationalism based on an impossible dream of international and cross-cultural harmony, the achievements of the Federal Republic in promoting cooperation and reconciliation should not be lightly discarded. These issues are bound to continue to influence cultural and intellectual debate as Germany bids farewell to the century in which it has frequently been a force for at least disruption and at worst evil. Changed by unification, Germany seeks to consolidate its place in a constantly evolving world.

STUART PARKES

See also German Democratic Republic; Stunde Null

Further Reading

Balfour, Michael, *Germany: The Tides of Power,* London and New York: Routledge, 1992

Buchner, Gerhard, *Die Bundesrepublik Deutschland,* Munich: Humboldt-Taschenbuchverlag, 1994

Glaser, Hermann, *Kleine Kulturgeschichte der Bundesrepublik Deutschland 1945–1989,* Munich: Hanser, 1991

Jeffery, Charlie, and Ruth Whittle, editors, *Germany Today: A Student's Dictionary,* London and New York: Arnold, 1997

Larres, Klaus, and Panikos Panayi, editors, *The Federal Republic of Germany since 1949,* London and New York: Longman, 1996

Merkl, Peter H., editor, *The Federal Republic of Germany at Forty-Five: Union without Unity,* New York: New York University Press, and Basingstoke: Macmillan, 1995

Parkes, K. Stuart, *Understanding Contemporary Germany,* London and New York: Routledge, 1997

Pulzer, Peter, *German Politics, 1945–1995,* Oxford and New York: Oxford University Press, 1995

Thränhardt, Dietrich, *Geschichte der Bundesrepublik Deutschland,* Frankfurt: Suhrkamp, 1986; expanded edition, 1996

Lion Feuchtwanger 1884–1958

Lion Feuchtwanger, who started his literary career as a journalist and a theater critic and who then tried his hand at writing plays, gained great popularity as the author of historical novels following the publication of *Die häßliche Herzogin Margarete Maultasch* (1923; *The Ugly Duchess*) and *Jud Süß* (1925; translated as *Jew Süß* and *Power*). Exiled during the Nazi regime, first in France, and then in the United States from 1940 to the end of his life, he was able to maintain his popularity through publications in exile publishing houses and in English translations. Because of his early leftist leanings, as expressed most forcefully in his travelogue *Moskau 1937: Ein Reisebericht für meine Freunde* (1937; *Moscow 1937: A Visit Described for My Friends*), and his antifascist stance, he was highly esteemed in Russia and, after World War II, in the GDR. As a result, he was hardly read during the Cold War era in the Federal Republic. It was not until West German television broadcast film versions of his novels *Exil* (1940; *Paris Gazette*) in 1981, *Die Geschwister Oppermann* (1933; *The Oppermanns*) in 1983, and *Erfolg: Drei Jahre Geschichte einer Provinz* (1930; *Success: Three Years History of a Province*) in 1992 that a true Feuchtwanger renaissance ensued. Above all, the 100th anniversary of Feuchtwanger's birth in 1984 gave occasion to the publication of a number of biographies and other scholarly works on the author. His preoccupation with the rise of fascism and the persecution of Jews through the ages has in particular contributed to the renewed popularity of his works in Germany today.

In his adaptation of the old-Indic play *Vasantasena* (1916), Feuchtwanger first dealt with the idea that the calm, contemplative wisdom of the East and its closeness to nature might ultimately triumph over Western culture and the Nietzschean philosophy of action. This Eastern attitude was then fully developed in the drama *Warren Hastings, Gouverneur von Indien* (1916; Warren Hastings, Governor of India). In 1927 Feuchtwanger reworked this play together with Bertolt Brecht, and it was then called *Kalkutta, 4. Mai* (1927). His drama about the 1918 German revolution, *Thomas Wendt* (1919; in 1934 reworked as *Neunzehnhundertachtzehn* [Nineteenhundredeighteen]), ends in the title hero's withdrawal from the world of politics. Several other dramas, including *Die Petroleuminseln* (1927; *Oil Islands*), *Wird Hill amnestiert* (1927; Will Hill Be Granted Amnesty), and, later, *Wahn; oder, Der Teufel in Boston* (1948; *The Devil in Boston*), deal with U.S. topics.

Feuchtwanger's fascination with history came out in a large number of historical novels. As he pointed out in his essays *Vom Sinn und Unsinn des historischen Romans* (1935; On the Sense and Nonsense of the Historical Novel) and *Das Haus der Desdemona; oder, Größe und Grenzen der historischen Dichtung* (1961; *The House of Desdemona; or, The Laurels and Limitations of Historical Fiction*), he believed that the historical novel should not just depict the past but deal with problems and topics of the present in historical garb. For Feuchtwanger, historical facts were merely a means of gaining distance from the present, of gaining a better perspective of current events. He did not consider historical accuracy important; the author is permitted to change the facts and to give his imagination free rein. Underlying all of Feuchtwanger's historical novels is the Enlightenment idea that history is a history of progress, that it will make use of cunning and accidents to promote its secret plan: the self-realization of reason. He therefore always tried to place his historical novels at the threshold of a new era. Thus, his first historical novel, *Jew Süß,* about the miraculous rise of the historical Josef Süß Oppenheimer, who in the 18th century became the powerful financial advisor of a Württemberg duke but was executed at the end, is placed at the time of transition from feudalism to the bourgeois money economy. Philosophically, the novel is still part of Feuchtwanger's preoccupation with Eastern philosophy. He wanted to show his title hero's inner road from action to inaction, from European to Indic philosophy, and from assimilation and career thinking to accepting his Jewish identity with all its consequences. His second, but first published novel, *The Ugly Duchess,* dealt with the fight of the ugly Duchess of Tyrol against the other European powers, which tried to take over her country. It is also the futile fight of an intelligent woman who tries to overcome her physical defects through reasonable actions and shrewd political behavior, but who ultimately resigns herself.

Toward the end of the Weimar Republic, Feuchtwanger began work on his *Wartesaal-Trilogie* (waiting-room trilogy), a series of three novels dealing with contemporary German history (1921–39). The first volume, *Success,* deals with the reactionary politics of Bavaria during the Weimar Republic, especially the machinations that agriculture and industry designed to control the government, including the attempt of a demagogue and a former General, obviously pointing at Hitler and Ludendorff, to carry out a coup d'état. The novel is thus a roman à clef about the rise of National Socialism in Germany. At the same time, it shows the transformation of a writer from an onlooker to a social-critical writer. In *The Oppermanns* (1933), published while he was already in exile in France, Feuchtwanger describes the fate of an upper-middle-class Berlin Jewish family from November 1932 to late summer 1933; they fall victim to National Socialist anti-Semitic politics shortly before and after their assumption of power. In *Paris Gazette* (1940), Feuchtwanger uses the figure of the composer Sepp Trautwein, who works for a German exile newspaper in Paris, to show the various attitudes of German intellectuals vis-à-vis National Socialism. In the course of the novel, Trautwein, whose son Hanns embraces communism, undergoes a change from a politically passive to an active role, and he even uses his art to this end. The novel constitutes Feuchtwanger's confession that art has a political responsibility and thus marks a clear change from his previously held views.

In other novels, Feuchtwanger also deals with the Third Reich, including the seemingly historical novel *Der falsche Nero* (1936; *The Pretender*), a largely satirical novel that takes place in Roman antiquity, and *Die Brüder Lautensack* (1944; *Double, Double, Toil and Trouble*), which tells the story of the clairvoyant Oskar Lautensack, who is ultimately liquidated by the Nazis whom he served. In both novels, Hitler and his followers are not taken seriously enough to be convincing.

Already in the first volume of his *Josephus* trilogy, *Der jüdische Krieg* (1932; *Josephus*), Feuchtwanger dealt with the question of nationalism versus cosmopolitanism. The title hero is the Jewish historiographer Flavius Josephus (A.D. 37 or 38–ca. 100), who undergoes a transformation from a Jewish nationalist to a Roman citizen of the world. In part 2, *Die Söhne* (1935; *The Jew of Rome*), the cosmopolitan Josephus believes that Rome can be defeated by introducing the spirit of Judaism to the Western world. In the third and final part, *Der Tag wird kommen* (1945; translated as *Josephus and the Emperor* and *The Day Will Come*), the author returns to his Jewish roots and patriotic thinking, although the cosmopolitan utopia is not given up. The novel is thus the expression of Feuchtwanger's own conclusions from the anti-Semitic persecutions of the Third Reich: in 1940, he himself finally embraced the ideal of a Jewish state, Israel.

Feuchtwanger's exile in France found expression not only in his autobiographical report *Der Teufel in Frankreich* (originally titled *Unholdes Frankreich* [1942; *The Devil in France*])—about the time of his internment there—but also in the play *Die Gesichte der Simone Machard* (1957; The Visions of Simone Machard), which he wrote together with Bertolt Brecht. He also produced a novel, *Simone* (1944; *Simone*), on the same topic, the resistance of a 15-year-old girl in occupied France.

Three other novels deal from various angles with the French Revolution. According to Feuchtwanger, the theme of the novel *Waffen für Amerika* (1947; *Proud Destiny* [This work was also published in two volumes in 1947–48 under the title *Die Füchse im Weinberg*]) is the interaction between progressive France and the U.S. War of Independence. Its main characters are the writer, businessman, and politician Beaumarchais, who supplies the rebel colonies with weapons, and the then congressional ambassador to France, Benjamin Franklin. According to Feuchtwanger, the actual hero is historical progress, which even uses the French King Louis XVI to provide the Americans with weapons against the British.

In *Goya; oder, Der arge Weg der Erkenntnis* (1951; *This Is the Hour*), Feuchtwanger traces Goya's transformation from a traditionalist court painter into a political artist. Its theme, therefore, is the political responsibility of the artist in his time.

In *Narrenweisheit; oder, Tod und Verklärung des Jean-Jacques Rousseau* (1952; *'Tis Folly to Be Wise; or, Death and Transfiguration of Jean-Jacques Rousseau*), Feuchtwanger takes up the theme of the French Revolution, dealing not only with the aging Rousseau as a fool who is ruled by his mother-in-law and cuckolded by his wife but also with the perpetuation of his legend and his work in and by the Revolution.

In the last years of his life, Feuchtwanger returned to the theme of Jewishness: in *Spanische Ballade* (1955; republished in the same year as *Die Jüdin von Toledo* [*Raquel, the Jewess of Toledo*]), he tells the story of the beautiful Jewess Raquel who in the 12th century falls in love with King Alfonso VIII of Castile, whose love for her makes him neglect his duties as a ruler. She is ultimately killed by his grandees, just like her father Jehuda, who had used his daughter to keep the king from fighting wars. By opposing figures symbolizing reason (Jehuda) and knightly fighting spirit (Alfonso), the new money economy and the old feudal order are contrasted, just as in Feuchtwanger's early novels.

In *Jefta und seine Tochter* (1957; *Jephta and His Daughter*), Feuchtwanger fashions the Old Testament story of the judge Jefta who sacrifices his daughter to fulfill a promise he made to God. At the end he understands his error and his guilt. Feuchtwanger uses Jefta to advocate reason and tolerance, but in dealing with the unification of the Jewish tribes, he points at the foundation of the state of Israel in his own time. The novel is thus again testimony to his idea that historical novels should treat themes taken from the present.

Hans Wagener

See also Jewish Culture and Literature

Biography

Born in Munich, 7 July 1884. Studied at the Universities of Berlin and Munich, 1903–7; Ph.D., 1907; freelance writer and theater critic, from 1907; moved to Berlin, 1925; exile in Sanary-sur-mer, French Riviera, 1933–39; internment in French detention camps, 1939–40; flight across the Pyrenees to Spain, Portugal, and the United States, 1940; settled in Los Angeles, California, 1941–58. National Prize, First Class for Art and Literature of the GDR, 1953; honorary doctorate from Humboldt University, Berlin (GDR), 1954. Died 21 December 1958.

Selected Works

Collections

Gesammelte Werke, 18 vols., 1935–48
Gesammelte Werke in Einzelausgaben, 14 vols., 1959–74
Gesammelte Werke in Einzelbänden, 16 vols., 1991–95

Fiction

Die Einsamen: Zwei Skizzen, 1903
Der tönerne Gott, 1910
Die häßliche Herzogin Margarete Maultasch, 1923; as *The Ugly Duchess*, translated by Willa and Edwin Muir, 1928
Jud Süß, 1925; as *Jew Süß: A Historical Romance*, translated by Willa and Edwin Muir, 1926 (also published as *Power*, 1926)
Erfolg: Drei Jahre Geschichte einer Provinz, 2 vols., 1930; as *Success: Three Years in the Life of a Province*, translated by Willa and Edwin Muir, 1930
Der jüdische Krieg, 1932; as *Josephus*, translated by Willa and Edwin Muir, 1932
Die Geschwister Oppermann (title temporarily changed to *Die Geschwister Oppenheim*), 1933; as *The Oppermanns*, translated by James Cleugh, 1934
Die Söhne, 1935; as *The Jew of Rome*, translated by Willa and Edwin Muir, 1936
Der falsche Nero, 1936; as *The Pretender*, translated by Willa and Edwin Muir, 1937
Marianne in Indien und sieben andere Erzählungen, 1934; as *Marianne in India*, translated by Basil Creighton, 1935; translation republished as *Little Tales*, 1935
Zwei Erzählungen, 1938
Exil, 1940; as *Paris Gazette*, translated by Willa and Edwin Muir, 1940
Die Brüder Lautensack, 1944; as *Double, Double, Toil and Trouble*, translated by Caroline Oram, 1943 (also published as *The Lautensack Brothers*, 1944)
Der Tag wird kommen, 1945; as *Josephus and the Emperor*, translated from the German manuscript by Caroline Oram, 1942 (also published as *The Day Will Come*, 1944); as *Simone*, translated by G.A. Herrmann, 1944
Venedig (Texas) und vierzehn andere Erzählungen, 1946
Waffen für Amerika, 1947; republished as *Die Füchse im Weinberg*, 2 vols., 1947; as *Proud Destiny*, translated by Moray Firth, 1947
Odysseus and the Swine and Other Stories, 1949; original German published as *Odysseus und die Schweine und zwölf andere Erzählungen*, 1950
Goya; oder, Der arge Weg der Erkenntnis, 1951; as *This Is the Hour*, translated by H.T. Lowe-Porter and Frances Fawcett, 1951
Narrenweisheit; oder, Tod und Verklärung des Jean-Jacques Rousseau, 1952; as *'Tis Folly to Be Wise; or, Death and Transfiguration of Jean-Jacques Rousseau*, translated by Frances Fawcett, 1953
Spanische Ballade, 1955, republished in the same year as *Die Jüdin von Toledo*; as *Raquel, the Jewess of Toledo*, translated by Eithne Wilkins and Ernst Kaiser, 1956
Jefta und seine Tochter, 1957; as *Jephta and His Daughter*, translated by Eithne Wilkins and Ernst Kaiser, 1958

Plays

Kleine Dramen, 2 vols., 1905–6
Der Fetisch, 1907
Ein feste Burg ist unser Gott, adaptation of a play by Arthur M. Müller, 1911
Julia Farnese (produced 1916), 1915
Warren Hastings, Gouverneur von Indien (produced 1916), 1916; reworked with Bertolt Brecht as *Kalkutta, 4. Mai* (produced 1928), 1925; as *Warren Hastings*, partially translated by Willa and Edwin Muir, in *Two Anglo-Saxon Plays*, 1928
Pierrots Herrentraum: Pantomime, with music by Adolf Hartmann-Trepka, 1916
Vasantasena: Nach dem Indischen des Königs Sudraka (produced 1916), 1916
Der König und die Tänzerin: Ein Spiel in vier Akten: Nach dem Indischen des Kalindasa (produced 1917), 1917
Appius und Virginia, adaptation of a play with the same title by John Webster, 1918
Friede: Ein burleskes Spiel: Nach den "Acharnern" und der "Eirene" des Aristophanes (produced 1954), 1917
Jud Süß (produced 1917), 1918
Die Kriegsgefangenen, 1919
Thomas Wendt: Ein dramatischer Roman, 1919
Der Amerikaner; oder, Die entzauberte Stadt: Eine melancholische Komödie, 1921
Der Frauenverkäufer: Ein Spiel in drei Akten nach Calderon (produced 1922), 1923
Der holländische Kaufmann (produced 1923), 1923
Wird Hill amnestiert? 1923
Leben Eduards des Zweiten von England (nach Marlowe): Historie, with Bertolt Brecht (produced 1924), 1924; edited by Reinhold Grimm, 1968; as *Edward II*, translated by Eric Bentley, 1966; as *The Life of Edward II of England*, translated by Jean Benedetti, in Bertolt Brecht, *Collected Plays*, vol. 1, 1970
Hill, 1925
Drei angelsächsische Stücke: Die Petroleuminseln (produced 1928) (includes *Die Petroleuminseln; Kalkutta, 4. Mai; Wird Hill*

amnestiert?), 1927; partially translated by Willa and Edwin Muir, in *Two Anglo-Saxon Plays*, 1928
Stücke in Prosa, 1936; partially translated by Emma D. Ashton as *Three Plays: Prisoners of War; 1918; The Dutch Merchant*, 1934
Wahn; oder, Der Teufel in Boston, edited by Ernst Gottlieb and Felix Guggenheim, 1948; as *The Devil in Boston*, 1948
Stücke in Versen, 1954
Die Witwe Capet (produced 1956), 1956; as *The Widow Capet*, 1956
Die Gesichte der Simone Machard (produced 1956), with Bertolt Brecht, 1957
Stücke in Prosa, 1957

Poetry
PEP: J.L. Wetcheeks amerikanisches Liederbuch, 1928; as *PEP: J.L. Wetcheek's American Songbook*, translated by Dorothy Thompson (and Sinclair Lewis), 1929

Other
Heinrich Heines "Der Rabbi von Bacharach": Eine kritische Studie, 1907
Die Aufgabe des Judentums, with Arnold Zweig, 1933
Moskau 1937: Ein Reisebericht für meine Freunde, 1937; as *Moscow 1937: A Visit Described for My Friends*, translated by Irene Josephy, 1937
Unholdes Frankreich: Meine Erlebnisse unter der Regierung Petain, 1942; later retitled *Der Teufel in Frankreich*; as *The Devil in France: My Encounter with Him in the Summer of 1940*, translated by Elisabeth Abbott, 1941
Centum Opuscula: Eine Auswahl, edited by Wolfgang Berndt, 1956
Das Haus der Desdemona; oder, Größe und Grenzen der historischen Dichtung, edited by Fritz Zschech, 1961; as *The House of Desdemona; or, The Laurels and Limitations of Historical Fiction*, translated by Harold A. Basilius, 1963

Translation
Die Perser des Aischylos (produced 1917), 1915

Further Reading
Arnold, Heinz Ludwig, editor, *Lion Feuchtwanger*, Text und Kritik, vol. 79/80, Munich: Edition Text und Kritik, 1983
Berendsohn, Walter A., *Der Meister des politischen Romans: Lion Feuchtwanger*, Schriften des deutschen Instituts der Universität Stockholm, vol. 3, Stockholm: Tyska Inst., 1976
Dietschreit, Frank, *Lion Feuchtwanger*, Stuttgart: Metzler, 1988
Huder, Walter, and Friedrich Knilli, editors, *Lion Feuchtwanger: ". . . für die Vernunft, gegen Dummheit und Gewalt,"* Berlin: Publica, 1985
Jaretzky, Reinhold, *Lion Feuchtwanger mit Selbstzeugnissen und Bilddokumenten*, Reinbek bei Hamburg: Rowohlt, 1984
Jeske, Wolfgang, and Peter Zahn, *Lion Feuchtwanger; oder, Der arge Weg der Erkenntnis: Eine Biographie*, Stuttgart: Metzler, 1984
Kahn, Lothar, *Insight and Action: The Life and Work of Lion Feuchtwanger*, Rutherford, New Jersey: Fairleigh Dickinson University Press, and London: Associated University Presses, 1975
Köpke, Wulf, *Lion Feuchtwanger*, Munich: Beck, Edition Text und Kritik, 1983
Kröhnke, Karl, *Lion Feuchtwanger, Der Ästhet in der Sowjetunion: Ein Buch nicht nur für seine Freunde*, Stuttgart: Metzler, 1991
Müller-Funk, Wolfgang, editor, *Jahrmarkt der Gerechtigkeit: Studien zu Lion Feuchtwangers zeitgeschichtlichem Werk*, Tübingen: Stauffenburg, 1987
Skierka, Volker, *Lion Feuchtwanger: Eine Biographie*, edited by Stefan Jaeger, Berlin: Quadriga, 1984
Spalek, John M., editor, *Lion Feuchtwanger: The Man, His Ideas, His Work: A Collection of Critical Essays*, University of Southern California Studies in Comparative Literature, vol. 3, Los Angeles: Hennessy and Ingalls, 1972
Sternburg, Wilhelm von, *Lion Feuchtwanger: Ein deutsches Schriftstellerleben*, Königstein/Ts.: Athenäum, 1984; expanded edition, Berlin: Aufbau, 1994
Wessler, Judith, *Lion Feuchtwangers "Erfolg": A "Großstadt" Novel*, Studies in Modern Literature, vol. 11, New York: Lang, 1989
Wagener, Hans, *Lion Feuchtwanger*, Köpfe des 20. Jahrhunderts, vol. 131, Berlin: Morgenbuch, 1996
Wolff, Rudolf, editor, *Lion Feuchtwanger: Werk und Wirkung*, Bonn: Bouvier, 1984

Jud Süß 1925

Novel by Lion Feuchtwanger

Lion Feuchtwanger initially encountered considerable difficulty interesting publishers in his first historical novel, *Jud Süß* (1925; translated as *Jew Süß* and *Power*). Major publishing houses refused the manuscript, reasoning that the historical novel was an outmoded genre or that the novel's political and Jewish themes were too controversial amid the anti-Semitic and nationalist turmoil of the Weimar Republic. In 1925 (over two years after the novel's completion), a small theater publisher, the Drei Masken Verlag in Munich, agreed to publish a small edition of Feuchtwanger's novel, which experienced an unexpected, meteoric success. Within five years after its initial publication, the work became an international best-seller and was translated into over 15 languages. Although *Jew Süß* enjoyed critical acclaim in the United States and Great Britain, German literary critics were loathe to acknowledge its artistic merits. Over the course of the 19th and early 20th centuries, the historical novel as a genre had been degraded to *Unterhaltungsliteratur* or *Trivialliteratur*, entertaining light fiction with mass appeal but little poetic value. The work's best-seller status further contributed to the skepticism of elite *Germanisten* and German literary critics. Only in recent years has *Jew Süß* gained acceptance into the canon of *Germanistik*, where it is now recognized as "one of three great novels of the Weimar period ranking among the greats of world literature"; it has earned Feuchtwanger credit for reviving the German historical novel as a serious literary genre (Klussmann). Recent critics read *Jew Süß* as an insightful study of German-Jewish identity, whereby the life story of Joseph Süß Oppenheimer mirrors the three phases of the history of Jews in Germany from Emancipation to the Weimar Republic: the journey out of the ghetto, the nearly complete assimilation with non-Jewish Germans, and the conscious return to Judaism and Jewish identity in the face of growing anti-Semitism and with the realization of a failed German-Jewish symbiosis (von der Lühe).

The historical novel *Jew Süß* was not Feuchtwanger's first attempt at a literary portrayal of the story of Joseph Süß Oppenheimer, the half-Jewish (he was the illegitimate child of a Jewish actress and a nobleman, but he was raised as a Jew) financial advisor to Prince Karl Alexander, who became the Duke of Württemberg in 1733. In 1917, Feuchtwanger published his play *Jud Süß*, which premiered in Munich in October of the same year. Although the play enjoyed relative success (after an initial ban by censors), Feuchtwanger was reportedly dissatisfied with his work, finding the dramatic genre inadequate for portraying the psychological development of his protagonists. In his 1929 essay "Über Jud Süß," Feuchtwanger writes that he became intrigued with the Joseph Süß material after reading in Manfred Zimmermann's 1874 biography of Josef Süß Oppenheimer (his main source for the novel) that Josef Süß, who was only half Jewish and not strictly observant, refused to convert to Christianity, although doing so could have saved his life. Süß's transformation from power-obsessed materialist to a man who embraced his own destruction exemplified for Feuchtwanger a new vision for Western civilization:

> the road from Europe to Asia, from Nietzsche to Buddha, from the old to the new covenant . . . the road past the narrow European doctrine of the will to power, through the Egyptian doctrine of the wish for immortality, to the Asian doctrine of sufferance and passivity.

Feuchtwanger believed that the "nature and fate of the Jew" was particularly well suited for demonstrating this development "because even his geographic origins offer him the blend of Asia and Europe, the West-Eastern traits that are characteristic of the type toward which history is progressing." In his 1935 defense of the historical novel, "Vom Sinn und Unsinn des historischen Romanes" (Of Sense and Non-Sense in the Historical Novel), Feuchtwanger recalls that he first tried to demonstrate the progression from "the European to the Asian philosophy of life" with the story of a Jewish-German contemporary, Walter Rathenau. Unsatisfied with this effort, he traveled back 200 years and with the story of Joseph Süß came "closer to his goal." In this essay, Feuchtwanger challenges the contemporary notion that the historical novelist was a "reactionary" who was guilty of evading contemporary problems and idealizing the past. He evokes the masters of historical literature (such as Homer, Shakespeare, and Tolstoy), whom, he observes, "intended nothing other than to express their own (contemporary) view of life, their subjective (by no means historicizing) view of life, and in this manner to communicate it to the reader." According to Feuchtwanger's conception of the historical novel, which bears an unmistakable affinity to Brecht's theatrical principles of alienation (*Verfremdung*), portrayals of contemporary people and things could too easily become clouded with the novelist's "insignificant and petty private experiences and interests," and thus risk losing the "equilibrium, which is the prerequisite for every work of art." The historical novelist chooses the "historical costume" to achieve critical distance, a more objective perspective.

Feuchtwanger was neither the first nor the last author to undertake a fictional portrayal of Joseph Süß Oppenheimer; Friedrich Knilli counts between 100 and 200 literary portrayals to date. The best-known predecessor of Feuchtwanger's novel was romantic author Wilhelm Hauff's mildly anti-Semitic novella of 1827. Of the over 20 Jud Süß portrayals produced in the 20th century, over half are based on Feuchtwanger's novel, including Ashley Duke's 1929 English-language drama, Paul Kornfeld's 1930 German-language dramatization of Feuchtwanger's novel, Mordechai Avi-Shaul's 1933 Hebrew-language drama, and director Lothar Mendes's film version of Feuchtwanger's novel (produced in England by the Gaumont-British Picture Corporation in 1934). Only one other 20th-century version of the Joseph Süß story, however, achieved the commercial success of Feuchtwanger's novel, namely, Veit Harlan's virulently anti-Semitic Nazi feature film *Jud Süß*, which premiered in Venice in 1940 and was an international box-office hit. Although the film was based (contrary to Feuchtwanger's assertion that it was a plagiarism of his novel) on Hauff's novella, Propaganda Minister Joseph Goebbels, who commissioned the film (which appeared in the same year as *The Eternal Jew* and *The Rothschilds* as part of a concerted effort to garner support for the "Final Solution"), likely expected to capitalize on the success of Feuchtwanger's novel.

ELIZABETH LOENTZ

Editions

First edition: *Jud Süß*, Munich: Drei Masken, 1925

Translations: *Jew Süß: A Historical Romance*, translated by Willa and Edwin Muir, London: Martin Secker, 1926 (also published as *Power*, New York: Modern Library, 1926)

Further Reading

Bathrick, David, "1925: *Jud Süß* by Lion Feuchtwanger Is Published," in *The Yale Companion to Jewish Writing and Thought in German Culture, 1096–1996*, edited by Sander L. Gilman and Jack Zipes, New Haven, Connecticut: Yale University Press, 1997

Feuchtwanger, Lion, "Über Jud Süß," *Freie Deutsche Bühne* 11, no. 1 (1929)

———, "Vom Sinn und Unsinn des historischen Romans," *Internationale Literatur* 9 (1935)

Huder, Walter, and Friedrich Knilli, editors, *Lion Feuchtwanger: ". . . für die Vernunft, gegen Dummheit und Gewalt,"* Berlin: Publica, 1985

Klussmann, Paul Gerhard, "Lion Feuchtwangers Roman *Jud Süß*: Gedichtete Psychologie und prophetischer Mythos des Juden," *Zeitschrift für deutsche Philologie* Sonderheft 97 (1978)

Koebner, Thomas, "Ein Denkmal für *Jud Süß*: Anmerkungen zu Lion Feuchtwangers Roman," in *Lion Feuchtwanger: Materialien zu Leben und Werk*, edited by Wilhelm von Sternburg, Frankfurt: Fischer Taschenbuch, 1989

Köpke, Wulf, "*Jud Süß*," in *Lion Feuchtwanger*, Munich: Beck, 1983

Milfull, John, "Juden, Christen, und andere Menschen: Sabbatianismus, Assimilation und jüdische Identität in Lion Feuchtwangers Roman *Jud Süß*," in *Im Zeichen Hiobs: Jüdische Schriftsteller und deutsche Literatur im 20. Jahrhundert*, edited by Gunter E. Grimm and Hans-Peter Bayerdörfer, Königstein: Athenäum, 1985

Petersen, Vibeke Rützou, "The Best of Both Worlds? Jewish Representations of Assimilation, Self, and Other in Weimar Popular Fiction," *German Quarterly* 68, no. 2 (1995)

Pischel, Joseph, "Lion Feuchtwangers *Jud Süß*: Lob der Asphaltliteratur," *Weimarer Beiträge* 19 (1983)

Small, William, "In Buddha's Footsteps: Feuchtwanger's *Jud Süß*, Walter Rathenau, and the Path to the Soul," *German Studies Review* 12 (1989)

von der Lühe, Barbara, "Lion Feuchtwangers Roman *Jud Süß* und die Entwicklung des jüdischen Selbstbewußtseins in Deutschland," in *Lion Feuchtwanger: Werk und Wirkung*, edited by Rudolf Wolff, Bonn: Bouvier, 1984

von Sternburg, Wilhelm, "*Jud Süß*," in *Lion Feuchtwanger: Ein deutsches Schriftstellerleben*, Berlin: Aufbau, 1994

Yuill, W.E., "*Jud Süß*: Anatomy of a Bestseller," in *Lion Feuchtwanger: The Man, His Ideas, His Work: A Collection of Critical Essays*, edited by John M. Spalek, Los Angeles: Hennessey and Ingalls, 1972

Hubert Fichte 1935–1986

Hubert Fichte's first novel, *Das Waisenhaus* (1965; *The Orphanage*), an autobiographical portrayal of the survival of a German-Jewish *Mischling* child during the Third Reich and stylistically his least experimental work, was awarded the *Hermann-Hesse Prize* in 1965. The young author then earned himself a scandal-ridden notoriety with his second novel, *Die Palette* (1968; the title is the name of a bar in Hamburg), which established the half-Jewish, openly gay Fichte as an experimental ethnographer of Hamburg's social and sexual margins. While *Die Palette* was still praised as one of the most genuine expressions of the rebellious 1968 *Zeitgeist* by critics such as Helmut Heißenbüttel and even Marcel Reich-Ranicki, Fichte's two subsequent novels, *Detlevs Imitationen Grünspan* (1971; *Detlev's Imitations*) and *Versuch über die Pubertät* (1974; Essay on Puberty), both autobiographical sequels to *The Orphanage,* signal the beginning of Fichte's engagement with black cultures in Brazil, West Africa, the Caribbean, Miami, and New York. Due to these "exotic" interests that take center stage in his subsequent oeuvre, as well as because of Fichte's interdisciplinary challenges to the literary and critical establishment in West Germany, the writing of the promising young *Gruppe 47* author of *Das Waisenhaus* was pronounced non-literary (Reich-Ranicki). After *Versuch über die Pubertät,* Fichte was known as the author of journalistic articles and radio plays on African-American and African trance religions, alternative psychiatry, Third World politics, and gay aesthetics. Throughout the 1970s and early 1980s, however, Fichte also worked on a *roman delta,* which consisted of eight novels written in close correspondence with his published essayistic, journalistic, and ethnographic writings. The novels, as well as compilations of essays and ethnographies, were, according to Fichte's detailed instructions, posthumously published under the umbrella title *Die Geschichte der Empfindlichkeit* (1987–93; The History of Sensibility). As the title indicates, Fichte's main interest was to seek to understand the intrapsychic dimensions of sensibility and identification. In this literary and anthropological project, he explored the hypothesis that male homosexuality coincides with a heightened sensibility and thus fosters the ability to identify with others and to develop intersubjective spaces, abilities which challenge the rigid and power-infused binary opposition of self and other.

Fichte's complex notion of the self as a space that is traversed by the non-self is an important contribution to the development of autobiographical writing in the 20th century. His texts are collages that draw on audio-visual techniques from films and radio plays. While Fichte's focus on his own autobiography and the centrality of the sexual and the private in his novels may be typical for the 1970s *New Subjectivity* movement, his use of New World African material within an autobiographical frame, combined with his complex, modernist-inspired formal experiments, exceeds and interrogates both the 1960s "turn outward" and the 1970s "turn inward." Thematically in proximity to Peter Weiss's, Hans Magnus Enzensberger's, and Hans Werner Henze's works on Cuba and Africa, Fichte's texts question the ideological suppression of the difficult aspects of self-other relations and sexuality and the simplifications in the Marxist writings of the late 1960s and early 1970s. Similar to Weiss, Fichte posits the Jewish Holocaust as the basis of all his identifications with Third World people. Unlike Weiss, however, Fichte explores those identifications self-critically. Similar to Enzensberger and Henze, Fichte seeks to integrate and interact with the literatures and cultures of Latin America. His engagement, however, exceeds that of Enzensberger and Henze both in scope and critical acumen. With respect to West German literature after the so-called *Tendenzwende* (shift in political trend), Fichte's increasing interest in external Latin American and African reality, his ethnographic precision, and his engagement with existing anthropological discourses constitute a break with the tendency toward anti-literary introspection in the generation of writers that immediately followed and opposed the "politicization" of the late 1960s (e.g., Verena Stefan, Peter Schneider, Karin Struck, and Bernward Vesper). Fichte's work, however, also breaks with aesthetic closure and postmodernist self-referentiality à la Peter Handke and the French Tel Quel group. In the face of postmodernist theories that seal language off from the facticity of the world, the experimental Fichte takes a surprisingly conservative, quasi-positivist stance.

Despite his anti-disciplinary proclivities (Fichte never even earned a high-school degree), Fichte's oeuvre directly engages, criticizes, and transcends a number of important literary and cultural discourses. In particular, the novel *Versuch über die Pubertät* formulates a response to the gay primitivism of Hans Henny Jahnn, an Expressionist German playwright and personal mentor of Fichte's. The novel *Platz der Gehenkten* (1989; Execution Square), set in Morocco, explicitly engages the modernist gay primitivisms of André Gide, Arthur Rimbaud, and Jean Genet. The Caribbean and Brazilian ethnographies in *Xango* (1976; Chango), *Petersilie* (1980; Parsley), and *Lazarus und die Waschmaschine* (1985; Lazarus and the Washing Machine) respond to European anthropological writings by Claude Lévi-Strauss, Marcel Mauss, Lucien Lévy-Bruhl, Michel Leiris, and Pierre Verger, as well as to surrealist thinkers such as Antonin Artaud, André Breton, and Georges Bataille. Fichte's most extensive writings on Brazil, the novel *Explosion* (1993; Explosion) and the ethnographic volume *Das Haus der Mina in São Luiz de Maranhão* (1989; The House of the Mina in São Luiz de Maranhão), engage with Latin American discourses of anti-Occidentalism (i.e., the Brazilian modernist *Cannibalist Movement* around Oswald de Andrade); Latin American anthropological theories of hybridity, transculturation, and racial integration (e.g., Edison Carneiro, Fernando Ortiz, and Lydia Cabrera); and Latin American testimonial literature of the 1960s and 1970s.

Since the late 1980s, Fichte's oeuvre has known a more thorough critical reception in Germany. After a decade of critical silence or rejection in the face of Fichte's cross-disciplinary challenges, the emerging fields of Cultural and Queer Studies within the German Academy have taken an interest in his oeuvre. Despite their limitations in dealing with Fichte's complex correspondence with Latin American discourses, Hartmut Böhme, Leo Kreuzer, Manfred Weinberg, D. Simo, and others have contributed to a better understanding of Fichte's difficult writings. The lack of critical attention to Fichte within German Cultural, Queer, and Postcolonial Studies in the United States is surprising since his oeuvre invites an analysis of the interface between many of the discourses that concern Cultural Studies: literature, politics, ethics, sexuality, psychoanalysis, and performativity. The recently published English translation of a collection of Fichte's essays on literature and homosexuality under the title *The Gay Critic,* as well as translations of his novels *The Orphanage* and *Detlev's Imitations,* will facilitate the reception of his writings in the English-speaking world.

CHRISTIAN GUNDERMANN

Biography

Born in Perleburg/Brandenburg, 21 March 1935. Since 1946, a child actor at various Hamburg theaters; from 1955–57 he was apprenticed in farming and agricultural techniques; worked as a farmer in Hannover and Sweden, and as a shepherd in Provence, France, from 1959–62; since 1963, worked as a freelance writer, journalist, and art critic; received various grants and stayed in Rome, 1967–68, in Brazil, Bahia, Haiti, and Trinidad, 1971–75, the United States, 1979, and lectured at the University in Bremen and Klagenfurt, 1979–80. Died (of AIDS) in Hamburg, 8 March 1986.

Selected Works

Collections
Die Geschichte der Empfindlichkeit, 18 vols., 1987–93

Novels
Das Waisenhaus, 1965; as *The Orphanage,* translated by Martin Chalmers, 1990
Die Palette, 1968
Detlevs Imitationen Grünspan, 1971; as *Detlev's Imitations,* translated by Martin Chalmers, 1992
Versuch über die Pubertät, 1974
Hotel Garni, 1987
Eine glückliche Liebe, 1988
Der Platz der Gehenkten, 1989
Forschungsbericht, 1989
Lil's Book, 1991
Explosion: Roman der Ethnologie, 1993

Short Stories
Aufbruch nach Turku, 1963

Ethnographies/Travelogues
Xango, 1976
Petersilie, 1980
Lazarus und die Waschmaschine, 1985
Das Haus der Mina in São Luiz de Maranhão, 1989

Essays
Deiner Umarmung süße Sehnsucht. Die Geschichte der Empfindungen. Intime Schriften des Grafen August von Platen-Hallermünde, 1985
Homosexualität und Literatur. 2 Bände, 1987–88; as *The Gay Critic,* translated by Kevin Gavin, 1996
Der kleine Hauptbahnhof oder Lob des Strichs, 1988

Radio Plays
Schulfunk (collection of radio plays), 1988

Interviews
Psyche, 1980
Genet, 1981

Other
Im Tiefstall, 1965
Baianas. Priesterinnen der Straße, 1985
Paraleipomena, 1991

Further Reading

Böhme, Hartmut, *Hubert Fichte: Riten des Autors und Leben der Literatur,* Stuttgart: Metzler, 1992
Böhme, Hartmut, and Nikolaus Tiling, editors, *Leben, um eine Form der Darstellung zu erreichen: Studien zum Werk Hubert Fichtes,* Frankfurt: Fischer Taschenbuch, 1991
——, editors, *Medium und Maske: Die Literatur Hubert Fichtes zwischen den Kulturen,* Stuttgart: M&P, 1995
Gilette, Robert, "On Not Writing Pornography: Literary Self-Consciousness in the Work of Hubert Fichte," *German Life and Letters* 48, no. 2 (1995)
Gundermann, Christian, "Between Ethnography and Poetry: Hubert Fichte's Brazilian Peregrinations," in *Vagabondage: The Poetics and Politics of Movement,* edited by Jeffrey Timon, Berkeley, California: Berkeley Academic Press, 1997
——, "Transforming Modernity's Primitivisms: Hubert Fichte's Queer Ethnography in the Postcolonial Latin American Context," Ph.D. dissertation, Cornell University, 1999
Heinrichs, Hans-Jurgen, *Die Djemma el-Fna geht durch mich hindurch, Oder wie sich Poesie, Ethnologie, und Politik durchdringen: Hubert Fichte und sein Werk,* Bielefeld: Pendragon, 1991
Kreutzer, Leo, *Literatur und Entwicklung: Studien zu einer Literatur der Ungleichzeitigkeit,* Frankfurt: Fischer Taschenbuch, 1989
Simo, D., *Interkulturalität und ästhetische Erfahrung: Untersuchungen zum Werk Hubert Fichtes,* Stuttgart: Metzler, 1993
Teichert, Torsten, *'Herzschlag aussen': Die poetische Konstruktion des Fremden und des Eigenen im Werk von Hubert Fichtes,* Frankfurt: Fischer Taschenbuch, 1987
Vocca, Robert Thomas, "Rites of Passage and the Construction of Masculinity in Hubert Fichte's Das Waisenhaus, Detlevs Imitationen Grünspan, Die Palette, and Versuch über die Pubertät," Ph.D. dissertation, Ohio State University, 1993
Weinberg, Manfred, *Akut, Geschichte, Struktur: Hubert Fichtes Suche nach der verlorenen Sprache einer poetischen Welterfahrung,* Bielefeld: Aisthesis, 1993

Johann Gottlieb Fichte 1762–1814

In 1798 the Romantic theoretician Friedrich Schlegel wrote that the French Revolution, Goethe's *Wilhelm Meisters Lehrjahre* (1795; *Wilhelm Meister's Apprenticeship*), and Fichte's *Wissenschaftslehre* (1810; The Science of Knowledge), "the first system of freedom," as Fichte called it, were the three most significant achievements of the age. Fichte has correctly been approached as the philosopher who sought to reconcile the Kantian dualism between freedom and necessity through the concept of a practically striving, nonderivative "I." His recognition of the unity between the process of knowing and the object of the knowing was doubtless his greatest, if never fully articulated intellectual achievement. Fichte considered such theoretical efforts necessary, for the practical disciplines of knowledge could only be established upon a sound philosophical foundation. But Fichte was more than merely a speculative philosopher. He was intimately involved in the pragmatic concerns of his age; among the topics he addressed were the desirability of revolution, the mission of the scholar, the economic system, the function of religion and aesthetics, patriotic nationalism, the concept of world history, and the organization of the university.

Fichte's philosophical career effectively began with the publication of his *Versuch einer Kritik aller Offenbarung* (1792; *Attempt at a Critique of All Revelation*). This generally well-received essay sought to demonstrate that the basis of revealed religion lies in the sovereignty of a nonempirical, spiritual law whose acknowledgment strengthens the moral law in humanity. In the following year, Fichte published anonymously two speeches: "Zurückforderung der Denkfreiheit von den Fürsten Europens, die sie bisher unterdrückten: Eine Rede" (A Discourse on the Reclamation of the Freedom of Thought from the Princes of Europe, Who Have Hitherto Suppressed It), in which he argues passionately and vehemently for freedom of the press and the legitimacy of social change, and "Beitrag zur Berichtigung der Urteile des Publikums über die französische Revolution: Erster Theil. Zur Beurteilung ihrer Rechtmäßigkeit" (A Contribution toward Correcting the Public's Judgment of the French Revolution), in which he reaffirms a nontraditional social organization in terms of the Rousseauian notion of contracts and Kantian autonomous ethics and even supports a right of active resistance against an incorrigibly unjust sovereign. These political essays contributed significantly to Fichte's reputation as a radical and laid the groundwork for future controversies.

At the age of 31, Fichte was invited to join the philosophy faculty at the University of Jena. In addition to his well-attended university lectures, he also delivered enormously popular public lectures, which were published (to counter the suspicion that they were subversive) as *Einige Vorlesungen über die Bestimmung des Gelehrten* (1794; Some Lectures concerning the Scholar's Vocation). Through cajoling, analysis, and exhortation, Fichte endeavored to convince his listeners that scholars and academics bear a responsibility for supervising the advancement of mankind and, hence, must be ethically pure. More than one listener subsequently documented Fichte's passionate plea for practical engagement, as expressed in the closing words of the lectures: "Act! Act! That is what we are here for!" Among those who held the lectures in high regard were Hölderlin, Novalis, Schiller, and Friedrich Schlegel.

"Über den Grund unsers Glaubens an eine göttliche Weltregierung" (1798; On the Foundation of Our Belief in a Divine Government of the Universe) precipitated the famous *Atheismusstreit,* which ultimately led to Fichte's departure from the University of Jena. In attempting to mediate F.K. Forsberg's more obvious denial of Christian divinity, Fichte apparently too closely identified God with a self-willed moral world order; in his account, religion seemed indistinguishable from philosophy. The conjunction of his ambiguous religious beliefs (although most scholars sided with his claim of theism), his political radicalness (it was rumored he had prophesied the demise of the nobility), and his confrontations with student unions provided an opportunity for the ecclesiastic and civic authorities, who feared the withdrawal of foreign students from the university, to dismiss him from the faculty despite his highly successful and innovative lectures.

Following his subsequent relocation to Berlin in 1799, Fichte's writing took on a decidedly popular tone. *Die Bestimmung des Menschen* (1800; *The Vocation of Man*) consciously attempts to overcome the obscurity or abstruseness of his earlier philosophical essays. (Schiller had rejected Fichte's "Über den Geist und Buchstab in der Philosophie: In einer Reihe von Briefen" [On the Spirit and Letter in Philosophy: In a Series of Letters] for publication in his journal *Die Horen* because Fichte, according to Schiller, harangued his reader.) In contrast, *The Vocation of Man* considers the needs and capabilities of the nonacademic, educated reader and weighs in a measured, dialogical manner the alternatives of doubt, knowledge, and faith before depicting the triumph over deterministic thinking. Fichte's clarity and concern for practical issues are likewise evident in "Idee für die innere Organization der Universität Erlangen" (Ideas concerning the Internal Organization of the University at Erlangen) and in his proposal for the establishment of a university in Berlin entitled "Deduzierter Plan einer zu Berlin zu errichtenden höheren Lehranstalt" (Deduced Plan to Create an Institute of Higher Learning in Berlin). In these works, Fichte shows himself to be opposed to traditional lecture practices; he wants students to become familiar with both the principles of intellectual life and the practical application of the principles.

Perhaps Fichte's most familiar essay is his *Reden an die deutsche Nation* (1808; *Addresses to the German Nation*). Based on lectures given in the amphitheater of the Berlin Academy beginning in December 1807, these talks lay out in a confident and even defiant tone Fichte's plan for educating Germans about their true identity and their place of leadership in world history. These essays restate Fichte's belief in the ethical educability of mankind, even if not all were equally educable, and in German nationalistic unity.

By all accounts, Fichte was a proud, forceful, and occasionally alienating personality, and his writings reflect his intensity. His essays vibrate with his contention that "the kind of philosophy one adopts depends upon the sort of man one is; for a philosophical system is not a lifeless piece of furniture that one might take or discard . . . but it is animated by the soul of the man who has it." As this dictum suggests, Fichte's writings, at times self-righteous, overly zealous, and abstruse, were aimed at purposeful, if not always aesthetically successful consciousness raising, with the goal that humanity should increase its freedom through reason. According to F.K. Forsberg, Fichte's first biographer, whereas Karl Reinhold, Fichte's predecessor in Jena, wanted to make men good, Fichte wanted to make great men. Although Fichte is seen as a Romantic philosopher—for his nationalism, idealism, subjectivism, and commitment to freedom—he was also attacked by the Romantics for his excessively intellectual conception of self-realization, his negative view of nature, and his overly moralistic view of the good life.

EDWARD T. LARKIN

See also Nationalism and Nationhood; Romanticism

Biography

Born in Rammenau, Saxony, 1762. Studied theology at the University of Jena, 1780–81, and Leipzig, 1781–84; because of financial hardship, held family tutorships from 1784–88; traveled to Zurich, 1788–89; professorship in Jena, 1793; moved to Berlin in 1799; dean of philosophical faculty at University in Berlin, 1810, and rector, 1811. Died (of typhus) in 1814.

Selected Works

Versuch einer Kritik aller Offenbarung, 1792; as *Attempt at a Critique of All Revelation,* translated by Garrett Green, 1978
Einige Vorlesungen über die Bestimmung des Gelehrten, 1794; as *Some Lectures concerning the Scholar's Vocation,* 1794; as *The Purpose of Higher Education,* translated by Jorn K. Bramann, 1988
Das System der Sittenlehre nach den Prinzipien der Wissenschaftslehre, 1798
Die Bestimmung des Menschen, 1800; as *The Vocation of Man,* translated by William Smith, 1925; translated by Roderick M. Chisholm, 1956; translated by Peter Preuss, 1987
Reden an die deutsche Nation, 1808; as *Addresses to the German Nation,* translated by R.F. Jones and G.H. Turnbull, 1979
Die Wissenschaftslehre, in ihren allgemeinen Umrisse dargestellt, 1810

Further Reading

Beiser, Frederick C., *The Fate of Reason: German Philosophy from Kant to Fichte,* Cambridge, Massachusetts: Harvard University Press, 1987
Breazeale, Daniel, "Fichte and Schelling: The Jena Period," in *The Age of German Idealism,* edited by Robert C. Solomon and Kathleen M. Higgins, London and New York: Routledge, 1993
Donougho, Martin, "Johann Gottlieb Fichte," in *Dictionary of Literary Biography,* vol. 89, Detroit, Michigan: Gale, 1989
Fichte, Johann Gottleib, *Fichte: Early Philosophical Writings,* edited and translated by Daniel Breazeale, Ithaca, New York: Cornell University Press, 1988
Gardiner, Patrick, "Fichte and German Idealism," in *Idealism, Past and Present,* edited by
Godfrey Vesey, Cambridge and New York: Cambridge University Press, 1982
Jacobs, Wilhelm G., *Johann Gottlieb Fichte,* Reinbeck bei Hamburg: Rowohlt, 1984
Lauth, Reinhard, "The Transcendental Philosophy of the Munich School," *Idealistic Studies* 11, no. 1 (1981)
Rockmore, Tom, *Fichte, Marx, and the German Philosophical Tradition,* Carbondale: Southern Illinois University Press, and London: Feffer and Simons, 1980

Film and Literature

In the course of its 100-year history, German cinema has been engaged in a highly complex intertextual relationship with literature. Despite their differences in production, signification, distribution, and communication, film and literature obviously share a common interest in narrative. Both forms generate and communicate ideas, values, and pleasures through simulating "reality" in fictional worlds; both forms construct national, cultural, and social histories through storytelling and by utilizing canonized characters, historical personalities, cultural icons, or motives. They also engage in transpositions from one medium to another: many movies are based upon novels and dramas, while 20th-century writers employ cinematographic techniques in their texts. Already in the 1910s and 1920s, however, the interplay between both artistic forms was not characterized by equivalence, polarity, and contiguity but by fierce economic competition and intellectual polarization. After their initial fascination with documentary and technical effects, slapstick, and the narration of shorter anecdotes, German cinematographers adapted longer narratives for the screen and turned to literature as a thematic source for their feature films. In addition, German cinema lured directors, actors, set designers, and writers away from the established theaters (including Max Reinhardt's); popular genre films satisfied the needs of the lower classes for entertaining distraction and threatened the production of trivial literature; and finally, the national film industry, with its reliance on modern technology, industrial production, and capital, challenged the aesthetic concepts of the bourgeois culture such as autonomous art and individual authorship.

The establishment of cinema as an institution for mass culture as well as the filmic replacement of poetic art with independent audiovisual works led to a heated controversy between the German *Bildungsbürger* (educated bourgeois) and the proponents of the new mass entertainment. During the so-called Kino-Debatte (debate on cinema) from 1909 to 1929, the modernist categorical distinction between high art and popular mass culture enforced the perception that, compared with literature, film was a form of lower cultural value because of its commodity relations and its specific modes of production and consumption. As the term *Literaturverfilmungen* (the filming of literature) indicates, the filmic adaptation of literary sources has almost always been judged critically by considering the film's faithfulness to the original text. While today conservative Germanists and critics still continue to subject film to the aesthetic criteria developed by poetics, British and American scholars have recently crossed the disciplinary border to film studies and have stressed the autonomy of film. By replacing notions of traditional literary criticism with the analysis of codes specific to the institution of cinema, they were able to generate an innovative field of research that paved the way for studying German culture beyond the boundaries set by canonical literature.

After years of importing French, Italian, American, and Danish films, German cinema received tremendous support from the government, the Deutsche Bank, and industrial concerns, which boosted the relatively small domestic production by founding the Universum-Film AG (UFA) in 1917. With this huge financial and institutional backing, UFA was able to create large-scale, well-equipped studios, which produced films that could compete on the international market. Often called the "Golden Age" of German cinema, the film production during the Weimar Republic is best known for its unprecedented innovation and experimentation. While most of the 5,000 films made between 1919 and 1933 were popular romances, comedies, adventure serials, and thrillers, the cinema of the 1920s also established a high-art film language that distinguished its films from the medium's plebeian image of fairground entertainment for the lower classes. Borrowing from the arts and literature, Expressionist films such as Robert Wiene's film *Das Cabinet des Dr. Caligari* (1919–20; *The Cabinet of Dr. Caligari*) emphasized visual stylization, mise-en-scène, narrative multiperspectivism, and the characters' expression over Hollywood's realism. The fascination that films such as Friedrich Wilhelm Murnau's *Nosferatu* (1921–22) or Fritz Lang's *Metropolis* (1925–26) have with the fantastic, not to mention the reappearance of E.T.A. Hoffmann's uncanny stories in numerous films, have led to Lotte Eisner's illuminating notion of the era's "haunted screen." But limiting Weimar cinema to its uneasy symbiosis between modern technology and Gothic/Romantic imagination does not do justice to the diverse richness of its genres, forms, and topics. Emerging from the *Kammerspielfilme,* street films and the films of the New Objectivity explored the different milieus of urban life, with its pressing social issues, and formulated a highly diverse critique of modernity; Ernst Lubitsch's comedies and Richard Oswald's educational films challenged patriarchal authority and its repressive sexual morals; and in *Geheimnisse einer Seele* (1926; *Secrets of a Soul*), Georg Wilhelm Pabst even brought psychoanalytic therapy to the screen. In their attempts to demonstrate that film could, indeed, become art, some filmmakers not only advanced the medium's technical capabilities—for example, the perplexing introduction of the mobile camera in Murnau's *Der letzte Mann* (1924; *The Last Laugh*) or the dramatic implementation of sound in Lang's *M* (1931)—but also tried to bring classic and modern literature on the screen. While a few films such as Murnau's free interpretation of *Faust* (1926), Pabst's *Die Büchse der Pandora* (1929; *Pandora's Box*), based on Frank Wedekind's plays, or Max Ophuls's adaptation of Arthur Schnitzler's *Liebelei* (1933) could survive the constant comparison to the more legitimate forms of theater, drama, and the novel, most adaptations and transformations came under criticism, which culminated in Bertolt Brecht's lawsuit against Pabst's filming of *Die Dreigroschenoper* (1931; *The Threepenny Opera*). For Brecht, who wrote the screenplay for the socialist film *Kuhle Wampe* (1932), as for Thomas Mann, Lion Feuchtwanger, and other writers, film supposedly trivialized the intellectual complexity of literature and distorted the authors' aesthetic or political intentions. Josef von Sternberg's *Der Blaue Engel* (1930; *The Blue Angel*) was dismissed because the film replaced the social criticism of Heinrich Mann's novel *Professor Unrat* (1905) with Marlene Dietrich's new incarnation of sex. Piel Jutzi's *Berlin Alexanderplatz* (1931) paradoxically displayed less cinematographic techniques (such as change of perspective, close-up, or montage) than were employed in Alfred Döblin's original novel. Although the script for the first German art film, Stellan Rye's *Der Student von Prag* (1913; *The Student of Prague*), was written by the best-selling author Hanns Heinz Ewers, many novelists and dramatists stayed away from film. On the one hand, Weimar cinema gave birth to the first professional scriptwriters such as Carl Mayer or the team of Fritz Lang and Thea von Harbou; on the other hand, the industry's business interests and control of production proved to be irreconcilable with many authors' belief in original creativity. By the end of the Weimar Republic, the increase in censorship, the flooding of the market with Hollywood films, and the exile of thousands who had worked in Germany's dynamic film industry suspended further artistic enterprises—a loss from which German cinema would never recover. Instead, historical costume films such as the popular *Fridericus Rex* series, as well as Arnold Fanck's prefascist mountain films, catered to the collective desire for resurrecting national myths. As the famous film critic and theoretician Siegfried Kracauer remarked, the psychological dispositions of German mentality were exposed on the screen.

Until fairly recently, Nazi cinema has been seen as the repulsive product of Joseph Goebbels's ministry of propaganda, which created the new party heroes (Hans Steinhoff's *Hitlerjunge Quex* [1933; *Hitler Youth Quex*]), celebrated the fascist formation of the masses (Leni Riefenstahl's *Triumph des Willens* [1934; *Triumph of the Will*]), and promoted anti-Semitic hate pamphlets (Veit Harlan's *Jud Süss* [1940; *Jew Süss*). But as Eric Rentschler points out, many of the 1,100 narrative films produced between 1933 and 1945 emanated from a sinister ministry of illusion: the Nazis systematically exploited and abused film's ability to mobilize emotions and immobilize the spectators' minds. The fantasies constructed by the film industry in the Third Reich were designed to inscribe totalitarian and racist ideology not only through chilling and horrendous propaganda films such as Harlan's last-minute war movie *Kolberg* (1945) but also through "unpolitical" comedies staging popular actors such as Heinz Rühmann, Willy Birgel, or Marika Rökk, musicals whose *Schlagers* (pop songs) made Zarah Leander famous, and melodramas that had a soothing effect on their audiences. Many opportunistic writers, directors, and actors helped National Socialism to govern its subjects with subtle persuasion by appealing to the imaginary, distracting audiences from the war and cultivating pleasurable hyper-kitsch. In his homecoming film *Der verlorene Sohn* (1934; *The Prodigal Son*), the Austrian actor/director Luis Trenker reinforced the *völkisch* blood-and-soil ideology by rejecting any alternative to one's provincial *Heimat* (homeland). Popular entertainments such as Paul Martin's *Glückskinder* (1936; *Lucky Kids*), with the dream couple Lilian Harvey and Willy Fritsch, copied comedies à la Hollywood and disseminated the illusion that film in the Nazi state escaped or even resisted the official doctrines on filmmaking, a belief still upheld in today's Germany. At the height of the war, Josef von Baky's color film *Münchhausen* (1943) took the spectators' minds off wartime realities and guided their escape into a space of fairy-tale special effects, where even war's tools become toys: the actor Hans Albers rides on a cannonball through the sky. In order to integrate German cultural heritage into the Nazi's aesthetic self-representation and to reach the educated middle class, Nazi cinema also mobilized the classics. One of its most compliant directors, Gustav Ucicky, collaborated with Weimar's famous actor Emil Jannings on their film adaptation of Heinrich von Kleist's *Der zerbrochene Krug* (1937; *The Broken Jug*). Hailed by contemporary as well as recent critics for its "faithful" transposition of the popular dramatic text into an entertainment film, the filmmakers' interpretation favored a slapstick approach to the ironic comedy and neglected Kleist's implicit critique of injustice and corruption. The intricate mixture of light amusement and indoctrinating affirmation of the Nazi ideology, exemplified in the waiting women who suffer for the nation's cause in Eduard von Borsody's blockbuster *Wunschkonzert* (1940; *Request Concert*), still continues to haunt and entertain German audiences: the legacy of Nazi cinema did not end with the regime's defeat.

After a short awakening with neorealistic and critical *Trümmerfilme* (rubble films) such as Wolfgang Staudte's *Die Mörder sind unter uns* (1946; *The Murderers Are among Us*), Germany's postwar cinema retreated to sentimental *Heimatfilme* (homeland movies) such as Hans Deppe's *Grün ist die Heide* (1951; *Green Is the Heather*) and to remakes of Weimar and Nazi classics. The latter efforts displayed an uncomfortable continuity: most of the directors, scriptwriters, and actors had come to fame under Goebbels's supervision. While in East Germany, the state-controlled Deutsche Film Gesellschaft (DEFA, 1946) produced antifascist films such as Staudte's original interpretation of Heinrich Mann's *Der Untertan* (1951; *The Subject*), the mediocre film production of the Adenauer era had no interest in enlightenment and could not even compete with the entertaining appeal of the "unpolitical" Nazi films shown on German television. Change came about in 1962, when a collective of young German filmmakers and authors issued the "Oberhausen Manifesto," which declared the need for creating a new German feature film freed from the conventions of the established industry: the New German Cinema was born. It not only wanted to challenge the Nazi past by revealing its impact on the present but also to speak a new cinematographic language. Supported by public money and, since 1971, by the cooperatively owned production and distribution company Filmverlag der Autoren (Authors' Film Publishing House), the New German Cinema was not a certain style or school but a unique experiment of independent filmmaking, which was, however, not free from political interference. Incorporating literature and critical theory into his films, Alexander Kluge might be considered the most intellectual director of the new era, which initiated the *Autorenkino* (auteur cinema). In his *Abschied von gestern* (1966; *Yesterday Girl*), based on the story of "Anita G." that was published in his collection *Lebensläufe* (1962; *Curricula Vitae*), Kluge testifies to Adorno's aesthetics of negativity through the subversion of visual pleasure (e.g., using alienation devices such as montage, direct address to the audience, and speeded-up sequences) and through the film's multiple layers of irony, criticism, and self-reflexivity. This formal resistance to conventional cinema is paralleled by the way in which the film tells the story of the displaced Jewish woman, who has been dispossessed of her past, as an integral part of German history. As in his later film *Die Patriotin* (1979; *The Patriot*), Kluge's filmic exploring and rewriting of Germany's repressed and obscured history is one of the trademarks of the New German Cinema. Hans Jürgen Syberberg's controversial *Hitler, ein Film aus Deutschland* (1977; *Hitler, a Film from Germany*); the political commentary to the terrorist hunt, *Deutschland im Herbst* (1977; *Autumn in Germany*), which was made by a collective of directors; Rainer Werner Fassbinder's private story as history *Die Ehe der Maria Braun* (1978; *The Marriage of Maria Braun*); feminist historiographies such as Helma Sanders-Brahm's *Deutschland, bleiche Mutter* (1980; *Germany, Pale Mother*) or Margarethe von Trotta's *Die bleierne Zeit* (1981; *Marianne and Juliane*); and Edgar Reitz's monumental 15-hour opus *Heimat* (1984) are just a few examples of the challenging return of history in film. Similar to the subsidized German television film production and because of their economic restrictions, virtually all of the directors of the New German Cinema used novels, short stories, and plays as the thematic source for their films. Volker Schlöndorff's *Der junge Törless* (1966; *Young Törless*) and his *Die Blechtrommel* (1979; *The Tin Drum*), Fassbinder's *Effi Briest* (1974), and Werner Herzog's *Woyzeck* (1978) also displayed apparent infatuations with literature. The crossroads of verbal art and film even led to surprising cooperations between writers and filmmakers. Heinrich Böll worked with Schlöndorff and von Trotta on the filming of his story *Die verlorene Ehre der Katharina Blum* (1977; *The Lost Honor of Katharina Blum*), while Wim Wenders and the Austrian writer Peter Handke teamed up for several films (e.g., *Falsche Bewegung* [1974; *Wrong Movement*]), with the result that Handke made his own movie, *Die linkshändige Frau* (1977; *The Left-Handed Woman*). Film also competed with the socially engaged literature of its time: Fassbinder's *Angst essen Seele auf* (1973; *Fear Eats the Soul*) uses love to break down boundaries of race and culture, Helke Sander's *Die allseitig reduzierte Persönlichkeit* (1977; *Redupers*) examines life in West Berlin from a feminist perspective, and Bernhard Sinkel's *Lina Braake* (1975) explores the way in which German society (mis)treats old people. Fassbinder's death in 1982 was seen as synonymous with the demise of the New German Cinema: similar to Wenders (*Paris, Texas* [1984] and *Der Himmel über Berlin* [1987; *Wings of Desire*]), many directors such as Herzog, Schlöndorff, and Petersen became international auteurs, shot their movies abroad, and seemed to have less spectators in Germany than elsewhere. Since Doris Dorrie's box office hit *Männer* (1985; *Men*) and since the restructuring of the postunification film industry, German cinema has been obsessed with comedies of sexual identity and displacement, which illustrate the new inferiority of German film.

STEPHAN K. SCHINDLER

See also Rainer Werner Fassbinder

Further Reading

Eisner, Lotte H., *The Haunted Screen: Expressionism in the German Cinema and the Influence of Max Reinhardt,* Berkeley: University of California Press, and London: Secker and Warburg, 1973

Elsaesser, Thomas, *New German Cinema: A History,* New Brunswick, New Jersey: Rutgers University Press, and London: British Film Institute, 1989

Jacobsen, Wolfgang, et al., editors, *Geschichte des deutschen Films,* Stuttgart: Metzler, 1993

Kaes, Anton, *Deutschlandbilder: Die Wiederkehr der Geschichte als Film,* Munich: Text and Kritik, 1987; as *From Hitler to Heimat: The Return of History as Film,* Cambridge, Massachusetts: Harvard University Press, 1989

Kaes, Anton, editor, *Kino-Debatte: Texte zum Verhältnis von Literatur und Film 1909–1929,* Tübingen: Niemeyer, and Munich: Deutscher Taschenbuchverlag, 1978

Knight, Julia, *Women and the New German Cinema,* New York and London: Verso, 1992

Koch, Gertrud, *Was ich erbeute, sind Bilder: Zum Diskurs der Geschlechter im Film,* Basel: Stroemfeld/Roter Stern, 1989

Kracauer, Siegfried, *From Caligari to Hitler: A Psychological History of the German Film,* Princeton, New Jersey: Princeton University Press, and London: Dobson, 1947

Petro, Patrice, *Joyless Streets: Women and Melodramatic Representation in Weimar Germany,* Princeton, New Jersey: Princeton University Press, 1989

Prinzler, Hans Helmut, *Chronik des deutschen Films, 1895–1994,* Stuttgart: Metzler, 1995

Rentschler, Eric, *The Ministry of Illusion: Nazi Cinema and Its Afterlife,* Cambridge, Massachusetts: Harvard University Press, 1996

Rentschler, Eric, editor, *German Film and Literature: Adaptions and Transformations,* New York: Methuen, 1986

Sandford, John, *The New German Cinema,* London: Wolff, and Totowa, New Jersey: Barnes and Noble, 1980

Schlüpmann, Heide, *Unheimlichkeit des Blicks: Das Drama des frühen deutschen Kinos,* Basel: Stroemfeld/Roter Stern, 1990

Schmidt, Klaus M., *Lexikon Literaturverfilmungen: Deutschsprachige Filme, 1945–1990,* Stuttgart: Metzler, 1995

Silberman, Marc, *German Cinema: Texts in Context,* Detroit, Michigan: Wayne State University Press, 1995

Caroline Auguste Fischer 1764–1842

Unlike her more famous contemporaries Caroline and Dorothea Schlegel, Caroline Auguste Fischer had no contact with the important literary circles of her day and no close ties with any well-known male German writer. Hence, her writings, published anonymously between 1801 and 1820 and well received at the time, were virtually forgotten after her death. Their eclectic combination of thematic and formal elements, drawn from a wide variety of 18th- and 19th-century literary and philosophical sources, including the novels of Richardson, Rousseau, and Sophie von La Roche, as well as Romanticism and the work of writers such as Goethe and Kleist, may appear derivative. Their originality lies, however, in the ways in which they undermine and ironize these elements, using them to question gender roles and to express a radical vision of the relations between the sexes and the disadvantages experienced by women in a patriarchal society in a fashion that is unmatched in the work of any other German writer of this period.

Apart from a few scattered references, mainly in encyclopedias of literary history, there was no serious critical reception of Fischer's work until the publication, in 1919, of Christine Touaillon's pioneering study of German novels by women. Touaillon devotes the whole of her last chapter to Fischer, whom she considers superior to all other women writers of her time. Paul Kluckhohn, in his 1922 treatise on the conception of love in German 18th-century and Romantic literature, also makes brief mention of Fischer's novels. No further work was done on her until the late 1980s, when her major works began to appear in photographic reprints. One of her stories has been included in a collection of 19th-century women's writing in German, a translation of another has appeared in a U.S. anthology of German women writers, and there is a modest but steadily growing body of secondary literature on Fischer in both German and English. This criticism attests to increasing interest in her writing, chiefly among feminist scholars in Germany, Britain, and the United States. While there is critical consensus on the tension between the radical implications and the conventional exterior of her work, there are differences of emphasis as to how far the former are qualified by the latter. No full-length, modern critical study of her work yet exists.

In all, Fischer published four novels, a farce, three fairy tales, nine other stories, and a series of journal articles. Her first novel, *Gustavs Verirrungen* (1801; The Errors of Gustav), charts the male protagonist's decline from youthful promise through debauchery to illness and death. Its stress on causal psychology anticipates Fischer's later narrative works, while its focus on the consequences of a sexually transmitted disease points forward to Ibsen. The farce *Vierzehn Tage in Paris* (1801; Fourteen Days in Paris), which likewise has a male hero, contains social criticism that implies the author's sympathy with the aims of the French Revolution. This is also true of the fairy tales; in addition, they include remarks on the relationship between the sexes of a type that later became a hallmark of Fischer's work.

The three epistolary novels *Die Honigmonathe* (1802; The Honeymoon), *Der Günstling* (1808; The Favorite), and *Margarethe* (1812) are Fischer's most substantial achievements. They center on male-female relationships, which are explored chiefly in the areas of marriage, art, and court life, and through the themes of passion, power, possession, self-sacrifice, renunciation, and premature death. The dominant passion in the first two novels is jealousy, and their violent denouement is implicit from the beginning. The third, which parodies the Romantic *Künstlerroman* (novel of the artist's life) and works by Goethe, especially his drama *Faust,* addresses the problems faced by women both as artists and as muse-figures or embodiments of the "eternal feminine," that is, as idealized, depersonalized objects subject to the male artistic gaze.

In different ways, both *Die Honigmonathe* and *Der Günstling* are highly critical of marriage as an institution, especially in a society divided by barriers of rank and gender. *Die Honigmonathe* mounts a blistering attack, from a female viewpoint, on the dependent status of married women in early 19th-century Germany, while also presenting a negative picture of Prussian militarism. *Der Günstling,* which is set in Russia, gives a novel slant to the well-worn themes of the powerful femme fatale, the man between two women, and the conflict between love and duty. The tragic ending—the death of the newly married couple on their wedding night in their marriage bed, poisoned by the jealous Tsarina—constitutes an unusual variation on the Romantic motif of the *Liebestod* and implies that marriage itself is fatal to love. In both works, whose titles are bitterly ironic, a rigid conception of gender roles leads to disaster. This is also the case in *Margarethe,* which, although set in Renaissance Florence, has obvious relevance to the Germany of Fischer's own day. In revealing the near impossibility of survival for a woman artist, the work implies a critique of the image of the female artist presented in Friedrich Schlegel's novel *Lucinde* (1799). It also highlights the problems posed by princely patronage and questions the idea that motherhood is a woman's only legitimate vocation.

Fischer's short stories, the majority of which were published in the collection *Kleine Erzählungen und romantische Skizzen* (1818; Short Stories and Romantic Sketches), continue the debate on gender roles begun in her earlier works. Here, women are the central focus of interest, and the subjects tackled include male violence against women (*Riekchen*), love across racial boundaries (*Wilhelm der Neger* [*William the Negro*]), incest (*Saphir und Mariah* [Saphir and Mariah]), and the woman artist (*Mathilde, Justine*). This last story contains the most devastating indictment of men's treatment of women to be found in any of Fischer's writings. All her significant works, however, have a single underlying theme: the conflict between women's need for independence and self-fulfillment on the one hand, and for love and security on the other. Under the conditions portrayed, this dilemma admitted no solution.

JUDITH PURVER

Biography

Born in Brunswick, 9 August 1764. In Copenhagen with her husband, Christoph Johann Rudolph Christiani, preacher to the Danish court and head of a German boys' school, early 1790s; left her husband and returned to Germany, 1799; divorced, 1801, and lived in Dresden with Christian August Fischer, 1801; moved to Heidelberg, 1803; moved to Würzburg and married Fischer, 1808; divorced Fischer and returned to Heidelberg, 1809; worked as a freelance writer and opened a girls' school in Heidelberg; ran a lending library in Würzburg, ca. 1820; admitted to a Würzburg hospital for mental illness, 1832. Died in Frankfurt, 25 May 1842.

Selected Works

Novels

Gustavs Verirrungen, 1801
Die Honigmonathe, 2 vols., 1802
Der Günstling, 1808 (dated 1809)
Margarethe, 1812

Stories

Kleine Erzählungen und romantische Skizzen, 1818; the story *William der Neger* as *William the Negro,* translated by Jeannine Blackwell, 1990

Further Reading

Kluckhohn, Paul, *Die Auffassung der Liebe in der Literatur des 18. Jahrhunderts und in der deutschen Romantik,* Halle: Niemeyer, 1922
Purver, Judith, "Caroline Auguste Fischer: An Introduction," in *Women Writers of the Age of Goethe,* vol. 4, edited by Margaret Ives, Lancaster: Department of Modern Languages, Lancaster University, 1991
———, "Passion, Possession, Patriarchy: Images of Men in the Novels and Short Stories of Caroline Auguste Fischer (1764–1842)," *Neophilologus* 79, no. 4 (1995)
———, "Die Erzählungen Caroline Auguste Fischers im Kontext ihrer Zeit," in *Schnittpunkt Romantik: Text- und Quellenstudien zur Literatur des 19. Jahrhunderts: Festschrift für Sibylle von Steinsdorff,* edited by Wolfgang Bunzel, et al., Tübingen: Niemeyer, 1997
Runge, Anita, "Wenn Schillers Geist einen weiblichen Körper belebt: Emanzipation und künstlerisches Selbstverständnis in den Romanen und Erzählungen Caroline Auguste Fischers," in *Untersuchungen zum Roman von Frauen um 1800,* edited by Helga Gallas and Magdalene Heuser, Tübingen: Niemeyer, 1990
———, "Die Dramatik weiblicher Selbstverständigung in den Briefromanen Caroline Auguste Fischers," in *Die Frau im Dialog: Studien zur Theorie und Geschichte des Briefes,* edited by Anita Runge and Liselotte Steinbrügge, Stuttgart: Metzler, 1991
———, *Literarische Praxis von Frauen um 1800: Briefroman, Autobiographie, Märchen,* Hildesheim: Olms-Weidmann, 1997
Touaillon, Christine, *Der deutsche Frauenroman des 18. Jahrhunderts,* Vienna: Braumüller, 1919; reprinted Bern: Lang, 1979
Zantop, Susanne, "Karoline Auguste Fernandine Fischer," in *German Writers in the Age of Goethe: Sturm und Drang to Classicism,* edited by James N. Hardin and Christoph E. Schweizer, Detroit, Michigan: Gale Research, 1990

Marieluise Fleißer 1901–1974

Arguably the best-known woman German playwright, Marieluise Fleißer was also a novelist and essayist. Her thousand-page corpus consists of five plays, an autobiographical novel, 33 short stories, 16 essays, and a travel report. Her best-known plays are *Fegefeuer in Ingolstadt* (1926; Purgatory in Ingolstadt), which depicts the trials of peer pressure during puberty, and *Pioniere in Ingolstadt* (1928; Pioneers in Ingolstadt), whose theme is power hierarchies in the military. These key literary texts address the sociopsychological origins and workings of fascism in small southern German towns. Despite being born and having died in her hometown, Ingolstadt, a provincial Bavarian town near Munich, Fleißer lived her life as an outcast, mostly due to her indictment of repressive Catholic mores and patriarchal values, and her critique of established social conventions.

In 1919 Fleißer moved to Munich where, against her father's wishes, she began to study German, philosophy, and theater art, a course of university education she never finished. While there she befriended Leon Feuchtwanger, who introduced her to Bertolt Brecht, the renowned Marxist dramatist, director, and filmmaker. Under Brecht's influence and tutelage, she moved in 1924 to Berlin, where she did most of her writing. Her style, informed by Brecht's theory of estrangement, offers a consciously unsentimental, markedly sparse prose that is a trademark of Neue Sachlichkeit (New Objectivity), a literary movement typified by its matter-of-factness, naturalistic claims, and focus on surface appearances and social realities. Typical for this genre, her characters function as types reading the cultural scripts assigned them (another Brechtian trademark that discourages audience identification with the characters). Yet unlike Brecht, her plays have little didacticism and portray the intimate side of relationships in the domestic sphere.

Fleißer's work depicts women, who, while ostensibly free to pursue their own longings and desires, nevertheless end up oppressed and downtrodden by society. Her first publication was the autobiographical story "Meine Zwillingsschwester Olga" (1923; My Twin Sister Olga), which was later revised as "Die Dreizehnjährigen" (1969; The Thirteen-Year-Olds). Drawing on her own life, Fleißer casts female protagonists in "narrative[s] of victimization" (Kosta, 1992) that illuminate the social disparities of the 1920s. While Fleißer's work predominantly concerns women's entry into the work force and their trials within the private (domestic) sphere, it also addresses the clash of expectations and lifestyles in the metropolis and in provincial towns, issues of sexuality, and the cult of the body. With her critical eye, Fleißer shows how women were caught in a double bind in the 1920s. Despite the new opportunities and ostensible freedoms open to them—specifically, the right to vote, and increased employment and educational opportunities—they remain limited by class and gender, stuck in inferior social positions, and trapped by rigid social structures. In her plays and stories as well as in her own life, power hierarchies continued to work against women.

In her texts, women are caught in a web of dependency, submissiveness, and helplessness. Fleißer's focus is on socially and historically disenfranchised working-class women. Her most famous play, *Pioniere in Ingolstadt,* unfortunately not yet translated into English, is a comic tragedy about the relationship between the sexes. Berta, the protagonist, loses her innocence and romantic hopes in a progression of love that ends (like all of Fleißer's works) in despair, failure, disillusionment, or even suicide. Fleißer sympathetically shows the woman's perspective: her psychological investment in this seemingly dismal setup between servant and master, and the necessity of illusory romantic and idyllic fantasies (of success and upward mobility, usually through marriage to the source of her pain) as shelter from despair. Fleißer's texts employ and then subvert these fantasies, exposing the psychic investments and cultural edifices that sexualize woman and uphold the power relations that perpetuate women's oppression.

While most of her writing was accomplished in Berlin, the literary capital of Weimar during the "Golden Twenties," a time known for its cultural innovation, Fleißer's plays and stories were frequently received with indignation, resentment, and outrage that a female playwright would explicitly thematize sexual relations, let alone criticize the exploitative relationships. After Brecht's production of *Pioniere in Ingolstadt* (1929) created a scandal due to the protagonist's loss of virginity on stage, a revision which Brecht insisted upon against Fleißer's wishes, Fleißer ended her friendship with him. For the next three decades, she lived in literary and social isolation. Fleißer's plight was sealed during the Nazi era. In 1935, the same year that the Nazis officially banned her work and forbade her from writing, Fleißer married Josef Haindl, a conservative tobacco merchant from her hometown. Her poverty and isolation continued after World War II, due mostly to her unhappy marriage to a tyrant who forbade her to write and her unpopularity in her hometown, where she nevertheless continued to live. Her works were out of print from 1932 to 1963; it was not until 1966 that one of her *Volksstücke* (folk plays), *Der starke Stamm* (1950; The Strong Stock), was produced.

Interest in Fleißer's dramas was renewed in Germany in the mid-1960s when Rainer Werner Fassbinder, the seminal figure of New German Cinema, staged *Fegefeuer in Ingolstadt* (1968) in Munich, dedicated his film *Katzelmacher* (1969) to her, and then filmed *Pioniere in Ingolstadt* (1979). With the feminist push in the 1970s for sociohistorical representations of and by women, Fleißer's oeuvre reentered academic and cultural circles. While still unknown outside of Germany, she has been cited as a major literary influence, along with Ödön von Horváth, for the socially critical *Volksstücke* of Fassbinder, Franz Xaver Kroetz, and Martin Sperr that were popular in Germany in the late 1960s and the 1970s. Her collected works were published by the distinguished publishing house Suhrkamp in 1972, two years before her death.

JILL GILLESPIE

Biography

Born in Ingolstadt, 23 November 1901. Studied drama in Munich; acquainted with Lion Feuchtwanger and Bertolt Brecht; temporary stay in Berlin; returned in 1933 to Ingolstadt and was prohibited to write in 1935; after her marriage, Fleißer discontinued writing until her husband's death in 1958, when she resumed her literary endeavors. Died 2 February 1974.

Selected Works

Collections

Gesammelte Werke, vols., 1–3, 1972; vol. 4, 1989
Das Mädchen Yella. Erzählungen, 1992

Plays

Fegefeuer in Ingolstadt, 1926
Pioniere in Ingolstadt, 1928; as *Purgatory in Ingolstadt,* in *The Divided Home/Land: Contemporary German Women's Plays,* 1992
Der Tiefseefisch, 1930
Karl Stuart, 1946
Der starke Stamm, 1950

Prose

Ein Pfund Orangen und neun andere Geschichten, 1929
Mehlreisende Frieda Geyer, 1931
Andorranische Abenteuer, 1932
Avantgarde, 1963
Abenteuer aus dem englischen Garten, 1969
Eine Zierde für den Verein. Roman, 1975
In der Enge geht alles. M. F.s Gang in die innere Emigration, 1984
"Purgatory in Ingolstadt," in *The Divided Home/Land: Contemporary German Women's Plays,* edited by Sue-Ellen Case, 1992
"The Athletic Spirit and Contemporary Art: An Essay on the Modern Type" [1929], in *Weimar Sourcebook,* edited by Anton Kaes, et al., 1994

Further Reading

Cocalis, Susan, "Weib ohne Wirklichkeit, Welt ohne Weiblichkeit: Zum Selbst-, Frauen- und Gesellschaftsbild im Frühwerk Marieluise Fleißers," *Entwürfe von Frauen in der Literatur des 20. Jahrhunderts,* edited by Irmela von der Lühe, Berlin: Argument, 1982
Herminghouse, Patricia, editor, *Frauen im Mittelpunkt: Contemporary German Women Writers,* New York: Suhrkamp, 1987
Hoffmeister, Donna L., "Growing Up Female in the Weimar Republic: Young Women in Seven Stories by Marieluise Fleißer," *German Quarterly* 56 (May 1982)

Joeres, Ruth-Ellen B., "Records of Survival: The Autobiographical Writings of Marieluise Fleißer and Marie Luise Kaschnitz," in *Faith of a (Woman) Writer*, edited by Alice Kessler-Harris and William McBrien, New York: Greenwood Press, 1988
Kosta, Barbara, "Employed Bodies: Female Servants in the Works by Marieluise Fleißer," *German Studies Review* 15 (1992)
Kraft, Friedrich, editor, *Marieluise Fleißer: Anmerkungen, Texte, Dokumente,* Ingolstadt: Donauer Courier, 1981
Marieluise Fleißer: Text und Kritik, vol. 64, edited by Heinz Ludwig Arnold, Munich: Text und Kritik, 1979
McGowan, Moray, *Marieluise Fleißer,* Munich: Beck, 1987

Paul Fleming 1609–1640

Paul Fleming's work falls into the early part of the Baroque era in German literature, which is usually considered to coincide more or less with the 17th century. At that time German writers had become conscious of the lack of a national literature in German-speaking lands and were striving to create works that might emulate the literatures of the European Renaissance established in countries such as Italy and France and emerging in England and the neighboring Low Countries. The first name associated with this development is Martin Opitz, whose *Buch von der deutschen Poeterey* (1624; Book of German Poesy) gave aspiring German poets the confidence to write verse in their own language. Until then most literary composition in Germany had been in Latin, and that was the way Opitz himself and many others began their practice as poets.

In his youth Fleming was already famous as a poet, being crowned *poeta laureatus* in 1632 during his student years and emerging as the first Saxon poet to match the excellence of Opitz and other contemporary Silesians. Despite spending so much of his short life on his travels, he remained in touch with German friends. When he died in 1640, only one year later than Opitz himself, his fame was already assured; later critics have concurred with the verdict of Fleming's contemporaries.

The first location associated with Fleming's poetry is the town of Leipzig. From 1622 he was a pupil at the famous Thomasschule, where a well-known poet and musician, Johann Hermann Schein, was the cantor. From 1623 onward he may have been present at lectures at the University of Leipzig, and in 1628 he took the oath and became a full-fledged student, remaining there until 1633. During these years he befriended Silesian students such as Georg Gloger and Martin Christenius, and through them he became acquainted with the principles of the Opitzian verse reform, notably the fundamental need for coincidence of metrical and natural rhythmic stress in German. Nevertheless, his first poetic attempts, like those of most humanist poets of the time, were in Latin. His poem *Jesu Christo S. Natalitium* (1631; On the Birth of Jesus Christ) enabled him to demonstrate his rhetorical expertise in religious subject matter as he recited it in the auditorium of the university, and, by contrast, in the same year he produced the extended love poem *Rubella* (1631; Rubella), a cycle lamenting the death of a Leipzig girl.

Many of Fleming's shorter poems were written for weddings and funerals, and the majority of these are in German; the "ode" (i.e., the song form that he began to cultivate) was to become his most famous contribution to German poetry. In more settled times Fleming might well have stayed in Leipzig, but the exigencies of the Thirty Years' War made travel attractive, and after the attainment of his degree of Magister in May 1633, he left Leipzig with a trade mission to Russia and Persia; thus, almost all of his subsequent poetry was composed outside Germany, away from the pressures of conventional surroundings, which may account for a certain originality of development.

During this time Fleming wrote his best-known poetry, some extended longer works, and many shorter items, especially sonnets and songs. The subject matter is varied, and much of it is still based on occasions such as weddings, funerals, and academic celebrations. It includes travel poems about the places in Russia and Persia that Fleming visited with the delegation, reflections on the state of affairs back in Germany, long pastoral works, such as the 1635 epithalamium for Reiner Brockmann, professor of Greek in Reval, reflections on his own poetic and personal destiny, and some superb religious poetry, such as the sonnet "An meinen Erlöser" (date uncertain; To My Redeemer). Although some of his poems, especially the longer ones, were published separately during his lifetime, the majority appeared in the collections that were put together by his friend Adam Olearius and came out posthumously in 1641, 1646, and later.

Above all Fleming was known then and has been known since for his love poetry, most of which was written for the Niehusen sisters in Reval, first for Elsabe and then for the younger Anna, to whom he became betrothed shortly before his death. Fleming disguises their names with a pseudonym and often hides the real name in the text with an acrostic. Like most love poetry of the 17th century, these are rooted in the Petrarchist tradition of the man's unceasing veneration of the woman. According to Hans Pyritz in a famous study, however, Fleming transcends this convention by insisting on a natural relationship and mutual love. It has since been recognized that this is a somewhat exaggerated judgment, since many of Fleming's love poems, especially the sonnets, use the rhetoric and topoi of the Petrarchist tradition intensively, albeit occasionally playfully. Certainly in his songs Fleming succeeds in fusing in an original way the language and attitudes of Petrarchism with a stress on fidelity and mutual love that may partly stem from the German folk-song tradition. Often he employs a stanza form that concludes with a two-line refrain, another feature reminiscent of the folk song. The Stoic tradition of bearing suffering willingly, popular in Protestant Germany at the time, is also introduced to help overcome the pain of separation from the beloved. All of this, allied with his sense of rhythm, creates a memorable and easy-flowing song. Famous examples of his songs include "Elsgens treues Hertz" (ca.

1636; Elsgen's Faithful Heart), "An Elsabe" (ca. 1636; To Elsabe), which unites many of the phenomena described above, "An Anemonen, nachdem er von ihr gereiset war" (1639; To Anemone, after He Had Traveled away from Her), with its stress on the eventual joy of reunion, and "An Anna aus der Ferne" (ca. 1639; To Anna from Afar). His contribution to German poetry in general and to song writing in particular is thus an original one, without transcending the parameters within which the poetry of the age finds its expression.

ANTHONY J. HARPER

Biography

Born in Hartenstein, in the Erzgebirge (Saxony), 1609. Studied liberal arts and medicine at the University of Leipzig, 1628–33; bachelor of arts degree, 1632; master of arts, 1633; participated in a commercial expedition sponsored by the Duke of Holstein-Gottorp, staying in Reval (now Tallinn, Estonia) and traveling through Russia and Persia, 1633–39; traveled from Reval to Leiden (Netherlands), 1639; doctorate in medicine, University of Leiden, 1640. Died in Hamburg, 1640.

Selected Works

Poetry
Jesu Christo S. Natalitium, 1631
Rubella, 1631
Gedichte auf . . . Reineri Brocmans . . . Hochzeit, 1635
Prodromus, edited by Adam Olearius, 1641
Teutsche Poemata, edited by Adam Olearius, 1646; as *Geist- und Weltliche Poemata,* 1651
Epigrammata Latina, edited by Adam Olearius, 1649
Lateinische Gedichte, edited by J.M. Lappenberg, 1863
Deutsche Gedichte, 2 vols., edited by J.M. Lappenberg, 1865

Further Reading

De Capua, Angelo George, "Paul Fleming," in *German Baroque Poetry: Interpretative Readings,* edited by Angelo George de Capua, Albany: State University of New York Press, 1973
Entner, Heinz, *Paul Fleming: Ein deutscher Dichter im Dreißigjährigen Krieg,* Leipzig: Reclam, 1989
Fechner, Jörg-Ulrich, "Paul Fleming," in *Deutsche Dichter des 17. Jahrhunderts: Ihr Leben und Werk,* edited by Benno von Wiese and Harald Steinhagen, Berlin: Schmidt, 1984
Harper, Anthony J., "Paul Fleming," in *German Baroque Writers 1580–1660,* Dictionary of Literary Biography, vol. 164, edited by James N. Hardin, Detroit, Michigan: Gale Research, 1996
Hoffmeister, Gerhart, "Paul Fleming," in *Deutsche Dichter 2. Reformation, Renaissance und Barock,* edited by Günter E. Grimm and Frank Rainer Max, Stuttgart: Reclam, 1988
Jones, G.L., "The Mulde's Half-Prodigal Son: Paul Fleming, Germany, and the Thirty Years' War," *German Life and Letters* 26 (1973)
Pyritz, Hans, *Paul Flemings Liebeslyrik: Zur Geschichte des Petrarkismus,* Göttingen: Vandenhoek und Ruprecht, 1963
Robert, Kyra, "Der Büchernachlaß Paul Flemings in der Bibliothek der Estnischen Akademie der Wissenschaften," *Daphnis* 22 (1993)
Schubert, Dietmar, "'Man wird mich nennen hören . . .': Zum poetischen Vermächtnis Paul Flemings," *Weimarer Beiträge* 30 (1984)
Sperberg-McQueen, Marian R., *The German Poetry of Paul Fleming: Studies in Genre and History,* Chapel Hill: University of North Carolina Press, 1990
———, "Leipzig Pastoral: Two Epithalamia by Martin Christenius, with a Note on Paul Fleming," *Chloe* 10 (1990)
Weevers, Theodor, "The Influence of Heinsius on Two Genres of the German Baroque," *Journal of English and Germanic Philology* 37 (1938)
Zon, Stephen, "Imitations of Petrarch: Opitz, Fleming," *Daphnis* 3 (1978)

Theodor Fontane 1819–1898

Among major novelists, Fontane is unique. In contrast to Goethe and Thomas Mann, who published their first novels in their mid-20s, he was 57 when *Vor dem Sturm* (1878; *Before the Storm*) appeared. Yet together with these two literary giants, Fontane has endured as the most widely read German novelist in his homeland. It took Fontane a lifetime to grow into a novelist, and for this reason, a look at his preparatory work is elucidating. Trained as a pharmacist, he left the profession two years after his accreditation in 1847 to live by his pen. By the age of 21, he had published the novella "Geschwisterliebe" and lyrics in several papers. He also translated *Hamlet.* In 1843, he joined the literary club "Tunnel über der Spree," a forum for his ballads, and in 1844, his military year, he took a trip to Britain, which yielded a travelogue. Fontane, whose "soul and body cried out for the love of woman," became engaged to Emilie Rouanet-Kummer the following year, who, similar to himself, was a descendant of Huguenots.

The period between 1845 and 1848 was one of discontent for Fontane since he did not earn enough to make good on the marital promise. He put the blame on von Manteuffel's government, which, in his opinion, had turned Prussia into a police state. Hence, in March 1848, Fontane mounted the barricades. His commitment to the revolution was stronger than he admits in retrospect for middle-class readers; in fact, he wrote two articles critical of the administration in the *Berliner Zeitungs-Halle* and the drama fragment *Karl Stuart,* and he was chosen as a delegate to the Berlin national assembly. Thereafter, he penned political essays for the *Dresdner Zeitung* and published two volumes of poetry, yet his finances were still precarious. Necessity made him enter Manteuffel's "Literary Cabinet." On that slim salary, he married Emilie, who bore him seven children and, although she did not appreciate his literary efforts, tirelessly transcribed his manuscripts. In 1855, as semiofficial press agent, he moved to London, where he familiarized himself with British society and its literature, especially Scott, Austen, and Thackeray. It also let him perceive social inequities in his favorite country—to which he had been alerted by Engels's *The Condition of the Working Class in England* (1845). The results of these years were two more travelogues.

Whatever Fontane tried as a writer, it was insufficient to meet the needs of his growing family. Neither the renowned *Wanderungen durch die Mark Brandenburg* (1862–82), his work for the *Kreuzzeitung,* nor his theater critiques for the *Voss'sche Zeitung,* where he distinguished himself as an interpreter of the contemporary German stage, nor his accounts of Bismarck's three wars, which led to German unity, put him on a financially solid footing. In 1876, he was appointed secretary of the Academy of Arts in Berlin, with a handsome salary, yet he resigned after three months. He wanted to know what he could do in the genre of the novel, perhaps to outreach his grasp. In the four decades preceding his career as a novelist, however, Fontane had become a genuine man of letters. His experiences lifted him above parochialism. An incident in *Effi Briest* (1895) displays his cosmopolitan tolerance. At a party at the home of a forest ranger, the company sings the anthem "I am a Prussian, do you know my colors," whereupon someone exclaims, "They don't have things like this in other countries." Yet Effi's husband, a Prussian official, replies, "No, in other countries they have something else."

Fontane's narrative work reflects the genealogy of the novel in late 18th- and early 19th-century Britain. It includes strains of the Gothic novel (ancestor to the detective story), historical novels, societal narratives, and novels of good society. The latter two forms constitute the core of Fontane's fiction and account for his longevity as a novelist. His detective stories, *Grete Minde* (1880), *Ellernklipp* (1881), *Unterm Birnbaum* (1885), and *Quitt* (1891), were written for monetary gain. Although Fontane wrote only two historical narratives, they figure prominently in his oeuvre. As his first novel, *Before the Storm* holds a special place. A "baggy monster," it portrays three main groups of characters during the winter of 1812–13, when the remnants of the "grande armée" straggled back from Russia. Since Fontane wished to counter the *Aventürenblech* (adventure rubbish) of the period's popular historical novelists, the only action in the narrative is an assault on the French garrison in Frankfurt-on-Oder. Instead of action, it conveys the mood of the country prior to the royally sanctioned uprising, and this is achieved splendidly through the conversations of his figures. They foreshadow the verbal exchanges of his novels of good society. *Before the Storm* also introduces social types seen in the later novels: the genial pastor and the eccentric schoolmaster.

Schach von Wuthenow (1882; *A Man of Honor*) is a different historical narrative: it is slender and focused on the hero's vanity and false concept of honor. The events occur one year before Prussia's crushing defeats in 1806 and reflect the ethical decline of the officer corps. There are two principal settings, the apartment of Frau von Carayon and her daughter Victoire, who are members of Berlin's Huguenot colony, and Château Wuthenow on Lake Ruppin. A captain of the elite cavalry regiment gendarmes, Schach woos the attractive mother, but he is prompted by an observation of a roguish prince to seduce the daughter, who is disfigured by pockmarks. The small number of characters, almost all of the nobility, and the themes of courtship, seduction, and marriage make this historical tale a novel of good society as well. Schach kills himself rather than be married to a woman of marred looks and thereby breaks his promise to her and his pledge to his sovereign. His suicide is not altogether surprising, for the text discloses Schach's ominous characteristics. He avoids being seen with Victoire, is horrified by the very word "wedlock," and cannot picture himself living as a country squire "en famille."

Late 19th-century Prussian society, the subject of all of Fontane's other novels, was certainly an anachronism, yet it was real enough. Although the nobility had fallen behind the bourgeoisie in wealth, it held on to power and its privileges. It observed a strict honor code. As late as the 1890s, two-thirds of the officer corps above the rank of colonel were aristocrats, whereas the majority of recruits hailed from rural areas, because rustics were thought to be uninfected with socialist ideas. In this society, the uniform played an exaggerated role, and the lieutenant, or *Vitzliputzli,* was adored as a sun and war god. Fontane's opinion of the nobility was ambiguous: he resented their selfishness yet found them aesthetically attractive. With advancing age, he viewed them ever more negatively.

He wrote four kinds of social novels. *Frau Jenny Treibel* (1892; *Jenny Treibel*) satirizes the bourgeoisie's false sentimentality, for if Fontane perceived the nobility ambiguously, he nursed a strong dislike for the bourgeoisie throughout his life. The posthumously published *Mathilde Möhring* (1906), the story of a woman of the lower middle class who after many trials succeeds in cutting out a professional life for herself, is an early example of feminine self-assertion. *Irrungen, Wirrungen* (1888; translated as *Trials and Tribulations, A Suitable Match,* and *Entanglements: An Everyday Berlin Story*) and *Stine* (1890) treat ill-starred loves between aristocratic officers and working girls. The main body of his oeuvre encompasses narratives about good society: *L'Adultera* (1882; *A Woman Taken in Adultery*), *Graf Petöfy* (1884), *Cécile* (1887), *Unwiederbringlich* (1892; *Beyond Recall*), *Effi Briest, Poggenpuhls* (1896; *The Poggenpuhl Family*), and *Der Stechlin* (1899; *The Stechlin*). As Peter Demetz has shown, these works were inspired by Austen's novels of manners, whose distinguishing features include a focus upon leisured society, a preponderance of conversation over action, and an exclusion of politics, history, and nature, which, since they can cause upheavals and threaten the protagonists' niches, can upset polite social interaction.

What Fontane adopted from Austen's model was spirited conversation, for he, too, was an outstanding "causeur." He also shared her exclusion of nature. Politics and history play important roles in his fiction, however, since Fontane appreciated Scott and Thackeray as well, in whose novels these forces are decisive. His own figures, members of the Prussian nobility, are steeped in tradition and involved in shaping their country's political present. In Austen's novels, conversation is an instrument to characterize figures by means of their relative verbal prowess or wit. For Fontane, conversation is equally important, yet it is charged with two additional functions. It is a dialogic instrument of assessing other characters after an event (e.g., a dinner), a technique that is also employed in Thackeray's *Vanity Fair* (1848), and it unmasks pompous intellectuals. Living in considerably different times than Austen, Fontane was self-conscious of finding the right tone for his figures. In his fiction, conversation constitutes an affirmation of the 18th-century humanism that recognized speech as the salient human trait. Even this claim, however, is relativized. In *Beyond Recall,* the Danish princess asserts, "the most human feature we have, is, after all, language," whereas Dubslav von Stechlin pushes this view to its logical conclusion with the ironic remark, "therefore, he who talks most is the purest human being."

The main flaws of Prussian society manifested themselves most glaringly in love and marriage, where the principle of comparable provenance was upheld. Moreover, in high society (which included the new bourgeoisie), marriages of convenience were usually arranged, as depicted in *A Woman Taken in Adultery, Cécile, Beyond Recall,* and *Effi Briest,* whereby age discrepancies of up to 30 years are not uncommon. All these texts chronicle failing marriages and, except for *A Woman Taken in Adultery,* close with the death of one spouse. The characteristic trope of these narratives is chiasmus, a reversal in the relations of the marriage partners. In *Cécile* and *Effi Briest,* it is the husband's concept of honor (although it has a different meaning for Colonel St. Arnaud and Baron von Instetten) that makes them fight a duel to the death with their wife's suitor, whereas Countess Holk is unable to forgive her husband on account of her narrow-minded religiosity and takes her own life. Effi Briest and Cécile die of broken hearts. Young Count von Haldern, who wishes to marry a seamstress, shoots himself when he learns that his family will not tolerate such a choice. Within the scope of the serious 19th-century novel, an unusually high number of major figures die in Fontane's works. The ubiquitous death of aristocrats in his fiction, which usually occurs because of the outdated moral code they uphold, suggests that for Fontane the time of this class has run out. Its beliefs had become hostile to life itself. Reacting to this stance, the divorced Effi Briest can say about her former spouse, who indoctrinated their mechanically responding daughter, "Weg mit Euch" (away with You). With this pronouncement, she dismisses the entire upper class, for her parents had also thought it necessary "to show their colors" and to bar her from their home for too long. They should have remembered that she was a 17 year old, snatched from the playground, and matched to a man 22 years her senior.

Fontane's art as a novelist also manifests itself in his treatment of objects. The very first page of *Effi Briest* offers a description of the round flower bed at the Briest mansion, with a sundial in the middle and a heliotrope growing round its edges. The sundial tells time on bright days, while the canna is a plant whose blossoms literally turn toward the sun. Heliotrope and sundial are coordinated with Effi, who is highly conscious of time and will soon turn to her fiancé, who has been chosen by her parents. In the closing scene of the narrative, the sundial has been replaced by Effi's gravestone. Time is no longer indicated; nor does it matter, for Effi has entered the realm of timelessness. Her parents, too, are outside of temporality, whereas the heliotrope, which has been spared, will have nowhere to turn since there will not be another day.

The reception of Fontane's novels provides an exciting story only when one considers the turnabout of his literary fortunes in Germany beginning in the 1960s. During his lifetime and up to the inception of the Expressionist movement, he was not widely popular. Even though *A Woman Taken in Adultery* caused a scandal because the author did not punish the adulterous couple, there was no increased interest in his subsequent works. For too long, he was considered a Prussian rather than a German writer. The aristocrats whom he depicted hardly read him; instead, as he wrote in a poem on his 75th birthday, his audience consisted of those descended from the biblical patriarchs, the real nobility.

Among writers, Fontane primarily influenced Thomas Mann, who called him in an homage "unser Vater." Mann borrowed sometimes from Fontane's works. The title for Mann's novel *Buddenbrooks,* his penchant for combining bourgeois German family names with exotic first names (Alonso Gieshübler and Tonio Kröger), and the conversational skills of Mann's figures all show Fontane's influence. By contrast, Broch's *Pasenow,* vol. 1 of *The Sleepwalkers* (1931), is a travesty of Fontane's Berlin novels. Fontane's unprecedented popularity in today's Germany has been the result of a symbiosis between publishers, reviewers, the reading public, and film producers. By the mid-1970s, this adulation raised him to the status of a classic, a phenomenon that Ulrike Tontsch has tried to explain. Cinematic works include Fassbinder's *Effi Briest* (1974), a television serial of *Der Stechlin* by Rolf Hädrich (1975), Gené's *Grete Minde* (1976), and F.J. Wild's *Jenny Treibel* (1981). It is not by chance that the title of Grass's monumental work *Ein weites Feld* (1996) is a borrowing from Fontane, who himself is given new life in the figure of "Fonty."

In Britain and the United States, he has remained a one-book author; *Effi Briest* has been his only generally accessible novel. Since its reissuing by Penguin in 1976, it had sold 60,000 copies worldwide by 1992. All of Fontane's societal novels have been translated, albeit in small, short-lived editions. Highly favorable reviews by luminaries in the foremost Anglo-Saxon literary journals have not brought about a change in the situation.

VOLKER DÜRR

See also Berlin

Biography

Born in Neuruppin, 30 December 1819. Military service, 1844; apprentice to an apothecary, Berlin, 1836–40; worked in Burg, Leipzig, Dresden, and Berlin, 1841–49; worked as a freelance writer; with the press bureau, Prussian government, 1851–55; London correspondent for Berlin newspapers, 1855–59; London editor of *Kreuzzeitung,* 1860–70; drama critic, *Vossische Zeitung,* 1870–89; secretary, Berlin Academy of Arts, 1876. Schiller prize (Prussia), 1891. Died 20 September 1898.

Selected Works

Collections

Sämtliche Werke, edited by Edgar Gross et al., 30 vols., 1959–75

Werke, Schriften, und Briefe, edited by Walter Keitel and Helmuth Nürnberger, 1962–

Romane und Erzählungen, edited by Peter Goldammer et al., 8 vols., 1969

Fiction

Vor dem Sturm, 1878; as *Before the Storm,* translated by R.J. Hollingdale, 1985

Grete Minde, 1880

Ellernklipp, 1881

L'Adultera, 1882; as *A Woman Taken in Adultery,* translated by Gabriele Annan, with *The Poggenpuhl Family,* 1979

Schach von Wuthenow, 1882; as *A Man of Honor,* translated by E.M. Valk, 1975

Graf Petöfy, 1884

Unterm Birnbaum, 1885

Cécile, 1887; as *Cecile,* translated by Stanley Radcliffe, 1992

Irrungen, Wirrungen, 1888; as *Trials and Tribulations,* 1917; as *A Suitable Match,* translated by Sandra Morris, 1968; as *Entanglements: An Everyday Berlin Story,* translated by Derek Bowman, 1986
Stine, 1890
Quitt, 1891
Unwiederbringlich, 1891; as *Beyond Recall,* translated by Douglas Parmée, 1964
Frau Jenny Treibel, 1892; as *Jenny Treibel,* translated by Ulf Zimmermann, 1976
Effi Briest, 1895; as *Effi Briest,* translated by Douglas Parmée, 1967; translated by Helen Chambers and Hugh Rorrison, 1995
Die Poggenpuhls, 1896; as *The Poggenpuhl Family,* translated by Gabriele Annan, with *A Women Taken in Adultery,* 1979
Der Stechlin, 1899; as *The Stechlin,* translated by William Zwiebel, 1995
Mathilde Möhring, 1906; revised version, 1969
Short Novels and Other Writings (includes *A Man of Honor; Jenny Treibel; The Eighteenth of March*), edited by Peter Demetz, 1982
Delusions Confusions; and The Poggenpuhl Family, edited by Peter Demetz, 1989

Poetry
Von der schönen Rosamunde, 1850
Männer und Helden, 1850
Gedicthe, 2 vols., 1851–75
Balladen, 1861
Die schönsten Gedichte und Balladen, 1982
Bilder und Balladen, edited by Werner Feudell, 1984

Other
Ein Sommer in London, 1854
Bilderbuch aus England, 1860; as *Journeys to England in Victoria's Early Days 1844–1859,* translated by Dorothy Harrison, 1939
Jenseit des Tweed, 1860; as *Across the Tweed,* translated by Brian Battershaw, 1965
Wanderungen durch die Mark Brandenburg, 4 vols., 1862–82
Kriegsgefangen, 1871
Aus den Tagen der Okkupation, 1872
Der Krieg gegen Frankreich, 1870–1871, 2 vols., 1873–76
Christian Friedrich Scherenberg und der literarische Berlin von 1840 bis 1860, 1885
Fünf Schlösser, 1889
Meine Kinderjahre (memoirs), 1894
Von Zwanzig bis Dreissig (memoirs), 1898
Aus dem Nachlass, edited by Joseph Ettlinger, 1908
Briefwechsel, with Wilhelm Wolfsohn, edited by Wilhelm Walters, 1910
Briefe, edited by Kurt Schreinert and Charlotte Jolles, 4 vols., 1968–71
Briefwechsel, with Paul Heyse, edited by Gotthard Erler, 1972
Briefe, edited by Gotthard Erler, 2 vols., 1980
Briefwechsel, with Theodor Storm, edited by Jacob Steiner, 1981
Ein Leben in Briefen, edited by Otto Drude, 1981
Autobiographische Schriften, edited by Gotthard Erler, Peter Goldammer, and Joachim Krueger, 3 vols., 1982
Briefe an den Verleger Rudolf von Decker, 1988

Further Reading

Bance, Alan, *Theodor Fontane: The Major Novels,* Cambridge and New York: Cambridge University Press, 1982
Craig, Gordon A., *Über Fontane,* Munich: C.H. Beck, 1997
Demetz, Peter, *Formen des Realismus: Theodor Fontane,* Munich: Hanser, 1964
Garland, Henry B., *The Berlin Novels of Theodor Fontane,* Oxford: Clarendon Press, and New York: Oxford University Press, 1980
Glass, Derek, "Fontane in English Translation: A Survey of the Publication History," in *Theodor Fontane: The London Symposium,* edited by Alan Bance et al., Stuttgart: Heinz/Akademischer Verlag, 1995
Mann, Thomas, "The Old Fontane," in *Essays of Three Decades,* translated by H.T. Lowe-Porter, New York: Knopf, and London: Secker and Warburg, 1947
Müller-Seidel, Walter, *Theodor Fontane: Soziale Romankunst in Deutschland,* Stuttgart: Metzler, 1975; 3rd edition, 1994
Nürnberger, Helmuth, *Fontane in Selbstzeugnissen und Bilddokumenten,* 21st edition, Reinbek bei Hamburg: Rowohlt, 1995
Pascal, Roy, *The German Novel,* Toronto: University of Toronto Press, and Manchester: Manchester University Press, 1956
Reuter, Hans-Heinrich, *Fontane,* 2 vols., Munich: Nymphenburger Verlag, 1968; 2nd edition, Berlin: Verlag der Nation, 1995
Tontsch, Ulrike, *Der "Klassiker" Fontane: Ein Rezeptionsprozeß,* Bonn: Bouvier, 1977
Wolff, Jürgen, "Verfahren der Literaturrezeption im Film, dargestellt am Beispiel der Effi-Briest-Verfilmungen von Luderer und Fassbinder," *Deutschunterricht* 33 (1981)
Zwiebel, William, *Theodor Fontane,* New York: Twayne, 1992

Effi Briest 1895

Novel by Theodor Fontane

Effi Briest, serialized between October 1894 and March 1895 as its author passed his 75th birthday, instantly became Theodor Fontane's most acclaimed and popular novel. One of the few 19th-century international classics by a German author, it is at once a pinnacle of realism, a *Zeitroman* that diagnoses Prussian moral and racial bigotry at the height of European imperialism, and a herald of the moderns which supplied Thomas Mann with the name for his grand saga of the decline of an age, *Buddenbrooks.*

Similar to his contemporaries Henrik Ibsen and Arthur Schnitzler, Fontane was already celebrated for his sympathetic depiction of strong women characters who fall victim either to men in unequal relationships or to the social restrictions imposed on their gender. In *Effi Briest,* he launches a searing attack from the perspective of a young bride on the institution of marriage as practiced in the upper echelons of Prussian society. Yet the novel is first and foremost a meticulously crafted work of art; this craft accounts for its immediate success and perennial popularity and also saves it from the denunciations made of an earlier masterpiece, *Irrungen, Wirrungen* (1888; translated as *Trials and Tribulations, A Suitable Match,* and *Entanglements: An Everyday Berlin Story*), which appeared to give value to the experience of a lower-class woman whom most of her contemporaries would have regarded as a prostitute.

The art in *Effi Briest* lies not just in the dialogues, the clearly delineated narrative progression, or the efficient characterization, but also in the use of detail, leitmotifs, and the role played by minor characters, some of the most important of whom appear for no more than a paragraph. In this classically centripetal text nothing is extraneous. There is no digression and no subplot. Each incident, encounter, anecdote, and character all enhance the plight of Fontane's enchanting heroine, who is destroyed by social conventions and expectations. At the end of the novel she is identified with the sacrificial female victims of the ancient Teutons, an image that recalls the scene at Stonehenge at the end of Thomas Hardy's *Tess of the d'Urbevilles,* which was published in the same year.

Effi, who retains her maiden name in the novel's title despite bearing her husband's for most of the novel, is the focus of Fontane's interest, rather than adultery, unequal marriages, or duelling. She is "a child of the air," an adolescent tomboy on the cusp of womanhood whose gender identity is not yet fixed when we first meet her. She is vivacious and just a little frivolous and has enjoyed home, schooling, her friends and parents, and, in fact, everything that a well-to-do country childhood had to offer. At the age of 17, she is then plucked from this happy environment by a man more than twice her age, who half a lifetime ago had courted her mother. She is taken to an unknown place, where she is neglected by her high-flying, career-minded husband. Effi's duty is to produce male children, but she gives birth to a daughter nine months to the day after her wedding. Her body then rebels against what is being done to her, and she fails to conceive for more than seven years. While she is on a "cure" for this failure in the spa town of Bad Ems, her husband Innstetten accidentally discovers incriminating letters from her lover Crampas and writes to tell her she may no longer return home, nor see her daughter.

While Effi is clearly on a downward slope before she is cast out, she does reach some sort of inner peace in the Berlin years that follow the disastrous period in provincial Kessin, a venue based on Fontane's happy childhood home of Swinemünde (now a stone's throw over the border in Poland). Effi's deception hardens her, and her knowledge of her sin robs her once and for all of her innocence, but she seems to have a premonition of the nature if not the extremity of her fate even before her marriage when she disturbs her foolish and ambitious mother with her sense of cynical resignation.

One of Fontane's greatest achievements in *Effi Briest* is that he does away with the need for a villain. Crampas, a vaudeville womanizer, hardly fits the bill, since he takes from Effi no more than what she wants to give. The heartless Innstetten, as husband a far more significant figure than Crampas as lover, is trapped by a repressive code of honor, which, as the novel makes clear, while no longer universally acknowledged, shapes his self-understanding and self-respect. He had been unable to marry his true love, Effi's mother, because of his lack of wealth and career success at the age of 20, which obliged her to settle for a man of means and property, her senior in years and inferior in wit. At the end of the novel, Innstetten is a sad and broken man who toys with the notion of emigrating to Africa to live among "pitch-black fellows" who have no understanding of honor or of the code of values that kill both Effi and Crampas and cripple him.

Fontane at his best is a best-selling populist who is not shy about employing melodramatic touches, including Innstetten's discovery of the letters and the duel between him and Crampas, or shamelessly tugging at his readers' heart strings, which he does in the novel's last phase. Apart from Effi, all the characters—the good and the bad, but especially the bad—are caricatures of one sort or another. What distinguishes Fontane from lesser novelists, however, is his "art of leaving things out" and his concentration on the moment either directly before or after the apparently big event. The reader does not witness Effi's wedding, for instance, and, far more tantalizingly, has to speculate on the degree of intimacy between her and Crampas. For this reason it is not often recognized that the adulterous couple, who meet outside on the beach in the middle of winter, are unlikely to have slept with one another.

One of the novel's most melodramatic motifs is the story of the Chinese ghost that Innstetten uses to control his new wife, scaring her, more than half-knowingly, about her burgeoning and unattended sexuality. A hidden theme emerges here, the Prussian projection of their own dread of sex onto foreigners: the Chinaman who is said to have eloped with the niece of a Kessin captain, the half-Polish Crampas, and the proto-lesbian Marietta Trippelli. Yet the characters who show sympathy to Effi, such as the Catholic Roswitha and the half-Portuguese Gieshübler, all diverge from the Prussian norm, which indicates how Fontane presents this moral malaise as particularly Prussian.

JULIAN PREECE

Editions

First edition: *Effi Briest,* Berlin: Friedrich Fontane, 1895
Critical edition: in *Werke, Schriften, und Briefe,* edited by Walter Keitel and Helmuth Nürnberger, Munich: Hanser, 1974
Translations: *Effi Briest,* translated by Douglas Parmée, London: Penguin, 1967; also translated by Helen Chambers and Hugh Rorrison, London: Angel Books, 1995

Further Reading

Greenberg, Valerie D., "The Resistance of Effi Briest: An (Un)told Tale," *Publications of the Modern Language Association of America* 103, no. 5 (1988)
Kempf, Franz R., "'Versteckt und gefährlich politisch': Hundert Jahre *Effi Briest*-Kritik," *Michigan German Studies* 17, no. 2 (1991)
Minden, Michael, "Realism Versus Poetry: Theodor Fontane, *Effi Briest,*" in *The German Novel in the Twentieth Century,* edited by David R. Midgley, Edinburgh: Edinburgh University Press, and New York: St. Martin's Press, 1993
Radcliffe, Stanley, "*Effi Briest* and the Crampas Letters," *German Life and Letters* 39 (1985–86)
Rainer, Ulrike, "*Effi Briest* und das Motiv des Chinesen," *Zeitschrift für Deutsche Philologie* 101 (1982)
Thanner, Josef, "Symbol and the Function of the Symbol in Theodor Fontane's *Effi Briest,*" *Monatshefte* 57 (1965)
Zimmermann, Gisela, "The Civil Servant as Educator: *Effi Briest* and *Anna Karenina,*" *Modern Language Review* 90, no. 4 (1995)

Der Stechlin 1899

Novel by Theodor Fontane

When Fontane offered his last, and perhaps best, novel to the editor of the journal *Über Land und Meer* for serial publication, he explained: "In the end an old man dies and two youngsters get married;—that is about all that happens in 500 pages. There are no complications and solutions, no entanglements of the heart or conflicts in general, no tensions or surprises." This narrative without an action or plot is the culmination of a tendency inherent in all of Fontane's novels: the displacement of action by conversation, which manifests itself as early as in *Vor dem Sturm* (1878; *Before the Storm*). On this premise, *Der Stechlin* (*The*

Stechlin), which is the novel most characteristic of Fontane, nevertheless introduces a new element into his fiction: contemporary politics. The narrative focuses on themes, locales, and figures whom it defines through discourse and their conduct. Whenever appropriate, the omniscient narrator provides insights.

In the absence of action, the themes hold the narrative together, and the most prominent is the contrast between the old generation of Dubslav Stechlin and the younger one of his son Woldemar, the woman the latter chooses as his spouse, and his fellow officer Czacko. The political views presented are tied to the generation gap. Personable and humane, the elder Stechlin stands for the preservation of traditional social order and customs, whereas his scion has been indoctrinated with the Christian-Social tenets of his mentor, the urbane pastor Lorenzen, a follower of the court-preacher Adolf Stöcker, without subscribing to the latter's anti-Semitism. Moreover, the elder Stechlin favors close ties with Russia, while his son looks toward England. Fontane also illustrates the importance of the Social Democratic party by describing a by-election to the Imperial Diet at Rheinsberg that pits the conservatives' Dubslav against the liberal-progressive Katzenstein and the socialist Torgelow. Dubslav does not give a single speech, but expects the mandate to be handed to him as a matter of course. Since most voters in the Rheinsberg district are farm hands and poor Glubsow glassblowers, the socialists win the day. Yet, the election results do not seem to affect Dubslav and his supporters, for they settle down to a sumptuous banquet.

The Stechlin has two principal settings. There is the decaying Stechlin manor, an adjacent village of the same name, and Lake Stechlin, which is endowed with the ability to respond to disturbances throughout the world with eruptions. The other main setting, the apartment of rich Count Barby in Berlin, serves as contrast to Dubslav's limited provincial circle of acquaintances. Altogether, country and city complement one another to present a full picture of Prussian society at the end of the 19th century. The novel displays a gamut of characters ranging from Dubslav's entourage of his servant Engelke (paralleled by Count Barby's attendant), his eccentric sister Adelheid, Domina of Cloister Wutz (a chauvinist Prussian), to the pauper child Agnes, who is brought in to divert the ailing Stechlin. There are also Kaztler, the forest supervisor, his wife of princely descent, young Stechlin's military comrades Rex and Czacko, the ambitious church supervisor Koseleger, the recently ennobled sawmiller von Gundermann and his "better half," Lorenzen, and the teacher Krippenstapel. The Berlin setting offers, aside from widowed Count Barby and his daughters, officers as well as artists and cultural critics who discredit themselves through their discourse.

Despite his election defeat, Dubslav towers above all other figures of the narrative through his discourse. Courteous, insightful, tolerant, and witty, he is a fictionalized alter ego of the author. Melusine, the vivacious elder daughter of Count Barby, a lady and *Frauenzimmer* in one, even toys with the idea of marrying him. Lovable as Dubslav and Melusine are, Fontane nevertheless believed that their time had run out, for he saw Germany's future in the fourth estate of the industrial workers. This seeming chiasm in his sociopolitical views is more outrightly expressed in his correspondence with Georg Friedlaender and, as Thomas Mann has pointed out, in his novel project the "Likedeelers" (North Sea pirates of the 16th century and communists), as well as in Fontane's letter to James Morris of 26 February 1896.

The apparent reversal of Fontane's social politics is no novelty, however; it signifies a recouping of his outbursts against the Prussian establishment between 1848 and the early 1850s, and of his dissent from Bismarck's (anti)-Socialist Legislation of 1878. It is all the more telling that he created the sympathetic Dubslav von Stechlin in order to demonstrate that his class was no longer the best instrument to run a united Germany. For all his wit and humane qualities (he picks up a plebeian drunk on his way home after the lost election), Dubslav does not really understand the everyday problems of the Glubsow workers. By contrast, his son, a much less impressive figure, yet always ready and able to mediate, who chooses the pale Armgard over her colorful sister Melusine, promises a better future for the denizens of the county in cooperation with a social democratic government.

The events described, including his son's wedding, are reinforced by a set of tropes and symbols that evoke the opening and closure of *Effi Briest* (1895). For like its predecessor, *The Stechlin* is a novel about time and temporality. Time is of utmost importance for Effi at the stage of her engagement to Innstetten, as well as in the discovery of her adulterous letters. In *The Stechlin,* the author prepares the hero's death in the chapter entitled "Sunset." Dubslav passes under the allegorical death-figure of a rococo clock tolling "twelve" and observes that at 12 it is all over. Yet this striking actually announces high noon. His exclamation, "But noon! . . . Where have you been hiding, sun!" turns the sun into the highest metaphor of power and happiness. Dubslav may be thinking of Nietzsche's "great midday" with the sun at the zenith of life's curve. Or he could remember that his happiest days came to an abrupt end with the death of his spouse one year after the birth of their son.

Instead of experiencing the sun directly, Dubslav has learned to take pleasure in its refracted light, in small things and amenities such as a letter from his daughter-in-law or a chaffinch whose trust comforts him. He is spiritually reassured by the thought that life has not been all bad. This is also his view of the "coming days," whether they are to be shaped by the Christian social consciousness of Woldemar and Armgard or by social democracy. According to Lorenzen, there will be a break with preformed or traditional society, but after a while some of the old social forces may reassert themselves and form asynthesis with the new ones. At that time, Lake Stechlin might once more jet up a fountain to inform the world of the good news.

It is too early to assess the ongoing reception of *The Stechlin.* Older critics, including Thomas Mann, consider *Effi Briest* as the culmination of Fontane's work, whereas some recent scholars rank Fontane's last novel among his finest narratives, if not his very best, notwithstanding some stylistic lapses observed by Demetz. Yet its humane generosity and tolerance have proved irresistible. In 1975, a German television serial, *Der Stechlin,* introduced Fontane's novel to an audience of millions. In 1995, an English translation was finally published.

VOLKER DÜRR

Editions

First edition: *Der Stechlin,* Berlin: Friedrich Fontane, 1899
Critical edition: in *Werke, Schriften, und Briefe,* edited by Walter Keitel and Helmuth Nürnberger, Munich: Hanser, 1974

Translation: *The Stechlin,* translated by William Zwiebel, Columbia, South Carolina: Camden House, 1995

Further Reading

Lützen,Wolf, and Wilhelm Pott, "*Stechlin* für viele: Zur historischen Verarbeitung einer literarischen Vorlage im Fernsehen," in *Literatur in den Massenmedien,* edited by Friedrich Knilli et al., Munich: Hanser, 1976

Müller-Seidel, Walter, "Fontane: *Der Stechlin,*" in *Der deutsche Roman,* edited by Benno von Wiese, vol. 2, Düsseldorf: Bagel, 1963

Strech, Heiko, *Theodor Fontane: die Synthese von Alt und Neu, "Der Stechlin" als Summe des Gesamtwerks,* Berlin: Schmidt, 1970

Wirsing, Sibylle, "Preußisches Märchen diskret: Zum Fernsehfilm über Fontanes *Stechlin,*" *Frankfurter Allgemeine Zeitung* (1 April 1995)

Louise von François 1817–1893

Louise von François, a writer of realist fiction and a contemporary of Theodor Fontane and Theodor Storm, has been hailed by literary commentators as one of Germany's most accomplished women writers. Self-educated and self-supported, François was driven by financial necessity to literary activity when she was almost 40 years old. She wrote secretly in her attic room, publishing anonymously at first, and remained throughout her life dismissive of the quality of her work. It was the celebrated author and critic Gustav Freytag who, in 1872, lifted François from obscurity when his generous praise for her novel *Die letzte Reckenburgerin* (1871; *The Last von Reckenburg*) made it an overnight success. The work was reprinted many times, enjoying international recognition in England, the United States, Denmark, and Holland, and was acclaimed both for its powerful narrative and its technical innovation.

François wrote two further novels—*Frau Erdmuthens Zwillingssöhne* (1873; Mrs Erdmuthen's Twin Sons) and *Die Stufenjahre eines Glücklichen* (1877; The Steps through the Years of a Lucky Fellow)—and some 20 novellas. Many of these are historical works, notable for their rich prose and psychological realism, and they demonstrate François's talent for originality of construction. The stories are peopled with unusual, colorful characters, many of whom, in the manner of Charles Dickens or Wilhelm Raabe, are given imaginative names. For François, however, fame and fortune proved elusive, and the solitary, ailing spinster lived out her years largely forgotten by the outside world.

François's literary achievement is closely molded to the shape of her life experience. Withdrawing from society at the age of 23 under the double blow of a broken engagement and an inheritance squandered by an unscrupulous guardian, the young woman entered on a lifetime of service as a nursemaid to a succession of infirm relatives. For all the arduousness and isolation of her existence, however, François nurtured the Enlightenment concepts of idealism and reason that had been instilled in her. With dogged perseverance, she was able to subvert the physical restrictions of her lot in life by turning them into an opportunity to broaden her mind. Thus, her fascination with history, together with her understanding of the concepts of honor and duty, which became essential to her life and work, were deepened by her elderly uncle's vivid tales of the Napoleonic Wars. Reading aloud to her blind stepfather, she further consolidated her knowledge of German history, and, in 1874, she published—pseudonymously—a history of the Wars of Liberation (1813–15), which became a recommended text for study by officers at the Prussian military academy.

The lifestyle of renunciation and selfless service that constituted François's everyday domestic reality is reflected in her stories, where the importance of moral behavior is repeatedly illustrated through depicting the classic conflict between duty and desire. The Reckenburg motto "In right and honor" encapsulates a challenging ethical code, which also informs many of her other works. Her writing has a strong didactic element, a sense of social conscience, and a commendation of productive activity and self-denial; all of these characteristics are easily ascribed to a woman who knew none of life's luxuries. Her fiction, however, is far from being a narrow call to asceticism. A writer with an independent, rationalistic mind and a sharp awareness of sociopolitical issues, François's humanistic worldview comes across, like that of other literary figures of the period, in her antipathy toward class prejudice and religious intolerance. By no means parochial in her concerns, moreover, a shrewd perception of history and politics led her to advocate the idea of a unified German nation in a manner that won her the respect of educated critics.

Conrad Ferdinand Meyer, who became her admirer and correspondent, aptly described her work in 1881 as a strange mixture of conservative tradition and liberal viewpoints. This is seen, for example, in the way in which she is patriotic, but nonetheless rejects anti-Semitism. Similarly, her standpoint is Christian, while betraying a strong element of humanism, and she espouses conventional notions about the roles of men and women yet focuses on the education of her heroines, often portraying strong, cerebral female characters. Her friend and fellow author Marie von Ebner-Eschenbach praised her ability, notwithstanding the seclusion in which she lived, to recognize and interpret the issues of her day. Similar to many of her realist contemporaries who published in decorous literary periodicals, however, François's work was circumscribed by aesthetic criteria of propriety and restraint; her work's implicit social criticism was only fully appreciated by later generations of commentators.

Interest in Louise von François subsided within a few years of her first novel's rise to prominence, but the Weimar Republic (1917–33), the beginning of which coincided with the celebration of the 100th anniversary of her birth, heralded a revival in her popularity. This was due in part to the patriotic, anti-French stance of *The Last von Reckenburg,* which, together with the qualities of fortitude and resilience embodied in its central character, appealed to the German mind-set in a postdefeat era. The

Insel publishing house brought out a five-volume edition of selected works by François in 1919, and her fiction became the object of increased scholarly attention. In the political period that followed, aspects of François's writing also appeared to match the Nazi emphasis on nationalism and motherhood, and so the fame of *The Last von Reckenburg* was preserved until 1945.

Subsequent reexaminations of François's work have opened up an interesting field of discussion. Although she was not an obvious candidate for analysis by feminist critics because the polemics of her work are often carefully veiled, recent years have seen a number of publications exploring the ambiguity of her writing from sociopolitical and feminist perspectives. Thus, an awareness of François's contribution in general to 19th-century realist literature and, more specifically, to women's writing at a seminal point in the movement toward female emancipation has been enhanced by recent scholarship. François's work has not benefited from the status of belonging to the established literary canon, but it has survived despite this, and it continues to yield stimulating matter for debate.

BARBARA BURNS

Biography

Born in Herzberg on the river Elster, 27 June 1817. Received little formal education, but was an avid reader, especially of history; lost her inheritance (her father was a Prussian military nobleman of Huguenot descent) through the mismanagement of a guardian, and led a frugal existence nursing elderly relatives; frequented Fanny Tarnow's literary salon in Weißenfels; began to publish in middle age. Awarded a pension by the Schiller Foundation in 1880. Died in Weißenfels, 25 September 1893.

Selected Works

Collections

Ausgewählte Novellen, 2 vols., 1868
Erzählungen, 2 vols., 1871
Hellstädt und andere Erzählungen, 3 vols., 1874
Natur und Gnade nebst andere Erzählungen, 3 vols., 1876
Phosphorus Hollunder - Zu Füßen des Monarchen, 1881
Das Jubiläum und andere Erzählungen, 1886
Gesammelte Werke in 5 Bänden, 5 vols., 1918
Gesammelte Werke in 2 Bänden, 2 vols., 1924

Novels

Die letzte Reckenburgerin, 2 vols., 1871; as *The Last von Reckenburg,* translated by S.M. Percival (Mary Joanna Safford), 1887
Frau Erdmuthens Zwillingssöhne, 2 vols., 1873
Die Stufenjahre eines Glücklichen, 2 vols., 1877

Play

Der Posten der Frau: Lustspiel in 5 Aufzügen, 1881

Essay

"Das Leben der George Sand," *Deutsches Museum* 6 (1856)

Nonfiction

Geschichte der preußischen Befreiungskriege in den Jahren 1813–1815: Ein Lesebuch für Schule und Haus, 1874

Further Reading

Fox, Thomas C., *Louise von François and "Die letzte Reckenburgerin": A Feminist Reading,* New York: Lang, 1988
Laane, Tiiu V., "Critical Perspectives of Society in Louise von François's Narratives," *European Studies Journal* 8, no. 2 (1991)
Marx, Leonie, "Der deutsche Frauenroman im 19. Jahrhundert," in *Handbuch des deutschen Romans,* edited by Helmut Koopmann, Düsseldorf: Bagel, 1983
Scheidemann, Uta, *Louise von François: Leben und Werk einer deutschen Erzählerin des 19. Jahrhunderts,* Frankfurt and New York: Lang, 1987
Schuch, Uta, *Die im Schatten stand: Studien zum Werk einer vergessenen Schriftstellerin, Louise von François,* Stockholm: Almqvist and Wiksell International, 1994
Thomas, Lionel, "Louise von François: 'Dichterin von Gottes Gnaden'," *Proceedings of the Leeds Philosophical and Historical Society* 11 (1964)
Worley, Linda Kraus, "The 'Odd' Woman as Heroine in the Fiction of Louise von François," *Women in German Yearbook* 4 (1988)

Frankfurt School

The Frankfurt School is "Frankfurt" in name from the address of the association of left-wing intellectuals that established the privately funded Frankfurt Institute for Social Research in the mid-1920s. A genuine "school," institutionally and intellectually, however, really only came into existence at the time of exile from Nazi Germany, during the American phase of operation of the former Frankfurt Institute's journal publication, the *Zeitschrift für Sozialforschung.* This school, then, was comprised of philosophers, literary critics, sociologists, psychologists, economists, and political scientists—of whom Theodor W. Adorno, Walter Benjamin, Erich Fromm, Max Horkheimer, Otto Kirchheimer, Leo Lowenthal, Herbert Marcuse, Franz Neumann, and Friedrich Pollock are the major figures. Benjamin alone did not make it to the United States on time. But before committing suicide in 1940 near the Spanish border that he could not get across, Benjamin had greatly influenced the school in the mid-1930s, although it largely took the strident form of limits testing versus editorial revisionism. The two essays that resulted from this in-house "dialectical" process, "Das Kunstwerk im Zeitalter seiner technischen Reproduzierbarkeit" ("The Work of Art in the Age of Mechanical Reproduction") and "Über einige Motive in Baudelaire" ("On Some Motifs in Baudelaire"), have proven to be the best-known parts of the legacy of the Frankfurt School. The trauma of Benjamin's parting in the wake of editorial cross fire installed his haunting influence in Adorno's subsequent works.

The geopolitical switch over of exile informs the U.S. work of the Frankfurt School. In retreat from the triumph of National

Socialism, which they had sought to understand and combat while still on location, they turned around to face U.S. mass culture, which they now read as on a continuum with National Socialism. The defeat that exile represented introduced a significant change in the terms of the school's lexicon: the upper hand that Marxist critique had enjoyed while in Germany gave way to what had only been up until that point "on the other hand," namely, psychoanalytic discourse. A phrase that cannot be assigned definitely to any one theorist—some say Adorno, others say Lowenthal—and that thus, in its anonymous circulation as Frankfurt School property, proves the existence of a school of thought, defines now National Socialism, now the U.S. culture industry as "psychoanalysis in reverse." This logo, applied simultaneously to two fronts or coasts, thus summarizes the multiple inside-out shifts that exile had introduced into Frankfurt School thought or, as Horkheimer named his formulation of it in the 1930s, "critical theory."

In the meantime, *critical theory* serves as a catchall term for a whole range of positions associated first with the Frankfurt Institute for Social Research, then with the Frankfurt School in U.S. exile. In name, the concept of critical theory derives from Kantian critical philosophy and from the school's redefinition of Marxism as a critique of ideology. Critique, in the Kantian sense, is an analysis of the conditions of possibility and the limits of rational faculties undertaken by reason itself: assuming a self-reflective or "transcendental" posture, reason analyzes and criticizes itself in the process of its world-constituting "legislating activity." The early mentors of the institute's members—Hans Cornelius, Martin Heidegger, Edmund Husserl, and Georg Lukács—belonged to a reception or revaluation of this Kantian meaning of critique, which had replaced science with cultural and social history as the primary theme of transcendental or critical self-reflection.

The other main source of critical theory, Marxism as ideology critique, refers both to the discovery of systematically concealed interests behind theories and to the explosive confrontation of the true and false dimensions of existing theories of reality. Because critique as self-criticism cannot generate all its terms out of itself, Marxism was required. In the works of Adorno and Benjamin, in particular, we see criticism operate according to the highest standard of self-criticism. In their account, no criticism can occur without reference to the critic's own words and work, not taken as a whole but as enmeshed between the lines of the allegorical accumulation of reformulation that accrues to the "collected work."

Within its redefinition of Marxism as ideology critique, the Frankfurt School made the further theoretical move from the critique of political economy to the critique of instrumental reason. This shift in critical theory responded to a change in the historical context, in which the domination of men over men and over nature was justified not by traditional bourgeois ideals but only by technological efficiency. This triumph of gadget love and the takeover of science and technology by ideology was referred to by Frankfurt School theorists as the "technological veil." Their critique of instrumental reason proceeded as a critique of politics, one that analyzed critically the new fetish of technological rationality in order to uncover the social dynamics fetishistically concealed. More specifically, according to this critique, the political-administrative domain takes the veil to avoid public scrutiny. At this point in time, man's control over nature, no longer a good thing, was seen as integral to the new ideology.

The third main resource that came to stand, last but not least, behind the men of the Frankfurt School was Freudian psychoanalysis. Indeed, the central agon of the leading players of the Frankfurt School (Adorno, Benjamin, and Marcuse) was the attempted coupling of Marxism and psychoanalysis. While their attempt was not new—some sort of merger between Freud's science and Marxism has been contemplated by numerous psychologists and sociologists ever since the end of World War I—the extent and rigor of Freud's coverage in this union in progress remains unparalleled within this genre of marriage of the two discursivities. It is, however, difficult, if not impossible, to imagine a merger with psychoanalysis going through that either would not already belong to Freud's science or would not bear a framing or division of labor between the two parties that would radically curtail or repress the full range of psychoanalytic application. Psychoanalysis is the critical discourse of contagion ("of" in the sense of "about," but also in the sense of "belonging to"). In other words, psychoanalysis, by virtue of always being in session, at the address of transference, gave another kind of site-specific materiality to Frankfurt School self-criticism, one that enabled these thinkers to know and include the location from which their discourse was addressing itself alongside its external topics. This recognition of the return address of these Frankfurt School interpretations can be distinguished from the contextless, history-less, and unidentified flying viewpoint of various kinds of positivism. The perspective that flies above everything that it scientifically qualifies or disqualifies, even or especially above the critical discourse itself, belongs ultimately to God.

Critics of Adorno and Horkheimer's attempt in *Dialektik der Aufklärung* (1944; *Dialectic of Enlightenment*) to rescue the Marxist philosophy of history through the turn to psychoanalysis point to a consequent dehistoricization of the dialectic, which in turn totalized the modern administered state of society doomed to be forever on the defensive. From a Marxian perspective, the Frankfurt School was thus heading itself off at the impasse, fascinated or mesmerized by the point of production of the total state apparatus and therefore unable to promote active or preventive measures in the reception area of effects and resistances. Paul Piccone summarizes how, in his view, the Frankfurt School got stuck doubling the totalization that was to be criticized or dismantled within the transitive dimension of its own discourse:

> Consequently, critical theory . . . retreats to defend particularity, autonomy and nonidentity against an allegedly totally administered society where thinking itself appears as a dispensable luxury. To the extent that the politicization of the productive process and the development of the culture industry lead to the colonization of consciousness, thus systematically ruling out any form of internal opposition, the logic of domination unfolds unchecked toward the even more disastrous manifestations of Auschwitz, the Gulag and Hiroshima. The psychoanalytic theory of socialization and the analysis of the "totally administered society" combine to checkmate all the remaining hopes of social emancipation.

From the psychoanalytic perspective, the Frankfurt School, through this turn inward, inside the psychoanalytic system, was able to raise the issue of state oppression in terms of the psychic resistance to change, the ambivalent character of all identification (which leads to the inside view of consumerism as another state of production), and the projective nature of our own inside out psychic apparatus. According to *Dialectic of Enlightenment,* we are in the first place in a haunted state; we either metabolize or monumentalize unacknowledged death wishes, those premier applications of our omnipotence of thoughts, our narcissism, which hand the force of command or action to the phantom issue of the loss accompanying a wish. The *Dialectic of Enlightenment* is grounded in our disturbed relations with the dead, which is always present tense, a present tension. This analytic grounding alone offers a stay against the claim that Adorno and Horkheimer addressed all of history on one continuum and thereby dehistoricized all contexts. But in addition to the psychoanalytic framing, the title also promotes, if only between the lines, a historical frame for the unconscious and for Freud's theory of the unconscious, the 18th through the 20th centuries, which again situates present tense or the tension of the dialectic right at the intersection between technology and the unconscious.

Secession from the psychoanalytic state of Frankfurt School thought is the diplomatic achievement of or the prerequisite for Jürgen Habermas's claim to be heir to this tradition. Habermas tries to get his tradition of criticism at a discount. He would discount, specifically, the dark side of his Frankfurt School precursors, the side associated with Nietzsche and Freud, in favor of a more active engagement with the details of our state of administration, a state that constitutively anticipates and requires moments of breakthrough or emancipation. Back to Kant? By application only and without mediation? How possible is it to elide the psychoanalytic phase of exile, which at the same time reconfigured the work of the Frankfurt School theorists Adorno, Benjamin, Horkheimer, and Marcuse? Habermas belongs to another Frankfurt School, in some parallel universe, one immediately but symptomatically cleansed of the dark side. Adorno and Horkheimer had held the dread of this darkness up to its light in *Dialectic of Enlightenment,* the light of the eternal or internal flame of repressed mourning.

Freud's understanding of group psychology contributes directly to Benjamin's notion of shock absorption in mass-media culture, to Adorno's highly ambivalent (or negative dialectical) reading of the mass reception of culture, and to Marcuse's identification of utopia with perversion. The psychology of groups, according to Freud, is both a force field of identifications, in which the violence that is a given of identification gets controlled and released, and a reformatting of our relations over and against the responsibilities of coupling and reproduction. In his 1932 *New Introductory Lectures,* Freud addresses the incompatibility of psychoanalysis with the worldviews of philosophy and Marxism. Since psychoanalysis has no worldview of its own, Freud entrusts it to the scientific worldview—the only one, by his account, that admits incompletion. Freud sends the impact of technology (and thus of group psychology) to the head of the classes historicized by Marx: progress and violence hold interchangeable places within a discontinuous shifting of power or fronts around each new media extension of the senses. But the psychoanalytic investment in the psychic and technological apparatus does not simply represent dehistoricization; instead, Freud in this lecture mounts a veritable genealogy of media:

> That does not sound very illuminating, but the first links at least in the chain are clearly recognizable. English politics were based on the security which was guaranteed by the seas that washed her coasts. In the moment at which Blériot flew across the Channel in his aeroplane this protective isolation was breached; and in the night during which (in peace-time and on an exercise) a German Zeppelin cruised over London the war against Germany was no doubt a foregone conclusion.

At the end of this lecture, Freud models a safeguarding of lingering emancipatory promises within the biological dimension, which characterizes the work of those Frankfurt School thinkers who cut the loss of Marxism with the intake of psychoanalysis. Freud raises, like a ghost, the issue of an independent cultural process or development, which, as is also always the case with the "individual" superego, remains largely impervious to social change, in particular change for the better, and in fact influences social factors. Nevertheless, however, this cultural development will on its own over time promote the scientific spirit. The latter point, that the craving for incompletion is part of the programming, represents the outside chance for social progress.

As an allegorical and melancholic discourse in its own right, in Freud's own writing, psychoanalysis gives shelter to the profound ambivalence of Frankfurt School thought. In a letter dated 2 August 1935, Adorno declares to Benjamin that it is always the recent past that comes back as primal, as linked to and separated from us by catastrophe. In their different ways, both Adorno and Benjamin sought to counter this repression of what just came before through some mode of identification that is irreducible to fast-food consumerism. For Adorno, it was the art of the past or, in the present, the contextless, nonreferential art that recalled this past; for Benjamin, it was outright allegorical rescue of artifacts comprising both the destruction and the preservation of the object of rescue. All the members of the Frankfurt School agreed that any attempt at a return to political or economic liberalism would, like all regression, have only monstrous consequences. At the same time, many members concentrated in their work on those aspects of liberal capitalist society that represented way stations in the process or even progress of human emancipation, moments to be remembered or retained as ruins that refer allegorically to a liberated future. While a few theorists of the Frankfurt School thus praised the achievements of liberalism in the sphere of politics and law, others who did not follow this particular move nevertheless produced analogous arguments in the context of art and philosophy. The latter judged the movement from the autonomous though undemocratic cultivation of high culture as an end in itself (*l'art pour l'art*) to mass culture in the same terms that the former members did the changing structure of political compromise. In both cases, what could be observed were the surrender of the last aspects of individual autonomy and the preparation of key elements of the fascist system. Frankfurt critical theory arose in the attempt to account theoretically for the authoritarian state, both in relationship to the liberalism it replaced and in the context of the traumatic experience of the victories of National Socialism. This context was also a contest in which the Frankfurt School's allegorical perspective vied with National Socialism's own melancholic condition, which was bent on bringing back what was past saving, a monstrous reanimation. According to Adorno, for example, fascism releases the subjectivity of destroyed subjects in outbursts of irrational, aggressive projection that are barely contained by a paranoid system. He saw the culture industry (in Weimar Germany as in southern California) repeating the group-psychological manipulations of fascism, in a world completely saturated with media technology with group members responding ultimately only to the commands of the culture industry. In like manner, Adorno sees fascism in charge of a certain insight into mass formation:

> It may well be the secret of fascist propaganda that it simply takes men for what they are: the true children of today's standardized mass culture, largely robbed of autonomy and spontaneity, instead of setting goals the realization of which would transcend the psychological status quo no less than the social one. Fascist propaganda has only to reproduce the existent mentality for its own purposes;—it need not induce change—and the compulsive repetition which is one of its foremost characteristics will be at one with the necessity for this continuous reproduction.

The fit between Freud's group psychology and the mass mobilizations of fascism, like that between a psychotic's delusional formation and Freud's theory of psychosis, can provoke paranoid reactions.

The psychoanalytic and allegorical discourse of Adorno and Benjamin has the quality of a historical act that cannot be completed—in such a manner that its inability to be completed is fundamentally related to its activeness, making it irreducible to fact or to information. Thus, while the systematics of German philosophy (from Kant to Marx) is constantly present in the background of their writing, in a manner that invites generalization and suggests that the substance of their work could have been expressed in the form of relatively systematic argument on the philosophical history of civilization, this stabilizing background operates in the thinkers of the Frankurt School only to the extent that they resolutely disavow the specific theorizing (Kant and Hegel in particular) from which their paradigms arise.

LAURENCE A. RICKELS

See also Theodor W. Adorno; Aestheticization of Politics; Walter Benjamin; Jürgen Habermas

Further Reading

Adorno, Theodor W., "Freudian Theory and the Pattern of Fascist Propaganda," in *The Essential Frankfurt School Reader,* edited by Andrew Arato and Eike Gebhardt, New York: Urizen, 1977; Oxford: Blackwell, 1978

Alford, C. Fred, *Narcissism: Socrates, the Frankfurt School, and Psychoanalytic Theory,* New Haven, Connecticut: Yale University Press, 1988

Buck-Morss, Susan, *The Origin of Negative Dialectics: Theodor W. Adorno, Walter Benjamin, and the Frankfurt Institute,* New York: Free Press, 1977

Freud, Sigmund, *New Introductory Lectures on Psycho-Analysis,* London: Hogarth Press, and New York: Norton, 1933

Jay, Martin, *The Dialectical Imagination: A History of the Frankfurt School and the Institute of Social Research, 1923–1950,* Boston: Little Brown, and London: Heinemann, 1973

Piccone, Paul, "General Introduction," in *The Essential Frankfurt School Reader,* edited by Andrew Arato and Eike Gebhardt, New York: Urizen, 1977; Oxford: Blackwell, 1978

Rickels, Laurence A., *The Case of California,* Baltimore, Maryland: Johns Hopkins University Press, 1991

Rose, Gillian, *The Melancholy Science: An Introduction to the Thought of Theodor W. Adorno,* New York: Columbia University Press, and London: Macmillan, 1978

Whitebook, Joel, *Perversion and Utopia: A Study in Psychoanalysis and Critical Theory,* Cambridge, Massachusetts: MIT Press, 1995

Karl Emil Franzos 1848–1904

Karl Emil Franzos was one of the most prominent German-language writers of Jewish origin in the last quarter of the 19th century. An aggressive and combative personality, he created a good deal of controversy, and his modern reputation is, if anything, even more embattled, but he developed an international standing as a writer of fiction and became a figure of importance as an editor, essayist, and literary scholar.

Franzos was born on 25 October 1848 while his family was hiding from the turmoil of the revolutionary year in Russian Podolia, just across the border from Czortow in the Austrian crown land of Galicia. His boyhood was spent in Czortow, where his father was district physician. There were many Jews in the area, but Franzos was raised aloof from them and grew to be critical of the culture of the *stetl* and especially of Hasidism. His father taught him a love of German language and culture, and he became of all German-Jewish writers perhaps the most militant assimilationist. Otherwise he developed a sympathy for the Ruthenians (western Ukrainians) in the area, whom he regarded as tyrannized by the Russians and the Poles. After his father's death in 1858, the family moved to Czernowitz, the vibrantly multicultural capital of the Bukovina. Beginning in 1867 he began to study law at the universities of Vienna and Graz, where he joined German nationalistic student organizations and got into trouble with the Austrian authorities. He abandoned his studies without taking a degree and subsequently became a free-lance writer.

Franzos was a passionate manuscript collector and achieved a coup with his discovery of the manuscript of Georg Büchner's *Woyzeck,* which he published in the first attempt at a critical edition of Büchner's works in 1879. Franzos's editorial work is not much admired today; he made many transcription errors, beginning with his misreading of the title as *Wozzeck* (taken over by Alban Berg for his opera, 1922), and he also harmed the manuscript by attempting to make it more legible with a chemical treatment. Nevertheless, he is an acknowledged pioneer in the modern discovery of Büchner. Franzos also found and published many letters of Heinrich Heine and wrote numerous essays, including a major contribution to the effort to establish Heine's birthdate. Through Crown Prince Rudolph he became an advisor to Empress Elisabeth, an admirer of Heine, in her effort to collect portraits and manuscripts. He would have liked to repeat his Büchner success by discovering Heine's mysterious memoirs, but this achievement eluded him.

Franzos opened his literary career with a series of novellas, beginning in 1869, that came to be collected under the title of *Die Juden von Barnow* (1877; *The Jews of Barnow*); Barnow is his fictionalization of Czortkow. Many of his stories relate experiences of Jews that are tragic or pathetic partly owing to environmental hostility but more important, in his view, to inadequately achieved emancipation and assimilation. His attitude was most succinctly expressed in the title of his widely read collection, *Aus Halb-Asien* (1876; From Half-Asia), *Half-Asia* being his pejorative term for eastern Europe and its ignorant, brutal Poles and superstitious Hasidic Jews (compared with the light and reason of German culture). This collection was followed by similar ones, such as *Vom Don zur Donau* (1878; From the Don to the Donau) and *Aus der großen Ebene* (1888, From the Great Plain), all subsequently published under the title *Aus Halb-Asien.* He also wrote a series of novels, among them *Moschko von Parma* (1880; Moschko of Parma), an epic of a Jew who tries to become a blacksmith but is drafted into the army, after which he lives in isolation on the periphery of his own community. This was followed by *Ein Kampf ums Recht* (1882; *For the Right*), *Der Präsident* (1884; *The Chief Justice*), *Die Reise nach dem Schicksal* (1885; The Journey toward Fate), and *Die Schatten* (1888; The Shadows).

Franzos worked as a newspaper editor, but in order to achieve editorial independence, he moved to Berlin in 1886 and founded a publishing house for his own works along with his own literary journal, *Deutsche Dichtung,* much of which he wrote himself until his death in 1904. In the journal Franzos shows himself to be distinctly unfriendly to modernism and literary experimentation; literary historians regard it as a conservative, rearguard periodical. His practice of saving postage by printing, with coded addressees, his letters of rejection has not found imitators. Once he sent a message in this manner to Rainer Maria Rilke advising him to write more clearly.

In Berlin he wrote several major novels and stories, including *Judith Trachtenberg* (1891), *Leib Weihnachtskuchen und sein Kind* (1896; Leib Weihnachtskuchen and His Child), and *Der Pojaz* (posthumous, 1905; The Clown). Why Franzos did not publish *Der Pojaz,* arguably his finest novel, during his lifetime is not certain; it was written more than a decade earlier, and a Russian version had appeared in 1895. It has been speculated that he was discouraged and disoriented in his allegiances by the rise of political anti-Semitism in the 1890s. *Der Pojaz* is the story of an orphan from Barnow who strives to emancipate himself from his abusive Orthodox environment, learn German, acquire a literary education, and pursue a career on the stage, at which he fails, eventually dying of consumption. It is a tragic Jewish Bildungsroman, its theme of an unachieved acting vocation evidently in succession to Karl Philipp Moritz's *Anton Reiser* (1785–90) and Goethe's *Wilhelm Meisters Lehrjahre* (1795–96; *Wilhelm Meister's Apprenticeship*).

After his death Franzos tended to be forgotten except as Büchner's editor, but more recently he has attracted considerable attention. Much of it, to be sure, has been hostile; his assimilationist allegiance to German culture has caused him to be charged with blindness, self-hatred, and even racism and anticipations of Nazism. Some of this critique appears overstated and anachronistic, although it is not unfair to regard him as an extremist on the spectrum of German-Jewish opinion of his time. But he was a vigorous and resourceful figure in literary life, a writer of ingenuity, force, and penetrating characterization; his ultimate evaluation may still be outstanding.

JEFFREY L. SAMMONS

Biography

Born in Podolia, Russia, 25 October 1848. Studied law at the University of Vienna, 1867–68, and the University of Graz, 1868–71; married the writer Ottilie Benedikt (pen name F. Ottmer), 1877 (died 1932); correspondent, journalist, and contributor for the *Neue freie Presse,* Vienna, along with numerous other Austrian, Hungarian, and German newspapers and periodicals; refounded and edited the journal *Deutsche Dichtung,* Berlin, 1886–1904. Died in Berlin, 28 January 1904.

Selected Works

Fiction

Aus Halb-Asien: Culturbilder aus Galizien, der Bukowina, Südrußland und Rumänien, 1876; revised, 1878; enlarged and revised, 1889
Die Juden von Barnow, 1877; enlarged, 1880, 1887; as *The Jews of Barnow,* translated by M.W. Macdowall, 1882
Vom Don zur Donau: Neue Culturbilder aus "Halb-Asien," 1878
Moschko von Parma: Geschichte eines jüdischen Soldaten, 1880
Ein Kampf ums Recht, 1882; as *For the Right,* translated by Julie Sutter, 1888
Der Präsident, 1884; as *The Chief Justice,* translated by Miles Corbet, 1890
Tragische Novellen, 1886
Aus der großen Ebene: Neue Kulturbilder aus Halb-Asien, 1888
Judith Trachtenberg, 1891; translated by L.P. and Charlton Thomas Lewis, 1891
Der Wahrheitssucher, 1893
Leib Weihnachtskuchen und sein Kind, 1896
Der alte Damian und andere Geschichten, 1905
Neue Novellen, 1905
Der Pojaz: Eine Geschichte aus dem Osten, 1905

Essays

Konrad Ferdinand Meyer: Ein Vortrag, 1899
Heines Geburtstag, 1900
Deutsche Fahrten: Reise- und Kulturbilder, 1903–5

Edited Works

Buchenblätter: Ein Jahrbuch für deutsche Literaturgestrebungen in der Bukowina, 1870
Georg Büchner, *Sämtliche Werke und handschriftlicher Nachlaß: Erste kritische Gesammt-Ausgabe,* 1879
Deutsches Dichterbuch aus Österreich, 1883
Die Geschichte des Erstlingswerks: Selbstbiographische Aufsätze, 1894

Aus dem neunzehnten Jahrhundert: Briefe und Aufzeichnungen, 1897–1900

Further Reading

Albert, Claudia, and Gregor Blum, "Des Sender Glatteis neue Kleider: Judentum und Assimilation bei Karl Emil Franzos (1848–1904)," *Die Horen* 30, 1, no. 137 (1985)

Bickel, Martha, "Zum Werk von Karl Emil Franzos," in *Juden in der deutschen Literatur: Ein deutsch-israelisches Symposium,* edited by Stéphane Moses and Albrecht Schöne, Frankfurt: Suhrkamp, 1986

Gay, Ruth, "Inventing the Shtetl," *American Scholar* 53 (1984)

Gelber, Mark H., "Ethnic Pluralism and Germanization in the Works of Karl Emil Franzos (1848–1904)," *German Quarterly* 56 (1983)

———, "Karl Emil Franzos," in *Dictionary of Literary Biography,* vol. 129, *Nineteenth-Century German Writers,* edited by James Hardin and Siegfried Mews, Detroit, Michigan and London: Gale Research, 1993

Hubach, Sibylle, *Galizische Träume: Die jüdischen Erzählungen des Karl Emil Franzos,* Stuttgart: Heinz, 1986

Pazi, Margarita, "Karl Emil Franzos' Assimilationsvorstellung und Assimilationserfahrung," in *Conditio Judaica: Judentum, Antisemitismus und deutschsprachige Literatur vom 18. Jahrhundert bis zum Ersten Weltkrieg,* edited by Hans Otto Horch and Horst Denkler, vol. 2, Tübingen: Niemeyer, 1989

Robertson, Ritchie, "Western Observers and Eastern Jews: Kafka, Buber, Franzos," *Modern Language Review* 83 (1988)

Sammons, Jeffrey L., "Rückwirkende Assimilation: Betrachtungen zu den Heine-Studien von Karl Emil Franzos und Gustav Karpeles," in *Von Franzos zu Canetti: Jüdische Autoren aus Österreich: Neue Studien,* edited by Mark H. Gelber, Hans Otto Horch, and Sigurd Paul Scheichl, Tübingen: Niemeyer, 1996

Schwarz, Egon, and Russell A. Berman, "Karl Emil Franzos: Der Pojaz (1905): Aufklärung, Assimilation und ihre realistischen Grenzen," in *Romane und Erzählungen des Bürgerlichen Realismus: Neue Interpretationen,* edited by Horst Denkler, Stuttgart: Reclam, 1980

Sommer, Fred, *"Halb-Asien": German Nationalism and the Eastern European Works of Karl Emil Franzos,* Stuttgart: Heinz, 1984

Steiner, Carl, *Karl Emil Franzos, 1848–1904: Emancipator and Assimilationist,* New York: Lang, 1990

Sigmund Freud 1856–1939

Together with Nietzsche and Marx, Freud belongs to the triumvirate of thinkers who have shaped almost every sphere of intellectual activity in the 20th century. As the so-called founding father of psychoanalysis—a term he first coined in 1896—Freud found followers, then opponents, in Sándor Ferenczi, Wihelm Stekel, Otto Rank, Alfred Adler, and, notoriously, Carl Jung. Freud saw himself as a successor to Copernicus (in cosmology) and Darwin (in biology), dealing a third and decisive psychological blow to the narcissistic pride of humanity.

Freud's work can be divided into four main periods. First, from 1886 to 1895, he moved from medicine to analysis. As his interest shifted from neurology to psychopathology, he began to use hypnotic suggestion and then free association in his practice. His "Entwurf einer Psychologie" (written 1895; known as "Project for a Scientific Psychology") gives a flavor of his early thinking, much of which was developed in correspondence with Wilhelm Fließ. Second, following the publication in 1895 of *Studien über Hysterie* (*Studies on Hysteria*) with Josef Breuer, with whom he soon broke, Freud began to formulate his major concepts, based largely on his own self-analysis. These reflections culminated in *Die Traumdeutung* (1900; *The Interpretation of Dreams*). Third, from 1900 to 1914, Freud elaborated his psychology, producing a theory of childhood sexual development and a series of papers on psychoanalytic technique, concentrating largely on the id, which "contains everything that is inherited, that is present at birth, that is laid down in the constitution—above all, therefore, the instincts which originate from the somatic organization and which find a first psychical expression here in forms unknown to us" (*Abriß der Psychoanalyse* [1938; *An Outline of Psycho-Analysis*]).

In 1908, the first International Congress of Psychoanalysis was held in Salzburg, Austria, and Freud's views began to be challenged from within the analytic community. Finally, in the wake of World War I, Freud extended and reformulated his earlier statements, concentrating now on the development of the ego: "The ego acts as an intermediary between the id and the external world" (*Outline*). Furthermore, Freud showed that psychoanalytic concepts could provide a useful tool for social and cultural critique. In particular, Freud turned his attention to religion and the origins of Judaism, the faith into which he had been born.

As this overview of his intellectual life suggests, Freud frequently revised and reworked his ideas, so that we can identify several different but overlapping models of the unconscious in his work. The first model can be described as the dynamic, in which Freud distinguishes between "primary process" (the mechanisms of condensation, displacement, symbolization, and irrational association, such as one finds in dreams) and "secondary process" (rational and logical thought and common sense). Correspondingly, the second, economic model distinguishes between the "reality principle" (governed by accommodation to external requirements) and the "pleasure principle" (governed by primary wish fulfillment). Both these models underpin Freud's view of the psyche in *The Interpretation of Dreams.* In "Das Unbewußte" (1915; "The Unconscious"), a tripartite structure of the psyche emerges, as Freud distinguishes between unconscious, preconscious, and conscious. This provided the basis for the third, topographical model, which Freud used in 1923 in *Das Ich und das Es* (*The Ego and the Id*): id, superego ("The long period of childhood, during which the growing human being lives in dependence on his parents, leaves behind it as a precipitate the formation in his ego or a special kind of agency in which this parental influence is prolonged" [*Outline*]), and ego. A fourth, cruder, and dualistic model can be found in such texts as *Jenseits des Lustprinzips* (1920; *Beyond the Pleasure Principle*), in which Freud's argument relies on a basic division of cosmic, or "archetypal," forces, consisting of Eros and Thanatos (the "death-drive").

One of the most striking examples of the inconsistency (some would say richness) of Freud's thought is his account of the origins of the ego. In *The Interpretation of Dreams* and *The Ego and the Id,* Freud outlined what has been called a "realist" account of the ego: it is a discrete agency whose cause must be strengthened and defended, or, as Freud put it in *Neue Folge der Vorlegsungen zur Einführung in die Psychoanalyse,* no. 31 (1933; *New Introductory Lectures on Psychoanalysis*), "Wo Es war, soll Ich werden" (Where id was, there ego shall be). By contrast, such works as "Zur Einführung des Narzißmus" (1914; "On Narcissism: An Introduction") and "Trauer und Melancholie" (1915; "Mourning and Melancholia") envisage the ego as a product of "narcissism," a psychic boundary established when the subject takes itself as its own love object. On this account, the subject is, in its very nature, divided.

Why did Freud evolve so many different and thus inconsistent models? Perhaps he did so to enable psychoanalysis to address the wide variety of issues that it did over the various periods of Freud's work. Whereas id psychology in the prewar period examined the problems of the self in its quest to obtain pleasure, avoid displeasure, and to the greatest possible extent, become free, the ego psychology of the postwar years concerned itself with the question of the social adaptation of the self. Likewise, the earlier models of the psyche informed (Freud claimed they were derived from) his theory of dreams and of childhood sexual development.

Freud called dreams the "royal road to a knowledge of the unconscious activities of the mind," taking as his basic principle the idea that "all dreams represent wish-fulfillment." Distinguishing between the "manifest content" of the dream (the images perceived) and its "latent content" (the hidden wish), Freud argued that dreams conceal our desires by means of such mechanisms as condensation (an "overdetermined" image, which signifies several different wishes), displacement (the desire for a forbidden object being expressed through the desire for a permitted one) and, of course, symbols (typically of a phallic nature).

Through his analysis of dreams, Freud developed his theory of the four stages of psychosexual development. According to this theory, the libido (Latin "desire") of the child undergoes a series of fundamental changes, corresponding to the zone of the body to which it is attracted. Initially, the libido of the infant lacks all structure in that the child is "polymorphously perverse." In the first, "oral" stage, the child obtains pleasure from sucking at the breast. In the second, "anal" stage, the child obtains pleasure from offering or withholding its feces. In the third, "phallic" stage, pleasure comes to be located in the genitals. In the case of males, this leads to the "Oedipus complex," in which the infant boy desires his mother but fears castration from the father. (Later, Jung invented an "Electra complex" for females). The resolution of the Oedipus complex closes the third stage and ushers in the fourth stage of latency, in which sexual desire (now psychically structured) awaits physical expression in puberty.

On the other hand, the later models of the psyche underpin Freud's critique of society, powerfully expressed in *Das Unbehagen in der Kultur* (1930; *Civilization and Its Discontents*). His starting point shared much with Schiller, who, in his *Briefe über die ästhetische Erziehung des Menschen* (1795; *Letters on the Aesthetic Education of Man*), had written, "Civilization, far from setting us free, in fact creates, with every power it develops in us, some new need." In this work, Freud diagnosed Western civilization as, in essence, neurotic. For if, on the one hand, the repression of such unconscious forces as Eros (the sexual aspect of libidinal energy) created a sense of unease or anxiety (*Unbehagen*), on the other the de-repression of our primal psychic forces threatened to unleash not only Eros but the death-drive as well. To solve this problem, civilization encourages "sublimation," or the recanalization of instinctual energies to noninstinctual purposes. Thus, far from arguing "make love not war," Freud saw the two activities as inextricably intertwined, and he can with good reason be labeled a pessimist. For, if the first edition ended with the vague hope that Eros might triumph over Thanatos, the 1931 edition ended on an even more ambiguous question mark.

Thus far, it would seem that Freud's oeuvre was largely abstract theorizing. Although much of it is, Freud claimed to find evidence for his theories in the clinical experiences he presented in his case studies. *The Interpretation of Dreams* included such examples as Freud's recollections of bed-wetting, of seeing his mother naked on a train journey (which, Freud believed, lay behind his dream of bird-headed men carrying his mother), his dream of "Irma's injection" (in fact, related to Emma Eckstein, a case that Freud and Fließ handled—and bungled), and a father's dream of a burning child while his son was actually being consumed by the flames next door. The correspondence with Fließ further confirms Freud's reliance on his own childhood experiences:

> A scene occurred to me which in the course of 25 years has occasionally emerged in my conscious memory without my understanding it. My mother was nowhere to be found; I was crying in despair. My brother Philipp . . . unlocked a wardrobe for me, and when I did not find my mother inside it either, I cried even more until, slender and beautiful, she came in through the door. What can this mean? (15 October 1897)

But *Studies on Hysteria* had contained the earliest of the famous case histories, that of "Anna O." (in reality, Bertha Pappenheim, the social worker and feminist), whose treatment Breuer called "the germ cell of the whole of psychoanalysis." Breuer claimed to have helped cure Anna O. by the "talking-cure" (or, as the patient termed it, "chimney-sweeping"), but his "cathartic method" collapsed when she hallucinated the belief that she was pregnant with his child. Perhaps the five most well known case histories are those referred to as "Little Dora," "Little Hans," "Rat Man," "Schreber," and "Wolf Man."

In "Bruchstück einer Hysterie-Analyse" (written 1900–1901, published 1905; "Fragment of an Analysis of a Case of Hysteria"), Freud analyzed a daughter and her relationships to her parents and another married couple, Frau K., with whom Dora's father was having a relationship, and Herr K., who had tried to seduce Dora. Notoriously, Freud argued in this paper that, in analysis, there are times when "'No' signifies the desired 'Yes.'" In "Analyse der Phobie eines fünfjährigen Knaben" (1909; "Analysis of a Phobia in a Five-Year-Old Boy"), Freud found in Hans's phobia about horses confirmation of his theory of infantile sexuality, the Oedipus complex, and castration anxiety. Described by Jung as "the first true insight into the psychology of the child," Freud's reliance on the reports of Hans's father and minimal contact with the actual patient later drew much criticism.

In "Bemerkungen über einen Fall von Zwangsneurose" (written 1907–9, published 1909; "Notes upon a Case of Obsessional Neurosis"), Freud presented the case of a lawyer tormented by various obsessions, including the fear that his father and his beloved would be subjected to a Chinese torture whereby a pot filled with live rats is attached to the buttocks of a victim. Presented as a case history at the first Congress for Psychoanalysis in Salzburg in 1908, it showed, according to Freud, that neurotic obsessions result from the repression of destructive wishes. After reading Denkwürdigkeiten eines Nervenkranken (1903; *Memoirs of My Nervous Illness*), written by a Leipzig judge, Daniel Paul Schreber, Freud wrote "Psychoanalytische Bemerkungen über einen autobiographisch beschriebenen Fall von Paranoia (Dementia paranoides)" (1911; "Psychoanalytic Notes on an Autobiographical Account of a Case of Paranoia [Dementia Paranoides]"), which explained the subject's illness in terms of repressed homosexuality.

Finally, in "Aus der Geschichte einer infantilen Neurose" (written 1914, published 1918; "From the History of an Infantile Neurosis"), Freud presented the case of a wealthy but neurotic Russian aristocrat, Sergei Pankeiev, who had a compulsion for women with large buttocks. From a childhood dream in which the subject saw several large, white wolves sitting in a tree outside his bedroom, Freud deduced that, as a child, his patient had witnessed the "primal scene": the sight of parental intercourse. Treatment of the "Wolf Man" lasted several years, and the extent of its success has been questioned.

Equally, the whole of Freud's work could be regarded as a series of attempts to answer a single question: Given the fact that we are unhappy, and assuming that unhappiness is caused by repression, what is the source of this repression? Concomitantly, this raises the therapeutic question: Can repression be overcome and thus happiness restored? Seen in this light, the claims of psychoanalysis are quite modest, for, as Freud wrote in "Zur Psychotherapie der Hysterie" (1895; "The Psychotherapy of Hysteria"), it tries to "take neurosis and turn it into ordinary misery."

Although educated at university in the mechanistic tradition of Ernst Brücke, Emil Du Bois-Reymond, Hermann von Helmholtz, and Carl Ludwig, Freud apparently arrived at his decision to matriculate in the faculty of medicine after attending a lecture at which Carl Brühl read "On Nature," a piece probably written by Tobler but attributed to Goethe. Indeed, much of Freud's work moves between a determinist acceptance of supposedly ineluctable psychic processes (here the influence of Schopenhauer is unmistakable) and a determined attempt to make the human will prevail. In "Eine Kindheitserinnerung des Leonardo da Vinci" (1910; "Leonardo da Vinci and a Memory of His Childhood"), in which he called Leonardo "the Italian Faust," Freud describes "the transformation of the instinct to investigate back into an enjoyment of life" as fundamental to the tragedy of Faust. In 1930, Freud was awarded the Goethe Prize of the City of Frankfurt, and, aside from the validity of psychoanalysis, the excellence of his prose style has never been in doubt.

Nor can there be any doubt about the extent of Freud's influence, for good or for bad. However, from a literary point of view, Freud deserves above all to be read within the context of Viennese modernism. That cultural period was, to a very great extent, governed by its reception of Nietzsche, whom Freud claimed never to have read properly. Yet the parallels between *Civilization and Its Discontents* and *Zur Genealogie der Moral* (1887; *On the Genealogy of Morals*) are, to say the least, remarkable. Both major and minor Viennese writers, from Hugo von Hofmannsthal, Arthur Schnitzler, and Stefan Zweig to Richard Beer-Hofmann and Leopold von Adrian, deal with such "Freudian" themes as the instability of personal identity and the significance of dreams, to say nothing of the use of sexual motifs in paintings of the Viennese Secession. The importance to his contemporaries of the view expressed in such papers as "Die 'kulturelle' Sexualmoral und die moderne Nervosität" (1908; "'Civilized' Sexual Morality and Modern Nervous Illness") cannot be underestimated. Nevertheless, caution should be taken regarding the extent to which any of their works represent a direct reception of psychoanalytic ideas. For example, Freud said that what Schnitzler had discovered through intuition, he (Freud) had discovered through research. However, Freud was apt to make such remarks in his correspondence.

Of course, Freud's influence extended beyond Vienna, and nearly all the major German-speaking, not to mention European, writers of the 20th century came under it. In "Freud und die Zukunft" (1936; "Freud and the Future"), Thomas Mann painted a portrait of a profound thinker who is nevertheless inclined toward mysticism. When Kafka had finished writing "Das Urteil" (written 1912, published 1916; "The Judgment"), he noted in his diary, "Thoughts about Freud, of course." Although Rilke protested against the debilitating effects of psychoanalysis on poetic creativity and rejected it as a therapy, he accepted its insights into what he called the "inner jungle, the primeval forest within." Rilke's ex-lover, Lou von Salomé, moved in psychoanalytic circles in Vienna and knew Freud well; indeed, her papers on psychoanalysis are notable for their acumen and elegance. Many of Hermann Hesse's fairy stories reveal his interest in psychoanalysis, although he was ultimately more attracted to Jung, one of whose followers analyzed him.

More generally, three developments of Freud's theories are especially noteworthy. First, Herbert Marcuse offered a synthesis of Marx and Freud in *Eros and Civilization* (1955). Marcuse's concept of "surplus repression"—a "cultural" repression found in capitalist society that could be abolished without complete derepression of humankind's destructive energies—offered a political interpretation of Freud that circumvented the latter's pessimistic outlook. Second, Freud's emphasis on the workings of language as conveyers, and betrayers, of desire is central to his importance for literary studies. Despite its title, *Der Witz und seine Beziehung zum Unbewußten* (1905; *Jokes and Their Relation to the Unconscious*) contains little that is amusing, but its insistence on the unconscious strategies revealed by language make the "return to Freud" of Jacques Lacan seem almost inevitable. Finally, Freud's attitude toward femininity is frequently held to be a chief weakness. According to Freud, "the sexual life of the mature woman is a dark continent for psychoanalysis"; he described "the nature of femininity" as a "riddle"; and famously he once asked Marie Bonaparte, "What does woman want?" Yet frequently feminists—both "dutiful daughters," such as Julia Kristeva, and "defiant women," such as Luce Irigaray—have had recourse to Freud (often through Lacan) to argue their cause, and psychoanalytic concepts are frequently mobilized to combat patriarchy.

Aside from the "continental" appropriation of psychoanalysis for theoretical purposes, Freud has been hailed by the American critic Harold Bloom as "prosified Shakespeare" because "Freud's vision of human psychology is derived, not altogether unconsciously, from his reading of the plays." Indeed, Bloom has gone so far as to suggest that "Shakespeare became Freud's hidden authority, the father he would not acknowledge." Finally, Freudianism has given rise to numerous worthy bon mots: Karl Kraus said that psychoanalysis is the disease of which it purports to be the cure, and Adorno claimed that the only thing true about psychoanalysis is its exaggerations.

PAUL BISHOP

See also Vienna

Biography

Born in Freiberg, Moravia, 6 May 1856. Studied at the University of Vienna, 1874–79, M.D., 1881; studied with Jean Charcot, Paris, 1885–86; worked at the Brücke Institute, 1881–82; worked at the General Hospital, Vienna, 1882–85; lecturer, University of Vienna, 1885; started a private practice in Vienna, 1886; visiting lecturer at Clark University, Worcester, Massachusetts, 1909; Huxley Lecturer, University of London, 1931; founder, with others, of the Vienna Psycho-Analytic Society, 1902, the International Psycho-Analytic Congress, 1908, the *Jahrbuch für psychoanalytische und psychopathologische Forschungen,* 1908, the *Internationale Zeitschrift für Psychoanalyse,* 1913, the *Jahrbuch der Psychoanalyse,* and the Internationaler Psychoanalytischer Verlag; emigrated to England, 1938. Awards: Goethe Prize, 1930; numerous honorary doctorates and memberships in professional organizations. Died in London, 23 September 1939.

Selected Works

Collections

Sammlung kleiner Schriften zur Neurosenlehre, 5 vols., 1906–22
Gesammelte Schriften, 12 vols., 1924–34
Collected Papers, 5 vols., 1924–50
The Basic Writings of Sigmund Freud, edited by A.A. Brill, 1938
Gesammelte Werke, 17 vols., 1940–52
The Standard Edition of the Complete Psychological Works of Sigmund Freud, James Strachey, general editor, 1953–74

Nonfiction

Zur Auffassung der Aphasien: Eine kritische Studie, 1891; as *On Aphasia: A Critical Study,* 1953
Studien über Hysterie, with Josef Breuer, 1895;as *Studies on Hysteria,* in *Standard Edition,* vol. 2
Die infantile Cerebrallähmung, 1897; as *Infantile Cerebral Paralysis,* 1968
Die Traumdeutung, 1900; as *The Interpretation of Dreams,* 1913; 8th revised edition, 1954
Zur Psychopathologie des Alltagslebens (Über Vergessen, Versprechen, Vergreifen, Aberglaube und Irrtum), 1904; as *Psychopathology of Everyday Life,* 1914
Der Witz und seine Beziehung zum Unbewußten, 1905; as *Wit in Its Relation to the Unconscious,* 1916; as *Jokes and Their Relation to the Unconscious,* 1960
Drei Abhandlungen zur Sexualtheorie, 1905; as *Three Contributions to the Sexual Theory,* 1910; as *Three Essays on the Theory of Sexuality,* 1949
Der Wahn und die Träume in W. Jensens Gradiva, 1907; as *Delusions and Dreams,* 1917
Selected Papers on Hysteria and Other Psychoneuroses, 1909
Über Psychoanalyse: Fünf Vorlesungen gehalten zur zwanzigjährigen Gründungsfeier der Clark University in Worcester, Massachusetts, September 1909, 1910; as "The Origin and Development of Psychoanalysis," in *Lectures and Addresses Delivered before the Departments of Psychology and Pedagogy in Celebration of the Twentieth Anniversary of the Opening of Clark University,* 1910
Eine Kinderheitserinnerung des Leonardo da Vinci, 1910; as *Leonardo da Vinci: A Psychosexual Study of Infantile Reminiscence,* 1916
Über den Traum, 1911; as *On Dreams,* 1914
Totem und Tabu: Über einige Übereinstimmungen im Seelenleben der Wilden und der Neurotiker, 1913; as *Totem and Taboo: Resemblances between the Psychic Drives of Savages and Neurotics,* 1917
"Zeitgemässes über Krieg und Tod," in *Imago* (Vienna), 4 (1915); as *Reflections on War and Death,* 1918; as "Thoughts for the Times on War and Death," in *Collected Papers,* vol. 4
Vorlesungen zur Einführung in die Psychoanalyse, 3 vols., 1916; as *A General Introduction to Psycho-analysis,* 1920; as *Introductory Lectures on Psycho-Analysis,* 1922
Jenseits des Lustprinzips, 1920; as *Beyond the Pleasure Principle,* 1922
Massenpsychologie und Ich-Analyse, 1921; as *Group Psychology and the Analysis of the Ego,* 1922
Das Ich und das Es, 1923; as *The Ego and the Id,* 1927
Eine Teufelsneurose im siebzehnten Jahrhundert, 1924; as "A Neurosis of Demoniacal Posession in the Seventeenth Century," in *Collected Papers,* vol. 4
Zur Technik der Psychoanalyse und zur Metapsychologie, 1924; translated in *Standard Edition*
Psychoanalytische Studien an Werken der Dichtung und Kunst, 1924; translated in *Standard Edition*
Kleine Beiträge zur Traumlehre, 1925; translated in *Standard Edition*
Hemmung, Symptom und Angst, 1926; as *Inhibition, Symptom and Anxiety,* 1927; as *Inhibitions, Symptoms and Anxiety,* 1936
Die Frage der Laienanalyse: Underredung mit einem Unparteiischen, 1926; as *The Problem of Lay-Analysis,* 1927; as *The Question of Lay-Analysis: An Introduction to Psycho-Analysis,* 1947
Die Zukunft einer Illusion, 1927; as *The Future of an Illusion,* 1928
Das Unbehagen in der Kultur, 1930; as *Civilization and Its Discontents,* 1930
Theoretische Schriften, 1931; translated in *Standard Edition*
Schriften zur Neurosenlehre und zur psychoanalytischen Technik (1913–1926), 1931; translated in *Standard Edition*
Kleine Schriften zur Sexualtheorie und zur Traumlehre, 1931; translated in *Standard Edition*
Vier psychoanalytische Krankengeschichten, 1932; translated in *Standard Edition*
Neue Folge der Vorlesungen zur Einführung in die Psychoanalyse, 1933; as *New Introductory Lectures on Psycho-Analysis,* 1933
Why War? with Albert Einstein, 1933
Der Mann Moses und de monotheistiche Religion: Drei Abhandlungen, 1939; as *Moses and Montheism,* 1939
Abriß derPsychoanalyse, 1940; as *An Outline of Psycho-Analysis,* 1949

Other

Selbstdarstellungen, 1925; as "An Autobiographical Study," in *The Problem of Lay-Analysis,* 1927; as *An Autobiographical Study,* 1935
The Origins of Psycho-Analysis: Letters to Wilhelm Fliess, Drafts and Notes, 1889–1902, edited by Anna Freud et al., 1954
Briefe 1873–1939, edited by E.L. Freud, 1960; as *Letters of Sigmund Freud 1873–1939,* 1961
Sigmund Freud/Oskar Pfister: Briefe 1909 bis 1939, edited by E.L. Freud and H. Meng, 1963; as *Psychoanalysis and Faith: Dialogues with the Reverend Oskar Pfister,* 1963

Sigmund Freud/Karl Abraham: Briefe 1907 bis 1926, edited by H.C. Abraham and E.L. Freud, 1965; as *A Psychoanalytic Dialogue: The Letters of Sigmund Freud and Karl Abraham, 1907–1926,* 1965
Sigmund Freud/Lou Andreas-Salomé, Briefwechsel, edited by E. Pfeiffer, 1966; as *Sigmund Freud and Lou Andreas-Salomé, Letters,* 1972
Briefwechsel von Sigmund Freud und Arnold Zweig, 1927–1939, edited by E.L. Freud, 1968; as *The Letters of Sigmund Freud and Arnold Zweig, 1927–1939,* 1970
Briefwechsel, with Carl Jung, edited by William McGuire and Wolfgang Sauerländer, 1974; as *The Freud/Jung Letters: The Correspondence between Sigmund Freud and C.G. Jung,* 1974
The Complete Letters of Sigmund Freud to Wilhelm Fliess, 1887–1904, edited by Jeffrey Moussaieff Masson, 1985

Further Reading

Bloom, Harold, "Freud: A Shakespearean Reading," in *The Western Canon,* New York: Harcourt Brace, and London: Macmillan, 1994
Jones, Ernest, *Sigmund Freud: Life and Work,* New York: Basic Books, 1953–57
Ellenberger, Henri, *The Discovery of the Unconscious: The History and Evolution of Dynamic Psychiatry,* New York: Basic Books, and London: Fontana, 1970
Grosz, Elizabeth A., *Jacques Lacan: A Feminist Introduction,* London and New York: Routledge, 1990
Horden, Peregrine, editor, *Freud and the Humanities,* London: Duckworth, and New York: St. Martin's Press, 1985
Mahony, Patrick J., *Freud as a Writer,* New York: International Universities Press, 1982; expanded edition, New Haven, Connecticut and London: Yale University Press, 1987
Marcus, Steven, *Freud and the Culture of Psychoanalysis,* New York and London: Norton, 1984
Mitchell, Juliet, *Psychoanalysis and Feminism,* London: Lane, 1974
Storr, Anthony, *Freud,* Oxford and New York: Oxford University Press, 1989
Sulloway, Frank, *Freud, Biologist of the Mind,* Cambridge, Massachusetts and London: Harvard University Press, 1979
Wright, Elizabeth, *Psychoanalytic Criticism: Theory in Practice,* London and New York: Methuen, 1984

Gustav Freytag 1816–1895

In the second half of the 19th century, a new generation of poets and writers emerged that was dedicated to the movement of realism. After the members of the Junges Deutschland (Young Germany) had failed to translate the revolutions of 1830 and 1848 into a democratic system, their successors increasingly turned to the material world surrounding them and adjusted to the new economic and political realities. Although Karl Marx and Ferdinand Lasalle, among others, continued to fight for their socialist theories, August Comte's positivism and Charles Darwin's evolutionary theory exerted the greatest influence on German intellectual life. The previous idealism supported by the followers of Hegel especially lost ground and was replaced by scientific and economic concepts. Beginning in the late 1840s, Gustav Freytag developed into one of the leading representatives of German literature who reflected upon these profound changes. His fundamental conviction was based on the belief that the bourgeoisie was destined to lead German society in the future. In his editorial to *Die Grenzboten,* he formulated, together with Julian Schmidt, that they would oppose dictatorial government, reject the ignorance of the masses, support education and science, and champion law and order. Enthusiastically advocating the Prussian monarchy from a liberal point of view, he argued for an authoritarian government that could fight the chaos that the proletarians could bring upon them through their revolutionary ideas. In his many historical novels, the author emphasized the responsibility of the individual for the well-being of society, and of subordinating one's own will under the collective good.

Freytag entertained a particular liking for the drama as a literary genre, and in his early years he composed several plays, including *Die Brautfahrt* (1844); *Der junge Gelehrte* (1847); *Die Valentine* (1847); *Graf Waldemar* (1850); the highly successful comedy *Die Journalisten* (1854), with its satirical treatment of the world of newspapers and its sharp criticism of the social corruption of society; and, finally, the poetic tragedy *Die Fabier* (1859), which led to a theoretical treatment in his *Technik des Dramas* (1863).

Nevertheless, his true literary abilities rested with the novel. In 1855, Freytag published the enormously popular *Soll und Haben* (*Debit and Credit*), in which he glorified the value of work as the highest German virtue and commercialism as the ideal profession for the bourgeoisie. Girded by sophisticated humor and witticism, broad moral statements, and a clear preference for the social middle class, Freytag's book captured the fascination of the bourgeois reading audience far into the 20th century, and it was reprinted over and over again until 1965, when it disappeared abruptly from the German book market. Fundamental changes in the socioeconomic and political conditions by then suddenly made Freytag appear an antiquated writer who had no longer anything to say to the modern generation. In the late 1970s, however, new editions appeared, and plans were made to create a film out of it. Since the early 1990s, almost all of the major texts by Freytag are available again in reprints or modern editions, which reflects a conservative reorientation of the reading public.

In *Debit and Credit* the protagonist Anton Wohlfahrt quickly moves up from being an apprentice in the trading house of T.O. Schröter to being its co-owner after having married the owner's daughter. In this novel, work for the company emerges as the highest ideal; it cannot be compensated with money, but it is considered a privilege. The individual has to subordinate all his feelings and desires to the demands of the company, which needs to survive in a tough global competition. The merchant, although not the producer of the wares that he buys and sells, makes the international exchange of goods possible by following the laws of capitalism and transforming these goods into fetishes that determine the behavior and thinking of the protagonists. At the same time, the novel subscribes to imperialistic ideas, projects highly negative images of Poland and its people, ruthlessly denigrates the Jews as cheaters and liars, and even ridicules the aristocrats as incompetent in business and economics. Freytag deliberately ignored the lower classes or included them only as loyal and humble workers with no particular needs and wishes for themselves.

Whereas Adalbert Stifter harshly criticized *Debit and Credit* as mediocre literary stuff for lending libraries, Theodor Fontane, among many other critics, praised Freytag's novel as the masterpiece of German Realism. Similarly, Berthold Auerbach, Felix Dahn, Wilhelm Dilthey, and Julian Schmidt gave Freytag's novel their highest accolades, and it proved to be an extraordinary best-seller for the next 100 years. To some extent Freytag's subsequent novel, *Die verlorene Handschrift* (1864; *The Lost Manuscript*), received similar praise, although it focuses on intellectuals and their interaction with the aristocracy. Between 1859 and 1867, Freytag began publishing his famous *Bilder aus der deutschen Vergangenheit,* narrative reflections upon German history that the author had thoroughly researched in archival studies. Beginning in 1872, Freytag composed his cycle of romances, *Die Ahnen,* in which he portrayed the historical development of Germany from the fourth century down to the Revolution of 1848, linking each epoch with the following one through family connections. These novels are somewhat tinged by a professorial didacticism and detailed explanations that are typical of late 19th-century historicism. In 1887, Freytag published his memoirs, *Erinnerungen aus meinem Leben* (*Reminiscences of My Life*), and in 1887, a volume of his critical essays appeared in print, followed by his collected works in 1888. In sum, Freytag portrayed in his texts the emerging bourgeoisie through his idealization of commerce and strict class structures, and his strong admiration for the Prussian state and German nationalism.

ALBRECHT CLASSEN

Biography

Born in Kreuzburg, Silesia (now Kluczbork, Poland), 13 July 1816. Studied German philology at the University of Breslau (now Wrocław), beginning 1835; moved to Berlin, where he studied with the famous philologist Karl Lachmann, 1838; Ph.D., 1839; taught at the University of Breslau, 1839–44; appointed, together with Julian Schmidt, as editor of the weekly *Die Grenzboten,* a nationalist literary paper, 1848; appointed court councillor by Duke Ernest of Sachsen-Coburg-Gotha, 1854; won election as a member of the North German Parliament representing the nationl liberal party of Thuringia, 1867; appointed reporter during the Franco-Prussian war by the Prussian crown prince, 1870; worked as a writer after 1879. Died in Wiesbaden, 1895.

Selected Works

Collections

Gesammelte Werke, 22 vols., 1887–88

Plays

Die Brautfahrt; oder, Kunz von der Rosen, 1844
Der junge Gelehrte, 1847
Die Valentine, 1847
Graf Waldemar, 1850
Die Journalisten, 1854; as *The Journalists,* translated by Herbert Leslie, 1904
Die Fabier, 1859

Novels

Soll und Haben, 3 vols., 1855; as *Debit and Credit,* translated by "Mrs. Malcolm," 1857; translated by "L.L.C.," 1858
Die verlorene Handschrift, 1864; as *The Lost Manuscript,* 1890
Die Ahnen, 6 vols., 1873–81

Nonfiction

Bilder aus der deutschen Vergangenheit, 5 vols., 1859–67
Die Technik des Dramas, 1863; as *Freytag's Technique of the Drama,* translated by Elias J. MacEwan, 1894
Erinnerungen aus meinem Leben, 1887; as *Reminiscences of My Life,* translated by Katharine Chetwynd, 1890

Further Reading

Aust, Hugo, *Literatur des Realismus,* Stuttgart: Metzler, 1977
Brinkmann, Richard, *Wirklichkeit und Illusion: Studien über Gehalt und Grenzen des Begriffs Realismus für die erzählende Dichtung des 19. Jahrhunderts,* Tübingen: Niemeyer, 1957; 3rd edition, 1977
Büchler-Hauschild, Gabriele, *Erzählte Arbeit: Gustav Freytag und die soziale Prosa des Vor- und Nachmärz,* Paderborn: Schöningh, 1987
Dove, Alfred, "Freytag, Gustav," in *Allgemeine Deutsche Biographie,* vol. 48, Berlin: Duncker und Humblot, 1904; reprint, 1971
Gubser, Martin, *Literarischer Antisemitismus: Untersuchungen zu Gustav Freytag und anderen bürgerlichen Schriftstellern des 19. Jahrhunderts,* Göttingen: Wallstein, 1998
Kienzle, Michael, *Der Erfolgsroman: Zur Kritik seiner poetischen Ökonomie bei Gustav Freytag und Eugenie Marlitt,* Stuttgart: Metzler, 1975
Klubertanz, Alex, *Ruinen voll Gefühl und Härte: Historisches Erzählen im 19. Jahrhundert zwischen glücklosen Liebhabern und machtvollen Erzählern,* Aachen: Shaker, 1992
Preisendanz, Wolfgang, *Wege des Realismus: Zur Poetik und Erzählkunst im 19. Jahrhundert,* Munich: Fink, 1977
Leppla, Rupprecht, *Gustav Freytag 1816–1895: Leben und Werk, Ausstellung,* Nuremberg: Stadtbibliothek, 1969
Schneider, Michael, *Geschichte als Gestalt: Formen der Wirklichkeit und Wirklichkeit der Form in Gustav Freytags Roman "Soll und Haben,"* Stuttgart: Heinz, 1981
Thomas, Lionel, *Bourgeois Attitudes: Gustav Freytag's Novels of Life in Nineteenth-Century Germany,* Leeds: Maney, 1973
Wirschem, Karin, *Die Suche des bürgerlichen Individuums nach seiner Bestimmung: Analyse und Begriff des Bildungsromans, erarbeitet am Beispiel von Wilhelm Raabes "Hungerpastor" und Gustav Freytags "Soll und Haben,"* Frankfurt and New York: Lang, 1986

Erich Fried 1921–1988

Erich Fried's significance for 20th-century literature lies particularly in his lyrical production, which is destined to have a lasting influence. As Walter Hinck pointed out in 1983, "It may be asserted that, with the exception of Bertolt Brecht, there is no other post-war poet with such a swarm of imitators as Erich Fried" (Hinck). This view was confirmed by the leading West German critic Marcel Reich-Ranicki, who noted "that no contemporary German lyric poet is imitated with such regularity as Erich Fried" (Reich-Ranicki).

Fried's lyrical production may be divided into three phases. The work of the early years, spent in exile in wartime London, is distinguished by traditional rhyme and meter coupled with a clearly political, and, at times, propagandistic content, which itself reflected Fried's activities in left-wing refugee groups. The poetry of these years thematizes aspects of the war and was obviously addressed to a specific refugee audience. The formal aspects of Fried's work substantiate the frequent assertion that exile literature of this period displays very conservative formal elements in contrast to the literary developments within the Weimar Republic. Fried, however, was still a young writer and his recourse to traditional forms such as the sonnet, folk songs, nursery rhymes, and biblical themes may be explained simply by the fact that he was still finding his literary feet. Fried's poetry volumes *Deutschland* (1944; Germany) and *Österreich* (1946; Austria) were well received by the exile press, and Fried was perceived as a promising young writer.

The second phase is characterized by the solipsistic and hermetic nature of Fried's work. In collections such as *Gedichte* (1958; Poems) and *Reich der Steine* (1963; Realm of Stones), complex imagery is linked to self-indulgent experiments with half rhymes and "serious puns"; the form frequently obscures the content to such a degree as to baffle the reader. The poems are marked by the poet's sense of sorrow about the Holocaust and by a vague feeling of unease at postwar political developments. Similarly, Fried's only novel, *Ein Soldat und ein Mädchen* (1960; A Soldier and a Girl), shows the writer attempting to come to terms with events in recent German history and provides a psychological exploration of human brutality. Fried was largely out of step with developments in postwar Germany, where the literary *Kahlschlag* marked much of the poetry being written. Swollen metaphors and similes and the use of educated classical and biblical references were abandoned by the late 1950s, as Bertolt Brecht's poetry became increasingly influential.

The final phase in the poet's work was inaugurated by the appearance of *Warngedichte* (1964; Warning Poems), in which the often esoteric nature of the earlier poems was replaced by a clarity and economy reminiscent of Brecht. The restraint Fried exercised means that the puns are more effective, particularly with the addition of concrete political subject matter. In *. . . und Vietnam und . . .* (1966; . . . and Vietnam and . . .), he combines skillful punning with criticism of the Vietnam War. In the controversial publication *Höre, Israel!* (1974; Hear, O Israel!), Fried attacks Zionist expansionism and draws parallels between Israel and Nazi Germany. Fried, himself a Jew and in exile, felt that the victims of yesterday had now become today's persecutors. Fried's position on the political left also made him an unwelcome commentator on developments in the Federal Republic, such as in *So kam ich unter die Deutschen* (1977; Thus I Found Myself among the Germans), which deals with the events surrounding the Baader-Meinhof terrorists. Fried's notion of politically committed poetry was challenged by other members of Gruppe 47, including Günter Grass, whose poem "Irgendwas machen" questions the integrity of Fried's protest literature and its constant search for new political engagements. In the 1970s and 1980s, Fried became extremely productive, publishing up to three volumes of poetry a year. He dealt with subjects as varied as Third World poverty, the situation in Nicaragua or Austria, and the arms race or the dogmatism of the German left wing. Additionally, Fried dwelt increasingly on the National Socialist past. This preoccupation is evident in titles such as *Gegen das Vergessen* (1987; Lest We Forget) and *Unverwundenes* (1988; Not Yet Overcome). While battling against cancer late in his life, Fried also thematized illness and death.

In his prose, Fried employs techniques of word association and punning but does so with less success than in his poetry. The writer's reputation as a political poet was equaled by his renown as a translator of English literature, including works by T.S. Eliot, Dylan Thomas, and William Shakespeare. His experience of exile not only made him an outsider capable of criticizing Germany and his native Austria, but also the ideal intermediary between two linguistic communities. Critical response to Fried's work has been mixed and, at times, has been determined by political rather than aesthetic criteria. Fried has been cited as having written some of the best and some of the worst German poetry. Despite his staggering productivity, there has been a paucity of secondary literature until recently.

Since his involvement with the student protest movement in the 1960s, Fried has enjoyed the support of an enthusiastic younger audience, and he may be credited with generating new interest in poetry, a genre that has traditionally been associated with the sphere of a cultural elite. Fried's work may almost certainly be found in the sparsely stocked poetry sections of German bookshops, and publications such as *Liebesgedichte* (1979; Love Poems) have sold in the hundreds of thousands. Some poems such as "Es ist was es ist" have struck a popular chord and are nigh endemic: they regularly appear daubed on walls or are cited in the lonely hearts columns of German newspapers. Formal recognition came late in Fried's life with the award of the prestigious Georg-Büchner-Preis (1987). Fried's literary and political importance was evidenced by the flurry of obituaries that appeared in 1988, by which time he had become one of the most prominent poets writing in the German language. In 1998, publishers such as Wagenbach and Suhrkamp are planning to bring out publications, and events have been organized to mark the anniversary of Fried's death.

STEVEN W. LAWRIE

Biography

Born in Vienna, Austria, 6 May 1921. Emigrated as Jewish refugee to London, 1938; worked variously as chemist, librarian, and editor; from 1952–68, worked as a program assistant and commentator for the BBC German Service; translated Greek, English, and American literature; lived as a freelance writer in London. Fördergabe des Schiller—Gedächtnispreises, 1965; International Publishers' Prize, 1977; Austrian

Würdigungspreis für Literatur, 1973; Bremer Literaturpreis, 1983; Ossietzky-Medaille, 1986; Georg Büchner Prize, 1987. Died in Baden-Baden, Germany, 22 November 1988.

Selected Works

Collections

Zeitfragen und Überlegungen, 1984
Fall ins wort: Ausgewählte Gedichte, 1944 bis 1983, 1985
Von bis nach Seit: Gedichte, 1945–58, 1985
Frühe Gedichte, 1986
Gründe: Gesammelte Gedichte, 1989
Einbruch der Wirklichkeit: Verstreute Gedichte 1927–1988, 1991
Gesammelte Werke, 1993
Erich Fried erzählt: Die schönsten Geschichten, 1997

Fiction

They Fight in the Dark: The Story of Austria's Youth, 1944
Ein Soldat und ein Mädchen: Roman, 1960
Kinder und Narren: Prosa, 1965; as *Children and Fools*, translated by Martin Chalmers, 1992
Fast alles Mögliche: Wahre Geschichten und gültige Lügen, 1975
Das Mißverständnis, 1982
Angst und Trost: Erzählungen und Gedichte über Juden und Nazis, 1983
Das Unmaß aller Dinge: 35 Erzählungen, 1982

Nonfiction

"Anmerkungen zu Verhaltensmustern," in *Intellektuelle und Sozialismus*, 1968
Und nicht taub und stumpf werden: Unrecht, Widerstand und Protest: Reden, Polemiken, Gedichte, 1984
Die da reden gegen Vernichtung: Psychologie, bildende Kunst und Dichtung gegen den Krieg, 1986
Mitunter sogar lachen: Zwischenfälle und Erinnerungen, 1986
Nicht verdrängen—nicht gewöhnen: Texte zum Thema Österreich, 1987
Gedanken in und an Deutschland, 1988
Anfragen und Nachreden: Politische Texte, 1994
Die Muse hat Kanten: Aufsätze und Reden zur Literatur, 1995

Drama

Izanagi und Izanami, 1960
Die Expedition, 1962
Indizienbeweise, 1966
Arden muß sterben: Eine Oper vom Tod des reichen Arden von Faversham in zwei Akten, 1967; as *Arden Must Die*, translated by Geoffrey Skelton, 1967
... und alle seine Mörder ...: Ein Schauspiel, 1984

Poetry

Deutschland: Gedichte, 1944
Österreich: Gedichte, 1946
Gedichte, 1958
Reich der Steine: Zyklische Gedichte, 1963
Überlegungen: Gedichte, 1964
Warngedichte, 1964
... und Vietnam und ...: 41 Gedichte, 1966
Anfechtungen: 50 Gedichte, 1967
Zeitfragen: Gedichte, 1967
Befreiung von der Flucht: Gedichte und Gegengedichte, 1968
Die Beine der größeren Lügen: 51 Gedichte, 1969
Unter Nebenfeinden: 50 Gedichte, 1970
Aufforderung zur Unruhe, 1972
Die Freiheit den Mund aufzumachen: 48 Gedichte, 1972
Gegengift: 49 Gedichte und ein Zyklus, 1974
Höre, Israel! 1974
So kam ich unter die Deutschen, 1977
Die bunten Getüme: 70 Gedichte, 1978
100 Gedichte ohne Vaterland, 1978; as *100 Poems without a Country*, translated by Stuart Hood, 1978
Liebesgedichte, 1979
Lebensschatten: Gedichte, 1981
Zur Zeit und zur Unzeit: Gedichte, 1981
Das Nahe suchen, 1982
Es ist was es ist: Gedichte, 1983
Beunruhigungen: Gedichte, 1984
Um Klarheit: Gedichte gegen das Vergessen, 1985
In die Sinne einradiert, 1985
Frühe Gedichte, 1986
Wächst das Rettende auch? Gedichte für den Frieden, 1986
Am Rand unserer Lebenszeit, 1987
Gegen das Vergessen, 1987
Vorübungen für Wunder, 1987
Unverwundenes: Liebe, Trauer, Widersprüche, 1988
Einblicke—Durchblicke: Fundstücke und Werkstattberichte aus dem Nachlaß von Erich Fried, 1993

Further Reading

Arnold, Heinz Ludwig, editor, *Erich Fried*, Munich: Edition Text und Kritik, 1986
Fried-Boswell, Catherine, and Volker Kaukoreit, editors, *Erich Fried: Ein Leben in Bildern und Geschichten*, Berlin: Wagenbach, 1996
Glenn, Jerry, "Erich Fried," in *Major Figures of Contemporary Austrian Literature*, edited by Donald G. Daviau, New York: Lang, 1987
Goodbody, Axel, "Erich Fried—German, Jew, British, and Socialist: The Composite Identity of an Austrian Emigré," in *From High Priests to Desecrators: Contemporary Austrian Writers*, edited by Ricarda Schmidt and Moray McGowan, Sheffield: Sheffield Academic Press, 1993
Grass, Günter, *Gesammelte Gedichte*, Darmstadt and Neuwied: Luchterhand, 1971; 8th edition, 1984
Heimann, Angelika, *"Bless thee! Thou art translated": Erich Fried als Übersetzer moderner englischsprachiger Lyrik*, Amsterdam: Grüner, 1987
Hinck, Walter, "Erich Fried: Die Freiheit den Mund aufzumachen," in *Germanistik als Literaturkritik: Zur Gegenwartsliteratur*, Frankfurt: Suhrkamp, 1983
Kane, Martin, "From Solipsism to Engagement: The Development of Erich Fried as a Political Poet," *Forum for Modern Language Studies* 21, no. 21 (1985)
Kaukoreit, Volker, *Vom Exil bis zum Protest gegen den Krieg in Vietnam: Frühe Stationen des Lyrikers Erich Fried, Werk und Biographie 1938–1966*, Darmstadt: Häusser, 1991
Lampe, Gerhard, *"Ich will mich erinnern an alles was man vergißt": Erich Fried, Biographie und Werk*, Cologne: Bund, 1989
Lawrie, Steven W., *Erich Fried: A Writer without a Country*, New York: Lang, 1996
Reich-Ranicki, Marcel, "Die Leiden des Dichters Erich Fried," *Frankfurter Allgemeine Zeitung*, no. 19, 23 January 1982
Schlund, Joern, editor, *"Habe Angst vor dem, der keine Zweifel kennt": Gespräche mit Erich Fried*, Basel: Z-Verlag, 1988
Wolff, Rudolf, editor, *Erich Fried: Gespräche und Kritiken*, Bonn: Bouvier, 1986

Max Frisch 1911–1991

The creative works of Max Frisch show a remarkable continuity from his earliest publications in the 1930s. The conflict between individual self-perception and the role imposed by society, the difficulty of decision making in interpersonal relationships, the burden of a sense of guilt and personal inadequacy that increase as life progresses, and a preoccupation with death—these themes, seen from a male perspective, are featured in his novels and plays. What Frisch called his *Zeitgenossenschaft* (being contemporary), his engagement as a writer with the issues of the age, is more manifest in his diaries and in his speeches and essays, where he confronts directly topics such as individual moral responsibility in war, the threat posed by the atomic bomb, and the encroachments of political and economic power on democratic rights and structures. As one of the most famous German-Swiss writers, he became a figure of moral authority for younger writers in Switzerland, but his attacks on aspects of Swiss life did not endear him to the general public there.

Frisch had the good fortune to have his first plays performed at the Zurich Schauspielhaus, which had acquired a prestigious reputation during World War II as the only major German-language stage not under Nazi control. *Nun singen sie wieder: Versuch eines Requiems* (1946; *Now They Sing Again*) and *Als der Krieg zu Ende war* (1949; *When the War Was Over*) are two of his first plays. They deal, respectively, with the shooting of hostages by German troops and the love of a German woman for a Russian officer in occupied Germany; both plays present a generalized view of human bestiality and prejudice that relativizes the historical situation they depict. *Graf Öderland* (1951; *Count Oederland*) and *Don Juan; oder, Die Liebe zur Geometrie* (1953; *Don Juan; or, The Love of Geometry*) examine bourgeois life in relation to individual longing that seeks to escape the restrictions of a social role that is perceived as imposed and limiting.

Tagebuch 1946–1949 (1950; *Sketchbook 1946–1949*) marked the start of Frisch's long association with the Frankfurt publishing house Suhrkamp, which was to play an important role in publishing the work of younger German-Swiss writers from the 1960s onward. *Sketchbook 1946–1949,* containing autobiographical reflections on art and politics, stories, anecdotes, and dramatic fragments, many of which were subsequently developed as individual works, defined both the political and moral stance that Frisch never abandoned. The work also established this form—an assemblage of sketches that yields meaning in the manner of a mosaic—as his preferred literary vehicle. Further, this first diary formulated the precept to which many of his literary themes relate: "Du sollst dir kein Bildnis machen" (You should not make an image unto yourself).

The novel *Stiller* (1954; *I'm Not Stiller*) depicts the failure of a minor sculptor, Anatol Ludwig Stiller, to come to terms with himself as either an artist or a man. Persuaded of his ineffectualness on both counts, Stiller has departed clandestinely from Switzerland in early 1946, and he is arrested when he returns with a false identity seven years later. The greater part of the novel consists of the notebooks, compiled by Stiller in prison, narrating the past and present lives of himself and three others who play crucial roles in his life. The figure of the artist serves to examine *Reproduktion,* the term in the novel for the way in which literature and the visual image determine both individual experience and expectations about behavior. Switzerland, trapped in endlessly recurring images of the past, becomes a fitting background for the fate of the artist who is insufficiently talented to break with the mass-produced stereotypes of the modern world. The problem of personal identity addressed by *I'm Not Stiller* related to the uncertainties foregrounded by French existentialism in the 1950s, and the novel's formal achievement established Frisch as a European novelist.

Homo Faber (1957; *Homo Faber*), a novel also depicting waste and death within a pattern of stereotyped thinking, complements *I'm Not Stiller.* The sculptor Stiller, in a manner that was to have considerable influence on attitudes in the German-Swiss novel after 1954, rejects inherited modes of perception but ultimately founders because he can himself establish no role; the engineer Faber, contemptuous of previous human knowledge, causes tragedy by adapting his perceptions and behavior to the role that he has cast for himself as a modern man who has no use for unquantifiable entities such as emotion. Rigidly ensconced in the world of technology, Faber is responsible, actually and symbolically, for the death of his daughter. Thus, Frisch completes the examination, begun with the character of the intellectual in the play *Die chinesiche Mauer* (1947; revised version, 1955; translated as *The Chinese Wall* and *The Great Wall of China*), of the role of three representative figures in modern society: the intellectual, the creative artist, and the technologist. All are characterized by inadequacy: the intellectual is helpless in the face of political power, the artist becomes the conduit of commercial pressures, and *homo faber,* traditionally the figure demonstrating man's ability to adapt, is destroyed by his inflexible attitude to the natural forces that he imagines he has conquered. The portrayal of all three reflects the intellectual pessimism of the uneasy 1950s.

The protagonists in Frisch's two best-known plays, which accorded him world fame, *Biedermann und die Brandstifter* (1958; translated as *The Fire Raisers* and *The Firebugs*) and *Andorra* (1962; *Andorra*), act out and defend roles that lead to disaster. Both plays achieved immense popularity largely because, as generalized parables, they lent themselves to interpretations that were in line with the cultural and historical prejudices of the spectator, a feature that Frisch himself later acknowledged to be a drawback. Thus, the vacillation and cowardice of Biedermann in face of the fireraisers, who install themselves in his home, which they eventually destroy, can always represent the shortcomings of someone other than the spectator. Similarly, the attitudes adopted by the inhabitants of the fictitious state of Andorra toward Andri, the young man whom they believe to be a Jew and for whose surrender to invading armed forces they are responsible, can provoke moral outrage at the behavior of a group to which the spectator does not belong. *The Fire Raisers,* and more especially *Andorra,* could be assimilated to generalized interpretations of recent history and could reinforce stereotyped thinking in a world dominated at the end of the 1950s by the black and white divisions of the Cold War and by the threat of nuclear disaster.

For his third major novel, Frisch returned to a theme from *Sketchbook 1946–1949:* the impossibility of narrating experience without creating fictions. *Mein Name sei Gantenbein* (1964; translated as *A Wilderness of Mirrors* and *Gantenbein*) presents a variety of possible stories that a narrator imagines about himself. In this work, the individual seeks to express himself in stories that convey his experience: "Ich probiere Geschichten an wie Kleider" (I am trying on stories like clothes). The attempt to transfer these possibilities from the novel to the stage took place with *Biografie: Ein Spiel* (1967; *Biography: A Game*), in which the protagonist Kürmann is offered the opportunity, under certain conditions, of taking in a different way the important decisions of his life. This "Drama der Permutation" (drama of permutation) relates to earlier plays such as *Santa Cruz* (1946; Santa Cruz) in its exploration of the unrealized elements of life, and to *The Chinese Wall,* in that the setting is the stage itself.

The decade from the mid-1960s to the mid-1970s were arguably the years of Frisch's most sustained engagement with contemporary political life. *Öffentlichkeit als Partner* (1967; Public as Partner) contains speeches on the role of the worker in the modern world and on aspects of contemporary Swiss culture and politics that were authoritative and respected statements from the standpoint of Frisch's fame. In the same period, a general revision of benevolent interpretations of the recent Swiss past began, and in this ethos of skepticism toward received views in the early 1970s, Frisch published three texts: *Wilhelm Tell für die Schule* (1971; Wilhelm Tell for Schools), a deconstruction of hallowed myths surrounding the origins of Switzerland; *Tagebuch 1966–1971* (1972; *Sketchbook 1966–1971*), his second major diary, in which the political comments are much less integrated into the literary structure than in the first diary, and in which themes of aging and death feature prominently; and *Dienstbüchlein* (1974; Army Service Booklet), a very unsentimental view of his military service and the atmosphere in Switzerland during World War II. This view had already found a more conventional expression in *Blätter aus dem Brotsack* (1940; Leaves from a Knapsack).

In the wake of the so-called privatization of literature in German in the early 1970s, when it was claimed that writing about individual experience promoted authenticity in literature, Frisch published the story *Montauk* (1975; *Montauk*). At one level, the narrative tells of a weekend spent together on Long Island by an aging writer Max and a young American woman Lynn; at another level, it inquires into the relationship between the writer and the first-person narrator he creates, examines themes such as guilt that manifest themselves in the writing of an individual, and, above all, highlights the fictions that the individual must create to communicate at all. Ironically, *Montauk,* far from demonstrating authenticity in a first-person narrative, underlines the constraints and limits upon communication.

Limitation features centrally in Frisch's last major play, *Triptychon: Drei szenische Bilder* (1978; revised version, 1980; *Tryptychon: Three Scenic Panels*), in which Frisch confronts modern embarrassment at the topic of death. As in *Now They Sign Again,* he brings the dead on to the stage and underlines the finality of their situation—where there are no more possibilities, no more stories for the individual to tell.

The last decade of Frisch's life was marked by a decline in literary activity, but he nonetheless published the spare narrative that takes a major place in the late work, *Der Mensch erscheint im Holozän* (1979; *Man in the Holocene*). During a few days of severe summer thunderstorms, Herr Geiser, a businessman who has retired to a small house in the Ticino, experiences the insubstantiality of his property and is sharply reminded of the limitations of all human knowledge and activity by his own diminishing grasp on interpreted reality. The ephemeral and marginal status of the elderly pensioner reflects the situation of man on the planet he temporarily inhabits. Theme and narrative combine to yield a very postmodernist text.

Blaubart (1982; *Bluebeard*), the last prose narrative, takes the form of a criminal investigation into the life of Felix Schaad, a doctor accused of murdering one of his six former wives. Acquitted at his trial, Schaad pursues his own investigation into his past, revealing more and more layers of guilt, perhaps not in a technical legal sense, but very definitely in a moral sense. Since there are narrative and situational elements that recall aspects of the four major novels—*I'm Not Stiller, Homo Faber, Mein Name sei Gantenbein,* and *Montauk*—*Bluebeard* represents a coda to the creative work, albeit a dark one, since the discovery of the real murderer provides no "solution," for Schaad's confession of guilt is not now accepted.

Toward the end of his life, Frisch unexpectedly involved himself for the last time in public life in a major way. In advance of the controversial referendum of 1989 seeking to abolish the Swiss army, he published *Schweiz ohne Armee? Ein Palaver* (1989; Switzerland without an Army? A Discussion), which, in a style and manner reminiscent of *Wilhelm Tell für die Schule,* seeks to demythologize a revered Swiss institution. This work achieved record sales in Switzerland and was performed in a stage version in the Zürich Schauspielhaus, *Jonas und sein Veteran* (1989; Jonas and His Veteran). It was the last manifestation of the *Zeitgenossenschaft* of a man who had played a major part in politicizing the role of the writer in Switzerland.

MALCOLM PENDER

Biography

Born in Zurich, Switzerland, 15 May 1911. Studied at the University of Zurich, 1930–33, and the Zurich Technische Hochschule, 1936–41; degree in architechture, 1941; service in the Swiss army, 1939–45; worked as a freelance journalist, 1933–42, architect, 1942–54, and then full-time writer; in Germany, France, and Italy, 1946; in Poland and Czechoslovakia, 1948; in Spain, 1950; in the United States and Mexico, 1951–52; in Rome, 1960–65. Raabe Prize, 1954; Schleussner Schüller Prize, 1955; Büchner Prize, 1958; Zurich Prize, 1958; Veillon Prize, 1958; Nordrhein-Westfalen Prize, 1962; Jerusalem Prize, 1965; Schiller Prize (Baden-Wüttemberg), 1965; Schiller Prize (Switzerland), 1974; German Book Trade Freedom Prize, 1976; Commonwealth Award, 1985; Neustadt International Prize, 1986; Heine Prize (Düsseldorf), 1989; honorary doctorates from numerous European and U.S. colleges and universities. Died 4 April 1991.

Selected Works

Plays

Nun singen sie wieder: Versuch eines Requiems (produced 1945), 1946; as *Now They Sing Again,* translated by David Lommen, in *Contemporary German Theatre,* edited by Michael Roloff, 1972

Santa Cruz (produced 1946), 1947

Die chinesische Mauer (produced 1946), 1947; revised version, 1955; as *The Chinese Wall,* translated by James L. Rosenberg, 1961; as *The Great Wall of China,* translated by Michael Bullock, in *Four Plays,* 1969

Als der Krieg zu Ende war (produced 1949), 1949; as *When the War Was Over,* translated by James L. Rosenberg, in *Three Plays,* 1967

Graf Öderland (produced 1951), 1951; as *Count Oederland,* translated by Michael Bullock, in *Three Plays,* 1962
Don Juan; oder, Die Liebe zur Geometrie (produced 1953), 1953; translated as *Don Juan; or, the Love of Geometry,* by James L. Rosenberg, in *Three Plays,* 1967; also translated by Michael Bullock, in *Four Plays,* 1969
Rip van Winkle (from the story by Washington Irving) (broadcast 1953), 1969
Biedermann und die Brandstifter (broadcast 1953; produced 1958), 1958; as *The Fire Raisers,* translated by Michael Bullock, in *Three Plays,* 1962, revised edition, 1985; as *The Firebugs,* translated by Mordecai Gorelik, 1963
Die grosse Wut des Philipp Hotz (produced 1958), 1958; as *The Great Rage of Philipp Hotz,* translated by James L. Rosenberg, in *Three Plays,* 1967; as *Philipp Hotz's Fury,* translated by Michael Bullock, in *Four Plays,* 1969
Andorra (produced 1961), 1962; translated as *Andorra,* by Michael Bullock, in *Three Plays,* 1962; also translated by Geoffrey Skelton, 1964
Stücke, 2 vols., 1962; enlarged edition, 1972
Three Plays (includes *The Fire Raisers; Count Oederland; Andorra*), translated by Michael Bullock, 1962
Zurich Transit (televised 1966), 1966
Biografie (produced 1968), 1967; as *Biography: A Game,* translated by Michael Bullock, in *Four Plays,* 1969
Three Plays (includes *Don Juan; or, the Love of Geometry; The Great Rage of Philipp Hotz; When the War Was Over*), translated by James L. Rosenberg, 1967
Four Plays (includes *The Great Wall of China; Don Juan; or, the Love of Geometry; Philipp Hotz's Fury; Biography: A Game*), translated by Michael Bullock, 1969
Triptychon: Drei szenische Bilder (produced 1979), 1978; revised edition, 1980; as *Triptych: Three Scenic Panels,* translated by Geoffrey Skelton, 1981
Jonas und sein Veteran (produced 1989)

Fiction
Jürg Reinhart: Eine sommerliche Schicksalsfahrt, 1934
Antwort aus der Stille: Eine Erzählung aus den Bergen, 1937
J'adore ce qui me brûle; oder, Die Schwierigen, 1943; revised edition as *Die Schwierigen; oder, J'adore ce qui me brûle,* 1957
Bin; oder, Die Reise nach Peking, 1945
Marion und die Marionetten: Ein Fragment, 1946
Stiller, 1954; as *I'm Not Stiller,* translated by Michael Bullock, 1958
Homo Faber, 1957; translated by Michael Bullock, 1959
Mein Name sei Gantenbein, 1964; as *A Wilderness of Mirrors,* translated by Michael Bullock, 1965; as *Gantenbein,* translated by Bullock, 1982
Wilhelm Tell für die Schule, 1971
Montauk, 1975; as *Montauk,* translated by Geoffrey Skelton, 1976
Der Mensch erscheint im Holozän, 1979; as *Man in the Holocene,* translated by Geoffrey Skelton, 1980
Blaubart, 1982; as *Bluebeard,* translated by Geoffrey Skelton, 1983

Other
Blätter aus dem Brotsack (diary), 1940
Tagebuch mit Marion (diary), 1947; revised edition, as *Tagebuch 1946–1949,* 1950; as *Sketchbook 1946–1949,* translated by Geoffrey Skelton, 1977
Achtung: Die Schweiz, 1955
Die neue Stadt: Beiträge zur Diskussion, 1956
Ausgewählte Prosa, 1961
Öffentlichkeit als Partner, 1967
Tagebuch 1966–1971, 1972; as *Sketchbook 1966–1971,* translated by Geoffrey Skelton, 1974
Dienstbüchlein (memoir), 1974
Stich-Worte (selection), edited by Uwe Johnson, 1975
Gesammelte Werke, edited by Hans Mayer and Walter Schmitz, 12 vols., 1976; same texts in 6 vols., 1976, with supplement, 1987
Erzählende Prosa 1939–1979, 1980
Forderungen des Tages: Porträts, Skizzen, Reden, 1943–82, edited by Walter Schmitz, 1983
Gesammelte Werke [Jubiläums edition], 7 vols., 1986
Schweiz ohne Armee? Ein Palaver, 1989
Schweiz als Heimat? Versuche über 50 Jahre, edited by Walter Obschlager, 1990

Further Reading

Bachmann, Dieter, editor, *DU: Die Zeitschrift der Kultur* [special Frisch issue] (December 1991)
Bircher, Urs, *Vom langsamen Wachsen eines Zorns: Max Frisch 1911–1955,* Zürich: Limmat, 1997
Butler, Michael, *The Novels of Max Frisch,* London: Oswald Wolff, 1976
——, *The Plays of Max Frisch,* London: Macmillan, 1985
Hage, Volker, *Max Frisch,* Reinbek bei Hamburg: Rowohlt, 1983; 10th edition, 1995
Petersen, Jürgen H., *Max Frisch,* Stuttgart: Metzler, 1988; 2nd edition, 1989
Probst, Gerhard F., and Jay F. Bodine, editors, *Perspectives on Max Frisch,* Lexington: University of Kentucky Press, 1982
Reich-Ranicki, Marcel, *Max Frisch: Aufsätze,* Zürich: Ammann, 1991
Schmitz, Walter, *Max Frisch: Das Spätwerk (1962–1982): Eine Einführung,* Tübingen: Francke, 1985
——, *Max Frisch: Das Werk (1931–1961): Studien zu Traditionen und Traditionsverarbeitung,* Bern and New York: Lang, 1985

G

Hans-Georg Gadamer 1900–

Hans-Georg Gadamer is arguably the most significant German philosopher in the 20th century except for Martin Heidegger. Gadamer is a philologist, philosopher, and literary critic, and he has written about some major poets in the German literary tradition, including Goethe, Hölderlin, Kleist, Stefan George, and Rilke, as well as less well known poets such as Hans Carossa and Hilde Domin. Although he began with thinking about Heidegger's work on interpretation (hermeneutics), Gadamer's best-known contribution emerged from his efforts to establish what he called "philosophical hermeneutics," and this project manifested in comprehensive fashion in *Wahrheit und Methode* (1960; *Truth and Method*). Thus, Gadamer needs to be seen as a figure within the tradition of hermeneutics, and as someone who helped to broaden the scope of hermeneutics beyond the problems and strategies of interpretation that were connected to biblical and classical studies.

Gadamer was Heidegger's student for a time, and he also had ties to the Stefan George Circle. For many literary critics and theorists, Heidegger is more interesting for his involvement with National Socialism than for his writings on poetry and language. With Gadamer, something of the opposite seems true; that is, despite Gadamer's own insistence on historicity in his writings about philosophical hermeneutics, almost no one has attended to Gadamer's history and his connections to National Socialism. Many, however, do know his writings on literature and philosophy and his concern with keeping philosophy aware of literature as its *other,* as that which resists, even refuses, philosophy's control.

Recently, some work has come out that seeks to clarify Gadamer's history during the National Socialist period, beginning in English with Robert Sullivan's *Political Hermeneutics* (1989) and elaborated by Teresa Orozco in *Platonische Gewalt: Gadamer's politische Hermeneutik der NS-Zeit* (1995; Platonic Power). Geoff Waite provides the salient details of this matter, and in an incisive manner he shows their continuing relevance for hermeneuticists (see his essays in *Gadamer at 100,* ed. Krajewski). Gadamer has not helped himself in at least one of his responses to questions about his activities during that time. In a reply to an essay by Robin May Schott in *The Philosophy of Hans-Georg Gadamer* (ed. Hahn, 1997), he remarks, "In the essay 'Über die politische Inkompetenz der Philosophie' (About the Political Incompetence of Philosophy), I illustrated with Plato and Heidegger what I myself think about the relation between philosophy and politics. With modesty I lay claim to the same incompetence." Elsewhere, Gadamer seems less dismissive of the political dimension in general than he does in the previous quote: "It would be insane to believe that the life devoted to theory would ever be independent of the political and social life and its constraints. The myth of the ivory tower where theoretical people live is an unreal fantasy. We all stand in the middle of the social system." Nonetheless, the comment about "political incompetence" opens up enormous questions, and an immediately pertinent one is explored by Sullivan and Waite, who devote themselves to foregrounding Gadamer's esotericism, which in turn assumes that Gadamer participates in an esoteric tradition that extends from Plato's *Seventh Letter* in the ancient world (a text Gadamer has written about, which is available in English in *Dialogue and Dialectic* [1980]) to Leo Strauss (with whom Gadamer had correspondence) in the modern. This esoteric tradition calls for a different kind of reading from the familiar textual methodologies currently available, which assume naively that almost everything is exoteric, and Gadamer himself acknowledges having occasionally produced a kind of writing between the lines, partly due to a keen awareness of specific political situations.

To view Gadamer working within the exo/esoteric tradition in relation to literature, one can turn to *Vom Geistigen Lauf des Menschen: Studien zu unvollendeten Dichtungen Goethes* (1949; On the Course of Human Spiritual Development: Studies of Goethe's Unfinished Writings), particularly Gadamer's reading of Goethe's "continuation" of Mozart's *Magic Flute:*

> And yet even Goethe was obviously able to see in the libretto a peculiar and deeper meaning. In speaking of it once, he said that one could be quite confident that the higher meaning of the work would be clear to the initiates. One way an attempt has been made to understand Goethe's remark is to consider the significance of Freemasonry both for Mozart's opera and Schikaneder's libretto.

While accepting Goethe's distinction between "initiates" and the uninitiated (uneducated?), a political move in its own right, Gadamer, in *Literature and Philosophy in Dialogue,* goes on to dismiss political readings of the *Magic Flute* or Goethe's "continuation" of it:

> Those who interpret the *Magic Flute* in a Masonic sense are not explicating the work, but rather reading meaning into it. The higher meaning of the events Goethe saw in the *Magic Flute* is certainly not to be interpreted in the narrow sense of a political pamphlet or a political apology for Freemasonry. . . . Not Freemasonry as such, but rather the problem of human morality and its relation to the spirit, constitutes the higher meaning of the events Goethe undoubtedly recognized in the opera.

"Higher" and lower ("narrow"?) meanings can be recognized, according to Gadamer, and these directions (not rules) for reading seem a short, practical guide to at least part of the content of philosophical hermeneutics.

Elsewhere, however, Gadamer has insisted on less hierarchical readings and more democratic understandings—to the point of eschewing esoteric and specialist readings. His book on Paul Celan's poetry, *Wer bin ich und wer bist du?* (1973; *Whom Am I and Who Are You?*), is exemplary on this point, precisely through the question that is the book's title. According to Gadamer, the poet and the poetry put the reader (the one addressed, the one questioned and questioning) in question, and it is not a question that will be settled once and for all. Literature, the poetic word, confounds readers, exposes them, opens horizons, leaves matters in the open, and asks readers to ponder not only who they are but where they are. Where do we stand with respect to all that has come down to us (tradition)? Literature can be a world of the otherwise, calling on those who encounter it to revise their thinking, and it is this revision that Gadamer calls hermeneutic experience. As Gerald Bruns has argued, that experience consists in an "acknowledgment of what is alien and refractory to one's categories."

In addition to the dialogue in his thought between philosophy and literature, Gadamer's attention to language and rhetoric makes him a significant figure for those interested in German literature. As he says in *Vernunft in Zeitalter der Wissenschaft* (1976; *Reason in the Age of Science*), "Hermeneutics may be precisely defined as the art of bringing what is said or written to speech again. What kind of art this is, then, we can learn from rhetoric." The "art of bringing what is said or written to speech again" consists of making the past speak again in the present, even if, at times, the encounter with the past renders us temporarily speechless and helps us to realize that we do not know a kind of undermining of knowledge that frees something else up. Freedom is, indeed, an issue here. Making sense of something, in this view, means being able to say something about the situation in which you and that something are relevant, to the point that your self-understanding becomes implicated in the situation.

The situation above is a dialogical one, and dialogue, as almost everyone knows by now, is central to Gadamer's thinking. This is something that perhaps could not be helped, since Gadamer has been a lifelong Plato scholar. In terms of literary interpretation, dialogue presupposes speaking *and* listening, and Gadamer's contribution has consisted of redirecting emphasis to the latter; he argues that what is more likely to happen in our encounter with literature is that we might be too garrulous, unable to hear what the poem, novel, or work of art wants to say. According to Gadamer, we have to be open to interruption, including interruptions in our attempts to master and to control the work, as the work attempts to work on us. An ethical relation resides within the dialogical situation, as if an obligation to attentiveness obtains. Poetry's strange, unsettling words ought, in most instances, to aid in making readers receptive to the otherness of words through a kind of resistance to control, immediate comprehension, and transparency of the sort that allows readers to look through or past words, instead of being stopped by unmanageable, dark language. Gadamer chose Celan, "one of the most inaccessible poets of world literature," because he was disappointed by what the experts had to say about the poetry. He wanted to hear what the poetry had to say and to participate in that hearing and that saying.

Language is the essence of hermeneutics. Gadamer's famous phrase, "Being that can be understood is language," indicates a primary relationship, at least, between language and understanding. Hardly anyone will be surprised that understanding takes place in language; the issue happens to be the ability of language to be shared. For Gadamer, conversations can be more or less successful, and ongoing conversations also have the feeling of something unfolding, even if continually unsettled. The famous phrase seems to include in its logic the possibilities of not understanding and misunderstanding, but Gadamer also seeks to remind us of the frequency of our communicative successes: "Social life depends on our acceptance of everyday speech as trustworthy. We cannot order a taxi without this trust. Thus understanding is the average case, not misunderstanding. . . . In literature there is a struggle to bring something to expression beyond what is already accepted." Literature turns out to be a special case, a point that separates Gadamer from a contemporary critical perspective that pushes almost anything into the category of "text."

Bruce Krajewski

See also Hermeneutics

Biography

Born in Marburg, 11 February 1900. Studied at the universities of Munich and Marburg; professor of philosophy, University of Marburg, 1937–39, University of Leipzig, 1939–47 (and rector, 1946–47), University of Frankfurt, 1947–49, and University of Heidelberg, 1949–68, where he was also professor emeritus; visiting professor at McMaster University, Hamilton, Ontario, 1972–75, and Boston College, 1976. Reuchlin-Preis, Pforzheim, 1971; Hegel-Preis, Stuttgart, 1979; member of the Academy of Leipzig, 1942, the Academy of Heidelberg, 1950, the Academy of Athens, the Academy of Rome, the Academy of Darmstadt, and Boston Academy.

Selected Works

Philosophical Works

Platos dialektische Ethik: Phänomenologische Interpretationen zum "Philebus," 1931
Plato und die Dichter, 1934
Regards sur l'histoire, Gadamer et al., 1941
Volk und Geschichte im Denken Herders (lectures), 1942
Bach und Weimar (lecture), 1946
Goethe und die Philosophie, 1947
Über die Ursprünglichkeit der Wissenschaft (lecture), 1947
Über die Ursprünglichkeit der Philosophie (lectures), 1948
Vom Geistigen Lauf des Menschen: Studien zu unvollendeten Dichtungen Goethes, 1949
Gedächtnisrede aus Oskar Schürer, 1952

Wahrheit und Methode: Grundzüge einer philosophischen Hermeneutik, 1960; as *Truth and Method,* 1975
Le Problème de la conscience historique (lectures), 1963
Dialektik und Sophistik im siebenten platonischen Briefe, 1964
Kleine Schriften, 4 vols., 1967–77; selections translated as *Philosophical Hermeneutics,* 1976
Platos dialektische Ethik und andere Studien zur platonischen Philosophie, 1968
Werner Scholz, 1968
Hegel, Hölderlin, Heidegger, Gadamer et al. (lectures), 1971
Die Begriffsgeschichte und die Sprache der Philosophie, 1971
Hegels Dialektik: Fünf hermeneutsiche Studien, 1971; as *Hegel's Dialectic: Five Hermeneutical Studies,* 1976
Wer bin ich und wer bist du? Ein Kommentar zu Paul Celans Gedichtfolge "Atemkristall," 1973; as *Who Am I and Who Are You?* translated and edited by Richard Heinemann and Bruce Krajewski, 1997
Idee und Wirklichkeit in Platos "Timaios" (lecture), 1974
Vernunft in Zeitalter der Wissenschaft: Aufsätze, 1976; as *Reason in the Age of Science,* 1981
Rhetorik und Hermeneutik (lecture), 1976
Poetica: Ausgewählte Essays, 1977
Die Aktualität des Schönen: Kunst asl Spiel, Symbol und Fest, 1977
Philosophische Lehrjahre, Gadamer with E. Ruckschau, 1977; as *Philosophical Apprenticeships,* 1985
Heidegger: Freiburger Universitätsvorträge zu seinem Gedenken, Gadamer et al., 1977; as *Heidegger Memorial Lectures,* edited by Werner Marx, 1982
Die Idee der Guten zwischen Plato und Aristoteles (lecture), 1978; as *The Idea of the Good in Platonic Aristotelian Philosophy,* 1986
Dialogue and Dialectic: Eight Hermeneutical Studies on Plato, 1980

Translation
Aristotle, *Metaphysics, Book XII,* translated, edited, and with commentary, 1970

Edited Works
Wilhelm Dilthey, *Grundriss der algemeinen Geschichte der Philosophie,* 1949
Ernst Hoffmann, *Platonismus und christliche Philosophie,* 1960
Beiträge zur Deutung der Phänemonologie des Geistes, 1966
Hegel-Tage, Royaumont, 1964, 1966
Deutscher Kongress für Philosophie: Das Problem der Sprache, 1967
Idee und Zahl, 1968
Hegel Tage, Urbino, 1965, 1969
Hermeneutik und Dialektik, 1970
Kurt Riezler, *Parmenides,* 1970
Truth and Historicity/Vérité et histoiricité, 1972

Further Reading

Bruns, Gerald L., *Hermeneutics, Ancient and Modern,* New Haven, Connecticut: Yale University Press, 1992
Gadamer, Hans-Georg, *Dialogue and Dialectic: Eight Hermeneutical Studies on Plato,* translated by P. Christopher Smith, New Haven, Connecticut and London: Yale University Press, 1980
———, *Reason in the Age of Science,* translated by Frederick G. Lawrence, Cambridge, Massachusetts and London: MIT Press, 1981
———, *Gesammelte Werke,* 10 vols., Tübingen: Mohr, 1985–95
———, *Literature and Philosophy in Dialogue: Essays in German Literary Theory,* translated by Robert H. Paslick, Albany: State University of New York Press, 1994
———, *Gadamer on Celan: "Who Am I and Who Are You?" and Other Essays,* edited and translated by Richard Heinemann and Bruce Krajewski, Albany: State University of New York Press, 1997
Hahn, Lewis Edwin, editor, *The Philosophy of Hans-Georg Gadamer,* Chicago: Open Court, 1997
Krajewski, Bruce, editor, *Gadamer at 100: Contingencies of Philosophical Hermeneutics,* Berkeley: University of California Press, 2000
Misgeld, Dieter, and Graeme Nicholson, editors, *Hans-Georg Gadamer on Education, Poetry, and History: Applied Hermeneutics,* Albany: State University of New York Press, 1992
Orozco, Teresa, *Platonische Gewalt: Gadamers politische Hermeneutik der NS-Zeit,* Hamburg: Argument, 1995
Sullivan, Robert R., *Political Hermeneutics: The Early Thinking of Hans-Georg Gadamer,* University Park: Pennsylvania State University Press, 1989

Gandersheim, Hrotsvith, *see* Hrotsvith von Gandersheim

Christian Fürchtegott Gellert 1715–1769

In the literature, as in the general culture of 18th-century Germany, the idea of human freedom was a powerful and, perhaps, the dominant factor. Eventually emerging in its full glory (and complexity) from 1770 onward, it was also a driving force in the German Enlightenment (*Aufklärung*), which had begun to emerge in the late 17th century, and took center stage in the late 1720s. In asserting the independent validity of the power of reason, and of nature (essentially, the rational principle as manifested in the universe as a whole), the movement at least implied the freedom of man, as it was proclaimed by Kant in the opening section of "Was ist Aufklärung?" (1784). But even Kant ends his essay with a paean of praise to Frederick the Great as the type of the enlightened despot. The urge to freedom, in the "enlightened" writer and thinker, was inhibited by a counter-impulse, which could be seen negatively as timidity and positively as an endorsement of the principle of order that informed nature itself. In the conditions of the earlier 18th century, in particular the 1740s, when most of his important work was done, Gellert can be seen as a prime example of the liberating and reforming tendency of the Aufklärung, and of its limitations.

Gellert, an educator by profession, remains a pedagogue in his writing, concerned to weed out the "false"; to cultivate the "true" entirely in the spirit of the *Aufklärung,* although without the pedantry and sharp polemical edge of a Gottsched; and (especially in his hymns and Moralische Gedichte such as "Reichtum und Ehre" or "Der Christ") to preach a morality that harmonized Christianity with rationalistic humanism, but without the satirical bite and rhetorical passion of a Haller. His was a conciliatory nature, a fact reflected in his most important contribution to the development of German literature, his style. We must look first, however, at his role in the rise of sentimentalism (Empfindsamkeit), which has led some to question his credentials as an *Aufklärer.*

It is true that this cult of the "heart" contains an element not just of human, but of individual self-assertion, which is potentially subversive of the strict hegemony of rationality that is the trademark of *Aufklärung* proper. It is in the lyric mode, the mode of individuality, that the danger is greatest, and this first truly made itself felt in the work of Klopstock. Gellert, who, like the majority of *Aufklärer,* lacked the lyrical vein, admired Klopstock but could not approve or enthuse, as his correspondence (especially with his friend J.A. Cramer) shows. But if the opportunity to indulge and, indeed, wallow in "Empfindung" could be found within the boundaries of rational legitimacy, Gellert was certainly all too willing to take advantage of it. Similar to many *Aufklärer,* he was wary of Pietism (cf. the comedy *Die Betschwester*), but by no means immune to its cult of self-examination. In particular, his novel *Leben der schwedischen Gräfin von G.* (1747, 1748; Life of the Swedish Countess of G.) and the comedy *Die zärtlichen Schwestern* (1747; The Tender-Hearted Sisters) bear eloquent witness to this. It is in the sentimental drama, whether "comic" or "tragic," in which the enlightened spectator could satisfy the demands of reason and at the same time thrill to the "philanthropic" goodness of his own heart by empathizing with and admiring the steadfast suffering of the deserving. This is the bourgeoisification of heroism, and the line leads on to Lessing, and eventually to Iffland, not to Klopstock, although the latter himself was not entirely immune and presents us with a little "bürgerliches Trauerspiel" in the Semida-Cidli episode in Canto IV of *Der Messias.*

This trend is not entirely absent from Gellert's most influential and effective literary production, namely, his fables and tales in verse (e.g., "Calliste," "Inkle und Yariko," or "Rhynsolt und Lucia," in which we are invited to join the revenging "hero" in shedding a "fromme Zähre" [pious tear]). But while such moral seriousness is sincere, Gellert is at his best when his touch can be consistently lighter ("leicht"), although it is never excessively frivolous ("frey"). Already an arbiter elegantarium in the field of epistolography, he handled the metrical and stylistic questions raised by the form of the short verse-narrative with a rational and poetic tact, which ensures a clear and graceful flow that in turn takes further and, perhaps, perfects the adaptation of Baroque forms to *Aufklärung* purposes begun by his hero Hagedorn. This is not yet true innovation: the rhetorical framework remains firmly in place. "Fire" must still operate within the confines of an intellectual "Witz" (cf. "Die Nachtigall und die Lerche"), just as Gellert's rationalism and moralism prevent his genuine sense of fun from allowing the sense of play to slip the leash and become, in Gellert's own phrase, "zu frey" (too free), an accusation he leveled at J.F. Löwen and from which he was not sure that even Hagedorn was immune. In the later stages of development of the *Aufklärung,* a much greater degree of liberation (of the not strictly rationalistic aspects of the human psyche) is observable in the rococo style of Wieland, of whose *Idris* (1768), say, Gellert could never have approved. But "timid" as he himself admits he is, there is a humor and a degree of elegance in Gellert, which could be said to represent a step in that direction. One can understand why Frederick the Great thought him "le plus raisonnable de tous les savants allemands," and there is a sense in which Wieland, who truly conquered the French heritage for 18th-century German poetry, can be said to be his inheritor.

ALAN MENHENNET

Biography

Born in Hainichen, near Freiburg, 1715. Studied at Leipzig University, 1734–38; private tutor, and qualified as lecturer, 1743; professor at Leipzig University, 1744; received by Friedrich II to recite his fables, Leipzig, 1760. Died in Leipzig, 1769.

Selected Works

Collections
Sämtliche Schriften, 1769–74
Gellerts Werke, Auswahl in zwei Teilen, edited by F. Behrend, 1910
Gesammelte Schriften, edited by B. Witte et al., vols. 3, 4, 1988, 1989

Poetry
Fabeln und Erzählungen, 1746, 1748
Geistliche Oden und Lieder, 1757

Comedies
Die Betschwester, 1745
Das Loos in der Lotterie, 1747
Die zärtlichen Schwestern, 1747
Pro comedia commovente, 1751

Novel
Leben der schwedischen Gräfin von G., 1747, 1748

Epistolography
Gedanken von einem guten Briefe, 1742
Briefe nebst einer praktischen Abhandlung von dem guten Geschmack in Briefen, 1751

Other
Briefwechsel, edited by J.F. Reynolds, 4 vols., 1983–96

Further Reading

Brüggemann, Fritz, *Gellerts "Schwedische Gräfin," der Roman der Welt- und Lebensanschauung des vorsubjektivistischen Bürgertums,* Aachen: Aachener Verlags- und Druckerei-Gesellschaft, 1925
May, Kurt, *Das Weltbild in Gellerts Dichtung,* Frankfurt: Diesterweg, 1928
Nickisch, Reinhard M.G., *Die Stilprinzipien in den deutschen Briefstellern des 17. und 18. Jahrhunderts,* Göttingen: Vandenhoeck und Ruprecht, 1969
Schlingmann, Carsten, *Gellert: Eine literarhistorische Revision,* Bad Homburg: Gehlen, 1967

Das Genie

For better and for worse, the notion of the creative genius (*das Genie*) has been wedded to German art and culture since Goethe's ascent to fame during the so-called genius-period (ca. 1755–75). The *Faust* author's early works explored the tragic fate of "ingenious" souls (e.g., *Werther, Tasso*), and later interpreters of modernity likewise sought to identify the destiny of German culture in superhuman possibility (Nietzsche), in decadent artistry (Thomas Mann), or in absolute leadership as racial re-creation (Hitler). With remarkable consistency, the catalyst for these various attempts to articulate the cultural ideal has been the affirmation of the *Genie* as creator of the new, the possible, of the future itself.

Parallel to the articulation of this ideal, one encounters an equally persistant discourse of critical skepticism and cultural antipathy, which culminates in the psychological diagnosis of genius as a degenerate and inherently dangerous gift. *Genie* signals an extraordinary possibility, and this underlies its peculiar association not just with modernity but also with a notion of Germanness whose archetype is Frankenstein, "the modern Prometheus." Even today, within an American culture that commonly associates the German with an efficiency tending from comical to brutal, the concept of "genius" is most frequently identified historically with figures from German-speaking culture, as in the popular notion that children who listen to Mozart as infants can grow up to become Einsteins. Hence an examination of the role played by the concepts of genius and *Genie* in German letters involves an indirect reflection on the history, and the fate, of German cultural identity.

The term *Genie* was adopted during the 17th and 18th centuries from the French *génie,* a word that combines the Latin terms *genius* (protective spirit, daemon) and *ingenium* (innate ability, talent, inventive capacity). Within the discourse of French Classicism, *génie* designates a creative passion, an inspiration or "fureur poetique" that seems to derive directly from heavenly sources. It provides the basis for the argument, in Charles Perrault's *Parallèle des anciens et des modernes* (1688; Parallels of Ancients and Moderns), that the artworks of the "ancients" are less to be imitated in their results than emulated in their creative impulse. The notion of *génie* sets forth an opposition between a tradition-bound, imitative standard of artistic excellence and a principle of creativity that draws more directly from nature. In the aesthetics of genius (Du Bos, Diderot), this turn to nature soon becomes a turn to the nature of creativity. Its proximity to nature sets *génie* apart from history and tradition, which enables it precisely to legitimate artworks that seek to challenge or depart from traditional standards of beauty and excellence. As a principle of the invention of the new, the concept of genius heralds the shift from the rationalistic notion of the creator of nature as divine mechanic to the romantic ideal of nature's creator as the first and most original artist.

The word *génie* passes into German language as a synonym both for *Witz* (wit), as the facility of poetic imagination or invention, and for *Geist* (spirit), which extends this facility metonymically to the overall mental capacity or character of the creative individual. Thus the Enlightenment critic and playwright Johann Christoph Gottsched, who advocated adherence to the strict norms of imitation and Aristotelian unities that governed classical French theater, deplored the term *Genie* as an "un-German thing." Countering Gottsched, Lessing argued that a new tradition in German poetics could arise only by following the example of tradition-breaking artistic innovators: "For a *genius* [*Genie*] can only be ignited by another *genius,* and most easily by one who seems to owe everything just to nature and isn't scared off by the laborious perfections of art." Significantly, Lessing stipulates that the art of genius still requires "laborious perfections," indeed that *Genie* should only "seem" entirely natural. For the same recourse to naturalness that legitimates a departure from traditional standards also could be taken to the extreme as an abandonment of tradition and perfection altogether. Concern about this tendency to excess informs the aesthetics of genius from Lessing to Kant.

For Lessing the foremost paradigm of poetic genius is found in Shakespeare. Indeed the reception of Shakespeare in German literary culture coincides with, and is largely framed by, the influence of English theories of "genius" that use the Bard as their primary example. The meaning of the English term follows from the Latin *ingenium;* "genius" is understood in relation to "humour" and "wit" as a special mental endowment, a talent or gift for invention in science as well as art. In the first English treatise specifically on "genius," Joseph Addison distinguishes between a merely learned, artificial talent and the "natural Genius" of great poets such as Homer, Pindar, and Shakespeare. Addison establishes the crucial notion that the innate originality of genius is not something one acquires or has, but that one simply "is." As a "poet of nature" Shakespeare must be understood as a natural force, not an imitator of nature but rather a creator *of* it. Direct influence on German thinking about poetic *Genie* also comes from Edward Young's essay "On Original Composition" (1759), which argues for the organic nature of "original genius," and Alexander Gerard's systematic "Essay on Genius" (1774), which situates the power of invention more specifically in "imagination." Along with Addison's treatise, these works inaugurate the problem-complex of imagination, nature, and reason that henceforth forms the centerpoint of German aesthetic and poetic theory.

In the science of aesthetics founded by Baumgarten and carried forth in the writings of Moses Mendelssohn, the concepts of *ingenium* and later *Genie* serve a decisive function. Baumgarten's psychological analysis of the creation and reception of works of art leads directly to an inward, purely subjective principle of invention as the ground and source of the "truth" of aesthetic experience. Mendelssohn further connects this principle of aesthetic truth to a Platonic ideal of the "perfection" of aesthetic experience. The idea of subjective creativity comes to be ever more closely aligned with, if not displacing, divine creativity. Brought forth from "the deepest secrets of the soul," *Genie* names the capacity of the artist-creator to draw upon "intuitive knowledge," to "feel with the intellect" and thus to reach an aesthetically "perfected" truth.

Following Lessing's critique of Gottsched's poetic rationalism, the Swiss theorists Bodmer and Breitinger develop a poetics of the inventive power and affective force of *Genie.* Citing Milton as well as Shakespeare as examples, Bodmer sets the highest artistic value upon a fantasy capable of producing a "wondrous" yet not improbable poetic "creation" which could produce a maximum emotional as well as intellectual effect on the reader. While Breitinger calls for a "writing-style that moves the heart," his contemporary Friedrich Gottlieb Klopstock argues that the poetic *Genie* must transform the representations of nature and fantasy into a total poetic "presentation" that is capable of moving nothing less than "the whole soul." In a programmatic treatise on sacred poetry, Klopstock declares: "Superior poetry is the work of a genius." The poetics of genius thus is brought into connection with the aesthetics of the sublime (Longinus, Burke), which describes how the intellectual appreciation of beauty in nature is superseded by emotional admiration for the creative force underlying it. Virtually substituted for nature as the object of poetic-aesthetic contemplation, the idea of *Genie* becomes the icon and standard for a newly discovered power of natural-artistic creativity, imbued with the capacity to found a new poetic tradition.

The culmination of the aesthetics of genius, Kant's *Critique of Judgment* (1790), articulates the dangers of an essentially self-legitimating concept of creativity. Evoking the oppositions of freedom and imitation, nature and artifice that governed preceding discourse, Kant defines *Genie* as "the innate mental predisposition (*ingenium*) through which nature gives the rule to art." As an innate capacity to bring forth unique yet exemplary works that continually redefine the standard of art, *Genie* creates "rules" for itself; it is unbound by the precedent of tradition and hence autonomous, free in its creative interplay of imagination and intellect. Kant describes the genius as "a favorite of nature" whose innate sense of formal expression communicates indirectly with the supersensory stratum and exhibits an "unnamable" quality in artistic experience which Kant calls "spirit" [*Geist*]. Yet because the spirit of genius alone cannot guarantee that its creativity will result in anything but a lawless freedom that produces nonsense and monstrosities, its autonomy must be harnessed by society through the discipline and cultivation of "taste" [*Geschmack*]. For Kant, the *conditio sine qua non* of "beautiful art" is taste, not genius; the wings of *Genie* must be clipped when necessary by good judgment. Thus Kant's "critical" notion of genius follows his critique of reason by confirming that the highest possibility of human creative achievement is grounded in an innate capacity of the human mind, yet still subject to regulation and cultivation by the rational intellect.

The so-called genius period (*Geniezeit*) in German literature is inaugurated with the publication in 1748 of the opening cantos of Klopstock's religious epic *Der Messias* (*The Messiah*) and extends through the 1760s, when it merges with the *Sturm und Drang* period. Already in Klopstock's first ode, "Der Lehrling der Griechen" (1747), the poet frames his calling in epochal terms as the "apprentice of the Greeks," "upon whom the gaze of the genius looked, as he was born / With a consecrating smile." Lessing's response to Klopstock—"because I recognize him as a great genius [*ein großes Genie*], I'm on my guard around him"—demonstrates how the artistic ideal of genius proved to be as problematic in its realization as it remained hopeful in its promise. The longing to discover a specifically German literary genius also must be viewed within the larger context of a newly ascendant bourgeois public sphere, which was seeking to emancipate itself culturally (as well as politically and economically) from an aristocratic and parochial social order, and at the same time to distinguish itself from the French-dominated poetics of Enlightenment. If original works of genius were by definition bound to defy the rational standards and traditional norms of critical taste, even more the very idea of genius was destined to become a magnet for the dissatisfaction and longing of an entire generation. This mood is famously captured in Goethe's *The Sorrows of Young Werther* (1773): "Oh, my friends! You ask why the torrent of genius so rarely pours forth, so rarely floods and thunders and overwhelms your astonished soul?" In Goethe's ambivalent icon of the self-destructive enthusiasm, the era of *Genie* finds perhaps its most sympathetic embodiment. But for many artists as well as critics, the reality of the "genius-epidemic" (*Genieseuche*) was far less tolerable. Goethe speaks of the many "bubbleheads" running about spouting tears and invectives; while Klinger, the nominal progenitor of Sturm und Drang, describes the "genius-, strength-, storm-and-stress-types" who, having failed as poets, turn into political revolutionaries.

Along with Klopstock and Goethe, the writings of Herder and Hamann during this period represent the cultural, historical, and spiritual dimensions of the program to produce a new German literary-artistic tradition. In this regard, it is important to trace the use of the term *der Genius* alongside *das Genie*. *Genius* evokes the Latin sense of a "protective spirit" which accompanies the destiny both of an individual and, by extension, the historical calling or "spirit" of a nation. The first meaning occurs explicity in Hamann's *Sokratische Denkwürdigkeiten* (1759; *Socratic Memorabilia*), which finds in Socrates's personal *daimonion* an icon for creative freedom from rules and rationality: "Socrates was well able to be unknowing: he had a genius." As a principle of inspired not-knowing, *der Genius* is invoked by Hamann as aesthetic resistance to the Enlightenment's rationalization and secularization of arts and intellect. By contrast, Herder's *Über die neuere deutsche Literatur* (1767; *Fragments on Recent German Literature*) invokes an antique notion of "genius" that transcends not only reason but individuality altogether, inhabiting the very language of a people and informing its historical self-expression: "Thus the genius of a language is also the genius of the literature of a nation." Herder's *Genius* is a principle of historical-cultural identity awaiting its instantiation in the work of poetic *Genie*. The identification of *Genius* and *Genie* becomes a lightning rod for efforts to articulate the conflicts inherent in a newly developing aesthetic-artistic sensibility: As Lavater declares, "Genie ist Genius."

The programmatic effort to synthesize these spiritual and nationalistic ideals of genius is exemplified in Goethe's early essay "On German Architecture" (1773). Inspired by an ongoing correspondence with Herder, Goethe contemplates and praises the Strasbourg cathedral as a model of German creative spirit: "Here was revealed to me in faint intuitings the genius [*der Genius*] of the great master-craftsman." Goethe's sense of revelation is attributed neither to the deity nor its earthly symbolization. Instead it is displaced—not without a hint of irony—onto the worker-artisan, whose "genius" is described in terms at once mundane and transcendent, closer to nature and yet at the pinnacle of cultural achievement, a paragon of individual creative subjectivity and yet representative of the artistic-spiritual "genius" of the German people as a whole.

Both within and beyond the *Geniezeit* it is hardly possible to separate the programmatic idea of genius in German literature from Goethe's own representations of it. His early works bring forth a virtually complete poetic realization of the psychology, symbolism, and social-historical fate of the creative *Genie*. For Goethe, the artist as genius culminates precisely in the artist of genius; the fate of genius is essentially to create itself, and to contemplate itself, as its own greatest work—"Like me!," as the 1773 hymn "Prometheus" concludes. In a similar way, in the opening of the ode "Wanderers Sturmlied" (1772), the poet evokes the spirit and style of Pindar, as well as the poetic self-appointment of his immediate predecessor Klopstock, in a moment of lyric self-contemplation: "Whom you do not abandon, genius." Framing his own poetic calling in relation to such mythical and historical predecessors, Goethe sets out to establish a new tradition under the sign of genius. Borrowing from Pindar and Homer, his early hymns and odes set forth a new metaphoric vocabulary of genius: the "flood" (force of nature, history) and "flame" (inner fire of passion and imagination), the "eagle" (symbol of freedom and national identity), and the "wanderer" (proximity to nature, loneliness, and social alienation). The myth of Prometheus, not only as inventor and transgressor but as one whose fate is to be eternally punished for his creative gift, is also central to the iconology of *Genie*. The theme of the extraordinary but somehow wounded individual characterizes virtually all of Goethe's early novels and plays, which systematically explore the tragic incompatibility of the *Genie* with the moral-social order, whether in the guise of the political leader (Götz von Berlichingen), the sensitive soul (Werther), the nobleman (Egmont), the artist (Tasso), the melancholy philosopher (Faust), or the hopeful young man (Wilhelm Meister). The latter works also exemplify how Goethe progressively distances himself from the tragic artistic ideal of *Genie* as his career evolves towards classicism and cosmopolitanism. Indeed one may view the poet's autobiography, *Dichtung und Wahrheit,* as the culminating work in the poet's lifelong encounter with the "poetry and truth" of his own creative genius.

In German Idealism and Romanticism, the concept of creative *Genie* is progressively universalized and driven into extremes of the absolute and the unconscious. Fichte's absolute *Ich* and Schiller's notion of "aesthetic eduction" raise the possibility of a transcendent-epochal work of art in which subject and object, freedom and nature, beauty and truth could be synthesized in the concrete identity of a *Genieprodukt.* In the "obscure concept of genius," Schelling sees the "obscure, unknown force" of fate realizing itself. For Friedrich Schlegel, genius is a fundamental condition of the human subject—"Intellect is mechanical, wit is chemical, and genius [*Genie*] is organic spirit." Schopenhauer sees the incomprehensibility of genius as manifestation instead of an ultra-objectivity, the "liberated excess of knowledge, [which has] now become the subject purified of will, the bright mirror of the essence of the world."

The fundamental ambivalence regarding such an extraordinary human possibility is charged with an additional historical-cultural dimension in the writings of Friedrich Nietzsche. The treatise *Human, All-too Human* (1878) contains his most systematic reflections on the cultural function of *Genie,* "a word that I request be understood without any mythological or religious aftertaste." Analyzing the social and moral function of *Genie* as a "sign of superior and inferior culture," Nietzsche sees it not as an ideal but as a problem of human creativity that arises from the cultural vanity and competitive jealousy of those confronted with greatness. This gives rise to the "cult" or "superstition of the genius," which attributes whatever is new or extraordinary to unnatural sources. Such superstition may even infect the genius himself (e.g., Napoleon, Wagner), leading him to regard his own superior creative power as an exceptional gift and thus to disregard or neglect the concentrated energy, self-critical discipline, and good fortune that make this superiority possible. The greatest philosophical fallacy for Nietzsche is to believe in *Genie* as a semi-divine "miracle," rather than to acknowledge it as the product of an "all too human" cultural process, as a "wound" that a culture inflicts upon itself as inoculation against its own weakness—what Nietzsche calls "ennoblement through degeneration."

The latest and perhaps last critical turn in the notion of genius can be traced through Nietzsche's own writings. Beginning with the early opposition between the rational, life-negating "genius" of Socrates and the rebirth of the affirmative, dionysian "spirit of music" embodied by Wagner, Nietzsche ultimately repudiated the latter as merely symptomatic of a self-delusory cult of the individual *Genie.* This leads directly to the call for an overcoming of humanity altogether in the *Übermensch.* With ominous irony, Nietzsche imagines such a "Genius der Kultur" whose tools would be "lies, violence, and the most ruthless self-interest," and who therefore only could be called a "demonic being."

The legacy of Nietzsche for the idea of genius in German literary and philosophical culture since Goethe is embodied as much in the career of the man as in his writings. The philosopher's notorious descent into insanity is seen to reflect the exuberant and excessive spirit of his thinking in a way that provides an uncanny double of Goethe's self-enactment of his own genius: from emblem of self-conscious artistic fulfillment, *Genie* reappears as a reciprocal symptomology of genius and madness. (In retrospect, the poet Hölderlin is seen to exemplify this tendency as well.) Contemporary with Nietzsche and in accord with his critique of *Genie,* European psychiatric theorists popularized the notion that hereditary physical and moral "degeneracy" in the form of pathological nervous illness must be the underlying cause of all extraordinary mental phenomena, creative as well as criminal, moral as well as immoral. The title of Cesare Lombroso's epochal study, *Genio e follia* (1864; Genius and Madness), indicates the degree to which the question of genius thereby shifts from aesthetic investigations of the creative principle underlying great works of art or invention to a psychological problem encompassing both individuals and cultural history in general. A further example of this shift is Freud's 1910 study of Leonardo da Vinci, whose artistic and scientific genius Freud traces directly to childhood sexual neurosis and repressed homosexuality. Yet even this progressive pathologization of genius as degeneracy finds itself rehabilitated as the self-legitimation of *Genie* under the sign of *Décadence* in the work of Thomas Mann. The crowning irony to be discovered in the sanitorium on Mann's *Magic Mountain* (1924) is that the "dignity" and "superiority" of man, indeed the progress of human culture itself, is due precisely to "genius [*Genie*], which as such is nothing other than disease!"

The intersection of mythology and pathology in the modern notion of genius finds its historically most perversely potent formulation in Goebbel's propaganda speeches for Hitler. Drawing directly from the tradition of *Genie* in German culture, Goebbels praises "the great political genius of this man" and declares, "A genius is building a new world!" In the figure of the failed artist become mass murderer, which itself is brought directly back into connection with the German cultural tradition in Mann's *Doktor Faustus* (1947), the demonic legacy of the *Genie*-concept reaches its anti-moral extreme. Its traces still informed the deep ideological suspicion that accompanied the concept throughout the 20th century. For the critical theorists of the Frankfurt

School, the "untruth" of the aesthetic concept of *Genie* lies in the "idealistic hubris" (Adorno) of believing that artworks might be somehow absolute, "original" creations rather than the products of a specific time, context, and person: "[Genius] turns more and more into ideology as the world becomes less a human one and as the spirit or consciousness of it is increasingly neutralized." Even the attribution of *Genie* to an author such as Goethe amounts to little more than a "title" that never can adequately express "a person's relationship to art as an essential one" (Benjamin). Such an ideological awareness also may be understood as a wariness about entrusting humanity with the responsibility for what it creates. The question of genius is in essence the dilemma of modernity itself: the anxiety of the present towards the future, towards the new, and ultimately towards the creative capacity of the human psyche. Or, as contemporary critic David Wellbery concludes in a psychoanalytic and semiotic deconstruction of Goethe's early "genius"-hymns: "Modernity is the wound of genius."

For contemporary literary criticism, an understanding of the dual concepts "genius" and "Genie" thus cannot be restricted to a purely aesthetic or philosophical viewpoint; *Genie* is no more of a viable ideal than "genius" a credible mythologeme. Yet even this awareness cannot quell entirely the sense of profound possibility that adheres to these ideas. "We cannot do justice to the meaning of the notion of genius if we characterize it quasi-philosophically 'in itself,' rather than understanding it from within its historical situation and its oppositions, that is, as the preferred instrument of a more comprehensive emancipatory striving" (Jochen Schmidt). The study of the history of these notions in German and European literature and philosophy must remain receptive to the "utopian trace" (Adorno) that inheres in these concepts as in the notion of culture itself.

ERIC J. SCHWAB

See also Romanticism

Further Reading

Kelling, Hans-Wilhelm, *The Idolatry of Poetic Genius in German Goethe Criticism,* Berne: Lang, 1970

Murray, Penelope, editor, *Genius: The History of an Idea,* Oxford and New York: Blackwell, 1989

Peters, Günter, *Der zerrissene Engel: Genieästhetik und literarische Selbstdarstellung im achtzehnten Jahrhundert,* Stuttgart: Metzler, 1982

Schlapp, Otto, *Kants Lehre vom Genie und die Entstehung der "Kritik der Urteilskraft,"* Göttingen: Vandenhoeck and Ruprecht, 1901

Schmidt, Jochen, *Die Geschichte des Genie-Gedankens in der deutschen Literatur, Philosophie, und Politik, 1750–1945,* 2 vols., Darmstadt: Wissenschaftliche Buchgesellschaft, 1985; 2nd edition, 1998

Schmidt-Dengler, Wendelin, *Genius: Zur Wirkungsgeschichte antiker Mythologeme in der Goethezeit,* Munich: Beck, 1978

Wellbery, David E., *The Specular Moment: Goethe's Early Lyric and the Beginnings of Romanticism,* Stanford, California: Stanford University Press, 1996

Stefan George 1868–1933

Stefan George created a body of superbly crafted and ideologically challenging poetry that exerted substantial influence on other poets and thinkers. His charismatic personality placed George at the center of an ever-evolving circle of writers, artists, and intellectuals who played significant, often tragic roles in Germany's cultural discourse and history.

Due in part to his origins near the French-German border, a gift for languages, and rigorous grounding in Latin and Greek, George was emphatic in his cosmopolitanism, as evidenced by his translations of major works of Dante, Shakespeare, and Baudelaire. His three earliest lyrical cycles, *Hymnen* (1890; *Odes*), *Pilgerfahrten* (1891; *Pilgrimages*), and *Algabal* (1892; *Algabal*) integrate dominant impulses of the period. We find the idealism of German Romanticism, the fugitive moods and fastidious musicality of the symbolists George encountered in England and France, and Baudelaire's amoral aestheticism. *Odes* and *Pilgrimages* trace the poet's way from initial consecration to a stringent muse to gradual disappointment with poetic idealism because it isolates him from life's vitality. He views his world with ambivalence, longing for its pleasures and skeptically ironic over the bourgeoisie's foibles. *Algabal,* a meditation on the Roman emperor Heliogabalus, who was at once brutal by nature and exquisitely decadent, explores and rejects aesthetic solipsism and fulfillment of every whim as a response to the tragic encounter between subjectivity and concrete, temporal circumstance.

Between 1892 and 1919, George and his friends published 12 volumes of *Blätter für die Kunst* (Leaves for Art), a journal purposely limited in circulation, in which George often published poems before they appeared in books. It initially propagated poetry, prose, drama, music, and art in the *Jugendstil* vein but increasingly came to convey George's visionary ethos of spiritual and cultural renewal. His claim to poetological leadership becomes evident in *Die Bücher der Hirten- und Preisgedichte, der Sagen und Sänge und der Hängenden Gärten* (1895; *The Books of Eclogues and Eulogies, of Legends and Lays, and of the Hanging Gardens*). The reader encounters here imagined cultural worlds and values, idealized very much in the Romantic spirit, that modern civilization has obscured: the elemental fatalism of the pastoral world, the faith and gallantry of medieval Europe, and the exotic amorousness of the *Arabian Nights*.

Das Jahr der Seele (1897; *The Year of the Soul*) had a more pronounced effect on the tone of German poetry than any other of George's verse cycles. In its melancholy autumnal opening, the year's dying coincides with the end of a crucial human relationship. The attendant moods and situations are conveyed through poems in which the inner and outer landscapes merge inextricably, objective and subjective reality intermingle in scrupulously wrought images of poignant color and beauty. Expressionists such as Trakl, Heym, Stadler and Benn learned these techniques from George and shared his preference for poetic forms with the stamp of the austere and classical. The volume closes on a note of exhaustion and disillusion over the cultivation of art for the sake of art and self-expression.

George was seeking a new purpose and direction for his poetry, a mission that would imbue it with a greater meaning and permanence than was possible within the social and literary context of the time, which seemed to offer as avenues of creativity only materialist social and political themes or the empty hedonism of the art nouveau or symbolist aesthetic. *Der Teppich des Lebens und die Lieder von Traum und Tod, mit einem Vorspiel* (1899; *The Tapestry of Life and the Songs of Dream and Death with a Prelude*) marks a turning point in George's life as a poet and thinker, but not the end of his quest. The "naked angel" whom the poet encounters in the *Vorspiel* is his higher, truer, authentic self, almost a Platonic daimon, that will henceforth guide his spiritual quest and let him reject the priority of the material, social world.

Like many adherents of Nietzsche's cultural pessimism, George believed that modern civilization was doomed to be succeeded by a new era. He felt obliged to be a prophet, condemning present depravity and exhorting his followers that a new generation would surpass humanity's past cultural achievements. George was convinced that humankind could transcend its existential limits, advancing on evolution's tightrope, as Nietzsche demanded, toward becoming *Übermensch* (over-man; super-man). He based this faith on his encounter with a beautiful and gifted young poet he called Maximin, who died of meningitis in 1904, just after turning 16. In his bereavement, George came to revere Maximin as the incarnation of a redemptive, mythic power. Commitment to a "new life," Dionysian in its creative energy, Apollonian in its assertion of discipline and form, now became the guiding principle of George's life and work. It was central to the artistic and cultural program for Germany that was being propagated by his disciples, the young academics at major universities who constituted George's circle, the *Kreis*.

George's three final books are imbued with this prophetic spirit. *Der Siebente Ring* (1907; *The Seventh Ring*), whose central section celebrates Maximin, begins with "Zeitgedichte" ("Poems of our Times") excoriating contemporary Germany and exalting true heroes and martyrs such as Goethe and Nietzsche. *Der Stern des Bundes* (1913; The Star of the Covenant) anticipates the new generation that will restore humanity's primal authority and obedience. *Das Neue Reich* (1928; *The Kingdom Come*) reflects deep sorrow over World War I, but also indomitable faith.

George's insistence on "eternal" aesthetic and cultural values and the background of his admirers in Germany's educated upper middle class have caused critics since 1965 to associate him with the forces of nostalgic antimodernism and political conservatism. Some commentators condemn aspects of his work as racist and authoritarian. Most recently, Stefan Breuer has characterized the outlook espoused by George as "aesthetic fundamentalism," the displacement of reason and ethics in favor of beauty and grandeur. A separation of the critical discourse on George's poetry from ideological and political concerns is unlikely for the foreseeable future.

Michael M. Metzger

See also Blätter für die Kunst

Biography

Born in Büdesheim, 12 July 1868. Traveled in England, Italy, Switzerland, France, Spain, Austria, Denmark, and Holland, 1888–95; studied Romance philology and literature at the University of Berlin, 1890–91; lived mainly in Berlin and Munich; moved to Switzerland, summer 1933. Died in Minusio, near Locarno, 4 December 1933.

Selected Works

Collections

Gesamt-Ausgabe der Werke, 18 vols., 1927–34
Werke, 2 vols., 1968
Sämtliche Werke in 18 Bänden, 1980–
Stefan George in fremden Sprachen, various translators, edited by Georg Peter Landmann, 1973
The Works of Stefan George, translated by Olga Marx and Ernst Morwitz, 2nd edition, 1974

Poetry

(All titles translated into English by Olga Marx and Ernst Morwitz in *The Works of Stefan George*)
Hymnen, 1890
Pilgerfahrten, 1891
Algabal, 1892
Die Bücher der Hirten- und Preisgedichte, der Sagen und Sänge und der Hängenden Gärten, 1895
Das Jahr der Seele, 1897
Der Teppich des Lebens und die Lieder von Traum und Tod, mit einem Vorspiel, 1899
Die Fibel, 1901
Der Siebente Ring, 1907
Der Stern des Bundes, 1913
Das Neue Reich, 1928

Translations

Charles Baudelaire, *Die Blumen des Bösen: Umdichtungen,* 1901
Zeitgenössische Dichter, 2 vols., 1905
William Shakespeare, *Sonnette,* 1909
Dante Alighieri, *Göttliche Komödie,* 1912

Further Reading

Benjamin, Walter, "Rückblick auf Stefan George," *Schriften,* vol. 2, Frankfurt: Suhrkamp, 1955
Bock, Claus Victor, *Wort-Konkordanz zur Dichtung Stefang Georges,* Amsterdam: Castrum Peregrini, 1964
Boehringer, Robert, *Mein Bild von Stefan George,* Munich: Bondi, 1951; 2nd edition, Munich: Küpper, 1968
Breuer, Stefan, *Ästhetischer Fundamentalismus: Stefan George und der deutsche Antimodernismus,* Darmstadt: Wissenschaftliche Buchgesellschaft, 1995
David, Claude, *Stefan George: Son oeuvre poétique,* Paris and Lyon: IAC, 1952; as *Stefan George: Sein dichterisches Werk,* Munich: Hanser, 1967
Goldsmith, Ulrich K., *Stefan George,* New York: Columbia University Press, 1970
Gundolf, Friedrich, *George,* Berlin: Bondi, 1920
Landmann, Georg Peter, *Stefan George und sein Kreis: Eine Bibliographie,* Hamburg: Hauswedell, 1960; 2nd edition, 1976
Landmann, Georg Peter, editor, *Der George-Kreis: Eine Auswahl aus seinen Schriften,* Cologne: Kiepenheuer und Witsch, 1965

Metzger, Michael M., and Erika A. Metzger, *Stefan George,* New York: Twayne, 1972
Morwitz, Ernst, *Kommentar zu dem Werk Stefan Georges,* Munich: Küpper, 1960; 2nd edition, Düsseldorf: Küpper, 1969
——, *Kommentar zu den Prosa- Drama- und Jugend-Dichtungen Stefan Georges,* Munich: Küpper, 1962
Salin, Edgar, *Um Stefan George: Erinnerung und Zeugnis,* Godesberg: Küpper, 1948; 2nd edition, 1954
Schonauer, Franz, *Stefan George in Selbstzeugnissen und Bilddokumenten,* Reinbek bei Hamburg: Rowohlt, 1960
Seekamp, H.J., et al., *Stefan George: Leben und Werk, Eine Zeittafel,* Amsterdam: Castrum Peregrini, 1972
Viereck, Peter, "Stefan George Rediscovered: Translations and Comments," *Parnassus: Poetry in Review* 14, no. 1 (1987)
Winkler, Michael, *Stefan George,* Stuttgart: Metzler, 1970
——, *George-Kreis,* Stuttgart: Metzler, 1972

Der Teppich des Lebens und die Lieder von Traum und Tod, mit einem Vorspiel 1899

Collection of Poems by Stefan George

Der Teppich des Lebens (*The Tapestry of Life*), marks a crucial transition in Stefan George's career as a poet and thinker. Its very title page, dated "1900," seems to herald a new era. By then, George had issued "public" editions of three books of poetry and was esteemed as a meticulous writer in the fashionable art nouveau style. As in George's earlier collections, the first edition of *The Tapestry of Life* consisted of 300 elaborately ornamented copies. A plainer second printing was soon made available to a larger audience. The poetry's style and ideology accorded with George's quest for more diverse readers. At this time he began to enlist those younger disciples who would form the "George-Kreis," the circle that was to project his influence within German thought and culture. More fervently than ever before, George asserts in this work the poet's right and obligation to act in the world not only as an artist but also as a priestly lawgiver whose mission is nothing less than spiritual reform. The poet draws his legitimacy from sacred poetic inspiration, yet he must exercise it solely through his power over language, seemingly the most fragile of instruments. In these formulations, George renews a conception of the poet previously postulated by Schiller, Hölderlin, and the Romantics, here radicalized by a Nietzschean license that makes the charismatic artist a force for change and places him beyond the conventions of good and evil.

Each of the three sections of *The Tapestry of Life* contains 24 poems, all articulated in four four-line stanzas. While symmetry had been a hallmark of George's earlier collections, such arithmetic uniformity anticipates the hieratic numerology of *Der Siebente Ring* (1907; *The Seventh Ring*) and *Der Stern des Bundes* (1913; *The Star of the Covenant*). The poems themselves, however, are not as uniform as this pronounced structural balance might suggest. While most are in iambic pentameter, there are fascinating prosodic departures and a variety of rhyme schemes. In their language, the poems characteristically suggest allegorical contexts and ranges of imagery whose precise references are never specified. This lends to them a sense of portentous mystery and, indeed, prophecy, which George's admirers revere as visionary but which more recent critics have deplored as being dangerously ambiguous, open categories. Like many of George's later works, some poems of *The Tapestry of Life* strike these readers as too liable, like the messages of oracles, to be given meanings shaped mainly by the interests of the interpreter, which may be primarily aesthetic or social and political.

The "Prelude" finds the poet in a crisis compounded of waning creativity, the loss of his youth and passion, and, ultimately, despair over the human condition. "A naked angel" that is a harbinger of *das schöne leben* (life in all its beauty) visits the poet. The expression is closest to the Greek *kalokagathia,* "the Good-Beautiful," with ethical as well as aesthetic meaning. The angel, who bears both biblical and classical Greek traits, is widely seen to represent the poet's own ideal, higher soul, a kind of Socratic daimon that transcends the pain of life and embodies an eternal, spiritual ideality of being and sacred truth. This redeeming "guide and friend" only promises the poet a painful, lonely struggle if he is to achieve the *ehrengift,* "honor's reward," for fulfilling his calling. The poet is to arouse in his own countrymen, but also in humanity as a whole, the will to carry out heroic deeds for the sake of what is noblest and most sublime in their souls. This can only be realized, however, by daring change, by transcending the values of the present, and by rising to new heights of achievement, whose nature, be it artistic or social, is not defined.

The middle section constitutes *The Tapestry of Life* itself. "The Tapestry" suggests a central tenet: in its initial inscrutability, a work of art, here a tapestry with many evocative figures, is a microcosmic exemplar of the mystery of human existence. True insight into art and life alike, the poem argues, lies in visionary revelation rather than in rational analysis, in a moment of grace received rather than in the philosophical exercises of an academy. The poems that follow celebrate elemental, archetypal relationships and deeds. George now believes that the authentic forces that determine human destiny reside in these archetypal acts. George's nostalgic antimodernism is also apparent in "Primeval Landscape," which hearkens back to the very rudiments of culture in archaic times. The *Tapestry*'s thematic threads, however, are more intricately interwoven than they seem. Several critics have remarked that, while certain poems can be read for their cultural, or even social or political messages, they also convey artistic points of view, arguments in favor of George's conception of poetry. "The Friend of the Fields," for example, describes how a devoted farmer lovingly cultivates his lands by bracing stalks, weeding, and testing the fruits. His effort results in a pastoral ideal: "Beneath his foot the region spills with flowers / And ripens to a harvest where he passes." The farmer has also been interpreted as an allegorical self-portrait of George, in which the poet describes his cultivation of the literary life of his circle—lending support to some, weeding out others. "Lambs" and "Brothers in Sorrow," while seemingly treating more universal experience, are also skillfully veiled allegories of George's deprecating view of the literary culture of Austria, a theme emphatically stated in the third section's "The Brothers." "The Disciple," "The Elect," and "The Outcast," which seem to present essential modes of thought and action that facilitate or hinder *das schöne leben,* also embody praise or condemnation of members of George's circle.

A tone of valediction dominates the "Songs of Dream and Death," in which George, his eyes on the visionary hope of the future, recalls with melancholy affection friendships that will soon lie behind him. The empathy that George here conveys for certain individuals and the spiritual and cultural qualities they symbolize, which he has nonetheless outlived, lends poignancy to the way in which he departs from them in order to encounter life's authentic beauty.

MICHAEL M. METZGER

Editions

First edition: *Der Teppich des Lebens und die Lieder von Traum und Tod, mit einem Vorspiel,* Berlin: Holten, 1899

Critical edition: in *Gesamt-Ausgabe der Werke,* vol. 5, Berlin: Bondi, 1932

Translation: *The Tapestry of Life and the Songs of Dream and Death with a Prelude,* in *The Works of Stefan George,* translated by Olga Marx and Ernst Morwitz, 2nd edition, Chapel Hill: University of North Carolina Press, 1974

Further Reading

Aler, Jan, "Stefan Georges Kunst der Komposition, veranschaulicht am 'Teppich des Lebens'," *Wirkendes Wort* 10, no. 3 (1960)

Breuer, Stefan, *Ästhetischer Fundamentalismus: Stefan George und der deutsche Antimodernismus,* Darmstadt: Wissenschaftliche Buchgesellschaft, 1995

David, Claude, *Stefan George: Son oeuvre poétique,* Paris and Lyon: Imprimerie Artistique en Couleurs, 1952; as *Stefan George: Sein dichterisches Werk,* Munich: Hanser, 1967

Hoffmann, Peter, *Stauffenberg: A Family History, 1905–1944,* Cambridge: Cambridge University Press, 1995

Manaster Ramer, Alexis, "Stefan George and Phonological Theory," *Phonology* 11, no. 2 (1994)

Marache, Maurice, "Du 'Tapis de la vie' à 'L'étoile d'alliance,' L'évolution de la pensée de Stefan George à la lumière des styles," *Etudes Germaniques* 21 (1966)

Morwitz, Ernst, *Kommentar zu dem Werk Stefan Georges,* Munich: Küpper, 1960; 2nd edition, Düsseldorf: Küpper, 1969

Pikulik, Lothar, "Stefan Georges Gedicht 'Der Teppich': Romantisch-Unromantisches einer wählerischen Kunstmetaphysik," *Euphorion* 80, no. 4 (1986)

Titzmann, Michael, "Der Teppich des Lebens und die Lieder von Traum und Tod mit einem Vorspiel," *Kindlers Literatur Lexikon im dtv,* edited by Wolfgang von Einsiedel, vol. 21, Munich: Deutscher Taschenbuch Verlag, 1974

Weber, Frank, "Stefan George und die Kosmiker," *Neue Deutsche Hefte* 35, no. 2 (1988)

German, Middle High, *see* Middle High German

German, Old High, *see* Old High German

German Democratic Republic

Books played a very special role in the German Democratic Republic (GDR). The country's politicians spoke of the GDR as a "country of readers" in order to emphasize that there was hardly a country in the world where more books were read. West German sociologists had no hesitation in referring to novels when looking for data on everyday life in the neighboring state. In the United States, specialists on GDR literature were regarded as experts on the whole country. The GDR Ministry for State Security (the "Stasi") expended great energy in their effort to control the written and the (un)printed word. And, subsequently, many authors boasted that their works had been their contribution to the collapse of the GDR. Are these all myths, paradoxes, or puzzles? In any event, we have here a series of questions for anyone looking back, after its demise in 1989–90, on the literature of the GDR.

To recapitulate the GDR's historical roots, in 1945, Germany was divided into four occupation zones. In May 1949, three of these combined to give birth to the Federal Republic of Germany, and in October of that year the German Democratic Republic emerged from the Soviet Occupation Zone. Its claim—made explicit in its title—was to be the foundation of the first truly democratic state on German soil: the reality was that the GDR was, from the very beginning, an attempt to shape this part of Germany on the Soviet model. Two groups were behind this development: the "Soviet Military Administration in Germany" and a group of German Communist Party officials led by Walter Ulbricht, who had been a member of the Reichstag in the Weimar Republic. The group returned with the Red Army from exile in Moscow.

Formally speaking, the GDR never became a Soviet Republic (based, that is, on soldiers' and workers' councils). In reality, however, the country was controlled by a single party, the SED (Socialist Unity Party of Germany). The party's structures and hierarchies (Central Committee, Politburo) took precedence over the state structures. The "leading role" of the party was in fact written into the constitution. Political activity was indelibly stamped by the contradiction between a superficial allegiance to the forms of parliamentary democracy (the GDR possessed a multiparty system, itself also dominated by the SED) and by the practical task of reconstructing society on socialist principles. It may be true that the population initially supported numerous decisions of principle in this restructuring, but these decisions were in fact taken by the new authorities. These authorities, however, were not prepared to take the risk of relying on unpredictable basis-socialism structures, and, as a result, their initial program, which had enjoyed wide acceptance, degenerated into an ideology whose sole function was the legitimation of power.

Writers and authors—in East and West Germany—had passionately warned against the political division of Germany. When this division had become inevitable, however, they quickly accepted the social functions that their respective political systems ascribed to them. There were differences of detail, of course, but these functions were characterized in both East and West Germany by the political weight that became attached to the "high office of the poet" (Karl Mickel). In both German states, the writers' role was marked by their experience of the National Socialist past. In West Germany, writers such as Heinrich Böll were obliged painfully to come to terms with this past, acting in the name of a society that conspicuously failed to do likewise. In East Germany, the overcoming of National Socialism was part of the public discourse, even though no honest reckoning with the past was sought for, since the victory of the Allied forces over Hitler's Germany had already been reinterpreted as a victory of the working classes over fascism. Writers participated in these reinterpretations, presenting—with hindsight—the supposed agents of this alleged revolution as enthusiastic followers of the goals of the revolution. Writers participated in this rewriting of history out of their belief that they were contributing to the construction of a more peaceful and just society. There were many reasons—historical as well as social and psychological—why these writers were ready to reorient their work in accordance with political and moral criteria in this way, but this activity took place at the cost of other significant dimensions of literary activity such as aesthetic concerns, experimentation, and entertainment.

It was not primarily the privileges that East Germany offered (for instance, higher food rations) that made many authors returning from exile settle in East Germany (including Bertolt Brecht, Stefan Heym, Anna Seghers, and Arnold Zweig). No less than writers returning home from the war (such as Franz Fühmann or Günter de Bruyn), these exiles' experiences of fascism had given them a personal conviction that the only way to avoid a repetition of the past lay in the socialist system. This is also true of the younger generation of writers who had grown up under National Socialism, among them Christa Wolf, Volker Braun, and Heiner Müller, and even for those born later, such as Christoph Hein. Their own experiences, their personal sense of guilt, and their own personal convictions—all these demanded of them a readiness to defend, almost at any cost, what was understood as a significant achievement of the postwar period: a political system based on opposition to fascism. There are many texts that also make clear, through their inception and the problems of their reception, the enormous moral and literary effort it took for writers to oppose even the distortions of socialism that they experienced in the GDR.

At the start, the cultural policy of the GDR aligned itself with the humanistic traditions of German culture—this was in keeping with the "Popular Front" strategy of the German Communist Party, which had aimed to bring together all progressive political forces under its leadership. Such was the declared aim of the "Kulturbund zur demokratischen Erneuerung Deutschlands" (Cultural Union for the Democratic Regeneration of Germany), founded in 1945 on an all-German basis. Its chairman, the poet-politician Johannes R. Becher (himself once a lyric poet in the Expressionist period, in the later years of the Weimar Republic the chairman of the BPRS—the Association of Proletarian-Revolutionary Writers—and, subsequently, minister for culture in the GDR), argued for a coalition of intellectuals and the state, while at the same time forcing writers to conform to traditional aesthetic norms. In publications in the immediate postwar years, Becher's traditionalism was in keeping with the personal aims and experiences of those writers returning from exile, as shown in the texts that had been written in exile. Anna Seghers' novel *Das siebte Kreuz* (1942; *The Seventh Cross*), for instance, which is the story of a successful escape from a concentration camp, although it is impressively compact in its plot and persuasive in its characterization, is highly conventional in its narrative form.

Traditionalism of this kind soon turned into a stick with which to beat modernism in art, a process that accompanied the major restructuring of social and economic life. After the founding of the GDR state in 1949, a series of reforms was forced through to turn GDR society toward a Soviet model. Soviet ideas and principles were the decisive factor, not merely in social and economic policy (where many collective, i.e., state, factories were set up, agriculture was collectivized, and the administration was centralized): the same process was carried out in cultural policy. In May 1951, the Central Committee of the SED demanded that a new national literature should provide "strong help for the German people in solving the great questions of its survival." This was a pedagogic rather than aesthetic program for literature, and yet many writers submitted to it. They were not entirely without complaint but driven by their grim recognition of the necessity—if they were to avoid of repetition of the recent past—of participating in the work of education and persuasion required by their particular historical situation. Prose writing played a key part in this pedagogic project. Novels—such as Eduard Claudius's *Menschen an unsrer Seite* (1951; *People at Our Side*)—portrayed the basic economic and social conflicts of the time and used simplified narrative techniques. Even Brecht seemed ready to adapt to these political necessities. After Paul Dessau's opera *Das Verhör des Lukullus* (1951; *The Trial of Lucullus*) had been taken out of the repertory, Brecht noted in his *Arbeitsjournal* (work-diary) on 25 March 1951: "It is to be expected that, in the face of such enormous upheavals, the arts will get into difficulty, even when they are to the fore in precipitating change."

In contrast to the claim that Marxist philosophy represented modernity, the art policies of the 1950s explicitly fought against modern and experimental ways of writing. They did so by reference to a definition of socialist art that the Hungarian philosopher and literary theoretician Georg Lukács had developed back in the 1930s. While his opponents—among them Brecht—had argued for a theory of literature that permitted a variety and openness of form, Lukács insisted on an understanding of socialist realism that was based exclusively on the further extension of a form of reproduction perfected in the golden age of bourgeois art—a process that went no further than simply to accommodate these art forms to the situations of the present. Authors such as James Joyce or John Dos Passos were rejected as being decadent, their works merely reflecting the decline of the bourgeois classes. A work of art was seen as being determined by the ideology of its author and by the author's ability to adapt to the canonized forms of 19th-century bourgeois art. Such an understanding of socialist realism reduced literature to a pedagogic activity. Despite the considerable efforts made in the late decades of the GDR to revise this view, Lukács's understanding of art determined the entire literary policy of the GDR.

The policies toward literature were organized by a central hierarchy. There were some 80 book and magazine publishers, 16 of which were exclusively responsible for imaginative literature. Their work was coordinated by the central office for publishers and the book trade in the Ministry for Culture. This office organized an annual plan according to the themes required, allocated paper supplies, checked manuscripts, and issued for each individual publication the license to print. So this office had the clear function, on one level, of censorship. Its possible actions ranged from reducing paper allocations to refusing the license to print. With hindsight, however, many of those who suffered at the hands of this agency saw it less as an arm of state power than as an institution in which experts negotiated the state's policy toward literature and in the process established the boundaries of that policy. This may be connected with the fact that the most contentious decisions were taken for the most part not in the Ministry of Culture but in the culture and media sections of the Central Committee of the SED and in the Politburo. If not there, decisions were made in the minds of the authors themselves, who had in the course of the years developed a sense of what was possible at a given moment. This internalized form of censorship contributed to the fact that for a long time the literature of the GDR was much more afraid of conflict than was the literature of neighboring East European states. The greatest factor was, however, fear of a possible revival of fascism. An amazingly large number of writers had accepted the use of Soviet tanks against the workers' uprising of 17 June 1953 because of their fear that the socialist experiment might come to an abrupt end. Only when they looked back on events in later years did many authors recognize in the use of violence against the allegedly sovereign people a first cause for doubts, doubts that had at the time of the uprising been buried under writers' consent to the political goals (if not the methods) of the time. These doubts were scarcely made public, of course. Questioning and personal scruples were generally hidden behind individual motifs and intertextual cross-references in literary works. Only later did two events alter this. First came the suppression of the Czech reform movement by Warsaw Pact troops (in August 1968), and, second, there was the expulsion of the political songwriter Wolf Biermann through the removal of his civil rights during his concert tour in the Federal Republic in November 1976. Up to that point, many writers' position had been one of critical loyalty, but these events made it easier for them to break out of what Wolfgang Emmerich has called the "loyalty trap" of socialist cultural policy.

Back in the 1950s, however, there was a sense of common purpose in working to create a new socialist literature. The first book written in the GDR to enjoy popular success was Bruno Apitz's *Nackt unter Wölfen* (1958; *Naked among Wolves*). This novel was not set in the socialist present but in a National Socialist concentration camp. Its conventional narrative form is well suited to the comforting certainties of an ideology that, on the basis of its antifascist past, was able to offer unambiguous positions. Explaining the present was more problematic, however. It was precisely to encourage the growth of a socialist literature about the present that party officials and creative writers met for a conference in Bitterfeld—in fact, in an electrochemical works. The topic was the relationships between literature and the world of work, and between writers and workers. The outcome of this and a follow-up conference held five years later was the program—known as the "Bitterfeld Way"—that was to determine state policy toward literature for the next ten years. The first conference focused on two topics: the first involved the need to change the role of the reader. Every reader was in principle meant to become a writer, to move from the consumption to the production of literature. The program—which operated under the slogan "Greif zur Feder, Kumpel" (pick up a pen, workmate)—stood in the tradition of the communist worker-correspondents movement and had the goal of encouraging individuals in the workforce to come to terms with their work environment through the process of writing. It led to a large quantity of *Brigadetagebücher* (diaries produced by the work brigades in the factories) and encouraged in addition other artistic forms of expression. A second focus concerned redefining the role of the writers. Authors were intended to learn firsthand about the production relations that were the basis of social praxis and, therefore, to spend time seconded to a factory, as it were, to adopt a factory. In essence, this program, with its insistence on writers recognizing the reality of contemporary experience in the GDR, contained a potential for interesting forms of modernization. After all, montage and reportage were established forms of socialist writing long before the war. If it had been taken seriously, the "Bitterfeld Way" could have led to the production of a literature of socialist modernism, which, by opening out the scope of literature, would have had clear implications for undermining ossified power structures. But since the initiators of the Bitterfeld program were not interested in genuine literary innovation, the program was doomed to fail. The familiar model of realism was not up for discussion. All that was sought were new contents and themes to put into conventional literary forms, with no other purpose than to reinforce the old cliché that the party's ideology had always insisted on: that there was no difference between the interests of the party, the collective, and the individual. Franz Fühmann—who was along with Christa Wolf one of the few leading writers to embark on the experiment of working in a factory—published a volume of reportages based on his experiences in a shipyard in Rostock

(*Kabelkran und Blauer Peter* [1961; Cable Crane and Blue Peter]), but at the same time in an open letter to the minister for culture he insisted on the unique and individual nature of his experiences. His excursion into the world of work might, he claimed, "enable me to engage in political debate, but not to be artistically productive." The second Bitterfeld conference finally buried this initiative. The representatives of the party argued that only people who understood the industrial world from their position as planners and managers, the officials, should be permitted to affect macrostructures. So, while the "Bitterfeld Way" initiated an interesting popular movement, of which the success of the famous Schwedt Workers Theater is an example, its most important result was to encourage the emergence of two socialist variants on traditional genres: the bildungsroman (novel of education) and the *Entwicklungsroman* (novel of development), which were both written from the point of view of party functionaries. The preoccupation with contemporary issues similarly gave rise to a new series of literary figures, made up of people who did not manage to achieve that identity of personal experience with the interests of the collective, which the party claimed to exist. Some of the characters came to grief precisely because they took literally Marxism's promise of self-fulfillment.

Erwin Strittmatter's *Ole Bienkopp* (1963) offers a good example of this trend. The central figure is a peasant who perishes in a conflict between his own personal impatience and the circumstances of his society, which are frozen in dogmatic rigidity. Strittmatter's narrative technique, in which the point of view of one character dominates all the others, points tentatively in the direction of a more subjective writing stance. Something similar can be seen in Christa Wolf's *Der geteilte Himmel* (1963; *The Divided Heaven*), where a more-or-less marginal action in the present allows the author to reconstruct the heroine's past by means of narrative flashbacks and monologues devoted to recollections. The conflicts with which this montage technique confronts the reader leave many questions unanswered. Hermann Kant's *Die Aula* (1965; The Auditorium) works with an apparently greater radicalism in the use of modern narrative techniques. His entertaining presentation of the founding years of the GDR leaves hardly a single modern narrative technique untried. The use of these techniques is deceptive, however, for, although the reader is constantly offered the chance of communication with the text, this communication never goes beyond affirmation and recognition of particular social experiences. Experiences that do not conform to this norm are, like all deviant perspectives on the future, implicitly devalued by a narrative stance that admits to no fallibility, since it is historically correct. Despite this, the formal and linguistic brilliance of Kant's novel made it one of the first GDR novels to achieve considerable success, both in the GDR and in translation in numerous other countries.

The "Bitterfeld Way" made it possible for authors to borrow—cautiously—some aspects of modern narrative techniques. Flashback, inner monologue and stream of consciousness, ironic breaks, and shifts in narrative perspective made their way into GDR prose, and in general the subjective ways of narrating began to relativize aspects of the narrated material and to differentiate it out. But radically new techniques still had no chance. Cultural politicians, as well as the censors and the agencies policing literary production, had a strong sense of the irreconcilability of "real existing socialism" and that deep skepticism articulated by modern art. Any literature that looked to support the idyll propagated by the party was by definition diametrically opposed to the claim of authenticity marking modern writing. Although from time to time efforts were made to establish modern writing techniques within socialist literary practice, the most important exponents of this could not be published inside the state. They form, nevertheless, an important part of the literature of the GDR. Uwe Johnson's novel *Mutmassungen über Jakob* (1959; *Speculations about Jakob*) is an inspired attempt at writing German-German realities into literary form, in a mixture of a search for truth, monologue, and report. In the special world of poetic fiction, Johnson manages to create a picture of the division of Germany that is still valid after the division itself has come to an end. No linear narrative could have remotely managed to grasp the paradoxical situation in Germany. However, Johnson's technique—the witnesses' statements and the conversations, reflections, and reports on events that took place at another time and place—creates the novel of an artificially divided land in which the lives of individuals, as well as their problems and worries, cross the frontier. No one can see a solution, least of all the author. His perplexity characterizes a book that lies between the frontiers, not merely those between the two German states but between those boundary lines that are drawn when types of texts are carefully kept apart and when particular literary forms are canonized or condemned for reasons of state policy.

Another example is Fritz Rudolf Fries's novel *Der Weg nach Oobliadooh* (1966; *The Road to Oobliadooh*). By the richness of the associations it evokes, the novel blurs the dividing line between content and form in narration and, using jazz as an analogy, suggests visions and projections of alternative lifestyles. A final example would be Irmtraut Morgner's novel *Rumba auf einen Herbst* (1992; Rumba as a Tribute to an Autumn), a text that originated in the 1960s but was for a long time thought to have been lost and was only recently pieced together from copies of the manuscript. The novel tells the story of a love affair, wild and fast moving, played out among scientists. Here, as in Fries's text, a deliberate role is given to a kind of music (rumba and blues) that, precisely because of its sensual and subversive qualities, was frowned on in the GDR at the time. The manuscript of this novel was rejected at the beginning of 1966, immediately after the notorious 11th plenary session of the Central Committee of the SED. The reasons given for this rejection made clear that the authorities had the crudest possible idea of the political effect of artistic devices. Among other criticisms, the fear was expressed that the techniques of inner monologue and flashback might lead directly to "unbridled individualism."

Where the content of texts offended the censors, the authorities reacted as they saw fit, on a case-by-case basis—or even arbitrarily. In the 1980s, a whole range of sensitive themes (flight from the GDR, the Stasi, the crimes of the Soviet Army, and environmental problems) came to be permitted. Texts with radical formal innovation that might open new perceptions to readers, however, were as a rule consistently blocked.

The hope to which many authors clung—that, as the political system was consolidated, literature might become free from tactical and pedagogic manipulation—was dashed. Even in the period after August 1961, when the building of the Berlin Wall made it feasible to think that a new socialist self-awareness might emerge without further political interference, the party kept art under its firm control. In 1962, the internationally renowned lyric poet Peter Huchel lost his job as the editor in chief of the periodical *Sinn und Form*. The SED secretary with responsibility for culture, Kurt Hager, explained that the periodical had not been unambiguous in its support for the Bitterfeld program. In 1963, the representatives of the GDR who attended an international conference in Liblice, in Czechoslovakia, declared that the work of Franz Kafka was of no interest to their country, since there was no experience there of the alienation that Kafka's work described. In December 1965, the 11th Plenary of the Central Committee of the SED took place, at which leading politicians strongly attacked the "modernism" and "nihilism" of Wolf Biermann, Werner Bräunig, Stefan Heym, Günter Kunert, Heiner Müller, and a whole series of film directors. Such an attack clearly stood in contradiction to Christa Wolf's cautious, if very brave, warning that literature should not be misunderstood as an instrument of civic education.

From the mid-1960s, if not earlier, it was evident that it was an illusion to hope that, within the consolidated socialist system, it might be possible for intellectuals and politicians to work together and to realize their utopia. Such a profound recognition of the irreconcilability of the aims of politics and literature stimulated the emergence of a literature that increasingly freed itself from the official discourse and thus gave a still stronger impulse to cultural life than the one that had come from the relative liberalization following the appointment of Erich Honecker as the successor to Walter Ulbricht. In a famous remark at the time of his inauguration, Honecker had promised a literature policy "without taboos." The year 1976 showed the reality, revealing the narrow limits to the SED's tolerance and readiness to talk. The way in which the SED dealt with the writers and artists (more than 100 in number) who protested in resolutions and open letters at the expulsion of Wolf Biermann from the GDR had an unmistakable message. State and party reacted with a whole range of punitive measures, running from arrest and house arrest, expulsion from the party or from the Writers' Association, disciplinary measures inside the party, and publication bans to the sudden encouragement to writers to leave the country. Many writers did in fact move to the West at this time (among others, Reiner Kunze, Jurek Becker, Klaus Schlesinger, Hans Joachim Schädlich, Sarah Kirsch, and Günter Kunert). Those who stayed continued with their efforts to liberate literature from political constraints—a course they had embarked upon in the mid-1960s. Their poems, plays, and novels actively supported the claims of the individual as against society. Conflicts were explicitly described, errors and mistakes were no longer confined to individuals but laid at the door of the state and the SED. Most of these texts, however, did not extend their critique of the party into matters of aesthetic form, although a whole series of writers (mostly lyric poets and dramatists) consciously left behind official paradigms and began to align themselves with negative models drawn either from Weimar classicism or from bourgeois realism. Heiner Müller was one of this group (with his 1965 publication of the plays *Philoktet* and *Der Bau—Construction* in the journal *Sinn und Form*): the lyric poets were represented not only by the older generation (Erich Arendt and Peter Huchel), whose long-established aesthetic position had meant that their response to the party's requirements had always been controversial, but also by representatives of the younger generation such as Volker Braun or Karl Mickel. Their personal discoveries were, on the one hand, Friedrich Hölderlin, Heinrich von Kleist, German Romanticism in general, Jean Paul, and Georg Büchner, or, on the other hand, the French avant-garde of the 19th century, particularly Charles Baudelaire and Arthur Rimbaud. The younger generation used these writers as models for their own work, reading back into these great writers of the past their own melancholy and the near schizophrenia of their own position.

In 1965, Christa Wolf published in the GDR a first cautious attempt at modern prose. Her short narrative text *Juninachmittag* (1967; *An Afternoon in June*) evokes a world richly shot through with digressions and visions and full of metaphors, associations, and reflections. In this text, Wolf was trying out the way of writing that, several years later, would cause such controversy in *Nachdenken über Christa T.*, (1968; *The Quest for Christa T.*). The later novel is a mixture of memories, dreams, inner monologues, streams of consciousness and diary entries, letters, and essayistic reflection, and it obviously goes back in style to Ingeborg Bachmann and Max Frisch. For Wolf, too, literature had become a search for identity, and since this ran counter to the dominant aesthetic, considerable barriers were put in the way of the novel's publication. Its author was subjected to the cross fire of political attacks. Such measures could not, however, prevent authors such as Wolf from acquiring an international following, which in turn strengthened her position at home and presented official cultural policy with a dilemma. At a time when the GDR was looking for international political recognition, its international reputation was also crucially important—as was the income in foreign currency that writers publishing abroad brought to the state.

While experiments in narrative techniques could be checked, they could not be stopped in the years that followed. More and more authors rediscovered techniques such as authorial reflection and discontinuity, together with genres such as fantasy and grotesque. Ulrich Plenzdorf (*Die neuen Leiden des jungen W.* [1973; *The New Sufferings of Young W.*]) treated the theme of the problems of young people in the GDR through the device of a disrespectful reworking of Goethe's *Werther*, while Irmtraud Morgner's witty tour de force, the novel *Leben und Abenteuer der Trobadora Beatriz* (1974; Life and Adventures of Trobadora Beatriz), portrayed the relationship between the sexes, switching times and points of view with true mastery. This play with literary forms came to perfection in her witches' novel, *Amanda*, in 1983. Wolf herself transposed her authorial self-reflections into literary history with her fictitious account of a meeting between Heinrich von Kleist and the Romantic writer Caroline von Günderrode (*Kein Ort. Nirgends* [1979; *No Place on Earth*]). Volker Braun in his *Hinze-Kunze-Roman* (1985) attempted to explore socialist writing's claim that it represented a literary avant-garde. His exploration of the master-servant relationship from a socialist perspective led him to write one of the most explosive modernist novels, which calls on all the techniques of modernist fiction—even the publisher's blurb on the book cover offers a confusing range of choices as to the novel's content, thus both appealing to the reader's imagination and playing games with the censor.

At the same time, a new type of realism was evolving, which sought neither to make the antifascist past heroic nor to work through the wishful thinking of socialism in the present. Jurek Becker's novel *Jakob der Lügner* (1969; *Jacob the Liar*) shed new light on the National Socialist persecution of the Jews. Wolf (*Kindheitsmuster* [1976; *Patterns of Childhood*]) had similarly attempted to open up the petit bourgeois milieu of the 1930s. Without explicit authorial commentary, this book exposed the structures of both thought and life of a group of people who were neither the victims nor the perpetrators of National Socialist atrocities and yet who by their attitudes had contributed to the success of German fascism. A similar intention lies behind Franz Fühmann's autobiographically colored essay *Zweiundzwanzig Tage oder die Hälfte des Lebens* (1973; *Twenty-Two Days or Half a Lifetime*), in which he relentlessly exposes such attitudes both in himself and in his time. By doing so, he could find his way back to still more distant historical periods. This led him to encounter Romanticism and Expressionism and to rediscover the themes and traditions of writing that conventional realism had obscured.

Gradually, not only literary-aesthetic taboos were being broken but also social and political ones. By the 1970s, literature—especially prose—had acquired a new function. It had become a substitute for the public sphere, which is to say that literature brought into public discussion issues and topics that the press ignored. Literature became one of the most important forums for the critical intellectuals within an authoritarian society. At a personal level, this was rewarding, but once again it mixed literary with political and moral issues. For writers to warn society and to uncover its ills merely continued their unsuccessful period as educators of the nation. Within the closed world of GDR literature, such a role brought many writers into conflict with the state but—in compensation almost—ensured them a prominent position in the society. Notwithstanding occasional stylistic innovations, writers were still locked in a literary discourse that was orientated to content, not form.

The central theme of prose writing in the 1970s and 1980s was alienation in an industrial society. Maxi Wander, Christoph Hein, Jurek Becker, Günter de Bruyn, Franz Fühmann, Harald Gerlach, Erich Loest, Helga Königsdorf, Klaus Schlesinger, and other writers found their themes in the everyday problems of a consumer society that had more or less stabilized itself, even if it remained economically less prosperous than the West. It was a society by now able to afford the luxury of debates about marriage, relationships, work as monotony (rather than as a heroic activity), and old age. As if in a time warp, GDR literature had discovered and reactivated the mode of socially critical writing that had dominated Western German literature in the 1960s. What is more, the use of familiar images, motifs, and characters suggested similarities in experiences across these two periods, particularly in personal relations. Similarities of historical experience were important, too, for there were historical and social factors that left their mark on individual experience no less strongly than did political programs and production relations. In terms of their literature, it seemed that the two German states were drawing closer together some time before the political end of their division.

Nevertheless, there remained a significant difference between East and West Germany: the continuing importance of authors and their texts in the East. On a personal level, this might be negative or favorable, but in the GDR, it was the content, the message, that was at the heart of writers' self-understanding. That was the way in which their works were read by the general public, the professional readers in the censorship and the Stasi, and literary critics. Only in Leipzig, Berlin ("Prenzlauer Berg"), and elsewhere did the youngest authors manage to create a literary milieu that ignored such matters, treated literature as an aesthetic game, and had no regard for the traditional rules (having to be a member of the Writers' Association or needing permission to get something printed). That two prominent members of this group—Sascha Anderson and Rainer Schedlinksi—were subsequently exposed as Stasi spies put these activities into an ironic light.

After the end of the GDR, many writers faced a dilemma when they attempted to define a new role for themselves. They were under attack in any case, not merely for particular social positions that they had taken up, whether as apologists or critics of the regime, but even for their utopian stances. They were obliged to find their feet as best they could in the new, Western-style literary scene, with its commissioning practices, book promotions, and its market shares—to say nothing of the network of influential critics already established in West Germany. They either established themselves afresh or lapsed into silence. It seems evident by now that unification did little to shake the importance of the individual and collective experiences that had been specific to the GDR. Even after the GDR has ceased to exist as society and state, there seems to be a need for what we might call a "virtual" GDR literature. Books such as the third volume of Strittmatter's trilogy *Der Laden* (1992; *The Shop*), Wolf's collection of essays *Auf dem Weg nach Tabou* (1994; *Parting from Phantoms*), and Kant's novel *Kormoran* (1994) enjoyed considerable commercial success, especially in the East. This suggests that local traditions of reading and writing continue unchanged, together with an insistence on content, a moral stance, and the cautious use of modern techniques. Such writing offers a chance for what Michael Rutschky has called "the GDR community of experience and writing" to prolong its existence or, as one might say more cynically, for the first time to acquire a genuine reality, albeit in the forms of nostalgia, post-hoc justifications of the GDR-state, aggressive isolationism, and all the variety of social-psychological ways in which the political and personal breaks of history can be knitted together—breaks that were merely papered over by the speed and violence of the unification process.

HANNES KRAUSS

See also Der Bitterfelder Weg; Socialist Realism

Further Reading

Atkins, Robert, and Martin Kane, editors, *Retrospect and Review: Aspects of the Literature of the GDR 1976–1990,* Amsterdam and Atlanta, Georgia: Rodopi, 1997

Bathrick, David, *The Power of Speech: The Politics of Culture in the GDR,* Lincoln: University of Nebraska Press, 1995

Cosentino, Christine, et al., editors, *DDR-Lyrik im Kontext,* Amsterdam: Rodopi, 1988

Emmerich, Wolfgang, *Kleine Literaturgeschichte der DDR,* Darmstadt: Luchterhand, 1981; revised edition, Leipzig: Kiepenheuer, 1996

Fehervary, Helen, "The Literature of the German Democratic Republic," in *The Cambridge History of German Literature,* edited by Helen Watanabe-O'Kelly, Cambridge and New York: Cambridge University Press, 1997

Fox, Thomas C., *Border Crossings: An Introduction to East German Prose,* Ann Arbor: University of Michigan Press, 1993
Grant, Colin B., *Literary Communication from Consensus to Rupture: Practice and Theory in Honecker's GDR,* Amsterdam and Atlanta, Georgia: Rodopi, 1995
Jäger, Manfred, *Kultur und Politik in der DDR: 1945–1990,* Cologne: Edition Deutschland Archiv, 1994
Lederer, Herbert, *Handbook of East German Drama, 1945–1985: DDR Drama Handbuch, 1945–1985,* New York: Lang, 1987
Reid, J.H., *Writing without Taboos: The New East German Literature,* Oxford and New York: Berg, 1990; distributed exclusively in the U.S. by St. Martin's Press
Tate, Dennis, *The East German Novel: Identity, Community, Continuity,* Bath: Bath University Press, 1984

German Language

German is a Germanic (Gmc) language. It is most closely related to the other West Germanic (WGmc) languages (English, Frisian, Dutch [Flemish in Belgium], and Afrikaans) and more distantly related to the North Germanic (Icelandic, Faroese, Norwegian, Swedish, and Danish) and East Germanic groups (represented by Gothic). In terms of its wider genetic affiliations, German is a member of the Indo-European (IE) group. Its salient archaic features include an inherited core vocabulary and a three-term gender system. By contrast, innovation characterizes the sound system and syntax in particular. The archaic features and innovative processes associated with German combine to give the impression of a language typologically very different from its close relative, English.

Writing in German began in the eighth century and helped shape a cultural identity that has always transcended transient political arrangements. But its pluricentricity means that German has never been a national language in the narrow sense. Until the emergence of the supraregional written standard during the course of the 18th century (New High German, NHG, 1750–present day), German was essentially regional in character, as the spoken language by and large still is. The dialects of Upper and Central German (UG, CG) in the south are primarily characterized by the Second (High German) Sound Shift. So words such as UG *Pfeffer* (pepper) and *Wasser* (water) contrast with northern (Low German, LG) *Pepper* and *Water* and serve to mark off UG and CG from LG, English, and the other Gmc languages. The major linguistic influence on German in the historical period is Latin, which, during the Middle Ages (Old High German, OHG, ca. 750–1050; Middle High German, MHG, 1050–1350) and the Early Modern period (Early New High German, ENHG, 1350–1750), functioned as the standard written medium in the German-speaking world. The history of written German can therefore be seen first in terms of its increasing distance from the spoken language and second in terms of its emancipation from Latin and the gradual assumption of its functions. Broadly speaking, the standardization process is characterized linguistically by a period of unconscious convergence of written regional varieties in the late Middle Ages and the elimination of competing regional forms. This period was followed, from the 16th century onward, by conscious codification, which eventually produced standard dictionaries and grammars. A major world standard language of extraordinary versatility and expressive power has resulted from this process.

For English readers, a series of contrasts with English will serve to characterize NHG and to highlight both its salient features and some of its stylistic possibilities. The spelling system, with capital letters for nouns (e.g., *der Text*), with the use of the umlaut to indicate plural and other grammatical features (e.g., *das Rad, die Räder* [the wheel, the wheels]), and with the contrast between *ss* and *ß* (*ich esse* [I eat] versus *ich aß* [I ate]), is merely a medium for recording the language, and it has been consistently overrated by commentators and authors, not just during the recent debate on spelling reform. Indeed, the German spelling that is now being modified was not standardized until 1901. Having said that, an important distinction is made in German studies between the standard written language (*Hochdeutsch, Schriftdeutsch* [High German]), the dialects (the indigenous forms of local speech furthest removed from the standard), and the idiom of everyday speech (German *Umgangssprache* [colloquial language]). In other words, the "ideology of the standard" is the written language rather than (as could be argued for British English) a spoken variety.

Colloquial German is a relatively recent phenomenon, having developed principally in the expanding urban areas during the ENHG period under the influence of the emerging standard language. Nowadays, the most linguistically conservative dialect speakers are located in rural communities, and statistics show that they are relatively more numerous in the south. All spoken German is regional to a greater or lesser extent, and speakers use forms closer to the dialects or closer to the standard language according to a number of factors, the most important of which is probably the degree of formality inherent in the situation. Especially in the south, regional features are not socially stigmatized, and speakers' own distinctions between dialect and High German do not always correspond to objective criteria. The ability to switch codes depends on factors such as the level of education and the degree of diatopic mobility enjoyed by a speaker.

German also contrasts with English in having preserved its inflectional character, but the change from the movable word accent of IE to the strong dynamic accent on initial syllables in Germanic has weakened the original endings considerably. One result is the gradual development from OHG onward of an accompanying article with nouns or an obligatory pronoun with verbs, and this development has shifted the functional load from the endings on the head word to the endings of the phrase as a whole. In NHG, grammatical categories are therefore expressed at phrase level. The noun phrase has a small set of endings that delimit each other within the phrase to express combinations of gender, number, and case: *n*, for example, has a number of possible functions, but in the context *den Lehrer-n* [(to) the teachers], it can only be dative plural. The verb phrase has taken this development furthest. Formally, German has two inflected tenses, the present (*er sieht* [he sees]) and the preterite (*er sah* [he saw]), supplemented by two inflected subjunctive forms (Konjunktiv I *er sehe* [he saw], which mainly marks reported speech, and Konjunktiv II *er sähe* [he would see], which mainly marks hypothetical situations). Further tense, modal, quasi-aspectual, transitivity, and focusing distinctions, if these meanings are not conveyed by particles (e.g., *doch, wohl*), are expressed periphrastically. The periphrasis uses either auxiliaries (*haben, sein, werden*) and nonfinite forms of the verb (e.g., perfect *ich habe gesehen* [I have seen]; future *ich werde sehen* [I will see]; the past tense of Konjunktiv I *er habe gesehen* [he said that he had seen]; and the past tense of Konjunktiv II *er hätte gesehen* [he would have seen]) or so-called function verbs, noun phrases, or prepositional phrases to express the lexical content of the verbal complex. For example, in *Hier entsteht eine neue Schule* (A new school is being built), the process is seen as a complete whole, whereas in *Die Schule ist noch in Entstehung begriffen* (which would translate the same way), the emphasis is on the perception that the process is incomplete. Distributional analysis reveals a larger number of parts of speech in German, with a richly developed system of particles, contrasting with an English ragbag class of "adverbs."

Word order in German, a misnomer because sentence constituents often contain more than one word, differs from English in that it never signals syntactic information. Both *Der Hund hat den Mann gebissen* and *Den Mann hat der Hund gebissen* mean "the dog has bitten the man." The verbal complex (in this case *hat . . . gebissen*) is often seen as providing a framework for declarative sentences (German *Satzrahmen* [sentence frame]) because the finite verb is placed in the second constituent position and any nonfinite elements are placed toward the end of the sentence. We therefore distinguish three positional fields: the *Vorfeld* before the finite verb, the *Mittelfeld* between the finite verb and other elements of the verbal complex, and the *Nachfeld* between the nonfinite elements and the end of the sentence. If word order does not signal syntactic information, what significance does it have? Within the constraints mentioned above, the position of nonverbal elements is largely determined by the degree to which they form common ground between the speaker/writer and the addressee—in Clark's words, "the sum of their mutual, common, or joint knowledge, beliefs, and suppositions." The *Vorfeld* usually marks a link with a previous text and therefore belongs unambiguously to common ground. The elements in the *Mittelfeld* are placed in order of decreasing commonality and therefore of increasing information value. That is why unstressed personal pronouns, which refer back to the last appropriate lexical item, come at the beginning, and new or unusual information comes at the end (*Gestern hat er mir zufälligerweise die zwei Bücher in die Hand gedrückt* [Yesterday, as chance would have it, he pressed the two books into my hand]); it is also why definite noun phrases precede indefinite ones (*Unglücklicherweise hat der Spion seinen Vorgesetzten vertrauliche Informationen weitergegeben* [Unfortunately, the spy passed on secret information to his superiors]). Conversely, moving elements to the right has the effect of increasing their information value, and, as phrase length tends to correlate positively with information value, the *Nachfeld* is typically used for subordinate clauses and other long elements. Intonation (*Satzmelodie*) is also determined by grammatical and pragmatic factors and generally lacks the attitudinal element characteristic of English.

Over the last two centuries, in many varieties and styles of written German, the relative frequency of verbs per sentence has declined, whereas the length of noun phrases (NPs) has increased. Noun phrases, too, appear to have a tripartite architecture supported by a nominal frame, which consists of a determiner (*der, ein, jeder*, etc.) and a noun. In contrast to this prototypical NP pattern, the absence of a determiner has developed significance, such as in the marking of indefinite plural NPs (*blaue Augen* [blue eyes]) and in the special use of abstracts (e.g., *Er fürchtet das Alter* [He's afraid of old age] versus *Alter schützt vor Torheit nicht* [Old age is no protection against stupidity, or, there's no fool like an old fool]). The *Vorfeld* may be occupied by a small set of so-called predeterminers (indeclinable *welch, solch, all,* or *so*), as in *welch ein Chaos* (what a mess). The *Mittelfeld* consists of adjectives such as *guter* in *mein guter Freund* (my good friend), which may also form the nucleus of an adjective phrase (AP), as in *mein sehr guter Freund* (my very good friend); the elements of the AP are marked by a lack of inflection. Such APs may be quite complex (e.g., *die in Richtung Koblenz nicht mehr befahrbare Autobahn* [the motorway/freeway that is no longer open in the direction of Koblenz]), for the inflection contrasts with use after the noun (e.g., *die Autobahn, in Richtung Koblenz nicht mehr befahrbar, . . .*). The *Nachfeld* typically contains structures dependent on nonadjectives (e.g., NPs, prepositional phrases, and relative clauses: *die Autobahnen der Nachkriegszeit, die Autobahn nach Koblenz, die Autobahn, die in Richtung Koblenz nicht mehr befahrbar ist*).

Correlating with the drift toward simple sentences containing one verbal and a set of often very large and complex nominal constituents, the number and variety of modern German noun and adjective derivations and compounds also contrast sharply with English. The verb *ziehen*, for which around 200 related derivations and 800 compounds have been counted, is not unique. Implicit derivation of the type often encountered in English (e.g., *the box* versus *to box*) is rarer in German, clear marking of word formation patterns being the norm (e.g., NHG *die Packung* vs. *packen*). New High German compounds are legendary for their complexity but in fact generally conform to the simple binary structure present since the preliterary period (e.g., Gmc *bruðiguman* [bridegroom]). The impression of complexity arises from the increased use in NHG of complex compositional elements: for instance, *Waffenstillstandserklärung* (cease-fire declaration) is made up of *waffenstillstand*, itself a compound, the second element of which is complex, and *erklärung*, a derivation. Even seemingly opaque ad hoc constructions such as *Kolonialwarenhändlerinsünden* (the sins of a grocer's wife [Grass]) conform to this pattern and are clear and apposite in context. Another salient lexical feature is the distinction between native and foreign words, amply illustrated in the *DUDEN Fremdwörterbuch*. Both the productivity of German word formation patterns, including occasional compounds, and the availability of alternative foreign and dialect expressions provide counterevidence to the notion that the lexicon of German is significantly smaller than English.

All these idiosyncratic features of German, as well as more general features such as length of sentence, number of adjectives, and nominal versus verbal constructions, have been used by German authors to stylistic effect. In the future, if emerging features of German usage are translated into longer-term developments, we may well see increasing linguistic distance between standard (written) and colloquial (spoken) German that produce tensions and motives for changes.

JONATHAN WEST

See also Middle High German; Old High German

Further Reading

Besch, Werner, et al., editors, *Dialektologie: Ein Handbuch zur deutschen und allgemeinen Dialektforschung,* 2 vols., Berlin and New York: de Gruyter, 1982

——, et al., editors, *Sprachgeschichte: Ein Handbuch zur Geschichte der deutschen Sprache und ihrer Erforschung,* 2 vols., Berlin and New York: de Gruyter, 1984

Clark, Herbert H., *Using Language,* Cambridge and New York: Cambridge University Press, 1996

Clyne, Michael, *The German Language in a Changing Europe,* Cambridge and New York: Cambridge University Press, 1995

Drosdowski, Günther, et al., editors, *Der Duden in 12 Bänden: Das Standardwerk zur deutschen Sprache,* Mannheim: Dudenverlag, 1984–93

Durrell, Martin, *Hammer's German Grammar and Usage,* London: Arnold; 2nd edition, 1991

Engel, Ulrich, *Deutsche Grammatik,* Heidelberg: Groos, 1988

Keller, Rudolf Ernst, *The German Language,* London: Faber, and Atlantic Highlands, New Jersey: Humanities Press, 1978

König, Werner, *dtv-Atlas zur deutschen Sprache: Tafeln und Texte mit Mundart-Karten,* Munich: Deutscher Taschenbuch Verlag, 1978; 10th edition, 1994

Ramat, Anna Giacalone, and Paolo Ramat, editors, *The Indo-European Languages,* London and New York: Routledge, 1998

Sowinski, Bernhard, *Deutsche Stilistik,* Frankfurt: Fischer Taschenbuch, 1972; revised edition, 1978

West, Jonathan, *Progressive Grammar of German,* 6 vols., Dublin: Authentik, 1992–94

Gesamtkunstwerk

The term *Gesamtkunstwerk* was coined by Richard Wagner in *Art and Revolution* (1849), the first of several seminal tracts written in Swiss exile and known as his "Zurich writings," which, under the influence of Ludwig Feuerbach's materialistic humanism and Pierre Proudhon's socialism, are essentially a continuation of Wagner's revolutionary aspirations in 1848–49. Others in which the theory is developed are *Das Kunstwerk der Zunkunft* (1849; *The Artwork of the Future*), *Oper und Drama* (1851; *Opera and Drama*), and *Eine Mitteilung an meine Freunde* (1851; *A Communication to My Friends*).

In his highly idealized reading, classical Greek drama is man's ultimate achievement, the self-expression of a whole people in its deepest and most noble aspect, a religious bonding ritual combining all the arts—notably poetry, music, and dance—in perfect synthesis (*diesem herrlich einen Kunstwerke*). Aeschylus is the supreme *Gesamtkünstler.* His *Prometheus* is the "most profound of all tragedies" and the *Oresteia* his most "conservative" creation, insofar as it unself-consciously preserves communal memory. What follows this brief flowering marks both the forward march of the human spirit and its inevitable fragmentation—the "revolutionary" Pericles, the Socratic world of reflective philosophy, Plato's suspicion of art, the decline of Athens. The great unified artwork of the Greeks (*das große griechische Gesamtkunstwerk*) dissolves into its constituent parts.

These individual arts are said to have survived both Roman barbarism and a quiescent Christian otherworldliness incompatible with artistic celebration. Yet Wagner believes their collective rebirth as the *dramma per musica* envisaged since the Renaissance has failed to materialize, while in our fallen world of industrial wage slavery, its degraded art the mere distraction of paid entertainment, theater offers only intrigue deprived of "the idealizing expression of music," while opera has long been a "chaos of unconnected sensual elements" (in Italy a "strumpet," in France a "coquette with a cold smile"). The main contemporary target of Wagner's rigorous aesthetic morality is the lack of organic integration—the "effects without causes" or spectacle insufficiently grounded dramatically—which he perceived in French grand opera, especially Meyerbeer. The total artwork must accordingly (like *Nothung*) be fashioned anew, he writes, not in slavish imitation of the Athenian model currently in vogue in Berlin's Court Theater (evidence of what has been called the continuing "tyranny of Greece over Germany" prevalent since Winckelmann), but reforged in the heat of universal social revolution. A fellowship of artists, indeed the *Volk* itself, will respond to the historical inevitability of its own demand, and the actor will be musician, poet and dancer in one, as were the Greeks. Wagner's early plans for an open-access festival theater on the banks of the Rhine are thus closer in spirit to those gargantuan public pageants—combining drama, poetry, and music with dance and all the visual arts—with which the French Revolutionaries attempted to cement true fraternity, than to the subsequent reality of Bayreuth.

In part, the argument that a soprano's vertiginous trills or a dancer's pirouettes pander to the jaded palates of opera-goers at the expense of "the overall dramatic purpose" is unexceptional. But Wagner also contends that, unless reunited, the separate arts in isolation are doomed to impotence and that Shakespearean drama and the Beethovenian symphony can be "redeemed" (as sculpture is "redeemed" in mime) only in musical drama. Even when understood as a dialectical progression beyond individual summits of achievement towards the integrated "artwork of the future" (and since Wagner's model here is Feuerbach's *Grundsätze der Philosophie der Zukunft* [1843; *Principles of the Philosophy of the Future*], the synthesis envisaged clearly owes more to the Young Hegelians than to Hegel's own abstract "absolute philosophy"), it is an audacious claim, vigorously mocked by his detractors.

Wagner never did put the theory into practice and soon dropped the grandiose term *Gesamtkunstwerk,* along with his "democratic" but unsustainable contention that all the arts should carry equal weight, implying a cumulative qualitative gain. His most memorable conclusion is that the drama, which should be the end, has become merely the means, while music, which should be the means, has become the end. But after reading Schopenhauer in 1854, "the great event of Wagner's life" (Thomas Mann), he became convinced—no doubt to his relief after five years of wrestling with these issues in which he wrote no music—that music did occupy a uniquely privileged place in the hierarchy of the arts, affording direct, non-mimetic access to the essence of the world. This flattered the composer and complemented a belief, shared by many of the Romantic generation (Novalis, Friedrich Schlegel) in instinctive reaction against French literary preeminence, that music was *the* German art. Musical forms might in turn be superimposed on sister arts. In his masque *Die Huldigung der Künste* (1805; The Homage of the Arts), Schiller even seems to have anticipated something akin to the *Gesamtkunstwerk:*

> As the magic rainbow in the sky
> Conjures its colors from the gorgeous sun,
> So will we, each for all, and all as one,
> With mystic sevenfold wealth of pageantry,
> Weave for thee, Lady, life's great tapestry.

And like many after Gluck's operatic reforms, Schiller could proclaim his "fixed confidence in opera, that out of it, as out of the choirs of the ancient festivals of Bacchus, tragedy in a noble form would erupt."

However, Wagner's newly felt confidence in his role as composer did not invalidate his earlier polemic in *Opera and Drama* against the "absolute" music of a Rossini for functioning in accordance with purely musical criteria, independently of the events on the stage. A reference to "acts of music made visible" in his essay *On the Designation Music Drama* (1872) is often cited as evidence of his conversion to the primacy of music, but though Wagner readily distinguished between his own earlier Romantic operas and subsequent "dramas" or "musical dramas" (terms he preferred to the soon ubiquitous references to *Musikdrama*), such theoretical distinctions seem sterile in the face of his own creative practice. Thus, "orchestral melody" (which Wagner habitually compared to the chorus in Greek tragedy), the emergence of the orchestra as protagonist and the symphonic web of "infinite melody" it spins over the whole work, the *leitmotif* technique as a solution to the problems of epic scale and recapitulation—these are more appropriate criteria with which to approach Wagner's genius than the *Gesamtkunstwerk,* described by his most trenchant critic, Eduard Hanslick (*Vom Musikalisch-Schönen* [1854; *The Beautiful in Music*]), as a musical dilettante's violation of music by words.

FRED BRIDGHAM

See also Richard Wagner

Further Reading

Aberbach, Alan David, *The Ideas of Richard Wagner,* Lanham, Maryland, and London: University Press of America, 1984

Laudon, Robert T., *Sources of the Wagnerian Synthesis,* Munich: Musikverlag Katzbichler, 1979

Millington, Barry, editor, *The Wagner Compendium,* London: Thames and Hudson, 1992

Tanner, Michael, "The Total Work of Art," in *The Wagner Companion,* edited by Peter Burbridge and Richard Sutton, London and Boston: Faber, 1979

Johann Wolfgang von Goethe 1749–1832

Goethe lived through a remarkable time in history. At his birth, Europe stood under the sway of Absolutism and Enlightenment. When he died, the French Revolution, the dissolution of the German Empire, and the fall of Napoleon belonged to the past; steam engines were beginning to change industrial production; and the Romantic movement dominated most literatures of the West. As a private person, as a minister of state, as a natural scientist, and not least as an author, Goethe closely observed and, at times, participated in the processes that brought about these changes.

In his autobiography *Aus Meinem Leben: Dichtung und Wahrheit* (1811–33; *The Autobiography of Goethe: Truth and Poetry*), Goethe reflects on the influence that his childhood environment had on him: his birthplace—Frankfurt am Main, an imperial city not subject to territorial rule—was a flourishing trade center strongly imbued with bourgeois values and one of the few places in Germany where Protestants, Catholics, and Jews coexisted. Goethe's well-to-do father, a Lutheran, had him educated by private tutors. Great weight was placed on religious instruction, with frequent and thorough reading of the Bible. Both the Old and the New Testament were present in Goethe's mind throughout his life. The same holds true for the moderate Enlightenment concepts in which he was brought up. A belief in the use of reason always guided him in his personal affairs, and tolerance was the steady hallmark of his responses to ideological and religious matters. Even in his last novel, *Wilhelm Meisters Wanderjahre* (1821; *Wilhelm Meister's Travels*), he continued to extol the benefits of a rationally oriented pedagogy.

The city of Leipzig, where Goethe studied jurisprudence for three years, was elegant and playful, filled with the spirit of the rococo and different from Frankfurt's conservative confines. Goethe inhaled this air with gusto, devoting himself to the theater and to painting and drawing lessons. He fell in love, wrote pastoral romances, and penned poetry in the spirit of Anacreon. Yet he also began to perceive the transiency of this world when he suffered a mental and physical breakdown at the end of his stay.

A further estrangement from his bourgeois upbringing occurred when Goethe became attracted to a group of anti-establishment writers, angry young men later known as *Stürmer und Dränger* (followers of the Sturm und Drang movement). Influenced by their philosophy, he claimed that the poet should be guided more by the strength of inner perception than by knowledge and skill. He led an unconventional life while he was completing his studies in Strasbourg and also afterward, when he served, halfheartedly, as an advocate to the jury court in his native city. His concerns were literary: he translated Macpherson's melancholy *Songs of Selma* and immersed himself in Shakespeare, who at the time was not yet well known in Germany. In a short prose piece, *Zum Schäkespears Tag* (1771; *On Shakespeare's Day*), he formulated his own Sturm und Drang credo: break with the rule—ridden French drama and its imitators and accept the supremacy of nature in life as well as in art. He wrote prodigiously, producing lyrics with a depth of feeling previously unknown in German letters and a series of dramatic drafts, among them the first scenes of *Faust* (1772–1831), the tragedy that would occupy him for his entire life. In his only completed play of the period, *Götz von Berlichingen mit der eisernen Hand* (1773; *Goetz of Berlichingen with the Iron Hand*), he resurrected the story of a 16th–century robber baron who confronted an emasculated age with the law of the strongest.

While still writing poetry in the Sturm und Drang vein, Goethe's interest was drawn to the thought and lifestyle of the Empfindsamen (adherents of the cult of Sensibility), young intellectuals who exulted in expressing their feelings, rejecting the rigorousness of their Enlightenment upbringing. His reading of authors such as Young, Sterne, Rousseau, and Klopstock encouraged him to look at the world in their way. Typically for his temperament, he responded to all these impressions with a work of his own, *Die Leiden des jungen Werthers* (1774; translated as *The Sorrows of Young Werther* and *The Sufferings of Young Werther*), an epistolary novel. Its persuasive expression of weltschmerz was widely embraced by a generation of sentimental readers and just as strongly opposed by the champions of rationalism.

After Goethe's move to Weimar in 1775, he turned to a more balanced manner of literary expression, gradually evolving classicist views. His ten-year service in the government of the Duchy of Sachsen-Weimar and a subsequent sojourn in Italy were decisive in this process of inner transformation. In tandem with his involvement in administrative responsibilities, he sought moderation in the conduct of his life: in pursuit of a *Streben nach Reinheit* (striving for purity), he measured his behavior against a yearned-for ideal, registering successes and failures. During his stay in Italy, he trained his eye to perceive the enduring principles of art embodied in Winckelmann's concept of the antique as noble, elevated, serene, and simple. Two dramas that reflect his search for inner balance, *Iphigenie auf Tauris* (1787; *Iphigenia in Tauris*) and *Torquato Tasso* (1789; *Torquato Tasso*), reached completion, and some scenes of *Faust* were born.

A breakthrough toward a distinctively formulated program of classicism occurred after 1794, when the poet Friedrich Schiller came to live in Jena and Weimar near Goethe. Their acquaintance developed into an intensive exchange of ideas, to the pleasure and benefit of both. Goethe moderated Schiller's tendency to philosophical speculation, and Schiller drew Goethe back toward literary efforts and away from the scientific studies that had been absorbing much of his energy. Goethe completed, among other works, the novel *Wilhelm Meisters Lehrjahre* (1795–96; translated as *Wilhelm Meister's Journeyman Years* and *Wilhelm Meister's Apprenticeship*) and the verse epic *Hermann und Dorothea* (1798; *Hermann and Dorothea*). Both in personal discussions and in writing, the two authors attempted to fashion classicist concepts of literature and art. The legacy of antiquity, a search for the typical, and a devotion to the "true, beautiful, and good" were taken to be the foundations of culture. Both Schiller's and Goethe's poetry and essays from this time are characterized by a tendency toward the didactic. Inner harmony is matched by an elegance and sublimity of form.

Goethe's activities in the years after Schiller's death in 1805 defy facile description, as the period until Goethe's own death in 1832 is characterized less by visible changes than by a steady devotion to his work. Aside from two journeys to the Rhein and Main region and sojourns in the spas of Bohemia, he remained in Weimar, concentrating on literary projects, critical writing, and scientific pursuits.

In his literary endeavors, Goethe completed works of major significance: a six-volume review of his life, with an emphasis, in *Truth and Poetry*, on his pre-Weimar years; the *West-oestlicher Divan* (1819; *West-Eastern Divan*), a cycle of more than 200 poems linking Persian traditions with his own concepts of love and wisdom; and two narratives, *Die Wahlverwandtschaften* (1809; *Elective Affinities*) and *Wilhelm Meister's Travels,* the first engaging delicate questions of marriage, the second treating issues of self-improvement and education. In *Faust,* which he completed in the last year of his life after it had occupied him for six decades, he turned the centuries—old story of the demonic magus into a panorama of human striving, erring, and finally salvation.

In his critical writings, Goethe evinced a growing receptivity to developments beyond Germany. The range of his interests extended from classical antiquity and Western Europe to the Slavic countries and even to China. He acknowledged that poetry stemmed from a regional background but felt nonetheless that the time of national literatures was past and that communication among writers would develop unhindered by state borders. To describe the process of interaction that he envisioned, he coined the term *Weltliteratur* (world literature). His cosmopolitan views were accompanied by a growing dissatisfaction with the younger generation of German writers, who liked to consider themselves Romantics. Their escape into a realm of dreams and illusions—once his own approach in *The Sorrows of Young Werther*—was alien to him now. He declared the Romantic to be the opposite of the natural, something artificial and sickly. On the other hand, he considered the classical to be genuine and healthy. Accepting such views, and in recognition of Goethe's and Schiller's towering accomplishments as writers, 19th-century literary critics identified the two as the *Klassiker* (classic authors) of German letters. The term *Weimarer Klassik* (Weimar classicism) was similarly accepted.

From about his 30th year on, Goethe had involved himself in geological and botanical observations, curious about their contexts. His stay in Italy had sparked his concept of the *Urpflanze* (primal plant), which he believed to contain the "principle of the original identity of all components of plants," the typical that exists unchangingly in all phenomena of nature. After summarizing his findings in the essay *Versuch die Metamorphose der Pflanzen zu erklären* (1790; *Attempt to Explain the Metamorphosis of Plants*), he drafted a *Metamorphose der Tiere* (Metamorphosis of Animals). In his later years, he extended his interests to almost all areas of scientific research known in his time. He doggedly pursued work on his *Zur Farbenlehre* (1810; *Theory of Colors*) until it grew into a treatise of over a thousand pages. In opposition to the English physicist Isaac Newton, who, correctly, had suggested that white light contains all other colors, Goethe believed that colors came into being as a result of the interaction of light and dark.

Typically, Goethe applied his concepts concerning natural phenomena to the world of thought. His emphasis on metamorphosis is a crucial element in many of his literary works, from *Iphigenia in Tauris* to *Faust*. Inherent components of life were *Polarität* and *Steigerung* (polarity and enhancement): polarity, a constant interplay of attraction and repulsion, occurred, he felt, not only in the material world but also in the human mind; enhancement took place when this interplay led to new entities. A case of polarity, for Goethe, was the confrontation of light and dark, as discussed in the *Theory of Colors;* in his literary oeuvre, polarity is recognizable in the dialogues between Faust and Mephistopheles. Enhancement is expressed in nature by the evolution of new forms; as depicted in *Faust,* it is evident in the stages of human *Streben* (striving).

Goethe's conviction that all change takes place by means of evolution determined his response to public events. In contrast to the enthusiasm with which many German intellectuals greeted the storming of the Bastille, he was unsettled by the unleashing of revolutionary forces. In several plays, as well as in the narrative *Unterhaltungen deutscher Ausgewanderten* (1795; *Conversations of German Refugees*), he dissociated himself from the idea of eliminating political abuses by means of violence. The unsuccessful invasion of France by German princes caused him to predict the breakdown of the Holy Roman Empire, and the French occupation of Germany, although it interrupted the balanced conditions of his personal life, did not appear to him to be a national catastrophe: unlike most of his compatriots, he recognized Napoleon's greatness, seeing in him an individual who could bring order to a politically torn continent. Ambitions of nationalistic self-sufficiency were alien to him, and he prophesied that the world would continue to bleed under them.

Goethe's concepts of religion, God, and humanity changed with the stages of his life. When he was 24, he combined in his *Brief des Pastors zu *** an den neuen Pastor zu **** (1773; *Letter from the Pastor in *** to the New Pastor in ****) an enlightened call for tolerance with criticism of the established church, the latter much in the spirit of the Sturm und Drang. *The Sorrows of Young Werther* reflects a poetically embellished pantheism. During the decades around the turn of the century, Goethe professed an ethical humanism. In his later years, the wide-ranging directions of his thought led him to regard any personal confession as restrictive. To questioning by a friend of his youth, Friedrich Heinrich Jacobi, he responded in an intentionally ambiguous manner:

> As a poet and artist I am a polytheist; as a scientist, however, I am a pantheist; and the one just as staunchly as the other. If I have need of a God for myself, as a moral human being, that is also provided for. Heavenly and earthly things form a realm so extensive it can only be grasped by the capabilities of all beings combined.

Less epigrammatic and thus more expressive is a comment to Sulpiz Boisserée, a confidant of his later years, concerning the Hypsistarians, a fourth-century sect in Asia Minor that claimed to take from pagans, Jews, and Christians the best each of them had to offer for inclusion in its own beliefs. Such an attitude, Goethe felt, could be his as well.

The reception of Goethe in Germany reflects in great part the nation's intellectual history. After the acclaim accorded *The Sorrows of Young Werther* by the sentimentalists of the 1770s and 1780s and after the approbation given *Hermann and Dorothea* at the turn of the century by a middle class that recognized itself in the epic's characters, he became an icon for many Romantics in the early 19th century, notwithstanding the fact that he himself had reservations about their philosophy. Both the first part of *Faust,* when it appeared in 1808, and *Wilhelm Meisters Apprenticeship* had an inspirational impact on them. Beethoven's and Schubert's compositions of his poems are indicative of the reverence in which he was held.

Later in the 19th century, Goethe was seen in a different light. The writers of *Das Junge Deutschland* (Young German School), Heine among them, who espoused liberal ideas in a time of government repression, admired his craft as a poet but decried his aloofness from the political environment. During the malaise after the failed revolution of 1848, public devotion to Weimar classicism was crucial in forming a sense of national identity among the Germans. After the unification of the German states and their industrial growth, respect for Goethe turned into an outright cult; knowledge of his writings became a must for those who wanted to be counted among the educated. He was seen as the Olympian of German letters. Soldiers entering into World War I carried *Faust* in their field packs.

The awakening experienced by German intellectual circles after that lost war brought a wave of creative interpretations of Goethe's oeuvre as well as suggestions that his views might lead to a spiritual renewal of the nation. However, all movement in this direction came to a standstill with the emergence of Hitler, whose followers, with limited success, tried to mold Goethe to their ideology. After their rule collapsed, renewed attempts were undertaken to capitalize on the dignity of Weimar's intellectual heritage, although with differing political undertones in the two parts of the then-divided nation. Celebrations in 1949 of the 200th anniversary of Goethe's birth illustrated this dichotomy: in the West the emphasis was on his humanistic and cosmopolitan views, whereas in the East he was seen as a component of the regime's *kulturelles Erbe* (cultural heritage), and his occasional criticism of feudal exploitation was accentuated. In the 1960s, students protesting the Federal Republic's educational system considered him part of the ballast that they wanted to jettison, but their voices gradually dwindled. Schools, universities, and theaters contributed to maintaining an interest in Goethe and his work. In a recent set of interviews undertaken by the weekly *Die Zeit,* representative intellectuals listed Goethe (with *Faust* and *Elective Affinities*) at the top of the canon of German writers, followed by Kafka (*Der Prozess* [1925; *The Trial*]) and Thomas Mann (*Buddenbrooks* [1901]). Currently, two major publishing houses, Suhrkamp and Hanser, are bringing out new critical editions of Goethe's works. For the 250th anniversary of his birth in 1999, celebrations took place in all parts of Germany, and the European Union designated Weimar a "European City of Culture."

Goethe's reception abroad was initially determined by two individuals: Madame de Staël in France and Thomas Carlyle in England. De Staël's comprehensive review of German culture in *De l'Allemagne* (1810; *Germany*) and Carlyle's translation of *Wilhelm Meister's Apprenticeship* (1824) contributed decisively to the creation of an image of the Germans as a "nation of poets and thinkers," with Goethe the *primus inter pares*. This view was adopted first by the Romantics in France and England, then also in many other countries, both in the Old and the New World. However, owing to the French and English use of the term *classic* for works of the 17th and 18th centuries, the German distinction between *Klassik* and *Romantik* for more recent developments was not acceptable in those countries. Consequently, outside of Germany, Goethe is identified as a genuine Romantic. Literary historians of those nations point out how much he shared a dedication to imagery, symbolism, and myth—crucial ingredients of the period—with such authors as Chateaubriand and Senancour, Byron and Wordsworth.

Much of the admiration for the Germans as a people of culture, and with it the interest in Goethe, collapsed in France after the war of 1870 and in other countries as a result of World War I. Since then, his works have been kept alive outside of Germany, mostly within the confines of academe. Wherever German literature is taught in schools and universities, his writings, mainly *The Sorrows of Young Werther* and the first part of *Faust*, belong to the bedrock of the curriculum. Scholars of many nations have analyzed his oeuvre, producing interpretations of the highest caliber, the latest being Nicholas Boyle's *Goethe, the Poet and the Age* (1991).

PETER BOERNER

See also Weimar

Biography

Born in Frankfurt, 28 August 1749. Studied law at Leipzig University, 1765–68, and in Strasbourg, 1770–71; law degree, 1771; practiced law in Frankfurt, 1771–72, and Wetzlar, 1772; joined the court of Duke Karl August in Weimar and served in various capacities, including director of the court theaters, 1775–1817; editor of numerous journals, including *Xenien, Die Propyläen, Kunst und Altertum,* and *Zur Naturwissenschaft;* chancellor of the University of Jena. Married Christiane Vulpius, 1806 (died 1816). Died in Weimar, 22 March 1832.

Selected Works

Collections

Schriften, 8 vols., 1787–90; as *Werke,* 13 vols., 1806–10, etc.; as *Werke* [Vollständige Ausgab letzter Hand], 60 vols., 1827–42
Complete Works [Bohn Standard Library], 14 vols., 1848–90
Werke [Weimar edition], 134 vols., 1887–1919
Sämtliche Werke [Jubiläum edition], edited by Eduard von der Hellen, 40 vols., 1902–7
Werke [Hamburg edition], edited by Erich Trunz et al., 14 vols., 1948–69
Gedenkausgabe der Werke, Briefe, und Gespräche, edited by Ernst Beutler, 27 vols., 1948–71
Goethe's Collected Works, edited by Christopher Middleton et al., translated by Michael Hamburger et al., 12 vols., 1983–89
Sämtliche Werke [Frankfurt edition], edited by Dieter Borchmeyer et al., 1985–
Sämtliche Werke nach Epochen seines Schaffens [Munich edition], edited by Karl Richter et al., 1986–

Novels

Die Leiden des jungen Werthers, 1774; revised 1787; as *The Sorrows of Werter,* translated by Richard Graves, 1780; as *The Sufferings of Young Werther,* translated by Bayard Quincy Morgan, 1976; as *The Sorrows of Young Werther,* translated by Elizabeth Meyer and Louise Bogan, 1973; translated by Victor Lange and Judith Ryan, in *Goethe's Collected Works,* vol. 11, 1988; translated by Michael Hulse, 1989
Wilhelm Meisters theatralische Sendung, written 1777–85, published 1911; as *Wilhelm Meister's Theatrical Calling,* translated by John R. Russell, 1996
Wilhelm Meisters Lehrjahre [and *Wanderjahre*], 1795–96 [1821]; as *Wilhelm Meister's Apprenticeship* [and *Travels*], translated by Thomas Carlyle, 1824–27; revised 1842, 1865; *Lehrjahre* as *Wilhelm Meister's Years of Apprenticeship,* translated by H.M. Waidson, 1977–79; as *Wilhelm Meister's Apprenticeship,* edited and translated by Eric A. Blackall in cooperation with Victor Lange, in *Goethe's Collected Works,* vol. 9, 1989; as *Wilhelm Meister's Journeyman Years,* translated by Krishna Winston, 1989
Die Wahlverwandtschaften, 1809; as *Kindred by Choice,* translated by H.M. Waidson, 1960; as *Elective Affinities,* translated by Elizabeth Mayer and Louise Bogan, 1963; translated by R.J. Hollingdale, 1971; translated by John Winkelman, 1987; translated by Victor Lange and Judith Ryan, in *Goethe's Collected Works,* vol. 11, 1988; translated by David Constantine, 1994
Novelle, 1826; as *Novella,* translated by Elizabeth Mayer and Louise Bogan, with *The Sorrows of Young Werther,* 1971; translated by Victor Lange and Judith Ryan, in *Goethe's Collected Works,* vol. 11, 1988

Plays

Götz von Berlichingen mit der eisernen Hand (produced 1774), 1773; as *Goetz of Berlichingen with the Iron Hand,* translated by Walter Scott, 1799; as *Ironhand,* translated by John Arden, 1965; as *Götz von Berlichingen,* translated by Charles E. Passage, in *Plays,* 1980
Clavigo (produced 1774), 1774; as *Clavidgo,* translated by Charles Leftley, 1798
Götter, Helden, und Wieland, 1774
Erwin und Elmire, music by Johann André (produced 1775), 1775; revised version, in verse, in *Schriften,* vol. 5, 1788
Stella, 1776; revised (produced 1806), in *Werke,* vol. 6, 1816; translated 1798
Claudine von Villa Bella (produced 1777), 1776; revised (produced 1789), in *Schriften,* vol. 5, 1788
Die Fischerin, music by Corona Schröter (produced 1782), 1782
Die Geschwister (produced 1776), in *Schriften,* vol. 1, 1787
Die Mitschuldigen (produced 1777), in *Schriften,* vol. 2, 1787; as *Fellow Culprits,* translated by Charles E. Passage, in *Plays,* 1980
Der Triumph der Empfindsamkeit (produced 1778), in *Schriften,* vol. 4, 1787; revised as *Proserpina,* music by Karl Eberwein (produced 1915), in *Werke,* 1808
Iphigenie (produced 1779; revised version, in verse, as *Iphigenie auf Tauris,* produced 1802), in *Schriften,* vol. 3, 1787; as *Iphigenia in Tauris,* translated by William Taylor, 1793; translated by Charles E. Passage, in *Plays,* 1980
Die Vögel (from Aristophanes) (produced 1780), 1787
Egmont (produced 1784), 1788; translated as *Egmont,* 1848; translated by Michael Hamburger, in *The Classic Theatre,* 1959; translated by F.J. Lamport, in *Five German Tragedies,* 1969; translated by Charles E. Passage, in *Plays,* 1980
Lili, music by Sigmund von Seckendorff (produced 1777), in *Schriften,* vol. 6, 1790

Das Jahrmarktsfest zu Plundersweilern (produced 1778), in *Schriften,* vol. 6, 1790
Jery und Bätely, music by Sigmund von Seckendorff (produced 1780), 1790
Torquato Tasso (produced 1807), in *Schriften,* vol. 6, 1790; translated by C. des Voeux, 1827; translated by A. Swanwick, in *Dramatic Works,* 1846; translated by John Prudhoe, 1979; translated by Charles E. Passage, in *Plays,* 1980; translated by Alan Brownjohn, 1985
Scherz, List und Rache (opera libretto; produced 1790), in *Schriften,* vol. 7, 1790
Der Gross-Cophta (produced 1791), 1792
Der Bürgergeneral (produced 1793), 1793
Mahomet (from Voltaire) (produced 1799), 1802
Tancred (from Voltaire) (produced 1801), 1802
Die natürliche Tochter (produced 1803), 1804
Die Laune des Verliebten (produced 1779), in *Werke,* vol. 4, 1806; as *The Lover's Whim,* translated by Charles E. Passage, in *Plays,* 1980
Paläophron und Neoterpe (produced 1800; revised version produced 1803), in *Werke,* 1808
Faust, Part One (produced 1819), in *Werke,* vol. 8, 1808; translated as *Faustus,* 1821; as *Faust,* translated by Walter Arndt, 1976, translated by Anna Swanwick, in *Faust, Part I; Egmont; Hermann and Dorothea,* 1982; translated by Stuart Atkins, in *Goethe's Collected Works,* vol. 2, 1984; translated by David Luke, 1987
Pandora, 1810
Romeo und Juliet (from Shakespeare) (produced 1812)
Des Epimenides Erwachen (produced 1815), 1815
Faust, Part Two (produced 1854), first complete publication in *Werke* [Vollständige Ausgabe letzter Hand], vol. 41, 1832; with Part One, as *Faust,* translated by Philip Wayne, 2 vols., 1949–59; translated by Stuart Atkins, in *Goethe's Collected Works,* vol. 2, 1984; translated by David Luke, 1994

Poetry

Neue Lieder mit Melodien, music by Bernhard Breitkopf, 1770
Gedichte, in *Schriften,* vol. 8, 1789
Römische Elegien, 1789; as *Roman Elegies,* translated by David Luke, 1977; translated by Michael Hamburger, 1996
Reineke Fuchs, 1794; as *Reynard the Fox,* translated by Thomas Arnold, 1855; as *Reineke Fox,* translated by A. Rogers, 1888
Hermann und Dorothea, 1798; as *Herman and Dorothea,* translated by Thomas Holcroft, 1801; translated by M. Teesdale, 1875; translated by Anna Swanwick, in *Faust, Part I; Egmont; Hermann and Dorothea,* 1982
West-oestlicher Divan, 1819; as *West-Easterly Divan,* translated by J. Weiss, 1876; as *West-Eastern Divan,* translated by Alexander Rogers,1890; also translated by E. Dowden, 1914; translated by John Whaley, 1998
Selected Verse (bilingual edition), edited by David Luke, 1964
Selected Poems (bilingual edition), edited by Christopher Middleton, translated by Michael Hamburger, et al., 1983
Erotic Poems, translated by David Luke, 1997

Other

Beiträge zur Optik, 1790
Versuch die Metamorphose der Pflanzen zu erklären, 1790; as *Goethe's Botany,* translated by Agnes Arber, 1946
Winkelmann und sein Jahrhundert, 1805
Zur Farbenlehre, 1810; as *Goethe's Theory of Colours,* translated by C.L. Eastlake, 1840
Aus meinem Leben: Dichtung und Wahrheit, 4 vols., 1811–33; as *Memoirs of Goethe; Written by Himself,* 1824; as *The Autobiography of Goethe: Truth and Poetry,* translated by John Oxenford, 1848; as *From My Life,* translated by Robert Heitner, in *Collected Works,* vol. 4, 1987
Italienische Reise, 1816–17; as *Travels in Italy,* translated by Alexander James Morrison, 1849; as *Italian Journey,* translated by W.H. Auden and Elizabeth Mayer, 1962; translated by Robert R. Heitner, 1989
Tag- und Jahreshefte, in *Werke,* vols. 31–32, 1830; as *Annals,* translated by Charles Nisbet, 1901
Gespräche mit Goethe, by Johann Peter Eckermann, 1836; as *Conversations with Goethe,* translated by S.M. Fuller, 1839; as *Conversations of Goethe with Johann Peter Eckermann,* edited by J.K. Moorhead (from John Oxenford's translation), 1998
Correspondence between Goethe and Thomas Carlyle, 1887
Die Schriften zur Naturwissenschaft, 1947
Amtliche Schriften, edited by Willy Flach and Helma Dahl, 3 vols., 1950–72
Briefe, edited by K.R. Mandelkow and B. Morawe, 6 vols., 1962–69
Gespräche, edited by W.F. and F. Von Biedermann, revised by Wolfgang Herwig, 3 vols., 1965–72
Goethe on Art, edited and translated by John Gage, 1980
Schriften zur Biologie, edited by Konrad Dietzfelbinger, 1982
Briefe aus Italien 1786 bis 1788, edited by Eugen Thurnher, 1985
Goethe's Botanical Writings, translated by Bertha Mueller, 1989
Correspondence between Goethe and Schiller (1794–1805), translated by Liselotte Dieckmann, 1994
Goethe on Science: A Selection, translated by Jeremy Naydler, 1996
Maxims and Reflections, translated by Elisabeth Stopp, 1998

Further Reading

Biedrzynski, Effi, *Goethes Weimar: Das Lexicon der Personen und Schauplätze,* Zurich: Artemis and Winkler, 1992; 3rd edition, 1994
Boerner, Peter, *Johann Wolfgang von Goethe,* Reinbek bei Hamburg: Rowohlt, 1964; 33rd edition, 1999
Boyle, Nicholas, *Goethe: The Poet and the Age,* vol. 1, *The Poetry of Desire,* Oxford: Clarendon, and New York: Oxford University Press, 1991
Conrady, Karl Otto, *Goethe: Leben und Werk,* 2 vols., Königstein: Athenäum, 1982
Dobel, Richard, editor, *Lexicon der Goethe-Zitate,* Zurich: Artemis, 1968
Friedenthal, Richard, *Goethe: His Life and Times,* Cleveland: World Publishing, and London: Weidenfeld and Nicolson, 1965
Hölscher-Lohmeyer, Dorothea, *Johann Wolfgang Goethe,* Munich: Beck, 1991
Seehafer, Klaus, *Mein Leben ein einzig Abenteuer: Johann Wolfgang Goethe Biographie,* Berlin: Aufbau, 1988
Williams, John R., *The Life of Goethe: A Critical Biography,* Oxford and Malden, Massachusetts: Blackwell, 1998
Wilpert, Gero von, *Goethe-Lexikon,* Stuttgart: Kröner, 1998
Witte, Bernd, et al., editors, *Goethe Handbuch,* 4 vols., Stuttgart: Metzler, 1996–98

Faust: Part I 1808, Part II 1832

Play by Johann Wolfgang von Goethe

For most of the last two centuries, Goethe's *Faust* has been the primary literary representative of German identity and for many the representative text of modernity as well. Based loosely on the legends first attached to Faust's name in the anonymous chapbook of 1587 (but not on Christopher Marlowe's *Dr. Faustus* of 1588, which Goethe encountered only in 1818), it draws on 3,000 years of literary, historical, artistic, mystical, and popular artifacts in an unmatched combination of dramatic, lyric, and epic forms. Thus, this paradigmatically German work emerges as a summa of the European tradition and testifies to Goethe's commitment to *Weltliteratur* (world literature). Because Goethe published this text of 12,000 lines in stages over some 60 years, it has mostly been considered in the 20th century as three more or less distinct texts—the *Urfaust* (Original Faust; a copy of Goethe's manuscript made around 1775), *Faust, Part I* (1808), and *Faust, Part II* (1832).

The *Urfaust,* discovered and published in 1887, is a document of the Sturm und Drang. All but its final prison scene, along with two scenes composed in 1788–89, were published with only slight revisions in 1790 as *Faust: Ein Fragment.* The often colloquial and abrupt language, the mixture of prose and verse, and the use of crowd scenes are Shakespearean features popularized by Goethe's own *Götz von Berlichingen mit der eisernen Hand* (1773; *Goetz of Berlichingen with the Iron Hand*), while the focus on the tragic seduction of Margarete is the most compelling German version of the so-called *bürgerliches Trauerspiel* (bourgeois tragedy), which was imported from England and popularized by Gotthold Ephraim Lessing. With its profound psychology, intense emotionalism, and rudimentary class consciousness, the *Urfaust* appealed to the vitalism of the late 19th century and contributed to its construct of "the young Goethe."

The text of *Faust, Part I*, composed primarily between 1797 and 1801, now constitutes the standard version of the play. Goethe returned to the drama at Friedrich Schiller's urging a year after finishing *Wilhelm Meisters Lehrjahre* (1795–96; translated as *Wilhelm Meister's Journeyman Years* and *Wilhelm Meister's Apprenticeship*). Like this bildungsroman, *Faust* pursues the theme of individual development, this time not in the context of social or class constraints, from all of which the drama frees itself in its prologue in Heaven, but solely in terms of the human condition as such. Most of the material from the *Urfaust* was revised into more regular verse and its significance was profoundly transformed by additions that doubled the length of the text and made the tragedy of the scholar, as the first half of the drama is known, equal in impact to the tragedy of Margarete. The additions include the three prologues, Faust's Easter walk, the pact scene, and the Walpurgis Night.

In this form *Faust* is the representative text of German Idealism. It oscillates between imprisoning cells and open spaces to embody the idealist dichotomies of subject and object, self and world, and self and the transcendental other or absolute. The resultant tensions play themselves out in the realms of memory, history, and art—all common loci of mediation in the dialectical systems of Romantic thinkers such as G.F.W. Hegel or Schiller. Goethe also reveals the heady implications of 18th-century historicism by converting the traditional pact with Mephistopheles into a bet that Faust will remain eternally unsatisfied: history as temporality opens to the active mind an infinite realm of experience. Because experience achieves its full significance for Goethe, as for Wordsworth, only in recollection, however, Faust's encounters with the world are transformed into "staged" enactments of such experiences, so that the drama becomes a series of plays-within-the-play, foremost among them the tragedy of Margarete. In its dialectical and historicist aspects, *Faust* reveals the possibilities and dangers of the secularization of European culture, which was virtually complete by the end of the 18th century. The grounding of identity exclusively in the self allows Faust the full development of his inherent capacities but also leaves him with no basis for a morality outside of the self. The dilemmas to which Rousseau and Kant had brought their century are here writ large.

Part II of the drama, written mostly 1825–31 and published according to Goethe's explicit wish only after his death in 1832, differs from the first part in its more openly allegorical style and its indifference to the unity of action, tone, or style. After a century of incomprehension, students of the play have come to understand both its thematic coherence and the ways in which it elaborates the implications of Part I. If the *Faust* of the 1790s focuses on the individual, Part II focuses on the trans-subjective implications of the idealist and historicist agendas and thus offers a sociological rather than an anthropological perspective. While the drama offers covert critiques of the state of European politics after the Restoration, most of its explicit discourse focuses on epistemological and aesthetic themes. The problem of representation organizes the first four acts, as Faust visits the court of the emperor, conjures the shade of Helen, reevokes her in more "natural" form during the classical Walpurgis Night, marries and has a son by her, and then returns to Germany to begin land reclamation projects. Goethe confronts his own convictions in favor of aesthetic autonomy with the representational nature of all social existence. History is no longer solely the locus of mediation but also the repetitive and relentless destroyer of all human achievement. Nowhere is Goethe's critique of his own historicist project more profound than in the play's encounter with classical antiquity. Since historicism had called into question the eternal classical ideal inherited by the 18th century, Goethe re-creates his Helena by setting her into the context of the development of antiquity from ancient Egypt on, and by dismissing her to the underworld when she has served her purpose. She is both the great achievement of 19th-century philhellenism and Goethe's warning monument to its transience. The drama's shift of focus to the future in act 5 is understood to be Goethe's dramatic critique of the pace and inhumanity of modernity, which he also makes in *Wilhelm Meisters Wanderjahre* (1821; *Wilhelm Meister's Travels*). Faust appears to lose his bet with Mephistopheles by savoring in anticipation the creative activity of his settlers, but ultimately he is saved to continue striving after death for an eternally receding ideal embodied in Margarete and labeled "das Ewig-Weibliche" (the eternal feminine). So complex is the web of irony, parody, and allusion in the final scenes that there is little agreement as to whether the ending is affirmative or nihilistic.

Faust dramatically increased the popularity of the Faust theme in literature from Goethe's time to our own; it also inspired a tradition of "world-historical" drama, of which the best-known practitioners are Henrik Ibsen, Adam Mickiewicz, and Imre Madách. The text has been illustrated innumerable times, most notably perhaps by Eugene Delacroix, Ernst Barlach, and Max Beckmann. The greatest impact of *Faust* has been in music, probably because of the operatic nature of Goethe's text. The most famous settings of songs from the play are by Franz Schubert, Ludwig van Beethoven, and Modest Mussorgsky. While Robert Schumann and Gustav Mahler both set scenes, Franz Liszt wrote a Faust symphony and Wagner a Faust overture. The best known of the numerous Faust operas are by Ludwig Spohr, Hector Berlioz, Charles Gounod, Arrigo Boito, and Ferruccio Busoni. With the exception of Boito's work, the operas typically revert to the damnation of the hero, so that Goethe's influence remains primarily in the seduction of Margarete and the Walpurgis Night. The same pattern prevails in F.W. Murnau's 1926 film, *Faust: Eine deutsche Volkssage,* which draws only to a limited extent on Goethe.

No other text has represented its nation both culturally and politically like *Faust,* which has been the carrier of German national identity. In his 17th *Literaturbrief* (Letter on Literature) of 1759, Lessing identified the Faust theme as the subject for a new German tragedy independent of the norms of French neoclassicism. Since Goethe had distinguished himself as the great genius of a renascent German literature with *Götz von Berlichingen* and especially with *Die Leiden des jungen Werthers* (1774; *The Sorrows of Young Werther*), the reports of his Faust play aroused immediate expectations for a specifically German masterpiece. By the time the *Fragment* appeared in 1790, however, the modern separation between high and popular art had already set in. Published here without its most moving scene of Margarete in the dungeon, *Faust* evoked little popular interest; nevertheless, it was embraced by the German Romantics as a masterpiece on the order of *Hamlet* or the *Divine Comedy.* They made it the center of their definition of modern philosophical tragedy, a position it has maintained in the modern liberal arts curriculum into the current generation.

After the publication of Part I in 1808 (after a delay occasioned by the Napoleonic Wars), reactions to *Faust* took on an ambivalence that was to remain characteristic. The play was greeted with respect, but as the masterpiece of a generation already past. This paradigmatic German tragedy was not staged for 20 years, and not staged uncut for 50 years after its first appearance. The German Idealists and their disciples enshrined it as an allegory of the quest for harmony between the absolute and the individual, while liberals rejected the author and his play for their solipsism, reactionary politics, and non-national stance. Part II was met with incomprehension and hostility for the same political reasons, and this reaction was compounded by resentment against the play's unfashionable allegories and against its author for having dominated German cultural life for 60 years. The play was popularized outside of Germany through Mme. de Staël's description, based mainly on the *Fragment,* in *De l'Allemagne* (1810), which makes Mephistopheles and Margarete the most important figures and stresses the vertiginous formlessness of the work. *Faust* was widely received as a model of Romantic diabolism in Europe and the United States and was simultaneously excoriated on religious grounds as immoral, even pagan. Political, moral, and aesthetic objections to it persisted for most of the 19th century despite the admiration expressed by figures such as Heinrich Heine, Adalbert Stifter, Friedrich Engels, Franz Liszt, Richard Wagner, and George Eliot. While Faust continued to be widely invoked as the representative figure of German culture, and while Goethe's *Faust* was called that culture's literary masterpiece, Margarete was the only element of Goethe's conception that penetrated into the popular conception of the legend.

The Second German Empire, established in 1870, adopted Goethe as its cultural father figure and promoted *Faust* to the status of the "second German Bible" (cited by Schwerte) and the symbol of the essence of Western culture (Oswald Spengler in his *Decline of the West*). Faust was no longer seen as Mme. de Staël's bored libertine but as a restless achiever whose pact with the devil opened the way to the fulfillment of his and the world's potential; his ultimate salvation validated the economic and political expansionism so wisely foreseen by the sage of Weimar. While *Faust* was invoked freely and in the same reading by all sides in the political debate throughout the Weimar Republic and the Nazi period, in 1933 Wilhelm Böhm tried for the first time to distinguish Goethe's *Faust* from the accretions of this reading in a book entitled *Faust, der Nichtfaustische* (Unfaustian Faust). After World War II, the revisionary reading of *Faust* as a kind of cosmopolitan modern morality play has built largely on the foundations laid by Erich Trunz's revaluation of Goethe's late work, particularly *Faust, Part II,* and Wilhelm Emrich's seminal study of its symbols (*Die Symbolik von Faust II*). *Faust* is no longer only the foundational text of the modern West but its prescient critique as well. This period also saw, however, a reemergence of the 19th-century ambivalence toward the text as the postwar generation began to question its cultural heritage. Despite revisionary readings, *Faust* has suffered some of the most hostile stagings and intense resentment of any German classic, now more for what is has been made to represent than for what it says. Its capacity to generate controversy testifies to its overwhelming stature in the German tradition.

JANE K. BROWN

Editions

First edition: *Faust: Ein Fragment,* in *Schriften,* vol. 7, Leipzig: Göschen, 1790; *Faust, der Tragödie I. Teil,* in *Werke,* vol. 8, and independently, Tübingen: Cotta, 1808; *Faust, der Tragödie zweiter Teil,* in *Werke* [Vollständige Ausgabe letzter Hand], vol. 41, Stuttgart and Tübingen: Cotta, 1832

Critical edition: in *Werke* [Weimar edition], vols. 14 and 15, edited by Erich Schmidt, Weimar: Böhlau, 1887–88

Translations: There are numerous translations of *Faust* that capture different aspects of the text; none is ideal. Of those currently available, the sense is most clearly and accurately rendered by Stuart Atkins, in *Goethe's Collected Works,* vol. 2, Cambridge, Massachusetts: Suhrkamp, 1984; meter, rhyme-scheme and specific images are best preserved by Walter Arndt, New York: Norton, 1976 (this translation also has an excellent commentary in English by Cyrus Hamlin); for general accuracy of tone and readability see David Luke's translation, Oxford: Oxford University Press, 1987 (Part I) and 1994 (Part II).

Further Reading

Atkins, Stuart Pratt, *Goethe's Faust: A Literary Analysis,* Cambridge, Massachusetts: Harvard University Press, 1958

Böhm, Wilhelm, *Faust, der Nichtfaustische,* Halle and Saale: Niemeyer, 1933

Brown, Jane K., *Goethe's Faust: The German Tragedy,* Ithaca, New York: Cornell University Press, 1986

Brown, Jane K., Meredith Lee, and Thomas P. Saine, editors, *Interpreting Goethe's "Faust" Today,* Columbia, South Carolina: Camden House, 1994

Emrich, Wilhelm, *Die Symbolik von Faust II: Sinn und Vorformen,* Berlin: Junker und Dünnhaupt, 1943; 5th edition, Königstein: Athenäum, 1981

Hamlin, Cyrus, editor, *Faust, a Tragedy: Backgrounds and Sources: The Author on the Drama, Contemporary Reactions, Modern Criticism,* translated by Walter Arndt, New York: Norton, 1976

Keller, Werner, editor, *Aufsätze zu Goethes "Faust I,"* Darmstadt: Wissenschaftliche Buchgesellschaft, 1974; 3rd edition, 1991

———, editor, *Aufsätze zu Goethes "Faust II,"* Darmstadt: Wissenschaftliche Buchgesellschaft, 1992

Kittler, Friedrich, "Die Gelehrtentragödie: Vorspiel auf dem Theater," in *Aufschreibesysteme 1800/1900,* Munich: Fink, 1987; as "The Scholar's Tragedy: Prelude in the Theater," in *Discourse Networks 1800/1900,* Stanford, California: Stanford University Press, 1990

Moretti, Franco, *Opere mondo: Saggio sulla forma epica dal "Faust" a Cent'anni di solitudine,* Turin: Giulio Einaudi, 1994; as *Modern Epic: The World-System from Goethe to Garcia Marquez,* London: Verso, 1996

Schwerte, Hans, *Faust und das Faustische: Ein Kapitel deutscher Ideologie,* Stuttgart: Klett, 1962

Trunz, Erich, editor, *Goethes Faust,* Hamburg: Wegner, 1949; 5th edition, 1959

Weinrich, Harald, "Faust's Forgetting," *Modern Language Quarterly* 55 (1994)

Die Leiden des jungen Werthers 1774

Novel by Johann Wolfgang von Goethe

Scarcely any other literary work written in the German language has been accorded as much acclaim by contemporaries as Goethe's novel *Die Leiden des jungen Werthers* (translated as *The Sorrows of Young Werther* and *The Sufferings of Young Werther*). Soon after the volume of barely more than 200 small pages was published in the fall of 1774, it sold out, and new printings appeared, followed by pirated editions. People read the book with tears in their eyes and passed it on, men and women alike. Some dressed in the fashion of the story's protagonists, Werther and Lotte. In Germany and then in other countries, the novel became at times the best-known book after the Bible. Cases of suicide were reported in connection with it, and there was talk about a Werther fever.

How to explain such a response to the apparently simple story of a young man who, in Goethe's own words, "was gifted with a deep sensitivity, lost himself in ecstatic dreams, was in addition shattered by unhappy passions, and finally put a bullet through his head"? The most frequently heard answer is the character of the reading audience in the last decades of the 18th century, mainly young intellectuals who rejected the rigidity of their Enlightenment upbringing and sympathized with the cult of Empfindsamkeit (sensibility). Influenced by the works of English writers, such as Edward Young's melancholic *Night Thoughts on Life, Death, and Immortality* (1742), Sterne's sensitive travel accounts, and Macpherson's sad-heroic songs published as Ossian's creations, as well as by Rousseau's idolization of nature, they became receptive to morbid delusions. Suicide, hitherto considered a scandalous offense but excused by Werther as "Krankheit zum Tode" ("sickness unto death"), a phrase later taken up by Kierkegaard, met with understanding. And a few, but persuasive, remarks on thoughtless attitudes of the upper class gave the novel a tilt toward social criticism that struck a responsive chord. However, the book must also be viewed as more than a reaction to contemporary conditions. In a manner that can be understood by people of all times, *The Sorrows of Young Werther* reveals a disproportion between the world and the God-imbued individual that leads to the latter's downfall: he cracks, without personal guilt, under the multiplicity of his emotions and thus under his innate character.

No less appealing than the intellectual message of the book are its dithyrambic language and, inspired by Samuel Richardson's epistolary novels, the power of its first-person narrative: in Goethe's hands, it becomes a direct dialogue between the narrator and the reader. The structure of the whole is forged by the interconnection of the individual scenes; delicate escalations lead from Werther's perception of a serene world in the first letters, past burgeoning love, to the gradual darkening of his mind. Parallels and contrasts of more tangible character heighten the dynamics of his inner experience: the jubilation of nature in the introductory pages gives way in the novel's latter part to storms and devastating floods; the mood changes with the seasons, from a blissful beginning in May to the shortest, most desolate day of the year; Ossian's somber visions overshadow and displace Homeric idylls.

With the appearance of Goethe's autobiographical account of his youth, *Aus Meinem Leben: Dichtung und Wahrheit* (1811–33; *The Autobiography of Goethe: Truth and Poetry*), almost four decades later, it became clear that the novel closely parallels events in the author's own life. Hesitantly but openly, he writes about these circumstances: while an intern at the Imperial Court of Chancery in Wetzlar in 1772, he was involved in a close friendship, like Werther, with a woman called Lotte and the man to whom she was engaged. His own solution for an increasingly difficult situation was abruptly to leave town, but an acquaintance who found himself in a similar predicament ended up by committing suicide. The shock of this news was the catalyst for the conception of the novel in 1774. Totally absorbed by it, Goethe completed it within four weeks, making, as he observed, Werther's and his own experiences almost indistinguishable.

As significant as the positive reactions to *The Sorrows of Young Werther* were the voices of criticism. Representatives of the Enlightenment's intellectual establishment, of the orthodox clergy, and of conservative governments recognized its anarchic sentiments, especially with regard to marital fidelity and suicide. Werther was seen as an outsider, a sick person whose destructive attitudes were a threat to the well-being of bourgeois society. Scathing rejoinders, calls for a ban, and outrageous parodies became almost as numerous as editions of the novel itself. However, by the end of the 1780s, such rejections began to lose their momentum. What remained was a steady endorsement, not only among the Romantics in Germany, but also abroad. Ugo Foscolo's *Ultime Lettere di Iacopo Ortis* (1802; *Last Letters of Iacopo Ortis*), Chateaubriand's *René* (1802; *René*), and Byron's *Manfred* (1817), among others, echoed the melancholy mood of *The Sorrows of Young Werther.* The French considered it a reflection of *mal du siècle* (illness of the century), much as German readers felt it to be the embodiment of weltschmerz.

Personal engagement with the novel diminished during the latter part of the 19th century, spawning Jules Massenet's melodramatic opera *Werther* (1886). However, more recent writers have again been affected by it. Thomas Mann responded to the Germans' obsession with the story's origins in his novel *Lotte in Weimar* (1939; *The Beloved Returns: Lotte in Weimar*), allowing Goethe and the Lotte of his Wetzlar encounter, now both aging, to renew their acquaintance. A contemporary author, Ulrich

Plenzdorf, in his play *Die neuen Leiden des jungen W.* (1972; The New Sufferings of Young W.), emphasized the modernity of the novel by retelling it from the point of view of a youthful citizen of the German Democratic Republic whose search for personal happiness conflicted with the restrictive conditions of the regime under which he had to live.

PETER BOERNER

See also Epistolary Novel

Editions

First edition: *Die Leiden des jungen Werthers*, Leipzig: Weygandsche Buchhandlung, 1774; new edition, revised by Goethe, *Leiden des jungen Werthers*, Leipzig: Georg Joachim Göschen, 1787

Critical edition: in *Sämtliche Werke* [Frankfurt edition], vol. 8, edited by Waltraud Wiethölter, Frankfurt: Deutscher Klassiker Verlag, 1994

Translations: *The Sorrows of Werter*, translated by Richard Graves, 1780; *The Sufferings of Young Werther*, translated by Bayard Quincy Morgan, London: Calder, 1976; *The Sorrows of Young Werther*, translated by Elizabeth Mayer and Louise Bogan, New York: Random House, 1971; translated by Victor Lange and Judith Ryan, edited by David E. Wellbery, in *Goethe's Collected Works*, vol. 11, New York: Suhrkamp, 1988; translated by Michael Hulse, London and New York: Penguin, 1989

Further Reading

Atkins, Stuart, *The Testament of "Werther" in Poetry and Drama*, Cambridge, Massachusetts: Harvard University Press, 1949

Grosse, Wilhelm, *Kommentar: Die Leiden des jungen Werthers*, Frankfurt: Suhrkamp, 1998

Hotz, Karl, editor, *Goethes "Werther" als Modell für kritisches Lesen: Materialien zur Rezeptionsgeschichte*, Stuttgart: Klett, 1974; 3rd edition, 1980

Jäger, Georg, *Die Leiden des alten und des neuen Werther: Kommentare, Abbildungen, Materialien zu Goethes "Leiden des jungen Werthers" und Plenzdorfs "Neuen Leiden des jungen W.,"* Munich: Hanser, 1984

Müller, Peter, *Zeitkritik und Utopie in Goethes "Werther,"* Berlin: Rütten und Loening, 1969; 3rd edition, 1983

Rothmann, Kurth, editor, *Johann Wolfgang Goethe: "Die Leiden des jungen Werthers,"* Stuttgart: Reclam, 1971; revised edition, 1987

Scherpe, Klaus R., *Werther und Wertherwirkung*, Bad Homburg: Gehlen, 1970; 3rd edition, Wiesbaden: Athenaion, 1980

Vaget, Hans Rudolf, "Die Leiden des jungen Werthers (1774)," in *Goethes Erzählwerk: Interpretationen*, edited by Paul Michael Lützeler and James E. McLeod, Stuttgart: Reclam, 1985

Die Wahlverwandtschaften 1809

Novel by Johann Wolfgang von Goethe

Die Wahlverwandtschaften (*The Elective Affinities*), which Goethe himself considered his "best book," grew out of a novella that was originally intended for *Wilhelm Meisters Wanderjahre* (1821; *Wilhelm Meister's Travels*); by 1807, however, it had become an independent project that would itself contain a novella and pieces of a diary. Goethe claimed later that it was his only project where he worked according to "an idea," although he never explicitly stated what this idea was and destroyed all of the work's sketches and drafts. Until recently, this idea has been associated with the chemical parable (*chemische Gleichnisrede*) in chapter 4 that also gave the novel its title. The term *elective affinity* originated in 1775, when the Swede Torbern Bergmann described a series of dissolutions and recombinations of different elements according to their attraction to one another. Thus, two compounds AB and CD could recombine into AC and BD. Bergmann's chemical theory, however, was already outdated by 1800, as Goethe knew. Indeed, the tricky parable only seems to resemble the events of the novel, in which a couple wants to break up to find new partners, but, more important, it also highlights the differences between human culture and natural laws rather than their similarities. While chemical substances can exchange partners without being destroyed, the human beings of the novel cannot perform these partner exchanges with the indifference of inanimate substances. Thus, recent views of the novel have stressed the specific organization and modernity of its cultural institutions, which arise in the restriction of an unlimited natural state (in particular, marriage, motherhood, self-consciousness, pedagogy, economics, medicine, art, and landscaping). The cultural process thereby appears as a "framing" or "freezing" of a fluid process to a mere image (or a fixed compound element). For example, nature only exists for the protagonists of the novel once it is transformed into a garden, and the self only exists as a fixed image of the self. Goethe developed this cultural program of images—a program toward which he remains critical throughout the novel—in his readings of Plotinus and Schelling.

Already, the beginning of the novel evokes the air of an experiment. Eduard, "as we shall call a well-to-do baron in the prime of his life," and his second wife, Charlotte, live in a country mansion where they spend their time with landscaping projects. Each is visited by a companion: Eduard by his friend the Captain (*Hauptmann*) and Charlotte by her niece Ottilie. It is here where the "elective affinities" seem to organize their behavior—Eduard falls in love with Ottilie and Charlotte with the Captain. With this in mind, Eduard and Charlotte commit a "double adultery." When they spend a night together each is thinking of their new love: "In the dim lamplight secret affections began to hold sway, and imagination took over from reality. Eduard clasped none other than Ottilie in his arms; Charlotte saw the Captain more or less distinctly before her mind's eye." The decisive power of images is revealed by the fact that the child conceived that night, Otto, will resemble the Captain and Ottilie, but not the biological parents.

Eduard and Charlotte react differently to the crisis of their marriage. Eduard, who "was not used to denying himself what he wanted," still wants a divorce, while the self-controlled Charlotte restricts herself and expects from Eduard the same self-denial (*Entsagung*). The novel presents their conflict as the dilemma of modern culture. While Eduard's narcissism is intolerable in its mere wish for expansion, Charlotte's self-mastery consists solely of self-restriction. Thus, her self-consciousness is not an act of self-knowing but merely the act of limiting herself to an image of what she should be.

Eduard, unable to bear the new bond to Charlotte created by the pregnancy, goes to war, while Charlotte and Ottilie remain at the mansion. Visitors come, among them Luciane, the devilish daughter of Charlotte, who is the masterpiece of a new pedagogical institute. Eduard himself returns only after the child's birth and secretly meets Ottilie with the infant in the park, where for the first time they exchange "free kisses." It is this emotional arousal of Ottilie that leads to the novel's most tragic scene. When Ottilie wants to return to the mansion, she crosses the lake with a boat, and the infant falls into the water; all attempts to revive Otto fail. Otto, the product of the "elective affinities" and already by his name the perfect mixture of all four (i.e., *Ott*ilie, Charl*otte,* and *Otto,* which is both the Captain's name and Eduard's real given name), proves instead to be a failed center of the four. Eduard hopes that this event will make a divorce possible, but now Ottilie withdraws. The paradox of a culture demanding self-restriction then finds its strongest expression in Ottilie; she stops speaking and starves herself to death. The villagers celebrate her displayed corpse like that of a martyr and attribute miracles to it. Eduard dies shortly afterwards, and the novel ends by expressing the hope that the couple will be united in a different world. Only with the help of religion can the regrouping according to the "elective affinities" take place.

The first readers of the novel reacted strongly against the display of a moral libertarianism tolerant of divorce, and they celebrated Ottilie as an image of angelic purity. More recent views of Ottilie have examined her construction as a martyr in an aestheticized cult. Thus, she plays the Virgin Mary in the *tableaux vivants* undertaken in the mansion (Goethe had seen some of these staged images by Lady Hamilton in Italy), the architect paints her face in the angels in a chapel, and even the scene of the drowning Otto uses the pictorial repertoire of Niobe weeping over her lost child. Ottilie figures as the ideal of a person frozen to a mere image, an ideal the novel displays as problematic but yet unavoidable in modern culture.

While the novel was only a moderate success at its publication, today it is seen as a key text that reflects the emergence of modernity, a modernity represented in the figures of the self-controlled Charlotte and the technically oriented Captain, as well as in the cultural institutions that guide and organize human behavior. The novel presents the disaster of the failed life of the four main characters, who are unable to step out of their bounds and limitations. The solution at which Goethe hints, as Walter Benjamin suggested, is presented in an embedded novella in which a couple escapes from its old and restricted life by jumping off a boat and finding an unexpected new beginning. A restrictive culture is corrected only by such a jump, which marks an entrance into history, the ultimate move of modernity. History, or "hope," as Benjamin said, exists only for the "hopeless."

FRITZ BREITHAUPT

Editions

First edition: *Die Wahlverwandtschaften,* 2 vols., Tübingen: Cotta, 1809

Critical edition: in *Sämtliche Werke nach Epochen seines Schaffens,* edited by Christoph Siegrist, vol. 9, Munich and Vienna: Carl Hanser, 1987

Translations: *Kindred by Choice,* translated by H.M. Waidson, London: Calder, 1960; as *Elective Affinities,* translated by Elizabeth Mayer and Louise Bogan, Chicago: H. Regnery, 1963; translated by R.J. Hollingdale, London: Penguin, 1971; with *The Sorrows of Young Werther,* translated by Victor Lange and Judith Ryan, edited by David E. Wellbery, in *Goethe's Collected Works,* vol. 11, New York: Suhrkamp, 1988; translated by David Constantine, 1994

Further Reading

Benjamin, Walter, "Goethes Wahlverwandtschaften," in *Gesammelte Schriften,* edited by Rolf Tiedemann and Hermann Schweppenhäuser, Frankfurt: Suhrkamp, 1972

Bolz, Norbert W., editor, *Goethes Wahlverwandtschaften: Kritische Modelle und Diskursanalysen zum Mythos Literatur,* Hildesheim: Gerstenberg, 1981

Buschendorf, Bernhard, *Goethes mythische Denkform: Zur Ikonographie der "Wahlverwandtschaften,"* Frankfurt: Suhrkamp, 1986

Härtl, Heinz, editor, *"Die Wahlverwandtschaften": Eine Dokumentation der Wirkung von Goethes Roman 1808–1832,* Weinberg: Acta Humanoria, 1983

Müller-Sievers, Helmut, *Self-Generation: Biology, Philosophy, and Literature around 1800,* Stanford, California: Stanford University Press, 1997

Wellbery, David E., "*Die Wahlverwandtschaften*: Desorganisation symbolischer Ordnungen," in *Goethes Erzählwerk*: *Interpretationen,* edited by Paul Michael Lützeler and James E. McLeod, Stuttgart: Reclam, 1985

Wilhelm Meisters Lehrjahre 1795/96

Novel by Johann Wolfgang von Goethe

When Goethe's novel *Wilhelm Meisters Lehrjahre* (1795/96; *Wilhelm Meister's Apprenticeship*) first appeared, Friedrich von Schlegel hailed it as one of the three "greatest tendencies of the age," juxtaposing its cultural significance to the political impact of the French Revolution. Comparable in influence only to his drama *Faust* (1808, 1832), Goethe's novel has continued to command a fascination not unlike that of Shakespeare's *Hamlet,* the discussion and performance of which form the central books of the work. The novel's most poetic characters, the exotic child Mignon and the tragic Harpist, have found their way into the literature of other nations and into fine arts; their songs have been set to music. Authors and scholars consider Goethe's *Wilhelm Meister's Apprenticeship* to be the prototype, the "unexcelled" embodiment (in the words of Hermann Hesse) of the ambiguous prose genre bildungsroman (novel of education and formative self-realization in society). Its multidimensional levels of meaning and wide range of themes have led to numerous interpretations, so that the history of German literary scholarship has sometimes been traced via the critical approaches applied to this work (Berghahn and Pinkerneil).

Authors of novels about an artist's development, from Novalis, Keller, Dickens, and Stifter to Thomas Mann, James Joyce, and later writers, have pondered the work's craftsmanship, probing its enchantment over the imagination and appeal to the inquisitive mind. In *Wilhelm Meister's Apprenticeship,* a broad, integrated spectrum of narratives, confessions, and poetry unfolds; types of theater and their history come alive; epic and drama, art works, and architecture play multiple roles. Religious, social, economic, educational, and philosophical issues move to the fore in the last three books. The major themes throughout the work, however, revolve around what Goethe called the "basis and center" of his existence, "productive imagination." In his bildungsroman, he delineates it as a gift requiring cultivation to at least the same degree as other human faculties. In this "totally symbolic" novel, the reader is expected to reflect thoroughly and discover "the more general and higher [meaning] hidden behind the characters."

During the 20 years of the work's composition, Goethe himself went through a major artistic metamorphosis. After the titanic subjectivity of his youth (*Die Leiden des jungen Werthers* [1774; *The Sorrows of Young Werther*], *Urfaust* [1887; Original Faust]), the author concentrated on "healing" himself by striving for greater objectivity, especially during his Italian journey (1786–88). There he immersed himself in the study of nature, the sciences, and the arts. He wrote home that everything he experienced and thought would be transformed and preserved in *Wilhelm Meister's Apprenticeship*. The novel has been called Goethe's ironically distanced "inner biography." On a symbolic-epistemological level, it delineates how the power of creative imagination is converted from a given incalculable aptitude to a maturing capability. Mastery, implied in the hero's name, is the challenge.

The novel's title character, talented, amiable, and highly imaginative, escapes his confining bourgeois environment as a child by reading fiction and by performing and writing dramas. At age 22, he falls deeply in love with Mariane, an actress, and fancies the stage to be his calling. He plans to elope with her, become a writer-actor, and found a national theater. His whole world falls apart when he erroneously believes that Mariane has betrayed him. The resulting life-threatening emotional and physical breakdown, which lasts for almost three years, indelibly affects his further development. Rejecting his poetic and theatrical endeavors, Wilhelm determines to become a businessman. But when his dearest aspirations, now rigged with guilt and self-doubt, are suppressed, they enter into the realm of unconscious creativity. Wilhelm joins wandering actors and appropriates the mysterious figures Mignon and the Harpist, his primary tragic doubles, whom his imagination incorporates into his aching heart.

Emerging from Wilhelm's longing for his lost love, the androgynous Mignon dances as the marionettes of his childhood danced. Not coincidentally, Wilhelm earlier had compared for Mariane the ecstasy of falling in love to the exuberant experience of his first marionette show as a ten-year-old. He had equated his pain after the puppet theater's sudden disappearance with the agony of a lover losing his "first and only" love. Mignon is as old (12 to 13 years) as the time span between his two momentous losses. Transformed into Wilhelm's "inner child" and guide, Mignon sings heart-rending songs of a past forfeited and of unending longing, all inspired by her "father" Wilhelm. Later, as he matures, she points to a higher resolution of the conflict and gradually loses her hold over his imagination. With profound psychological insight, Goethe makes Wilhelm attract another doppelgänger, the Harpist, into his "little family." The Harpist's guilt-ridden and fatalistic songs, his mentally incestuous solipsism and destructive fantasies, symbolize the perilous potentials of Wilhelm's power of imagination.

Wilhelm, however, also surrounds himself with burlesque, picaresque, and life-affirming characters. Foremost is Philine, a delightful embodiment of the gracious, sensual enjoyment of the present. Outwardly she resembles his lost love. Later, Wilhelm recognizes his natural son by Mariane. His name and association with Mariane indicating a fortunate future, Felix (felicity) is almost sacrificed by the Harpist, an obvious symbolic event. Felix continues Philine's healing function on a higher level and guides his father to his ultimate goal, Natalie, the noblest and most beautiful of various female figures surrounding the hero. She represents complementary balance, recognized natural laws, as well as the highest ethical standards and practices. She is, in fact, the personified model of dynamic and flexible equilibrium in nature and mankind, worth emulating.

To become cognizant of her, Wilhelm requires beneficial educational "detours." Thrilled by the splendor and refinement of the aristocracy, he soon discovers its superficial aspects (book 3). His association with a professional theater teaches him about human and worldly relationships, the power of illusions, and the need for self-knowledge. Significantly, his studies of Shakespeare (books 4 and 5) sharpen his aesthetic sense for form and lead to his insight that great art is based on the truth of reality. By analyzing and playing the role of Hamlet on the stage, he finally overcomes his identification with Shakespeare's melancholic prince. Hamlet represents the last of Wilhelm's literary doubles and marks his transition to a nontragic conception of life. Book 6, the religious "Confessions of a Beautiful Soul," constitutes another mirroring narrative within the novel. It parallels Wilhelm's search for a focus in life but also pinpoints the dangers of excessive introversion. Slowly, by trial and error, he learns to differentiate between his own projections and an outside reality composed of coincidence and necessity. Their discernment is, for Goethe, one of the prerequisites for mastering the imagination and creating lasting works.

Wilhelm's initiation into the Tower Society, an association of socially progressive thinkers and leaders modeled after 18th-century secret societies, brings him closer to emotional and cognitive maturity (books 7 and 8). These new friends help him overcome his perennial vacillation, which is the distinguishing feature of fantasy without direction. His imagination now becomes solidly founded and integrated. For the mature Goethe—and Wilhelm—this requires the assistance of critical analysis, down-to-earth and far-reaching activity, sensibility, knowledge, and "higher intuition." The Tower Society members representing these strengths need Wilhelm as much as he needs them. Thus, in symbolic-allegorical code, the novel contains a "critique of productive imagination," which Goethe thought was missing in Kant's *Critiques* (letter to Maria Poulowna, 3 January 1817).

In the realm of the Tower, there is no need for fatalism or unfulfilled longing. After Wilhelm belatedly receives Mariane's letters of clarification and grief, he recognizes that her death was partially caused by his former reliance on appearances and fears rather than fact. According to the epistemologically rigorous logic of the novel, the fear- and fancy-driven Harpist now commits suicide and Mignon withers away. Wilhelm and his helpers, symbolically his new collective identity, transform Mignon's body into a work of art. In her distanced objectification, Wilhelm masters his past. Enshrined in the "hall of the past, present, and future" of Natalie's castle, which exhibits the classical features of unity, variety, and the dynamic interaction of high art and society, Mignon testifies to the uniqueness of the artist's creation.

Poetologically, Goethe's novel includes a metafictional rendition of the creative author's ability to grow beyond subjectivity, to become knowledgeable about nature's laws, the writer's craft, human affairs, and his own strengths and weaknesses. Goethe's mature ethos no longer permits a Wertherian rift between head and heart. By introducing the "sick prince" motif and the Tower Society into the revised novel, Goethe emphasized the healing process of Wilhelm Meister. "Master" (Meister), the hero's last name, is the ironically tinged but nevertheless undeniable *indicium* of his potential and ultimate aim, just as his first name, Wilhelm, is not coincidentally allied with that of his "patron," "friend," and spiritual "father," William Shakespeare.

HELLMUT AMMERLAHN

See also Bildungsroman

Editions

First edition: *Wilhelm Meisters Lehrjahre,* Berlin: Unger, 1795/96
Critical editions: *Goethes Werke. Hamburger Ausgabe*, vol. 7, edited and annotated by Erich Trunz, Hamburg: Wegner, 1950; *J.W. Goethe, Sämtliche Werke* (Frankfurt Edition), vol. 9, edited and annotated by Wilhelm Voßkamp, Frankfurt: Deutscher Klassiker Verlag, 1992
Translation: *Wilhelm Meister's Apprenticeship*, edited and translated by Eric A. Blackall in cooperation with Victor Lange, in *Goethe's Collected Works*, vol. 9, New York: Suhrkamp, 1989

Further Reading

Ammerlahn, Hellmut, "Wilhelm Meisters Mignon: Ein offenbares Rätsel: Name, Gestalt, Symbol, Wesen und Werden," *Deutsche Vierteljahrsschrift* (DVLG) 42, no. 1 (1968)
——, "Goethe's *Wilhelm Meisters Lehrjahre:* An Apprenticeship toward the Mastery of Exactly What?" *Colloquia Germanica* 30, no. 2 (1997)
Berger, Albert, *Ästhetik und Bildungsroman: Goethes "Wilhelm Meisters Lehrjahre,"* Vienna: Braumüller, 1977
Berghahn, Klaus L., and Beate Pinkerneil, *Am Beispiel Wilhelm Meister: Einführung in die Wissenschaftsgeschichte der Germanistik,* 2 vols., Königstein: Athenäum, 1980
Blackall, Eric A., *Goethe and the Novel,* Ithaca, New York: Cornell University Press, 1976
Fick, Monika, *Das Scheitern des Genius: Mignon und die Symbolik der Liebesgeschichten in Wilhelm Meisters Lehrjahren,* Würzburg: Königshausen und Neumann, 1987
Graham, Ilse, "An Eye for the World: Stages of Realisation in 'Wilhelm Meister'," in *Goethe: Portrait of the Artist,* by Ilse Graham, Berlin and New York: de Gruyter, 1977
Hoffmeister, Gerhart, editor, *Goethes Mignon und ihre Schwestern: Interpretationen und Rezeption,* New York: Lang, 1993
Lange, Victor, "Goethe's Craft of Fiction," *Publications of the English Goethe Society* 22 (1952–53)
Lukács, Georg, "Wilhelm Meisters Lehrjahre," in *Goethe und seine Zeit,* Bern: A. Francke, 1947; translated in *Goethe and His Age,* London: Merlin Press, 1968; New York: Grosset and Dunlap, 1969
Muenzer, Clark S., *Figures of Identity: Goethe's Novels and the Enigmatic Self,* University Park: Pennsylvania State University Press, 1984
Reiss, Hans Siegbert, *Goethes Romane,* Bern and Munich: Francke, 1963; as *Goethe's Novels,* London: Macmillan, and New York: St. Martin's Press, 1969
Roberts, David, *The Indirections of Desire: Hamlet in Goethe's "Wilhelm Meister,"* Heidelberg: Winter, 1980
Sagmo, Ivar, *Bildungsroman und Geschichtsphilosophie: Eine Studie zu Goethes Roman "Wilhelm Meisters Lehrjahre,"* Bonn: Bouvier, 1982

Claire Goll 1891–1977

Claire Goll's reputation has been linked almost entirely to her role in subordinating her career to that of her idolized husband, Yvan Goll, and then in editing his work and protecting his image. Her early poetry, the outspoken product of a young political activist, has been largely forgotten—despite her often successful adoption of fashionable styles and influences. Backed by Franz Pfemfert, the editor of the Expressionist periodical *Die Aktion,* most of her poetry reflects outspoken feminism. Attention has been focused not on her poetry, however, but on her autobiographies. *Education barbare* (1941; Barbarous Education) gives an account of her childhood up to the suicide of her brother, which was caused by the sadism of her mother. *Traumtänzerin* (1971; Dream Dancer) relates her upbringing and short marriage in 1917 to Heinrich Studer, whom she left. Above all, *La poursuite du vent* (1976; In Pursuit of the Wind) attacks leading modernists such as Pablo Picasso, Salvador Dali, André Malraux, and James Joyce and provides sensational revelations about her own life and that of other famous literary figures. This last work created the aura of a femme fatale who suffered greatly from abuse at various levels.

That Goll was an ardent pacifist and feminist journalist during World War I is also generally forgotten. Her depiction of suffering and humiliated human beings and her attacks on the conditions of modern life were partly the result of hatred by and toward her mother, violent physical abuse, and withdrawal into her own imaginary worlds. Such traumas also explain psychologically the themes and style of her writing, particularly her prose works. Her experiences as an adult included a first unhappy marriage, divorce, and the loss of custody of her children; these experiences were compensated by a life on the edge of the surrealist movement in Paris and then by living with a genius poet and friend of some of the leading avant-garde figures of the day. She was idealized by such writers as Rainer Maria Rilke, with whom she had a short-lived affair in 1921, and by Yvan Goll, whom she first met in 1917. She appeared as an enigmatic, unattainable woman, not least because of the celebration of lesbian love in her two stories *Der gläserne Garten* (1919; The Glass Garden), which owed much to her temporary relationship with the actress Elisabeth Bergner. In the 1930s, her closeness to Yvan Goll was marred by her hatred for his eight-year liaison with the poet Paula Ludwig.

Continued passionate concern for social causes led Goll to write a series of social novels (e.g., *Une perle* [1929; A Pearl]), where the central women figures are portrayed as victims of society. Her bouts of despair after Yvan's death, punctuated by visions and hearing voices, were only partly relieved by her removing Paula Ludwig from her memory, and her attempted suicide in 1938 was the culmination of years of protest and deep suffering. Verena Mahlow has shown the interweaving of triviality and fate in Goll's novels, where cliché images are used to highlight protests against the impossibility that many women could attain dignity and self-identity against the cruelty of sexual deceit (see *Une crime en Provence* [1932; A Crime in Provence]). Her involvement with more general issues is shown in *Der Neger Jupiter raubt Europa* (1926; The Negro Jupiter Rapes Europe), where, as Moray McGowan has shown (in Robertson and Vilain), an attempt was made to come to terms with such themes as the interdependence of black and white cultures, the complicity of Third World elite classes, and European prejudices and stereotyping. The Europa myth serves both as a structural device and to point up hidden fears that reflect those of European Jews.

The relative lack of professional interest so far in Goll's work is exacerbated by the difficulties with the unpublished documents held in the Deutsches Literaturarchiv Marbach and also by the episode in the 1950s when she accused Paul Celan of plagiarizing Yvan Goll's posthumous volume of poetry *Traumkraut* (1951; Soporific) in his collection *Mohn und Gedächtnis* (1952; Poppy and Memorial). Details of Paul Celan's reactions to her accusatory letters to him are in the Marbach Catalogue *Fremde Nähe: Celan als Übersetzer* (1997; Distant Proximity: Celan as Translator).

Despite attempts to decry her as a writer because of her aggressive and sharp-tongued self-defense, her obvious indebtedness to Rilke and Yvan Goll, and her writing mainly in French after 1920, Goll's German works should not be overlooked. Anna Rheinsberg sums up these achievements as a new and unusual tone: "Pathos und Engagement. Sozialrealismus plus Hintertreppe und Jargon" (Pathos and engaged writing. Social realism plus backstairs gossip and jargon). Her final years were also marked by scandals and self-publicity. The chaos of her life is reflected in the wide scope and ambivalence of her work; it has also led to prejudice against her reputation as a person and as a writer.

Brian Keith-Smith

Biography

Born in Nuremberg, 29 October 1891. Studied at Leipzig University before 1917; married to Heinrich Studer, 1911–16; moved to Switzerland, 1917, where she met Yvan Goll and joined the Zurich Dadaist group; lived for a few weeks in Munich with the poet Rainer Maria Rilke; from 1919, lived with Yvan Goll in Paris, where among her circle were André Malraux, Jean Breton, James Joyce, Fernand Léger, Jean Cocteau, Salvador Dali, and Marc Chagall; married Yvan Goll and went with him to New York, 1939–47; after his death in 1950, lived in Ascona (Switzerland) and Paris. Süddeutscher Rundfunk Prize, 1952; Société des Gens de Lettres Prize, 1959; Mandat de Poètes Prize, 1960; Katherine Mansfield Prize, 1965; Prize of the Deutsche Akademie Darmstadt, 1966. Died in Paris, 30 May 1977.

Selected Works

Novels

Une Allemande à Paris, 1924; German version, 1927
Der Neger Jupiter raubt Europa, 1926
Une perle, 1929; German version as *Ein Mensch ertrinkt,* 1931
Un crime en Provence, 1932; German version as *Arsenik,* 1933; revised as *Jedes Opfer tötet seinen Mörder,* 1977
Education barbare, 1941
Le tombeau des amants inconnus, 1941
Le ciel volé, 1958; German version, 1962
Un amour du Quartier latin, 1959

Poetry

Mitwelt, 1919
Lyrische Films, 1922
Poèmes d'amour, with Yvan Goll, 1925; revised version, 1930
Poèmes de jalousie, with Yvan Goll, 1926
Poèmes de la vie et de la mort, with Yvan Goll, 1927
Chansons malaises, with Yvan Goll, 1935; German version, 1967
Dix milles aubes, with Yvan Goll, 1951; German version, 1954
Les Larmes pétrifiées, 1951; German version, 1952
Das tätowierte Herz, 1957
Klage um Ivan, 1960
L'ignigère, 1969

Short Fiction

Die Frauen erwachen, 1918
Der gläserne Garten, 1919
Journal d'un cheval. Les mémoires d'un moineau, 1925; German version of the *Journal d'un cheval,* 1950
Ménagerie sentimentale, 1930
Blanchisserie chinoise, 1943; German version, 1953
L'inconnue de la Seine. Le Diner de 500 Francs, 1944
Die Taubenwitwe, 1951
Nouvelles petites fleurs de Saint Francois, 1952; German version, 1952
Apollon sans bras, 1956
Jeanne d'Arc deux fois brulée, 1961
La Récolte de Huitres, 1961
Les confessions d'un moineau de siècle, 1963; German version, 1969
Le suicide d'un chien, 1964
La Correction, 1968
Zirkus des Lebens, 1976

Other

Traumtänzerin: Jahre der Jugend, 1971
La poursuite du vent, 1976; German version as *Ich verzeihe keinem: Eine literarische Chronique scandaleuse unserer Zeit,* 1978; new editions, 1980, 1994

Further Reading

Blumenthal, Bernhardt, "Rilke and Claire Goll," *Modern Austrian Literature* 15, no. 3/4 (1982)
———, "Claire Goll's Prose," *Monatshefte* 75 (1983)
Brinker-Gabler, Gisela, *Deutsche Dichterinnen vom 16. Jahrhundert bis zur Gegenwart,* Frankfurt: Fischer Taschenbuch, 1978
Döhl, R., "Geschichte und Kritik eines Angriffs: Zu den Behauptungen gegen Paul Celan," *Deutsche Akademie für Sprache und Dichtung Darmstadt Jahrbuch* (1960)
Gabrisch, A., "'Ich verzeihe keinem,'" *Sinn und Form* 33, no. 2 (1981)
Glauert, Barbara, "'Liliane': Rainer Maria Rilke und Claire Studer in ihren Briefen 1918–1925," *Börsenblatt für den Deutschen Buchhandel* 7 (23 January 1976)
Hausdorf, Anna, "Claire Goll und ihr Roman *Der Neger Jupiter raubt Europa,*" *Neophilologus* 74 (1990)
Mahlow, Verena, *"Die Liebe, die uns immer zur Hemmung wurde . . .": Weibliche Indentitätsproblematik zwischen Expressionismus und Neuer Sachlichkeit am Beispiel der Prosa Claire Golls,* Frankfurt and New York: Lang, 1996
Naumann, Helmut, "Claire Golls Erinnerungen an Rainer Maria Rilke," *Blätter der Rilke-Gesellschaft* 9 (1992)

Neumann, Michael, "Claire Golls letztes Buch," *Westermanns Monatshefte,* January (1978)
Rheinsberg, Anna, "Claire Goll, 1890–1977," in *Wie bunt entfaltet sich mein Anderssein,* Mannheim: Persona, 1993
Robertson, Eric, and Robert Vilain, editors, *Yvan Goll—Claire Goll: Texts and Contexts,* Amsterdam and Atlanta, Georgia: Rodopi, and London: Institute of Germanic Studies, 1997
Schultz, Joachim, "Das Afrika- und 'Neger'-Bild in den Werken von Claire und Ivan Goll," in *Proceedings of the XIIth Congress of the International Comparative Literature Association,* vol. 2, edited by Roger Bauer, Munich: Iudicum, 1988
Serke, Jürgen, "Claire Goll," in *Die verbrannten Dichter,* Weinheim: Beltz und Gelberg, 1977

Yvan Goll 1891–1950

Yvan Goll's singular characteristic as a writer was his multilingualism. In a famous summing-up of his life in 1920 he wrote (originally in German): "Yvan Goll has no home: by fate a Jew, by chance born in France, by a stamped piece of paper claimed as a German citizen. Yvan Goll has no age: his childhood was sucked away by old people whose blood had gone. The god of war assassinated the young man." Steeped in international culture, he wrote in German as an Expressionist until 1924, in French until his death, in English during his years in America, and in German again during his last few years. The homelessness of modern man, suffered by him personally, was to become the main general theme of his works.

He published his first poems in French in Switzerland during World War I with other pacifist writers, and his works pay tribute to those on both sides who had been killed or wounded. Afterward, he took part in prolonged discussions with Viking Eggeling about the theoretical principles for the first abstract film *Symphonie diagonale* (Diagonal Symphony). In 1920, he was one of the first to suggest the concept of surrealism in the foreword to his "Überdramen" *Die Unsterblichen* (The Immortals). Four years later, praising in particular the poetry of Apollinaire, he applied the principles of cubism to literature in his periodical *Surréalisme.* Despite his radically different views, which predated those of André Breton, he included Breton among other famous avant-garde writers in his French-American literary periodical *Hemispheres* (1943–46). Typical of his industrious literary activity was his own translation into German of his novel *Lucifer vieillisant* (1934; The Aging Lucifer), perhaps the only novel he wrote of lasting importance. However, *Die Eurokokke* (1927; The Eurococcus), with its portrayal of the collapse of modern city life through the corruption of culture, humanity, and the body, and the Balzacian portrayal of avarice in *Le microbe de l'or* (1927; The Microbe of Gold) both effectively evoke grotesque extremes in Parisian society. More significant was his stage satire *Methusalem; oder, Der ewige Bürger* (1922; Methusalem; or, The Eternal Bourgeois), which was a link between the French dramatist Jarry's grotesque pieces and the Rumanian Ionesco's theater of the absurd. In the foreword, Goll defines his aims in drama as unmasking man as a self-made puppet while using a superreal style. He reveals in dreamlike sequences the infinite possibilities or extensions of human consciousness through a mass of unrelated details. Antilogical links between apparently unrelated thoughts are used to give the semblance of a new order, including a manic energy where cupidity, snobbery, jealousy, and revolutionary ideals are mimed and bizarrely presented within the confines of the sketch or revue form.

Goll's aim in his lyric poetry was to explore and establish such order. In the early cycles from 1914–20, he experimented with the current vogue of dithyrambic Expressionism, and from 1920 to 1924, with cubism. The cycle *Der Panama-Kanal* (1914; The Panama Canal), which had seven different versions, combines vitalist excitement with a detached, almost ironic attention to detail; in this work, the canal engineering project becomes a unifying force for the chaos of nature and man. Goll refined and never totally abandoned his interest in Expressionism, and his attention to order was to govern all his often reworked later works. Words and images increasingly became pointers to hidden levels of meaning that were precise yet visionary. The early collections reached their essential poetic high point in *Le nouvel Orphée* (1918; The New Orpheus) and *Der Eiffelturm* (1924; The Eiffel Tower); in these works, the Orpheus figure and the impersonal bustle of the modern city provide leitmotifs in a series of surprising images and montages from newspaper headings. A series of delicately phrased love poems followed (*Poèmes d'amour* [1925; Love Poems] was written together with his wife, and *Chansons malaises* [1935; Malaysian Songs] celebrates his affair with the poetess Paula Ludwig). Out of the threats of loneliness, decay, and death, he fashioned a new fragile order in relationships and love. His masterpiece came in the cycle of ballads *La Chanson de Jean sans terre* (1936; Song of Homeless John), where, in his search for poetic identity, he turned his own fate into a myth. After his flight to America in 1939 with his wife Claire, occult and cabalistic influences in his writings supported his fascination with death and increasingly referred to his awareness of suffering from leukemia. In the two volumes *Le char triomphal de l'Antimoigne* (1949; The Chariot of Triumph of the Antimoigne) and *Les cercles magiques* (1951; The Magic Circles), alchemy and magic underscore a personal mythology. *Traumkraut* (1951; Dreamweed) and *Abendgesang* (1954; Evening Song) articulate the various stages of his illness. It is noteworthy that whereas most of his French poetry is rhymed, nearly all his German poetry is unrhymed; this is not a sign of superior facility in either language, but of genuine feeling for the potentials of internal rhyming, repetitions, and wordplay. In the later collections, compression and concentration allow him to highlight essential poetic elements. References to fairy tales, magic, and myth extend and intensify normal verbal meaning so that Goll's poetry is one of the richest in German literature that exploits such techniques. Using French poetic traditions to create broader visions in German also made his poetry unique, and this work inspired later writers such as Paul Celan. For Goll, poetry implied working with language in order to produce the most evocative word or image.

Goll's works have been accepted by many writers and critics as among the most significant of modern times, yet because of his often intense and hermetic use of language, they remain largely inaccessible to and generally unknown by the general reading public. This is also partly the result of their piecemeal editing by his widow; however, the four-volume edition of his poetry that appeared in 1966 opened the way to fresh understandings and interpretations. Robert Vilain has also pointed to the several special factors that have contributed to the neglect of Goll's works: his love of self-publicity, his wife's scandalous autobiography, his multilingualism, the unreliability of accurate information about his life and writing, and the instability of his authorial persona. This instability is also marked by his use of several pseudonyms, his frequent revisions of his works, and his coauthorship with his wife of several individual poems.

BRIAN KEITH-SMITH

Biography

Born in St. Dié in the Vosges, 29 March 1891. Studied law at Strassburg University; continued his studies in Lausanne, 1915–18, where he met Romain Rolland's pacifist circle and the Zurich Dadaist group; from 1919, lived with Claire Studer in Paris at the center of a modernist group including André Malraux, Jean Breton, James Joyce, Fernand Léger, Jean Cocteau, Salvador Dali, and Marc Chagall; married Claire Studer and collaborated with her on love poems; began an affair with the Austrian poetess Paula Ludwig, 1931; fled with his wife to New York, 1939, returning to Paris in 1947. Died of leukemia in Paris, 27 February 1950.

Selected Works

Collections

Der Eiffelturm: Gesammelte Dichtungen, 1924
Quatre Études. Oeuvres choisies, 1956
Dichtungen. Lyrik. Prosa. Drama, edited by Claire Goll, 1960
Ausgewählte Gedichte, edited by Georges Schlocker, 1962
Die Lyrik, edited by Barbara Hesse-Glauert, 4 vols., 1966
L'Antirose: Gedichte von Ivan und Claire Goll, 1967
Gedichte. Eine Auswahl. Mit vierzehn Gedichten von Claire Goll, edited by René A. Strasser, 1968
Oeuvres, edited by Claire Goll and Francois Xavier Jaujard, 2 vols., 1968–70
Gedichte 1924–50, edited by Horst Bienek, 1976
Gefangen im Kreise. Auswahl, edited Klaus Schumann, 1988

Novels

Die Eurokokke, 1927
Le microbe d'or, 1927
À bas l'Europe, 1928
Agnus Dei, 1929
Sodom et Berlin, 1929
Lucifer viellissant, 1934

Poetry

Films. (Verse), 1914
Der Panama-Kanal, 1914
Requiem. Für die Gefallenen von Europa, 1917
Der Torso, 1918
Dithyramben, 1918
Der neue Orpheus, 1918
Die Unterwelt, 1919
Astral. Ein Gesang, 1920
Poèmes d'amour, with Claire Goll, 1925; revised version, 1930
Poèmes de jalousie, with Claire Goll, 1926
Poèmes de la vie et de la mort, with Claire Goll, 1927
Noemi, 1929
Chansons malaises, with Claire Goll, 1935; German version, 1967
La Chanson de Jean sans terre, 1936
Métro de la mort, 1936
Deuxième livre de Jean sans terre, 1938
Troisième livre de Jean sans terre, 1939
Fruit from Saturn, 1946
Le mythe de la roche percée, 1947
Elégie d'Ihpétonga, suivie de Masques de Cendre, 1949
Le char triomphal de l'antimoigne, 1949
Les cercles magiques, 1951
Dix milles aubes (with Claire Goll), 1951; German version as *Zehntausend Morgenröten,* 1954
Les Géorgiques Parisiennes, 1951; German version by Claire Goll as *Pariser Georgika,* 1956
Traumkraut: Gedichte aus dem Nachlaß, 1951
Abendgesang. (Neila). Letzte Gedichte. Aus dem Nachlaß, 1954
Multiple femme, 1956
Jean sans terre, 1958

Drama

Die Unsterblichen: Zwei Possen, 1920
Die Chapliniade: Eine Kinodichtung, 1920
Methusalem; oder, Der ewige Bürger. Ein satirisches Drama, 1922
Der Stall des Augias: Tragödie in fünf Akten, 1924
Royal Palace: Oper in einem Akt (music by Kurt Weill), 1926
Phèdre: Opéra en cinq scénes (music by Marcel Mihalovici), 1948
Melusine: Ein Stück in vier Akten, 1956

Other Writings

Lothringische Volkslieder. *Nachdichtungen,* 1912
Elégies Internationales. Pamphlets contre cette guerre, 1915
Requiem. Für die Gefallenen von Europa, 1917
Die drei guten Geister Frankreichs (essays on Diderot, Cézanne, and Mallarmé), 1919
Germaine Berton, die rote Jungfrau (report), 1925
Pascin, 1929
Briefe. Iwan Goll Claire Goll, 1966
Ich sterbe mein Leben: Briefe 1934–1940 (correspondence with Paula Ludwig), 1993

Translations

Translated anthologies, works by Walt Whitman, Henri Barbusse, Voltaire, Pierre Hamp, Blaise Cendrars, Francois Mauriac, René Fraudet, Albert Londres, Rafael Schermann, Mirko Jelusich, Franz Werfel, and Fritz von Unruh

Further Reading

Carmody, Francis J., *The Poetry of Yvan Goll: A Biographical Study,* Paris: Caractères 1956
Dohl, R., "Geschichte und Kritik eines Angriffs. Zu den Behauptungen gegen Paul Celan," *Veröffentlichungen der Deutschen Akademie für Sprache und Dichtung* 7 (1960)
Exner, Richard, "Yvan Goll. Zu seiner deutschen Lyrik," *German Life and Letters* 8 (1955)
———, "Surrealist Elements in Yvan Goll's Franco-German Poetry," *Symposium* 11 (1957)
———, "Yvan Golls Werk seit 1930. Oden, Jean sans Terre und Hiob, Surrealismus, Liebeslyrik," in *Yvan Goll Dichtungen,* edited by Claire Goll, Darmstadt: Helmut Luchterhand, 1960
Heselhaus, Clemens, "Yvan Golls Symbol-Verschränkung," in Clemens

Heselhaus, *Deutsche Lyrik der Moderne: Von Nietzsche bis Yvan Goll,* Düsseldorf: Bagel, 1961
Menz, Egon, "Yvan Goll. Der Panama-Kanal," in *Gedichte der Menschheitsdämmerung,* edited by Horst Denkler, Munich: Fink, 1971
Müller, Burkhard, "Yvan Goll. Das lyrische Werk," in *Hauptwerke der deutschen Literatur 2. Vom Vormärz bis zur Gegenwartsliteratur,* Munich: Kindler, 1994
Müller, Joachim, *Yvan Goll im deutschen Expressionismus,* Berlin: Akademie-Verlag, 1962
Parmée, M.A., *Ivan Goll: The Development of His Poetic Themes and Their Imagery,* Bonn: Bouvier, 1981
Perkins, Vivien, *Yvan Goll: An Iconographical Study of His Poetry,* Bonn: Bouvie, 1970
Phillips, James, *Yvan Goll and Bilingual Poetry,* Stuttgart: Akademischer Verlag H.-D. Heinze, 1984
Profit, Vera B., *Interpretations of Iwan Goll's Late Poetry with a Comprehensive and Annotated Bibliography of the Writings by and about Iwan Goll,* Bern and Las Vegas, Nevada: Lang, 1977
Robertson, Eric, and Robert Vilain, editors, *Yvan Goll—Claire Goll: Texts and Contexts,* Amsterdam and Atlanta, Georgia: Rodopi, 1997
Schaefer, Dietrich, "Yvan Goll," in *Expressionismus als Literatur: Gesammelte Studien,* edited by Wolfgang Rothe, Bern and Munich: Francke, 1969
Uhlig, Helmut, "Yvan Goll," in *Expressionismus: Gestalten einer literarischen Bewegung,* edited by Hermann Friedmann and Otto Mann, Heidelberg: Rothe, 1956
———, "Yvan Golls Werk bis 1930," in *Yvan Goll Dichtungen,* edited by Claire Goll, Darmstadt: Luchterhand, 1960

Gottfried von Straßburg fl. 1200

The personal and professional life of Gottfried von Straßburg remains a mystery, but the same can be said in large part for every other major author of the German High Middle Ages. Those biographies that have been attempted are based on the evidence of his one major extant work, *Tristan und Isold,* and the occasional allusion to his person by later poets such as Ulrich von Türheim and Heinrich von Freiberg. These writers set themselves the task of completing Gottfried's fragmented romance, the former between 1235 and 1243, the latter about 1290. Gottfried is also accorded high praise as a stylist by Konrad von Würzburg, Rudolf von Ems, Konrad von Stoffeln, and Johann von Würzburg. In contrast to many of his literary contemporaries, he was, in all likelihood, not a knight. When he is accorded a title by other medieval poets, it is "meister," which could have several meanings, among them the academic designation of *Magister.* It has also been maintained that his text evinces a marked anti-knightly bias (although this should not be misunderstood as antipathy on his part toward the cultivated manners of the court per se). With his knowledge of various disciplines, which is so abundantly displayed in *Tristan und Isold,* he most assuredly attended a cathedral or monastery school and quite likely enjoyed a university education. It has also been variously suggested that he was either a municipal or clerical official, perhaps even a schoolteacher or a member of the legal community in Straßburg (later poets and the language of the romance provide evidence that Straßburg was, in fact, Gottfried's home), but no conclusive evidence has ever been produced to substantiate any of the aforementioned theories regarding his profession.

While known primarily (and in many instances *only*) for the romance *Tristan,* Gottfried has also been designated in the *Große Heidelberger Liederhandschrift C* (the *Manesse Manuscript*) as the author of a six-stanza *Minnelied,* a panegyric to Mary and Christ in 63 stanzas, and a 13-stanza didactic poem on poverty. Scholars have contended, however, that none of these can be attributed to Gottfried. The allusion by Rudolf von Ems in his *Alexander* to Gottfried's authorship of an epigram dealing with "daz glesîn gelücke" ("glassy [fragile] fortune") has, on the other hand, a basis in fact. A stanza with this precise theme is to be found in the *Große Heidelberger Liederhandschrift C,* although it is attributed to Ulrich von Lichtenstein. Together with the preceding strophe, however, this epigram is now considered to be part of Gottfried's literary corpus. An analysis of their form and content demonstrates compelling similarities to what one finds in *Tristan und Isold.*

Gottfried's *Tristan* is generally dated to ca. 1210. As is the case with most medieval romances and epics, however, a precise time of composition is impossible to ascertain. The work's plot itself is certainly older. Gottfried claims to have derived his knowledge of it from Thomas of Brittany, although the most well-known version of the tale outside Germany was undoubtedly that by the Norman author Béroul (ca. 1200). Specific allusions within the work point to the likelihood that Gottfried was engaged in some sort of feud regarding both stylistics and substance with his contemporary, Wolfram von Eschenbach, the author of *Parzival,* whom Gottfried called one of those "vindaere wilder maere" (inventors of wild tales). Gottfried prided himself in rendering faithfully into Middle High German the adulterous tale of Tristan and Isolde as it had been recorded by Thomas of Brittany (ca. 1160). Both Gottfried's and Thomas's versions have survived as fragments, with the intriguing coincidence that Thomas's work picks up the story at almost the very moment that Gottfried's breaks off—at that point when, just prior to wedding Isolde of the White Hands, Tristan begins to despair over his love for the fair Isolde of Ireland and to doubt that the latter has any idea of the suffering he is experiencing. For all intents and purposes, then, we have the complete tale at our disposal in what has been passed down both by Gottfried's version and by the source on which he claims to have based his work.

If anonymity characterizes Medieval German heroic epic, self-identification is a common feature of the courtly romance of the period. Gottfried does not, however, name himself. Whether or not the initial letter "G" in the acrostic of his prologue is intended as an allusion to the author remains debatable. In view of the fact that *Tristan und Isold,* which consists of 19,548 verses composed in rhyming couplets (to be found in around two dozen manuscripts and partial manuscripts), remained fragmentary, however, it is quite possible that Gottfried would have named himself had he completed his work.

At the core of the story, regardless of the particular stage of its development, is the illicit love affair between Tristan and Isolde, the nephew and wife, respectively, of King Mark of Cornwall. The High Medieval versions of the romance have the added motif of the magic love potion, which, consumed unwittingly by the lovers, frees them from subjective guilt. Older versions of the tale were shorter, although always culminating in the death of Tristan and Isolde following the discovery of the lovers in a forest. Later versions add the sections dealing with Isolde's return to Mark's court, Tristan's banishment, and his eventual marriage to Isolde of the White Hands, as well as an introduction recounting the story of Tristan's parents, Riwalin and Blanscheflur. The romance—with these additions, commonly referred to as the *Estoire*—had probably assumed the form in which we now know it about the year 1150 and was quite possibly written down at the court of Eleonore of Poitou, certainly the grandest patron of the arts at that time. The *Estoire* was the basis for the troubadour-like version of the tale produced by the French writer Béroul, as well as for the more courtly rendition by Thomas of Brittany. The first German version of *Tristan* was that of Eilhart von Oberge (ca. 1170–75), who tended to follow Béroul, while Gottfried's masterpiece, as the narrator himself makes abundantly clear, used Thomas as his source.

Tristan und Isold has its roots in history, myth, fairy tales, and diverse literary traditions. The Morolt episode has been traced to the Picts of the ninth century, and the name of the major protagonist, Tristan, is patterned upon the name of Drust, the son of the Pict king Talorc, who ruled in northern Scotland at the end of the eighth century. A King Mark is documented as existing in Cornwall during the sixth century, and classical literary influence can be detected in the Isolde of the White Hands section (the saga of Paris and Oenone; saga of Theseus). Scholars have also pointed to the significance of the late classical *Apollonius* for the *Tristan* romance, and compelling parallels have been discovered between the story of Tristan and Isolde of the White Hands and the Arabic poet Kais ibn Doreidsch in the seventh century.

Tristan und Isold was justifiably characterized by the late Joseph Campbell as *the* romantic love tale of the Middle Ages. With his definition of the "noble hearts" (for whom he had written the tale)—those beings who accepted and perhaps even sought out the dichotomy between joy and sorrow—Gottfried allows his romance to break with the standard cyclical structure of the Arthurian romance, which may be described as follows: a harmonious (or apparently harmonious) state gives way to one of crisis that serves as a catalyst for questing knights, sent forth from Arthur's court, to participate in adventures and/or tests, the successful outcome of which culminates in the restoration of joy and harmony in Arthurian society. Typical examples of this structure can be found in Wolfram von Eschenbach's *Parzival* (ca. 1220) and Hartmann von Aue's *Erec* (1180/85) and *Iwein* (ca. 1200). By contrast, the love of Tristan and Isolde—forbidden, illicit, and not without a demonic tinge—precludes any "fairy-tale" happy ending. In some respects, it may appear to have much in common with the love of Lancelot and Guinevere, which ultimately plays a pivotal role in the demise of the Arthurian realm. Yet Tristan and Isolde's love is described as altogether transcending this world. The symbolism that attaches to it has prompted some scholars to suggest that Gottfried was promoting nothing less than a new "religion" of love.

Viewed from a modern, psychological perspective, Tristan and Isolde may be seen as having succumbed to the archetype of romantic love, with its unrealistic anima and animus projections. Robert A. Johnson has suggested that the two characters are more in love with the idea of love itself rather than with each other as mortal, fallible human beings. A transformation from "being in love" to "loving," which might be described as a process of "domesticating" love, is an impossible expectation for this pair of lovers. Their union is of an otherworldly nature, tragic and condemned in this world; perhaps, however, their union is sanctified in the next.

Romantic love, and in particular the romantic love experienced by Tristan and Isolde, has been viewed as an expression of individuality that was unique to the High Middle Ages. In one sense, namely, the demonstration of feelings of *amor* between two individuals, this is correct; it was an alternative to the arranged marriages sanctioned and promoted by the Church and State. Archetypes are, however, autonomous, controlling the individual rather than vice versa (this may be what the magic potion consumed by Tristan and Isolde, which unleashes their love, was meant to convey). In this regard, one could argue that the lovers have exchanged the tyranny of the arranged marriage for the tyranny of the archetype.

Gottfried's achievement lies in the unique way in which he was able to combine form and content to produce a literary masterwork, which, rich in unorthodox ideas, represented, in the genre of romance, truly a *unicum* in its time. Aesthetics and ethics are combined to constitute a plot that must have run counter to all contemporary expectations. Tristan's artistry is evident in his command of languages, his skill at chess, his knowledge of excoriation practices, his musical talent, and, above all, his success as a lover/deceiver. The deception practiced by Tristan and Isolde, an element that each, in his or her own way, has inherited from immediate forebears, has its sinister side—the murderous action contemplated against Brangane being, perhaps, the most poignant example. Yet there is no unequivocal condemnation by the narrator/author of that element; on the contrary, one gains the impression that the behavior of Tristan and Isolde is sanctioned throughout as essential to the "coming," higher man. Gottfried even borrows from the language of the Eucharist at the conclusion of his prologue to describe the symbolism of their love, their devotion to one another, and their deaths: "Their life, their death are our bread. Thus lives their life, thus lives their death. Thus they live still and yet are dead, and their death is the bread of the living" (Hatto).

The story of Tristan and Isolde has clearly retained its power of attraction throughout the centuries since the Middle Ages. While later Spanish, Italian, Russian, and English versions (including that by Sir Thomas Malory in his *Morte d'Arthur* [1469]) are based on a 13th-century prose rendering in French, a 15th-century German prose version (chapbook) employs Eilhart as its source. In the 16th century, Hans Sachs dealt with the Tristan and Isolde tale in both his *Meisterlieder* and in a *Tragedia*. C.H. Myller's Gottfried edition of 1785, appearing on the threshold of Romanticism, ushered in a new wave of interest in the tale, but this, as Michael S. Batts has underscored, did not culminate in the appearance of any specifically "Romanticist" version of the work. The "immorality" of the plot evidently created reservations within the Romanticist community, and these evolved into scathing criticism of the story on the part of several scholars of the period and the one immediately following. Apart from the incomplete verse epic by Karl Lebrecht Immermann, which he worked on between 1832 and 1840, no attempted literary reworking of the Tristan and Isolde plot from the 19th century is particularly noteworthy. In the 20th century, Thomas Mann parodied the dilettante artist Detlev Spinell in his paradoxically titled novella *Tristan* (1903). The modern world, however, knows the story of the lovers for the most part through the beautiful, if haunting, strains of Wagner's *Tristan und Isolde* (premiered on 10 June 1865 in Munich under the direction of Hans von Bülow, the first husband of Wagner's later wife, Cosima). The opera is based on Gottfried's version as recorded in a translation produced by Hermann Kurtz (1844). The medieval masterpiece has also been available since 1960 to English-speaking readers in the superlative translation by A.T. Hatto.

Given its clear advocacy of an adulterous relationship—consider what that would have signified for members of any royal family at the height of the Middle Ages—Gottfried's *Tristan und Isold* represents one of the most enigmatic and, to the modern interpreter, challenging works of the time. The question begs itself as to how such a tale, which was meant to be read, or read aloud, would have been accepted by the literate in early 13th-century Germany, most of whom would have been church-affiliated or at least church-educated. How would they have understood or reacted to the remark by the narrator in Isolde's "ordeal" scene that Christ was "as pliant as a windblown sleeve"? This, in turn, raises the question as to the extent that Gottfried can be taken literally, or whether we are not more justified in viewing him as a master of irony. There are no conclusive answers to such questions, but that is assuredly part of the attraction of this tale, authored by one of the most original and controversial literary figures of early 13th-century Germany.

WINDER MCCONNELL

Biography

Flourished in Alsace, 1200. Died ca. 1210.

Selected Works

Poetry

Tristan und Isolt, 13th-century manuscript; in *Sammlung deutscher Gedichte aus dem 12., 13., und 14. Jahrhundert,* vol. 2, edited by Christoph Heinrich Müller, 1785; edited by Karl Marold, 1906; edited by Rüdger Krohn, 1995–96; as *Tristan,* translated by A.T. Hatto, 1982

Further Reading

Batts, Michael S., *Gottfried von Strassburg,* New York: Twayne, 1971
Bekker, Hugo, *Gottfried von Strassburg's Tristan: Journey through the Realm of Eros,* Columbia, South Carolina: Camden House, 1987
Chinca, Mark, *Gottfried von Strassburg, Tristan,* Cambridge and New York: Cambridge University Press, 1997
Jackson, W.T.H., *The Anatomy of Love: The Tristan of Gottfried von Strassburg,* New York: Columbia University Press, 1971
Jaeger, C. Stephen, *Medieval Humanism in Gottfried von Strassburg's Tristan und Isolde,* Heidelberg: Winter, 1977
Johnson, Robert A., *We, Understanding the Psychology of Romantic Love,* San Francisco: Harper and Row, 1983
McDonald, William C., *The Tristan Story in German Literature of the Late Middle Ages and Early Renaissance: Tradition and Innovation,* Lewiston, New York: Mellen Press, 1990
Ranke, Friedrich, *Die Allegorie der Minegrotte in Gottfrieds "Tristan,"* Berlin: Deutsche Verlagsgesellschaft für Politik und Geschichte, 1925
Schröder, Werner, *Über Gottfried von Strassburg,* Stuttgart: Hirzel, 1994
Thomas, Neil, *Tristan in the Underworld: A Study of Gottfried von Strassburg's Tristan Together with the Tristan of Thomas,* Lewiston, New York: Mellen Press, 1991
Weber, Gottfried, *Gottfrieds von Strassburg Tristan und die Krise des hochmittelalterlichen Weltbildes um 1200,* Stuttgart: Metzler, 1953
Weber, Gottfried, and Werner Hoffman, *Gottfried von Strassburg,* Stuttgart: Metzler, 1962; 5th revised edition, 1981
Wolf, Alois, *Gottfried von Strassburg und die Mythe von Tristan und Isolde,* Darmstadt: Wissenschaftliche Buchgesellschaft, 1989
Wolf, Alois, editor, *Gottfried von Strassburg,* Wege der Forschung 320, Darmstadt: Wissenschaftliche Buchgesellschaft, 1973

Jeremias Gotthelf 1797–1854

Jeremias Gotthelf (whose real name was Albert Bitzius) was a Swiss Protestant country parson by vocation, but by the time of his death in 1854 he had become a widely admired author in Germany and Switzerland. In his first novel, *Der Bauernspiegel* (1837; *The Mirror of Peasants*), he blended autobiography and a realistic setting with bildungsroman elements; in the dozen that followed during the remaining 17 years of his life, he looked beyond himself to depict the joys and tribulations of the peasantry around him. With *Uli der Knecht* (1841; *Ulric the Farm Servant*) his fame spread beyond Switzerland to Germany, France, and Scandinavia. Later masterpieces from *Geld und Geist* (1843; translated as *Wealth and Welfare* and *Soul and Money*) and *Anne Bäbi Jowäger* (1843–44) to *Uli der Pächter* (1849; Uli the Tenant-Farmer) and *Zeitgeist und Bernergeist* (1852; The Spirit of the Times and the Spirit of Bern) illustrate his readiness to use fiction to address the problems raised by the changes taking place around him. Modern criticism has shown how, as his art matured, his view of the world darkened. With mounting concern, his later works focus on the growing conflict between the materialism of the new industrial age and the traditional values of both the patrician city of Bern and the patriarchal peasant society of the nearby Emmental, the part of Switzerland he knew best.

The many shorter stories Gotthelf also found time to write, such as *Die Erbbase* (1849; The Rich Cousin), *Barthli der Korber* (1852; Barthli the Basket-Maker), and *Der Besenbinder von Rychiswyl* (1852; The Broom-Maker of Rychiswyl), show his appreciation of the close links between skilled labor and self-respect at a time when rural crafts were already threatened, as he realized, by mass production and the railways that were spreading into Switzerland in the 1850s. Gotthelf may sometimes seem a gloomy writer; as a man of God, however, he was not inclined to short-term pessimism, and he saw things on a broader time scale or, indeed, *sub specie aeternitatis.* His robust faith and linguistic verve have sometimes caused him to be likened to Luther, and he certainly benefited from a legacy of oral and written narrative in the Alemannic area that went back to the *Schwank:* his *Kalendergeschichten* or almanac stories are second only to J.P. Hebel's. Like his religious faith, this rootedness in popular narrative culture gives the narrative art of this Swiss 19th-century realist a dimension that even his major contemporaries—Honoré de Balzac, George Eliot, and Charles Dickens—lack, while his affirmation of life, his recognition of the divine in nature, and his confidence in the innate goodness of most human beings and in the redemptive power of God stand in marked contrast to Thomas Hardy's tragic skepticism and the stark naturalism of Zola's accounts of country life in the second half of the 19th century.

Many of Gotthelf's best-loved shorter prose works are high-spirited and light-hearted. This is particularly the case with his three tales of country courtship, *Wie Joggeli eine Frau sucht* (1840; Joggeli in Search of a Wife), *Wie Christen eine Frau gewinnt* (1845; How Christen Won a Wife), and *Michels Brautschau* (1850; Michael Looks for a Bride), in which the theme of the young farmer trying to find himself a suitable wife is traced with narrative skill and increasing psychological subtlety. Even the large-scale novels contain high-spirited episodes that show the genial verve of a great humorist. But Gotthelf was equally capable of evoking the mysterious innocence of childhood and fairy tale in works such as *Das Erdbeeri-Mareili* (1852; *Little Mareili, the Strawberry-Picker*), and of invoking the darker visions of the Old Testament prophet whose name he borrowed for his nom de plume in works such as *Die Wassernot im Emmental* (1838; The Inundation in the Emmental), a powerful amalgam of documentary and apocalyptic writing and perhaps his most elemental work. His pseudonym's second component, "Gotthelf," suggests the omnipresent concepts of love and redemption that underlie his finest works; *Wealth and Welfare* is a penetrating study of marital breakdown whose reassuring subtitle is *Die Versöhnung* (The Reconciliation).

Like Dickens, Jeremias Gotthelf did not hesitate to reveal individual foibles or lay bare the flaws in society: his urge to castigate follies and right injustices places him in a long line of satirists and links him both to Thomas Murner in the 16th century and Friedrich Dürrenmatt in the 20th. Unlike his contemporaries, however, Gotthelf was reluctant to carry his readers into the lives and homes of middle-class characters. His work is therefore far removed from what in France, England, and even Russia is regarded as the mainstream of 19th-century prose fiction. Like Balzac, however, Gotthelf did learn from his generation's literary hero, Sir Walter Scott—and from his own observations as a parish parson—that human beings are conditioned by factors outside themselves, such as their place and function in a community with a historical past. As a historical writer his range is wide: stories such as *Die Gründung Burgdorfs* (1841; The Foundation of Burgdorf) reach back in time and reveal his mythopoetic imagination as he re-creates legends in ways that prefigure modern concepts of historicizing interpretation. Others, such as *Kurt von Koppingen* (1844) and *Der letzte Thorberger* (1840–41; The Last of the Thorbergers) are set in the Middle Ages. The famous story *Elsi, die seltsame Magd* (1843; Elsi, the Strange Maid) takes place in the recent past of Gotthelf's own childhood.

Gotthelf's achievements in the historical mode have been unduly if understandably overshadowed by his well-deserved popularity as a chronicler of peasant life. In the latter, he has few counterparts. For him, the countryside did not possess nostalgic charm, and his work therefore lacks the sentimental note of the peasant novels Berthold Auerbach and George Sand were writing at the same time; nor was he preoccupied with the tensions between peasantry and landowners that frame much contemporaneous British and Russian writing. For Gotthelf, the tenant and freehold peasant farmers of the Emmental constitute a complex society with inherent tensions and contrasts of light and shade; he explores this society most notably in *Anne Bäbi Jowäger,* his large-scale study of the disastrous workings of ignorance and superstition where education is defective and medical ignorance rife. Sometimes the rural and the historical, the two essential dimensions of his oeuvre, merge, as in his towering masterpiece, *Die schwarze Spinne* (1842; *The Black Spider*), which in its brief compass conjures up the specters of the past and confronts the nature of evil by placing both in a delightful country setting, which enhances the tensions between present and past. Gotthelf's ability to bring together contrasting elements is also immediately evident in his language and style. Here, too, his range is enormous. Homeric descriptions, resonant with biblical echoes, endow his descriptions of the natural world with a timeless quality; yet the moment his peasants start to banter, argue, or woo, his command of the Emmental dialect of German-speaking Switzerland arrests the reader's ear. In Germany, his works require linguistic adaptation for their German readers; in Switzerland, however, their popularity still mainly depends upon their vernacular quality.

PETER SKRINE

Biography

Born in Murten, Switzerland, 4 October 1797. Theology student, Bern Academy, 1814–20; studied at Göttingen University for one year; ordained, 1820; curate, Utzenstorf, 1820, and 1822–24, Herzogenbuchsee, 1824–29, and transferred to Bern, 1829–31; pastor, Lützelflüh, Emmental, 1832–54; local education official, 1835–45. Died in Lützelflüh, 22 October 1854.

Selected Works

Collections

Gesammelte Schriften, 24 vols., 1856–58
Gesamtausgabe, edited by Rudolph Hunziker, Hans Bloesch, et al., 24 vols., 1911–32; supplementary vols., 1922–
Werke, edited by Walter Muschg, 20 vols., 1948–53

Fiction

Der Bauernspiegel; oder, Lebensgeschichte des Jeremias Gotthelf, 1837; as *The Mirror of Peasants,* translated by Mary Augusta Ward, in *Macmillans Magazine,* 1883
Wie fünf Mädchen im Branntwein jämmerlich umkamen, 1838
Die Wassernot im Emmental, 1838
Leiden und Freuden eines Schulmeisters, 1839; as *The Joys and Griefs of a National Schoolmaster,* translated by Mary Augusta Ward, in *Macmillans Magazine,* 1883; as *The Joys and Sorrows of a Schoolmaster,* 1864
Dursli, der Brannteweinsäufer; oder, Der Heilige Weihnachtsabend, 1839
Wie Uli der Knecht glücklich wird, 1841
Ein Sylvester-Traum, 1842
Die schwarze Spinne, 1842; as *The Black Spider,* translated by Mary Hottinger, in *Nineteenth Century German Tales,* 1958; also translated by H.M. Waidson, 1958
Bilder und Sagen aus der Schweiz (stories), 6 vols., 1842–46
Wie Anne Bäbi Jowäger haushaltet, 1843–44
Geld und Geist; oder, Die Versöhnung, 1843; as *Wealth and Welfare,* 1866; as *Soul and Money,* translated by Julia Guarterick Vere, 1872
Wie Christen eine Frau gewinnt, 1845
Uli der Knecht, 1846; as *Ulric the Farm Servant,* translated by Julia Firth, 1866
Der Geldstag; oder, Die Wirtschaft nach der neuen Mode, 1846
Der Knabe des Tell, 1846
Jakobs, des Handwerksgesellen, Wanderungen durch die Schweiz, 2 vols., 1846–48
Käthi die Grossmutter, 1847; as *The Story of an Alpine Valley; or, Katie the Grandmother,* translated by L.G. Smith, 1896
Hans Joggeli der Erbvetter, 1848
Uli der Pächter, 1849
Die Erbbase, 1849
Die Käserei in der Vehfreude, 1850
Erzählungen und Bilder aus dem Volksleben der Schweiz, 1850–55
Hans Jakob und Heiri; oder, Die beiden Seidenweber, 1851
Zeitgeist und Bernergeist, 1852
Erlebnisse eines Schuldenbauers, 1854
Das Erdbeeri-Mareili, 1858
Elsi, die seltsame Magd, 1858

Other

Bericht über die Gemeinde Utzenstorf, 1824
Die Armennot, 1840
Jeremias Gotthelf und Karl Rudolf Hagenbach; ihr Briefwechsel aus den Jahren 1841 bis 1853, edited by Ferdinand Vetter, 1910
Familienbriefe Jeremias Gotthelfs, edited by Hedwig Wäber, 1929

Further Reading

Fehr, Karl, *Jeremias Gotthelf,* Zurich: Büchergilde Gutenberg, 1954
——, *Jeremias Gotthelf (Albert Bitzius),* Stuttgart: Metzler, 1967; 2nd edition, 1985
Günther, Werner, *Jeremias Gotthelf: Wesen und Werk,* Berlin: Schmidt, 1954
Holl, Hanns Peter, *Gotthelf im Zeitgeflecht,* Tübingen: Niemeyer, 1985
——, *Jeremias Gotthelf: Leben, Werk, Zeit,* Zurich: Artemis, 1988
Muschg, Walter, *Gotthelf: Die Geheimnisse des Erzählers,* Munich: Beck, 1931; revised edition, 1967
Waidson, H.M., *Jeremias Gotthelf: An Introduction to the Swiss Novelist,* Oxford: Blackwell, 1953

Johann Christoph Gottsched 1700–1766

Gotthold Ephraim Lessing's 17th *Letter on Literature* (1759) effectively determined Johann Christoph Gottsched's reputation for the following two centuries. Quoting a contemporary critic's assertion that "No one will deny that the German stage owes its initial improvement in large measure to Professor Gottsched," Lessing added, "I am this No One. I deny it absolutely." His attack, part of a younger generation's revolt against the established poetics, is still familiar to students of German literature. Forgotten are Gottsched's genuine achievements. Admittedly, the older man's vanity and zeal made him an easy target, but his accomplishments were considerable, and he deserves better.

His *Erste Gründe der gesammten Weltweisheit* (1733–34; First Principles of a Complete Philosophy), based on Christian Wolff's writings, made him the most widely read German philosopher of his time, and his *Versuch einer critischen Dichtkunst vor die Deutschen* (1730; Attempt at a Critical Poetics for Germans) provided Germany's most influential articulation of Early Enlightenment aesthetics. More than any other 18th-century works, his various books on rhetoric and grammar helped to codify the German language and to make it a respectable medium of expression, while his translations and his six-volume anthology of plays provided Germans with important models for Enlightened theater. Of his own dramas, *Sterbender Cato* (1732; Dying Cato), a tragedy in alexandrines that celebrated republican virtues, was particularly successful. His poetry, too, was respected, if not admired, and one of his odes became the basis for J.S. Bach's cantata, "Lass, Höchster, lass der Hoffnung Strahl." But his influence extended even further. The two moral weeklies and three critical journals that he edited, the various learned societies that he organized, and the popular lectures that he delivered for over 40 years as a professor at the University of Leipzig all played a central role in German intellectual life. His many other publications include editions of the first popular German encyclopedia and a translation of Bayle's *Dictionaire.* He was also elected rector of his university five times. At the same time, he was willing to reach beyond the academic world and even helped to enact his theatrical reforms by joining forces with Caroline Neuber's acting company, a daring step at the time. Contrary to his later reputation as a retrograde curmudgeon, Gottsched championed women's rights and education and enthusiastically supported the literary efforts of his first wife, Luise Adelgunde, known to literary history as *die Gottschedin* (the Gottschedess).

Above all, Gottsched was a German patriot who was intent on creating public spaces for the emerging middle class. Hoping to provide his fellow Germans with models of proper speech and reasonable behavior, he tried to fashion a theater that avoided the aristocratic courts' French and Italian traditions, but that also shunned the crude performance practices of wandering troupes and puppeteers. Aristotelian poetics and French models of taste and reason underlay these reforms, but their ultimate goal was to promote the German language and bourgeois values. By the former, Gottsched meant clear, unaffected expression in conformity with educated speech; by the latter, he meant practicality, forthrightness, and common sense. With his support, his wife and followers developed the tradition of Saxon Comedy. Satirical works associated with this tradition embodied his ideals: the primacy of the text, the traditional three unities, and the conventional distinctions between laughter and tears. In these plays, people of common sense pillory vices such as religious intolerance, hypocrisy, misogyny, francophilia, irrational enthusiasms, and the employment of Latinate constructions.

He set forth most of his aesthetic theories in his *Versuch einer critischen Dichtkunst vor die Deutschen,* which was published in four editions from 1730 to 1751. Although an amalgamation of established French aesthetics, it broke new ground in Germany by defining the poetic temperament at least partly in terms of imagination, feeling, and national character. Because succeeding generations expanded these concepts in ways that Gottsched found objectionable, we tend to underestimate the newness of his approach, but later developments in fact depended on his work. At the same time, however, the *Versuch einer critischen Dichtkunst vor die Deutschen* was mostly prescriptive, rigidly defining genres and assigning them appropriate themes and forms. Above all, it characterized literature as the imitation of nature, and as bounded by reason and confined largely to the service of moral improvement. The primacy of art's mimetic function left little room for representations of the imaginary. Certain genres, such as the fable or anacreontic poetry, could portray "possible worlds," but only if they remained "probable," with a transparent causality available in everyday life. To Gottsched, poetic imagination was the capacity to invent images that evoke conceivably real experiences. Stage performances were particularly limited in terms of the imaginary, and Professor Gottsched, as he was always known, reserved particular disdain for opera, the most improbable form of all.

Contrary to the claims of most literary histories, Gottsched commanded broad respect throughout his life, and new editions of his works continued to appear even after his death. But in the area of poetics, developments started to pass him by in the 1740s, and the revolt against his influence became inevitable. His negative assessment of Milton, Shakespeare, and the notion of genius led to a feud with Bodmer and Breitinger that divided the German literary world briefly into the "Leipzig" and "Zurich" camps. But even Gottsched's followers eventually chafed under his rigid prescriptions. When some of them began to mix sentiment with comedy, he saw himself betrayed by an ungrateful younger generation. Lessing's attack 15 years later, part of a more radical mutiny joined by Friedrich Nicolai, was the final blow that colored most subsequent appraisals. Not until the 1960s did scholars begin to reassess Gottsched's contributions, as well as to make his works available in a critical edition.

BRUCE DUNCAN

See also Aufklärung

Biography

Born 2 February 1700 in Juditten, near Königsberg. Studied theology, philosophy, and poetics at the University of Königsberg, 1714–23; exceptionally tall and thus vulnerable to conscription into the king's regiment of "Long Fellows," fled Prussia for Leipzig, 1723; began teaching at the University of Leipzig, 1725; appointed Professor of Poetics, 1730; Professor of Logic and Metaphysics, 1734; married Luise Adelgunde Victoria Kulmus (1713–62) in 1735; married Ernestine Susanne Katharina Neunes, 1765. Died in Leipzig, 12 December 1766.

Selected Works

Collections

Gesammelte Schriften, 6 vols., 1903–6
Ausgewählte Werke, 12 vols., edited by Joachim Birke and P.M. Mitchell, 1968–95

Periodicals

Die vernünftigen Tadlerinnen, 1725–26
Der Biedermann, 1727–29
Beyträge zur critischen Historie der deutschen Sprache, Poesie und Beredsamkeit, 1732–44
Neuer Büchersaal der schönen Wissenschaften und freyen Künsten, 1745–50
Das Neueste aus der anmuthigen Gelehrsamkeit, 1751–62

Plays

Sterbender Cato, 1732
Die deutsche Schaubühne nach den Regeln und Exempeln der alten Griechen und Römer eingerichtet, 6 vols., 1741–45
Atalanta; oder, Die bezwungene Sprödigkeit, 1742
Agis, König zu Sparta, 1753

Poetry

Gedichte, edited by Johann Joachim Schwabe, 1736; 2nd enlarged edition, 2 vols., 1751

Treatises

Versuch einer critischen Dichtkunst vor die Deutschen, 1730; 4th revised edition, 1751
Erste Gründe der gesammten Weltweisheit, 2 vols., 1733–34; 7th enlarged and revised edition, 1762
Grundlegung einer Deutschen Sprachkunst, nach den Mustern der besten Schriftsteller des vorigen und jetzigen Jahrhunderts, 1748; 3rd revised and enlarged edition, 1752
Beobachtungen über den Gebrauch und Misbrauch vieler deutscher Wörter und Redensarten, 1758

Further Reading

Bormann, Dennis R., "Gottsched's Enlightened Rhetoric: The Influence of Christian Wolff's Philosophy on Johann Gottsched's Ausführliche Redekunst," Ph.D. dissertation, University of Iowa, 1968
Connor, David, "Johann Christoph Gottsched and the Growth of German Literature," Ph.D. dissertation, Yale University, 1969
Freier, Hans, *Kritische Poetik: Legitimation und Kritik der Poesie in Gottscheds Dichtkunst,* Stuttgart: Metzler, 1973
Gühne, Ekkehard, *Gottscheds Literaturkritik in den "Vernünftigen Tadlerinnen" (1725–26),* Stuttgart: Heinz, 1978
Hiebel, Hans H., *Gottsched (1700–1766),* Munich: Beck, 1979
Horch, Hans Otto, *Das Wunderbare und die Poetik der Frühaufklärung: Gottsched und die Schweizer,* Darmstadt: Wissenschaftliche Buchgesellschaft, 1988
Johansson, Peter Carl, "Two Aspects of Gottsched's Deutsche Sprachkunst: The Phonetic Norm and the Idea of the 'Best Writers,'" Ph.D. dissertation, University of California, Santa Barbara, 1977
Kawatsu, Susanne, "Love and Reform: Johannn Christoph Gottsched and *Die Deutsche Schaubuehne,*" Ph.D. dissertation, University of Chicago, 1996

Meier, Georg Friedrich, *Beurteilung der Gottschedischen Dichtkunst,* Halle: Hemmerde, 1747–48; reprint, Hildesheim and New York: Olms, 1975

Mitchell, P.M., *Gottsched and the Middle Ages,* Göppingen: Kümmerle, 1988

———, "Johann Christoph Gottsched (1700–1766)," in *German Writers from the Enlightenment to Sturm und Drang, 1720–1764,* Dictionary of Literary Biography, vol. 97, edited by James Hardin and Christoph E. Schweitzer, Detroit, Michigan: Gale Research, 1990

———, *Johann Christoph Gottsched (1700–1766): Harbinger of German Classicism,* Columbia, South Carolina: Camden House, 1995

Rieck, Werner, *Johann Christoph Gottsched: Eine kritische Würdigung seines Werkes,* Berlin: Akademie, 1972

Romboy, Dieter, "Gottsched: Myth and Fact," Ph.D. dissertation, University of Utah, 1974

Schatzberg, Walter, "Gottsched as a Popularizer of Science," *Modern Language Notes* 83 (1968)

Unger, Thorsten, *Handeln im Drama: Theorie und Praxis bei J. Chr. Gottsched und J.M.R. Lenz,* Göttingen: Vandenhoeck and Ruprecht, 1993

Wetterer, Angelika, *Publikumsbezug und Wahrheitsanspruch: Der Widerspruch zwischen rhetorischem Ansatz und philosophischem Anspruch bei Gottsched und den Schweizern,* Tübingen: Niemeyer, 1981

Versuch einer critischen Dichtkunst vor die Deutschen 1730

Treatise by Johann Christoph Gottsched

Versuch einer critischen Dichtkunst vor die Deutschen (Attempt at a Critical Poetics for Germans) is a treatise on literature by Johann Christoph Gottsched, which was first published in 1730. The second edition, with a complete reprint of Horace's *Ars Poetica,* was printed in 1737; this was followed by a third edition in 1742 and a fourth enlarged edition in 1751, which was reprinted in 1962 and 1977. Gottsched's work has to be evaluated in relation to his attempts to further the German language and literature and to return German theater to the rules established by the ancients (*Grundsätze der Alten*). His work was intended as a corrective measure that responded to the pompous style of Baroque theater and poetics. The two central ideas on which Gottsched based his own poetics were the Aristotelian concept of *mimesis* (*Naturnachahmung* [verisimilitude]) and *aut prodesse volunt aut delectare poetae* (the poet's goal is either the useful or the pleasing) from Horace's *Ars Poetica*. The *Versuch einer critischen Dichtkunst vor die Deutschen* is divided into two parts: the first 12 chapters provide the theoretical foundation and are followed by 12 main chapters (*Hauptstücke*) on literary genres that are pedantically separated from one another.

For Gottsched, as he points out in his introduction, the source for all poetic work lies in the human emotions (*Gemüthsneigungen des Menschen*). Emotions, however, have to be controlled by form and reason. Gottsched stresses that a poet cannot rely solely on the imagination—this choice would result in a lower lyrical form—but also needs intellect (*Witz*), docility (*Gelehrsamkeit*), and taste (*Geschmack*). Even taste is not a subjective element, for it is only good if it corresponds to the rules that are established by nature and can be perceived by reason. A work of art, therefore, becomes an imitation (Nachahmung) of nature. Mimesis in this context does not necessarily mean realism; it is only supposed to restrict the miraculous and extraordinary elements (*das Wunderbare*) within the framework of probability (*Wahrscheinlichkeit*), thus leaving room for some fictitious elements as an expression of hypothetical but probable alternative worlds (Leibnitz, Wolff). Each literary work also needs a fable to exemplify a moral goal (*nützliche moralische Wahrheit*). Based on this concept, Gottsched demands a strict adherence to the three unities of classical drama and despises the involvement of magical figures (i.e., Harlequin) and gods in drama. His poetical approach culminates in the following recipe for the production of a tragedy:

> The poet selects a moral doctrine, which he intends to imprint on his audience in a sensual manner. In order to accomplish this goal, he invents a general plot that sheds light on the truth of the selected doctrine. The next step is to find famous historical characters who had similar experiences. The poet should use the names of these characters to increase the importance of his plot. He then invents all the subplots or episodes in a way that gives probability to the main plot. The poet then divides the final product into five pieces of about equal length.

In the second part of *Versuch einer critischen Dichtkunst vor die Deutschen,* Gottsched discusses individual literary genres. In spite of assigning a somewhat higher artistic value to prose works, he still considers the epic to be the highest form of poetic expression. His concepts of drama are mainly based on French examples, which he considers to be closest to the classical ideas. Only in the fourth edition does Gottsched discuss the novel, whose artistic value he considers to be very low. For Gottsched, the novel is only a "bastard cousin" of the epic, which neither adheres to (his) poetic rules nor realizes the qualities of good prose.

The *Versuch einer critischen Dichtkunst vor die Deutschen* found its earliest critics in Johann Jakob Bodmer (*Critische Abhandlung von dem Wunderbaren in der Poesie* [1740; Critical Treatise on the Miraculous in Poetry]) and Johann Jakob Breitinger (*Critische Dichtkunst* [1740; Critical Poetics]), who argued strongly against the limitations of poetry proposed by Gottsched and against his exclusion of "das Wunderbare." Lessing's harsh critique in *Hamburgische Dramaturgie* (Sammelausgabe 1768–69) was probably the decisive factor that curbed Gottsched's influence. Lessing not only disagreed with Gottsched about the quality of French drama—according to him, Racine, Corneille and Voltaire produced only "das kahlste, wäßrigste, untragischste Zeug" (watered-down, undramatic stuff)—but also produced a series of misinterpretations of Aristotle's poetics that had led to Gottsched's stressing of form (i.e., the unities).

In spite of Bodmer's, Breitinger's, and Lessing's criticisms, however, one still has to see Gottsched's work in a more positive light today. His writings triggered change in the perception of theater and literature in Germany and led to reforms that represent an important step toward Weimar Classicism.

BERNHARD R. MARTIN

Editions

First edition: *Versuch einer critischen Dichtkunst vor die Deutschen,* Leipzig: Breitkopf, 1730

Further Reading:
Blanck, Karl, *Der französische Einfluss im zweiten Teil von Gottscheds critischer Dichtkunst,* Göttingen: Kaestner, 1910
Bodmer, Johann Jakob, *Critische Betrachtungen und freye Untersuchungen zum Aufnehmen und zur Verbesserung der deutschen Schaubühne: Mit einer Zuschrift an die Frau Neuberin,* Bern: 1743
Braitmaier, Friedrich, *Die poetische Theorie Gottsched's und der Schweizer,* Tübingen: Laupp, 1879
Bruck, Jan, "Der aristotelische Mimesisbegriff und die Nachahmungstheorie Gottscheds und der Schweizer," Ph.D. diss., Friedrich Alexander Universität, 1972
Brüggemann, Fritz, *Das Weltbild der Deutschen Aufklärung: Philosophische Grundlagen und literarische Auswirkung: Leibniz, Wolff, Gottsched, Brockes, Haller,* Leipzig: Reclam, 1935; reprint, Darmstadt: Wissenschaftliche Buchgesellschaft, 1966
——, *Gottscheds Lebens- und Kunstreform in den zwanziger und dreißiger Jahren: Gottsched, Breitinger, die Gottschedin, die Neuberin,* Darmstadt: Wissenschaftliche Buchgesellschaft, 1966
Brüggemann, Fritz, editor, *Reihe Aufklärung,* Leipzig: Reclam, 1938
Danzel, Theodor Wilhelm, *Gottsched und seine Zeit: Auszüge aus seinem Briefwechsel,* Leipzig: Dyk, 1848; reprint, New York: Olms, 1970
——, *Gesammelte Aufsätze,* Leipzig: Dyk, 1855; reprint, Frankfurt: Klotz, 1998
Gottsched, Johann Christoph, *Sterbender Cato: Ein Trauerspiel, nebst des Herrn Erzbischops von Cambray, Fenelons Gedanken von Trauerspielen, und einem critischen Anhange,* Leipzig: Teubner, 1757
Heitmüller, Franz Ferdinard, *Hamburgische Dramatiker zur Zeit Gottscheds und ihre Beziehungen zu ihm: Ein Beitrag zur Geschichte des Theaters und Dramas im 18. Jahrhundert,* Wandsbeck: Puvogel, 1890
Hiebel, Hans, *Individualität und Totalität: Zur Geschichte und Kritik des bürgerlichen Poesiebegriffs von Gottsched bis Hegel anhand der Theorien über Epos und Roman,* Bonn: Bouvier, 1974
Hollmer, Heide, *Anmut und Nutzen: Die Originaltrauerspiele in Gottscheds "Deutscher Schaubühne,"* Tübingen: Niemeyer, 1994
Pizer, John David, *The Historical Perspective in German Genre Theory: Its Development from Gottsched to Hegel,* Stuttgart: Akademischer, 1985
Steinmetz, Horst, *Das deutsche Drama von Gottsched bis Lessing: Ein historischer Überblick,* Stuttgart: Metzler, 1987

Luise Adelgunde Victorie Gottsched 1713–1762

Luise Adelgunde Victorie Gottsched, praised by Empress Maria Theresa as the most learned woman in Germany, was undoubtedly one of the most active literary personalities in the German-speaking world during the first half of the 18th century. As the wife and lifelong assistant of Johann Christoph Gottsched (1700–1766), who was Germany's leading proponent of the early Enlightenment and an influential reformer of German literature and language, she played a key role in the implementation and defense of her husband's rationalistic literary and linguistic theories. Through the translation of important works by English and French Rationalists, and through the publication of her plays and correspondence, L.A.V. Gottsched contributed substantially not only to the education of the German reading public, but also to the development of two literary genres: the comedy and the letter.

From the very beginning of her marriage to Johann Christoph Gottsched in 1735 until her death, L.A.V. Gottsched (known as "die Gottschedin") acted primarily as her husband's right hand and industrious helper. She took an active role in virtually all his literary endeavors. Not only did she listen to Johann Christoph's lectures (from behind the door), learn Latin, and study musical composition, but she also cataloged his library, conducted research for his anthology *Nöthiger Vorrath* (1746–47; Basic Supply) and his prodigious project *Die deutsche Sprachkunst* (1748; German Linguistics), wrote correspondence in his name, and corrected the galley proofs of virtually all his publications. L.A.V. Gottsched translated most of the articles in Addison and Steele's *The Spectator* (1739–43), 330 of the 635 articles in her husband's edition of Pierre Bayle's *Dictionnaire historique et critique* (1741–44; Historical Critical Dictionary), Alexander Pope's *Rape of the Lock* (1744), parts of Gottfried Wilhelm Leibniz's *Theodizee* (1744; Theodicy), and all of Addison's moral weekly *The Guardian* (1745). In addition, she translated ten plays, seven of them for *Die Deutsche Schaubühne* (1741–45; The German Stage), her husband's six-volume collection of exemplary works, which were to bring literate drama to the German stage as well as to serve as model guides to domestic writers.

Encouraged by her husband, she wrote *Die Pietisterey im Fischbein-Rocke* (1736; *Pietism in Petticoats*), an adaptation of Guillaume-Hyacinthe Bougeant's play *La femme docteur* (1731; The Lady Scholar), making her the first woman playwright in Germany since the Middle Ages. Published anonymously to protect the author from repercussions, the play—which was seen as a vicious attack against the movement of German Pietism—caused a serious religious uproar in Danzig, was confiscated in Königsberg and Berlin, and led to a sharpening of the Prussian censorship laws. With this play, however, and her original contributions to *Die Deutsche Schaubühne,* Gottsched founded the tradition of the Saxon comedy, a dramatic genre in which coarse wit and satire must serve to bring reason to triumph over irrationality and human folly. In *Die ungleiche Heirat* (1743; *The Mésalliance*), she satirized both the vanity of the upper middle classes and the foolishness of the lower nobility. Greed and rivalry are attacked in *Das Testament* (1745; *The Last Will*), and a toplofty university student becomes the target of ridicule in *Der Witzling* (1745; *The Witling*). Gottsched's plays (including her only tragedy, *Panthea* [1745]) were soon criticized for their overbearing moral didacticism, their total absence of character development, and their often offensive vulgarity. In his *Hamburgische Dramaturgie* (1767–68; *Hamburg Dramaturgy*), G.E. Lessing objected most strongly to her comedy *Die Hausfranzösinn* (1744; *The French Housekeeper*), which he found "not only low, and flat, and cold, but on top of that filthy, disgusting, and insulting in the highest degree." Still, her plays would become instrumental to the dramatic and dramaturgical writings of later playwrights, including J.C. Krüger, C. Mylius, C.F. Gellert, J.E. Schlegel, and G.E. Lessing.

Gottsched's private correspondence with her husband and with Dorothea Henriette von Runckel (1724–1800), her most intimate friend and confidante in the last decade of her life, are of special interest to literary and cultural historians. Stylistically, her letters (published by Runckel the year after Gottsched's death) are unprecedented in the New High German language for their clarity, emotional immediacy, and elegance. Thematically, they reveal the triumphs and hardships of a highly sensitive woman of great intelligence, wit, and grace. They also betray her ambiguous attitude toward her demanding and egocentric husband and toward her own role as a hard-working but dependent woman who destroyed her health in a life of almost ceaseless writing.

Despite these inner struggles and the fact that, already during her lifetime, Gottsched was considered the most formidable woman on the German literary scene, she remained aloof from other women writers, such as Christiana Mariane von Ziegler (1695–1760) and Sidonia Hedwig Zäunemann (1714–40). According to her own account, she disapproved of learned women, though her statement may well have been intended to advocate merely modest, rather than ostentatious, behavior. She decided not to see Voltaire, in whom she saw a pompous blasphemer, and she refused to pay her respects to King Frederick the Great during his visit to Leipzig in 1757 because she was angered by the grief Prussia was causing in the Seven Years' War.

Having been frail and in poor health for much of her adult life, L.A.V. Gottsched spent the last two years of her life in constant sickness and suffering, to the extent that she could barely eat and drink and was unable to read or write. She died on 26 June 1762.

CHRISTOPH LOREY

Biography

Born Luise Adelgunde Victorie Kulmus in Danzig, 11 April 1713. Educated privately; began to write poetry at the age of 12; learned English from her half-brother and French from her mother; translated Mme. de Lafayette's *La princesse de Clèves* (1678) at age 15; married Johann Christoph Gottsched, 1735. Died 26 June 1762.

Selected Works

For a comprehensive list of L.A.V. Gottsched's works, most of which appeared anonymously, under a cryptonym, or under her husband's name, see Sanders.

Collections

Der beste Fürst. Der Frau Luise Adelgunde Victoria Gottschedinn, geb. Kulmus, Sämmtliche Kleinere Gedichte, 1763

Briefe der Frau Luise Adelgunde Victorie Gottsched gebohrne Kulmus, 3 vols., 1771–72

Die Lustspiele der Gottschedin, 2 vols., edited by Reinhard Buchwald and Albert Köster, 1908–9

Pietism in Petticoats and Other Comedies, translated by Thomas Kerth and John R. Russell, 1994

Plays

Die Pietisterey im Fischbein-Rocke; oder, Die doctormässige Frau, 1736; as *Pietism in Petticoats,* in *Pietism in Petticoats and Other Comedies,* translated by Thomas Kerth and John R. Russell, 1994

Triumph der Weltweisheit, 1739

Die ungleiche Heirat, 1743; as *The Mésalliance,* in *Pietism in Petticoats and Other Comedies,* translated by Thomas Kerth and John R. Russell, 1994

Die Hausfranzösinn; oder, Die Mamsell, 1744; as *The French Housekeeper,* in *Pietism in Petticoats and Other Comedies,* translated by Thomas Kerth and John R. Russell, 1994

Panthea, 1745

Das Testament, 1745; as *The Last Will,* in *Pietism in Petticoats and Other Comedies,* translated by Thomas Kerth and John R. Russell, 1994

Herr [also *Der*] *Witzling,* 1745; as *The Witling,* in *Pietism in Petticoats and Other Comedies,* translated by Thomas Kerth and John R. Russell, 1994

Translations

Anonymous, *Chevy-Jagd,* 1739 (translation of *The Hunting of the Cheviot*)

Joseph Addison and Richard Steele, *Der Zuschauer,* 9 vol., 1739–43 (translation of articles from *The Specator*)

Mlle. Barbier, *Cornelia, die Mutter der Gracchen,* 1741 (translation of *Cornélie, mère des Gracques*)

Joseph Addison, *Das Gespenst mit der Trommel; oder, Der wahrsagende Ehemann,* 1741 (translation of Destouches's French version of Addison's *The Drummer*)

Néricault Destouches, *Der poetische Dorfjunker,* 1742 (translation of *La fausse Agnés; ou, Le poète campagnard*)

Molière, *Der Menschenfeind,* 1742 (translation of *Le Misanthrope*)

Néricault Destouches, *Der Verschwender; oder, Die ehrliche Betrügerinn,* 1742 (translation of *Le dissipateur*)

Charles Dufresny, *Die Widerwillige,* 1742 (translation of *L'esprit de contradiction*)

Voltaire, *Alzire; oder, Die Amerikaner,* 1743 (translation of *Alzire; ou, Les Américains*)

Alexander Pope, *Herrn Alexander Popens Lockenraub,* 1744 (translation of *The Rape of the Lock*)

Neue Sammlung auserlesener Stücke, aus Popens, Eachards, Newtons, und andrer Schriften, 1749 (translation anthology)

Mme de Grafigny, *Cenie; oder, Die Großmuth im Unglücke,* 1753 (translation of *Cénie*)

Satirical Writing

"Das ein rechtschaffener Freund ein Philosoph sein müsse," 1739

"Das Lob der Spielsucht," 1739

"Auf den Namenstag eines guten Freundes, nach Art gewisser grossen Geister zusammengeschrieben," 1739

Horatii, als eines wohlerfahrnen Schiffers treumeynender Zuruff an alle Wolffianer von X.Y.Z., 1740

Further Reading

Becker-Cantarino, Barbara, *Der lange Weg zur Mündigkeit: Frauen und Literatur in Deutschland (1500–1800),* Stuttgart: Metzler, 1987

Duncan, Bruce, "Luise Adelgunde Gottsched (1713–62)," in *Bitter Healing: German Women Writers from 1700 to 1830: An Anthology,* edited by Jeannine Blackwell and Susanne Zantop, Lincoln: University of Nebraska Press, 1990

Hecht, Wolfgang, "Materialien zum Verständnis der Texte," in *Luise Adelgunde Viktorie Gottsched Der Witzling: Ein deutsches Nachspiel in einem Aufzuge,* edited by Wolfgang Hecht, Berlin: de Gruyter, 1962

Heuser, Magdalene, "Das Musenchor mit neuer Ehre zieren: Schriftstellerinnen zur Zeit der Frühaufklärung," in *Deutsche Literatur von Frauen,* edited by Gisela Brinker-Gabler, vol. 1: *Vom Mittelalter bis zum Ende des 18. Jahrhunderts,* Munich: Beck, 1988

Kerth, Thomas, and John R. Russell, "Introduction," in *Pietism in Petticoats and Other Comedies,* by Luise Adelgunde Victorie Gottsched, translated by Thomas Kerth and John R. Russell, Columbia, South Carolina: Camden House, 1994

Kord, Susanne, "Eternal Love or Sentimental Discourse? Gender Dissonance and Women's Passionate 'Friendships'," in *Outing Goethe and His Age,* edited by Alice A. Kuzniar, Stanford, California: Stanford University Press, 1996

———, "Luise Gottsched (1713–1762)," in *Women Writers in German-Speaking Countries: A Bio-Bibliograhical Critical Sourcebook,* edited by Elke P. Frederiksen and Elizabeth G. Ametsbichler, Westport, Connecticut: Greenwood Press, 1998

Martens, Wolfgang, "Nachwort," in *Die Pietisterey im Fischbein-Rocke: Komödie,* by Luise Adelgunde Victorie Gottsched, edited by Wolfgang Martens, Stuttgart: Reclam, 1968

Richel, Veronica C., *Luise Gottsched: A Reconsideration,* Bern: Lang, 1973

Sanders, Ruth H., "'Ein kleiner Umweg': Das literarische Schaffen der Luise Gottsched," in *Die Frau von der Reformation zur Romantik: Die Situation der Frau vor dem Hintergrund der Literatur- und Sozialgeschichte,* edited by Barbara Becker-Cantarino, Bonn: Bouvier, 1980

Waters, Michael, "Frau Gottsched's 'Die Pietisterey im Fischbein-Rocke': Original, Adaptation or Translation?" *Forum for Modern Language Studies* 11 (1975)

Christian Dietrich Grabbe 1801–1836

In German cultural history, Christian Dietrich Grabbe's work coincides with the Biedermeier period, the transitional phase between the end of classicism and Romanticism on the one hand and the rise of realism on the other. In the context of German political history, it falls into the "Restauration" or "Vormärz" era, which began with the defeat of Napoléon in 1815 and closed with the revolutions of March 1848. Sigmund Freud described Grabbe as "an original and rather peculiar poet," Heinrich Heine called him "a drunken Shakespeare," and Karl Immermann saw him as having both "a wild, ruined nature" and "an outstanding talent." Although his image as a flawed genius lingers, he is now also hailed as one of Germany's major experimental dramatists, and the irregularities of his plays are regarded as an integral part of their originality.

The only child of the local jailer, Grabbe felt oppressed and alienated in his provincial hometown of Detmold where, as he wrote to Ludwig Tieck, "an educated person is looked upon as an inferior kind of fattened ox." Physically frail and psychologically unstable, he seemed the archetype of the dissolute bohemian artist, oscillating between sullen shyness and aggressive self-assertion, imperiously demanding recognition but refusing to please or to conform, performing erratically in his duties as army legal officer, staying in a destructive marriage, and precipitating his fatal decline by excessive drinking. While it is uncertain to what extent his "bizarreness" was natural and to what extent it was cultivated to shock his middle-class contemporaries, the "Grabbe myth" soon became confused with, and has often overshadowed, his work.

After his death, Grabbe was condemned to oblivion by classically oriented criticism, until both the nationalists and naturalists of the late 19th century rediscovered him as a kindred soul. In the 20th century, the Expressionists celebrated him as a fellow outcast of bourgeois society, the Dadaists and surrealists welcomed him as another rebel against rationality, the Nazis exalted him as a prophet of "blood and soil," Brecht placed him alongside Georg Büchner in the "non-Aristotelian" tradition leading from the Elizabethans to his own Marxist "Epic Theater," and more recent commentators have stressed his affinities with postmodernism. On the German stage, he was first adopted in the 1870s, revived in the early 1920s and late 1930s, and finally included in the established repertory—primarily with *Scherz, Satire, Ironie und tiefere Bedeutung* (1827; *Jest, Satire, Irony, and Deeper Meaning*) and *Napoleon; oder, Die hundert Tage* (1831; *Napoléon; or, The Hundred Days*)—in the 1950s. Outside Germany he is still unknown to most readers and theatergoers.

In philosophical terms, Grabbe and contemporaries such as Lord Byron, Alphonse Lamartine, Giacomo Leopardi, and Heinrich Heine were products of an age in which idealism gave way to materialism, leaving young intellectuals in a spiritual void and delivering them to post-Romantic skepticism and melancholy. His early plays—notably the sadomasochistic melodrama *Herzog Theodor von Gothland* (1827) and the black comedy *Jest, Satire, Irony*—convey, in his own words, the despair of "intellect spent and emotion shattered." A similar disillusionment kindles superhuman desires in *Don Juan und Faust* (1829; *Don Juan and Faust*), which "glorifies the tragic fall of the sensualist and the metaphysician" alike. Nihilistic moods also underlie his later plays—particularly *Napoleon* and *Hannibal* (1835)—which blend a longing for powerful heroes with a debilitating sense of the impermanence of all things and the "immeasurable chaos of baseness."

Current social and political affairs were of little interest to Grabbe. He abandoned his fashionably patriotic *Hohenstaufen* (1829–30; The Hohenstaufen Dynasty) cycle after only two installments on Barbarossa and Heinrich VI, and his last play, *Die Hermannsschlacht* (1838; Arminius's Battle), was inspired by his "best childhood memories" of its setting—the Teutoburg Forest near Detmold—rather than by the nationalism traditionally associated with the topic. Nevertheless, his cynicism, pessimism, and iconoclasm may well be interpreted as a protest against the constricting cultural and political conditions of his era.

By consensus Grabbe's supreme achievement consists of his innovations in historical drama. Unlike the historical plays of Schiller and his followers, which were classical in style and idealistic in content, Grabbe's historical plays are prosaic in language, episodic in structure, and realistic in outlook. Above all, they present history as determined not by abstract ideas or outstanding personalities but by mass movements and the contingencies of time, place, circumstance, and chance. Foreshadowed in *Marius und Sulla* (1827), carried further in the two *Hohenstaufen* pieces, and culminating in *Napoleon* and *Hannibal,* Grabbe's ability to re-create the broad sweep of history has been much admired. Speaking of *Napoleon,* he rightly claimed to have accomplished "a dramatic-epic revolution," although he might well have included his other historical plays in that remark.

Grabbe's "revolution" in historical drama was accompanied by a revolutionary approach to drama in general. Once dismissed as signs of incompetence, capriciousness, or a sick psyche, his methods now seem eminently modern. Full of incongruities and distortions, deliberately avoiding any appearance of harmony or beauty, his disjointed actions, ambiguous characters, dissonant dialogues, and tragicomic moods not only reflect the social, intellectual, and aesthetic tensions of his own age but also anticipate the "open" form and "absurd" content favored by many dramatists in ours. Long before the cinema was invented, he also foreshadowed many of its techniques.

With the exception of *Don Juan and Faust,* none of Grabbe's plays was performed in his lifetime. Commenting again on *Napoleon,* he declared: "I haven't taken any trouble over its shape as a drama. The present stage doesn't deserve it." But he also observed: "Drama is not bound to the stage. . . . The proper theater is the imagination of the reader." We cannot tell whether he was expressing seriously considered doubts about the suitability of the theater for any literary creation, or simply giving vent to his resentment of the specific theatrical conventions of his period, which provided no scope for his particular gifts. In either case, the paradoxical conflict between a born dramatist and the theater may ultimately account for both the successes and the failures of this remarkable nonconformist in the history of German drama.

LADISLAUS LÖB

Biography

Born in Detmold, Westphalia, 11 December 1801. Studied law at Leipzig University, 1820–22; attempted a career as an actor in Dresden, Hanover, Brunswick, and Bremen, 1822–24; legal practice in Detmold, 1824; worked in the legal branch of the army, Detmold, 1826–34; in Frankfurt, 1834; in Düsseldorf at the invitation of the writer Karl Immermann, 1834–36; wrote for the journals, *Hermann* and *Düsseldorfer Fremdenblatt.* Died in Detmold, 12 September 1836.

Selected Works

Collections

Sämtliche Werke, 4 vols., 1902–3
Sämtliche Werke, 6 vols., 1912
Werke und Briefe. Historisch-kritische Gesamtausgabe, edited by Alfred Bergmann, 6 vols., 1960–73
Werke, edited by Roy C. Cowen, 3 vols., 1975–77
Grabbe über seine Werke, edited by Ladislaus Löb, 1991

Plays

Herzog Theodor von Gothland (produced 1892); in *Dramatische Dichtungen,* 1827
Scherz, Satire, Ironie und tiefere Bedeutung (produced 1876); in *Dramatische Dichtungen,* 1827; as *Comedy, Satire, Irony, and Deeper Meaning,* translated by Barbara Wright, 1955; as *Jest, Satire, Irony, and Deeper Significance,* translated by Maurice Edwards, 1966
Marius und Sulla (produced 1936); in *Dramatische Dichtungen,* 1827
Nannette und Maria (produced 1914); *Dramatische Dichtungen,* 1827
Dramatische Dichtungen, 2 vols., 1827
Don Juan und Faust (produced 1829 with music by Albert Lortzing), 1829; translated 1963
Die Hohenstaufen I: Kaiser Friedrich Barbarossa (produced 1875), 1829
Die Hohenstaufen II: Kaiser Heinrich der Sechste (produced 1875), 1830
Napoleon; oder, Die hundert Tage (produced in a shortened version, 1869; complete version produced 1895), 1831
Aschenbrödel (produced 1937), 1835
Hannibal (produced 1918), 1835
Die Hermannsschlacht (produced 1936), 1838

Essays

Über die Shakespearo-Manie, in *Dramatische Dichtungen,* 1827
Das Theater zu Düsseldorf, 1835

Further Reading

Broer, Werner, and Detlev Kopp, editors, *Christian Dietrich Grabbe (1801–1836): Ein Symposium,* Tübingen: Niemeyer, 1987
Cowen, Roy C., *Christian Dietrich Grabbe,* New York: Twayne, 1972
Ehrlich, Lothar, *Christian Dietrich Grabbe: Leben und Werk,* Leipzig: Reclam, 1986
Freund, Winfried, editor, *Grabbes Gegenentwürfe: Neue Deutungen seiner Dramen,* Munich: Fink, 1986
Hegele, Wolfgang, *Grabbes Dramenform,* Munich: Fink, 1970
Höllerer, Walter, *Zwischen Klassik und Moderne: Lachen und Weinen in der Dichtung einer Übergangszeit,* Stuttgart: Klett, 1958
Kopp, Detlev, *Geschichte und Gesellschaft in den Dramen Christian Dietrich Grabbes,* Frankfurt: Lang, 1982
Kopp, Detlev, editor, *Christian Dietrich Grabbe: Ein Dramatiker der Moderne,* Bielefeld: Aisthesis, 1996
Kopp, Detlev, and Michael Vogt, editors, *Grabbe und die Dramatiker seiner Zeit: Beiträge zum II. Internationalen Grabbe-Symposium 1989,* Tübingen: Niemeyer, 1990
Kutzmutz, Olaf, *Grabbe: Klassiker ex negativo,* Bielefeld: Aisthesis, 1995
Löb, Ladislaus, *Christian Dietrich Grabbe,* Stuttgart: Metzler, 1996
McInnes, Edward, "'Die wunderlose Welt der Geschichte': Grabbe and the Development of Historical Drama in the Nineteenth Century," *German Life and Letters* 32 (1978–79)

Nicholls, Roger A., *The Dramas of Christian Dietrich Grabbe,* Paris: Mouton, 1969

Porrmann, Marianne, *Grabbe, Dichter für das Vaterland: Die Geschichtsdramen auf deutschen Bühnen im 19. und 20. Jahrhundert,* Lemgo: Wagener, 1982

Schneider, Manfred, *Destruktion und utopische Gemeinschaft: Zur Thematik und Dramaturgie des Heroischen im Werk Christian Dietrich Grabbes,* Frankfurt: Athenäum, 1973

Wiese, Benno von, *Die deutsche Tragödie von Lessing bis Hebbel,* Hamburg: Hofmann, 1948

Oskar Maria Graf 1894–1967

Although Germany's main literary development between 1910 and 1950 has left some traces in his works, Oskar Maria Graf was basically a solitary figure who does not fit into any literary period. He made his writer's debut in 1914 with poems that appeared in *Die Aktion* and in other Expressionist journals. His first two books were collections of lyrical poetry: *Die Revolutionäre* (1918; The Revolutionaries) and *Amen und Anfang* (1919; Amen and a Beginning). These were followed by a few books of art criticism and several collections of stories, which reflect the author's intimate knowledge of life in a small Bavarian village and in the large city of Munich. At age 16, Graf had run away from his small-town home to the near-by capital of Bavaria in order to escape the tyranny of his oldest brother, who had become the head of household after the death of their father; Graf related these experiences in *Frühzeit* (1922; Early Youth), a blunt and unadorned autobiography. Following several works that have regional Bavarian settings (novels, fairy tales, and collections of short stories), Graf achieved sudden fame with his revised and greatly expanded new autobiography, *Wir sind Gefangene* (1927; *Prisoners All*), in which a large portion of the added second part is devoted to the depiction of the author's Schweik-like undermining of Germany's war effort as a soldier in World War I and his participation in the revolutionary events of 1918 in Munich and in the two short-lived Bavarian Soviet Republics of 1919. Thomas Mann hailed the "indelible value" of this work. His and other writers' judgments have contributed to the book's fame and its translation into other languages, as well as its periodic republication in German. Following Hitler's ascent to power in 1933, the Nazis singled out *Prisoners All* as unacceptable, unlike the author's other works, which they recommended to German readers in their propagation of a blood and soil literature.

A closer reading of Graf's novels and short stories, which fill one dozen volumes published between 1922–32, shows that they are anything but the glorification of a patriotic peasantry and the country idylls favored by the Nazis. In the large two volume anthology *Kalender-Geschichten* (1929; Calendar Tales), one of Graf's best works, which contains 50 stories about Bavarian village and city life, the peasants and city workers are portrayed with stark realism as helpless figures fighting against the historical adversities under which they are either crushed or survive only with deceit and cunning. Similar to Bertolt Brecht at this time, who like Graf used the old literary form of the calendar tale to express modern political and moral thought (a tradition that in German literature has its origin in the folk literature of the 17th century), Graf struck a happy medium between his intended social criticism and popular appeal. Graf's stories were also compared to Brecht's writings on a different level by Walter Benjamin, who averred that Graf's calendar tales, like Brecht's dramas, pioneered a new school of modern writing called "epic" literature. In one of his novels of this time, *Bolwieser* (1931; *The Station Master*), Graf depicts the morally corrupt and politically apathetic society of a Bavarian small town that, during the 1920s, became the fertile ground for the fomentation of Nazi ideology. Another of his novels, *Einer gegen Alle* (1932; *The Wolf*), with its reflections on the negative consequences of war, belongs into the same tradition of antiwar literature that Graf had set into motion with *Prisoners All.* This tradition yielded a large crop of pacifist novels, of which Erich Maria Remarque's *Im Westen nichts Neues* (1929; *All Quiet on the Western Front*) is the best known. While Graf's socially critical works were well received by the prominent critics of the Weimar Republic, however, it is another book, which Graf had written in a state of financial need, that, to his own embarrassment, became his most popular work: *Das bayrische Dekameron* (1928; The Bavarian Decameron). This work's fame and notoriety has sometimes even overshadowed his reputation as a serious and socially responsible writer. The tales in this book bear some resemblance to Boccaccio's work, but their eroticism is rather tame by today's measure and is infested with many putrid elements.

Graf had to forego a number of started literary projects—among them a planned work focusing on the life of his greatest literary example, the Russian writer Leo Tolstoy—when he left Germany shortly after Hitler's coming to power, but he was able to save the manuscript of his novel *Der harte Handel* (1935; The Difficult Deal), which he had written in Munich. He eventually published it in exile. In May of 1933, Graf wrote his famous letter "Verbrennt mich" ("Burn Me Too"), in which he speaks out against the recommendation of most of his books by the Nazis, and which today is considered one of the key texts of German exile literature. Subsequently, he wrote a number of novels depicting the advent of National Socialism in Germany and the weak and ineffective resistance of many German people and their political parties. In *Anton Sittinger* (1937), the protagonist is a government employee who between 1918 and 1933 repeatedly changes his party affiliation until he is almost left out in 1933 when Hitler becomes chancellor of Germany; but he is saved by his equally opportunistic wife who, without his knowledge, has registered him with the Nazi party. The most important work of Graf's exile period and perhaps the best of his entire oeuvre is *Das Leben meiner Mutter* (1946; first published in English in 1940 as *The Life of My Mother: A Biographical Novel*). In this work, he uses both biographic and autobiographic events to depict, in slightly fictionalized form, the steadily growing interaction between the slow life in the country and the political storms that threatened Germany from Bismarck to Hitler. Another exile novel, *Unruhe um einen Friedfertigen* (1947; Unrest Surrounding a Peaceful Man), unmasks the false basis of German anti-Semitism by representing the story of a Jewish cobbler who is fully integrated into a Bavarian village but is finally murdered by the Nazis. Graf also tried his hand at the utopian novel, a quickly emerging subgenre after the war, in *Die Eroberung der Welt* (1949; The Conquest of the World, republished as *Die Erben des Untergangs* [1959; The Heirs of the Collapse]); and he depicted the life of a German exile group in New York in *Die Flucht ins Mittelmäßige: Ein New Yorker Roman* (1959; Escape into Average Life: A New York Novel).

Like other exile writers, Graf only slowly regained the German book market after the war. Renewed interest in his work was first kindled outside Germany by scholars of exile literature; this interest eventually coincided with the growing German interest in dialect and provincial literature. Although Graf's works are not written in dialect, they bear some of the typical signs of the Bavarian dictum and show the problems of the larger world in the microcosm of a provincial setting. A younger generation of writers who have consciously focused upon the life of people in small towns and villages, among them Martin Sperr, Franz Xaver Kroetz, and Herbert Achternbusch, have conceded their indebtedness to Graf's literary example. Similarly, the renewed interest of people in *Heimat* (native background) has helped Graf's works experience a renaissance from 1970 to 1990.

While previously some of his works and political actions inspired other authors—Graf's "Verbrennt mich!" became the subject of Bertolt Brecht's exile poem "Die Bücherverbrennung" ("The Book Burning")—more recently, several film adaptations have been made of Graf's novels and short stories, among them Rainer Maria Fassbinder's *Bolwieser.* As Germany not only reflects upon her past but also tries to separate her high-quality regional literature of the 1920s—seeing its value along with big-city literature of the same period—from the pseudo-provincial literature of the conservative right, Graf's influence continues to grow. The International Oskar Maria Graf Society was founded on the occasion of the author's 100th birthday in Munich, and the List Verlag of Munich has published an almost-complete edition of his collected works, with more selective collected editions available from the Büchergilde Gutenberg and the Deutscher Taschenbuch-Verlag.

HELMUT F. PFANNER

Biography

Born in Berg on Lake Starnberg, Bavaria, 22 July 1894. Apprenticeship as a baker in oldest brother's bakery; lived in Munich, 1911–33; joined the anarchistic syndicate group "Die Tat" in Munich, 1911, and visited an anarchist colony in the Tessin region of Switzerland, 1912; hunger strike and feigned insanity as a soldier on the eastern front, 1915; imprisoned on account of his participation in the Bavarian Soviet experiments of 1919 and released upon the intervention of the poet Rainer Maria Rilke; held a number of odd jobs until he became a freelance writer in 1921; member of the German PEN Club and other literary organizations of the Weimar Republic; exile in Vienna, 1933–34; co-editor of the German exile journal *Neue deutsche Blätter,* 1933–35; witnessed uprising of Austrian workers against Dollfuß, 1934, and continued exile in Brno, Czechoslovakia; participated in First Congress of Socialist Writers, Moscow, 1934; fled to New York, 1958, where he lived until his death; chairman of the German-American Writers Organization, 1939–40, and frequent speaker before German-American groups in New York and in other American cities; his naturalization as a U.S. citizen repeatedly delayed because he was maligned by other exiles as a communist sympathizer, and he refused to sign the defence clause of the Oath of Allegiance; following the exceptional removal of the clause in 1958, four visits to Germany between 1958 and 1965. Honorary doctorate from Wayne State University, Michigan, 1960. Died 28 June 1967.

Selected Works

Die Revolutionäre, 1918
Amen und Anfang, 1919
Georg Schrimpf, 1919; new and expanded text, 1923
Maria Uhden, 1921
Ua Pua . . . ! Indianergeschichten, 1921
Frühzeit: Jugenderlebnisse, 1922
Zur freundlichen Erinnerung: Acht Erzählungen, 1922
Bayrisches Lesebücherl: Weißblaue Kulturbilder, 1924; expanded edition, 1966
Die Traumdeuter: Aus einer alten bayrischen Familienchronik, 1924
Die Chronik von Flechting: Ein Dorfroman, 1925
Die Heimsuchung: Roman, 1925
Finsternis: Sechs Dorfgeschichten, 1926
Im Winkel des Lebens, 1927
Licht und Schatten: Eine Sammlung zeitgemäßer Märchen, 1927
Wir sind Gefangene: Ein Bekenntnis aus diesem Jahrzehnt, 1927; as *Prisoners All,* translated by Margaret Green, 1928
Wunderbare Menschen: Heitere Chronik einer Arbeiterbühne nebst meinen drolligen und traurigen Erlebnissen dortselbst, 1927
Das bayerische Dekameron, 1928; expanded edition, 1951
Kalender-Geschichten, 1929; expanded edition, 1975
Bolwieser: Roman eines Ehemannes, 1931; edited as *Die Ehe des Herrn Bolwieser: Roman aus Niederbayern,* 1967; as *The Station Master: A Novel,* translated by Margaret Goldsmith, 1933
Dorfbanditen: Erlebnisse aus meinen Schul- und Lehrlingsjahren, 1932; expanded as *Größtenteils schimpflich: Von Halbstarken und Leuten, welche dieselben nicht leiden können,* 1962
Einer gegen Alle: Roman, 1932; as *The Wolf,* translated anonymously, 1934
Notizbuch des Provinzschriftstellers Oskar Maria Graf 1932: Erlebnisse, Intimitäten, Meinungen, 1932
Der harte Handel: Ein bayrischer Bauern-Roman, 1935
Der Abgrund: Ein Zeitroman, 1936; new revised edition as *Die gezählten Jahre,* 1980
Anton Sittinger: Roman, 1937
Der Quasterl, 1938; expanded edition as *Der Quasterl und andere Erzählungen,* 1945; further expanded as *Mitmenschen,* 1950; excerpts under the title *Menschen aus meiner Jugend auf dem Dorfe: Drei Erzählungen,* 1953
Das Leben meiner Mutter, 1946; as *The Life of My Mother: A Biographical Novel,* translated anonymously, 1940
Unruhe um einen Friedfertigen: Roman, 1947
Die Eroberung der Welt: Roman einer Zukunft, 1949; revised edition as *Die Erben des Untergangs: Roman einer Zukunft,* 1959
Der ewige Kalender: Ein Jahresspiegel, 1954
Die Flucht ins Mittelmäßige: Ein New Yorker Roman, 1959
An manchen Tagen: Reden, Gedanken, und Zeitbetrachtungen, 1961
Der große Bauernspiegel: Dorfgeschichten und Begebnisse von einst und jetzt, 1962
Altmodische Gedichte eines Dutzendmenschen, 1962; as *Old-fashioned Poems of an Ordinary Man,* Partially translated by Elisabeth Bayliss, 1967
Er nannte sich Banscho: Der Roman einer Gegend, 1964
Gelächter von außen: Aus meinem Leben, 1966
Beschreibung eines Volksschriftstellers, with previously unpublished texts edited by Wolfgang Dietz and Helmut F. Pfanner, 1974

Reise in die Sowjetunion 1934, with letters by Sergej Tretjakov, edited by Hans-Albert Walter, 1974; newly edited by Rolf Recknagel as *Reise nach Sowjetrußland 1934,* 1977
Oskar Maria Graf in seinen Briefen, edited by Gerhard Bauer and Helmut F. Pfanner, 1984
Jedermanns Geschichten, with an epilogue by Gert Heidenreich, 1988
Reden und Aufsätze aus dem Exil, edited by Helmut F. Pfanner, 1989

Further Reading

Bauer, Gerhard, *Gefangenschaft und Lebenslust: Oskar Maria Graf in seiner Zeit,* Munich: Süddeutscher Verlag, 1987
Bollenbeck, Georg, *Oskar Maria Graf: Mit Selbstzeugnissen und Bilddokumenten,* Reinbek bei Hamburg: Rowohlt, 1985
Johnson, Sheila, *Oskar Maria Graf: The Critical Reception of His Prose Fiction,* Bonn: Bouvier, 1979
Kaufmann, Ulrich, and Detlev Ignasiak, *Oskar Maria Graf: Rebell, Erzähler, Weltbürger: Studien und Materialien,* Munich: Kirchheim, 1994
Recknagel, Rolf, *Ein Bayer in Amerika: Oskar Maria Graf, Leben und Werk,* 2nd edition, Berlin: Verlag der Nation, 1978
Schoeller, Wilfried F., *Oskar Maria Graf: Odyssee eines Einzelgängers: Texte, Bilder, Dokumente,* Frankfurt: Büchergilde Gutenberg, 1994

Günter Grass 1927–

In the work of Günter Grass, discourses of mourning, migration, and the vicissitudes of the Enlightenment as master narrative of the Western world form a complex web of interrelated issues. The narrative techniques Grass employs for his literary production are thoroughly grounded in the modern aesthetic tradition, although elements of postmodernism can be discerned in some of his texts, most notably already in *Die Blechtrommel* (1959; *The Tin Drum*).

Keeping up the work of mourning and remembrance after the Shoah motivates Grass's production. He became simultaneously one of the most prominent and the most troublesome commentators on 20th-century German history when he combined this impulse with a continuing critique of how minorities and people considered as "other" have been treated by the Germans. He traces the mechanisms of oppression, hate, violence, and repression inherent in German history back to the Enlightenment, thereby providing his own account of a dialectics of enlightenment that resembles that of Horkheimer and Adorno. However, in opposition to the Frankfurt School theorists, Grass still pays tribute to a kind of primal Christianity that serves as a source for utopian hope.

Coming from a multiethnic family background of German, Polish, and Keshubian ancestry and born during the interwar period, Grass experienced the contingencies of 20th-century German history and commented on them in manifold ways of literary and artistic expression. Grass is a typical product of the war and postwar period in Germany. Subjected to Nazi propaganda and education during his childhood and youth, he experienced the shock of disillusion and horror after the end of World War II. As a result, he developed a genuine distrust of ideology and subscribed to Albert Camus's version of the philosophy of the absurd. Among the books Grass talks about when he looks back at the decisive influences of his life, Camus's *Le Mythe de Sisyphe* (1942; *The Myth of Sisyphus*) figures most prominently. However, this did not prevent him from becoming the most politically engaged West German writer. A personal friend of Willy Brandt and a supporter of "Democratic Socialism," he started campaigning for the Social Democratic Party in the 1960s, supported the Green Party in the 1980s, criticized the way in which minorities were treated in unified Germany, and became a target of right-wing violence in the 1990s.

In an essay on Grass, Salman Rushdie has pointed out the threefold loss that shaped the German writer: the loss of home, or *Heimat,* in Danzig (today in Poland); the loss of his native language, which had been compromised and contaminated by the Nazis; and the disruption of the social fabric that Grass had known in his childhood and youth. According to Rushdie, Grass is a "double migrant: a traveler across borders in the self, and in Time." Grass himself has reflected on the losses he has suffered in a speech he gave in 1992, entitled *Rede vom Verlust* (1990; *Speech about Loss*). He confirms Rushdie's contention that it was the loss of his home that laid the foundation for his literary imagination. In addition, Grass argues, the rise of German fascism and the guilt associated with the atrocities committed by Germans became the driving force for his writing. Thus, Auschwitz became the central metaphor for his work, as he states in retrospect in his lecture *Schreiben nach Auschwitz* (1990; *Writing after Auschwitz*).

The *Danziger Trilogie* (*Danzig Trilogy*), consisting of *The Tin Drum, Katz und Maus* (1961; *Cat and Mouse*), and *Hundejahre* (1963; *Dog Years*), traces the rise and fall of German fascism and the continuation of fascist mentalities into postwar West Germany. Spanning the period from the mid-1920s to the late 1950s, the *Danzig Trilogy* follows a cast of members of the German middle class and views them from the perspective of outsiders who double as narrators of the texts. These first-person narrators (Oskar Matzerath in *The Tin Drum,* Pilenz in *Cat and Mouse,* and Brauxel/Liebenau/Matern in *Dog Years*) are driven by their feelings of guilt, shame, and responsibility and keep up the work of mourning and remembrance. Unlike the novels and short stories of his contemporary Heinrich Böll, which highlight the Germans as suffering from the war, the *Danzig Trilogy* foregrounds the other as victim. In many of Grass's texts, it is the other who is granted a narrative voice and the status of victim. In *The Tin Drum,* the Jewish toy dealer Sigismund Markus commits suicide during the pogrom of the Night of Broken Glass. After the war, Oskar meets a Jew named Fajngold, whose entire family has been murdered. In *Dog Years,* Brauxel is identical with Amsel, the Jewish childhood friend of Matern, whom Matern had brutally beaten up with a group of storm trooper thugs. *Aus dem Tagebuch einer Schnecke* (1972; *From the Diary of a Snail*) combines a fictional diary of Grass that comments on the election campaign of 1969 with a minute rendering of the fate of the Danzig Jewish community from 1929 to 1945.

Even before Günter Grass challenged the literary establishment of postwar West Germany in 1959 with the publication of *The Tin Drum,* he had laid the groundwork for his literary career. Many of the motifs that would gain prominence in his later writings had been introduced in his poetry and theater production in the 1950s. To name just one example, the idea to write a novel narrated from the perspective of a dwarf had come to Grass when he wrote the poem "Der Säulenheilige" in 1952. Although the early poems and especially his plays have received little attention, knowledge of them is decisive for understanding Grass's work. The three volumes of poetry *Die Vorzüge der Windhühner* (1956; The Advantages of Windfowl), *Gleisdreieck* (1960; Railroad-Track Triangle), and *Ausgefragt* (1967; *New Poems*) provide indispensable insights into Grass's use of language, metaphor, and intertextual references.

Time and again, Grass has insisted on the interdependence of his literary production and other means of artistic expression. In *Vier Jahrzehnte: Ein Werkstattbericht* (1991; Four Decades: A Workshop Report), Grass has documented how his writing interacted with his drawing, etching, and sculpting. Having been trained as an artist at the art academies of Düsseldorf and Berlin from 1948 to 1952 and 1953 to 1956, Grass discovered writing as just one more way of expressing himself. From 1956 to 1960, he lived in Paris, where *The Tin Drum* was written. In 1958, Grass was awarded the prize of the Gruppe 47 for the still unfinished manuscript of *The Tin Drum.* He would become one of the most productive and controversial members of the group until it was dissolved in 1967.

Beginning in the 1970s, Grass concentrated his efforts more and more on problems he saw emerging out of certain deficiencies connected with the process of enlightenment. Global threats such as the arms race, the destruction of the environment, and the widening gap between the rich industrial nations and the Third World, resulting in mass migration, took center stage in his literary writings as well as in his political work.

In *Der Butt* (1977; *The Flounder*), Grass undertook the monumental task of rewriting 3,000 years of male-dominated history. This ironic account teams up a first-person narrator who is present through the ages with a mythical flounder who doubles as a manifestation of various forms of the Hegelian *Weltgeist,* although in the final analysis every attempt at making sense in human history is bound to fail. Not even radical feminism—represented by an all-female tribunal that accuses the flounder of having betrayed the primal matriarchy and of having established a male "history"—can save the world from the aberrations of an enlightenment gone wild.

Doubts in the potential of enlightenment as master narrative of the Western world are also expressed in *Die Rättin* (1986; *The Rat*), *Kopfgeburten; oder, Die Deutschen sterben aus* (1980; *Head Births; or, The Germans Are Dying Out*), *Zunge zeigen* (1988; *Show Your Tongue*), and *Totes Holz: Ein Nachruf* (1990; Dead Woods: An Obituary), the latter combining drawings of dead forests with quotations from a report of the German Ministry of Agriculture and Forestry. Whereas *The Rat* focuses on the destruction of the environment and the specter of nuclear war, in *Head Births* and *Show Your Tongue,* Grass makes use of his firsthand experience traveling in Third World countries. *Show Your Tongue* is a literary by-product of a six-month stay in India, where Grass had found uncanny resemblances with his native German history (e.g., in the person of the Indian leader, or *Führer,* Subhas Chandra Bose).

The 1990s are, according to Grass, a time when unified Germany once again had to face its past. Grass, who sees himself as a defender of the Basic Law (in the sense of what Habermas has called *Verfassungspatriotismus,* or patriotism for the constitution), criticizes tendencies that in his view weaken the Basic Law and bring about the loss of the social dimension in the political fabric of the Federal Republic of Germany. In a series of public statements, he condemns the way in which German unification was handled by the West German political and economic elite, specifically the work of the Treuhandanstalt (Trust Agency for the People's Property) and the failure or, rather, the unwillingness on the part of German politicians to work out a new constitution for the unified Germany.

The generally hostile reaction toward his novel *Ein weites Feld* (1995; Too Far Afield) can be explained at least in part by the fact that after 1989 Grass put his finger on the deficiencies and injustice that the process of unification produced for the population of East Germany. The political and literary establishment could not forget that it was Grass who had declared that the memory of Auschwitz should be an insurmountable obstacle to a unified Germany that would try to establish itself within the international community as a nation enjoying a newfound "normalcy," for Grass believed that such an assertion of normalcy would only complete the revisionist tendencies of the 1980s that had found their expression in Ronald Reagan's visit to Bitburg and the so-called historians' debate (*Historikerstreit*).

With *Ein weites Feld,* Grass tried to work through German unification and its shortcomings. The protagonists of the novel are Theo Wuttke, also called Fonty, who is at the same time a *revenant* of Theodor Fontane, and Hoftaller, a literary resurrection of the main character of Hans-Joachim Schädlich's 1986 novel *Tallhover.* During their walks through Berlin and in their conversations, these two compare the two German unifications: the one accomplished by Bismarck in 1870–71, which Fontane witnessed, and the one in 1990. Just as both unifications are the outcome of questionable historic decisions, both characters have a troubled past. Wuttke became involved in Nazi propaganda during the war, and Hoftaller had been an operative for the East German secret service, the Stasi. (In Schädlich's novel, Tallhover was the quintessential German spy and informer, a by-product of the German state and its paranoia toward potential political enemies.) The building in which Wuttke works symbolizes the anti-Democratic tradition that Grass sees at work to the present day; it housed in sequence Göring's Ministry of Aviation (Reichsluftfahrministerium) during the Third Reich, then the House of Ministries (Haus der Ministerien) of communist East Germany, and finally the Treuhandanstalt after unification.

The reception of Grass reached a new climax (and created a minor scandal) when the most influential German contemporary literary critic, Marcel Reich-Ranicki, condemned *Ein weites Feld* as ill-conceived, cumbersome, and boring and when the magazine *Der Spiegel* printed a cover showing Reich-Ranicki literally tearing the book apart. Although the negative reception of *Ein weites Feld* was largely politically motivated, Grass continued with unshaken resolve to observe recent political developments in unified Germany. Out of protest against the amendment of the asylum law—for Grass one of the pillars of the Basic Law—he canceled his membership in the Social Democratic Party. He protested against the fetishization of economics and the apparent abandonment of a political consensus that for more than 40 years had been the foundation of the West German welfare state (*Rede über den Standort,* 1997).

The critical debate on Grass at home reaches from initial admiration and glorification (after *The Tin Drum* had appeared and had put contemporary German literature at the center of international attention) to increasing irritation during the 1970s and 1980s and outright rejection and condemnation after German unification. After 1989, conservative critics maintained that Grass had lost touch with political realities and that he appeared to be an angry old man whose aesthetics were just as outdated as his political beliefs. Many left-wing intellectuals had already rejected Grass since the late 1960s, when he had attempted to criticize the student movement's revolutionary tendencies and had upheld his belief in Social Democratic revisionism. On the other hand, Grass and his work had been heralded by writers such as John Updike, John Irving, and Salman Rushdie and a host of international critics and scholars. In 1997, a symposium on the occasion of Grass's 70th birthday was headed "Appreciated Abroad—Hated at Home?" The title indicates the mixed and troubled reception of one of the most important contemporary German writers.

THOMAS W. KNIESCHE

Biography

Born in Danzig (now Gdansk, Poland), 16 October 1927. Studied at the Academy of Art, Düsseldorf, 1948–52, and at the State Academy of Fine Arts, Berlin, 1953–56; served in World War II; prisoner of war, Bavaria, 1945–46; farm worker, miner, stonecutter, jazz musician; in Paris, 1956–59; worked as artist and illustrator; co-editor of *L'76,* since 1976; editor for L'80, publishers, since 1980; member of Gruppe 47. Gruppe 47 Prize, 1958; Foreign Book Prize (France), 1962; Büchner Prize, 1965; Fontane Prize, 1968; Mondello Prize (Palermo), 1977; International Literature Prize, 1978; Feltrinelli Prize, 1982; Premio Grinzane Cavour (Italy), 1992; Literature Prize of the Bavarian Academy of Fine Arts, 1992; Premio Hidalgo (Madrid), 1993; Kavel-Copek-Prize (Prague), 1994; Sonning-Prize (Denmark) 1996; Nobel Prize for literature, 1999. Various honorary doctorates and memberships in scholarly societies. Currently lives in Behlendorf/Schleswig-Holstein.

Selected Works

Fiction

Danziger Trilogie, 1980; as *The Danzig Trilogy,* translated by Ralph Manheim, 1987
Die Blechtrommel, 1959; as *The Tin Drum,* translated by Ralph Manheim, 1962; screenplay, with Volker Schlöndorff, 1979
Katz und Maus, 1961; as *Cat and Mouse,* translated by Ralph Manheim, 1963; screenplay, 1967
Hundejahre, 1963; as *Dog Years,* translated by Ralph Manheim, 1965
Örlich betäubt, 1969; as *Local Anaesthetic,* translated by Ralph Manheim, 1970
Aus dem Tagebuch einer Schnecke, 1972; as *From the Diary of a Snail,* translated by Ralph Manheim, 1973
Der Butt, 1977; as *The Flounder,* translated by Ralph Manheim, 1978
Das Treffen in Telgte, 1979; as *The Meeting at Telgte,* translated by Ralph Manheim, 1981
Kopfgeburten; oder, Die Deutschen sterben aus, 1980; as *Headbirths; or, The Germans Are Dying Out,* translated by Ralph Manheim, 1982
Die Rättin, 1986; as *The Rat,* translated by Ralph Manheim, 1987
Unkenrufe, 1992; as *The Call of the Toad,* translated by Ralph Manheim, 1992
Ein weites Feld, 1995

Plays

Hochwasser (produced 1957; produced as radio play, 1977), 1965; as *Flood,* translated by Ralph Manheim, in *Four Plays,* 1967
Onkel, Onkel, (produced 1958), 1965; as *Onkel, Onkel,* translated by Ralph Manheim, in *Four Plays,* 1967
Noch zehn Minuten bis Buffalo (produced 1959; produced as a radio play, 1962), in *Theaterspiele,* 1970; as *Only Ten Minutes to Buffalo,* translated by Ralph Manheim, in *Four Plays,* 1967
Beritten hin und zurück (produced 1959)
Die bösen Köche (produced 1961), in *Theaterspiele,* 1970; as *The Wicked Cooks,* translated by A. Leslie Willson, in *Four Plays,* 1967
Die Plebejer proben den Aufstand (produced 1966), 1966; as *The Plebeians Rehearse the Uprising,* translated by Ralph Manheim, 1966
Four Plays (includes *Flood; Onkel, Onkel; Only Ten Minutes to Buffalo; The Wicked Cooks*), 1967
Davor (produced 1969), in *Theaterspiele,* 1970; as *Max,* translated by A. Leslie Willson and Ralph Manheim, 1972
Theaterspiele (includes *Noch zehn Minuten bis Buffalo; Hochwasser; Onkel, Onkel; Die Plebejer proben den Aufstand; Davor*), 1970

Poetry

Die Vorzüge der Windhühner, 1956
Gleisdreieck, 1960
Selected Poems, translated by Michael Hamburger and Christopher Middleton, 1966; as *Poems of Günter Grass,* 1969
Ausgefragt, 1967; as *New Poems,* translated by Michael Hamburger, 1968
Gesammelte Gedichte, 1971
Mariazuehren/Hommageàmarie/Inmarypraise, 1973; as *Inmarypraise,* translated by Christopher Middleton, 1974
In the Egg and Other Poems (bilingual edition), translated by Michael Hamburger and Christopher Middleton, 1977
Ach, Butt, dein Märchen geht böse aus, 1983
Die Gedichte 1955–1986, 1988
Novemberland: 13 Sonette, 1993; as *Novemberland: Selected Poems, 1956–1993,* translated by Michael Hamburger, 1996

Other

Die Ballerina, 1963
Dich singe ich Demokratie (pamphlets), 5 vols., 1965
Der Fall Axel C. Springer am Beispiel Arnold Zweig, 1967
Briefe über die Grenze; Versuch eines Ost-West-Dialogs, with Pavel Kohout, 1968
Über meinen Lehrer Döblin und andere Vorträge, 1968
Über das Selbstverständliche: Reden, Aufsätze, Offene Briefe, Kommentare, 1968; revised and enlarged as *Über das Selbstverständliche: Politische Schriften,* 1969; translated in part by Ralph Manheim, as *Speak Out! Speeches, Open Letters, Commentaries,* 1969
Der Bürger und seine Stimme, 1974
Denkzettel: Politische Reden und Aufsätze 1965–76, 1978
Die Blechtrommel als Film (screenplay), with Volker Schlöndorff, 1979

Aufsätze zur Literatur, 1957–1979, 1980
Zeichnen und Schreiben: Das bildnerische Werk des Schriftstellers Günter Grass:
I. Zeichnungen und Texte 1954–1977, 1982; as *Drawings and Words 1954–*
1977, translated by Michael Hamburger and Walter Arndt, 1983
II. Radierungen und Texte 1972–1982, 1984; as *Etchings and Words 1972–*
1982, translated by Michael Hamburger and others, 1985
Die Vernichtung der Menschheit hat begonnen, 1983
Widerstand lernen: Politische Gegenreden 1980–1983, 1984
On Writing and Politics, 1967–1983 (selection), translated by Ralph Manheim, 1985
In Kupfer, auf Stein: Die Radierungen und Lithoprophien 1972–1986, 1986
Werkausgabe, edited by Volker Neuhaus, 10 vols., 1987
Es war einmal ein Land: Lyrik und Prosa, Schlagzeug und Perkussion, with Günter "Baby" Sommer, 1987
Zunge Zeigen (travel), 1988; as *Show Your Tongue,* translated by John E. Woods, 1989
Skizzenbuch, 1989
Wenn wir von Europa sprechen: Ein Dialog, with Françoise Giroud, 1989
Alptraum und Hoffnung: Zwei Reden vor dem Club of Rome, with T. Aitmatow, 1989
Deutscher Lastenausgleich: Wider das dumpfe Einheitsgebot: Reden und Gespräche, 1990; as *Two States—One Nation? The Case against Reunification,* translated by Krishna Winston and A.S. Wensinger, 1990
Totes Holz: Ein Nachruf, 1990
Deutschland, einig Vaterland? Ein Streitgespräch, with Rudolph Augstein, 1990
Ein Schnäppchen namens DDR: Letzte Reden vorm Glockengeläut, 1990
Rede vom Verlust, 1990; translated in *The Future of German Democracy,* edited by Robert Gerald Livingson and Volkmar Sander, 1993
Schreiben nach Auschwitz: Frankfurter Poetik-Vorlesung, 1990
Gegen die verstreichende Zeit: Reden, Aufsätze, und Gespräche 1989–1991, 1991
Vier Jahrzehnte: Ein Werkstattbericht, edited by G. Fritze Margull, 1991
Die Deutschen und ihre Dichter, edited by Daniela Hermes, 1995
Gestern, vor 50 Jahren: Ein deutsch-japanisches Briefwechsel, with [O]e Kenzabur[o], 1995
Fundsachen für Nichtleser, 1997
Rede über den Standort, 1997
Günter Grass liesst "Die Blechtrommel" [sound recording], 1997
Werkausgabe, edited by Volker Neuhaus and Daniela Hermes, 16 vols., 1997
Angestiftet, Partei zu ergreifen, edited by Daniela Hermes, 1998

Further Reading

Hayman, Ronald, *Günter Grass,* London and New York: Methuen, 1985
Keele, Alan Frank, *Understanding Günter Grass,* Columbia: University of South Carolina Press, 1988
Labroisse, Gerd, and Dick van Stekelenburg, editors, *Günter Grass: Ein europäischer Autor?* Amsterdam and Atlanta, Georgia: Rodopi, 1992
Neuhaus, Volker, *Günter Grass,* Stuttgart: Metzler, 1979; revised edition, 1993
O'Neill, Patrick, editor, *Critical Essays on Günter Grass,* Boston: Hall, 1987
Reddick, John, *The "Danzig Trilogy" of Günter Grass,* New York and London: Harcourt Brace Jovanovich, 1975
Rushdie, Salman, "On Günter Grass," *Granta* 15 (1985)
Stolz, Dieter, *Vom privaten Motivkomplex zum poetischen Weltentwurf: Konstanten und Entwicklungen im literarischen Werk von Günter Grass (1956–1986),* Würzburg: Königshausen und Neumann, 1994

Die Blechtrommel 1959

Novel by Günter Grass

Written between 1953 and 1959, published in 1959, and later defined as part of the *Danziger Trilogie,* Günter Grass's *Die Blechtrommel* (*The Tin Drum*) is a local novel immortalizing lost Danzig and its dialect. It is a political novel, insistently demolishing Nazi racialism by exploring the ethnic appellations in Danzig's hinterland in the 1930s. It is a topical satire on the Federal Republic, referring particularly to the economic miracle. It is a social novel in which the vocabulary, smells, and eccentrics of Danzig in the 1930s, and the new start in Düsseldorf, make a stuffy petit bourgeois reality with lifelike secondary characters. It is a study of abnormal psychology. It uses myth and märchen allusions, and it goes back two generations through reminiscences that are quasi-legend; Grandmother Anna Bronski is an Earth Goddess with four seasons (her skirts) and four elements as she squats on the ground by her bonfire in the rain under the wide sky. Finally, it is a metaliterary novel, in which the figure of Bebra (Oskar's mentor), an entertainer with ideas of resistance but in reality dependent on pleasing the powerful, hopes to have the influence of the court jester but in fact has to compromise with evil. Oskar is heir to his guilt, although he ironizes it.

Grass totally transcends surface realism in order to deal with National Socialism commensurately. His narratorial and linguistic virtuosity makes the literary work an autonomous object—not a recapitulation of fact, but an opposing, artificial, and significant order of reality. This virtuosity short-circuits the difficulty of the inevitable disproportion between historical events of 1933–45 and any literary reflection of them. Similar to Rabelais' Gargantua, Oskar Matzerath is born already with critical, adult awareness; at age three he decides to grow no further and artificially stunts his growth by falling through a trapdoor. As a consequence, he can crawl in anywhere and comment intelligently on what he discovers. He remains a special case, a construct, a *Märchengestalt* with miraculous powers—he has the ability to break glass with his voice. Oskar the literary device has three levels: on the immanent level he is a fictive figure who develops psychologically, on the symbolic level he enacts the moral outrages of the era in his person, and on the metaliterary level he reacts to them as an artist. The levels are mutually contradictory—the artist mourns for actions for which the criminal has no intention of atoning—but only this technique allows Grass to collect all he has to say in one work.

The immanent plot is largely about an unintegrated personality who develops a psychotic anxiety state, identifying himself with Jesus and fearing impending crucifixion. Grass invites accusations of blasphemy by building up parallels of Jesus and Oskar: in two episodes (one wartime, one postwar), Oskar takes the place of the child Jesus in the arms of the Madonna. He also wishes to return to the womb (the grandmother's skirts) or to the cupboard, which he connects with the nurse Dorothea (nurses obsess him, a theme Grass explores with titillating detail).

Oskar—a liar and murderer—reproduces in an individual way the era's destructiveness: that voice, for instance, is referred to as *Wunderwaffe* (miracle weapon) at the moment when the V2 rocket is topical. He is responsible for the deaths of both his putative and real fathers, and he confesses this to Bebra—but only to enter the future unencumbered with guilt (in this perhaps representing postwar Germans).

Oskar's first art form is drumming, with which he influences the present or conjures up the past and exorcises the ghosts of Nazism, neutralizing evil: postwar Germans are served onions in a restaurant, while Oskar drums the past and enables them to weep. This is the artist's function for Grass. The second art form is writing, a conscious process of transposing his drum solos into language.

Grass spins a dense web of allusions, symbols, and interconnections. The eponymous drum—a character per se, determining the action—is painted red and white, the Polish national colors; German-Polish relations are hinted at in the games of skat continually played in the Matzerath-Bronski household; to get a new drum, Oskar goes to the city center on 31 August 1939; and there the final symbolic skat game proceeds as World War II starts. Individual fates such as that of the grocer Greff are linked in multiple, ambiguous ways with the fate of Germany.

Telling episodes exemplify society's indefensible ethical priorities: one character is expelled from the storm troopers, executors of *Kristallnacht,* for cruelty to cats. Like Döblin in *Wallenstein,* Grass leaves historical facts in uninterpreted chaos. He juxtaposes different contemporary actions, gives breathless listings, alternates hints and exactitude, develops associations of images, and repeats words in artful stuttering: for instance, the word *Unglück* (misfortune), repeated, is gradually revealed to mean joining the SA (Sturmabteilung). Grass glories in words for their sensuous and concrete possibilities, and he shows a virtuosity reminiscent of Döblin.

The novel has parallel chronologies between its narrated time (1925–53) and its time of narration (1953–55). Generally, Oskar's perspective is employed, but this is broken by a dramatic scene and twice by chapters narrated by other characters whose versions may differ from Oskar's. This relativizes Oskar's viewpoint.

The Tin Drum was fought over by publishers and eagerly awaited by the public after Grass's reading of excerpts at the Gruppe 47 in 1958 made a stir and gained him the group's prize. Immediate, sensational success with enthusiastic or at least appreciative reviews in the leading newspapers was followed by allegations of blasphemy and pornography; church and youth workers and conservative-minded critics engaged in fierce arguments with proponents of modern literature and uncompromising honesty. Grass was refused the Bremen Literature Prize of 1962 by an image-conscious municipality that overruled the unanimous jury. Nevertheless this was the major novel that established *Bewältigung der Vergangenheit* (coming to terms with the past) as a literary and public reality. It also established Grass as a public figure and a serious author who was interviewed and written about in the general and specialist press along with Böll, Frisch, and the rest. Both a best-seller and a long-seller, the novel has reached a total print run of over 4 million copies. It has an unrivalled reputation abroad (the English translation appeared in 1962, the French one in 1961) as the major work of one of the major post-1945 German authors. (Indeed, both García Márquez and Rushdie admit to having learned from him.)

Filming by Volker Schlöndorff (1979) cemented its fame; Grass accepted him as a director who could find visual equivalents for his verbal style. The film jettisons the narratorial stance of the mad Oskar and allows a much more positive, empathetic view of the child Oskar (played by the attractive David Bennent). It also lessens the role of fantasy and irony, but it is able to bring out the historical main lines clearly, insisting on the endemic violence of pre-war Danzig as the precondition of the catastrophe of 1945. The period after 1945, however, remains outside the film's scope.

The novel is a frequent object of academic study. Although early criticism attempted to find some traditional definition (such as picaresque or novel of development) to classify the long, tortuous text, the novel defies classification either by genre or literary school. Favored aspects for study include narrative perspectives, mythic elements, sources for different episodes, the treatment of Nazism, and the relationship of the novel to historical actuality.

ALFRED D. WHITE

Editions

First edition: *Die Blechtrommel,* Neuwied: Luchterhand, 1959

Translation: *The Tin Drum,* translated by Ralph Manheim, London: Secker and Warburg, 1962; New York: Pantheon, 1963; in *The Danzig Trilogy* [also includes *Cat and Mouse* and *Dog Years*], translated by Ralph Manheim, New York: Pantheon, 1987

Further Reading

Head, David, "Volker Schlöndorff's *Die Blechtrommel* and the *Literaturverfilmung* Debate," *German Life and Letters* 38 (1982–83)

Krumme, Detlef, *Günter Grass: "Die Blechtrommel,"* Munich: Hanser, 1986

McElroy, Bernard, "Lunatic, Child, Artist, Hero: Grass's Oskar as a Way of Seeing," *Forum for Modern Language Studies* 22 (1986)

Neuhaus, Volker, *Günter Grass: "Die Blechtrommel": Interpretation,* Munich: Oldenbourg, 1982

Thomas, Noel L., *Grass: "Die Blechtrommel,"* London: Grant and Cutler, 1985

Catharina Regina von Greiffenberg 1633–1694

Catharina Regina von Greiffenberg is known as the greatest woman poet of the German Baroque period. During her lifetime, her reputation was guaranteed by the high level of respect accorded to her by her literary contemporaries. As Sigmund von Birken, her mentor, wrote about the woman he called the "Teutsche Uranie" (German Urania) in a 1666 letter to Caspar von Lilien: "This woman is indeed a wonder of our time . . . her memory, filled with well-read knowledge and accompanied by the most mature powers of judgment, makes her highly eloquent. Her power of reason sees to the depth and the heart of all circumstances at the same time" (Spahr).

For her contemporaries, Catharina embodied the Baroque principle of dichotomy: she was admired both as a woman and as a poet for her erudition and reason as well as for her spiritual piety. While Catharina is best known today for her poetry, she achieved significant recognition in her own lifetime through her eight volumes of *Andachtsbücher* (Books of Meditation). In style, her meditative poems and songs are excellent examples of the expressive language and intensification of poetic imagery characteristic of the Nuremberg poets with whom she was allied. Typical of the high Baroque is her preference for artistic sonnets, alexandrines, involved syntax, and, particularly, her pleasure in composite nouns such as "Herzgrundrotes Meer" (a sea as red as the depths of the heart) and "Himmels-Herzheit" (Heart of Heaven). The musicality of her language is striking: "Jauchzet / Bäume / Vögel singet! danzet / Blumen / Felder lacht!" (Rejoice, trees / Sing, birds! Dance, flowers / Laugh, fields!) But her poetic voice is unique for the period because of its personal immediacy and emotional intensity; equally unusual is the frequent close identification between the poet and her subject. Her writings affirm the sacred aspect of the body. Catharina is a deeply sensual poet who celebrates the world as God's physical manifestation; the role of man, and especially of the poet, is to act as sensory organs to perceive the divine in nature through seeing, hearing, tasting, smelling, and feeling. Her religious convictions show a strong affinity to mysticism. Her *Andachtsbücher,* while belonging to a devotional genre popular in the 17th century, are exceptional for their highly individualized expressions of religious experience and for the absence of religious didacticism and orthodoxy.

Born in Castle Seisenegg near Amstetten in Lower Austria, Catharina came from a Lutheran family of recent nobility. The circumstances of her life as a devout Protestant in the midst of the Austrian Counter Reformation figure significantly in her writing. Following the death of her younger sister in 1651, she dedicated her life and work entirely to the glory of God. She received an excellent education in the spirit of the Renaissance, first from her mother and then from her uncle, Rudolph Freiherr von Greiffenberg, who became her guardian at her father's death in 1641.

In 1663, Catharina left Austria for Nuremberg because of the imminent threat of a Turkish invasion. While in exile in 1663–64, she wrote her heroic poem, *Sieges-Seule der Busse und Glaubens, wider den Erbfeind Christlichen Namens* (1675; Triumphal Column of Penance and Faith, Against the Archenemy of Christian Belief). This long and erudite work of over 7,000 alexandrines portrays the historic struggle of Christianity against Islam, which the poet views as the scourge sent by God to unite Christians in one last—Protestant—crusade under the House of Habsburg. Although she begins her poem with the admonition "Jungfrauen sollen schweigen" (women should remain silent), Catharina nevertheless considered her poetry as a weapon to be used against the Turks. In a strikingly modern sense of equality, the poet advocated the responsibility of women as well as men to engage in cultural, religious, and sociopolitical issues of the day. Her lifelong efforts to convert the Holy Roman Emperor to Protestantism, while destined to fail, are a good example of her personal commitment to action.

Viewing herself as a poet chosen by God to complete His work, she dedicated her life to meditation and writing. Shortly after her move to Nuremberg, however, her uncle Rudolph, 30 years older than Catharina, proposed marriage. Only when her uncle tried to obtain approval from the Catholic Church in exchange for a reconversion to Catholicism did she finally agree to the marriage. The couple was married in 1664 in Nuremberg through a special dispensation from the Protestant margrave of Brandenburg-Bayreuth. Her marriage to a blood relation was to be a source of embarrassment and legal difficulties for the poet throughout her life. When her husband died in 1676, a decade after the couple returned to Castle Seisenegg to live, Catharina lost most of her estate through the intrigues of family and creditors. In 1680 she returned to Nuremberg where she remained until her death in 1694.

Catharina was active in the literary life of the day; her home became a meeting place for intellectuals in Germany and Austria. In Austria she was part of a pastoral circle of noblemen and noblewomen, the *Ister-Nymphen-Gesellschaft* (Ister Society of Nymphs). There she met her future mentor, Johann Wilhelm von Stubenberg. He brought her poetry to the attention of the Nuremberg poet Sigmund von Birken, who invited her to join the important literary circle the *Pegnesischer Blumenorden* (Pegnitz Order of Flowers). Birken, who became a close personal friend, wrote the 20-page introduction to her cycle of 250 sonnets and 52 songs, *Geistliche Sonette, Lieder, und Gedichte* (Spiritual Sonnets, Songs, and Poems), and saw to its publication in Nuremberg in 1662. Birken also arranged the contact between Catharina and Duke Anton Ulrich von Braunschweig, who dedicated volume V of his novel *Aramena* to her. Catharina was also the first female member of Phillip von Zesen's Nuremberg *Deutschgesinnte Genossenschaft* (German Patriotic Society).

Details of Catharina's life emerge from the collection of 250 letters and other archival material in the Germanic Museum in Nuremberg, re-cataloged by Blake Lee Spahr in 1960. There has been a revival of interest in her life and works, particularly since the 300th anniversary of her death in 1994. Recent feminist studies affirm her importance not only for literary history but also for the tradition of women's religious discourse.

MARILYN SCOTT LINTON

Biography

Born at Castle Seisenegg, near Amstetten, in Lower Austria, 7 September 1633. Lived in Nuremberg, 1663–65; returned to Austria, 1665–80; back in Nuremberg, 1680–94, where she became an active participant in literary and intellectual life. Died in Nuremberg, 8 April 1694.

Selected Works

Collections

Sämtliche Werke, edited by Martin Bircher and Friedhelm Kemp, 10 vols., 1983

Writings

Geistliche Sonette, Lieder, und Gedichte, 1662

Des allerheiligst- und allerheilsamsten Leidens und Sterbens Jesu Christi: Zwölf andächtige Betrachtungen, 1672

Sieges-Seule der Buße und Glaubens, wider den Erbfeind Christlichen Namens, 1675

Der allerheiligsten Menschwerdung, Geburt, und Jugend Jesu Christi: Zwölf Andächtige Betrachtungen, 1678

Der allerheiligsten Lebens Jesu Christi: Sechs Andächtige Betrachtungen von dessen Lehren und Wunderwercken, 1693

Des allerheiligsten Lebens Jesu Christi: Ubrige Sechs Betrachtungen von dessen heiligem Wandel, Wundern, und Weissagungen, von- und biß zu seinem allerheiligsten Leiden und Sterben: Denen auch eine Andacht vom Heiligen Abendmahl hinzugefügt, 1693

Further Reading

Becker-Cantarino, Barbara, *Der lange Weg zur Mündigkeit: Frau und Literatur (1500–1800),* Stuttgart: Metzler, 1987

———, "Frauen in den Glaubenskämpfen: Öffentliche Briefe, Lieder und Gelegenheitsschriften," in *Deutsche Literatur von Frauen,* 2 vols., edited by Gisela Brinker-Gabler, Munich: Beck, 1988

Browning, Robert Marcellus, *German Baroque Poetry, 1618–1723,* University Park: Pennsylvania State University Press, 1971

Cerny, Heimo, *Catharina Regina von Greiffenberg, geb. Freiherrin von Seisenegg (1633–1694): Herkunft, Leben und Werk der größten deutschen Barockdichterin,* Amstetten: Stadtgemeinde Amstetten, 1983

———, "Neues zur Biographie der Catharina Regina von Greiffenberg," in *Literatur in Bayern* 38 (December 1994)

Daly, Peter M., *Dichtung und Emblematik bei Catharina Regina von Greiffenberg,* Bonn: Bouvier, 1976

———, "Catharina Regina von Greiffenberg," in *Deutsche Dichter des 17. Jahrhunderts: Ihr Leben und Werk,* edited by Harald Steinhagen and Benno von Wiese, Berlin: Erich Schmidt, 1984

Foley-Beining, Kathleen, *The Body and Eucharistic Devotion in Catharina Regina von Greiffenberg's "Meditations,"* Columbia, South Carolina: Camden House, 1997

Frank, Horst-Joachim, *Catharina Regina von Greiffenberg: Leben und Welt der barocken Dichterin,* Göttingen: Sachse und Pohl, 1967

Gnädinger, Louise, "Ister-Clio, Teutsche Uranie, Coris die Tapfere. Catharina Regina von Greiffenberg (1633-1694). Ein Portrait," in *Deutsche Literatur von Frauen,* 2 vols., edited by Gisela Brinker-Gabler, Munich: Beck, 1988

Kimmich, Flora, *Sonnets of Catharina von Greiffenberg: Methods of Composition,* Chapel Hill: University of North Carolina Press, 1975

Mehl, Jane M., "Catharina Regina von Greiffenberg: Modern Traits in a Baroque Poet," in *South Atlantic Bulletin* 45 (1980)

Spahr, Blake Lee, *The Archives of the Pegnesischer Blumenorden,* Berkeley: University of California Press, 1960

Franz Grillparzer 1791–1872

Critics of the most divergent schools and ideologies—conservative, nationalist (even National Socialist), liberal, socialist, and feminist—have paid homage to Franz Grillparzer, the most important 19th-century Austrian dramatist, in various attempts to appropriate his name for their causes. Indeed, Grillparzer and his work dramas, narrative prose, notebooks, diaries, and lyric poetry present readers with paradoxes and puzzles and prompt biased readings. Officially retired from his career as a dramatist at Vienna's court theater after the terrible failure of his comedy *Weh dem, der lügt!* (1840; *Thou Shalt Not Lie*) in 1838, Grillparzer remained until his death the most celebrated Viennese poet of his time.

Troubled by the ambivalence he ascribed to Grillparzer, the man and his work, Hans Weigel in *Flucht vor der Grösse* questioned the quality of Grillparzer's work. Weigel interprets Grillparzer's openness as a lack of rigor and decisiveness and doubts that he deserved his inordinate fame given his shortcomings as a poet. Comparing Grillparzer's language to Adalbert Stifter's disciplined, carefully chiseled prose, Weigel claims that Grillparzer lacked those foremost Austrian qualities, formal perfection and subtlety. Yet, precisely because of its stylistic inconsistencies and unevenness, Grillparzer's oeuvre expresses the tensions and contradictions of the Habsburg monarchy that was in the process of establishing itself separate from Northern Germany and was in search of a national discourse. With a remarkable attentiveness to detail, which reflects his legal background and intimate knowledge of state affairs, Grillparzer's works suggest the turmoil of his era, which was overshadowed by the aftermath of the French Revolution, the Napoleonic occupation, and the Vienna Congress. Grillparzer was a key figure in shaping a new Austrian discourse that mirrored the period's fast-paced social and political developments and its simultaneous desire to hold on to tradition. During the despotic regime of Franz I, the Viennese sympathizers of the prerevolutionary *Vormärz,* among them Grillparzer, had to be more on guard than authors elsewhere. Under the watchful eye of Metternich's secret police, the rigid censorship laws were strictly enforced. The unsuccessful revolution of 1848 and the days of civil war were followed by the reign of Franz Joseph and a court that favored the reactionary clergy and opposed the emancipation movements of the 19th century. The end of the Age of Grillparzer coincided with the foundation of the German Empire in 1871, which the poet viewed with extreme pessimism. The triumph of the German national paradigm ended his cosmopolitan dream of a multinational, unified Central and Eastern Europe. As he remarked, "The course of modern learning leads from humanism via nationalism to bestiality."

Grillparzer's basic concerns and issues, his internal geography and reference points, are distinct from those of his German contemporaries, conservatives or liberals. Rather than national, Grillparzer's sense of identity is regional: his home is the "land around the Kahlenberg" (the highest mountain in Vienna), and his focus is the individual. To authors such as Heinrich von Kleist, Clemens Brentano, and Gustav Freytag, the concept of German nationhood is foremost, and they combine this notion in the later part of the century with visions of Germany as a colonial, military, and industrial power: hence, their emphasis on national traits and cultural coherence. Grillparzer, by contrast, followed the Enlightenment legacy of Joseph II and was suspicious of the collectivist ideals of the postrevolutionary era. Early in his career, he had joined the popular anti-French sentiment and expressed intense dislike of Napoléon, but he came to resent German nationalism and the xenophobia it promoted, and he despised the soldier-like ethos set forth by Clausewitz and Fichte. In *König Ottokars Glück und Ende* (1825; *King Ottokar, His Rise and Fall*), the defeated king denounces war and the toll that it takes on the individual human being. Moreover, Grillparzer had nothing but contempt for the Romantics' sentimentalized vision of the *Volk,* the common people, and frequently satirized this concept in works such as *Thou Shalt Not Lie.* He dismissed also the Romantics' predilection for Roman Catholicism, which he considered a repressive force that was unsuited to function as a universal myth through which the fragmented post-Enlightenment world could be synthesized. Most of all, however, Grillparzer rejected Hegel's philosophy of history and German Idealism, which cast Protestant Northern Europe as the cultural realm at the cutting edge, the only one possessing world historical significance. Statements in which Grillparzer characterized himself as a Catholic poet have to be understood in this context: they define a cultural position in opposition to German nationalism and Prussia's hegemonic ambitions.

German philosophers forged the German national discourse, but Austrian poets, first and foremost Grillparzer and Stifter, articulated an Austrian identity and shaped an Austrian literary language. The abdication of the last emperor of the Holy Roman Empire of German Nation had made the Habsburg Austrian project a necessity. Grillparzer's vision of a multi-nation state, in which Germans, Austrians, Hungarians, Italians, Czechs, and Poles could exist side by side united by the ruling dynasty, was so powerful that Austrians invoked it again and again in times of crisis, as Claudio Magris describes in *Der habsburgische Mythos in der österreichischen Literatur.* Despite his relentless criticism of particular rulers and governments, Grillparzer expressed a strong allegiance toward the multination state and its capital. Nowhere are these feelings more obvious than in his memoir of the revolution and in a controversial poem in which he condemns the uprising of 1848 and celebrates the subjugation of the rioters by Field Marshall Radetzky's army. At the same time, his works convey a strong distaste for a social order that sanctions aristocratic privileges and absolutism. The condemnation of tyranny in the public as well as the private sphere is obvious in *Ein treuer Diener seines Herrn* (1830; *A Faithful Servant to His Master*). The posthumously produced drama *Libussa* (1874; published 1872) provides an excellent representation of Grillparzer's position. Expressing unequivocal admiration for personal freedom, equality, and justice for all under the leadership of a caring, enlightened ruler, the work also shows the limitations of a system that relies on a rational, mature, and tolerant majority. Driven by greed and resentment, those whose former privileges are diminished, the men and the rich, call for a strong authoritarian leader. *Libussa* summarizes in a nutshell the fundamental dynamics of Austrian history since Joseph II.

Beginning with his somewhat atypical Gothic drama *Die Ahnfrau* (1817; *The Ancestress*), and the novella *Das Kloster bei Sendomir* (1828; The Monastery Near Sendomir), cultural diversity is an important element in Grillparzer's writing. For the most part, his works deal with conflicts that involve gender and gender roles, class, and cultural difference, regardless whether the respective piece is set in Central Europe, as in *King Ottokar, His Rise and Fall,* in classical antiquity, as in the trilogy *Das goldene Vlies* (1822; *The Golden Fleece*), or in ancient Germanic times, as in *Thou Shalt Not Lie.* Most of the interchanges between persons of different background end tragically. Nonetheless, at least initially most of characters show considerable willingness to experience diversity. They engage in intimate encounters with the Other, and they display an interest in being cosmopolitan and in opening themselves up to the unknown. Often Grillparzer inscribes the Other as feminine, as is the case in *The Golden Fleece* and *Die Jüdin von Toledo* (1872; *The Jewess of Toledo*), dramas that thematize the relationship between European men, members of conquering nations, and women. Because of their culture, their religion of origin, and their physical appearance—black hair and black eyes—these women are stigmatized by man's society and treated as pariahs while becoming disenfranchised from their native environment. The sensitivity with which Grillparzer constructs these women figures and the language he ascribes to them—German with an unmistakable Austrian tinge, in contrast to their opponents' proper High German—suggest an affinity on the poet's part for these figures. Through them, his dissatisfaction with the dominant culture and the prevailing social conditions is revealed.

Writers such as Grillparzer, especially dramatists, had to be careful when criticizing the moral code and the religious or political establishment. Grillparzer was particularly vulnerable since the less rigid regulations of the suburban theaters (*Vorstadttheater*), the domain of Ferdinand Raimund and Johann Nestroy, did not apply to the *Hofburgtheater* inside Vienna's city walls. Grillparzer did come in conflict with the office of censorship more than once. In order to get around the strict rules that forbade the representation of the clergy, illicit relationships between men and women, and contemporary politics on stage, Grillparzer resorted to historical and antique subjects and to a highly symbolic, allusive language. In *Libussa,* for example, the heroine's broken belt, her ruined veil, her scattered jewelry, and a change of clothes that apparently took place without her being aware of it, strongly suggest that a rape may have occurred, or, at least, that Libussa has lost her virginity. This suggestion also accounts for her ineligibility to retreat from worldly affairs, as do her two sisters.

The external constraints imposed on Austrian poets produced a seemingly apolitical body of literature devoted to private problems, a literature often referred to as Biedermeier. Upon closer inspection, however, it becomes obvious that the private concerns in Grillparzer's works, including his frequently debated prose work *Der arme Spielmann* (1847; *The Poor Fiddler*), his literary contribution to the year of the revolution, are thoroughly political. The private world of Jakob, the novella's protagonist, is the perfect expression of the stunted human development that is produced by an oppressive regime. Prevented by class barriers to find a fulfilling, simple occupation, Jakob fails as an artist, a lover, and a citizen. The resulting passive aggression, most glaringly expressed by his cacophonous music, causes him to disappoint not only the expectations of authority figures but also the hopes of a simple girl whom he loves and who wishes to marry him. Through Jakob, Grillparzer exposes the destructive effects of the kind of oppression he experienced as a poet, intellectual, and individual, and which he often deplored in his autobiographical texts. *The Poor Fiddler* characterizes not only his own predicament as an Austrian artist but that of his entire class, the bourgeoisie, which was deprived of its political rights. Similar to Jakob, Grillparzer never married—although he was engaged to his fiancée, Katharina Fröhlich, until he died—and he considered his poetic achievement flawed, as flawed as the music of his protagonist.

In Grillparzer's analysis of 19th-century power structures, the category of gender is foremost. Already *The Ancestress* and *Das Kloster bei Sendomir* examine the patriarchal double standard that prevents women from making their own life choices, notably, from choosing their partner. The ghost of the woman murdered by her jealous husband, which appears whenever disaster is about to strike again, is more than a Gothic stock character. Indeed, the curse afflicting the House of Borotin symbolizes the socially sanctioned violence that continues to breed more violence. Peace and justice are impossible to achieve when half of the population are oppressed because of their sex. In his later works, Grillparzer undermines gender stereotypes by exposing the discrepancy between biological sex and socially constructed gender roles. Many of his female characters, including Erny in *A Faithful Servant to His Master* and Barbara in *The Poor Fiddler,* display a boldness and determination traditionally cast as masculine, while their male partners appear feminine. Most important, contrary to most dramatists of his time (e.g., Friedrich Hebbel), Grillparzer fails to validate the qualities associated with manliness. Aging and defeated, King Ottokar recognizes his limitations as a man and a human being. At that point, he begins to understand and value the type of pacifist caring ethic that makes Grillparzer's matriarchal queen Libussa so admirable and so vulnerable. Similarly, one of his most complex figures, Emperor Rudolf in *Ein Bruderzwist in Habsburg* (1872; *Family Strife in Hapsburg*), a withdrawn mystic and intellectual, may not be superior to his brother Matthias as a politician and military leader, but despite his flaws, he does come across as the better monarch and the better man.

Grillparzer's approach to theater differs from that of dramatists such as Hebbel, who use the stage to a didactic end, to convey their social or historical theories, or, in Hebbel's case, Hegel's dialectic. Grillparzer's dramatic figures and conflicts are complex, calling to mind Shakespeare rather than classical French drama. Grillparzer, as Gerhard Scheit points out, stands in the tradition of Austrian opera and the popular drama. He mixes the elements and devices of high culture and popular literature, and the moods in his plays change fast. The dimensions of Grillparzer's historical drama are epic, but all of his works aim at creating a balance between entertainment and instruction, the Horatian *prodesse et delectari.* Thus, they engage the viewers and appeal to their critical faculties. Grillparzer does not present conventional villains, heroes, saintlike role models, or scapegoats. All of his characters possess positive and negative qualities so that they must be assessed within the larger context of the drama. Overall, Grillparzer's works raise problems, ask questions, and point toward solutions; nowhere do they present easy answers to complex problems. The significance of actions or a character tends to be revealed *ex negativo,* in processes that propose more, or less, desirable scenarios. A similarly experimental proclivity is also present in Grillparzer's use of language. His style lacks the certainty and clarity of the classical period, a result of Grillparzer's attempt to come to terms with the tensions of early modernity and the major cause of the multifaceted character of his oeuvre, an oeuvre of rare integrity that is a brilliant document of an era.

DAGMAR C.G. LORENZ

See also Biedermeier Period

Biography

Born in Vienna, Austria, 15 January 1791. Law student at the University of Vienna, 1807–11; tutored the nephew of Count von Seilern in law, 1812; volunteer assistant in a court library, 1813; civil servant, from 1814; appointed Theaterdichter in Vienna, 1818; in Italy, 1819, and Germany, 1826; director of court archives, 1832; retired, 1856; member of the upper house of the Austrian parliament, 1861; founder of the Austrian Academy of Sciences, 1847; honorary doctorate, University of Leipzig, 1859. Died 21 January 1872.

Selected Works

Collections

Sämtliche Werke: Historisch-kritische Gesamtausgabe, edited by August Sauer and Reinhold Backmann, 42 vols., 1909–48

Sämtliche Werke: Ausgewählte Briefe, Gespräche, Berichte, edited by Peter Frank and Karl Pörnbacher, 4 vols., 1960–65

Werke, edited by Helmut Bachmaier, 1986–

Plays

Die Ahnfrau (produced 1817), 1817; as *The Ancestress,* translated by Herman L. Spahr, 1938

Sappho (produced 1818), 1819; translated by J. Bramsen, 1820; translated by E.B. Lee, 1846; translated by Lucy C. Cumming, 1855; translated by E. Frothingham, 1876; translated by Arthur Burkhard, 1953

Das goldene Vlies (trilogy) (produced 1821), 1822; vol. 3 as *Medea,* translated by F.W. Thurstan and S.A. Wittmann, 1879; translated byArthur Burkhard, 1941; trilogy as *The Golden Fleece,* translated by Burkhard, 3 vols., 1942

König Ottokars Glück und Ende (produced 1825), 1825; as *Ottokar,* translated by Thomas Carlyle, 1840; as *King Ottokar, His Rise and Fall,* translated by G. Pollack, 1907; translated by Arthur Burkhard, 1932; translated by Henry H. Stevens, 1938

Ein treuer Diener seines Herrn (produced 1828), 1830; as *A Faithful Servant to His Master,* translated by Arthur Burkhard, 1941

Des Meeres und der Liebe Wellen (produced 1831), 1839; edited by E.E. Pabst, 1967; edited by Mark Ward, 1981; as *Hero and Leander,* translated by Henry H. Stevens, 1938; translated by Arthur Burkhard, 1962; as *The Waves of Sea and Love,* translated by Samuel Solomon, in *Plays on Classic Themes,* 1969

Melusina, music by Konradin Kreutzer (produced 1833), 1833

Der Traum ein Leben (produced 1834), 1840; edited by W.E. Yuill, 1955; as *A Dream Is Life,* translated by Henry H. Stevens, 1947

Weh dem, der lügt! (produced 1838), 1840; as *Thou Shalt Not Lie,* translated by Henry H. Stevens, 1939

Esther (produced 1868), in *Sämmtliche Werke,* 1872; translated by Arthur Burkhard, with *The Jewess of Toledo,* 1953

Ein Bruderzwist in Habsburg (produced 1872), in *Sämmtliche Werke,* 1872; edited by Bruce Thompson, 1982; as *Family Strife in Hapsburg,* translated by Arthur Burkhard, 1940

Die Jüdin von Toledo (produced 1872), in *Sämmtliche Werke,* 1872; as *The Jewess of Toledo,* translated by George Henry Danton and Annina Periam Danton, in *German Classics of the Nineteenth and Twentieth Centuries,* edited by Kuno Francke, vol. 6, 1914; translated by Arthur Burkhard, with *Esther,* 1953

Libussa (produced 1874), in *Sämmtliche Werke,* 1872; translated by Henry H. Stevens, 1941

Fiction

Das Kloster bei Sendomir, in *Aglaja,* 1828

Der arme Spielmann, in *Iris,* 1847; as *The Poor Musician,* translated by A. Remy, 1914; translated by J.F. Hargreaves and J.G. Cumming, in

German Narrative Prose, edited by E.J. Engel, 1965; as *The Poor Fiddler,* translated by Alexander and Elizabeth Henderson, 1969

Poetry
Tristia ex Ponto, in *Vesta,* 1827
Gedichte, edited by P. von Matt, 1970

Other
Selbstbiographie, 1872
Erinnerungen an das Revolutionsjahr 1848, in *Sämtliche Werke,* 1887
Gespräche und Charakteristiken seiner Persönlichkeit durch die Zeitgenossen, edited by August Sauer, 6 vols., 1904–16; supplementary volume, edited by Reinhold Backmann, 1941
Tagebücher und Reiseberichte, edited by Klaus Geissler, 1981

Further Reading

Bachmaier, Helmut, editor, *Franz Grillparzer,* Frankfurt: Suhrkamp, 1991
Bernd, Clifford A., editor, *Grillparzer's "Der Arme Spielmann": New Directions in Criticism,* Columbia, South Carolina: Camden House, 1988
Coenen, Frederic Edward, *Franz Grillparzer's Portraiture of Men,* Chapel Hill: University of North Carolina Press, 1951
Denscher, Bernhard, and Walter Obermaier, editors, *Grillparzer; oder, Die Wirklichkeit der Wirklichkeit,* Vienna: Historisches Museum der Stadt Wien, 1991
Fink, Humbert, *Franz Grillparzer,* Innsbruck: Pinguin, 1990
Hagl-Catling, Karin, *Für eine Imagologie der Geschlechter: Franz Grillparzers Frauenbild im Widerspruch,* Frankfurt and New York: Lang, 1997
Klettenhammer, Sieglinde, editor, *Zwischen Weimar und Wien: Grillparzer, ein Innsbrucker Symposion,* Innsbruck: Institut für Germanistik, 1992
Lorenz, Dagmar C.G., *Grillparzer, Dichter des sozialen Konflikts,* Vienna: Böhlau, 1986
Magris, Claudio, *Der habsburgische Mythos in der österreichischen Literatur,* Salzburg: Müller, 1966
Modern Austrian Literature 28, no. 3/4, special Franz Grillparzer issue (1995)
Politzer, Heinrich, *Franz Grillparzer; oder, Das abgründige Biedermeier,* Vienna, Munich, and Zurich: Molden, 1972
Scheit, Gerhard, *Franz Grillparzer,* Reinbek bei Hamburg: Rowohlt, 1989
Thompson, Bruce, *Franz Grillparzer,* Boston: Twayne, 1981
Wagner, Eva, *An Analysis of Franz Grillparzer's Dramas: Fate, Guilt, and Tragedy,* Lewiston, New York: Mellen Press, 1992
Weigel, Hans, *Flucht vor der Grösse,* Vienna: Wollzeilen Verlag, 1960; as *Flight from Greatness,* translated by Lowell A. Bangerter, Riverside, California: Ariadne Press, 1998
Wells, George Albert, *The Plays of Grillparzer,* London and New York: Pergamon Press, 1969
Yates, W.E., *Grillparzer: A Critical Introduction,* London and Cambridge: Cambridge University Press, 1972

Der arme Spielmann 1847

Novella by Franz Grillparzer

Franz Grillparzer has long been considered the leading Austrian dramatist of the 19th century, but *Der arme Spielmann* (*The Poor Musician*) is his only work of prose whose reputation has matched that of his plays. Initially neglected by critics and still occasionally omitted from general studies of his work, *The Poor Musician* has in recent years been the object of detailed scrutiny and many conflicting interpretations.

On the surface, the story told is a simple one. While visiting a famous fair in the Viennese suburb of Brigittenau, the narrator becomes fascinated by a musician who cannot play a recognizable tune but reveals traces of a good education. When the narrator seeks out the musician in his humble home, he hears Jakob's story of a well-to-do upbringing but increasing hardship and failure, not least the loss of his inheritance to an unscrupulous secretary. In turn, this loss puts an end to the somewhat tentative relationship that he has formed with the daughter of a neighboring shopkeeper. In the midst of these disappointments, Jakob's one source of solace is his music. After a number of years, the narrator returns to discover that Jakob has died in the floodwaters that inundated the Leopoldstadt district.

Critical attention was initially focused on Jakob, and it is the character of the musician that has prompted the greatest range of conflicting interpretations. On the one hand, he has been viewed as the "absolutely pure soul" (by the writer Gottfried Keller in 1871), as the "disembodied good will" (Stern), and as a saint or martyr. Jakob is undoubtedly a man of noble qualities and moral integrity, as revealed in his honesty and simple piety, his refusal to see anything but goodness in relatives and acquaintances, and his selfless desire to help others. Critics who emphasize such characteristics in Jakob have argued that his failures are irrelevant or the inevitable result of his saintliness remaining unappreciated by others; as John M. Ellis concludes, "we should all choose to lean in the Spielmann's direction." However, opposing views have been stated with increasing frequency since Benno von Wiese's (1956) depiction of Jakob as a distorted, even grotesque figure of failure and incompetence, and the musician has been seen as excessively naive, impractical, and impossibly unrealistic in trusting those who do not deserve such trust. He appears totally isolated from the everyday social reality represented by the crowds at the fair, and his pedantic desire for order causes him to overlook the underlying logicalities of existence or is ignored by others, as symbolized most poignantly in the chalk line dividing his half of the room from that inhabited by two young apprentices. His general inability to distinguish between the important and the unimportant also leads to his death: at the height of the floods, he first saves children from drowning but then catches a chill by going back into the water to rescue documents and a small amount of money.

At the heart of the ambiguity of Jakob's character is his moral approach to music. He seeks to play only the good notes, to avoid all discord, and even (as he says) to play the good Lord. He intends his music to have an ennobling effect, and he leaves the festival before sunset lest his music encourage dancing or unruly revelry. As a result, his music might be thought to represent a purity that sinful mortals cannot understand and as such underlining his qualities as a saint or martyr. At the other extreme, Jakob's music has been variously described as a parable of the biblical fall (Politzer) and as a sign of selfishness, solipsism, or sublimated sexuality. Undoubtedly, his music mirrors his failure to grasp ordinary reality: he goes home at the time when his performance might start to earn money, but this in turn is unlikely because his music, based on complex musical theories that he has only half understood, results not in goodness and purity but in what the narrator describes as a "hellish concert," a cacophony that is a torture for all who hear it.

However, whether the narrator is qualified to assess the musician has often been debated. In the long opening section, we meet a self-styled successful dramatist and keen observer of humanity who describes the festival as an occasion when the usual divisions and hierarchies in society are overcome. Yet his ideas are presented in an elaborate, self-conscious, and occasionally pompous language that might make one question his philanthropic credentials, and his interest in society and equality is quickly deflected by his new fascination with Jakob. A number of similarities exist between two such apparently different characters, but the narrator is reluctant to admit this affinity and instead hides behind ironic condescension and the would-be objectivity of the sociologist. It has been argued that his depiction of Jakob is distorted and unreliable, even that he is a complete impostor (Ellis); to others he appears benevolent and understanding, preventing the musician's story from being too ridiculous or sentimental.

Surprisingly little attention has been paid to questions of genre, although *The Poor Musician* has frequently been included in studies of the German *Novelle.* Almost all the many investigations of the narrative technique ultimately return to the ambiguities and psychological complexities in both narrator and musician that might be seen to constitute the principal excellence of the work. The affinity between the two main characters derives in part from the autobiographical features in both, and, with its suggestion that noble intentions might be a cause of artistic and personal failure, *The Poor Musician* undoubtedly provides echoes of the sense of failure that is often expressed in Grillparzer's diaries. With its depiction of the gulf between ideals and practical reality, the story also sheds an interesting light on many characters in Grillparzer's plays: the eponymous Libussa, Rudolf II in *Ein Bruderzwist in Habsburg,* and Bishop Gregor in the comedy *Weh dem, der lügt! The Poor Musician* influenced writers such as Stifter, whose *Kalkstein* was originally titled *Der arme Wohltäter,* Storm (*Der stille Musikant*), and Kafka, who was fascinated by the story. Even in 1988, the adjective in the label "neglected masterpiece" (Roy C. Cowen in Bernd) was perhaps already an exaggeration, and its vital place among Grillparzer's most significant works has now been fully acknowledged.

Ian F. Roe

Editions

First edition: *Der arme Spielmann,* published in the magazine *Iris: Deutscher Almanach für 1848* (1847)
Critical editions: in *Sämtliche Werke: Historisch-kritische Gesamtausgabe,* edited by August Sauer and Reinhold Backmann, vol. 1/13, Vienna: Schroll, 1930; in *Sämtliche Werke: Ausgewählte Briefe, Gespräche, Berichte,* edited by Peter Frank and Karl Pörnbacher, vol. 3, Munich: Hanser, 1964
Translation: *The Poor Musician,* translated by J.F. Hargreaves and J.G. Cumming, in *German Narrative Prose,* edited by E.J. Engel, London: Wolff, 1965

Further Reading

Bernd, Clifford Albrecht, editor, *Grillparzer's "Der arme Spielmann": New Directions in Criticism,* Columbia, South Carolina: Camden House, 1988
Ellis, John M., "Grillparzer's *Der arme Spielmann,*" *German Quarterly* 45 (1972)
Politzer, Heinrich, *Franz Grillparzers "Der arme Spielmann,"* Stuttgart: Metzler, 1967
Roe, Ian F., *An Introduction to the Major Works of Franz Grillparzer,* Lewiston, New York and Lampeter: Mellen, 1991
Stern, J.P., "Beyond the Common Indication: Grillparzer," in *Re-Interpretations: Seven Studies in Nineteenth Century Literature,* London: Thames and Hudson, 1964
Swales, Martin, *The German Novelle,* Princeton, New Jersey: Princeton University Press, 1977
Wiese, Benno von, "Grillparzer: *Der arme Spielmann,*" in *Die deutsche Novelle von Goethe bis Kafka,* Düsseldorf: Bagel, 1956

Die Jüdin von Toledo 1872

Play by Franz Grillparzer

Die Jüdin von Toledo (*The Jewess of Toledo*) by Franz Grillparzer was published posthumously, as were *Libussa* (1872) and *Ein Bruderzwist in Habsburg* (1872; *Family Strife in Hapsburg*). *The Jewess of Toledo*, based on Lope de Vega's (1562–1635) comedy *Las paces de los reyes y Judía de Toledo* (The Peace of the Kings; or, The Jewess of Toledo), is set in 12th-century Spain. The topic of Lope's play is an illicit love affair between the Spanish king Alfonso VIII and a beautiful Jewish woman, which ends in the latter's death and the reconciliation of the royal couple. Without deviating from the plot line, Grillparzer changed the trajectory by designating his play a *Trauerspiel* with the title figure, the Jewess Rahel—brutally murdered at the end of act III by the queen's co-conspirators—as the heroine. Early readers of Grillparzer balked at ascribing tragic stature to a post-biblical Jewish woman who neither embodies the conventional female virtues nor the heroic traits of the classical virgin heroine. In keeping with the misogynist and anti-Semitic discourses of their times, Friedrich Gundolf and Johannes Volkelt, following the reading proposed by Grillparzer's contemporary and director of the Vienna Hofburgtheater, Heinrich Laube, interpreted the king's paramour as a sensual creature lacking grandeur and moral significance. According to them, she was a catalyst that the play employs to trace the king's psychological and intellectual growth. Indeed, if read as a play about gender and gender relationships or the way in which love and romance contribute to the maturation process of a young man, *The Jewess of Toledo* would appear profoundly flawed. Yet later critics such as Heinz Politzer used a psychoanalytical approach to validated their interpretation of the play, thereby overlooking Grillparzer's anticlerical and social-critical intent.

The Jewess of Toledo revolves around the issues of power and marginalization as they relate to status, position, gender, and culture. The play reveals basic injustices and inequities that were deeply embedded in 19th-century Austrian society and the larger Christian European culture. The difficulties arising from the character of Rahel made critics wonder whether Grillparzer's drama was a tragedy at all; some of them tried to establish a character other than Rahel as the tragic hero. Joachim Kaiser opted for King Alfonso, disregarding the fact that the king does survive the dramatic crisis by allowing himself to be co-opted by the murderers and, when he is partially restored to his former authority, leads a jubilant army into the war against the Muslims. The notion that Queen Eleonore might be the tragic heroine was introduced as well.

Harold Lenz was the first to take Grillparzer's subversive dramatic strategies fully into account by focusing on the wider ramifications of a Christian ruler's transgression against the established code of conduct. Alfonso becomes involved with a Jewish woman, a social and religious pariah from the Spanish point of view, who spurns Christian morality and gender roles by acting on her sexual desires and social ambitions. Yet, in her last words on stage, as her murderers are setting out to kill her and she has nothing left to lose, she does declare her love for the king: "Und hab ihn, Schwester, wahrhaft doch geliebt" ("And, Sister, I did truly love him"). Grillparzer's favorable representation of the sincere, rebellious, and beautiful Jewess coincides with his positive remarks about the dancer Lola Montez, née Eliza Gilbert, the mistress of Ludwig I of Bavaria. The affair, a major factor in Ludwig's abdication in 1848, is one of Grillparzer's reference points and must be taken into consideration when examining the significance of rank, culture, gender, and ethnicity in *The Jewess of Toledo.*

The poet's own diary and notes reveal critical attitudes that are restated in the play as well. The encounter between a wealthy Jewish child-woman and an immature king who grew up without a mother among soldiers and married a prudish English princess is the point of departure for political commentary. The major political debates of Grillparzer's era were the emancipation of the Jews, women, the middle class, and the proletariat. A Josephinian, Grillparzer was critical of the suppression of the liberal forces by the Habsburg court and apprehensive of German nationalism. In *The Jewess of Toledo,* he focuses on the rights of the individual regardless of his or her group identity, and he places Rahel, a Jew and a woman, into the center of his tragedy.

Rahel acts in accordance with the ideals of the French Revolution, denouncing the double standard for men and women, challenging anti-Semitic regulations, and transgressing against social barriers. She is forceful and, at the same time, childlike and naive, trusting that a determined individual such as herself will prevail. Physically enticed by her, the king indulges her. He is confident that he will keep the upper hand both with her and his subjects. It is obvious to the viewer and to Rahel that he considers his mistress a mere toy. Thus, it comes as a shock to him that because of his affair he is excluded from his community, his family, the Spanish court, and Christianity; that his authority is diminished; and that Rahel is accused of being a witch and seductress and finds herself in mortal danger. Finally, despite his first impulse to avenge his murdered mistress, the king ends up agreeing with the conspirators, who dispute Rahel's merits as a woman and a human being.

Contrary to the majority of his contemporaries, Grillparzer refrains from drawing unambiguous characters, good or evil. He attributes to his Jewish and Christian *dramatis personae* convincing characteristics and motives. The queen, for example, lacks sexual experience, which only increases her spite and jealousy; furthermore, she also has very real family concerns and ambitions. In the case of Rahel's father, Isaac, a life of oppression, poverty, and social marginalization motivates greed; in the case of Garceran, the king's friend, a love of adventure and pleasure engenders recklessness; and in the case of Esther, Rahel's sister, it is hinted that her modesty and prudence are the results of being the older, less wealthy, and less attractive sister. An analysis of the many personalities in Grillparzer's dramatic universe leads to the conclusion that Rahel, despite her obvious shortcomings, is the most humane and genuine character of the play. It is tragic, indeed, that along with her the principles for which she stands—the love of life and spiritual and physical freedom—are destroyed and that the Spaniard's warlike ethos, the hatred of the other, and the precepts of patriarchy emerge triumphant.

DAGMAR C.G. LORENZ

Editions

First edition: *Die Jüdin von Toledo: Historisches Trauerspiel in fünf Aufzügen,* Stuttgart: Cotta, 1872

Critical edition: in *Sämtliche Werke,* edited by August Sauer and Reinhold Backmann, Vienna: Schroll, 1924

Translations: *The Jewess of Toledo,* translated by George Henry Danton and Annina Periam Danton, in *German Classics of the Nineteenth and Twentieth Centuries,* edited by Kuno Francke, vol. 6, New York: German Publication Society, 1914; *The Jewess of Toledo: Historical Tragedy in Five Acts,* translated by Arthur Burkhard, Yarmouth Port, Massachusetts: Register Press, 1953

Further Reading

Geissler, Rolf, *Ein Dichter der letzten Dinge: Grillparzer heute: Subjektivismuskritik im dramatischen Werk, mit einem Anhang über die Struktur seines politischen Denkens,* Vienna: Braumüller, 1987

Hagl-Catling, Karin, *Für eine Imagologie der Geschlechter: Franz Grillparzers Frauenbild im Widerspruch,* Frankfurt and New York: Lang, 1997

Kind, Frank, "Was sie verunziert es ist unser Werk: Frank Grillparzer und das Judentum: Biographische, werk- und rezeptionsgeschichtliche Aspekt," Ph.D. dissertation, Frankfurt: 1993

Lenz, Harold F.H., *Franz Grillparzer's Political Ideas and Die Jüdin von Toledo,* New York: published privately, 1938

Lindsey, Barbara, "The Wasteland Revisited: Death of the Garden in Grillparzer's *Die Jüdin von Toledo,*" *Modern Austrian Literature* 28, no.3/4 (1995)

Lorenz, Dagmar C.G., "'Schafe im Wolfspelz' oder die Bösewichte, die keine waren: Die Juden in Grillparzers *Die Jüdin von Toledo,*" *Jahrbuch der Grillparzer-Gesellschaft,* 3rd series, vol. 15 (1983)

———, "Die schöne Jüdin in Stifters *Abdias* und Grillparzers *Die Jüdin von Toledo,*" *Jahrbuch der Grillparzer-Gesellschaft,* 3rd series, vol. 19 (1996)

McCrary, Susan Niehoff, *A Comparative Study of Lope de Vega's 'Las paces de los reyes y judia de Toledo' and Franz Grillparzer's 'Die Jüdin von Toledo,'* Norfolk, Virginia: Old Dominion University Research Foundation, 1988

Volkelt, Johannes, *Franz Grillparzer als Dichter des Tragischen,* Nördlingen: Beck, 1888

Wedel-Parlow, Ludolf von, *Die Jüdin von Toledo und Kaiser Karls Geisel eine stilvergleichende Betrachtung,* Heidelberg: Hahn, 1927

Wittkowski, Wolfgang, "Motiv und Strukturprinzip in Grillparzers Jüdin von Toledo," *Modern Austrian Literature* 28, no.3/4 (1995)

Jacob Grimm 1785–1863 and Wilhelm Grimm 1786–1859

Few names in German cultural history are as well known as those of the brothers Jacob Ludwig Carl and Wilhelm Carl Grimm. They were the two oldest sons of Philipp Wilhelm Grimm, a lawyer, and Dorothea (née) Zimmer, daughter of a city councilman in Kassel. Three of their children died, and five boys and one girl survived. Their father, who had by then become a district judge, died at the age of 44 in 1796, leaving his wife and children largely dependent on support from Dorothea's family. Jacob and Wilhelm were diligent students at the Lyzeum in Kassel, graduating at the head of their classes in 1802 and 1803, respectively.

Nevertheless, being of insufficiently high social standing, both needed special permission to study law at the University of Marburg, where one of their law professors was Friedrich Carl von Savigny. Jacob attended Savigny's lectures in the winter semester 1802–3 and remained one of his most diligent students. Savigny left Marburg in the summer of 1804 to pursue research at the Bibliothéque Nationale in Paris on the history of Roman law in the Middle Ages. It quickly became clear to Savigny that he needed an assistant, and he offered the opportunity to Jacob Grimm, who eagerly accepted. The friendship and collaboration with Savigny represented an essential stimulus for two reasons: Savigny's ideas on the historicity of law and the meticulous research habits that Jacob Grimm learned from Savigny. The notions that laws are formed for a particular time, place, and people; that they are not necessarily immutable and universal; and that studying their historical evolution would allow us to gain important insights into the habits and habits of mind of our ancestors underlie the impulse of the Grimms not only to collect folk materials but also to produce many of the first editions of Old High and Middle High German literature. Almost incidentally, they laid the foundation for what was to become the discipline of Germanic philology.

The legal background also led to Jacob's publication in 1828 of *Deutsche Rechtsalterthümer* (Ancient German Law). Searching for, copying (by hand), and cataloging medieval Latin law codices (the grunt work for Savigny's history of law) was transferred by Jacob Grimm in particular to other collecting activities that soon took a different direction from the legal work of their teacher. In a letter of 18 December 1807, after having turned down Savigny's offer to help him obtain a position at a library in Munich, Jacob wrote to Savigny about his and Wilhelm's contribution to the second and third volume of *Des Knaben Wunderhorn,* the first major collection of German folk poetry.

The Grimms had contributed to this important work because of their friendship with Savigny, the brother-in-law of Clemens Brentano, who in turn was a close collaborator and friend of Achim von Arnim. Brentano and Arnim had begun collecting folk poetry in June 1802 and published the first volume of *Des Knaben Wunderhorn* in 1805 (imprint 1806). The contributions of the Grimms were integrated into the second and third volumes of the collection in 1807. With the genre of the folk song covered well, it was to some extent a logical next endeavor to collect folktales.

When the plan to collect folktales started to take shape, the brothers were in their early 20s. Sketches from around 1812, the time of the first volume of the first edition of the *Kinder- und Hausmärchen* (in scholarly jargon known as *KHM;* 1215–15; many translations), show mustachioed, dashing young men. Savigny was a mere six or seven years older than the brothers. Collecting the folk materials was thus the idea and the project of young men and women. The impulse for collecting did not come from some sort of vague notion of the virtue of the unwashed and unlettered but, in addition to the scholarly example set by Savigny and the urging of Arnim and Brentano, against the background of the desperate political state of affairs of the German-speaking lands at the time.

Soon after French troops crossed the Rhine in 1792, the initial enthusiasm of Germans with hope for social progress and democratic aspirations, such as a written constitution, was dashed. The French did not bring with them *liberté, fraternité,* and *égalité.* To be sure, the *Code Napoléon* brought a measure of progress in civil law, but contemporary sources document amply the life of a conquered people. Beethoven's undoing his dedication to Napoléon of his "Eroica" symphony is only a banner signaling a widespread disillusionment with social progress imported at the tip of a bayonet.

From many comments that the Grimms made in letters and notes, it is clear that the frustration of being so thoroughly victimized is part of the motivation to study or preserve what they did possess, namely, a common culture that was articulated in poetry, philosophy, music, and painting. The beginning of the Grimms's work is at least contiguous with the desire for liberation from French occupation, not some sort of jingoistic nationalism. Kassel, the brothers' home, had become part the kingdom of Westphalia, with Jérôme Bonaparte, the brother of who was now the emperor, installed as king; Jacob's experience in Paris and especially his language skills helped him receive a post in the king's library in 1808.

Tale collecting involved circles of friends and neighbors; in the end there were over 80 "informants" or sources for the complete *KHM.* Nor did the collecting efforts stop with the first edition. While in Vienna in 1815 as secretary to the Hessian delegation to the Congress of Vienna, Jacob wrote, had printed, and began to send out a *Circular wegen Aufsammlung der Volkspoesie* (Open Letter concerning the Collecting of Folk Poetry), soliciting contributions of folk poetry, sagas, superstitions, proverbs, plays, and what would generally be described as the material of folk life: ceremonies at the occasions of birth, marriages, deaths, and so on. Of particular importance for the first edition of the *KHM* are the informants who were close to the Grimms's ideal of the tale tellers, virtually unlettered but equipped with intelligence and prodigious memory. Dorothea Viehmann was one of those. She was a peasant woman who came to Kassel regularly to sell produce, and after the Grimms heard about her tale-telling talent, they invited her to come and visit them in their apartment, and, on receiving a glass of wine and something to eat, she would reel off stories. Jacob and Wilhelm took turns writing down the stories as accurately as they could, and a few of their transcripts do exist. Thirty-five stories are traceable to *die Viehmännin.* The idea that the Grimms themselves traipsed through the countryside sitting at the feet of doughty peasant tale tellers is pure fiction.

What is true is that, between the first volume of the first edition of 1812 and the seventh edition of 1857, the collection grew from the initial 86 tales to 210. It is also true that many tales underwent changes, ranging from adding an occasional "Once upon a time" to lengthy additions and embellishments. And some tales were omitted in later editions. Of the copies available before Christmas 1812 in German bookstores, relatively few were sold. Initially a project for a fairly learned if not scholarly audience, it took a considerable time for the tales to gain popularity. In 1822, a volume of notes to the tales appeared, charting sources and analogs to the then 200 tales. To be sure, the attributions are sometimes misleading, creating the impression of collecting on-site when, for example, a tale is said to come "From Hessia" or some other region. Most likely, one of the more than 80 informants sent a written version to the Grimms. They (especially Wilhelm) edited, added, omitted, or standardized many tales. The changes from the earliest versions (especially the so-called *Ölenberg* manuscript) to the seventh edition make a fascinating subject of scholarship. The charge that they pursued a nationalistic or authoritarian agenda misreads the (Victorian) times or demonizes what is in reality the floundering beginning of the study of folklore. Furthermore, many of the important informants were of French Huguenot background, underlining the fact that the tales are part of a European tradition.

The tales caught on in England fairly quickly, after the first anonymous translation with illustrations by George Cruikshank appeared in London in 1823. By the time Walter Crane illustrated the *Household Stories from the Collection of the Brothers Grimm,* translated by Lucy Crane (1882), the success story of the tales was well underway and has not stopped in the 20th century, when the films of Disney took up many of the tales, although these are based mainly on Charles Perrault's *Contes de Fées* (1697).

Considering the overall accomplishment of the brothers, the *KHM* are rather peripheral. At the center of their life's work were linguistic studies and pioneering editions. Their monumental *Deutsches Wörterbuch* (equivalent to the *Oxford English Dictionary*), charting the history and meanings of all words the Grimms could find documentation for, was published from 1854 (volume 1 [*A-Biermolke*]) onward, its last volume appearing in 1961. Their works include crucial studies of the development of Germanic languages and establish the key notions that are the cornerstone of our understanding of *Germanic Grammar* (1819–37; *Deutsche Grammatik*) and *The History of the German Language* (1848; *Gedichte der deutschen Sprache*).

The bibliography of their works, both joint and individual authorship, is immense. The scope of their work is wide ranging, from old Danish heroic epics, Scottish songs, a translation of a Serbian grammar, a spate of editions of Old High and Middle High German texts, treatises on older literature, Germanic mythology, and what seem uncountable speeches, volumes of correspondence, political pamphlets, and evidence of lively involvement in the political life of the time.

Besides the *KHM* and scholarly books and articles, the Grimms gained fame or notoriety on two occasions. In 1837 the Grimms were professors at the University of Göttingen, part of the kingdom of Hannover, ruled by the king of England and Hannover, William IV. When William IV died in June of 1837 leaving no male heir, Victoria was crowned queen of England, and William's 66-year-old brother, Ernst August, duke of Cumberland, became king of Hannover. He abrogated privileges established by his predecessor in 1833 and declared the constitution of 1819 to be in effect. Seven professors, the Grimms among them, refused to submit a *Dienst- und Huldigungsrevers,* a loyalty oath on the old constitution required of all civil servants. In December 1937, all seven were dismissed from the university.

The group became known as the Göttingen Sieben, and the principled stance they took garnered them considerable fame in Europe and beyond. Their refusal, explained in a letter to the Universitäts-Kuratorium, comparable to a university board of trustees, was couched in what now might seem exceedingly subservient language. Nevertheless, the seven articulated a principle at least contiguous to the notion of academic freedom that was to become a crucial aspect of German university life and, inasmuch as German universities were—at least in the 19th and early 20th centuries—model institutions, important for universities elsewhere as well. The argument of the seven came down to this: shifting loyalties willy-nilly from one constitution to another, without any acceptable reason, and taking steps backward in rights and responsibilities would undermine both the credibility of the professoriate among the students and the ideals of the university. It reads almost as if it were a contemporary event when the investigation launched into the behavior of the seven focuses initially not on the principles of the argument but on the charge that they leaked their letter of defense to the French and British press.

The seven were not only dismissed from the university but also banished from Göttingen. It reads almost like a Gilbert and Sullivan operetta when three of the banished leave Göttingen, cross the bridge over the river Werra, and enter Hessia in Witzenhausen to be greeted by supporting students who have rushed ahead to welcome them.

The last, but by no means least, accomplishment of Jacob Grimm was his election as a deputy of the 29th district for the national assembly that began meeting in St. Paul's cathedral in Frankfurt on 18 May 1848. The stenographic record of meetings and motions, as well as contemporary paintings, show Jacob in the midst of debates, drafting, among other things, his own version of articles 1 to 4 of the proposed Basic Law. Although voted down (205 to 192), it clearly shows the libertarian sentiments of the Grimms, arguing for civil liberties and vocal against slavery. Jacob's contribution to this effort of democracy, although unsuccessful at the time, characterizes the fundamental attitudes of the Grimms: patriotic, to be sure (but not jingoistic), and democratic and progressive, groping for ways toward a new political order. However, the legacy of the two remarkable brothers rests mainly on their folkloristic and linguistic work, which, despite all its shortcomings, represents a monumental effort and accomplishment, laying the foundation for two new disciplines.

MICHAEL BACHEM

See also Fairy Tales; German Language

Biographies

Jacob Ludwig Carl Grimm

Born in Hanau, 4 January 1785. Studied law at the University of Marburg, 1802–5; researcher for Friedrich Carl von Savigny in Paris, 1805; secretary of the War Office, Kassel, 1806; librarian for the private library of King Jérôme Bonaparte, Wilhelmshöhe, 1808–14; co-editor, with his brother Wilhelm, of *Altdeutsche Wälder,* 1813–16; legation secretary for the Hessian delegation at the Congress of Vienna,

1814–15; librarian in Kassel, 1816; chairman, archaeology and librarianship departments, University of Göttingen, Hanover, 1830–37; dismissed from the university for political reasons, 1837; in Kassel, 1837–41; president of the Conferences of Germanists, Frankfurt, 1846, and Lubeck, 1847; elected to the Frankfurt parliament, 1848. Order of Merit, 1842; member of the Academy of Science, Berlin, 1841; honorary doctorates from the University of Marburg, 1819, Berlin University, 1828, and Breslau University, 1829. Died 20 September 1863.

Wilhelm Carl Grimm

Born in Hanau, 24 February 1786. Studied law at the University of Marburg, 1803–6; law degree, 1806; co-editor, with his brother Jacob, of *Altdeutsche Wälder,* 1813–16; assistant librarian in the electoral library, Kassel, 1814–29; professor at the University of Göttingen, 1830; dismissed from the university for political reasons, 1837; in Kassel, 1837–41. Member of the Academy of Science, Berlin, 1841; honorary doctorate from the University of Marburg, 1819. Died 16 December 1859.

Selected Works (both authors)

Collections

Complete Works, 62 vols., 1974–
Die älteste Märchensammlung der Brüder Grimm, edited by Heinz Rölleke, 1975
Grimm's Tales for Young and Old: The Complete Stories, translated by Ralph Manheim, 1977
The Complete Fairy Tales of the Brothers Grimm, edited and translated by Jake Zipes, 2 vols., 1987

Fiction

Kinder- und Hausmärchen, 2 vols., 1812–15; revised editions, 3 vols., 1819–22 (includes *Anmerkungen zu den einzelnen Märchen*), 1837, 1840, 1843, 1850, 1857; edited by Friedrich Panzer, 1975, and by Heinz Rölleke, 1982; numerous subsequent translations, including as *German Popular Stories,* translated by Edgar Taylor, 2 vols., 1823–26; revised edition as *Gammer Grethel; or, German Fairy Tales and Popular Stories,* 1839; as *Home Stories,* translated by Matilda Louisa Davis, 1855; as *Grimm's Popular Stories,* 1868; as *Grimm's Fairy Tales,* translated by H.H.B. Paull, 1872; translated by L.L. Weedon, 1898; translated by Edgar Lucas, 1900; translated by Beatrice Marshall, 1900; translated by N.J. Davidson, 1906; Ernest Beeson, 1916; translated by Peter Carter, 1982; as *Grimm's Goblins,* 1876; as *The Complete Grimm's Fairy Tales,* translated by Margaret Hunt, 1944.
Deutsche Sagen, 1816–18; as *The German Legends of the Brothers Grimm,* edited and translated by Donald Ward, 1981

Other

Deutsches Wörterbuch, with others, 32 vols., 1854–1961
Freundesbriefe von Wilhelm und Jacob Grimm: Mit Anmerkungen, edited by Alexander Reifferscheid, 1878
Briefwechsel des Freiherrn K.H.G. von Meusebach mit Jacob und Wilhelm Grimm, 1880
Briefwechsel zwischen Jacob und Wilhelm Grimm aus der Jegendzeit, edited by Herman Grimm and Gustav Hinrichs, 1881; revised edition, edited by Wilhelm Schoof, 1963
Briefwechsel der Gebrüder Grimm mit nordischen Gelehrten, edited by Ernst Schmidt, 1885
Briefwechsel zwischen Jacob und Wilhelm Grimm, Dahlmann und Gervinus, edited by Eduard Ippel, 2 vols., 1885–86
Briefe der Brüder Jacob und Wilhelm Grimm an Georg Friedrich Benecke aus den Jahren 1808–1829, edited by Wilhelm Müller, 1889
Briefwechsel F. Lückes mit den Brüdern Jacob und Wilhelm Grimm, 1891
Briefe der Brüder Grimm an Paul Wigand, edited by Edmund Stengel, 1910
Briefwechsel Johann Kaspar Bluntschlis mit Jacob Grimm, 1915
Briefe der Brüder Grimm, edited by Albert Leitzmann and Hans Gürtler, 1923
Briefwechsel der Brüder Jacob und Wilhelm Grimm mit Karl Lachmann, edited by Albert Leitzmann, 2 vols., 1927
Briefwechsel zwischen Jacob Grimm und Karl Goedeke, edited by Johannes Bolte, 1927
Briefe der Brüder Grimm an Savigny, edited by Wilhelm Schoof, 1953
Unbekannte Briefe der Brüder Grimm, edited by Wilhelm Schoof, 1960
John Mitchell Kemble and Jacob Grimm: A Correspondence 1832–1852, 1971
Briefwechsel der Bruder Grimm mit Hans Georg von Hammerstein, edited by Carola Gottzmann, 1985

Translation

Thomas Croften Croker, *Irische Elfenmärchen,* 1826

Edited Works

Die beiden ältesten deutschen Gedichte aus dem achten Jahrhundert: Das Lied von Hildebrand und Hadubrand und das Weissenbrunner Gebet, 1812
Lieder der alten Edda, 1815
Hartmann von Aue, *Der arme Heinrich,* 1815

Selected Works by Jacob Grimm

Collections

Reden und Aufsätze, edited by Wilhelm Schoof, 1966
Selbstbiographie: Ausgewählte Schriften, Reden und Abhandlungen, 1984

Fiction

Irmenstrasse und Irmensäule: Eine mythologische Abhandlung, 1815
Deutsche Mythologie, 3 vols., 1835–37; as *Teutonic Mythology,* translated by James Stevens Stallybrass, 4 vols., 1883–88
Frau Adventiure klopft an Beneckes Thür, 1842
Der Fundevogel: Ein Märlein, 1845

Other

Über den altdeutschen Meistergesang, 1811
Deutsche Grammatik, 4 vols., 1819–37
Zur Recension der deutschen Grammatik, 1826
Deutsche Rechtsalterthümer, 1828
Hymnorum veteris ecclesiae XXVI interpretation Theodisca nunc primum edita, 1830
Bericht . . . an die Hannoversche Regierung, 1833
Reinhart Fuchs, 1834
Über meine Entlassung (pamphlet), 1838
Sendschreiben an Karl Lachmann über Reinhart Fuchs, 1840
Über zwei entdeckte Gedichte aus der Zeit des deutschen Heidenthums, 1842
Grammatik der Hochdeutschen Sprache unserer Zeit, 1843
Deutsche Grenzalterthümer, 1844
Über Dipthonge nach weggefallnen Consonanten, 1845
Über Iornandes und die Geten: Eine in der Akademie der Wissenschaften am 5. März 1846 von Jacob Grimm gehaltene Vorlesung (lecture), 1846
Geschichte der deutschen Sprache, 2 vols., 1848
Über Marcellus Burdingalensis, 1849
Das Wort des Besitzes: Eine linguistische Abhandlung, 1850
Rede auf Lachmann, gehalten in der öffentlichen Sitzung der Akademie der Wissenschaften am 3. Juni 1851 (lecture), 1851
Über den Liebesgott: Gelesen in der Akademie am 6. Januar 1851 (lecture), 1851
Über den Ursprung der Sprache, 1851

Über Frauennamen aus Blumen, 1852
Über die Namen des Donners, 1855
Über die Marcellischen Formeln, with Adolf Pictet, 1855
Über den Personenwechsel in der Rede, 1856
Über einige Fälle der Attraction, 1858
Von Vertretung männlicher durch weibliche Namensformen, 1858
Über Schule, Universität, Academie, 1859
Über das Vebrennen der Leichen: Eine in der Academie der Wissenschaften am 29 November 1849 . . . (lecture), 1859
Rede auf Schiller, gehalten in der feierlichen Sitzung der König, 1859
Rede auf Wilhelm Grimm und Rede über das Alter, edited by Herman Grimm, 1863
Kleinere Schriften, edited by Karl Victor Müllenhoff and Eduard Ippel, 8 vols., 1864–90
Briefwechsel zwischen Jacob Grimm und Friedrich David Graeter aus den Jahren 1810–1813, edited by Hermann Fischer, 1877
Briefe an Hendrik Willem Tydeman: Mit einem Anhange und Anmerkungen, edited by Alexander Reifferscheid, 1883
Briefwechsel von Jacob Grimm und Hoffmann von Fallersleben mit Henrik van Wyn: Nebst anderen Briefe zur deutschen Literatur, edited by Karl Theodor Gaedertz, 1888
Kopitars Briefwechsel mit Jakob Grimm, edited by Max Vasmer, 1938

Translation
Vuk Stefanovic Karadzic, *Kleine serbische Grammatik,* 1824

Edited Works
Silva de romances viejos, 1815
Zur Recension der deutschen Grammatik, 1826
Taciti Germania edidit et qua as res Germanorum pertinere videntur e reliquo Tacitino oere excerpsit, 1835
Lateinische Gedichte des X. und XI. Jahrhunderts, edited with Andreas Schmeller, 1838
Andreas und Elene, 1840
Gedichte des Mittelalters aus König Friedrich I., dem Staufer, und aus seiner, sowie der nächstfolgenden Zeit, 1844

Selected Works by Wilhelm Grimm

Writings
Über deutsche Runen, 1821
Grâve Ruodolf: Ein Altdeutsches Gedicht, 1828
Zur Literatur der Runen, 1828
Bruchstücke aus einem Gedicht von Assundin, 1829
Die deutsche Heldensage, 1829
De Hildebrando antiquissimi carminis teutonici fragmentum, 1830
Die Sage vom Ursprung der Christusbilder, 1843
Exhortatio ad plebem christianam Glossae Cassellanae: Über de Bedeutung der deutschen Fingernamen, 1848
Über Freidank: Zwei Nachträge, 1850
Altdeutsche Gespräche: Nachtrag, 1851
Zur Geschichte des Reims, 1852
Nachtrag zu den Casseler glossen, 1855
Thierfabeln bei den Meistersängern, 1855
Die Sage von Polyphem, 1857
Kleinere Schriften, edited by Gustav Hinrichs, 4 vols., 1881–87
Unsere Sprachlaute als Stimmbildner, 1897

Translations
and editor, *Drei altschottische Lieder,* 1813
Altdänische Heldenlieder, Balladen und Märchen, 1811
Thomas Crofton Croker, *Irische Land-und Seenmärchen,* edited by Werner Moritz and Charlotte Oberfeld, 1986

Edited Works
Vridankes Bescheidenheit, 1834
Der Rosengarten, 1836
Ruolandes Liet, 1838
Wernher vom Niederrhein, 1839
Konrad von Würzburg, *Goldene Schmiede,* 1840
Konrad von Würzburg, *Silvester,* 1841
Athis und Prophilias: Mit Nachtrag, 2 vols., 1846–52
Altdeutsche Gespräche: Mit Nachtrag, 2 vols., 1851
Ludwig Achim von Arnim, *Sämtliche Werke,* edited with Bettina von Arnim and Karl August Varnhagen von Ense, 22 vols., 1853–56; revised edition, 21 vols., 1857
Bruchstüche aus einem unbekannten Gedicht vom Rosengarten, 1860

Further Reading

Antonsen, Elmer H., et al., editors, *The Grimm Brothers and the Germanic Past,* Amsterdam and Philadelphia, Pennsylvania: J. Benjamins, 1990
Bettelheim, Bruno, *The Uses of Enchantment: The Meaning and Importance of Fairy Tales,* New York: Knopf, and London: Thames and Hudson, 1976
Dégh, Linda, "Grimm's *Household Tales* and Its Place in the Household: The Social Relevance of a Controversial Classic," *Western Folklore* 38, no. 2 (1979)
Dundes, Alan, editor, *Cinderella, a Casebook,* Madison: University of Wisconsin Press, 1988
Franz, Marie-Luise von, *The Interpretation of Fairy Tales,* Boston and New York: Shambhala, 1996
Haase, Donald, "Motifs: Making Fairy Tales Our Own: Yours, Mine, or Ours? Perrault, the Brothers Grimm, and the Ownership of Fairy Tales," in *Once upon a Folktale: Capturing the Folklore Process with Children,* edited by Gloria T. Blatt, New York: Teachers College Press, 1993
Haase, Donald, editor, *The Reception of Grimms' Fairy Tales: Responses, Reactions, Revisions,* Detroit, Michigan: Wayne State University Press, 1993
Harvey, Brett, "Grimm Tidings: New Spins on Old Yarns," in *Village Voice Literary Supplement,* November 1988
Kamenetsky, Christa, *The Brothers Grimm and Their Critics: Folktales and the Quest for Meaning,* Athens: Ohio University Press, 1992
Neumann, Siegfried, "The Brothers Grimm as Collectors and Editors of German Folktales," in *The Reception of Grimm's Fairy Tales: Responses, Reactions, Revisions,* edited by Donald Haase, Detroit, Michigan: Wayne State University Press, 1993
Ohles, Frederik, *Germany's Rude Awakening: Censorship in the Land of the Brothers Grimm,* Kent, Ohio: Kent State University Press, 1992
Rölleke, Heinz, "New Results of Research on Grimms' Fairy Tales," in *The Brothers Grimm and Folktale,* edited by James M. McGlathery, Urbana: University of Illinois, 1988
Rusch-Feja, Diann D., *The Portrayal of the Maturation Process of Girl Figures in Selected Tales of the Brothers Grimm,* Frankfurt and New York: Lang, 1995
Tatar, Maria M., *The Hard Facts of the Grimms' Fairy Tales,* Princeton, New Jersey: Princeton University Press, 1987
——, *Off with Their Heads! Fairy Tales and the Culture of Childhood,* Princeton, New Jersey: Princeton University Press, 1992
Zipes, Jack David, "The Enchanted Forest of the Brothers Grimm: New Modes of Approaching the Grimm's Fairy Tales," *Germanic Review* 62, no. 2 (1987)
——, *The Brothers Grimm: From Enchanted Forest to the Modern World,* New York: Routledge, 1988; London and New York: Routledge, 1989

Hans Jakob Christoffel von Grimmelshausen 1622–1676

The image of Grimmelshausen as the "teutsch" (i.e., plain, unvarnished) satirist in the "realist" tradition of the 16th century has been opposed in more recent scholarship by that of a sophisticated writer who was at ease with allegory and fully prepared to indulge in Baroque "play" with meanings and realities. Both images contain an important truth; neither, however, is adequate to the complex phenomenon that is Grimmelshausen's work as a whole. His life, perhaps, points toward an understanding. He was clearly gifted above the average, both aesthetically and intellectually, but was deprived of his parents in his early years, and of a proper education and settled social existence by age 13 at the latest. He was also exposed to and involved in the vagaries of the Thirty Years' War in a way for which there is no parallel elsewhere for an author of 17th-century German literature. Even after he had managed to educate himself to some extent and to climb back to a relatively comfortable situation, he does not seem to have felt, or, perhaps, even wished, himself to be located in a secure niche within the rigidly stratified and hierarchical social and literary systems of his time. He thought as a "Baroque man" and believed in the existing order, but while he shunned identification with the common man or the *picaro,* he had absorbed enough of the earthiness and vitality of the former and of the latter's sense of freedom and involvement in the broad reality of life to locate himself in a place apart. What emerges from his writing, in particular from the cycle of "Simplician" novels for which he is chiefly remembered, is a sense of dualism. And it is the achievement of what he himself designated as a "Simplician" outlook and style that enables him to make that dualism a productive and dynamic interaction rather than a destructive dichotomy and to create a world of constant movement and, ultimately, coherence.

At what point Grimmelshausen definitively worked out his "simplicianische Manier" is not certain. He began as a fairly conventional satirist and novelist (*Satyrischer Pilgram* and *Keuscher Joseph,* respectively, both 1666), but it is likely that he had at that time also begun work on his masterpiece, *Der abentheurliche Simplicissimus Teutsch* (1668; *Simplicius Simplicissimus*), in which the new style is triumphantly established. Here, the impact of the two most important influences on Grimmelshausen, J.M. Moscherosch's satirical *Philander von Sittewald* (1640–50) and Charles Sorel's comic novel *Francion* (German translation 1662) is evident, yet that impact is presented in a highly Simplician manner: they stand side by side, but there is no attempt to harmonize them. The moral seriousness of satire and the essentially nonjudgmental response to the comic in the world coexist as aspects of life itself. In that sense, the "Simplician author" (Grimmelshausen's own phrase) is a realist of a kind, but the sense of immediate coherence and consistency that one expects of artistic realism is lacking. Homogeneity is foreign to the Simplician vision: it deliberately cultivates a sense of multiplicity of perspective (including the allegorical and religious) and a sense of the odd ("seltzam" and "abentheurlich"). A striking example of this is the way in which, after the success of *Simplicissimus,* Grimmelshausen felt able to "Simplicianize" works such as the *Keuscher Joseph* (second version, 1670) and the *Ratio Status* (an attack on the "Machiavellian" tendency, published in 1670, but probably written earlier) simply by adding to them, with only the most tenuous, indeed, derisory of linkages, material (the "Sabud" story) that is radically different in nature. More striking still, perhaps, is the change in literary technique and style. Narrative, hitherto essentially a shell, becomes itself the kernel, and we feel that this part of the work is not merely in form but also in substance "lustig entworffen" (i.e., written to entertain). Not that Grimmelshausen is a mere entertainer: the disclaimer in the opening chapter of the "Continuation" of *Simplicissimus* (book 6 of the cycle) is genuine and justified. As can be seen above all from the *Simplicissimus,* Grimmelshausen can convey profound moral and religious reflection within narrative form. But it is as a storyteller that he is most effective and most himself.

The Simplician manner, once established, is capable of being effectively deployed in more discursive treatises (the *Teutsche Michel* [on language] and *Rathstübel Plutonis* [on wealth] stand out), but the remainder of the space here is devoted to the novels of the Simplician cycle, in which Grimmelshausen adapts the picaresque form to his own purpose, which could be defined as an attempt to present a panoramic picture of a world of almost Faustian scope. In addition to the five books of *Simplicissimus,* this effort comprises the *Continuatio* or "Conclusion" of that work (1669), *Trutz Simplex; oder, Ausführliche und wunderseltzame Ertzbetrügerin und Landstörtzerin Courasche* (*The Runagate Courage*) and *Der seltzame Springinsfeld* (*The Singular Life Story of Heedless Hopalong*) (both 1670), and the two books of *Das wunderbarliche Vogelnest* (1672 and 1675, respectively; The Miraculous Birdnest). As Grimmelshausen himself points out in the preface to the last of these works, this makes a sequence of ten books, which he claims need to be read together. Only the *Continuatio* (which shows Simplicius the ex-picaro in penitent mood) can be seen as a "sequel" of the main novel (many critics see *Simplicissimus* as a six-book corpus); the others are satellites rather than sequels. *The Runagate Courage,* the story of an unrepentant sinner, is a deeply serious, yet highly entertaining exercise in irony; *Springinsfeld,* the robust tale of an old soldier, plays a pivotal role in the cycle by juxtaposing the settled citizen with the rootless vagrant; and the two *Vogelnest* novels bring the sequence to a close on a characteristically dualistic examination of the theme of magic. While there is a more-or-less logical progression in terms of the situation of the various narrators, and of the character Simplicissimus himself, who from the *The Runagate Courage* onward ages and becomes primarily an observer of rather than a participant in life, the characters in the narrated material move independently in time and space, occasionally crisscrossing in a kind of network that suggests the natural chance of life itself rather than a calculated plan.

In general, the cycle has the scope, and the variegated nature, of life itself. Although the narration is firmly located in the late 1660s and early 1670s, the period of time covered by the *narrative* stretches back to the early 17th century. The area covered extends from the Balkans to North Germany, Paris, and Russia (not to mention the Indian Ocean), and the style and mood varies between graphically realized physical action (including the sexual variety), always animated and often funny, and static, serious, and sometimes allegorical episodes of spiritual reflection in which the perspective of the here and now is balanced by that of eternity. Grimmelshausen sees this earth as simultaneously a world of fun and sin, but if one aspect is to have priority, then the balance must clearly come down on the religious side; hence, the conclusion of the whole cycle is an almost liturgical renunciation of the world, the flesh, and the devil. But just as the most sinful (and vital) of all Grimmelshausen's characters, the "arch-deceiver and vagrant Courasche" (the name itself is the result of a sexual double entendre), is entirely aware of her sinfulness but psychologically unable to repent of it, the conclusion should not be taken as a final renunciation of, and hermit-like withdrawal from, life.

ALAN MENHENNET

Biography

Born in Gelnhausen, near Frankfurt, Germany, 1622. Studied at Lutheran Latin School, Gelnhausen, 1627. In the imperial army, 1637; garrison soldier in Offenburg, 1639; regimental office clerk, 1645; regimental office secretary, 1648; steward for the von Schauenburgs, Gaisbach bei Oberkirch, 1649; married Katharina Henninger, 1649; inkeeper, Gaisbach, 1658, 1665; steward for Dr. Küeffer, 1662; mayor of Renchen, 1667. Died 17 August 1676.

Selected Works

Collections

Gesammelte Werke in Einzelausgaben, edited by R. Tarot et al., 13 vols., 1966–76

Werke, edited by D. Breuer, 3 vols., 1997

Writings

Der abentheurliche Simplicissimus Teutsch, 1668; with *Continuatio des abentheurlichen Simplicissimi; oder, Schluß desselben,* 1669; as *Der abentheurliche Simplicissimus Teutsch und Continuatio des abentheurlichen Simplicissimi,* edited by Rolf Tarot, 1967; as *The Adventurous Simplicissimus,* translated by A.T.S. Goodrick, 1912; as *Simplicissimus the Vagabond,* 1924; as *The Adventures of a Simpleton,* translated by Walter Wallich, 1962; as *Simplicius Simplicissimus,* translated by Monte Adair, 1986

Trutz Simplex; oder, Ausführliche und wunderseltzame Lebensbeschreibung der Ertzbetrügerin und Landstörtzerin Courasche, 1670; edited by Wolfgang Bender, 1967; as *Mother Courage,* translated by Walter Wallich, 1965; as *The Runagate Courage,* translated by Robert L. Hiller and John C. Osborne, 1965

Des vortrefflich keuschen Josephs in Egypten . . . , enlarged edition, 1670; edited by Wolfgang Bender, 1968

Der seltzame Springinsfeld, 1670; edited by Frank Günter Sieveke, 1969; as *The Singular Life Story of Heedless Hopalong,* translated by Robert L. Hiller and John C. Osborne, 1981

Das abenteuerlichen Simplicissimi ewigwährender Calender, 1671; edited by Klaus Haberkamm, 1967

Das wunderbarliche Vogelnest, 1672, 1675; edited by Rolf Tarot, 1970

Rathstübel Plutonis, 1672; edited by Wolfgang Bender, 1975

Dess Weltberuffenen Simplicissimi Pralerey und Gespräng mit seinem teutschen Michel, 1673; edited by Rolf Tarot, 1976

Further Reading

Feldges, Mathias, *Grimmelshausens "Landstörtzerin Courasche": Eine Interpretation nach der Methode des vierfachen Schriftsinnes,* Bern: Francke, 1969

Hayens, Kenneth, *Grimmelshausen,* Oxford: Oxford University Press, 1932

Könnecke, Gustav, *Quellen und Forschungen zur Lebensgeschichte Grimmelshausens,* Leipzig: Insel, 1926–28; reprint, Hildesheim: Olms, 1977

Meid, Volker, *Grimmelshausen: Epoche, Werk, Wirkung,* Munich: Beck, 1984

Menhennet, Alan, *Grimmelshausen the Storyteller,* Columbia, South Carolina: Camden House, 1997

Negus, Kenneth, *Grimmelshausen,* New York: Twayne, 1974

Parker, Alexander A., *Literature and the Delinquent,* Edinburgh: Edinburgh University Press, 1967

Streller, Siegfried, *Grimmelshausens Simplicianische Schriften: Allegorie, Zahl, und Wirklichkeitsdarstellung,* Berlin: Rütten und Loening, 1957

Weydt, Günther, *Nachahmung und Schöpfung im Barock,* Bern: Francke, 1968

Der abentheurliche Simplicissimus Teutsch 1668

Novel by Hans Jakob Christoffel von Grimmelshausen

In *Der abentheurliche Simplicissimus Teutsch* (various translations, including *Simplicius Simplicissimus*), a novel in five books, Hans Jakob Christoffel von Grimmelshausen uses as his basic form the retrospectively narrated picaresque novel, but he adapts it to suit his own tastes and view of life. The homogeneity of a continuous forward flow of specific events in "everyday" reality and time is frequently interrupted by static passages of satirical or religious contemplation (e.g., the *Ständebaum* [Tree of Social Classes] allegory of society in Book I, chapters 15–18), which shift the perspective from the nose-to-the-ground "realism" of the picaresque (also present in large measure) to something more universal, often transcendental. Sometimes "reality' is patently flouted, as in the *Mummelsee* episode (Book V, chapters 11–17), in which Simplicissimus is transported to the underwater world of the sylphs. At other times, it is flouted by the rhetorical intensification of an overtly realistic description such that the description becomes quasi-allegorical, as in the banquet scene in Book I (chapter 30), which articulates, momentarily at least, a reflection on gluttony, thanks to the naïve lad's concern for the *edle Seelen* (noble souls) of the revelers. All the deadly sins are reflected upon at some point or other in the book, which is as religious as it is realistic, as serious as it is comic.

The book is set during the Thirty Years' War (which acts as a kind of ground and a source of constant movement) and the years immediately following. Its overall "plot" is indicated on the title page: an ignorant young lad without even a name is thrown by the war into the company of a hermit (as it turns out, his natural father), who turns him from a *Bestia* (beast) into a *Christenmensch* (Christian). After the hermit's death, the lad enters the *Welt* (world), in which he goes through a wide variety of experiences, eventually bidding farewell to the world (in a long rhetorical passage adapted from the Spaniard Guevara [see Weydt, 1962]) and withdrawing again to the *Wald* (forest) to live as a hermit. He does this, however, with the proviso that the withdrawal may not be permanent. Indeed, impermanence (*Wechsel, Veränderung, Unbestand*) is a constant factor in this earthly life: nothing is "more constant than inconstancy." Here, as on many other occasions, a transcendental reality comes into play, and the attraction of the hermit's life (associated with constancy and devotion to God) and its quasi-emblematic status become clear.

At the same time, even if one isolates the 1668 *Simplicissimus* from the rest of the Simplician cycle (see the general article on Grimmelshausen) on the grounds, perhaps, that it may have been written before the idea of the cycle became clear in Grimmelshausen's mind, the idea that its message is rejection of the world is not sustainable. The transcendental reality (which clearly has ideological priority) is ever-present and often impinges on that of the material world, and there have been attempts to use this fact as a key to the "meaning" of the book. Günther Weydt, for example, offers an impressively scholarly astrological interpretation (in his "Planetensymbolik"), and others (e.g., Triefenbach) have approached the work through medieval exegetic methods (above all, the "fourfold sense of scripture") that would still have been familiar in the 17th century, and no doubt known to Grimmelshausen. But such attempts, for all that they add to our knowledge of the book's variety and scope, eventually leave us unsatisfied as "keys," for while they unlock possible areas of appreciation, they also tend not to deny, but to lock out what is perhaps the most important one of all, namely, the vitality that is our main reason for reading Grimmelshausen today and that for him, at least, coexists quite easily with the text's more serious aspects. Most valuable of all, perhaps, is his achievement as a comic author: not the equal of Cervantes, admittedly, but in the same league. The episode in Lippstadt (Book III, chapter 21), where the "godless" Simplicissimus acquires his first wife through a comic misunderstanding, is a fine example of the polar duality of the other-worldly and worldly perspectives that, in the last analysis, give *Simplicissimus* its distinctive "Simplician" quality.

The *Continuatio des abentheurlichen Simplicissimi* (1669) purports to be both a continuation of the original novel and *der Schluß desselben* (the conclusion thereof), but whether it should be seen as an integral part of a six-book novel is debatable. The appearance of the word "conclusion" on the title page is not itself conclusive. True, Simplicissimus, who has been routed out of his sylvan retreat and sent on further wanderings and adventures, seems determined at the "end" of *his* narrative (chapter 23) to remain as a hermit on the desert isle on which he has eventually been shipwrecked. Conclusiveness, however, is a quality that does not sit easily with the basic principle of "Simplician" structure, which expresses the openness and flexibility of life itself. The work does, after all, indulge in fanciful play with the concept of an ending: it has two "ends" and a *Beschluß* (conclusion), each by a different hand, and the last of these (which emanates from Grimmelshausen himself, after he has shuffled off two other authorial *personae*) gives a clear indication of further Simplician writings to come. The debate will no doubt continue, but it is perhaps more fruitful to see the *Continuatio* in the context of the whole Simplician cycle, because the idea for writing the cycle was probably already in Grimmelshausen's mind at that time.

Seen in this light, we can characterize this book as one of contrast, perhaps of corrective balance, to the original novel. It begins with a strong plea to be seen not as entertainment and certainly not as comedy, but as moral satire (see chapter 1). This statement is a better guide to interpreting what follows than what has gone before. While the characteristic Simplician liveliness and quirkiness is by no means totally absent, the tone is undeniably more austere: there is more sin than fun in this world, and thoughts of the next bulk larger. The culmination of Simplicissimus's own narrative seems almost to prefigure the confessional atmosphere and contrition in which the whole cycle culminates at the end of *Das wunderbarliche Vogelnest* (1672, 1675; The Miraculous Birdnest). The sentiments are no doubt sincere, but the book should not be taken on its own as an expression of Grimmelshausen's final philosophy; rather, it is a necessary patch of darker color on a wider canvas.

ALAN MENHENNET

Editions

First edition: *Der abentheurliche Simplicissimus Teutsch,* Nuremberg: Wolff Eberhard Felssecker, 1668; with *Continuatio des abentheurlichen Simplicissimi; oder, Schluß desselben,* 1669

Critical edition: *Der abentheuerliche Simplicissimus Teutsch und Continuatio des abentheuerlichen Simplicissimi,* edited by Rolf Tarot, Tübingen: Niemeyer, 1967

Translation: *Simplicius Simplicissimus,* translated by Monte Adair, Lanham, Maryland: University Press of America, 1986

Further Reading

Menhennet, Alan, "Grimmelshausen, the Picaresque, and the Large Loose Baggy Monster," *The Seventeenth Century* 1 (1986)

Triefenbach, Peter, *Der Lebenslauf des Simplicius Simplicissimus: Figur, Initiation, Satire,* Stuttgart: Klett-Cotta, 1979

Valentin, J.-M., "Grimmelshausen zwischen Albertinus und Sorel," *Simpliciana* 12 (1990)

Weydt, Günther, "Adjeu Welt: Weltklage und Lebensrückblick bei Guevara, Albertinus und Grimmelshausen," *Neophilologus* 46 (1962)

———, "Das Problem Simplicissimus" and "Planetensymbolik im barocken Roman," in *Nachahmung und Schöpfung im Barock,* Bern: Francke, 1968

Weydt, Günther, editor, *Der Simplicissimusdichter und sein Werk,* Darmstadt: Wissenschaftliche Buchgesellschaft, 1969

Gruppe 47

Following the measures taken by the American authorities against *Der Ruf,* which he had coedited with Alfred Andersch, Hans Werner Richter convened the first meeting of the Gruppe 47 at the Bannwaldsee near Füssen in September 1947. Fifteen people connected with the banned periodical were present, a figure that expanded to 25 by the second meeting in November. From these modest beginnings, the group established itself as the leading literary force in the Federal Republic until its de facto demise in 1967. Publishers especially thought that it was in their interests to stress any connection between their authors and the group.

Despite the significance that the group gained in public consciousness, in part through Richter's promotional skills, it remains difficult to categorize the Gruppe 47. Whatever the implications of the word *group,* it is impossible to talk of membership in any normal sense. As an institution, it only fully existed during its brief meetings, which until 1955, with one exception, occurred biannually and thereafter, usually annually. The prime purpose of these meetings was for writers to present and discuss their works. In all, around 200 authors read from their work, ranging from the popular novelist Johannes Mario Simmel through the major figures of post-1945 literature, including Bachmann, Grass, Enzensberger, and Walser, to now almost-forgotten names. In later years, younger authors such as F.C. Delius and Elisabeth Plessen made their debuts.

Attendance was only possible upon the receipt of an invitation from Richter, whose postcards gained almost iconic status. Some people attended on virtually all occasions; others, often seen as key participants in the group, such as Böll, Walser, and even Andersch, experienced periods of alienation; and others only attended once, because they were never invited again or had no wish to repeat the experience. The most famous name in the second category is Paul Celan, whose work was subjected to the most grotesque criticism at the 1952 gathering at Niendorf, even being compared in its tone to the rhetoric of Joseph Goebbels.

Immediate criticism, to which authors were not allowed to respond, became a central part of meetings, with a number of professional critics, including Walter Höllerer, Walter Jens, Joachim Kaiser, Marcel Reich-Ranicki, and Hans Mayer, gradually gaining a quasi-official status. In addition, those present, led by Richter, would show their reactions to a reading by raising or lowering their thumbs. Given the effect that a negative reaction could have on literary careers, it is no wonder that the name "electric chair" was given to the place from which the authors presented their work.

Although it is difficult to define the Gruppe 47 in terms of a consistent membership, a look at its detractors may help to explain its essence. For a number of older writers at the time, most significantly Thomas Mann, the ambiance of its meetings was crude and undignified. In the light of such views, the group can be seen as the voice of a generation, which, since the days of *Der Ruf,* saw itself as having a prime role to play both politically and culturally in the postwar world. As such, it was resisted by older generations and then became an object of derision for the next generation. The last regular meeting at the Pulvermühle in 1967 was interrupted by students, who vociferously showed their contempt for literature at a time of perceived political ferment. They also highlighted the growing tensions within the group, which were an additional factor in its decline. Moreover, the group was also the target of criticism from official cultural circles in the GDR, few of whose authors, with the exception of Johannes Bobrowski, attended on anything like a regular basis. In particular, the ideal of the writer as a nonconformist outsider favored by Richter and many colleagues was anathema to people who wanted to incorporate culture into the mainstream of society. To these critics, the group was seen as seeking to subvert the GDR in the same way as the West German government was.

Although such a claim has to be seen as an expression of ideological paranoia, the group did increasingly develop into a kind of literary establishment. Along with increasing numbers of publishers, television cameras began to appear at meetings, which suggests the many links between the group and the media. The two meetings in Berlin in 1962 and 1965 were in a villa owned by the Sender Freies Berlin, and many group participants worked regularly in radio. Richter was also happy to accept invitations to take the group abroad—where it was often seen as the "official" voice of German literature. Meetings took place in Sweden in 1964 and, much more controversially, Princeton in 1966. Left-wing writers were particularly incensed given the American involvement in Vietnam, even if some claimed that Princeton was a center of protest. Unease with Richter's control was expressed in 1964, when Walser, to Richter's annoyance, suggested that the group should be "socialized" and thus taken out of Richter's control. At Princeton, the young Peter Handke, in his admittedly aesthetic rather than political criticisms of the group, prefigured the German student protests a year later. At the same time, he was using the group's fame to draw attention to himself.

More recent criticisms of the group have pointed to the way in which it dealt with individual authors, especially its attitude toward women, who, irrespective of their talents, were, it is claimed, largely treated by Richter as little more than decorations to gain further attention for his organization. That Ilse Aichinger won the group's prize in 1952 and Ingeborg Bachmann did so a year later is also viewed as part of this strategy. Critics of the group also point out that many authors whose work is now often held in particularly high esteem never became involved. This category includes Arno Schmidt and Wolfgang Koeppen, although the latter did once set out for a meeting but turned back en route. Another particularly serious reproach aimed at the group is that it failed to address adequately issues surrounding the Nazi past. Even in *Der Ruf,* both Andersch and Richter refused to accept that their generation carried any responsibility for the crimes of National Socialism. Both had been members of Hitler's army, and Richter, at least, held views that were open to the charge of nationalism. It was even felt by some that the atmosphere of group meetings resembled a gathering of "Obergefreite" (lance corporals), something that showed itself in the participants' attitude not only to women but also to alcohol.

Although there is substance in these criticisms, there are achievements to stress as well. In his own writing, Richter was a traditional realist; nevertheless, he did not seek to tie the group to one kind of writing. On a number of occasions, especially after being cajoled by Andersch, he invited writers whose modernistic works were not to his liking. If the work of the group's prizewinners is considered, then it is difficult to discern a bias toward realism. Martin Walser won the prize in 1955 for the story "Templones Ende" ("Templone's End"), which, like all his work at that time, owed much to Kafka, a name that cropped up endlessly at early group meetings. Grass's success with extracts from *Die Blechtrommel* (*The Tin Drum*) three years later can undoubtedly be put down to his linguistic and stylistic originality. Moreover, this was a work that did deal openly with the Nazi past. Finally, the last winner of the prize in 1967 was Jürgen Becker, none of whose work falls into the category of straightforward realism.

Westernization is one possible term that might be used to sum up the literature most closely connected with the group. Just as the creation of the Federal Republic provided a framework for the westernization of German politics, the literature of the time became open to Western influences such as the philosophical movements of existentialism and phenomenology and, in the realm of aesthetics, the various forms of modernism. Nazism had, of course, cut Germany off from these developments, which were also mistrusted in the East, where "formalism" was condemned as "bourgeois decadence."

Despite the possible links between literary and other developments in the west of Germany, we should not assume that group members, who were not solely German, were always in harmony with those in positions of power in the early years of the Federal Republic. Insofar as they took any interest in cultural affairs, those close to the Adenauer government certainly did not favor modernism, especially if works of literature contained explicit treatment of sexual themes, as in Grass's work. The status gained by the group led the Christian Democrat politician Josef Hermann Dufhues to describe it in 1963 as "a secret *Reichsschrifttumskammer,*" a reference to the body that controlled literature in the Nazi era. This outburst had undoubtedly much to do with the politics of leading members of the group. In this connection, it should be remembered that *Der Ruf* had been launched primarily as a political journal and that Richter in particular never abandoned politics. In the 1950s, he founded the Grünwalder Kreis, which was dedicated to fighting militarism and neo-Nazism, and at the end of the decade, he joined the antinuclear movement.

Direct political activity that can be associated with the Gruppe 47 includes a variety of open letters. In 1960, for instance, the group wrote in support of French intellectuals opposed to the Algerian War and, in the same year, against the abortive plans of the Adenauer administration to create a centralized television channel that would have been largely in the control of the government. The group also happened to be meeting in Berlin when one of the worst scandals in the history of the Federal Republic, the *Spiegel* Affair of 1962, began with the searching of the *Spiegel* magazine's offices and the arrest of journalists, who were accused of having committed treason by revealing military secrets. About half of those present in Berlin joined in the chorus of protest that led to a government crisis and, ultimately, to a victory for press freedom. Some group members, however, balked at one sentence in the resolution that proclaimed that betraying military secrets was a moral duty in the nuclear age. Similarly, three years later, a resolution on Vietnam, framed at the group's gathering, did not gain universal approval—with Richter and Grass refusing to sign—another example of the group's growing fragility.

Initially, the group was associated with outright opposition to the Adenauer government, although for the Austrian Ingeborg Bachmann, its stance was never very radical, when compared to stances of intellectuals in other European countries. The nature of its political activity certainly changed in the 1960s, when many writers aligned themselves with the increasingly reformist Social Democratic Party (SPD). Walser edited a volume in support of the SPD before the 1961 federal election, and Richter did the same four years later. When this party joined in a Grand Coalition with the Christian Democrats a year later, however, many intellectuals were disillusioned, yet another sign of splits within their ranks. Nevertheless, the change of mood in the Federal Republic that led to the forming of an SPD-led government in 1969 can be attributed in part to the activities of writers and intellectuals associated with the group. In this way, they can be said to have helped to make the Federal Republic a "normal" democracy.

In 1979, Grass published the story *Das Treffen in Telgte* (*The Meeting at Telgte*), ostensibly about a gathering of writers seeking to contribute to a renewal of Germany at the end of the Thirty Years' War, but in many ways a tribute to the achievements of the Gruppe 47 and its guiding spirit, Hans Werner Richter. While recent research has revealed its undoubted flaws, Grass was right to see the institution in a positive light. It provided a literary focus in a new country that lacked a cultural capital, encouraged many talented writers of different types, and contributed to much-needed democratic development.

STUART PARKES

See also Alfred Andersch; Der Ruf

Further Reading

Arnold, Heinz Ludwig, editor, *Die Gruppe 47: Ein kritischer Grundriß,* Munich: Text und Kritik, 2nd edition, 1987

Cofalla, Sabine, editor, *Hans Werner Richter: Briefe,* Munich and Vienna: Hanser, 1997

Fetscher, Justus, et al., editors, *Die Gruppe 47 in der Geschichte der Bundesrepublik,* Würzburg: Königshausen und Neumann, 1991

Lettau, Reinhard, editor, *Die Gruppe 47: Bericht, Kritik, Polemik. Ein Handbuch,* Neuwied and Berlin: Luchterhand, 1967

Mandel, Siegfried, *Group 47: The Reflected Intellect,* Carbondale and Edwardsville: Southern Illinois University Press, and London: Feffer and Simons, 1973

Neunzig, Hans A., editor, *Hans Werner Richter und die Gruppe 47,* Munich: Nymphenburger, 1981

———, editor, *Lesebuch der Gruppe 47,* Munich: Deutscher Taschenbuchverlag, 1983; 2nd edition, 1997

Richter, Hans Werner, editor, *Almanach der Gruppe 47,* Reinbek bei Hamburg: Rowohlt, 1962

Richter, Toni, editor, *Die Gruppe 47 in Bildern und Texten,* Cologne: Kiepenheuer und Witsch, 1997

Andreas Gryphius 1616–1664

Andreas Gryphius is the most famous writer of the German Baroque and has often been compared with Shakespeare. Growing up during the Thirty Years' War gave him keen, pessimistic insights into the human condition, especially into religious conflict and the worlds of politics and learning. Desiring to bring German literature up to the standards set by other European nations, Gryphius accepted in general the principles for form and style established by Martin Opitz in his influential *Buch von der deutschen Poeterey* (1624; *Book of German Poetry*), but he differs from Opitz in his stoical sense of the futility of all earthly endeavors in the face of death and eternity. Deep melancholy laced with sarcastic wit characterizes his works. Like most contemporary writers, Gryphius prided himself on his learning and looked to literary models in Dutch, Spanish, French, and English, all of which he was familiar with (as well as Latin, Greek, and Hebrew). Gryphius mastered all of the lyrical genres of the European canon—sonnets, odes, and epigrams—steeped as he was in the poetry of Martial, John Owen, Pierre de Ronsard, Daniel Heinsius, and Opitz.

Although Gryphius worked in multiple genres, most of his writings are barely known today; only a few texts have achieved lasting fame. Four or five poems are commonly cited as embodying the essence of the Baroque worldview. Poems such as "Es ist alles eitel" ("All Is Vanity") or his sonnets that meditate on the war or transitoriness are fixtures in German poetry collections. He also wrote plays, which were performed until the 18th century. The decline of his reputation as a dramatist had more to do with the history of the German theater than with the quality of his plays. The poetic power of Gryphius's dramatic language, which is distinguished by rich, emblematic metaphors embedded in an elaborately rhetorical style, is the most significant characteristic of his plays. This brought them the greatest admiration during the 17th century but caused them to fall out of favor in the 18th century, when a more natural, "reasonable" style came into favor. Today only his comedy *Absurda Comica; oder, Herr Peter Squenz* (1658; Absurd Farce; or, Master Peter Squentz) is associated with Gryphius. It is based on the familiar play-within-a-play of Shakespeare's *A Midsummer Night's Dream,* possibly augmented by German adaptations of Ovid's "Pyramus and Thisbe." What attracts audiences today is the richness of its humor in satirizing the malaprop pretensions of an ignorant schoolmaster claiming to be a playwright and director. On the other hand, the protagonist's calm in ignoring his own failure and the direct manner he uses toward the king and his court charm the spectator with the artist's autonomy and self-possession. By implication, in this work Gryphius is also satirizing earlier German playwrights, mainly Hans Sachs in Nuremberg, and condemning the acting style of the English comedians and their German imitators.

Other comedies of Gryphius, though largely neglected, are worthy of note. In *Horribilicribrifax* (1663), Gryphius holds up the mirror of irony to the attempts of soldiers and ordinary citizens after the Thirty Years' War to come to terms with rebuilding social relations following a catastrophe. While the extravagantly polyglot manners and morals are ridiculed, they also reflect the author's tragically ironic sense of the chaotic state of human affairs and the nakedness of power exploiting the weak, who have only their wits to help them survive. Social concerns are also evident in *Verliebtes Gespenst/Die geliebte Dornrose* (1661; A Ghost in Love/The Beloved Thornrose). Individual scenes of this intricate double play alternate, presenting side by side two distinct plots involving characters from different worlds and classes. Parts of *Die geliebte Dornrose* are spoken in the Silesian popular dialect, interpolating the traditions of folk theater into the comedic style more usual for educated audiences. Other comedies—*Majuma* (1657; Majuma), *Piastus* (1660; Piastus), and *Der schwermende Schäffer Lysis* (1661; The Deluded Shepherd Lysis), the last adapted from Thomas Corneille—were commissioned for special occasions. These plays praise the ruler and affirm things as they are, but to later readers they again reveal deep conflicts in the 17th-century mind in relation to authority, erudition, and the performance of social roles. The deluded Lysis, for instance, is an inexperienced young man who must find his place in a world that is everywhere cruel and selfish, be it at court, in the city, or in the country.

As a tragedian, Gryphius emulated classical Greek and Roman models of dramatic style and structure. He observed the Aristotelian unities of time, place, and decorum and included such theatrical devices as prologues, choruses, and a five-act structure, setting the standard that dramatists such as Daniel Casper von Lohenstein would follow. At the center of Gryphius's chief tragedies, which caused admirers to call him a "German Sophocles," stands the figure of the martyr. Modifying the dictum that tragedies could feature only gods and kings, Gryphius included figures from the upper bourgeoisie and lower nobility, as in *Cardenio und Celinde; oder, Unglücklich Verliebete* (1657; Cardenio and Celinde or the Unhappy Lovers). The work brings together the motifs of martyr and tragic hero of less-than-royal rank as the murdered Marcello is sacrificed by the lovers' passions, a fate that brings them to their senses. Walter Benjamin distinguishes between a German Baroque *Trauerspiel* (play of sorrows) and *Tragödie* (tragedy); he counted *Cardenio und Celinde* as one of the former. Yet a cathartic purging of emotion seems to operate in the service of Christian-stoic morality, calling such categorizations into question. Cardenio and Celinde resign themselves to the impossibility of marrying the people they desire, preserving the honor and marriage of Olympia and Lysander at the end and averting further tragedy. The surviving characters learn from the tragic fates of others; the lessons of the grave lead to the *Weg zum Leben* (way to life) because of a pervasive, tragic awareness of death's constant imminence.

A murdered Byzantine king is the subject of Gryphius's earliest tragedy, *Leo Armenius; oder, Fürsten-Mord, Trauerspiel* (1650; Leo Armenius: A Tragedy). Leo came to power by deposing his predecessor. In turn, he is assassinated while worshiping on Christmas Eve by hirelings of his general. Gryphius poses the moral question of whether murder becomes a kind of divine right when kingship is involved. Does Leo deserve to suffer his fate as retribution for his sins, or does his royal station, even if unjustly won, place him above the law and biblical injunctions to mercy? Leo seals his own fate by hesitating out of Christian charity to destroy his enemies, thus ironically becoming a sacrifice to his faith. Martyrdom in the name of Christianity is the principal theme in Gryphius's second tragedy, *Catharina von Georgien; oder, Bewehrete Beständigkeit* (1657; Catharina of Georgia; or, Constancy Preserved), which he based on an event in recent history. In 1624, the Christian queen of Georgia died as a prisoner of the shah of Persia. Gryphius expands this into an impressive object lesson in martyred constancy: rather than gain her freedom by becoming the shah's bride, she chooses to be faithful to her dead husband and her religion and suffers a gruesome execution. The shah, compelled to kill the woman he loved, goes mad, tormented by her triumphant ghost.

Only about a year after the English under Oliver Cromwell shocked Europe by executing King Charles I, Gryphius published a tragedy in response: *Ermordete Majestät; oder, Carolus Stuardus, König von Groß Britannien* (1657; second version 1660–63; *Murdered Majesty; or, Charles Stuart, King of Great Britain*). It is one of Gryphius's most appreciated and puzzling works. Though a Catholic himself, Charles had been related to the German Protestant Elector Palatine Frederick V, the unfortunate "Winter King" of Bohemia; Gryphius was acquainted with members of his family. *Murdered Majesty* reflects a corresponding political bias in its passionate defense of a king's God-given inviolability, which even the people's right to rebel against injustice must not defile. Although the play presents arguments in favor of the deed, it depicts the execution as a horrendous crime that cries out for revenge. In 1660, after the Stuart Restoration, Gryphius revised the tragedy, playing down the political aspects and casting the king as a martyr who willingly chose to emulate Christ's sacrifice. For the Protestant Gryphius, the well-being of the monarchy was in the people's best interest. The events in England aroused only dark forebodings of the future in those who, like Gryphius, believed in the destiny of the Holy Roman Empire and royalty's prerogatives.

In his last tragedy, *Großmütiger Rechts-Gelehrter; oder, Sterbender Ämilius Paulus Papinianus* (1659; The Valiant Jurist; or, The Death of Aemilius Paulus Papinianus), Gryphius, himself an attorney, describes how an honorable man must act when coerced by powerful and corrupt rulers. The hero is a Roman lawyer who served Marcus Aurelius and Caracalla. Caracalla has murdered his brother and his friends and asks Papinianus to invent legal grounds to justify this deed. Papinianus refuses and is executed, but only after hearing that the emperor has also had Papinianus's little boy abducted and killed. Papinianus could have saved himself but chooses to die for what he considers to be *heiliges Recht* (holy justice). Christian martyrdom is displaced here by the stoic-patristic tradition. Thus, *Papinianus* reflects political conflicts that Gryphius and his fellow officials faced in trying to reconcile the conflicting demands of rulers and their subjects according to moral and religious notions of justice. Students frequently performed *Papinianus* at schools in Germany and Switzerland; it was clearly valued as an instructive and inspirational drama.

His deeply religious, apocalyptic vision of the world caused Gryphius to regard concrete reality as a complex revelation. Its phenomena are not "nature" but images that are emblematic of truths that man must strive to understand, aided by the poet's art. Modern critics have characterized his basic philosophy and religious position as embodied in a *Klagegestus* (attitude of perpetual lamentation) that pervades his dramas and poetry alike. The personal note of his poetry is so affecting that it is hard to resist identifying with the "ich" (I) speaking in his verses, with Gryphius himself. His metaphysically witty poems to the mysterious "Eugenie" provide an excellent example of how he could blend intellect with human warmth. Gryphius published his *Lissaer Sonette* (1637; Sonnets from Lissa) at the age of 21, promising that he would publish much more soon. Amid the occasional poetry, love poems, and satirical sonnets addressed mainly to his teachers, friends, and patrons, however, we find "Tears of the Fatherland," his immortal lament on the war, then in its 18th year. The war devastated Germany and its institutions, but it especially affected ordinary men and women, taking away their faith and hope, their *Seelen-Schatz* (treasure of the soul). In comparison with Opitz and the playful, musical, "galant" direction that lyrical poetry received from the Renaissance, Gryphius's poems, such as those on Rome, are meditative and deeply serious, even when they are not expressly religious. His reflections on biblical stories and above all on the life, death, and resurrection of Jesus Christ express his fervent desire to believe, to conquer his profound skepticism about life, this *todten Gruft* (house of the dead).

But Gryphius also wrote very personal poems, such as "An sich selbst" ("To Myself") and "Threnen in schwerer Kranckheit" ("Tears in Severe Illness"). In the latter he laments but also transcends illness and human frailty, expressing gratitude for the grace of healing. He commemorates special occasions, as in "Der Autor über seinen Geburtstag" ("The Author on His Birthday"). He ponders his loneliness in the sonnet "Einsambkeit" ("Solitude") and the often heartbreaking stories of persons close to him, as in "An einen guten Freund / über das Absterben seiner Tochter" ("To a Good Friend on the Death of His Daughter"). This very human touch in his writing has kept the poet's voice alive. Reading Andreas Gryphius today means to enter the world of an individual worthy of our attention and to share in his struggles.

ERIKA A. METZGER

See also Baroque

Biography

Born in Glogau, Silesia, 2 October 1616. Studied at Glogau, 1631, Goerlitz, Fraustadt, and Danzig, 1632–36; tutor for the children of Georg von Schönborn, Freistadt, 1636–38; studied and lectured at the University of Leyden, 1638–42; on a grand tour, 1644–47; lived in France and Italy; married Rosina Deutschländer, 1649; secretary to the estates, Glogau, 1650. Died 16 July 1664.

Selected Works

Collections

Dramatische Dichtungen, edited by Julius Tittmann, 4 vols., 1870
Lustspiele, Trauerspiele, Lyrische Gedichte, edited by Hermann Palm, 3 vols., 1878–84
Werke, edited by Marian Szyrocki, 1963
Gesamtausgabe der deutschprachigen Werke, edited by Marian Szyrocki and Hugh Powell, 8 vols., 1963–83

Plays

Ermordete Majestät; oder, Carolus Stuardus, König von Gross Britannien (produced 1650), 1657, 1663; as *Murdered Majesty; or, Charles Stuart, King of Great Britain,* edited by Hugh Powell, 1955
Leo Armenius; oder, Fürsten-Mord, Trauerspiel (produced 1651), 1650; excerpts as *Leo Armenius: A Tragedy,* translated by Janifer Gerl Stackhouse, 1992
Die sieben Brüder; oder, Die Gibeoniter, from the play by Joost van den Vondel (produced 1652), 1698
Majuma, 1657
Catharina von Georgien; oder, Bewehrete Beständigkeit (produced 1655), 1657
Beständige Mutter; oder, Die Heilige Felicitas (produced 1657), 1657
Cardenio und Celinde; oder, Unglücklich Verliebete (produced 1661), 1657
Absurda Comica; oder, Herr Peter Squentz, 1658
Freuden und Trauer-Spiele, auch Oden und Sonnette sampt Herr Peter Squentz, 1658
Großmüthiger Rechts-Gelehrter; oder, Sterbender Ämilius Paulus Papinianus (produced 1660), 1659
Verliebtes Gespenst and *Die geliebte Dornrose,* 1661
Horribilicribrifax (produced 1674), 1663

Poetry

Lissaer Sonnete, 1637
Sonn-und Feiertags- Sonnete, 1639

Sonnete, 1643
Oden, 1643
Epigrammata, 1643
Olivetum, 1646
Teutsche Reim-Gedichte, 1650
Kirchhofsgedanken, Oden, 1657
Andreae Gryphii Deutscher Gedichte Erster Theil, 1657
Epigrammata; oder, Bey- Schrifften, 1663

Other
Fewrige Freystadt, 1637
Dissertationes funebres; oder, Leich-Abdankungen, bey unterschiedlichen hoch- und ansehnlichen Leich-Begängnüssen gehalten. Auch nebenst seinem letzten Ehren-Gedächtnüss und Lebens-Lauff, 1683

Translations
Thomas Corneille, *Der schwermende Schäffer Lysis,* 1661
Girolamo Razzi, *Seugamme, oder Untreues Hausgesinde,* 1663
Richard Baker, *Frag-Stück und Betrachtungen über das Gebett des Herren,* 1663

Further Reading

Bekker, Hugo, *Andreas Gryphius: Poet between Epochs,* Bern and Frankfurt: Lang, 1973
Benjamin, Walter, *Ursprung des deutschen Trauerspiels,* Berlin: Rowohlt, 1928
Browning, Robert Marcellus, *German Baroque Poetry, 1618–1723,* University Park: Pennsylvania State University Press, 1971
Gillespie, Gerald Ernest Paul, editor, *German Theater before 1750,* New York: Continuum, 1992
Manheimer, Victor, *Die Lyrik des Andreas Gryphius: Studien und Materialien,* Berlin: Weidmannsche Buchhandlung, 1904
Mannack, Eberhard, *Andreas Gryphius,* Stuttgart: Metzler, 1968; 2nd edition, 1986
Metzger, Erika A., and Michael M. Metzger, *Reading Andreas Gryphius: Critical Trends 1664–1993,* Columbia, South Carolina: Camden House, 1994
Pascal, Roy, *Shakespeare in Germany,* Norwood, Pennsylvania: Norwood Editions, 1937; New York: Octagon Books, 1971
Schindler, Marvin S., *The Sonnets of Andreas Gryphius: Use of the Poetic Word in the Seventeenth Century,* Gainesville: University of Florida Press, 1971
Spahr, Blake Lee, *Andreas Gryphius: A Modern Perspective,* Columbia, South Carolina: Camden House, 1993
Stackhouse, Janifer Gerl, *The Constructive Art of Gryphius' Historical Tragedies,* Bern and New York: Lang, 1986
Szyrocki, Marian, *Andreas Gryphius: Sein Leben und Werk,* Tübingen: Niemeyer, 1964

Karoline Friederike Louise Maximiliane von Günderrode 1780–1806

The place of Karoline von Günderrode (pseudonym: Tian or Ion) among her contemporaries is still open to dispute. Christa Wolf argues that her strongest affinities were to the tormented spiritual world of Heinrich von Kleist. Rehm, by contrast, aligned her convictions with those of Clemens and Bettina von Brentano and the Romantic philosopher and mystic Friedrich Creuzer. Goethe called her first collection of poems and prose a truly "remarkable" publication. Perhaps because Günderrode pursued a career as an artist in her own ardent way, however, she could never join Goethe's circle of literary women.

Günderrode's language reveals how attuned she was with the German poetic tradition from the Baroque to Goethe and Schiller. Reticence, reserve, and artistic discipline characterize Günderrode's style and diction. Her poem "Hochrot" (Bright Red), included in many German anthologies, represents a rare exception. It conveys the single idea that love must be as vibrant as the brilliant color red "bis an den Tod" (until death). It illustrates what Margaret Fuller, the first American critic to admire Günderrode's work, called the "silvery spiritual clearness of an angel's lyre."

Clemens Brentano criticized as "eigenmächtig" (idiosyncratic) Günderrode's desire to depict subjective events through vivid metaphors that center on peculiarly exalted phenomena, as in "Der Kuß im Traum" (The Kiss in a Dream), "Die Töne" (Sounds), or "Der Caucasus" (The Caucasus), whose peaks she imagines to be enveloped in eternal sublimity, in tragic contrast to humanity's turmoil. "Der Dom zu Cölln" (Cologne Cathedral) and, amazingly apt and contemporary, "Der Luftschiffer" (The Balloonist) convey man's existential loneliness and his striving to transcend earthly limits. The balloonist is carried back to earth by "das Gesetz der Schwere" (law of gravity). He must acknowledge that he cannot share in the power of the stars toward which he has traveled. Günderrode also authored such poetic dialogues as "Des Wandrers Niederfahrt" (The Pilgrim's Subterranean Descent) and "Die Manen" (Souls of the Dead). She wrote the plays *Mahomed, der Prophet von Mekka* (1805; Mohammed, the Prophet of Mecca), and *Udohla* (1806). *Hildgund,* the only drama of hers that was ever performed (1990), deplores the oppression of women by men (Burwick).

Günderrode's letters to Bettina von Arnim (née von Brentano) were preserved through the efforts of her friend, who used them, augmented by many poems, as the basis for the first biography of Günderrode. Critics point out that here we have the first printed exchange of letters between two young German women writers. The work has been seen as a novel and a "utopian text," "a first highlight in the history of a female literary tradition" (Frederiksen), even if, as has been suggested, Bettina von Arnim composed some of these letters 35 years later. In her letters, Karoline von Günderrode reveals herself to be an avid student of history, philosophy, and mythology. She is attentive to life around her; for instance, she provides a sharp vignette of Goethe's mother at the theater. Her insights, too, are telling: she declares Bettina to be a person who lives a life of poetry filled with a "musikalischer Urgeist" (essence of music). Günderrode admires the powers of nature in her friend's soul and declares her own poems to be nothing but "Balsam auf Unerfüllbares im Leben" (balm for unrealized dreams).

In her prose narratives, which intend to convey a moral or philosophical message, Günderrode shared with Goethe and other German Romantics, such as Novalis, Joseph Görres, and Friedrich Schlegel, a leaning toward the exotic. Her stories often feature Middle Eastern settings. "Geschichte eines Braminen" (Story of a Brahmin), originally published in a journal edited by Sophie von La Roche, also reflects Günderrode's own childhood. Reversing her experiences with her widowed mother, she tells of Almor, whose father neglected him following his mother's death. She argues that children are wounded for life if they are unloved.

In this story of education and enlightenment, Almor, first imbued with the Koran's teachings and the great religions of the past, travels to India to be the disciple of a Brahmin. He comes to see all faiths only as crutches for established customs and moral behavior and to learn that human beings live on three levels: animal-like as earthly beings, human in relationships with others, and on a spiritual level in connection with the infinite and eternal. Only by living on all three levels does a person find his true calling. This story is remarkable for the philosophical questions that Günderrode touches upon. Even the act of suicide is discussed: one character rejects it as harmful to society, and Almor argues that the individual has the freedom to take his own life.

Judging by her publications between 1804 and 1806, which branch out into many genres of literature at once, the young Günderrode had a brilliant future as a writer. Her passionate encounter with Creuzer, a married man who raised her hopes and then betrayed them, plunged her into despair and caused her to lose sight of her larger purpose. A dramatic poem, "Wandel und Treue" (Change and Constancy), written before she knew Creuzer, reveals Günderrode's sense of tragic necessity in the antithesis between the self-absorbed masculine spirit, Narziß (Narcissus), and the loving, rooted feminine principle of self-sacrifice, Violetta. Narziß demands from each relationship nothing but the perfect moment and after that complete freedom for himself. Violetta remains behind empty-handed. The poem seems eerily to prefigure the blatant egoism that Günderrode now encountered at Creuzer's hands, victim of circumstances though he might have been.

Creuzer's final renunciation of Günderrode, together with her constitutional melancholy, became too much to bear. Unlike her character Hildgund, she felt unable to take revenge. Now more keenly than ever aware of the social penalties of being female, she deplored that she was not born a man. Such utterances suggest that carefully analyzing Günderrode's texts in order to understand the complexities of her psychological state is the most important task for students of her work. Unlike Bettina von Brentano, Günderrode was possessed by—and had expressed in her work—that legendary Romantic longing for death (Rehm). In ending her own life, Günderrode left her work unfinished in its first budding and its fate undecided. Creuzer, her unhappy lover, withdrew Günderrode's last collection, *Melete* (1806), shortly after it had gone to print and destroyed several of her manuscripts because he no longer wanted to be connected with her works after her unseemly death.

ERIKA A. METZGER

Biography

Born in Karlsruhe, 11 February 1780. Daughter of a court official who died in 1786; entered a Protestant convent for poor female members of nobility in Frankfurt am Main, 1797; friendship with Bettina and Clemens von Brentano, Friedrich Carl von Savigny, and Friedrich Creuzer. Died (suicide) in Winkel on the Rhine, 26 July 1806.

Selected Works

Collections

Gedichte und Phantasien, 1804
Poetische Fragmente, 1805
Melete von Ion, 1806
Gesammelte Dichtungen, edited by Friedrich Götz, 1857
Gesammelte Werke, edited by Leopold Hirschberg, 3 vols., 1920–22; reprint, 1970
Gesammelte Dichtungen, edited by Elisabeth Salomon, 1923
Der Schatten eines Traumes: Gedichte, Prosa, Briefe, Zeugnisse von Zeitgenossen, edited by Christa Wolf, 1979; reprint, 1981
Gedichte, edited by Franz Joseph Goertz, 1985
Sämtliche Werke und ausgewählte Studien, edited by Walter Morgenthaler, et al., 1991

Other

Die Liebe der Günderode: Friedrich Creuzers Briefe an Caroline von Günderode, edited by Karl Preisendanz, 1912; reprint, 1974
The Defiant Muse: German Feminist Poems from the Middle Ages to the Present, A Bilingual Anthology, edited and translated by Susan L. Cocalis, 1986
Bitter Healing: German Women Writers 1700–1830, An Anthology, edited by Jeannine Blackwell and Susanne Zantop, translated by Walter Arndt and Marjanne E. Goozé, 1990
'Ich sende Dir ein zärtliches Pfand': Die Briefe der Karoline von Günderrode, edited by Birgit Weißenborn, 1992

Further Reading

Burdorf, Dieter, "'Diese Sehnsucht ist ein Gedanke, der ins Unendliche starrt': Über Karoline von Günderrode—aus Anlass neuer Ausgaben ihrer Werke und Briefe," *Wirkendes Wort: Deutsche Sprache in Forschung und Lehre* 43, no. 1 (1993)
Burwick, Roswitha, "Liebe und Tod in Leben und Werk der Günderode," *German Studies Review* 3 (1980)
Figueira, Dorothy M., "Karoline von Günderrode's Sanskrit Epitaph," *Comparative Literature Studies* 26, no. 4 (1989)
Frederiksen, Elke, editor, *Women Writers of Germany, Austria, and Switzerland: An Annotated Bio-Biographical Guide,* New York: Greenwood Press, 1989
Gnüg, Hiltrud, and Renate Möhrmann, editors, *Frauen, Literatur, Geschichte: Schreibende Frauen vom Mittelalter bis zur Gegenwart,* Stuttgart: Metzler, 1985
Hoff, Dagmar von, "Aspects of Censorship in the Work of Karoline von Günderrode," *Women in German Yearbook: Feminist Studies in German Literature and Culture* 11 (1995)
Kuhn, Anna K., "The 'Failure' of Biography and the Triumph of Women's Writing: Bettina von Arnim's 'Die Günderode' and Christa Wolf's 'The Quest for Christa T.'," in *In the Shadow of Olympus: German Women Writers around 1800,* edited by Katherine R. Goodman and Edith Waldstein, Albany: State University of New York Press, 1990
Lazarowicz, Margarete, *Karoline von Günderrode: Portrait einer Fremden,* Frankfurt and New York: Lang, 1986
Obermeier, Karin, "Private Matters Made Public: Love and the Sexualized Body in Karoline von Günderrode's Texts," *Dissertation Abstracts International* 56, no. 3 (1995)
———, "Karoline von Günderrode (1780–1806) Germany," in *Women Writers in German-Speaking Countries: A Bio-Bibliographical*

Critical Sourcebook, edited by Elke P. Frederiksen and Elisabeth G. Ametsbichler, Westport, Connecticut: Greenwood Press, 1998
Patterson, Rebecca, "Emily Dickinson's Debt to Günderrode," *Midwest Quarterly* 8 (1967)
Rehm, Walter, "Über die Gedichte der Karoline von Günderrode," in *Goethe-Kalender auf das Jahr 1942,* Leipzig: Frankfurter Goethe Museum, 1941
Solbrig, Ingeborg, "The Contemplative Muse: Karoline von Günderrode's Religious Works," *Germanic Notes and Reviews* 18 (1987)
Susman, Margarete, *Frauen der Romantik*, 3rd edition, Cologne: Melzer, 1960
Toegel, Edith, "Margaret Fuller, Bettina von Arnim, Karoline von Günderrode: A Kinship of Souls," *Yearbook of German-American Studies* 23 (1988)
Winkle, Sally A., "In Search of a Lost Friend: Death and Absence in Bettine von Arnim's Günderrode," *Selecta: Journal of the Pacific Northwest Council on Foreign Languages* l3 (1992)

Karl Gutzkow 1811–1878

Karl Gutzkow was the youngest of the group of writers known as Das Junge Deutschland (Young Germany) and was two years older than Georg Büchner, whom he can be said to have discovered. Both in terms of his abiding concern with religious, sexual, and political emancipation, and the manner in which he interacted with the emerging capitalist literary market of 19th-century Germany, Gutzkow represents a new secularized generation in German letters. Born in Berlin of humble parentage, he recorded in *Aus der Knabenzeit* (1852; From My Boyhood) the impact of poverty and cramped living conditions on family life, especially for women. Profiting from the Prusso-German scholarship system designed to attract able minds to the establishment, Gutzkow studied theology and philosophy at Berlin; his teachers included Hegel and Friedrich Schleiermacher. The Paris revolution of July 1830 determined his future career. Now not the Protestant church but the periodical press would supply him with his pulpit. In over 40 years of active life as a journalist, critic, and author, Gutzkow would produce over 2,600 texts in journals and newspapers, and he and his work attracted some 2,000 articles from contemporaries. He was one of the first Germans to set out to earn his living exclusively from his pen, without the support of a bourgeois profession or family connections. He aspired to be a journalist and critic in the manner of his West European contemporaries and saw the writer as the conscience of society. Robespierre, declared Heine, was but the hand of Rousseau, and for all his jealousy of his more gifted older contemporary, Gutzkow too believed passionately in the power of the written word to change society. He had the misfortune to embark on his career at one of the worst periods of repressive censorship in Germany's history. He was briefly incarcerated and his works were banned (along with those of Heine, Laube, Wienbarg, and Mundt) by the Diet of the German Confederation following the publication of *Wally, die Zweiflerin* (1835; Wally, the Doubter), Gutzkow's "scandalous" novel of sexual and religious emancipation featuring a "female Job" (Kruse).

Most literary histories still tend to identify Gutzkow almost exclusively with the Young Germans in the 1830s and with the work that attracted the most notoriety from contemporaries, his polemical and provocative *Wally.* But Gutzkow's range was much broader, his central concern as a writer being the liberation of the secular imagination, which he explored in many genres. He wrote novels, novellas, and short stories, tragedies and comedies, autobiography and travel literature, essays and sketches, trying, as so many of his generation did, to create for Germany the type of critical public discourse that had long existed in France and Britain. To a considerable extent Gutzkow did embody that aspiration in his person, attracting some 750 reviews of his own work and a further 720 reviews of his dramas. Gutzkow's dramatic oeuvre is long forgotten, but he was once a great box-office success, notably for his comedies, *Das Urbild des Tartüffe* (1844; The Model for Tartuffe) and *Zopf und Schwert* (1844; *Sword and Queue*), and for his drama, *Richard Savage; oder, Der Sohn einer Mutter* (1839; Richard Savage; or, The Son of a Mother). This play, with its fashionable "English" hero and German theme of the problems of the contemporary writer, was on the repertoire of some 18 German theaters within six months of its first performance. Perhaps Gutzkow's best dramatic work was his verse tragedy *Uriel Acosta* (1848), so admired by contemporaries, which recounts the struggle of a Jewish freethinker against prejudice and bigotry, ending in the hero's humiliating submission to superior force. (The parallels with some of the Young Germans' own lives cannot be overlooked.) Based on his novella *Der Sadduzäer von Amsterdam* (1834; The Sadducee of Amsterdam), the play marks a midway stage in German writing on Jewish subjects between Lessing's *Nathan der Weise* (1779) and Schnitzler's *Professor Bernhardi* (1912). Like Tieck and Immermann before him and Laube later, Gutzkow was one of a group of bourgeois directors who exercised considerable influence on the repertory and on performance styles of the mid-19th-century German-language theater.

"Brilliant journalist, who would try his hand as a poet"—Fontane's judgment is not wholly fair. Hebbel correctly observed that one needed to judge Gutzkow's achievement from more than one angle. A tireless editor of journals, many of them opinion leaders (such as Campe's *Telegraph für Deutschland,* which he edited 1837–42), Gutzkow showed his capacity to operate successfully in the business world with his magazine *Unterhaltungen am häuslichen Herd* (1852–62; Entertainments at the Fireside), modeled on Dickens' *Household Words.* Unlike Dickens, whom he much admired, Gutzkow did not appreciate his own talent for comedy, well displayed in his comic novels (*Seraphine* [1837] and *Blasedow und seine Söhne* [1838; Blasedow and His Sons]) and in stories such as *Der Ring oder die Nihilisten* (1852–53; The Ring or the Nihilists). He invested immense energy in two long novels of contemporary life but little realism, *Die Ritter vom Geiste* (1850–51; The Knights of the Spirit) and *Der Zauberer vom Rom* (1858–61; The Sorcerer of Rome), designed to illustrate his new concept of the novel *des Nebeneinander* (of simultaneity). Fontane praised the idea (not, however, properly realized) of taking the age as the novel's hero; he undoubtedly learned from it for his own first novel, *Vor dem Sturm* (1878; *Before the Storm*). But it is as a critic and a literary phenomenon that Gutzkow best deserves to be remembered. No one has as yet paid him the compliment of a critical edition, but since the appearance of Wolfgang Rasch's exemplary bibliography, students of literature and of the media in 19th-century Germany have an opportunity of appreciating what a ubiquitous and influential figure he once was.

EDA SAGARRA

See also Das Junge Deutschland

Biography

Born in Berlin, 17 March 1811. Educated at Friedrichwerdersches Gymnasium in Berlin; studied theology and philosophy in Berlin; founded journal *Forum der Journal-Literatur,* 1831; lived in Berlin, Leipzig, Frankfurt, Hamburg; first to recognize Büchner's genius, publishing his *Dantons Tod* and *Leonce und Lena;* served as general secretary of Schillerstiftung in Weimar, 1862–64; suffered in later life from acute paranoia, spending extended periods in a mental asylum and making several suicide attempts. Died in Frankfurt, 16 December 1878.

Selected Works

Collections

Vermischte Schriften, 4 vols., 1842
Dramatische Werke, 9 vols., 1842–57
Gesammelte Werke, 13 vols., 1845–52
Dramatische Werke, 20 vols., 1862–63
Gesammelte Werke, 12 vols., 1873–76
Karl Gutzkows ausgewählte Werke, 12 vols., edited by Heinrich Hubert Houben, 1908

Writings

Briefe eines Narren an eine Närrin, 1832
Maha Guru: Geschichte eines Gottes, 2 vols., 1833
Novellen, 2 vols., 1834
Wally, die Zweiflerin, 1835; as *Wally the Skeptic,* translated by Ruth-Ellen Boetcher-Joeres, 1974
Börne's Leben, 1840
Uriel Acosta, 1848; translated by M.M., 1860
Die kleine Narrenwelt, 3 vols., 1856–57
Reiseeindrücke aus Deutschland, der Schweiz, Holland und Italien (1832–73), 1876

Further Reading

Jones, Roger, "Gutzkow and the Catholic Issue," in *Vormärzliteratur in europäischer Perspektive,* vol. 1, *Öffentlichkeit und nationale Identität,* edited by Helmut Koopmann and Martina Lauster, Bielefeld: Aisthesis, 1996

Jones, Roger and Lauster, Martina, editors, *Gutzkow To-day,* Bielefeld: Aisthesis, 2000

Kruse, Joseph A., "Gutzkows *Wally* und der verbotsbeschluß," in *Das Junge Deutschland: Kolloquium zum 150. Jahrestag des Verbots vom 10. Dezember 1835,* edited by Joseph A. Kruse and Bernd Kortländer, Hamburg: Hoffmann and Campe, 1987

Lauster, Martina, "Reflections on the Public Sphere in the Critical Writings of Bulwer-Lytton, Sainte-Beuve and Gutzkow," in *Vormärzliteratur in europäischer Perspektive,* vol. 1, *Öffentlichkeit und nationale Identität,* edited by Helmut Koopmann and Martina Lauster, Bielefeld: Aisthesis, 1996

Plett, Bettina, "Zwischen 'gemeinem Talent' und 'Anempfindungskunst': Zwiespalt und Übergang in Karl Gutzkows Erzählungen," in *Geschichtlichkeit und Gegenwart: Festschrift für Hans Dietrich Irmscher zum 65. Geburtstag,* edited by Hans Esselborn and Werner Keller, Cologne: Böhlau, 1994

Rasch, Wolfgang, *Bibliographie Karl Gutzkow,* 2 vols., Bielefeld: Aisthesis, 1998

Sammons, Jeffrey, L., *Six Essays on the Young German Novel,* Chapel Hill: University of North Carolina Press, 1972

H

Jürgen Habermas 1929–

Jürgen Habermas's work as a social and critical theorist first gained wide attention in 1968, when he published *Erkenntnis und Interesse* (*Knowledge and Human Interests*). With this book he became recognized as the heir to such earlier Frankfurt theorists as Theodor Adorno, Max Horkheimer, and Herbert Marcuse. Habermas's work, however, has subsequently become much more Kantian in inspiration than that of these forebears.

Prior to *Knowledge and Human Interests,* Habermas had published a series of essays (later collected in *Theory and Practice*) and his first book, *Strukturwandel der Öffentlichkeit* (1962; *The Structural Transformation of the Public Sphere*). The essays, which treat a variety of topics from Hobbes to education, concern the capacity of social theory to account for the conditions under which it arises and is applied. This issue was basic to Marx's critique of ideology, since in order to engage in such a critique one must first make sure that one is not ideological oneself. But Habermas gives this idea a somewhat different twist. The basic condition for any kind of social theory is, of course, the free exchange of ideas, so any theory that would account for itself must at least in part be a theory of human interaction. But even Marx, a key figure in many of the book's essays, failed to see this communicative side of social theory—hence, he narrowed his emancipatory concerns merely to the liberation of work.

The precise nature of and conditions for truly free discussion are not easy to discern, and specifying them has occupied much of Habermas's work. His first major book, *The Structural Transformation of the Public Sphere,* carries these themes within a largely historical account of the rise—and fall—of the "public sphere," a space for informal but free social discussion that flourished in the bourgeois world of the 18th century.

Knowledge and Human Interests is also concerned with the capacity of knowledge to reflect upon its own genesis and applications. Its discussions of a broad range of 19th-century thinkers (including Hegel, Marx, Comte, Pierce, Dilthey, and Nietzsche, as well as Freud) amount to a major critique of positivism—the view that only the sciences can provide knowledge. For Habermas, what is inaccessible to science after the positivist or scientistic "disavowal of reflection" is the human interests that underlie knowledge. There are, he argues, three such interests. The sciences are underscored by an interest in technical control, but hermeneutic interpretation also aims at sustaining mutual understanding in ordinary language communication and in action. And the critical sciences seek to free us from dependence on hypostatized powers: they seek to serve an emancipatory interest. An example of this is psychoanalysis—when freed from the "scientistic" cast given to it by Freud himself.

Determining the precise way in which these interests are rooted in human nature proved to be problematic. Although Habermas had always found thought and reason to be realized primarily in language, he increasingly took a linguistic turn, as evidenced in essays such as "Some Distinctions in Universal Pragmatics," "Toward a Theory of Communicative Competence," and "Theories of Truth." These studies culminated in his most important single book, *Theorie des kommunikativen Handelns* (1982; *The Theory of Communicative Action*).

A work of immense scope, *The Theory of Communicative Action* views language and, indeed, all forms of human communication in terms of the "validity claims" they raise. When I say (or write) anything whatsoever to another person, Habermas argues, I am implicitly claiming that what I say is true; socially appropriate, and thus in conformity to whichever social codes govern the situation in which I speak; and sincere, so that my utterance truthfully expresses what I think and feel. These three validity claims refer me to an intersubjective sphere; as *validity* claims, however, they cannot not be warranted true merely by my saying so. Hence, if any of them is challenged by a hearer, I must try and show that they are valid. When this is undertaken, the situation turns from being one of communicative action to one of "discourse." And in order for discourse to justify anything, it must itself conform to certain principles: no claim can be declared exempt from discourse's scrutiny, no one can be excluded from speaking, all must have an equal chance to speak, and (what the other three principles are to guarantee) the force of the better argument must prevail.

The upshot of this is the important claim that all language is implicitly rational—not just in the sense that syntax exhibits logical structure, a fact known even to "positivists," but in the sense that language conveys, with each utterance, a commitment to rationality. For in everything I say, I commit myself, if challenged, to move to a speech situation that is structured on the principles of inclusivity, universality, and equality. The structure of this situation is Habermas's image of autonomy and freedom; a society can be criticized by seeing how closely the ways it reaches decisions approximate this picture.

There are two main ways in which they may not. The first is when decision-making patterns in society are reached via "strategic" actions that aim simply at influencing others in order to achieve some end. In such actions, the speaker's goals are not open to challenge by others; indeed, they may not even be made known to others. Strategic action, in fact, stands under no norms or constraints: the speaker simply does whatever works. Such action often moves by way of "money" and "power," two important mechanisms that get people to do things without convincing them rationally that they should. These "steering mechanisms," anchored in political and economic structures, are antithetical to communicative action and its home in the everyday "life world." Their progressive takeover of human affairs in the modern era is referred to by Habermas as the "colonization" of the life world.

The other way in which decision-making patterns in society may deviate from Habermas's communicative norms is when they are truncated: when, for example, only one sort of validity claim is allowed to be challenged and discussed. This is where *The Theory of Communicative Action* joins up with Habermas's earlier critique of positivism, for under a positivist regime, truth is the only thing in which we can have a rational interest, and rational disputes are all solely disputes about truth.

The Theory of Communicative Action thus presents a life world structured by the rational principles of communicative action and the discourse to which it leads. It is increasingly challenged, however, by the "steering mechanisms" of money and power; it is also increasingly disabled by the reduction of rationality to the positive sciences. It is in such a life world, then, that *The Theory of Communicative Action* has itself come to be; and in reflecting on the conditions of the book's own existence, Habermas sees the origins of the life world in the historical process of modernization. In modernization, which Habermas conceives following the example of Max Weber, the three validity claims have become increasingly distinct, and, with this shift, the unified premodern human world has differentiated into three distinct domains. Each domain has its own patterns of argumentation and separate social sphere: the "objectivating" rationality present in the sciences is geared to the production of technological means for the pursuit of various ends. In the modern world, it has been set off against the "moral-practical" rationality that is socially embedded in the legal system and ethical norms of a society and against the "aesthetic-practical" rationality embedded primarily in the institutions of the art world.

The Theory of Communicative Action thus in part reflects on history. It is not the actual events of history that Habermas meditates upon, however, but the history of the social theories that seek, in turn, to comprehend those events and their results. Hence, the book contains major discussions of Weber, as well as Mead, Durckheim, and Talcott Parsons. What Habermas seeks to show with all this is that the differentiation of validity claims into the three claims recognized by modernity was not merely a contingent happening but a "learning process" that teaches us something about how reason "really" is.

The view that history can make progress in this way—and that only through such historical progress can we gain knowledge of ourselves—is a basically Hegelian view, and, to that extent, Habermas may be seen as operating in the tradition of Hegel. His concern with autonomy and the structures to which we are always rationally committed, however, is suggestive of Kant, and this Kantian strand in Habermas's thought comes increasingly to the fore after *The Theory of Communicative Action*. It leads him in two directions: toward more concrete developments of the guiding themes of *The Theory of Communicative Action* and into polemics against what he considers to be foes of enlightenment, both in Germany and abroad.

Habermas fleshes out *The Theory of Communicative Action* in two main ways: by developing what he calls "discourse ethics" and by discussing issues in social philosophy, particularly those that concern law and democracy. Habermas's Kantianism is especially clear in his approach to ethics, which is summed up in *The Theory of Communicative Action* (vol. 2) as follows:

> What was intended by the categorical imperative can be made good by projecting a will-formation under the idealized conditions of universal discourse. Subjects capable of moral judgment cannot test each for himself alone whether an established or recommended norm is in the general interest . . . but can do so only in community with all others affected.

For Kant, the moral realm, with its categorical imperative, was grounded in a noumenal world—one that we do not sense and therefore cannot know, but whose idea we can construct via rational "recipes." Habermas keeps the basic content of Kant's philosophical idea but he changes its status: the categorical imperative is no longer grounded in a noumenal world but in the basic ideals presupposed by human interaction. With this move, Habermas both gains and loses: on the one hand, many vexed questions concerning the status of Kant's "noumenal" realm are circumvented; on the other hand, the universality that Kant had achieved for his ethics by removing it from everything empirical becomes problematic for Habermas. How do we know that our patterns of communication and, by extension, their presuppositions are universal?

In *Faktizität und Geltung* (1992; *Between Facts and Norms*), Habermas returns to a concrete analysis of modern society, and, in particular, to the public sphere. Seeking to find concrete realizations of his "idealized . . . universal discourse," he distinguishes between "weak publics" and "strong publics." Weak publics are the kind of informal "nongovernmental organizations" of the types that he had discussed in *The Structural Transformation of the Public Sphere*, while "strong publics" such as parliaments, actually make legally binding decisions. The book contains extensive discussions of various theories on the normative force of law.

Like Kant, Habermas is a vigorous polemicist, arguing forcefully against those who would deny the "project of enlightenment" that so deeply inspires his own thought. The most public form this has taken was in his engagement in the *Historikerstreit* of the 1980s, in which Habermas entered the fray against various forms of Holocaust denial. He has also written courageously on German identity during and after the reunification of the two Germanys.

JOHN MCCUMBER

See also Historians' Debate

Biography

Born in Düsseldorf, 18 June 1929. Studied at the University of Göttingen; Ph.D., University of Bonn, 1954; further study at the University of Marburg, 1961; lecturer in philosophy, University of Heidelberg, 1962–64; professor of philosophy and sociology, University of Frankfurt, 1964–71, and honorary professor, 1974; codirector, Max-Planck-Institut zur Erforschung der Lebensdingungen der wissenschaftlich-technischen Welt, Starnberg, West Germany, 1971–81; returned as professor of philosophy and sociology, University of Frankfurt, since 1983. Hegel Prize, Stuttgart, 1974; Sigmund Freud Prize, 1976; Adorno Prize, 1980; Geschwister Scholl Prize, 1985. Currently lives in Frankfurt.

Selected Works

Philosophical and Sociological Works

Strukturwandel der Öffentlichkeit, 1962; as *The Structural Transformation of the Public Sphere: An Inquiry into a Category of Bourgeois Society,* translated by Thomas Burger, 1989

Theorie und Praxis (essays), 1963; as *Theory and Practice,* translated by J. Viertel, 1973

Zur Logik der Sozialwissenschaften, 1967; as *On the Logic of the Social Sciences,* translated by Shierry Weber Nicholsen and Jerry A. Stark, 1988

Erkenntnis und Interesse, 1968; as *Knowledge and Human Interests,* translated by Jeremy J. Shapiro, 1971

Legitimationsprobleme im Spätkapitalismus, 1973; as *Legitimation Crisis,* translated by Thomas McCarthy, 1975

Theorie des kommunikativen Handelns, 2 vols., 1982; as *The Theory of Communicative Action,* translated by Thomas McCarthy, 2 vols., 1984–87

Moralbewusstsein und kommunikatives Handeln, 1983; as *Moral Consciousness and Communicative Action,* translated by Christian Lenhardt and Shierry Weber Nicholsen, 1990

Vorstudien und Ergänzungen zur Theorie des Kommunikativen Handelns, 1984

Der philosophische Diskurs der Moderne, 2nd edition, 1985; as *The Philosophical Discourse of Modernity,* translated by Frederick Lawrence, 1987

Nachmetaphysisches Denken, 1988; as *Postmetaphysical Thinking,* translated by William Mark Hohengarten, 1992

Vergangenheit als Zukunft, 1990; as *The Past as Future,* translated and edited by Max Pensky, 1994

Faktizität und Geltung, 1992; *Between Facts and Norms,* translated by William H. Rehg, 1996

Die Normalität einer Berliner Republik, 1995; as *A Berlin Republic: Writings on Germany,* translated by Steven Rendall, 1997

Die Einbeziehung des Anderen, 1996; as *The Inclusion of the Other,* edited by Ciaran Cronin and Pablo De Greif, 1998

Further Reading

Benhabib, Seyla, *Critique, Norm, and Utopia,* New York: Columbia University Press, 1986

Braaten, Jane, *Habermas's Critical Theory of Society,* Albany: State University of New York Press, 1991

Geuss, Raymond, *The Idea of a Critical Theory,* Cambridge and New York: Cambridge University Press, 1981

McCarthy, Thomas, *The Critical Theory of Jürgen Habermas,* Cambridge, Massachusetts: MIT Press, 1978

Rasmussen, David M., *Reading Habermas,* Oxford and Cambridge, Massachusetts: Blackwell, 1990

Thompson, John B., and David Held, *Habermas: Critical Debates,* Cambridge, Massachusetts: MIT Press, and London: Macmillan, 1982

White, Stephen K., *The Recent Work of Jürgen Habermas,* Cambridge: Cambridge University Press, 1987; New York: Cambridge University Press, 1988

Strukturwandel der Öffentlichkeit 1962

Philosophical/Historical Study by Jürgen Habermas

In Germany of the 1960s, the second generation of critical sociologists was coming of age, and perhaps no work is more closely identified with its maturation than Jürgen Habermas's *Strukturwandel der Öffentlichkeit* (*The Structural Transformation of the Public Sphere*), published in 1962. With this work, Habermas began to establish himself as perhaps the most important intellectual voice of postwar Germany and to promote the public sphere as one of its most significant sociological categories.

According to Habermas's historical account, the public sphere (*Öffentlichkeit*) emerged concomitant and intertwined with the bourgeois culture of the 18th and 19th centuries. As a sociological category or "ideal type" definitive of modernity, it has two distinct components. *Historically,* it comprised artistic, literary, journalistic, and other institutions that, beginning in England and moving later to the continent, were spurred on by the rising autonomy of the bourgeois citizen as a private person in an economically marked civil society that was, in turn, increasingly separated structurally from the state through private law. *Normatively,* the public sphere was a space open to all. Habermas therefore ascribes to the public sphere the potential for rational discourse, in which private individuals discuss issues of common or conflicting interest and seek to reach consensus free of both state and economic interference. The public sphere thus presented an incipient communicative arena—distinct from the state, the intimate sphere, and the economic domain—where individual needs and interests could be mutually formulated and negotiated free of power relations or heteronomous regulation.

In place of the display and spectacle that defined the "representative publicness" of manorial authority, a newly emerging "authentic public sphere" relied not on hierarchical distinctions between participant and observer of public representations but rather on secured distinctions between public and private spheres of life. As the public authority of the complex apparatus and institutions of state organization and control grew during the 17th and 18th centuries, self-representation at the court lost its significance as a form of public authority and was transformed into an essentially private activity. In addition, this new category of privacy was also crucial for the development of the self-assertion of the new bourgeois class. For from here, it could launch the institutions of civil society that would become the home for unregulated political will formation in the public sphere.

Within civil society, therefore, the solidified category of privacy provided the precondition for a new and "authentic" concept of publicness. For here, the establishment of private law that regulated economic interaction as opposed to public law that secured the negative rights and the personal and national safety of citizens was accompanied historically by the emergence of the intimate sphere of bourgeois family life. Privacy thus allowed for freedom *from* state intervention as well as for the development of an interior subjectivity that was a main focus of the bourgeois novel. Reliant on and ideologically justified by this new form of subjectivity, the public sphere emerged as a domain of collective private engagement in opposition to state authority. Distinct from the state, the marketplace, and the intimate sphere of the family, it was constituted in a lively culture of coffeehouses, salons, reading organizations, a critical press, and learned societies, in which forms of expression, especially artistic forms, were rendered increasingly autonomous of their formerly religious or "representative public" functions.

Crucial to Habermas's normative understanding of this sphere are three institutional criteria shared by these venues: first, hierarchies were leveled by the practice of an open discourse, in which better arguments secured parity among participants; second, the content of dialogue was no longer restricted, as issues of common interest no longer belonged to the province of the state or the Church; and third, the public was composed of a discrete group that was, however, potentially infinitely inclusive of all who wished to engage in public discourse. Thus, the public sphere must be understood not only in its historically specific relation to bourgeois society but also normatively in relation to the constitutional rights that it virtually embodied as a bulwark against state intervention both in the economy as well as in the communicative activities of the public sphere itself. Therefore, the bourgeois public sphere contained an essential self-contradiction. By providing a domain for the democratic formation of political will within civil society, the historical public sphere was preparing the normative grounds for the deliberative legal procedures later secured by liberal democratic constitutions, and hence, for its own institutional obsolescence.

Ideologically, as the derivative of liberal structures of civil society, the bourgeois public sphere also mimicked the laissez-faire practices of the free market. While as an ideal the bourgeois public sphere fulfilled the cosmopolitan dream of Kant's Perpetual Peace, which has fascinated Habermas throughout his career, it also relied on the fictional identity between the roles of its members as human beings most generally (*homme*) and as property owners (*bourgeois*), which both became increasingly untenable toward the end of the 19th century. Marx was thus correct in noting that the unity of public interests manifested in the public sphere with the modes of discourse practiced there were not supported by the objective structure of society that was, in truth, wracked with the incommensurability of interests determined by deep class divisions.

Only a democratization of the liberal economic base that provided the social conditions of the public sphere would be able to address the structural crises of monopoly capitalism's "neo-mercantilism." Moreover, only an activist state with a well-developed bureaucratic apparatus could respond to the subsequent demands for regulations of labor practices and for deep intervention into the social realm in order to treat the acute ills associated with poverty, health, civil rights, and later, the environment of an entire populace. Accompanying this "refeudalization" by the state of the formerly independent social domain was also a loss of integrity in the border between public and private life, as the state once again became the exclusive voice of public interests, which it had lost with the historical emergence of the public sphere.

In addition, the activities of the public institutions of this reinvigorated state began to resemble those of private citizens, entering into contractual agreements in order to provide social services. And, at the same time, those political parties that existed formerly as independent constituents of civil society became inseparable from the state itself, cooperating with it in the production and manipulation of public opinion, with the goal of ensuring an undisrupted continuity between preparliamentary and parliamentary discussions that had once been distinctly separate. Today, publicity and public opinion, Habermas has concluded, are adduced only as a post factum rationalization of the exercise of social and political power from a centralized authority rather than from a dispersed public deliberation.

Open public deliberation is replaced, therefore, by a voting public whose opinion results from public relation techniques borrowed from marketing and advertising strategies and delivered by mass media. With this, the historical public sphere that belonged to the age of the bourgeois constitutional state lost even a residue of its emancipatory function. In the social-welfare state that has privatized the public domain and incorporated social interests into the state, the liberal guarantee of state noninterference in free expression no longer suffices to ensure the grounds of a democratic society. For a future public sphere, not only rights but also participation needs to be guaranteed. The reading public needs to be transformed into one more directly involved in the building of political consensus. In addition, only by securing institutional structures for this can there be determinate features of public opinion that would allow one to distinguish between a consensus that is the product of reasonable communication and one that merely reflects irrational conformity.

This conformity is assured by state colonization of unregulated public debate and by the collapse of public and private spheres. Even the workplace, once clearly demarcated from both the private and the public spheres, is transformed into an "occupational sphere," as the working populace becomes dominated by wage-earning specialists rather than by owners of the economic means of their own subsistence through small-scale production or agriculture. The company town, the corporatization of social benefits, and the determination of social ties based on work rather than status or voluntary participation by private citizens in a public deliberation on cultural and political issues all contributed to the occlusion of the historical public sphere. In addition, individual socialization formerly excluded to the intimate familial domain was attenuated by the introduction of mandatory schooling. And, most important, the "man of letters" was reduced from a participant in the production of public discourse to a mere consumer of entertainment, and leisure activities were created for his relaxation rather than cultivation. Habermas would agree here with Herbert Marcuse that the critical, public character of social life was replaced by the "repressive desublimation" of the culture industry. Instead of offering public spaces into which private people can enter to participate in a common discussion, mass media now channel culture into the pseudoprivate sphere, thereby obviating the distinction between public and private spheres that was the precondition for an authentically democratic polity. In the place of a shared productive activity with a political quality, public communication devolves into "acts of individuated reception" that serve merely as a "tranquilizing substitute for action."

Thus, the historical public sphere became a victim of the socioeconomic transformations entailed in the historical development from a liberal to a social-welfare state and the technologization of communicative media. Yet even as the historical public sphere has shrunk and become politically superfluous, the prospects for a new public sphere remain unclear. The hope Habermas evinces of establishing procedures outside or on the margins of the state, which would guarantee a political will constituted by democratic deliberation rather than "mediatized" conformity, rests on a highly abstracted structure: "Under conditions of a large social-welfare state the communicative interconnectedness of a *public* can be brought about only in this way: through a critical publicity brought to life within intraorganizational public spheres, the completely short-circuited circulation of quasi-public opinion would be linked to the informal domain of the hitherto non-public opinions." How to construe these intraorganizational public spheres is left unexplained. In his later work Habermas seeks to translate its normative content, which he vaguely formulates in these formal terms, into rationally secured forms inherent in all speech and, especially, in the domain of multileveled deliberation inherent in the procedural legitimization of law. Here, however, he leaves open the question of whether the public sphere, without being utopian, can be more than a "negative constant"—a regulative fiction—in today's world; or whether, as a historical category, it can find a new place for itself.

Through Habermas's work, the conceptualization of the public sphere reached a new level of sociological subtlety and complexity. Not surprisingly, it also encountered several strains of criticism, one of which is represented by Oskar Negt, an assistant to Habermas, and Alexander Kluge, a student of Adorno's, in their *Public Sphere and Experience* (1972). Here, along with a new emphasis on concrete "life contexts" associated with the precarious concept of experience (*Erfahrung*), Negt and Kluge reject the hegemony of a singular public sphere. Along with what they call "counter-public spheres," they emphasize the multiplicity of public spheres, each of which must be understood in more complex ways as aggregation of experiences and phenomena rather than normatively defined. This critique resonates with the work of Geoff Eley, who, after Habermas's work was finally translated into English in 1989, was joined by Nancy Fraser, Carole Pateman, Mary Ryan, and others in pointing out the gender specificity of the historical public sphere, which not only excluded women but served empirically as sites of specifically masculinized cultural practices.

Negt and Kluge also maintain that the homogenized, ideal form of the public sphere that Habermas propagated was unnecessarily narrowly defined in a way that led to an inexorable diagnosis of decline and disintegration that might be less dire if greater emphasis were placed on the heterogeneity of its contents and forms. In addition, Jean Cohen and Andrew Arato have asserted that Habermas's overreliance on Marx's ideological-critical view of the public sphere compelled him to formulate the public sphere in more exclusionary terms than he would have had he relied on more liberal guides. But they also point out that Habermas later ultimately rejected both Marxist and liberal versions of a renewed public sphere. Even if in his later work Habermas did suggest that the integrative and communicative features of law in a deliberative democracy reproduce the normative content of the public sphere, however, it is clear that a historical variant has yet to be realized.

BRETT R. WHEELER

Editions

First edition: *Strukturwandel der Öffentlichkeit: Untersuchungen zu einer Kategorie der bürgerlichen Gesellschaft,* Neuwied: Luchterhand, 1962

Translation: *The Structural Transformation of the Public Sphere: An Inquiry into a Category of Bourgeois Society,* translated by Thomas Burger, Cambridge, Massachusetts: MIT Press, and London: Polity Press, 1989

Further Reading

Calhoun, Craig J., editor, *Habermas and the Public Sphere,* Cambridge, Massachusetts: MIT Press, 1992

Cohen, Jean L., and Andrew Arato, *Civil Society and Political Theory,* Cambridge, Massachusetts: MIT Press, 1992

Hohendahl, Peter Uwe, *The Institution of Criticism,* Ithaca, New York: Cornell University Press, 1982

Jäger, Wolfgang, *Öffentlichkeit und Parlamentarismus: Eine Kritik an Jürgen Habermas,* Stuttgart: Kohlhammer, 1973

Keane, John, editor, *Civil Society and the State,* London and New York: Verso, 1988

Knödler-Bunte, Eberhard, "The Proletarian Public Sphere and Political Organization," *New German Critique* 4 (Winter 1974)

Landes, Joan B., *Women in the Public Sphere in the Age of the French Revolution,* Ithaca, New York: Cornell University Press, 1988

Lottes, Günther, *Politische Aufklärung und plebejisches Publikum: Zur Theorie und Praxis des englischen Radikalismus im späten 18. Jahrhundert,* Munich: Oldenbourg, 1979

Negt, Oskar, and Alexander Kluge, *Öffentlichkeit und Erfahrung: Zur Organisationsanalyse von bürgerlicher und proletarischer Öffentlichkeit,* Frankfurt: Suhrkamp, 1972; as *Public Sphere and Experience: Toward an Analysis of the Bourgeois and Proletarian Public Sphere,* translated by Peter Labanyi et al., Minneapolis: University of Minnesota Press, 1993

Robbins, Bruce, editor, *The Phantom Public Sphere,* Minneapolis: University of Minnesota Press, 1993

Strum, Arthur, "A Bibliography of the Concept Öffentlichkeit," *New German Critique* 61 (Winter 1994)

Wehler, Hans Ulrich, *Deutsche Gesellschaftsgeschichte,* Munich: Beck, 1987

Ida von Hahn-Hahn 1805–1880

Both Ida von Hahn-Hahn's life and work were marked by radical changes in the late 1840s. The 1848 revolution and the death of her friend and lifelong partner, Baron Adolf von Bystram, in 1849, stirred up anxieties that made her turn to the Catholic Church. Religion and the church became major factors in her personal life, and this combination is reflected in the themes of most of her later works.

Ida Marie Luise Gustave, Countess von Hahn-Hahn (née Hahn; married Hahn), was born on 22 June 1805, in Tressow/Mecklenburg, into a family of impoverished aristocrats. Her parents divorced when she was four years old, and her mother raised her and her three siblings under tight financial circumstances. Hahn-Hahn received little formal education. During her teenage years, however, she read widely and began to experiment with writing poems. A marriage of convenience to her cousin Friedrich Adolf von Hahn-Basedow was arranged in 1826, but it soon ended in divorce (1829), leaving Hahn-Hahn so disillusioned with marriage that she vowed never to marry again. While she had not questioned marriages of convenience earlier, she now started to search for happier alternatives for the women of her time. In 1829 she entered into a "free" relationship with Baron Adolf von Bystram, and the heroines of her novels that were published prior to her conversion to Catholicism (1850) usually demand more rights for women, question conventions, and challenge patriarchy. As a result, some contemporary critics considered Hahn-Hahn a frivolous rebel whose demands could easily undermine social "morale" (in this context, morale was equated to male dominance). These early novels were clearly targeted at a female audience, or, more specifically, a female audience that could appreciate accounts of the boredom, frustrations, and suffering of aristocratic young women; many show autobiographic traits. *Aus der Gesellschaft* (1838; *Society of High Life in Germany;* republished in 1845 as *Ilda Schönholm*), *Der Rechte* (1839; The Right Man), *Gräfin Faustine* (1841; *The Countess Faustina*), *Ulrich* (1841; *Ulrich: A Tale*), *Sigismund Forster* (1843), *Cecil* (1844), *Zwei Frauen* (1845; *Two Women*), *Clelia Conti* (1846), *Sibylle: Eine Selbstbiographie* (1846; Sibylle: An Autobiography), and *Levin* (1848) all share many common themes. First, they all criticize arranged marriages. Second, the works' female protagonists break with traditions and conventions in order to escape suffering and frustrations. Third, in these works, talented women artists (writers, painters, or musicians) are torn between the obligation to stay faithful to an unloved and/or unloving husband and the desire to follow a soul mate who would help to foster their talents and accept them as equal partners in "free" and/or platonic relationships. Fourth, the convent is seen as a final refuge from society. Even though the titles of some of these novels could suggest that Hahn-Hahn wanted to place men in the center of her novels, each novel clearly focuses on the actions and reflections of a female protagonist. In some instances, well-known characters from one novel even reappear in another novel (e.g., Ilda Schönholm reappears in *Ulrich,* characters from *Sigismund Forster* resurface in *Cecil,* and Tranquillina, the daughter of the heroine in *Clelia Conti,* returns in *Levin*).

All of these early novels were quite successful, although *The Countess Faustina* received most of the attention. In this work, Hahn-Hahn for the first time openly challenges the rules of conduct in a patriarchal society by creating a female protagonist who is financially independent, openly lives with her lover, and rejects gender-related hierarchical thinking.

Hahn-Hahn also made a name for herself as a travel writer. Between 1835 and 1847, she traveled to several European countries and was one of the first German-speaking women to travel to the Near East and to write about her experiences. She published several travelogues that were well received between 1840 and 1844; the most successful was her *Orientalische Briefe* (1844; translated as *Letters of a German Countess: Written during her Travels in Turkey, Egypt, the Holy Land, Syria, Nubia, etc. in 1843–34,* also *Letters from the Holy Land,* and *Letters from the Orient; or, Travels in Turkey, the Holy Land, and Egypt*). Originally published in three volumes, this travelogue compiles letters that she had sent to close family members and a friend. Lengthy descriptions of the environment are intertwined with reflections upon topics that were already important to her back home: the status of women within society and within relationships. While Hahn-Hahn paid much attention to the "female sphere" in other cultures, and while one can sense a certain amount of empathy in these reflections, they nevertheless clearly show limitations. Hahn-Hahn was very much a child of her own time; she believed in the superiority of the white race.

During the years 1848 and 1849, almost everything changed in Ida von Hahn-Hahn's life. The threat that democratic and republican forces within society could restrict or even abolish the privileges of the nobility and the death of her lover made her search for a new meaning in life. For her, the Catholic Church became a refuge that stood for preservation and in itself symbolized an antidemocratic structure. Hahn-Hahn explained the reasons for her conversion in great detail in *Von Babylon nach Jerusalem* (1851; *From Babylon to Jerusalem*). In 1854 Hahn-Hahn founded and financed a convent "Zum guten Hirten" (To the Good Shepard) in Mainz, where she created a refuge for unwed mothers. Even though Hahn-Hahn never became a nun, she spent the last 26 years of her life there. She died on 12 January 1880.

All of Hahn-Hahn's books that were written after her conversion differ tremendously from the books she had published before. Most of the works that were published between 1851 and 1860 depict the lives of people who had served within the church, retell legends, or glorify the life of the Virgin Mary. Hahn-Hahn clearly distanced herself from her pre-1850 publications and even objected to a 21-volume edition of her "Protestant" (pre-1850) books, which was put on the market against her will in 1851. After 1860 Hahn-Hahn resurfaced as a novelist and wrote 14 "Catholic" novels. Among these novels, *Nirwana* (1875) stands out. Here, Hahn-Hahn portrays lax and hypocritical Catholics; she was heavily criticized by the Catholic Church for doing so. A complete edition of Hahn-Hahn's "Catholic" works (45 volumes) was published between 1902 and 1905.

Hahn-Hahn was one of the most widely read 19th-century female novelists in Germany, and many of her works were soon translated into other languages. Looking at the official reception during her lifetime, however, suggests that most critics either objected to ideas she promoted or simply labeled her writings as nothing more than *Unterhaltungsliteratur* (escapist literature). Among the women critics of her time, the comments of Fanny Lewald and Minna Cauer (a leftist advocate for women's rights) stand out. Both of them criticized Hahn-Hahn for focusing almost exclusively on her own class and for demanding women's rights based on individual change alone, while rejecting a democratization of society. Lewald, who was also involved in a personal feud with Hahn-Hahn over a man (Heinrich Simon), even went so far to ridicule Hahn-Hahn openly in her novel *Diogena: Roman von Iduna Gräfin H. . . . H. . . .* (*Diogena, a Novel by Iduna Countess H. . . . H. . . .*), which was published anonymously in 1847.

Regarding the scholarly reception of Hahn-Hahn's works, it must be stated that almost every study on this author either focuses exclusively on the pre-1850 or the post-1850 literary production, which explains why Hahn-Hahn has been ascribed many different labels that seem contradictory: they range from titles such as "the German George Sand" to depictions that stress nothing but the author's ultramontane point of view. While Hahn-Hahn did not receive much scholarly attention during the 20th century until the late 1970s, her early novels and her travelogues were rediscovered by feminist literary and sociohistorical scholarship and by modern research on travel literature.

STEFANIE OHNESORG

Biography

Born in Tressow/Mecklenburg, 22 June 1805. Daughter of Count Karl Friedrich von Hahn-Neuhaus and Sophie von Behr; married cousin, Count Adolf von Hahn-Basedow, 1826; marriage dissolved, 1829; birth of a mentally handicapped daughter, 1829; began relationship with Adolf Baron Bystram, 1829; birth of son, 1830; traveled to Switzerland, Spain, France, Scandinavia, Turkey, Near East, England, 1835–47; felt threatened by the events of the 1848 revolution; converted to Catholicism, 1850; lived in Mainz, from 1850; founded convent "Zum guten Hirten in Mainz, 1854. Died in Mainz, 12 January 1880.

Selected Works

Collections

Gedichte und neue Gedichte, 2 vols., 1835
Aus der Gesellschaft: Gesammt-Ausgabe der Romane (bis 1844), 8 vols., 1845 [vol.1: *Ilda Schönholm*, vol. 2: *Der Rechte*, vols. 3 and 4: *Gräfin Faustine*, vols. 5 and 6: *Ulrich*, vol. 7: *Sigismund Forster*, vol. 8: *Cecil*]
Gesammelte Schriften, 21 vols., 1851
Lichtstrahlen aus den Werken, edited by H. Keiter, 1881
Gesammelte Werke: Mit einer bibliographisch-literarischen Einleitung von Otto von Schaching, 45 vols., 1902–5
Perlen aus Gräfin Ida Hahn-Hahn's Werken, edited by J.G., 1905
Heiligenlegenden von Ida Hahn-Hahn, edited by Anton Georg Weber, 1914

Fiction

Aus der Gesellschaft, 1838; newly published in German as *Ilda Schönholm,* 1845; as *Society of High Life in Germany,* 1854
Der Rechte, 1839
Ulrich, 2 vols., 1841; as *Ulrich: A Tale,* translated by J.B.S., 2 vols., 1845
Gräfin Faustine, 1841; as *The Countess Faustina,* translated by H.N.S., 1844; as *Faustina: A Novel,* 1872
Sigismund Forster, 1843
Cecil, 2 vols., 1844
Die Brüder, 1845
Zwei Frauen, 2 vols., 1845
Sibylle: Eine Selbstbiographie, 2 vols., 1846
Clelia Conti, 1846
Levin, 2 vols., 1848
Maria Regina: Eine Erzählung aus der Gegenwart, 2 vols., 1860
Doralice: Ein Familiengemälde aus der Gegenwart, 2 vols., 1861
Zwei Schwestern: Eine Erzählung aus der Gegenwart, 2 vols., 1863
Peregrin: Ein Roman, 2 vols., 1864
Die Geschichte eines armen Fräuleins, 2 vols., 1869
Die Glöcknerstochter, 2 vols., 1871
Die Erzählung des Hofraths, 2 vols., 1872
Vergib uns unsere Schuld!, 2 vols., 1874; as *Dorothea Waldgrave, A Tale,* 1875 translated by Mary Elizabeth and Court Herbert, 1875
Nirwana, 2 vols., 1875
Eine reiche Frau, 2 vols., 1877
Der breite Weg und die enge Straße: Eine Familiengeschichte, 2 vols., 1877
Wahl und Führung, 2 vols., 1878

Travel Writing

Jenseits der Berge, 2 vols., 1840; revised edition, 1845
Reisebriefe, 2 vols., 1841
Erinnerungen aus und an Frankreich, 2 vols., 1842
Ein Reiseversuch im Norden, 1843; as *Travels in Sweden: Sketches of a Journey to the North,* translated by J.B.S., 1845
Orientalische Briefe, 3 vols., 1844; 1 vol. abridged version, edited by Gabriele Habinger, 1991; as *Letters of a German Countess: Written during Her Travels in Turkey, Egypt, the Holy Land, Syria, Nubia, etc. in 1843–44,* 3 vols., 1845, 1846; as *Letters from the Holy Land,* translated by Samuel Phillips, 1845, 1849; as *Letters from the Orient: or, Travels in Turkey, the Holy Land, and Egypt,* 1844
Meine Reise in England, edited by Bernd Goldmann, 1981

Poetry

Gedichte, 1835
Neue Gedichte, 1836
Venezianische Nächte, 1836
Lieder und Gedichte, 1837
Astralion: Eine Arabeske, 1839
Das Jahr der Kirche, 1854

Other

Die Kinder auf dem Abensberg: Eine Weihnachtsgabe, 1843
"Vorwort," *Lichtstrahlen aus der Gemüthswelt: Zur Erweckung und Erquickung für Blinde* [also contains three poems not published elsewhere], selected and edited by A. Lindau, 1845
Unsrer lieben Frau: Marienlieder, 1850
Von Babylon nach Jerusalem, 1851; as *From Babylon to Jerusalem,* translated by Elizabeth Atcherley, 1851
Aus Jerusalem, 1851
Die Liebhaber des Kreuzes, 2 vols., 1852
Ein Büchlein vom guten Hirten: Eine Weihnachtsgabe, 1853; as *A Few Words about the Good Shepherd,* 1858
co-editor, *Legende der Heiligen,* 3 vols., 1854–56
Bilder aus den drei ersten Jahrhunderten der christlichen Kirche, 4 vols., 1856–66 [vol. 1: *Die Märtyrer*, vol. 2: *Die Väter der Wüst*, vols. 3 and 4: *Die Väter der orientalischen Kirche*]; vol. 2 as *Lives of the Fathers of the Desert,* translated by Emily F. Bowden, 1867
Vier Lebensbilder: Ein Papst, ein Bischof, ein Priester, ein Jesuit, 1861
Orsini, Abbé (Mathieu), *The Life of the Blessed Virgin Mary: With the History of the Devotion to her from the French of the Abbé Orsini; to which is added Meditations on the Litany of the Virgin from the French of the Abbé E. Barthe; also Poems on the Litany of Loretto from the German of the Countess Hahn-Hahn,* 1862
Ben-David: Ein Phantasiegemälde von Ernest Renan, 1864
Eudoxia, die Kaiserin: Ein Zeitgemälde aus dem fünften Jahrhundert, 2 vols., 1866; as *Eudoxia: A Picture of the Fifth Century,* 1869
Sanct Augustinus: Die Kirchenväter, 1866
Teresa of Avila [Teresa de Jesús], *Das Leben der heiligen Teresa von Jesus: Von ihr selbst geschrieben,* translated from Spanish to German by Ida von Hahn-Hahn, 1867
Teresa of Avila [Teresa de Jesús], *Das Buch der Klostergründungen nach der reformierten Carmeliter-Regel,* translated from Spanish to German by Ida von Hahn-Hahn, 1868
Die Erbin von Cronenstein, 2 vols., 1868; as *The Heiress of Cronenstein,* translated by Mary H.Allies, 1900
"Briefwechsel der Gräfin Ida Hahn-Hahn und des Fürsten Pückler-Muskau," in *Briefwechsel des Fürsten Pückler-Muskau I,* edited by Ludmilla Assing, 1873; reprint, 1971
Das Leben des heiligen Wendelinus, 1876 [excerpt from *Bilder aus der Geschichte der Kirche,* 1856–66]
Die heilige Zita: Dienstmagd zu Lucca im 13. Jahrhundert, 1878
Der heilige Karl Borromäus, Erzbischof von Mailand: ein Lebensbild, 1909
Frauenbriefe von und an Hermann Fürsten Pückler-Muskau: aus dem Nachlaß neu herausgegeben, edited by G. Müller, 1912
Melchior von Diepenbrocks Briefwechsel mit Ida Hahn-Hahn vor und nach ihrer Konversion, edited by A. Nowak, 1931

Further Reading

Chambers, Helen, "'Ein schwer definierbares Ragout': Ida Hahn-Hahn's 'Gräfin Faustine': Vapours from the 'Hexenküche' or Social and Psychological Realism?" in *Perspectives on German Realist Writing: Eight Essays,* edited by Mark G. Ward, Lewiston, New York: Mellen Press, 1995

Esterházy, Péter, *The Glance of Countess Hahn-Hahn: Down the Danube,* translated from Hungarian by Richard Aczel, London: Weidenfeld and Nicholson, 1994; Evanston, Illinois: Northwestern University Press, 1998

Geiger, Gerlinde Maria, *Die befreite Psyche: Emanzipationsansätze im Frühwerk Ida Hahn-Hahns (1838–1848),* Frankfurt and New York: Lang, 1986

———, "Hahn-Hahn, Ida Marie Luise Gustave von" in *Women Writers of Germany, Austria, and Switzerland: An Annotated Bio-Bibliographical Guide,* edited by Elke Frederiksen, New York: Greenwood Press, 1989

Herminghouse, Patricia A., "Seeing Double: Ida Hahn-Hahn (1805–1880) and Her Challenge to Feminist Criticism," *Amsterdamer Beiträge zu Neueren Germanistik* 28 (1989)

Kraft, Helga W., "Ida Hahn-Hahn (1805–1880)," in *Women Writers in German-Speaking Countries: A Bio-Bibliographical Critical Sourcebook,* edited by Elke P. Frederiksen and Elizabeth G. Ametsbichler, Westport, Connecticut: Greenwood Press, 1998

Möhrmann, Renate, *Die andere Frau: Emanzipationsansätze deutscher Schriftstellerinnen im Vorfeld der Achtundvierziger-Revolution,* Stuttgart: Metzler, 1977

Möhrmann, Renate, editor, *Emanzipation im Vormärz: Texte und Dokumente,* Stuttgart: Reclam, 1978

Munster, Katrien van, *Die junge Ida, Gräfin Hahn-Hahn,* Graz: Stiasny, 1929

Oberembt, Gert, *Ida Gräfin Hahn-Hahn, Weltschmerz und Ultramontanismus: Studien zum Unterhaltungsroman im 19. Jahrhundert,* Bonn: Bouvier, 1980

Ohnesorg, Stefanie *Mit Kompaß, Kutsche, und Kamel: (Rück-)Einbindung der Frau in die Geschichte des Reisens und der Reiseliteratur,* St. Ingbert: Röhrig Universitätsverlag, 1996

Sagarra, Eda, "Gegen den Zeit- und Revolutionsgeist: Ida Gräfin Hahn-Hahn und die christliche Tendenzliteratur im Deutschland des 19. Jahrhunderts," in *Deutsche Literatur von Frauen, II: 19. und 20. Jahrhundert,* edited by Gisela Brinker-Gabler, Munich: Beck, 1988

Schmid-Jürgens, Erna Ines, *Ida Gräfin Hahn-Hahn,* Berlin: Ebering, 1933; reprint, Nendeln, Lichtenstein: Kraur, 1967

Albrecht von Haller 1708–1777

Haller presents a unique combination of great scientist and important poet; yet, in a sense, this double distinction characterizes the culture of Europe during the Age of Reason. In all his work, whether literary or scientific, the spirit of inquiry runs in almost always harmonious parallel with the assumption that the universe makes sense and that all the organisms inhabiting it, including humans, have a purpose. Haller the botanist was eager to collect and collate the flora of a "new" world, the high Alps, which he explored on a botanizing expedition in 1728. In 1742 he published his *Enumeratio methodica stirpium Helvetiae indigenarum* (*Methodical Enumeration of Switzerland's Indigenous Plants*), a reference work later superseded by his even more comprehensive *Historia stirpium Helvetiae inchoata* (1768; *Incomplete History of Switzerland's Indigenous Plants*). Haller the poet was struck by the grandeur of the landscape he had encountered and by the simplicity and self-sufficient contentment of its inhabitants. The contrast between "civilized" urban society and this unpolluted, unspoiled way of life provides the central argument of *Die Alpen* (1729; *The Alps*), the large-scale discursive and descriptive poem for which he is most famous. This pioneering masterpiece, which links the Baroque age and European Romanticism, made its first appearance in the single, groundbreaking collection of poems with scientific honesty and characteristic modesty, he published anonymously and titled *Versuch schweizerischer Gedichten* (1732; An Essay in Swiss Verse). By 1777, the year of Haller's death, it had been enlarged, undergone countless emendations and additions, and run to 11 editions.

Haller can be regarded as the most gifted, important, and widely influential of the many notable figures Switzerland produced during the 18th century. He was born in Bern, the son of a lawyer who occupied a modest status in a city proud of its patrician elite. He lost his mother early, and his father died when he was 12. However, neither these childhood bereavements nor his weak constitution affected his rapid intellectual development. He entered Tübingen University at the age of 16 but soon moved to Leiden. A qualified medical doctor by 1727, he visited England and then returned to Switzerland until 1736, when he was offered the chair in anatomy, surgery, and botany at the new university at Göttingen. His years there saw him become a principal figure of the Age of Enlightenment. His rapid rise was due primarily to his authoritative research on human physiology. His standard handbook of the subject was first published in Latin (1747; translated as *First Lines in Physiology*) and then translated into German and expanded into an eight-volume treatment of the subject titled *Elementa physiologiae corporis humanae* (1757–66; *Principles of the Physiology of the Human Body*). These and his many other publications in many scientific fields encouraged a spate of research throughout Europe, especially in the domain of neurology, which Haller had made his own.

Haller's poetic career was extremely short. Most of his poetry was the immediate product of the relatively short period between 1728 and 1736, the year in which he lost his first wife, Marianne, a bereavement that affected him deeply. Coming as it did just four weeks after his arrival at Göttingen, this blow inspired two of his finest poems, *Unvollkommenes Gedicht über die Ewigkeit* (An Incomplete Poem on Eternity) and *Trauer-Ode* (*Threnody*), in which personal experience adds an intense lyrical urgency and expressiveness to a complex of ideas that he had already explored in *Über den Ursprung des Übels* (1734; *On the*

Origin of Evil) and the earlier *Die Falschheit menschlicher Tugenden* (1730; *The Falseness of Human Virtues*) and *Gedanken über Vernunft, Aberglauben und Unglauben* (1729; *Thoughts on Reason, Superstition, and Unbelief*). In all four poems, Haller's powerful moral imagination and questioning mind wrestle with language as he voices his thoughts on the feasibility of reconciling a rational view of the world with all the evidence to the contrary. In his case, faith alone could effect this reconciliation; great experimenter and researcher that he was, he discovered that Christianity provided a rationale by which he could live and die.

Haller's great reflective poems broached profound topics in language of a resonance and profundity not heard in German verse since Gryphius over half a century before and that recommended them forcefully to Bodmer, Klopstock, Kant, Lessing, and Herder. Schiller, a trained doctor himself, felt especially close to his Swiss precursor, and his last major work, the drama *Wilhelm Tell,* owes much to the man who not only helped him rise to the challenge of its Swiss subject but also played some part in generating the views of society, community, and individual that permeate it. Although he had largely abandoned poetry by 1736, he did not abandon literature. Between 1745 and 1779, he reviewed scores of books in the influential *Göttingische Zeitungen von Gelehtrten Sachen,* which he also edited from 1747, drawing his German readership's attention to new writers such as Richardson and Rousseau. In the early 1770s, he published three political novels: *Usong* (1771), *Alfred, König der Angel-Sachsen* (1773; *The Moderate Monarchy*), and *Fabius und Cato* (1774), in which he deployed fictional Chinese, English, and Roman historical settings to examine, respectively, the advantages and shortcomings of enlightened autocracy, constitutional monarchy, and republican oligarchy. Thus, Haller became a link between the political novelists of the 17th century, such as Lohenstein and Weise, and the political writers of the Sturm und Drang and Romantic periods. The fact that his achievements in these fields have been unaccountably neglected does not diminish their stimulating originality.

Haller was capable of a lighter touch than his *Gedankenlyrik* and political novels suggest. In his early years, he had staked a claim to be the most entertaining and pungent of German-language satirists with poems in the manner of Pope (whom he greatly admired), such as *Die verdorbenen Sitten* (1731; *Spoilt Manners*) and *Der Mann nach der Welt* (1733; *The Man of the World*), while his amorous poem *Doris* (1730) charmed generations of pre-Romantic readers. For posterity, however, his name was indelibly linked to *Die Alpen,* the poem that "discovered" a whole new poetic landscape.

PETER SKRINE

Biography

Born in Bern, Switzerland, 16 October 1708. Studied medicine at Tübingen University, 1724–25, and Leiden University, 1725–27, and mathematics at Basel, 1728; practiced medicine in Bern until appointed to a chair of anatomy, surgery, and medicine at Göttingen University; returned to Bern in 1753 to take up administrative posts; published widely in the fields of botany, physiology, and neurology; editor of and reviewer for the *Göttingische Zeitungen von gelehrten Sachen;* member of the Royal Society, 1740; ennobled, 1749. Died in Bern, 12 December 1777.

Selected Works

Poetry

Versuch schweizerischer Gedichte[n], 1732; enlarged 1734, 1743, 1748, 1751, 1768

Novels

Usong. Eine morgenländische Geschichte, 1771; as *Usong: An Eastern Narrative,* 1772; as *Usong: An Oriental History,* 1773

Alfred, König der Angel-Sachsen, 1773; as *The Moderate Monarchy; or, Principles of the British Constitution, Described in a Narrative of the Life and Maxims of Alfred the Great and His Counsellors,* translated by Francis Steinitz, 1849

Fabius und Caro, ein Stück der römanischen Geschichte, 1774

Other

Tagbücher seiner Reisen nach Deutschland, Holland, und England, 1723–1727, edited by Erich Hintzsche, 1948 and 1971

Tagebuch seiner Beobachtungen über Schriftsteller und über sich selbst, edited by Johann Georg Heinzmann, 1787, reprint 1971

Further Reading

Albrecht von Haller zum 200. Geburtstag, Göttingen: Vandernhoeck und Ruprecht, 1977

Balmer, Heinz, *Albrecht von Haller,* Bern: Haupt, 1977

Cleve, John van, "Social Commentary in Haller's *Die Alpen,*" *Monatshefte* 72 (1980)

Guthke, Karl S., *Haller und die Literatur,* Göttingen: Vandenhoeck und Ruprecht, 1962

———, "Albrecht von Haller," in *Deutsche Dichter des 18. Jahrhunderts,* edited by Benno von Wiese, Berlin: Schmidt, 1977

Häny, Arthur, *Die Dichter und ihre Heimat,* Bern: Franke, 1978

Kempf, Franz R., *Albrecht von Hallers Ruhm als Dichter,* Bern: Lang, 1986

Kohlschmidt, Werner, *Dichter, Tradition, und Zeitgeist,* Bern: Francke, 1965

Menhennet, Alan, "Order and Freedom in Haller's *Lehrgedichte: On the Limitations and Achievements of Strict Rationalism within the Aufklärung,*" *Neophilologus* 56 (1972)

Siegrist, Christoph, *Albrecht von Haller,* Stuttgart: Metzler, 1967

Wiswall, Dorothy R., *A Comparison of Selected Poetic and Scientific Works of Albrecht von Haller,* Bern: Lang, 1981

Johann Georg Hamann 1730–1788

The influence of Johann Georg Hamann, the so-called Magus in Norden, on the development of German literature and philosophy is inestimable, despite the fact that he is the least known of the group of writers who stand at the forefront of modern German literature: Gotthold Ephraim Lessing, Johann Joachim Winckelmann, and Johann Gottfried Herder. Traditionally known as the "father of Sturm und Drang" and a progenitor of the Romantic movement, Hamann was a principal influence on Herder and, through his mediation, on the young Goethe. Among contemporaries who felt Hamann's influence were Theodor Gottlieb von Hippel, Johann Caspar Lavater, Matthias Claudius, and, above all, Friedrich Heinrich Jacobi. Further, it was Hamann who called the attention of Immanuel Kant to Hume's philosophy, thus contributing to the arousal of Kant from his "dogmatic slumber." Jean Paul (Johann Paul Friedrich Richter) owed much to Hamann, and Søren Kierkegaard hailed him as a decisive influence on his life and philosophy. In the 20th century, Martin Buber, Ernst Jünger, and Johannes Bobrowski found profound stimulus in Hamann's writings.

Despite Hamann's anti-Newtonian stance—which misled earlier interpreters to regard him as an "irrationalist"—it is now generally recognized that he, too, was a child of the Enlightenment. He developed a view of natural science that later came to fruition in Goethe's scientific endeavors. Early in his career he wrote, "Ein sorgfältiger Ausleger muss die Naturforscher nachahmen" (A careful interpreter must imitate the natural scientists). The scientists he had in mind, however, were the 18th-century chemists, not the physicists, and he made bold to claim that he followed their procedure in his writings, which, according to Kant, are indeed informed by "anschauende Vernunft" (intuitive reason).

In his youth, Hamann had espoused and enthusiastically publicized ideals of the Enlightenment, such as the belief in progress and the power of trade and commerce to promote peace, liberty, and civic virtue. He believed these humanitarian goals could be achieved through the power of reason alone, but all that was to undergo a sea change, for in his 27th year, he underwent a religious experience that was to determine the future course of his life and to radically change his outlook. This break with his earlier views resulted in the *Sokratische Denkwürdigkeiten* (1759; *Hamann's Socratic Memorabilia*), an eloquent and multidimensional manifesto that not only attacked the prevailing biases of the Enlightenment but also presented an original apologia for his newly found faith. The narrative proceeds on three levels: first, there is an account of the life and teachings of the historical Socrates; second, there is the typological interpretation of the daimonic Socrates as a prolepsis of Christ; third, the narrative serves as a mask for Hamann himself in his contest with the Enlighteners. Appealing to Hume, he challenges the basic metaphysical assumptions of the Enlightenment. In regard to art, he maintains that true creativity springs from genius, not from the observance of rules.

Stylistically, the Socratic essay also marks a new beginning, for it is the first example of his notoriously difficult style. Hamann's writing is characterized by a succession of more-or-less extended aphorisms (whose causal connections are not immediately obvious), the drawing of startling parallels from the most disparate sources (the Bible, ancient and contemporary literature, theology, philosophy, science, history, and economics), quotations in ancient and modern languages, and footnotes that often appear to have no connection to the text. These characteristics appear in *Hamann's Socratic Memorabilia* and are the hallmark of his style in subsequent writings.

Three years later, in the *Aesthetica in nuce* (1762; Aesthetics in a Nutshell)—which is vintage Hamann—he comes to terms with the rationalistic approach to the Bible and, by extension, to literature in general. Since "Poesie ist die Muttersprache des Menschengeschlechts" (Poetry is the mother-tongue of the human race), God condescends to speak to human beings, in the "books" of nature, history, and Scripture in that language, not in the abstract language of the philosophers. The head and forefront of the offense was Johann David Michaelis, whose biblical hermeneutics ruled out all levels of meaning in Scripture except the literal. His counterparts among the natural scientists were those who, like Newton, interpreted "the text of nature" in purely mathematical terms, thus robbing it of its "beauties and riches." If Hamann had established the existence of an external world through faith in the *Socratic Memorabilia,* in the *Aesthetica in nuce* he establishes its nature as "text." These two essays taken together constitute Hamann's most powerful attack on the Enlightenment and provided the main stimulus for the Sturm und Drang. Most of his subsequent works can be considered as expanded commentaries on ideas contained in these two essays, at least in part.

In *Des Ritters von Rosenkreuz letzte Willensmeynung über den göttlichen und menschlichen Ursprung der Sprache* (1772; The Knight of the Rose-Cross's Last Will and Testament on the Divine and Human Origin of Language), Hamann rejects Herder's thesis that man invented language, holding that language is a *given* for human thought and involves an interplay of divine and human energy and ideas. A decade later Hamann, in his *Metakritik über den Purismum der Vernunft* (1800; Metacritique of the Purism of Reason), argued that Kant's *Kritik der reinen Vernunft* (1781; *Critique of Pure Reason*) ignores the fact that there is no thought apart from language. Unusual for his time are Hamann's frequent frank references to sexuality, often bordering on the scatological, but quite serious was his emphasis on the sexual component in cognition, and in the *Versuch einer Sibylle über die Ehe* (1775; Essay of a Sibyl on Marriage), he boldly attempts to relate the erotic and spiritual elements of marriage to the Christian doctrine of the Trinity. In *Golgatha und Scheblimini!* (1784; Golgatha and Scheblimini) he counters the argument of Moses Mendelssohn that the spheres of church and state can be sharply delimited in order to avoid conflict. For a thinker such as Hamann, who always insisted on the wholeness or interrelatedness of all human affairs, such a division as that proposed by Mendelssohn would constitute a violation of the divine order. Hegel considered this late work of Hamann's his greatest.

Hamann's correspondence, which is much easier to understand than his published writings, is essential for a full understanding of his thought, especially his extensive correspondence with Herder and Friedrich Heinrich Jacobi. Without his letter of 18 December 1784 to Christian Jacob Kraus, we would not have his critique of Kant's essay "What Is Enlightenment?" which is currently the subject of considerable interest.

It is paradoxical that both Goethe and Hegel admired Hamann, but for very different reasons: the former for his fidelity to sense perception, the latter for his dialectic. According to Johann Peter Eckermann, these differences came into sharp focus in a friendly conversation, when Hegel was Goethe's guest, each spiritedly defending his position. Epistemologically speaking, however, the true heirs of Hamann, mutatis mutandis, are Goethe and Nietzsche.

JAMES C. O'FLAHERTY

Biography

Born in Konigsberg, 27 August 1730. Matriculated at the University of Königsberg in theology, 1746, later transferring to law and economics; read widely in classics and *belles lettres* and collaborated on *Daphne,* a weekly for women; in 1752, he left the university without a degree and became a tutor in the Baltic area; sojourn in London, 1757–58, where he underwent a decisive religious experience and wrote *Tagebuch eines Christen* and *Gedanken über meinen Lebenslauf;* unemployed in the home of his father, 1759–63, where he wrote the important works *Sokratische Denkwürdigkeiten* and *Aesthetica in nuce,* among others; entered into a common-law marriage, 1763, with Anna Regina Schumacher and became a copyist in the municipal administration, transferring to the Prussian Department of War and Crown Lands; Herder became his pupil in Italian and English, 1763; accompanied a *Hofrat* to Warsaw as secretary, 1765–67; employed in the Prussian tax administration under Frech tax collectors, 1767, and became superintendant of customs warehouse, 1777–87; guest of Princess Amalia von Gallitzin, Münster, Westphalia, 1787–88; visited Friedrich Heinrich Jacobi. Died in Münster, 21 June 1788.

Selected Works

Sokratische Denkwürdigkeiten, 1759; as *Hamann's Socratic Memorabilia,* translated by James C. O'Flaherty, 1967
Die Magi aus Morgenlande zu Bethlehem, 1760
Kreuzzüge des Philologen, 1762
Aesthetica in nuce, first published in *Kreuzzüge des Philologen,* 1762
Des Ritters von Rosenkreuz letzte Willensmeynung über den göttlichen und menschlichen Ursprung der Sprache, 1772
Philologische Einfälle und Zweifel, 1772
Versuch einer Sibylle über die Ehe, 1775
Konxompax: Fragmente einer apokryphischen Sibylle über apokalyptische Mysterien, 1779
Golgatha und Scheblimini! 1784
A-Ω Entkleidung und Verklärung. Ein Fliegender Brief an Niemand den Kundbaren, 1785
Metakritik über den Purismum der Vernunft, 1800

Further Reading

Alexander, W.M., *Johann Georg Hamann: Philosophy and Faith,* The Hague: Nijhoff, 1966
Bayer, Oswald, *Zeitgenosse im Widerspruch: Johann Georg Hamann als radikaler Aufklärer,* Munich: Piper, 1988
Dickson, Gwen Griffith, *Johann Georg Hamann's Relational Metacriticism,* Berlin and New York: de Gruyter, 1995
Dunning, Stephen Northrop, *The Tongues of Men: Secular versus Biblical Language in the Interpretation of History: A Study of G.W.F. Hegel and J.G. Hamann: A Thesis,* Cambridge, Massachusetts: Dunning, 1977
Henkel, Arthur, "Goethe und Hamann: Ergänzende Bemerkungen zu einem denkwürdigen Gegengespräch," *Euphorion* 77 (1983)
Hoffman, Volker, *Johann Georg Hamanns Philologie,* Stuttgart: Kohlhammer, 1972
Jørgensen, Sven-Aage, "Zu Hamanns Stil," *Germanisch-Romanische Monatsschrift,* Neue Folge 16 (1966)
Merlan, Philip, "From Hume to Hamann," *The Personalist* 33 (1951)
Nadler, Josef, *Johann Georg Hamann: Der Zeuge des Corpus Mysticum,* Salzburg: Müller, 1949
O'Flaherty, James C., *Johann Georg Hamann,* Boston: Twayne, 1979
Schuman, Detlev W., "The Latecomer: The Rise of German Literature in the Eighteenth Century," *German Quarterly* 39 (1966)
Smith, Ronald Gregor, *J.G. Hamann 1730–1788: A Study in Christian Existence,* New York: Harper, and London: Collins, 1960
Swain, Charles W., "Hamann and the Philosophy of David Hume," *Journal of the History of Philosophy* 5 (1967)

Peter Handke 1942–

In 1966, Peter Handke made an inflammatory and widely publicized speech at the meeting of the Gruppe 47 in Princeton. Nearly all the Handke reception of the next 25 years has made this story of a young writer who bearded the established postwar writers and critics (Ilse Eichinger, Hans Werner Richter, Günter Grass, Heinrich Böll, Ingeborg Bachmann, and others) into the major early event of Handke's biography. His critique of his colleagues' "new realism" and his reminder that "literature is made with language and not with the things that are described with language" sounded themes that have been constants in his work.

In that same year, Handke's play *Publikumsbeschimpfung* (1966; *Offending the Audience*) achieved critical success in Frankfurt. Claus Peymann directed the "speech play," a cerebral and profane exploration of theatrical representation that inverts the focus from the stage to the audience. Two years later, Peymann directed Handke's *Kaspar* (1968), which takes its title from the unsocialized, speechless Kaspar Hauser who appeared on the streets of Nürnberg early in the 19th century. As Kaspar learns to speak in Handke's play, he finds that language helps him to order his life; simultaneously, however, he comes to understand that language is an arbitrary system through which violence can be done to those who challenge the system. The play's positive assertion in a context of negation, its undermining of what it proposes, sets up a dialectic that may be Handke's most basic and long-lasting formal signature.

In the ensuing three decades, Peymann has premiered most of Handke's plays, including, most recently in Vienna's Burgtheater, three plays that continue to investigate the dialectical possibilities of meaning in a contingent world: *Das Spiel vom Fragen; oder, Die Reise zum sonoren Land* (1989; *Voyage to the Sonorous Land; or, The Art of Asking*), the silent play *Die Stunde da wir nichts voneinander wußten* (1992; *The Hour We Knew Nothing of Each Other*), and *Zurüstungen für die Unsterblichkeit* (1997; Preparations for Immortality).

Handke's novel *Die Angst des Tormanns beim Elfmeter* (1970; *The Goalie's Anxiety at the Penalty Kick*) was his first prose work to reach a large readership (Wim Wenders filmed the novel two years later). With a structure partially determined by conventions of the detective novel, *The Goalie's Anxiety* features an ex-goalie, Josef Bloch, who swings between a world so mediated by language that it has no reality and a world so unmediated that it threatens his existence. This theme continues in several other works, including *Der kurze Brief zum langen Abschied* (1972; *Short Letter, Long Farewell*), in which a character travels across the United States searching for his potentially dangerous wife and for ways to give order to a hostile world; *Wunschloses Unglück* (1972; *A Sorrow beyond Dreams*), an attempt to "make sense" of the life of the author's mother after she committed suicide; *Die Stunde der wahren Empfindung* (1975; *A Moment of True Feeling*), whose main character, an Austrian working in France, loses all linguistic and moral connection with his surroundings and battles to find, finally, lifesaving meaning in an arbitrary constellation of things on the ground; and *Die linkshändige Frau* (1976; *The Left-Handed Woman*), which depicts a woman who voluntarily gives up the life structured by her husband and then struggles to cobble together another sort of life from the various possibilities available to her. Handke also directed a film of *The Left-Handed Woman* (1977), and he has since filmed his novel *Die Abwesenheit* (1987; film 1992; *Absence*), with Jeanne Moreau, Sophie Semin, and Bruno Ganz in three of the leading roles.

With his *Slow Homecoming* tetralogy (comprised of *Langsame Heimkehr* [1979; *The Long Way Around*], *Die Lehre der Sainte-Victoire* [1980; *The Lesson of Mont Sainte-Victoire*], *Kindergeschichte* [1981; *Child Story*], and the "dramatic poem" *Über die Dörfer* [1981; *Walk about the Villages*]), Handke continued to try out aesthetic forms as disparate as Greek tragic theater, the German Romantic novel, and Cezanne's paintings. In his 1985 interview with Zarko Radakovic, Handke spoke at length about his desire, after Nazi brutalizations of the language, to reconstitute certain words and the perspectives they allow: words such as "nature," "God," "history," "beauty," "grace," "holiness," and "Volk." A word such as "Volk" can tend, Handke argued, to a constructive unity, and he hoped to reconstruct the nonmetaphysical "material idea" of a *Volk*. Nazi rhetoric and state religion provide the negative backdrop for this positive attempt, a backdrop Handke himself painted a warning red; but he was determined to work beyond that into a dialectic, or, as he put it, a "weaving," to reintroduce lost words onto the literary and political stage. Martin Heidegger (with qualification) and Paul Celan (poet and Jew, without qualification) were claimed as ancestors in this venture.

Child Story, for example, presents a father living in Parisian exile who enrolls his daughter in a Jewish school so that she, the actual and linguistic child of historically damned speakers of German, will experience a meaningful tradition that he himself is unable to pass on. As a consequence, she,

> by birth and language a descendant of murderers who seemed condemned to flounder for all time, without aim or joy, metaphysically dead, would learn the binding tradition, would go her way with others of her kind, and embody that steadfast, living earnestness which he, who had been rendered incapable of tradition, knew to be necessary but forfeited day after day to frivolous caprice.

This kind of reclaiming, although it may seem archeological, etymological, or aimed at a metaphysically grounded beginning, takes place in the context of Handke's sense of the arbitrariness of language and of the constant threat posed by metaphysical certainty. For example, the reclaiming will take place in stories and not in religious or political tracts: "Odd, that the word 'God' does not disturb me (in fact, it moves me) in, for example, *Parzival*, the epic; with Meister Eckhart, in a treatise, however, it does: it even inhibits me" (*Phantasien der Wiederholung* [1983; Fantasies of Repetition]). The word to be rehabilitated will be contested even in the assertion: "How can the word 'angel' still be used?—Together with 'battle' (in every written text there ought to be felt the 'battle with the angel')" (*Phantasien der Wiederholung*). And it will have paradox as constant companion: "Once again I succeeded in denying myself: and the rooster inside me crowed happily. When I am especially strongly he who I am, I succeed in saying that I am not he who I am" (*Die Geschichte des Bleistifts* [1982; The Story of the Pencil]).

Handke's work on this tricky (non)metaphysical "ground" has been attacked by critics as a sellout to a cheap metaphysics. Peter Strasser, perhaps Handke's most interesting reader, has admitted that Handke attempts to show his readers "that in some moments of a life Heaven is possible and real, which is what his critics have suspected." Strasser continues, however, by pointing out that "if one wants to do justice to Handke, one must read him doubly, ambiguously, as it were."

In this vein, the novels *Die Wiederholung* (1986; *Repetition*) and *Absence* both examine narration, as opposed to systematic philosophy, as a vehicle for what might be called "post-metaphysical metaphysics." In *Repetition*, for example, the young Filip Kobal, traveling through northern Yugoslavia in search of his lost brother, learns that "the empty forms both of the cow paths and of the blind windows could be relied on; they were the seal of our right." A seal is generally the stamp of authority, a sign from above that guarantees or assures. The genius of these particular seals is that they are empty forms, forms that question while asserting, that stimulate a contingent production of meaning. In their blindness, arbitrariness, and emptiness, these signs are in fact no different from any other sign. Their power lies in the way their emptiness asserts contingency while they act, simultaneously, as productive, meaning-producing signs.

Handke continued his formal philosophical experiments with a series of essays, the genre Theodor Adorno once called the most dialectical of all genres. These include three long essays on seemingly mundane topics, *Versuch über die Müdigkeit* (1989; *Essay on Tiredness*), *Versuch über die Jukebox* (1990, 1995; *Essay on the Jukebox*), and *Versuch über den geglückten Tag* (1991; *Essay on the Successful Day*); a book of short travel essays *Noch einmal für Thukydides* (1990; *Once Again for Thucydides*), about scenes experienced while traveling along the Dalmatian coast, Spain, and Japan; and three political/travel essays written about (and against) the breakup of Yugoslavia: *Abschied des Träumers vom Neunten Land* (1991; Departure of the Dreamer from the Ninth Country), *Eine winterliche Reise zu den Flüssen Donau, Save, Morawa und Drina; oder, Gerechtigkeit für Serbien* (1996; *A Journey to the Rivers—Justice for Serbia*), and *Sommerlicher Nachtrag zu einer winterlichen Reise* (1996; A Summer's Addendum to a Wintery Journey).

In *Essay on the Successful Day*, Handke's narrator describes a song by Van Morrison and then partially corrects his flawed description in the course of the essay. Mistakes must be made, the essay seems to say. Misreadings are necessary. "Reality" must be represented and thus misrepresented. And through this hesitant process, postmetaphysical achievement—whatever form that takes—becomes possible. The writer doesn't act as a mirror that reproduces Van Morrison's reproduction of his satisfying day but essays his own thoughts on the basis of his memory of that song. His mistakes help remind the reader that the dream of the achieved day is not something the narrator has found but rather something he has made: "except that instead of *having* it, I've *made* it in this essay. Look at my eraser, so black and small, look at the pile of pencil shavings below my window."

Similar to his other essays, Handke's intensely debated *A Journey to the Rivers* is an exploratory exercise in dialectic. After an attack on journalists of the *Frankfurter Allgemeine Zeitung* (among others) for their simplistic, one-sided, and rhetorically charged reporting on the Yugoslavian civil wars, and for their nondialectical rhetoric, which may have contributed to those wars, Handke's narrator turns to a travel account in which he focuses on people and things in Serbia. The prose of this account is difficult, syntactically convoluted, and, above all, self-questioning:

> But isn't it, finally, irresponsible, I thought there at the Drina and continue to think it here, to offer the small sufferings in Serbia . . . while over the border a great suffering prevails, that of Sarajevo, of Tuzla, of Srebrenica, of Bihać? . . .
>
> Finally, to be sure, I thought each time: but that's not the point. My work is of a different sort. To record the evil facts, that's good. But something else is needed for a peace, something not less important than the facts.

This something else, this something beyond facts, this something that might contribute to peace, and this dialectical narrative are all central themes in Handke's two most recent novels as well, the massive *Mein Jahr in der Niemandsbucht* (1994; *My Year in the No-Man's-Bay*) and the story of a mushroom-gathering pharmacist, *In einer dunklen Nacht ging ich aus meinem stillen Haus* (1997; On a Dark Night I Left My Quiet House). A single example from the former will demonstrate one more formal innovation that carries on a thematic constant in Handke's work.

"I would like to be calm and composed," Handke said in a *Spiegel* interview after the publication of *My Year in the No-Man's-Bay,* "but each of my paragraphs still ends bitingly. I would like to be an Epicurean, but I am one who is thrown back and forth." To keep his narrative from ending cynically, to shepherd his self-reflective fairy tale along its 365-day route, and to "experience fragmentarily while dreaming wholly," Handke's narrator links his sentences and paragraphs with a remarkable series of "ands," hundreds of them, which move the narration along, coordinate it, introduce a second idea, and announce a new beginning, a new attempt. The "ands" ensure that the new is not radically new and simultaneously deny a radical return to an origin. And as the book approaches its end, the narrator repeatedly raises the question: "And what then?"

Perhaps that is a fitting question here, as the conclusion of a description of the work of a dialectical writer at the height of his abilities: And what then?

Scott Abbott

See also Neue Subjektivität

Biography

Born in Griffen, Carinthia, 6 December 1942. Studied at the University of Graz, 1961–65; full-time writer, 1966–; cofounder, Verlag der Autoren, 1969; in Paris, 1969; in Kronberg, near Frankfurt, 1971; in Paris, 1973; in Salzburg, 1979–87; travel to Yugoslavia, Greece, Egypt, Spain, and Japan, 1987–90. Hauptmann Prize, 1967; Büchner Prize, 1973 (returned, 1999); Kafka Prize (refused), 1979; Grillparzer Prize, 1991; Schiller-Memorial Prize, 1995. Currently lives in Chaville, France.

Selected Works

Plays

Publikumsbeschimpfung (produced 1966); included in *Publikumsbechimpfung und andere Sprechstücke,* 1966; as *Offending the Audience,* in *Kaspar and Other Plays,* translated by Michael Roloff, 1969

Kaspar (produced 1968), 1968; as *Kaspar* in *Kaspar and Other Plays,* translated by Michael Roloff, 1969

Der Ritt über den Bodensee (produced 1971); as *The Ride across Lake Constance* in *The Ride across Lake Constance and Other Plays,* translated by Michael Roloff, 1976

Über die Dörfer: Dramatisches Gedicht (produced 1982), 1981; as *Walk about the Villages: A Dramatic Poem,* translated by Michael Roloff, 1996

Das Spiel vom Fragen; oder, Die Reise zum sonoren Land (produced 1990), 1989; as *Voyage to the Sonorous Land; or, The Art of Asking,* translated by Gitta Honegger, 1996

Die Stunde da wir nichts voneinander wußten: Ein Schauspiel (produced 1992), 1992; as *The Hour We Knew Nothing of Each Other,* translated by Gitta Honegger, 1996

Zurüstungen für die Unsterblichkeit, Ein Königsdrama (produced 1997), 1997

Fiction

Die Hornissen, 1966

Die Angst des Tormanns beim Elfmeter, 1970; as *The Goalie's Anxiety at the Penalty Kick,* translated by Michael Roloff, 1972

Der kurze Brief zum langen Abschied, 1972; as *Short Letter, Long Farewell,* translated by Ralph Manheim, 1974

Wunschloses Unglück, 1972; as *A Sorrow beyond Dreams,* translated by Ralph Manheim, 1975

Die Stunde der wahren Empfindung, 1975; as *A Moment of True Feeling,* translated by Ralph Manheim, 1977

Die linkshändige Frau, 1976; as *The Left-Handed Woman,* translated by Ralph Manheim, 1978

Langsame Heimkehr, 1979; as *The Long Way Around,* 1985

Die Lehre der Sainte-Victoire, 1980; as *The Lesson of Mont Sainte-Victoire,* translated by Ralph Manheim, 1985

Kindergeschichte, 1981; as *Child's Story,* translated by Ralph Manheim, 1985

Phantasien der Wiederholung, 1983

Der Chinese des Schmerzes, 1983; as *Across,* translated by Ralph Manheim, 1986

Die Wiederholung, 1986; as *Repetition,* translated by Ralph Manheim, 1987

Nachmittag eines Schriftstellers, 1987; as *The Afternoon of a Writer,* translated by Ralph Manheim, 1989

Die Abwesenheit, 1987; as *Absence,* translated by Ralph Manheim, 1990

Mein Jahr in der Niemandsbucht: Ein Märchen aus den neuen Zeiten, 1994; as *My Year in the No-Man's-Bay,* translated by Krishna Winston, 1998

In einer dunklen Nacht ging ich aus meinem stillen Haus, 1997

Poetry
Die Innenwelt der Aussenwelt der Innenwelt, 1969; as *The Innerworld of the Outerworld of the Innerworld,* translated by Michael Roloff, 1974
Gedicht an die Dauer, 1986

Other
Das Gewicht der Welt: Ein Journal (November 1975–März 1977), 1977; as *The Weight of the World,* translated by Ralph Manheim, 1984
Die Geschichte des Bleistifts, 1982
Phantasien der Wiederholung, 1983
Versuch über die Müdigkeit, 1989; as *Essay on Tiredness,* translated by Ralph Manheim, 1994
Versuch über die Jukebox, 1990; as *Essay on the Jukebox,* translated by Krishna Winston, 1994
Noch einmal für Thukydides, 1990, 1995; as *Once Again for Thucydides,* translated by Tess Lewis, 1998
Abschied des Träumers vom Neunten Land: Eine Wirklichkeit, die vergangen ist: Erinnerung an Slovenien, 1991
Versuch über den geglückten Tag, 1991; as *Essay on the Successful Day,* translated by Ralph Manheim, 1994
Eine winterliche Reise zu den Flüssen Donau, Save, Morawa und Drina; oder, Gerechtigkeit für Serbien, 1996; as *A Journey to the Rivers—Justice for Serbia,* translated by Scott Abbott, 1997
Sommerlicher Nachtrag zu einer winterlichen Reise, 1996
Am Felsfenster morgens (und andere Ortszeiten 1982–1987), 1998

Translations
Walker Percy, *Der Kinogeher,* 1980
Florjan Lipuš, *Der Zögling Tjaz,* 1981
Emmanuel Bove, *Meine Freunde,* 1981
Francis Ponge, *Das Notizbuch vom Kiefernwald,* 1982
Georges-Arthur Goldschmidt, *Der Spiegeltag,* 1982
Gustav Januš, *Gedichte,* 1983
Emmanuel Bove, *Bécon-les-Bruyères,* 1984
Marguerite Duras, *Die Krankheit Tod. La Maladie de la Mort,* 1985
Aischylos, *Prometheus, gefesselt,* 1986
Julien Green, *Der andere Schlaf,* 1988
William Shakespeare, *Das Wintermärchen,* 1991

Films
Die linkshändige Frau (screenplay and direction), 1977
Der Himmel über Berlin (screenplay), with Wim Wenders, 1987; as *Wings of Desire,* 1987
Die Abwesenheit (screenplay and direction), 1992

Further Reading
Abbott, Scott, "'The Material Idea of a *Volk*': Peter Handke's Dialectical Search for a National Identity," in *1945–1995: Fünfzig Jahre deutschsprachige Literatur in Aspekten,* edited by Gerhard P. Knapp and Gerd Labroisse, Amsterdam and Atlanta, Georgia: Rodopi, 1995
———, "Postmetaphysical Metaphysics? Peter Handke's *Repetition,*" in *Themes and Structures: Studies in German Literature from Goethe to the Present,* edited by Alexander Stephan, Columbia, South Carolina: Camden House, 1997
Fuchs, Gerhard, and Gerhard Melzer, editors, *Peter Handke: Die Langsamkeit der Welt,* Graz: Droschl, 1993
Klinkowitz, Jerome, and James Knowlton, *Peter Handke and the Postmodern Transformation,* Columbia: University of Missouri Press, 1983
Pütz, Peter, *Peter Handke,* Frankfurt: Suhrkamp, 1982
Strasser, Peter, *Der Freudenstoff: Zu Handke eine Philosophie,* Salzburg: Residenz, 1990
Vollmer, Michael, *Das gerechte Spiel: Sprache und Individualität bei Friedrich Nietzsche und Peter Handke,* Würzburg: Königshausen und Neumann, 1995

Publikumsbeschimpfung 1966

Play by Peter Handke

On 8 June 1966, Peter Handke's play *Publikumsbeschimpfung* (*Offending the Audience*) had its world premiere during the theater festival *Experimenta I* in Frankfurt am Main, Germany. Directed by a then-unknown Claus Peymann (who would go on to become one of the major theater directors in Germany and Austria) at the Theater am Turm, the production made the 23-year-old Austrian author and playwright famous virtually overnight. The play has no plot, no characters, no costumes, no props, no dialogues, and (with the exception of two passages at the beginning and end) no stage directions. Written for an ensemble of four actors, the play offers unlimited possibilities for dividing up the text among them; it is a 30-page-long address to the audience in 67 paragraphs. Peymann's actors turned this body of text into a virtuoso performance using chorus and solo speaking, different rhythms, and a wide range of vocal activity.

In this play, Handke verbally dismantles the conventions of classical realist theater that became the norm in the 18th century and that have retained much of their influence into the 20th century. The play also challenges audience expectations and norms of behavior that go hand in hand with—and help perpetuate—such bourgeois theater practices, which were still very much in place in 1960s German theater. In that sense, the whole work is a sustained act of offending the audience, even though the actual *Beschimpfung,* the directing of invectives at the spectators, only makes up the final ten percent of the play. The emphasis on signification and language rather than on content and establishing a fictional reality firmly places *Offending the Audience* not only in Handke's early period, with his other *Sprechstücke* (speaking plays, or speak-ins) of the late 1960s, but also in his oeuvre as a whole. For Handke, theater and literature in general are about words, not reality.

Much of the play can be characterized by what it tells the audience at one point: "You recognized that we negate something. You recognized that we repeat ourselves. You recognized that we contradict ourselves." The opening of the play creates a deliberately formal setting of pleasurable anticipation. After addressing typical audience expectations and behavior, the text moves on to a sustained refutation of everything that theater usually offers, in particular its representational dimension and illusionist quality: "The emptiness of this stage is no picture of another emptiness. . . . This is not the world as a stage." The text then offers a reversal of the traditional positions of audience vis-à-vis the actors by assigning the central position to the audience: "You are the subject matter. You are the center of interest. . . . You are the heroes and the villains of this piece." Throughout, the play offers critical reflections and exposures of verbal and social patterns and clichés. Eventually, the actors launch into their final "offense," an imaginative and intriguing range of insults mixed with tongue-in-cheek praise for the spectators' fine performance.

While Handke's *Offending the Audience* is similar to Brecht's *Threepenny Opera* in allowing the audience to derive aesthetic pleasure from being maligned, Handke's play is distinctly anti-Brechtian: his purpose is not to present a staged social reality in need of change, and his formalist, language-oriented approach has roots in Dadaism, Wittgensteinian language philosophy, and absurd theater. As he explains in a "Letter on Theater" in *Theater Heute* (1967), it was not his intention to create a manifesto or a scandal: "More than anything else, my focus was the formal dimension, the rhythm. . . . The words and sentences of *Offending the Audience* are a result of my search for reasonable words and sentences that could be addressed to persons sitting in a theater." In the same vein, his "Rules for the Actors" that precede the play text start with the following: "Listen to the litanies in the Catholic churches. Listen to football teams being cheered on and booed. Listen to the rhythmic chanting at demonstrations."

Handke's play is full of contradictions, as critics have pointed out: it is an antitheater treatise presented as theater, a 1960s happening that became a canonical classic, and an intellectual disquisition presented as rhythmic montage. Moreover, its insults are rendered innocuous by wordplay and, perhaps most vexingly, its call to action for the spectators leaves no space for the interaction it purports to encourage, leaving audience members unsure whether to revolt against the traditional spectator role or to sit back and savor the aesthetic spectacle of the performance. The very presentation of the assault on the "fourth wall" between performers and spectators thus serves to reinforce that barrier. In that sense, audience reactions to the first two performances mark the gamut of possible responses: at the premiere, only a few audience members left, there were a couple of brief and polite interruptions, and at the end the audience applauded wildly. On the following night, however, audience members took up the play's call for action by interrupting the actors, dragging table and chairs onstage, and nearly derailing the performance. In other words, each group responded to one of the paradoxically conflicting imperatives of Handke's play.

On the whole, Handke's provocation was well received, and audiences were inclined to enjoy being offended. Theater critics focused on the performance rather than the issues raised by Handke's text, calling it "a triumph," "theater pure," and "the greatest theater event of the year." Dissenting voices—"a marketing ploy," "the theater bluff of the year"—were in the minority. Mildly scandalized audiences and critics made *Offending the Audience* one of the most successful plays of the late 1960s, with many major German theaters mounting productions of the play. As a provocation, it was short-lived—in fact, by the end of the 1960s, critics felt its message was passé. Moreover, with the exception of Günther Büch's production at the Berlin Forum-Theater, which premiered in April 1967 (and ran to more than 700 performances), few directors complied with Handke's emphasis on language rather than theatrics, which prompted the author to withdraw his permission for new productions of the play in 1969, stating that in future it should only be presented in the form of staged readings. He relaxed his injunction later, and the 1980s and 1990s have seen a smattering of productions that tend to be more relaxed and playful than the earlier ones, resurrecting the piece as a classic rather than as a play that caused furors with its 1960s productions.

SABINE GROSS

Editions

First edition: *Publikumsbeschimpfung,* in *Publikumsbeschimpfung und andere Sprechstücke,* Frankfurt: Suhrkamp, 1966

Translation: *Offending the Audience,* in *Kaspar and Other Plays,* translated by Michael Roloff, New York: Farrar, Straus, and Giroux, 1969

Further Reading

Schenkel, Martin, "Peter Handke: *Publikumsbeschimpfung,*" in *Lessings Poetik des Mitleids im bürgerlichen Trauerspiel "Miss Sara Sampson": Poetisch-poetologische Reflexionen: Mit Interpretationen zu Pirandello, Brecht, und Handke,* Bonn: Bouvier, 1984

Schlueter, June, *The Plays and Novels of Peter Handke,* Pittsburgh, Pennsylvania: University of Pittsburgh Press, 1981

Terhorst, Christel, "*Publikumsbeschimpfung,*" in *Peter Handke: Die Entstehung literarischen Ruhms,* Frankfurt and New York: Lang, 1990

Valentin, Jean-Marie, "Reine Theatralität und dramatische Sprache," in *Peter Handke,* edited by Raimund Fellinger, Frankfurt: Suhrkamp, 1985

Wiles, Timothy, "Afterword: *Offending the Audience* and Embracing It," in *The Theater Event: Modern Theories of Performance,* Chicago: University of Chicago Press, 1980

Wunschloses Unglück 1972

Novel by Peter Handke

Peter Handke's *Wunschloses Unglück* (*A Sorrow beyond Dreams*) is a biography of his mother, Maria Siutz Handke, who spent most of her life in the small town of Griffen in southern Austria. Handke's male narrator describes Maria's birth and suicide, her poor Austrian and Slovenian ancestors, and her life as a woman ("For a woman to be born into such surroundings was in itself deadly"). He remarks on the first, fleeting sense of self and pride that the Nazi movement provides for her, and the communal experiences occasioned by the war. He describes the married German soldier whom she loves, and the German soldier who marries her although she carries the other's child (Peter, born in 1942 in Griffen). Then come the war years in Berlin and the new but still limited possibilities for self-development. And finally there is postwar life in Griffen, where village and religious rites and customs eradicate whatever individuality she (may have) achieved in Berlin.

Maria makes several vain attempts to break out of the linguistic/cultural prison house that has become her lot. In the books she reads, for example, Handke's mother finds no possible future, but only roles she might have played. Socialist politics prove to be a dead end. A neurologist is somewhat helpful, as is a vacation in Yugoslavia. But finally, inexorably, she sinks into the "wunschloses Unglück"—a sorrow beyond desire—that gives the book its title.

As the story reaches the suicidal end it began with, after describing the funeral rituals that further depersonalize Maria, the book—which has been a fairly integrated if self-reflexive text—finally breaks into a series of short fragments related only by juxtaposition. "From this point on," the narrator writes, "I shall have to be careful to keep my story from telling itself."

Although *A Sorrow beyond Dreams* is obviously biographical, the subtitle classifies it as a "story." With this word Handke reminds his readers that they are not reading his mother's life, but an always-incomplete reconstruction under distorting generic restraints. The narrator's life as a writer, then, is limited in ways similar to his mother's. Where she finds little recourse against the ready formulations in which a rural Austrian woman lived her life ("At least in its merrymaking, country society thought of itself as classless—as long as you were NEAT, CLEAN, AND JOLLY"), the writer must turn to stock forms and ideas as well: "Accordingly, I compare, sentence by sentence, the stock of formulas applicable to the biography of a woman with my mother's particular life; the actual work of writing follows from the agreements and contradictions between them."

Handke has often emphasized the destructive and/or productive nature of language (in *Die Angst des Tormanns beim Elfmeter* [1970; *The Goalie's Anxiety at the Penalty Kick*], for instance, or later in *Langsame Heimkehr* [1979; *The Long Way Around*]), so it is no surprise to find the language-related forms of culture described here as both inhibiting and enabling.

Although the narrator precipitately cuts off the fictional, fragmented, and failed biography to avoid the lie of closure, he has, in fact, written the book; and he ends it with the final promise: "Someday I shall write about all this in greater detail." This double movement of assertion and critique at work in *A Sorrow beyond Dreams* is, for Handke, the essence of art: "only this, the saying what is the case with failing voice, the liminal word, will be heard in eternity" (*Phantasien der Wiederholung;* 1983; Fantasies of Repetition).

A Sorrow beyond Dreams was identified by early readers as a manifestation of what they called the New Subjectivity in postwar German literature. Some critics used this designation to attack Handke and to such others as Karin Struck, Rolf Dieter Brinkmann, and Botho Strauß as apolitical writers indifferent to social reality. It may be more productive, however, to read even Handke's early work as a kind of sociopolitical *Kahlschlag* (clear cutting) in which *all* language is stripped of supposed metaphysical character by emphasizing its totalizing, terrorizing character. Kaspar, for example, in Handke's early drama of that name, finds that while language is a useful way of ordering the world, it is also intimately connected with the violence used to force others into that same order.

In a recent insightful reading, Matthias Konzett has described *A Sorrow beyond Dreams* as a postideological text (in the context of work by the philosophers of the Frankfurt School and the thinking of Hannah Arendt) that focuses on the necessity of individual reflective narration, of developing personal ways of speaking/experiencing the world so that community life is possible beyond the objectifying relationships ideologies impose on members of a community.

A Sorrow beyond Dreams is one of Peter Handke's most popular and enduring books. The rural Austrian themes of the (auto)biography have continued to engage the author, and he has returned to them in works as diverse as the play *Über die Dörfer* (1981; *Walk about the Villages*), the novel *Die Wiederholung* (1986; *Repetition*), and the essay *Versuch über die Müdigkeit* (1989; *Essay on Tiredness*).

SCOTT ABBOTT

Editions

First Edition: *Wunschloses Unglück*, Salzburg: Residenz, 1972
Translation: *A Sorrow beyond Dreams,* translated by Ralph Manheim, New York: Farrar, Straus, and Giroux, 1975

Further Reading

Abbott, Scott, "'The Material Idea of a *Volk*': Peter Handke's Dialectical Search for National Identity," *Amsterdamer Beiträge zur neueren Germanistik,* 38/39 (1995)
DeMeritt, Linda C., *New Subjectivity and Prose Forms of Alienation: Peter Handke and Botho Strauss,* New York: Lang, 1987
Konzett, Matthias, "Cultural Amnesia and the Banality of Human Tragedy: Peter Handke's *Wunschloses Unglück* and Its Postideological Aesthetics," *Germanic Review* 70, no. 2 (1995)
Schmiedt, Helmut, "Analytiker und Prophet: Die Wiederholung in Peter Handkes Prosatexten *Wunschloses Unglück* und *Die Wiederholung,*" *Text und Kritik* 24 (1989)
Varsava, Jerry A., "Auto-Bio-Graphy as Metafiction: Peter Handke's *A Sorrow Beyond Dreams,*" *Clio* 14, no. 2 (1985)

Hartmann von Aue 1160–ca. 1210

Hartmann is the most prolific of all the poets who flourished during the high courtly era in Germany (ca. 1170–1240). As an epic and lyric poet, he also produced the most varied body of work of this period. His allegorical tract *Die Klage* (The Lament), is a disputation between the heart and body of a young man suffering the pangs of unrequited love. *Erec,* the first Arthurian work in German, is an adaptation of Chrétien de Troyes' *Erec et Enide. Gregorius,* an adaptation of the Old French *La vie de Saint Grégoire,* is a saint's life with an incestuous twist. Other works include *Der arme Heinrich* (Heinrich the Wretched), a tale about a nobleman stricken with leprosy, and *Iwein,* an adaptation of Chrétien's *Le chevalier au lion.* Hartmann also composed several poems of courtly love as well as crusading lyric.

Hartmann produced a body of work whose volume and thematic scope would have been impressive in any age. Thus it is odd that until roughly the past 20 years he suffered from benign neglect on the part of medieval scholars. This was not the case in the Middle Ages. Hartmann was honored and revered by his contemporaries and by poets of succeeding generations. Although many writers praised him, it is the encomium of his contemporary, Gottfried von Straßburg, that provides the best appreciation of Hartmann as a poet. In the section of his *Tristan* known as the "poetic excursus," Gottfried digresses from the tale of the ill-fated lovers and provides a critical review of many of his contemporaries. About Hartmann, he says:

> Hartmann, [the one] from Aue, ah, how he illuminates and adorns [the] tale both outside [i.e., externally] and in with language and with meaning! How he pinpoints exactly the sense [i.e., real meaning] of the adventure! How clear and precise are his crystalline words, and so they will always remain! They approach one decorously and prefer the one who knows how to understand them correctly. Whoever is able to comprehend masterful language well and precisely, he must grant the man from Aue his wreath and his laurels!

Gottfried provides an important insight into Hartmann the poet. The poet is able, in Gottfried's judgment, to render his sources precisely with words externally (with the *colores,* the rhetorical devices) and with meaning internally. Hartmann is so clear because he has understood the true meaning, the "sense," of his source. Thus, he was a master stylist as well as a consummate poet who infused his works with substance as a result of his gift of correctly "understanding" his sources. And these texts, too, seek only those who will also understand them "correctly." In addition to his appreciation of Hartmann, Gottfried also opens a window on the medieval understanding of poetic genius. Unlike the modern perception of what constitutes originality, the medieval perspective held that the true poet had a source, indeed that one could basically translate a source and still be considered a poet. Undeniably this is what Hartmann did with the two Arthurian romances, *Erec* and *Iwein,* and with *Gregorius.* Although the source of the *Der arme Heinrich* is not known, he certainly followed the same practice in that work. The medieval poet never boasts of writing something new, and in this respect Hartmann is no exception. In his *Gregorius,* for example, he states: "He who prepared [i.e., adapted] this tale and put it into German was Hartmann von Aue." Likewise in *Der arme Heinrich* he states: "Now he [Hartmann] will begin to relate a tale that he found written down." Interesting in the preceding statement is the word "relate" (Middle High German *diuten*). While "relate" or "narrate" are the most common translations, *diuten* can also be rendered as "explain" or "interpret," which moves the accomplishment of the poet from the merely mechanical task of translating to mediating between the foreign text and the German listener and, thereby, reshaping the work to fit the expectations of his audience. That is the genius of Hartmann and, indeed, of all the great medieval poets.

While Gottfried offers a glimpse into the aesthetic Hartmann and his literary influence, one must depend on the poet himself for information about the individual, Hartmann von Aue. He identifies himself in each of his epic works with the exception of *Erec,* which is, however, missing an indeterminate number of lines at the beginning where Hartmann's introduction of himself was doubtless to be found. In *Iwein* Hartmann describes himself and his activity as poet as follows:

> A knight, who was so learned
> that he read books
> whenever he could not
> better pass the time,
> and even wrote poetry
> (he expended great effort
> on those things
> that one liked to hear;
> his name was Hartman
> and he was from Aue)
> —he composed this tale.

We learn several important things about Hartmann from the above few lines. He was a knight and, thus, a layperson and a warrior. He had the privilege of an education, which points to a childhood residence in a monastery school—possibly Reichenau—where he studied the *trivium* and possibly the *quadrivium.* In other words, he learned Latin (Grammar), the universal language; he studied rhetoric using the works of such Roman masters as Virgil and Cicero; and he also learned the art of disputation (dialectic). The lines from *Iwein* provide a further insight into Hartmann, namely his view of his role of poet. It is, as he says, something to pursue when he has nothing better to do, for he is first and foremost a knight. Lastly, Hartmann reveals that he is from Aue, an otherwise unidentifiable place.

The prologue of *Der arme Heinrich* adds one further bit of information: Hartmann identifies himself as a *dienstman* of Aue, in other words a ministerial and standing on a very specific rung of the ladder of nobility. It can also be assumed, then, that he was not landed, but rather occupied a position at court. That is the extent of Hartmann's biography. Nonetheless, when compared with the known facts about other poets of the courtly period, it represents an abundance of riches.

Locating Hartmann chronologically can also not be precisely determined, but it is generally assumed that he was literarily active from ca. 1180–ca. 1205. He is believed to have died about 1210. In roughly two-and-a-half decades, Hartmann fundamentally changed the German literary landscape. It is fair to say that he was ahead of his age in almost every respect. His first epic work, *Die Klage,* is a disputation of 1,644 verses in rhyming couplets followed by a declaration of love formulated by the heart for the lady, which is comprised of 270 lines in rhyme pairs arranged over 15 strophes, the first of which has 32 lines and the last four. In the progression from first to last, each strophe loses two lines. Even in this youthful work, Hartmann is an innovator, for although allegorical disputations were known in Latin poetry, the vernacular *Klage* is isolated both rhetorically and artistically at this time. His songs of courtly love, written during the early 1180s, similarly demonstrate a penchant for experimentation. A generation before Walther von der Vogelweide, arguably the greatest of the German courtly lyric poets, repudiated the rigid conventions of courtly love in favor of a more spontaneous and natural expression, Hartmann also humorously rejected the distant, rebuffing woman in favor of the natural, loving girls of the village ("Many a man greets me thus: 'Hartmann, let's go look at courtly ladies!' Let him rush off to the ladies! All I get from [the experience] is tired feet!"). To be sure, Walther's repudiation is on a more substantive level, both in form as well as content. Nonetheless, Hartmann's poem represents the first experimentation—in German—with the rigidity of content in the courtly lyric.

In his epic tales, Hartmann depicts the journey of individuals, men and women alike, toward the fulfillment of their unique destinies. The Arthurian knights, Erec and Iwein, struggle to discover the true essence of rulership. The Lord Heinrich, stricken with leprosy, finally comes to the realization that God, not he, is the center of the universe. The knight Gregorius, the product of and unwitting participant in incest, spends 17 years atoning on an island until called to become Pope. In three of the works—*Erec, Der arme Heinrich,* and *Gregorius*—female characters, too, undergo trials and progress toward self-realization. In the Arthurian romance, Enite, like Erec, must learn that the essence of ruling is to serve the court, that individual desires must accede to the demands of the great society. By learning to be queen, she is able to assist Erec in his progress toward kingship. In *Gregorius,* the title character realizes that he must atone to God for his sin of incest with his mother, ignorant though he was of that fact. His mother, too, must undertake a penitential journey and lead an ascetic life to atone not only for incest with her son, but also for incest with her brother, a union that produced Gregorius. In the end, after both mother and son have sincerely repented, they are led into reconciliation with God and each other. Similarly in *Der arme Heinrich,* Heinrich and the maiden must move away from their solipsistic existence to the awareness that the good of the other is truly the only good. Like Gregorius and his mother, Heinrich and the maiden must put God back into their lives. Only then will Heinrich be cured of his leprosy and the maiden of her pride.

Though respected by his contemporaries, in the modern period until the 1970s Hartmann was generally neglected by critics in favor of his seemingly more robust peers, Wolfram von Eschenbach, Gottfried von Straßburg, and the anonymous *Nibelungenlied* poet. Nonetheless, Hartmann's works have not been without their effect. Already in the 13th century, *Iwein* inspired a series of frescoes in Rodeneck, a castle near Brixen in South Tyrol, in the Hessenhof in Schmalkalden, and in Burg Runkelstein. *Der arme Heinrich* and *Gregorius* have captured the fancy of many modern authors and composers. Perhaps the most noteworthy modern version of *Gregorius* is the novel *Der Erwählte* (1951; *The Holy Sinner*), by Thomas Mann. *Der arme Heinrich* has undergone lyric reworkings by Chamisso and Longfellow, and has been made into an opera by Hans Pfitzner, a novella by Ricarda Huch, and dramas by Gerhart Hauptmann and, most recently, Tankred Dorst.

The closing years of the 20th century witnessed a genuine Hartmann renaissance in scholarship, which demonstrates that Gottfried von Straßburg was right on the mark with his enthusiastic appreciation of Hartmann and his genius.

FRANCIS G. GENTRY

See also Arthurian Romance

Biography

Born in Swabia, 1160. Educated in a monastery; minister to a lord; participant in a crusade, 1189–90 or 1197. Died between 1210 and 1220.

Selected Works

Collections

Selections from Hartmann von Aue, translated by Margaret F. Richey, 1962

Das Hartmann-Liederbuch, edited by Richard Kienast, 1963

Werke, 2 vols., edited by E. Schwarz, 1967

Die Lieder Hartmanns von Aue, edited by Ekkehard Blattmann, 1968

The Narrative Works of Hartmann von Aue, translated by R.W. Fisher, 1983

Poetry

Der arme Heinrich, edited by Johann Gustav Büsching, 1810; edited by Jacob and Wilhelm Grimm, 1815; edited by Karl Simrock, 1830; edited by W. Wackernagel, 1835; edited by Franz Kocian, 1878; edited by H. Raul, 1882; edited by J.G. Robertson, 1895; edited by E. Gierach, 1911; edited by C.H. Bell, 1931; edited by F. Maurer, 1958; edited by Helmut de Boor, 1967; revised edition by H. Henne, 1987; translated by R.W. Fisher in *The Narrative Works of Hartmann von Aue,* 1983

Iwein, edited by G.F. Benecke and K. Lachmann, 1827; edited by A. Pernhoffer, 1857; translated by J.W. Thomas, 1979; translated by R.W. Fisher, in *The Narrative Works of Hartmann von Aue,* 1983; translated by Patrick M. McConeghy, 1984

Gregorius, edited by Karl Lachmann, 1838; edited by Hermann Paul, 1873; edited by F. Neumann, 1958; as *Gregorius: A Medieval Oedipus Legend,* translated by Edwin H. Zeydel, 1955; as *Gregorius: The Good Sinner,* translated by Sheema Zeben Buehne, 1966; as *Gregorius,* translated by R.W. Fisher, in *The Narrative Works of Hartmann von Aue,* 1983

Erec, edited by Moriz Haupt, 1839; revised edition by Moriz Haupt, 1871; edited by O. von Heinemann, 1898; edited by Albert Leitzmann, 1939; revised edition by Albert Leitzmann, 1972; translated by J.W. Thomas, 1979; translated by R.W. Fisher, in *The Narrative Works of Harmann von Aue,* 1983; translated by Michael Resler, 1987; translated by Thomas L. Keller, 1987

Gedichte, edited by Fedor Bech, 1867

Die Klage, edited by Herta Zutt, 1968

Das Klagenbüchlein: Hartmann von Aue und das zweite Büchlein, edited by Ludwig Wolff, 1972; edited and translated by Thomas L. Keller, 1986

Das Büchlein, edited by Petrus, W. Tax, 1979

Further Reading

Cormeau, Christoph, and Wilhelm Störmer, *Hartmann von Aue: Epoche, Werk, Wirkung,* Munich: Beck, 1985

Hasty, Will, *Adventures in Interpretation: The Works of Hartmann von Aue and Their Critical Reception,* Columbia, South Carolina: Camden House, 1996

Jackson, W.H., *Chivalry in Twelfth-Century Germany: The Works of Hartmann von Aue,* Cambridge and Rochester, New York: Brewer, 1994

Kaiser, Gert, *Textauslegung und gesellschaftliche Selbstdeutung: Die Artusromane Hartmanns von Aue,* 2nd edition, Wiesbaden: Akademische Verlagsgesellschaft Athenaion, 1978

Kuhn, Hugo, and Christoph Cormeau, editors, *Hartmann von Aue,* Darmstadt: Wissenschaftliche Buchgesellschaft, 1973

McFarland, Timothy, and Silvia Ranawake, editors, *Hartmann von Aue, Changing Perspectives: London Hartmann Symposium, 1985,* Göppingen: Kümmerle, 1988

Mertens, Volker, *Gregorius Eremita: Eine Lebensform des Adels bei Hartmann von Aue in ihrer Problematik und ihrer Wandlung in der Rezeption,* Munich: Artemis, 1978

———, *Laudine: soziale Problematik im Iwein Hartmanns von Aue,* Berlin: Schmidt, 1978

Neubuhr, Elfriede, *Bibliographie zu Hartmann von Aue,* Berlin: Schmidt, 1977

Tobin, Frank J., *Gregorius and Der arme Heinrich: Hartmann's Dualistic and Gradualistic Views of Reality,* Bern: Lang, 1973

Wapnewski, Peter, *Hartmann von Aue*, Stuttgart: Metzler, 1962

Walter Hasenclever 1890–1940

Walter Hasenclever was one of the prominent playwrights of German Expressionism, along with Georg Kaiser and Ernst Toller. In the theater, Expressionism rebelled against the massive, detailed sets and realistic language of naturalism. Thematically, Expressionism signified a revolt against war, the values and social institutions of the older generation, and the mechanization and dehumanization caused by modern urban, industrialized society. Hasenclever's play *Der Sohn* (1914; *The Son*) was the first German Expressionist drama to be performed (30 September 1916, in Prague). He also wrote poetry, two autobiographical novels, a few shorter prose pieces, essays, and film scenarios; toured Germany reading from his works; occasionally directed a play; and acted on stage and screen.

In *The Son,* which was influenced by Nietzsche, Schopenhauer, and the activism of Kurt Hiller, Hasenclever rebelled not only against the abusive treatment he received from his own father but also, similar to the other playwrights of his generation, against all authoritarian restrictions imposed by the state, the schools, and society. The dramatis personae are Expressionistic character types (the Son, the Father, the Friend, etc.), and all events are portrayed from the perspective of the central character. In Richard Weichert's landmark 1918 production in Mannheim, the actor portraying the Son was in the middle of a minimalist black-and-white set under a glaring overhead spotlight while the other characters moved in and out of the light. The actor accentuated his speeches with exaggerated, angular gestures, which came to be considered Expressionistic acting. *The Son* struck a responsive chord in Hasenclever's contemporaries, who could relate to his rebellion against his father and all for which his generation stood.

Similar to many of his contemporaries, Hasenclever had greeted the outbreak of World War I as the beginning of the end for the hypocritical old order, but during his military service he became a convinced pacifist. In his play *Antigone* (1917), King Creon's misuse of power leads to the destruction of the nation while Antigone opposes the principle of violence and war with the moral principle of love and humanity. Creon represents Kaiser Wilhelm II and the heroine in her apocalyptic fervor embodies the desires of the younger generation to live in a "new world" of peace, freedom, and international understanding. *Antigone* is an appeal to the people to rise up against tyrants, the state, and war itself for the achievement of such a world.

As a result of *The Son, Antigone,* and the volume of earlier poems and prose pieces published in 1919 as *Der politische Dichter* (The Political Poet), Hasenclever was celebrated as a political writer even after he had turned away from political themes. Following his military service, he entered into a mystical period, influenced by Emanuel Swedenborg and Buddhism, during which he wrote dramas such as *Die Menschen* (1918; *Humanity*), *Die Entscheidung* (1919; The Decision), and *Jenseits* (1920; *Beyond*), in which dialogue is reduced to a minimum. In *Humanity,* a murdered man goes through the world seeking salvation. The staccato speech and the juxtaposition of short scenes in *Humanity*—along with its emphasis on expressive gestures and lighting effects, as outlined in Hasenclever's 1916 essay *Das Theater von morgen* (The Theater of Tomorrow)—reflect his lifelong interest in the medium of film. The play, which was performed by the Living Theater in New York in 1991, formed the basis of Detlev Müller-Siemens's 1990 opera *Die Menschen.*

In the 1920s, Hasenclever and other playwrights of his generation turned to the satirical comedy as a vehicle for their criticism of society. *Ein besserer Herr* (1926; Man of Distinction) was particularly successful and continued to be performed after World War II in Germany, Edinburgh, and New York. The "better sort of gentleman" is Hugo Möbius, a gigolo who falls in love with the daughter of a prominent industrialist after reading about her search for a husband in a classified advertisement. Another popular comedy, *Ehen werden im Himmel geschlossen* (1928; Marriages Are Made in Heaven), involved Hasenclever in a lawsuit in which he was accused of blasphemy. *Napoleon greift ein* (1929) was performed on Broadway as *Her Man of Wax* (1933). The comedy *Christoph Columbus; oder, Die Entdeckung Amerikas* (1931; *Christopher Columbus*), written in collaboration with Kurt Tucholsky, served as the basis for Jura Soyfer's *Broadway Melody 1492* (1937).

In exile, Hasenclever turned to historical themes such as Münchhausen, Mary, Queen of Scots, and the biblical story of Queen Esther. His correspondence in the 1930s reflects his mostly unsuccessful efforts to earn money by writing new plays and film scenarios that were to be produced in England or the United States. The novel *Die Rechtlosen* (The Outcasts, or The Pariahs), which portrays the experiences of the German exiles in France, and the autobiographical novel *Irrtum und Leidenschaft* (Error and Passion) were published posthumously.

CHARLES H. HELMETAG

Biography

Born in Aachen, 8 July 1890. Educated at Oxford University, 1908, the University of Lausanne, Switzerland, 1908–9, the University of Leipzig (where his lifelong friendship with Kurt Pinthus began), 1909–14, and the University of Bonn, 1914–15; served during World War I first as a translator, then as a staff officer on the eastern front; co-editor (with Heinar Schilling) of the periodical *Menschen,* 1920–22; Paris correspondent for the Berlin newspaper *8 Uhr Abendblatt,* 1924–28; in Berlin, 1928–32; in Hollywood, June–September 1930, translating screenplays of major films into German for MGM; left Germany in January 1933 and spent his exile years in Paris, Nice, London, near Dubrovnik in Yugoslavia, Lastra a Signa in Italy, and finally Cagnes sur Mer near Nice; interned in September 1939 and again in June 1940. Kleist Prize, 1917. Died (suicide), in the internment camp at Les Milles, near Aix-en-Provence, 21 June 1940.

Selected Works

Collections

Gedichte, Dramen, Prosa, edited by Kurt Pinthus, 1963

Sämtliche Werke, 5 volumes, edited by Dieter Breuer and Bernd Witte, 1990–97

Plays

Nirwana, 1909

Das unendliche Gespräch (lyrical scene), 1913

"Die Hochzeitsnacht" (screenplay), in *Das Kinobuch,* edited by Kurt Pinthus, 1914

Der Sohn (produced 1916), 1914; as *The Son,* translated by Henry Marx, 1986

Antigone, 1917; as *Antigone,* translated by J.M. Ritchie, 1969
Die Menschen (produced 1920), 1918; as *Humanity,* translated by Walter H. and Jacqueline Sokel, 1963
Die Entscheidung (comedy), 1919
Der Retter (produced 1919), 1919
Die Pest (screenplay), 1920; as *The Plague,* 1923
Jenseits, 1920; as *Beyond,* translated by Rita Matthias, 1925
Gobseck, 1922
Mord, 1926
Ein besserer Herr (comedy), 1926
Ehen werden im Himmel geschlossen (comedy), 1928
Napoleon greift ein (comedy) (produced 1930), 1929; as *Her Man of Wax,* translated by Julian Thompson, 1933
Kommt ein Vogel geflogen (comedy), 1931
Münchhausen (produced 1948), in *Gedichte, Dramen, Prosa,* 1963
Der Froschkönig (farce), restored by Peter Hacks, 1975
Christoph Columbus; oder, Die Entdeckung Amerikas (comedy) (produced 1932), in collaboration with Kurt Tucholsky, 1985; as *Christopher Columbus,* translated by Max Spalter and George E. Wellwarth, 1972
Sinnenglück und Seelenfrieden (produced 1936), in *Sämtliche Werke,* 1990
Ehekomödie (comedy) (produced in London as *What Should a Husband Do?* translated by Hubert Griffith, 1937), in collaboration with Robert Klein, in *Sämtliche Werke,* 1990
Konflikt in Assyrien (comedy) (produced 1939 in London as *Scandal in Assyria,* translated by Robert Klein; produced in Germany, 1957), in *Sämtliche Werke,* 1990
Bourgeois bleibt Bourgeois (comedy) (produced 1929), in collaboration with Ernst Toller, 1992

Poetry
Städte, Nächte und Menschen, 1910
Der Jüngling, 1913
Tod und Auferstehung, 1917
Der politische Dichter, 1919
Gedichte an Frauen, 1922

Novels
Die Rechtlosen, in *Gedichte, Dramen, Prosa,* 1963
Irrtum und Leidenschaft, 1969

Translation
Emanuel Swedenborg: Himmel, Hölle, Geisterwelt, selections, 1925

Other
Dichter und Verleger: Briefe von Wilhelm Friedrich an Detlev von Liliencron, edited and introduction by Hasenclever, 1914
Briefe 1907–1940, edited by Bert Kasties and Dieter Breuer, 1994
Ich hänge, leider, noch am Leben: Briefwechsel mit dem Bruder, edited by Bert Kasties, 1997

Further Reading

Breuer, Dieter, editor, *Walter Hasenclever 1890–1940,* Aachen: Alano, 1990; 2nd edition, 1996
Elwood, William R., "Hasenclever and Brecht: A Comparison of Two *Antigones,*" *Educational Theatre Journal* 24 (1972)
Helmetag, Charles H., "Walter Hasenclever in Hollywood," *Seminar* 16 (1980)
——, "Walter Hasenclever: A Playwright's Evolution as a Film Writer," *German Quarterly* 64 (1991)
Hoelzel, Alfred, *Walter Hasenclever's Humanitarianism: Themes of Protest in His Works,* Bern and New York: Lang, 1983
Kasties, Bert, *Walter Hasenclever: Eine Biographie der deutschen Moderne,* Tübingen: Niemeyer, 1994
Knobloch, Hans-Jörg, *Das Ende des Expressionismus: Von der Tragödie zur Komödie,* Frankfurt and Bern: Lang, 1975
Wilder, Ania, *Die Komödien Walter Hasenclevers: Ein Beitrag zur Literatur der Zwanziger Jahre,* Frankfurt: Lang, 1983

Wilhelm Hauff 1802–1827

Wilhelm Hauff's strength was in his ability to tell good stories. They have attracted a wide readership to this day and have been published in many new editions, translated repeatedly, and used for movies and musical compositions. At the same time, he was not one of the great innovative authors, nor did he pursue ideological issues. His characters and their fates are easily understood. The world Hauff presents is post-Romantic, one in which such conservative values as hard work, antimaterialism, honesty, and plain goodness prevail. With its many realistic details, his work belongs to the Restoration period.

Under the name of H. Clauren, which was actually the pseudonym of the best-selling author Karl Heun, Hauff published in 1825 *Der Mann im Mond* (The Man in the Moon), a parody of Heun's novels. Hauff surpassed Heun's kitsch, thus making the spoof a successful novel in the 19th century. The lawsuit that followed furthered Hauff's reputation as an author. Even though his publisher lost the case, sales of *Der Mann im Mond* increased significantly because of the scandal.

Also in 1825 *Mitteilungen aus den Memoiren des Satan* (a second part appeared in 1826; Extracts from the Memoirs of Beelzebub) appeared; in this work, a rather subdued devil surveys in an ironic manner certain aspects of German life. Hauff pokes fun at student life and German politics, criticizes religious bigotry as well as the practices at the Frankfurt stock market, and reviews the contemporary literary scene.

We find much more unity of focus in *Lichtenstein: Romantische Sage aus der würtembergischen Geschichte* (1826; *The Banished: A Swabian Historical Tale*). Hauff's aim was to do for Germans what Walter Scott had done for his countrymen: make his readers proud of and interested in their own heritage. The novel is centered around the life of Ulrich, Duke of Württemberg (1487–1550), and the 15th-century castle in Lichtenstein, which had been replaced in Hauff's time by a hunting lodge, but which was made into a castle again soon after his death. Ulrich's unstable character is put in contrast to the faithfulness of his subjects, the simple folk. Hauff adds a love story between the daughter of the master of the Lichtenstein castle and a young knight. The novel represents a valiant effort to make history come alive and contains beautiful passages celebrating the Swabian landscape, but *The Banished* moves on a rather superficial level.

Also mixing history and fiction is the novel *Jud Süß* (1827; The Jew Suss), which deals with the all-powerful and much-feared 18th-century Württemberg finance minister Joseph Süß-Oppenheimer. Leon Feuchtwanger was later to write on the same subject. In Hauff's novel, the young protagonist fails to come to Süß's aid in a critical moment. Süß's daughter commits suicide after her father's execution, leaving her lover, the young protagonist, to spend the rest of his life an unhappy man.

Hauff has remained a popular author on the basis of his three *Märchenalmanache* (1826–28; *Die Karawane* [*The Caravan*], *Der Scheik von Alessandria* [*The Sheik of Alexandria*], and *Das Wirtshaus im Spessart* [The Inn in the Spessart]). They are collections of tales that mix realistic detail with the supernatural in the form of fairies, magicians, and the devil. Some of the stories are placed in the Orient, reveal the influence of *The Thousand and One Nights,* and show Hauff's idealized vision of Arab wisdom and magnanimity. All tales stress adventure and excitement, and some add a humorous element: for instance, the two protagonists of *Die Geschichte vom Kalif Storch* (*The Tale of Caliph Stork*) are in danger of remaining storks forever because they have forgotten the magic formula that will turn them back into human beings. Equally humorous is "Der Affe als Mensch" (translated as "The Young Englishman" and *A Monkey's Uncle*), in which the citizens of a small German town swoon over a monkey who has been trained by his master to act the dandy. Hauff is a master at creating suspense by a variety of narrative techniques. Thus, in *Das Wirtshaus im Spessart,* a group of travelers try desperately to stay alert by having each one tell a story. They know the innkeeper is about to betray them to a band of robbers who are waiting outside. In addition to the various voices of the narrators, characters appear both in the frame narrative and in the story, and some of the stories are interrupted at crucial moments so as to make the reader all the more anxious about the outcome.

Hauff is also the author of several novellas, among them *Das Bild des Kaisers* (1828; *The Emperor's Picture*), in which both Napoléon's admirers and detractors have their say on this much-debated figure. In *Die Bettlerin vom Pont des Arts* (1826; *The Beggar Girl of the Pont des Art*), romantic elements such as love at first sight and duplication between an old portrait and the protagonist's beloved give way to such realistic details as problems with a steam engine, divorce, and converting to Protestantism to make the marriage of true lovers possible.

Hauff's last and stylistically best novel is *Phantasien im Bremer Rathskeller* (1827; *The Wine-Ghosts of Bremen*), in which the narrator celebrates the many wonderful varieties of wine, conjures up the dead, and experiences haunting memories in the spooky night atmosphere of the cellar.

Hauff was well acquainted with Goethe and Schiller, but the Romantics, among them Tieck, Fouqué, and especially E.T.A. Hoffmann, were closest to his own way of writing. Hauff, however, lacks the analytical depth of a Hoffmann and stays rather on the level of the well-told story with many realistic aspects that are easily enjoyed; these types of stories have remained the favorites of generations of readers to this day.

CHRISTOPH E. SCHWEITZER

Biography

Born in Stuttgart, 29 November 1802. Studied theology at Tübingen University but started to write even before the completion of his studies; tutor in the family of the minister von Hügel; grand tour through France, Belgium, the Netherlands, and northern Germany, 1826; editor of Cotta's *Morgenblatt für gebildete Stände,* 1827. Died in Stuttgart, 18 November 1827.

Selected Works

Collections

Sämtliche Werke, edited by S. von Steinsdorff and U. Schweikert, 1970

Fiction

Der Mann im Monde, 1825
Mitteilungen aus den Memoiren des Satan, 2 vols., 1825–26
Lichtenstein: Romantische Sage aus der würtembergischen Geschichte, 1826; as *The Banished: A Swabian Historical Tale,* edited by James Morier, 1839
Jud Süß, 1827

Further Reading

Beckmann, Sabine, *Wilhelm Hauff: Seine Märchenalmanache als zyklische Kompositionen,* Bonn: Bouvier, 1976
Hinz, Ottmar, *Wilhelm Hauff: Mit Selbstzeugnissen und Bilddokumenten,* Reinbek bei Hamburg: Rowohlt, 1989
Hofacker, Erich P., "Wilhelm Hauff," in *German Writers in the Age of Goethe, 1789–1832,* Dictionary of Literary Biography, vol. 90, edited by James Hardin and Christoph E. Schweitzer, Detroit, Michigan: Gale Research, 1989
Martini, Fritz, "Wilhelm Hauff," in *Deutsche Dichter der Romantik,* edited by Benno von Wiese, Berlin: Schmidt, 1971, 2nd edition, 1983
Mayer, Mathias, and Jens Tismar, *Kunstmärchen,* Stuttgart: Metzler, 1977; 3rd edition, 1997
Schwarz, Egon, "Wilhelm Hauff: *Der Zwerg Nase, Das kalte Herz,* und andere Erzählungen (1826–27)," in *Romane und Erzählungen zwischen Romantik und Realismus,* edited by Paul Michael Lützeler, Stuttgart: Reclam, 1983

Gerhart Hauptmann 1862–1946

The centenary edition of Gerhart Hauptmann's *Sämtliche Werke* (1962–74) demonstrates in its almost 14,000 pages the author's mastery of numerous genres: drama, novel, novella, verse epic, lyric poetry, essay, aphorism, and theoretical writing. Hauptmann has been acclaimed by critics as both the "last German classical author" (during his lifetime, his works were included in the public school curriculum beside those of Goethe and Schiller) and a "seismograph of his age," whose works reflect such literary movements as naturalism and neo-Romanticism, but also less tangible national characteristics such as the proclivity for Romantic mysticism and, especially during World War II, the sense of catastrophic pessimism. The recipient of the 1912 Nobel Prize for literature, his works were translated into 39 languages, including Chinese and Esperanto. Especially renowned as a playwright, he has maintained a prominent place in the German theater repertoire for the past century. Although less well remembered in the United States, where his greatest success was the fairy-tale play *Die versunkene Glocke* (1896; *The Sunken Bell*), he was, for a time, the most popular dramatist in Russia and exerted a strong influence on that country's stage history. Especially admired for his true-to-life characters, Hauptmann's popular appeal is confirmed by the more than 50 film and television adaptations of his works—more than any other German author.

Despite his vigorous protestations against being subsumed under the naturalist label, it is Hauptmann's naturalistic dramas that have been most favorably received. The essence of German Naturalism (approximately 1880–92) is best characterized by referring to its most extreme theoretician, Arno Holz. Starting from Zola's famous equation "art = nature – *x*," in which *x* represents the individuality of the artist, Holz, who rejected the concept of artistic genius, aimed at minimizing the *x;* he thus tended to reduce literature to a photographically, phonographically accurate rendering of reality. It was in his *Papa Hamlet* (1889), coauthored with Johannes Schlaf, that Hauptmann discovered the efficacy of a hyperrealistic language, capable of exposing inner depths of character; this discovery inspired his first successful drama, *Vor Sonnenaufgang* (1889; *Before Sunrise*).

It was not so much the language as the allegedly scandalous content of this drama, however, that made its author an instant celebrity. The decadent lifestyle of a nouveau riche family—featuring hereditary alcoholism and suggestions of incest—and the leftist proclivities of the play's hero provoked an immediate rift between a generally older, conservative audience and the younger progressive naturalists.

Having caught the public's attention, Hauptmann soon retreated from a reliance on sensational Zola-esque content, applying his linguistic virtuosity instead to a more Ibsenian dissection of bourgeois family life. Both *Das Friedensfest* (1890; *The Coming of Peace*) and *Einsame Menschen* (1891; *Lonely Lives*) demonstrate his firm belief in the primacy of character over plot; they have come to be seen as early examples of the psychologizing of modern drama. Both also exemplify their author's lifelong tendency to transmute personal experience into art. *The Coming of Peace* was inspired by a father-son conflict of his (erstwhile) friend, the author Frank Wedekind, while *Lonely Lives* draws upon the marriage difficulties of his brother Carl. On a still more personal level, both also feature the recurrent Hauptmannian theme of a gifted individual trying to reconcile his calling with family demands.

Hauptmann's next play, *Die Weber* (1892; *The Weavers*), treats the capitalist exploitation of a group of Silesian weavers. Because of its politically charged content and emotional intensity, the play carried the author's reputation far beyond the borders of Germany. (Translated into Russian by Lenin's sister, it was almost immediately exploited as agitprop in that country's political struggles.) While ostensibly based on an aborted weavers' revolt of 1844, the horrible conditions it depicts were identical to those still prevailing, and so it remained as topical as ever. The play's formal innovations, such as the use of masses of people as a collective hero, an epic structure that substitutes a series of tableaux for a traditional plot, and a reliance on historical documents, foreshadowed Expressionism, Brecht, and the documentary drama of postwar years.

With *Der Biberpelz* (1893; *The Beaver Coat*), Hauptmann showed that naturalism was not limited to depressing subject matter. Frequently ranked with Lessing's *Minna von Barnhelm* and Kleist's *Der zerbrochene Krug* as one of the three greatest comedies of German literature, it satirizes Prussian bureaucracy and features a pompous official whose blind admiration for a thieving washerwoman only increases as she deceives him with ever greater impunity.

Of Hauptmann's later naturalistic dramas, the following deserve special mention: the historical drama *Florian Geyer* (1896; *Florian Geyer*); *Fuhrmann Henschel* (1898; *Drayman Henschel*); *Michael Kramer* (1900), an artist drama greatly admired by James Joyce and Thomas Mann; *Rose Bernd* (1903) and *Die Ratten* (1911; *The Rats*), both involving themes of motherhood and illegitimacy; and *Vor Sonnenuntergang* (1932; Before Sunset), which illuminates the conditions in the Weimar Republic shortly before the Nazi takeover.

Generally less favored by present-day audiences are those plays in which Hauptmann gave rein to his ever-present Romantic and metaphysical temptations. They include *Hanneles Himmelfahrt* (1893; *Hannele*), with its melodramatic dream sequences; the neo-Romantic *The Sunken Bell* mentioned previously; and *Und Pippa tanzt!* (1906; *And Pippa Dances*), which nicely balances a naturalistic style and mystical content. The reputation of Hauptmann's last ambitious effort, *Die Atriden-Tetralogie* (1941–48), a reworking of the Agememnon myth written during World War II, which reflects that era's dismal zeitgeist, has also suffered since its initial critical acclaim.

Of Hauptmann's prose fiction, several works continue to enjoy critical and popular favor. Foremost among these is *Bahnwärter Thiel* (1888; *Lineman Thiel*). Described by one critic as "a symphony in prose," this novella is frequently included in anthologies of masterpieces of German fiction for its seamless amalgamation of naturalism, mysticism, nature description, and social criticism. Deriving from the author's lifelong preoccupation with religion, *Der Narr in Christo, Emanuel Quint* (1910; *The Fool in Christ, Emanuel Quint*) remains one of the finest treatments of the "Jesus redivivus" motif in world literature. Together with the long novella *Der Ketzer von Soana* (1918; *The Heretic of Soana*), a kind of Dionysian continuation of the novel, the two works represent Hauptmann's view that Christianity must learn to accommodate sexuality and the life of the flesh.

WARREN R. MAURER

See also Naturalism

Biography

Born in Ober-Salzbrunn, Silesia, 15 November 1862. Studied sculpture at the Royal College of Art, Breslau, 1880–82; studied at the University of Jena, 1882–83; worked as a sculptor in Rome, 1883–84; worked as an actor in Berlin; joined the literary group *Durch.* Grillparzer prize, 1896, 1899, 1905; Goethebünde Schiller Prize, 1905; Nobel Prize for literature, 1912; Ordre pour le Mérite, 1922; Goethe Prize (Frankfurt), 1932; honorary degrees from the University of Oxford, 1905, the University of Leipzig, 1909, the University of Prague, 1921, Columbia University, 1932. Died 8 June 1946.

Selected Works

Collections

Dramatic Works, edited by Ludwig Lewisohn, translated by Lewisohn et al., 9 vols., 1912–29
Gesammelte Werke, 12 vols., 1922
Sämtliche Werke, edited by Hans-Egon Hass, 11 vols., 1962–74

Plays

Vor Sonnenaufgang (produced 1889), 1889; as *Before Dawn,* translated by Leonard Bloomfield, 1909; translated by Richard Newnham, in *Three German Plays,* 1963; as *Before Daybreak,* translated by Peter Bauland, 1978; as *Before Sunrise,* translated by James Joyce, edited by Jill Perkins, 1978
Das Friedenfest (produced 1890), 1890; as *The Coming of Peace,* translated by Janet Achurch and C.E. Wheeler, 1900; as *The Reconciliation,* in *Dramatic Works,* 1914
Einsame Menschen (produced 1891), 1891; as *Lonely Lives,* translated by Mary Morrison, 1898
Die Weber (produced 1893), 1892; edited by M. Boulby, 1962; as *The Weavers,* translated by Mary Morrison, 1899; translated by Theodore H. Lustig, in *Five Plays,* 1961 (also published in *Plays,* 1994); translated by Frank Marcus, 1980
Kollege Crampton (produced 1892), 1892; as *Colleague Crampton,* translated by Roy Temple House and Ludwig Lewisohn, in *Dramatic Works,* 1914
Der Biberpelz (produced 1893), 1893; as *The Beaver Coat,* translated by Ludwig Lewisohn, 1912; also translated by T.H. Lustig, in *Five Plays,* 1961
Hanneles Himmelfahrt (produced 1893), 1893; as *Hannele,* translated by William Archer, 1894; also translated by Charles Henry Meltzer, 1908; translated by T.H. Lustig, in *Five Plays,* 1961
Florian Geyer (produced 1896), 1896; as *Florian Geyer,* translated by Bayard Quincy Morgan, in *Dramatic Works,* 1929
Die versunkene Glocke (produced 1896), 1896; as *The Sunken Bell,* translated by Mary Harned, 1898; translated by Charles Henry Meltzer, 1899
Fuhrmann Henschel (produced 1898), 1898; as *Drayman Henschel,* translated by Marion A. Redlich, in *Dramatic Works,* 1913; also translated by T.H. Lustig, in *Five Plays,* 1961
Schluck und Jau (produced 1900), 1900; as *Schluck and Jau,* translated by Ludwig Lewisohn, in *Dramatic Works,* 1919
Michael Kramer (produced 1900), 1900; translated by Ludwig Lewisohn, in *Dramatic Works,* 1914
Der rote Hahn (produced 1901), 1901; as *Conflagration,* translated by Ludwig Lewisohn, in *Dramatic Works,* 1913
Der arme Heinrich (produced 1902), 1902; as *Henry of Auë,* translated by Ludwig Lewisohn, in *Dramatic Works,* 1914
Rose Bernd (produced 1903), 1903; as *Rose Bernd,* translated by Ludwig Lewisohn, in *Dramatic Works,* 1913; translated by T.H. Lustig, in *Five Plays,* 1961
Elga (produced 1905), 1905; translated by Mary Harned, in *Dramatic Works,* 1919
Und Pippa tanzt! (produced 1906), 1906; translated as *And Pippa Dances,* 1907
Die Jungfrau vom Bischofsberg (produced 1907), 1907; as *Maidens of the Mount,* translated by Ludwig Lewisohn, in *Dramatic Works,* 1919
Kaiser Karls Geisel (produced 1908), 1908; as *Charlemagne's Hostage,* translated by Ludwig Lewisohn, in *Dramatic Works,* 1919
Griselda (produced 1909), 1909; translated by Alice Kauser, in *Dramatic Works,* 1919
Die Ratten (produced 1911), 1911; as *The Rats,* translated by Ludwig Lewisohn, in *Dramatic Works,* 1913
Gabriel Schillings Flucht (produced 1912), 1912; as *Gabriel Schilling's Flight,* translated by Ludwig Lewisohn, in *Dramatic Works,* 1919
Festspiel in deutschen Reimen (produced 1913), 1913; as *Commemoration Masque,* translated by Bayard Quincy Morgan, in *Dramatic Works,* 1919
Der Bogen des Odysseus (produced 1914), 1914; as *The Bow of Ulysses,* translated by Bayard Quincy Morgan, in *Dramatic Works,* 1919
Winterballade (produced 1917), 1917; as *A Winter Ballad,* translated by Edwin and Willa Muir, in *Dramatic Works,* 1925
Der weisse Heiland (produced 1920), 1920; as *The White Savior,* translated by Edwin and Willa Muir, in *Dramatic Works,* 1925
Indipohdi (produced 1920), 1920; translated by Edwin and Willa Muir, in *Dramatic Works,* 1925
Peter Bauer (produced 1921), 1921
Veland, 1925; translated by Edwin Muir, in *Dramatic Works,* 1929
Dorothea Angermann (produced 1926), 1926
Spuk; oder, Die schwarze Maske und Hexenritt (produced 1929), 1929
Vor Sonnenuntergang (produced 1932), 1932
Die goldene Harfe (produced 1933), 1933
Hamlet in Wittenberg (produced 1935), 1935
Ulrich von Lichtenstein (produced 1939), 1939
Die Tochter der Kathedrale (produced 1939), 1939
Die Atriden-Tetralogie: Iphigenie in Aulis; Agamemnons Tod; Elektra; Iphigenie in Delphi (produced 1940–44), 4 vols., 1941–48
Magnus Garbe (produced 1942), 1942
Die Finsternisse, 1947
Herbert Engelmann, completed by Carl Zuckmayer (produced 1952), 1952
Five Plays, translated by Theodore H. Lustig, 1961

Fiction

Fasching, 1887
Bahnwärter Thiel, 1888; as *Lineman Thiel,* translated by Stanley Radcliffe, 1989
Der Apostel, 1890
Der Narr in Christo, Emanuel Quint, 1910; as *The Fool in Christ, Emanuel Quint,* translated by Thomas Seltzer, 1911
Atlantis, 1912; as *Atlantis,* translated by Adele and Thomas Seltzer, 1913
Lohengrin, 1913
Parsival, 1914; as *Parsifal,* translated by Oakley Williams, 1915
Der Ketzer von Soana, 1918; as *The Heretic of Soano,* translated by Bayard Quincy Morgan, 1923
Phantom, 1922; as *Phantom,* translated by Bayard Quincy Morgan, 1923
Die Insel der grossen Mutter, 1924; as *The Island of the Great Mother,* translated by Edwin and Willa Muir, 1925
Wanda, 1928
Buch der Leidenschaft, 1930
Die Hochzeit auf Buchenhorst, 1931
Das Meerwunder, 1934
Im Wirbel der Berufung, 1936
Der Schuss im Park, 1939
Das Märchen, 1941
Mignon, 1944
Lineman Thiel and Other Tales, translated by Stanley Radcliffe, 1989

Poetry

Promethidenlos, 1885
Das bunte Buch, 1888

Anna, 1921
Die blaue Blume, 1924
Till Eulenspiegel, 1928
Ährenlese, 1939
Der grosse Traum, 1942
Neue Gedichte, 1946

Other
Griechischer Frühlung, 1908
Ausblicke, 1922
Um Volk und Geist, 1932
Gespräche, edited by Josef Chapiro, 1932
Das Abenteuer meiner Jugend, 2 vols., 1937
Italienische Reise 1897; Tagenbuchaufzeichnungen, edited by Martin Machatzke, 1976
Diarium 1917 bis 1933, edited by Martin Machatzke, 1980
Notiz-Kalender 1889 bis 1891, edited by Martin Machatzke, 1982
Gerhart Hauptmann—Ludwig von Hofmann: Briefwechsel 1894–1944, edited by Herta Hesse-Frielinghaus, 1983
Otto Brahm, Gerhart Hauptmann: Briefwechsel 1889–1912, edited by Peter Sprengel, 1985
Tagebuch 1892 bis 1894, edited by Martin Machatzke, 1985
Tagebücher 1897 bis 1905, edited by Martin Machatzke, 1987

Further Reading
Daiber, Hans, *Gerhart Hauptmann oder der letzte Klassiker,* Vienna: Molden, 1971
Guthke, Karl Siegfried, *Gerhart Hauptmann: Weltbild im Werk,* Göttingen: Vandenhoeck und Ruprecht, 1961; 2nd edition, Munich: Francke, 1980
Hilscher, Eberhard, *Gerhart Hauptmann: Leben und Werk,* Frankfurt: Athenäum, 1988
Hoefert, Sigfrid, *Gerhart Hauptmann,* Stuttgart: Metzler, 1974; 2nd edition, 1982
Kipa, Alfred A., *Gerhart Hauptmann in Russia, 1889–1917: Reception and Impact,* Hamburg: Buske, 1974
Maurer, Warren R., "Gerhart Hauptmann in the United States," in *The Fortunes of German Writers in America: Studies in Literary Reception,* edited by Wolfgang Elfe et al., Columbia: University of South Carolina Press, 1992
——, *Understanding Gerhart Hauptmann,* Columbia: University of South Carolina Press, 1992
Osborne, John, *The Naturalist Drama in Germany,* Manchester: Manchester University Press, and Totowa, New Jersey: Rowman and Littlefield, 1971
Schrimpf, Hans Joachim, editor, *Gerhart Hauptmann,* Darmstadt: Wissenschaftliche Buchgesellschaft, 1976
Sprengel, Peter, and Philip A. Mellen, editors, *Hauptmann-Forschung: Neue Beiträge,* Frankfurt and Bern: Lang, 1986; as *Hauptmann Research: New Directions,* New York: Lang, 1986

Die Weber 1892

Play by Gerhart Hauptmann

Triggering what has been deemed the most spectacular case of political censorship in the history of German literature, Gerhart Hauptmann's *Die Weber* (*The Weavers*) is a prime example of naturalist drama at its most strident. The play represents a milestone in its genre because of the way in which it adopts a collective rather than an individual hero, and the revolutionary import of this proletarian tragedy ensured an immediate succès de scandale. Although *The Weavers* ostensibly was historical, documenting the Silesian weavers' revolt of 1844, it in fact addresses ongoing injustices in an uncompromising manner, which inevitably caused it to meet with opposition. Not only was the play the subject of a protracted legal battle in Germany but public performances were also at first banned in France, Austria, Italy, and Russia; performances of the play even led to trouble in the United States.

But what was to the authorities a dangerously socialist work, which incited public disorder and violence, was for its writer an honest engagement with the plight of the oppressed. As mechanization heralded the death of the hand-loom industry, Hauptmann had personally witnessed the appalling conditions endured by the rural pieceworkers existing at the mercy of ruthless factory owners who paid them barely enough for survival. While the play is compelling evidence of his social concern, its exact political implications have long been a topic for debate. By the 1890s, the naturalist writers were expressing reservations about some of their affinities with the socialist movement, and Hauptmann, anxious to avoid party politics, described *The Weavers* as "social, but not socialist." The reactions of influential observers, however, clearly revealed the perceived significance of the work. As Emperor Wilhelm II angrily canceled his subscription to a permanent box at the Deutsches Theater, Lenin arranged for the play's publication and circulation in Russia, having edited a translation of it by his own sister.

One of *The Weavers*'s striking qualities is Hauptmann's accomplishment in his portrayal of the working classes. Unlike some other naturalist playwrights, he eschews an intellectual, middle-class perspective, thus preventing sentimentality. Critics have applauded his skill in combining a sensitive depiction of individual characters, whose dignity and separate identity are preserved, with a remarkable psychological insight into the masses of the weavers, a community of downtrodden workers united by their poverty and their rebellion. Some commentators nevertheless, dissatisfied with the play's "slice-of-life" emphasis, have felt the lack of a single protagonist who symbolizes the struggle and whose fortunes are followed through to a conclusion.

Critical attention has focused most controversially on the role of old Hilse, the figure who dominates the fifth act of the play. His opposition to the uprising, springing from his pietistic stance of patient endurance and nonviolence, lends an ambiguity to the ending. Theodor Fontane leads one school of thought by arguing that this portrayal balances out the revolutionary tone of the first four acts and alters the message of the play. But later critics have interpreted Hilse, like the other weavers, as a product of his environment who has been controlled by the church—representative of a hollow middle-class morality—which has taught him to accept his lot in the prevalent social order. His quietism, therefore, is construed as a form of compensation for suffering and as an anachronism in the context of modern capitalist exploitation.

The language of *The Weavers* has, ironically, proved both its greatest strength and its ultimate weakness. A salient feature of naturalist drama was the endeavor to render spoken language with total realism, and Hauptmann was also at pains to reaffirm the dignity and range of dialect that, in his view, was too often employed in literature as a curiosity or condescendingly exploited for comic effect. The first version of the play, entitled *De Waber,* was written entirely in dialect, and even in the second, High German version—revised to exclude the most controversial content—a substantial vernacular element was retained. This vernacular element enabled Hauptmann to underpin the moral of the play by harnessing the vitality of local speech rhythms and to differentiate characters across the social spectrum according to linguistic expression. The problem for modern audiences, however, is that the Silesian dialect has now virtually disappeared—the area was subsumed into Poland after World War II—and the work loses much of its original force when the dialect passages are adapted into more accessible vernaculars.

The Weavers quickly validated itself as a classic treatment of deprivation and social unrest. Its dramatization of the move from subservience to collective confidence in revolt has found resonance throughout over a century of workers' protests in many countries. A highly acclaimed silent film version, directed by F. Zelnik, was made in 1927, and as an established text in the literary canon of the Soviet Union, the work was influential in the emergence of socialist realism. The play continues to be performed today and to attract media interest in both the aesthetic and the polemical issues it raises. A notable example is B. Findlay's Scots translation, premiered in 1997, which seeks through the use of old Angus Scots to recapture the former intention and spirit of the play through the use of dialect.

The unprecedented visual power of certain images in *The Weavers* has resulted in many now-familiar imitations on both stage and screen. Images such as the starving child collapsing at the employer's feet, the undernourished worker whose stomach can no longer tolerate the luxury of a piece of dog meat, or the band of marauding weavers who, after breaking into the manufacturer's house, fall silent in awe of the luxurious furnishings, have been identified by Peter Skrine as highly influential effects first conceived by Hauptmann and often repeated in 20th-century film and drama.

Thus, from the early, somewhat discredited position of scandalous success, *The Weavers* has come to enjoy the status of a seminal work with international recognition. It is widely regarded as the most outstanding achievement not only of Hauptmann himself, but also of German naturalist drama as a whole.

BARBARA BURNS

Editions

First edition: *Die Weber,* Berlin: Fischer, 1892
Critical edition: edited by M. Boulby, London: Harrap, 1962
Translation: *The Weavers,* translated by Theodore H. Lustig, in *Plays,* edited by Reinhold Grimm and Caroline Molina y Vedia, The German Library, vol. 57, New York: Continuum, 1994

Further Reading

Cowen, Roy C., *Hauptmann-Kommentar zum dramatischen Werk,* Munich: Winkler, 1980
Guthke, Karl S., *Gerhart Hauptmann: Weltbild im Werk,* Göttingen: Vandenhoeck und Ruprecht, 1961; 2nd edition, 1980
Hildebrandt, Klaus, *Naturalistische Dramen Gerhart Hauptmanns,* Munich: Oldenbourg, 1983
Hilscher, Eberhard, *Gerhart Hauptmann,* Berlin: Verlag der Nation, 1969
Hoefert, Sigfrid, *Gerhart Hauptmann,* Stuttgart: Metzler, 1974; 2nd revised edition, 1982
Osborne, John, *The Naturalist Drama in Germany,* Manchester: Manchester University Press, and Totowa, New Jersey: Rowman and Littlefield, 1971
Praschek, Helmut, editor, *Gerhart Hauptmanns "Weber": Eine Dokumentation,* Berlin: Akademie-Verlag, 1981
Sinden, Margaret J., *Gerhart Hauptmann: The Prose Plays,* Toronto: University of Toronto Press, 1957
Skrine, Peter N., *Hauptmann, Wedekind, and Schnitzler,* Basingstoke: Macmillan, and New York: St. Martin's Press, 1989
Sprengel, Peter, *Gerhart Hauptmann: Epoche, Werk, Wirkung,* Munich: Beck, 1984
Tank, K.L., *Gerhart Hauptmann in Selbstzeugnissen und Bilddokumenten,* Reinbek bei Hamburg: Rowolt, 1959
Tschörtner, H.D., *Ungeheures erhofft: Zu Gerhart Hauptmann—Werk und Wirkung,* Berlin: Buchverlag Der Morgen, 1986

Friedrich Hebbel 1813–1863

Born two years before the defeat of Napoléon and dying eight years before the foundation of the Second German Reich, Friedrich Hebbel lived in an age marked in philosophy by the transition from idealism to positivism and in politics by the victory of conservative authoritarianism over radical democratic aspirations. Although he also wrote stories, poems, and comedies, he is remembered above all for his tragedies. Seeking to reconcile the earlier approaches of German classicism with the new methods of realism, he argued that works of art should be records of empirical observation as well as symbols of transcendental truth. He defined drama as "the art of mixing the general and the particular" in such a way that "the law which is obeyed by all living things" never appears "naked" and is never "completely missed," and he regarded the tragic mode as supreme, since "in all great crises history itself turns into tragedy." Despite his acute awareness of psychological and social forces, he frequently resorted to abstruse metaphysical speculation in his cerebral search for meaning in an existence that he instinctively believed to be meaningless. As Brecht put it: "Wherever German playwrights started thinking, like Hebbel and before him Schiller, they started contriving."

The son of a poor North German stonemason, Hebbel suffered a great deal of deprivation and humiliation. He also hurt others—particularly Elise Lensing, a seamstress who supported him for ten years and bore him two sons before he abandoned her in order to marry the celebrated Viennese actress Christine Enghaus. It was not until his fifth and last decade that he achieved fame and moderate wealth, although he never became popular with the broad public, and his work is rarely performed today. Awkwardly self-educated, touchy but arrogant, obstinate, quarrelsome, humorless, and depressive, he had a profoundly pessimistic outlook. In his diaries he notes that "all life is a struggle of the individual against the universe" and that "there is only one necessity, which is that the world should exist; how individuals fare in the world is immaterial." In his treatise *Mein Wort über das Drama* (1843; My Word on Drama), he argues that individuals are obliged by their very nature to incur the—existential rather than moral—guilt of self-assertion and must be destroyed to preserve the universal order. Although at times he tried to find solace in the reflection that the destruction of the individual contributed to the dialectical progress of the universe, he mostly emphasized the uncertainty, insecurity, and misery of the human condition. These ideas, which occasionally reveal the influence of Hegel, Schelling, Gotthilf Heinrich Schubert, and Ludwig Feuerbach, are at the center of his concept of tragedy.

In all of Hebbel's major plays, the confrontation of overbearing men and resentful women reflects both his personal experiences and his Kantian maxim: "Using a human being as a means to an end: the worst sin." He is most penetrating in his depictions of the sadomasochistic battle of the sexes, which anticipate Ibsen and Strindberg, but he tends to lessen their impact by adding incongruous episodes proclaiming his theories about the evolution of history. In *Judith* (1840), the notion that the Jewish widow, by killing the Assyrian general Holofernes, will help to replace the era of idolatry with that of monotheism is uneasily tied to the work's exploration of a woman's confusion between her sense of divine mission and her personal revenge on a brutal lover. In *Herodes und Mariamne* (1850; *Herod and Mariamne*), the advent of Christianity, due to supplant Judeo-Roman despotism, seems an inconsequential afterthought to the play's analysis of possessiveness, devotion, hostility, and incompatible desires in marriage, which combine to destroy the heroine and leave the hero in lonely desolation. In *Gyges und sein Ring* (1856; *Gyges and His Ring*), the study of the fatal consequences of the Lydian king's neurotic desire to flaunt the beauty of his excessively modest Indian-born queen appears more plausible than the work's message of a cultural synthesis between tradition and innovation, which is embodied in their Greek successor to the throne. In the trilogy *Die Nibelungen* (1862; *The Nibelungs*)—which became Hebbel's greatest theatrical success in his lifetime when it was performed in Weimar in 1861—the vengeance of Brunhild and Kriemhild for the affronts of Siegfried and Hagen fails to blend with the play's allusion to the impending defeat of heathendom by Christianity.

In two instances, however, Hebbel manages to avoid theorizing. In *Agnes Bernauer* (1852), a historical tragedy set in the 15th century, a barber's daughter marries the son of a ruler, who has her assassinated in order to prevent a war of succession. The proposition that the citizen must always be sacrificed to the state demonstrates Hebbel's conservative ideology, which became more pronounced after the 1848 revolutions, but the contest of love and politics fuses concrete human reality with abstract thought in a dramatically convincing manner. In *Maria Magdalena* (1844), any abstract thought is totally absorbed in vital drama. Set in Hebbel's own time, this domestic tragedy—as he argues in his renowned preface—represents a significant advance in the genre since the days of Lessing and Schiller, in that the tragic events derive no longer from the clash of the middle and upper classes but from the prejudices of the petty bourgeoisie itself. As the provincial joiner's daughter, after becoming pregnant, is driven to suicide by the desertion of her mercenary seducer and the threats of her puritanical father, the compelling portrayal of unfortunate individuals and their claustrophobic personal circumstances unites with a merciless criticism of an inhuman society to produce not only Hebbel's masterpiece but one of the outstanding works of European realism as a whole.

With regard to dramatic structure, Hebbel's preference for the classically "closed" form is liable to distort his realistic insights. With regard to language, he is most effective when writing contemporary prose, while his blank verse is prone to clumsiness, bombast, and anticlimax. At their worst, his plays are hysterical in atmosphere, extravagant in characterization, artificial in situation, and tortuous in argument. At their best, however, they rise to powerful, tragic conflicts that memorably reflect both the contradictions of the age and the perplexities of an idiosyncratic artist who was doggedly determined to overcome a daunting array of intellectual, emotional, and social odds.

LADISLAUS LÖB

Biography

Born in Wesselburen, Holstein, Denmark (now Germany), 18 March 1813. Servant and clerk to a local official, 1827–35; studied at the University of Heidelberg, 1836, and in Munich, 1836; in Hamburg, 1839; doctorate, University of Erlangen, 1844; worked as a freelance writer in Munich, 1836–39, and Hamburg, 1839–43; a travel grant from the king of Denmark allowed him to live in Paris, 1843–44, and Rome, 1844–45; in Vienna from 1845; honorary court librarian, Weimar, 1863. Schiller Prize, 1863. Died 13 December 1863.

Selected Works

Collections

Sämtliche Werke, edited by Richard Maria Werner, 27 vols., 1904–22
Werke, edited by Gerhard Fricke, Werner Keller, and Karl Pörnbacher, 5 vols., 1963–67

Plays

Judith (produced 1840), 1840; translated by Carl van Doren, 1914
Genoveva (produced 1849), 1843
Maria Magdalena (produced 1846), 1844; translated by Barker Fairley, in *Three Plays*, 1914; translated by Carl Richard Mueller, 1962; translated by Sarah Somekh, 1990
Der Diamant (produced 1852), 1847
Julia (produced 1903), 1848
Herodes und Mariamne (produced 1849), 1850; as *Herod an Mariamne*, translated by L.H. Allen, in *Three Plays*, 1914
Der Rubin (produced 1849), 1851
Michel Angelo (produced 1861), 1851
Ein Trauerspiel in Sizilien (produce 1907), 1851
Agnes Bernauer (produced 1852), 1852; translated by L. Pattee, in *Poet Lore*, 1909
Gyges und sein Ring (produced 1889), 1856; as *Gyges and His Ring*, translated by L.H. Allen, in *Three Plays*, 1914
Die Nibelungen (produced 1861), 2 vols., 1862; as *The Nibelungs*, translated by H. Goldberger, 1921
Demetrius (from Schiller) (produced 1869), 1864
Ein Steinwurf, 1883

Three Plays (includes *Maria Magdalena; Herod and Marianmne; Gyges and His Ring*), translated by L.H. Allen and Barker Fairley, 1914

Fiction
Schnock: Ein niederländisches Gemälde, 1850
Erzählungen und Novellen, 1855

Poetry
Gedichte, 1842
Neue Gedichte, 1848
Gedichte, 1857
Mutter und Kind, 1859

Other
Mein Wort über das Drama!, 1843
Über den Stil des Dramas, 1857
Tagebücher, edited by F. Bamberg, 2 vols., 1885–87
Der einsame Weg (diaries), edited by Klaus Geissler, 1996
Briefe, edited by U. Henry Gerlach, 2 vols., 1975–78

Further Reading

Fenner, Birgit, *Friedrich Hebbel zwischen Hegel und Freud,* Stuttgart: Klett-Cotta, 1979
Flygt, Sten Gunnar, *Friedrich Hebbel,* New York: Twayne, 1968
Garland, Mary, *Hebbel's Prose Tragedies,* Cambridge: Cambridge University Press, 1973
Grundmann, Hilmar, and Ludger Lütkehaus, editors, *Friedrich Hebbel: Neue Studien zu Werk und Wirkung,* Heide: Westholsteinische Verlagsanstalt Boyens, 1982
Kaiser, Herbert, *Friedrich Hebbel: Geschichtliche Interpretation des dramatischen Werks,* Munich: Fink, 1983
Koller-Andorf, Ida, editor, *Hebbel, Mensch und Dichter im Werk: Jubiläumsband 1995 mit Symposionsreferaten,* Vienna: Friedrich-Hebbel-Gesellschaft, 1995
Kraft, Herbert, *Die Poesie der Idee: Die tragische Dichtung Friedrich Hebbels,* Tübingen: Niemeyer, 1971
Kreuzer, Helmut, editor, *Hebbel in neuer Sicht,* Stuttgart: Kohlhammer, 1963
———, editor, *Friedrich Hebbel,* Darmstadt: Wissenschaftliche Buchgesellschaft, 1989
Matthiesen, Hayo, *Friedrich Hebbel in Selbstzeugnissen und Bilddokumenten,* Reinbek bei Hamburg: Rowohlt, 1970
Meetz, Anni, *Friedrich Hebbel,* Stuttgart: Metzler, 1962
Müller, Joachim, *Das Weltbild Friedrich Hebbels,* Halle: Niemeyer, 1955
Purdie, Edna, *Friedrich Hebbel: A Study of His Life and Work,* Oxford and London: Oxford University Press, 1932
Sengle, Friedrich, "Friedrich Hebbel (1813–1863)," in *Biedermeierzeit: Deutsche Literatur im Spannungsfeld zwischen Restauration und Revolution, 1815–1848,* 3 vols., Stuttgart: Metzler, 1971
Stern, J.P., "Friedrich Hebbel: In Search of the Absolute," in *Idylls and Realities: Studies in Nineteenth-Century German Literature,* London: Methuen, and New York: Ungar, 1971
Stolte, Heinz Hermann, *Friedrich Hebbel: Welt und Werk,* Hamburg: Holsten, 1965
Wiese, Benno von, *Die deutsche Tragödie von Lessing bis Hebbel,* Hamburg: Hoffmann und Campe, 1948
Ziegler, Klaus, *Mensch und Welt in der Tragödie Friedrich Hebbels,* Berlin: Junker und Dünnhaupt, 1938; Darmstadt: Wissenschaftliche Buchgesellschaft, 1966

Johann Peter Hebel 1760–1826

Johann Peter Hebel is one of the most attractive figures of the German Enlightenment. He wrote no novels or plays, but he is the author of one of the most celebrated of all *Bildungsgedichte* or poems of personal development (featuring, we should note, a female protagonist). And he succeeded like no other writer of his time in turning the ordinary living room into a "Moralischer Anstalt" or ethical institution. His works have exerted an influence far exceeding their girth, and they have counted among their admirers some of the greatest stylists in German. Because he wrote in genres usually considered minor, yet achieved such consummate mastery in them, he can be said to have expanded the expressive range of German literature.

Hebel was born to relatively humble parents in 1760. His mother was a native of the *Wiesenthal,* and it was in her language that he wrote his first book, the *Alemannische Gedichte* (1803; Poems in the Alemannic Dialect). By this stage he was living in linguistic exile near the court in Karlsruhe. There seems little doubt that the book was inspired at least partly by feelings of nostalgia. Yet despite the presence in them of various hobgoblins and will-o'-the-wisps, of a ruined castle and pervasive personification, these poems are not Romantic in spirit, and their form has little to do with folk song. On the contrary, they are largely classical, expressing a view of the world that is benign but not sentimental, indebted to pastoral but informed by an inimitable plasticity, self-evidently but not dogmatically Christian, committed to the project of enlightenment, but by no means unaware of darkness, death, and loss. And the form, from the hexameters of the great narrative pieces to the exquisitely crafted tetrameters and trimeters of the smaller lyrics, is indebted to, and need not fear comparison with, the greatest models of antiquity.

In other words, Hebel's recourse to dialect was not a spontaneous outpouring of natural feeling, but sprang from a conscious, philological ambition to elevate what he regarded as one of the wellsprings of the German language to a status equivalent to Homer's. And in this he succeeded so well that his work is generally regarded as the fountainhead of dialect poetry in German, and it can stand alongside even such celebrated contemporaries as Robert Burns. Unfortunately, however, the image of Hebel as a simple—not to say simpleminded—countryman has proved hard to dispel. In the German context, of course, such an image can prove especially damaging. And in Hebel's particular case the problem is compounded by his adoption in another of his masterpieces of the persona of the *Rheinländischer* or *Rheinischer Hausfreund* (Rhenisch Fireside Companion).

Such was the title under which the Lutheran State Almanach for Baden was re-launched under Hebel's editorship in 1808. The stories, anecdotes, riddles, tips, and practical information that Hebel contributed to the almanac and that later went to make up the *Schatzkästlein des rheinischen Hausfreundes* (1811; *The Treasure Chest*) are often described as the best-loved texts of German literature. Because of a persistent tendency to identify Hebel with the *Hausfreund*, however, this popularity was until comparatively recently attributed to Hebel's personality rather than to his sophisticated literary technique. In fact it is the skilful manipulation of the relationship between the "Calendar Man" and his readers that enables Hebel to impart information and moral instruction without falling into the trap of didacticism. (One telling indication of this is the frequent disjunction between the implicit and explicit "morals" of these stories.) The artful marriage of the procedures of classical rhetoric with syntactic peculiarities derived from dialect create the impression of spontaneous immediate speech. And the judicious deployment of scientific and moral authority creates a relationship of trust that is the nearest literary equivalent of teaching by example. Writers who came after Hebel were not always able to emulate this art of concealing art. But all of them, from Gotthelf and Graf to Brecht, Benjamin, and Kafka, found inspiration in Hebel, without whom the particular form of the *Kalendergeschichte*, the anecdote or the very short story, would almost certainly have been confined to obscurity.

It is symptomatic of the spirit that Hebel sought to convey and of the complicated context in which he was working that one of his stories, which pleads for the precedence of faith over confession, fell foul of the Catholic authorities and had to be withdrawn. It must have been particularly gratifying, then, that his *Biblische Geschichten* (1824; *Hebel's Bible Stories*) should have proved acceptable to, although they were never actually adopted by, that same Catholic Church. They share the same qualities of rationalism, clarity, and vividness as the almanac pieces. And although they have recently begun to attract attention for their theological complexities, they remain among the masterpieces of children's literature in German. Similar to the work of Charles and Mary Lamb in English, Hebel's versions of the Bible define their own literary genre and stand out as literary works in their own right.

Johann Peter Hebel died of cancer in 1826. In his lifetime, he published three books, some eight almanac annuals, and a number of other occasional pieces. But it was not until after his death that a further great masterpiece was added to the canon in the form of his collected letters (*Briefe* [1939]). In their tone and their tact, their variety, their exuberance, and their sheer virtuosity, they bear eloquent testimony to Hebel's capacity for literary friendship. Yet just as the *Hausfreund* was merely a persona, so in the letters there is so much role playing that the real Hebel remains tantalizingly unknowable. And that, of course, is what makes his work so endlessly fascinating.

ROBERT GILLETT

Biography

Born in Basel, 10 May 1760. Studied theology in Erlangen; ordained 1780; taught at Hertingen and Lörrach before being called to the staff of his old school in Karlsruhe, where he was also subdeacon; rose to position of headmaster, prelate of the Lutheran Church, parliamentarian, and synod member. Died in Schwetzingen 22 September 1826.

Selected Works

Collections

Sämtliche Schriften, edited by Adrian Braunbehrens, Gustav Adolf Penrath, and Peter Pfaff, 1990–

Writings

Alemannische Gedichte, 1803; edited by Wilhelm Zentner, 1960; 1820 edition edited by Helmut Bender, 1990

Schatzkästlein des rheinischen Hausfreundes 1811; edited by Winfried Theiß, 1981; as *The Treasure Chest*, translated by John Hibberd, 1994

Biblische Geschichten für die Jugend bearbeitet 1824; edited, with an afterword by Ivo Camartin, 1982; as *Hebel's Bible Stories*, translated by Emily Anderson, illustrated by Susan Sims, 1961

Briefe, edited by Wilhelm Zentner, 2 vols., 1957

Further Reading

Däster, Ulrich, *Johann Peter Hebel in Selbstzeugnissen und Bilddokumenten*, Reinbek bei Hamburg: Rowohlt, 1973

Feger, Robert, *Annäherung an einen Prälaten: Fragestellungen zu Leben und Werk von Johann Peter Hebel*, Lahr: Schauenburg, 1983

Forster, Leonard, "Johann Peter Hebel and 'Die Vergänglichkeit,'" *German Life and Letters* 29 (October 1975)

Hibberd, John L., "J.P. Hebel's *Allemannische Gedichte* and the Idyllic Tradition," *Forum for Modern Language Studies* 8 (1972)

———, "Johann Peter Hebel," in *German Writers in the Age of Goethe, 1789–1832*, Dictionary of Literary Biography, vol. 90, edited by James Hardin and Christoph E. Schweitzer, Detroit, Michigan: Gale Research, 1989

Hopwood, Elin Mererid, *Johann Peter Hebel and the Rhetoric of Orality*, Stuttgart: Heinz, 1994

Knopf, Jan, *Geschichten zur Geschichte: Kritische Tradition des "Volkstümlichen" in den Kalendergeschichten Hebels und Brechts*, Stuttgart: Metzler, 1973

Kully, Rolf Max, *Johann Peter Hebel*, Stuttgart: Metzler, 1969

Magill, C.P., "Pure and Applied Art: A Note on J.P. Hebel," *German Life and Letters* 10 (1957)

Oettinger, Klaus, *Ulm ist überall: Essays und Vorträge zu Johann Peter Hebel*, Constance: Universitätsverlag Konstanz, 1990

Rohner, Ludwig, *Kalendergeschichte und Kalender*, Wiesbaden: Athenaion, 1978

Georg Wilhelm Friedrich Hegel 1770–1832

Hegel's philosophy has never been well understood. Part of the problem is the difference between his first major work, *Die Phänomenologie des Geistes* (1808; *Phenomenology of Spirit*), and his later or "systematic" writings. While the former appears to be a dialectical meditation on the history of humanity or, at least, of Western culture, the later writings seem to shift toward an ahistorical version of metaphysics or even theology.

The *Phenomenology* concerns the adventures of something called *consciousness* as it advances from sensory experience to *Absolute Knowing* (*das absolute Wissen*). *Consciousness* (*Bewußtsein*) is a term basic to Kant, so it is reasonable to suppose that the book deals with the Kantian structures of consciousness—the categories that Kant maintained structure human cognition. In this view, Hegel is showing how the categories arise in and through a certain kind of experience. The prime category involved in this for Hegel is truth, since "truth" designates the proper relation between subject and object. Each section of the *Phenomenology* therefore begins with a definition of what "truth" is taken to be. Consciousness then goes through an "experience" (*Erfahrung*) in which this "certainty" is first applied and then breaks down, leading to a new definition—and a new section. Although occupied in this way with definitions, the *Phenomenology* is not merely a theoretical enterprise: the idea of the proper relation between subject and object includes ethical and social dimensions as well.

The book contains several sections. In the first, "Consciousness" (taken in a stricter sense), consciousness (in the broader sense) confronts an object that is not itself conscious: sense-contents, things, or forces. In the rest of the book, the object of consciousness is another consciousness. As this kind of relation begins, in "Self-Consciousness," the relation of consciousness to its object is antagonistic. This section includes some of the most famous parts of the *Phenomenology,* including "Independence and Dependence of Consciousness," made central to Hegel interpretation by Alexandre Kojève; "Lordship and Bondage," a clear inspiration for Marx's analysis of capitalism; and "The Unhappy Consciousness," which prefigures existentialist and particularly Kierkegaardian themes.

At the end of "The Unhappy Consciousness," consciousness no longer sees truth as residing in an antagonistic relationship to another consciousness, and cooperative efforts begin. At first, in "Reason," these are cognitive in nature: this section discusses Hegel's version of the scientific community. In "Spirit," they become ethical, and the ethical community evolves until all antagonism finally vanishes in the forgiveness of evil (in oneself as well as in the other). It then reaches out, in "Religion," to ultimate reality, developing increasingly adequate and complex concepts of, and relations to, God. When the last otherness between God and humans falls away, consciousness knows that to explain ultimate reality is also to unfold itself, and the *Phenomenology* closes with a very cryptic chapter on "Absolute Knowing."

Although its specific nature is highly unclear, Absolute Knowing seems to closely resemble Hegel's approach to philosophy, and the point of the *Phenomenology* appears to be to show that all alternatives to its way of achieving truth must fail. Thus, the beginning of the book—"Sense-Certainty"—is concerned with the way of achieving truth that is farthest removed from Hegel's own. The problems encountered at each stage force consciousness into a form that is a bit closer to Hegel's own until at last there is no alternative to his philosophy.

It is thus no surprise to learn that Hegel published the *Phenomenology,* at the age of 38, in an effort to get a professorial position (at Jena). The effort failed, but four years later, in 1812, he renewed it with the publication of the first volume of the *Science of Logic,* which was followed by a second in 1816. This work at last got him a professorship at Heidelberg.

The *Wissenschaft der Logik* (1812–16; *Science of Logic*), the most demanding of Hegel's works, is an abstract procession of concepts in which each is defined in terms of those that went before and then in turn helps define those that come after. Perhaps because of its abstractness, it has not drawn the attention that the *Phenomenology* has, but it has had many defenders, and Hegel himself clearly regarded it as the keystone of his system. The book begins with "The Logic of Being," in which concepts come singly: Being, as the first concept, has no definition, and this absence is called Nothing; the movement from Being to Nothing and back can be called Becoming—and so on. The book's second section, which is called "The Logic of Essence," deals with pairs of concepts, including Essence and Accident, Cause and Effect, and other pairs. The last section, "The Logic of the Notion," deals with triads of concepts that mutually define one another. When all the concepts of the metaphysical tradition have been defined in this way, the book ends by calling for a move to reality.

Hegel's *Realphilosophie* is developed in his writings after the *Science of Logic.* All of these writings are concerned with Hegel's lectures at Heidelberg and Berlin, and they fall into two groups. The *Encyklopädie der philosophischen Wissenschaften im Grundrisse* (1817, 1827, 1830; *Encyclopedia of Philosophy*) and *Grundlinien der Philosophie des Rechts* (1821; *The Philosophy of Right*) were written as handbooks to his lectures. Students would buy them and follow along as Hegel first read a paragraph from the book; they would then take notes as he expatiated upon it. The other group of writings, much more numerous, has been put together from the student notes themselves. In such an enterprise, much depends on the editor—and even more on the student who originally took the notes. Hence, these lecture courses must be used with great caution. (Uncritical use of the *Vorlesungen über die Philosophie der Geschichte* [1837; *Lectures on the Philosophy of History*], in particular, has caused great harm to Hegel interpretation.)

The first part of the *Realphilosophie,* the *Philosophy of Nature,* uses the concepts defined in the *Logic* to comprehend nature. The difference is that, while the *Logic* constructs a very tight "logical space" of relations among its various concepts, natural space is wholly unstructured. There is no reason for the entire universe not to be, say, three feet or three miles east of where it is; the same holds for almost everything within it. Space thus introduces an element of randomness that was missing in the *Logic,* and the importance of this contingency for Hegel cannot be overstated (that Eskimos live farther from the sun than do Arabs has enormous effects on their respective cultures, for example). Being thus conditioned by contingency, natural objects never fully exemplify the rational structures developed in the

Logic. But they must have an impulse to do so, for otherwise there would be no structure of any kind in the universe. The *Philosophy of Nature* traces this impulse insofar as it is natural from mechanics through biology.

The *Philosophy of Spirit* takes the story up at the moment that the organism is able to organize and reorganize itself. An animal cannot shift the size and placement of its body parts to meet new challenges, but human beings can do precisely this with their cultural heritage, and in the case of its linguistic component they do it all the time, rearranging the inherited words of their language to convey new meanings. The *Philosophy of Spirit* is thus divided into three stages: "Subjective Spirit" (comprising anthropology, phenomenology—a puzzle, since Hegel had, of course, already written a book by that name—and psychology), "Objective Spirit," and "Absolute Spirit." The latter two have been extremely influential—Objective Spirit because Hegel wrote a separate work, *The Philosophy of Right,* to convey its content, and Absolute Spirit because of his lecture on its components (primarily art and religion).

The *Philosophy of Right,* Hegel's mature social philosophy, is a rational presentation of the structures of the modern state. It begins with a discussion of the basic moralizing force in a society, law; then it moves to discuss the individual moral agent. Its longest section is concerned with "Ethical Life," which is basically defined as the social mores and governmental organisms that constitute the modern state. The *Philosophy of Right* presents these aspects as a mutually reinforcing set, each aspect of which has evolved to meet certain challenges and none of which can be changed in isolation. Hegel's political philosophy has therefore been taken to be very conservative in character. It could also be, however, that he took the other way out from his recognition that serious change can only be global, and thus was an early revolutionary. This view has received support from recent discoveries of student notes and early drafts of the *Philosophy of Right,* in which Hegel is vehemently critical of many aspects of life in the modern state. Most of these were eliminated, apparently for political reasons, from the published version of *The Philosophy of Right.*

In the *Phenomenology,* art and religion are dealt with together: art is essentially characterized as a form of religion. In the later writings, art negates the political sphere, and religion does the same for art. Hegel's treatments of both are exhaustive, containing a sizable fraction of what was actually known in his time. He seeks in each case to arrange his material on rational principles that will, as in the *Philosophy of Right,* show all of the phenomena of art and religion to be mutually reinforcing and historically developed.

Hegel's philosophy as a whole has generally been considered too preposterous to be taken seriously. From the time he arrived in Berlin, he has been one of the most ridiculed of all philosophers and stands for many—particularly in the English-speaking world—as a shining example of what not to do in philosophy. Many parts of his thought, however, have attained great credence. The *Phenomenology* has had a decisive influence on thinkers as diverse as Marx and Kierkegaard, and Hegel's innovative discussion of civil society, in the *Philosophy of Right,* as a sphere distinct from that of the state has also been widely accepted, as has his general schematization of history into Ancient, Medieval, and Modern periods. His accounts of individual artworks such as the pyramids and the *Antigone* have achieved classic status themselves, as have his articulation and defense of Lutheranism in the *Vorlesungen über die Philosophie der Religion* (1832; *Lectures on the Philosophy of Religion*).

But the irony is palpable, for Hegel himself would have maintained that the individual insights he proffered could be understood and validated only by his overall thought, which generated them. Western culture's almost constant return to parts of Hegel's system, coupled with its flagrant disregard for the unified enterprise from which they derive, would shock him. This suggests that there is still much work to be done in appropriating and digesting this very difficult philosopher.

JOHN MCCUMBER

See also Romanticism

Biography

Born in Stuttgart, 1770. Studied at Tübingen, 1788–93; many years of financial and personal difficulty; worked as a private tutor in Berne and Frankfurt, as an unpaid lecturer at Jena, as editor of the *Bamberger Zeitung,* and as a high school principal in Nuremberg; professor at Heidelberg, 1817; moved to Berlin, where he became a rector. Died (in cholera epidemic), 1832.

Selected Works

Collections

Werke, edited by Eva Moldenhauer and Karl Markus Michel, 20 vols., 1970–71

Philosophy

Die Phänomenologie des Geistes, 1808; as *Phenomenology of Spirit,* translated by A.V. Miller, 1977

Wissenschaft der Logik, 1812–16; as *Science of Logic,* translated by A.V. Miller, 1976

Encyklopädie der philosophischen Wissenschaften im Grundrisse, 1817; 2nd edition, as *Encyclopädie,* 1827; 3rd edition, 1830; as *Encyclopedia of Philosophy,* translated by Gustav Emil Mueller, 1959

Grundlinien der Philosophie des Rechts, 1821; as *The Philosophy of Right,* translated by S.W. Dyde, 1896

Vorlesungen über die Philosophie der Religion, 1832; as *Lectures on the Philosophy of Religion,* translated by E.B. Spiers and J. Burdon Sanderson, 3 vols., 1895

Vorlesungen über die Geschichte der Philosophie, 3 vols., 1833–36; as *Lectures on the History of Philosophy,* translated by Elizabeth S. Haldane and Frances H. Simson, 3 vols., 1892–96

Vorlesungen über die Philosophie der Geschichte, 1837; as *Lectures on the Philosophy of History,* translated by J. Sibree, 1857

Hegels theologische Jugendscrhiften, edited by Herman Nohl, 1907; as *Early Theological Writings,* translated by T.M. Knox, 1948

Hegel Reader, edited by Stephen Houlgate, 1998

Further Reading

Avineri, Shlomo, *Hegel's Theory of the Modern State,* Cambridge and London: Cambridge University Press, 1972

Burbidge, John W., *On Hegel's Logic: Fragments of a Commentary,* Atlantic Highlands, New Jersey: Humanities Press, 1981

Fackenheim, Emil, *The Religious Dimension in Hegel's Thought,* Bloomington: Indiana University Press, 1967

Flay, Joseph C., *Hegel's Quest for Certainty,* Albany: State University of New York Press, 1984

Hyppolite, Jean, *Genesis and Structure of Hegel's "Phenomenology of Spirit,"* translated by Samuel Cherniak and John Heckman, Evanston, Illinois: Northwestern University Press, 1974

Kojève, Alexandre, *Introduction to the Reading of Hegel,* translated by James Nichols, New York: Basic Books, 1969

McCumber, John, *The Company of Words,* Evanston, Illinois: Northwestern University Press, 1993
Mure, G.R.G., *A Study of Hegel's Logic,* Oxford: Clarendon Press, 1950
Pinkard, Terry P., *Hegel's Dialectic: The Explanation of Possibility,* Philadelphia, Pennsylvania: Temple University Press, 1988
Pippin, Robert B., *Hegel's Idealism: The Satisfactions of Self-Consciousness,* Cambridge and New York: Cambridge University Press, 1989
Rockmore, Tom, *Hegel's Circular Epistemology,* Bloomington: Indiana University Press, 1986
Taylor, Charles, *Hegel,* Cambridge and New York: Cambridge University Press, 1975

Martin Heidegger 1889–1976

Martin Heidegger is one of the 20th century's leading thinkers. Heidegger's academic career commenced in 1919, when he held seminars at Freiburg University as an unpaid lecturer (*Privatdozent*) and acted as assistant to Edmund Husserl. The publication of Heidegger's magnum opus *Sein und Zeit* (1927; *Being and Time*) marked his rapid climb to fame. Yet, Heidegger's notoriety as a stringent thinker was already established among students. From 1923, Heidegger lectured at Marburg University and succeeded Husserl at Freiburg in 1928. Despite the respectful dedication in *Being and Time* to Husserl "in reverence and friendship," Heidegger adapted Husserl's phenomenological approach to suit his own brand of "phenomenological ontology." Initially, critical efforts to account for the originality of Heidegger's thought led to the close association of his ideas with Karl Jaspers's philosophy of existence.

In the early 1930s, the theoretical approach of these leading thinkers was heralded as the inspiration for the philosophical movement of existentialism. However, it soon transpired that existentialism applied to a poeticized version of Heidegger's concepts, a view that was underlined by Jean-Paul Sartre's enthusiastic response in *Being and Nothingness* to Heidegger's philosophy. Sartre's work sparked off an enduring critical resonance for Heidegger's thought in France. In the postwar era, Jean Beaufret, among others, continued the French interest in Heidegger's endeavors. By contrast, Heidegger's credibility in his native Germany was irrevocably damaged, mainly because of his actions on Hitler's rise to power. The practical approach to Heidegger's thought, which gained popularity after Heidegger's death in 1976, provoked a scholarly debate that quickly escalated into controversy. Inside Germany and abroad, Heidegger's reputation was scrutinized to determine the significance of what some critics represented as an implicit correlation of Heidegger's thinking with National Socialist ideology of the time.

When *Being and Time* appeared, it aroused controversial reactions. Heidegger's approach involved a captivating brand of hermeneutics that was meant to extrapolate from the given facts of life the foundations of Being itself. What aroused widespread interest was Heidegger's predilection for coining new ways of expressing his ideas, such as the hyphenation of his terms, which impressed on his audience an innovative style of language that frequently dazzled by its *unvergleichliche Suggestionskraft* (incomparable power of suggestion) (Gadamer). Heidegger's particular method of "destruction" was to analyze Being, which he argued was cast in oblivion (*Seinsvergessenheit*) by Platonic metaphysics. His endeavor in *Being and Time* was to isolate *Sein* (Being) from the given ontical plain, *Seiendheit,* that is, the sheer prospect of being there, *Da-sein.* Heidegger (in *Sein und Zeit*) turned his gaze *zu den Sachen selbst* (to the things themselves). He scrutinized the ontological difference of earthly life from what he called humanity's "throwness" (*Geworfenheit*) into Being.

In Heidegger's postwar essay collection, *Holzwege* (1950; Woodpaths), the essential difference of *In-der-Welt-Sein* (Being-in-the-world) from Being itself is taken a step further. Heidegger refers to Being as an obscure manner of *Ek-sistenz.* The reference sets existence apart from the facts of life in a way that Heidegger later referred to in his essay *Identität und Differenz* (1957; *Identity and Difference*) as a "happening" (*Ereignis*) that intrinsically connects humans with their true sense of natality. Heidegger's exaggerated ways of writing Being as "Seyn" or "Sein," literally crossed out, as in *Zur Seinsfrage* (1956; *The Question of Being*), underline his view that Being "stands out" (*Ek-sistenz*) from merely being here (*Da-sein*). Heidegger was no less inventive in *Being and Time* in his bid to secure an adequate expression of his vision of Being as a layer of *Existenzialen*— "existentialist" terms—such as *Man* (the "they"), as *Sorge* (care), or as *Sein zum Tode* (Being-towards-death). These terms are distinct from the mundane incidence of life, but Heidegger's breakthrough to "existentialist" facts of authentic existence did not reconcile his conception of Being with human mortality, that is, with the temporal constraint of Time as historicity.

Heidegger's attempt to reverse his analysis and provide an exposition of Being from the temporality of "existentialist" conditions was considered by him unsuccessful. A pause occurred in his published work after the inaugural lecture at Freiburg University, *Was ist Metaphysik?* (1929; "What Is Metaphysics?"). This comparatively silent period is partly explained by a shift in Heidegger's thinking away from the pursuit of Being to a preoccupation with language and, more precisely, with Hölderlin's poetry. In 1936, Heidegger traveled to Rome, where he lectured on Hölderlin. At around the same time, from 1936 to 1940, he lectured on Nietzsche's thought, although these lectures were not published until 1961.

Heidegger's preoccupation with Nietzsche and his lectures in the early 1940s on Hölderlin's hymns explored a new direction that is elaborated on in the important essay *Der Ursprung des*

Kunstwerkes (*The Origin of the Work of Art*), first published in *Holzwege* (1950). A comparison is drawn between poetry and thinking to suggest that, in Heidegger's view, the artist and the thinker discover compatible ways to disclose the truth of Being as *Unverborgenheit* (unconcealment). Being comes to light as *Lichtung* (a clearing). The title reference to *Holzweg* is not a "dead-end trail" but a metaphor, "like the woodcutter whose occupation lies in the woods, treads paths that he has himself beaten" (Arendt). Heidegger's emphasis on the Greek conception of truth as "aletheia" (unconcealment) relates to his attempt to return, inspired by his study of Hölderlin, to text fragments of the pre-Socratic thinkers, such as Heraclitus and Parmenides. Heidegger commented on his shift of focus in his first postwar publication, a letter to Beaufret, *Der Brief über den Humanismus* (1947; *Letter on Humanism*). What had occurred was a *Kehre* (reversal), but the reversal was also Heidegger's admission of his inability to consider Being from its temporal conditions. Heidegger highlighted his predicament as based on a failure to overcome the metaphysical terms that still characterized his thinking. After the "reversal," he considered language itself as the "abode" of Being (*Haus des Seins*).

Heidegger's preoccupation with language also coincided with the disastrous aftermath of his failure as rector of Freiburg University from 1933 to 1934. This distressing episode was followed by Heidegger's increasing withdrawal from public life to the solitary confines of his *Hütte,* the wooden cabin that was built near Todtnauberg. Heidegger's solitary lifestyle was in stark contrast to the notoriety he had attracted when he accepted the rectorship of Freiburg University on 21 April 1933. Heidegger marked his elevation in the world with a controversial address, *Die Selbstbehauptung der deutschen Universität* (1933; *The Self-Assertion of the German University*). Heidegger's speech demonstrated his support for Hitler's regime by appropriating pro-Nazi terminology, insofar as he spoke up for what he saw then as a moment of epiphany for the German *Volk* and the German philosophical tradition. That Heidegger relinquished the rectorship a year later, in April 1934, was obscured by his membership in the Nazi party from 1 May 1933. A number of official and incriminating documents survive as indisputable evidence of his political involvement with the prevailing ideology of the time. Understandably, Heidegger's position was seriously tarnished by his brief and disastrous flirtation with Nazism. On Jaspers's recommendation, the French occupying authorities banned Heidegger from his teaching post at Freiburg between 1945 and 1951, although, as Jaspers advised, he was still able to publish and was later reinstated as emeritus professor from 1952.

Nevertheless, Heidegger's actions cast a dark shadow over his scholarly reputation. He sought to overcome this by sanctioning critical scrutiny of the practical implications of his ideas when he instructed the newsweekly *Der Spiegel* to publish an exclusive interview after his death. Heidegger's remarks posthumously elaborated on his analysis in 1933 of Hitler's rise to power as a moment of assertion for the German university as a powerful embodiment of the Greek metaphysical spirit and the potential ruling force of ideas. Yet, Heidegger's apologia hardly satisfied the critics. Notably, in *Heidegger et le Nazisme* (1987; *Heidegger and Nazism*), Victor Farias dogmatically unfolded the thesis that Heidegger was a "*radical* Nazi" (Wolin). Farias's work forced a reappraisal of Heidegger's thought in France, where interest in his work was sustained in "deconstructionist" theories of Jacques Derrida, Michel Foucault, and others. Farias's bitter attack on Heidegger for conspicuously failing to retract his support for Nazism was echoed by the biographical studies of the historian Hugo Ott. Interestingly, the variety of opinions prevailing among Heidegger's former pupils—Karl Löwith, Herbert Marcuse, Hans Georg Gadamer, and Hannah Arendt—paved the way to the polemics following Heidegger's death.

In the immediate postwar period, Löwith and Marcuse concluded that Heidegger's philosophy went hand in hand (Löwith, in Wolin) with the political situation in Nazi Germany. On the occasion of Heidegger's 80th birthday, Arendt struck a decidedly conciliatory tone and cautiously referred to Heidegger's political error by claiming that he had never read *Mein Kampf* (Arendt). Arendt was not necessarily intending to pose as Heidegger's apologist for, like Karl Jaspers, she endeavored to prevent Heidegger's personal shortcomings and political mistakes from overshadowing what each considered Heidegger's significant contribution to German philosophy in the 20th century. Heidegger's turn in his later writings to consider the connection of the poetic art of language with the truth of Being seemed to confirm the wayward direction of his project in *Being and Time,* which he regarded as a fragment of the more complex endeavor to appreciate Western metaphysical thought by returning to the pre-Socratic thinkers before Plato and Aristotle.

Heidegger's increasing preoccupation with the poetic art was enthusiastically received by the author Ernst Jünger, who attempted to establish a dialogue with Heidegger in his essay of dedication to their friendship, *Über die Linie* (1950; On the Meridian). The aesthetic appeal of Heidegger's metaphysical enquiries is apparent in a series of speeches that were first given in Bremen in 1949 to convey Heidegger's views on technology, which he captured by referring to the symbol of the *Ge-stell* ("Enframing"). The entity of the *Ge-stell* conveys the essence of technology in much the same way as the metaphor of the *Holzweg* touched on an experience of the trail as equally important as the task of reflecting on its possible meaning. In *Die Frage nach der Technik* (1955; *The Question concerning Technology*), Heidegger's reflections on technology represent the *Gestell* not necessarily as a demonic structure but as a process that is potentially liberating for humankind in the context of bringing forth rapid technological advance.

Heidegger's reference in his *Letter on Humanism* to a shift in his approach corresponds to a curious mode of indebtedness that arises in his examination of thinking as a mode of giving thanks. In *Was heisst Denken?* (1954; *What Is Called Thinking?*), Heidegger draws a connection between thinking and thanking, not in the sense of indebtedness as a form of guilt, a subject that Heidegger briefly dealt with in *Being and Time* as a subjective problem. Rather, Heidegger's discussion of an attitude of thanks is for its connection with the gift of what provokes thought, that is, the memory, or the ability to recall. The extent to which Heidegger's tentative correlation of thinking and thanking is linked with the view expressed in *Gelassenheit* (1959; *Discourse on Thinking*) that a meditative stance, an attitude of letting-be, is necessary to understand his own reversal and attempt to come to terms with his support for Nazism remains an open question. In his letter to the rector of Freiburg

University of 4 November 1945, Heidegger was careful to observe that his works were effectively censured and that he had been under surveillance by the Gestapo from 1934. Nevertheless, the startling characterization by Arendt of Heidegger's legacy as "passionate thinking" pertinently reflects the difficulties of reconciling Heidegger's standing as a leading intellectual with his enthusiastic response to one of the darkest episodes of contemporary politics.

SUZANNE KIRKBRIGHT

See also Fascism and Literature

Biography

Born in Messkirch, 26 September 1889. Ph.D., University of Freiburg, 1914; lecturer and then assistant to Edmund Husserl, 1916–23, associate professor, 1923–28, University of Marburg; professor, 1928–45, rector, 1933–34, and professor emeritus, 1951–58, University of Freiburg (banned from teaching by French occupation forces, 1945–51). Hebel Prize, 1960; member, Academy of Fine Arts, Berlin; member, Academy of Sciences, Heidelberg; member, Bavarian Academy of Fine Arts. Died 26 May 1976.

Selected Works

Collections

Gesamtausgabe, 1975–
Martin Heidegger: Basic Writings: From Being and Time (1927) to The Task of Thinking (1964), edited by David Farrell Krell, 1977

Philosophy

Die Lehre vom Urteil im Psychologismus: Ein kritisch-positiver Beitrag zur Logik, 1914
Die Katagorien- und Bedeutungslehre des Duns Scotus, 1916
Sein und Zeit: Erste Hälfte, 1927; as *Being and Time,* translated by John Macquarrie and Edward Robinson, 1962
Kant und das Problem der Metaphysik, 1929; as *Kant and the Problem of Metaphysics,* translated by James S. Churchill, 1962
"Vom Wesen des Grundes," in *Festschrift für Edmund Husserl,* 1929; as *The Essence of Reasons,* translated by Terence Malick, 1969
Was ist Metaphysik? 1929; as "What Is Metaphysics?" translated by R.F.C. Hull and A. Crick, in *Existence and Being,* edited by Werner Brock, 1949
Die Selbstbehauptung der deutschen Universität, 1933; as *The Self-Assertion of the German University,* 1983
Vom Wesen der Wahrheit, 1943; as "On the Essence of Truth," translated by R.F.C. Hull and A. Crick, in *Existence and Being,* edited by Werner Brock, 1949
Erläuterungen zu Hölderlins Dichtung, 1944; selection as "Hölderlin and the Essence of Poetry," translated by D. Scott, in *Existence and Being,* edited by Werner Brock, 1949
Platons Lehre von der Wahrheit: Mit einem Brief über den "Humanismus," 1947; as "Plato's Doctrine of Truth" and "Letter on 'Humanism,'" in *Philosophy in the Twentieth Century,* edited by William Barrett and Henry D. Aiken, vol. 2, 1962
Holzwege, 1950; *Der ursprung des Kunstwerkes* as *The Origin of the Work of Art,* translated by Albert Hofstadter, in *Poetry, Language, Thought,* 1971
Der Feldweg, 1953
Einführung in die Metaphysik, 1953; as *An Introduction to Metaphysics,* translated by Ralph Manheim, 1959
Aus der Erfahrung des Denkens, 1954
Vorträge und Aufsätze, 3 vols., 1954
Was heisst Denken? 1954; as *What Is Called Thinking?* 1968
Was ist das—die Philosophie? 1956; as *What Is Philosophy?* translated by William Kluback and Jean T. Wilde, 1958
Über "Die Linie," 1955; as *Zur Seinsfrage,* 1956; as *The Question of Being,* translated by William Kluback and Jean T. Wilde, 1958
Der Satz vom Grund, 1957
Identität und Differenz, 1957; as *Identity and Difference,* translated by Joan Stambaugh, 1969
Hebel—Der Hausfreund, 1957
Gelassenheit, 1959; as *Discourse on Thinking,* translated by John M. Anderson and E. Hans Freund, 1966
Unterwegs zur Sprache, 1959; as *On the Way to Language,* translated by Peter D. Hertz, 1971
Nietzsche, 2 vols., 1961; as *Nietzsche,* translated by David Farrell Krell, 4 vols., 1979–87
Die Technik und die Kehre, 1962; in *The Question concerning Technology and Other Essays,* translated by William Lovitt, 1977
Die Frage nach dem Ding: Zu Kants Lehre von den transzendentalen Grundsätzen, 1962
Kants These über das Sein, 1963
Wegmarken, 1967
Zur Sache des Denkens, 1969; selections in *The End of Philosophy,* 1973
Heraklit: Seminar Wintersemester 1966/67 (with Eugen Fink), 1970; as *Heraclitus Seminar, 1966–67,* translated by Charles H. Seibert, 1979
Phänomenologie und Theologie, 1970
Frühe Schriften 1912–16, 1972
Die Grundprobleme der Phänomenologie, 1975; as *The Basic Problems of Phenomenology,* translated by Albert Hofstadter, 1982
Early Greek Thinking (selected essays), 1975
Logik: Die Frage nach der Wahrheit, 1976
The Piety of Thinking: Essays by Martin Heidegger, 1976
Prolegomena zur Geschichte des Zeitbegriffs, 1979; as *History of the Concept of Time: Prolegomena,* translated by Theodore Kisiel, 1985

Further Reading

Arendt, Hannah, "Martin Heidegger at Eighty," in *Heidegger and Modern Philosophy: Critical Essays,* edited by Michael Murray, New Haven, Connecticut, and London: Yale University Press, 1978
Farias, Victor, *Heidegger et le Nazisme,* Lagrasse: Verdier, 1987; as *Heidegger and Nazism,* Philadelphia, Pennsylvania: Temple University Press, 1989
Franzen, Winfried, *Martin Heidegger,* Stuttgart: Metzler, 1976
Gadamer, Hans Georg, *Heideggers Wege: Studien zum Spätwerk,* Tübingen: Mohr, 1983
Heidegger, Martin, "Nur ein Gott kann uns noch retten," *Der Spiegel* 23 (31 May 1976); as "Only a God Can Save Us," in *The Heidegger Controversy: A Critical Reader,* edited by Richard Wolin, Cambridge, Massachusetts, and London: MIT Press, 1993
Jaspers, Karl, *Notizen zu Heidegger,* edited by Hans Saner, Munich: Piper, 1978
Löwith, Karl, "Martin Heidegger Denker in dürftiger Zeit," *Neue Rundschau* 63 (1952)
Mehta, J.L., *The Philosophy of Martin Heidegger,* Varanasi: Banaras Hindu University Press, 1967; revised edition, New York: Harper and Row, 1971
Ott, Hugo, *Martin Heidegger: Unterwegs zu seiner Biographie,* Frankfurt and New York: 1988; as *Martin Heidegger: A Political Life,* translated by Allen Blunden, London and New York: Harper Collins, 1993
Pöggeler, Otto, and Annemarie Gethmann-Siefert, editors, *Heidegger und die praktische Philosophie,* Frankfurt: Suhrkamp, 1988
Safranski, Rüdiger, *Ein Meister aus Deutschland: Heidegger und seine Zeit,* Munich and Vienna: Hanser, 1994
Wolin, Richard, editor, *The Heidegger Controversy: A Critical Reader,* Cambridge, Massachusetts, and London: MIT Press, 1993

Der Ursprung des Kunstwerkes 1950

Essay by Martin Heidegger

Written by Martin Heidegger in 1935, just after his infamous Nazi engagement (1933–34) and at the beginning of the *Kehre* or "turn" in his thought, the essay *Der Ursprung des Kunstwerkes* (*The Origin of the Work of Art*) has been called a work of "passage" from the early to the late Heidegger. It goes far beyond the aesthetic realm narrowly conceived to present controversial political views and even the framework for a new ontology.

In *Being and Time*'s earlier (1927) version of Heidegger's ontology, things are either "present at" or "ready to" hand (*vor-* and *zuhanden*). Something ready to hand is encountered in use, and using it requires us to be explicitly open, not to the thing itself, but to contexts of significance that extend far beyond it: when I am writing a letter, I am thinking of the envelope into which I will put it, and of the friend who will read it. But I am not aware of the pen with which I am actually writing. Something present at hand, by contrast, is encountered as an object of explicit awareness, independently of any context whatsoever.

A work of art, as Heidegger claims in *The Origin of the Work of Art,* crosses these ontological categories. Using phenomenological descriptions of a Van Gogh painting and a Greek temple, Heidegger argues that we are explicitly aware of a work of art even as it appropriates itself to larger contexts of significance. In doing this, the work of art not only "gathers" (*sammelt*) the components of a world, but, when it is sufficiently innovative in this, actually founds or "sets up" (*aufstellt*) a world. In such a founding, contexts of significance that to some extent preexist the work are made explicit. To make something explicit is to make it a topic for possible speech, and so a work of art—great art, at least—changes the linguistic capacities of those who experience it. It opens up the basic vocabulary within which a community can articulate its life and decide its fate. The primary function of the work of art is linguistic, and the originary art is poetry.

The later Heidegger's concern with poetry is thus broached here. Also present is his characteristic avoidance of vulgar racism: as founded upon works of art, human communities cannot be founded upon blood or land. His later concern with the "Fourfold" of earth, sky, mortal, and immortals is foreshadowed by the "Twofold" (*Zweifalt*) of earth and world.

What Heidegger here calls "earth" is traditionally called the "material" or "medium" out of which a work of art is made—the stone of a statue, the pigments of a painting, or the preexisting language in which a poem is written. In Heidegger's radically new conception, the quiescent material of the philosophical tradition is replaced by an "earth," which actively seeks to close itself off from the explicating activity of art. The "world"—the overarching context of significance into which the work of art comes to take its stand—is in strife (*Streit*) with this earth. The work of art is thus not to be conceived as a harmonious reconciliation of form and matter, then, but as the instigation of a *polemos* or strife.

Such instigation cannot, Heidegger claims, be grasped as the work of a "creator" in the traditional sense. Working from his own (idiosyncratic) version of Greek etymology (that of *technê,* which cannot reliably be translated as either "art" or *Kunst*) and from his view that the thematizing of preexisting content is a "setting to the work" (*Ins-Werk-Setzen*) of truth itself, Heidegger displaces the artist from the center of that event:

> It is not the "N.N. Fecit" that is to be known. Rather, the simple "factum est" is to be held forth into the Open by the work: namely this, that unconcealedness of what is has happened here, and that as this happening it happens here for the first time.

As important to the work as the artist is the community that "preserves" the work: the people who experience its gathering of phenomena as the setting-up of a [new] world, and who seek to carry this experience into their own lives. No general rules can be given for this, since preservation must be guided by the uniqueness of that which it preserves. But in it, the new contexts opened up by a work of art come to ground the language and, as a consequence, the very selfhood of a community. It is in this way that art also comes to ground history. The "origin" of the work of art is thus one that the work *is*, not one that it *has*.

The Origin of the Work of Art is, in sum, a series of challenges to traditional philosophical categories—those of matter and form and of their reconciliation, and those of artistic creativity and subjective pleasure. In its discussion of the activity of preserving the work of art, the essay anticipates the "reader response criticism" developed later in the twentieth century by Wolfgang Iser, Hans-Robert Jauss, and others. In its treatments of both artist and spectator, it also challenges the presupposition of self-enclosed subjectivity on which modern philosophy itself—not just aesthetics—is built. And its view of a primordial strife between the "sky" of public significance and the unfathomable "earth" on which it rests find echoes in deconstruction.

As Jürgen Habermas and others have argued, Heidegger's discussion of the "founding" role of artwork isolates a distinct level of human affairs in relation to which traditional argumentation and justification are lacking. Since Heidegger includes not only works of art but "the deed which grounds the state" on that level, the political implications of this essay—especially during the Nazi period—are gloomy indeed. However, not all reason is lost. The founding of new contexts happens only on the most general level, and it must at least strike a responsive chord among possible preservers.

JOHN MCCUMBER

Editions

First edition: "Der Ursprung des Kunstwerkes," in *Holzwege*, Frankfurt: Klostermann, 1950. This remains the standard German edition

Translation: "The Origin of the Work of Art," in *Poetry, Language, Thought,* translated by Albert Hofstadter, New York: Harper and Row, 1971

Further Reading

Biemel, Walter, "Poetry and Language in Heidegger," in *On Heidegger and Language,* edited by Joseph J. Kockelmans, Evanston, Illinois: Northwestern University Press, 1972

———, *Martin Heidegger in Selbstzeugnissen und Bilddokumenten,* Reinbek bei Hamburg: Rowohlt, 1973; as *Martin Heidegger: An Illustrated Study,* translated by J.L. Mehta, New York: Harcourt Brace Jovanovich, 1976; London: Routledge and Kegan Paul, 1977

Dallmayr, Fred, *The Other Heidegger,* Ithaca, New York: Cornell University Press, 1993

Gadamer, Hans-Georg, "Being, Spirit, God," in *Heidegger Memorial Lectures,* by Hans-Georg Gadamer et al., Pittsburgh, Pennsylvania: Duquesne University Press, 1982

Kockelmans, Joseph J., *Heidegger on Art and Art Works,* Dordrecht and Boston: Nijhoff, 1985

Schwan, Alexander, *Politische Philosophie im Denken Heideggers,* Cologne and Opladen: Westdeutscher Verlag, 1965; 2nd edition, 1989

Heimatroman

Although the German *Heimatroman* is associated with a specific movement and with a programmatic periodical first published in 1900, the concepts of *Heimatroman, Heimatkunst,* and *Heimatdichtung* (the regional novel, art, and poetry) are generically difficult to pin down and somewhat imprecise. Furthermore, they have also acquired a negative reputation, linked as they are with the nationalism that, taken to extremes, led to the Blut- und Bodenliteratur (literature of blood and soil) of the Third Reich. Some representatives of the genre such as Hermann Löns (who was killed at the very start of World War I) were claimed by the Nazis (rightly or wrongly) as nationalist heroes, while others such as Gustav Frenssen actually *did* write books and pamphlets in their support. The genre in the narrowest sense is thus frequently omitted from literary histories altogether, although it has to be said that this is not entirely for political reasons. This omission has just as much to do with the fact that, although the genre as a whole and some of the individual novels were extremely popular in their time (and thus of great interest in terms of reception history), the writers associated most closely with the movement were not striking enough to rise sufficiently above the somewhat narrow limits of the genre so as to stand the literary test of time. And yet the *Heimatroman* was part of a broad German cultural context (and not just German), and it had much-read antecedents, so if it led to excesses in one direction, it has also helped to provoke an interesting reaction in recent literature.

The movement was placed on a theoretical basis by Adolf Bartels and Friedrich (Fritz) Lienhard, who produced with the publisher Georg-Heinrich Meyer the periodical *Heimat* (Homeland); other similar periodicals soon followed. The philosophy of the movement was initially one of reaction; the slogan "los von Berlin" (away from Berlin) summarized a deliberate distancing from the city as theme (and, hence, in literary terms, away from the naturalist *Großstadtroman,* or city novel) and a move toward a concentration on the countryside, farming, and peasant life. Rural life involved struggles but represented health against the sickness of the decadent city. In style, the *Heimatroman* utilized some of the devices of naturalism (such as dialect), but it was at a considerable remove from many naturalist writers in political terms. The approach was essentially Romantic and nationalistic and, above all, conservative, although Bartels claimed in the title of an essay published in *Heimat* that it was "konservativ, nicht reaktionär" (conservative without being reactionary). Yet it completely rejected elements perceived as inherently associated with the city; these included socialism and what *Heimatroman* writers saw as a rootless Jewish dominance, from which view the stress on German national purity fostered by the Nazis was developed. Bartels, in particular, was markedly anti-Semitic in his literary histories of the period. The *Heimatroman* was also largely reactionary in its stress against the modernity of the machine and in its the approval of folk customs and the old ways. One of the flaws in the whole philosophy is that a city can also be a *Heimat,* and a great deal of literature is rooted in the land of the writer's origins. The stress, however, was on the drive that came from the regional earth and that was in the blood of the local people, and *Schollendichtung* (poetry of the sod) became a key term, although the phrase Blut und Boden itself also dates from 1902.

Bartels (1862–1944) came from Dithmarschen, Lienhart (1866–1929) came from Alsace, and both wrote novels associated with these regions. The best-sellers of the movement, however, were first of all Frenssen (1863–1945), also from Dithmarschen, and then Löns (1866–1914), from the *Lüneburger Heide.* Frenssen's long and rambling novel *Jörn Uhl* (1901; *Jörn Uhl*) chronicles the life of a young man struggling against odds to maintain his farm, while his *Hilligenlei* (1906; *Holyland,* the name of a *Hallig,* a small low island off Schleswig-Holstein) sets up a contrast with Berlin. Hermann Löns had an even greater success with *Der Wehrwolf* (1910; *Harm Wulf*), a novel set in the Thirty Years' War but depicting the defense of the land in vigorous fashion. Jethro Bithell refers to it as "essentially a boy's book, like *Hereward the Wake,*" and it was much praised by the Nazis. Löns, however, although clearly nationalistic in some of his writing, was essentially a nature writer, observing and writing about the animals and birds of the Heath, a region for which he had genuine and lasting affection, either as straight descriptions (*Mein grünes Buch* [1901; My Green Book]) or in peasant novels such as *Da hinten in der Heide* (1910; Out There on the Heath). Löns's nationalism led him to enlist in 1914, and he was killed within weeks; his war diary shows his continuing interest in nature and (both ironically and symbolically) the destruction of the pastoral. Whether he deserves the posthumous reputation conferred by the Nazis is debatable, but he is one of the few members of the central group perhaps worthy of reconsideration.

Most areas of Germany had their representatives, and there are too many writers to note in detail. The most closely associated figures include Timm Kröger (1844–1918) from Schleswig-

Holstein; from the same area came both the more interesting Gorch Fock (Jakob Kinau [1880–1916]), who was killed at Jutland, and Helene Voigt-Diederichs (1875–1952). Indeed, women are relatively well represented in the *Heimatroman* genre: Lulu von Strauß und Torney (1873–1948), from Westphalia, continued writing for a long time, and Clara Viebig (1860–1952), from the Eifel, is interesting in her own right. Viebig (whose works are now being reprinted) examines psychosexual drives and the role of women in her own landscape, notably in the novels *Das Kreuz im Venn* (1908; The Cross on the Moor) and *Das Weiberdorf* (1900; Village of Women). The north and the southern regions are the most fully represented, however; Switzerland and the Black Forest produced (among many others) Rudolf von Tavel (1866–1934), Jakob Christoph Heer (1859–1925), and Ernst Zahn (1867–1952). The latter was the butt of one of Robert Neumann's brief but telling parodies, and the fact that the style could easily be parodied is significant. Neumann's squib observes someone struggling to eat up his *Knödel* (noodles), with a brief disquisition on the precise locality of this dish and a selection of suggested variations.

Bavaria and Austria had Ludwig Ganghofer (1855–1920) and (Rudolf) Hans Bartsch (1873–1952), respectively, and some writers championed regions eventually lost to Germany: Josef Ponten (1883–1941) from Eupen is one such author, as is Hermann Stehr (1864–1940) from Silesia. To these may be added the Austrian Adam Müller-Guttenbrunn (1852–1923); he is now forgotten, but he was notable for writing about the struggles of German nationals in Hungary, a theme that would recur. That the names are now virtually all forgotten underscores the fact that this particular movement produced no writer comparable, say, with Thomas Hardy in English. Hardy, however, has a far broader range of themes; he uses his Wessex setting as a support for moral issues rather than concentrating on one aspect of morality and associating it with the local earth.

The roots of a conscious concentration on specific regions, although without the insistence on the soil, reach back some distance in history. Even roughly contemporary German writers whose interest was regional, however, frequently presented broader themes against a local background. As a simple example, although Adrienne Thomas's *Die Katrin wird Soldat* (1930; *Cathérine Joins Up*) is subtitled *Ein Roman aus Elsaß-Lothringen* and the region of Alsace is highly relevant to the work, it is in no respects a *Heimatroman*. Much of it is set in a town (Metz), and the latter part, dealing with World War I, transcends the issue of regionality.

Leaving aside claims of a literary ancestry that goes back to works such as the later medieval *Meier Helmbrecht* (*Helmbrecht*), which is essentially a conservative sermon on the appropriateness of the estates, or even to Virgil's *Georgics* and the classical idyll, the earliest relevant influences on the *Heimatroman* are perhaps the *Novellen* of J.P. Hebel, the *Schwarzwälder Dorfgeschichten* (*Black Forest Village Stories*) of Berthold Auerbach, and works by writers of the stature of Jeremias Gotthelf, Theodor Storm, Gottfried Keller, and Adalbert Stifter, who were all from different regions. Closer still are the Low German dialect writings of Fritz Reuter and the works of the Bavarian Ludwig Thoma. These, however, do not exhibit the programmatic insistence on the soil, and both Reuter, in his tales of Uncle Bräsig, and Thoma, in his short stories, have the dimension of a self-ironizing humor, which the *Heimatroman* proper so often lacks. Nor does either place a positive emphasis on peasant life. Most closely related of all, however, is the *Dorfgeschichte* (village tale) as such, which derives largely from Auerbach, Jean Paul, and others, and its chronologically closest representative, the work of Peter Rosegger (1843–1918) from Styria. In a sense, however, the *Dorfgeschichte* bypasses the *Heimatroman:* its interest is in the people rather than their relationship with the land, and it has recent echoes in story collections such as Siegfried Lenz's *So zärtlich war Suleyken* (1955; How Sweet Was Suleyken), which, however, is not only comic-ironic but has a new dimension, the backward look at a lost rural-regional *Heimat* (in Lenz's case Masuria). Recent history has added nostalgia as an element. Indeed, the paths first struck by Adam Müller-Guttenbrunn have a modern resonance in works such as Gudrun Pausewang's *Rosinkawiese* (1980; Rosinka Meadow), which looks back at a kind of alternative living in the Sudetenland in the 1920s; but that again is a retrospective ecological idyll.

Discussion of the later development of the *Heimatroman* must take account of the *Heimatfilm*. Again, the Nazis developed the genre and played up the perceived intrinsic link between the territory and the spiritual development of those living there; film titles such as *Ewiger Wald* (1936; The Eternal Forest) and *Der Berg ruft* (1937; The Call of the Mountain) make their own point. After the war, the genre developed rather differently into heavily sentimentalized and largely unrealistic idylls, with the hero realizing at the end the charms of his rural home (usually in Bavaria) and the forester's pretty dirndl-wearing daughter. Again, film titles such as *Einmal noch die Heimat seh'n* (1958; To See Home Just Once More) speak for themselves. Here, the (South-) German *Heimat* becomes a scenically beautiful myth, but there are still occasional overtones of Blut und Boden. Edgar Reitz's monumental film sequence *Heimat* (1980; published as a *Filmroman* with Peter Steinbach in 1984), however, opened up a new direction for the genre by concentrating on the lives of a group of people in the Hunsrück throughout the century, thereby offering a mirror of recent history.

Awareness of the *Heimatroman* (even if they are now hardly read) has contributed most recently to a reaction, although to talk of a specific *anti-Heimatroman* is perhaps to attribute too much importance to the original form. Rather, the whole notion of *Heimat* and the stress on the pastoral scene has undergone changes (and continues to do so) in post–World War II society, both in political and ecological terms. Reactions to the insistence on regional rurality as a healthy world can take the form of parody, as in works by Jutta Schütting and others, although the finest parody of the regional novel in general (and highly relevant in comparative terms in spite of the distance of culture) remains a work originally in Irish, Flann O'Brien's *The Poor Mouth* (1941). Reaction can also take the form of a deliberate attack on the idyll and the unthinking transfiguration of the countryside. Thomas Bernhard (1931–89) makes the regional landscape into something ugly and threatening in *Frost* (1964; *Frost*), and Franz Innerhofer's (1944–) novel *Schöne Tage* (1974; *Beautiful Days*) refers to the rural situation as a "Bauern-KZ" (concentration camp for peasants). Similar points are made by Josef Winkler (1953–) in his trilogy *Das wilde Kärnten* (1979–82; Wild Carinthia). Beyond the novel, the inherent possibility that fascism can be linked intrinsically with insistent regionalism is attacked in what are effectively responses not to the *Heimatroman* but to the

Volksstück (the [southern] popular theater). These attacks can be seen in plays by Elfriede Jelinek (1946–), Peter Turrini (1944–), Rainer Werner Fassbinder (1945–82), including *Katzelmacher* (1963; *Katzelmacher*), and Martin Sperr (1944–), whose *Bayrische Trilogie* (1966–71; Bavarian Trilogy) moves from a village in Niederbayern to Landshut, and then to Munich.

BRIAN MURDOCH

See also Fascism and Literature

Further Reading

Bithell, Jethro, *Modern German Literature 1880–1950,* 3rd edition, London: Methuen, 1959

Höfig, Willi, *Der deutsche Heimatfilm 1947–1960,* Stuttgart: Enke, 1973

Mahrholz, Werner, *Deutsche Dichter der Gegenwart,* Berlin: Wegweiser, 1926; as *Deutsche Literatur der Gegenwart,* edited by Max Wieser, Berlin: Siebe-Stäbe, 1930

Polheim, Karl Konrad, editor, *Wesen und Wandel der Heimatliteratur am Beispiel der österreichischen Literatur seit 1945,* Bern and New York: Lang, 1989

Pott, Hans-Georg, editor, *Literatur und Provinz: Das Konzept 'Heimat' in der neueren Literatur,* Paderborn: Schöningh, 1986

Rossbacher, Karlheinz, *Heimatkunstbewegung und Heimatroman: Zu einer Literatursoziologie der Jahrhundertwende,* Stuttgart: Klett, 1975

Seliger, Helfried W., editor, *Der Begriff 'Heimat' in der deutschen Gegenwartsliteratur,* Munich: Iudicium, 1987

Waldinger, Ernst, "Über Heimatkunst und Blut- und Bodenideologie," *German Life and Letters* 10 (1956–57)

Christoph Hein 1944–

Christoph Hein has come to epitomize many aspects of postwar German literature. His texts, both the historical texts and those set in the everyday life of the present, offer a chronology of recent German history, including scenes, problems, and conflicts typical of the life of a generation that, although it never experienced National Socialism at first hand, lives its life under the burden of this legacy. Strangely enough, the recent German past seems to be stamped more indelibly on writers too young to have experienced war or the immediate postwar years than on the work of writers from the previous generation such as Heinrich Böll or Christa Wolf, whose work grew out of their personal experience of National Socialism. Christoph Hein's work is an unusual fusion of the National Socialist past, the day-to-day reality of the GDR, and his personal experiences of childhood and adolescence. The resulting mixture casts a stark light not only on the two halves of a divided Germany but also on the present state of the united Germany. His work contains the preferred images of the two systems, together with the various forms of official optimism about the future, and it confronts these with everything that has been repressed and kept silent: it confronts them with the threadbare self-deceits of antifascist attitudinizing and with the banal realities of social existence. The recurring theme of Hein's fiction, dramas, and essays is the disconcerting mixture of breaks and continuities within subjective and collective experience. In each of these genres, his mastery is evident when he highlights a fresh dimension to his overall theme.

We cannot make sense of Hein's work and its impact without considering briefly the situation of postwar literature. Germany was divided after 1945 by a demarcation line, which forced the two German states to become models of their respective power blocks. This meant, in turn, that writers on both sides were forced into social roles that were defined not only by literary criteria but by the political weighting of their profession. Political polarization of this kind did serve a useful and essential purpose in that it initiated those discourses (demanding basic democratic rights or analyzing National Socialism) that many institutions in East and West Germany would have refused to countenance, but its effects were not all positive. Politicization burdened writers with a responsibility that they could not always live up to. The uncompromising reflective process of coming to terms with the National Socialist past and the deliberate involvement of writers in public matters became institutionalized, a kind of trademark for postwar German writers who wished to demonstrate both their moral and literary quality.

This background is reflected in the contradictions of Hein's biography. His way through the education system was complicated by the fact that, as the son of a Protestant minister, Hein was at first not permitted to attend the higher-grade schools. Yet, paradoxically, as early as 1973, Hein was working as resident dramatist to an East Berlin theater; from 1979, he was able to live on his work as a writer, and in 1982, he received one of the most prestigious literary awards of the GDR: the Heinrich Mann prize. His name was known to a wider public with the unexpected success of his novella *Der fremde Freund* (1982; *The Distant Lover*) in both the GDR and the Federal Republic. Despite his conflicts with the socialist state (whether in the context of his education, his difficulties in getting his plays performed, or in the efforts of the state to prevent the publication of his prose works), Hein never became a dissident, and he was never provoked into joining the constant stream of writers leaving the GDR in the 1970s and 1980s. His sense of identification with the political ideals that had constituted the state (but in no way with their actual manifestations) was too deep for that. This basis—the literary historian Wolfgang Emmerich writes of the GDR's antifascism as one of its "founding myths"—seemed to Hein to offer a guarantee that the horrors of fascism would not be repeated. Hein represents a type of writer that has become increasingly uncommon in Germany: morally committed, always ready to become involved, but never dogmatic—indeed, his literary works are marked by coolness and reserve. He has always strongly resisted attempts to tie him to particular political stances. It was to be expected that he would deal with the victors in the process of German unification with the same reserve with which he treated the socialist authorities.

Hein's work accepts the routinely negative experiences of daily life, yet it expresses a doubting and skeptical hope for liberation. This hope cannot be dismissed as sentimentality: indeed, it seems more durable even than Hein's disillusionment. His writing neither offers grandiose visions of a better future nor portrays a spectacular day of reckoning. It is content merely to present a dilemma. Hein is an extraordinarily political writer, but his works are not concerned with political agitation. His themes are expressed with literary means alone: in his dramas, these are the techniques of historical parables; in prose, Hein works through artificially simple scenes of daily reality. His use of language is clever, accomplished, and precise, never emotional. His texts cut through to the reality of situations, but they never go in for interpretation. In the face of the catastrophes, great and small, with which his works deal, Hein's optimistic insistence on the power of words to achieve understanding can sometimes seem a little anachronistic.

More than once Hein has claimed to be a dramatist who writes prose merely as a writing exercise, but despite such remarks it is his prose that has ensured his international success. With the sensational impact of *The Distant Lover,* Hein became one of the most important of contemporary writers. It was not only in the GDR that this short text won many readers, with its portrayal of an unspectacular, dislocated relationship. The conflicts of everyday life are recorded here in a lucid and accurate language by an author who is himself without illusions and, therefore, close to the sufferings and problems of his characters. It is the story of a doctor, Claudia (told in the first person), whose lover, Henry, has lost his life in a stupid accident. In this story (and more clearly still in the childhood memories of Claudia, which are interspersed through the text, and which reveal her claims to be at peace with herself as a pretense), the text uncovers the processes and structures of alienation of a society that is shaped not merely by its socialist program but by its industrial production processes and its history. Hein writes in such a way as to compel his readers to adopt the stance of an equally detached observer. But the reader who wishes to go deeper will discover in the multiplicity of historical, philosophical, and literary references (references, among others, to Martin Luther, Christa Wolf, Sigmund Freud, and Walter Benjamin) an account of the complex cultural and historical backgrounds to the conflicts Hein portrays, circumstances that have their roots in the early phase of bourgeois society and are far from being resolved in the transitional socialist society of the GDR.

Hein followed this theme consistently in his succeeding books. In the novel *Horns Ende* (1985; The Death of Horn), he relentlessly focuses his attention on the repressive German educational tradition, with its anxious shunning of aliens. The story is placed in a small town in Saxony in the 1950s. It deals from a number of perspectives with a series of events that culminate in the suicide of a museum director who has previously been dismissed from a post in the city and transferred to the provinces. The portrait is of a colorless, petty-bourgeois respectability, which (as is made clear by flashback memories) had served the National Socialist period well, and which still had its uses in the phase of socialist reconstruction. The novel offers a personal microcosm of German history in the 1950s, and not simply that of the GDR. Hein's prose is concerned with the psychological dimensions of history, and this focus means that his fictional world, whose inhabitants display a coldness and inability to love, refers to more than the social system in which it is set—this remains true, despite Hein's repeated insistence that he was writing only about the GDR. In the novel *Der Tangospieler* (1989; *The Tango Player*), for instance, the specific references to the GDR are unmistakable—the novel is set in 1968 shortly before Warsaw Pact troops occupied Czechoslovakia. Yet the images and themes of the book (expressed through the resignation and alienation of a university history teacher who has been unjustly imprisoned and who has subsequently lost both his job and his will to work) are more than familiar to readers from other social circumstances.

We may take a different approach to Hein's works between 1982 and 1989 and see them as an attempt to use literature to free up, despite the fossilization of society, the discussion of themes declared by the state to be taboo and even criminal. "Education in silence" is one of the central themes of *The Distant Lover,* and this and subsequent texts try to break with the official silence as to the continuities of German history. *The Distant Lover* focuses on the damage done to the individuals by the traumas of childhood and uses intertextual references to this end. This strategy illuminated the links between individual growth and political education. *Horns Ende* explores the theme of continuity in the context of the 1950s, a theme that *The Tango Player* provocatively identifies in the political oppression of the 1960s. It is true of all these texts that political issues are expressed primarily in private experience, in the situation of individual characters. But there is no shortage of clear political statements in Hein's texts, mostly in reference to those philosophers to whom he felt close: notably the historical materialists such as Walter Benjamin and Theodor W. Adorno who were no longer able to share the unbridled historical optimism of Marx and Engels.

It is evident that, with the end of the German socialist state, Hein's themes have not vanished. The instruments of social criticism that sharpened during the GDR years have served him well in his attacks on the new injustices, as in his novel *Das Napoleon-Spiel* (1993). A motiveless murder is used as a metaphor for life in a consumerist industrial society that social ideology can no longer contain. The form of this work brings together, in an exciting mixture of narrative and essay, sharply contoured episodes from the first-person narrator's life and his own thoughts on aging, sexuality, politics, and billiards.

Hein's most recent work to date—a collection of highly autobiographical childhood episodes, which he places in the 1950s and 1960s—shows how much more focused this perspective on an overall German experience has become. The foreground is autobiographical, but the tone of this work is set by an approach to German postwar history that suspends previous political certainties in a set of poetic differentiations.

For all their differences to the prose works, Hein's plays have been no less effective in creating new styles and periods in the GDR. Here, too, we may observe the way in which Hein's moral commitment is constrained by the discipline of style. His plays are less laconic than his prose, and in their virtuosity they stand in a great tradition, from Shakespeare to Brecht. While his prose plumbs the psychological and social depths of history, Hein's dramas belong in the intellectual traditions of the Enlightenment, and of necessity they acquire a didactic quality that does not detract from their vitality. At the center of his plays there is a philosophical questioning of the driving forces of history and a process of reflection about those revolutions that came to nothing in the course of history. Hein's idea of history is certainly a Marxist one ("In world-history . . . everything is a consequence of a consequence of a consequence"), but any dogmatic historical optimism gives way to a skepticism, which behind each individual progress catches sight of fresh catastrophes to come. Hein draws his skepticism both from his own historical experience and indirectly from the work of Walter Benjamin, and it means that Hein's historical plays are more than historical tableaux. Oliver Cromwell in *Cromwell* (1978) and Ferdinand Lassalle in *Lassalle fragt Herrn Herbert nach Sonja* (produced 1980) are presented as prototypes of revolutionaries who are brought low by circumstances or by their themselves. Historical events and the fate of prominent individuals in world history are of little interest to Hein without this prototypical quality. Because his plays ask more basic questions, they inevitably point to the issues of the present. Hein's principal interest lies with the role of intellectuals in the process of social change. This can be seen in the comedy *Schlötel; oder, Was solls* (produced 1974), which tells of an intellectual's failed attempt to shake the working class from its lethargy, and equally in the play *Passage* (1987), which tells of the helplessness of intellectuals in dealing with the National Socialists. (At the same time, the play is an homage to Walter Benjamin, marking an intellectual debt to Benjamin that can be traced throughout Hein's entire work.) The problem of intellectuals and power is most forcibly shown in *Die wahre Geschichte des Ah Q* (1983; *The True Story of Ah Q*). The scene (a dilapidated house) is reminiscent of the works of Samuel Beckett. In this house, the two intellectuals Ah Q and Wang are waiting for the revolution. When it finally arrives it seems not to affect them at all. One of them is too busy philosophizing, and the other is caught up in his business sidesteps. Indeed, if it were not for an absurd misunderstanding that costs Ah Q his life, they might not even have noticed that the revolution had taken place. This play is a bringing together, by no less a talent, of Beckett's theater with Brechtian traditions to create a new standard of contemporary drama. The lesson is, once again, historical pessimism, presented in an entertaining and instructive manner.

Hein's work in fiction and drama is rounded off by his extensive essays. Their appeal lies in a laconic precision, and here, too, Hein shows himself to be a committed and highly original thinker. The themes are familiar: art and politics, the individual and history, the power of language and of thought, the deformations of personal development, and political education. Of particular interest is the speech that Hein made in 1987 at the Tenth Writers Congress of the GDR, in which he demanded the abolition of censorship. The speech marks the final point of Hein's tireless struggle against GDR taboos. Following German unification, Hein has not abandoned the awkward stance of a person thinking and writing against the grain of his times. In 1998, after many years of bitter argument, the German branches of the PEN-Club were united, and Christoph Hein was elected president of the new organization, representing both East and West Germany. No better candidate could have been chosen.

HANNES KRAUSS

Biography

Born in Heinzendorf/Silesia, 8 April 1944; grew up in Saxonia (GDR). Educated at a West Berlin Gymnasium, 1958–60; completed the Abitur as an evening student in East Berlin; worked as a book dealer, factory worker, actor, and director's assistant; studied philosophy and logic at the universities of Leipzig and East Berlin (Humboldt), 1967–71; served as artistic director, literary adviser, and playwright for the Volksbühne, East Berlin, 1971–79. Heinrich Mann Prize, 1982; West German Critic's Prize, 1983; City of Hamburg Prize, 1986; Lessing Prize, 1989; Andres Prize, 1989; Fried Prize, 1990. Currently lives in Berlin.

Selected Works

Fiction

Einladung zum Lever Bourgeois, 1980; as *Nachtfahrt und früher Morgen,* 1982

Der fremde Freund, 1982; as *Drachenblut,* 1983; as *The Distant Lover,* translated by Krishna Winston, 1989

Horns Ende, 1985

Der Tangospieler, 1989; as *The Tango Player,* translated by Philip Boehm, 1991

Das Napoleon-Spiel, 1993

Exekution eines Kalbes, 1994

Von allem Anfang an, 1997

Plays

Vom hungrigen Hennecke (produced 1974)

Schlötel; oder, Was solls (produced 1974), 1981

Cromwell (produced 1980), 1978

Lassalle fragt Herrn Herbert nach Sonja: Die Szene ein Salon (produced 1980), 1981

Der neue Menoza; oder, Geschichte des kumbanischen Prinzen Tandi (adaptation of the play by Jakob Michael Reinhold Lenz) (produced 1982), 1981

Die wahre Geschichte des Ah Q, based on a novel by Lu Hsun (produced 1983), 1983; as *The True Story of Ah Q* (produced 1990)

Passage (produced 1987), 1987

Die Ritter der Tafelrunde (produced 1989), 1989

Randow (produced 1994), 1994

Bruch (produced 1999), 1999

Other

Das Wildpferd unterm Kachelofen (for children), 1984

Öffentlich arbeiten: Essais und Gespräche, 1987

Als Kind habe ich Stalin gesehen: Essais und Reden, 1990

Die fünfte Grundrechenart: Aufsätze und Reden 1987–1990, 1990

Further Reading

Arnold, Heinz Ludwig, editor, *Christoph Hein,* Munich: Edition Text und Kritik, 1991

Baier, Lothar, editor, *Christoph Hein: Texte, Daten, Bilder,* Frankfurt: Sammlung Luchterhand, 1990

Fischer, Bernd, *Christoph Hein: Drama und Prosa im letzten Jahrzehnt der DDR,* Heidelberg: Winter, 1990

Grunenberg, Antonia, "Geschichte und Entfremdung: Christoph Hein als Autor der DDR," *Michigan Germanic Studies* 8 (1985)

Hell, Julia, "Christoph Hein's *Der fremde Freund/Drachenblut* and the Antinomies of Writing under 'Real Existing Socialism'," *Colloquia Germanica* 25, no. 3/4 (1992)

Janssen-Zimmermann, Antje, *Gegenwürfe: Untersuchungen zu Dramen Christoph Heins,* Frankfurt and New York: Lang, 1988

McKnight, Phillip S., "'Alltag', Apathy, Anarchy: GDR Everyday Life as a Provocation in Christoph Hein's Novella *Der fremde Freund,*" in *Studies in GDR Culture and Society,* volume 8, Lanham, Maryland: University Press of America, 1988

Murray, Janice, and Mary-Elizabeth O'Brien, "Interview with Christoph Hein, *New German Review* 3 (1987)

Heinrich Heine 1797–1856

Heine's life and work spans the period from the Romantics, through Junges Deutschland (Young Germany) and Vormärz (anticipation of the March revolution of 1848), and into the later phases of Biedermeier and realism. It is not only the changing contexts of his work that make it difficult to assign him to a particular movement: in many ways he is instrumental in defining the changing styles of the day. The critical essay *Die Romantische Schule* (1836; *The Romantic School*), for example, was the first account to give popular coherence to the various writers grouped under the name of Romanticism. Although he is often critical of Romantic writing and parodies its styles, Heine recognized himself in the title "romantique défroqué" (unfrocked Romantic). In the autobiographical *Geständnisse* (1854; *Confessions*), he claims "mit mir ist die alte lyrische Schule der Deutschen geschlossen, während zugleich die neue Schule, die moderne deutsche Lyrik von mir eröffnet ward" (with me the old lyric German school closed, while at the same time the new school, the modern German lyric was inaugurated by me). When he returns to the themes and forms of Romantic poetry, it is to demonstrate both the exhaustion of its imagery and the continuing contemporary significance, for political reasons, of its interests in folk song, myth, and legend.

Heine also identified the central position of Goethe and repeatedly associated the end of a whole cultural epoch, the "period of art" ("das Ende der Kunstperiode"), with Goethe's death. This acknowledges the unavoidable dominance of the older poet in the earlier part of Heine's career, as well as his own allegiance to Goethe as his successor and competitor. In his critical competition with the "tendentious" political poets ("Tendenzdichter") of the Vormärz, by contrast, he defines and then transcends a current propagandist style. Similar to many contemporaries—Grabbe in Germany or Stendhal in France—he saw in the passing of great figures such as Goethe or Napoleon the end of an heroic age, which was succeeded by mediocrity and limitation.

Whatever he may set out to write about, Heine constantly writes about himself. His first public successes, the sketches collected in *Reisebilder* (1826–31; *Pictures of Travel*), create within the loose framework of the travelogue a half-fictional and half-autobiographical persona who returns in different guises and disguises throughout his work. This personal dimension of Heine's writing attracted both prurient curiosity and sharp criticism among contemporaries and subsequent readers alike. The first collections of *Reisebilder* (1826, 1830) established Heine's reputation as a master of comic ridicule, even though his ridicule was often condemned as frivolity; the poems collected in *Buch der Lieder* (1827; *Book of Songs*) yielded his image as a poet of unrequited love and inner self-division (so called Zerrissenheit).

Despite his conversion to Lutheranism in 1825, Heine was unable as a Jew to find suitable employment in public administration or the universities. In response to the July Revolution, he moved to Paris in May 1831, and became both a high-profile exile moving in the literary circles of the French capital and an acute commentator on its cultural and political life. When his health finally collapsed in 1848 and he was left bedridden, a third image of Heine was constructed both by his visitors and by Heine himself—as a man who courageously endured his "mattress grave" ("Matratzengruft") with his mind and spirits unimpaired.

Although his early poetry gained steadily in popularity through the 19th century, his reputation was damaged by the rejection of Stefan George, who valued only the atmospheric aspects of Heine's poetry, and not its incisive wit. Karl Kraus's essay "Heine und die Folgen" (1910; Heine and the Consequences) laid the blame for the worst of contemporary journalism at Heine's door and effectively blocked his further reception for a generation. After 1945, his work was claimed as a socialist heritage by critics in the GDR, while liberal interpretations developed in the West during the 1960s. Both the major Düsseldorf edition of the complete works (16 volumes, 1973–97) and the wide distribution of Briegleb's *Hanser* edition (6 volumes, 1968–1976) provide ample evidence of Heine's standing as a classic. His bicentenary year produced a crop of conferences and their proceedings around the world, although the *relatively* small amount of new work perhaps indicates that Heine's reception has entered its final and saturated phase.

Three issues have dominated critical discussion of Heine's work: the extent and significance of the autobiographical element in his writings; the nature of his political commitments; and the extent to which his response to political censorship, on the one hand, and the radical pressure to conform, on the other, can be successfully deciphered as a coherent discourse. The poems of *Buch der Lieder* parade themselves as the product of unrequited love, supposedly first for his Hamburg cousin Amalie and then for her sister Therese. The chronological inconsistency of this explanation in relation to the genesis of the poems, however, has been apparent at least since William Rose's inquiry, *The Early Love Poetry of Heinrich Heine* (1962). Instead, the poems are now seen as variations on a Petrarchan theme; the carefully arranged illusion of autobiography that they create explores the conventions of the "lyric of experience" (Erlebnislyrik) as defined by Goethe's love poetry and his novel *Die Leiden des jungen Werther* (1774; *The Sorrows of Young Werther*). In reworking the conventional terms of individual experience, however, the *Buch der Lieder* also measures Heine's sense of exclusion from the social world of the grande bourgeoisie in Hamburg; Heine's Jewish origins also excluded him from the public world of politics and the academy.

If social criticism is nevertheless marginal to Heine's early poetry, political questions are both implicit and explicit in *Neue Gedichte* (1844; *New Poems*). After poems recalling the sarcastic-sentimental mixture of the first collection, the sequences entitled "Verschiedene" (Sundry Women) consider a more modern, Parisian eroticism addressed in "sundry" idioms, but they testify, above all, to Heine's engagement with the fleshly and emancipationist materialism of Saint Simon. In the "Zeitgedichte" (Poems of the Times), Heine develops a political aesthetic designed to drum up opposition to Prussian authoritarianism without giving way to the "vague and unproductive pathos" (Preface to *Atta Troll*) that he detected in the work of his contemporaries. The verse satire *Atta Troll: Ein Sommernachtstraum* (1847; *Atta Troll: A Midsummer Night's Dream*), similar to its companion piece *Deutschland: Ein Wintermärchen* (1844; *Germany: A Winter's Tale*), makes fun of the liberal aspirations and national sentiments of Vormärz poets such as Freiligrath and Herwegh. Heine resists their attempts to convert political belief into poetic allegory, a form that he particularly subverts in *Atta Troll*. According to Heine, the freedom to which they all aspire is not to be found in the generalized political slogans of the struggle against feudalism, but it can be preserved for the time being in the utopian space of poetry itself. In his later poetry, *Romanzero* (1851) and the posthumous *Gedichte 1853–54* (*Poems 1853–54*), Heine again reworks some of the traditional forms he had exploited before, but he uses the romance and the historical ballad in this case ("Historien") to express the disappointment of radical expectations after 1848 ("Karl I") and the apostasy of other writers on the left. In these works, Heine also locates himself and his bedridden existence in relation to the disenchantments of modern urban life in Paris, "die leuchtende Hauptstadt der Welt" ("this world capital of light"); the late poems on the biblical "Lazarus" theme indicate a theological—although never orthodox—turn in his thought and feeling.

An analysis of religious ideas laid the foundation for Heine's two critical books on German literature and thought. *The Romantic School* and *Zur Geschichte der Religion und Philosophie in Deutschland* (1835; *On the History of Religion and Philosophy in Germany*) constitute a progressive account of the state of German intellectual life that responds to Madame de Staël's *De l'Allemagne*. In these works, Heine identifies in Christianity the oppressive principle of "spiritualism," which in elevating the soul, condemns the flesh; against this principle, he sets the "sensualism" that vindicates the full and physical rights of humanity. According to Heine, German thought has progressed through the religious and philosophical revolutions of the Reformation and idealism; what must now complete the development is the social and political revolution. In literary terms, the two principles are realized in Romanticism, with its allegorical view of reality, and, by contrast, in the classical ideal of immediate and fully realized individuality, which Heine also identifies with the experience of modernity. Its heroes are Luther, who liberated thought; Lessing, who promoted the Enlightenment critique of religion; and Voß, who polemicized against the wave of conversions to Roman Catholicism.

Heine was determined to mediate between German *thought* and French social *action*, and his Paris journalism in *Französische Maler* (1833; *French Painters*) and *Französische Zustände* (1833; *Conditions in France*) reported on cultural and political developments in France. Like almost all of Heine's writing, his accounts of French and German culture and politics encountered the restrictions of censorship. (In 1835, the decree of the German Federal Parliament [Bundestagsbeschluß] banned his works along with those of "Das Junge Deutschland," and in Prussia, all his writings, past *and* future, were banned.) Heine quickly responded to this situation by developing both techniques of self-censorship and an indirect discourse that invites the reader to recognize an "esoteric" meaning in the most harmless details. In *Die Harzreise* (1826; *The Harz Journey*), for example, the narrow "philistine" world of the German bourgeoisie is contrasted with a true freedom found in nature, which politicizes the Romantic cliché. Subsequent *Reisebilder* (*Travel Pictures*) are more explicit in their celebration of Napoleon as the representative of revolutionary politics—in *Ideen: Das Buch Le Grand* (1827; *Ideas: The Book of Le Grand*)—or in the polemics of Heine's response to Platen's anti-Semitic attack on his work in *Die Bäden von Lucca* (1830; *The Baths at Lucca*). Here, too, Heine's vicious remarks about Platen's homosexuality are designed as a broader attack on Bavarian aristocracy and clericalism. In later journalism on the culture and politics of Paris, collected as *Lutezia* (1854), as in his earlier writings on Berlin, London, and Paris, Heine generates a complex web of allusion; he thus invites his readers to observe successive attempts to give allegorical meaning to the cultural life of the city, and to read these signs of the times for themselves.

Ludwig Börne: Eine Denkschrift (1840; *Ludwig Börne: Portrait of a Revolutionist*) returns to the contrasts of the spiritual and the sensual (under the guise of the Nazarenic and Hellenic). Shortly after Börne's death, Heine responded with extraordinary virtuosity to the exiled republican's criticism that he was not a true patriot and that mere talent overwhelmed any moral character in his work. Within the range of Heine's prose, from his largely unsuccessful attempts at fiction such as *Der Rabbi von Bacherach* (1826–40; *The Rabbi of Bacherach*) through the *Reisebilder* to his critical essays and journalism, the Börne book draws together themes of exile and marginalization, while its structure and rhetoric brilliantly transcend the limitations of what passed for liberal politics in the Vormärz.

The many settings by Schumann and Brahms, among others, of poems from the "Lyrisches Intermezzo" and "Heimkehr" (Lyric Intermezzo; The Homecoming) sections of *Buch der Lieder* have sustained Heine's reception. Since the 1960s, however, it has been the later poetry and, particularly, *Romanzero* that has held critical attention. This collection and the later and posthumous poems reveal remarkable affinities with the work of younger contemporaries such as Baudelaire. As the huge editorial efforts of the Düsseldorf edition are assimilated, Heine's significance in relation to the politics of modern urban experience in Paris and his profound exploration of the relations between Judaism and modernity have both already been underlined. Heine wanted to be thought of as the "first man of the [19th] century," and he cheerfully modified the date of his birth (to 31 December 1799) to accommodate this desire: the extraordinary political and satirical finesse of his writing will continue to guarantee his central position as the first truly *modern* author writing in the German language.

ANTHONY PHELAN

See also Das Junge Deutschland

Biography

Born in Düsseldorf, probably 13 December 1797. Apprenticed to a banking house and to a grocery dealer, Frankfurt, 1815; worked in his uncle's bank, Hamburg, 1816; ran a textile business, 1818–19; studied law, University of Bonn, 1819–20, University of Berlin, 1821–24, and University of Göttingen, 1820–21, 1824–25; doctor of law, University of Göttingen, 1825; worked as a writer in Lüneberg and Hamburg, 1825–27; coeditor, *Neue Allgemeine Politische Annalen,* Munich, 1827–28; in Italy, 1828; in Hamburg and Berlin, 1829–31; in Paris from 1831; correspondent for Augsburg *Allgemeine Zeitung.* Died 17 February 1856.

Selected Works

Collections

Sämtliche Werke, edited by Ernst Elster, 7 vols., 1887–90
Works, translated by Charles Geoffrey Leland et al., 16 vols., 1905
Sämtliche Schriften, edited by Klaus Briegleb et al., 6 vols., 1968–76
Säkularausgabe: Werke, Briefwechsel, Lebenszeugnisse, 1970–
Historisch-kritische Gesamtausgabe der Werke, edited by Manfred Windfuhr, 16 vols., 1973–97
Selected Works, translated by Helen M. Mustard and Max Knight, 1973
The Complete Poems of Heinrich Heine, edited and translated by Hal Draper, 1982
Selected Prose, edited and translated by Ritchie Robertson, 1993

Poetry

Gedichte, 1822
Tragödien nebst einem lyrischen Intermezzo (includes the plays *Almansor* and *William Ratcliff*), 1823
Buch der Lieder, 1827; revised edition, 1844; as *Book of Songs,* translated by J.E. Wallis, 1856; translated by Charles Godfrey Leland, 1864; translated by Stratheir, 1882; translated by Theodore Martin and E.A. Bowring, 1884; translated by John Todhunter, 1907; translated by R. Levy, 1909; translated by Robert R. Garran, 1924; translated by Hal Draper, in *The Complete Poems of Heinrich Heine,* 1982; selections in *Songs of Love and* Grief (bilingual edition), translated by Walter W. Arndt, 1995
Neue Gedichte, 1844; revised edition, 1851; as *New Poems,* translated by Margaret Armour, 1910
Deutschland: Ein Wintermärchen (separate issue from *Neue Gedichte*), 1844; as *Germany: A Winter's Tale,* translated by H. Salinger, 1944; translated by Hal Draper, in *The Complete Poems of Heinrich Heine,* 1982; as *Deutschland: A Winter's Tale,* translated by T.J. Reed, 1986; as *Deutschland, Deutschland: An Unsentimental Journey,* translated by Reed, 1987
Atta Troll: Ein Sommernachtstraum, 1847; as *Atta Troll: A Midsummer Night's Dream,* translated by Thomas Selby Egan, in *Atta Troll and Other Poems,* 1876; translated by Herman Scheffauer, 1913
Romanzero, 1851; translated as *Romancero,* 1905
Paradox and Poet: The Poems, translated by Louis Untermeyer, 1937
The Lazarus Poems (bilingual edition), translated by Alistair Elliott, 1979
Jewish Stories and Hebrew Melodies, translated by Charles Godfrey Leland, Frederic Ewen, and Hal Draper, 1987

Other

Reisebilder (includes *Die Harzreise; Die Heimkehr; Die Nordsee; Ideen: Das Buch Le Grand; Reise von München nach Genua; Die Bäden von Lucca; Die Stadt Lucca, Englische Fragmente*), 4 vols., 1826–31; as *Pictures of Travel,* translated by Charles Godfrey Leland, 1855; translated by Russell Davis Gilmann, 1907; as *Travel Pictures,* translated by F. Storr, 1887; as *The Italian Travel Sketches,* translated by Elizabeth A. Sharp, 1892
Französische Zustände, 1833; as *French Affairs,* 1889
Zur Geschichte der neueren schönen Literatur in Deutschland, 1833; as *Die Romantische Schule,* 1836; as *The Romantic School,* translated by S.L. Fleishman, 1882
Der Salon, 4 vols., 1834–40
Shakespeares Mädchen und Frauen, 1839; as *Heine on Shakespeare,* translated by Ida Benecke, 1895
Ludwig Börne: Eine Denkschrift, 1840; as *Ludwig Börne: Portrait of a Revolutionist,* translated by T.S. Egan, 1881
Der Doktor Faust (ballet scenario), 1851; as *Doctor Faust: A Dance Poem,* translated by Basil Ashmore, 1952
Vermischte Schriften (includes *Geständnisse, Lutezia*), 3 vols., 1854
Memoiren and neugesammelte Gedichte, Prosa, und Briefe, edited by Eduard Engel, 1884; as *Memoirs,* translated by T.W. Evans, 1884; translated by G. Cannon, 1910
Works of Prose, edited by Hermann Kesten, translated by E.B. Ashton, 1943
Poetry and Prose, edited by Frederic Ewen, translated by Ewen, Louis Untermeyer et al., 1948
Briefe, edited by Friedrich Hirth, 6 vols., 1950–51
The Sword and the Flame (selected prose), edited by Alfred Werner, 1960
Begegnungen mit Heine: Berichte der Zeitgenossen, edited by Michael Werner, 2 vols., 1973
Poetry and Prose, edited by Jost Hermand and Robert C. Holub, 1982
The Romantic School and Other Essays, edited by Jost Hermand and Robert C. Holub, 1985
Heinrich Heine und die Musik: Publizistische Arbeiten und poetische Reflexionen (selections), edited by Gerhard Müller, 1987

Further Reading

Altenhofer, Norbert, *Die verlorene Augensprache: Über Heinrich Heine,* edited by Volker Bohn, Frankfurt: Insel, 1993
Bayerdörfer, Hans-Peter, "Politische Ballade: Zu den 'Historien' in Heines *Romanzero,*" *Deutsche Vierteljahrsschrift* 46 (1972)
Höhn, Gerhard, *Heine-Handbuch: Zeit, Person, Werk,* Stuttgart: Metzler, 1987; revised edition, 1997
Kruse, Joseph A., et al., editors, *Ich Narr des Glücks,* Stuttgart: Metzler, 1997
Reeves, Nigel, *Heinrich Heine: Poetry and Politics,* London: Libris, 1974; revised edition, 1997
Robertson, Ritchie, *Heine,* London: Halban, and New York: Grove Press, 1988
Sammons, Jeffrey L., *Heinrich Heine: The Elusive Poet,* New Haven, Connecticut, and London: Yale University Press, 1969
———, *Heinrich Heine: A Modern Biography,* Princeton, New Jersey: Princeton University Press, 1979

Buch der Lieder 1827

Collection of Poems by Heinrich Heine

Heinrich Heine's first self-contained collection of poetry, which he called *Buch der Lieder* (*Book of Songs*), at once established his reputation as one of Germany's leading lyric poets. As he proudly proclaimed in poem no. 13 of the cycle "Homecoming": "I am a German poet, Within my own land famed; If the best names are cited, Then mine is also named." Though still deeply indebted to the preceding Romantic generations, and especially to Clemens Brentano and Achim von Arnim's influential anthology *Des Knaben Wunderhorn* (1805–8; The Boy's Magic Horn), Heine was to prove his independence as a poet and to exhibit his own style. As he later declared: "With me the old lyrical school of the Germans was brought to a close, whilst at the same time the new school of modern German lyric poetry was opened by me."

He found the lure of the Romantic tradition hard to resist, but chose to borrow from its outer trappings and effects, to parody and play with Romantic imagery. This early collection already displays a high degree of self-conscious artistry and formal mastery, which slips readily into opalescent irony and those willful breaks in mood for which Heine became famous. In this he follows the then-prevalent fashion for Byronic posing, literary affectation, and a penchant for bathos, the use of impure rhyme, and dissonant diction. The young poet's ever-divided self reveled in the disharmonies and torn emotions of a disaffected victim of *mal de siècle,* and never with more self-indulgence than when caught in the bittersweet anguish of love. The book's first cycle, entitled *Junge Leiden* (Youthful Sufferings), includes poem after poem on the subject of unrequited or disappointed love, many in the form of dreams and visions, others in the guise of romances, others again in sonnet form. Though, like Goethe, Heine sensed that there was something psychologically unhealthful about many of the Romantics' morbid and mystical leanings, none could more effectively exploit in his poetry the intimate connection between the afflictions of body and mind than Heine. The representative poem ("That is the ancient fairy wood!") with which he introduced the third edition contains the sensual dream-image of the Sphinx, whose voluptuous embrace is both "delicious torture and blissful pain." The deep affinities between beauty and pain, the fickleness and cruelty of woman (the Lorelei figure), the sweet torments of the wounded heart, the satedness of the voluptuary, or the interconnection of pain and pleasure are all further refinements of Romantic sensibility which Heine explored more fully than his predecessors; this made him a precursor of Baudelaire and Rimbaud.

What distinguishes Heine from most German Romantics, and places him closer to the French, is an intellectual clarity of vision, a perspicacity that combats illusion. This is most evident in his treatment of the dream and dreaming. The cycle "Traumbilder" (Dream Images) contains poems that almost inevitably involve a rude awakening to sober insight. For this poet, dreams exist mainly as illusion: they are there to be shattered. Since they serve as evidence of man's self-delusion and folly, their true function is to confront the dreamer with an irreducible reality. The opposing voices of the Romantic dreamer and the down-to-earth rationalist are shown to be irreconcilable in the witty "Chat upon Paderborn Heath."

Heine characteristically planned and composed his poems in cyclical form so that their effectiveness in some measure rests upon motivic links and composite patterns. These early cycles, which were later arranged to form *The Book of Songs,* had already been published at intervals between 1817 and 1826. The entire book was ordered chronologically and shows a distinct development within the poetic persona it contains, offering, as Heine noted, "a psychological picture" of the author. The pervasive presence and self-projection of this essentially fictive persona is focal to the design of the whole collection. The subjective accents of a distinctive voice are conspicuous throughout, and its fluctuations of tone and mood range from tearful sentiment or anguished self-pity to spirited irony and biting satire. Heine's lucid, critical mind and polemical temperament predestined him from the outset for a career as a public poet, and the urgent, rhetorical voice which engages with an envisaged readership may already be heard in such poems as "Yet the Castrati Grumbled" or "Black Frock Coats and Silken Stockings." The social satire is also evident in "I Dreamt That I Was God Himself," "They Sat Drinking Tea at the Table," and "I Called the Devil and He Came."

Georg Brandes famously observed that "Heine introduced a new style, the combination of sentiment and humor in lyric poetry, and a new idea, the introduction of prose into poetry." The novelty of this combination of disparate elements and the boldness with which prosaic and informal idiom is employed set this poetry apart in its day and contributed to its great popularity. The strain of pure lyricism was no less at the poet's command, as many of the poems show, and numerous composers were drawn to the collection throughout the 19th century and beyond. Schubert's *Schwanengesang* (1828; Swan Song) embraced settings of six of the poems, including the theatrical lyricism of "The Double." Mendelssohn immortalized "On the Wings of Song," while Schumann's musical and critical gifts would seem to have predestined him as Heine's most congenial Lieder composer in *Dichterliebe* (1840; Poet's Love) and Liederkreis Op. 24 (1840). The free verse forms, fluctuating rhythms, and impressionistic technique which Heine employed for the concluding "North Sea Songs" proved no less influential. They served Wagner as models for his libretti and found imitators in Russia, where Tyuchev's and Fet's translations first ushered in free verse as a form.

ALEXANDER STILLMARK

Editions

First edition: *Buch der Lieder,* Hamburg: Hoffmann und Campe, 1827

Critical editions: in *Säkularausgabe,* vol. 1, Berlin and Paris: Akademie-Verlag, 1970; also in *Sämtliche Schriften,* vol. 1, edited by Klaus Briegleb, Munich: Hanser, 1968

Translations: in *The Complete Poems of Heinrich Heine,* translated by Hal Draper, Boston: Suhrkamp/Insel, 1982; selections in *Songs of Love and Grief* (bilingual edition), translated by Walter W. Arndt, Evanston, Illinois: Northwestern University Press, 1995

Further Reading

Lüdi, Rolf, *Heinrich Heines "Buch der Lieder": Poetische Strategien und deren Bedeutung,* Bern: Lang, 1979

Perraudin, Michael, *Heinrich Heine, Poetry in Context: A Study of the Buch der Lieder,* Oxford: Oxford University Press, and New York: Berg, 1989

Prawer, Siegbert Salomon, *Heine: Buch der Lieder,* London: Arnold, 1960

Reeves, Nigel, *Heinrich Heine: Poetry and Politics,* London: Oxford University Press, 1974

Robertson, Ritchie, *Heine,* London: Halban, and New York: Grove, 1988

Rose, William, *The Early Love Poetry of Heinrich Heine: An Inquiry into Poetic Inspiration,* Oxford: Clarendon Press, 1962

Sammons, Jeffrey L., *Heinrich Heine, the Elusive Poet,* New Haven, Connecticut: Yale University Press, 1969

Deutschland: Ein Wintermärchen 1844

Collection of Poems by Heinrich Heine

Heine's comic epic *Deutschland: Ein Wintermärchen* (1844; *Deutschland: A Winter's Tale*) left its earliest readers in no doubt about his political intentions. Conservatives were outraged by its satire of religion and smutty jokes (*Zoten*); the Prussian government banned the volume *Neue Gedichte* (*New Poems*) in which it appeared and sought to extend this proscription throughout the German federal states. More liberal critics welcomed the precision and wit of Heine's mockery, while the early socialists among Heine's Paris friends, including Karl Marx, granted the poem canonical status as an expression of "the humanist principle" (Marx).

Marx arranged for a reprint in *Vorwärts* (*Forward*), and some critics (particularly those in the GDR) have claimed to identify his direct influence. In spite of the close friendship that developed between Marx and Heine toward the end of 1843 when *Deutschland* was being written, there is no evidence that Marx had anything to do with its composition. On the contrary, Heine's critique of religion as *Das Eiapopeia vom Himmel* (the lullaby about heaven [canto 1]) and of the role of nationalist ideologies actually anticipates some of the later work of Marx and Engels.

The framework of a journey from Aachen to Hamburg allows the poem to address the question of German identity and national unity. *Deutschland* faces opposition on two fronts. The feudal and reactionary view of Germany appears in successive cantos under the guise of the Prussian army and its uniforms, the *Zollverein* (German Customs Union), the Cologne cathedral, and various figures of myth and legend, including Heine's dream of the once and future Kaiser, Barbarossa. Because an ideal of German national unity was also promoted by democrats such as Gutzkow (who had attacked Heine's supposed lack of political commitment before), the poem simultaneously attacks liberal fantasies of national emancipation, preferring an internationalist politics of which Germany is to be the mouthpiece and exemplar.

Heine is able to accommodate this wide range of material and argument through the form of a verse *Reisebild,* or travel picture. In prose, this form had first brought him to public notice with *Die Harzreise* (1826; *The Harz Journey*). Heine's travel pictures allow a kind of ambling, associative writing, which can include both local detail and imaginative flights of fancy or dreams. Developing the political travelogue outlined in the last part of his "Tannhäuser" poem (1836), *Deutschland: A Winter's Tale* recasts the *Reisebild* as verse. The resulting form initiated a new genre with both a loose structure and the possibility of movement between local color and sharp political reflection. Heine gives his work satirical bite through the wonderfully conversational tone of his four-line folk-stanza and his sometimes outrageous rhymes.

Heine models the poem on his journey to Hamburg in the period from October to December (and not "in the sad month of November") 1843, deriving the itinerary as the reverse of his route back to France. The border crossing of the opening cantos (cantos 1 and 2) provides the perspective of the exile's view of patriotism in his own land. Passing through customs also alerts the reader to hidden meanings, especially the contraband concealed in the traveler's head. The journey is exclusively on Prussian territory, so the Prussian heraldic eagle becomes a leitmotif of threat and oppression. Other set pieces have a more immediate contemporary resonance: Friedrich Wilhelm IV's national project to complete the building of Cologne cathedral, Father Rhine's complaints about Becker's "Rheinlied" ("Rhine Song") in response to the diplomatic "Rhine-crisis" of 1840, and the erection of a Hermann Memorial in Teutoburg Forest are hardly *concealed* themes. Other parts of the poem on Hagen and Unna in Westphalia (cantos 8–10) and large parts of the Hamburg section (canto 43) avoid overtly political issues and prefer culinary and gastronomic matters.

Local color and personal recollections enable the traveler/Heine to position himself in the two cantos that lead up to the central retelling of the Barbarossa legend and to attack both the monarchy in general and the pseudo-medievalism of Heine's contemporaries. Canto 12 sees the carriage halted and surrounded by wolves. Heine here reasserts his political sympathy with the Left, insisting that he had always been a wolf—even though he occasionally had to don sheep's clothing. As in the Preface to *Deutschland*, Heine's polemics on political style in the companion poem *Atta Troll: Ein Sommernachtstraum* (1847; *Atta Troll: A Midsummer Night's Dream*) and against republican hypocrisy in his memoir of *Ludwig Börne* also proclaim that his deepest convictions are radical. This has been understood as the beliefs he shared with other liberal writers of the *Vormärz,* or as his fundamental sympathy for the working class and its socialist representatives. In the following canto (13), however, the traveler addresses a wayside crucifix as "my poor cousin," which underlines Heine's marginal position in the spectrum of contemporary politics—both as a Jew and as an idealist *Menschheitsretter* (savior of humanity). When Heine sees his doppelgänger, or double, earlier in the Cologne dream of cantos 6 and 7, this position of distance becomes the model for the intellectual's role. His critical thought is aggressively realized by other, related forces in the real world.

The final cantos were thought particularly scandalous: the poet receives a vision of the future by gazing into the chamber pot of Hammonia, the Rubenesque tutelary goddess of Hamburg. She promises that the reactionary idyll of German feudalism is coming to an end and that the rumblings of a revolutionary *Spektakelstück* (spectacle-drama) are drawing closer. The final section commits the poet to youth and the future and, like *Atta Troll,* vindicates the power of poetry over political control.

The flexibility of Heine's travel picture in verse encouraged many imitations. The best of these in recent times is Wolf Biermann's *Deutschland: Ein Wintermärchen* (1972), which renews the exile's point of view from the perspective of the GDR. The topographical framework of Heine's poetic self-definition provides a subtler point of departure for Peter Rühmkorf's third self-portrait, "Selbst III / Mit den Jahren" (Self III / With the Years), from *Einmalig wie wir alle* (1988; *Unique Like All of Us*).

Anthony Phelan

Editions

First edition: *Deutschland: Ein Wintermärchen,* in *Neue Gedichte,* Hamburg: Hoffmann und Campe: 1844

Critical edition: in *Historisch-kritische Gesamtausgabe der Werke,* vol. 4, edited by Winfried Woesler, Hamburg: Hoffmann und Campe, 1985

Translation: *Deutschland: A Winter's Tale,* translated by T.J. Reed, London: Angel Books, 1986; as *Germany: A Winter's Tale,* translated by Hal Draper, in *The Complete Poems of Heinrich Heine,* Oxford: Oxford University Press, 1982

Further Reading

Atkinson, Ross, "Irony and Commitment in Heine's *Deutschland: Ein Wintermärchen,*" *Germanic Review* 50 (1975)

Dethlefsen, Dirk, "Die 'unstäte Angst': Der Reisende und sein Dämon in Heines *Deutschland: Ein Wintermärchen,*" *Heine-Jahrbuch* 28 (1989)

Höhn, Gerhard, "*Deutschland: Ein Wintermärchen,*" in *Heine-Handbuch: Zeit, Person, Werk,* Stuttgart: Metzler, 1987; 2nd edition, 1997

Prawer, S.S., *Heine, the Tragic Satirist,* Cambridge: Cambridge University Press, 1961

Heinrich von Veldeke ca. 1150– ca. 1210

Heinrich von Veldeke is one of only a handful of medieval German poets to enjoy a reputation as a composer of both love songs (Minnesang) and narrative literature. In both, he is a pivotal figure; he introduced German audiences to many aspects of the courtly culture that had been flourishing in France and Provence, while preserving some features of the native German traditions, which were presumably appreciated by his patron and his public. He can be localized in a region that accords well with this intermediary role: in the Limburg province of modern Belgium, an area in which in Veldeke's day both French and German were spoken and through which cultural developments in Paris found their way to Germany. The name Veldeke is attested among documents of the Counts of Loon, but it is not sure whether Veldeke belonged to the family bearing the name or was simply named after the estate. He later became one of the first poets to enjoy the patronage of Landgrave Hermann of Thuringia, who was famous for his association with other notable German poets, including Wolfram von Eschenbach and Walther von der Vogelweide.

The dates of Veldeke's literary activity can be established with some precision and are in fact a useful orientation point in the history of courtly culture in Germany. From the evidence of his narrative *Eneas,* he must have been composing already in the early 1170s, and he was able to complete the narrative after 1184, the date of Friedrich Barbarossa's court celebration in Mainz, at which Veldeke claims to have been present (*Eneas*). For dating his Minnesang, one likewise assumes the period 1170–90, but for the third work known for certain to have been written by Veldeke, an account of the life and miracles of a local saint, Servatius of Tongeren, no precise dating is possible. This last work is the only one that survives in manuscripts written in Veldeke's own Limburg dialect, although in some modern editions, scholars have reconstructed his Minnesang corpus and the *Eneas* in that dialect as well; there has been considerable debate about whether the High German versions surviving in the manuscripts go back to Veldeke himself or were transcribed later.

Veldeke's corpus of perhaps 40 love songs offers the clearest evidence of his indebtedness to both local German traditions and the new romance ideas. Most of the songs consist of one stanza, unlike those of later poets who increasingly composed several stanzas in the same meter (i.e., to the same melody), which might then be sung together. Yet 75 percent of Veldeke's stanzas have the tripartite structure (*Stollenstrophe*) characteristic of romance influence; in addition, most of his rhymes are full rhymes rather than the simple assonance typical of early German poets. This attention to form is evident in the continuation of rhymes throughout the stanza in over half of Veldeke's corpus.

As far as their content is concerned, his songs are also typical of the "transitional" poets. Veldeke has a fondness for nature, which he brings to life rather more vividly than many of his successors, and which he incorporates not only as an introduction to the song. Further indicating the emerging new fashion, very few of his songs are composed from the woman's point of view (only nos. II and XXXVIII, one stanza in XXXII, and possibly one stanza in VII). The male longing for "hohe Minne" (lofty love), which dominates by the end of the 12th century, is already obvious in many of Veldeke's songs, no more so than in no. I, which begins with a reference to the joys of nature that the singer cannot hope to match. It then unfolds as a lament at his foolishness for jeopardizing earlier joy by expecting a physical response from the embodiment of beauty.

Veldeke's narrative *Eneas* is an adaptation of an anonymous French work that was probably written at the Anglo-Norman court of Henry II. Both the medieval French and Veldeke's version bear witness to the popularity of Virgil's epic in the Middle Ages. While retaining much of the pagan mythology in retelling the story of the Roman hero, both medieval poets brought the subject matter up to date for a Christian courtly audience. Thus, the warriors are now knights, the battle tactics and equipment are those of late 12th-century warfare, and the extensive descriptions of fine clothes, feasting, and etiquette are clearly meant to appeal to a courtly audience capable of appreciating such matters. The political perspective is also rather different; at the end of his narrative, Veldeke extends the genealogy of Eneas down to the birth of Christ, thus establishing a link between the pagan Roman Empire and the contemporary Christian one and endowing Friedrich Barbarossa and 12th-century knighthood with all the authority of "history."

But Veldeke's public, like that of his Anglo-Norman source, must also have appreciated the way in which he catered to another central preoccupation of courtly society, namely, love. Both medieval poets considerably expand the Dido episode by dwelling on the demonic, elemental aspects of her desperate passion, many of which attest to the poets' acquaintance with Ovid. In addition, they balance this emphasis in the second half of the work with similar descriptions of the love between the hero Eneas and his future wife Lavinia, so that the narrative as a whole has a double climax that focuses on love. At the same time, the warrior and love themes are interwoven in a manner that becomes typical of many later romances, since Eneas's combat with Turnus determines the validity of his love as well as the future of Rome.

Comparisons between Veldeke's *Eneas* and his French source used to be bedeviled by inappropriate nationalism. Recent scholarship suggests that Veldeke's narrative technique is less spontaneous, which may have made for a less lively impact on his public, and it has long been recognized that he is generally more concerned about courtly etiquette. In addition, he seems to have introduced a narrator's perspective that goes beyond the Anglo-Norman poet's close identification with his characters.

ROD FISHER

Biography

Born in Belgium, ca. 1150. Active in the lower Rhineland area; possible patrons include Countess Agnes of Loon (modern Looz), Countess Margaret of Cleves, Count Palatine (later Landgrave) Hermann of Thuringia. Died before 1210.

Selected Works

Narrative

Eneasroman, modern German translation by Dieter Kartschoke, 1986; edited and with modern German translation by Hans Fromm, 1992; as *Eneas,* translated by Rodney W. Fisher, 1992

Songs

Lieder, in *Des Minnesangs Frühling,* edited by Hugo Moser and Helmut Tervooren, 1988; in *Mittelhochdeutsche Minnelyrik,* edited and with modern German translations by Günther Schweikle, 1993

Further Reading

Cormier, Raymond, "Classical Continuity and Transposition in Two Twelfth-Century Adaptations of the 'Aeneid'," *Symposium* 47, no. 4 (1993/94)

Deist, Rosemarie, "The Kiss of Ascanius in Vergil's 'Aeneid,' the 'Roman d'Enéas' and Heinrich von Veldeke's 'Eneide'," *German Quarterly* 67, no. 4 (1994)

Emberson, Jane, *Speech in the Eneide of Heinrich von Veldeke,* Göppingen: Kümmerle, 1981

Fisher, Rodney W., *Heinrich von Veldeke: Eneas,* Bern and New York: Lang, 1992

Groos, Arthur, "Amor and His Brother Cupid: The 'Two Loves' in Heinrich von Veldeke's 'Eneit'," *Traditio* 32 (1976)

Kaplowitt, Stephen, "Heinrich von Veldeke's Song Cycle of 'Hohe Minne'," *Seminar* 11, no. 3 (1975)

Kartschoke, Dieter, *Heinrich von Veldeke, Eneasroman: Mittelhochdeutsch / Neuhochdeutsch,* Stuttgart: Reclam, 1986

Kasten, Ingrid, "Herrschaft und Liebe: Zur Rolle und Darstellung des 'Helden' im 'Roman d'Eneas' und Veldekes Eneasroman," *Deutsche Vierteljahrsschrift für Literaturwissenschaft und Geistesgeschichte* 62, no. 2 (1988)

Kistler, Renate, *Heinrich von Veldeke und Ovid,* Tübingen: Niemeyer, 1993

Sayce, Olive, *The Medieval German Lyric, 1150–1300: The Development of Its Themes and Forms in Their European Context,* Oxford: Clarendon Press, and New York: Oxford University Press, 1982

Schieb, Gabriele, *Henric van Veldeken: Heinrich von Veldeke,* Stuttgart: Metzler, 1965

Schweikle, Günther, *Mittelhochdeutsche Minnelyrik,* Darmstadt: Wissenschaftliche Buchgesellschaft, 1977; new edition, Stuttgart: J.B. Metzler, 1993

Johann Jakob Wilhelm Heinse 1746–1803

Wilhelm Heinse is one of the most important representatives of Sturm und Drang (Storm and Stress). This movement, which reached its height in the 1770s and 1780s, is also known as the *Geniezeit* (age of genius) because of its turning away from the rationalism of the Enlightenment and from any theoretical copybook learnedness. Outstanding individuals, creatively rooted in their own time and place, were raised to almost godlike status. Shakespeare headed the list, to which Heinse added Rubens as the depicter of *höchstes Leben* (life at its fullest, stormiest). Heinse did this in two long letters of 1776–77, the *Gemäldebriefe,* in which he discusses art theory and vividly describes paintings from the Düsseldorf Gallery. These letters are now recognized as an aesthetic manifesto of Sturm und Drang.

The young Goethe with his *Die Leiden des jungen Werthers* (1774; translated as *The Sorrows of Werter* and *The Sufferings of Young Werther*) had presented the *Gefühlsmensch* (man of feeling) of Sturm und Drang. In Heinse's most famous work, *Ardinghello und die glückseeligen Inseln* (1787; Ardinghello and the Islands of Happiness), he created Werther's counterpart, the *Tatenmensch* (man of deeds) Ardinghello. Among the doomed figures of rebellion typical of Sturm und Drang drama or novels, Ardinghello stands out as the only positive hero and survivor, a dazzling sunlit Renaissance universal man endowed with an 18th-century mind, an ardent searcher after beauty in all its manifestations, a proclaimer of a grandiose and ecstatic aesthetic-erotic vision of the cosmos.

As early as 1769 in his *Musikalische Dialogen* (published posthumously, 1805; Musical Dialogues), Heinse raised his voice in the often radical verbal attack by Sturm und Drang on the misuse of power and the rigidity of social structures, as well as on religion, morals, politics, education, and the position of women. In true Sturm und Drang spirit, he also celebrates the great outdoors, youth, and simplicity along the lines of Rousseau's Noble Savage, raised above tainted civilization, pedantry, and French mincing artificiality. However, though quintessentially part of Sturm und Drang, Heinse does not fit into its mainstream image. The movement had no serious interest in art or music. Yet Heinse is unquestionably the informed and authoritative writer on art and music of his generation. Another striking difference from Sturm und Drang norm is that Heinse's writing never exhibits the fragmented, forced, explosive style characteristic of the movement. His stylistic Sturm und Drang boldness lies rather in pushing semantic structures to the limit at times, as if reveling in newly discovered possibilities of the German language. The result is—even for today's reader—a style of exhilarating freshness and immediacy, without wordiness. In the *Gemäldebriefe* his language frequently so matches the brushwork perceived as to become a work of art in its own right. Other art and nature descriptions, particularly the three Rhine Falls descriptions from his Italian journey of 1780–83, still seek their equal as high points of the expressiveness of German.

Unfortunately, no substantial part of Heinse's oeuvre has so far been translated into English. Also, a large section of the 7,000 or so pages of notes left by him still awaits publication. These notes, which are now being assessed text-critically and chronologically, are generally acknowledged as being of central importance for a balanced appraisal of his work. Wilhelm Heinse has had 200 years of mixed reception, ranging from highest acclaim by some contemporaries, even Goethe, and by many avant-gardists since, to moral outrage. Heinse's often misunderstood aesthetic-erotic stance, not to mention his highly advanced ideas on a free sex-life, the emancipation of women, and joyous sensous existence, were all coldly rejected for instance by Schiller and much 19th-century literary criticism. Lack of financial support from Germany meant failure for a planned venture that might really have suited him: an art journal from Italy for his compatriots back home.

The difficulty of squeezing Heinse's multifaceted talent into a single convenient pigeonhole for the purpose of literary historical classification has contributed much to his undeserved obscurity. He has been cast as a late Enlightenment man, a classicist, a writer looking back to the Baroque, a forerunner of the Romantics, an 18th-century Nietzsche, an Impressionist, an Expressionist, and more. No conventional novelist, Heinse used the form as a vehicle to accommodate his insight into art and music, his ideas about politics and morals, or his vitalistic, materialistic philosophy.

For his first novel, *Laidion; oder, Die eleusinischen Geheimnisse* (1774; Laidion; or, The Mysteries of Elysium), Heinse followed the grecizing rococo mode of his unloved teacher Christoph Martin Wieland, but broke its playful mold for good by a first attempt at elemental realism in an appended long poem, the so-called *Stanzen* (The Stanzas). In 1773 he had claimed a writer's right to such freedom in the foreword to his translation of Petronius's *Satyricon*.

He learned much from Johann Joachim Winckelmann's classicistic writings on art, yet fervently castigated him for promoting the imitation of bygone Greek perfection. Today art historians consider Heinse to be Winckelman's most formidable adversary.

In 1795–96 Heinse published the "music novel" *Hildegard von Hohenthal,* unique with its detailed, knowledgeable discussions of the music heard in his day. The first critical edition of Heinse's music writings, based on the novel, was scheduled for publication in 2000 and is expected to illuminate some significant aspects of music in 18th-century Germany for the first time.

Interest in Heinse, rekindled by Max L. Baeumer in the 1960s, continues to grow. A first book-length study concerning Heinse appeared in 1996. At a 1996 Weimar colloquium celebrating Heinse's 200th birthday, his important influence on Hölderlin was recognised; and Heinse's quirky last work, *Anastasia und das Schachspiel* (1803; Anastasia and the Game of Chess), was found to fit meaningfully into his oeuvre, as a reflection of the Aristotelean self-reliance of his reclusive years at court.

The scarcity and inadequacies of the 1902–25 Schüddekopf/ Leitzmann edition of Heinse's works make the available critical editions of important sections of his work the more welcome. Others will follow in due course, proof that this fascinating and strikingly modern writer and thinker is coming into his own at last.

ROSEMARIE ELLIOTT

Biography

Born in Langewiesen, near Ilmenau, 15 February 1746. Studied law, literature, and philosophy, universities of Jena and Erfurt, 1768–71; tutor in Halberstadt with von Massow family, 1772–74; co-editor of Johann Georg Jacobi's ladies' journal *Iris,* Düsseldorf, 1774–76; in Italy, 1780–83; obtained post at Mainz court of Elector and Archbishop Friedrich Karl Joseph von Erthal, 1786; privy councillor and court librarian, 1788; moved to Aschaffenburg Castle, 1794. Died in Aschaffenburg, 22 June 1803.

Selected Works

Collections

Sämmtliche Werke, edited by Carl Schüddekopf and Albert Leitzmann, 12 vols., 1902–25

Novels

Laidion; oder, Die eleusinischen Geheimnisse, 1774
Ardinghello und die glückseeligen Inseln, 2 vols., 1787
Hildegard von Hohenthal, 3 vols., 1795–96
Anastasia und das Schachspiel, 2 vols., 1803

Letters

Über einige Gemälde der Düsseldorfer Gallerie, in *Der Teutsche Merkur,* 1776–77; published in *Frühklassizismus: Position und Opposition: Winckelmann, Mengs, Heinse,* edited by Helmut Pfotenhauer, et al., 1995
Briefe zwischen Gleim, Wilhelm Heinse und Johannes von Müller, edited by Wilhelm Körte, 2 vols., 1806

Essays

Musikalische Dialogen (written 1769), edited by J.F.K. Arnold, 1805
Zur Erfindung der Buchdruckerkunst in Mainz, in Max L. Baeumer, *Heinse-Studien,* 1966

Further Reading

Baeumer, Max L., *Das Dionysische in den Werken Wilhelm Heinses: Studie zum dionysischen Phänomen in der deutschen Literatur,* Bonn: Bouvier, 1964
———, *Heinse-Studien: Mit einer bisher unveröffentlichten Schrift Heinses Zur Erfindung der Buchdruckerkunst in Mainz,* Stuttgart: Metzler, 1966
———, *Winckelmann und Heinse: Die Sturm-und-Drang-Anschauung von den bildenden Künsten,* Stendal: Winckelmann-Gesellschaft, 1997
Dick, Manfred, *Der junge Heinse in seiner Zeit: Zum Verhältnis von Aufklärung und Religion im 18. Jahrhundert,* Munich: Fink, 1980

Elliott, Rosemarie, "Wilhelm Heinse—'eines beßern Schiksals werth,'" *Publications of the English Goethe Society* 61 (1991)
———, "Goethe and the Image of Wilhelm Heinse," in *Weltbürger, Textwelten,* edited by Leslie Bodi et al., Frankfurt am Main and New York: Lang, 1995
———, *Wilhelm Heinse in Relation to Wieland, Winckelmann, and Goethe: Heinse's Sturm und Drang Aesthetic and New Literary Language,* Frankfurt and New York: Lang, 1996
Klinger, Uwe R., "Wilhelm Heinse's Ardinghello: A Re-Appraisal," *Lessing Yearbook* 7 (1975)
———, "Wilhelm Heinse's Socio-Political Ethos," *Lessing Yearbook* 8 (1976)
———, "Heinse's Perception of Nature," *Lessing Yearbook* 10 (1978)
Terras, Rita, "The Power of Masculinity: Wilhelm Heinse's Aesthetic," in *Eighteenth-Century German Authors and Their Aesthetic Theories: Literature and the Other Arts,* edited by Richard Critchfield and Wulf Koepke, Columbia, South Carolina: Camden House, 1988
———, "Wilhelm Heinse's 'Musikalische Dialogen,'" *Goethe Yearbook* 6 (1992)
———, *Wilhelm Heinses Ästhetik,* Munich: Fink, 1972
Theile, Gert, editor, *Das Maß des Bacchanten: Wilhelm Heinses Über-Lebenskunst,* Munich: Fink, 1998

Helmut Heißenbüttel 1921–1996

Helmut Heißenbüttel's attempt to construct poetry and literature in a new, unexpected way, which rejected established categories such as emotion, identification, and atmosphere, resulted in a radical poetic shift toward the investigation of language and its meaning. This shift to more "experimental" forms and motifs is already visible in the titles of his first two collections of poems, *Kombinationen* (1954; Combinations) and *Topographien* (1956; Topographies). Here the trained Germanist explicitly states the necessity to "penetrate language, to break it apart and to question its hidden connections." Accordingly, the language of the poems itself breaks the rules and patterns of syntax in order to question the structure and content of traditional communication and to reveal its underlying constructedness. Heißenbüttel's strictly scientific method of writing is indicative of his presumption that literature consists of language only and not of images, imagination, opinions, etc. This assessment brought him much criticism not only in his early days but throughout the second half of the 20th century. Self-consciousness and the scientific method were the cornerstones of his poetic and theoretical writings, both of which were largely influenced by Ludwig Wittgenstein's theories.

In the realm of lyric poetry, Heißenbüttel's linguistic experiments and concerns with the inner structure of language were particularly shocking in the context of Germany in the 1950s. Although trying to free itself from the Nazi past, German poetic style and content stayed mostly with traditional forms and motifs; personal experiences and reflections were often thematically central to individual and collected poems. After Heißenbüttel's first public reading at one of the famous gatherings of the Gruppe 47 in 1955, rejection and noncomprehension became standard reactions to his works, which he continuously referred to as "texts" rather than "poems." Even those critics who did find his work interesting failed to understand the fact that he was not simply an immature young author but one who had instead developed a revolutionary approach to writing that was diametrically opposed to the current norm and was later termed *konkrete Poesie* (concrete poetry).

Perhaps owing to the widespread criticism of his poems and readers' lack of comprehension, Heißenbüttel accompanied his poems—particularly those that appeared in the series of *Textbuch I* to *Textbuch VI* (Textbook, 1960–67)—with notes, arguments, references, and explanations, which often prevented critics from ever dealing with the poems (or "texts") themselves, since they became engaged in the debate on poetics. Of course, Heißenbüttel had thereby achieved what he had sought: reflection by his readers, if not concerning language itself, then at least on poetics. Many of these theoretical and critical writings are assembled in *Über Literatur* (1966; On Literature). Ultimately, Heißenbüttel's penetration of language results in a questioning of the subject matter itself and thus of an individually perceived reality—an approach later formulated by French literary theorists. He frequently provoked his readers by using quotes and juxtaposing familiar material in montage technique. This style was ultimately well received in the case of "Deutschland 1944" (Germany 1944) from *Textbuch VI* (1967), where he used newspaper articles, philosophical writings, Hitler speeches, etc., to construct a text that presented all of these elements in a new, shocking context.

Having introduced the basic concepts of his literary approach in theoretical writings and poetry, Heißenbüttel crafted *D'Alemberts Ende* (1970; D'Alembert's End), which has the formal elements of an extensive novel but was instead termed *Projekt Nr. 1* (Project No. 1). For the first time there seems to be an actual story line. In part 1, nine people from the literary and artistic world meet on 25 July 1968. Part 2 recounts their conversations on the following day; Marx and Freud are the topics discussed, especially their views on society, modern art, literature, and other subjects typical for the late 1960s. Part 3 deals with the death of the art critic D'Alembert and with the various stages leading to that death: a mosaic of dreams, hallucinations, and memories. Again, as in many of his earlier texts, *D'Alemberts Ende* chiefly consists of a montage of quotations, and it is often unclear which parts originally stem from the author and which do not. The entire *Projekt Nr. 1* can be read as a satire on intellectuals, their concerns, and their use of language.

Despite Heißenbüttel's criticism of language, he nevertheless privileged literature, because he believed language—without which literature is inconceivable—to be prerequisite for all knowledge. Heißenbüttel paid tribute to the significance of language when he republished his *Textbücher I–VI* into one collection that he called *Das Textbuch* (1970). Here, the texts are arranged in methodological rather than chronological order, as in the earlier version. The very fact that he presents the material in a more user-friendly fashion shows Heißenbüttel's perhaps hidden but deep desire to be understood in terms of his philosophy of language.

This concern with the function of language also motivated Heißenbüttel's 1973 collection of poems, edited together with Franz Mon, entitled *Antianthologie.* The texts in the *Antianthologie* are arranged according to choice of words rather than by author or subject matter, which results in a rich and playful structure of interacting texts.

Many of Heißenbüttel's writings were originally conceived as radio plays, a format that allowed him to continue with linguistic experimentation. By imagining a text as spoken, he deconstructs it and often uncovers the inherent loss of meaningful content. For instance, *Zwei oder drei Portraits* (1970; Two or Three Portraits) is a collage of sentences from *D'Alemberts Ende,* arranged according to the length of the words, unveiling the absence of content in popular intellectual jargon. Similarly, *Was sollen wir überhaupt senden* (1970; What Should We Even Broadcast), a collage of authentic broadcast material, points out the absence of meaning and relevance in much of today's communication. Often a text that was originally conceived as a radio play is later presented as a poem, such as the 13 texts in *Projekt Nr. 2,* also entitled *Das Durchhauen des Kohlhaupts* (1974; Cutting through the Cabbage). Heißenbüttel's play with language here also produces a play with different genres, which exemplifies his virtuosity as a literary critic, poet, and philosopher of language.

AGNES C. MUELLER

See also Concrete Poetry

Biography

Born in Rustringen, near Wilhelmshaven, 21 June 1921. Wounded as soldier in World War II; studied German literature and art history in Dresden, Hamburg, and Leipzig; worked in publishing and radio broadcasting; awarded a guest professorship on poetics at the Universität Frankfurt, 1963; co-editor of the literary magazine *Hermannstraße 14,* 1978–81. Died September 1996.

Selected Works

Poems and Texts
Kombinationen: Gedichte, 1951–54, 1954
Topographien: Gedichte, 1956
Ohne weiteres bekannt, 1958
Textbuch 1, 1960
Texte, ohne komma, 1960
Textbuch 2, 1961
Textbuch 3, 1962
Textbuch 4, 1964
Textbuch 5, 1965
Textbuch 6, 1967
Das Textbuch, 1970
Die Freuden des Alterns, 1971
Gelegenheitsgedichte und Klappentexte, 1973
Das Durchhauen des Kohlhaupts: Projekt Nr. 2, 1974
Texts, translated by Michael Hamburger, 1977
Eichendorffs Untergang und andere Märchen: Projekt 3/1, 1978
Wenn Adolf Hitler den Krieg nicht gewonnen hätte: Projekt 3/2, 1979
Die goldene Kuppel des Comes Arbogast; oder, Lichtenberg in Hamburg, 1979
Das Ende der Alternative: Projekt 3/3, 1980
Ödipuskomplex made in Germany: Gelegenheitsgedichte, Totentage, Landschaften 1965–1980, 1981
Alles was ich weiß, 1983
Textbuch 8, 1981–1985, 1985
Textbuch 9, 1981–1984, 1986
Textbuch 10: Von Liebeskunst, 1986
Textbuch 11 in gereinigter Sprache, 1987

Essays
Über Literature, 1966
Briefwechsel über Literatur, 1969
Was ist das Konkrete an einem Gedicht, 1967
Projekt Nr. 1: D'Alemberts Ende, 1970
Zur Tradition der Moderne, 1972
Der fliegende Frosch und das unverhoffte Krokodil, 1976
Die Erfindung der Libido, 1981
Von fliegenden Fröschen, libidinösen Epen, vaterländischen Romanen, Sprechblasen und Ohrwürmern, 1982
Versuch über die Lautsonate von Kurt Schwitters, 1983

Further Reading

Arnold, Heinz Ludwig, "Synthetische Authentizität: Helmut Heißenbüttels 'Projekt Nr. 1, D'Alemberts Ende'," in *Brauchen wir noch die Literatur? Zur literarischen Situation in der Bundesrepublik,* edited by Heinz Ludwig Arnold, Düsseldorf: Bertelsmann Universitätsverlag, 1972
Endres, Elisabeth, "Helmut Heißenbüttel," in *Deutsche Dichter der Gegenwart,* edited by Benno von Wiese, Berlin: 1973
Fülleborn, Ulrich, "Helmut Heißenbüttel," in *Die deutsche Lyrik, 1945–1975,* edited by Klaus Weissenberger, Düsseldorf: Bagel, 1981
Helmut Heißenbüttel, Munich: Edition Text und Kritik, 1981
Weiss, Christina, editor, *Schrift, écriture, geschrieben, gelesen: Für Helmut Heißenbüttel zum siebzigsten Geburtstag,* Stuttgart: Klett-Cotta, 1991
Weyrauch, Wolfgang, "Was die Uhren geschlagen haben: Über die Methoden des Schriftstellers Helmut Heißenbüttel," *Welt der Literatur* 7, no. 1 (1965)

Heliand ca. 830
Epic Poem

Two great epic works mark the beginning of German literature, both telling the story of Christ but each going a different way in language, style, form, and thought. One is Otfrid's *Evangelienharmonie,* which points, with its end rhyme and allegorical interpretations, to the future of medieval literature. The other is the *Heliand,* which harks back to pagan Germanic poetry.

Like Otfrid's work, the *Heliand* is a synoptic narration of the Gospels based on the second-century *Diatessaron* by Tatian and stands in the long tradition growing from that seminal book. The *Heliand*'s uniqueness is in its adaptation of the story to an audience that had just been converted to Christianity.

The Saxons, a Germanic tribal group that inhabited the northwestern part of what is now Germany and that had participated in the Anglo-Saxon migration to England, had been conquered and incorporated into Charlemagne's Frankish Empire in a series of wars that dragged on for more than 30 years. By a decree of Charlemagne (779), they had been forcefully converted to Christianity, but as late as the middle of the ninth century, there were sporadic rebellions and trends of reverting to paganism. Much missionary work remained to be done. To this end, Emperor Louis the Pious commissioned a prominent Saxon poet to render the Bible in poetic form and in the Saxon dialect.

This task was carried out splendidly by the author. He built a bridge between Christianity and Saxon folkways by replacing the Gospels' Palestinian setting largely with a northern ambience. The Sea of Galilee, for example, appears as the North Sea, fishing boats become Viking longboats, the wine at Cana turns into apple cider, and the town of Bethlehem becomes a hill fort. Most important, Christ is depicted as a Germanic lord or chieftain with the disciples as his warriors and retainers around him.

Beyond this outward appearance, however, the Christian message has not been altered. To be sure, some of Christ's prescriptions that might have seemed too shocking to Teutonic ears, such as the admonitions to offer the other cheek and to leave father and mother, are omitted, whereas those virtues that are congruent with Germanic values central to the retinue system, such as loyalty, service, and trust, are emphasized. The poet also puts great store in the Germanic concept of predetermined fate, and he gives Christ's miracles a flair of magic and spells. However, the author does not compromise Christian principles, such as humility, charity, and peaceableness, and he criticizes warrior virtues, such as pugnacity, love of glory, and hubris. The Christian message remained unchanged, but clad in a Saxon coat it must have looked less foreign to its Germanic audience.

The surface structure of the *Heliand* is simple enough. The plot is chronological. The narrative itself is divided into 71 chapters (so-called *fitts*). Attempts to discover a numerological-symbolic construction have not met with general acceptance, but there is common agreement that the poem has a clearly symmetric structure with the Sermon on the Mount as its centerpiece.

The poet was obviously very familiar with late-Germanic, especially Anglo-Saxon, literary style. He used the powerful Germanic alliterative meter (a long line of four stressed and a variable number of unstressed syllables in which two, three, or four stressed syllables start with the same consonant or a vowel). However, he adapted the Germanic stichic verse junction to his longer narrative by making extensive use of enjambments, thus avoiding monotony.

The main stylistic feature of the *Heliand* is also one that stems from Germanic poetry. It is the device of variation, a repetition of sentence elements, such as subject or object, with paraphrases and metonymies. This poetic device is used so extensively in the poem that it can disturb a modern reader trying to read speedily. However, when the poem is read slowly and aloud, this variation gives it a sermonic character that synergizes with the alliterative verse to increase the dignified air of the narration. This solemnity is intensified by extensive use of formulaic expressions known from heroic poetry and is balanced by vivid imagery and quick changes between direct and indirect speech that keep the narration lively. In addition, some vestiges of musical notation in one manuscript suggest that the poem might have been recited with a musical component (chant or instrument). The following illustration will give the reader an impression of the *Heliand*'s style:

> [mano] uuanod ohto uuahsid. Sô dôd an thesaro uueroldi hêr,
> an thesaru middilgard mennisco barn:
> farad endi folgod, frôde sterƀad,
> uuerðad eft iunga aftar kumane,
> uueros auuahsane, unttat sie eft uurð farnimid.

> [The moon] wanes or waxes. So do in this world here,
> in this Middle Realm the children of men:
> they go away and follow, the old die,
> again arise young ones coming after,
> growing men, until again Fate takes them away.

Little is known with certainty about the genesis of the *Heliand.* The author is unknown, as is the exact place and time of composition. However, a Latin introduction that was added to the poem still in Carolingian times gives us some hints. It mentions the commission by Emperor Louis the Pious that sets a time frame of 814–40; this and additional arguments have led to a commonly agreed-upon date of about 830. No person has ever been plausibly identified with the poet mentioned in the introduction, but the common view is that the author was a man of upper-class origin with a military and political background and ecclesiastic-theological training. The place of writing has also been searched for extensively, the monastery at Fulda remaining the most likely place as it was here that the poem's main sources (Tatian and the Matthew commentary of Hrabanus Maurus) and its literary models and inspirations (through Fulda's links to the Anglo-Saxon realm) existed together.

The poem has survived in two manuscripts and the fragments of three others. Four of these copies date from the second half of the ninth century, and the most complete manuscript (written in England and kept in the British Library in London) is 100 years younger. It comprises about 6,000 lines with a (presumably) short passage missing at the end. The manuscripts are untitled; the name *Heliand* (cognate with *holy, heal, hale,* and *hail* and meaning "savior/healer") was given to the poem by its first modern editor.

Because of its language and its specific purpose, the *Heliand*'s currency was limited in space and time. However, judging from the fact (unusual for the time) that the poem was still copied 100 years later (and in England as well), one can assume that the work had significant effect and reach. In addition, since the *Heliand*'s first modern edition in 1830, the unique clothing of the Gospel in a Germanic dress has always greatly impressed its readers. Thus, criticism focused mainly on the question of "Germanization" and its extent. The prevailing position, until adopted and discredited by Nazi ideology, was that the poem presented a new Germanic Christianity. The opposite position has been dominant since then, namely, that the *Heliand* has only a very superficial Germanic tinge because the poet used traditional formulas, by needs used the existing prefeudal vocabulary, and followed the old metaphoric concept of the "Soldier of Christ." Recently, G.R. Murphy has advocated a more balanced view. In his spirited translation and commentary, he shows that the *Heliand,* in reimaging the Gospels and accommodating them to the Germanic literary and conceptual arsenal, is an intercultural work of art that certainly is medieval and Christian but in which we can hear a clear echo of Germanic life and thought.

WOLFGANG HEMPEL

Editions

Edition of original text: *Heliand,* edited by Burkhard Taeger, Altdeutsche Textbibliothek 4, Halle: Niemeyer, 1984

Modern German translation: *Heliand und die Bruchstücke der Genesis,* translated into modern German by Felix Genzmer, with commentary and an afterword by Bernhard Sowinski, Stuttgart: Reclam, 1989

English translation: *The Heliand: The Saxon Gospel: A Translation and Commentary,* translated by G. Ronald Murphy, Oxford and New York: Oxford University Press, 1992

Further Reading

Eichhoff, Jürgen, and Irmengard Rauch, editors, *Der Heliand,* Darmstadt: Wissenschaftliche Buchgesellschaft, 1973

Liebermann, Anatoly, "Heliand," in *German Writers and Works of the Early Middle Ages: 800–1170,* Dictionary of Literary Biography, vol. 148, Detroit, Michigan: Gale Research, 1995

Murphy, G. Ronald, *The Saxon Savior: The Germanic Transformation of the Gospel in the Ninth-Century Heliand,* Oxford and New York: Oxford University Press, 1989

Rathofer, Johannes, *Der Heliand: Theologischer Sinn als tektonische Form,* Cologne: Böhlau, 1962

Taeger, Burkhard, "Heliand," in *Die deutsche Literatur des Mittelalters: Verfasserlexikon,* vol. 3, Berlin: de Gruyter, 1981

Zanni, Roland, *Heliand, Genesis und das Altenglische,* Berlin and New York: de Gruyter, 1980

Henschke, Alfred, *see* Klabund (Alfred Henschke)

Johann Gottfried Herder 1744–1803

Johann Gottfried Herder was one of those fascinating German intellectuals in the 18th century who, together with Kant, Lessing, Goethe, Schiller, Wieland, and others, were instrumental in creating the emancipatory idea of a modern middle-class culture. Herder made substantial contributions not only to one but to all those epochs in Germany of which he was a contemporary, that is, the Age of Enlightenment (*Aufklärung*), Sturm und Drang, classicism (*Klassik*), and Romanticism (*Romantik*). He is considered the forerunner and "father" of Sturm und Drang and Romanticism and is credited with being the founder of a philosophy of humanity as well as the German version of the philosophy of history. It was he who contextualized the Bible exegesis within a poetological framework and who opened his contemporaries' eyes on the then undiscovered values of popular culture. It is the irony of the fate of Herder's oeuvre that his innovative ideas and concepts were received very favorably by his contemporaries as well as his posterity but that, in the course of this process of reception, his name became separated from his legacy. One of the results today is that Herder's name is still remembered; however, very often this remembrance does not associate the name with Herder's specific achievements.

Herder's comprehensive oeuvre is characterized above all by the vast array of fields covered by his writings. Literary criticism, general philosophy, philosophy of history, aesthetics, theology, pedagogy, poetry, translation, art history, and anthropology (ethnology as well as philosophical anthropology), to name the most obvious ones, were the realms to which he made substantial contributions. Intellectual versatility is one of Herder's hallmarks, as is his being someone who intentionally did not separate distinctly philosophy and poetry and thus created a discourse of "poetic philosophy" in which well-defined concept and oscillating metaphor intermingle. Finally, Herder has been characterized as an eternal fragmentist, with some of his writings reaching the multivolume dimension of monumental fragments.

Recent research has contributed to a revaluation of this author. Older scholarship used to acknowledge some of his achievements, such as his idea of the state, as well as a work of art being organic, his new concepts of humanity and individuality, and his idea of a nation in a historical era in which Germany did not yet exist as a nation and even the modern idea of a nation only came into being. However, despite all this recognition, Herder also used to be considered a thinker who was intellectually incapable of following the then new developments, especially Kant's new philosophical paradigm of transcendentalism from 1781 on. From this perspective of older scholarship, Herder is an "irrationalist." However, more recent research has tried to understand Herder's way of thinking and writing in its own right and as a new way of self-enlightening enlightenment as well as a valid alternative to the Kantian philosophy. From this perspective, Herder is considered a holistic thinker whose philosophy is capable of conceiving of the human being as a complex entity, keeping body and soul together in a new concept of humanity (*Humanität*).

Herder started his public career with writings in the field of literary criticism. At the age of 22, he published anonymously three volumes of *Über die neuere deutsche Literatur* (1767; *Fragments on Recent German Literature*). With these publications, he entered the German intellectual arena at the highest level. The main purpose of the *Fragments,* as well as several later writings, was to help constitute a German literature of its own within the European context. His ideas about the particularity of the German language in comparison with other languages, modern and ancient, and his reflections about the interrelationship between language and literature provide the fundament for Herder's ideas about German and "Germanic" literature. As his comparisons with ancient and modern foreign literature demonstrate, Herder was not aiming at an aggressive version of a nationalist paradigm of German cultural superiority. Rather, he suggested learning from other national literatures through translating and imitating to adopt their best, detecting the specificity of German language and literature, and smoothening them in a peaceful competition of cultures. His essay *Ossian,* although taking Macpherson's pseudotranslations from the Gaelic at face value, as well as his essay on *Shakespeare* (both 1773), aimed basically in the same direction as his *Fragments.* At the same time, Herder developed the groundbreaking idea that authentic culture can only be popular culture, that is, culture of the people. From Herder on, *the people* (*das Volk*) no longer will be identified with *populace* or *mob* but will lose its negative connotations. Thus, Herder is the founder of folklore in Germany. His criticism of the culture of the nobility, especially the French and their German imitators, together with the German reception of Rousseau's cultural criticism, laid the groundwork for a new concept of middle class and popular culture that was enthusiastically adopted by the Sturm und Drang movement and later by the Romantics, most of them without referring to its inventor.

In 1772, Herder received the highly competitive prize of the Prussian Academy of the Sciences for his *Abhandlung über den Ursprung der Sprache* (*Essay on the Origin of Language*). Despite the title, Herder does not search in this essay for a historical or an ontological origin but for a "genetic reason" for human language. He does not find it in the idea of language as a divine gift and does not agree with the hypotheses of Rousseau and Condillac about the "cry of nature." Herder finds the origin of human language in the human being as a social animal itself, in his or her *Besonnenheit* (reflection), which constitutes an ever-developing dialectics of language and thinking. Herder later received three more academy awards, two of the Prussian Academy (1775 and 1780) and one of the Bavarian Academy (1778).

One of Herder's most popular publications and a substantial contribution to the constitution of folklore are his two volumes of *Volkslieder* (1778–79; Folk Songs). Although most of this collection was taken from the old oral tradition of folk songs from a variety of countries, some of the lieder are poems written by contemporary poets such as Matthias Claudius and Johann Wolfgang von Goethe. The reason for Herder's selection was to show not only that popular culture is an affair of a distant (and anonymous) past but also that the source for popular culture is still alive, even in the philosophical Age of Enlightenment.

A literary critic and theorist of the highest quality, Herder was also a poet. Most of his poems did not survive his times, with one exception: his epic adaptation *Der Cid* (1802; *The Cid*).

In 1769, Herder had already made a vigorous attempt to escape his bourgeois environment in Riga and engaged in a sea journey to France. He wrote *Journal meiner Reise im Jahr 1769* (1846; *Journal of My Travels in the Year 1769*), which was a manifesto of an intellectual who wanted to leave behind all ossified tradition and dead erudition. Above all, that text is a comprehensive catalog of new fields of knowledge to explore, be it in, for example, the natural sciences, anthropology, geography, philosophy, or pedagogy.

One of these new fields of knowledge was the philosophy of history, a term that had been coined just some years before (1765) by Voltaire. Herder authored two philosophies of history. The earlier one was published anonymously: *Auch eine Philosophie der Geschichte zur Bildung der Menschheit* (1774; Yet Another Philosophy of History for the Education of Humanity). The later one is considered Herder's masterpiece, a four-volume monumental fragment titled *Ideen zur Philosophie der Geschichte der Menschheit* (1784–91; translated as *Outlines of a Philosophy of the History of Man* and *Reflections on the Philosophy of the History of Mankind*). Herder's basic question formulates the new project of the philosophy of history. He asks himself "whether, as everything in the world has its philosophy and science, there must not also be a philosophy and science of what concerns us most closely, of the history of humankind at large?"

The philosophical approach to history was supposed to discover an underlying order to the apparently contingent experience of history, and it had to be a philosophy of the history of humankind (as opposed to the history of a state or a dynasty). In the 1774 version, Herder approached this complex field more speculatively by applying analogously the development of the individual to the history of humankind. In the elaborated version of 1784–91, he based his reflections on a huge amount of historical, ethnological, geographical, and other data. He came to the conclusion that the history of humankind is the history of the development of humanity/humaneness (*Humanität*). According to Herder, each human action anywhere on Earth, be it disastrous or positive, helps develop and improve the faculties and disposition of all humans. Just like ignoring the natural laws, ignoring the laws of history would be lethal.

Herder's opus maximum remained a fragment, but he started another huge project in 1793 that can be considered a pragmatic sidepiece to his latter philosophy of history: ten collections of *Briefe zu Beförderung der Humanität* (1793–97; Letters for the Advancement of Humanity). In a fictitious one-sided correspondence, Herder creates a cosmopolitan republic of letters, inserting every now and then biographies of exemplary personalities (e.g., Benjamin Franklin, Martin Luther, and Joseph II). In these collections, Herder is gathering examples from all times and cultures that should prove that there is an "advancement of humanity," as was already supposed in his philosophy of history. Toward the end of his life, Herder edited and authored *Adrastea* (1802–3), a periodical with a programmatic title, as Adrastea is the other name for Nemesis. Nevertheless, the title does not indicate the old-Herder-turned-pessimist because, from Herder's point of view, Nemesis/Adrastea is not the ancient goddess of retribution but rather that of meting out truth and justice.

Herder's philosophical work is by no means limited to history. He equally made important contributions to the development of general aesthetics. In the tradition of the founder of aesthetics as a philosophical discipline, Alexander Gottlieb Baumgarten, Herder conceived aesthetics as a general theory of sensate perception and cognition. Thus, aesthetics occupied a crucial position in Herder's ideas about human culture and civilization. Early on, he developed a very differentiated philosophy of the senses and spent a good deal of his attention to the traditionally neglected senses, especially the haptic sense in his essay *Plastik* (1769–78; *Sculpture*). Furthermore, he developed a fundamental theory of the interrelationship between sensation and cognition. In his essay *Vom Erkennen und Empfinden der menschlichen Seele* (1774–78; On Cognition and Sensation of the Human Soul), Herder insists that there is no cognition without sensation, one of Herder's many polemic attacks against a current of one-eyed and dogmatic representatives of enlightenment.

Herder's ambivalent but mostly critical stance toward Kant's transcendental philosophy developed as early as Herder was a student of Kant in Königsberg (1762–64). The relationship became almost intolerable when Kant mercilessly criticized Herder's philosophy of history. Toward the end of his life, Herder waged war against Kant's transcendentalism in his *Metakritik* (1799; Metacritique) against Kant's *Critique of Pure Reason,* as well as in his *Kalligone* (1800) against Kant's *Critique of Judgment.* Only recent research has tried to make evident that Herder, as the "loser" in the course of the development of philosophy, was not necessarily wrong and, in turn, that the "winner," Kant, was not necessarily right.

Last, but not least, Johann Gottfried Herder was a Protestant theologian and a very successful preacher by profession. Large parts of his writings relate to this spectrum of his activities. He read the Bible, especially the Old Testament, within its original cultural and historical context and suggested that the Bible be read in a mythological and poetological perspective to discover the historical form of knowledge of these texts. He applied the same hermeneutical principles to the Bible as he did to any other literary text. His *Die Älteste Urkunde des Menschengeschlechts* (1774–76; Oldest Record of Humankind) as well as *Vom Geist der ebräischen Poesie* (1782; *The Spirit of Hebrew Poetry*) and others thoroughly document Herder's intention to show that the Bible is not some kind of immediate revelation of God's intentions but that it has a human linguistic and, moreover, poetic form.

As present discussions about Herder demonstrate clearly, he is not undisputed and there is still much to discover. This is true both because no edition yet covers his entire oeuvre and because of the way in which he developed a subtle anti-intellectualist but not antirationalist position.

Hans Adler

See also Weimar

Biography

Born in Mohrungen, East Prussia, 1744. Studied theology and philosophy at Königsberg University; teacher at the cathedral school, Riga, 1764; traveled to France, 1769, where he was a traveling tutor to the prince of Holstein-Eutin; met Goethe in Strasburg, 1770; court preacher to the court at Schaumburg-Lippe, Bückeburg, 1771; moderator in Weimar, 1776; in Italy, 1788; returned to Weimar, 1789. Married Caroline Flachsland, 1773. Died in Weimar, 1803.

Selected Works

Collections

Sämtliche Werke, edited by Bernhard Suphan et al., 33 vols., 1877–1913

Briefe: Gesamtausgabe 1763–1803, edited by Wilhelm Dobbek and Günter Arnold, 10 vols., 1977–96

Werke, edited by Wolfgang Pross, 2 vols., 1984–87

Werke in zehn Bänden, edited by Günter Arnold et al., 1985–

Selected Early Works 1764–1767: Addresses, Essays, and Drafts; "Fragments on Recent German Literature," edited by Ernest A. Menze and Karl Menges, translated by Ernest A. Menze and Michael Palma, 1992

Against Pure Reason: Writings on Religion, Language, and History, translated and edited by Marcia Bunge, 1993

On World History: Johann Gottfried Herder, an Anthology, edited by Hans Adler and Ernest A. Menze, translated by Ernest A. Menze and Michael Palma, 1997

Writings

Über die neuere deutsche Literatur, 1767; edited by Regine Otto, 1985; as *Fragments on Recent German Literature,* in *Selected Early Works 1764–1767,* translated by Ernst A. Menze and Michael Palma, 1992

Kritische Wälder, 3 vols., 1769; edited by Regine Otto, 2 vols., 1990

Abhandlung über den Ursprung der Sprache, 1772; as *Essay on the Origin of Language,* translated by John H. Moran and Alexander Gode, 1966

Auch eine Philosophie der Geschichte zur Bildung der Menschheit, 1774

Die Älteste Urkunde des Menschengeschlechts, 1774–76

Volkslieder, 1778–79

Vom Geist der ebräischen Poesie, 1782

Ideen zur Philosophie der Geschichte der Menschheit, 4 vols., 1784–91; edited by Heinz Stolpe, 2 vols., 1965; as *Outlines of a Philosophy of the History of Man,* translated by T.O. Churchill, 1800; 2nd edktin, 2 vols., 1803; as *Reflections on the Philosophy of the History of Mankind,* abridged by Frank E. Manuel, 1968; in *On World History: An Anthology,* translated by Ernest A. Menze and Michael Palma, 1997

Briefe zu Beförderung der Humanität, 1793–97; edited by Heinz Stolpe, Hans-Joachim Kruse, and Dietrich Simon, 2 vols., 1971

Eine Metakritik zur Kritik der reinen Vernunft, 1799

Journal meiner Reise im Jahr 1769, 1846; edited by Katharina Mommsen, Momme Mommsen, and Georg Wackerl, 1976; as *Journal of My Travels in the Year 1769,* translated by John Francis Harrison, 1953

Further Reading

Adler, Hans, *Die Prägnanz des Dunklen: Gnoseologie, Ästhetik, Geschichtsphilosophie bei Johann Gottfried Herder,* Hamburg: Meiner, 1990

———, "Johann Gottfried Herder's Concept of Humanity," in *Studies in Eighteenth-Century Culture,* edited by Carla H. Hay and Syndy M. Conger, vol. 23, East Lansing, Michigan: Colleagues Press, 1994

Bollacher, Martin, editor, *Johann Gottfried Herder: Geschichte und Kultur,* Würzburg: Königshausen und Neumann, 1994

Clark, Robert Thomas, *Herder: His Life and Thought,* Berkeley and Los Angeles: University of California Press, 1955; 2nd edition, 1969

Gaier, Ulrich, *Herders Sprachphilosophie und Erkenntniskritik,* Stuttgart and Bad Canstatt: Frommann-Hoolzboog, 1988

Haym, Rudolf, *Herder nach seinem Leben und seinen Werken,* 2 vols., Berlin: Gaertner, 1877–85; reprint, Berlin: Weidmann, 1880–85; reprint, Berlin: Aufbau, 1958

Herder Jahrbuch / Herder Yearbook, edited by Karl Menges, Wulf Koepke, Wilfried Malsch (1992); Wilfried Malsch, Wulf Koepke (1994); Wilfried Malsch, Hans Adler, Wulf Koepke (1996); Hans Adler, Wulf Koepke (1998), Columbia, South Carolina: Camden House, 1992 (vol. 1); Stuttgart and Weimar: Metzler, 1994–

Irmscher, Hans Dietrich, "Beobachtungen zur Funktion der Analogie im Denken Herders," *Deutsche Vierteljahrsschrift für Literaturwissenschaft und Geistesgeschichte* 55 (1981)

Koepke, Wulf, editor, *Johann Gottfried Herder: Language, History, and the Enlightenment,* Columbia, South Carolina: Camden House, 1990

——, editor, *Johann Gottfried Herder: Academic Disciplines and the Pursuit of Knowledge,* Columbia, South Carolina: Camden House, 1996

Koepke, Wulf, and Samson B. Knoll, editors, *Johann Gottfried Herder: Innovator through the Ages,* Modern German Studies, vol. 10, Bonn: Bouvier, 1982

Mueller-Vollmer, Kurt, editor, *Herder Today: Contributions from the International Herder Conference, Nov. 5–8, 1987, Stanford, California,* Berlin and New York: de Gruyter, 1990

Otto, Regine, editor, *Nationen und Kulturen: Zum 250. Geburtstag Johann Gottfried Herders,* Würzburg: Königshausen und Neumann, 1996

Pénisson, Pierre, *J.G. Herder: La raison dans les peuples,* Paris: Éditions du Cerf, 1992

Sauder, Gerhard, editor, *Johann Gottfried Herder: 1744–1803,* Studien zum achtzehnten Jahrhundert, vol. 9, Hamburg: Meiner, 1987

Shichiji, Yoshinori, editor, *Herder-Studien,* Tokyo: Herder-Gesellschaft Japan, 1995–

Ideen zur Philosophie der Geschichte der Menschheit 1784–1791

Essays by Johann Gottfried Herder

Reflections on the Philosophy of the History of Humankind is Johann Gottfried Herder's opus maximum, also known as his "Weimarian philosophy of history" (as opposed to his Bückeburg philosophy of history, *Auch eine Philosophie der Geschichte zur Bildung der Menschheit* [1774; Yet Another Philosophy of History for the Education of Mankind]). Despite its 800 to 900 pages (depending on the printing format), the *Reflections* remained a monumental fragment. Herder's efforts to accomplish his task were part of a new project that European philosophers had embarked on during the last third of the 18th century, a project for which Voltaire coined the term *philosophy of history* in 1765. From the point of view of the dominating philosophical paradigm, this new paradigm was a provocation because the term *philosophy of history* unites two levels of discourse that were strictly separated before that time. Either "history" was considered the multitude of contingent events that follow God's will and thus are ordered according to a principle (religious/theological) that eludes human rational comprehension—in which case the form of a "universal history" under God's regime was the appropriate form of representation—or "history" was nothing but a multitude of apparently unstructured events that could be arranged along a supposed time line (e.g., in the form of a chronicle). At that time, there was no discourse of history organized around an intrinsic principle of human history, that is, without reference to an almighty God or as more than a mere bookkeeping of so-called facts in time. From the perspective of the 18th-century philosophical theory of knowledge (epistemology), *historical knowledge* was the technical term for the lowest level of cognition, which was defined as "cognition of that which is or happens." On the other hand, "philosophy" was expected to explain things, not simply to record them. Thus, the project named "philosophy of history" consisted of a crucial effort of Enlightenment philosophers and historians to explain human history without using arguments that were out of the reach of human rational knowledge (e.g., miracles or truths of faith).

Herder's central question is "whether, as everything in the world has its philosophy and science, there must not also be a philosophy and science of what concerns us most closely, of the history of humankind at large." As a matter of fact, states Herder, "philosophy of history . . . is the true history of humankind" itself because without philosophical explanations, all events in their contingency constitute nothing but terrifying strange things and "rubble."

However, what Herder calls "philosophy" is not lofty speculation. He wants facts that demonstrate visibly that there *are* laws that govern human history. In the four volumes, consisting of 20 sections called "books," which in turn are divided into 115 chapters, the reader is overwhelmed by the sheer volume of information provided by Herder. However, remaining true to his original project, Herder again and again inserts lengthy passages of reflection on the factual knowledge to find an order in history and to formulate the laws that govern these allegedly contingent facts. The methodological approach that Herder applies in his *Reflections* (as he does often throughout his entire oeuvre) is a blend of induction and analogy, looking for laws that become evident when finding similarities between different facts and events and trying to understand history in terms of knowledge borrowed from the natural sciences.

The entire first volume of *Reflections* is devoted to determining the physical, mental, and emotional endowment and position of the human being and to infer a possible human future from that position and endowment. Earth is a planet in a "middle position," and the human being is, accordingly, a "middle being" (*ein Mittelwesen*). This means that human beings are equipped to live under mesocosmic conditions and that they adapt like other creatures to their environment because they are in large part identical with the elements of this environment—a clearly ecological statement at the beginning of an attempt to explain history.

The organic difference between animals and human beings lies in the latter's unique stature, which allows for upright posture. In turn, walking upright made possible the development of the arms as tools, of a previously unknown overview, and the right angle of the vertebral column in relation to the skull—the necessary condition for the development of the specific structure of the human brain and speech organs. Thus, Herder develops the fundament of his philosophy of history from an anthropological perspective, based on the principles of comparative anatomy (comparing apes and humans from a non-Darwinian point of view), and he is the first to do so. With this approach, Herder affirms his idea of principles being equally at work in the realms of nature *and* culture, that is, that human nature is based on natural laws. Everything that constitutes human culture, such as reason (*Vernunft*) and language, is considered not an original and complete endowment but a result of permanent development. "We are what we have become," is one of Herder's succinct formulations of this idea.

The second volume of *Reflections* starts with an extensive ethnological overview of the peoples living close to the North Pole; of those living in Central Asia, the Middle East, Africa, and the islands of the Pacific Ocean; and of the native Americans. While registering the variety of differences between the peoples, Herder soon comes back to his project of a history of humankind by showing what all human beings have in common as well as the reasons of and conditions for the differences between them.

Beginning with the last section of the second volume (book 10), Herder launches historical investigations in the narrower sense, speculating first about the origin of humankind as presented in old mythologies that he confronts with then-recent research results from different disciplines, such as biology, geology, geography, and others.

Volume 3 of *Reflections* presents overviews of the ancient history of Asia (book 11), the Near East (book 12), Greece (book 13), and the Roman Empire (book 14). The final section of this volume (book 15) is crucial for the whole project of *Reflections.* Here, Herder summarizes his findings and draws conclusions from them, thus reaching a higher level of philosophical reflection on history. The central assumption is that humanity/humaneness (*Humanität*) "is the purpose of human nature of our own species." According to Herder's understanding, neither reason nor humanity/humaneness are given from the outset of human history, so that they need to be simply "developed." It is in the cause of human history that those dispositions gain shape through experience. Just as the purpose of nature is to produce the maximum of variety of organisms, the purpose of history is to try out all possibilities of the human faculties, including the destructive ones. Herder is convinced that behind all events and developments in history and nature there is an all-encompassing blueprint that will eventually lead human history to a state of reason and equity (*Vernunft und Billigkeit*). With this idea, Herder presents himself as one of the majority of those philosophers who shared the optimism of the Enlightenment. This was not only a theoretical attitude, as can be seen from Herder's harsh rejection of any form of racism, slavery, and oppression as well as from his frequently uttered conviction that every individual has a right to his or her own life. Again and again, Herder applies this principle of the unalienable right of the individual to individual nations and epochs.

With the fourth volume of *Reflections,* Herder turns to the ancient history of the peoples of Europe beyond the Romans (book 16, the fourth chapter of which about "Slavic Peoples" made Herder especially famous in East European countries) and to the development of Christianity (book 17), Germanic peoples (book 18), and Catholicism and Arab culture (book 19). Herder ends his book (without closing the history) with reflections on Europe in the Middle Ages and on the fringe of the Renaissance (book 20). Thus, *Reflections* stops, from a historical vantage point, about 300 years before the author's present, and even Herder's outline for another volume does not go beyond the 16th century.

Herder's *Reflections* were received very critically by Kant, who read the book as an attack not only on his own ideas about anthropology and history but also on his philosophy as a whole. Goethe took great interest in the conception and writing of *Reflections,* especially because he shared with Herder a set of assumptions on the methodological level. *Reflections* has been translated and retranslated into many languages, and more recent research has emphasized the amazing modernity in this text, especially concerning Herder's methodology and his ideas about the right of the individual, the different cultures, and his bringing together of anthropology and world history.

HANS ADLER

Editions

First edition: *Ideen zur Philosophie der Geschichte der Menschheit,* 4 vols., Riga and Leipzig: Johann Friedrich Hartknoch, 1784–91

Critical edition: in *Sämtliche Werke*, edited by Bernhard Suphan et al., 33 vols. Berlin: Weidmann'sche Buchhandlung 1877–1913; annotated edition in *Werke in Einzelausgaben,* edited by Heinz Stolpe, 2 vols., Berlin and Weimar: Aufbau-Verlag, 1965; annotated edition in *Werke in zehn Bänden,* edited by Günter Arnold et al., vol. 6, Frankfurt: Deutscher Klassiker Verlag, 1989

Translations: *Outlines of a Philosophy of the History of Man,* translated by T.O. Churchill, London: [J. Johnson], 1800; 2nd edition, 2 vols., London: [J. Johnson], 1803; *Reflections on the Philosophy of the History of Mankind,* abridged and with an introduction by Frank E. Manuel, Chicago: University of Chicago Press, 1968; in *On World History: An Anthology,* translated by Ernest A. Menze and Michael Palma, edited by Hans Adler and Ernest A. Menze, Armonk, New York: M.E. Sharpe, 1997

Further Reading

Adler, Hans, *Die Prägnanz des Dunklen: Gnoseologie, Ästhetik, Geschichtsphilosophie bei Johann Gottfried Herder,* Hamburg: Meiner, 1990

———, "Ästhetische und anästhetische Wissenschaft: Kants Herder-Kritik als Dokument moderner Paradigmenkonkurrenz," *Deutsche Vierteljahrsschrift für Literaturwissenschaft und Geistesgeschichte* 68 (1994)

Breysig, Kurt, *Die Meister der entwickelnden Geschichtsforschung,* Breslau: Marcus, 1936

Grawe, Christian, *Herders Kulturanthropologie: Die Philosophie der Geschichte der Menschheit im Lichte der modernen Kulturanthropologie,* Bonn: Bouvier, 1967

Jørgensen, Sven-Aage, "Fortschritt und Glückseligkeit in Herders *Ideen,*" in *Herders Idee der Humanität: Grundkategorie menschlichen Denkens, Dichtens, und Seins: Materialien des internationalen Symposiums zum Thema "Johann Gottfried Herder—Leben und Wirkung,"* edited by Jan Watrak and Rolf Bräuer, Szczecin, 1995

Nisbet, Hugh B., "Herders anthropologische Anschauungen in den *Ideen zur Philosophie der Geschichte der Menschheit,*" in *Anthropologie und Literatur um 1800,* edited by Jürgen Barkhoff and Eda Sagarra, Munich: Iudicium, 1992

Hermeneutics

In its mythical origin, hermeneutics—from the Greek *hermeneuein:* to interpret, to translate in one's own idiom, or to make understandable—referred to a communicative activity. Hermes, the messenger of the Greek gods, transmitted and explained their warnings and prophecies to the mortals. This auxiliary function of deciphering expressions or signs in search for their correct or intended meaning also defined the role of textual interpretation in the referred tradition of theology, law, and philology. Whereas ancient hermeneutics was confined to following normative rules of interpretation to get access to the auctorial intention, modern hermeneutics participated in epistemological debates and challenged traditional methods for retrieving the "true" meaning of a word, sentence, and text. By establishing a methodological framework, hermeneutics eventually emerged as a theory: what was traditionally conceived as the art or technique of interpretation transformed into a methodology for the human sciences and into a general philosophy of understanding as well. Although it is advisable not to present the history of hermeneutics as a teleological process (as the historian of hermeneutics Wilhelm Dilthey had done), certain paradigmatic developments and transformations can be outlined by alluding to those prominent theologians, philologists, and philosophers whose concepts of understanding positioned hermeneutics as one of the most influential theories in German intellectual history.

In antiquity and in the Middle Ages, theological and literary critical hermeneutics developed several conflicting techniques of interpretation. Most of these techniques followed either the rules of the historical-grammatical method, which establishes what the words of a passage say (*sensus litteralis*), or those of the allegorical method, which attempts to find out what the passage means (*sensus spiritualis*). Although the Latin term *hermeneutica* did not emerge until the 17th century, some theoretical principles of modern biblical hermeneutics (*hermeneutica sacra*) were already formulated during the Reformation and its aftermath. Martin Luther, for example, questioned the interpretive authority of the ecclesiastical hierarchy by claiming that the Holy Scripture is intelligible and univocal and thus functions as its own interpreter ("sacra scriptura sui ipsius interpres"). Although Luther's primacy of the *sola scriptura* did not address the problem of the Bible's obscure passages, his follower Matthias Flacius insisted on the possibility of a universally valid interpretation that would clarify even those biblical passages in dispute. He not only emphasized the importance of grammatical knowledge of the Bible as a universal key for interpretation but also drafted what became later known as the "hermeneutic circle": to get access to the meaning of a passage, one must understand the dialectic relation between the whole of the text and its individual parts.

The first systematic exposition of Enlightenment hermeneutics written in German can be found in Johann Martin Chladenius's *Einleitung zur richtigen Auslegung vernünfftiger Reden und Schrifften* (1742; *Introduction to the Correct Interpretation of Reasonable Discourses and Books*). His theory of secular interpretation (*hermeneutica profana*) was based on a pedagogical impetus to provide students with techniques and strategies for decoding the meaning of those parts of speech or written work that are obscure and difficult to understand. By categorizing various kinds of obscurity and by assigning specific techniques for their correction, Chladenius was able to separate philological critique (editing, revising, and correcting ancient texts) and the application of grammatical knowledge from the new philosophical hermeneutics. Regarding the separate issue of interpretation, he emphasized that the art of interpretation (*Auslegekunst*) must reach beyond understanding the straightforward meaning of a passage to grasp its underlying concepts (*Begriffe*). Chladenius asserted that complete understanding is possible only if one knows the historical subject matter, the context, and the specific perspective of an utterance or text. By taking into consideration that writers/readers conceive things and ideas in different ways, Chladenius's theory of a viewpoint (*Sehe-Punckt*) prepared the way for the universal perspectivism of today's hermeneutics.

In the early 19th century, the many emerging concepts of rationalistic and Romantic hermeneutics were synthesized in Friedrich Schleiermacher's system of universal hermeneutics. The Protestant theologian has been credited with formulating the first general theory of interpretation, which was not limited to clarifying obscure passages or to revealing the already established meaning of a biblical or classical text as the former specialized hermeneutics had done. Instead, Schleiermacher extended the task of hermeneutics to every linguistic object (text, conversation, speech, etc.) as a potential object for interpretation when he premised that the fundamental operation of understanding—the cornerstone of his theory—must precede any possible experience of misunderstanding. In his view, hermeneutics was not supposed to end with the decoding of a given meaning but to become creative deconstruction through reversing the grammar and composition of speech or text. To really comprehend something said or written, the interpreter must transcend the subject matter by reproducing the author's original creative act, which includes reconstructing the author's viewpoint and his or her individual use of language. Schleiermacher developed two modes of interpretation and redefined the role of the hermeneutic circle in both of them. The "grammatical" interpretation is concerned with the objective linguistic material and with the relation of an individual speech/text to the totality of language, whereas the "technical" ("psychological") interpretation considers the given discourse as a manifestation of its author's individual thoughts in relation to the whole of his or her life. Schleiermacher emphasized this "divinatory" (guessing) character of the latter because he regarded the author's inner thoughts, hidden behind an utterance or text, as the real target of interpretation. Although his idealistic aim of hermeneutics suggested that the interpreter is able to understand an author better than he or she had understood him- or herself, he was also aware of the fact that every interpretation represents an asymptotic and infinite task, that is, always approaching but never reaching the totality of meaning.

Schleiermacher's substantial contributions to the theory of interpretation, his emphasis on the linguisticality of understanding, and his broad definition of hermeneutics as the art and science of understanding and interpretation had a significant effect on the dramatic transformation of hermeneutics into a metascience. It was mainly Dilthey who bridged the gap between 19th-century hermeneutics, which was still embedded in theology, philology, or history, and 20th-century hermeneutical philosophy and methodology. Dilthey has been criticized for overemphasizing Schleiermacher's speculative psychological subjectivism of interpretation by introducing the notion of *Einfühlung* (empathy with the producer of the text, projecting oneself into the soul of the other) into hermeneutics. However, he was able to universalize hermeneutics only because he neglected the linguistic method of grammatical interpretation in favor of his own concept of understanding as a "category of life" (*Lebenskategorie*). According to Dilthey, the understanding of human as cultural expressions is rooted in an *Erlebnis* (lived experience), the ultimate unit of consciousness that links the subject's inner world with external objects and with other subjects' spirits. In his view, living itself is interpreting because all understanding of cultural meaning is the translation of manifestations of life into the spiritual inwardness from which they emerged. This vitalist foundation of understanding enabled Dilthey to consider hermeneutics as the definitive methodology for the humanities (*Geisteswissenschaften*). Against the positivists' attempt to borrow their methods from the natural sciences, Dilthey claimed that both sciences differ not only in their objects of investigation but also in their modes of knowledge: understanding (*Verstehen*) of historic events and cultural objects in the human sciences versus explanation (*Erklären*) of causes and effects in the natural sciences.

Whereas Dilthey still retained a somewhat restricted definition of hermeneutics as a technique for the understanding of cultural memorials within the framework of the human sciences, Martin Heidegger broadened the horizon within which understanding belongs when he conceived hermeneutics as the ontological foundation of existential philosophy. In his seminal book *Sein und Zeit* (1927; *Being and Time*), Heidegger rejected the romantic notion of the author's/reader's sovereign subjectivity as well as Dilthey's idea of imaginative sympathy with another person's mind as a basis for understanding. Instead, he grounded his concept of hermeneutics in the individual's primordial self-understanding of "being-in-the-world." This preunderstanding precedes all understanding, which is no longer a methodological concept or an ideal of human experience but the original form of the realization of *Dasein* ("there-being," existence), its practical mode of being concerned with its own being. By expanding the realm of understanding to everyday life, the hermeneutical circle attains universal validity: when everything is embedded in a temporal world and in language, everything is involved in the circular structure of the process of understanding. In this way, Heidegger reversed the relationship between understanding and interpretation. Traditionally, the telos of interpretation was to facilitate understanding; now interpretation extends understanding and aids to make preunderstanding and self-understanding transparent. Following this model, the interpretation of literature is concerned less with the author's thoughts or intentions and more with the text itself as the representation of a specific worldview. Heidegger's definition of hermeneutics as the disclosure of the basic existential structures of human existence has had far-reaching consequences not only for academic philosophy but also for literary criticism and the social sciences. However, due to Heidegger's enigmatic style of writing and his involvement in National Socialism, his philosophical hermeneutics had to be reintroduced into the theoretical debate by his student, Hans-Georg Gadamer, to gain broader attention.

In his magnum opus, *Wahrheit und Methode* (1960; *Truth and Method*), Gadamer investigated the paradigmatic tension between the scientific concept of methodological objectivity and the hermeneutic understanding of truth, which is mediated through the experience of art, philosophy, and the historical tradition. His comprehensive inquiry into the history of hermeneutic concepts accentuated the historicality and linguisticality of understanding, which he considered to be universal and not simply a methodology for the human sciences. Because the individual is always already situated in language and tradition, every interpreter of the past or of cultural artifacts is guided by his or her particular *Vorurteile* (prejudices), which are not purely negative in nature but are formed by a historical set of values, cognitions, judgments, or cultural conditions. These prejudices are the quasi-transcendental prerequisite of all understanding insofar as they constitute the historical reality of the individual's being. Through interpretation, that is, through the self-critical confrontation of one's own prejudices with the otherness of the phenomenon (people, artifacts, and cultures), the interpreter's horizon is supposed to be transformed and ultimately united with the horizon of the phenomenon. This "fusion of horizons" (*Horizontverschmelzung*) is expedited through the individual's awareness of being part of effective history (*Wirkungsgeschichte*), the continuum that bridges the gap between present and past. Thus, understanding means that the historically effective consciousness is participating in the changing happenings of intersubjective tradition and in the continuation of an ongoing dialogue that precedes it. Following his linguistic principle of understanding, Gadamer projected an answer-question relationship between the interpreter and the *interpretandum,* that is, between the interpreter and his or her soul's inner striving. It is this dialogical structure of understanding and interpretation on which Gadamer established his hermeneutic critique of propositional logic: finding the truth of a proposition is possible only through continuously questioning its presuppositions.

Over the last 30 years, Gadamer's rejuvenation of universal hermeneutics has generated an intense international theoretical discussion. On the one hand, scholars such as Peter Szondi, Manfred Frank, and the founders of the Konstanz School of the aesthetics of reception, Wolfgang Iser and Hans Robert Jauss, have tried to use Gadamer's concepts to redirect hermeneutics to its traditional application in the humanities and especially in literary criticism; on the other hand, hermeneutics' claim to universality has aroused opposition. The jurist Emilio Betti criticized existential hermeneutics' departure from methodologism and from objectivity, whereas the sociologist Jürgen Habermas attacked Gadamer's overemphasis on tradition and called for an integration of psychoanalysis and the critique of ideology into a theory of critical hermeneutics. However, Habermas soon learned to work Gadamer's basic hermeneutic category of dialogical understanding into his own communicative theory of universal mutual agreement (*Verständigung*) as both scholars united in common front against deconstruction and postmodernism. The recent poststructuralist critique of hermeneutics has pointed out that the subject's attempt to understand texts or the Other is constantly subverted by his or her failure to master language, which has inscribed itself into the very structure of subjectivity because the subject itself is an effect of language. Furthermore, philosophers such as Jacques Derrida suggested that the metaphysical will to power is the striving force behind the dialogical model of understanding, which represses difference and dissidence in its attempt to reach consensus. Initiatives to diffuse the emotionally charged confrontation between French deconstruction and German hermeneutics (e.g., Manfred Frank's reintroduction of a nonmetaphysical subjectivity into poststructuralism or Paul Ricoeur's return to the letter in his structural hermeneutics) seem to have failed to cross the borders, although the critical hermeneutic concept of establishing a dialogical community could have advanced the notion of pluralism and difference favored by deconstruction.

STEPHAN K. SCHINDLER

See also Criticism; Wilhelm Dilthey; Hans Georg Gadamer; Friedrich Schleiermacher

Further Reading

Chladenius, Johann Martin, *Einleitung zur richtigen Auslegung vernünftiger Reden und Schriften,* Düsseldorf: Stern, 1969
Dilthey, Wilhelm, *Der Aufbau der geschichtlichen Welt in den Geisteswissenschaften,* Frankfurt: Suhrkamp, 1981; as *Introduction to the Human Sciences,* Detroit, Michigan: Wayne State University Press, 1988
Frank, Manfred, *Das individuelle Allgemeine: Textstrukturierung und -interpretation nach Schleiermacher,* Frankfurt: Suhrkamp, 1977
———, *Das Sagbare und das Unsagbare: Studien zur neuesten französischen Hermeneutik und Texttheorie,* Frankfurt: Suhrkamp, 1980
Gadamer, Hans-Georg, *Wahrheit und Methode,* Tübingen: Mohr, 1960; as *Truth and Method,* New York: Continuum, 1975
Grondin, Jean, *Einführung in die philosophische Hermeneutik,* Darmstadt: Wissenschaftliche Buchgesellschaft, 1991; as *Introduction to Philosophical Hermeneutics,* New Haven, Connecticut: Yale University Press, 1994
Habermas, Jürgen, *Zur Logik der Sozialwissenschaften,* 5th edition, Frankfurt: Suhrkamp, 1982; as *On the Logic of the Social Sciences,* Cambridge, Massachusetts: MIT Press, 1988
Heidegger, Martin, *Sein und Zeit,* Halle: Niemeyer, 1927; Tübingen: Niemeyer, 1980; as *Being and Time,* New York: Harper and Row, 1962
Iser, Wolfgang, *Der Akt des Lesens: Theorie ästhetischer Wirkung,* Munich: Fink, 1976; as *The Act of Reading: A Theory of Aesthetic Response,* Baltimore, Maryland: Johns Hopkins University Press, and London: Routledge, 1978
Jauss, Hans Robert, *Ästhetische Erfahrung und literarische Hermeneutik,* Munich: Fink, 1977; as *Aesthetic Experience and Literary Hermeneutics,* Minneapolis: University of Minnesota Press, 1982
Müller-Vollmer, Kurt, editor, *The Hermeneutics Reader,* New York: Continuum, 1985; Oxford: Blackwell, 1986
Ricoeur, Paul, *From Text to Action: Essays in Hermeneutics II,* Evanston, Illinois: Northwestern University Press, and London: Athlone, 1991
Schleiermacher, Friedrich, *Hermeneutics: The Handwritten Manuscripts,* Missoula, Montana: Scholars Press, 1977
———, *Hermeneutik und Kritik,* Frankfurt: Suhrkamp, 1977
Szondi, Peter, *Einführung in die literarische Hermeneutik,* Frankfurt: Suhrkamp, 1975; as *Introduction to Literary Hermeneutics,* Cambridge and New York: Cambridge University Press, 1995

Theodor Herzl 1860–1904

Although Theodor Herzl was during his lifetime a renowned feuilletonist, foreign correspondent, and editor, as well as a respected dramatist, his literary and journalistic achievements have been eclipsed in public memory by his role as the founder of the modern Zionist movement.

Historians now generally dismiss Herzl's claim to have undergone an almost spontaneous conversion to Zionism upon witnessing the Dreyfus trials while a foreign correspondent in Paris; they instead agree that his metamorphosis from assimilated Austrian Jew with German nationalist leanings (demonstrated by his membership in the German nationalist dueling student-fraternity *Albia*) to Zionist was a gradual process. Growing anti-Semitism, both in Vienna (exemplified in Georg Schönerer's anti-Semitic pan-German movement, and the election of Viennese Mayor Karl Lueger on an anti-Semitic platform) and abroad (exemplified not only by the Dreyfus trials, but also by ritual murder trials in Germany and Hungary, pogroms in Eastern Europe, and the widespread popularity of racially anti-Semitic literature such as Drumont's 1886 best-seller, *La France Juive*) led Herzl to consider other radical solutions to the "Jewish Question" (including the mass public baptism of Jews, the mass enlistment of Jews in the cause of socialism, and challenging leading anti-Semites to duels) before publishing his Zionist manifesto, *Der Judenstaat* (1896; *The Jewish State: An Attempt at a Modern Solution of the Jewish Question*).

In *The Jewish State,* Herzl concluded that the Jews were one people and that the "Jewish Question" was a national question that could be solved only by political means. According to Herzl, Jewish emancipation and the assimilationist strategy long favored by most Western and Central European Jews had failed, because the majority would not allow Jews to integrate fully. Jews could therefore achieve total equality only by founding an autonomous nation with its own national territory. Although the sentiments expressed in Herzl's pamphlet were not new (they had been advanced by a number of predecessors: Leon Pinsker, Moses Hess, Rabbi Zevi Hirsch Kalischer, and Nathan Birnbaum), Herzl is generally considered the founder of the modern Zionist movement. Unlike his predecessors, he succeeded (thanks certainly in part to his renown as journalist and dramatist) in uniting disparate factions of Zionists worldwide at the first World Zionist Congress in 1897, where the World Zionist Organization was founded. Herzl chaired the Congress and served as president of the WZO until his death.

Herzl embarked on his literary career at an early age. While still in Budapest he formed the school literary society Wir (1876); started an epistolary novel; and composed satires, essays, poems, and book and theater reviews, some of which were accepted by the respected newspaper *Pester Lloyd.* After studying law in Vienna and serving one year at the district courts of Vienna and Salzburg, Herzl, realizing that as a Jew his chances for advancement in Habsburg civil service were limited, devoted himself full-time to his literary and journalistic career. Herzl worked several years as freelance contributor to a number of newspapers and, in 1887, served as feuilleton editor of the

Wiener Allgemeine Zeitung. In 1891, he became the Paris foreign correspondent for the Vienna *Neue Freie Presse,* the most distinguished Austrian newspaper of the time. Afraid of being labeled a *Judenblatt* (Jew-paper) by anti-Semites and of alienating the majority of German-speaking Jews, who preferred assimilationism over Jewish nationalism, Herzl's superiors prohibited coverage of the Zionist movement in the paper. While Herzl remained at the *Neue Freie Presse* (primarily for financial reasons) until his death, he also founded in 1897 the Zionist weekly, *Die Welt,* which he programmatically dubbed a *Judenblatt,* seeking a positive revaluation of the anti-Semitic slur.

Parallel to his journalistic activities, Herzl pursued a career as dramatist, writing at least 19 dramas and one libretto. Several of these works were never staged, and few enjoyed much critical or commercial success. Literary scholars of recent years have been quick to dismiss the bulk of Herzl's plays as superficial social comedies with one-dimensional, underdeveloped characters; they also fault him for continuing in the tradition of the French society play when the German stage had moved on to realism and, later, naturalism. Nonetheless, five of Herzl's plays (*Die Wilddiebe* [1887; produced 1889; The Poachers], *Der Flüchtling* [1887; produced 1890; The Fugitive], *Die Dame in Schwarz* [produced 1891; The Lady in Black], *Tabarin* [1884; produced 1885], and *I Love You* [produced 1900]) were staged at the Vienna Burgtheater, considered the pinnacle of the German-language stage. The reception of these plays was mixed. *Die Dame in Schwarz* and *I Love You* were critical and popular flops, whereas *Die Wilddiebe,* a romantic comedy about three playboys in pursuit of beautiful women, was shown at the Burgtheater 57 times and appeared in over 50 German cities. Herzl's strongly autobiographical work *Das neue Ghetto* (1895; produced 1894; *The New Ghetto*), the literary precursor to *The Jewish State,* has received much more attention from scholars than any of Herzl's other dramas. In *The New Ghetto,* Herzl demonstrates that while legal emancipation had freed Jews from the old ghetto, it left them trapped in a "new ghetto," impeded both by growing anti-Semitism (supposedly inflamed by the increased public and economic presence of emancipated Jews) and by the Jewish self-hatred inherent in their assimilationist strategy; the play, however, stops short of offering the Zionist solution to the "Jewish Question." Despite help from Arthur Schnitzler, the play was not staged until 1898. Numerous theaters rejected *The New Ghetto* on the grounds that it was too controversial—they argued that Jews would be offended by Herzl's stereotypically negative portrayal of Jews and that anti-Semites would find the play too Jewish.

Herzl completed only two novels: *Die Brunner auf Hagenau* (1882), which appeared in installments in the *Neue Freie Presse* in 1900, and his best-known literary work, the utopian novel *Altneuland* (1902; *Old New Land*), which portrays Palestine of 1923 as a secular, multilingual Jewish state that is exemplary in its tolerance, scientific and technological advances, and "mutualistic" economic order. The novel was widely read and translated, but it was rejected by many Zionists, who objected to the novel's (Western) Eurocentric tenor and disregard for modern Hebrew. Literary scholars have also recently taken an aesthetic interest in Herzl's diaries, which he referred to as the "serial novel of my life."

While Herzl's place in the annals of the German literary canon may still not be secure, this founder of the Zionist movement achieved a stature in world history and popular memory matched by few of his literary contemporaries. Almost immediately after Herzl's untimely death, the Zionist movement fashioned Herzl into an infallible myth, portraying him as either the embodiment of the heroic Zionist new man or a tortured Messiah (see Berkowitz). Although Herzl did not witness the realization of his Zionist project in Israel, the state of Israel continues to honor his memory. One of the first official acts of the state of Israel was to reinter Herzl's remains on Mount Herzl in Jerusalem. The anniversary of Herzl's death was named a national memorial day in Israel. The city of Herzliyyah is named after Herzl, and Tel Aviv takes its name from the title of the Hebrew translation of *Altneuland.* In 1997, the centennial of the First Zionist Congress, Israeli and Swiss organizations held jointly a *Theodor Herzl Jubiläum* in Basel.

ELIZABETH LOENTZ

See also Zionism

Biography

Born in Bupdapest, 2 May 1860. Studied law in Vienna, 1878–84; received law degree, 1884; worked as legal clerk in Vienna and Salzburg, 1884–85; first publication in Vienna, 1894; plays produced at Burgtheater in Vienna, from 1894; Paris correspondent for *Neue Freie Presse,* including coverage of trial of Capt. Alfred Dreyfus, 1891–95; founded weekly Zionist newspaper, *Die Welt,* 1897; convened First World Zionist Congress in Basel, 1897. Died in Edlach, Austria, 3 January 1904.

Selected Works

Essays

Der Judenstaat, 1896; as *The Jewish State: An Attempt at a Modern Solution of the Jewish Question,* translated by Sylvie d'Avigdor, 1896; translated by Harry Zohn, 1970
Zionistische Schriften, 1905; as *Zionist Writings: Essays and Addresses,* translated by Harry Zohn, 1973–75
Philosophische Erzählungen, 1900
Feuilletons, 1904
Gesammelte Zionistische Werke, 5 vols., 1934–1935
Der Baseler Congress, 1897; as *The Congress Address,* translated by Nell Straus, 1917

Plays

Tabarin (produced 1885), 1884
Seine Hoheit (produced 1888), 1888
Der Flüchtling (produced 1890), 1887
Die Wilddiebe (produced 1889), 1887
Die Glosse: Lustspiel in einem Act, 1894
Das neue Ghetto (produced 1894), 1895; as *The New Ghetto,* translated by Heinz Norden, 1955
Unser Kätchen: Lustspiel in 4 Acten, 1898

Fiction

Altneuland, 1902; as *Old-New Land,* translated by Jacob de Haas, in *The Maccabaean,* 1902–3; translated by Lotta Levensohn, 1941; revised edition, 1960 (also published as *Old new Land,* edited by jacques Kornberg, 1987); translated by Paula Arnold, 1960

Other

Tagebücher, 1895–1904, 3 vols., 1922–23; as *Complete Diaries of Theodor Herzl,* translated by Harry Zohn, 1960

Further Reading

Bein, Alex, *Theodore Herzl: A Biography,* Philadelphia, Pennsylvania: Jewish Publication Society of America, 1940

Beller, Steven, *Herzl,* London: Halban, and New York: Grove Weidenfeld, 1991
Berkowitz, Michael, *Zionist Culture and West European Jewry before the First World War,* Cambridge and New York: Cambridge University Press, 1993
Brude-Firnau, Gisela, "The Author, Feuilletonist, and Renowned Foreign Correspondent Theodor Herzl Turns toward Zionism and Writes the Manifesto *The Jewish State*," in *Yale Companion to Jewish Writing and Thought in German Culture, 1096–1996*, edited by Sander L. Gilman and Jack Zipes, New Haven, Connecticut and London: Yale University Press, 1997
Bunzl, Matti, "The Poetics of Politics and the Politics of Poetics: Richard Beer-Hofmann and Theodor Herzl Reconsidered," *German Quarterly* 69, no. 3 (1996)
Dethloff, Klaus, editor, *Theodor Herzl, oder, der Moses des Fin de siècle,* Vienna: Böhlau, 1986
Elon, Amos, *Herzl,* New York: Holt, Rinehart and Winston, 1975
Kornberg, Jacques, *Theodor Herzl: From Assimilation to Zionism,* Bloomington: Indiana University Press, 1993
Leser, Norbert, *Theodor Herzl und das Wien des Fin de siècle,* Vienna: Böhlau, 1987
Leser, Norbert, and Edward Timms, editors, *Theodor Herzl and the Origins of Zionism,* Edinburgh: Edinburgh University Press, 1997
Robertson, Ritchie, "The Problem of 'Jewish Self-Hatred' in Herzl, Kraus, and Kafka," *Oxford German Studies* 16 (1985)
Schoeps, Julius H., *Theodor Herzl: Wegbereiter des politischen Zionismus,* Göttingen: Musterschmidt, 1975

Altneuland 1902

Novel by Theodor Herzl

Stymied in his efforts to persuade wealthy, influential European Jews to support the securing of a site where destitute, primarily Eastern European Jews could relocate, unable to come to an agreement with the Turkish sultan on a charter to establish Jewish colonies in Palestine (over which the Ottoman empire ruled), and disputing with oppositional forces within Zionism about the location and constitution of a Jewish state, the Zionist leader Theodor Herzl mapped out his vision of a new society for the Jewish people in his only novel, *Altneuland* (1902; *Old New Land*), in order to vent his frustrations and to win over new believers. Six years earlier, Herzl had expounded slightly different ideas in the pamphlet *Der Judenstaat* (1896; *The Jewish State: An Attempt at a Modern Solution of the Jewish Question*). Then, he had feared that ideas expressed in novel form would be dismissed as a fairy tale. Now, the erstwhile feuilletonist and dramatist resorted to a genre that he had previously rejected as an appropriate medium for positing political and social programs: the utopian novel that had become popular—among Jewish authors, as well—in the late 19th century. In *Old New Land,* plot and character development are subordinate to Herzl's Zionist ideals.

The first of five books in this novel depicts the Jewish milieu in Vienna that Herzl had criticized in his successful drama, *Das neue Ghetto* (produced 1894; *The New Ghetto*). There he maintained that prejudice and limited opportunities lay at the root of middle-class Jews' preoccupation with money and their desire to ape the manners and tastes of Gentile society. Mortally wounded in a duel defending Jewish honor, the hero cries out his desire to escape the ghetto, a ghetto bound not by walls, but rather by economic, social, and psychic constraints. *Old New Land* contains a theme prevalent in Jewish-German literature of the period: the generational conflict between fathers, who had worked arduously in trade and commerce to improve the lot of their offspring, and their university-educated, unemployed sons, "a kind of superior proletariat." Arthur Schnitzler would describe this generational difference far more artistically in the novel *Der Weg ins Freie* (1908; *The Road into the Open*). Through the eyes of Herzl's main protagonist, Friedrich Loewenberg, an unemployed young lawyer who has recently lost his two best friends, one to yellow fever while founding a Jewish labor camp in Brazil and the other to suicide, Herzl expresses loathing for Jewish parvenus who dismiss Zionism and the idea of Palestine as a homeland with superficial witticisms. When the young woman Friedrich has been courting becomes engaged to an unattractive, but decidedly more solvent, provincial merchant, Friedrich responds to an ad in the newspaper for "an educated, desperate young man" and agrees to accompany the cynical, misanthropic Mr. Kingscourt, né Koenigshoff—a German nobleman and former military officer who made his fortune in America—to spend the rest of his years on a South Sea island. Before his departure, Friedrich uses the money Kingscourt offers him to settle his accounts and to aid the Littwak family, impoverished Galician Jews. This upright family represents the need (*Judennot*) of the Eastern European Jews that Zionism would ameliorate. Herzl's contempt for the Viennese society of which he was a part has been characterized as "Jewish self-hatred," but Herzl believed prejudice had stunted Jews morally and psychologically, no matter how assimilated they perceived themselves to be.

En route to their island, Kingscourt and Friedrich stop at Jaffa. Recent critics note the discourse of colonialism that describes Palestine as a barren, swampy, and desolate land (to be filled) and that characterizes the population of its decaying, filthy towns as indolent, beggarly, and hopeless (to be cleansed). But Friedrich fails to respond to Kingscourt's suggestion that this land needs the Jews to bring it water and shade and does not register the promise of the already-existing settlements. When the pair returns to Palestine in 1923, David Littwak, now a prominent member of Old-New-Land, initiates a tour of the flourishing, prosperous Jewish colony. Founded by the New Society, Old-New-Land is a large cooperative association, not a state. It is managed by technocrats, rather than politicians, and governmental functions are kept to a minimum. As a secular society, Old-New-Land invites people from many nations and of all faiths to contribute to the enterprise—"a Mosaic mosaic," Kingscourt quips. The main square in Haifa is called "The Place of the Nations," and in Jerusalem the new "Palace of Peace"—there is no army—serves as counterpoint to the revered Jewish, Moslem, and Christian religious sites. Palestinians have benefited from the New Society's improvements of the land. Indeed, Reschid Bey, the Berlin-educated Moslem engineer, is grateful to the Jewish people for building up his country.

In this novel, Herzl expresses the 19th century's great optimism about the power and the beneficence of technology. Electricity—used for irrigation, cultivation, transportation, refrigeration, manufacturing, and communications—plays a major role in making the land habitable. At Passover the visitors hear the voice of Joe Levy, general director of the Department of Industry and master of American know-how, narrating on the phonograph how the 20th-century exodus was made possible by modern machinery and Jewish entrepreneurship—now viewed positively since it threatens no one. Large department stores have replaced small traders and peddlers, occupations on which many Jews in the Diaspora subsisted for lack of other opportunities. Stemming from a belief in meritocracy, public education is free, and pupils wear uniforms to prevent distinctions in wealth.

Even though the functions of the society are centrally planned, the economic system is not doctrinaire. The cooperatives provide "the mean between individualism and collectivism. The individual is not deprived of the stimulus and pleasures of private property, while . . . he is able, through union with his fellows, to resist capitalist domination." Herzl regarded his Zionist plan as an alternative to the socialism feared by so many bourgeois liberals of his age who distrusted the masses. Detractors of the novel regard its economic program as primitive and, insofar as Old-New-Land opens new markets for goods produced in Europe, consider the plan an imperialist system in the service of capitalism.

Although *Old New Land* was printed in many languages, it did not enjoy the resonance Herzl had desired. Instead, it further fueled the controversy among the Zionists he sought to address, prompting an attack by the cultural Zionist Ahad Ha-am (Asher Ginzberg), who believed the build-up of the New Society was too fantastic both in terms of technology and rapid settlement. Above all, Ahad Ha-am and his followers, including Martin Buber, Berthold Feiwel, and Chaim Weizmann, believed Zionism should address the spiritual crisis of Jewry and revive the national sentiment. Ahad Ha-am saw little that was distinctly Jewish in the New Society—an essentially correct observation that nevertheless overlooks certain Messianic discourse, references to some historic Jewish figures and literature, the Passover celebration (a stock scene in German texts treating Jewish life), and David Littwak's assertion that only the Jews could have created this New Society, since their moral sufferings were as much a necessary element as their commercial experience and cosmopolitanism. Nevertheless, Friedrich observes affirmatively, "the New Society can exist anywhere—in any country," and Professor Steineck is working on a cure for malaria so that a homeland may be opened up in Africa for "despised and hated" Negroes in the Diaspora.

When the novel was reissued in the early 1960s to commemorate the 100th anniversary of Herzl's birth, illustrations and annotations highlighted how many of Herzl's dreams had become reality—a decidedly pro-Israeli perspective. Of late the text has enjoyed close critical readings that point out the inherent tensions within the novel between Herzl's assimilationist predisposition and his separatist vision of a Zionist homeland for the Jews (Kornberg). Indeed, the two come together in the notion that Old-New-Land serves as a vent to take pressure off Europe by relieving it of the excess population. Analyses of the variety of discursive practices Herzl deployed in his argument point in particular to the competing spatial dimensions of the literary landscape (utopia) and concrete territories (geopolitics) and to the masculinist discourse of Prussian nationalism that Herzl brought to bear on the founding of the New Society (Stolow and Press).

While there are surprisingly few studies devoted solely to this novel, *Old New Land* is one of the core texts of Zionism. As such, it will continue to be a lightning rod of controversy as long as conflict at the site of Old-New-Land prevails.

IRENE STOCKSIEKER DI MAIO

Editions

First edition: *Altneuland: Roman,* Leipzig: Hermann Seemann Nachfolger, 1902

Critical editions: *Altneuland,* in *Gesammelte Zionistische Werke,* vol. 5, Berlin: Jüdischer Verlag, 1934; *Altneuland: Roman,* published under the auspices of the Herzl Centenary Committee Jerusalem, Haifa: Haifa Publishing Co., 1962

Translations: translated by Jacob de Haas, in *The Maccabaean,* 1902–3; *Old New Land,* edited by Jacques Kornberg, translated by Lotta Levensohn, New York: Markus Wiener, and the Herzl Press, 1987 (Levensohn's translation was originally published as *Old-New Land* by Bloch Publishing Company, New York, 1941, and revised with a new preface by Emanuel Neumann, 1960).

Further Reading

Bunzl, Matti, "The Poetics of Politics and the Politics of Poetics: Richard Beer-Hofmann and Theodor Herzl Reconsidered," *German Quarterly* 69, no. 3 (1996)

Gelber, Mark H., "Theodor Herzl, Martin Buber, Berthold Feiwel, and the Young-Jewish Viennese Poets," in *Turn-of-the-Century Vienna and Its Legacy: Essays in Honor of Donald G. Daviau,* edited by Jeffrey B. Berlin et al., Riverside, California: Ariadne Press, 1993

Halbrook, Stephen, "The Class Origins of Zionist Ideology," *Journal of Palestine Studies* 2, no. 1 (1972)

Kornberg, Jacques, *Theodor Herzl: From Assimilation to Zionism,* Bloomington: Indiana University Press, 1993

Laqueur, Walter, *A History of Zionism,* New York: Holt, Rinehart, and Winston, 1972

Press, Jacob, "Same-Sex Unions in Modern Europe: *Daniel Deronda, Altneuland,* and the Homoerotics of Jewish Nationalism," in *Novel Gazing: Queer Readings in Fiction,* edited by Eve Kosofsky Sedgwick, Durham, North Carolina: Duke University Press, 1997

Shimoni, Gideon, *The Zionist Ideology,* Hanover, New Hampshire: University Press of New England, 1995

Stolow, Jeremy, "Utopia and Geopolitics in Theodor Herzl's *Altneuland,*" *Utopian Studies* 8, no. 1 (1997)

Hermann Hesse 1877–1962

The family into which Hermann Hesse was born was one of devout Pietist faith, steeped in the ideal of unselfish service to others and antagonistic to any form of egoism or self-will. His parents were especially sensitive to issues concerning self-emancipation or going one's own way in defiance of Christian imperatives. Hesse's personal development was generated by conscious opposition. In the same way that, as a boy, he rebelled in opposition to the orthodox demands of parents and teachers, so later, in his years as a nascent writer, he was defining himself in opposition to the prevailing literary trends of his day. In 1895, German literature appeared in his judgment to be dominated by the naturalist drama and novel, both of which were contrary to his Romantic sensibility because of their preoccupation with the seamy and degenerate side of life. The novel of this period was characterized by psychological analysis and the dissection of various forms of decadence and mental aberration. Measuring the present state of literature against the works of the past, Hesse found himself to be "reactionary" in his literary ideals, thus setting the stage for his receptivity to Novalis, the Romantics, and an incipient neo-Romanticism. His aversion to drama, naturalism, and socialism was the outgrowth of his aversion to notions of the collective.

The experiences that went into Hesse's first prose work, *Eine Stunde hinter Mitternacht* (1899; An Hour beyond Midnight), were adventures of the mind rather than actual personal relations with the outside world. The work is a clear reflection of his association of art with religion, nourished by German Romanticism; his need to revere and venerate; and his readiness to genuflect before the exalted figures of his imagination. Woman in this work is not associated with the sexual. Her role is one of muse, awakening in man the religious and the aesthetic impulse. This is a quality that woman will retain throughout most of Hesse's works: that of a teacher who helps man to rediscover some quality in himself that has been lost or forgotten. It is in essence already a prefiguration of Carl Jung's concept of the anima. *Peter Camenzind* (1904) was a foray that depicted life in the big city after the sojourn in *Eine Stunde hinter Mitternacht* portrayed life on an island retreat remote from all reality. *Peter Camenzind* depicts a failed attempt of the would-be artist at social integration, and it draws on the Romantic conflict between life in the idyllic rural countryside and the questionable haute culture of the big city. Nature and individuality emerge as victorious, but at the expense of withdrawal and isolation.

It was in Jungian psychology that Hesse found an interpretive frame of reference into which he could fit his own past development. He informed *Demian* (1919) with constructs borrowed from Jung, but the story he was telling was his own. Here, the significance of the androgyny motif emerges for the first time. The polarity of the sexes is dissolved and replaced by the idea of the interdependence of the sexes. Sinclair's encounters with the shadow and the anima are confrontations with aspects of the self that have been projected on other persons. Only after the dark side of the self, the shadow, with its potential for evil and destructiveness, has been acknowledged and internalized can Emil Sinclair pass through the second stage in which he is guided by the anima who inspires him to artistic creativity and self-discovery. If *Demian* was the story of adolescent crisis, *Klein und Wagner* (1919), which foreshadowed *Der Steppenwolf* (1927; *Steppenwolf*), depicts a phase of crisis at midlife. It is the most explicitly psychoanalytical tale in all of Hesse's fiction. Its very structure and execution is informed and sustained by an analytic method that gradually reveals psychological conflicts and their origins. Klein discovers the murderer within himself; this narrative also exemplifies Hesse's use of the shadow motif. Teresina, with whom Klein has a brief but adventurous affair, is the embodiment of the negative anima in that she draws out his dark and pathological side.

Hesse's novels all have a strong didactic component, a heritage of the German bildungsroman (novel of education). The protagonist invariably learns that his concept of himself or his destiny is erroneous. In *Steppenwolf,* Harry Haller discovers that his conception of himself as part man and part wolf is the product of a self-indulgent and oversimplified persona. In the Magic Theater, the notion of a dual personality is replaced by the idea of a multiple personality with infinite groupings of components, which in turn is symbolized in the chess game. The motif of false destiny figures in *Narcissus und Goldmund* (1930; translated as *Death and the Lover* and *Narcissus and Goldmund*). Goldmund discovers that his true calling is not that of the monk, a representative of the father world of spirit, but that of the artist. The very process of artistic creativity is a synthesis of the father and mother worlds, of spirit and matter, of Logos and Eros. The androgyny principle is expanded here to embrace artistic creativity itself. Goldmund's development reflects Hesse's experience that the total integration of life's polarities was possible only in art; in life, by contrast, the realization of this goal could only be approximate, destined to remain imperfect.

In *Die Morgenlandfahrt* (1932; *The Journey to the East*), Hesse sought to effect a synthesis of individuality and collectivity, but this merger becomes aborted, since the development of the narrator, the musician H.H., culminates instead in the personal concern of overcoming despair and gaining integrity. The same synthesis was attempted in *Das Glasperlenspiel* (1943; translated as *Magister Ludi* and *The Glass Bead Game*), but the outcome was in essence the same: life in the collective, the rarefied realm of *Geist* (spirit) in Castalia, ultimately gives way to issues of individuation. Hesse's efforts to rid himself of or even subordinate egoism to the collective—a dictum he was admonished to follow by his father during his adolescent years—was bound to fail, for the lifeblood of his work was the autobiographical impulse. However much he may have wanted to transcend the level of psychological individuation to the ethical plane of social commitment, the impulse to concentrate interest on the self rather than the external social world and its problems proved to be stronger.

The peaks and valleys in the critical and popular reception of Hesse's works appear to correlate largely with external circumstances. His works have consistently appealed to youth during times of social crisis, most particularly in the immediate aftermath of World Wars I and II and, in the United States, during and after the Vietnam War. There are a number of themes and motifs in Hesse's works with which youth can identify: the questioning of parental, church, and state authority, and the quests for the definition and realization of the self and for authenticity in one's personal philosophy and lifestyle. While external events may trigger the enthusiasm among youth for Hesse, the motifs that appear to draw the young to his works are archetypal, which suggests that the primary factor in his popular success may be the character of universality in his writings. This is reflected in Hesse's worldwide readership. In the 1970s, Hesse was being read in all the major countries of Western and Eastern Europe and in the Middle and Far East. It should also not be overlooked that Hesse commanded the respect of such writers and luminaries as Rilke, Kafka, Freud, Jung, Martin Buber, T.S. Eliot, André Gide, Romain Roland, and Peter Weiss, among others.

Academic interest in Hesse prior to 1950 was minimal. During the early 1930s, he was attacked from both political extremes. The Nazis denounced him for his antinationalism and espousal of Jewish writers, while emigrants reproached him for continuing to publish in German periodicals. The award of the Nobel Prize in 1946 sparked some scholarly interest, which was appreciative but descriptive and low-key. In 1957, Hesse was denounced by Karlheinz Deschner in his *Kitsch, Convention, and Art,* which characterized him as a second- or even third-rate writer devoid of a single original thought, and which described his style as epigonic and mediocre in the extreme. Deschner's book was followed in 1958 by a cover story in *Der Spiegel* that depicted Hesse as a vegetable gardener who also happened to be a writer. The sharp descent of Hesse's popularity in Germany in the late 1950s coincided with a steady rise of appreciation of his work in the United States that culminated in the Hesse boom of the 1960s and 1970s. This spilled over in the 1970s into renewed enthusiasm for the author in Germany. In the 1970s, film adaptations of both *Siddhartha* (1922) and *Steppenwolf* were produced.

Since the early 1980s, critics have not appreciably enlarged our perspective on Hesse in terms of new insights, reevaluations, or interpretive methods. Perhaps the most significant development in recent criticism is the establishment of Jungian archetypal psychology as a legitimate approach for interpreting Hesse's works during the critical years of his career (1916–27), in which he wrote works such as *Demian, Steppenwolf,* and *Narcissus and Goldmund*. According to David Richards's observations of the scene in the mid-1990s, "a new wave may be forming, one that can be surfed via the Hesse news group on the Internet."

Don Nelson

Biography

Born in Calw, Württemberg, 2 July 1877. Volunteer editor of books and magazines for prisoners of war in Switzerland during World War I; apprentice in a clock factory, Calw, 1894–95; apprentice, 1895–98, and then assistant, 1898–99, Heckenhauer bookshop, Tübingen; worked for bookdealers in Basle, 1899–1903; freelance writer from 1903; co-editor of *März,* 1907–12; co-editor, *Vivos Voco,* 1919–21; editor of a publisher's book series, 1910s–1920s; regular writer for *Carona* and *Bonniers Litterära Magasin,* 1930s; in Gaienhofen, 1904–12, near Bern, Switzerland, 1912–19, and Montagnola, Switzerland, 1919–62. Bauernfeldpreis (Vienna), 1904; Fontane Prize (refused), 1919; Keller Prize, 1936; Nobel Prize for literature, 1946; Goethe Prize, 1946; Raabe Prize, 1950; German Book Trade Peace Prize, 1955; honorary doctorate, University of Bern, 1947. Died 9 August 1962.

Selected Works

Collections

Gesammelte Dichtungen, 6 vols., 1952; enlarged edition as *Gesammelte Schriften,* 7 vols., 1957
Werkausgabe, edited by Volker Michels, 12 vols., 1970; supplement, 2 vols., 1972
Gesammelte Briefe, edited by Ursula and Volker Michels, 4 vols., 1972–86

Fiction

Hinterlassene Schriften und Gedichte von Hermann Lauscher, 1901; revised edition as *Hermann Lauscher,* 1907
Peter Camenzind, 1904; translated by W.J. Strachan, 1961; also translated by Michael Roloff, 1969
Unterm Rad, 1906; as *The Prodigy,* translated by W.J. Strachan, 1957; as *Beneath the Wheel,* translated by Michael Roloff, 1968
Diesseits: Erzählungen, 1907; revised edition, 1930
Nachbarn: Erzählungen, 1908
Gertrud, 1910; as *Gertrude and I,* translated by Adèle Lewisohn, 1915; as *Gertrude,* translated by Hilda Rosner, 1955
Umwege: Erzählungen, 1912
Anton Schievelbeyns ohn-freywillige Reise nacher Ost-Indien, 1914
Der Hausierer, 1914
Rosshalde, 1914; translated by Ralph Manheim, 1970
Knulp: Drei Geschichten aus dem Leben Knulps, 1915; as *Knulp: Three Tales from the Life of Knulp,* translated by Ralph Manheim, 1971
Am Weg, 1915
Schön ist die Jugend: Zwei Erzählungen, 1916
Hans Dierlamms Lehrzeit, 1916
Alte Geschichten: Zwei Erzählungen, 1918
Zwei Märchen, 1918; revised edition, 1946; as *Strange News from Another Star and Other Tales,* translated by Denver Lindley, 1972
Demian: Geschichte einer Jugend, 1919; as *Demian,* translated by N.H. Priday, 1923; also translated by W.J. Strachan, 1958; also translated by Michael Roloff and Michael Lebeck, 1965
Im Pressel'schen Gartenhaus, 1920
Klingsors letzter Sommer: Erzählungen, 1920; as *Klingsor's Last Summer,* translated by Richard and Clara Winston, 1970
Siddhartha: Eine indische Dichtung, 1922; as *Siddhartha,* translated by Hilda Rosner, 1951
Psychologia balnearia; oder, Glossen eines Badener Kurgastes, 1924; as *Kurgast,* 1925
Die Verlogung: Erzählungen, 1924
Der Steppenwolf, 1927; as *Steppenwolf,* translated by Basil Creighton, 1929; revised edition by Joseph Mileck and Horst Frenz, 1963; revised translation by Walter Sorell, 1963
Narziss und Goldmund, 1930; as *Death and the Lover,* translated by Geoffrey Dunlop, 1932; as *Goldmund,* 1959; as *Narcissus and Goldmund,* translated by Ursule Molinaro, 1968; translated by Leila Vennewitz, 1993
Die Morgenlandfahrt, 1932; as *The Journey to the East,* translated by Hilda Rosner, 1956
Kleine Welt: Erzählungen, 1933
Fabulierbuch: Erzählungen, 1935
Das Glasperlenspiel, 1943; as *Magister Ludi,* translated by Mervyn Savill, 1949; as *The Glass Bead Game,* translated by Richard and Clara Winston, 1969
Der Pfirsichbaum und andere Erzählungen, 1945
Traumfährte: Neue Erzählungen und Märchen, 1945
Berthold: Ein Romanfragment, 1945
Glück (collection), 1952

Zwei jugendliche Erzählungen, 1956
Freunde: Erzählungen, 1957
Geheimnisse: Letzte Erzählungen, 1964
Erwin, 1965
Aus Kinderzeiten und andere Erzählungen, 1968
Stories of Five Decades, edited by Theodore Ziolkowski, translated by Ralph Manheim, 1972
Die Erzählungen, 2 vols., 1973
Six Novels, with Other Stories and Essays, 1980
Pictor's Metamorphoses and Other Fantasies, edited by Theodor Ziolowski, translated by Rika Lesser, 1982

Poetry
Romantische Lieder, 1899
Gedichte, 1902
Unterwegs, 1911
Musik des Einsamen: Neue Gedichte, 1915
Ausgewählte Gedichte, 1921
Krisis: Ein Stück Tagebuch, 1928; as *Crisis: Pages from a Diary*, translated by Ralph Manheim, 1975
Trost der Nacht: Neue Gedichte, 1929
Vom Baum des Lebens: Ausgewählte Gedichte, 1934
Das Haus der Träume, 1936
Stunden im Garten: Eine Idylle, 1936
Neue Gedichte, 1937
Die Gedichte, 1942
Der Blütenzweig: Eine Auswahl aus den Gedichten, 1945
Bericht an die Freunde: Letzte Gedichte, 1960
Die späten Gedichte, 1963
Poems, translated by James Wright, 1970
Hours in the Garden and Other Poems, translated by Rika Lesser, 1979

Other
Eine Stunde hinter Mitternacht, 1899
Boccaccio, 1904
Franz von Assisi, 1904
Aus Indien: Aufzeichnungen von einer indische Reise, 1913
Zum Sieg, 1915
Brief ins Feld, 1916
Zarathustras Wiederkehr: Ein Wort an die deutsch Jugend, 1919
Kleiner Garten: Erlebnisse und Dichtungen, 1919
Wanderung: Aufzeichnungen, 1920; as *Wandering: Notes and Sketches*, translated by James Wright, 1972
Blick ins Chaos: Drei Aufsätze, 1920; as *In Sight of Chaos*, translated by Stephen Hudson, 1923
Elf Aquarelle aus dem Tessin, 1921
Sinclairs Notizbuch, 1923
Erinnerung an Lektüre, 1925
Bilderbuch: Schilderungen, 1926
Der schwere Weg, 1927
Die Nürnberger Reise, 1927
Betrachtungen, 1928
Eine Bibliothek der Weltliteratur, 1929; revised edition, 1946
Zum Gedächtnis unseres Vaters, with Adele Hesse, 1930
Gedenkblätter, 1937
Aus der Kindheit der heiligen Franz von Assisi, 1938
Der Novalis: Aus den Papieren eines Altmodischen, 1940
Kleine Betrachtungen: Sechs Aufsätze, 1941
Dank an Goethe, 1946
Der Europäer, 1946
Krieg und Frieden: Betrachtungen zu Krieg und Politik seit dem Jahr 1914, 1946; revised edition, 1949; as *If the War Goes On . . . : Reflections on War and Politics*, translated by Ralph Manheim, 1971
Stufen der Menschwerdung, 1947
Frühe Prosa, 1948
Berg und See: Zwei Landschaftsstudien, 1948
Gerbersau, 2 vols., 1949
Aus vielen Jahren, 1949
Späte Prosa, 1951
Briefe, 1951; revised editions, 1959, 1964
Eine Handvoll Briefe, 1951
Über das Alter, 1954
Briefe, with Romain Rolland, 1954
Aquarelle aus dem Tessin, 1955
Beschwörungen: Späte Prosa, neue Folge, 1955
Abendwolken: Zwei Aufsätze, 1956
Aus einem Tagebuch des Jahres 1920, 1960
Aerzte: Ein paar Erinnerungen, 1963
Prosa aus dem Nachlass, edited by Ninon Hesse, 1965
Neue deutscher Bücher, 1965
Kindheit und Jugend vor Neunzehnhundert, edited by Ninon Hesse, 1966
Briefwechsel, with Thomas Mann, edited by Anni Carlsson, 1968; revised edition, 1975; edited by Hans Wysling, 1984; as *The Hesse/Mann Letters: The Correspondence of Herman Hesse and Thomas Mann, 1910–1955*, translated by Ralph Manheim, 1975
Briefwechsel 1945–1959, with Peter Suhrkamp, edited by Siegfried Unseld, 1969
Politische Betrachtungen, 1970
Eine Literaturgeschichte in Rezensionen und Aufsätzen, edited by Volker Michels, 1970
Beschreibung einer Landschaft, 1971
Lektüre für Minuten, edited by Volker Michels, 1971; as *Reflections*, translated by Ralph Manheim, 1974
Mein Glaube, edited by Siegfried Unseld, 1971; as *My Belief: Essays on Life and Art*, edited by Theodore Ziolkowski, translated by Denver Lindley and Ralph Manheim, 1974
Zwei Autorenporträts in Briefen 1897 bis 1900: Hesse—Helene Voigt-Diederichs, 1971
Eigensinn: Autobiographische Schriften, edited by Siegfried Unseld, 1972; as *Autobiographical Writings*, edited by Theodore Ziolkowski, translated by Denver Lindley, 1972
Briefwechsel aus der Nähe, with Karl Kerenyi, edited by Magda Kerenyi, 1972
Die Kunst des Müssiggangs: Kurze Prosa aus dem Nachlass, edited by Volker Michels, 1973
Hermann Hesse, R.J. Humm: Briefwechsel, edited by Ursula and Volker Michels, 1977
Politik des Gewissens: die politische Schriften 1914–1932, edited by Volker Michels, 2 vols., 1977
Die Welt im Buch, edited by Volker Michels, 1977
Briefwechsel mit Heinrich Wiegand, 1924–1934, edited by Klaus Pezold, 1978
Hermann Hesse/Hans Sturzenegger: Briefwechsel, edited by Kurt Bächtold, 1984
Bodensee: Betrachungen, Erzählungen, Gedichte, edited by Volker Michels, 1986
Soul of the Age: The Selected Letters, 1891–1962, edited by Theodore Ziolkowski, 1991

Edited Works
Der Lindenbaum, deutsche Volkslieder, edited with others, 1910
Der Zauberbrunnen: Die Lieder der deutschen Romantik, 1913
Matthias Claudias, *Der Wandsbecker Bote*, 1916
Alemannenbuch, 1919
Ein Schwabenbuch für die deutschen Kriegsgefangenen, edited with Walter Stich, 1919
Xaver Schnyder von Wartensee, *Ein Luzerner Junker vor hundert Jahren*, 1920
Solomon Gessner, *Dichtungen*, 1922
Mordprozesse, 1922

Novellino: Novellen und Schwänke der ältesten italienischen Erzähler, 1922
Novalis: Dokumente seines Lebens und Sterbens, edited with Karl Isenberg, 1925
Hölderlin: Dokumente seines Lebens, edited with Karl Isenburg, 1925
Geschichten aus dem Mittelalter, 1925
Ziya' al-Din Nakhshabi, *Sesam: Orientalische Erzählungen,* 1925

Further Reading

Marrer-Tising, Carlee, *The Reception of Hermann Hesse by the Youth in the United States,* Bern and Las Vegas, Nevada: Lang, 1982
Mileck, Joseph, *Hermann Hesse and His Critics,* Chapel Hill: University of North Carolina Press, 1958
———, *Hermann Hesse: Life and Art,* Berkeley: University of California Press, 1978
Pfeifer, Martin, editor, *Hermann Hesses weltweite Wirkung,* 3 vols., Frankfurt: Suhrkamp, 1991
Richards, David G., *The Hero's Quest for the Self: An Archetypal Approach to Hesse's "Demian" and Other Novels,* Lanham, Maryland: University Press of America, 1987
Ziolkowski, Theodore, *The Novels of Hermann Hesse: A Study in Theme and Structure,* Princeton, New Jersey: Princeton University Press, 1965
Ziolkowski, Theodore, editor, *Hesse: A Collection of Critical Essays,* Englewood Cliffs, New Jersey: Prentice Hall, 1973

Der Steppenwolf 1927

Novel by Hermann Hesse

Hermann Hesse's Steppenwolf image is the symbolic expression of a negative form of the self that surfaces after a long period of suppression and that expresses itself in various forms of hostility and destructive urges. *Der Steppenwolf* (*Steppenwolf*), however, is not just personal pathology; it is also social criticism. Harry Haller's existential crisis is not something separate from the tumultuous times in which he lives, and this aspect of the work was immediately noticed in the novel's earliest critical reviews. The wolf in Haller has its analogue in the murders and assassinations in the new Weimar Republic of the early 1920s, a decade pregnant with coming disaster, as Germany marched relentlessly toward fascism. Hesse was convinced that Germany was running its course out of fateful necessity, a course that could not be checked by any amount of resistance. The 1920s, in his estimation, were without any moral or spiritual base from which one could check the process of disintegration. He saw technology and the irrational politics of the Right Wing poisoning the atmosphere and setting Germany on its suicidal course. He continued to see Oswald Spengler's *Decline of the West* (1918) as the only meaningful intellectual work of the day. And in 1924, shortly before publication of *Steppenwolf,* Thomas Mann had published his novel *The Magic Mountain,* in which the diseased clientele of a remote Swiss sanitarium became a metaphor for a diseased German nation, if not the entire European international community.

Haller's dual personality of wolf and man—a combination of an antisocial animal and a man who cherishes the domestic comforts of an orderly bourgeois existence—is a reflection of the polarity of destructiveness and creativeness that Hesse sought to integrate within himself. These opposing tendencies existed, however, not only within the self but in the external world as well, in the opposition between the Weimar government's voice of reason and moderation and the violence and assassination unleashed by the ill-fated regime's opponents.

The prose novel *Steppenwolf* was preceded by the composition of the *Crisis* poems (1928). Hesse referred to them as a kind of "lyrical diary"—recorded experiences that were later to be incorporated into *Steppenwolf.* Because of their greater immediacy of expression and undisguised autobiographical character, the poems served a cathartic function for Hesse. The *Crisis* poems did not, however, satisfy his own standards for a work of art; he attributed little or no aesthetic value to them. In a response to criticism of the poems, he wrote in a letter of 14 October 1926 to Heinrich Wiegard,

> What I have been writing is not imaginative literature, but confession. I am like a man who is drowning or has just discovered that he has been poisoned and who is therefore not concerned with his hair-style or with the modulation of his voice, but simply cries out in distress.

Both Hesse and his biographer, Hugo Ball, anticipated a negative response to the novel, especially from more chauvinistic readers, because of its strident antiwar and antinationalist notes. The reception turned out to be much more positive and laudatory than expected, but Hesse was disappointed about the lack of appreciation for its careful craftsmanship.

The internal structure of the work is divided into three main sections: the preliminary material, the action, and the magic theater. The preliminary material, in turn, is further subdivided into the introduction, Haller's narrative, and the Treatise. The actual plot makes up the second section. The three sections of the introduction serve to illuminate Haller's character from three different perspectives. The first perspective is that of an editor who represents the strait-laced yet curious bourgeois mentality; this is followed by Haller's own view of himself, which is shown in the following Treatise to be a drastic misconception. The Treatise thus functions both as a corrective and a prefiguration of Haller's destiny, which suggests what he must experience to achieve self-realization; namely, encountering his true self. This foreshadows Haller's experiences in the Magic Theater, the final section of the book.

A major hermeneutic problem for interpreters of *Steppenwolf* is the question about the distinction between the "real" and the symbolic—with respect to both the figures in the novel and the action. The concept of "double perspective" or "double perception" has been introduced to resolve the problematic question of the interplay or simultaneity of the real and the imagined. According to Theodore Ziolkowski, "By means of double perception almost any given action of the book may be interpreted on two distinct levels. . . . This produces the effect of simultaneity or concomitance of the two planes or melodic lines." From the time Haller reads the Treatise, Ziolkowski argues, it becomes "necessary throughout the remainder of the book to make a sharp distinction between two levels of reality: the everyday plane of the *Bürger* or the placard-bearer, and the exalted, supernal plane of the Immortals and the magic theater."

David Richards suggests an alternative approach, which is "based on Jungian psychology and Hesse's claim that all his figures are parts of himself." According to this view, the figures in the novel are largely projections from Haller's unconscious, parts of himself with which he must engage in dialogue. Perhaps the most important and also problematic character in the novel is Hermine. Her name is the feminine counterpart to the author's name, just as Harry Haller bears his initials. On the level of ordinary reality she is a prostitute, but in the protracted dialogues, she talks in a style that is hardly to be differentiated from that of the intellectual Haller. In fact, Haller notes that "all of these, it seemed to me, were perhaps not her own thoughts, but mine, which the clairvoyant girl had read and breathed in and which she was now restoring to me so that they had form and stood before me as though new."

Ralph Freedman considers the figures and scenes in the novel to have both an objective reality and a symbolic character. He notes that the encounter with the self is often equivalent to the self-reflection that is manifest in the many examples of mirroring in the work. For Freedman, the symbolic mirror becomes "the center around which the novel is built."

For critics of Jungian persuasion, the double-perspective approach is most vulnerable in its assumption that an external reality or "real world" actually exists outside the fictional one. According to Richards, "it would be more accurate to speak of different levels of internal reality and to see Haller as a mask or "persona" of the author and part of his symbolic world, just as Hermine, Maria, Pablo, and Mozart are." Such a view is also in accord with fundamental aspects of the literary art of Expressionism. In this view, the characters in *Steppenwolf* are projections of Haller's cast of characters within his unconscious. They are functional rather than independently operating persons with objective realities and individual personalities. They are externalizations of Haller's inner voices and fantasies, rendered visible in order that he may dialogue with them. Seen within a Jungian framework, however, Hermine is the anima, the functional agent who furthers Haller's development, while the persona—Haller's construction of an artificial, dual personality of wolf and man—constitutes the initial obstacle to individuation. Hermine's influence is salutary in that it works against Haller's identification of the ego with the persona. She "seduces" Haller away from thoughts of suicide by teaching him the art and joy of living through dancing as a medium.

The critical reception of *Steppenwolf* exhibits an interesting history. The earliest criticism praised the novel for the honesty and forthrightness of the author's confessions, although some, mostly close friends of the author, were embarrassed, believing that he had carried the element of confession and eroticism too far. In the late 1950s, Mileck did not include *Steppenwolf* among the three Hesse novels that he predicted would achieve lasting fame, an assessment that he reversed 20 years later. By the early 1980s, the novel was considered by U.S. critics to be the author's main work in terms of its artistry and immediacy. Criticism in the mid-1960s United States countered the predominantly biographical approach of earlier German criticism by focusing more on Hesse's craftsmanship: the novel's analogies that use the musical form of the sonata, its juxtaposition of the real and the imaginary, and its relation to a new form of the romantic fairy tale, associated with E.T.A. Hoffmann, in which a fantasy is situated in a specific time and place. Egon Schwarz notes parallels to Goethe's Faust: in both works, an aging man disillusioned with learning and disgusted with life is at the point of committing suicide; both figures are saved from death by entering into questionable "pacts" and are led into a new life by a young woman.

A film version of *Steppenwolf,* with Max von Sydow in the role of Haller, was produced in the 1970s and enjoyed a modicum of success. The name "Steppenwolf" found its way into U.S. popular culture in a variety of forms, including a bookshop "Steppenwolf" in Aspen, a "Steppenwolf" bar in Berkeley, the rock quintet "Steppenwolf," and the Chicago theater troupe of that name.

Don Nelson

Editions

First edition: *Der Steppenwolf,* Berlin, Fischer, 1927

Translation: *Steppenwolf,* translated by Basil Creighton and revised by Joseph Mileck and Horst Frenz, New York: Bantam, 1963

Further Reading

Freedman, Ralph, *The Lyrical Novel: Studies in Hermann Hesse, Andre Gide, and Virginia Woolf,* Princeton, New Jersey: Princeton University Press, 1963

Michels, Ursula, and Volker Michels, editors, *Gesammelte Briefe,* vol. 2, Frankfurt: Suhrkamp, 1979

Richards, David G., *Exploring the Divided Self: Hermann Hesse's Steppenwolf and Its Critics,* Columbia, South Carolina: Camden House, 1996

Schwarz, Egon, "Zur Erklärung von Hesses 'Steppenwolf'," *Monatshefte* 53 (1968)

Stefan Heym 1913–

Stefan Heym's fiction has been consistently motivated by ideological and social factors, a fact that has led to a politically oriented reception throughout his long career. Beginning as a poet and journalist in Berlin of the early 1930s, Heym fled Germany shortly after the Reichstag fire (1933), survived as a journalist in Prague for two years, and then won a scholarship to the University of Chicago. Changing to English as one of his languages of composition, he continued to write poems and newspaper articles, becoming chief editor in 1937 of a small German paper for exiles in New York. Failing to find success as a dramatist, he launched into fiction with a novel on Nazi-occupied Prague, a thriller detective story with a clear interest in psychology and an obvious political message (*Hostages,* 1942). Thereafter, until the early 1970s, English was his first language of literary composition and fiction his preferred medium. He has translated a number of his works from and into German and has proved one of the most successful self-translators of our age.

Heym's fiction is almost exclusively in the realist tradition and owes much to his wide-ranging experience as an investigative and reflective journalist. He has a good eye for detail and the gripping plot and can develop his themes through a telling use of confrontation and dialogue. His preferred subject is the struggling, often idealist intellectual, who is used as a focus for broad questions on the nature of truth, power, and the forces in history. He regularly portrays the reaction of individuals in crisis and in revolution, the temptations to compromise, and the risks associated with idealism. Partly to overcome problems getting published in the German Democratic Republic (GDR), Heym turns to historical material in a number of works, all of which reveal detailed knowledge of a wide range of primary and secondary sources and some of which include historical documents. The perspective is always socialist.

Heym's most successful novel was that based on his experiences as a U.S. soldier in World War II; his ironically entitled *The Crusaders* (1948) traces the U.S. advance in Europe until the establishment of a semicorrupt postwar society. In addition to portraying much American bravery and castigating immoral Nazi behavior, the author probes numerous American weaknesses: materialism, selfishness, and lack of certainty over war aims. Idealists are seen in a minority that is constantly threatened. The critical reception of the novel was largely enthusiastic, but the positive evaluation of the Soviet forces at the end of the novel led to distinct unease in some reviews. However, Heym's following novel, *The Eyes of Reason* (1951), provoked an angry reception as a result of its positive evaluation of the Communists' rise to power in Prague in 1948 and its argument that certain minor freedoms need to be restricted to ensure the preservation of greater ones. The attack on capitalism was more severe in *Goldsborough* (1953), which focused on the U.S. miners' strike of 1949–50. Fearful of McCarthy persecution, by this point Heym had settled in the GDR, where he was soon to prove equally controversial as a result of his outspoken criticism of bureaucratic incompetence and, later, party oppression.

Heym has always reached a mass audience through his ability to combine drama and tension with serious questioning of issues relevant to our own age. His works have also carried force through his ability to incorporate much historical detail, and in this respect his novels are thoroughly researched investigations; his scholarship has covered such widely differing events as the pillorying of Daniel Defoe and the Baden revolution of 1849. He has also shown a particular interest in treating the lives of problematic socialist figures, such as Ferdinand Lassalle and Karl Radek, as well as taboo moments of socialist history, such as the short-lived German socialist republic of Schwarzenberg (1945) and the workers' uprising in East Berlin (1953). Personal experience has regularly informed his works, and dramatic moments of his career are as striking in his early panoramic treatment of war in *The Crusaders* as they are in his late study of Stalinist elements in the GDR (*Collin*, 1979), all of which are treated fully in his remarkably successful autobiography *Nachruf* (1988; Obituary).

The two works to draw the most critical attention are both biblical in inspiration but are centrally concerned with problems of modern socialism, a point often reinforced by their linguistic echoes. *Der König-David-Bericht* (1972; *The King David Report*) subtly exposes the contradictions of the books of Samuel and the books of Kings as the author reinterprets biblical evidence to suggest the relevance of ancient power politics for several societies beyond that of ancient Israel. Parody of biblical style enriches the humor of this troubling and often moving investigation of primitive totalitarianism. In *Ahasver* (1981; *The Wandering Jew*), Heym treats the legend of the Wandering Jew, exploring anti-Semitism, questions of religious and secular order, and forms of idealistic dissent. Ahasver is seen as a fallen angel in revolt against God and his failure to intervene decisively in the development of the world. The author uses the legend of Ahasver to interpret features of modern and medieval society, religious history, and the creation and end of the world (a warning against atomic warfare). Satire of institutionalized bigotry and ruthless adherence to dogma are paralleled with contemporary events in the GDR.

Throughout his career, Heym has revealed considerable courage in his preparedness to stand against what he felt to be unacceptable in a succession of different societies (National Socialism, U.S. imperialism, Stalinism, dogmatism), a stand that provided considerable material for his fiction, short stories, and journalism. He has been a consistent advocate of democratic socialism, and he played an important role as dissenter in the GDR; the reception of his works in both the East and the West was determined partly by this status. His vigorous journalistic activities and fearless remarks on the reform of socialism led to his being hailed as one of several literary heroes of the bloodless GDR revolution of 1989.

PETER HUTCHINSON

Biography

Born in Chemnitz, 10 April 1913. Studied at the University of Berlin; M.A. from the University of Chicago, 1935; editor, *Deutsches Volksecho*, New York, 1937–39; salesman, New Union Press, 1939; became a United States citizen, 1943; service in the U.S. Army, 1943–48; expelled from GDR Writers' Union, 1977; fined for publishing outside the GDR without government permission, 1979. Heinrich Mann Prize, 1953; GDR National Prize; Jerusalem Prize, 1993. Honorary doctorates from the University of Berne, 1990, and the University of Cambridge, 1991; elected member of the Bundestag, 1994 (resigned 1995). Currently lives in Berlin-Grünau.

Selected Works

Fiction

Hostages, 1942; as *The Glasenapp Case*, 1962; as *Der Fall Glasenapp*, 1958
Of Smiling Peace, 1944
The Crusaders, 1948; as *Kreuzfahrer von heute*, 1950; as *Der bittere Lorbeer*, 1950
The Eyes of Reason, 1951; as *Die Augen der Vernunft*, 1955
Goldsborough (in English), 1953; translated into German, 1954
Die Kannibalen und andere Erzählungen, 1953; as *The Cannibals and Other Stories*, 1958
Schatten und Licht: Geschichten aus einem geteilten Lande, 1960; as *Shadows and Lights: Eight Short Stories*, 1963
Die Papiere des Andreas Lenz, 1963; as *Lenz; oder, Die Freiheit*, 1965; as *The Lenz Papers*, 1964
Lassalle, 1969; as *Uncertain Friend*, 1969
Die Schmähschrift; oder, Die Königin gegen Defoe, 1970; as *The Queen against Defoe and Other Stories*, 1974
Der König-David-Bericht, 1972; as *The King David Report*, 1973
5 Tage im Juni, 1974; as *5 Days in June*, 1977
Erzählungen, 1976
Die richtige Einstellung und andere Erzählungen, 1976
Collin, 1979; in English, 1980
Ahasver, 1981; as *The Wandering Jew*, 1984
Schwarzenberg, 1984
Gesammelte Erzählungen, 1984
Auf Sand gebaut: Sieben Geschichten aus der unmittelbaren Vergangenheit, 1990
Radek, 1995

Immer sind die Weiber weg und andere Weisheiten, 1997
Pargfrider, 1998

Play
Tom Sawyers grosses Abenteuer, with Hanus Burger, 1952

Other
Nazis in U.S.A.: An Exposé of Hitler's Aims and Agents in the U.S.A., 1938
Forschungsreise ins Herz der deutschen Arbeiterklasse, 1953
Offene Worte: So liegen die Dinge, 1953
Reise ins Land der unbegrenzten Möglichkeiten, 1954; as *Keine Angst vor Russlands Bären*, 1955
Im Kopf sauber: Schriften zum Tage, 1954
Offen Gesagt: Neue Schriften zum Tage, 1957
Das kosmische Zeitalter, 1959; as *A Visit to Soviet Science*, 1959; as *The Cosmic Age: A Report*, 1959
Casimir und Cymbelinchen: Zwei Märchen (for children), 1966
Cybelinchen; oder, Der Ernst des Lebens: Vier Märchen für kluge Kinder, 1975
Das Wachsmuth-Syndrom, 1975
Erich Hückniesel, und das fortgesetzte Rotkäppchen, 1977
Wege und Umwege: Streitbare Schriften aus fünf Jahrzehnten, edited by Peter Mallwitz, 1980
Atta Troll: Versuch einer Analyse, 1983
Münchner Podium in den Kammerspielen '83: Reden über das eigene Land Deutschland, 1983
Märchen für kluge Kinder (for children), 1984
Reden an den Feind, 1986
Nachruf (autobiography), 1988
Meine Cousine, die Hexe und weitere Märchen für kluge Kinder (for children), 1989
Stalin verläßt den Raum: politische Publizistik, 1990
Einmischung: Gespräche, Reden, Essays, 1990
Filz: Gedanken über das neueste Deutschland, 1992

Translation
Mark Twain, *King Leopold's Soliloquy*, 1961

Edited Works
Auskunft 1–2; Neue Prosa aus der DDR, 2 vols., 1974–78; enlarged, 1985
Die sanfte Revolution, edited with Werner Heiduczek, 1990

Further Reading

Ecker, Hans-Peter, *Poetisierung als Kritik: Stefan Heyms Neugestaltung der Erzählung vom Ewigen Juden*, Tübingen: Narr, 1987
Hutchinson, Peter, "Problems of Socialist Historiography: The Example of Stefan Heym's *King David Report*," *Modern Language Review* 81 (1986)
——, *Stefan Heym: The Perpetual Dissident*, Cambridge and New York: Cambridge University Press, 1992
Lauckner, Nancy, "Stefan Heym's Revolutionary Wandering Jew: A Warning and a Hope for the Future," in *Studies in GDR Culture and Society: Selected Papers from the Ninth New Hampshire Symposium on the German Democratic Republic*, edited by Margy Gerber et al., Lanham, Maryland: University of America Press, 1984
——, "Stefan Heym's *5 Tage im Juni* and *Schwarzenberg*: Two Visions of the Past in the light of the 1989–90 Events in the GDR," in *The End of the GDR and the Problems of Integration: Selected Papers from the Sixteenth New Hampshire Symposium on the German Democratic Republic*, edited by Margy Gerber and Roger Woods, Lanham, Maryland: University of America Press, 1993
Pender, Malcolm, "Popularising Socialism: The Case of Stefan Heym," in *Socialism and the Literary Imagination: Essays on East German Writers*, edited by Martin Kane, Oxford and New York: Berg, 1991; distributed in the U.S. by St. Martin's Press
Tait, Meg, "Stefan Heym's Radek: The Conscience of a Revolutionary," *German Life and Letters* 51, no. 4 (1998)
Zachau, Reinhard K., *Stefan Heym*, Munich: Beck, 1982

Paul Heyse 1830–1914

During much of the latter part of the 19th century, Paul (Johann Ludwig) Heyse, Germany's first winner of the Nobel Prize for literature, enjoyed immense popularity. Heyse was regarded by many as the foremost representative of German literature, a master of classical form and language, and thus Goethe's legitimate successor. An exceptionally prolific author—Thomas Mann called him "almost indecently productive," and Fontane remarked "every two years a child, every year a drama, every half year a story"—Heyse wrote numerous poems, around 50 plays, 177 prose and verse novellas, 8 novels, several fairy tales, essays, and critical literary studies. He also kept extensive diaries; corresponded with Fontane, Keller, Storm, Mörike, Burckhardt, and other major cultural figures; edited anthologies; and translated, mainly from Italian (Leopardi, Manzoni, Giusti, and others).

Heyse was brought up in a liberal, cultured environment (his father was a philologist, and his mother was related to the Mendelssohn-Bartholdy family). An extended visit to Italy in 1852 was to have a lasting impact on the "Italianissimo," as he was known to his friends. Italy acts as a background to many of the stories throughout his writing career. Titles such as *Lieder aus Sorrent, Italienische Novellen, Geschichten aus Italien, Novellen vom Gardasee,* and *Meraner Novellen* refer to the country of his literary choice.

Heyse's early mentor and great influence was the poet Emanuel Geibel, whose example of perfectly executed verse he followed, based on the study of ancient classical models and Goethe. At Geibel's recommendation, Maximilian II, king of Bavaria, offered him a titular professorship and a lifetime stipend. As a leader of the Munich Poets' Circle, he enjoyed professional and popular success.

Heyse's primary interest was drama. Although his carefully constructed plays were produced throughout Germany, he never achieved the public and literary success that he had hoped for. A number of his dramatic works deserve to be reexplored, among them the patriotic play *Colberg* and the historical drama *Hans Lange*.

Heyse's success is mainly due to his novellas. He regarded this genre as inferior to drama, but he addressed the demands of the time as the novella generally developed into the preferred form of narrative fiction. As its principal and most imaginative exponent, Heyse exercised considerable influence on his fellow authors.

One of his first novellas, *L'Arrabbiata* (1852), was characterized by Storm as "an extraordinary pearl," and Fontane praised it as an "exemplary model of simplicity, clarity and depth." His many other unquestionable masterpieces include the following: *Andrea Delfin* (1860), a description of corrupt and deceitful society, places him in the great tradition of Keller and other realists. *Die Stickerin von Treviso* (1868; The Embroideress of Treviso) is a classical framework novella, allegedly based on an old chronicle. *Das Mädchen von Treppi* (1855; The Girl from Treppi) is stylistically similar to *L'Arrabbiata.* In *Die Dichterin von Carcassone* (1880; The Poetess of Carcassone), the artistic vanity of a poet leads to a catastrophe. *Die Kaiserin von Spinetta* (1875; The Empress of Spinetta), based on a historical anecdote, is a burlesque with a tragic ending. *Judith Stern* (1875) is a story of passion and unconditional devotion.

In 1871, Heyse began publishing the highly successful anthology *Deutscher Novellenschatz* (Treasury of German Novellas), which he coedited with Hermann Kurz. In his introduction, Heyse states the criteria for his selection and reviews the development of the genre. In that context, he points out the genre's specific and distinguishing characteristics, including a clearly delineated narrative core and the necessity for an inward conflict culminating in an abrupt turning point. This change should be represented by a concrete symbol (as illustrated by the "falcon" in a Boccaccio story)—although Heyse does not define the genre dogmatically.

Heyse was celebrated and read, but he was also met with unprecedented hostility, especially from the supporters of radical naturalism, who sighted Heyse as the main target of their iconoclastic attacks. They rebuked him for his alleged unrealistic overidealization, self-righteous aesthetic indulgence, and shunning of social questions. Heyse did not yield, arguing his standpoint. In novellas such as *Die Witwe von Pisa* (1866; The Widow from Pisa), *Der letzte Centaur* (1860; The Last Centaur), and the later novels *Merlin* (1892) and *Geburt der Venus* (1909; Birth of Venus), he developed his aesthetic convictions, voicing his pronounced opposition to the tenets of naturalism and subscribing to classical balance and restraint. He demanded "that literature should see life in an ideal light that would transfigure reality." Heyse was fundamentally not an antirealist, but he rejected the realist extremes advocated by the naturalists.

Although Heyse's novels avoid pronounced political and sociological views, they show a more detailed social and cultural picture than the novellas, which have a strong dramatic element. Indebted to the tradition of the German bildungsroman, with its emphasis on the self-fulfillment of the hero, the novels tend to be polemical and topical, taking issue with the moral and aesthetic problems of the day.

The phase of the struggle between church and state under Bismarck is the background to Heyse's first novel, *Kinder der Welt* (1872; Children of the World). In the person of the private scholar Edwin, who composes a philosophical treatise on civic liberty, Heyse repudiates dogmatic orthodoxy and advocates "nature," individual freedom, and enlightened tolerance instead.

Jugenderinnerungen und Bekenntnisse (1900; Memories of My Youth and Confessions) is a valuable social document that gives a detailed account of the first four decades of the author's life.

On the occasion of Heyse's 60th birthday, Fontane expressed the opinion that "some day this literary epoch will probably be named after him." Fontane's tentative prophecy has not come true. By the turn of the 20th century, Heyse had been to a large extent forgotten, and the fact that in 1910 he was awarded the Nobel Prize for literature "as a tribute to the consummate artistry, permeated with idealism, which he demonstrated during his long productive career as a lyric poet, dramatist, novelist and writer of world-renowned short stories," was felt by most as an anachronistic act. Heyse died in the year of the outbreak of World War I, the year in which his world—the European culture of the 18th and 19th century—finally collapsed.

The negative or indifferent attitude toward Heyse's work that still prevails is partially due to the repercussions of his opponents' polemical verdict. Reference works and literary histories tend to repeat and endorse this predominant judgment or use Heyse as a negative contrast to the great realists of that era. Although Heyse remains almost totally unknown to a wider readership, there are signs of a reappraisal and a rekindled research interest in this important but unjustly marginalized author.

HERMANN RASCHE

Biography

Born in Berlin, 5 March 1830. Studied classics and then Romance languages in Berlin and Bonn; after a year's stay in Italy was summoned by King Maximilian II to Munich; lived in Munich from 1854; founded the literary society Krokodil; regular travels to Italy; accepted into the Order of Maximilian, 1871; committee member of newly found Goethe Society, 1885; made nobleman by the King of Bavaria, 1885. Schiller Prize, 1884; Nobel Prize in literature, 1910. Died 2 February 1914.

Selected Works

Collections

Jugenderinnerungen und Bekenntnisse, 1912
Gesammelte Werke, edited by Erich Petzet, 1924; reprinted, with an afterword by Norbert Miller, 1984–91
Novellen, edited by Manfred Schunicht, 1970
Paul Heyse: Werke, 2 vols., 1980

Further Reading

Bernd, Clifford A., editor, *Theodor Storm—Paul Heyse: Briefwechsel,* Berlin: Schmidt, 1969
Erler, Gotthard, editor, *Der Briefwechsel zwischen Theodor Fontane und Paul Heyse,* Berlin: Aufbau, 1972
Hillenbrand, Rainer, "'In die Poesie verbannt': Poetologisches in Paul Heyses Novellen," *Michigan Germanic Studies* 20 (1994)
———, *Heyses Novellen: Ein literarischer Führer,* Frankfurt: Lang, 1998
Hillenbrand, Rainer, editor, *Ein Gefühl der Verwandtschaft: Paul Heyses Briefwechsel mit Eduard Mörike,* Frankfurt and New York: Lang, 1997
Krausnick, Michail, *Paul Heyse und der Münchner Dichterkreis,* Bonn: Bouvier, 1974
Kroes-Tillmann, Gabriele, *Paul Heyse Italianissimo: Über seine Dichtungen und Nachdichtungen,* Würzburg: Königshausen und Neumann, 1993
Mahr, Johannes, "Paul Heyse," in *Deutsche Dichter,* edited by Gunter Grimm and Frank Rainer Max, Stuttgart: Reclam, 1989
Martin, Werner, *Paul Heyse: Eine Bibliographie,* Hildesheim and New York: Olms, 1978
Moisy, Sigrid von, *Paul Heyse: Münchner Dichterfürst im bürgerlichen Zeitalter,* Munich: Beck, 1981

Mülheim, Hubert, "'Viele hundert Fuß über der bürgerlichen Welt': Zum Problem der Subjektivität in den Novellen Paul Heyses," *Literatur für Leser* 4 (1986)
Petzet, Erich, *Der Briefwechsel von Jakob Burckhardt und Paul Heyse,* Munich: Lehmann, 1916
Spies, Bernhard, "'Der Luxus der Moral': Eine Studie zu Paul Heyses Novellenwerk," *Literatur für Leser* 3 (1982)
Stähli, Fridolin, *"Du hast alles, was mir fehlt . . .": Gottfried Keller im Briefwechsel mit Paul Heyse,* Zürich: Gut, 1990

Das Hildebrandslied ca. 800–820

Epic Poem

Handbooks on older German literature refer to *Das Hildebrandslied* (*The Lay of Hildebrand*) as the only existing example of alliterative heroic poetry in German from the Germanic migration period. This designation underlines the work's unique position in the history of German literature and draws attention to some of its problematic aspects: dating, origin, evolution, and survival as a literary text. The link to the Germanic period, based on the references to Theodoric (ca. 454–526), or Dietrich von Bern (Verona), king of the Ostrogoths, and Odoacer (ca. 435–93), Germanic chieftain, provides no substantial historical evidence for the origin of the poem or for its central figures, Hildebrand and Hadubrand. The coupling of Dietrich and Hildebrand as lord and vassal in other Germanic heroic works, however, suggests at least a literary relationship between the two figures and links *The Lay of Hildebrand* with the legendary material surrounding the name of Dietrich von Bern.

The dating of the text in its current fragmentary form, based on internal linguistic evidence, assumes an earlier Bavarian version written down in the last decades of the eighth century. A later stage, dated variously from the beginning of the ninth century up to as late as 840, places the text in Fulda, where orthographic evidence suggests the collaboration of two scribes. The Fulda version of the work was inscribed on the first and last pages of a Latin manuscript. Subsequent dating efforts posited the existence of a pre-Bavarian Lombardic version, for which there is no concrete evidence. References to Theodoric (Dietrich) suggest the possibility of an even earlier Gothic version. The two leaves of the Hildebrandslied fragment were stolen at the end of World War II, taken to the United States, and subsequently returned separately (in 1954 and 1972) to their original home in Bad Wildungen; they are now in the Landesbibliothek in Kassel, Germany.

The Lay of Hildebrand is generally linked to the group of Indo-European hero tales incorporating the theme of a father-son conflict. Similar versions are Sohrab and Rustum (Persian), Ilya Muromets (Russian), Cu Chulainn (Irish), and the post-Homeric legend of Telegonus and Odysseus. The absence of some of the more traditional themes in the Lay of Hildebrand—for example, the illegitimacy of the son, the recognition token left behind by the father, the son's search for his father—has suggested to some an independent tradition. The similarities, however, outweigh the differences and anchor *The Lay of Hildebrand* in a literary tradition that reaches beyond national boundaries.

Despite the fragmentary nature of the manuscript, *The Lay of Hildebrand* exhibits characteristics indicative of its literary context: Germanic heroic alliterative poetry. While the alliterative style cannot be compared favorably with the strict metrical standards of Anglo-Saxon alliterative poetry, the use of rhyming patterns for initial consonants, though inconsistent, has led to the suggestion that the work belongs perhaps to the period of decline of this metrical style. The lay's literary merits may be sought more profitably in techniques such as the use of direct and indirect speech to provide narrative structure, the possibility of interior monologue to introduce a different point of view, the use of the in medias res narrative technique, and the subsequent blending of past and present through shifting perspectives in narrative.

The Germanic-heroic ethos provides a context for the confrontation between two warriors revealed by means of narrative exposition to be father and son, a fact that the father recognizes early on but that the son persistently refuses to acknowledge. The probability of the blood relationship is reinforced by references to an extended family (Heribrand, Hildebrand, Hadubrand, an abandoned wife-mother) and biographical revelations that draw attention to the potential for tragedy as the verbal confrontation moves inevitably toward physical combat. The impact of the narrative is not lessened by the father's early recognition of his opponent as his son. To the contrary, the ironic dimension to his thoughts, gestures, and his necessarily futile efforts at reconciliation all serve to raise the lay above the level of a typical heroic narrative of judicial combat.

The protestations of the son, Hadubrand, asserting his acceptance of the reports of his father's death, are less convincing as personal narratives than as vehicles for the introduction of the summarized biography of Hildebrand, his father. The ironic posture of the father, who must listen to the story of his death as narrated by his own son and recognize the commitment of the son to accept that death as factual truth, is the essence of tragedy. Hildebrand's fateful lament—"welaga nu, waltant got, wehwurt ski-hit"—(let destiny take its course!)—underlines his helplessness, while drawing attention to his painful awareness of his own role in the destruction of his family, past and present. His measured responses to Hadubrand's insulting retorts, the offer of arm rings, perhaps a remnant of the recognition token in other versions, and the reluctance of Hildebrand to accept the unavoidable reality all combine to set him apart as the tragic figure who is destined to have to bear the heaviest burden a father could have: knowledge of his role in the death of his own son. The logical movement toward such an outcome makes the account of the actual battle seem almost irrelevant; the loss of the part of the manuscript containing the ending of the poem has little or no effect on its narrative impact. The reciprocal verbal exchanges of father and son, whether viewed as spoken narrative or interior monologue, provide the reader/listener access to a remarkable delineation of personal characteristics and resulting personal dilemmas that are universal in scope, perspective, and significance.

The Germanic warrior context of *The Lay of Hildebrand* reflects an acceptance of the role of fate, the importance of personal honor, and the possibility of having to choose between loyalty to one's lord and one's love for wife and child, which seem to be well-defined and meaningful parts of an identifiable social posture. The efforts of adaptations from the 13th to 16th centuries to retain these aspects while eliminating the tragic aspect, emphasizing reconciliation of father and son, seem to compromise both the integrity of the poem and the cultural ethos it represents.

RICHARD ERNEST WALKER

See also Old High German

Editions

First edition: *Commentarii de rebus Franciae orientalis I,* 1729
First modern edition: *Die beiden ältesten deutschen Gedichte aus dem achten Jahrhundert, zum ersten Mal in ihrem Metrum dargestellt und herausgegeben durch die Brüder Grimm,* 1812
Translation: *The Hildebrandslied,* translated by Francis A. Wood, Chicago: University of Chicago Press, 1914

Further Reading

Elliot, R.W., "Byrhtnoth and Hildebrand: A Study in Heroic Technique," *Comparative Literature* 14 (1962)
Groseclose, J. Sidney, and Brian Murdoch, *Die althochdeutschen poetischen Denkmäler,* Stuttgart: Metzler, 1976
Hatto, A.T., "On the Excellence of the Hildebrandslied," *Modern Language Review* 68 (1973)
Hoffman, W., "Das Hildebrandslied und die indogermanischen Vater-Sohn-Kampf-Dichtungen," *Paul-Braune- Beiträge* 92 (1970)
McLintock, D.R., "The Language of the Hildebrandslied," *Oxford German Studies* 1 (1966)
——, "The Politics of the Hildebrandslied," *New German Studies* 2 (1974)
Murdoch, Brian, *Old High German Literature,* Boston: Twayne, 1983
Northcott, K.J., "Das Hildebrandslied: A Legal Process?" *Modern Language Review* 56 (1961)
Pickering, F.P., "Notes on Fate and Fortune (for Germanisten)," in *Festschrift for Fredrick Norman,* London: Institute of Germanic Studies, 1965

Hildegard von Bingen 1098–1179

In 1998, the 1,000th anniversary of Hildegard's year of birth was celebrated in many parts of the world. Even today, this famous medieval mystical writer continues to enjoy a tremendous recognition as a visionary and a musical composer, as a poet and as a scientist, as a medical doctor and as a religious leader. Her works have been translated into many different languages and have provided significant insight into medieval women's spirituality, medicine, music, and poetry. Hildegard was not only dignified through her divine visions, she also gained widespread renown as a politician, a leader of her convent, and an expert in medicinal herbs. She was so famous during her time that she corresponded with such personalities as the Popes Eugenius III, Anastasius IV, Adrian IV, and Alexander III, and also with the German Emperors Konrad III and Frederick Barbarossa.

Her life began in Bermersheim in Hesse near Alzey as the child of the knight Hildebert, who served Meginhard, the Count of Spanheim. In 1104 her parents entrusted Hildegard to the care of the anchoress Jutta, sister of Count Meginhard, who taught her the basics of reading and writing, how to sing in Latin, and textile craft. Soon other women joined the small group of encloistered anchorites, and they formed a Benedictine convent attached to a monastery at Disibodenberg. When Jutta passed away in 1136, Hildegard was unanimously elected as abbess of this women's convent.

At the age of 15 she experienced her first vision, and her visions then continued throughout the years until her death. In 1141 Hildegard received, as she claimed, a call from God to copy down her revelations, and after initial hesitation she set to work with the help of the scribe Volmar and her favorite convent sister, Richardis of Stade. Soon a copy of an excerpt got into the hands of Pope Eugenius III, who participated at a synod of bishops in Trier during the winter of 1147–48. He was deeply impressed by Hildegard's visionary power, read the text out loud, and publicly acknowledged it as being divinely inspired. This provided her with the highest possible authority to continue recording her revelations as messages directly derived from God.

Sometime between 1147 and 1150, after having received a command from God to move away, Hildegard split from the Disibodenberg monastery and decided to found her own convent. Abbot Kuno struggled long and hard against her departure because it undermined the financial well-being of his monastery, which had profited tremendously from her international reputation as a mystic, but in the end he had to let her go. Hildegard founded the new monastery at Rupertsberg near Bingen. This became the location where she lived for the rest of her life—apart from the many trips that she took throughout Germany and Europe. On those trips, she always preached to large crowds and gained strong respect as a visionary. In 1165 Hildegard founded a second convent at Eibingen across the Rhine near Bingen.

As in the case of many other mystical writers, Hildegard's confessions are both religious revelations and literary documents of the highest aesthetic caliber. Whereas the religious components remain inaccessible to all outsiders who have not experienced visions themselves, the texts, composed in Latin, are astoundingly expressive and beautiful literary works, and their illuminations have artistic excellence and significance. Hildegard wrote her first three mystical books between 1141 and 1151 under the title *Scivias* (May You Know the Way). Her more autobiographical work, *Liber vitae meritorum* (The Book of the Life of Meritorious Works), appeared between 1158 and 1163. Finally, Hildegard also composed a *Liber divinorum operum simplicis hominis* (The Book of the Divine Works of a Simple Man) between 1163 and 1173.

Scivias contains Hildegard's cosmic visions of the universe and of God as the creator and discusses her concept of the interaction between macrocosm and microcosm. The text contains extensive descriptions of genesis, the fall of man, his salvation, the victory of Ecclesia over Synagoga, and the sacraments. The oldest manuscript, extent until 1945 when it was destroyed in an aerial raid on Dresden, was written between 1165 and 1173 in Rupertsberg and was lavishly illuminated with 35 marvelous miniatures that Hildegard might have created herself. It seems more likely, however, that they were painted in the convent's scriptorium. An excellent photocopy had been produced in 1927, and between 1927 and 1933 the nuns of Eibingen manually created a facsimile that closely reflects the great artistic skills of the original miniatures (*Riesenkodex,* Hessische Landesbibliothek, Wiesbaden, cod. 2).

In the *Liber vitae meritorum,* Hildegard examines the character and meaning of the various virtues and vices as they influence people's lives and then describes the responsibilities of each individual in this world and the mystical relationship between man and God. The author develops highly vivid images of allegorical figures representing vices and virtues, and relates extremely realistic visions of the Godhead. In the *Liber divinorum operum simplicis hominis,* Hildegard outlines her dogmatic and ascetic ideals and presents her visions of the cosmic unity of creation, where all beings are intimately related to each other by way of a macrocosmic and microcosmic order.

In her treatise *Physica* (1150–58), Hildegard outlines her understanding of the physical world, and in her medical treatise *Causae et curae* (1150–60; Causes and Cures), she examines a wide range of herbs, fruit, roots, leaves, and even stones as remedies against sickness. Hildegard perceived the human body in holistic terms and treated it always both in its physical and spiritual dimensions. Some of the most interesting chapters deal with human sexuality, pregnancy, menstruation, sleep patterns, blood circulation, and holistic nutrition. Some of her teachings represent typical misconceptions of the Middle Ages; others are considered, even today, to be highly effective.

Finally, Hildegard also composed *vitae* (lives) of the saints Disibodi and Rupert. Her theological work includes *Explanatio symboli Sancti Athanasii* (Explanation of the Symbol of Saint Athanasius) and *Explanatio regulae Sancti Benedicti* (Explanation of the Rule of Saint Benedict). In addition, Hildegard composed approximately 70 sequences of hymns, antiphons, and responsories, which were collected in her *Symphonia armonie celestium revelationum* (The Harmonious Symphony of Heavenly Revelations). She also created one of the first liturgical plays, *Ordo virtutum* (Order of the Virtues).

Although Hildegard enjoyed considerable respect and authority as the leader of her convent and as a visionary, as an expert medical doctor and as a composer of liturgical songs, she was also deeply embroiled in imperial and church politics and in personal conflicts, as her extensive correspondence indicates. When her former friend and fellow sister Richardis of Stade was appointed abbess of Bassum in 1151, Hildegard strove to prevent her election because she did not want to lose her beloved secretary and helper. Even the pope, however, supported the nomination and rejected Hildegard's intervention. Tragically, when Richardis finally felt penitent and was about to return to Rupertsberg, she suddenly died on 29 October 1152. In 1164, Hildegard vehemently opposed Emperor Frederick Barbarossa in his decision to support the anti-Pope Alexander III, because it created a schism within the Church. The same happened in 1168, and Hildegard continued with her struggle against Frederick, who was determined to assert his authority over the church through appointing the pope. In 1164, she also composed a vitriolic tract condemning the Cathars, whom she considered to be dangerous heretics. Finally, in 1178, a bitter controversy over the burial of a previously excommunicated nobleman caused her convent to be censured by the church, meaning that the convent was denied communion for more than six months.

Hildegard is highly acclaimed both as a literary writer of great skill and as an artist. Her scientific contributions to medicine and physics are considered to be masterpieces of her time. Her visions and revelations also qualify her as one of the most important mystics in medieval Europe. Quite fittingly, she was often called the "Teutonic prophetess," the "jewel of Bingen," and the "sibyl of the Rhine."

ALBRECHT CLASSEN

See also Mysticism

Biography

Born in Bermersheim, 1098. Educated at Benedictine monastery, from 1106; entered convent between 1112–15; prioress of convent at Disibodenberg near Bingen, from 1136; began to record her mystic visions, from 1141. Confirmed as visionary and writings deemed acceptable to the Church by synod at Trier, 1147–48. Died in Rupertsberg bei Bingen, 17 September 1179.

Selected Works

Theological Works

Scivias, 1141–51; as *Scivias,* translated by Columba Hart and Jane Bishop, with plates redrawn from the copy of the Rupertsberg manuscript, 1990

Liber vitae meritorum, 1158–63; as *Hildegard of Bingen: The Book of the Rewards of Life,* translated by Bruce W. Hozeski, 1994

Liber divinorum operum, or *De operatione Dei,* 1163–73; as *Hildegard of Bingen's Book of Divine Works with Letters and Songs,* edited by Matthew Fox, 1987

Other

Causa et curae, 1150–60

Physica, 1150–58

Musical Compositions
Ordo virtutum, 1158; performance edition, with English translation, edited by
Audrey Ekdahl Davidson, 1984
Symphonia harmoniae caelestium revelationum, 1151–58; as *Symphonia: A Critical Edition of the Symphonia armonie celestium revelationum [Symphony of the Harmony of Celestial Revelations],* edited by Barbara Newman, 1988

Translations in German
Schriften der Heiligen Hildegard von Bingen, selected and translated by Johannes Bühler, 1922
Heilkunde, das Buch von dem Grund und Wesen und der Heilung der Kranken, 1957
Übersetzung der Hauptwerke, Salzburg, 1953–82
Gott ist am Werk, 1958
Heilkraft der Natur: Physika, 1991
Heilen mit der Kraft der Seele, 1993
Wisse die Wege, 1997

Further Reading
Davidson, Audrey Ekdahl, editor, *The "Ordo Virtutum" of Hildegard of Bingen: Critical Studies,* Kalamazoo: Medieval Institute Publications, Western Michigan University, 1992
Flanagan, Sabina, *Hildegard of Bingen, 1098–1179: A Visionary Life,* London and New York: Routledge, 1989
Forster, Edeltraud, editor, *Hildegard von Bingen: Prophetin durch die Zeiten: zum 900. Geburtstag,* Freiburg: Herder, 1997
Gossmann, Elisabeth, *Hildegard von Bingen: Versuche einer Annährung,* Munich: iudicium, 1995
Kastinger Riley, Helene M., *Hildegard von Bingen,* Reinbek bei Hamburg: Rowohlt, 1997
Kraft, Kent, "The German Visionary Hildegard of Bingen," in *Medieval Women Writers,* edited by Katharina M. Wilson, Athens: University of Georgia Press, 1984
Lehrbach, Heike, *Katalog zur Internationalen Ausstellung "Hl. Hildegard von Bingen 1179–1979" aus Anlass des 800. Todestages der Heiligen,* Bingen: Museumspädagogisches Zentrum des Römisch-Germanischen Zentralmuseums, 1979
McInerney, Maud Burnett, editor, *Hildegard of Bingen: A Book of Essays,* New York: Garland, 1998
Schipperges, Heinrich, *Hildegard of Bingen: Healing and the Nature of the Cosmos,* translated by John A. Broadwin, Princeton, New Jersey: Wiener, 1996
Termolen, Rosel, *Hildegard von Bingen: Biographie,* Augsburg: Pattoch, 1990
Weeks, Andrew, *German Mysticism from Hildegard of Bingen to Ludwig Wittgenstein: A Literary and Intellectual History,* Albany: State University of New York Press, 1993

Wolfgang Hildesheimer 1916–1991

Wolfgang Hildesheimer is essentially a satirist. Deeply pessimistic and living in dark times, he wrote prose and plays that reflect the experiences of a cosmopolitan European Jew during the Nazi era. The appellation "German" applies only to his birthplace and his language: he spent almost two-thirds of his life in exile and treated German culture with bitter irony and compulsive parody. But he used the language with clarity and elegance, as if to cleanse it of bureaucratic and academic accretions and to preserve it in pure culture. Hildesheimer's oeuvre divides itself into three periods: a primarily satiric phase (1950–60), in which he produced short stories, plays for stage and radio, and a comic novel with serious undertones; a much darker period (1961–74), in which he wrote his two major works of fiction, *Tynset* and *Masante,* and other prose works of a monologic, retrospective nature; and an essayistic phase (1975–91), in which he published a large-scale psychobiography of Mozart and the ingenious mock biography *Marbot: Eine Biographie* (1981; *Marbot: A Biography*), as well as essays on literature and the arts, particularly his programmatic speech, *The End of Fiction.* In his later years, he addressed himself increasingly to problems of the environment and overpopulation.

His early works are written in a humorous vein but often reveal deeper meanings. He began to publish short prose sketches in the early 1950s when he was in his mid 30s; these works gained him entry into Gruppe 47. Entitled *Lieblose Legenden* (1952; Loveless Legends), they ridicule social climbers and their cultural pretensions while also probing the alienation of the outsider. These stories are among his best. In "Die zwei Seelen" (1951; The Two Souls), Hildesheimer uses a well-known quotation from Goethe's *Faust* to debunk the so-called German-Jewish symbiosis: in this work, German and Jew, poet and critic, and the tragic and ironic voices cannot coexist. Common characteristics seen in these stories include first-person narration, the passivity of the protagonist, and the predilection for inventing biographies. Mock biography helps the author build fiction out of facts, parody a problematic genre, express opinions in a voice not his own, and examine his own life through the prism of another. Hildesheimer's only novel, *Paradies der falschen Vögel* (1953; Paradise of Dissemblers), has a chronologically told plot, but it is also a mock biography that deals with art forgers. Underneath its comic surface Hildesheimer treats questions of authenticity, deception, and creative failure. The setting, a small Balkan state, enables him to show the pernicious effects of national pride.

Even though Hildesheimer excelled at writing prose, he wrote many plays for stage and radio. They tend to be rather literary and display a fine use of language, verbal wit, little action or character development, literary allusions, adaptation of older themes, and unmasking technique. His early comedy *Der Drachenthron* (1955; Throne of Dragons), one of his several versions of the Turandot story and perhaps his most effective play, transmutes the contest between the Chinese princess and her suitor into a verbal duel: the prince, an impostor but genuine in the author's terms, defeats her and then renounces her and the imperial title, leaving Turandot and China to the virile and brutal military conqueror—an ending worthy of Shaw. The sinister one-act play *Nachtstück* (1963; *Nightpiece*) depicts the gradual destruction of the solitary protagonist by an intruder and by his own fears. The two characters are prototypes of the victim and his pursuer—a theme that preoccupied Hildesheimer intensely.

After going into exile again in 1957, this time voluntarily, Hildesheimer wrote in a markedly darker vein. His voice turned inward and less ironic. Haunted by what he had heard as an interpreter at the Nuremberg Trials and disturbed by the failure, as he saw it, of the Federal Republic to come to grips with the Nazi past, he wrote works of reflective prose that deal with the situation of the persecuted Jew during the Third Reich. These works were foreshadowed by several plays, which have been labeled theater of the absurd. Although Hildesheimer identified himself with this genre in his programmatic speech *Über das absurde Theater* (1960; On Theater of the Absurd), his plays have a political message, a literary ambience and a satiric-parodic quality that differentiate them from the canonical theater of the absurd—an opinion not shared by most critics.

Hildesheimer's writings between 1961 and 1974 are dominated by two extensive and conjoined prose monologues, *Tynset* (1965) and *Masante* (1973). (Tynset and Masante are places in Norway and Italy, respectively, which define the narrator's remove from Germany.) Told by a sophisticated, world-weary narrator, they are the night thoughts of a witness to our age, a German Jew who has retreated from the terrors of the 20th century. Comparing himself with Hamlet, his favorite literary figure, he finds himself unable to cope with the schemes of evil men. Both pursuer and victim transcend the specific and become, in Hildesheimer's vivid prose, eternal types. In a world ruled by pursuers, there is no place for this narrator. At the end of *Masante,* he loses his way in the desert, a suicide that signals the end of the author's interior journey.

With *Tynset* and *Masante,* Hildesheimer settled accounts with Germany and exhausted the possibilities of reflective narration. In 1975, he grandly declared "the end of fiction." In a speech given in English and delivered in Ireland in homage to James Joyce, the English-speaking writer he most admired after Shakespeare, Hildesheimer argued that it is the writer's function in our post-Auschwitz age to transcend or sublimate reality into a universal statement about the human condition and that only intensely subjective writers such as Joyce, Marcel Proust, Franz Kafka, and Samuel Beckett have achieved this goal. Having gone as far as he could in this direction, Hildesheimer turned to biographical writing. His choice of subject was Mozart. He delved into Mozart's character and motivations and examined his letters and his relationships. The book is selective and not chronological, and it corrects or dismisses much previous writing on the composer. It is Hildesheimer's best-known book, and it has brought him international recognition. He characterized the book as an escape from the 20th century.

This characterization also applies to the other half of his biographical diptych, the mock biography *Marbot.* Hildesheimer's preoccupation with biographical writing stemmed from his gift for analytic prose, his interpretive flair, his psychoanalytic orientation, and his withdrawal from large-scale fiction. By inventing his subject, an English art critic of the early 19th century, Hildesheimer attempted to objectify himself, but this work is also a mock autobiography disguised as an essay in the psychology of art, as well as a critique of European culture in the Romantic age. Discussions of *Mozart* and *Marbot,* his best-known works in the English-speaking world, revolve around the subjectivity of his biographical writing, his mingling of fact and fiction, and his psychoanalytic stance.

In 1983, Hildesheimer announced that he would stop writing because the state of the world made it seem frivolous, but one suspects that he had said what he wanted to say. In his last years, he returned to graphic art, with which he had begun as a young man. A few months before his death, he appealed to a group of high school students to care for the earth and all its creatures; this address was his last work. Hildesheimer translated or adapted several English plays for the German stage, and he translated numerous English prose works into German. His reputation in Germany may have been affected by his irreverent wit and his sardonic view of German culture.

HENRY A. LEA

Biography

Born in Hamburg, 9 December 1916. Emigrated to England and then to Palestine, 1933; trained as a carpenter and interior decorator in Jerusalem, 1934–37; studied art and stage design in Salzburg, 1937, and in London, 1937–39; English teacher at the British Institute in Tel Aviv, 1940–42; information officer in the British Public Information Office in Jerusalem, 1943–46; interpreter at the Nuremberg war crimes trials, 1946–49; artist and freelance writer, from 1950; member of Gruppe 47, from 1951; emigrated to Switzerland in 1957; honorary Swiss citizen, 1982. Bremen Literature Prize, 1966; Büchner Prize, 1966; Bundesverdienstkreuz (Order of Merit of the German Federal Republic), 1983. Died in Poschiavo, Switzerland, 21 August 1991.

Selected Works

Collections

Das Ende der Fiktionen: Reden aus fünfundzwanzig Jahren (includes original speech given in English as *The End of Fiction*), 1984
The Collected Stories of Wolfgang Hildesheimer, translated by Joachim Neugroschel, 1987
Die Hörspiele, 1988
Die Theaterstücke, 1989
Gesammelte Werke in sieben Bänden, 1991

Fiction

Lieblose Legenden, 1952
Paradies der falschen Vögel, 1953
Hamlet, 1961
Der Ruf in der Wüste, 1963
Tynset, 1965
Masante, 1973
Marbot: Eine Biographie, 1981; as *Marbot: A Biography,* translated by Patricia Crampton, 1983

Plays

(Note: Hildesheimer adapted some of his plays for the radio and some of his radio plays for the stage. Each play is listed according to its initial version.)

Stage Plays

Der Drachenthron, 1955
Spiele, in denen es dunkel wird (includes *Pastorale oder die Zeit für Kakao, Landschaft mit Figuren,* and *Die Uhren*), 1957
Die Herren der Welt, 1958
Die Verspätung, 1961
Nachtstück, 1963; as *Nightpiece,* translated by Wolfgang Hildesheimer, 1967
Mary Stuart: Eine historische Szene, 1970; as *Mary Stuart,* translated by Christopher Holme, 1972

Radio Plays
Das Ende kommt nie, 1952
Das Opfer Helena, 1955; as *The Sacrifice of Helen,* translated by Jacques-Leon Rose, 1968
Herrn Walsers Raben, 1960
Unter der Erde, 1962
Monolog, 1964
Hauskauf, 1974
Biosphärenklänge, 1977

Biography
Bleibt Dürer Dürer? 1971
Mozart, 1977; as *Mozart,* translated by Marion Faber, 1982
Der ferne Bach, 1985

Literary Criticism
Über das absurde Theater, 1960
Büchners atemlose Melancholie, 1966
Frankfurter Poetik-Vorlesungen (includes *Die Wirklichkeit des Absurden, Die Wirklichkeit des Reaktionäre,* and *Das absurde Ich*), 1967
The End of Fiction, 1975
Die Subjektivität des Biographen, 1982
The Jewishness of Mr. Bloom, 1984

Other
Vergebliche Aufzeichnungen, 1962
Zeiten in Cornwall, 1971
Mein Judentum, 1978
Mitteilungen an Max über den Stand der Dinge und anderes, 1983; as *Missives to Max,* translated by Joachim Neugroschel in *The Collected Stories of Wolfgang Hildesheimer,* 1987
Klage und Anklage (includes *Klage und Anklage, Notat eines Verlierers, In den Wind geschrieben,* and *Herr, gib ihnen die ewige Ruhe nicht*), 1989
Rede an die Jugend, 1991

Translations
Djuna Barnes, *Nachtgewächs,* 1959
Übersetzung und Interpretation einer Passage aus "Finnegans Wake" von James Joyce, 1969

Further Reading

Hanenberg, Peter, *Geschichte im Werk Wolfgang Hildesheimers,* Frankfurt: Lang, 1989
Hildesheimer, Wolfgang, *"Ich werde nun schweigen": Gespräch mit Hans Helmut Hillrichs in der Reihe "Zeugen des Jahrhunderts,"* edited by Ingo Hermann, Göttingen: Lamuv, 1993
Jehle, Volker, *Wolfgang Hildesheimer: Werkgeschichte,* Frankfurt: Suhrkamp, 1990
Koebner, Thomas, "Entfremdung und Melancholie: Zu Hildesheimers intellektuellen Helden," in *Über Wolfgang Hildesheimer,* edited by Dierk Rodewald, Frankfurt: Suhrkamp, 1971
Lea, Henry A., *Wolfgang Hildesheimers Weg als Jude und Deutscher,* Stuttgart: Heinz, 1997
Loquai, Franz, "Hildesheimer, Hamlet und die Häscher: Von der Suche nach Wahrheit zum Ende des Exils," in *Wolfgang Hildesheimer,* edited by Volker Jehle, Frankfurt: Suhrkamp, 1989
Nef, Ernst, "Die absurde Geschichte; die Fälscher; die Häscher; der Melancholiker," *Schweizer Monatshefte* 55 (1975)
Sacker, H.D., "Hildesheimer's Vision of Literature," *Hermathena* 121 (1976)

Edgar Hilsenrath 1926–

Beginning with the controversial ghetto novel *Nacht* (1964; *Night*) and ending with the autobiographical novel *Die Abenteuer des Ruben Jablonski* (1997; The Adventures of Ruben Jablonski), the works of the Shoah survivor Edgar Hilsenrath, who returned to Germany after living in New York for almost 20 years, are informed by the author's experiences of an age of atrocities. A comparison between Hilsenrath's earlier and later prose suggests that, for Hilsenrath, writing has been a way of processing the past. Compared to *Night,* which is replete with violence, brutality, and horrors, the most recent work reads like a picaresque novel. Under the guise of fiction, the author's story is told as if by a young boy, and it reviews the boy's childhood years in Leipzig, his escape from Nazi Germany to his extended family in Romania, his imprisonment in the ghetto, his liberation by the Red Army, his adventurous journey to Palestine, and his reunion with his family.

Hilsenrath's works, some abjectly sinister, others satirical and humorous but always mixing grotesque, horrible, and amusing elements, revolve around the Holocaust. They examine the absurd and tragic fates of men and women persecuted because of their alleged otherness even though they are assimilated and indistinguishable from the mainstream. Having been excluded from his cultural roots as a German Jew, Hilsenrath's literary language, German, shows evidence of a type of critical deflation characteristic of most post-Shoah German Jewish writing. Traditional concepts of identity and belonging, psychology and character, are constantly undermined, as are the values specific to the dominant culture. Few other authors, except perhaps Jerzy Kosinski, Jean Améry, and Jakov Lind, have written as compellingly as Hilsenrath about the effects of the Holocaust on the individual and collective psyche, including language and the perception of reality. Although Hilsenrath's existence came unhinged when he was still a child, his dream, which he shared with Jakov Lind, whom he met in Palestine, was to be an author—a German author. Hilsenrath tells the story of the destruction of the European Jews in the language of those most intimately involved, yet their language, the German language, continues to resist this part of history as it does no other.

In 1938, the family life and the formal education of Edgar Hilsenrath, the son of a Jewish businessman, came to an end when his parents, prompted by the anti-Semitic legislation and violence, separated. His father left with the intention of meeting his wife and children at a later date in Paris; his mother took the two sons to her native Romania, where Hilsenrath, having grown up in an assimilated urban environment, encountered traditional Judaism and life in the country for the first time. This short period of peacetime living in the Bukowina is reflected in the nostalgic passages about East European Jewish life in *Jossel Wassermanns Heimkehr* (1993) and in the premodern setting of *Das Märchen vom letzten Gedanken* (1989; *The Story of the Last Thought*). Although associated with Turkish-Armenia, the rural patriarchal lifestyle calls to mind Elias Canetti's childhood account and seems inspired by Hilsenrath's own memories of the Bukowina prior to being deported to the ghetto Moghilev-Podolsk.

Hilsenrath began his first novel, *Night*, after his liberation, which was followed by his journey from Bucharest to Paris. It was completed in New York. *Night* reveals in shocking detail the intellectual and moral deterioration of a man named Ranek, one of the Jews left to starve by the Nazis in a burned-out town. The situation is one of total chaos: lack of food, space, and goods. Without the direct intervention of concentration camp guards or the SS, the hungry men and women create a social Darwinist hierarchy. Everyone, at least every male, seems to forget his peacetime socialization, including religion, love, and loyalty, and takes advantage of those weaker than himself. The rivaling males engage in atavistic power plays, the object of which is the conquest and subjugation of females and weaker males. Hilsenrath's unflattering portrayal of human beings trying to survive under extreme duress contradicts versions of the Holocaust experience in books that ascribe a higher meaning or a humanist lesson to the genocide.

In West Germany of the 1960s, the Shoah was an uncomfortable topic, and Hilsenrath's novel, varying greatly from the conciliatory and aesthetically palatable Holocaust literature that found favor with the public, met with outrage. His representation of Jews as individuals capable of the full range of emotions and actions—Hilsenrath's female protagonist Deborah was moral and altruistic, and Ranek was amoral and callous—challenged the stereotype of Jews as victims. Possibly, Hilsenrath's focus on the body and the instrumentalization of its functions, notably sex, for the purpose of asserting power and establishing identity, caused his first publisher, Kindler, to produce only a small edition of *Night*. Two years later, *Night* appeared in English translation, but only after the success of *Der Nazi und der Friseur* (1977; *The Nazi and the Barber*) was it published in Germany again, this time by the Literarischer Verlag Braun.

The Nazi and the Barber, just as the stories in *Zibulsky; oder, Antenne im Bauch* (1983; Zibulsky; or, Antenna in the Belly), stands in the tradition of Jewish satire that had become almost extinct after the destruction of German Jewish culture. In his bawdy parodies and jokes, Hilsenrath satirizes the perpetrators of the Holocaust, many of whom, like his protagonist, the mass murderer Max Schulz, posed as Nazi victims after the war. Cognizant of the pacifist European Jewish legacy, Hilsenrath portrays Israel's militant fighter ethos in highly critical terms. He describes how easy it is for Schulz to slip into an assumed Jewish identity and to become a respected Israeli citizen. Hilsenrath draws into question the concepts of identity and ethnicity altogether by poking fun at ethnic markers and racial stereotypes, notably those of 19th- and 20th-century anti-Semitic literature, and he satirizes German postwar fiction about the Nazi past, including Günter Grass's *Die Blechtrommel* (1959; *The Tin Drum*). Hilsenrath's novel implies that, because of its failure to properly address anti-Semitism and the Shoah, this type of literature is flawed.

Hilsenrath's literary devices include bizarre characters, grotesque misunderstandings, and astute discourses about individuals written off by the dominant culture. In *Bronskys Geständnis* (1980; Bronsky's Confessions), he traces the German Jewish exile experience in the United States, and in *The Story of the Last Thought,* he connects Holocaust themes with a story about the genocide perpetrated by the Young Turks against the Armenians. Here, Hilsenrath addresses, as he does in *Jossel Wassermanns Heimkehr,* the discrepancy between the experience of everyday people and sanitized official versions of history. In all of his works, his main focus is the suffering of the average person. He describes the brutality applied to the human body during torture, revealing that the destruction of lives goes along with lust and sexual gratification.

Hilsenrath exposes connections between the phenomena of sadism and politics, war, and genocide. He discusses these phenomena not only in the context of Nazi Germany, but also relates them to other cultures and periods. By doing so, he deliberately transgresses against established taboos that prevent a reexamination of "human nature" by scholars and humanists. Hilsenrath's derisive portrayal of the competitive and cruel behavior on the part of human beings, particularly males, that is fostered by social systems validating authoritarian excesses suggests that humans are mistaken to ascribe "humane" qualities to their own species. Hilsenrath communicates his profoundly moralistic messages in an explicit language, which he sets deliberately apart from the bland rhetoric of the desk murderers and the sentimental bombast of charismatic leaders. He writes about the misery of the weak and oppressed, women, children, the sick, the hungry, the poor, and the impoverished in the direct and simple language of the streets.

DAGMAR C.G. LORENZ

See also Holocaust (Shoah) Literature

Biography

Born in Leipzig, 2 April 1926. Emigrated in 1938 and joined Jewish relatives in Romania; deported to the ghetto Moghilev-Podelsk (Ukraine), 1941; returned to Bucharest, 1944, and emigrated to Palestine and eventually to the United States, 1951. Currently lives in Berlin.

Selected Works

Nacht, 1964; as *Night,* translated by Michael Roloff, 1966
Der Nazi und der Friseur, 1977; as *The Nazi and the Barber,* translated by Andrew White, 1971 [sic]
Gib acht Genosse Mandelbaum, 1979
Bronskys Geständnis, 1980
Zibulsky, oder, Antenne im Bauch, 1983
Das Märchen vom letzten Gedanken, 1989; as *The Story of the Last Thought,* translated by Hugh Young, 1990
Moskauer Orgasmus: Roman, 1992
Joseph Wassermanns Heimkehr, 1993
Die Abenteuer des Ruben Jablonski: Ein autobiographischer Roman, 1997

Further Reading

Gilman, Sander L., "Jüdische Literaten und deutsche Literatur: Antisemitismus und verborgene Sprache der Juden am Beispiel von

Jurek Becker und Edgar Hilsenrath," *Zeitschrift für Deutsche Philologie* 107, no. 2 (1988)
Kraft, Thomas, editor, *Edgar Hilsenrath: das Unerzählbare erzählen,* Munich: Piper, 1996
Lorenz, Dagmar C.G., "Social Darwinism in Edgar Hilsenrath's Ghetto Novel Nacht," in *Insiders and Outsiders: Jewish and Gentile Culture in Germany and Austria,* edited by Dagmar C.G. Lorenz and Gabriele Weinberger, Detroit, Michigan: Wayne State University Press, 1994
Moeller, Susann, "Politics to Pulp a Novel: The Fate of the First Edition of Edgar Hilsenrath's Novel *Nacht,*" in *Insiders and Outsiders: Jewish and Gentile Culture in Germany and Austria,* edited by Dagmar C.G. Lorenz and Gabriele Weinberger, Detroit, Michigan: Wayne State University Press, 1994
Stenberg, Peter, "Memories of the Holocaust: Edgar Hilsenrath and the Fiction of Genocide," *Deutsche Vierteljahrsschrift für Literaturwissenschaft und Geistesgeschichte* 56, no. 2 (1982)
———, "Edgar Hilsenrath and Jakov Lind Meet at the Employment Office in Netanya, Palestine, Discuss Literature, and Contemplate Their Recent Past," in *Yale Companion to Jewish Writing and Thought in German Culture,* edited by Sander L. Gilman and Jack Zipes, New Haven, Connecticut and London: Yale University Press, 1997
Taylor, Jennifer L., *Writing as Revenge: Jewish German Identity in Post-Holocaust Germany: Reading Survivor Authors Jurek Becker, Edgar Hilsenrath, and Ruth Klüger,* Ph.D. dissertation, Cornell University, 1995

Historians' Debate

On 11 July 1986, *Die Zeit* published an article by the philosopher Jürgen Habermas in which he castigated the apologetic tendencies of some German contemporary historians. He particularly criticized Michael Stürmer, Andreas Hillgruber, Klaus Hildebrand, and Ernst Nolte. Stürmer had repeatedly pleaded for a renationalization of the West German identity through historiography. This, according to Stürmer, would only be possible by circumventing the Nazi period in German history, as an alleged "guilt-obsession" with the latter would otherwise prevent Germans from reaching a more balanced assessment of the national past. Hillgruber, in a little booklet entitled *Zweierlei Untergang,* had, according to Habermas, heeded Stürmer's advice by writing the history of the final months of World War II at the eastern front from the perspective of and identifying with the German soldiers who, according to Hillgruber, heroically defended the German civilians from the threatening Red Army. Hillgruber juxtaposed this vignette with a much briefer and more sober and "scientific" description of the extermination of European Jewry that lacked all moral commitment. Finally, Nolte was accused by Habermas of rewriting the history of National Socialism so as to allow for a more positive identification of Germans with their past. Nolte, according to Habermas, relativized the singularity of the Holocaust by comparing it with other genocides in history and by arguing that Hitler was only responding to the earlier "class genocide" committed by Stalin in the Soviet Union. Hildebrand was primarily criticized for recommending Nolte's work. Together with Stürmer and Hagen Schulze, he formed part of a liberal-conservative camp of historians who were bitter rivals of a left-liberal group headed by the doyens of German historical social science, Hans Ulrich Wehler and Jürgen Kocka. Habermas, in alliance with these left-liberal historians, called on German contemporary historians to reject all attempts to homogenize and renationalize German national identity. Instead, he insisted on a healthy pluralism of historical interpretations and on the enlightening function of history writing. Rather than return to national identity, Habermas argued, Germans should learn to develop "constitutional patriotism" (*Verfassungspatriotismus*), i.e. adhere to the values and sentiments enshrined in the constitution of the Federal Republic.

Habermas's article was the start of a national debate that lasted for more than a year and that has witnessed several rebirths since. Those who had been attacked by Habermas and his allies at first attempted to reduce the issue "to the defence of professional pedantries" (Eley): they denounced Habermas as a nonhistorian, distanced themselves from the obvious link between history and politics, and legitimated Nolte's and Hillgruber's views with reference to a healthy professional pluralism. The debate, however, soon had repercussions far beyond the circle of professional historians and involved journalists, writers, and academics from other disciplines. All major and minor newspapers and journals reported on the controversy, and the debate was carried out on radio and television. Conferences were held on the topic, and a provisional bibliography on the theme, published in 1991, included over 1,200 titles (Donat et al.). The debate was also widely noted abroad—with many foreign historians and writers joining the debate or commenting on it. Anxious questions were being asked about whether the world would witness a new revisionism in the writing of the history of National Socialism. The debate focused on a wide range of themes, many of which had originated in Habermas's original attack.

There was, above all, concern with the relativization of the Holocaust. In Nolte's writings, in particular, Hitler's anti-Semitism appeared as the legitimate response to the Stalinist threat to exterminate the European middle classes. The extreme dimensions of the Holocaust were rooted, according to Nolte, in Stalin's liquidation of the kulak class in the Soviet Union. Nolte's wild theories had their motives in his desire to allow for the return of Germans to a "normal" national identity. Such a return, however, was only possible if one could successfully remove the stumbling block of the Third Reich and, more specifically, of the Holocaust from its central place in the historical self-understanding of Germans. Hence, any attempt to "normalize" the national sentiment in Germany had to downplay the

National Socialist period in German history. There was widespread consensus in the mid-1980s that such a relativization should not be attempted, and with the exception of a minority of far right-wing historians such as Nolte or Helmut Diwald, most historians rejected any such efforts.

Attempts to revitalize the theory of totalitarianism to equate the National Socialist dictatorship with the Communist dictatorships in Eastern Europe were more widespread than contemporary approval for Nolte's philosophical speculations. Even moderate center-right historians continued to use the concept—sometimes pointing out that comparison between the National Socialist and the Communist dictatorships did not necessarily mean equating the two regimes. Other conservatives such as Stürmer and Joachim Fest wanted to revive the "antitotalitarian consensus" of the postwar period, which allegedly was drowned out in the obsession with "coming-to-terms-with-the-past" concerns that began in the 1960s. In light of the continued "Soviet threat" and its "fifth column" in the form of the German peace movement, the revival of antitotalitarianism seemed welcome to conservative historians and politicians alike. Nevertheless, as the concept of totalitarianism had been such a blatant ideological tool of anticommunism in the Cold War, many left-liberal historians found it useless for interpreting either National Socialism or Communism.

The question of German unity was of central importance in the debate. The preamble of the Basic Law obliged every German government to seek German unity as its most urgent priority. By the 1980s, however, many on the center-left in West Germany argued that the time had come to accept the division of Germany. Historians such as Heinrich August Winkler argued that the brief period of a unified German nation state between 1871 and 1945 was not the most happy period of German history and that historians should cease to understand 1871 as their "natural" reference point for the writing of national history. On the other hand, the political change in 1982, which saw Helmut Kohl replace Helmut Schmidt as West German chancellor, brought renewed emphasis on national sentiment. Next to family values and issues of law and order, the "fatherland" and its rhetoric scored high on Kohl's list of priorities. Would German historians under such political conditions return to the Prussianism of the 19th century? Would they begin to champion the national idea once again, as they had done for almost 100 years from the mid-19th to the mid-20th century? Stürmer, for one, argued that only such renationalization would prevent Germany from drifting into "civil war" in the face of the alleged double threat constituted by the peace movement and Soviet Communism. On this issue of German unity, mainstream historians tended to be divided between center-right and center-left historians. It was, to a large extent, a party-political division between those conservative historians with some attachment to the Christian Democratic Parties (CDU/CSU) and those left liberals who were broadly sympathetic to the Social Democratic Party (SPD). While the former accused the Left of an almost pathological antinationalism, the latter responded by castigating neonationalist tendencies among the center right.

There were also fears on the center-left that any return to the nation state might endanger the degree of Westernization achieved by the Federal Republic after 1949. The political and, above all, the intellectual link with the West had ended the German "special path" (*Sonderweg*) and brought the Federal Republic closer to the political culture of the West European democracies, notably Great Britain and France. Historians on the center-left perceived a return to the ideology of the *Sonderweg*. For instance, there had been attempts to revive geopolitics (the notion that modern German history can largely be explained by reference to Germany's position in the center of Europe), as well as efforts to lay the blame for Hitler's success at the door of the Allies, who not only had imposed the Treaty of Versailles on the Germans in 1919 but were also responsible for appeasing the dictator in the 1930s. Furthermore, there had been signs that center-right politicians and historians were interpreting the end of World War II in Europe on 8 May 1945 as a defeat rather than as a liberation. The 40-year anniversary of the end of World War II in 1985 had provided plenty of opportunities to reflect on the suffering of Germans in World War II and thereafter—with particular emphasis on the division of the country at Yalta and the result of the Allied bombing campaign in the war. By contrast, center-left historians stressed the opportunities inherent in the defeat of Nazi Germany. At long last, they argued, at least one part of Germany, the FRG, could embark on the road to the successful democratization and modernization of its society along the lines of other West European nation states.

The controversy was extended to include the question of the general remit of historical writing. Was it legitimate for historians to seek to bring about or stabilize identity? Or should its aim be to allow critical self-understanding and to enlighten (*aufklären*) citizens? Again the division was broadly marked between the center-right and the center-left of German historians. The debate was extended to include plans of the West German government to build two new historical museums in Bonn and Berlin that would depict the history of the FRG (Bonn) and German national history (Berlin), respectively. Center-left historians suspected an attempt by the center-right government to use the opportunity and to present the public with a homogenized and "official" national history and identity that would not allow space for alternative interpretations.

As center-right historians tended to be more present among political and diplomatic historians while center-left historians dominated the areas of social history and the history of everyday life, methodological questions were also discussed. Was diplomatic and political history an antiquated thing of the past? Or were the representatives of German social history attempting to establish themselves as the new orthodoxy, which was unwilling to accept other forms of history writing? Did domestic policy influence foreign policy or vice versa? How useful was the concept of the German *Sonderweg,* which was so central to the German social history sponsored by the so-called Bielefeld school of historians surrounding Hans Ulrich Wehler and Jürgen Kocka? Methodological questions, however, were never the focus of the historians' debate. It was primarily a political controversy about the way Germans should define their identity within a post–National Socialist period in which the National Socialist past would not (and, as historians on the center-left argued, should not) go away.

By way of conclusion, the historians' controversy cannot be adequately understood without reference to its political context. It was an attempt by parts of the center-left to stem the tide of political neoconservatism after the so-called *Wende* in 1982, to which context the revival of the national idea firmly belonged. Stürmer was a close political advisor of Chancellor Helmut Kohl in the mid-1980s, and the CDU/CSU's political agenda included the return to an allegedly "healthy" national identity. The ideological context of the historians' debate also includes the Bitburg affair of May 1985, which attempted symbolically to close the books on Nazi Germany. Furthermore, the debate incorporated the renewed wave of anticommunism in the wake of the German peace movement's vigorous campaign for disarmament in the first half of the 1980s. In referring to an alleged consensus on national matters that had existed before the neoconservative revival, critics of historiographic nationalism were adhering themselves to homogenizing strategies and disallowing alternative discourses that had questioned the rationale of Westernization from the standpoint of the Left. After all, both Habermas and Stürmer strongly defended the FRG's commitment to NATO against neutralist tendencies in the German peace movement. Furthermore, left-liberal historians were revealing their own strong (if often negative) attachments to issues of national history and national identity.

By the late 1980s, it seemed as though the center-left historians, led by Habermas, had been successful in regaining the intellectual high ground: any relativization of the Holocaust had been averted, and plans to return to "healthy" national identity had been thwarted. Nolte and his followers were marginalized and retained credibility only on the far right-wing margins of political and historiographic discourse. Complex modern societies, center-left historians such as Hans Mommsen and Bernd Faulenbach argued, had to live with competing social and political identities rather than waste time in artificially developing consistent and homogenous ones. History writing was about enlightenment rather than about building identities.

The collapse of the GDR in 1989 and the unexpected reunification of the country in 1990, however, changed all that and saw the themes and topics that had been central to the historians' debate return to haunt Germany with renewed vigor and urgency. As the controversies surrounding the Wehrmacht exhibition of the Hamburg Institute for Social Research, Daniel Jonah Goldhagen, or Martin Walser demonstrate, German historical culture continues to be a bitterly divided one.

STEFAN BERGER

See also Jürgen Habermas

Further Reading

Baldwin, Peter, editor, *Reworking the Past: Hitler, the Holocaust, and the Historians' Debate,* Boston: Beacon Press, 1990

Berger, Stefan, "Historians and Nation-Building in Germany after Reunification," *Past and Present* 148 (1995)

———, "Challenge by Reunification: The 'Historical Social Science' at Era's End," *Tel Aviver Jahrbuch für deutsche Geschichte* 25 (1996)

Diner, Dan, and Wolfgang Benz, editors, *Ist der Nationalsozialismus Geschichte? Zu Historisierung und Historikerstreit,* Frankfurt: Suhrkamp, 1987

Donat, Helmut, et al., editors, *Auschwitz erst möglich gemacht? Überlegungen zur jüngsten konservativen Geschichtsbewältigung,* Bremen: Donat, 1991

Eley, Geoff, "Nazism, Politics, and the Image of the Past: Thoughts on the West German *Historikerstreit,* 1986–1987," *Past and Present* 121 (1988)

Evans, Richard J., *In Hitler's Shadow: West German Historians and the Attempt to Escape from the Nazi Past,* London: I.B. Tauris, and New York: Pantheon, 1989

Forever in the Shadow of Hitler? Original Documents of the Historikerstreit, the Controversy Concerning the Singularity of the Holocaust, Atlantic Highlands, New Jersey: Humanities Press, 1993

Gerstenberger, Heide, and Dorothea Schmidt, editors, *Normalität oder Normalisierung? Geschichtswerkstätten und Faschismusanalyse,* Münster: Westfälisches Dampfboot, 1987

Hillgruber, Andreas, *Zweierlei Untergang: Die Zerschlagung des deutschen Reiches und das Ende des europäischen Judentums,* Berlin: Siedler, 1986

Kühnl, Reinhard, editor, *Vergangenheit, die nicht vergeht: Die 'Historiker-Debatte': Darstellung, Dokumentation, Kritik,* Cologne: Pahl-Rugenstein, 1987

Maier, Charles S., *The Unmasterable Past: History, Holocaust, and German National Identity,* Cambridge, Massachusetts: Harvard University Press, 1988

Mommsen, Hans, *Auf der Suche nach historischer Normalität,* Berlin: Argonverlag, 1987

Nolte, Ernst, "Between Myth and Revisionism? The Third Reich in the Perspective of the 1980s," in *Aspects of the Third Reich,* edited by H.W. Koch, London: Macmillan, and New York: St. Martin's Press, 1985

———, *Das Vergehen der Vergangenheit: Antwort an meine Kritiker im sogenannten Historikerstreit,* Berlin: Ullstein, 1987; 2nd edition, 1988

Puhle, Hans-Jürgen, "Die neue Ruhelosigkeit: Michael Stürmers nationalpolitischer Revisionismus," *Geschichte und Gesellschaft* 13 (1987)

Streitfall deutsche Geschichte: Geschichts- und Gegenwartsbewußtsein in den 80er Jahren, Essen: Hobbing, 1988

Wehler, Hans Ulrich, *Entsorgung der deutschen Vergangenheit? Ein polemischer Essay zum "Historikerstreit,"* Munich: C.H. Beck, 1988

Historiography

History as an academic discipline that critically reconstructs past events originated at the University of Göttingen between 1760 and 1800. Göttingen historians such as Johann Christian Gatterer (1727–99), August Ludwig Schlözer (1735–1809), and Ludwig Timotheus Spittler (1752–1810) for the first time formed an intellectual community that defined methodological ground rules for the writing of history and that made history writing distinct from other forms of writing. Professional standards were set that established the discipline of history as a "science" (*Wissenschaft*). The Göttingen historians wrote predominantly regional, social, and economic history, but the rise of the doctrine of nationalism in the 19th century cut short those promising beginnings of a German social history. From the second half of the 19th century onward, the hegemonic discourse of German historiography came to rest on the twin pillars of nationalism and historicism.

Historicism refers to a concept, represented most prominently by Leopold von Ranke (1795–1886), that understands all political order within its own historical context. To understand the nature of any historical phenomenon (be it an institution or an idea), the historicist argues, one has to consider its historical development, the changes it undergoes over a period of time. Historical epochs, Ranke claimed, should not be judged according to predetermined contemporary values or ideas. Rather, they had to be understood on their own terms by empirically establishing "how it actually was" (*wie es eigentlich gewesen*). Some of historicism's key elements had already been defined before Ranke, but Ranke came to embody historicism, largely because he practiced what he preached in such superior fashion. He emphasized both "individuality" and "development" in history. Every historical phenomenon, historical epoch, and historical event had its own individuality, and it was the task of the historian to establish its essence. To do this, historians, according to Ranke, had to immerse themselves in the epoch, to "extinguish" their own personality.

This individualizing approach to the writing of history went hand in hand with a notion of historical development that, according to Ranke, was sanctioned by God's will. This Protestant element in Ranke's historical thinking should be taken very seriously. It made historicism inherently conservative by justifying what had historically triumphed and by condemning historical losers. It also robbed historians of any norms and values against which they could judge historical events. The major problem with historicism was not, as Friedrich Nietzsche (1844–1900) had surmised, its "antiquarianism," or its alleged lack of interest in the present, but its relativism, which often essentially served to legitimate the present.

If Ranke was the godfather of historicism, Johann Gottfried Herder (1744–1803) and Johann Gottlieb Fichte (1762–1814) were the godfathers of the national turn in German historiography. Herder's idea that every people had an essential ethnic core (*Volksseele, Volksgeist*) that separated it from all others and Fichte's notions that a people finds its true expression only through language and that nations are "natural" linguistic communities all became commonplaces among German historians. These commonplaces helped to produce a dangerous cocktail of ethnic, cultural, and linguistic nationalism that came to characterize the mainstream of German historiography until at least 1945.

The power of the state in particular came to fascinate national-liberal Protestant North German historians, who looked to Prussia for the fulfillment of their dream of a unified German nation-state. Prussian historiography (*Borussismus*), however, was caught in a dilemma: its proponents were all liberals who championed the idea of a constitutional state, yet Prussia was the epicenter of illiberalism and absolutism in the German lands. The Prussian traditions had to be united with liberal aspirations. The idea of freedom had to be linked to the necessity of a powerful state. In the 1848 revolution such a merger failed, and in 1871, the majority of Prussian historians convinced themselves that any liberal deficits of the newly founded nation-state would, in the medium term, be overcome. In Imperial Germany, Prussian historiography sought to merge Prussian state traditions and liberal principles by adhering to the concept that a "constitutional monarchy" was the form of government best suited to the needs of Germany. Parliamentary government, which came to be identified with the West European nations, would mean weak government. Given that Germany was not yet a consolidated nation and that its geographical position in the middle of Europe (*Mittellage*) meant that it was potentially surrounded by external enemies, it needed a strong monarchical government that could mediate between the different sectional interests in society.

Around the turn of the century, historians increasingly came to criticize Prussianism for its openly one-sided and politicized writing of history. Stressing instead that the historian should be committed to the ideal of objectivity, historians such as Max Lenz (1850–1932) and Erich Marcks (1861–1938) aimed at returning to Ranke as the great model for any historian. The nation-state, it seemed to them, had been established. Therefore, the major aim of Prussianism had been achieved, and now historians could once again write history more dispassionately. Beneath the surface of this claim to greater objectivity, however, neo-Rankean historiography provided the essential justification for Germany's *Weltpolitik* under Wilhelm II. In this respect, neo-Rankean historiography simply expanded Prussia's mission in Germany to Germany's mission in the world. For this very reason one could argue that neo-Rankeanism not only represents a break with Prussianism but that it also, to a large extent, continued Prussianism. Its championing of social Darwinism, its continued concern with the "great men" in history, its Bismarck cult, its antisocialism, and its focus on the state came to characterize neo-Rankeanism. Neo-Rankeans can be divided into a more conservative section represented by Dietrich Schäfer (1845–1929) and a more liberal variant embodied by Friedrich Meinecke (1862–1954) or Hermann Oncken (1869–1945).

Three important challenges to the dominance of historicism and nationalism in late 19th- and early 20th-century German historiography can be identified. First, Catholic historians criticized Prussia for dividing the nation. They did not adhere to the predominant "small-German"(*kleindeutsch*) conceptions of history. Instead, they championed "greater German" (*großdeutsch*) ideas that maintained the right of Austrians (and other ethnic Germans outside the borders of the German Reich) to belong to the German nation. Second, established historians such as Karl Lamprecht (1856–1915), Eberhard Gothein (1853–1923), and Otto Hintze (1861–1940) became dissatisfied with historicism's sole concern with the political, the individual, and the specific. Lamprecht sought to employ ethnic-psychological criteria to explore social history. Gothein attempted to introduce cultural history, while Hintze aimed to establish a sociological understanding of the state, using general typologies to explore economic, structural, and comparative history. The Lamprecht controversy around the turn of the century was a major effort by mainstream historicism to retain the methodological and thematic homogeneity of the profession, and Lamprecht's opponents succeeded in delaying the introduction of social, cultural, and comparative history for another half century. Third, Marxist historians outside the profession, above all Franz Mehring (1846–1919), practiced social history. The close association between social history and socialist history made it even more difficult for social history to become established at German universities, which remained bulwarks of antisocialism (at least in the FRG) until well after World War II.

After 1918, German historiography was preoccupied with defending the nation against the war guilt clause of the Versailles Treaty. The profession cultivated antirepublican, "antisystem" sentiments that were powerfully underpinned by the notion of a German *Sonderweg*. It perceived the German nation-state as superior in comparison with its West European neighbors. In particular, the Prussian idea of the state as standing above society and party politics prevented a more widespread endorsement of parliamentary democracy. The historicist concept of "understanding" (*Verstehen*) was still regarded as superior to the various normative approaches of "Western" historiography. A handful of committed republicans could only be found among the younger generation of historians, which included Eckart Kehr (1902–33), Arthur Rosenberg (1889–1943), G.W.F. Hallgarten (1901–75), and Hajo Holborn (1902–69).

Their challenge to the dominant mixture of nationalism and historicism was rivaled by the challenge of *Volkshistoriker* such as Hans Freyer (1880–1969) and Gunther Ipsen (1899–1984). By establishing sociological categories for the writing of history, the *Volkshistoriker* were aiming to widen the horizon of historians to encompass social and cultural history. Their nostalgia for premodern communities and their espousal of a crude and blatant racism, however, tainted their conceptualization of social history. Their focus ensured, of course, that *Volksgeschichte* was popular under National Socialism, especially with a younger generation of historians who willingly cooperated with the Nazi regime in planning the future map of a German-dominated Europe and, most horrifically, the extermination of European Jewry. But the older generation of historians also served the regime well enough to prevent the Nazis from attempting any major institutional changes.

The key pillars of German historiography remained intact both in 1933 and 1945—at least in West Germany. In the GDR, the break with the German tradition was sharper and more thorough. The small dissident Marxist tradition of German history writing became the prescribed new orthodoxy. The more traditional historians, but also some Marxists who found it hard to conform to the dogmatism espoused by the SED, were driven out of the universities and out of the country. In subsequent decades, East German social history stimulated important debates on a variety of topics, including class formation, revolution, the working class, and the labor movement. Initially, the rejection of the national heritage promised a break with the traditions of German historiography, but already after 1951 GDR historians developed their own nationalist narratives, and their Marxist theory often was little more than a gloss laid over rather traditional historicist studies of the (overwhelmingly) nationalist past. The 1980s even saw marked efforts to integrate a sense of positive national identity into the historical consciousness of a self-professed socialist society. The "heritage and tradition" (*Erbe und Tradition*) debate aimed to legitimate the "socialist German nation" of the GDR.

After 1945, the doyens of West German historiography such as Meinecke and Gerhard Ritter (1888–1967) upheld both the historicist paradigm and the notion of a "good nationalism," which was routinely contrasted to the National Socialist perversion of it. A delayed break with the historiographic tradition only occurred in the late 1950s and early 1960s. While a younger group of historians championed by Theodor Schieder (1908–84) and Werner Conze (1910–86) were attracted to social history, the publication of Fritz Fischer's (1908–) books on the outbreak of World War I marked the end of the nationalist consensus in German historiography. A new historical social science (*Gesellschaftsgeschichte*) was championed by, among others, Hans-Ulrich Wehler (1931–) and Jürgen Kocka (1941–). Methodologically, it built on Max Weber's (1864–1920) "ideal types" and Hintze's "generalizing methods" in order to put forward a more theoretically informed way of writing history. They investigated structures and processes, and particular emphasis was given to explaining the rise of National Socialism from within German society. Historical social science replaced the politics of the nation with the politics of emancipation. Its project was to contribute, through the writing of history, to the bringing about of a genuine civic society.

German historiographic discourse was genuinely pluralized in the 1970s and 1980s. While traditional historicist approaches continued to inform the writing of much political history, historical social science itself came under intense criticism from proponents of a history of everyday life (*Alltagsgeschichte*). They attacked what they regarded as reductionist modernization theory underpinning historical social science. They accused its proponents of leaving the people out of their histories and producing sterile teleologies of modernization in which human agency disappeared behind structures and processes. A History Workshop Movement united thousands of mostly lay historians, unattached to the profession, who began unearthing a rich stream of local and regional history. Women's and gender history provided new fields of historical investigation and reinterpreted older ones with refreshing new perspectives. Postmodern approaches to the writing of history, and in particular the so-called linguistic turn, have drawn attention both to the tenuous borderline between history as a "science" and literature and to the importance of language in the constitution of social "reality."

The collapse of the GDR in 1989 and reunification of the country in 1990 reinvigorated attempts (which had already begun in the mid-1980s, with the historians' debate) to renationalize German historical consciousness. A self-declared "new right" has called for the establishment of a "self-confident nation." New-right historians have criticized German historiography for its alleged anti-Germanism. They have attempted to marginalize what was essential about National Socialism, namely, its extreme racism, and instead they have foregrounded the allegedly modern aspects of the Nazi regime. Furthermore, they have been concerned with shifting the history of National Socialism into the background by concentrating on the history of the "second German dictatorship," the GDR. The old Federal Republic is interpreted by the new right as an unpalatable provincial *Sonderweg,* the traditions of which have to be abandoned in the pursuit of a "normal," post-1990 nation-state. Finally, the new right has attempted to portray the nation-state as the "natural" focus of identity for people at the end of the 20th century. More mainstream conservative historians share parts of the new right's rhetoric of "normalization" and "national identity," and some prominent representatives of historical social science have declared their willingness to return to the category of the nation. The continued methodological plurality and conceptual variety of history writing in contemporary Germany, however, is a hopeful sign that any new *Sonderweg* of German historiography belongs firmly to the past.

STEFAN BERGER

Further Reading

Berger, Stefan, *The Search for Normality: National Identity and Historical Consciousness in Germany since 1800,* Providence: Berghahn, 1997

Burleigh, Michael, *Germany Turns Eastwards: A Study of*

Ostforschung in the Third Reich, Cambridge and New York: Cambridge University Press, 1988

Eley, Geoff, "Is All the World a Text? From Social History to the History of Society Two Decades Later," in *The Historic Turn in the Human Sciences*, edited by Terrence J. McDonald, Ann Arbor: University of Michigan Press, 1996

Evans, Richard J., *In Defence of History*, London: Granta, 1997; as *In Defense of History*, New York: Norton, 1999

Geyer, Michael, and Konrad H. Jarausch, "The Future of the German Past: Transatlantic Reflections for the 1990s," *Central European History* 22 (1989)

Iggers, Georg G., *The German Conception of History: The National Tradition of Historical Thought from Herder to the Present*, Middletown, Connecticut: Wesleyan University Press, 1968; revised edition, 1983

———, *Marxist Historiography in Transformation: East German Social History in the 1980s*, New York: Berg, 1991

———, *Historiography in the Twentieth Century: From Scientific Objectivity to the Postmodern Challenge*, Hanover, New Hampshire: Wesleyan University Press, 1997

Lambert, Peter, "German Historians and Nazi Ideology: The Parameters of the *Volksgemeinschaft* and the Problem of Historical Legitimation, 1930–45," *European History Quarterly* 25 (1995)

Lehmann, Hartmut, and James van Horn Melton, editors, *Paths of Continuity: Central European Historiography from the 1930s to the 1950s*, Washington, D.C.: German Historical Institute, and Cambridge and New York: Cambridge University Press, 1994

Lipp, Carola, "Writing History as Political Culture: Social History versus 'Alltagsgeschichte': A German Debate," *Storia della Storiografia* 17 (1990)

Lüdtke, Alf, editor, *The History of Everyday Life: Reconstructing Historical Experiences and Ways of Life*, Princeton, New Jersey: Princeton University Press, 1995

Maier, Charles S., *The Unmasterable Past: History, Holocaust, and German National Identity*, Cambridge, Massachusetts: Harvard University Press, 1988

Moses, John Anthony, *The Politics of Illusion: The Fischer Controversy in German Historiography*, London: Prior, and New York: Barnes and Noble, 1975

Oberkrome, Willi, *Volksgeschichte: Methodische Innovation und völkische Ideologisierung in der deutschen Geschichtswissenschaft, 1918–1945*, Göttingen: Vandenhoek und Ruprecht, 1993

Oexle, Otto Gerhard, *Geschichtswissenschaft im Zeichen des Historismus: Studien zu Problemgeschichten der Moderne*, Göttingen: Vandenhoek und Ruprecht, 1996

Ritter, Gerhard Albert, *The New Social History in the Federal Republic of Germany*, London: German Historical Institute, 1991

Schöttler, Peter, editor, *Geschichtsschreibung als Legitimationswissenschaft, 1918–1945*, Frankfurt: Suhrkamp, 1997

Sheehan, James J., "What Is German History? Reflections on the Role of German History and Historiography," *Journal of Modern History* 53 (1981)

Weber, Wolfgang, "The Long Reign and the Final Fall of the German Conception of History: A Historical-Sociological View," *Central European History* 21 (1988)

Ernst Theodor Amadeus Hoffmann 1776–1822

Among readers in the English-speaking world, there is a distinct vagueness about the work and the reputation of E.T.A. Hoffmann. If one has heard of him at all, it is often in the context of Jacques Offenbach's opera *Les contes d'Hoffmann* (1881; *Tales of Hoffmann*), which is based on his stories and whose mention conjures up romantic notions of jolly tavern scenes, unrequited love, and a gentle gondola ride to the accompaniment of the famous "Barcarolle." Some might know that Hoffmann was the literary inspiration for Tchaikovsky's *Nutcracker* suite and for another famous ballet, Delibes's *Coppelia*. But as far as his writings and the circumstances of his life are concerned, there is considerable ignorance—apart from a vague sense that he was a rather unbalanced character, fond of alcohol and prone to fantastic dreams and visions. Walter Scott, one of the first British readers of Hoffmann, was responsible for giving Hoffmann bad press in this regard and for contributing to the persisting view of Hoffmann as a drunk and a writer of ephemeral horror-stories. Whatever the extent of Scott's influence on the image of Hoffmann in the English-speaking world, particularly in the 19th century, it is certainly true that Hoffmann's influence on English literature has been minimal compared with the scale of his reputation in France and Russia.

Within Germany he was regarded as an effective storyteller in the 19th century, but not until the latter half of the 20th century was he considered a serious writer. The 19th-century view of Hoffmann was strongly influenced by the publication of *Aus Hoffmann's Leben und Nachlass* (1823; Hoffmann's Life and Unpublished Works), which includes a combination of original letters and diary entries compiled by Hoffmann's friend Julius Eduard Hitzig. For the most laudable of motives—he wished to preserve the memory of his friend—Hitzig provided a detailed account of the many stages of Hoffmann's life and activities. However, he could not conceal his disapproval of what he regarded as Hoffmann's suspect behavior and character, especially his drinking. This moralistic tone gained currency as Hitzig's work was constantly reprinted, and the relevance of its conclusions was not restricted to Hoffmann's life; what relevance could be ascribed to the characters and situations that a man created under the influence of drink? This judgment, together with that of Walter Scott, was not without its effect even on Goethe who, like Heinrich Heine, tended to dismiss Hoffmann as a writer of sensational and second-rate stories. With the onset and growth of realism in the course of the 19th century, interest in the Romantic period remained dormant until the end of the century, although Hoffmann, ironically, may be regarded as a forerunner of realism in his choice of locations.

Thus, although Hoffmann's work was never out of print, it was rarely assumed that he had anything very important to say. It was recognized that his most successful stories, such as the "Märchen" *Der Goldne Topf* (1814; *The Golden Pot*) were a virtuoso weave of the fantastic and the realistic and swept the reader along by the skillful interchange of perspective and the grotesqueness of the humorous effects. His skill in creating terrifying situations was also generally recognized (he was widely known as "Gespenster-Hoffmann" [Hoffmann of the ghost stories]), but the verdict of the literary society, and in particular of the academic world, was that, compared with some of his contemporaries, he did not have anything very profound to say about the human condition.

In the past 30 years, there has been a considerable change of opinion. It is now recognized that, with regard to both content and form, there are many modern elements in Hoffmann and that to have consigned him to the category of a writer of Gothic potboilers was to underestimate his contribution to German literature. Some of his work is seen to contain a psychological depth and realism that was quite remarkable for his time and to betray a deep interest in the motivation for human action. In narrative technique, Hoffmann is now seen as a skilled and subtle practitioner who is just as concerned with establishing the credibility and veracity of his story as he is with creating startling effects. This is not to doubt that, where some of his stories are concerned (this includes the group entitled *Nachtstücke* [1816–17; Night Pieces], of which *Der Sandmann* [*The Sandman*] is the opening story), Hoffmann's prime motivation was to produce what the public wanted and to earn money. (His professional career as a lawyer in the Prussian civil service had been cut short in 1806 by the Napoleonic occupation, and his alternative source of income as a musician was not particularly lucrative.) Thus there is an inconsistency in the quality of his work.

One of the fascinating aspects of many of his stories is the way in which contemporary urban life is present as the starting point for the narrative; the fact that the fantastic and romantic elements tend to monopolize the reader's attention can sometimes obscure the point that the "unreal" world grows out of the real one and is unthinkable without it. Berlin is the city most closely associated with Hoffmann since he spent more time there than anywhere else, leading, in the eight years up to his death, an active social life with other writers and artists and establishing his reputation as a liberal-minded lawyer and particularly as a writer. But, where the *Nachtstücke* are concerned, the experience of Bamberg is crucial and provides a context in which many of his motifs and themes can be more fully understood.

Hoffmann moved to Bamberg in 1808, two years after declining to take an oath of allegiance to Napoleon and thus barring himself from further employment as a lawyer in the civil service. He was already becoming known as a composer and in 1805 had completed his "Singspiel" *Die lustigen Musikanten* (The Merry Musicians), the Mass in D minor and the Symphony in E-flat major. The post of kapellmeister at the theater in Bamberg seemed initially to offer him the chance to devote himself to music, to which he was drawn above all else (he had changed his middle name from Wilhelm to Amadeus in homage to Mozart), and at the same time to earn a decent living in a period of considerable political and social fluidity in Germany. But within a year Hoffmann had resigned from his post and was earning his living as a freelance music teacher. When a new general manager of the theater was appointed in 1810, Hoffmann was persuaded to return as a theater composer and stage designer, but he maintained his independent source of income, which was now augmented by his contributions to the *Allgemeine Musikalische Zeitung,* published in Leipzig. One of these contributions was his first story, *Ritter Gluck,* published in 1809, which begins in an entirely realistic setting, a Berlin street-café, and describes an encounter between the narrator and a figure who ultimately reveals himself to be the composer Christoph Willibald von Gluck. The fact that Gluck has been dead some 20 years in no way detracts from the reality of the experience for the narrator, and the reader is introduced to the manner, to become typical of Hoffmann, in which the world of tangible phenomena can be transformed into an imaginative experience which is just as real but which cannot be explained in rational terms.

The move to Bamberg meant that for the first time in his life, Hoffmann was able to develop his talents as a musician and a writer. With his review of Beethoven's Fifth Symphony he also established himself as a music critic of first rank, a view which was later to be confirmed by his interpretation of Mozart's *Don Giovanni.* Hoffmann was only too glad not to be tied to what was to him the soul-destroying burden of a professional routine, and he found time to develop his talents as a conductor, voice-trainer, singer (he had a light tenor voice), stage designer, and painter. But the central experiences of the Bamberg period which were to leave an indelible mark on his literary work are connected, on the one hand, with his activities as a music teacher, and, on the other, with the contacts he made among the medical profession and the monks of the Franciscan order in Bamberg. Of great significance for the sense of social estrangement typical of many of his characters was his relationship with one of his pupils.

Julia Marc was 14 years old when she began taking singing lessons with Hoffmann. She is reputed to have had a glorious voice, and Hoffmann fell totally in love with her. There is little evidence that his love was reciprocated; it was certainly never consummated. After a full-scale row during which Hoffmann insulted Julia's betrothed, the contact was broken. Julia eventually married her merchant fiancé and left for Hamburg. There is no doubt that the motif of the unattainable beloved that is characteristic of Hoffmann's work derives from this experience, as does the sense in which the artist is portrayed as being essentially apart from a society in which he and his art are misunderstood or rejected. This rejection, indeed this inherent inability to adapt and conform, is most clearly illustrated by the figure of Johannes Kreisler, one of Hoffmann's most famous creations, a gifted yet restless musician who is drawn to society—indeed, in the novel *Lebensansichten des Kater Murr* (1820–22; *The Life and Opinions of Kater Murr*) to a girl called Julia—but who lacks the balance and equanimity to conform. Kreisler first appears in short prose pieces written during the Bamberg period and, in his restlessness and his inability to break out of the "Kreis" which is symbolic of his personality and reflected in his name, he is akin to Nathanael in *The Sandman.* In some of his "Märchen" Hoffmann allows his characters to attain to the ideal world of art beyond the restraints of everyday existence, but both Johannes Kreisler and Nathanael are denied this solution.

Hoffmann could be sociable, and in Bamberg he established friendships that influenced his writing. Although not a religious person in any conventional sense, he became friendly with the abbot of the local Capuchin monastery, not least because of the wine that was freely available there, and acquainted himself with the ascetic routine of the monks. His first novel, *Die Elixiere des Teufels* (1815–16; *The Devil's Elixir*), written in the style of the Gothic novel and heavily influenced by Lewis's *The Monk,* drew upon his experiences in Bamberg and immediately precedes and then coincides with work on the *Nachtstücke*. The themes of the novel and the hero's sense of an ineluctable fate prove interesting parallels to the shorter stories.

Despite their reliance upon inexplicable and frightening events and phenomena, it is the depiction of characters under stress that gives these works their remarkable quality and enables them to transcend the limitations of the conventional literary forms in which they are written. From an early age both Medardus, the central character in *The Devil's Elixir,* and Nathanael have struggled against a force that prevents them from finding a secure and lasting place within society, whether it is an unblemished career in holy orders where Medardus is concerned, or the attainment of a conventional life and a contented relationship with Clara in Nathanael's case. In the novel, the preponderance of twists of fate and cases of mistaken identity tends to obscure the picture of Medardus's personality and, in any case, it is not easy for the average reader to identity with the monk. Nathanael, however, is a student and possesses traits that can be generally appreciated. The lasting fascination of the story resides in no small measure in the fact that, although Nathanael's fate is not shared by those around him, what happens to him is presented as entirely credible in psychological terms.

Among Hoffmann's acquaintances in Bamberg was the physician Adalbert Friedrich Marcus, whose interest in psychological illnesses and in animal magnetism had made him famous beyond the bounds of Bamberg. Like many writers of the Romantic period, Hoffmann was fascinated by the causes of psychological disorder and had read much of the popular literature of the period on the subject, such as Gotthilf Heinrich Schubert's *Ansichten von der Nactseite der Naturwissenschaften* (1808; Views on the Dark Side of the Natural Sciences) and Johann Christian Reil's *Rhapsodien über die Anwendung der psychischen Curmethode auf Geisteszerrüttungen* (1803; Thoughts on the Psychological Treatment of Mental Breakdown). Hoffmann the lawyer also had a professional interest in the extent to which the individual was responsible for his actions, and it is remarkable how the themes of free will and determinism, which characterize the novels and dramas of the Naturalist period later in the century, are prefigured in the work of this late-Romantic writer. He employs motifs of the contemporary fate tragedy and resorts to traditional Romantic motifs such as mistaken identity in order to enhance the effectiveness of his stories, but underlying the familiar surface is the realization that the individual, in his egocentric existence, often experiences great difficulty in establishing a healthy relationship with the outside world. In some stories this tension is described and resolved through humor and understanding; in others, the resolution is a tragic one.

Hoffmann's final years (1814–22) were spent in Berlin, where he resumed his legal career. He became a counsellor in the Prussian Supreme Court and, in his spare time, frequented the literary salons. In 1818 he was required to investigate subversive political activities against the state. Although he carried out his duties with characteristic efficiency, he was moved to satirize—in the figure of Knarrpanti in *Meister Floh* (1822; *Master Flea*)—the abuse of state power, particularly on the part of the Director of Police in Berlin. (Hoffman died before the ensuing investigation into his conduct was completed.) This work, written as Hoffmann gradually succumbed to paralysis, is remarkable too for the intricate interweaving of past and present, the contrast between internal self-awareness and external perception, and the issue of psychological control and manipulation. These themes are central to most of Hoffmann's works that end tragically. The fact that they are presented here in the form of a "Märchen," linking the tale in theme and form to the more famous *The Golden Pot,* emphasizes the degree to which he was capable of objectivity, courage, and good humor in the most appalling physical circumstances.

David H.R. Jones

Biography

Born in Königsberg, 24 January 1776. Studied law, University of Königsberg, 1792–95; civil service posts in Glogau, 1796–98; Berlin, 1798–1800; Posen, 1800–2; Plozk, 1802–4; Warsaw, 1804–8; house composer and designer, Bamberg Theater, 1810–12; conductor for Sekonda Company, Leipzig and Dresden, 1813–14; composer of operas and editor of music by Beethoven, Mozart, Gluck, and others, 1809–21. Died 25 June 1822.

Selected Works

Collections

Werke, edited by Georg Ellinger, 15 vols., 1912; 2nd edition, 1927
Sämtliche Werke, edited by Walter Müller-Seidel et al., 5 vols., 1960–65
Gesammelte Werke, edited by Rudolf Mingau and Hans-Joachim Kruse, 1976–
Sämtliche Werke, edited by Wulf Segebrecht, Hartmut Steinecke et al., 1985–

Fiction

Fantasiestücke in Callots Maniet, 4 vols., 1814–15
Die Elixiere des Teufels, 1815–16; as *The Devil's Elixir,* translated by R. Gillies, 1824; as *The Devil's Elixirs,* translated by Ronald Taylor, 1963
Nachtstücke, 2 vols., 1816–17
Seltsame Leiden eines Theater-Direktors, 1819
Klein Zaches genannt Zinnober, 1819
Die Serapions-Brüder: Gesammelte Erzählungen und Märchen, 4 vols., 1819–21; edited by Wulf Segebrecht, 1995; as *The Serapion Brethren,* translated by Alexander Ewing, 1886–92
Lebensansichten des Kater Murr, 1820–22
Prinzessin Brambilla, 1821
Meister Floh, 1822; as *Master Flea,* translated by G. Sloane, in *Specimens of German Romance,* vol. 2, 1826
Die letzten Erzählungen, 2 vols., 1825
Tales of Hoffmann, edited by Christopher Lazare, 1946
The Tales of Hoffmann, translated by Michael Bullock, 1963
Tales of Hoffmann, translated by James Kirkup, 1966
The Best Tales of Hoffmann, edited by E.F. Bleiler, 1967
Tales, edited by Victor Lange, 1982
Tales of Hoffmann, edited and translated by R.J. Hollingdale et al., 1982

Play

Die Maske, edited by Friedrich Schnapp, 1923

Poetry

Poetische Werke, edited by Gerhard Seidel, 6 vols., 1958

Other

Die Vision auf dem Schlachtfelde bei Dresden, 1814
Briefwechsel, edited by Hans von Müller and Friedrich Schnapp, 3 vols., 1967–69
Selected Writings, edited and translated by Leonard J. Kent and Elizabeth C. Knight, 2 vols., 1969
Tagebücher, edited by Friedrich Schnapp, 1971

Juristische Arbeiten, edited by Friedrich Schnapp, 1973
Selected Letters of E.T.A. Hoffmann, edited and translated by Johanna C. Sahlin, 1977

Further Reading

Feldges, Brigitte, and Ulrich Stadler, *E.T.A. Hoffmann: Epoche, Werk, Wirkung,* Munich: Beck, 1986
Hewett-Thayer, Harvey W., *Hoffmann: Author of the Tales,* Princeton, New Jersey: Princeton University Press, 1948
Hitzig, Julius Eduard, *Aus Hoffmann's Leben und Nachlass,* Berlin: Dümmler, 1823; as *E.T.A. Hoffmanns Leben und Nachlass,* edited by Wolfgang Held, Frankfurt: Insel, 1986
Kaiser, Gerhard R., *E.T.A. Hoffmann,* Stuttgart: Metzler, 1988
Köhn, Lothar, *Vieldeutige Welt: Studien zur Struktur der Erzählungen E.T.A. Hoffmanns und zur Entwicklung seines Werkes,* Tübingen: Niemeyer, 1966
McGlathery, James M., *E.T.A. Hoffmann,* London: Prentice Hall, and New York: Twayne, 1997
Safranski, Rüdiger, *E.T.A. Hoffmann: Das Leben eines skeptischen Phantasten,* Munich: Hanser, 1984
Segebrecht, Wulf, *Autobiographie und Dichtung: Eine Studie zum Werk E.T.A. Hoffmanns,* Stuttgart: Metzler, 1967
Wright, Elzabeth, *E.T.A. Hoffmann and the Rhetoric of Terror: Aspects of Language Used for the Evocation of Fear,* London: University of London, Institute of Germanic Studies, 1978

Das Fräulein von Scuderi 1819

Novella by Ernst Theodor Amadeus Hoffmann

Drawing on Pitaval and Voltaire respectively, this story by Ernst Theodor Amadeus Hoffmann constructs a more-than-usually solid historical basis of reality for what is, on the surface, a tense murder mystery, but at a deeper level, primarily a psychological and spiritual study. Madeleine de Scudéry, a 73-year-old woman of letters universally respected for her grace and virtue, is, for the first time, drawn into contact with the world of crime and vice which seems to counterpoint the brilliant culture of the Paris of Louis XIV and Madame de Maintenon. Will Scudéry's erstwhile protégé, Olivier, be tortured and executed for the apparent murder of the ultrarespectable goldsmith Cardillac, who, it turns out, is mentally unbalanced and criminal? Olivier is reprieved, thanks not to Scudéry's analytical powers of deduction, but to her ability to confront and defeat the powers of darkness within her own heart and mind, and the moral (and artistic) force she can bring to bear to persuade the King.

Mystery (not infrequently allied to criminality) was nothing new in German literature. It is familiar from the Gothic tradition, originating in the 18th century, which certainly strongly influenced Hoffmann. But the frequent references to the heavenly and the hellish, angelic and diabolical to be found in this text are more than Gothic clichés. They are part of a densely woven fabric of motifs whose unifying theme is the duality endemic to the universe, which preoccupies Hoffmann as it does so many other Romantics and which usually takes the form of an examination of the delicate and easily disturbed balance of a material dimension and a transcendental dimension that meet and interact in the human mind—or at least in those minds that are not deadened by philistinism. Occasionally, Hoffmann develops this theme in mythical form (e.g., *Der goldene Topf* [*The Golden Pot*] or *Prinzessin Brambilla*), but even in a work such as *Scuderi,* where the carefully created historical setting adds "realistic" ballast, the basic framework is clearly discernible. This is most obvious, perhaps, in the formulaic "angel" figure of Madelon, Cardillac's daughter and Olivier's beloved, who constitutes Scudéry's principal material "evidence" for the faith that seems momentarily to be confounded by the "facts" in the important Conciergerie scene. The crucial battle against the "höllische Macht auf Erden" (power of hell on earth), in whose reality Hoffmann certainly believes, and which attacks Scudéry and threatens, not her physical, but her spiritual life—her *Glaube an Tugend und Treue* (faith in virtue and fidelity)—can become manifest in the human world only through the human mind and will. The old lady's acceptance of the subsequent interview with Olivier represents her heroic victory in the battle and deepens and enriches the *Anmut* (grace) and *Würde* (dignity) that are the outward and visible signs of that victory. She is no longer "zerrissen" (torn apart) or in danger of being so.

Cardillac, on the other hand, has lost the battle. While not perhaps himself a devil, he is beset by devils. In spite of a (probably deliberate) parallel with Kleist's opening paragraph of *Michael Kohlhaas* (1810), he is no Kohlhaas, and the chance of a final reconciliation which might save his soul is not open to him. As an artist, he has not lost the awareness of a higher ideal, but he cannot achieve the balance between the conflicting inner feelings to which all artists are subject. He may try to shift the blame on to a "böser Stern" (evil star) or entertain the superstitious hope that Scudéry can somehow "save" him, but he is a lost soul, a creature of the dark (the duality of day and night forms an important thread in the story's structural fabric). He may admire the grace and dignity encapsulated in the epigram of Scudéry ("Un amant qui craint les voleurs n'est point digne d'amour" [a lover who is afraid of thieves is not at all worthy of love])—a detail culled from Wagenseil's "Nuremberg Chronicle" of 1697, which was in a way the seed from which the whole story grew—but to redeem him, it must arise from within. And since it cannot, he is irredeemably split—a fact reflected outwardly in the contradiction between a rigidly enforced social virtue and an inner criminality, and in an unattractive and rather ridiculous eccentricity which contrasts with Scudéry's genuine humor. This humor is reflected most notably in her handling of the conceit of the "Goldschmiedsbraut" which forms the launching-pad of her successful attempt to move the King, the representative of God on earth, to mercy. She begins by making him laugh, and then works through the force of her personality and a narrative imbued with genuine poetic skills ("[die] Gewalt des lebendigsten Lebens" [the power of the liveliest of life]) which belong to Hoffmann's, rather than to the historical, Scudéry. It is right that the story should bear her name, for it is above all in the creation of this figure of *Anmut und Liebenswürdigkeit* (grace and amiability), whom Hoffmann himself contrasts with the person who presided in the 17th century over a "bureau d'esprit" in the Rue St Honoré, that it succeeds, as the Serapiontic Brotherhood agrees, in becoming "wahrhaft serapiontisch, weil sie auf geschichtlichem Grund gebaut, doch hinaufsteige ins Fantastische" (truly serapiontic, because, although it is built on a historical foundation, it nevertheless ascends into the realm of the fantastic).

If it does not represent Hoffmann at his most complex and profound (and perhaps because of that), this story is a fine example of his narrative art and has always been popular.

ALAN MENHENNET

Editions

First edition: in *Taschenbuch der Liebe und Freundschaft gewidmet,* 1819; also in *Die Serapions-Brüder,* 1819–21

Critical edition: in *Die Serapionsbrüder,* edited by Wulf Segebrecht, Munich: Artemis und Winkler, 1995

Translation: in *Tales of Hoffmann,* translated by R.J. Hollingdale et al., Harmondsworth: Penguin, 1982

Further Reading

Ellis, J.M., "E.T.A. Hoffmann's *Das Fräulein von Scuderi,*" *Modern Language Review* 64 (1969)

Himmel, Helmut, "Schuld und Sühne der Scuderi: Zu Hoffmanns Novelle," *Mitteilungen der E.T.A. Hoffmann-Gesellschaft* 7 (1960)

Kanzog, Klaus, "E.T.A. Hoffmanns Erzählung *Das Fräulein von Scuderi* als Kriminalgeschichte," *Mitteilungen der E.TA. Hoffmann-Gesellschaft* 11 (1964)

Thalmann, Marianne, "E.T.A. Hoffmanns *Fräulein von Scuderi,*" *Monatshefte* 41 (1949)

Der Sandmann 1817

Novella by Ernst Theodor Amadeus Hoffmann

Ernst Theodor Amadeus Hoffmann's story *Der Sandmann* (*The Sandman*), written in 1815 and published in 1817 in his second collection of stories entitled *Nachtstücke* (Night Pieces), was not well received by his contemporaries. The gruesome tale about the traumatic experiences of the child Nathanael, who is punished by the sinister advocate Coppelius for spying on adults performing chemical experiments, evoked confusion in readers because of the story's interplay between reality perception and imagination. Sir Walter Scott shaped the story's negative reception, which continued throughout the 19th century, when he dismissed *The Sandman* as the ominous creation of a sick and crazy intellect. Scott attributed what he considered an unbearable poetic flop to the erratic or even drugged mind of the musician, civil servant, and writer E.T.A. Hoffmann. This devastating judgment, which was echoed in a milder tone by prominent readers such as Georg Wilhelm Friedrich Hegel and Johann Wolfgang von Goethe, was based on Hoffmann's fictionalization of madness. Critics felt appalled by the aesthetic representation of the dreadful evil that emanates from the story's terrifying figures, who torment the hero Nathanael until he seeks escape from the abyss of insanity through suicide.

As in many of his other stories such as the *Der Magnetiseur* (1814; *The Magnetizer*), *Das Gelübde* (1817; *The Pledge*), *Das öde Haus* (1817; *The Deserted House*), or *Der unheimliche Gast* (1821; *The Uncanny Guest*), Hoffmann utilizes his broad knowledge of contemporary psychiatry (Mesmer, Pinel, Reil) in order to represent the crisis of modern rationality by depicting the bewilderment of the madman's perception, identification, and relationships. While many narratives of the late-Romantic period disclose the nightmares of reason as a different source of privileged knowledge—and in that way question the authority of enlightened rationality—the provocation of *The Sandman* derives from additional sources. On the one hand, the story blurs the distinction between the real and the imagined through its complex narrative relativism (which includes letters, change of perspectives, and the narrator's commentary on storytelling); on the other hand, it creates an uncanny effect by intertwining disturbing themes and motifs (childhood trauma, occult science, voyeurism, and fetishism) with the familiar (domestic happiness, love, and poetry).

It took more than 100 years until *The Sandman* met a competent reader who was able to disperse the disputable clichés lingering over the story and its author. In his intriguing analysis *Das Unheimliche* (1919; *The Uncanny*), Sigmund Freud pays much more attention to the story's leitmotif: the fear of losing one's eyes. Nathanael identifies the sandman, the folklore character who makes children sleep by sprinkling sand in their eyes, with Coppelius, who not only dislocates his limbs but also threatens to take the boy's eyes out for his mysterious endeavors. This primal scene has a long-lasting effect on Nathanael's life in terms of the development of his psychotic behavior. Later in life when he is a student, Nathanael encounters Coppelius's double in the barometer seller Coppola, who convinces him to purchase a pocket spyglass through which Nathanael observes Olimpia, the daughter of his science professor Spalanzani. Attracted by her beauty, Nathanael falls in love with her and neglects his fiancée, the domestic and rational Clara, until he discovers that Olimpia is in fact a lifeless automaton created by Spalanzani and Coppola. They appear to have continued the experiments initiated by Coppelius and Nathanael's father because Spalanzani claims that Coppelius/Coppola stole Nathanael's eyes in order to insert them into Olimpia's empty eye sockets. Freud reads this reoccurrence of Nathanael's early childhood fear (dismemberment, disfiguration, and the loss of eyes) as a symbolic displacement of the hero's enslavement to his castration complex, and he argues that Nathanael splits his father-imago into the good, loving father (his natural father/Spalanzani) and the bad, punishing father (Coppelius/Coppola). The psychoanalytical interpretation concludes that Olimpia and Nathanael are identical: the automatic doll represents "a materialization of Nathaniel's [*sic*] feminine attitude towards his father," which renders him "incapable of loving a woman." Freud's thought-provoking commentary on the story's obsession with vision, his credits to Hoffmann's prepsychoanalytical insights, but also his ignorance toward the text's narrative structures sparked a new interest in the story.

Since the 1970s, subsequent interpretations of *The Sandman* have either extended or rejected Freud's reading. Approaches following Lacanian psychoanalytic thought see the text as an implicit critique of the new family ideology; after all, Nathanael's bourgeois home with its emphasis on socialization through storytelling is the place where the fear of the sandman is inscribed into the child. The modern practice of subject formation through imaginary identification with the other creates the fantasized doppelgänger, the object of Nathanael's narcissistic desire as well as his voyeurism and fetishism. Opponents of such views have pointed out that the narrative complexities of *The Sandman* defy psychological categorization. According to these critics, the intellectual uncertainty produced by the text might not be a manifestation of Nathanael's paranoid fantasies; rather, this uncertainty might result from a conspiracy staged against the innocent victim. The textual ambiguities and ironies support such a thesis, because the narrator/author himself diffuses the borderline between reality and hallucination in his much-quoted phrase: "Then, O my reader, you may come to believe that nothing can be stranger or weirder than real life, and that the poet can do no more than capture the strangeness of reality, like the dim reflection in a dull mirror." Hoffmann's satiric interventions in the story open an even wider range of possible readings. If, for example, the public figure Coppelius/Coppola is the "real" cause for the destruction of Nathanael's family happiness, then he might as well be seen as a menacing representative of the ancien régime that reestablished its authority after Napoléon's fall and then intervened repressively in private life. The diverse multitude of scholarly interpretations establishes *The Sandman* as a masterpiece of modern European literature; it still provokes the reader's capabilities to understand the truth of fiction.

Hoffmann's spooky story also experienced many adaptations in different forms of art. By the end of the 19th century, *The Sandman* became better known to readers outside of German-speaking countries through its musical dramatization in the first act of Jacques Offenbach's opera *Les contes d'Hoffmann* (1881; *Tales of Hoffmann*). Recently, the uncanniness associated with the story also entered popular cinema when David Lynch used analogous structures of perceptual ambiguity and sexual perversion in his film *Blue Velvet* (1986).

STEPHAN K. SCHINDLER

Editions

First edition: in *Nachtstücke,* Berlin: Verlag der Realschulbuchhandlung, 1817

Critical edition: *E.T.A. Hoffmann: Der Sandmann: Textkritik, Edition, Kommentar,* edited by Ulrich Hohoff, Berlin: de Gruyter, 1988

Translations: in *The Golden Pot and Other Tales,* translated and edited by Ritchie Robertson, Oxford: Oxford University Press, 1992; in *Selected Writings of E.T.A. Hoffmann,* vol. 1, edited and translated by Leonard J. Kent and Elizabeth C. Knight, Chicago: University of Chicago Press, 1969 (also published in *Tales,* edited by Victor Lange, New York: Continuum, 1982)

Further Reading

Ellis, John M., "Clara, Nathanael, and the Narrator: Interpreting Hoffmann's *Der Sandmann,*" *German Quarterly* 54, no. 1 (1981)

Freud, Sigmund, *The Uncanny,* in *The Standard Edition of the Complete Psychological Works of Sigmund Freud,* edited and translated by James Strachey, London: Hogarth Press, 1953

Jennings, Lee B., "Blood of the Android: A Post-Freudian Perspective on Hoffmann's *Sandmann,*" *Seminar* 22, no. 2 (1986)

Kittler, Friedrich A., "'Das Phantom unseres Ichs' und die Literaturpsychologie: E.T.A. Hoffmann, Freud, Lacan," in *Urszenen: Literaturwissenschaft als Diskursanalyse und Diskurskritik,* edited by Friedrich A. Kittler and Horst Turk, Frankfurt: Suhrkamp, 1977

Kremer, Detlef, *Romantische Metamorphosen: E.T.A. Hoffmanns Erzählungen,* Stuttgart: Metzler, 1993

Kuzniar, Alice A., "Ears Looking at You: E.T.A. Hoffmann's *The Sandman* and David Lynch's *Blue Velvet,*" *South Atlantic Review* 54, no. 2 (1989)

Scott, Sir Walter, "On the Supernatural in Fictitious Composition; and Particularly on the Works of Ernest Theodore William [*sic*] Hoffmann," *Foreign Quarterly Review* 1 (1827)

Tatar, Maria M., "E.T.A. Hoffmann's *Der Sandmann:* Reflection and Romantic Irony," *Modern Language Notes* 95, no. 3 (1981)

Wawrzyn, Lienhard, *Der Automaten-Mensch: E.T.A. Hoffmanns Erzählung vom "Sandmann,"* Berlin: Wagenbach, 1976

Hugo von Hofmannsthal 1874–1929

When Hofmannsthal died in 1929, many contemporaries felt that a literary and cultural epoch had come to an end. Modernism had lost one of its foremost figureheads, and soon people would talk about the youngest classic author in German literature.

But which of his works have classical stature? The lyrical drama *Der Tor und der Tod* (1894; *Death and the Fool*) fascinated a whole generation and molded the image of the author; the indestructible *Jedermann* (1911; translated as *The Play of Everyman* and *The Salzburg Everyman*) has proven the centerpiece of the Salzburg Festival; and *Der Rosenkavalier* (1910; translated as *The Rose-Bearer* and *The Cavalier of the Rose*), the libretto of Richard Strauss's most popular opera, has charmed music lovers all over the world. But not many other writings of Hofmannsthal's live on in the general consciousness of the present. The fame of the author remains uncontested, but the richness and diversity of his work are virtually unknown.

Hofmannthal's oeuvre can be divided into three periods. First, there are his youthful works of the 1890s through the turn of the century: his poems and lyrical plays are unmatched in their beautiful language and precocious profundity. They are followed by a period in which the author gave up poetry and tried to conquer the "real stage" with works that connected with the great dramatic traditions of the past—Greek tragedy, Shakespearean drama, and the Spanish Baroque theater—until he found his preferred genre in comedy and musical drama. World War I marked the transition to the third phase of his production. Anxious about the destruction of the historical Austria, the Habsburg Empire, and wishing to stem the chaotic social, political, and intellectual tide with visionary images, Hofmannsthal turned more and more to his Austrian roots. But neither the productivity of the young poet nor the work of the author of the second or third period provide sufficient grounds for assessing Hofmannsthal as a classic writer. It is his entire poetic development, the three steps and levels of his creativity, and his permanent drive to express the problems of his time and to find solutions for them that give his personality and his oeuvre their representative character and classical stature.

Hofmannsthal's external life lacks dramatic events. His rich inner biography, however, is reflected in his works and correspondence, as well as in memories of numerous friends and contemporaries. The young student was considered by many as the preeminent representative of Jung Wien (Young Vienna), a group of distinguished modern writers that included Arthur

Schnitzler, Hermann Bahr, Richard Beer-Hofmann, and others. The leading German poet of the fin de siècle, Stefan George, tried to win young Hofmannsthal for his exclusive circle and wished to exercise with him a "salutary dictatorship" over German letters. Hofmannsthal's social nature resisted this approach, and the author strived more and more to overcome his own aestheticism and his fascination with the principle of *l'art pour l'art* and to combine poetry with general human concerns. His service in the Austrian army and his marriage to the amiable Austrian-Jewish Gerty Schlesinger in 1901 contributed to this development. But for many he remained the esoteric youth of his early years. World War I inspired him to political and social activities, speeches, essays, and editorial projects aimed at a large audience. His later works, although innovative in form as well as content, constitute conservative cultural and social statements, when compared with the zealous plays of the Expressionists or the manifestos of the literary leftists. His death appeared to create a new regard from readers and scholars, but the political affairs in Germany and Austria strangled this interest, and a Hofmannsthal renaissance in the 1950s was needed to reestablish his position.

Hofmannsthal's poems, particularly those that he collected himself in 1903 and thereafter, fascinate by their individual tone. Through the change of sound, rhythm, metaphor, and symbol, the author seems to fashion in each of them a genre of its own. They are not biographical but nonetheless very personal. One of them is called *Weltgeheimnis* (Mystery of the World, Mystery of Life), a title that characterizes them all.

The playlets of the young author thrive on the splendor of their language to such an extent that readers to this day tend to neglect their serious content. Most of them, however, challenge unsuitable or immoral ways of living. Life, or the intensity of living, appears in them—in concurrence with Nietzsche and the whole epoch—as the highest value. But only the figures in *Das kleine Welttheater* (1903 [written in 1897]; *The Little Theatre of the World*) appear to be happy with themselves and their world. All others must learn that they are pursuing life in the wrong manner. In *Gestern* (1891), Hofmannsthal's first play, it is the lack of commitment, the impressionistic indulgence in fleeting pleasures, which is refuted; in *Der Tod des Tizian* (1892; *The Death of Titian*), art and aestheticism prevent the students of Tizian from confronting "real life"; *Der weiße Fächer* (1906 [written in 1897]) demonstrates how the proud resolution to be moral, to be "better than life," can cause one not only to miss out on life but to become guilty. *Death and the Fool* is only the most famous example of these early plays, which examine various ways of living. Claudio is called a fool because he did not learn the principles of life until he encounters Death. His aestheticism and dilettantism, his fruitless reflection, and his wordy commentary on life hide his fear of reality and keep him isolated from his fellow human beings and unfulfilled. Many contemporaries found their own problems reflected in this play and/or identified the author with his hero. *Der Kaiser und die Hexe* (1897; *The Emperor and the Witch*) and two uncanny, almost Kafkaesque narratives, *Das Märchen der 672. Nacht* (1895) and *Reitergeschichte* (1899), round out this group of works. The plays *Der Abenteurer und die Sängerin* and *Die Hochzeit der Sobeide* (*The Marriage of Sobeide*), which premiered in 1899 at the Burgtheater of Vienna and, at the same time, at the Deutsche Theater in Berlin, mark the transition to the real stage.

On the threshold to Hofmannsthal's second period we find a document called *Ein Brief* (1902; *The Lord Chandos Letter*), which has continuously grown in importance in the scholarly discussion of modernity. It is the author's most famous essay or, rather, a fictitious letter of a Lord Chandos to Francis Bacon about his inability to continue writing: he has lost all confidence first in words and then in abstract or generalizing thought. The questioning of the authenticity of language and the exposure of the frivolous use of words, which culminates here, is an issue that runs through Hofmannsthal's works from the early essays to his comic masterpiece *Der Schwierige* (1921; *The Difficult Man*). Critics consider *Ein Brief* a document of a new era—one of the most important turning points in the development of modernism.

Hofmannsthal's Greek tragedies *Elektra* (1904; *Electra*) and *Ödipus und die Sphinx* (1906) grew out of the author's encounter with the Berlin theater director Max Reinhardt and his acting staff, whose request for antique plays that were less *gipsern,* or sterile, coincided with Hofmannsthal's own wishes. He revived the old mythology with the spirit and the psychology of the turn of the century (Bachofen, Rohde, and Freud) and created uncanny works of immense theatrical power. *Electra,* which was written as a counterpart to Goethe's "devilishly humane" *Iphigenie,* particularly intrigues through its dark, inscrutable portrait of suffering, pride, and vengeance. The composer Richard Strauss was so much attracted to this play that he asked Hofmannsthal's permission to set it to music, thereby starting a long and fruitful working relationship between the poet and the musician.

A completely different world opens up in Hofmannsthal's morality plays *The Play of Everyman* and *Das Salzburger große Welttheater* (1922; *The Salzburg Great Theatre of the World*). When the poet got hold of the medieval English morality play *Everyman,* he felt that the spirit of the medieval and Baroque European theater tradition could be revived for the present, particularly in Austria and Southern Germany, where it had survived in popular allegorical plays over centuries. In response to critics who dismissed the work as religiously dogmatic, Hofmannsthal emphasized that the story of the worldly Everyman who is rescued from eternal damnation through Belief and Good Works does not represent belief in a Catholic or Protestant creed but rather a "humanly absolute" Christian fairy tale. When in 1918–19, Hofmannsthal in conjunction with Max Reinhardt founded the Salzburg Festival for the celebration of theater and music of the past and the present, *Jedermann* became the centerpiece of this undertaking, and it has remained, in Reinhardt's brilliant staging, a main attraction until today. *The Salzburg Great Theatre of the World,* based on Calderon, was expressly written for the Salzburg Festival. It features more modern ideas than *Jedermann,* such as revolutionary action, but culminates in a similar medieval-Baroque solution.

Hofmannsthal's last tragedy, *Der Turm* (1925–27; *The Tower*), a rich and complex vision of his tumultuous epoch projected into a mythical Poland of the 18th century, is not only a "dark reflection on his time" but a stylistically enthralling play, because it combines the spirit and motifs of the Greek tragedies with those of the morality plays in a new expressive form. The first version has a hopeful ending and can be read in context with Hofmannsthal's renowned speech *Das Schrifttum als geistiger Raum der Nation* (1926), in which the author advocates a "conservative revolution." The final pessimistic version expresses, in Hofmannsthal's own words, the "actual mercilessness of our reality."

The sensitive author himself suffered from the gloominess of his tragedies and felt much more comfortable with his comedies. Beginning with *Gestern* and *Der weiße Fächer,* Hofmannsthal explored the comic genre, and in 1908 he wrote his first comedy, *Cristinas Heimreise* (1910; *Cristina's Journey Home*), which, similar to *Der Abenteurer und die Sängerin,* is based on the famous memoirs of Casanova. *The Difficult Man* is his comic masterpiece; in this play, he creates a subtle language that distinguishes the characters according to class, personality, and circumstances rendering not only the obvious but also the unspoken and unspeakable relations between the figures. The comedy describes the aristocratic Austrian society, which was eliminated by World War I, in all its weakness and charm. The happy ending is a tenuous attempt to find a way out of frailty and destruction. A second prose comedy of Hofmannsthal's late period, *Der Unbestechliche* (1956 [written in 1923]), is more robust and more directly embedded in the comical tradition.

The majority of Hofmannsthal's librettos for Richard Strauss also belong, in many ways, to the genre of comedy. *Der Rosenkavalier* is subtitled "comedy for music," *Ariadne auf Naxos* (1912; *Ariadne on Naxos*) represents the combination of a societal comedy with a Baroque mythological opera, and *Arabella* (1933 [written in 1929]) is called a "lyrical comedy." The other librettos, *Die Frau ohne Schatten* (1919; *The Woman without a Shadow*) and *Die ägyptische Helena* (1928; *Helen in Egypt*), are a musical fairy tale and a witty mythological-psychological tale, respectively. After *Electra,* the poet refused to write another tragic work for his composer.

Der Rosenkavalier, the first libretto that Hofmannsthal wrote in real collaboration with Strauss, is a full literary play, but the author accommodated his style to the needs of the composer and left enough space for the music so that the "unspeakable" or unspoken nuances of the interaction between the characters could be expressed by the musical score. By re-creating Vienna at the time of the Empress Maria Theresia, Hofmannsthal tried to write a counterpart to Richard Wagner's *Die Meistersinger von Nürnberg.* But the work that Hofmannsthal himself liked best among his librettos was *Ariadne on Naxos,* an ingenious combination of various genres and different epochs, which discusses and in some measure resolves a major dilemma of his: the antinomies of being and becoming, of faithfulness and change, and of persisting and forgetting.

Hofmannsthal's work is so rich that only some of the most important titles could be mentioned here. The author's incomplete novel *Andreas* (1930 [written in 1917–18]; *Andreas*) is considered by many as one of the most important prose works of its epoch. The complex fairy tale *Die Frau ohne Schatten* (1919), which was written in tandem with the opera of the same title, recalls the style of Goethe's *Märchen* and Mozart's *Die Zauberflöte.* Several ballets and his dance poems, and numerous translations and adaptations of works by Molière, Calderón, and many others document Hofmannsthal's wish to revive the great theater tradition of the past. His many essays and speeches supplement and amplify his poetic works. The new Critical Hofmannsthal Edition *Sämtliche Werke,* which is close to completion, has revealed many new aspects of the work and will be an invaluable tool for future Hofmannsthal scholarship.

WOLFGANG NEHRING

See also Austria: Late Habsburg Literature in Vienna; Jung Wien

Biography

Born in Vienna, Austria, 1 February 1874. Law student, 1892–94, student of romantic philology at the University of Vienna, 1895–97; Ph.D., 1897; served in sixth Dragoon Regiment in Göding, 1894–95; full-time writer from 1901; lived in Rodaun, near Vienna; librettist for operas by Richard Strauss, from 1909; editor, Österreichische Bibliothek, 1915–17; cofounder, with Max Reinhardt, of the Salzburg Festival, 1919. Died in Rodaun, Austria, 15 July 1929.

Selected Works

Collections

Die Gedichte und Kleinen Dramen, 1911
Rodauner Nachträge, 1918
Gesammelte Werke, 6 vols., 1924; revised edition, 3 vols., 1934
Gesammelte Werke in Einzelausgaben, edited by Herbert Steiner, 15 vols., 1945–59
Selected Writings: Prose, Poems and Verse Plays, Plays and Libretti, edited by Mary Hottinger, Tania and James Stern, and Michael Hamburger, 3 vols., 1952–63
Gesammelte Werke in zehn Einzelbänden, edited by Bernd Schoeller, 1979
Sämtliche Werke, edited by Heinz Otto Burger et al., 1975–

Plays

Gestern (produced 1928), 1891
Der Tod des Tizian, 1892; as *The Death of Titian,* translated by John Heard, 1914
Der Tor und der Tod (produced 1898), 1894; as *Death and the Fool,* translated by Max Batt, 1913; translated by Michael Hamburger, in *Selected Writings,* vol. 2, 1961; translated by Alfred Schwarz, in *Three Plays,* 1966
Die Frau im Fenster (as *Madonna Dianora,* produced 1898); in *Theater in Versen,* 1899; as *Madonna Diaonora,* translated by Harriet Betty Boas, 1916
Theater in Versen, 1899
Der Abenteurer und die Sängerin (produced 1899); in *Theater in Versen,* 1899; revised version, 1909
Die Hochzeit der Sobeide (produced with *Der Abenteurer und die Sängerin,* 1899); in *Theater in Versen,* 1899; as *The Marriage of Sobeide,* translated by Bayard Quincy Morgan, in *German Classics of the Nineteenth and Twentieth Centuries,* edited by Kuno Francke and William G. Howard, vol. 20, 1920; as *The Marriage of Zobeide,* translated by Christopher Middleton, in *Selected Writings,* vol. 2, 1961
Der Kaiser und die Hexe (written 1897; produced 1926), in *Die Insel,* 1900; as *The Emperor and the Witch,* translated by Christopher Middleton, in *Selected Writings,* vol. 2, 1961
Das kleine Welttheater; oder, Die Glücklichen (written 1897), 1903; as *The Little Theatre of the World,* translated by Walter R. Eberlein, 1945; translated by Michael Hamburger, in *Selected Writings,* vol. 2, 1961
Elektra (produced 1903), 1904; revised version, music by Richard Strauss (produced 1909), 1908; as *Electra,* translated by Arthur Symons, 1908; translated by Alfred Schwarz, in *Selected Writings,* vol. 3, 1964, and in *Three Plays,* 1966
Das gerettete Venedig (from the play *Venice Preserved,* by Otway; produced 1905), 1905
Ödipus und die Sphinx (produced 1906), 1906
Der weisse Fächer (written 1897; produced 1927), 1906
Kleine Dramen, 1906; enlarged edition, 2 vols., 1907
König Ödipus (from the play by Sophocles; produced 1910), 1907

Vorspiele, 1908
Alkestis (from the play by Euripides; written 1893–94; produced 1916), 1909; arranged for music by Egon Wellesz, 1923
Cristinas Heimreise (produced 1910), 1910; as *Cristina's Journey Home,* translated by Roy Temple House, in *Poet Lore,* vol. 28, 1917
Die Heirat wider Willen (from a play by Molière), 1910
Der Rosenkavalier (music by Richard Strauss; produced 1911), 1911; as *The Rose-Bearer,* translated by Alfred Kalisch, 1912; as *The Cavalier of the Rose,* translated by Christopher Holme, in *Selected Writings,* vol. 3, 1963
Jedermann: Das Spiel vom Sterben des reichen Mannes (produced 1911), 1911; as *The Play of Everyman,* translated by G. Sterling, 1917; as *The Salzburg Everyman,* translated by M.E. Tafler, 1929
Ariadne auf Naxos (music by Richard Strauss; produced 1912), 1912; revised edition (produced 1916), 1916; as *Ariadne on Naxos,* translated by Alfred Kalisch, 1913, 1922
Josephslegende (ballet scenario), with Harry Graf Kessler (music by Richard Strauss; produced 1914), 1914
Die Lästigen (from a play by Molière; produced 1916), 1917
Prima Ballerina (ballet scenario), 1917
Der Bürger als Edelmann, (from a play by Molière; music by Richard Strauss; produced 1918), 1918
Die Frau ohne Schatten (music by Richard Strauss; produced 1919), 1919; as *The Woman without a Shadow,* 1927
Dame Kobold (from a play by Pedro Calderón de la Barca; produced 1920), 1920
Der Schwierige (produced 1921), 1921; as *The Difficult Man,* translated by Willa Muir, in *Selected Writings,* vol. 3, 1963
Das Salzburger große Welttheater (from a play by Pedro Calderón de la Barca; produced 1922), 1922; as *The Salzburg Great Theatre of the World,* translated by Vernon Watkins, in *Selected Writings,* vol. 3, 1963
Die Ruinen von Athen (produced 1924), 1925
Die grüne Flöte (ballet scenario; music by Wolfgang Amadeus Mozart; edited by Einar Nilson; produced 1916), 1925
Der Turm, 1925; revised edition (produced 1928), 1927; as *The Tower,* translated by Michael Hamburger, in *Selected Writings,* vol. 3, 1963; translated by Alfred Schwarz, in *Three Plays,* 1966
Die ägyptische Helena (music by Richard Strauss; produced 1928), 1928; as *Helen in Egypt,* translated by Alfred Kalisch, 1928
Semiramis—Die beiden Götter, (written 1905–9 and 1917), 1933
Das Bergwerk zu Falun (written 1899), 1933; as *The Mine at Falun,* translated by Michael Hamburger, in *Selected Writings,* vol. 2, 1961
Arabella (music by Richard Strauss; produced 1933), 1933; translated by John Gutman, 1955; translated by Nora Wydenbruck and Christopher Middleton, in *Selected Writings,* vol. 3, 1963
Danae; oder, Die Vernunftheirat, 1933
Dramatische Entwürfe aus dem Nachlass, edited by Heinrich Zimmer, 1936
Der Unbestechliche (produced 1923); 1956
Silvia im Stern, (written 1907), edited by Martin Stern, 1959
Three Plays, translated by Alfred Schwarz, 1966
Timon der Redner (written 1917–25), 1975 (in *Sämtliche Werke*)

Fiction
Reitergeschichte, 1899
Das Märchen der 672. Nacht und Andere Erzählungen (includes *Das Märchen der 672. Nacht; Reitergeschichte;* and *Erlebnis des Marschalls von Bassompierre*), 1905
Prinz Eugen der edle Ritter, 1915
Die Frau ohne Schatten, 1919
Andreas; oder, Die Vereinigten, (written 1912–14), 1930; as *Andreas; or, The United,* translated by Marie D. Hottinger, 1936
Four Stories, edited by Margaret Jacobs, 1968

Poetry
Ausgewählte Gedichte, 1903; revised edition, 1904
Die gesammelten Gedichte, 1907
Die Gedichte und kleinen Dramen, 1911
Lyrical Poems, translated by Charles Wharton Stork, 1918
Gedichte, 1922
Nachlese der Gedichte, 1934

Essays, Criticism, Letters
Ein Brief, in *Der Tag,* 18–19 October 1902; as *The Lord Chandos letter,* translated by Michael Hofmann, 1995
Studie über die Entwicklung des Dichters Victor Hugo, 1901; as *Victor Hugo,* 1904; as *Versuch über Victor Hugo,* 1925
Die prosaischen Schriften gesammelt, 2 vols., 1907; vol. 3, 1917
Charakteristiken deutscher Dichter, 1925
Reden und Aufsätze, 1921
Buch der Freunde, 1922; edited by Ernst Zinn, 1965
Loris: Die Prosa des jungen Hofmansthals, 1930
Die Berührung der Sphären, 1931
Briefe, 2 vols., 1935–37
Briefwechsel, with Anton Wildgans, edited by Joseph A. von Bradisch, 1935; revised edition, edited by Norbert Altenhofer, 1971
Briefwechsel, with Stefan George, edited by Robert Boehringer, 1938; revised edition, 1953
Briefwechsel, with Richard Strauss, edited by Franz and Alice Strauss, 1952; revised editions, edited by Willi Schuh, 1954–78; as *Correspondence,* translated by Hans Hammelmann and Ewald Osers, 1961
Briefe der Freundschaft, with Eberhard von Bodenhausen, edited by Dora von Bodenhausen, 1953
Briefwechsel, with Rudolf Borchardt, edited by Marie Luise Borchardt and Herbert Steiner, 1954
Briefwechsel, with Carl J. Burckhardt, edited by Burckhardt, 1956; revised edition, 1991
Briefwechsel, with Arthur Schnitzler, edited by Theresa Nickl and Heinrich Schnitzler, 1964
Briefwechsel, with Helene von Nostitz, edited by Oswalt von Nostitz, 1965
Briefwechsel, with Edgar Karl von Bebenburg, edited by Mary E. Gilbert, 1966
Briefe, to Marie Herzfeld, edited by Horst Weber, 1967
Briefwechsel, with Leopold von Andrian, edited by Walter Perl, 1968
Briefwechsel, with Willy Haas, edited by Rolf Italiaander, 1968
Briefwechsel, with Harry Graf Kessler, edited by Hilde Burger, 1968
Briefwechsel, with Josef Redlich, edited by Helga Fußgänger, 1971
Briefwechsel, with Richard Beer-Hofmann, edited by Eugene Weber, 1972
Briefwechsel, with Max Rychner, Samuel and Hedwig Fischer, Oscar Bie, and Moritz Heimann, 1973
Briefwechsel, with Ottonie Gräfin Degenfeld, edited by Marie Therese Miller-Degenfeld, 1974
Briefwechsel 1899–1925, with Rainer Maria Rilke, edited by Rudolf Hirsch and Ingeborg Schnack, 1978
Briefwechsel, with Max Mell, edited by Margret Dietrich and Heinz Kindermann, 1982
Briefwechsel, with Ria Schmujlow-Claasen, 1982
Briefwechsel, with Paul Zifferer, edited by Hilde Burger, 1983
Briefwechsel, with Insel-Verlag, edited by Gerhard Schuster, 1991

Edited Works
Hesperus: Ein Jahrbuch, with Rudolf Borchardt and Rudolf Alexander Schröder, 1909
Deutsche Erzähler, 4 vols., 1912
Österreichischer Almanach auf das Jahr 1916, 1916
Österreichische Bibliothek, 26 vols., 1913–16

Deutsches Lesebuch, 2 vols., 1922–23; revised edition, 1926
Neue Deutsche Beiträge, 1922–27
Deutsche Epigramme, 1923
Wert und Ehre deutscher Sprache, 1927

Further Reading

Alewyn, Richard, *Über Hugo von Hofmannsthal,* Göttingen: Vandenhoeck und Ruprecht, 1958; 4th edition, 1967
Bennett, Benjamin, *Hugo von Hofmannsthal: The Theatres of Consciousness,* Cambridge and New York: Cambridge University Press, 1988
Brinkmann, Richard, "Hofmannsthal und die Sprache," *Deutsche Vierteljahrsschrift für Literaturwissenschaft und Geistesgeschichte* 35 (1961)
Broch, Hermann, *Hofmannsthal und seine Zeit,* Frankfurt: Suhrkamp, 1974; as *Hugo von Hofmannsthal and His Time: The European Imagination 1860–1920,* translated by Michael P. Steinberg, Chicago: University of Chicago Press, 1984
Coghlan, Brian, *Hofmannsthal's Festival Dramas: Jedermann, Das Salzburger große Welttheater, Der Turm,* Cambridge: Cambridge University Press, 1964
Erken, Günther, *Hofmannsthals dramatischer Stil: Untersuchung zur Symbolik und Dramaturgie,* Tübingen: Niemeyer, 1967
Fiechtner, Helmut, editor, *Hugo von Hofmannsthal: Der Dichter im Spiegel der Freunde,* Bern: Francke, 1963
Kobel, Erwin, *Hugo von Hofmannsthal,* Berlin: de Gruyter, 1970
Mauser, Wolfram, *Hugo von Hofmannsthal: Konfliktbewältigung und Werkstruktur: Eine psychosoziologische Interpretation,* Munich: Fink, 1977
Mayer, Mathias, *Hugo von Hofmannsthal,* Stuttgart: Metzler, 1993
Nehring, Wolfgang, "Hugo von Hofmannsthal," in *Deutsche Dichter des zwanzigsten Jahrhunderts,* edited by Hartmut Steinecke, Berlin: Schmidt, 1994
Rey, William H., *Weltentzweiung und Weltversöhnung in Hofmannsthals griechischen Dramen,* Philadelphia: University of Pennsylvania Press, 1962
Rösch, Ewald, *Komödien Hofmannsthals: Die Entfaltung ihrer Sinnstruktur aus dem Thema der Daseinsstufen,* Marburg: Elwert, 1963; 3rd edition, 1975
Rudolph, Hermann, *Kulturkritik und konservative Revolution,* Tübingen: Niemeyer, 1971
Schorske, Carl E., *Fin-de-siècle Vienna: Politics and Culture,* New York: Knopf, 1979
Tarot, Rolf, *Hugo von Hofmannsthal: Daseinsformen und dichterische Struktur,* Tübingen: Niemeyer, 1970
Volke, Werner, *Hugo von Hofmannsthal in Selbstzeugnissen und Bilddokumenten,* Reinbek bei Hamburg: Rowohlt, 1967; 2nd edition, 1992
Wiethölter, Waltraud, *Hofmannsthal; oder, Die Geometrie des Subjekts: Psychostrukturelle und ikonographische Studien zum Prosawerk,* Tübingen: Niemeyer, 1990
Wunberg, Gotthart, editor, *Hofmannsthal im Urteil seiner Kritiker: Dokumente zur Wirkungsgeschichte Hofmannsthals in Deutschland,* Frankfurt: Athenäum, 1972

Ein Brief 1902

Essay by Hugo von Hofmannsthal

Since its first appearance, Hugo von Hofmannsthal's "imaginary" letter has been regarded as one of his most important works. The precise nature of its importance, however, remains the subject of critical debate, for the unassuming title of the text belies the complexity of its content.

Ein Brief (1902; *The Lord Chandos Letter*) purports to be a letter written in 1603 by the (fictional) Lord Philipp Chandos to his erstwhile mentor, the English scientist and philosopher Francis Bacon (1561–1626). In it the 26-year-old Chandos, author of neoclassic pastorals and a learned treatise in Latin, attempts to explain his two-year silence and his failure to realize earlier literary plans. Among these plans was the ambitious project of an encyclopedic work combining classical myths and modern observations, which was to have borne the title *Nosce te ipsum* (the Delphic injunction, "know thyself"). Chandos describes how his loss of faith in language has made such self-knowledge through literature impossible. He relates how his command of language inexplicably eroded until he was no longer capable of apprehending the world conceptually. This process began with a reluctance to use general or abstract terms and gradually became a disgust that spread to everyday language; the process eventually rendered Chandos incapable of passing judgments, and, ultimately, deprived him of the ability to speak or even think coherently. This is Chandos's seemingly irreversible condition when he writes to Bacon and is the reason for his renunciation of literary activity.

Although Chandos's state is one of agonizing deprivation, it is periodically relieved by involuntary moments of bliss in which he seems to transcend his subjectivity and become one with all things. These quasi-religious moments of illumination can be caused by everyday and even absent objects. Chandos is unable to account for his epiphanies, however, which by their nature defy rational linguistic characterization. Thus, he can only suggest the quality of his condition by allusions to classical myth and literature, leaving it to Bacon's superior intellect to explain the phenomenon.

The critical reception of *The Lord Chandos Letter* encompasses a range of diverse and not always compatible interpretations. Early readings tended to concentrate on the autobiographical significance of the text, occasionally going so far as to identify Hofmannsthal with Chandos. Such readings are based on the evidence of Hofmannsthal's own periodic artistic crises and the similarities between the author and his creation. Like Chandos, Hofmannsthal was a precocious literary talent and had produced a considerable body of (mainly lyrical) work during the 1890s. After 1900, Hofmannsthal's lyrical output decreased, and he turned to such social and non-linguistic forms as drama, ballet, and mime; Chandos, moreover, is the same age as Hofmannsthal was in 1900. Thus, the letter has been seen as the veiled confession of a crisis that led to the author's own renunciation of lyric poetry.

While such readings are not completely unfounded, exclusively or predominantly autobiographical interpretations of the text can only be sustained at the expense of its historical setting, which then becomes an unnecessary distraction from the author's "confession." They also fail to account for the fact that Chandos's crisis leads not merely to a change of literary genre but to a total renunciation of literature. Furthermore, Hofmannsthal's documented crisis preceding the writing of the text was no isolated phenomenon. During the 1890s, he suffered many such periods of creative stagnation and, more importantly, throughout the decade expressed a recurrent concern with the limits of language. Nevertheless, autobiographical interpretations remain part of the critical mythology surrounding Hofmannsthal's life and work.

The text has also been read as symptomatic of a more widespread *Wertverlust* (loss of value) around the turn of the century. Some critics have seen the disintegration of Chandos's world as being essentially linguistic, and thus closely linked to skeptical analyses of the relationship between language and the world, such as the one advanced in Fritz Mauthner's *Beiträge zu einer Kritik der Sprache* (1901–2), the first volume of which Hofmannsthal knew. Others have interpreted Chandos's state as reflecting more fundamental problems of epistemology raised by the radical empiricism of Ernst Mach, whose philosophical account of personal identity as a fiction was extremely influential in the literary circles of turn-of-the-century Vienna. This second line of interpretation has also been used to explain Hofmannsthal's choice of Francis Bacon, the father of empiricist philosophy, as the addressee of the letter. This view explains Chandos's curiously modern problems as the result of pursuing Baconian proto-empiricism to its Machian conclusion. Seen in this light, the disintegration of Chandos's world into ever smaller, unrelated parts is a literary correlative of Mach's atomistic empiriocriticism.

A number of critical readings have focused on the significance of the historical Francis Bacon, revealing that Chandos's unrealized plans correspond to works actually written by Bacon. While this can be taken as showing Chandos's crisis to be the consequence of Baconian philosophy, it has also been contended that his loss of the ability to think coherently marks a radical departure from empiricism. In a recent hermeneutic interpretation, Jost Bomers has argued that the understanding of mythology that underlies Chandos's abandoned plans is essentially that of Bacon, who regarded myths as allegorical expressions of general truths. In its resistance to rational "decoding," the use of myth in the second half of the text is, by contrast, symbolic and represents the only adequate means of expressing Chandos's existential condition. In its analysis of the poetological function of the letter as a self-reflexive literary text, Bomers's interpretation has opened a new perspective in Hofmannsthal studies.

The number and diversity of critical readings indicate the importance of *The Lord Chandos Letter* in Hofmannsthal's oeuvre, and it remains a key text in the canon of turn-of-the-century German literature. Its presentation of quasi-mystical moments of illumination is related to the notion of epiphany in the early aesthetic of James Joyce, and Chandos's horror in the face of the void behind language foreshadows 20th-century existentialist philosophy and the literature of the absurd. In its paradoxically eloquent explanation of silence, the text is a forerunner of a modern literary tradition that includes Samuel Beckett and Paul Celan.

Steve Rizza

Editions

First edition: *Ein Brief,* in *Der Tag,* Berlin, 18–19 October 1902
Critical edition: in *Sämtliche Werke,* vol. 31, edited by Ellen Ritter, Frankfurt: Fischer, 1991
Translation: *The Lord Chandos Letter,* translated by Michael Hofmann, London: Syrens, 1995

Further Reading

Alewyn, Richard, "Hofmannsthals Wandlung," in *Über Hugo von Hofmannsthal,* by Richard Alewyn, Göttingen: Vandenhoeck und Ruprecht, 1958; 4th edition, 1967
Bennett, Benjamin, "Chandos and His Neighbours," *Deutsche Vierteljahresschrift für Literaturwissenschaft und Geistesgeschichte* 49 (1975)
Bomers, Jost, *Der Chandosbrief: Die Nova Poetica Hofmannsthals,* Stuttgart: Verlag für Wissenschaft und Forschung, 1991
Brinkmann, Richard, "Hofmannsthal und die Sprache," *Deutsche Vierteljahresschrift für Literaturwissenschaft und Geistesgeschichte* 35 (1961)
Busch, Walter, and Hansgeorg Schmidt-Bergmann, "Der Gestus des Verstummens—Hugo von Hofmannsthals Chandosbrief," *Literatur für Leser* 4 (1986)
Daviau, Donald G., "Hugo von Hofmannsthal and the 'Chandos Letter,'" *Modern Austrian Literature* 4 (1971)
Härter, Andreas, *Der Anstand des Schwiegens: Bedingungen des Redens in Hofmannsthals "Brief,"* Bonn: Bouvier, 1989
Kuna, Franz, "The Expense of Silence: Sincerity and Strategy in Hofmannsthal's 'Chandos Letter,'" *Publications of the English Goethe Society* N.S. 40 (1970)
Morton, Michael, "Chandos and His Plans," *Deutsche Vierteljarhesschrift für Literaturwissenschaft und Geistesgeschichte* 62 (1988)
Pauget, Michèle, "Der Brief des Lord Chandos in seinem Verhältnis zum mythischen Denken," in *Österreichische Literatur des 20. Jahrhunderts,* edited by Sigurd Paul Schleichl and Gerald Stieg, Innsbruck: Institut für Germanistik der Universität Innsbruck, 1986
Schulz, H. Stefan, "Hofmannsthal and Bacon: The Sources of the Chandos Letter," *Comparative Literature* 13 (1961)
Wunberg, Gotthart, "Francis Bacon—Der Empfänger des Lord Chandos Briefes von Hugo von Hofmansthal," *German Life and Letters* 15, no. 2 (1962)

Johann Christian Friedrich Hölderlin 1770–1843

Friedrich Hölderlin's emergence as a writer occurred against the grain of the two movements that defined German literature of his time: Weimar classicism and early (Jena) Romanticism. Although befriended and supported by Schiller in his beginnings during the 1790s (Goethe was never anything but cool toward him, and he had only fleeting acquaintance with Herder), Hölderlin avoided classicism's strictures of harmonious form and theme in his mature work and also adopted an increasingly less tranquil view of Greek antiquity and its art. And although briefly present in Jena in 1794 and susceptible to Fichte's powerful influence there (Plato, Kant, and Rousseau were other early philosophical influences) and the recipient of a positive review of several of his poems by Friedrich Schlegel in 1799, Hölderlin lacked the Jena Romantics' fascination with irony and the most modern tendencies of prose fiction. Thus, he remained an obscure and underpublished figure during his lifetime, with only single editions of his novel *Hyperion* (1797–99) and his translations of two Sophocles tragedies and some 70 poems in journals appearing during his years of independence and sanity. The second half of his life was spent in mental illness.

Despite this unpromising literary biography, Hölderlin has subsequently been received as a major author of his age—ranked with Goethe and Kleist—and of German and, indeed, European modernity in its entirety. He is recognized above all as a poet of unprecedented imagistic, syntactic, figurative, and narrative originality. He is increasingly also understood as a literary theorist of profound originality as well as a seminal contributor to early idealist philosophy. (Hölderlin was a schoolmate and friend of Hegel and Schelling at Tübingen's Lutheran theological seminary [*Stift*], and he continued to have important exchanges with them, in conversation and by letter, during the formative years of their philosophical developments; Hegel dedicated a revealing sublime poem, "Eleusis," to Hölderlin in 1796.) Admired early by Mörike, then by Nietzsche, Rilke, Hesse, and many German Expressionists, he has been repeatedly reedited and translated throughout the 20th century and has become the object of broad public appropriation and celebration, including propagandistic manipulation during the Nazi period. He has also been the subject of some of the most demanding and scrupulous literary scholarship that German and international scholars have produced on any author. The major philosophical readers of German literature—Benjamin, Heidegger, Adorno, Maurice Blanchot, and Paul de Man—privilege Hölderlin as perhaps the most important German poet of modernity (the most important poet altogether for Heidegger), and Celan draws on no German poet more than Hölderlin for his own explorations of the continued possibilities of modern poetry.

Such an elevated stature for a once-neglected author cannot be explained by reference to the juvenile work that was the first of Hölderlin's writings to be published. His early hymns and odes were of a self-consciously Schillerian kind, praising lofty themes (e.g., Greece and nature) with a smooth but artificial rhetoric of declamation. His epistolary novel *Hyperion,* which preoccupied its author over four years (1792–96; published in two parts in 1797 and 1799), is interesting above all for the philosophical meditation on ancient Greece and the attractions of its historical and cultural foreignness that it initiates in Hölderlin's oeuvre. However, in its prose style and tone, its characterizations, and its powers of emplotment, it lacks almost any literary significance; were this novel, about a modern man wandering in Greece as if it were still ancient, the major publication that Hölderlin had bequeathed to posterity, he would justly be reduced to a minor footnote in the history of German Hellenism.

Instead, where the Schillerian normative poetry of praise and the novelistic casting of ideas of Hellenism break off—where they fail—is precisely where the originality of Hölderlin's literary contributions begins. His mature writings date from the completion of *Hyperion,* and the first of these (from what is sometimes called his middle period, although this is misleading for a career that was both so rapid in its development and so short-lived in its duration) include an unfinished tragedy, *Der Tod des Empedokles* (1798–1800), many highly achieved odes and elegies, and a series of fragmentary "poetological" writings. In each of these genres, Hölderlin is in a different way attempting to recast his and his contemporaries' attitudes toward ancient Greece away from those of imitation and nostalgic (what Schiller called "sentimental") longing and toward strategies of sacrifice alternating with vigorous reappropriation. Hölderlin is undertaking to celebrate a past that had to have become lost to yield historical differentiation and at the same time to articulate this past's discontinuous narrative across its "successor" cultures of Western Christianity and a German future that has yet to arrive, not even, especially, in Weimar classicism and its humanism.

The *Empedokles* play, which underwent three versions, was abandoned in 1799 and never published in Hölderlin's lifetime; its significance resides less in its energetic verse monologues and more in the philosophical concerns with the theorization of tragedy that it inaugurates. These emerge in the essay "Grund zum Empedokles," which marked the abandonment of the project; they are contemporary with important work by Schelling and Hegel on tragedy and anticipate Hölderlin's own later translations of Sophocles and his accompanying notes on the tragedies (1803).

The many fragmentary poetological essays of this same, so-called Homburger period (from Hölderlin's residence in the town during 1799) begin to sketch a complicated doctrine of what he calls "the change of tones" between genres—with respect to their individual modes of presentation, their basic themes or ideas, and their overarching "spirits" or achieved meanings—as well as between the basic impulses and aims of Greek and modern literature. This theory of poetics has been searchingly interpreted as dialectical in the sense that every element of literary structure (e.g., an aspect of style) or historical periodization (e.g., a feature of Greek literature) is answered by an opposing force from another structural or historical element that in turn creates a further dialectical counterforce across the time of a work's functioning or a period's historical dissolution. Nonetheless, what keeps this nascent theory from being satisfactorily understood as thoroughly dialectical is that Hölderlin radically resists both any systematic resolution of the incoherences of form, theme, and metaphor within the literary genres and any positively secured position of self-conscious knowledge within the philosophical modality of reflexive thought.

This same period (1798–1800) sees Hölderlin's first great poems in the form of odes and elegies. In the odes "Heidelberg" and "Rousseau," and then in slightly later ones (the dating is uncertain) such as "Dichterberuf," "Stimme des Volkes," "Der blinde Sänger," "Dichtermut," and "Blödigkeit," Hölderlin's long-standing effort to transpose intricate Greek metric forms into German verse combines with a major new concern: how to tell of a poet's role and achievement in the face of an audience and a historical moment that, at a time of revolutionary upheaval and anticipation (Hölderlin is an enthusiast of the French Revolution), are, strictly speaking, not yet there. Any present action, however heroic it might be, is suspended between a past still powerfully present in memory and ruin and a future full of historical and divine promise. This suspension—the failure to be grounded in anything but the act of poetic witness and utterance—constitutes precisely the tragic heroism of the poet and the individual poems. The elegy "Brot und Wein," one of the most achieved and admired poems of the German language (1800–1801, subsequently revised and published in its entirety only in 1894), casts this problem over the entire landscape of ancient Greece and its gods (above all, Dionysus), Christianity, and modern Germany. Its elegant triadic formal arrangement, its remarkable narrative sinuosity as it weaves from present to past and back to present, and its powerful syntactic inversions, metaphoric inventions, and apophthegmatic utterances all establish the signature features of Hölderlin's mature poetry. A slightly later elegy, "Heimkunft" (1801), is his other most celebrated example of this form.

The influence of Klopstock's enraptured Christian poetry of praise (the *Messias*) and of Swabian Pietism as well had been important in Hölderlin's development thus far, but more decisive for his remaining work were his experiences in translating Pindar, begun in 1799–1800 and continued through 1803. The distinction between odes and hymns becomes vague and ultimately invisible for Hölderlin (he called Pindar's triadic odes "hymns" after the Greek term for "song"), and his poetic style—already masterfully exploiting the German language's resources for syntactic inversion, semantic polyvalence, and neologistic compounding—develops rapidly into what his first scholarly editor, Norbert von Hellingrath, named (following Dionysius of Halicarnassus) the "austere or rough articulation" (*harte Fügung*) of Pindaric verse. A paratactic style of syntactic and grammatical juxtaposition without subordination, a multiplying of tropes such as transposed or broken word order (hyperbaton and asyndeton), a wild display of adversative conjunctions (*aber, doch*) that might be an adaptation of Pindar's fluid use of Greek particles, and finally an utterly unique use of German nouns that, in their compounded forms and etymological resonances, function as especially vivid metaphors and images—these features transform Hölderlin's poetic language in the wake of his experience of translating and commenting on Pindar.

Beginning in late 1799, with the unfinished poem "Wie wenn am Feiertage . . . ," Hölderlin's major poems—called "vaterländische Gesänge" by him and later editors—are exceedingly adventurous in their formal and narrative ambitions. Sometimes hundreds of lines in length and comprising 15 strophes, they attempt to tell mythohistorical narratives of signifying exchanges between gods and men ("Friedensfeier," "Der Einzige," "Patmos," and "Mnemosyne") or between natural landscapes and their historical and divine reverberations ("Am Quell der Donau," "Der Rhein," and "Der Ister"—these latter among Hölderlin's distinctive subgenre of so-called river poems). Dionysiac Greece and Apollo's "fire from heaven," the powerfully epiphanic and apocalyptic speech acts of Christ and his apostles, and the landscapes and historical acts of early modern Germany and contemporary revolutionary Europe conjoin—often violently—in encounters and ruptures of breathtaking visual imagery, verbal pathos, and religious and political hope. Many of these poems underwent several versions or constant revisions; many others ("An die Madonna," "Das Nächste Beste," and "Kolomb") are unfinished; none were published during Hölderlin's sane years. "Der Rhein" and "Patmos" are surely among the greatest of the *vaterländische Gesänge* and of any long German poems. And once, with "Andenken" (1803–5), Hölderlin brought together a singular form (five strophes with shortened lines) and a combination of subject matters—geographical differentiation, the personal experiences of adventure undergone and love lived and lost, and the binding efforts of remembering—into a poem of such originality and beauty that it is unlike anything else in his oeuvre, in German literature, or in world poetry. No Hölderlin poem has been the object of more voluminous commentary (thousands of pages), both philosophical and philological. And, together with his short and imagistically dense poem "Hälfte des Lebens," "Andenken" anticipates and, indeed, discovers the vein of crystalline brilliance that then runs through modern poetry from Dickinson and Mallarmé to Trakl and Celan.

Poets from Mörike onward, and especially Rilke, René Char, and Celan, take Hölderlin with the utmost seriousness because of his figurative and syntactic originality, his success at articulating the modern poet's tenuous balance between a despairing alienation from the social-historical world and an equally desperate ecstatic intimation of divine illuminations and afterimages, and his philosophically important themes and arguments, especially those regarding the possibilities of mediation of all kinds. The latter have also attracted many major German philosophers, from Heidegger and his student Hans-Georg Gadamer to the dean of German Idealist scholarship, Dieter Henrich. As well, Hölderlin has a wide audience of nonspecialist readers, some of whom have been drawn by reasons of religious piety or nationalist fervor (especially during the 1930s and 1940s) that are only poorly borne out by his texts themselves. The fascination with the surprising originality of the language and the pathos of the biography has ensured an ongoing reception, both popular and literary (Peter Weiss's play and Peter Haertling's novel, both titled *Hölderlin*). The unfinished state of so many of Hölderlin's mature poems also continues to confront his historical-critical editors with challenges to an entire tradition's assumptions about what constitutes a finished work or an author's intention. Thus, the current Frankfurter Ausgabe of Hölderlin's *Sämtliche Werke* challenges the previous and still-standard Grosse Stuttgarter Ausgabe by editing and printing the poems as fluid "processes" rather than as more or less fixed "versions."

In most of these matters, the issue is not and cannot be one of decisive resolution. Just as it is fruitless and ultimately pointless to ask whether Hölderlin's "madness" informed his mature writing (a view held by Schelling, among others) or whether his brilliantly original writing drove him mad (the view of many of his Romantic and modern mythologizers), so is it uncertain whether he is "Romantic" or "modern," Graecophilic or "nationally" (*vaterländisch*) Germanophilic, resolutely literary against the systematic philosophies of German Idealism, or philosophically profound unlike any other German literary author. What alone seems certain is that, more than Goethe, Rilke, or Celan, Hölderlin wrote some 20 poems of such daring, influence, and beauty that he stands as the preeminent poet of the German language and one of the most admired and influential authors of all modern Western literature.

TIMOTHY BAHTI

Biography

Born in Lauffen, 20 March 1770. Studied at the Tübingen Seminary, 1788–93, and received his master's degree, 1790; worked as a private tutor, Waltershausen, 1793–94, Weimar and Jena, 1794–95, Frankfurt,

1796–98, Hauptwil, Switzerland, 1801, and Bordeaux, France, 1802; librarian, Homburg, 1804–6; in a clinic for mental illness, Tübingen, 1806–7; privately cared for after 1807. Died 7 June 1843.

Selected Works

Collections

Historisch-Kritische Ausgabe, edited by Norbert von Hellingrath et al., 6 vols., 1914–23

Sämtliche Werke [Große Stuttgarter Ausgabe], edited by Friedrich Beissner and Adolf Beck, 8 vols., 1943–85

Sämtliche Werke [Frankfurter Ausgabe], edited by Dietrich E. Sattler, 1975–

Poetry

Gedichte, edited by Gustav Schwab and Ludwig Uhland, 1826

Poems and Fragments (bilingual edition), translated by Michael Hamburger, 1966

Selected Poems (bilingual edition; with *Selected Poems* by Mörike), translated by Christopher Middleton, 1972

Hymns and Fragments (bilingual edition), translated by Richard Sieburth, 1984

Play

Der Tod des Empedokles (incomplete), in *Gedichte,* 1826; numerous subsequent editions, including the one edited by M.B. Benn, 1968

Fiction

Hyperion; oder, Der Eremit in Griechenland, 2 vols, 1797–99; as *Hyperion; or, The Hermit in Greece,* translated by Willard R. Trask, 1965

Hyperion and Selected Poems, edited by Eric L. Santner, 1990

Other

Essays and Letters on Theory, translated by Thomas Pfau, 1988

Translations

Sophocles, *Die Trauerspiele des Sophokles,* 2 vols., 1804–6

Pindar, *Hölderlins Pindar-Übertragungen,* edited by Norbert von Hellingrath, 1910

Further Reading

Adorno, Theodor W., "Parataxis: Zur späten Lyrik Hölderlins," in *Noten zur Literatur,* Frankfurt: Suhrkamp, 1965; 4th edition, 1996; translated as *Notes to Literature,* New York: Columbia University Press, 1991–92

Bahti, Timothy, "Lightning Bolts, Arrows, Weather Vanes, and the Crux of Soullessness: Directions and Ends of the Poetic Image in Three Hölderlin Poems," in *Ends of the Lyric: Direction and Consequence in Western Poetry,* Baltimore, Maryland: Johns Hopkins University Press, 1996

Böschenstein, Bernhard, *"Frucht des Gewitters": Hölderlins Dionysos als Gott der Revolution,* Frankfurt: Insel, 1989

De Man, Paul, "Heidegger's Exegeses of Hölderlin," in *Blindness and Insight: Essays in the Rhetoric of Contemporary Criticism,* New York: Oxford University Press, 1971; 2nd edition, Minneapolis: University of Minnesota Press, and London: Methuen, 1983

———, "Wordsworth and Hölderlin," in *The Rhetoric of Romanticism,* New York: Columbia University Press, 1984

Heidegger, Martin, *Erläuterungen zur Hölderlins Dichtung,* Frankfurt: Klostermann, 1944; 6th expanded edition, 1996

Henrich, Dieter, *The Course of Remembrance and Other Essays on Hölderlin,* Stanford, California: Stanford University Press, 1997

Kurz, Gerhard, *Mittelbarkeit und Vereinigung: Zum Verhältnis von Poesie, Reflexion und Revolution bei Hölderlin,* Stuttgart: Metzler, 1975

Sieburth, Richard, introduction to *Hymns and Fragments,* by Friedrich Hölderlin, translated by Richard Sieburth, Princeton, New Jersey: Princeton University Press, 1984

Szondi, Peter, *Hölderlin-Studien,* Frankfurt: Insel, 1967; 3rd edition, Frankfurt: Suhrkamp, 1977

Unger, Richard, *Hölderlin's Major Poetry,* Bloomington: Indiana University Press, 1975

Hyperion; oder, Der Eremit in Griechenland 1797–1799

Novel by Johann Christian Friedrich Hölderlin

Hölderlin's one and only novel was a long time in gestation; the initial idea went back as far as 1792. The final version adopts the epistolary form, as does the only other version available to Hölderlin's contemporaries, the "Fragment von Hyperion," which appeared in Schiller's journal *Thalia* in 1794. Also extant are fragmentary nonepistolary versions, one in prose ("Hyperions Jugend") and one metrical. Common to all, however, is that they confront us with a first-person narrator who tells the story of his past life and comments on it in the process. The use of the epistolary convention in the final version is unusual and innovative. Similar to Goethe's *Werther,* the novel consists of a one-way correspondence addressed to a friend of whom we know little or nothing. Unlike *Werther,* however, the narrative within the letters is not written from the immediacy of the present or near present; it relates events from Hyperion's life that predate the actual writing by a considerable length of time. These events culminate in an experience of pantheistic union with nature, which occurs shortly before he takes up his pen, but which is narrated a year later. *Hyperion* is thus effectively an epistolary autobiography, a form for which there are 18th-century precedents (e.g., Pierre Marivaux, *La vie de Marianne* [1731–36], or John Cleland, *Fanny Hill* [1749]).

Following his predecessors, Hölderlin exploits the form's possibilities, juxtaposing the narrative with critical reflections from the perspective of the present. But he goes further by emphasizing the dimension of the narrator, giving that dimension an observable extension in time, so that we are offered not simply the stages of the hero's development within his own narrative but also insights into the evolving consciousness of the narrator himself, as he confronts his own past. Hölderlin skillfully exploits the resulting tension between the narrator and his subject matter. It is a tension that would not be possible in this degree without the appreciable temporal distance between the narrated events and the narrator's present. In the first half of the novel, we have a gloomy or even despairing narrator relating essentially happy to blissful experiences from his own past; in the second half, an increasingly calm, almost serene narrator tells of grief and disaster.

That the development of the narrator should be regarded as the major focus of the novel is indicated by the subtitle, *Der*

Eremit in Griechenland. For it is the hermit, in his self-imposed isolation, who produces these letters. They document how he came to turn his back on humanity, but also, more significantly, how through an evolving process of reflection he begins to discover pattern and meaning in his experiences by the very act of mediating and articulating them. What starts out as a private (and initially, almost reluctant) confession to an intimate becomes the realization (in all senses) of a poetic vocation. At the end of the novel, Hyperion's first creation, we find a narrator who has emerged from his misanthropic isolation and, instead of turning away from his fellow men, is now addressing them; he will, no doubt, have more to say in future works. The final words, "Nächstens mehr" ("More soon"), remind us that the narrator has a developing, open-ended present. They also point us back to the beginning, for they oblige us to ask what happened next in the narrator's life—the answer being that he returned home to embark on the narrative we have just been reading.

The novel thus provides us with an ingenious combination of linearity and circularity, perhaps the most perfect realization in German literature of Friedrich Schlegel's Romantic program (*progressive Universalpoesie*)—although it is only in recent years that it has been recognized as such. It was really not until Lawrence Ryan's study in 1965 that critics' eyes began to open to the novel's narrative sophistication. That it is written in rhythmic prose of often stunning beauty had tended to lead to its being regarded as an example of lyric genius misapplied. Now we can see that one of the work's great qualities is that it is as tightly structured as a poem.

Hölderlin's friend and mentor, Stäudlin, had advised the young poet to insert into his novel "versteckte Stellen über den Geist der Zeit" (cryptic passages about the spirit of the age). That spirit was one of revolutionary turmoil and upheaval, and it is indeed reflected in the novel in a number of telling ways. Hölderlin situates his novel in Greece, the classical home of democratic ideals; significantly, however, it does not depict ancient Greece, but the Greece of the near present. The novel's background is the unsuccessful 1770 insurrection against the occupying Turkish power. It is in the wake of his crushing failure as a man of action that Hyperion goes into exile in Germany, subsequently returning to Greece to take up his hermitic existence. The aspirations of the revolutionary free spirit are, however, most completely embodied in the figure of (the somewhat Fichtean) Alabanda, with whom Hyperion strikes up a close relationship in the first half of the novel. After a temporary rupture, Hyperion joins forces with Alabanda in the second half of the novel, having been persuaded to take part in the abortive rebellion. Alabanda's alienation is counterbalanced by the harmony with the world of nature, which Hyperion's beloved Diotima mediates to him.

Both Diotima and Alabanda have to die, but before they do so they are given final speeches in which they articulate their ideals and beliefs. Alabanda's is concerned with the indestructibility of the individual spirit and emphasizes freedom from external restraint; Diotima's speech concerns what is common to all life and makes it of equal value in all its forms—it is "Freiheit" and "Gleichheit" that resonate in their respective swan songs. Hyperion's hymn to nature, with which the novel (provisionally) concludes, echoes both of these watchwords of the French Revolution, together with a third watchword in the adjective "brüderlich." The implication would seem to be that Alabanda's freedom and Diotima's equality come together in the fraternity that Hyperion must then realize among his fellow men. He is equipped to do so, not as the man of action or lover, but as the poet he has become in the course of his writing. In attempting to recover and articulate the experience of oneness with all creation with which the novel "ends" ("einiges, ewiges, glühendes Leben ist Alles"), Hyperion achieves the resolution of the dissonances voiced by the foreword, both in himself and in his readership. Poetry redeems and makes whole. The answer to the problems and conundrums adumbrated in the novel is the novel itself.

HOWARD GASKILL

Editions

First edition: *Hyperion; oder, Der Eremit in Griechenland,* Tübingen: Cotta, 1797–99

Critical editions: *Sämtliche Werke* [Große Stuttgarter Ausgabe], vol. 3, edited by Friedrich Beißner and Adolf Beck, Stuttgart: Kohlhammer, 1957; *Sämtliche Werke* [Frankfurter Ausgabe], vols. 10, 11, edited by D.E. Sattler, Frankfurt: Verlag Roter Stern, 1982

Translation: *Hyperion; or, The Hermit in Greece,* translated by Willard E. Trask, adapted by David Schwarz, in *Hyperion and Selected Poems,* edited by Eric L. Santner, New York: Continuum, 1990

Further Reading

Gaskill, Howard, *Hölderlin's "Hyperion,"* Durham: University of Durham, 1984

Knaupp, Michael, editor, *Friedrich Hölderlin: "Hyperion": Erläuterungen und Dokumente,* Stuttgart: Reclam, 1997

Prignitz, Chistoph, "Die Bewältigung der Französischen Revolution in Hölderlins *Hyperion,*" *Jahrbuch des freien deutschen Hochstifts* (1975)

Ryan, Lawrence, *Hölderlins "Hyperion": Exzentrische Bahn und Dichterberuf,* Stuttgart: Metzler, 1965

Der Tod des Empedokles 1826

Play by Johann Christian Friedrich Hölderlin

Friedrich Hölderlin's dramatic fragments, *Der Tod des Empedokles* (The Death of Empedokles), include three versions written during the period of time that he spent in Homburg trying unsuccessfully to establish himself as an independent writer. He left the household of the Frankfurt banking family, the Gontards, in September 1798 under difficult personal circumstances and sought refuge and new hope in the vicinity of his friend Isaak von Sinclair, a liberal and influential intellectual then in the employ of the ruling family of the small principality of Homburg. Hölderlin attempted to enlist Goethe and Schiller as well as other prominent German intellectuals and writers in a journal project for which he had even found a publisher, and he tried as well to write or complete a number of literary pieces, including a drama based on third century accounts of Empedocles that were drawn from Diogenes Laertius. These half historical, half legendary tales tell of the philosopher Empedokles, much revered in his homeland Agrigent, a city-state in Sicily, who was driven out by a public discontented with their mentor's constant unhappiness about the apparently comfortable conditions of life in the city and then restored to favor, only to be driven into exile again by a portion of the populace led by the high priest, Hemokrates. Empedokles, upon his second exile, ends his life by jumping into Mount Aetna, sacrificing himself for the welfare of his fellow countrymen.

Hölderlin wrote his first and longest version of this story in 1798–99 (two complete acts) and depicts Empedokles suffering from his great sensitivity to the people's lack of awareness of the need for change in both moral and political spheres of life. Although the city-state is prospering, the philosopher has warned the population repeatedly that this assumed happiness is superficial and will soon disappear unless the population rejects its attachment to its own shallow life and resumes its earlier awareness of the great future, which only an equally great awareness and moral will can bring about.

A second version, written in 1799, breaks off after the third scene of the first act and includes a small portion of the end of the second act. This second version develops a sharpening perception of the motivations of the party led by the priest, Hemokrates. By pointing out Empedokles's willfully heightened subjectivity and his insistence on his own extreme individualism, this version suggests the extent of the philosopher's own hubris. At the same time, the social contradictions that have so agitated the philosopher-protagonist are also emphasized.

A third version, written in 1799–1800, includes only the first three scenes and several outlines for further portions of the work. In this version, Empedokles is driven out of the city by his own brother and looks inward at the flawed relationship that he has developed with the people of Agrigent. His death, in this latest fragment, serves the now-clearer function of sacrifice: Empedokles realizes that his own individual awareness of the situation of his city-state and its people must be translated through sacrificial death into a greater awareness. In this realization he has been able to take into account his own hubris and his flawed relationship with the people themselves.

The fragments reflect the context of Hölderlin's own life during these years. Separated by social class and by the law from his idealized beloved (and wife of his employer), Susette Gontard, and failing to establish himself as an independent writer and intellectual, Hölderlin also labored under the difficult political circumstances in the German states at that time. The end of the Rastatt Congress (1797–99) and the resultant Second Coalition War, which began in 1799, put an end to the hopes of the South German liberals to whose sphere of influence both Sinclair and Hölderlin belonged—hopes that greater liberalization, at least in the South German states, would take place. The proclamation of a Helvetian Confederation in several of the Swiss cantons had raised these hopes, and, through Sinclair, Hölderlin had been introduced into oppositional circles whose plans for French assistance were dashed not only by the Congress of Rastatt but by the growing imperialism of the French regime itself. Trapped among these triply dashed hopes, Hölderlin composed *The Death of Empedokles* as an artistic and moral solution both to his own increasingly hopeless personal and artistic situation and to the perceived gap between an avant-garde art and the general population that could not yet understand the purpose of that art. The notion of sacrifice—the intentional death of the philosopher-artist as a sacrifice for his still blind and beloved people—represented the highest aspiration for the young poet whose own personal life offered him only increasing contradictions and grievous personal setbacks.

There has been an ongoing avant-garde enthusiasm for Hölderlin's works, but this fragmentary drama in particular has fascinated literary scholars and theater producers as a document of the failed aspirations and hopes for a new and revolutionary social and political situation for Germans that would have been brought about by the direct intervention and influences of the French Revolution and its early Napoleonic aftermath. The political but also the psychological portrayal of the writer's impossible position—the loss of his muse and his lover, Susette (the Diotima of some of his finest verse), possibly due in part to his own fear of a sexual relationship, and the loss of his own political and larger German cultural ambitions—was accompanied by a sense of personal failure. This sense of failure encompassed Holderlin's failure to resolve the relationship with Susette, to escape his dependency on his mother, and to establish himself financially and artistically, thus ensuring that he would not have to take up the career of village pastor so ardently wished for him by his mother. *The Death of Empedokles,* although remaining only a fragment, is thus one of the most personal and political of all of Hölderlin's many works, but it is also imbued with that same attention to artistic detail that is characteristic of the writer. The verse forms and the meters are consistent with Hölderlin's unparalleled ability to compose classical verse forms in the German language, giving to that language outside of what is otherwise considered to be the classical component of German letters of that period, a literary grandeur commensurate with the idealism of the contents and its author.

DUNCAN SMITH

Editions

First edition: incomplete, in *Gedichte,* 1826

Critical editions: in *Sämmtliche Werke* [Große Stuttgarter Ausgabe], vol. 4, edited by Friedrich Beißner, Stuttgart: Kohlhammer, 1943–1985; edited by M.B. Benn, London: Oxford University Press, 1968

Further Reading

Bertaux, Pierre, "Was Hölderlin Mentally Ill?" *Philosophy Today* 37, no. 4 (Winter 1993)

Birkenhauer, Theresia, *Legende und Dichtung: Der Tod des Philosophen und Hölderlins Empedokles,* Berlin: Vorwerk 8, 1996

Constantine, David, "Mythologie und Vernunft: Vier philosophische Studien zu Friedrich Holderlin by Uwe Beyer," *Modern Language Review* 91 (1996)

Dilthey, Wilhelm, "Hölderlin and the Causes of His Madness," *Philosophy Today* 37, no. 4 (Winter 1993)

Grätz, Katharina, *Der Weg zum Lesetext: Editionskritik und Neuedition von Friedrich Hölderlins Der Tod des Empedokles,* Tübingen: Niemeyer, 1995

Kuzniar, Alice A., "Friedrich Hölderlin: Narrative Vigilance and the Poetic Imagination by Eric L. Santner," *Germanic Review* 64, no. 2 (1989)

Rush, Fred L., Jr., "The Unity of Reason: Essays in Kant's Philosophy: The Course of Remembrance and Other Essays on Hölderlin," *Journal of Philosophy* 95, no. 3 (March 1998)

Holocaust (Shoah) Literature

When in 1968 the Library of Congress catalog introduced the disputed English term *Holocaust* (from the Greek *Holokauston,* or whole burnt)—instead of the Hebrew *Shoah* (catastrophe, destruction)—as a subject category for the systematic Nazi destruction of European Jewry ("Holocaust, Jewish 1939–1945"), literary approaches to the morally challenging topic had already met considerable resistance. Theodor W. Adorno's famous dictum—"to write a poem after Auschwitz is barbaric"—articulates the concerns many authors, critics, and readers had raised about how to represent the Holocaust adequately. In the 1950s and 1960s, the subject was virtually taboo, a consequence of the universally affirmed *Stunde Null* (zero hour), and writing the Holocaust was left to respectful historical research that reconstructed the political, legal, social, or military ramifications of the German extermination of Jewish people. For many critics, the incomprehensible enormity of the event was incompatible with the Western literary tradition, for it evoked the limits of aesthetic concepts, signified the irrevocable loss of (the German) language, and rendered art as "trivial and impertinent" (George Steiner, *Language and Silence,* 1967). With its stress on individual subjectivity, its imaginative construction of utopian worlds and beautiful apparition, or its interplay of fact and fiction, literature is not well equipped to deal with mass suffering, mass murder, and inexpressible loss. Nazi concentration camps constituted such a terrific assault on religious, humanistic, moral, and philosophical values that narratives emerging from or propagating ethical standards became speechless vis-à-vis the factual horror of extreme genocide. Furthermore, an "aesthetic" response to Auschwitz seems to destroy the horrifying singularity of the event by transfiguring the real suffering of its victims into an object of aesthetic pleasure, which could indeed satisfy sadomasochistic desires. Even the survivor and writer Elie Wiesel asserted that the term *Holocaust literature* is a contradiction because "Auschwitz negates all literature as it negates all theories and doctrines" (*A Jew Today,* 1978).

Despite all these crucial reservations and their potentially silencing effects, women and men have written about life in ghettos, on transports, or in camps and have depicted conditions of starvation, torture, epidemics, and murder. The result has been that Holocaust literature has emerged as one of "the most compelling literatures of our day" (Rosenfeld), as a quintessentially (post-)modern, international, and deeply engaging body of work. By employing narrative devices that concentrate on the individual, Holocaust literature presents multiple perspectives associated with the victims and generates a plurality of meaning by using the imaginative faculties of rhetorical and figurative language in a wide variety of literary forms. Following the classical narrative formula of historical novels, private stories (*Geschichten*), for example, make the political history (*Geschichte*) of the Holocaust transparent for an audience that for some time had felt quite comfortable with shelving the memory of the Jewish genocide in abstract histories. Instead of freezing the event in the anonymity of the murder of 6 million Jews, autobiographical as well as fictional accounts of the Holocaust rehumanize the vast number of victims by facilitating an understanding of the individual physical and psychological suffering involved in the Holocaust. Through writing, many Holocaust survivors also give testimony to the world, express their grief over lost ones, and attempt to restore singular identities of victims through names and personal voices. Furthermore, narrating unique situations and distinctive miseries mediates the specific details of individual traumas by confronting the reader with previously unknown personal experiences in unimaginable spaces of horror, survival, and death. Besides its documentary and educational functions in regard to the most violent and dehumanized deaths in history, Holocaust literature also transforms and transcends the Shoah by questioning those values and paradigms of Western civilization that could neither prevent nor explain the genocide.

Literary testimonies in the form of diaries, memoirs, or autobiographical stories were initially considered the only appropriate, "authentic," and ethically responsible way of representing the historic event to which they give personal evidence. Their specific narrative forms shift the focus from the horrendous deeds of the perpetrators to the subjectivity of the storyteller whose writing of individual experiences affirms his or her existence as a witness. By describing the daily fears in hiding places, the tormenting journey on cattle trains, and the fatal realities in the various localities of the camps, some of these texts have established tropes in the topography of the Holocaust and have become "classics" of its genre. Anne Frank's posthumously published *The Diary of a Young Girl* (1947), for example, provides a sense of the haunted life of Jews in occupied Holland. Written between 1942 and 1944 while Anne hid in Amsterdam, the intimate notes about the typical problems and experiences of adolescence give detailed descriptions of the persecution and how it affected Anne's daily life. In addition, the diary informs the reader how much information was available about the Nazi atrocities even to people in hiding. Anne was deported to Auschwitz and Bergen-Belsen, where she died of starvation and disease. Her book became a best-seller, and it serves as an introduction to the Holocaust, especially for young readers who can relate to the ideas, feelings, and worries of a young girl. The readers' knowledge of her fate, however, might influence a compassionate reading that inflicts violence on the text/author: feeling good about oneself (the pleasure of reading) through symbolic participation in the pain of others (the problem of pity). Because it is based on a narcissistic pattern of object relations, this kind of sentimental identification with the victims perpetuates the incapacity to recognize or perceive the suffering of the real victims.

Like Frank's diary, Elie Wiesel's memoir *Night* (1958) is a short but complex presentation of the Holocaust through the personal experiences of a (religious) Jewish boy from Hungary (one-third of all Holocaust victims were children under the age of 16). This realistic narrative with a personal voice depicts single characters with specific functions, avoids any psychological commentary of the narrating "I," and places emphasis on the victims rather than on the survivors. The main character describes the torture of several deportations—thirst, heat, hunger, claustrophobia, and even murder in the cattle wagon—and the nightmare of atrocities in the camps (Auschwitz, Buchenwald). The differentiated depiction of Auschwitz draws the readers' attention to the selection procedures on the ramp, the differences between the camps (Birkenau, Monowitz/Buna), the daily routine (roll call, forced labor), and the struggle for survival, which is introduced as a matter of chance. After the death of his father, the story comes to an end: the narrator has lost his entire family and is even alienated from his own body/identity. By questioning his belief in God, Wiesel presents religion's limitations in explaining mass murder.

In *Survival in Auschwitz* (1958; also as *If This Is a Man*), the Italian chemist Primo Levi presents his memoirs with a very detailed "blow-by-blow" description of deprivation. His work explores the discursive and logistical space of Auschwitz, its social structure, and its administrative rituals in order to show that the absurdity of the camp society had a complex structure. On one hand, the laws of the outside world are magnified: social and ethnic hierarchies determine one's identity (class system); the privileged oppress the underprivileged (political system); the accumulation of material goods provides power (free market system); the status of one's health, age, and skills regulates job opportunities (employment system); and the dehumanization, exploitation, and killing of people is not arbitrary but follows administrative guidelines (bureaucratic system). On the other hand, the camp has its own laws: critical rationality is abolished; the system of destroying people through regulated starvation, inhuman labor and living conditions creates absurdities (e.g., the ill are taken into hospitals in order to kill them more slowly); and human solidarity is very fragile because the victims are forced to become collaborators and to lose their morals in order to survive. Levi confronts this system that denies both life and the principles of a human society with his determination to preserve his identity and dignity as a moral human being. He utilizes his dreams and memories about his home to keep the belief alive that there has been and will be another world. His solidarity with fellow Italian prisoners provides shelter, security, comfort, and material goods. Within an absurd world that attempts to destroy individual integrity, Levy recognizes that even banal activities such as washing and shaving can become a tool for moral stability and self-esteem. But it is primarily his analytical mind that allows him to recall the reasoning of the outside world and apply it to the camp. Understanding the structure of the camp, understanding and anticipating the behavior of others, and developing communicative skills are indispensable strategies for his own survival.

In his collection of short stories *This Way for the Gas Ladies and Gentlemen* (1959), the non-Jewish Polish survivor Tadeusz Borowski adds a new perspective to the complex process of victimization in Auschwitz by depicting the dehumanization but also the brutality and ruthlessness of "privileged" prisoners who were forced to collaborate with their oppressors. The realistic, detailed description of the arrival, selection, and killing of Jews at the ramp conveys the clash of different realities of Auschwitz, where the collaborators had to suspend the laws and moral concepts that govern the outside world. While removing corpses from the freight trains and watching the random murder of Jews, gentile prisoners act as the vultures of the camp who obtain material goods from Jewish victims in order to guarantee their own survival. Within the limited space of the genre, Borowski can explore neither the psychological development of a character nor the prolonged unfolding of an event. Instead of transcending physical torture, he presents single situations that provide a perplexing insight into the complicated relationships between victims and perpetrators and among different victims. Borowski's matter-of-fact narration and his use of "camp slang" and grim irony increase the brutality of what is narrated and reinforce the cruel inexorability of concentration camp reality in order to confront the reader with same exact images the observer had to face.

Although some critics have associated Holocaust literature essentially with testimonies of survivors, whose stories guarantee their own truth by using first-person, realistic narratives, many authors—Jew or gentile, survivor or observer—have adhered to a more imaginative approach to the Shoah. The fragile boundary between memoir literature and documentary fiction (history represented in stories) becomes even more blurred when the Holocaust is represented in the novel, a genre that is more or less built upon the absolute freedom of the writer's imagination. This foundation for creative writing confronts novelists with a formal and moral dilemma. When the magnitude of the historical fact itself surpasses its fictional reconstruction, what is there left for the novel to represent? In order to do justice to the subject, are the entertaining qualities of the novel supposed to be suspended? How can a post-Auschwitz imagination solve the conflict between aesthetic innovations and ethical limitations? Writers from very diverse traditions have addressed these challenging questions with various success. In his critically acclaimed novel *The Last of the Just* (1959), André Schwarz-Bart locates the Holocaust within the history of anti-Semitism and as the history of Jewish martyrdom by rewriting the Jewish legend of the Just Men. The author takes great liberties with the legend when he portrays the Just Men in a continuum of willing sufferers that culminates in the story of Ernie Levy, the last of the Just Men, who is killed in Auschwitz. While the inevitability of martyrdom seems to be the organizing principle of the novel, Ernie's choice to die with and for his people departs from the narrated chronology of Jewish destiny and defines him as a martyr out of human passion. The depiction of Ernie's last moments when he comforts the children and his lover Golda is one of the very few literary accounts of the deaths in the gas chambers. This scene of narrative imagination, however, avoids the illustration of the gruesome realities and instead portrays Ernie's compassion and mercy toward fellow victims.

Whereas Schwarz-Bart utilizes the traditional codes of lamentation literature in order to evoke infinite sadness, Jerzy Kosinski's controversial *The Painted Bird* (1965) draws upon nihilistic worldviews and presents a demonic universe in which only evil succeeds. Fusing innocent adolescence with the most horrifying adult experiences, the novel exhibits the corruption of childhood during World War II. A young nameless boy—perhaps a Jew or a Gypsy—wanders alone through Slav villages in a continuing struggle for self-preservation. He experiences separation from his family, abuse, fear of death, and physical and psychological torture; he observes an endless stream of suffering of others (beatings, murder, and rape); and, finally, he engages himself in violent acts. While his memory of his parents and of an ethical society is fading, the boy gradually learns to conform to the laws of his hostile environment. Identifying with the brutality of the aggressors and with what he calls "the powers of evil," he adopts hate as his guiding principle in a destructive world and thereby transforms himself from victim into victimizer. Despite Kosinski's mention that his own experiences had informed his writing, the novel has been criticized for its graphic depiction of sadism and its obscene aesthetics of violence.

When they are confronted with unbearable atrocities, the characters in the realistic novel *An Estate of Memory* (1969), which was written by the survivor Ilona Karmel, exhibit a radically different response. Following the tradition of great prison novels, Karmel tells the story of four Jewish women incarcerated in a concentration camp who develop a system of coexistence, mutual support, and intimate bonding. Following Primo Levi's emphasis on the importance of solidarity, Karmel undermines the assumption that only selfishness guarantees survival. Under the unnatural conditions of Nazi imprisonment, the four protagonists—Barbara Grünbaum, Tola Ohrenstein, Aurelia Katz, and the adolescent Alinka—not only share food, clothes, comfort, and their diverse memories, but also their hopes for freedom and life, with which they confront the inversion of the human society in the camp. Despite their gradual physical deterioration and the tensions emerging from their unique individualities, the love between these women is so strong that they even manage to hide the birth of Aurelia's child and to smuggle the infant out of the camp. While the altruistic efforts of these women's friendship save the child and Alinka, the novel does not engage, however, in the clichés of wishful thinking. Its psychological exploration of the characters' disappointments, conflicts, and individual failures; its constant changes of narrative perspective; and its painful depiction of life at the limits of humanity all help construct a very complex narration of plausible and possible human experiences in borderline situations.

Many fictional works have addressed one of the basic philosophical questions of the postwar era: how can the survivors manage to continue their lives with their memories of the Holocaust? In Isaac Bashevis Singer's *Enemies, a Love Story* (1966–72), a novel about companionship, desire, and memory in a New York community of Jewish refugees, all the protagonists realize that they can not escape the past, which continues to structure their daily lives and their relationships. Depicting personalities with distinct character traits, Singer portrays the complexities that evolve from the interdependencies between historical events and individual reaction. The main character, Herman Broder, who survived the Holocaust by hiding in a hayloft, is surrounded by women—his savior and second wife, the Polish Catholic and now converted Yadwiga, his first wife Tamara, and his lover Masha—who nurture him, save him, love him, and control him to the extent that he allows his entire existence to be managed by others. While he survived sheltered in hiding, the women in his life endured the occupation and the death camps, joined the Jewish underground, or outlasted Stalinist incarceration. Although Herman is personally bound to the past (Yadwiga/Tamara), he tries to escape his memory through love (to Masha). His attempt fails because his own life philosophy as well as his reactions to the world surrounding him are based on the past. As a result of the Holocaust, he mistrusts Western ideas (from Leibniz to Husserl) that could not prevent atrocities. He only reads the old Jewish books, identifies with biblical figures, and invents a religious philosophy of history based on lust and desire. Haunted by the ghosts of the past, he journeys through a self-built labyrinth of deception, and his story comes to closure when he vanishes again in hiding while the two wives he leaves behind form a bond of solidarity in order to raise his child.

While Singer stresses the suffering women had to endure during the Holocaust, some novels exploit the atrocities of the Holocaust in order to provoke their audience or to expose the moral dilemma of our times. The most disputable example of this kind of text is William Styron's *Sophie's Choice* (1979). Here fiction and historical fact are mixed to the extent that a Polish Catholic woman becomes the main character representing the Jewish victims of Auschwitz. Furthermore, after having survived the camp, she becomes the victim of sexual abuse in New York, and one of her cruel lovers is Jewish. Although the novel illuminates the twisted sexuality of the Western world (there are other examples of mutilated woman who survived the camps and then become sex objects for men), it touches upon one of the ultimate taboos: the reversal of victim and perpetrator through the female body.

Over the last 20 years a new Holocaust literature has emerged, which is written by the survivors' children who articulate their confrontation with the Holocaust as part of their family history. One of the most controversial texts of the second generation is Art Spiegelman's *Maus: A Survivor's Tale* (1986), which is continued in *Maus II: And Here My Troubles Began* (1991). Utilizing a traditionally "low" genre, the comic book, this postmodern response to the Holocaust challenges the view that a grave theme (mass murder) demands a serious genre (such as epic or tragedy) for its proper representation. In *Maus,* pity and terror are held at a distance through the devices of the cartoon and its humorous image of the mouse, which permits an intellectually more active response than angst and lament. The artistic reduction of the Germans to cats, the Jews to mice, the Poles to pigs, the French to frogs, and Americans to dogs (etc.) offers an intentional simplification that at first glance seems to mimic Nazi practices of dehumanization, but this miniaturizing on the level of character identification allows for multiple narratives through diverse text types. The images are always accompanied by dialogue boxes, commentaries, maps, diagrams of hideouts, real photographs from the family archive, plans of crematoria, an exchange table about the value of goods in Auschwitz, or a shoe-repair manual; all of these allow the reader to move through different times and places of persecution and survival, not to mention postwar daily life in New York. In addition, *Maus* portrays several perspectives. The story of the Polish survivor Vladek Spiegelman is told in aesthetic representation by his son Artie, who himself struggles to understand his family origins, his father's idiosyncracies, and his own life. Working through the traumatic past—the narrated death of his brother Richieu, the suicide of his mother Anja in 1968, and the murder of the European Jews—the text addresses questions of Jewish trauma and guilt and of the transmission of these conflicts from one generation to the next. Although both Artie and his father come out looking more like beasts than human beings, this ironic and bewildered view of the Holocaust is one of the most moving narrative accounts of the subject. The cat-and-mouse iconography provokes and alienates its readers and draws new attention to an old story by using comic ambiguity that embraces life.

Compared with the international production, dissemination, and reception of Holocaust literature, there has been very little cultural encouragement in Germany to come to terms with its past. Instead of speaking openly about their involvement with the Nazi regime and about the collectively committed atrocities, Germans silenced, forgot, and denied the Holocaust. It took until the end of the 1970s for the general public in Germany to gain a full and collective awareness of the Holocaust and empathy with its victims. In 1979 the broadcast of the NBC adaptation of Gerald Green's sentimental novel *Holocaust: The Story of the Family Weiss* (1978) created a new collective historical consciousness in the "land of the guilty," which neither political documentaries nor critical literature had been able to achieve: for the first time the majority of Germans seemed to overcome their "inability to mourn" (Alexander and Margarete Mitscherlich) by identifying with the victims of their own history. In comparison, Claude Lanzmann's nine-hour documentary film *Shoah* (1985) was mostly seen by intellectuals. His gruesome interviews with survivors, former guards, and onlookers reconstruct in detail the process of extermination and the "unspeakable." Visiting the rails and sites of Auschwitz, Treblinka, and Chelmno, the survivors recall what happened to human beings, while the perpetrators articulate their terrible detachment by getting lost in technical details or in the rhetoric of repression and denial. Even in the 1990s, the German public was mainly reached through traditional filmed narratives of the Holocaust, including Agnieszka Holland's *Hitlerjunge Salomon* (1991; *Europa, Europa*) and Steven Spielberg's filming of Thomas Keneally's 1982 historical novel *Schindler's List* (1993). Unlike the internationally shaped visual representations of the Holocaust, literature in the German language had to face another dilemma. The Nazi's linguistic and metaphorical perversion of language, which was the discursive accompaniment to their attempt to dehumanize the Jewish people, had tainted the German language to the extent that in the context of the Holocaust, German was merely seen as "Nazi-Deutsch," a language whose syntax, style, and symbolic associations extended Nazi racism and ideology into every area of cultural expression. In spite of these obstacles, however, a literature of the Holocaust written in the German language has appeared and has even gained some international appreciation.

Many autobiographic, poetic, dramatic, or fictional approaches to the Holocaust have been composed in German, including Ilse Aichinger's *Eine größere Hoffnung* (1948; *Herod's Children*), Bruno Apitz's *Nackt unter Wölfen* (1958; *Naked among Wolves*), Jakov Lind's *Eine Seele aus Holz* (1962; *Soul of Wood*), Rolf Hochhuth's *Der Stellvertreter* (1963; *The Deputy*), and Jurek Becker's *Bronsteins Kinder* (1986; *Bronstein's Children*)—but only a few have had a significant influence on the genre as a whole. Already in the early postwar years, the Holocaust survivors Paul Celan (Paul Antschel) and Nelly Sachs—the latter also wrote the biblical mystery play *Eli* (1943)—chose poetry as a medium in which language neither surrendered to the Nazi corruption of the symbolic nor affirmed the ideology of silence. Their poems translate the gassing of the Jews into hermetic metaphors that resist the hermeneutic practices of the advancing consumer culture and that "transmuted the ugly realities into work of aesthetic perfection without detracting from the horror" (Ezrahi). In Celan's poem "Todesfuge" (Fugue of Death), for example, neologistic expressions such as "black milk," "grave in the air," "ashen hair," and "death is a master from Germany" all capture the agony and the physicality of the torment in the simplicity of mundane words, which appear obscure, dense, dark, and ambiguous. Written in musical form, the poem depicts life and death in the camps, German atrocities, and the Jewish suffering with which Celan identified when he wrote in the first person plural. By juxtaposing two literary figures—the blonde German Margarete (Goethe's Gretchen) and the ashen-haired biblical Shulamite (the cremated Jewess)—the poem also reveals Celan's struggle with his cultural identity after the Holocaust. Like many other poets and authors, Celan was "contending with a silent God" (Rosenfeld), and the poem enunciates the spiritual void evoked by the shattering of Jewish beliefs. In his almost blasphemous poem "Psalm" (1963), he forms his fatalistic theology by negating biblical sentences: "No one moulds us again out of earth and clay, / no one conjures our dust. / No one."

A similar silence and finality of life can be found in the poems of Nelly Sachs, the 1966 Nobel Prize winner who sought to "represent the tragedy of the Jewish people" throughout her work. Poems such as "O die Schornsteine" (1967; O, the Chimneys) deal with finding a language that transforms the unutterable and the screams of the victims into transcendental truth, which for Sachs is deeply embedded in the larger history of Jewish martyrdom. In Sachs's poetic universe, images of the Holocaust—"burnt body," "dust," or "dead child"—do not stand by themselves but are interconnected with those of the Hasidic and Cabalistic tradition. Celan's and Sachs's use of hermetic metaphors, abstract language, and complex cultural references has made their poems quite inaccessible to some of today's readers, but for the literary critic they seem to have found an appropriate language to represent the so-called unrepresentable.

In his drama *Die Ermittlung* (1965; *The Investigation*), Peter Weiss demonstrates how to represent the "unimaginable hell" of Auschwitz by using the cold, factual language of the documentary theater. Although embraced by some critics as one of the best plays written about the Holocaust, this theatrical reenactment of the Auschwitz trials in Frankfurt (1963–65) poses a political issue, because it constructs a causal nexus between capitalism and Auschwitz. In an attempt to challenge bourgeois political assumptions about Auschwitz through the representation of the condensed "facts," Weiss systematized authentic material from the trial proceedings into an artistic montage of selected reality bites. His Marxist understanding of historical events, however, transforms Jewish victims into political and national victims (socialists, Soviet prisoners) who are persecuted by monopoly capitalism in its worst historic stage. The confrontations of the witnesses and the accused, and of the prosecution and the defense counsel, are presented as completely emotionless (with the exception of the hellish laughter of the accused) and are staged from the victims' perspectives. The nine witnesses, who represent the hundreds of witnesses at the actual trial, are kept in anonymity and are only identified by the numbers one through nine so as to symbolize the loss of identity in Auschwitz. The accused, however, bear their original names, which stand for their gruesome involvement in the evil system. Weiss uses a linear structure of narration (not the structure of the trial) in order to recall the times and sites the victims had encountered in Auschwitz (the ramp, entering the camp, camp life, the gas chamber, and the crematorium), but he also dramatizes the narration by organizing the material in 11 "songs," which recalls the third part of Dante's *Divina Commedia.* The reversal of Dante's paradise into the hell of Auschwitz is grounded in Weiss's skepticism in regard to any kind of redemption. Unlike the trial, the play does not end with a verdict and the sentencing of the accused but with the last speech of a perpetrator, who uses West Germany's capitalistic success to legitimize forgetting the Holocaust. Written for a German audience that had tried to return to "normality" by successfully repressing its Nazi past, the play had several didactic purposes: to protest against attempts to legitimize opportune behavior under the Nazi regime, to make public that the companies that had contributed to the postwar economic success were also involved in the Holocaust (IG Farben, Krupp, Siemens, etc.), to provide a rational explanation for Auschwitz within a sociohistorical interpretation of exploitation, and to claim that the German conscience and its reliance on fulfilling duties had not changed.

Jakob der Lügner (1969; *Jacob the Liar*), written by Jurek Becker, a survivor of the Lodz ghetto and several concentration camps, is one of the few German fictional accounts of the Holocaust that has gained international attention. The novel describes one man's spiritual triumph in the midst of the Holocaust. The main character, Jacob Heym, stumbles into the role of an encourager for the inmates of a Polish ghetto where hopelessness and a high suicide rate dominate daily life. After having left a German police station miraculously unharmed, Jacob tells his fellow men that he has overheard the news that the Red Army has advanced closer to the ghetto. To be credible and not to be seen as a collaborator, Jacob pretends that he secretly owns a radio, a possession that not only puts him but the entire ghetto at risk. People begin to listen and the suicide rate in the ghetto drops to zero. After his first lie Jacob finds himself in the role of having to provide further information; thus, he invents many more promising news reports. Finally, he gets fed up with creating stories and in an attempt to give up his entire charade he tells his oldest friend the truth, who in an act of despair hangs himself. This combination of the tragic with the comic and satirical is distinctive to Becker's approach to the Holocaust. Although the ending of the novel shows the terrible realities of the Holocaust, the very engaging tale nevertheless provides hope amid despair. It demonstrates the will to live through the example of an ordinary man and restores the humanity of victims by telling their unique stories. Becker's novelistic invention of the characters, places, and events in his story has been praised as a successful narrative attempt to write fiction about the Holocaust.

In the early 1990s, German literary circles were so fascinated or stunned by one Holocaust memoir that they awarded one of Germany's highest literary prizes to its author. Ruth Klüger's *Weiter leben: Eine Jugend* (1992; Continue to Live: A Youth) is a literary autobiography of a survivor of Theresienstadt, Auschwitz, and Groß-Rosen who became a professor of German literature in the United States. Because of her reflections on international Holocaust literature, literary criticism, feminism, and theories of fascism, Klüger presents a critical metadiscourse that exceeds the narrow definition of memoirs. She implicitly dismisses all theories that judge the aesthetic representation of the Holocaust in strictly moralistic terms and rather refers to another tradition of writings by Holocaust survivors, which she seeks to expand with her critical feminist voice. Her complex narrative (flashbacks, poetry and prose, and reflections on writing) reconstructs the story of a rebellious young girl from the Viennese Jewish middle class. After her father is abducted and killed by the Nazis, she and her mother are persecuted and forced into the camps during the most important and formative phases of the young girl's life. Despite the extreme circumstances of her upbringing, she nevertheless develops a strong identity as a Jewish woman who witnesses the victimization of women, their mutual support for survival, and their traumatic memory of the Holocaust. Klüger's remembering of her and her family's suffering is constantly intertwined with reflections about other survivors' memories and texts; in this way, she stages a dialogue with specific historical and discursive traditions. Written for a German-speaking audience, the book also explores the barriers between German gentiles and Jews, between amnesia and memory, and urges the reader to copy what the text does best: to differentiate.

Although Holocaust literature is challenged in regards to its historical authenticity and its realistic narration about an "unimaginable" world, its task cannot be literally to reproduce or mirror the reality of the Holocaust, something even historical writing or documentation is unable to achieve when it relies heavily on the sources of the perpetrators. The literary participation in the imaginative reconstruction of a true event, on which all collective memory depends, transmits various historical, psychological, and philosophical truths about the unprecedented atrocities of the German war against the Jewish people. Being more scrutinized than other literatures, Holocaust literature faces the complex task of undoing historical amnesia while simultaneously avoiding the tendency to mythicize or to trivialize the Holocaust. Written in many languages and literary genres, Holocaust literature is still not yet on the canon of literature and is rarely taught. Some readers have attempted to universalize Holocaust literature as a part of a larger humanitarianism instead of localizing it to the Jewish catastrophe; others have denied its broader significance and pushed it into a literary "ghetto." These reactions have to be seen in light of the new challenges Holocaust literature poses for literary criticism. Reading Holocaust literature, audiences have to adopt ethical values and to apply literary categories (aesthetic and critical standards) in order to be able to judge what is acceptable: "The scholar's task is to show both its relevance and its specificity, to give it a context and a place in our literary histories and theories without lessening the impact of its unique contribution" (Angress). Holocaust literature not only reminds us of the individual suffering of Jewish people but restores the humanity of the victims by showing compelling variations of human behavior.

STEPHAN K. SCHINDLER

See also Hannah Arendt; Paul Celan; Exile Literature; Jewish Culture and Literature

Further Reading

Angress, Ruth K., "Discussing Holocaust Literature," *Simon Wiesenthal Center Annual* 2 (1985)

Cernyak-Spatz, Susan E., *German Holocaust Literature,* New York: Lang, 1985

Conter, Claude, editor, *Literatur und Holocaust,* Bamberg: Universität Bamberg, 1996

Ezrahi, Sidra DeKoven, *By Words Alone: The Holocaust in Literature,* Chicago: University of Chicago Press, 1980

Friedman, Saul S., editor, *Holocaust Literature: A Handbook of Critical, Historical, and Literary Writings,* Westport, Connecticut: Greenwood Press, 1993

Insdorf, Annette, *Inedible Shadows: Film and the Holocaust,* New York: Random House, 1983

Klüger, Ruth, *Weiter leben: Eine Jugend,* Göttingen: Wallstein, 1992

Lang, Berel, and Aron Applefeld, editors, *Writing and the Holocaust,* New York: Holmes and Meier, 1988

Lorenz, Dagmar C.G., *Verfolgung bis zum Massenmord: Holocaust-Diskurse in deutscher Sprache aus der Sicht der Verfolgten,* New York: Lang, 1992

Rosenfeld, Alvin H., *A Double Dying: Reflections on Holocaust Literature,* Bloomington: Indiana University Press, 1980

Young, James Edward, *Writing and Rewriting the Holocaust: Narrative and the Consequences of Interpretation,* Bloomington: Indiana University Press, 1988

Arno Holz 1863–1929 and Johannes Schlaf 1862–1941

Arno Holz and Johannes Schlaf owe their place in the history of German literature to the works that they produced in five years of close collaboration from 1887 to 1892. In a small number of self-consciously experimental prose sketches and one drama, they pushed the mimetic dimension of prose writing to an extreme beyond which further development was scarcely possible. Quite different in terms of temperament and literary interest, they brought distinct but mutually complementary talents to the joint venture; from 1898 onward, however, they became embroiled in an unseemly quarrel over the relative scope and importance of their respective contributions. Their subsequent independent work is illustrative of the modernist possibilities opened up by the naturalist project in which they had been major participants.

Like many of the German Naturalists, Holz and Schlaf came from a provincial background: Holz was born in East Prussia, Schlaf in Magdeburg, and both moved to Berlin during the period of industrial expansion following the foundation of the Second Empire in 1871. Holz was the first to make his mark as a writer through his contributions to the naturalist lyric anthology edited by Wilhelm Arent, *Moderne Dichtercharaktere* (1885; Modern Poetic Personalities), and in the following year, he was widely acclaimed as the leading naturalist poet for his *Buch der Zeit: Lieder eines Modernen* (1886; Book of the Age: Songs of a Modern Man). Except in the "Phantasus" poems of the *Buch der Zeit,* there is little attempt at formal innovation in these early works, but the social critical poems herald the concern of the writers of his generation. These poems' response to problems arising from rapid urban growth and, more specifically, their Berlin setting also anticipate the works written together with Schlaf.

At the time at which these poems were written, Holz was beginning to play an important role in the literary life of the capital, which had been given a new direction in the early 1880s by the Hart brothers, as a contributor to the new literary journals and as a member of the Verein Durch, the literary society that brought together the early pioneers of naturalism. Schlaf, who first encountered the new literary tendency along with Hermann Conradi in Magdeburg, moved to Berlin after having begun his studies in Halle. In 1887, he settled with Holz in Pankow, where an intense period of collaboration began.

By this time, Holz had become convinced that the literary revolution of the early 1880s would remain insubstantial unless it became a stylistic revolution. For Holz, this meant the development of a theory of literature based on deterministic principles derived from the natural sciences, which would be more radical than Zola's theory of the experimental novel from which he took his point of departure. Holz insisted that the extensive theoretical speculations, documented in the two volumes *Die Kunst: Ihr Wesen und ihre Gesetze* (1891; Art: Its Essence and Its Laws), were undertaken in order to improve the practice of writing; they began to bear fruit in the "konsequenter Realismus" (consistent realism) of the works written together with Schlaf.

The first of these works was a collection of prose sketches, *Papa Hamlet,* which was published in 1889 under the pseudonym Bjarne P. Holmsen in order to exploit and satirize what the two authors perceived as a current prejudice in favor of foreign (especially Scandinavian) writing. In addition to *Papa Hamlet,* the collection contains *Der erste Schultag* (The First Day at School), the story of a boy experiencing a very frightening first day at school, and *Ein Tod* (A Death), which describes the vigil of two students at the bedside of a friend who was fatally wounded in a duel. These works were followed by the drama *Die Familie Selicke* (1890; The Selicke Family), produced by the Berlin Freie Bühne (Free Theatre) in 1890, and a further collection of prose sketches, published under the title *Neue Gleise* (1892; New Tracks).

The story *Papa Hamlet* was a reworking of a previously unpublished text by Schlaf, *Ein Dachstubenidyll* (1890; A Garret Idyll). A comparison of the texts shows the advances made by what the authors described as the *Sekundenstil* in the precise rendition in verbal form of intensely observed details of the material environment and in the phonetic reproduction of everyday speech. Both of these features recur in the drama, where in the contemporary working-class setting they underline significantly the theme of social determinism. In the story, however, the emphasis on the main character as an unemployed actor and the interweaving of quotations from *Hamlet* to indicate his delusory identification with a particular role introduce a subjective perspective. This perspective is less prominent in Holz's theory but is also manifest in both the use of free indirect speech in *Der erste Schultag* and the creation of a sense of shared entrapment in *Ein Tod.* Notwithstanding the implicit intentions of its theoretical basis, the style developed by Holz and Schlaf proved no less appropriate to the kind of work that is realistic only in the sense that it shows how certain people experience reality.

This ambivalence was exploited to good effect by Schlaf in a further play in the naturalist style, *Meister Oelze* (1892; Master Oelze), but in his later work, the refinement of the *Sekundenstil* was used to express the subjective fascination of the male gaze with female eroticism and vitality (*Die Suchenden* [1902; The Seekers], *Der Kleine* [1904; The Little One]) and to overcome naturalism by bringing an element of mysticism back into literature (*Frühling* [1896; Spring]).

Holz, by contrast, was to pursue the theoretical line, focusing increasingly on the crisis of language in literary modernism, applying his insights in revisions and extensions to his "Phantasus," and "fathering" a substantial tradition of experimental writing from Döblin to Heißenbüttel.

JOHN OSBORNE

Biographies

Arno Holz

Born in Rastenburg, East Prussia, 26 April 1863. Journalist; edited the journal *Freie Bühne;* collaboration with Johannes Schlaf in Berlin, 1887–92. Died in Berlin, 26 October 1929.

Johannes Schlaf

Born in Querfurt, Saxony, 21 June 1862. Studied classical philology and German literature Universities of Halle and Berlin; collaboration with Arno Holz in Berlin, 1887–92; in Weimar, 1904. Died in Querfurt, 2 February 1941.

Selected Works (both authors)

Collections
Papa Hamlet, 1889
Neue Gleise, 1892

Short Fiction
Papa Hamlet, 1889
Der erste Schultag, 1889
Ein Tod, 1889
Die papierne Passion, 1890

Play
Die Familie Selicke (produced 1890), 1890

Selected Works by Holz

Collections
Das Werk, edited by Hans W. Fischer, 10 vols., 1924–25
Werke, edited by Wilhelm Emrich and Anita Holz, 7 vols., 1961–64

Poetry
Klinginsherz! Lieder, 1883
Buch der Zeit: Lieder eines Modernen, 1886
Phantasus, 1898–99
Dafnis, 1904

Plays
Sozialaristokraten (produced 1897), 1896
Sonnenfinsternis, 1908
Ignorabimus, 1913

Other
Die Kunst: Ihr Wesen und ihre Gesetze, 1891
Revolution der Lyrik, 1899

Selected Works by Schlaf

Collections
Novellen, 3 vols., 1899–1901
Ausgewählte Werke, 2 vols., 1934, 1940

Plays
Meister Oelze (produced 1894), 1892
Die Feindlichen, 1899

Short Fiction
Ein Dachstubenidyll, 1890
In Dingsda, 1892
Frühling, 1896

Novels
Die Suchenden, 1902
Der Kleine, 1904

Further Reading

Arnold, Susanne, and Elke Mohr, "Über die Dekadenz zum neuen Menschen in den frühen Romanen von Johannes Schlaf," in *Dekadenz in Deutschland: Beiträge zur Erforschung der Romanliteratur um die Jahrhundertwende,* edited by Dieter Kafitz, Frankfurt and New York: Lang, 1987
Burns, Rob, *The Quest for Modernity: The Place of Arno Holz in Modern German Literature,* Frankfurt and Bern: Lang, 1981
Chevrel, Yves, *Le Naturalisme,* Paris: Presses Universitaires de France, 1982
Cowen, Roy C., *Der Naturalismus: Kommentar zu einer Epoche,* Munich: Winkler, 1973
Döblin, Alfred, "Grabrede auf Arno Holz," in *Aufsätze zur Literatur,* Olten: Walter, 1968
Heißenbüttel, Helmut, "Vater Arno Holz," in *Über Literatur,* Olten: Walter, 1966
Holz, Arno, and Johannes Schlaf, *Papa Hamlet: Ein Tod,* edited by Fritz Martini, Stuttgart: Reclam, 1966
Kafitz, Dieter, *Johannes Schlaf, Weltanschauliche Totalität und Wirklichkeitsblindheit: Ein Beitrag zur Neubestimmung des Naturalismus-Begriffs und zur Herleitung totalitärer Denkformen,* Tübingen: Niemeyer, 1992
Martini, Fritz, "Arno Holz: Papa Hamlet," in *Das Wagnis der Sprache: Interpretationen deutscher Prosa von Nietzsche bis Benn,* Stuttgart: Klett, 1954; 5th edition, 1964
Osborne, John, *Gerhart Hauptmann and the Naturalist Drama,* Amsterdam: Harwood Academic, 1998
Pascal, Roy, "Arno Holz, *Der erste Schultag:* The Prose-Style of Naturalism," in *"Erfahrung und Überlieferung": Festschrift for C.P. Magill,* edited by Hinrich Siefken and Alan Robinson, Cardiff: University of Wales Press, 1974
Scheuer, Helmut, *Arno Holz im literarischen Leben des ausgehenden 19. Jahrhunderts (1883–1896): Eine biographische Studie,* Munich: Winkler, 1971
Schulz, Gerhard, *Arno Holz: Dilemma eines bürgerlichen Dichterlebens,* Munich: Beck, 1974
Turner, David, "Die Familie Selicke and the Drama of Naturalism," in *Periods in German Literature: Texts and Contexts,* II, edited by James Macpherson Ritchie, London: Wolff, 1969

Homosexuality and Literature

Within a comparatively short time, the social and literary history of homosexuality has moved from condemnation and taboo to acceptance and postmodern repositioning. During the same period, the perception and treatment of women have undergone comparably radical changes, which in turn have had a critical effect on notions of lesbianism. Such transformations, of course, are neither straightforward nor complete; furthermore, they are characteristic of Western Europe as a whole rather than Germany in particular. Nonetheless, rather than listing out authors or outing listed ones, the intention here is to present some German instances of the process.

As in the rest of Europe, the history of homosexuality in German-speaking countries has been indelibly marked by the tendentious atrocities of the Christian Church. One of the most influential of the Christian theologians living in what is now Germany was Albertus Magnus (1193–1280). For him, homosexuality was a sin against procreation and, hence, against nature and God. It was particularly terrible because it was inherently disgusting, a manifestation of unrestrained libido, stubborn, and similar to a contagious disease. Elsewhere in medieval literature, homosexuality is volubly characterized as unspeakable. And the merest suggestion of it could ruin reputations, as, for example, in the moment when a queen in Heinrich von Veldeke's 12th-century version of the *Aeneid* trumpets her reluctance to say what her daughter's beloved allegedly does with other men.

Albertus's text explicitly includes what we would now call lesbianism. Just as, in a tradition that includes Luther, homosexuality was a convenient charge to lay against the fanatically celibate—thus effectively equating homosexuality and heresy—by misogynistic extension, lesbianism became associated with witchcraft, as in another influential Latin text written in what is now Germany: the *Malleus Maleficarum,* or Witches' Hammer of 1487.

It is indicative of the persistence of such views that a disgust similar to that voiced by Albertus Magnus was apparently still available to Heine when he read Platen's poems in 1828. Similarly, the tautological relationship between illicit love and promiscuity is stressed in Hans Kaltneker's play about lesbianism, *Die Schwester* (1924; The Sister). The analogy of homosexuality and disease not only gave rise to the ongoing search for a cure but also dominated the writings of sexologists such as Karl Friedrich Otto Westphal (1833–90) and Richard von Krafft-Ebing (1840–1902).

These inventors of modern homosexuality are heirs to two traditions that are deeply damaging to homosexuals, and women in particular. In one, the discourse of nature is applied to gender, constructing women as essentially weak and stupid. In the other, the search for symptoms is specifically linked to possibilities of punishment, which helps explain the prominence of sexologists in the debate concerning the infamous Section 175.

Section 175 was the section of the 1871 penal code that outlawed sexual acts between men. The Nazis extended its scope and severity but retained the number. Symptomatically, the Federal Republic adopted the Nazi version and even sought to tighten it up: hence, the presentation of homosexuals as fair game in Martin Sperr's *Jagdszenen aus Niederbayern* (1966; Hunting Scenes from Lower Bavaria). The GDR reverted to the older law, but an adherence to scientific positivism made it possible for professor Günter Dörner (1929–) to experiment with rats' hormones and to declare the aberration treatable.

The exclusion of women from Section 175 reflects their marginalization in society at large at that time. The sexologists, and even the German language, tend to treat lesbianism as a mere analog to male homosexuality. For centuries women's access to literature had been severely restricted; lesbians had nonetheless been made the object of the male gaze in imaginative writing. The most famous example of this is Countess Geschwitz in Wedekind's *Lulu* plays (1885–1902), but the effect of the double bind, in terms of the difficult access to language, the elaboration of the butch-femme model, and the interiorization of prejudice can still be traced in contemporary lesbian novels such as Luise Pusch's pseudonymous *Sonja* of 1981.

Because of this radically unconducive context, expressions of same-sex love in German literature have been subject to certain characteristically ambiguous paradigms. The source for most of them is to be found in classical Greek literature, particularly Plato. Indeed, it is not the least of Thomas Mann's achievements in *Der Tod in Venedig* (1912; *Death in Venice*) that he conjured and gave the lie to so many of the fraudulent platitudes widely associated with Greek love. Thus, just as Tadzio is aged at the onset of puberty, so there is a recurrent tradition of sublimated pedophilia in German that encompasses both the "Gemeinschaft der Eigenen" (Company of the Special) of Benedict Friedländer (1866–1908) and the circle around Stefan George (1868–1933). And even where the relationship is not between a man and a boy, a difference of age is very often decisive, as in Stefan Zweig's "Verwirrung der Gefühle" (1927; Emotional Turmoil) or the works by Christa Winsloë on which the film *Mädchen in Uniform* (1931; *Children in Uniform*) is based. In the Zweig, the Winsloë, and Plato, the basis of the relationship is a pedagogical one, and it founders on a combination of one-sidedness and internalized prejudice. In many other texts, such relationships symbolically flirt with death or fail because one of the partners eventually finds his or her way back to heterosexuality. The famous episode with the fisher boy in Goethe's *Wilhelm Meisters Wanderjahre* (1829; *Wilhelm Meister's Years of Travel*) combines both motifs, which are also prominent in texts about lesbianism such as Anna Elisabet Weirauch's *Der Skorpion* (1919, 1921, 1931; *The Scorpion*) and Maria Eichhorn's *Fräulein Don Juan* (1903; Miss Don Juan).

Equally, the fact that Mann's Aschenbach, on first seeing Tadzio, is reminded of Greek sculpture clearly refers back to the tradition of Winckelmann (1717–68). His attempt to emulate the boy's beauty in his writing also takes up the theme of aestheticizing sublimation that runs like a leitmotif through much of the homosexual literature in German, including Paul Heyse's "David und Jonathan" (1882), Elisabeth Dauthendey's *Vom neuen Weibe und seiner Liebe* (1903; Of the New Woman and Her Love), and the anonymous letter to Karl Philipp Moritz's *Magazin für Erfahrungsseelenkunde* (1791; Journal of Applied Psychology), in which it is suggested that the best cure for lovesickness is friendship.

Precisely because of the moral imperative to separate love from its realization, this notion of "friendship" becomes notoriously ambiguous in German. As a result it is difficult to reach agreement on whether the expressions of passionate attachment between, say, Caroline von Günderrode and Bettina von Arnim (1805–6) or between Goethe and Friedrich Heinrich Jacobi (1846) are to be treated as homosexual. By the same token, because they arise from a necessity for concealment, it is difficult to prove and easy to deny that certain textual strategies adopted by Heinrich von Kleist (1777–1811) or Franz Kafka (1883–1924) reflect the distortions required of homosexuals by a homophobic society. And it is only because they later came out and admitted to them that we can recognize in gay, male, gender-neutral, or heterosexual texts by Christa Reinig (1926–), or Marlene Stenten (1935–) a coded reflection of lesbian experience.

Of course, processes of internalization and equivocation are not the only possible response to homophobia, and an impressive number of German writers have had the courage to combat the phenomenon. The tradition begins in the Enlightenment, when the view was put forward by Voltaire and his followers that severely punishing a crime that claimed no victims was incompatible with reason. In Heinrich Zschokke's "Eros" (1821), a passionate apologist is allowed his say, although not the last word. In Johann Ludwig Casper's *Klinische Novellen* (1864; News from the Clinic), homosexuality is discussed openly and fairly.

A tireless campaign against criminalization was begun by Karl Heinrich Ulrichs (1825–95), who coined the notion of a "third sex," which was characterized by a "woman's soul in a man's body." This campaign was continued by Magnus Hirschfeld (1868–1935), who organized one of the first and most powerful homosexual rights movements in Europe, which in 1910 prevented Section 175 being extended to women, and in 1929 very nearly managed to remove it altogether. And just as Hirschfeld fully acknowledged the contribution made by lesbians to his cause, so in a novella by Alfred Meebold, *Dr Erna Redens Thorheit und Erkenntnis* (1900; Dr. Erna Reden's Folly and Realization), the eponymous heroine, according to Jeanette Foster, "returns to Germany full of crusading zeal against those who persecute homosexuals."

Following the destruction of Hirschfeld's work by the Nazis and their successors, an attempt was made by Kurt Hiller (1885–1972) to reinvigorate the movement. While his attempt failed, however, the struggle has been taken up by the sober scientist Rudolf Klimmer (1905–77) in the East, and the flamboyant filmmaker Rosa von Praunheim (1942–) in the West.

In a sense, of course, apologists of various forms of same-sex love also presuppose and prolong the homophobic tradition. The best possible counterweight to that tradition, therefore, would be the truthful and unapologetic treatment of homosexuality in literature, and despite the difficulties, this has, at certain times and under certain conditions, proved possible. Thus, behind the Baroque facade of Daniel Casper von Lohenstein's *Agrippina* (1666) there lurks an astonishingly frank depiction of nonstandard forms of sexuality. Here and there in the voluminous oeuvre of Johann Wolfgang von Goethe—in the essay on Winckelmann (1805), for example, or the poems of the *West-östlicher Divan* (1819; *West-Eastern Divan*) and the second part of *Faust* (1832)—certain homosexual phenomena appear wonderfully unashamed. The polyglot diaries of August von Platen (1796–1835) contain passages of similarly undistorted sensuality; so, too, do the poems of Marie Madelaine, Baroness von Puttkamer (b. 1881), and Aimée Duc's *Sind es Frauen?* (1901; Are These Women?) allows its lesbians a positive presentation and a rare happy ending.

Other groundbreaking lesbian novels in German suffered suppression and delayed publication. Johanna Moosdorf's *Die Freundinnen* (The Girlfriends) was written in the late 1960s but not published until 1977. Waltraud Lewin's story, "Dich hat Amor gewiß . . ." ("Love, to Be Sure . . ."), although written in 1974, was not published until 1983. In Ingeborg Bachmann's "Ein Schritt nach Gomorrha" (1961; "Step toward Gomorrha"), the possibility of lesbian feminist liberation is raised, which was subsequently realized in Verena Stefan's *Häutungen* (1975; *Shedding*).

The nexus of sexuality, violence, and problems of language touched upon in Stefan's novel is also to be found in the work of erotic writers such as Regina Nössler (1964–) and lesbian crime writers such as Claudia Gelien (1966–) and Thea Dorn (1971–). It is of central importance, too, in the work of two major gay writers: Hans Henny Jahnn (1894–1959) and Hubert Fichte (1935–86). The latter in particular has created an oeuvre of searing honesty in which the realities of his own life and times are brilliantly and unflinchingly reflected. And the same clarity of vision is to be found in the work of Detlev Meyer (1950–), although his tone is radically different.

In the last volume of his trilogy *Biographie der Bestürzung* (1985–89; Consternation: A Biography), Meyer is concerned with the subject of AIDS. While it may seem paradoxical to include AIDS literature under the heading of "islands of affirmation," and although the earlier, autobiographical accounts make depressing reading, there is a quality of humor, self-deprecation, and sheer spirit about the works of, say, Stefan Reichert or Napoleon Seyfarth that successfully defy tragedy and, with it, conventional patterns of thought.

Immediately after the emergence of the AIDS syndrome, whole sections of the community, in Germany as elsewhere, could be heard muttering that it was God's judgment on gays for their stubborn pursuit of an unnatural, sick, sinful, disgusting, and promiscuous way of life. And sufferers felt constrained to adopt strategies of concealment and camouflage comparable to those adopted earlier by practically all homosexuals. Instead of being accepted as the norm and the orthodoxy, however, these homophobic reactions now seem increasingly like embarrassing aberrations. And instead of the old garrulous silence, there is now a strident public discussion of all the issues involved. As a result, we can hope that neither homosexuality nor literature will ever be quite the same again.

ROBERT GILLETT

Further Reading

Berlin Museum, *Eldorado: Homosexuelle Frauen und Männer in Berlin 1850–1950: Geschichte, Alltag, und Kultur,* Berlin: Fröhlich und Kaufmann, 1984; 2nd edition, Berlin: Edition Hentrich, 1992

Campe, Joachim, *Andere Lieben: Homosexualität in der deutschen Literatur: Ein Lesebuch,* Frankfurt: Suhrkamp, 1988

Derks, Paul, *Die Schande der heiligen Päderastie: Homosexualität und Öffentlichkeit in der deutschen Literatur 1750–1850,* Berlin: Verlag Rosa Winkel, 1990

Detering, Heinrich, *Das offene Geheimnis: Zur literarischen Produktivität eines Tabus von Winckelmann bis zu Thomas Mann,* Göttingen: Wallstein, 1994

Dietrich, Hans, *Die Freundesliebe in der deutschen Literatur,* Leipzig: W. Hellbach, 1931; 2nd edition, Berlin: Verlag Rosa Winkel, 1996

Fadermann, Lillian, and Brigitte Eriksson, editors, *Lesbians in Germany 1890's–1920's,* Tallahassee, Florida: Naiad Press, 1990

Forum: Homosexualität und Literatur (Journal) 1987–

Foster, Jeanette, *Sex Variant Women in Literature: A Historical and Quantitative Survey,* London: Muller, 1958

Frank, Miriam, "Lesbian Life and Literature: A Survey of Recent German-Language Publications," *Women in German Yearbook* 10 (1994)

Hacker, Hanna, *Frauen und Freundinnen: Studien zur "weiblichen Homosexualität" am Beispiel Österreich 1870–1938,* Weinheim: Beltz, 1987

Hohmann, Joachim Stephen, editor, *Der heimliche Sexus: Homosexuelle Belletristik in Deutschland der Jahre 1920–1970,* Frankfurt: Foerster, 1979

Jackson, David, editor, *Taboos in German Literature,* Providence, Rhode Island: Berghahn, 1996

Jones, James W., *"We of the Third Sex": Literary Representations of Homosexuality in Wilhelmine Germany,* New York: Lang, 1990

Kowalski, Gudrun von, *Homosexualität in der DDR: Ein historischer*

Abriß, Marburg: Verlag Arbeiterbewegung und Gesellschaftswissenschaft, 1987
Kuzniar, Alice A., editor, *Outing Goethe and His Age,* Stanford, California: Stanford University Press, 1996
Marti, Madeleine, *Hinterlegte Botschaften: Die Darstellung lesbischer Frauen in der deutschsprachigen Literatur seit 1945,* Stuttgart: Metzler, 1991
Popp, Wolfgang, *Männerliebe: Homosexualität und Literatur,* Stuttgart: Metzler, 1992
Richter, Simon, *Laocoon's Body and the Aesthetics of Pain: Winckelmann, Lessing, Herder, Moritz, Goethe,* Detroit, Michigan: Wayne State University Press, 1992
Spreitzer, Brigitte, *Die Stumme Sünde: Homosexualität im Mittelalter,* Göppingen: Kümmerle, 1988
Steakley, James D., *The Homosexual Emancipation Movement in Germany,* New York: Arno Press, 1975
Summers, Claude J., editor, *The Gay and Lesbian Literary Heritage,* New York: Holt, 1995

Barbara Honigmann 1949–

Born after the end of World War II, Barbara Honigmann is one of a group of Jewish authors writing in German who have created a new body of German Jewish literature, especially since the mid-1980s. The overarching topic that makes such a collective designation of disparate and distinct texts legitimate is their exploration of the tenuous contemporary identity of German Jews and, through this lens, the critical illumination of contemporary German society in relation to its anti-Semitic legacy and the Shoah. This is the issue that "has her," as Honigmann has put it, and that defines her literary and artistic production (she is also a painter). She shares this fraught topic with others of her generation, yet her texts offer an unmistakably unique literary voice and style, which is described alternately by critics as banal or highly sophisticated, simplistic or exquisitely clear. Guy Stern designates Honigmann's stylistic control and her skill in mediating her "semi-fictional world through revelatory but utterly commonplace detail" as characteristics of postmodern writing; influential reviewers Reinhart Baumgart and Marcel Reich-Ranicki champion her artistic naïveté. Her narrative prose, the basis of her critical acclaim since the publication of *Roman von einem Kinde* in 1986, is replete with autobiographical gestures, and the shorter texts of *Roman von einem Kinde: Sechs Erzählungen* (Novel of a Child: Six Short Stories), as well as the later *Eine Liebe aus Nichts* (1991; A Love Made of Nothing), feature a strong first-person female narrator, which has led some readers unduly to conflate the author with her narrative personas. In *Soharas Reise* (1996; Soharas's Journey), Honigmann narrates the story of the title character in the third person and, through manipulation of narrative conventions and subtle humor, plays with suggestions of an authorial voice that is refracted through several characters. Honigmann has discussed her work as autobiographical fiction. Her narratives incorporate reflections upon the dilemmas and continuous challenges of creating and shaping viable stories of the self and upon the role that writing often plays in those processes (most explicitly in the title story of *Roman von einem Kinde* and in *Eine Liebe aus Nichts*).

In Honigmann's narratives, commanding parental stories of persecution, exile, and return hold sway over the children of Jewish survivors of persecution as they strive to relate their own stories of identity. Literal and metaphoric journeys with which characters trace or resist the paths of the parents, simultaneously seeking their own independent directions and access to familial and collective history and traditions, recur in many of Honigmann's texts. The journey as a figure of narrative itself is underscored in her titles, including "Wanderung" (Hiking Tour), in *Roman von einem Kinde* and *Soharas Reise.* These travels often entail delineations and crossings of borders that function as markers of division and as seams of connection, as sites that both separate and bind. Honigmann's texts also explore both the perception and negotiation of geographic, political, linguistic, generational, and historical borders and the ways their traversal or lack thereof informs the manner in which her characters struggle to articulate their religious and cultural identities. Spatial descriptions of her characters' inner and outward search for a locus of identity and of the unsettling but fundamental condition of nomadism are important in Honigmann's texts. In *Roman von einem Kinde,* the narrator desires recognition of "die Stelle des Übergangs, die Grenze, an der die Zustände wechseln;" in "Wanderung," the depiction of the characters' vacation travels and their experiences of foreignness parallels that of their impassioned debates on the political and personal histories of their parents and their self-positioning in the GDR. *Doppeltes Grab* (Double Grave) relates a visit with Gerschom Scholem and reflects on his double life, commemorated by two tombstones, one in Berlin and one in Jerusalem, as signs of his dual and ultimately incompatible identities as a German and a Jew. Scholem's example and his tales of the dispersal of the Jewish library, the home of the foundational texts of Jewish learning and identity, strengthen the narrator's decision to leave the GDR in search of a place where she can be a Jew in a thriving Jewish community. In "Bonsoir Madame Benhamou," she describes her experience of herself as foreign in her newly chosen home in France and her integration into the structures of the Jewish community that motivated and sustained her move. Mirroring Honigmann's own decision to leave the GDR and Germany and to settle in Strasbourg near the river border between France and Germany, the longer narrative *Eine Liebe aus nichts* follows the stations of its narrator's journey from East Berlin to France. After she draws radical borders between herself and the country of her birth in search of a place of belonging as a Jew in another land, she then goes back again across the French and German borders to Weimar in order to attend her father's funeral. Her travels in search of a new home coincide with her ventures into personal and collective memory and with her confrontation with the impassable threshold of death, which she seeks, nonetheless, to bridge through writing. *Soharas Reise* approaches travel, Jewish nomadism, and the experience of exile from the perspective of the title character, an Orthodox Sephardic Jew, for whom the Ashkenazim, the "Elite des Leidens," and their stories of persecution and exile are foreign and in many respects incomprehensible. Sohara's identity is radically called into question as her criminal husband abducts her children and abandons her; the text explores Sohara's own emancipatory journey of personal, religious, and cultural identity and portrays the female cultivation of traditions and of a home in relation to experiences of motherhood and the support of a community of women.

The critical reception of Honigmann's texts as part of the new German Jewish literature has been firmly established since the publication of her stories in 1986; her earlier dramatic pieces of the 1980s ("Das singende springende Löweneckerchen," "Don Juan," and "Der Schneider von Ulm") and the radio plays based on them did not find a wide critical resonance. Honigmann's essays and other short prose pieces were recently collected under the title *Am Sonntag spielt der Rabbi Fußball* (1998; The Rabbi Plays Soccer on Sunday).

CLAIRE BALDWIN

Biography

Born in East Berlin, 1949, as the daughter of assimilated, communist Jewish parents. Studied drama in Berlin and began her artistic career as a playwright and director; freelance writer and painter since 1975; moved with her family to Strasbourg, 1984, with its visible and active Jewish community, in search of a Jewish identity "beyond the perpetual discourse on anti-Semitism" prevalent in Germany; received critical attention for *Roman von einem Kinde* as an important figure in Germany's newly emerging Jewish literatures. *aspekte* Literature Prize, 1986; Nicolas Born Prize, 1994.

Selected Works

Roman von einem Kinde: Sechs Erzählungen, 1986
Eine Liebe aus Nichts, 1991
Soharas Reise, 1996
Am Sonntag spielt der Rabbi Fußball, 1998
Damals, dann und danach, 1999

Further Reading

Feinberg, Anat, "Abiding in a Haunted Land: The Issue of Heimat in Contemporary German-Jewish Writing," *New German Critique* 70 (1997)

Fries, Marilyn Sibley, "Text as Locus, Inscription as Identity: On Barbara Honigmann's Roman von einem Kinde," *Studies in Twentieth Century Literature* 14, no. 2 (1990)

Herzog, Todd, "Hybrids and Mischlinge: Translating Anglo-American Cultural Theory into German," *German Quarterly* 70, no. 1 (1997)

Lorenz, Dagmar C.G., *Keepers of the Motherland: German Texts by Jewish Women Writers,* Lincoln: University of Nebraska Press, 1997

Nolden, Thomas, *Junge jüdische Literatur: Konzentrisches Schreiben in der Gegenwart,* Würzburg: Königshausen und Neumann, 1995

Remmler, Karen, "En-gendering Bodies of Memory: Tracing the Genealogy of Identity in the Works of Esther Dischereit, Barbara Honigmann, and Irene Dische," in *Reemerging Jewish Culture in Germany,* edited by Sander L. Gilman and Karen Remmler, New York: New York University Press, 1994

Stern, Guy, "Barbara Honigmann: A Preliminary Assessment," in *Insiders and Outsiders: Jewish and Gentile Culture in Germany and Austria,* edited by Dagmar C.G. Lorenz and Gabriele Weinberger, Detroit, Michigan: Wayne State University Press, 1994

Die Horen 1795–1797

Die Horen, edited by Schiller with the enthusiastic support of Goethe, appeared on a monthly basis for three years and is the most celebrated journal of Weimar Classicism. Yet it is surrounded by paradoxes. Appearing in its publicity to be nonpolitical, it in fact espoused an educational program that was indirectly but intensely political. Containing some of the most impressive works of Classicism, it nevertheless was a commercial failure from the outset. Taking for its title the Horae, the Greek goddesses of order, justice, and peace—and thus asserting the classical values of balance and harmony—it became a focus for bitter literary and personal controversy among its own contributors as well as its many opponents.

Schiller had planned a new literary and philosophical journal since 1788. His intention was to recruit a cadre of the best writers and thinkers and so replace the numerous minor periodicals available in Germany. The new journal would achieve national status and, like the schemes for a national theater put forward by Lessing and others, would counteract the provincial fragmentation of intellectual life in a Germany still divided on particularist lines. Schiller acknowledged that his wish to unite a wide and disparate public dictated that the contributions be both profound and accessible. The aim of creating a new vehicle for communal debate was also a reason for preserving neutrality in religious and political matters. Yet it was the aftermath of the French Revolution that finally convinced Schiller that his journal should eschew any direct discussion of contemporary politics.

The appeal for contributors of June 1794 states that all discussion of "state religion and political constitutions" shall be "absolutely prohibited" in *Die Horen*—constitutional matters, it should be noted, not politics in general. In the "Announcement" with which he prefaced the first issue of *Die Horen,* he went into more detail. The new journal would offer respite from "universal harassment by the demon of critical analysis of the state" and would ban from its columns "all references to the present course of events and the immediate expectations of mankind." Literary historians have persistently interpreted this declaration as an abandonment of politics—noble or irresponsible according to their own ideological perspectives—in favor of a retreat into the ivory tower of culture. Such interpretations fail to take account of the context of Schiller's arguments. Developments in France had precipitated a torrent of polemical debate in Germany about the relative merits of monarchy and republicanism and the ideal form of constitution. It was these often vituperative and, as Schiller saw them, futile controversies that he wished to avoid. However, in the opening "Announcement" he did not exclude abstract discussion of political principles with the aim of devising philanthropic forms of government, and he expressly committed *Die Horen* to the continuing search for the "ideal of ennobled humanity." There was simply to be no partisan reference to current events and particular regimes.

The Schiller who had written a series of Sturm und Drang plays denouncing aristocratic misuse of power was initially sympathetic to the aims of the French Revolution. By 1793, however, following the execution of Louis XVI and the descent of the French into internecine violence, he was describing the revolutionaries as "the miserable lackeys of executioners." In letters to the Duke of Augustenburg over the following months, published subsequently in *Die Horen* as "Über die ästhetische Erziehung des Menschen" (*On the Aesthetic Education of Man*), Schiller set out the anthropological and ideological conclusions that he drew from events in France. He continued to believe in democratic principles but maintained that their French exponents had not possessed the integrity and maturity to put them into effect. The French Revolution was a missed opportunity, in which "a corrupt generation" had reverted to uncivilized self-interest and brutality. It followed, crucially, that there was no point in constitutional change—and no point in discussing it—unless and until a reform of the human character had been effected which would ensure altruistic behavior. This "ennobled humanity" was feasible only through a process of education of the human spirit, and such education could best be carried out through the medium of aesthetic experience and by refinement of sensibility. It was such education, in the broadest terms, that was to be the task of *Die Horen.* Thus Schiller writes in the "Announcement" that his journal will occupy itself with "the construction of better conceptions, purer principles and nobler morals, on which in the end all true amelioration of social conditions depends."

Goethe's *Unterhaltungen deutscher Ausgewanderten* (*Conversations of German Emigrants*), a series of short stories narrated by a German family displaced by French revolutionary armies, appeared in early issues of *Die Horen* and did not seem to accord with Schiller's program on more than one count. Nor did Goethe's interminable and turgid translation of the memoirs of Benvenuto Cellini. Much more appropriate was his cycle of erotic poems in classical hexameters and pentameters, the *Römische Elegien* (*Roman Elegies*). Yet their joyous and unabashed celebration of sexuality encountered only the incomprehension of a pedantic and prudish literary establishment. Goethe's essay "Literarischer Sansculottismus" ("Literary Sansculottism") echoes Schiller's regret over German provincialism: to attack individual German authors for failing to produce great works under such adverse conditions is analogous to French sans-culottes assaulting individual aristocrats rather than the social conditions that support privilege. Schiller's own contributions to *Die Horen,* as well as *On the Aesthetic Education of Man* and the treatise *Über naive und sentimentalische Dichtung* (*On Naive and Sentimental Poetry*), in which he seeks to divide ancient and modern literature into two fundamental categories, included two of his most important philosophical poems: "Das Ideal und das Leben" ("The Ideal and Life") and "Der Spaziergang" ("The Walk"). Hölderlin also contributed two poems: "Der Wanderer" ("The Wanderer") and "Die Eichbäume" ("The Oak Trees"). Other authors included Herder, Alexander and Wilhelm von Humboldt, Sophie Mereau, August Wilhelm Schlegel, and Fichte.

Fichte contributed an essay to the first issue with the title *Über Belebung und Erhöhung des reinen Interesses für Wahrheit* (*On Activation and Intensification of Pure Interest in Truth*) in which he placed intellectual rigor above all forms of literary pleasure and entertainment. Such material, together with Schiller's philosophical treatises, constituted a dauntingly ascetic agenda and contradicted Schiller's declared aim in the "Announcement" of making *Die Horen* "comprehensible to common sense." The first reviews were almost exclusively negative. A further contribution by Fichte, who had been part of a small editorial board, was rejected by Schiller on grounds of excessive political content, which led to Fichte's withdrawal from *Die Horen.* Herder also became alienated from Schiller and submitted no further contributions. The publisher, Cotta, had begun by printing 2,000 copies of *Die Horen,* of which initially 1,800 were sold, but by 1797 the circulation barely reached 1,000 copies and the journal had to be abandoned. The collapse of *Die Horen* seemed to Schiller and Goethe only to demonstrate the lack of standards in German intellectual life that had caused them to launch it in the first place. In a surrender to siege mentality, they turned on their critics and denounced the entire spectrum of the cultural establishment in a series of barbed satirical epigrams, the *Xenien.*

Perhaps a sufficiently sophisticated readership never did exist; perhaps the content of *Die Horen* was pitched too high for a journal aiming at a wide public. Certainly Schiller as an editor underestimated the time and effort needed to manage a monthly publication and never attracted a sufficient number of independent contributions. In the end, he and Goethe wrote nearly 50 percent of *Die Horen* themselves. The elitism and purism of a liberal intellectual who rejected "everything [. . .] which is marked by vulgar factionalism," as Schiller wrote in the "Announcement," was not conducive to a collaborative, national venture. Perhaps *Die Horen* is best regarded as a splendid failure.

RICHARD LITTLEJOHNS

See also Journals; Friedrich von Schiller

Editions

Published monthly from 1795 to 1797, Tübingen, J.G. Cotta
Facsimile edition: *Die Horen,* 12 vols., Stuttgart: Cotta, 1959

Further Reading

Bruford, Walter Horace, *Culture and Society in Classical Weimar, 1775–1806,* London: Cambridge University Press, 1962

Köpke, Wulf, "'. . . das Werk einer glücklichen Konstellation': Schillers 'Horen' und die deutsche Literaturgeschichte," in *Friedrich Schiller: Kunst, Humanität und Politik in der späten Aufklärung,* edited by Wolfgang Wittkowski, Tübingen: Niemeyer, 1982

Reed, T.J., "Ecclesia Militans: Weimarer Klassik als Opposition," in

Unser Commercium: Goethes und Schillers Literaturpolitik, edited by Wilfried Barner, Stuttgart: Cotta, 1984

Schulz, Günter, *Schillers Horen: Politik und Erziehung, Analyse einer deutschen Zeitschrift,* Heidelberg: Quelle und Meyer, 1960

Weisinger, Kenneth D., "Fathering the Canon: The Correspondence between Goethe and Schiller," in *A Reassessment of Weimar Classicism,* edited by Gerhart Hoffmeister, Lewiston, New York: Mellen Press, 1996

Ödön von Horváth 1901–1938

Ödön von Horváth was arguably the most critically astute of the young authors of the 1920s who adapted the genres of popular theater to the interests of intellectually sophisticated audiences. He is also remembered for two novels that were published in the year of his death, which depict the attitudes prevalent in Nazi Germany.

In his earliest plays, Horváth experimented with a variety of theatrical styles. *Die Bergbahn* (1927–28; The Mountain Railway) treats issues of class conflict in a predominantly naturalistic vein, but it also draws on the atmospheric devices of Expressionist theater to evoke the vulnerability and ultimate futility of human life. *Rund um den Kongress* (1929; Round about the Congress), which vacillates between seriousness and flippancy in its treatment of the issue of prostitution, shows signs of the contemporary interest in turning the theater into a forum for debate and uses devices for the disruption of theatrical illusion similar to those found in Brecht's early plays. But in *Sladek; oder, Die schwarze Armee* (1928; Sladek; or, The Black Army)—a satirical exposé of the underground militia tolerated by officialdom during the Weimar period, which reached the stage only in a muted form in 1929—Horváth can already be seen to be developing the style of dialogue that was to become his hallmark. In this play, he brings out the latent tensions in the mentalities and motivation of characters by segmenting the dialogue in such a way as to underscore the revealing changes of direction in a character's train of thought.

In his one extant piece of programmatic writing, the *Gebrauchsanweisung* (1932; Instructions for Use), Horváth describes the intention behind such pointed structuring of his scenes as the "unmasking of consciousness"; each scene, he writes, shows a character undergoing a transition, and the pregnant pauses that segment the dialogue mark the moments in which the conscious mind can be seen to be struggling with the unconscious. In the same text he also speaks of the "Bildungsjargon," the ready-made discourse of preformed social expectations, which molds the way his characters express themselves, and his best work reveals his acute ear for the self-deluding nature of such speech. The textual history of his plays further shows how he increasingly focused on lower middle-class settings, where he found the most theatrically effective instances of the masking of underlying impulses by social convention and aspiration. The result was a variation on the traditional 19th-century *Volksstück,* with admixtures that suggest the influence of Wedekind and the South German popular comedy of Horváth's own lifetime, in which the conventional expectations associated with that genre—wishful thinking as a dynamic element in the plot, fairy-tale happy endings, and an implicit acceptance of the status quo in the denouement—are ironized and subverted.

The play for which Horváth was awarded the Kleist Prize in 1931, and which made him a target for Nazi agitation in subsequent years, *Italienische Nacht* (1930; Italian Night), is a political comedy that satirizes the complacency of the Social Democrat establishment in a small-town setting. The Italian theme of the gala night held by the local SPD is the vehicle for unmasking this group's blindness to the "night" of fascism that threatens them. It was in the plays that he went on to write in the next few years that Horváth developed the potential of the "critical *Volksstück*" to the full. *Geschichten aus dem Wiener Wald* (1931; *Tales from the Vienna Woods*) uses several devices of popular legend, including the waltzes of Johann Strauss, to evoke the atmosphere of Vienna and its environs, but the play undercuts the Romantic expectations associated with these devices with the exposure of mean-spiritedness and self-regard at work in the reality of social relations. *Kasimir und Karoline* (1932; *Kasimir and Karoline*) presents the corrosive interaction of personal motives and stereotypical expectations in a sequence of kaleidoscopically shifting emotional relationships set among the festivities of the Munich Oktoberfest, whose atmosphere has been soured by the onset of the Great Depression. In *Glaube, Liebe, Hoffnung* (1932; *Faith, Hope, and Charity*) the social perspective becomes bleaker still. The young female protagonist, who is shown already in the opening scene trying to raise money by selling her body—not for sex, but for medical experimentation after her death—undergoes a relentless experience of criminalization and stigmatization at the hands of characters identified with one kind of official role or another.

Horváth's best-known plays established a model of theater that resembles Epic Theater in Brecht's sense but that shows a stronger emphasis on psychological factors. This model of theater enjoyed a powerful surge of interest during the period of renewed social and political questioning in West Germany in the late 1960s and early 1970s. Critical opinion differs, however, over whether Horváth's works provide an interpretation of the social tendencies of the 1920s that can really be said to transcend the limitations of their petty bourgeois settings. His frequent stylization of young women as the victims of social forces has been criticized for satisfying the demands of dramatic presentation rather than those of social and gender analysis.

Horváth's writings were banned in Germany in 1933, and the loss of Berlin audiences made his earlier style of work unsustainable. As the holder of a Hungarian passport, however, he was able to move more freely in and out of Germany than the German nationals who had opted for exile, and in 1934–35, he obtained official approval to work as a writer of film dialogue in Nazi Germany—until it again became clear that conditions were hostile to his kind of work. He used his firsthand knowledge to describe the brutal atmosphere of Nazi Germany in two novels published in Amsterdam in 1938: *Jugend ohne Gott* (*Youth without God*), in which a schoolmaster tells of the erosion of humanist values around him, and *Ein Kind unserer Zeit* (*A Child of Our Time*), in which a soldier loyal to the regime reveals the ideological conditioning of his outlook, in a manner that is similar to the self-presentation of characters in Horváth's earlier plays, through the clichés in which he expresses himself. Horváth was killed by the falling branch of a tree in Paris later the same year.

Among the studies that have been done on his late works, it depends largely on critical expectations as to whether the emphasis comes to fall on the ironization of political disillusionment, as has been seen in *Figaro lässt sich scheiden* (first produced 1937; first published 1959; *Figaro Gets a Divorce*), which travesties the prerevolutionary themes of Mozart's opera, or on the retreat to questions of existential guilt as a response to the situation of the 1930s, which can be found in *Don Juan kommt aus dem Krieg* (1936; *Don Juan Comes Back from the War*) and *Der jüngste Tag* (first produced 1937; first published 1955; *Judgment Day*). Other critics focus upon the characteristic figures of thought that suggest an underlying psychological continuity between Horváth's early and late writings.

David Midgley

Biography

Born in Fiume (now Rijeka), Austro-Hungarian Empire, 9 December 1901. Studied at the University of Munich, 1919–22; writer from 1922; wrote for various newspapers and journals; in Berlin, 1926; freelance writer from 1929; attacked by the Nazis from 1931; dialogue writer for German films, 1934; left Germany to retain Hungarian citizenship, 1933; in Berlin briefly in 1933 and 1934–35; in Austria until the German annexation; emigrated to Zurich, Switzerland, 1934. Kleist Prize, 1931. Died 1 June 1938.

Selected Works

Collections

Stücke, edited by Traugott Krischke, 1961
Gesammelte Werke, edited by Traugott Krischke, Walter Huder, and Dieter Hildebrandt, 4 vols., 1970
Gesammelte Werke: Kommentierte Werkausgabe in Einzelbänden, edited by Traugott Krischke and Susanna Foral-Krischke, 1983–
Gesammelte Werke, edited by Traugott Krischke, 4 vols., 1988

Plays

Das Buch der Tänze (libretto; produced 1922), 1922
Revolte auf Côte 3018 (produced 1927), 1927; as *Die Bergbahn* (produced 1929), 1928
Zur schönen Aussicht (produced 1969), 1927
Sladek; oder, Die schwarze Armee (produced 1972), 1928; revised version, as *Sladek, der schwarze Reichswehrmann* (produced 1929), 1929
Rund um den Kongress (produced 1959), 1929
Italienische Nacht (produced 1931), 1930; edited by Ian Huish, 1986
Geschichten aus dem Wiener Wald (produced 1931), 1931; edited by Hugh Rank, 1980; edited by Traugott Krischke, 1986; as *Tales from the Vienna Woods*, translated by Christopher Hampton, 1977
Kasimir und Karoline (produced 1932), 1932; edited by Traugott Krischke, 1973; as *Kasimir and Karoline*, translated by Violet B. Ketes, in *Four Plays*, 1986
Glaube, Liebe, Hoffnung (as *Liebe, Pflicht und Hoffnung*, produced 1936), 1932; edited by Traugott Krischke, 1973; edited by Ian Huish, 1986; as *Faith, Hope, and Charity*, translated by Paul Foster and Richard Dixon, in *Four Plays*, 1986; translated by Christopher Hampton, 1989
Die Unbekannte aus der Seine (produced 1949), 1933
Hin und Her (produced 1934), in *Gesammelte Werke*, 1970
Mit dem Kopf durch die Wand (produced 1935), 1935
Figaro lässt sich scheiden (produced 1937), 1959; as *Figaro Gets a Divorce*, translated by Roger Downey, in *Four Plays*, 1986; as *Figaro Gets Divorced*, translated by Ian Huish, in *Two Plays*, 1991
Der jüngste Tag (produced 1937), 1955; edited by Ian Huish, 1985; as *Judgment Day*, translated by Martin and Renate Esslin, in *Four Plays*, 1986
Ein Dorf ohne Männer (from a novel by Koloman van Mikszáth) (produced 1937), in *Gesammelte Werke*, 1970
Himmelwärts (produced 1950), in *Gesammelte Werke*, 1970
Don Juan kommt aus dem Krieg (produced 1952), in *Stücke*, 1961; as *Don Juan Comes Back from the War*, translated by Christopher Hampton, 1978
Pompeji (produced 1959), in *Stücke*, 1961
Four Plays, various translators (includes *Kasimir and Karoline; Faith, Hope, and Charity; Figaro Gets a Divorce; Judgment Day*), 1986
Two Plays (includes *Don Juan Comes Back from the War* and *Figaro Gets Divorced*), translated by Ian Huish and Christopher Hampton, 1991

Fiction

Der ewige Spiesser, 1930
Ein Kind unserer Zeit, 1938; as *A Child of Our Time*, translated by R. Wills Thomas, 1938
Jugend ohne Gott, 1938; as *Zeitalter der Fische*, 1953; as *The Age of the Fish*, 1939

Further Reading

Balme, Christopher B., *The Reformation of Comedy: Genre Critique in the Comedies of Ödön von Horváth*, Dunedin: Department of German, University of Otago, 1985
Bance, Alan, "Ödön von Horváth: Sex, Politics, and Sexual Politics," *German Life and Letters* 38, no. 3 (1985)
Bartsch, Kurt, et al., editors, *Horváth-Diskussion*, Kronberg: Scriptor, 1976
Gamper, Herbert, *Horváths komplexe Textur, dargestellt an frühen Stücken*, Zurich: Ammann, 1987
Haag, Ingrid, "Das 'traurige Happy-End': Zur Struktur der 'Fräuleinstücke' Ödön von Horváths," *Austriaca* 6 (1978)
Huish, Ian, *A Students' Guide to Horváth*, London: Heinemann, 1980
Krischke, Traugott, editor, *Ödön von Horváth*, Frankfurt: Suhrkamp, 1981
———, editor, *Horváth auf der Bühne, 1926–1938*, Vienna: Verlag der Österreichischen Staatsdruckerei, 1991
Midgley, David, "Ödön von Horváth: The Strategies of Audience Enticement," *Oxford German Studies* 14 (1983)
Nolting, Winfried, *Der totale Jargon: Die dramatischen Beispiele Ödön von Horváths*, Munich: Fink, 1976
Schnitzler, Christian, *Der politische Horváth: Untersuchungen zu Leben und Werk*, Frankfurt and New York: Lang, 1990
Winston, Krishna, *Horváth Studies: Close Readings of Six Plays (1926–1931)*, Bern, Frankfurt, and Las Vegas, Nevada: Lang, 1977

Geschichten aus dem Wiener Wald 1931

Play by Ödön von Horváth

Geschichten aus dem Wiener Wald (1931; *Tales from the Vienna Woods*) is perhaps the most prominent of the social dramas written by Ödön von Horváth during the last years of the Weimar Republic; the play is also the most representative of his aims and techniques in transforming the traditional *Volksstück*. In their portrayal of the milieu and everyday life of a stratum of society seen as representative of the broad mass of the people, Horváth's plays are a conscious attempt—shared in different ways by Fleißer and Brecht—to find a dramatic form and language that could articulate the realities of individual existence in mass culture by reinvesting with a new critical force what had become a trivialized and commercialized theatrical genre. In the 1930s, Horváth (Krischke, 1970) spoke in Freudian terms of dramatizing the alienation of individual from society as the battle of consciousness and subconsciousness, of presenting a dialogue that confronts the spectator with an "unmasking of consciousness" and that draws the public into the catharsis of recognizing their own repressed or unknown instinctive drives in the fiction. Horváth's *Volksstück* became a drama of false consciousness, but what distinguishes his project, and in particular *Geschichten aus dem Wiener Wald,* from other attempts to reinvent a theater of the people is that his critique of individual and social consciousness is realized satirically, through invoking the debased norms of common culture on which the traditional *Volkstück* itself rests. The conventions and assumptions of the genre become an ironic metaphor, in Horváth's portrayal, for the debilitating hold of the collective over the individual, of the power of the given over the hope of what might be. In this sense it is Horváth, rather than Brecht, whom Adorno (1974) sees as the practitioner of a progressive anti-*Volksstück,* one that recovers the original potential of the genre—to resist the "filthy flood of bourgeois idealism"—by refuting what its degenerate form has come to stand for: the pernicious deceit of a *schöne heile Welt* (a safe and secure world) that escapes the deformation of human relations in modern society. Thus, when Horváth speaks of both renewing and destroying the *Volksstück,* he is signalling his satiric intention to use the dramatic form (and its ideology) against itself. Horváth himself rejected the term *parody,* with its suggestion of comic caricature, in relation to his work, but what is implied is a principle of ironic quotation. That principle is realized here in the very title, *Geschichten aus dem Wiener Wald,* and the settings of picturesque "old Vienna," but also in the never-ending flow of the musical flotsam and jetsam of waltzes and songs and, above all, in the language of a *Volk* of *Kleinbürger* (petite bourgeoisie): a mix of poetic, pseudo-learned, and colloquial jargon, a multilayered amalgam of fragments of speech with which the characters vainly seek to find expression. It is their inability to escape, or even, mostly, to recognize the emptiness of that jargon that leads both to the final enslavement of the one character who tries to rebel against this closed and asphyxiating world, and to the murder of her child.

The first performance of *Geschichten aus dem Wiener Wald* in Berlin in November 1931, one week after Horváth was awarded, on Carl Zuckmayer's recommendation, the prestigious Kleist prize, confirmed Horváth's position as one of the leading young dramatists of the day. German critics generally praised the distinctive quality of the work: for Kurt Pinthus it was "the most bitter, the most brutal, and the most bitterly brutal play in recent literature," while Erich Kästner and others recognized the satiric ambivalence of this "Viennese Volksstück against the Viennese Volksstück" (Krischke, 1983). Outright condemnation, however, came from nationalists, who were already enraged by the fact that the man targeted by the Nazi party paper as a "Salonkulturbolschewik" (upper-class cultural Bolshevic) should receive the highest German literary honor. Perhaps predictably, the Viennese response to this picture of what the Neue Freie Presse called a "degenerate and repulsive Vienna" (Krischke, 1983) remained cool. Not until 1948 did the play receive its Viennese premiere, and it met with a stormy reception and critical wrath at its supposed defamation of Austrian life, often in terms strongly reminiscent of those employed by right-wing commentaries of the 1930s. Only 20 years later, after Horváth's work in general had experienced a renaissance on the German and Austrian stage, did this *Volksstück* finally find favor in the city it depicted. In the meantime, television productions were making a wider public familiar with the play. Michael Lehmann's production for Bavarian television in 1964 was followed in 1980 by Erich Neuberg's production for Austrian television, while the English stage premiere of 1977, translated by Christopher Hampton and directed by Maximilian Schell, became the basis of the screenplay they wrote for the German commercial film that was released in 1979.

By the late 1960s, the reaction against the perversions of Nazi *Heimatliteratur* and against the *Heimatfilm* of postwar Germany, in which the trivialized and ideologically corrupted *Volksstück* celebrated its apotheosis, had brought the issues addressed by Horváth, Fleißer, and Brecht more than a generation before back to the center of cultural debate. In particular, Horváth's contribution to a modern drama of *Bewußtseinskritik* and *Sprachkritik* (the critique of language and consciousness) began to gain recognition and to influence a new generation of writers and filmmakers. Ironically, it was Horváth, rather than Brecht, who seemed to have most to tell us about the "womb" from which, according to Brecht's poem *Germany, Pale Mother,* the beast of National Socialism "crawled." For Peter Handke (1972), Brecht's "glib model of social contradictions" appeared lightweight and simplistic against Horváth's "models of malice, helplessness, confusion." The new champions of a critical Volksstück, Franz Xaver Kroetz, Wolfgang Bauer, Martin Sperr, and Peter Turrini, sought to follow and adapt the lead given by their predecessors in the Weimar years, and their work on the stage was matched by the anti-*Heimatfilm* of the New German Cinema—by Peter Fleischmann, Volker Schlöndorff, Reinhard Hauff, and, on stage and screen, Rainer Werner Fassbinder. Fundamental to the new departures was the perception of a society at the mercy of its own *Sprachnot* (crisis of language), where the manipulation of consciousness and social practice was generated and reflected in mechanisms of linguistic alienation. Kroetz traces his "proletariat of the speechless" directly to Horváth's *Kleinbürger* and the jargon that entraps them. He argues, however, that there is a significant change: unlike the tradition of inherited phraseology on which the petite bourgeoisie of the 1920s could still draw, his working-class protagonists are condemned to the helplessness of literal silence, and their crimes follow with the "compulsion of the production line" (1972). For Kroetz, silence represents the linguistic deprivation produced by social and economic exploitation, but in Horváth's principle of ironic quotation, silence fulfills a very different function: it reveals the possibility of otherness, of a speech that departs from the anonymity and automatism of the flow of rhetoric. Here, perhaps, the socialist radicalism of the 1960s and 1970s is in danger of leading the new *Volksstück* to a linguistic determinism, which in turn may even obscure the processes of the domination of the individual by society. What Horváth hears in the language of his *Volk,* and what becomes increasingly audible as the electronic media establish ever-wider and tighter networks of communication, is the very ease with which the fictions and "tales" of ready-made speech are disseminated and reproduced. With the exception of Fassbinder, it is arguable whether Horváth's successors of the 1960s and 1970s were always able to build on the insight implicit in the silences and ironic hesitations in his dialogue. However desperate the conclusion of *Geschichten aus dem Wiener Wald,* those moments, albeit barely heeded by the protagonists in the play, offer a glimpse of potential reflection and resistance without which the modern *Volkstück* would consign its society, and itself, to a doctrine of hopelessness. The fact that the ambivalent simplicity of Horváth's drama demands a response from the spectator, yet prescribes none, is probably why it remains one of the most performed works on the German and Austrian stage and has proved so adaptable to the screen.

ANTHONY COULSON

Editions

First edition: *Geschichten aus dem Wiener Wald: Volksstück in drei Teilen,* Berlin: Popyläen, 1931

Critical edition: *Gesammelte Werke: Kommentierte Werkausgabe in Einzelbänden,* edited by Traugott Krischke and Susanna Foral-Krischke, Frankfurt: Suhrkamp, 1986

Translation: *Tales from the Vienna Woods,* translated by Christopher Hampton, London: Faber, 1977

Further Reading

Adorno, Theodor W., "Reflexion über das Volksstück," in *Noten zur Literatur,* Schriften, vol. 11, edited by Rolf Tiedemann, Frankfurt: Suhrkamp, 1974

Arntzen, Helmut, "Horváth: *Geschichten aus dem Wiener Wald,*" in *Zur Sprache kommen: Studien zur Literatur- und Sprachreflexion, zur deutschen Literatur und zum öffentlichen Sprachgebrauch,* Münster: Aschendorff, 1983

Best, Alan, "Ödön von Horváth: The *Volksstück* Revived," in *Modern Austrian Writing: Literature and Society after 1945,* edited by Alan Best and Hans Wolfschütz, London: Wolff, and Totowa, New Jersey: Barnes and Noble, 1980

Emrich, Wilhelm, "Die Dummheit oder das Gefühl der Unendlichkeit," in *Materialien zu Ödön von Horváth,* edited by Traugott Krischke, Frankfurt: Suhrkamp, 1970

Handke, Peter, "Horváth und Brecht," in *Ich bin ein Bewohner des Elfenbeinturms,* Frankfurt: Suhrkamp, 1972

Huish, Ian, *A Student's Guide to Horváth,* London: Heinemann, 1980

Krischke, Traugott, editor, *Horváth's "Geschichten aus dem Wiener Wald,"* Frankfurt: Suhrkamp, 1983

Kroetz, Franz Xaver, "Horváth von heute für heute," in *Über Ödön von Horváth,* edited by Dieter Hildebrandt and Traugott Krischke, Frankfurt: Suhrkamp, 1972

Hrotsvit von Gandersheim ca. 930– ca. 1000

Hrotsvit von Gandersheim is considered the first woman poet in the Middle Ages in Europe. She is also the first person in this era to write drama, and she made her mark as the first historian in Germany: she wrote a rhymed history of the convent of Gandersheim, *Coenobii Gandersheimensis,* and a chronicle of Otto I, *Carmen de gestis Oddonis I. imperatoris.* All her works are written in Latin, the language of the church and of intellectuals at her time. Her creative works include biblical poems, legends on women, and dramas. Hrotsvit's legends are the only ones in medieval times written by a woman. As canoness of the Benedictine convent of Gandersheim, she had the opportunity to study Latin and was able to draw on Roman literature and Bible stories for poetical inspiration.

It is assumed that her plays and legends were used as teaching materials for her students at the convent and were perhaps read aloud. Some scholars are convinced that her plays were performed during Hrotsvit's lifetime (Butler). Reference works note that her works were forgotten and rediscovered by Conrad of Celtis only in the 15th century. It must now be assumed, however, that her work was known before this discovery, since recently, manuscripts were located in various places in Germany and Austria.

The main themes of Hrotsvit's writings focus on miraculous salvation, the triumphs of martyrs even over death, and the powers of chastity. In one of her hagiographies, a new major topic of Western literature emerges for the first time: the Faust theme. The writer's concern with this topic during the tenth century indicates an unusual sensibility, which prefigures a popular discourse on spiritual principles that circulated at a much later time.

The works of Hrotsvit are increasingly recognized, especially her dramatic work. Viewed from a postmodern standpoint, the author's six dramas (*Gallicanus, Dulcitius, Calimachus, Abraham, Pafnutius,* and *Sapientia*) constitute an unusual intellectual achievement as well as a stylistic one. She experimented with rhymed prose and transformed the dramas of the Roman writer Terence into Christian morality plays that were situated during the period of Roman rule. In addition, she created a precarious tension between the martyr theme and a humorous, even slapstick style, which she borrowed from her Roman model. She also introduces antiauthoritarian attitudes and the notion of the empowerment of the meek. The ultimate threat from authority, death for disobedience, is rendered ineffective. The martyrs are mostly women, and although some critics see a triumph of the patriarchal order at the end of her plays (e.g., Sperberg-McQueen), Hrotsvit subtly subverts this very male centered institution at the same time.

In the plays, women are in the center of the action and their agency decides the outcome of the plot (Case). All women ascertain their self-determination as they reach beyond their inscribed social identity. The fathers and potential lovers in most of the plays want to kill the women who resist their will, especially in sexual matters. The importance of sexuality or its suppression constitutes a consistent undercurrent of the plays. Chastity is an all-important empowering commodity for young women. Men want to take it away, and those women who resist are often thrown into whorehouses as punishment. The women, however, also slyly use the prescribed chastity rule of their society (both Roman and Christian) as a shield for their disobedience. These attitudes, thematized in the plays, give women above all the strength to reject sexual and other submissions imposed by men. If they cannot determine their own lives, women in Hrotsvit's plays wish nothing better than death in order to reach the promised Christian paradise, where they will be united with the man of their own choice: Jesus. The Christian concepts that life on earth is only a virtual life and that life begins after death are thus taken literally. This paradox undermines patriarchal dominance. With masochistic zeal, Hrotsvit's women yearn to be tortured and burnt at the stake because as martyrs they will quickly reach true life. To be dead or alive in Hrotsvit's works are also blurred categories. Some of the dead victims come back to life, and the theme of necrophilia is present as well. Although Christian virtue triumphs, women's traditional role in society is undermined.

Perhaps the writer worked through her own situation with these plays. She lived in a rich Benedictine convent. Here, she was relieved of all duties as a daughter, wife, or mother who had to serve either a father or a husband in order to be protected in society. Although in the convent she was bound to duties prescribed by Church, she was able to lead a life in which she could pursue her own interests, a privilege usually only reserved for men. The Christian enclave permitted her to promote her intellect and to receive an education equivalent to that of a highly educated man. To be Christian and to be chaste in essence aided in her emancipation.

Thus, many women in her play are wise and educated; the heathen men, by contrast, are mostly uneducated and uncouth. In the play *Sapientia,* the learned protagonist is able to confuse the heathen emperor with a long treatise on mathematics. Wisdom is for Hrotsvit—as it was for Saint Augustine—a revelation of God's essence. Human beings who study can participate in it and can move closer to God than others.

However, the situation of learned women is class specific. In the play, Sapientia is of high birth. Women of the lower classes, by contrast, were doing menial work in the convent. Hrotsvit was only able to become canoness because she came from a noble family. She was not a nun and did not have to swear the oath of poverty, and she could leave the convent at any time to get married.

Until recently, critics considered Hrotsvit's plays as epigonal works based on Terence. They granted a lively dialogue, but missed the unity of plot, time, and place. Non-Aristotelian theater has conquered our theaters in the meantime, and some critics now see her dramatic work as a precursor to Brechtian epic theater. Her plays were successfully performed in the 1970s and 1980s, and the dramatist Peter Hacks used the material of these plays and Hrotsvit's life to write the drama *Rosie träumt* (1976; Rosie Dreams).

HELGA W. KRAFT

Biography

Born in central Germany, near present-day Brunswick, ca. 930. Educated in a Benedictine convent, where she studied religion, Latin prosody, mathematics, astronomy, and music; taught at the convent and began writing; canoness in the convent and, by the age of 30, widely known as a writer. Died after 973, perhaps as late as 1002.

Selected Works

Collections

Hrotsvit: Patrologiae cursis completus, 1853
Die Dramen der Roswitha von Gandersheim, 1889
Sämtliche Dichtungen [complete works], introduction by Bert Nagel, 1966
Hrotsvithae opera, 1970
Werke in deutsche Übertragung [von] Hrotsvita von Gandersheim, 1973
The Plays of Hrotswitha of Gandersheim, translated by Larissa and Warren Bonfante, 1979
The Dramas of Hrotsvit of Ganderscheim, 1985
Hrotsvit of Gandersheim: A Florilegium of Her Works, 1998

Plays

Gallicanus
Dulcitius
Calimachus
Abraham
Pafnutius
Sapientia

Legends

The Martyrdom of St. Gangolf
The Youthful St. Pelagius
Theophilus
St. Basil
St. Dionysius
St. Agnes

Biblical Poetry

Leben Mariens
Von der Himmelfahrt des Herrn

Historical Writing

Carmen de gestis Oddonis I. imperatoris
Carmen de Primordiis
Coenobii Gandersheimensis

Further Reading

Butler, Mary Marguerite, *Hrotsvitha: The Theatricality of Her Plays,* New York: Philosophical Library, 1960
Case, Sue Ellen, "Re-Viewing Hrotsvit," *Theatre Journal* 35, no. 4 (December 1983)

Hacks, Peter, *Das Jahrmarktsfest zu Plunderweilern; Rosie träumt: Zwei Bearbeitungen nach J.W. von Goethe und Hrosvith von Gandersheim,* Berlin: Aufbau, 1976; 2nd edition, 1982
Haight, Anne Lyon, *Hroswitha of Gandersheim: Her Life, Times, and Works, and a Comprehensive Bibliography,* New York: Hroswitha Club, 1965
Kraft, Helga, "Am Anfang war die Dramatikerin: Hrotsvith von Gandersheim," in *Ein Haus aus Sprache: Dramatikerinnen und das andere Theater,* Stuttgart: Metzler, 1996
Kuhn, Hugo, "Hrotsviths von Gandersheim: Dichterisches Programm," *Deutsche Vierteljahrsschrift für Literaturwissenschaft und Geistesgeschichte* 24 (1950)
Lerner, Gerda, *The Creation of Feminist Consciousness: From the Middle Ages to 1870,* Oxford and New York: Oxford University Press, 1993
Nagel, Bert, *Hrotsvit von Gandersheim,* Stuttgart: Metzler, 1965
Sperberg-McQueen, M.R., "Whose Body Is It? Chaste Strategies and Reinforcement of Patriarchy in Three Plays by Hroswitha von Gandersheim," *Women in German Yearbook* 8 (1992)
Wilson, Katharina M., "The Saxon Canoness: Hrotsvit of Gandersheim," in *Medieval Women Writers,* Athens: University of Georgia Press, 1984
———, *Hrotsvit of Gandersheim: Rara avis in Saxonia? A Collection of Essays,* Ann Arbor, Michigan: Medieval and Renaissance Collegium, 1987
———, *Hrotsvit of Gandersheim: The Ethics of Authorial Stance,* Leiden, and New York: Brill, 1988
Wilson, Katharina M., editor, *The Plays of Hrotsvit of Gandersheim,* New York: Garland, 1989

Peter Huchel 1903–1981

Peter Huchel's literary career spanned the period from the late 1920s through the 1970s. He made his literary debut during the Weimar Republic, and he continued to write during the Third Reich until his conscription into the armed forces in 1941. After his release from a Soviet prisoner of war camp in 1945, Huchel worked for the Berliner Rundfunk (Berlin Radio), then edited the literary magazine *Sinn und Form* (Meaning and Form).

Huchel was one of the collaborators on the newspaper *Die Kolonne: Zeitung der Jungen Gruppe Dresden* (The Crew: Newspaper of the Young Group Dresden), which appeared from 1929 until 1932. It was here that he published his poems. He won the *Kolonne* prize in 1932 for his poem "Der Knabenteich" (1932; The Boy's Pond). *Die Kolonne* served as a mouthpiece for a new and decidedly unpolitical type of poetry, a conscious break with the critical and political overtones of Expressionism. At this time, Huchel developed friendships with Ernst Bloch and Alfred Kantorowicz. From 1935 to 1940 Huchel wrote radio plays, an activity that would influence his career after the war.

In 1945 Huchel was held at the Soviet prisoner of war camp at Rüdersdorf where he underwent his antifascist reeducation. While in the camp he displayed his artistic talents, leading to a position developing the radio play department. He then rose to become cultural director of the Soviet-licensed Berliner Radiofunk, a position he held until 1949. Despite his indoctrination into communism at the prisoner of war camp, Huchel was not an activist. At the time, ideological purity was not necessary for cultural work. Huchel's lack of commitment to Communist Party ideology would later prove to be his downfall.

In 1949 the literary magazine *Sinn und Form* was founded and published under the auspices of the Akademie der Künste (Academy of Arts). Johannes R. Becher, the Culture Minister, appointed Huchel chief editor. This was an interesting choice because Huchel was not a Marxist, a fact that contributed to the content that *Sinn und Form* would have in the ensuing years. Under Huchel's leadership, *Sinn und Form* gained preeminent status in German literary life. He courted Western literature and succeeded in publishing a great deal of it. Huchel also refused to print Party maxims and avoided reviewing contemporary works. This enabled him to be independent of the constantly changing Party-influenced campaigns.

Huchel was dismissed from his post at *Sinn und Form* in 1962, but he had actually fallen into disgrace much earlier. He was first dismissed in 1952, but was reinstated in 1953 through the intervention of Bertolt Brecht. In 1959, Huchel was condemned at the Bitterfeld conference. Huchel's final dismissal occurred because he did not support socialist realism and the Bitterfelder Weg movement initiated by the cultural functionaries of the German Democratic Republic. Instead, he chose to publish a number of West German writers in his literary magazine at a time when the GDR was trying to solidify and define its own contributions to the cultural sphere. Huchel tended to think more in a *Gesamtdeutsch* or even European context.

Following the construction of the Berlin Wall in August 1961, the GDR was able to shut itself off culturally. This enabled the party functionaries to dismiss Huchel as a perpetrator of "Westernisms." He retained his post long enough to publish the final double issue of 1962. He managed to publish Brecht's "Rede über die Widerstandskraft der Vernunft" (Speech About the Resistance Strength of Reason). Further, Huchel published six of his own poems. In 1963 the culture minister, Kurt Hager, denounced the literary magazine for not having taken a stance in favor of the GDR. The Akademie der Künste replied that although the journal was supportive of the GDR, the section responsible for language and literature always deferred to Huchel's wishes.

Huchel's ideological distance from GDR cultural policies also played a role in his own texts. His early poetry can be classified as nature poetry, influenced by the time he spent at his grandfather's country estate during his childhood and youth. As time went on, he changed the focus of his poetry to reflect nature as the showplace for history, using nature metaphors to represent human and social conditions. Huchel was unable to reconcile his poetic works to the political-cultural ideology of the GDR. His works from the 1950s on display a cultural pessimism directly opposed to the GDR's promotion of progress. Following his dismissal from *Sinn und Form,* Huchel was isolated artistically. His texts grew increasingly dark and he left the nature themes behind, turning his attention to mythological and historical motifs. This remaining poetry was published in the West only after his emigration. Huchel's works did have considerable influence on subsequent generations of poets in the GDR, including Heinz Czechowski, Wulf Kirsten, and Uwe Grüning.

Following his firing, Huchel's house in Wilhelmshorst was watched and he was not permitted to travel. Indeed, even visitors were unwelcome. In 1971, he was again permitted to travel; he went first to Rome and then emigrated to West Germany, where he died in April 1981. In December 1981, there was again a changing of the guard at *Sinn und Form,* and Wilhelm Girnus stepped down as editor. In his departing message, he made no mention of Huchel. Girnus's successor, Paul Wiens, took up this gauntlet in the first issue of 1982 and published four of Huchel's poems. In the annotation, Wiens also indicated Huchel's tenure as chief editor of the magazine.

CAROL ANNE COSTABILE-HEMING

Biography

Born in Berlin, 3 April 1903. Studied literature in Berlin, Freiburg, and Vienna; contributor to the literary magazines *Die literarische Welt, Die Kolonne,* and *Das innere Reich,* 1930; served in World War II, 1940–45, and was captured by the Russians; worked for the Berlin Broadcasting Company in various editorial and supervisory functions, 1945–48; editor-in-chief for the prominent East German literary magazine *Sinn und Form,* 1949–62; during the 1960s, Huchel was prohibited from leaving the country and placed under restricted visitation rights; moved to Rome, 1971, and eventually settled in West Germany. Austrian State Prize for European Literature, 1971. Died 30 April 1981.

Selected Works

Collections
Ausgewählte Gedichte, 1973
Selected Poems, translated by Michael Hamburger, 1974
The Garden of Theophrastus and Other Poems, translated by Michael Hamburger, 1983
Gesammelte Werke in zwei Bänden, 2 vols., edited by Axel Vieregg, 1984
Thistle in His Mouth: Poems, translated by Henry Beissel, 1987

Poetry
Gedichte, 1948
Chausseen Chausseen, 1963
Die Sternenreuse: Gedichte 1925–1947, 1967
Gezählte Tage, 1972
Der Tod der Büdner, 1976
Unbewohnbar die Trauer, 1978
Die neunte Stunde, 1979
Margarete Minde: Eine Dichtung für den Rundfunk, 1984

Edited Work
Marie Luise Kaschnitz, *Gedichte,* 1975

Further Reading

Best, Otto F., editor, *Hommage für Peter Huchel: Zum 3. April 1968,* Munich: Piper, 1968
Dolan, Joseph P., "The Politics of Peter Huchel's Early Verse," *University of Dayton Review* 13, no. 2 (1978)
Freytag, Cornelia, *Weltsituationen in der Lyrik Peter Huchels,* Frankfurt: Lang, 1998
Hilton, Ian, "Peter Huchel's Poetic Vision," in *Neue Ansichten: The Reception of Romanticism in the Literature of the GDR,* edited by Howard Gaskill, et al., Amsterdam and Atlanta, Georgia: Rodopi, 1990
Mayer, Hans, editor, *Über Peter Huchel,* Frankfurt: Suhrkamp, 1973
Nijssen, Hub, *Der heimliche König : Leben und Werk von Peter Huchel,* Würzburg: Königshausen and Neumann, 1998
Parker, Stephen, "Collected—Recollected—Uncollected? Peter Huchel's *Gesammelte Werke,*" *German Life and Letters* 40, no. 1 (1986)
——, "Visions, Revisions and Divisions: The Critical Legacy of Peter Huchel," *German Life and Letters* 41, no. 2 (1988)
——, "Peter Huchel and Sinn und Form: The German Academy of Arts and the Issue of German Cultural Unity," in *German Writers and the Cold War, 1945–61,* edited by Rhys W. Williams, et al., Manchester and New York: Manchester University Press, 1992
——, *Peter Huchel: A Literary Life in 20th-Century Germany,* Bern: Lang, 1998
Schoor, Uwe, *Das geheime Journal der Nation: Die Zeitschrift "Sinn und Form": Chefredakteur, Peter Huchel, 1949–1962,* Berlin and New York: Lang, 1992
Siemes, Christof, *Das Testament gestürzter Tannen: Das lyrische Werk Peter Huchels,* Freiburg im Breisgau: Rombach, 1996
Vieregg, Axel, "The Truth about Peter Huchel?" *German Life and Letters* 41, no. 2 (1988)
Vieregg, Axel, editor, *Peter Huchel, Suhrkamp Taschenbuch Materialien,* Frankfurt: Suhrkamp, 1986
Walther, Peter, editor, *Peter Huchel: Leben und Werk,* Frankfurt: Insel, 1996

Richard Huelsenbeck 1892–1974

Richard Huelsenbeck is remembered first and foremost as a participant in the Dada movement in Zurich and Berlin between 1916 and 1920, and as a key figure in the revival of interest in that movement in Germany and the United States following World War II. Prior to and during his activities as a Dadaist, Huelsenbeck wrote Expressionist fiction and poetry; between 1923 and his exile in 1936, he combined careers as a medical doctor and as a journalist and travel writer. Abandoning writing almost completely for his first dozen years in the United States, he resumed creative activity as a poet and painter around 1949.

Huelsenbeck's first three books of fiction fall clearly within the narrative tradition of Expressionism. *Azteken; oder, Die Knall-*

bude (1918; Aztecs), a novella written in 1913, depicts the plight of a naive enlisted man who is trapped by the hierarchy and class structure of the German military. Its implied criticism of Wilhelmine military and civilian society anticipates the author's strong antiwar stance and his leftist orientation during the Dada years. *Verwandlungen* (1918; *Transformations*) depicts a love triangle that includes Jamaika, a woman with romantic dreams of a theatrical life; her husband Kakadu, a journalist of respectable background and intellectual pretensions; and her lover Butterweg, a circus performer who tempts Jamaika with the pleasures of the demimonde. While the situation of the novella borders on literary cliché, it also includes elements of the absurd that link it to Dada parody: Butterweg, who considers himself a great artist, specializes in swallowing live frogs; the rapid turns in the plot and the transformations in the power relationships among the characters, moreover, occur with little motivation and almost at random. Huelsenbeck's third book of fiction, *Doctor Billig am Ende* (1921; Doctor Billig at the End of His Rope), is the first of his fictional books to approach the length of a true novel. The title character, another respectable German bourgeois character fatally attracted to the demimonde, finds his downfall in the prostitute Margot, through whom he becomes entrapped in a web of criminal activity. Similar to the characters in the two earlier novellas, Billig's fate is absolute humiliation.

During the early years of World War I, Huelsenbeck became involved in proto-Dada activities in Berlin with his friend Hugo Ball; he participated in antiwar readings and lectures and composed manifestos attacking both German militarism and the complicity of many of the Expressionists in the war. Following Ball into Swiss exile in 1916, Huelsenbeck was one of the early members of the budding Dada movement in Zurich. His most celebrated contributions to the Cabaret Voltaire evenings were his primitivistic performance poems, which were collected as *Phantastische Gebete* (1916; *Fantastic Prayers*). Unlike Ball's sound poems, all but one of the *Fantastic Prayers* are firmly grounded in the German language. They make liberal use of collage technique, incorporating fragments from newspaper advertisements and articles and interpolating bruitistic syllables that conjure images of tribal chants. The imagery of the poems is at times violent, and many of the poems added to the expanded Berlin edition of 1920 refer directly to the brutal events of World War I and the November Revolution. Huelsenbeck's recitations of the *Fantastic Prayers* in Zurich became legendary; flailing a cane and accompanying himself with drumbeats, the author's incantational style underlined the violence of the poems. Also dating from the Zurich Dada period was the apocalyptic poem *Schalaben, Schalabai, Schalamezomai* (1916) and several collaborative works, including the trilingual "simultaneous poem" entitled "L'Amiral cherche une maison à louer" (1916; The Admiral Looks for a House to Rent), which he composed with Marcel Janco and Tristan Tzara.

Returning to Berlin in January 1917, Huelsenbeck became involved with the antiwar Neue Jugend group that included George Grosz, John Heartfield, Wieland Herzfelde, and other young writers and artists. It was through Huelsenbeck's participation that this group evolved into Berlin Dada, which was a far more overtly political movement than its Swiss counterpart. Huelsenbeck wrote a number of the group's major pamphlets and manifestos. The longest of these, *Deutschland muß untergehen* (1920; Germany Must Fall), is a bitter recapitulation of the defeat of the November Revolution by anticommunist forces. But by 1920, when three of his books were published by Herzfelde's Malik-Verlag, Huelsenbeck had begun distancing himself from the increasingly doctrinaire communism of some of the Berlin Dadaists and was casting himself as a chronicler and anthologist of the international Dada movement. In that same year, Huelsenbeck published *Dada siegt!* (Dada Is Victorious!), a critical assessment; *En avant Dada*, the first book-length history of the movement; and *Dada Almanach* (*The Dada Almanac*), an international anthology. He also attempted (unsuccessfully) to publish a second anthology, *Dadaco*.

For several years after 1920, Huelsenbeck focused his attention on his medical career, publishing only a few poems and essays. A second phase of literary activity began in 1923, when he received his first appointment as a ship's doctor. Throughout the late 1920s and early 1930s, Huelsenbeck became known as a prolific travel writer, producing for Berlin newspapers numerous accounts of his experiences in Africa, Asia, and the United States. Also dating from this period are a number of travel books and novels with foreign settings, including *Afrika in Sicht* (1928; Africa in View), *Der Sprung nach Osten* (1928; The Leap Eastward), *China frißt Menschen* (1930; China Devours People), and *Der Traum vom großen Glück* (1933; The Dream of Great Happiness).

Exile in the United States meant another hiatus in Huelsenbeck's literary career, as he struggled to establish himself as a psychoanalyst in New York. He became an important member of Karen Horney's American Institute for Psychoanalysis, and he published several articles in English on creativity and psychoanalysis. Following the war, he resumed his creative activities, publishing two new verse collections that were largely based on his responses to life in New York: *Die New Yorker Kantaten* (1952; The New York Cantatas) and *Die Antwort der Tiefe* (1954; The Answer of the Depths). He also began painting and participated in group exhibitions with his wife Beate and his son Tom.

But in the long run, Huelsenbeck became best known for his contributions to the Dada revival of the 1950s and 1960s. As a relatively fluent English speaker who had participated in both Zurich and Berlin Dada, he was much in demand for lectures and essays that interpreted the early 20th-century movement for a new generation. His 1920 history of Dada was translated for Robert Motherwell's seminal anthology *The Dada Painters and Poets* (1951). His own background as a psychoanalyst and his strong interest in French existentialism led him to portray Dada in a way that gained him the enmity of many of his old comrades. In fact, Tzara and others reacted so vehemently to Huelsenbeck's "Dada Manifesto 1949," which was intended for Motherwell's anthology and depicted historical Dada as a sort of precursor of existentialism, that the publisher bowed to their pressure and issued the manifesto as a separate pamphlet. Here and in other writings of the 1940s and 1950s, Huelsenbeck disclaimed the political (communist) aspect of Dada, downplayed the importance of Berlin Dada in relation to Zurich Dada, and portrayed the movement as one that affirmed the positive, creative side of the individual. This revisionist approach to the history and interpretation of Dada culminated in Huelsenbeck's memoir, *Mit Witz, Licht und Grütze* (1957; *Memoirs of a Dada Drummer*).

TIMOTHY SHIPE

See also Dadaism

Biography

Born in Frankenau, 23 April 1892. Studied medicine, German literature, philosophy, and art history at various universities in Germany, France, and Switzerland, 1911–17; participated in Expressionist circles in Munich and Berlin, 1913–15; discharged after three months service in World War I for reasons of health, October 1914; active in the Dada movement in Zurich and Berlin, 1916–20. Completed examinations in Medicine, 1920; practiced medicine in Gdansk, 1920–23, and Berlin, 1923–24; worked as ship's doctor and newspaper correspondent, traveling extensively in Asia, America, and Africa, 1924–33; practiced medicine in Berlin, 1934–36; emigrated to the United States, 1936; practiced medicine in New York City and on Long Island, 1936–39. Changed name to Charles R. Hulbeck, ca. 1938. Joined American Institute for Psychoanalysis, 1942; first exhibition of paintings in New York, 1944; a key figure in the revival of interest in Dada, from 1949; film collaborations with Hans Richter, 1956; settled in Minusio, Switzerland, 1969. Died in Muralto, Switzerland, 20 April 1974.

Selected Works

Fiction

Verwandlungen, 1918; as *Transformations,* translated by Matthew Josephson, 1923
Azteken; oder, Die Knallbude, 1918
Doctor Billig am Ende, 1921
China frißt Menschen, 1930
Der Traum vom großen Glück, 1933
Die Sonne von Black-Point (originally published in serial form), 1934–35; 1996

Poetry

Schalaben, Schalabai, Schalamezomai, 1916
Phantastische Gebete, 1916; expanded edition, 1920; as *Fantastic Prayers,* translated by Malcolm Green in *Blago Bung Blago Bung Bosso Fataka!: First Texts of German Dada,* 1995
Die New Yorker Kantaten, 1952
Die Antwort der Tiefe, 1954

Drama

Warum lacht Frau Balsam?, with Günther Weisenborn, 1932

Nonfiction Prose

Dada siegt!: Eine Bilanz des Dadaismus, 1920
En avant Dada: Eine Geschichte des Dadaismus, 1920; as *En avant Dada: A History of Dadaism,* translated by Ralph Manheim in *The Dada Painters and Poets,* 1951
Deutschland muß untergehen, 1920
Afrika in Sicht, 1928
Der Sprung nach Osten, 1928
Mit Witz, Licht und Grütze, 1957; as part of *Memoirs of a Dada Drummer,* translated by Joachim Neugroschel, 1974
Sexualität und Persönlichkeit, 1959
Dada, eine literarische Dokumentation, 1964
Reise bis ans Ende der Freiheit: Autobiographische Fragmente, edited by Ulrich Karthaus and Horst Krüger, 1984
Wozu Dada: Texte 1916–1936, edited by Herbert Kapfer, 1994
Weltdada Huelsenbeck: Eine Biografie in Briefen und Bildern, edited by Herbert Kapfer and Lisbeth Exner, 1996

Edited Work

Dada Almanach, 1920; as *The Dada Almanac,* translated by Malcolm Green, et al., 1993

Further Reading

Esman, Aaron H., "Richard Huelsenbeck," *American Imago* 32, no. 4 (1975)
Feidel-Mertz, Hildegard, editor, *Der junge Huelsenbeck: Entwicklungsjahre eines Dadaisten,* Giessen: Anabas, 1992
Füllner, Karin, "The Meister-Dada: The Image of Dada through the Eyes of Richard Huelsenbeck," in *New Studies in Dada: Essays and Documents,* edited by Richard Sheppard, Driffield: Hutton Press, 1981
——, *Richard Huelsenbeck: Texte und Aktionen eines Dadaisten,* Heidelberg: Winter, 1983
Nenzel, Reinhard, *Kleinkariete Avantgarde: Zur Neubewertung des deutschen Dadaismus: Der frühe Richard Huelsenbeck: Sein Leben und sein Werk bis 1916 in Darstellung und Interpretation,* Bonn: Nenzel, 1994
Sheppard, Richard, *Richard Huelsenbeck,* Hamburg: Christians, 1982
——, "Richard Huelsenbeck (1892–1974): Dada and Psychoanalysis," *Literaturwissenschaftliches Jahrbuch* 26 (1985)

Humanism

Humanism—the word was coined in 1808 for a program of studies based on classical authors—may be defined as the spirit of the humanities. The *studia humanitatis* (studies of humanity) originated as a curriculum around 1400 in the northern Italian schools and designated a rather narrowly focused corpus of liberal arts subjects. It included grammar, rhetoric, poetics, history, and ethics, while excluding other subjects belonging to the universal medieval curriculum: the mathematical *quadrivium* (arithmetic, geometry, astronomy, and music), logic, metaphysics, theology, jurisprudence, natural philosophy, and medicine. The teachers and scholars of this "new learning" were called "humanists" by association with the word *humanitas* (humanity) found in Cicero's remarks on liberal education. Ethical and aesthetic considerations were foundational to the new learning. Petrarch, the "father of humanism," urged students not to settle, as the Aristotelian scholastics did, with *defining* virtue but to explore the anthropological *causes* behind our striving for and pleasure in virtue. For Petrarch, the answer was elegance. A truth badly stated does not attract our desire to know it; how then can it be true? What is worth knowing will somehow engage the natural human affinity to study and know it; truth is beauty, beauty truth. Humanist knowledge is selective knowledge—thus, the abbreviated curriculum. In one of humanism's finest hours, Leonardo Bruni, the renowned chancellor of Florence in the early quinquecento, extended these ideas into the practice of civic humanism. Bruni believed that the cultivation of the humanities perfected and adorned humans in both their private and public roles and that the collective result of these individual enhancements made the republic strong.

Although the new learning did not begin to spread north of the Alps until well into the 15th century, the close political relationship between the Habsburgs and Italy occasioned a first flowering of German humanism very early at the Bohemian court of Charles IV ("protohumanism," 1350–1400). Prague possessed at the time Europe's premier botanical garden, was a center for the study of the natural sciences, and attracted some of Europe's best legal minds, including the chief expert in Roman law, Bartolo Sassaferrato. Of particular import for the history of German humanism, however, were the visits of Cola di Rienzi, a political visionary, and Petrarch himself. Rienzi's fantastical notion to restore the Roman Empire under Charles would be exploited 150 years later by nationalist-humanists such as Ulrich von Hutten during the ideological struggle between Germanists and Romanists. From Petrarch's conversations in Prague and his subsequent correspondence with Chancellor Johannes von Neumarkt, a vernacular imitation was construed that provided the basis for the first prose masterpiece in modern German, Johannes von Tepl's *Der Ackermann aus Böhmen* (1401; The Plowman of Bohemia). These two foci demonstrate the intrinsic connection in early humanism between politics and poetry. Why this excellent birth did not continue to mature owed both to the illiberal political environment after 1400 (persecution of the Hussites), as well as to the fact that the *studia humanitatis* had not yet been implemented north of the Alps.

After 1400, several developments prepared the efflorescence of humanist studies in Germany ("early humanism," 1440–80), the period that opens the first main chapter of German humanism, a part of the larger movement of northern humanism, sometimes called transalpine humanism. A lively period of student wandering brought thousands of Germans to Italian universities, where they gained firsthand acquaintance with the new learning, which they would later champion back home. Conversely, the ecclesiastical reform councils at Constance (1414–18) and Basel (1431–49) brought many Italian humanists, who were in papal service, across the Alps and to the direct attention of northern intellectuals and patrons. Proliferation of financial markets and the rapid growth of northern urban centers made it not only possible but desirable to support the requisites of higher culture. Most significant, Gutenberg's invention of the printing press revolutionized the speed with which humanist books and ideas could be disseminated abroad. This technological advancement proved to be timely for the spread of humanist patriotism and reformism, both of which would soon join similar currents gaining momentum on the religious and political fronts to create the great tide of German Reformation.

The surge of humanist patriotism at midcentury was occasioned by the publication of a cultural-geographical history of Germany, *De ritu, situ, moribus et conditione Germaniae* (1457; On the Customs, Geography, Habits, and Condition of Germany) by the Italian humanist Enea Silvio Piccolomini (later Pope Pius II). With its elegant description of the natural wonders of the German lands and peoples, the book struck a chord of intense national longing within humanist circles ("nationalist humanism"), which would continue to resonate among the Baroque language and literary reformers, the Enlightenment legal scholars, and the Storm and Stress patriots, until it eventually succumbed to imperial sentimentality around 1800. Piccolomini's book also provided the Germans with a proud image of their ancestors, based on his use of Tacitus, who had been rediscovered in the 1420s. This first-century Roman historian expressed admiration in his *Germania* for the honesty, loyalty, and genius of the Germanic peoples; in his *Annals,* he praised their courage and love of liberty embodied in the tribal leader Arminius, who had successfully defied the Roman legions. Suddenly, the early humanist idea of *renovatio imperii* (empire restored) was more than a fiction, and the rationale was available for German nationalist assertion against Rome. The driving force for this assertion was reformism.

Reformism constitutes the heart of German "high humanism" (1480–1530). During this half-century in Germany, humanism rose from its fringe position within the Renaissance cosmos to a full partnership in the German nationalist movement toward intellectual, educational, artistic, and ecclesiopolitical autonomy. The concept of the *studia humanitatis,* introduced in Germany at the University of Heidelberg in 1456 by the wandering humanist Peter Luder, was propagated with missionary zeal throughout greater Germania over the following decades. In a poetic appeal in 1486 to Apollo to "leave fair Helicon and . . . hasten to our shores," Conrad Celtis expressed the feeling shared by increasing numbers of his contemporaries that Rome had forfeited its moral and intellectual privilege and that Germany should now assume this role. Inspired by this idea, influential societies, or sodalities, for the cultivation of humanist poetic and ethical ideals sprang up around leading humanists in cities such as Augsburg (Conrad Peutinger), Nuremberg (Willibald Pirckheimer), Erfurt (Eobanus Hessus), and, especially, Heidelberg (Johannes von Dalberg) and Vienna (Celtis). German humanists displayed greater interest in mathematics and the natural sciences than their Italian predecessors did; and as their concern with reform penetrated into the social and religious spheres, political and even theological studies were added to the recommended areas of humanist expertise. The German humanist involvement in religious affairs was to prove most fateful.

A distinction must be drawn, however, between the religious inclinations of the earlier German humanists, on the one hand, and those who participated more fully in the 16th-century Reformation, on the other. Men such as Celtis had little interest in the affairs of the church and articulated their religious sentiments only obliquely, usually in terms of the divinity of nature. Luther and other reformers suspected them of paganism. But another distinction must be drawn here, as well, between matters of doctrine and morality. As a group the humanists focused on the moral revival of the individual and institutions; doctrine itself was almost a nonissue. Thus, the more doctrinaire Lutheran reformers accused the humanistically trained Huldrych Zwingli and his Swiss brethren of theological laxity; Zwingli responded that Luther's insistence on justification by faith alone threatened the necessity of moral renewal and, as a consequence, social reform. As far as the question of confessing one's faith went, however, the generation of humanists implicated in the religious conflicts of the early 16th century expressed their Christianity openly ("Christian humanism"). Erasmus's entire reform agenda, indeed, rested squarely upon a Christian foundation, the *philosophia Christi* (philosophy of Christ), which for him was synonymous with the original message of Jesus. The humanists sought to recover the true and original meaning of Scripture by applying the modern philological method, which consisted in retracing the Latin, Greek, and Hebrew manuscript witnesses, comparing and rejecting false readings, until the earliest and most reliable one, the critical text, finally "revealed itself." Often, false readings were shown to have been responsible for false (read: Catholic) doctrines. Seen in this light, Luther's translation of the Bible, which repeatedly repudiated the Latin Vulgate in use in the Catholic Church, was a revolutionary act, and one in which the humanist philologists were in complicity.

The fundamental irritation between the religious and humanist reformers, however, mounted steadily until it reached a critical juncture in the mid-1520s, with the publication of Erasmus's *De libero arbitrio diatribe* (A Disquisition on Free Will) and Luther's bitter reply. With this exchange, a fundamental gulf between the reforming sides became apparent. The optimistic anthropology behind Erasmus's thesis of human volition in the act of grace was disavowed by Luther, who viewed man as hopelessly fallen. Thereafter—and particularly because the humanists held the Evangelicals responsible for certain excesses (iconoclasm, secularization of monasteries and nunneries, and acquiescence in the suppression of the peasants by the nobility in 1524–25)—many humanists either abandoned Luther (some such as Pirckheimer returned to the Catholic fold) or sought to avoid further tangible engagement with ecclesiastical reform. As this inconsistency between humanist thought and action during the Reformation illustrates, the humanist propensity for the life of contemplation sometimes muted the call to public action. The question may therefore be raised: Was the integration of politics and intellect in men such as Bruni and Hutten more of an option than an inevitability in humanism? Some recent criticism has cast doubt on the philosophical sincerity of humanism, arguing that it derived its authority and principles in part superficially from the imitation of individual great men—an opinion that echoes the cult of personality in Jacob Burckhardt's *Die Kultur der Renaissance in Italien* (1859; The Civilization of the Period of the Renaissance in Italy).

The years between 1530 and 1555 witnessed the consolidation of Lutheranism in Germany ("Lutheran humanism"). Of the few humanists who remained active in this practical endeavor, none had more lasting impact than Philipp Melanchthon. His name is especially identified with two major accomplishments: the reform of the education system along the lines of Lutheran doctrine; and the Christianization of rhetoric, by which he simultaneously filled the categories of rhetorical argument with biblical content and reduced the system of Lutheran theology to accessible principles (*Loci Communes,* 1521–59; *Augsburg Confession,* 1530–31).

Looking back on the second half of the 16th century, as the Lutheran Reformation, the Catholic Counter Reformation, and growing numbers of Protestant offshoots hardened into ideological camps and as confessional wars engulfed Germany, two distinct but complementary streams of humanist activity emerged: one secular, the other spiritual in emphasis ("late humanism," 1555–1600 and beyond). Humanist scholars of *Reichspublizistik* (public law) came into demand in the territories to help sort out the administrative and constitutional problems that derived from the terms of the Peace of Augsburg (*cuius regio eius religio* [whose territory, his religion]). In addition to these domestic issues, others affected Germany's role in Europe and required the counsel and intervention of scholars of broad erudition and experience. Two of the most urgent issues were the renewed papal claim to supreme imperial authority and the reinvocation by certain political philosophers, most notably Jean Bodin, of the French racial claim to the empire of Charles V. Since these threats to German religion and sovereignty could be dissolved only through a united front, which, in the first place, meant repairing the tattered confessional fabric, many humanists—most identified themselves with the new Reform Church or as Calvinists or moderate Lutherans—threw their efforts into working out a politics of conciliation based on Erasmian principles of toleration and peace. Key to the success of this so-called Second Reformation was to reduce the number and importance of doctrinal differences, a goal admirably realized in the Heidelberg Catechism of 1563. A steady production of irenic (peace) writings can be followed deep into the 17th century. Chief among these religious humanists were Zacharias Ursinus and Caspar Olevianus. A book by Ursinus's disciple David Pareus, the *Irenicum* (1614; The Book of Peace), offered a blueprint for confessional unity that continued to inspire hope for peace through the dark days of the Thirty Years' War.

MAX REINHART

See also Sebastian Brant

Further Reading

Baron, Hans, *The Crisis of the Early Italian Renaissance,* 2 vols., Princeton, New Jersey: Princeton University Press, 1955; revised edition, 1966

Bernstein, Eckhard, *Die Literatur des deutschen Frühhumanismus,* Stuttgart: Metzler, 1978

———, *German Humanism,* Boston: Twayne, 1983

Bolgar, R.R., *The Classical Heritage and Its Beneficiaries,* Cambridge: Cambridge University Press, 1954

Borchardt, Frank, *German Antiquity in Renaissance Myth,* Baltimore, Maryland: Johns Hopkins University Press, 1971

Bradshaw, Brandon, "Transalpine Humanism," in *The Cambridge History of Political Thought,* edited by J.H. Burns, Cambridge and New York: Cambridge University Press, 1991

Buck, August, editor, *Die Rezeption der Antike: Zum Problem der Kontinuität zwischen Mittelalter und Renaissance,* Hamburg: Hauswedell, 1981

Burger, Heinz Otto, *Renaissance, Humanismus, Reformation,* Bad Homburg: Gehlen, 1969

Füssel, Stephan, editor, *Deutsche Dichter der frühen Neuzeit, 1450–1600,* Berlin: Schmidt, 1993

Grafton, Anthony, and Lisa Jardine, *From Humanism to the Humanities: Education and Liberal Arts in Fifteenth- and Sixteenth-Century Europe,* Cambridge, Massachusetts: Harvard University Press, and London: Duckworth, 1986

Hoffmeister, Gerhart, editor, *The Renaissance and Reformation in Germany: An Introduction,* New York: Ungar, 1977

Kristeller, Paul Oskar, *Renaissance Thought and Its Sources,* edited by Michael Mooney, New York: Columbia University Press, 1979

Nauert, Charles Garfield, *Humanism and the Culture of Renaissance Europe,* Cambridge and New York: Cambridge University Press, 1995

Reinhart, Max, editor, *German Writers of the Renaissance and Reformation, 1280–1580,* Dictionary of Literary Biography, vol. 179, Detroit, Michigan: Gale Research, 1997

Roloff, Hans-Gert, "Neulateinische Literatur," in *Renaissance und Barock, 1400–1700,* Propyläen Geschichte der Literatur, vol. 3, Berlin: Propyläen, 1984

Schilling, Heinz, editor, *Die reformierte Konfessionalisierung in Deutschland: Das Problem der "Zweiten Reformation,"* Gütersloh: Mohn, 1986

Schmidt, Josef, editor, *Renaissance, Humanismus, Reformation,* Stuttgart: Reclam, 1976; expanded edition, 1983

Spitz, Lewis, *The Religious Renaissance of the German Humanists,* Cambridge, Massachusetts: Harvard University Press, 1963

Tracy, James D., "Erasmus among the Postmodernists: *Dissimulatio, Bonae Literae,* and *Docta Pietas* Revisited," in *Erasmus' Vision of the Church,* Sixteenth Century Essays and Studies, edited by Hilmar M. Pabel, vol. 33, Kirksville, Missouri: Sixteenth Century Journal Publishers, 1995

Trunz, Erich, "Der deutsche Späthumanismus um 1600 als Standeskultur," reprinted in *Deutsche Barockforschung: Dokumente einer Epoche,* edited by Richard Alewyn, Cologne: Kiepenheuer, 1965; 4th edition, 1970

Wiesner, Merry E., *Gender, Church, and State in Early Modern Germany: Essays,* London and New York: Longman, 1998

Wilhelm von Humboldt 1767–1835

Wilhelm von Humboldt's family ascended the ranks of the municipal and state administration and those of the diplomatic and officer corps; eventually, it became part of the nobility in 1738. Living at Schloß Tegel, Wilhelm and his younger brother Alexander were privately educated by the school reformer Johann Heinrich Campe, Christian Kunth, a collaborator of the Prussian reformer von Stein, and other prominent Berlin academics. Wilhelm studied law in Frankfurt/Oder and Göttingen, where he expanded his knowledge of Kantian philosophy, began his study of classical languages, and met Georg Forster. In 1789 he traveled with his former teacher, Campe, to Southern Germany, Switzerland, and Paris, where he witnessed the French Revolution, the decisive event of his life and the axis around which most of his political and social reflections revolve, as evidenced by his antiabsolutist work *Ideen zu einem Versuch, die Grenzen der Wirksamkeit des Staates zu bestimmen* (written in 1792; first published 1851; *The Sphere and Duties of Government*). Humboldt believed the state, acting as the "vicar of the nation," should be confined to exercising the necessary protective and legal functions, which would allow its citizens to achieve the higher goal of a free and fully developed individuality. His conception of the state, which was greatly influenced by Herder and German Romanticism, attached the highest importance to the concepts of the supraindividual and a historically conditioned nationality. Like Fichte, he viewed nationality as only a part of universal divine life and only an individual expression of humanity.

In 1801 he joined the Prussian State Department and received a seven-year diplomatic assignment to the Vatican. His extended stay in Rome gave him the opportunity to further his study of classical ideals and what he saw as the edifying influence of art. Neohumanistic images subsequently became the cornerstone of his elitist and conservative humanistic ideal of the German *Bildungsbürgertum* and his subsequent education reforms. Under his guidance in 1809, the Prussian Ministry of Culture and Education put the educational system under state control. At this time, the universal requirement to attend school was introduced, and schooling from elementary school to the university was transformed: his design for a democratic, holistic, and multidisciplinary humanities curriculum replaced the trade and class training so prevalent in the Enlightenment. Modeled on the humanistic ideals of classical Greece and the German neoclassicists and inspired by Fichte, Nicolovius, Friedrich Schleiermacher, Wilhelm Süvern, and Pestalozzi, his educational reforms also included the creation of the classical humanistic gymnasium and the establishment of a new university in Berlin, which he describes in his *Über die innere und äussere Organisation der höheren wissenschaftlichen Anstalten in Berlin* (1810; Regarding the Internal and External Organization of Higher Technical Institutions in Berlin). Humboldt University, with its emphasis on both teaching and research, on *Wissenschaft* as well as the classics, provided Germany not only with an academic center but also with a model for the modern public research university. Only now is Humboldt's educational model being supplanted in higher education by a technological institution that is responsive primarily to corporate concerns for productivity and market value.

After reactionary members of government forced him out of office in 1810, Humboldt joined the diplomatic service and took over the Prussian Foreign Service in Vienna, where he attempted to unite Kaiser Franz and Metternich against Napoléon. Along with Hardenberg, he represented Prussia in 1814–15 at the Congress of Vienna. Later in Berlin as the minister of domestic affairs, he worked on creating constitutions for Germany (1813) and Prussia (1819). In these constitutions he, like Baron von Stein, advocated a liberalism that preserved the historical traditions and independence of the local states, provinces, and regions and hoped to fit the constitution to the "genius of the national character." Although he admitted certain fundamental individual rights, he did not follow the French revolutionaries in deriving the state from the isolated wills of individuals. Nor did he, like the conservatives, wish to revive the old feudal estates; he called instead for a "traditional liberalism" that allowed regional self-governing bodies to take part in the old monarchical bureaucratic state through district representation. These endeavors were frustrated by political reactions in 1819, when he was dismissed from the Prussian State Department for his criticism of the reactionary Karlsbad Decrees.

He returned to Schloß Tegel where, until his death, he continued his research in art history and linguistics. In addition to his earlier linguistic study of the Basque language, which he conducted in 1799, he wrote a groundbreaking study of the Javanese language of Kawi, *Über die Kawi-Sprache auf der Insel Java* (1836–40; Regarding the Kawi Language on the Island of Java), an unfinished study that made him one of the pioneers of historical and comparative linguistics and linguistic philosophy. For Humboldt, language is the foundation of the human soul, a dynamic "organism" consisting of forms that shape subjective experience and the operations of the mind. These linguistic structures give expression to particular worldviews and mold the institutions that shape national cultures. Both Wilhelm Dilthey and Ernst Cassirer acknowledged Humboldt for restoring language to its place at the heart of the human sciences.

Much of the representational thinking that characterizes Humboldt's theories of the state, identity, education, and language have been criticized by poststructuralist thinkers such as Derrida, Foucault, and Deleuze. Humboldt's conception of these categories presupposes a certain internal sameness and consistency and a coherence between the thinking subject and its concepts—all of which are antithetical to postmodern conceptions of the self. And his depiction of the philosopher's relation to the state, particularized in the relation between the university and government, has also been called into question by Marxist critics. Ideally, Humboldt University was to supply the "spiritual and moral training of the nation." This training was to result from relating and testing matters in relation to both ideals and a posited original conception of truth. By deriving everything from an original principal of truth and by relating everything to the ideal of justice, the individual, Humboldt theorized, would become morally enlightened and unified with the state. Habermas reconsiders such idealistic identifications of part and whole in his discussion of "consensus." Feminists influenced by deconstruction theories, including Hélène Cixous and Luce Irigaray, have also attacked such phallogocentric notions of the state, while other more contemporary comparisons could be drawn to Deleuze and Guattari and the "arborescent model" of thought, where modern-day Platos lecture to students under the boughs of some proudly erect tree.

JENNIFER HAM

See also Universities

Biography

Born in Potsdam, 22 June 1767. Both Wilhelm and his younger brother, Alexander, the famous naturalist, as sons of a well educated and wealthy Huguenot family, were privately educated by some of the most reputable Enlightenment tutors in Berlin. Studied law with an emphasis on philosophy, particularly that of Kant, in Frankfurt/Oder, 1787, and Göttingen, 1788–89. Traveled to Paris, 1789, where he witnessed the French Revolution, to Southern Germany and Switzerland and Erfurt, where he met and married Karoline von Dacheröden, 1791. Lived in Weimar and Jena for several years and spent time with Goethe and Schiller, from 1791. Lived in Paris, 1797–1801. Acted as Minister in Prussian Legation in Rome, also studying ancient history, 1803–8. Served as director of culture and education in Ministry of the Interior, 1809–10. Served as prussian ambassador to Vienna, 1810–15. Appointed ambassador to London, 1817; resigned, 1819. Lived in Thuringia in a kind of self-imposed exile, were he concentrated entirely on his writings, from 1819. Died in Tegel, Berlin, 8 April 1835.

Selected Works

Collections

Gesammelte Schriften, 15 vols., ed. by A. Leitzmann, et.al., 1903–36

Essays and Treatises

Ideen zu einem Versuch, die Grenzen der Wirksamkeit des Staates zu bestimmen (published in excerpted essay form), 1792; as *The Sphere and Duties of Government,* translated by Joseph Coulthard, 1996

Über das Studium des klassischen Altertums, 1793

Über die innere und äussere Organisation der höheren wissenschaftlichen Anstalten in Berlin, 1810

Betrachtungen über die Weltgeschichte, 1818

Other

Über die Kawi-Sprache auf der Insel Java, 3 vols., 1836–40

Further Reading

Freese, Rudolf, editor, *Wilhelm von Humboldt: Sein Leben und Wirken, dargestellt in Briefen, Tagebüchern, und Dokumenten seiner Zeit,* Darmstadt: Wissenschaftliche Buchgesellschaft, 1985

Hartke, Werner, and Henny Maskolat, editors, *Wilhelm von Humboldt, 1767–1967,* Halle: Niemeyer, 1967

Kaehler, Siegfried August, *Wilhelm von Humboldt und der Staat,* Munich: Oldenburg, 1927; revised edition, Göttingen: Vandenhoeck und Ruprecht, 1963

Sauter, Christina M., *Wilhelm von Humboldt und die deutsche Aufklärung,* Berlin: Duncker and Humblot, 1989

I

Irony, Romantic

Around the turn of the 19th century, the concept of irony, which as a rhetorical figure and mode of discourse had been part of the repertoire of European writing since antiquity, was substantially modified to assist in the solution of crucial Romantic problems. Taking its name from the Greek *eironeia* ("dissimulation"), irony consists of purporting a meaning of an utterance or a situation that is different, often opposite, to the literal one. Its intellectual and didactic function lies in its oppositional nature, which requires a constructive independent involvement from the addressee, who must infer the latent meaning. It was this oppositional nature and the constructive reaction it demands that attracted the Romantic thinkers.

The Romantic endeavor to avoid one-dimensional approaches in its search to achieve a vision of totality utilized irony to express opposites together without neutralizing them. Romantic irony aims at a perpetual dialectic dynamic that does not allow its own process to stop. The roots for the need to do this lie in Romantic literary theory, which is closely linked to Romantic philosophy (i.e., German Idealism), in this case especially J.G. Fichte's subjective idealism, as expressed in his *Grundlage der gesammten Wissenschaftslehre* (1794–95; *Foundation of the Science of Knowledge*). Contemporary theorists of irony include Karl Solger (1780–1819) and Adam Müller (1779–1829), but most of the theoretical foundation for this concept of irony has been attributed to Friedrich Schlegel (1772–1829), whose definition of (Romantic) literature in his seminal 116th *Athenäums-fragment* (1798; *Athenaeum Fragment*) as "progressive Universalpoesie" (progressive universal poetry), a perpetual all-inclusive process that "ewig nur werden, nie vollendet sein kann" (can only be perpetually becoming, never be completed to perfection), demands a means by which this can be achieved. This means is irony, which he defines in the earlier, 108th *Lyceums-fragment* (1797; *Lyceum Fragment*) as follows:

> In it [this irony] everything should be all jest and all seriousness, everything guilelessly open and deeply hidden. . . . It contains and arouses a sense of the indissoluble antagonism between the absolute and the relative, between the impossibility and the necessity of complete communication. It is the freest of all licences, because through it one transcends oneself, but at the same time it is the most prescribed, because [it is] absolutely necessary.

This elevates irony from the confines of belonging to an arsenal of rhetorical devices to the independent status of a means of philosophical inquiry and revelation. It is obvious that this theory is, because of its abstractly all-inclusive claims, difficult to pin down into a concrete definition or to put into literary practice. To a large degree this is its audacious point: by offering the means for its own explosion, it guaranteed its very indestructibility in a never-ending process of reflective distancing. As such, Romantic irony is the intellectual response of the (Romantic) human mind finding itself alone and without external guidance in an infinitely complex and ultimately unknowable world in which the only way to assert any kind of independence and authority is to engage in the conscious act of hovering between opposites (which irony allows), affirming and negating at the same time. Although the paradoxical totality afforded by this approach strives toward divine omniscience, it equally engenders the absolute relativity of all values and opens the door to nihilism. A melancholic, even desperate, viewpoint developed quickly that understands irony as a last resort to make bearable the Romantically contradictory experience of existence, which, in its negative manifestation, finds expression in the notion of *weltschmerz*.

Romantic irony found its most immediate and tangible expression in the authors' practice to distance themselves from their writing by casting an ironic question mark over the assumed universal claim to authority—that "this is how it is"—of what is being expressed. This leads to a plurality of values regarding content and to a perspectivism regarding the approach to content. Schlegel saw Romantic irony realized in Goethe's *Wilhelm Meisters Lehrjahre* (1795–96; *Wilhelm Meister's Apprenticeship*) and tried his own hand at it in his novel *Lucinde* (1799; *Lucinde*). Other examples can be found in the works of Ludwig Tieck, E.T.A. Hoffmann, and the theoretical and literary writings of Jean Paul. However, far from being limited to these Romantic contemporaries, this kind of literary irony has exerted a pervasive influence on 19th- and especially 20th-century literary theory and practice. It occupied the Danish philosopher Søren Kierkegaard at the beginning of his philosophical career and is evident in the work of Heinrich Heine. Importantly, it has been recognized as having paved the way for modernist approaches to literary writing as found, for example, in Thomas Mann's or James Joyce's work; for much structuralist thought;

and for modern theories of communication with their emphasis on the arbitrary nature of the relation between the signifier and the signified. However, the early 19th-century developers of this notion of irony did not see themselves as its inventors. Schlegel pointed to Socrates, Boccacio, Cervantes, and Shakespeare as practitioners of this ironic approach, from whom he gleaned his ideas and with whose works as evidence he sought to establish this approach as typologically archetypal rather than merely historical. This, however, must not detract from the historical quality of this concept occurring at this particular juncture in intellectual history: it emerged within the shift from Enlightenment to Romanticism, when the prevalence of Enlightened forms of classical irony, present in the employment of the much-prized 18th-century wit, had made it an easily available basis from which to develop a modified concept to address the newly developed intellectual situation, in which the universal certainty of the Enlightened frame of mind had been replaced by the self-conscious "Romantic" awareness of the persistent possibility of doubt. In the former situation, irony could be used to make visible definite answers and solutions and in the latter to reflect the shifting movements of an ever-progressing intellectual inquiry.

MAIKE OERGEL

See also Romanticism

Further Reading

Alford, Steven E., *Irony and the Logic of the Romantic Imagination,* New York: Lang, 1984

Behler, Ernst, *German Romantic Literary Theory,* Cambridge and New York: Cambridge University Press, 1993

Finlay, Marike, *The Romantic Irony of Semiotics: Friedrich Schlegel and the Crisis of Representation,* Berlin and New York: de Gruyter, 1988

Furst, Lilian, *Fictions of Romantic Irony in European Narrative, 1760–1857,* London: Macmillan, and Cambridge, Massachusetts: Harvard University Press, 1984

Garber, Frederick, editor, *Romantic Irony,* Budapest: Akadémiai Kiado, 1988

Muecke, D.C., *The Compass of Irony,* London: Methuen, 1969; reprint, 1980

Schlegel, Friedrich, "Lyceumsfragmente" and "Athenäumsfragmente," in *Charakteristiken und Kritiken I (1796–1801),* edited by Hans Eichner, Munich: Schönigh, 1967

Simpson, David, *Irony and Authority in Romantic Poetry,* London: Macmillan, and Totowa, New Jersey: Rowman and Littlefield, 1979

Strohschneider-Kohrs, Ingrid, *Die romantische Ironie in Theorie und Gestaltung,* Tübingen: Niemeyer, 1960; 2nd edition, 1977